COLLINS

POCKET ITALIAN DICTIONARY

ITALIAN ▶ ENGLISH   ENGLISH ▶ ITALIAN

HarperCollins*Publishers*

second edition/seconda edizione 1996

latest reprint 1998

HarperCollins Publishers
P.O. Box, Glasgow G4 ONB, Great Britain
ISBN 0 00 470399-5

Pubblicato in Italia dalla
Arnoldo Mondadori Editore, Milano
ISBN 88-04-41581-9

Catherine E. Love • Michela Clari

contributors to second edition/hanno collaborato alla seconda edizione
Bob Grossmith • Gabriella Bacchelli

editorial staff/segreteria di redazione
Joyce Littlejohn

series editor/collana a cura di
Lorna Sinclair Knight

Typeset by Morton Word Processing Ltd, Scarborough

*Printed and bound in Great Britain by
Caledonian International Book Manufacturing Ltd, Glasgow, G64*

INTRODUCTION

We are delighted that you have decided to buy the Collins Pocket Italian Dictionary, and hope you will enjoy and benefit from using it at home, at school, on holiday or at work.

The innovative use of colour guides you quickly and efficiently to the word you want, and the comprehensive wordlist provides a wealth of modern and idiomatic phrases not normally found in a dictionary this size.

In addition, the supplement provides you with guidance on using the dictionary, along with entertaining ways of improving your dictionary skills.

We hope that you will enjoy using it and that it will significantly enhance your language studies.

I marchi registrati

I termini che a nostro parere
costituiscono un marchio
registrato sono stati designati
come tali. In ogni caso, né la
presenza né l'assenza di tale
designazione implicano alcuna
valutazione del loro reale stato
giuridico.

Note on trademarks

Words which we have reason to
believe constitute trademarks have
been designated as such. However,
neither the presence nor the
absence of such designation should
be regarded as affecting the legal
status of any trademark.

COME USARE IL DIZIONARIO COLLINS POCKET

Per imparare ad usare in modo efficace il dizionario è importante comprendere la funzione delle differenziazioni tipografiche, dei simboli e delle abbreviazioni usati nel testo. Vi forniamo pertanto qui di seguito alcuni chiarimenti in merito a tali convenzioni.

I lemmi

Sono le parole in **rosso** elencate in ordine alfabetico. Il primo e l'ultimo lemma di ciascuna pagina appaiono al margine superiore.

Dove opportuno, informazioni sull'ambito d'uso o il livello di formalità di certe parole vengono fornite tra parentesi in corsivo e spesso in forma abbreviata dopo la trascrizione fonetica (es. (*comm*), (*inf*)).

In certi casi più parole con radice comune sono raggruppate sotto lo stesso lemma. Tali parole appaiono in neretto ma in un carattere leggermente ridotto (es. **dolce, dolcezza; accept, acceptance**).

Esempi d'uso del lemma sono a loro volta in neretto ma in un carattere diverso dal lemma (es. **to be cold**).

La trascrizione fonetica

La trascrizione fonetica che illustra la corretta pronuncia del lemma è in parentesi quadra e segue immediatamente il lemma (es. **mezzo** ['mɛddzo]; **knead** [niːd]). L'elenco dei simboli fonetici è alle pagine xiv-xv.

Le traduzioni

Le traduzioni sono in carattere tondo e se si riferiscono a diversi significati del lemma sono separate da un punto e virgola. Spesso diverse traduzioni di un lemma sono introdotte da una o più parole in corsivo in parentesi tonda: la loro funzione è di chiarire a quale significato del lemma si riferisce la traduzione. Possono essere sinonimi, indicazioni di ambito d'uso o di registro del lemma (es. **party** (POL) (*team*) o (*celebration*), **laid back** (*inf*) etc.).

Le "parole chiave"

Un trattamento particolare è stato riservato a quelle parole che, per frequenza d'uso o complessità, necessitano una strutturazione più chiara ed esauriente (es. **da, di, avere** in italiano, **at, to, be, this** in inglese). Il simbolo ◆ e dei numeri sono usati per guidarvi attraverso le varie distinzioni grammaticali e di significato e, dove necessario, ulteriori informazioni sono fornite in corsivo tra parentesi.

Informazioni grammaticali

Le parti del discorso (noun, adjective ecc.) sono espresse da abbreviazioni convenzionali in corsivo (*n, adj* ecc) e seguono la trascrizione fonetica del lemma.

Eventuali ulteriori informazioni grammaticali, come ad esempio le forme di un verbo irregolare o il plurale irregolare di un sostantivo, precedono tra la parentesi la parte del discorso (es. **fall** (*pt* **fell**, *pp* **fallen**) *n*; **man** (*pl* **men**) *n*).

USING YOUR COLLINS POCKET DICTIONARY

A wealth of information is presented in the dictionary, using various typefaces, sizes of type, symbols, abbreviations and brackets. The conventions and symbols used are explained in the following sections.

Headwords
The words you look up in a dictionary — "headwords" — are listed alphabetically. They are printed in **red type** for rapid identification. The two headwords appearing at the top of each page indicate the first and last word dealt with on the page in question.

Information about the usage or form of certain headwords is given in brackets after the phonetic spelling. This usually appears in abbreviated form and in italics (e.g. *(fam)*, *(COMM)*).

Where appropriate, words related to headwords are grouped in the same entry (**illustrare, illustrazione; accept, acceptance**) in a slightly smaller bold type than the headword.

Common expressions in which the headword appears are shown in a different bold roman type (e.g. **aver freddo**).

Phonetic spellings
Where the phonetic spelling of headwords (indicating their pronunciation) is given, it will appear in square brackets immediately after the headword (e.g. **calza** ['kaltsa]; **knead** [niːd]). A list of these symbols is given on pages xiv-xv.

Translations
Headword translations are given in ordinary type and, where more than one meaning or usage exists, these are separated by a semi-colon. You will often find other words in italics in brackets before the translations. These offer suggested contexts in which the headword might appear (e.g. **duro** *(pietra)* or *(lavoro)*) or provide synonyms (e.g. **duro** *(ostinato)*).

"Key" words
Special status is given to certain Italian and English words which are considered as "key" words in each language. They may, for example, occur very frequently or have several types of usage (e.g. **da, di, avere; at, to, be,**

this). A combination of lozenges and numbers helps you to distinguish different parts of speech and different meanings. Further helpful information is provided in brackets and in italics.

Grammatical information

Parts of speech are given in abbreviated form in italics after the phonetic spellings of headwords (e.g. *vt, av, cong*).

Genders of Italian nouns are indicated as follows: *sm* for a masculine and *sf* for a feminine noun. Feminine and irregular plural forms of nouns are also shown (**dottore, essa; droga, ghe**).

Feminine adjective endings are given as are plural forms (**opaco, a, chi, che**).

ABBREVIAZIONI

ABBREVIATIONS

abbreviazione	**abbr**	abbreviation
aggettivo	**adj**	adjective
avverbio	**adv**	adverb
amministrazione	**ADMIN**	administration
aeronautica, viaggi aerei	**AER**	flying, air travel
aggettivo	**ag**	adjective
agricoltura	**AGR**	agriculture
amministrazione	**AMM**	administration
anatomia	**ANAT**	anatomy
architettura	**ARCHIT**	architecture
articolo definito	**art def**	definite article
articolo indefinito	**art indef**	indefinite article
attributivo	**attrib**	attributive
ausiliare	**aus, aux**	auxiliary
l'automobile	**AUT**	the motor car and motoring
avverbio	**av**	adverb
aeronautica, viaggi aerei	**AVIAT**	flying, air travel
biologia	**BIOL**	biology
botanica	**BOT**	botany
inglese della Gran Bretagna	**BRIT**	British English
consonante	**C**	consonant
chimica	**CHIM, CHEM**	chemistry
commercio, finanza, banca	**COMM**	commerce, finance, banking
comparativo	**compar**	comparative
informatica	**COMPUT**	computers
congiunzione	**cong, conj**	conjunction
edilizia	**CONSTR**	building
sostantivo usato come aggettivo, non può essere usato né come attributo, né dopo il sostantivo qualificato	**cpd**	compound element: noun used as adjective and which cannot follow the noun it qualifies
cucina	**CUC, CULIN**	cookery
davanti a	**dav**	before
articolo definito	**def art**	definite article
determinativo: articolo, aggettivo dimostrativo o indefinito etc	**det**	determiner: article, demonstrative etc
diminutivo	**dimin**	diminutive
diritto	**DIR**	law
economia	**ECON**	economics
edilizia	**EDIL**	building
elettricità, elettronica	**ELETTR, ELEC**	electricity, electronics
esclamazione	**escl, excl**	exclamation
femminile	**f**	feminine
familiare (! da evitare)	**fam(!)**	informal usage (! particularly offensive)
ferrovia	**FERR**	railways

ABBREVIAZIONI

ABBREVIATIONS

figurato	**fig**	figurative use
fisiologia	**FISIOL**	physiology
fotografia	**FOT**	photography
(verbo inglese) la cui particella è inseparabile dal verbo	**fus**	(phrasal verb) where the particle cannot be separated from main verb
nella maggior parte dei sensi; generalmente	**gen**	in most or all senses; generally
geografia, geologia	**GEO**	geography, geology
geometria	**GEOM**	geometry
impersonale	**impers**	impersonal
articolo indefinito	**indef art**	indefinite article
familiare (! da evitare)	**inf(!)**	informal usage (! particularly offensive)
infinitivo	**infin**	infinitive
informatica	**INFORM**	computers
insegnamento, sistema scolastico e universitario	**INS**	schooling, schools and universities
invariabile	**inv**	invariable
irregolare	**irreg**	irregular
grammatica, linguistica	**LING**	grammar, linguistics
maschile	**m**	masculine
matematica	**MAT(H)**	mathematics
termine medico, medicina	**MED**	medical term, medicine
il tempo, meteorologia	**METEOR**	the weather, meteorology
maschile o femminile, secondo il sesso	**m/f**	either masculine or feminine depending on sex
esercito, linguaggio militare	**MIL**	military matters
musica	**MUS**	music
sostantivo	**n**	noun
nautica	**NAUT**	sailing, navigation
numerale (aggettivo, sostantivo)	**num**	numeral adjective or noun
	o.s.	oneself
peggiorativo	**peg, pej**	derogatory, pejorative
fotografia	**PHOT**	photography
fisiologia	**PHYSIOL**	physiology
plurale	**pl**	plural
politica	**POL**	politics
participio passato	**pp**	past participle
preposizione	**prep**	preposition
pronome	**pron**	pronoun
psicologia, psichiatria	**PSIC, PSYCH**	psychology, psychiatry
tempo passato	**pt**	past tense
qualcosa	**qc**	
qualcuno	**qn**	
religione, liturgia	**REL**	religions, church service
sostantivo	**s**	noun

ABBREVIAZIONI

ABBREVIATIONS

	sb	somebody
insegnamento, sistema scolastico e universitario	**SCOL**	schooling, schools and universities
singolare	**sg**	singular
soggetto (grammaticale)	**sog**	(grammatical) subject
	sth	something
congiuntivo	**sub**	subjunctive
soggetto (grammaticale)	**subj**	(grammatical) subject
superlativo	**superl**	superlative
termine tecnico, tecnologia	**TECN, TECH**	technical term, technology
telecomunicazioni	**TEL**	telecommunications
tipografia	**TIP**	typography, printing
televisione	**TV**	television
tipografia	**TYP**	typography, printing
inglese degli Stati Uniti	**US**	American English
vocale	**V**	vowel
verbo	**vb**	verb
verbo o gruppo verbale con funzione intransitiva	**vi**	verb or phrasal verb used intransitively
verbo riflessivo	**vr**	reflexive verb
verbo o gruppo verbale con funzione transitiva	**vt**	verb or phrasal verb used transitively
zoologia	**ZOOL**	zoology
marchio registrato	®	registered trademark
introduce un'equivalenza culturale	≈	introduces a cultural equivalent

TRASCRIZIONE FONETICA

PHONETIC TRANSCRIPTION

Consonants   Consonanti

NB The pairing of some vowel sounds only indicates approximate equivalence/La messa in equivalenza di certi suoni indica solo una rassomiglianza approssimativa.

Vowels   Voca

NB p, b, t, d, k, g are not aspirated i Italian/sono seguiti da un'aspirazione i inglese.

puppy	**p**	*padre*	
baby	**b**	*bambino*	
tent	**t**	*tutto*	
daddy	**d**	*dado*	
cork kiss	**k**	*cane che*	
chord			
gag guess	**g**	*gola ghiro*	
so rice kiss	**s**	*sano*	
cousin buzz	**z**	*svago esame*	
sheep sugar	**ʃ**	*scena*	
pleasure beige	**ʒ**		
church	**tʃ**	*pece lanciare*	
judge general	**dʒ**	*giro gioco*	
farm raffle	**f**	*afa faro*	
very rev	**v**	*vero bravo*	
thin maths	**θ**		
that other	**ð**		
little ball	**l**	*letto ala*	
	ʎ	*gli*	
rat brat	**r**	*rete arco*	
mummy comb	**m**	*ramo madre*	
no ran	**n**	*no fumante*	
	ɲ	*gnomo*	
singing bank	**ŋ**		
hat reheat	**h**		
yet	**j**	*buio piacere*	
wall bewail	**w**	*uomo guaio*	
loch	**x**		

Vowels / Voca

heel bead	**iː i**	*vino idea*	
hit pity	**ɪ**		
	e	*stella edera*	
set tent	**ɛ**	*epoca eccetto*	
apple bat	**æ a**	*mamma*	
		amore	
after car calm	**ɑː**		
fun cousin	**ʌ**		
over above	**ə**		
urn fern work	**ɜː**		
wash pot	**ɔ**	*rosa occhio*	
born cork	**ɔː**		
	o	*ponte ognuno*	
	ø	*föhn*	
full soot	**u**	*utile zucca*	
boon lewd	**uː**		

Diphthongs   Dittonghi

ɪə	*beer tier*
ɛə	*tear fair there*
eɪ	*date plaice day*
aɪ	*life buy cry*
au	*owl foul now*
əu	*low no*
ɔɪ	*boil boy oily*
uə	*poor tour*

Miscellaneous   Varie

* per l'inglese: la "r" finale viene pronunciata se seguita da una vocale.

' precedes the stressed syllable/precede la sillaba accentata.

ITALIAN PRONUNCIATION

Vowels

Where the vowel **e** or the vowel **o** appears in a stressed syllable it can be either open [ɛ], [ɔ] or closed [e], [o]. As the open or closed pronunciation of these vowels is subject to regional variation, the distinction is of little importance to the user of this dictionary. Phonetic transcription for headwords containing these vowels will therefore only appear where other pronunciation difficulties are present.

Consonants

c before "e" or "i" is pronounced *tch*.

ch is pronounced like the "k" in "kit".

g before "e" or "i" is pronounced like the "j" in "jet".

gh is pronounced like the "g" in "get".

gl before "e" or "i" is normally pronounced like the "lli" in "million", and in a few cases only like the "gl" in "glove".

gn is pronounced like the "ny" in "canyon".

sc before "e" or "i" is pronounced *sh*.

z is pronounced like the "ts" in "stetson", or like the "d's" in "bird's-eye".

Headwords containing the above consonants and consonantal groups have been given full phonetic transcription in this dictionary.

NB All double written consonants in Italian are fully sounded: e.g. the *tt* in "tutto" is pronounced as in "ha*t t*rick".

ITALIANO - INGLESE
ITALIAN - ENGLISH

A a

a (*a+il* = **al**, *a+lo* = **allo**, *a+l'* = **all'**, *a+la* = **alla**, *a+i* = **ai**, *a+gli* = **agli**, *a+le* = **alle**) *prep* **1** (*stato in luogo*) at; (: *in*) in; **essere alla stazione** to be at the station; **essere ~ casa/~ scuola/~ Roma** to be at home/at school/in Rome; **è ~ 10 km da qui** it's 10 km from here, it's 10 km away

2 (*moto a luogo*) to; **andare ~ casa/~ scuola** to go home/to school

3 (*tempo*) at; (*epoca, stagione*) in; **alle cinque** at five (o'clock); **~ mezzanotte/ Natale** at midnight/Christmas; **al mattino** in the morning; **~ maggio/ primavera** in May/spring; **~ cinquant'anni** at fifty (years of age); **~ domani!** see you tomorrow!

4 (*complemento di termine*) to; **dare qc ~ qn** to give sth to sb

5 (*mezzo, modo*) with, by; **~ piedi/ cavallo** on foot/horseback; **fatto ~ mano** made by hand, handmade; **una barca ~ motore** a motorboat; **~ uno ~ uno** one by one; **all'italiana** the Italian way, in the Italian fashion

6 (*rapporto*) a, per; (: *con prezzi*) at; **prendo 500.000 lire al mese** I get 500,000 lire a *o* per month; **pagato ~ ore** paid by the hour; **vendere qc ~ 500 lire il chilo** to sell sth at 500 lire a *o* per kilo

abbacchi'ato, a [abbak'kjato] *ag* downhearted, in low spirits
abbagli'ante [abbaʎ'ʎante] *ag* dazzling; **~i** *smpl* (*AUT*): **accendere gli ~i** to put one's headlights on full (*BRIT*) *o* high (*US*) beam
abbagli'are [abbaʎ'ʎare] *vt* to dazzle; (*illudere*) to delude; **ab'baglio** *sm* blunder; **prendere un abbaglio** to blunder, make a blunder
abbai'are *vi* to bark
abba'ino *sm* dormer window; (*soffitta*) attic room
abbando'nare *vt* to leave, abandon, desert; (*trascurare*) to neglect; (*rinunciare a*) to abandon, give up; **~rsi** *vr* to let o.s. go; **~rsi a** (*ricordi, vizio*) to give o.s. up to; **abban'dono** *sm* abandonment; neglect; (*SPORT*) withdrawal; (*fig*) abandon; **in abbandono** (*edificio, giardino*) neglected
abbas'sare *vt* to lower; (*radio*) to turn down; **~rsi** *vr* (*chinarsi*) to stoop; (*livello, sole*) to go down; (*fig: umiliarsi*) to demean o.s.; **~ i fari** (*AUT*) to dip *o* dim (*US*) one's lights
ab'basso *escl*: **~ il re!** down with the king!
abbas'tanza [abbas'tantsa] *av* (*a sufficienza*) enough; (*alquanto*) quite, rather, fairly; **non è ~ furbo** he's not shrewd enough; **un vino ~ dolce** quite a sweet wine, a fairly sweet wine; **averne ~ di qn/qc** to have had enough of sb/sth
ab'battere *vt* (*muro, casa*) to pull down; (*ostacolo*) to knock down; (*albero*) to fell; (: *sog: vento*) to bring down; (*bestie da macello*) to slaughter; (*cane, cavallo*) to destroy, put down; (*selvaggina, aereo*) to shoot down; (*fig: sog: malattia, disgrazia*) to lay low; **~rsi** *vr* (*avvilirsi*) to lose heart; **abbat'tuto, a** *ag* (*fig*) depressed
abba'zia [abbat'tsia] *sf* abbey
abbece'dario [abbetʃe'darjo] *sm* primer
abbel'lire *vt* to make beautiful; (*ornare*) to embellish
abbeve'rare *vt* to water; **~rsi** *vr* to drink
'abbia *etc vb vedi* **avere**
abbicci [abbit'tʃi] *sm inv* alphabet;

(*sillabario*) primer; (*fig*) rudiments *pl*

abbi'ente *ag* well-to-do, well-off ♦ *smpl*: **gli ~i** the well-to-do

abbi'etto, a *ag* = abietto

abbiglia'mento [abbiʎʎa'mento] *sm* dress *no pl*; (*indumenti*) clothes *pl*; (*industria*) clothing industry

abbigli'are [abbiʎ'ʎare] *vt* to dress up

abbi'nare *vt*: ~ **(a)** to combine (with)

abbindo'lare *vt* (*fig*) to cheat, trick

abbocca'mento *sm* talks *pl*, meeting

abboc'care *vt* (*tubi, canali*) to connect, join up ♦ *vi* (*pesce*) to bite; (*tubi*) to join; ~ **(all'amo)** (*fig*) to swallow the bait

abboc'cato, a *ag* (*vino*) sweetish

abbona'mento *sm* subscription; (*alle ferrovie etc*) season ticket; **fare l'~** to take out a subscription (*o* season ticket)

abbo'narsi *vr*: ~ **a un giornale** to take out a subscription to a newspaper; ~ **al teatro/alle ferrovie** to take out a season ticket for the theatre/the train; **abbo'nato, a** *sm/f* subscriber; season-ticket holder

abbon'dante *ag* abundant, plentiful; (*giacca*) roomy

abbon'danza [abbon'dantsa] *sf* abundance; plenty

abbon'dare *vi* to abound, be plentiful; ~ **in** *o* to be full of, abound in

abbor'dabile *ag* (*persona*) approachable; (*prezzo*) reasonable

abbor'dare *vt* (*nave*) to board; (*persona*) to approach; (*argomento*) to tackle; ~ **una curva** to take a bend

abbotto'nare *vt* to button up, do up

abboz'zare [abbot'tsare] *vt* to sketch, outline; (*SCULTURA*) to rough-hew; ~ **un sorriso** to give a hint of a smile; **ab'bozzo** *sm* sketch, outline; (*DIR*) draft

abbracci'are [abbrat't∫are] *vt* to embrace; (*persona*) to hug, embrace; (*professione*) to take up; (*contenere*) to include; **~rsi** *vr* to hug *o* embrace (one another); **ab'braccio** *sm* hug, embrace

abbrevi'are *vt* to shorten; (*parola*) to abbreviate

abbreviazi'one [abbrevjat'tsjone] *sf* abbreviation

abbron'zante [abbron'dzante] *ag* tanning, sun *cpd*

abbron'zare [abbron'dzare] *vt* (*pelle*) to tan; (*metalli*) to bronze; **~rsi** *vr* to tan, get a tan; **abbronza'tura** *sf* tan, suntan

abbrusto'lire *vt* (*pane*) to toast; (*caffè*) to roast

abbru'tire *vt* to exhaust; to degrade

abbu'ono *sm* (*COMM*) allowance, discount; (*SPORT*) handicap

abdi'care *vi* to abdicate; ~ **a** to give up, renounce

aberrazi'one [aberrat'tsjone] *sf* aberration

a'bete *sm* fir (tree); ~ **rosso** spruce

abi'etto, a *ag* despicable, abject

'abile *ag* (*idoneo*): ~ **(a qc/a fare qc)** fit (for sth/to do sth); (*capace*) able; (*astuto*) clever; (*accorto*) skilful; ~ **al servizio militare** fit for military service; **abilità** *sf inv* ability; cleverness; skill

abili'tato, a *ag* qualified; (*TEL*) which has an outside line; **abilitazi'one** *sf* qualification

a'bisso *sm* abyss, gulf

abi'tacolo *sm* (*AER*) cockpit; (*AUT*) inside; (: *di camion*) cab

abi'tante *sm/f* inhabitant

abi'tare *vt* to live in, dwell in ♦ *vi*: ~ **in campagna/a Roma** to live in the country/in Rome; **abi'tato, a** *ag* inhabited; lived in ♦ *sm* (*anche*: *centro abitato*) built-up area; **abitazi'one** *sf* residence; house

'abito *sm* dress *no pl*; (*da uomo*) suit; (*da donna*) dress; (*abitudine, disposizione, REL*) habit; **~i** *smpl* (*vestiti*) clothes; **in ~ da sera** in evening dress

abitu'ale *ag* usual, habitual; (*cliente*) regular

abitu'are *vt*: ~ **qn a** to get sb used *o* accustomed to; **~rsi a** to get used to, accustom o.s. to

abitudi'nario, a *ag* of fixed habits ♦ *sm/f* regular customer

abi'tudine *sf* habit; **aver l'~ di fare qc** to be in the habit of doing sth; **d'~** usually; **per ~** from *o* out of habit

abo'lire *vt* to abolish; (*DIR*) to repeal

abomi'nevole *ag* abominable

abo'rigeno [abo'ridʒeno] *sm* aborigine

abor'rire *vt* to abhor, detest

abor'tire *vi* (*MED: accidentalmente*) to miscarry, have a miscarriage; (: *deliberatamente*) to have an abortion; (*fig*) to miscarry, fail; **a'borto** *sm* miscarriage; abortion; (*fig*) freak

abrasi'one *sf* abrasion; **abra'sivo, a** *ag*, *sm* abrasive

abro'gare *vt* to repeal, abrogate

A'bruzzo *sm*: **l'~, gli ~i** the Abruzzi

'abside *sf* apse

a'bulico, a, ci, che *ag* lacking in will power

abu'sare *vi*: ~ **di** to abuse, misuse; (*alcool*) to take to excess; (*approfittare, violare*) to take advantage of; **a'buso** *sm* abuse, misuse; excessive use

a.C. *av abbr* (= *avanti Cristo*) B.C.

a'cacia, cie [a'katʃa] *sf* (*BOT*) acacia

'acca *sf* letter H; **non capire un'~** not to understand a thing

acca'demia *sf* (*società*) learned society; (*scuola: d'arte, militare*) academy; **acca'demico, a, ci, che** *ag* academic ♦ *sm* academician

acca'dere *vb impers* to happen, occur; **acca'duto** *sm*: **raccontare l'accaduto** to describe what has happened

accalappi'are *vt* to catch; (*fig*) to trick, dupe

accal'care *vt* to crowd, throng; **~si** *vr*: **~si (in)** to crowd (into)

accal'darsi *vr* to grow hot

accalo'rarsi *vr* (*fig*) to get excited

accampa'mento *sm* camp

accam'pare *vt* to encamp; (*fig*) to put forward, advance; **~rsi** *vr* to camp

accani'mento *sm* fury; (*tenacia*) tenacity, perseverance

acca'nirsi *vr* (*infierire*) to rage; (*ostinarsi*) to persist; **acca'nito, a** *ag* (*odio, gelosia*) fierce, bitter; (*lavoratore*) assiduous, dogged; (*fumatore*) inveterate

ac'canto *av* near, nearby; ~ **a** *prep* near, beside, close to

accanto'nare *vt* (*problema*) to shelve; (*somma*) to set aside

accapar'rare *vt* (*COMM*) to corner, buy up; (*versare una caparra*) to pay a deposit on; **~rsi qc** (*fig: simpatia, voti*) to secure sth (for o.s.)

accapigli'arsi [akkapiʎ'ʎarsi] *vr* to come to blows; (*fig*) to quarrel

accappa'toio *sm* bathrobe

accappo'nare *vi*: **far ~ la pelle a qn** (*fig*) to bring sb out in goose pimples

accarez'zare [akkaret'tsare] *vt* to caress, stroke, fondle; (*fig*) to toy with

acca'sarsi *vr* to set up house; to get married

accasci'arsi [akkaʃ'ʃarsi] *vr* to collapse; (*fig*) to lose heart

accat'tone *sm/f* beggar

accaval'lare *vt* (*gambe*) to cross; **~rsi** *vr* (*sovrapporsi*) to overlap; (*addensarsi*) to gather

acce'care [attʃe'kare] *vt* to blind ♦ *vi* to go blind

ac'cedere [at'tʃedere] *vi*: ~ **a** to enter; (*richiesta*) to grant, accede to

accele'rare [attʃele'rare] *vt* to speed up ♦ *vi* (*AUT*) to accelerate; ~ **il passo** to quicken one's pace; **accele'rato** *sm* (*FERR*) slow train; **accelera'tore** *sm* (*AUT*) accelerator; **accelerazi'one** *sf* acceleration

ac'cendere [at'tʃɛndere] *vt* (*fuoco, sigaretta*) to light; (*luce, televisione*) to put o switch o turn on; (*AUT: motore*) to switch on; (*COMM: conto*) to open; (*fig: suscitare*) to inflame, stir up; **~rsi** *vr* (*luce*) to come o go on; (*legna*) to catch fire, ignite; **accen'dino** *sm*, **accendi'sigaro** *sm* (cigarette) lighter

accen'nare [attʃen'nare] *vt* to indicate, point out; (*MUS*) to pick out the notes of; to hum ♦ *vi*: ~ **a** (*fig: alludere a*) to hint at; (: *far atto di*) to make as if; ~ **un saluto** (*con la mano*) to make as if to wave; (*col capo*) to half nod; **accenna a piovere** it looks as if it's going to rain

ac'cenno [at'tʃenno] *sm* (*cenno*) sign; nod; (*allusione*) hint

accensi'one [attʃen'sjone] *sf* (*vedi accendere*) lighting; switching on; opening; (*AUT*) ignition

accen'tare [attʃen'tare] *vt* (*parlando*) to stress; (*scrivendo*) to accent

ac'cento [at'tʃento] *sm* accent; (*FONETICA, fig*) stress; (*inflessione*) tone (of voice)

accen'trare [attʃen'trare] *vt* to centralize

accentu'are [attʃentu'are] *vt* to stress, emphasize; **~rsi** *vr* to become more noticeable

accerchi'are [attʃer'kjare] *vt* to surround, encircle

accerta'mento [attʃerta'mento] *sm* check; assessment

accer'tare [attʃer'tare] *vt* to ascertain; (*verificare*) to check; (*reddito*) to assess; **~rsi** *vr*: **~rsi (di)** to make sure (of)

ac'ceso, a [at'tʃeso] *pp di* **accendere** ♦ *ag* lit; on; open; (*colore*) bright

acces'sibile [attʃes'sibile] *ag* (*luogo*) accessible; (*persona*) approachable; (*prezzo*) reasonable; (*idea*): **~ a qn** within the reach of sb

ac'cesso [at'tʃesso] *sm* (*anche INFORM*) access; (*MED*) attack, fit; (*impulso violento*) fit, outburst

acces'sorio, a [attʃes'sɔrjo] *ag* secondary, of secondary importance;**~i** *smpl* accessories

ac'cetta [at'tʃetta] *sf* hatchet

accet'tabile [attʃet'tabile] *ag* acceptable

accet'tare [attʃet'tare] *vt* to accept; **~ di fare qc** to agree to do sth;**accettazi'one** *sf* acceptance; (*locale di servizio pubblico*) reception; **accettazione bagagli** (*AER*) check-in (desk)

ac'cetto, a [at'tʃetto] *ag*: **(ben) ~** welcome; (*persona*) well-liked

accezi'one [attʃet'tsjone] *sf* meaning

acchiap'pare [akkjap'pare] *vt* to catch

acci'acco, chi [at'tʃakko] *sm* ailment

acciaie'ria [attʃaje'ria] *sf* steelworks *sg*

acci'aio [at'tʃajo] *sm* steel

acciden'tale [attʃiden'tale] *ag* accidental

acciden'tato, a [attʃiden'tato] *ag* (*terreno etc*) uneven

acci'dente [attʃi'dɛnte] *sm* (*caso imprevisto*) accident; (*disgrazia*) mishap; **non si capisce un ~** it's as clear as mud; **~i!** (*fam: per rabbia*) damn (it)!; (*: per meraviglia*) good heavens!

accigli'ato, a [attʃiʎ'ʎato] *ag* frowning

ac'cingersi [at'tʃindʒersi] *vr*: **~ a fare** to be about to do

acciuf'fare [attʃuf'fare] *vt* to seize, catch

acci'uga, ghe [at'tʃuga] *sf* anchovy

accla'mare *vt* (*applaudire*) to applaud; (*eleggere*) to acclaim;**acclamazi'one** *sf* applause; acclamation

acclima'tare *vt* to acclimatize; **~rsi** *vr* to become acclimatized

ac'cludere *vt* to enclose;**ac'cluso, a** *pp di* **accludere** ♦ *ag* enclosed

accocco'larsi *vr* to crouch

accogli'ente [akkoʎ'ʎɛnte] *ag* welcoming, friendly;**accogli'enza** *sf* reception; welcome

ac'cogliere [ak'kɔʎʎere] *vt* (*ricevere*) to receive; (*dare il benvenuto*) to welcome; (*approvare*) to agree to, accept; (*contenere*) to hold, accommodate

accol'lato, a *ag* (*vestito*) high-necked

accoltel'lare *vt* to knife, stab

ac'colto, a *pp di* **accogliere**

accoman'dita *sf* (*DIR*) limited partnership

accomia'tare *vt* to dismiss; **~rsi** *vr*: **~rsi (da)** to take one's leave (of)

accomoda'mento *sm* agreement, settlement

accomo'dante *ag* accommodating

accomo'dare *vt* (*aggiustare*) to repair, mend; (*riordinare*) to tidy; (*conciliare*) to settle; **~rsi** *vr* (*sedersi*) to sit down; **s'accomodi!** (*venga avanti*) come in!; (*si sieda*) take a seat!

accompagna'mento [akkompaɲ-ɲa'mento] *sm* (*MUS*) accompaniment

accompa'gnare [akkompaɲ'ɲare] *vt* to accompany, come *o* go with; (*MUS*) to accompany; (*unire*) to couple; **~ la porta** to close the door gently

accomu'nare *vt* to pool, share; (*avvicinare*) to unite

acconcia'tura [akkontʃa'tura] *sf* hairstyle

accondi'scendere [akkondiʃ'ʃendere] *vi*: **~ a** to agree *o* consent to;**accondi-'sceso, a** *pp di* **accondi-scendere**

acconsen'tire *vi*: ~ **(a)** to agree o
consent (to)
acconten'tare *vt* to satisfy; **~rsi di** to be
satisfied with, content o.s. with
ac'conto *sm* part payment; **pagare una
somma in** ~ to pay a sum of money as a
deposit
accoppia'mento *sm* coupling, pairing
off; mating; (*TECN*) coupling
accoppi'are *vt* to couple, pair off; (*BIOL*)
to mate; **~rsi** *vr* to pair off; to mate
acco'rato, a *ag* heartfelt
accorci'are [akkor'tʃare] *vt* to shorten;
~rsi *vr* to become shorter
accor'dare *vt* to reconcile; (*colori*) to
match; (*MUS*) to tune; (*LING*): ~ **qc con qc**
to make sth agree with sth; (*DIR*) to grant;
~rsi *vr* to agree, come to an agreement;
(*colori*) to match
ac'cordo *sm* agreement; (*armonia*)
harmony; (*MUS*) chord; **essere d'~** to
agree; **andare d'~** to get on well together;
d'~! all right!, agreed!
ac'corgersi [ak'kordʒersi] *vr*: ~ **di** to
notice; (*fig*) to realize; **accorgi'mento** *sm*
shrewdness *no pl*; (*espediente*) trick,
device
ac'correre *vi* to run up
ac'corso, a *pp di* **accorrere**
ac'corto, a *pp di* **accorgersi** ♦ *ag*
shrewd; **stare** ~ to be on one's guard
accos'tare *vt* (*avvicinare*): ~ **qc a** to
bring sth near to, put sth near to;
(*avvicinarsi a*) to approach; (*socchiudere:
imposte*) to half-close; (: *porta*) to leave
ajar ♦ *vi* (*NAUT*) to come alongside; **~rsi a**
to draw near, approach; (*fig*) to support
accovacci'arsi [akkovat'tʃarsi] *vr* to
crouch
accoz'zaglia [akkot'tsaʎʎa] (*peg*) *sf* (*di
idee, oggetti*) jumble, hotchpotch; (*di
persone*) odd assortment
accredi'tare *vt* (*notizia*) to confirm the
truth of; (*COMM*) to credit; (*diplomatico*) to
accredit; **~rsi** *vr* (*fig*) to gain credit
ac'crescere [ak'kreʃʃere] *vt* to increase;
~rsi *vr* to increase, grow; **accresci'tivo,
a** *ag*, *sm* (*LING*) augmentative;
accresci'uto ,**a** *pp di* **accrescere**

accucci'arsi [akkut'tʃarsi] *vr* (*cane*) to lie
down
accu'dire *vt* (*anche: vi*: ~ *a*) to attend to
accumu'lare *vt* to accumulate
accumula'tore *sm* (*ELETTR*) accumulator
accura'tezza [akkura'tettsa] *sf* care;
accuracy
accu'rato, a *ag* (*diligente*) careful;
(*preciso*) accurate
ac'cusa *sf* accusation; (*DIR*) charge; **la
pubblica** ~ the prosecution
accu'sare *vt*: ~ **qn di qc** to accuse sb of
sth; (*DIR*) to charge sb with sth; ~
ricevuta di (*COMM*) to acknowledge
receipt of
accu'sato, a *sm/f* accused; defendant
accusa'tore, 'trice *sm/f* accuser ♦ *sm*
(*DIR*) prosecutor
a'cerbo, a [a'tʃerbo] *ag* bitter; (*frutta*)
sour, unripe; (*persona*) immature
'acero ['atʃero] *sm* maple
a'cerrimo, a [a'tʃerrimo] *ag* very fierce
a'ceto [a'tʃeto] *sm* vinegar
ace'tone [atʃe'tone] *sm* nail varnish
remover
A.C.I. ['atʃi] *sigla m* (= *Automobile Club
d'Italia*) ≈ A.A.
'acido, a ['atʃido] *ag* (*sapore*) acid, sour;
(*CHIM*) acid ♦ *sm* (*CHIM*) acid
'acino ['atʃino] *sm* berry; ~ **d'uva** grape
'acne *sf* acne
'acqua *sf* water; (*pioggia*) rain; **~e** *sfpl* (*di
mare, fiume etc*) waters; **fare** ~ (*NAUT*) to
leak, take in water; ~ **in bocca!** mum's
the word!; ~ **corrente** running water; ~
dolce fresh water; ~ **minerale** mineral
water; ~ **potabile** drinking water; ~
salata salt water; ~ **tonica** tonic water
acqua'forte (*pl* **acque'forti**) *sf* etching
a'cquaio *sm* sink
acqua'ragia [akkwa'radʒa] *sf* turpentine
a'cquario *sm* aquarium; (*dello zodiaco*):
A~ Aquarius
acqua'santa *sf* holy water
ac'quatico, a, ci, che *ag* aquatic;
(*SPORT, SCIENZA*) water *cpd*
acqua'vite *sf* brandy
acquaz'zone [akkwat'tsone] *sm*
cloudburst, heavy shower

acque'dotto *sm* aqueduct; waterworks *pl*, water system

'acqueo, a *ag*: **vapore ~** water vapour

acque'rello *sm* watercolour

acqui'rente *sm/f* purchaser, buyer

acqui'sire *vt* to acquire

acquis'tare *vt* to purchase, buy; (*fig*) to gain; **a'cquisto** *sm* purchase; **fare acquisti** to go shopping

acqui'trino *sm* bog, marsh

acquo'lina *sf*: **far venire l'~ in bocca a qn** to make sb's mouth water

a'cquoso, a *ag* watery

'acre *ag* acrid, pungent; (*fig*) harsh, biting

a'crobata, i, e *sm/f* acrobat

acu'ire *vt* to sharpen

a'culeo *sm* (*ZOOL*) sting; (*BOT*) prickle

a'cume *sm* acumen, perspicacity

a'custica *sf* (*scienza*) acoustics *sg*; (*di una sala*) acoustics *pl*

a'cuto, a *ag* (*appuntito*) sharp, pointed; (*suono, voce*) shrill, piercing; (*MAT, LING, MED*) acute; (*MUS*) high-pitched; (*fig: dolore, desiderio*) intense; (: *perspicace*) acute, keen

ad (*dav V*) *prep* = **a**

adagi'are [ada'dʒare] *vt* to lay *o* set down carefully; **~rsi** *vr* to lie down, stretch out

a'dagio [a'dadʒo] *av* slowly ♦ *sm* (*MUS*) adagio; (*proverbio*) adage, saying

adatta'mento *sm* adaptation

adat'tare *vt* to adapt; (*sistemare*) to fit; **~rsi (a)** (*ambiente, tempi*) to adapt (to); (*essere adatto*) to be suitable (for)

a'datto, a *ag*: **~ (a)** suitable (for), right (for)

addebi'tare *vt*: **~ qc a qn** to debit sb with sth; (*fig: incolpare*) to blame sb for sth

ad'debito *sm* (*COMM*) debit

adden'sare *vt* to thicken; **~rsi** *vr* to thicken; (*nuvole*) to gather

adden'tare *vt* to bite into

adden'trarsi *vr*: **~ in** to penetrate, go into

ad'dentro *av* (*fig*): **essere molto ~ in qc** to be well-versed in sth

addestra'mento *sm* training

addes'trare *vt* to train; **~rsi** *vr* to train; **~rsi in qc** to practise (*BRIT*) *o* practice (*US*) sth

ad'detto, a *ag*: **~ a** (*persona*) assigned to; (*oggetto*) intended for ♦ *sm* employee; (*funzionario*) attaché; **~ commerciale/stampa** commercial/press attaché; **gli ~i ai lavori** authorized personnel; (*fig*) those in the know

addì *av* (*AMM*): **~ 3 luglio 1978** on the 3rd of July 1978 (*BRIT*), on July 3rd 1978 (*US*)

addi'accio [ad'djattʃo] *sm* (*MIL*) bivouac; **dormire all'~** to sleep in the open

addi'etro *av* (*indietro*) behind; (*nel passato, prima*) before, ago

ad'dio *sm, escl* goodbye, farewell

addirit'tura *av* (*veramente*) really, absolutely; (*perfino*) even; (*direttamente*) directly, right away

ad'dirsi *vr*: **~ a** to suit, be suitable for

addi'tare *vt* to point out; (*fig*) to expose

addi'tivo *sm* additive

addizio'nare [addittsjo'nare] *vt* (*MAT*) to add (up); **addizi'one** *sf* addition

addob'bare *vt* to decorate; **ad'dobbo** *sm* decoration

addol'cire [addol'tʃire] *vt* (*caffè etc*) to sweeten; (*acqua, fig: carattere*) to soften; **~rsi** *vr* (*fig*) to mellow, soften

addolo'rare *vt* to pain, grieve; **~rsi (per)** to be distressed (by)

ad'dome *sm* abdomen

addomesti'care *vt* to tame

addormen'tare *vt* to put to sleep; **~rsi** *vr* to fall asleep, go to sleep

addos'sare *vt* (*appoggiare*): **~ qc a qc** to lean sth against sth; (*fig*): **~ la colpa a qn** to lay the blame on sb; **~rsi qc** (*responsabilità etc*) to shoulder sth

ad'dosso *av* (*sulla persona*) on; **mettersi ~ il cappotto** to put one's coat on; **non ho soldi ~** I don't have any money on me; **~ a** (*sopra*) on; (*molto vicino*) right next to; **stare ~ a qn** (*fig*) to breathe down sb's neck; **dare ~ a qn** (*fig*) to attack sb

ad'dotto, a *pp di* **addurre**

ad'durre *vt* (*DIR*) to produce; (*citare*) to cite

adegu'are *vt*: ~ **qc a** to adjust *o* relate sth to; **~rsi** *vr* to adapt; **adegu'ato, a** *ag* adequate; (*conveniente*) suitable; (*equo*) fair

a'dempiere *vt* to fulfil, carry out

adem'pire *vt* = **adempiere**

ade'rente *ag* adhesive; (*vestito*) close-fitting ♦ *sm/f* follower; **ade'renza** *sf* adhesion; **aderenze** *sfpl* (*fig*) connections, contacts

ade'rire *vi* (*stare attaccato*) to adhere, stick; ~ **a** to adhere to, stick to; (*fig*: *società, partito*) to join; (: *opinione*) to support; (*richiesta*) to agree to

ades'care *vt* to lure, entice

adesi'one *sf* adhesion; (*fig*) agreement, acceptance; **ade'sivo, a** *ag*, *sm* adhesive

a'desso *av* (*ora*) now; (*or ora, poco fa*) just now; (*tra poco*) any moment now

adia'cente [adjat ʃen'te] *ag* adjacent

adi'bire *vt* (*usare*): ~ **qc a** to turn sth into

adi'rarsi *vr*: ~ (**con** *o* **contro qn per qc**) to get angry (with sb over sth)

a'dire *vt* (*DIR*): ~ **le vie legali** to take legal proceedings

'adito *sm*: **dare ~ a** to give rise to

adocchi'are [adok'kjare] *vt* (*scorgere*) to catch sight of; (*occhieggiare*) to eye

adole'scente [adoleʃ'ʃɛnte] *ag*, *sm/f* adolescent; **adole'scenza** *sf* adolescence

adope'rare *vt* to use; **~rsi** *vr* to strive; **~rsi per qn/qc** to do one's best for sb/sth

ado'rare *vt* to adore; (*REL*) to adore, worship

adot'tare *vt* to adopt; (*decisione, provvedimenti*) to pass; **adot'tivo, a** *ag* (*genitori*) adoptive; (*figlio, patria*) adopted; **adozi'one** *sf* adoption

adri'atico, a, ci, che *ag* Adriatic ♦ *sm*: **l'A~, il mare A~** the Adriatic, the Adriatic Sea

adu'lare *vt* to adulate, flatter

adulte'rare *vt* to adulterate

adul'terio *sm* adultery

a'dulto, a *ag* adult; (*fig*) mature ♦ *sm* adult, grown-up

adu'nanza [adu'nantsa] *sf* assembly, meeting

adu'nare *vt* to assemble, gather; **~rsi** *vr* to assemble, gather; **adu'nata** *sf* (*MIL*) parade, muster

a'dunco, a, chi, che *ag* hooked

a'ereo, a *ag* air *cpd*; (*radice*) aerial ♦ *sm* aerial; (*aeroplano*) plane; ~ **a reazione** jet (plane); ~ **da caccia** fighter (plane); ~ **di linea** airliner; **ae'robica** *sf* aerobics *sg*; **aerodi'namica** *sf* aerodynamics *sg*; **aerodi'namico, a, ci, che** *ag* aerodynamic; (*affusolato*) streamlined; **aero'nautica** *sf* (*scienza*) aeronautics *sg*; **aeronautica militare** air force; **aero'plano** *sm* (aero)plane (*BRIT*), (air)plane (*US*); **aero'porto** *sm* airport; **aero'sol** *sm inv* aerosol

'afa *sf* sultriness

af'fabile *ag* affable

affaccen'dato, a [affatt ʃen'dato] *ag* (*persona*) busy

affacci'arsi [affat'tʃarsi] *vr*: ~ (**a**) to appear (at)

affa'mato, a *ag* starving; (*fig*): ~ (**di**) eager (for)

affan'nare *vt* to leave breathless; (*fig*) to worry; **~rsi** *vr*: **~rsi per qn/qc** to worry about sb/sth; **af'fanno** *sm* breathlessness; (*fig*) anxiety, worry; **affan'noso, a** *ag* (*respiro*) difficult; (*fig*) troubled, anxious

af'fare *sm* (*faccenda*) matter, affair; (*COMM*) piece of business, (business) deal; (*occasione*) bargain; (*DIR*) case; (*fam*: *cosa*) thing; **~i** *smpl* (*COMM*) business *sg*; **Ministro degli A~i esteri** Foreign Secretary (*BRIT*), Secretary of State (*US*); **affa'rista, i** *sm* profiteer, unscrupulous businessman

affasci'nante [affaʃʃi'nante] *ag* fascinating

affasci'nare [affaʃʃi'nare] *vt* to bewitch; (*fig*) to charm, fascinate

affati'care *vt* to tire; **~rsi** *vr* (*durar fatica*) to tire o.s. out

af'fatto *av* completely; **non ... ~** not ... at all; **niente ~** not at all

affer'mare *vt* (*dichiarare*) to maintain, affirm; **~rsi** *vr* to assert o.s., make one's name known; **affermazi'one** *sf* affirmation, assertion; (*successo*) achievement

affer'rare *vt* to seize, grasp; (*fig: idea*) to grasp; **~rsi** *vr*: **~rsi a** to cling to

affet'tare *vt* (*tagliare a fette*) to slice; (*ostentare*) to affect; **affet'tato, a** *ag* sliced; affected ♦ *sm* sliced cold meat

affet'tivo, a *ag* emotional, affective

af'fetto *sm* affection; **affettu'oso, a** *ag* affectionate

affezio'narsi [affettsjo'narsi] *vr*: **~ a** to grow fond of

affian'care *vt* to place side by side; (*MIL*) to flank; (*fig*) to support; **~ qc a qc** to place sth next to *o* beside sth; **~rsi a qn** to stand beside sb

affia'tato, a *ag*: **essere molto ~i** (*coppia*) to get on very well; (*gruppo, amici*) to make a good team

affibbi'are *vt* (*fig: dare*) to give

affi'dabile *ag* reliable

affida'mento *sm* (*DIR: di bambino*) custody; (*fiducia*): **fare ~ su qn** to rely on sb; **non dà nessun ~** he's not to be trusted

affi'dare *vt*: **~ qc o qn a qn** to entrust sth *o* sb to sb; **~rsi** *vr*: **~rsi a** to place one's trust in

affievo'lirsi *vr* to grow weak

af'figgere [af'fiddʒere] *vt* to stick up, post up

affi'lare *vt* to sharpen

affili'are *vt* to affiliate; **~rsi** *vr*: **~rsi a** to become affiliated to

affi'nare *vt* to sharpen

affinché [affin'ke] *cong* in order that, so that

af'fine *ag* similar; **affinità** *sf inv* affinity

affio'rare *vi* to emerge

affissi'one *sf* billposting

af'fisso, a *pp di* **affiggere** ♦ *sm* bill, poster; (*LING*) affix

affit'tare *vt* (*dare in affitto*) to let, rent (out); (*prendere in affitto*) to rent; **af'fitto** *sm* rent; (*contratto*) lease

af'fliggere [af'fliddʒere] *vt* to torment; **~rsi** *vr* to grieve; **af'flitto, a** *pp di* **affliggere**; **afflizi'one** *sf* distress, torment

afflosci'arsi [afflɔʃ'ʃarsi] *vr* to go limp; (*frutta*) to go soft

afflu'ente *sm* tributary; **afflu'enza** *sf* flow; (*di persone*) crowd

afflu'ire *vi* to flow; (*fig: merci, persone*) to pour in; **af'flusso** *sm* influx

affo'gare *vt*, *vi* to drown; **~rsi** *vr* to drown; (*deliberatamente*) to drown o.s.

affol'lare *vt* to crowd; **~rsi** *vr* to crowd; **affol'lato, a** *ag* crowded

affon'dare *vt* to sink

affran'care *vt* to free, liberate; (*AMM*) to redeem; (*lettera*) to stamp; (: *meccanicamente*) to frank (*BRIT*), meter (*US*); **~rsi** *vr* to free o.s.; **affranca'tura** *sf* (*di francobollo*) stamping, franking (*BRIT*), metering (*US*); (*tassa di spedizione*) postage

af'franto, a *ag* (*esausto*) worn out; (*abbattuto*) overcome

af'fresco, schi *sm* fresco

affret'tare *vt* to quicken, speed up; **~rsi** *vr* to hurry; **~rsi a fare qc** to hurry *o* hasten to do sth

affron'tare *vt* (*pericolo etc*) to face; (*assalire: nemico*) to confront; **~rsi** *vr* (*reciproco*) to come to blows

af'fronto *sm* affront, insult

affumi'care *vt* to fill with smoke; to blacken with smoke; (*alimenti*) to smoke

affuso'lato, a *ag* tapering

a'foso, a *ag* sultry, close

'Africa *sf*: **l'~** Africa; **afri'cano, a** *ag*, *sm/f* African

afrodi'siaco, a, ci, che *ag*, *sm* aphrodisiac

a'genda [a'dʒɛnda] *sf* diary

a'gente [a'dʒɛnte] *sm* agent; **~ di cambio** stockbroker; **~ di polizia** police officer; **agen'zia** *sf* agency; (*succursale*) branch; **agenzia di collocamento** employment agency; **agenzia immobiliare** estate agent's (office) (*BRIT*), real estate office (*US*); **agenzia pubblicitaria/viaggi** advertising/travel agency

agevo'lare [adʒevo'lare] *vt* to facilitate, make easy

a'gevole [a'dʒevole] *ag* easy; (*strada*) smooth

agganci'are [aggan'tʃare] *vt* to hook up; (*FERR*) to couple

ag'geggio [ad'dʒeddʒo] *sm* gadget, contraption

agget'tivo [addʒet'tivo] *sm* adjective

agghiacci'ante [aggjat'tʃante] *ag* (*fig*) chilling

agghin'darsi [aggin'darsi] *vr* to deck o.s. out

aggior'nare [addʒor'nare] *vt* (*opera, manuale*) to bring up-to-date; (*seduta etc*) to postpone; **~rsi** *vr* to bring (*o keep*) o.s. up-to-date; **aggior'nato, a** *ag* up-to-date

aggi'rare [addʒi'rare] *vt* to go round; (*fig: ingannare*) to trick; **~rsi** *vr* to wander about; **il prezzo s'aggira sul milione** the price is around the million mark

aggiudi'care [addʒudi'kare] *vt* to award; (*all'asta*) to knock down; **~rsi qc** to win sth

aggi'ungere [ad'dʒundʒere] *vt* to add; **aggi'unto** [ad'dʒunto] *ag* assistant *cpd* ♦ *sm* assistant; **sindaco aggiunto** deputy mayor

aggius'tare [addʒus'tare] *vt* (*accomodare*) to mend, repair; (*riassettare*) to adjust; (*fig: lite*) to settle; **~rsi** *vr* (*arrangiarsi*) to make do; (*con senso reciproco*) to come to an agreement

agglome'rato *sm* (*di rocce*) conglomerate; (*di legno*) chipboard; **~ urbano** built-up area

aggrap'parsi *vr:* **~ a** to cling to

aggra'vare *vt* (*aumentare*) to increase; (*appesantire: anche fig*) to weigh down, make heavy; (*fig: pena*) to make worse; **~rsi** *vr* (*fig*) to worsen, become worse

aggrazi'ato, a [aggrat'tsjato] *ag* graceful

aggre'dire *vt* to attack, assault

aggre'gare *vt:* **~ qn a qc** to admit sb to sth; **~rsi a** to join; **~rsi a** to join, become a member of

aggressi'one *sf* aggression; (*atto*) attack, assault

aggres'sivo, a *ag* aggressive

aggrot'tare *vt:* **~ le sopracciglia** to frown

aggrovigli'are [aggroviʎ'ʎare] *vt* to tangle; **~rsi** *vr* (*fig*) to become

complicated

agguan'tare *vt* to catch, seize

aggu'ato *sm* trap; (*imboscata*) ambush; **tendere un ~ a qn** to set a trap for sb

agguer'rito, a *ag* fierce

agi'ato, a [a'dʒato] *ag* (*vita*) easy; (*persona*) well-off, well-to-do

'agile ['adʒile] *ag* agile, nimble; **agilità** *sf* agility, nimbleness

'agio ['adʒo] *sm* ease, comfort; **vivere negli ~i** to live in comfort; **mettersi a proprio ~** to make o.s. at home *o* comfortable

a'gire [a'dʒire] *vi* to act; (*esercitare un'azione*) to take effect; (*TECN*) to work, function; **~ contro qn** (*DIR*) to take action against sb

agi'tare [adʒi'tare] *vt* (*bottiglia*) to shake; (*mano, fazzoletto*) to wave; (*fig: turbare*) to disturb; (*: incitare*) to stir (up); (*: dibattere*) to discuss; **~rsi** *vr* (*mare*) to be rough; (*malato, dormitore*) to toss and turn; (*bambino*) to fidget; (*emozionarsi*) to get upset; (*POL*) to agitate; **agi'tato, a** *ag* rough; restless; fidgety; upset, perturbed; **agitazi'one** *sf* agitation; (*POL*) unrest, agitation; **mettere in agitazione qn** to upset *o* distress sb

'agli ['aʎʎi] *prep* + *det vedi* **a**

'aglio ['aʎʎo] *sm* garlic

a'gnello [aɲ'ɲɛllo] *sm* lamb

'ago (*pl* **'aghi**) *sm* needle

ago'nia *sf* agony

ago'nistico, a, ci, che *ag* athletic; (*fig*) competitive

agoniz'zare [agonid'dzare] *vi* to be dying

agopun'tura *sf* acupuncture

a'gosto *sm* August

a'graria *sf* agriculture

a'grario, a *ag* agrarian, agricultural; (*riforma*) land *cpd*

a'gricolo, a *ag* agricultural, farm *cpd*; **agricol'tore** *sm* farmer; **agricol'tura** *sf* agriculture, farming

agri'foglio [agri'fɔʎʎo] *sm* holly

agrimen'sore *sm* land surveyor

agritu'rismo *sm* farm holidays *pl*

'agro, a *ag* sour, sharp; **~dolce** *ag* bittersweet; (*salsa*) sweet and sour

a'grume *sm* (*spesso al pl: pianta*) citrus; (*: frutto*) citrus fruit

aguz'zare [agut'tsare] *vt* to sharpen; ~ **gli orecchi** to prick up one's ears

a'guzzo, a [a'guttso] *ag* sharp

'ai *prep* + *det vedi* **a**

'Aia *sf*: **l'~** the Hague

'aia *sf* threshing floor

ai'rone *sm* heron

aiu'ola *sf* flower bed

aiu'tante *sm/f* assistant ♦ *sm* (*MIL*) adjutant; (*NAUT*) master-at-arms; ~ **di campo** aide-de-camp

aiu'tare *vt* to help; ~ **qn (a fare)** to help sb (to do)

ai'uto *sm* help, assistance, aid; (*aiutante*) assistant; **venire in ~ di qn** to come to sb's aid; ~ **chirurgo** assistant surgeon

aiz'zare [ait'tsare] *vt* to incite; ~ **i cani contro qn** to set the dogs on sb

al *prep* + *det vedi* **a**

'ala (*pl* **'ali**) *sf* wing; **fare ~** to fall back, make way; ~ **destra/sinistra** (*SPORT*) right/left wing

'alacre *ag* quick, brisk

a'lano *sm* Great Dane

a'lare *ag* wing *cpd*

'alba *sf* dawn

Alba'nia *sf*: **l'~** Albania

al'batro *sm* albatross

albeggi'are [albed'dʒare] *vi*, *vb impers* to dawn

alberghi'ero, a [alber'gjɛro] *ag* hotel *cpd*

al'bergo, ghi *sm* hotel; ~ **della gioventù** youth hostel

'albero *sm* tree; (*NAUT*) mast; (*TECN*) shaft; ~ **genealogico** family tree; ~ **a gomiti** crankshaft; ~ **di Natale** Christmas tree; ~ **maestro** mainmast; ~ **di trasmissione** transmission shaft

albi'cocca, che *sf* apricot; **albi'cocco, chi** *sm* apricot tree

'albo *sm* (*registro*) register, roll; (*AMM*) notice board

'album *sm* album; ~ **da disegno** sketch book

al'bume *sm* albumen

'alce ['altʃe] *sm* elk

al'colico, a, ci, che *ag* alcoholic ♦ *sm* alcoholic drink

alcoliz'zato, a [alcolid'dzato] *sm/f* alcoholic

'alcool *sm* alcohol; **alco'olico** *etc* = **alcolico** *etc*

al'cuno, a (*det: dav sm*: **alcun** +*C*, *V*, **alcuno** +*s impura, gn, pn, ps, x, z*; *dav sf*: **alcuna** +*C*, **alcun'** +*V*) *det* (*nessuno*): **non ... ~** no, not any; **~i, e** *det pl* some, a few; **non c'è ~a fretta** there's no hurry, there isn't any hurry; **senza alcun riguardo** without any consideration ♦ *pron pl*: **~i, e** some, a few

aldilà *sm*: **l'~** the after-life

alfa'beto *sm* alphabet

alfi'ere *sm* standard-bearer; (*MIL*) ensign; (*SCACCHI*) bishop

'alga, ghe *sf* seaweed *no pl*, alga

'algebra ['aldʒebra] *sf* algebra

Alge'ria [aldʒe'ria] *sf*: **l'~** Algeria

ali'ante *sm* (*AER*) glider

'alibi *sm inv* alibi

a'lice [a'litʃe] *sf* anchovy

alie'nare *vt* (*DIR*) to alienate, transfer; (*rendere ostile*) to alienate; **~rsi qn** to alienate sb; **alie'nato, a** *ag* alienated; transferred; (*fuor di senno*) insane ♦ *sm* lunatic, insane person; **alienazi'one** *sf* alienation; transfer; insanity

ali'eno, a *ag* (*avverso*): ~ **(da)** opposed (to), averse (to) ♦ *sm/f* alien

alimen'tare *vt* to feed; (*TECN*) to feed; to supply; (*fig*) to sustain ♦ *ag* food *cpd*; **~i** *smpl* foodstuffs; (*anche: negozio di ~i*) grocer's shop; **alimentazi'one** *sf* feeding; supplying; (*gli alimenti*) diet

ali'mento *sm* food; **~i** *smpl* (*cibo*) food *sg*; (*DIR*) alimony

a'liquota *sf* share; (*d'imposta*) rate

alis'cafo *sm* hydrofoil

'alito *sm* breath

all. *abbr* (= *allegato*) encl

'alla *prep* + *det vedi* **a**

allacci'are [allat'tʃare] *vt* (*scarpe*) to tie, lace (up); (*cintura*) to do up, fasten; (*due località*) to link; (*luce, gas*) to connect; (*amicizia*) to form

alla'gare *vt* to flood; **~rsi** *vr* to flood

allar'gare *vt* to widen; (*vestito*) to let out; (*aprire*) to open; (*fig: dilatare*) to extend

allar'mare *vt* to alarm

al'larme *sm* alarm; ~ **aereo** air-raid warning

allar'mismo *sm* scaremongering

allat'tare *vt* to feed

'alle *prep* + *det vedi* **a**

alle'anza [alle'antsa] *sf* alliance

alle'arsi *vr* to form an alliance; **alle'ato, a** *ag* allied ♦ *sm/f* ally

alle'gare *vt* (*accludere*) to enclose; (*DIR: citare*) to cite, adduce; (*denti*) to set on edge; **alle'gato, a** *ag* enclosed ♦ *sm* enclosure; **in allegato** enclosed

alleg'gerire [alleddʒe'rire] *vt* to lighten, make lighter; (*fig: sofferenza*) to alleviate, lessen; (*: lavoro, tasse*) to reduce

alle'gria *sf* gaiety, cheerfulness

al'legro, a *ag* cheerful, merry; (*un po' brillo*) merry, tipsy; (*vivace: colore*) bright ♦ *sm* (*MUS*) allegro

allena'mento *sm* training

alle'nare *vt* to train; ~**rsi** *vr* to train; **allena'tore** *sm* (*SPORT*) trainer, coach

allen'tare *vt* to slacken; (*disciplina*) to relax; ~**rsi** *vr* to become slack; (*ingranaggio*) to work loose

aller'gia, gie [aller'dʒia] *sf* allergy; **al'lergico, a, ci, che** *ag* allergic

alles'tire *vt* (*cena*) to prepare; (*esercito, nave*) to equip, fit out; (*spettacolo*) to stage

allet'tare *vt* to lure, entice

alleva'mento *sm* breeding, rearing; (*luogo*) stock farm

alle'vare *vt* (*animale*) to breed, rear; (*bambino*) to bring up

allevi'are *vt* to alleviate

alli'bire *vi* to be astounded

allibra'tore *sm* bookmaker

allie'tare *vt* to cheer up, gladden

alli'evo *sm* pupil; (*apprendista*) apprentice; (*MIL*) cadet

alliga'tore *sm* alligator

alline'are *vt* (*persone, cose*) to line up; (*TIP*) to align; (*fig: economia, salari*) to adjust, align; ~**rsi** *vr* to line up; (*fig: a idee*): ~**rsi a** to come into line with

'allo *prep* + *det vedi* **a**

al'locco, a, chi, che *sm* tawny owl ♦ *sm/f* oaf

allocuzi'one [allokut'tsjone] *sf* address, solemn speech

al'lodola *sf* (sky)lark

alloggi'are [allod'dʒare] *vt* to accommodate ♦ *vi* to live; **al'loggio** *sm* lodging, accommodation (*BRIT*), accommodations (*US*); (*appartamento*) flat (*BRIT*), apartment (*US*)

allontana'mento *sm* removal; dismissal

allonta'nare *vt* to send away, send off; (*impiegato*) to dismiss; (*pericolo*) to avert, remove; (*estraniare*) to alienate; ~**rsi** *vr*: ~**rsi (da)** to go away (from); (*estraniarsi*) to become estranged (from)

al'lora *av* (*in quel momento*) then ♦ *cong* (*in questo caso*) well then; (*dunque*) well then, so; **la gente d'**~ people then *o* in those days; **da** ~ **in poi** from then on

allor'ché [allor'ke] *cong* (*formale*) when, as soon as

al'loro *sm* laurel

'alluce ['allutʃe] *sm* big toe

alluci'nante [allutʃi'nante] *ag* awful; (*fam*) amazing

allucinazi'one [allutʃinat'tsjone] *sf* hallucination

al'ludere *vi*: ~ **a** to allude to, hint at

allu'minio *sm* aluminium (*BRIT*), aluminum (*US*)

allun'gare *vt* to lengthen; (*distendere*) to prolong, extend; (*diluire*) to water down; ~**rsi** *vr* to lengthen; (*ragazzo*) to stretch, grow taller; (*sdraiarsi*) to lie down, stretch out

allusi'one *sf* hint, allusion

al'luso, a *pp di* **alludere**

alluvi'one *sf* flood

al'meno *av* at least ♦ *cong*: (**se**) ~ if only; (**se**) ~ **piovesse!** if only it would rain!

a'logeno, a [a'lɔdʒeno] *ag*: **lampada ~a** halogen lamp

a'lone *sm* halo

'Alpi *sfpl*: **le** ~ the Alps

alpi'nismo *sm* mountaineering, climbing; **alpi'nista, i, e** *sm/f* mountaineer, climber

al'pino, a *ag* Alpine; mountain *cpd*

al'**quanto** *av* rather, a little; **~, a** *det* a certain amount of, some ♦ *pron* a certain amount, some; **~i, e** *det pl, pron pl* several, quite a few

alt *escl* halt!, stop! ♦ *sm*: **dare l'~** to call a halt

alta'**lena** *sf* (*a funi*) swing; (*in bilico, anche fig*) seesaw

al'**tare** *sm* altar

alte'**rare** *vt* to alter, change; (*cibo*) to adulterate; (*registro*) to falsify; (*persona*) to irritate; **~rsi** *vr* to alter; (*cibo*) to go bad; (*persona*) to lose one's temper

al'**terco, chi** *sm* altercation, wrangle

alter'**nare** *vt* to alternate; **~rsi** *vr* to alternate; **alterna'tiva** *sf* alternative; **alterna'tivo, a** *ag* alternative; **alter'nato, a** *ag* alternate; (*ELETTR*) alternating; **alterna'tore** *sm* alternator

al'**terno, a** *ag* alternate; **a giorni ~i** on alternate days, every other day

al'**tezza** [al'tettsa] *sf* height; width; breadth; depth; pitch; (*GEO*) latitude; (*titolo*) highness; (*fig: nobiltà*) greatness; **essere all'~ di** to be on a level with; (*fig*) to be up to *o* equal to; **altez'zoso, a** *ag* haughty

al'**ticcio, a, ci, ce** [al'tittʃo] *ag* tipsy

altipi'**ano** *sm* = altopiano

alti'**tudine** *sf* altitude

'**alto, a** *ag* high; (*persona*) tall; (*tessuto*) wide, broad; (*sonno, acque*) deep; (*suono*) high(-pitched); (*GEO*) upper; (*: setten-trionale*) northern ♦ *sm* top (part) ♦ *av* high; (*parlare*) aloud, loudly; **il palazzo è ~ 20 metri** the building is 20 metres high; **ad ~a voce** aloud; **a notte ~a** in the dead of night; **in ~** up, upwards; at the top; **dall'~ in o al basso** up and down; **degli ~i e bassi** (*fig*) ups and downs; **~a fedeltà** high fidelity, hi-fi; **~a finanza** high finance; **~a moda** haute couture; **~a società** high society

alto'**forno** *sm* blast furnace

altolo'**cato, a** *ag* of high rank

altopar'**lante** *sm* loudspeaker

altopi'**ano** (*pl* altipi'ani) *sm* plateau, upland plain

altret'**tanto, a** *ag, pron* as much; (*pl*) as many ♦ *av* equally; **tanti auguri! — grazie, ~** all the best! — thank you, the same to you

'**altri** *pron inv* (*qualcuno*) somebody; (*: in espressioni negative*) anybody; (*un'altra persona*) another (person)

altri'**menti** *av* otherwise

'**altro, a** *det* **1** (*diverso*) other, different; **questa è un'~a cosa** that's another *o* a different thing

2 (*supplementare*) other; **prendi un ~ cioccolatino** have another chocolate; **hai avuto o notizie?** have you had any more *o* any other news?

3 (*nel tempo*): **l'~ giorno** the other day; **l'altr'anno** last year; **l'~ ieri** the day before yesterday; **domani l'~** the day after tomorrow; **quest'~ mese** next month

4 : **d'~a parte** on the other hand ♦ *pron* **1** (*persona, cosa diversa o supplementare*): **un ~, un'~a** another (one); **lo farà un ~** someone else will do it; **~i, e** others; **gli ~i** (*la gente*) others, other people; **l'uno e l'~** both (of them); **aiutarsi l'un l'~** to help one another; **da un giorno all'~** from day to day; (*nel giro di 24 ore*) from one day to the next; (*da un momento all'altro*) any day now

2 (*sostantivato: solo maschile*) something else; (*: in espressioni interrogative*) anything else; **non ho ~ da dire** I have nothing else *o* I don't have anything else to say; **più che ~** above all; **se non ~** at least; **tra l'~** among other things; **ci mancherebbe ~!** that's all we need!; **non faccio ~ che lavorare** I do nothing but work; **contento? — ~ che!** are you pleased? — and how!; *vedi* **senza; noialtri; voialtri; tutto**

al'**tronde** *av*: **d'~** on the other hand

al'**trove** *av* elsewhere, somewhere else

al'**trui** *ag inv* other people's ♦ *sm*: **l'~** other people's belongings *pl*

altru'**ista, i, e** *ag* altruistic

al'**tura** *sf* (*rialto*) height, high ground;

(*alto mare*) open sea; **pesca d'~** deep-sea fishing

a'**lunno, a** *sm/f* pupil

alve'**are** *sm* hive

'**alveo** *sm* riverbed

al'**zare** [al'tsare] *vt* to raise, lift; (*issare*) to hoist; (*costruire*) to build, erect; ~**rsi** *vr* to rise; (*dal letto*) to get up; (*crescere*) to grow tall (*o* taller); ~ **le spalle** to shrug one's shoulders; ~**rsi in piedi** to stand up, get to one's feet; **al'zata** *sf* lifting, raising; **un'alzata di spalle** a shrug

a'**mabile** *ag* lovable; (*vino*) sweet

a'**maca, che** *sf* hammock

amalga'**mare** *vt* to amalgamate

a'**mante** *ag*: ~ **di** (*musica etc*) fond of ♦ *sm/f* lover/mistress

a'**mare** *vt* to love; (*amico, musica, sport*) to like

amareggi'**ato, a** [amared'dʒato] *ag* upset, saddened

ama'**rena** *sf* sour black cherry

ama'**rezza** [ama'rettsa] *sf* bitterness

a'**maro, a** *ag* bitter ♦ *sm* bitterness; (*liquore*) bitters *pl*

ambasci'**ata** [ambaʃ'ʃata] *sf* embassy; (*messaggio*) message; **ambascia'tore,** '**trice** *sm/f* ambassador/ambassadress

ambe'**due** *ag inv*: ~ **i ragazzi** both boys ♦ *pron inv* both

ambien'**tare** *vt* to acclimatize; (*romanzo, film*) to set; ~**rsi** *vr* to get used to one's surroundings

ambi'**ente** *sm* environment; (*fig: insieme di persone*) milieu; (*stanza*) room

am'**biguo, a** *ag* ambiguous; (*persona*) shady

am'**bire** *vt* (*anche: vi*: ~ **a**) to aspire to

'**ambito** *sm* sphere, field

ambizi'**one** [ambit'tsjone] *sf* ambition; **ambizi'oso, a** *ag* ambitious

'**ambo** *ag inv* both

'**ambra** *sf* amber; ~ **grigia** ambergris

ambu'**lante** *ag* travelling, itinerant

ambu'**lanza** [ambu'lantsa] *sf* ambulance

ambula'**torio** *sm* (*studio medico*) surgery

a'**meno, a** *ag* pleasant; (*strano*) funny, strange; (*spiritoso*) amusing

A'**merica** *sf*: **l'~** America; **l'~ latina** Latin America; **ameri'cano, a** *ag, sm/f* American

ami'**anto** *sm* asbestos

a'**mica** *sf vedi* **amico**

ami'**chevole** [ami'kevole] *ag* friendly

ami'**cizia** [ami'tʃittsja] *sf* friendship; ~**e** *sfpl* (*amici*) friends

a'**mico, a, ci, che** *sm/f* friend; (*amante*) boyfriend/girlfriend; ~ **del cuore** *o* **intimo** bosom friend

'**amido** *sm* starch

ammac'**care** *vt* (*pentola*) to dent; (*persona*) to bruise; ~**rsi** *vr* to bruise

ammaes'**trare** *vt* (*animale*) to train; (*persona*) to teach

ammai'**nare** *vt* to lower, haul down

amma'**larsi** *vr* to fall ill; **amma'lato, a** *ag* ill, sick ♦ *sm/f* sick person; (*paziente*) patient

ammali'**are** *vt* (*fig*) to enchant, charm

am'**manco, chi** *sm* (*ECON*) deficit

ammanet'**tare** *vt* to handcuff

ammas'**sare** *vt* (*ammucchiare*) to amass; (*raccogliere*) to gather together; ~**rsi** *vr* to pile up; to gather; **am'masso** *sm* mass; (*mucchio*) pile, heap; (*ECON*) stockpile

ammat'**tire** *vi* to go mad

ammaz'**zare** [ammat'tsare] *vt* to kill; ~**rsi** *vr* (*uccidersi*) to kill o.s.; (*rimanere ucciso*) to be killed; ~**rsi di lavoro** to work o.s. to death

am'**menda** *sf* amends *pl*; (*DIR, SPORT*) fine; **fare ~ di qc** to make amends for sth

am'**messo, a** *pp di* **ammettere** ♦ *cong*: ~ **che** supposing that

am'**mettere** *vt* to admit; (*riconoscere: fatto*) to acknowledge, admit; (*permettere*) to allow, accept; (*supporre*) to suppose

ammez'**zato** [ammed'dzato] *sm* (*anche: piano* ~) mezzanine, entresol

ammic'**care** *vi*: ~ **(a)** to wink (at)

amminis'**trare** *vt* to run, manage; (*REL, DIR*) to administer; **amministra'tivo, a** *ag* administrative; **amministra'tore** *sm* administrator; (*di condominio*) flats manager; **amministratore delegato** managing director; **amministrazi'one** *sf* management; administration

ammiragli'**ato** [ammira'ʎʎato] *sm*

admiralty
ammi'raglio [ammiˈraʎʎo] *sm* admiral
ammi'rare *vt* to admire; **ammira'tore,**
'trice *sm/f* admirer; **ammirazi'one** *sf*
admiration
ammissi'one *sf* admission;
(*approvazione*) acknowledgment
ammobili'ato, a *ag* furnished
am'modo *av* properly ♦ *ag inv*
respectable, nice
am'mollo *sm*: **lasciare in ~** to leave to
soak
ammo'niaca *sf* ammonia
ammoni'mento *sm* warning;
admonishment
ammo'nire *vt* (*avvertire*) to warn;
(*rimproverare*) to admonish; (*DIR*) to
caution
ammon'tare *vi*: **~ a** to amount to ♦ *sm*
(*total*) amount
ammorbi'dente *sm* fabric conditioner
ammorbi'dire *vt* to soften
ammortiz'zare [ammortidˈdzare] *vt*
(*ECON*) to pay off, amortize; (*: spese
d'impianto*) to write off; (*AUT, TECN*) to
absorb, deaden; **ammortizza'tore** *sm*
(*AUT, TECN*) shock-absorber
ammucchi'are [ammukˈkjare] *vt* to pile
up, accumulate
ammuf'fire *vi* to go mouldy (*BRIT*) *o*
moldy (*US*)
ammutina'mento *sm* mutiny
ammuti'narsi *vr* to mutiny
ammuto'lire *vi* to be struck dumb
amnis'tia *sf* amnesty
'amo *sm* (*PESCA*) hook; (*fig*) bait
a'modo *av* = **ammodo**
a'more *sm* love; **~i** *smpl* love affairs; **il**
tuo bambino è un ~ your baby's a
darling; **fare l'~** *o* **all'~** to make love; **per**
~ o per forza by hook or by crook; **amor**
proprio self-esteem, pride; **amo'revole**
ag loving, affectionate
a'morfo, a *ag* amorphous; (*fig: persona*)
lifeless
amo'roso, a *ag* (*affettuoso*) loving,
affectionate; (*d'amore: sguardo*) amorous;
(*: poesia, relazione*) love *cpd*
ampi'ezza [amˈpjettsa] *sf* width, breadth;

spaciousness; (*fig: importanza*) scale, size
'ampio, a *ag* wide, broad; (*spazioso*)
spacious; (*abbondante: vestito*) loose;
(*: gonna*) full; (*: spiegazione*) ample, full
am'plesso *sm* (*eufemismo*) embrace
ampli'are *vt* (*ingrandire*) to enlarge;
(*allargare*) to widen
amplifi'care *vt* to amplify; (*magnificare*)
to extol; **amplifica'tore** *sm* (*TECN, MUS*)
amplifier
am'polla *sf* (*vasetto*) cruet
ampu'tare *vt* (*MED*) to amputate
amu'leto *sm* lucky charm
anabbagli'ante [anabbaʎˈʎante] *ag* (*AUT*)
dipped (*BRIT*), dimmed (*US*); **~i** *smpl* dipped
(*BRIT*) *o* dimmed (*US*) headlights
a'nagrafe *sf* (*registro*) register of births,
marriages and deaths; (*ufficio*) registry
office (*BRIT*), office of vital statistics (*US*)
analfa'beta, i, e *ag, sm/f* illiterate
anal'gesico, a, ci, che [analˈdʒɛziko]
ag, sm analgesic
a'nalisi *sf inv* analysis; (*MED: esame*) test;
~ grammaticale parsing; **ana'lista, i, e**
sm/f analyst; (*PSIC*) (psycho)analyst
analiz'zare [analidˈdzare] *vt* to analyse;
(*MED*) to test
analo'gia, 'gie [analoˈdʒia] *sf* analogy
a'nalogo, a, ghi, ghe *ag* analogous
'ananas *sm inv* pineapple
anar'chia [anarˈkia] *sf* anarchy;
a'narchico, a, ci, che *ag* anarchic(al)
♦ *sm/f* anarchist
'ANAS *sigla f* (= *Azienda Nazionale
Autonoma delle Strade*) national roads
department
anato'mia *sf* anatomy; **ana'tomico, a,**
ci, che *ag* anatomical; (*sedile*) contoured
'anatra *sf* duck
'anca, che *sf* (*ANAT*) hip; (*ZOOL*) haunch
'anche [ˈanke] *cong* (*inoltre, pure*) also,
too; (*perfino*) even; **vengo anch'io** I'm
coming too; **~ se** even if
an'cora¹ *av* still; (*di nuovo*) again; (*di
più*) some more; (*persino*): **~ più forte**
even stronger; **non ~** not yet; **~ una**
volta once more, once again; **~ un po'** a
little more; (*di tempo*) a little longer
'ancora² *sf* anchor; **gettare/levare l'~** to

cast/weigh anchor; **anco'raggio** *sm* anchorage; **anco'rare** *vt* to anchor; **ancorarsi** *vr* to anchor

anda'mento *sm* progress, movement; course; state

an'dante *ag (corrente)* current; *(di poco pregio)* cheap, second-rate ♦ *sm (MUS)* andante

an'dare *sm*: **a lungo ~** in the long run ♦ *vi* to go; *(essere adatto)*: **~ a** to suit; *(piacere)*: **il suo comportamento non mi va** I don't like the way he behaves; **ti va di andare al cinema?** do you feel like going to the cinema?; **andarsene** to go away; **questa camicia va lavata** this shirt needs a wash *o* should be washed; **~ a cavallo** to ride; **~ in macchina/aereo** to go by car/plane; **~ a fare qc** to go and do sth; **~ a pescare/sciare** to go fishing/skiing; **~ a male** to go bad; **come va?** *(lavoro, progetto)* how are things?; **come va? — bene, grazie!** how are you? — fine, thanks!; **va fatto entro oggi** it's got to be done today; **ne va della nostra vita** our lives are at stake; **an'data** *sf* going; *(viaggio)* outward journey; **biglietto di sola andata** single *(BRIT) o* one-way ticket; **biglietto di andata e ritorno** return *(BRIT) o* round-trip *(US)* ticket; **anda'tura** *sf (modo di andare)* walk, gait; *(SPORT)* pace; *(NAUT)* tack

an'dazzo [an'dattso] *(peg) sm*: **prendere un brutto ~** to take a turn for the worse

andirivi'eni *sm inv* coming and going

'andito *sm* corridor, passage

an'drone *sm* entrance hall

a'neddoto *sm* anecdote

ane'lare *vi*: **~ a** *(fig)* to long for, yearn for

a'nelito *sm (fig)*: **~ di** longing *o* yearning for

a'nello *sm* ring; *(di catena)* link

a'nemico, a, ci, che *ag* anaemic

a'nemone *sm* anemone

aneste'sia *sf* anaesthesia; **anes'tetico, a, ci, che** *ag, sm* anaesthetic

anfite'atro *sm* amphitheatre

an'fratto *sm* ravine

an'gelico, a, ci, che [an'dʒɛliko] *ag*

angelic(al)

'angelo ['andʒelo] *sm* angel; **~ custode** guardian angel

anghe'ria [ange'ria] *sf* vexation

an'gina [an'dʒina] *sf* tonsillitis; **~ pectoris** angina

angli'cano, a *ag* Anglican

angli'cismo [angli'tʃizmo] *sm* anglicism

anglo'sassone *ag* Anglo-Saxon

ango'lare *ag* angular

angolazi'one [angolat'tsjone] *sf (FOT etc, fig)* angle

'angolo *sm* corner; *(MAT)* angle

an'goscia, sce [an'gɔʃʃa] *sf* deep anxiety, anguish *no pl*; **angosci'oso, a** *ag (d'angoscia)* anguished; *(che dà angoscia)* distressing, painful

angu'illa *sf* eel

an'guria *sf* watermelon

an'gustia *sf (ansia)* anguish, distress; *(povertà)* poverty, want

angusti'are *vt* to distress; **~rsi** *vr*: **~rsi (per)** to worry (about)

an'gusto, a *ag (stretto)* narrow; *(fig)* mean, petty

'anice ['anitʃe] *sm (CUC)* aniseed; *(BOT)* anise

a'nidride *sf (CHIM)*: **~ carbonica/ solforosa** carbon/sulphur dioxide

'anima *sf* soul; *(abitante)* inhabitant; **non c'era ~ viva** there wasn't a living soul

ani'male *sm, ag* animal; **~ domestico** pet

ani'mare *vt* to give life to, liven up; *(incoraggiare)* to encourage; **~rsi** *vr* to become animated, come to life; **ani'mato, a** *ag* animate; *(vivace)* lively, animated; (: *strada*) busy; **anima'tore, 'trice** *sm/f* guiding spirit; *(CINEMA)* animator; *(di festa)* life and soul; **animazi'one** *sf* liveliness; *(di strada)* bustle; *(CINEMA)* animation; **animazione teatrale** amateur dramatics

'animo *sm (mente)* mind; *(cuore)* heart; *(coraggio)* courage; *(disposizione)* character, disposition; **avere in ~ di fare qc** to intend *o* have a mind to do sth; **perdersi d'~** to lose heart

'anitra *sf* = **anatra**

anna'cquare *vt* to water down, dilute

annaffi'are *vt* to water; **annaffia'toio** *sm* watering can

an'nali *smpl* annals

annas'pare *vi* to flounder

an'nata *sf* year; (*importo annuo*) annual amount; **vino d'~** vintage wine

annebbi'are *vt* (*fig*) to cloud; **~rsi** *vr* to become foggy; (*vista*) to become dim

annega'mento *sm* drowning

anne'gare *vt, vi* to drown; **~rsi** *vr* (*accidentalmente*) to drown; (*deliberatamente*) to drown o.s.

anne'rire *vt* to blacken ♦ *vi* to become black

an'nesso, a *pp di* **annettere** ♦ *ag* attached; (*POL*) annexed; **... e tutti gli ~i e connessi** and so on and so forth

an'nettere *vt* (*POL*) to annex; (*accludere*) to attach

annichi'lire [anniki'lire] *vt* = **annichilare**

anni'darsi *vr* to nest

annien'tare *vt* to annihilate, destroy

anniver'sario *sm* anniversary

'anno *sm* year

anno'dare *vt* to knot, tie; (*fig: rapporto*) to form

annoi'are *vt* to bore; (*seccare*) to annoy; **~rsi** *vr* to be bored; to be annoyed

an'noso, a *ag* (*problema etc*) age-old

anno'tare *vt* (*registrare*) to note, note down; (*commentare*) to annotate; **annotazi'one** *sf* note; annotation

annove'rare *vt* to number

annu'ale *ag* annual

annu'ario *sm* yearbook

annu'ire *vi* to nod; (*acconsentire*) to agree

annul'lare *vt* to annihilate, destroy; (*contratto, francobollo*) to cancel; (*matrimonio*) to annul; (*sentenza*) to quash; (*risultati*) to declare void

annunci'are [annun't∫are] *vt* to announce; (*dar segni rivelatori*) to herald; **annuncia'tore, 'trice** *sm/f* (*RADIO, TV*) announcer; **l'Annunciazi'one** *sf* the Annunciation

an'nuncio [an'nunt∫o] *sm* announcement; (*fig*) sign; **~ pubblicitario** advertisement; **~i economici** classified advertisements; small ads

'annuo, a *ag* annual, yearly

annu'sare *vt* to sniff, smell; **~ tabacco** to take snuff

'ano *sm* anus

anoma'lia *sf* anomaly

a'nomalo, a *ag* anomalous

a'nonimo, a *ag* anonymous ♦ *sm* (*autore*) anonymous writer (*o painter etc*); **società ~a** (*COMM*) joint stock company

anores'sia *sf* (*MED*) anorexia

anor'male *ag* abnormal ♦ *sm/f* subnormal person; (*eufemismo*) homosexual

ANSA *sigla f* (= *Agenzia Nazionale Stampa Associata*) press agency

'ansa *sf* (*manico*) handle; (*di fiume*) bend, loop

'ansia *sf* anxiety

ansietà *sf* = **ansia**

ansi'mare *vi* to pant

ansi'oso, a *ag* anxious

'anta *sf* (*di finestra*) shutter; (*di armadio*) door

antago'nismo *sm* antagonism

an'tartico, a, ci, che *ag* Antarctic ♦ *sm*: **l'A~** the Antarctic

An'tartide *sf*: **l'~** Antarctica

antece'dente [antet∫e'dɛnte] *ag* preceding, previous

ante'fatto *sm* previous events *pl*; previous history

antegu'erra *sm* pre-war period

ante'nato *sm* ancestor, forefather

an'tenna *sf* (*RADIO, TV*) aerial; (*ZOOL*) antenna, feeler; (*NAUT*) yard; **~ parabolica** satellite dish

ante'prima *sf* preview

anteri'ore *ag* (*ruota, zampa*) front; (*fatti*) previous, preceding

antia'ereo, a *ag* anti-aircraft

antia'tomico, a, ci, che *ag* antinuclear; **rifugio ~** fallout shelter

antibi'otico, a, ci, che *ag, sm* antibiotic

anti'camera *sf* anteroom; **fare ~** to wait (for an audience)

antichità [antiki'ta] *sf inv* antiquity; (*oggetto*) antique

antici'pare [antitʃi'pare] *vt* (*consegna, visita*) to bring forward, anticipate; (*somma di denaro*) to pay in advance; (*notizia*) to disclose ♦ *vi* to be ahead of time; **anticipazi'one** *sf* anticipation; (*di notizia*) advance information; (*somma di denaro*) advance; **an'ticipo** *sm* anticipation; (*di denaro*) advance; **in anticipo** early, in advance

an'tico, a, chi, che *ag* (*quadro, mobili*) antique; (*dell'antichità*) ancient; **all'~a** old-fashioned

anticoncezio'nale [antikontʃettsjo'nale] *sm* contraceptive

anticonfor'mista, i, e *ag, sm/f* nonconformist

anti'corpo *sm* antibody

an'tidoto *sm* antidote

anti'furto *sm* (*anche: sistema ~*) anti-theft device

anti'gelo [anti'dʒelo] *ag inv:* (*liquido*) **~** (*per motore*) antifreeze; (*per cristalli*) de-icer

An'tille *sfpl:* **le ~** the West Indies

antin'cendio [antin'tʃendjo] *ag inv* fire *cpd*

antio'rario [antio'rarjo] *ag:* **in senso ~** anticlockwise

anti'pasto *sm* hors d'œuvre

antipa'tia *sf* antipathy, dislike; **anti'patico, a, ci, che** *ag* unpleasant, disagreeable

antiquari'ato *sm* antique trade; **un oggetto d'~** an antique

anti'quario *sm* antique dealer

anti'quato, a *ag* antiquated, old-fashioned

antise'mita, i, e *ag* anti-Semitic

anti'settico, a, ci, che *ag, sm* antiseptic

antista'minico, a, ci, che *ag, sm* antihistamine

antolo'gia, 'gie [antolo'dʒia] *sf* anthology

anu'lare *ag* ring *cpd* ♦ *sm* third finger

'anzi ['antsi] *av* (*invece*) on the contrary; (*o meglio*) or rather, or better still

anzianità [antsjani'ta] *sf* old age; (*AMM*) seniority

anzi'ano, a [an'tsjano] *ag* old; (*AMM*) senior ♦ *sm/f* old person; senior member

anziché [antsi'ke] *cong* rather than

anzi'tutto [antsi'tutto] *av* first of all

apa'tia *sf* apathy, indifference

a'patico, a, ci, che *ag* apathetic

'ape *sf* bee

aperi'tivo *sm* apéritif

a'perto, a *pp di* **aprire** ♦ *ag* open; **all'~** in the open (air)

aper'tura *sf* opening; (*ampiezza*) width, spread; (*POL*) approach; (*FOT*) aperture; **~ alare** wing span

'apice ['apitʃe] *sm* apex; (*fig*) height

ap'nea *sf:* **immergersi in ~** to dive without breathing apparatus

a'postolo *sm* apostle

a'postrofo *sm* apostrophe

appa'gare *vt* to satisfy; **~rsi** *vr:* **~rsi di** to be satisfied with

ap'palto *sm* (*COMM*) contract; **dare/prendere in ~ un lavoro** to let out/undertake a job on contract

appan'nare *vt* (*vetro*) to mist; (*metallo*) to tarnish; (*vista*) to dim; **~rsi** *vr* to mist over; to tarnish; to grow dim

appa'rato *sm* equipment, machinery; (*ANAT*) apparatus; **~ scenico** (*TEATRO*) props *pl*

apparecchi'are [apparek'kjare] *vt* to prepare; (*tavola*) to set ♦ *vi* to set the table; **apparecchia'tura** *sf* equipment; (*macchina*) machine, device

appa'recchio [appa'rekkjo] *sm* piece of apparatus, device; (*aeroplano*) aircraft *inv;* **~ televisivo/telefonico** television set/telephone

appa'rente *ag* apparent; **appa'renza** *sf* appearance; **in** *o* **all'apparenza** apparently, to all appearances

appa'rire *vi* to appear; (*sembrare*) to seem, appear; **appari'scente** *ag* (*colore*) garish, gaudy; (*bellezza*) striking

ap'parso, a *pp di* **apparire**

apparta'mento *sm* flat (*BRIT*), apartment (*US*)

appar'tarsi *vr* to withdraw; **appar'tato, a** *ag* (*luogo*) secluded

apparte'nere *vi:* **~ a** to belong to

appassio'nare *vt* to thrill; (*commuovere*) to move; **~rsi a qc** to take a great interest in sth; to be deeply moved by sth; **appassio'nato, a** *ag* passionate; (*entusiasta*): **appassionato (di)** keen (on)

appas'sire *vi* to wither

appel'larsi *vr* (*ricorrere*): **~ a** to appeal to; (*DIR*): **~ contro** to appeal against; **ap'pello** *sm* roll-call; (*implorazione, DIR*) appeal; **fare appello a** to appeal to

ap'pena *av* (*a stento*) hardly, scarcely; (*solamente, da poco*) just ♦ *cong* as soon as; **(non) ~ furono arrivati ...** as soon as they had arrived ...; **~ ... che** *o* **quando** no sooner ... than

ap'pendere *vt* to hang (up)

appen'dice [appen'ditʃe] *sf* appendix; **romanzo d'~** popular serial

appendi'cite [appendi'tʃite] *sf* appendicitis

Appen'nini *smpl*: **gli ~** the Apennines

appesan'tire *vt* to make heavy; **~rsi** *vr* to grow stout

ap'peso, a *pp di* **appendere**

appe'tito *sm* appetite; **appeti'toso, a** *ag* appetising; (*fig*) attractive, desirable

appia'nare *vt* to level; (*fig*) to smooth away, iron out

appiat'tire *vt* to flatten; **~rsi** *vr* to become flatter; (*farsi piatto*) to flatten o.s.; **~rsi al suolo** to lie flat on the ground

appic'care *vt*: **~ il fuoco a** to set fire to, set on fire

appicci'care [appittʃi'kare] *vt* to stick; (*fig*): **~ qc a qn** to palm sth off on sb; **~rsi** *vr* to stick; (*fig: persona*) to cling

appi'eno *av* fully

appigli'arsi [appiʎ'ʎarsi] *vr*: **~ a** (*afferrarsi*) to take hold of; (*fig*) to cling to; **ap'piglio** *sm* hold; (*fig*) pretext

appiso'larsi *vr* to doze off

applau'dire *vt, vi* to applaud; **ap'plauso** *sm* applause

appli'care *vt* to apply; (*regolamento*) to enforce; **~rsi** *vr* to apply o.s.; **applicazi'one** *sf* application; enforcement

appoggi'are [appod'dʒare] *vt* (*mettere contro*): **~ qc a qc** to lean *o* rest sth

against sth; (*fig: sostenere*) to support; **~rsi** *vr*: **~rsi a** to lean against; (*fig*) to rely upon; **ap'poggio** *sm* support

appollai'arsi *vr* (*anche fig*) to perch

ap'porre *vt* to affix

appor'tare *vt* to bring

apposita'mente *av* specially; (*apposta*) on purpose

ap'posito, a *ag* appropriate

ap'posta *av* on purpose, deliberately

appos'tarsi *vr* to lie in wait

ap'prendere *vt* (*imparare*) to learn; (*comprendere*) to grasp

appren'dista, i, e *sm/f* apprentice

apprensi'one *sf* apprehension; **appren'sivo, a** *ag* apprehensive

ap'presso *av* (*accanto, vicino*) close by, near; (*dietro*) behind; (*dopo, più tardi*) after, later ♦ *ag inv* (*dopo*): **il giorno ~** the next day; **~ a** (*vicino a*) near, close to

appres'tare *vt* to prepare, get ready; **~rsi** *vr*: **~rsi a fare qc** to prepare *o* get ready to do sth

ap'pretto *sm* starch

apprez'zabile [appret'tsabile] *ag* noteworthy, significant

apprezza'mento [apprettsa'mento] *sm* appreciation; (*giudizio*) opinion

apprez'zare [appret'tsare] *vt* to appreciate

ap'proccio [ap'prɔttʃo] *sm* approach

appro'dare *vi* (*NAUT*) to land; (*fig*): **non ~ a nulla** to come to nothing; **ap'prodo** *sm* landing; (*luogo*) landing-place

approfit'tare *vi*: **~ di** to make the most of, profit by

approfon'dire *vt* to deepen; (*fig*) to study in depth

appropri'arsi *vr*: **~ di qc** to appropriate sth

appropri'ato, a *ag* appropriate

approssi'marsi *vr*: **~ a** to approach

approssima'tivo, a *ag* approximate, rough; (*impreciso*) inexact, imprecise

appro'vare *vt* (*condotta, azione*) to approve of; (*candidato*) to pass; (*progetto di legge*) to approve; **approvazi'one** *sf* approval

approvvigio'nare [approvvidʒo'nare] *vt*

to supply; **~ qn di qc** to supply sb with sth

appunta'mento *sm* appointment; (*amoroso*) date; **darsi ~** to arrange to meet (one another)

appun'tato *sm* (*CARABINIERI*) corporal

ap'punto *sm* note; (*rimprovero*) reproach ♦ *av* (*proprio*) exactly, just; **per l'~!, ~!** exactly!

appu'rare *vt* to check, verify

apribot'tiglie [apribot'tiʎʎe] *sm inv* bottle opener

a'prile *sm* April

a'prire *vt* to open; (*via, cadavere*) to open up; (*gas, luce, acqua*) to turn on ♦ *vi* to open; **~rsi** *vr* to open; **~rsi a qn** to confide in sb, open one's heart to sb

apris'catole *sm inv* tin (*BRIT*) *o* can opener

a'quario *sm* = **acquario**

'aquila *sf* (*ZOOL*) eagle; (*fig*) genius

aqui'lone *sm* (*giocattolo*) kite; (*vento*) North wind

A'rabia Sau'dita *sf*: **l'~** Saudi Arabia

'arabo, a *ag, sm/f* Arab ♦ *sm* (*LING*) Arabic

a'rachide [a'rakide] *sf* peanut

ara'gosta *sf* crayfish; lobster

a'rancia, ce [a'rantʃa] *sf* orange; **aranci'ata** *sf* orangeade; **a'rancio** *sm* (*BOT*) orange tree; (*colore*) orange ♦ *ag inv* (*colore*) orange; **aranci'one** *ag inv*: (**color**) **arancione** bright orange

a'rare *vt* to plough (*BRIT*), plow (*US*)

a'ratro *sm* plough (*BRIT*), plow (*US*)

a'razzo [a'rattso] *sm* tapestry

arbi'trare *vt* (*SPORT*) to referee; to umpire; (*DIR*) to arbitrate

arbi'trario, a *ag* arbitrary

ar'bitrio *sm* will; (*abuso, sopruso*) arbitrary act

'arbitro *sm* arbiter, judge; (*DIR*) arbitrator; (*SPORT*) referee; (*: TENNIS, CRICKET*) umpire

ar'busto *sm* shrub

'arca, che *sf* (*sarcofago*) sarcophagus; **l'~ di Noè** Noah's ark

ar'cangelo [ar'kandʒelo] *sm* archangel

ar'cata *sf* (*ARCHIT, ANAT*) arch; (*ordine di* *archi*) arcade

archeolo'gia [arkeolo'dʒia] *sf* arch(a)eology; **arche'ologo, a, gi, ghe** *sm/f* arch(a)eologist

ar'chetto [ar'ketto] *sm* (*MUS*) bow

architet'tare [arkitet'tare] *vt* (*fig: ideare*) to devise; (*: macchinare*) to plan, concoct

archi'tetto [arki'tetto] *sm* architect; **architet'tura** *sf* architecture

ar'chivio [ar'kivjo] *sm* archives *pl*; (*INFORM*) file

arci'ere [ar'tʃɛre] *sm* archer

ar'cigno, a [ar'tʃiɲɲo] *ag* grim, severe

arci'vescovo [artʃi'veskovo] *sm* archbishop

'arco *sm* (*arma, MUS*) bow; (*ARCHIT*) arch; (*MAT*) arc

arcoba'leno *sm* rainbow

arcu'ato, a *ag* curved, bent; **dalle gambe ~e** bow-legged

ar'dente *ag* burning; (*fig*) burning, ardent

'ardere *vt, vi* to burn

ar'desia *sf* slate

ar'dire *vi* to dare ♦ *sm* daring; **ar'dito, a** *ag* brave, daring, bold; (*sfacciato*) bold

ar'dore *sm* blazing heat; (*fig*) ardour, fervour

'arduo, a *ag* arduous, difficult

'area *sf* area; (*EDIL*) land, ground

a'rena *sf* arena; (*per corride*) bullring; (*sabbia*) sand

are'narsi *vr* to run aground

areo'plano *sm* = **aeroplano**

'argano *sm* winch

argente'ria [ardʒente'ria] *sf* silverware, silver

Argen'tina [ardʒen'tina] *sf*: **l'~** Argentina; **argen'tino, a** *ag, sm/f* Argentinian

ar'gento [ar'dʒento] *sm* silver; **~ vivo** quicksilver

ar'gilla [ar'dʒilla] *sf* clay

'argine ['ardʒine] *sm* embankment, bank; (*diga*) dyke, dike

argo'mento *sm* argument; (*motivo*) motive; (*materia, tema*) subject

argu'ire *vt* to deduce

ar'guto, a *ag* sharp, quick-witted;

ar'guzia *sf* wit; (*battuta*) witty remark

'aria *sf* air; (*espressione, aspetto*) air, look; (*MUS: melodia*) tune; (*: di opera*) aria; mandare all'~ qc to ruin *o* upset sth; all'~ aperta in the open (air)

'arido, a *ag* arid

arieggi'are [arjed'dʒare] *vt* (*cambiare aria*) to air; (*imitare*) to imitate

ari'ete *sm* ram; (*MIL*) battering ram; (*dello zodiaco*): A~ Aries

a'ringa, ghe *sf* herring *inv*

'arista *sf* (*CUC*) chine of pork

aristo'cratico, a, ci, che *ag* aristocratic

arit'metica *sf* arithmetic

arlec'chino [arlek'kino] *sm* harlequin

'arma, i *sf* weapon, arm; (*parte dell'esercito*) arm; chiamare alle ~i to call up (*BRIT*), draft (*US*); sotto le ~i in the army (*o* forces); alle ~i! to arms!; ~ da fuoco firearm

ar'madio *sm* cupboard; (*per abiti*) wardrobe; ~ a muro built-in cupboard

armamen'tario *sm* equipment, instruments *pl*

arma'mento *sm* (*MIL*) armament; (*: materiale*) arms *pl*, weapons *pl*; (*NAUT*) fitting out; manning

ar'mare *vt* to arm; (*arma da fuoco*) to cock; (*NAUT: nave*) to rig, fit out; to man; (*EDIL: volta, galleria*) to prop up, shore up; ~rsi *vr* to arm o.s.; (*MIL*) to take up arms; ar'mata *sf* (*MIL*) army; (*NAUT*) fleet; arma'tore *sm* shipowner; arma'tura *sf* (*struttura di sostegno*) framework; (*impalcatura*) scaffolding; (*STORIA*) armour *no pl*, suit of armour

armeggi'are [armed'dʒare] *vi*: ~ (intorno a qc) to mess about (with sth)

armis'tizio [armis'tittsjo] *sm* armistice

armo'nia *sf* harmony; ar'monica, che *sf* (*MUS*) harmonica; ~ a bocca mouth organ; ar'monico, a, ci, che *ag* harmonic; (*fig*) harmonious; armoni'oso, a *ag* harmonious

armoniz'zare [armonid'dzare] *vt* to harmonize; (*colori, abiti*) to match ♦ *vi* to be in harmony; to match

ar'nese *sm* tool, implement; (*oggetto indeterminato*) thing, contraption; male in ~ (*malvestito*) badly dressed; (*di salute malferma*) in poor health; (*di condizioni economiche*) down-at-heel

'arnia *sf* hive

a'roma, i *sm* aroma; fragrance; ~i *smpl* (*CUC*) herbs and spices; aromatera'pia *sf* aromatherapy; aro'matico, a, ci, che *ag* aromatic; (*cibo*) spicy

'arpa *sf* (*MUS*) harp

ar'peggio [ar'peddʒo] *sm* (*MUS*) arpeggio

ar'pia *sf* (*anche fig*) harpy

arpi'one *sm* (*gancio*) hook; (*cardine*) hinge; (*PESCA*) harpoon

arrabat'tarsi *vr* to do all one can, strive

arrabbi'are *vi* (*cane*) to be affected with rabies; ~rsi *vr* (*essere preso dall'ira*) to get angry, fly into a rage; arrabbi'ato, a *ag* rabid, with rabies; furious, angry

arraf'fare *vt* to snatch, seize; (*sottrarre*) to pinch

arrampi'carsi *vr* to climb (up)

arran'care *vi* to limp, hobble

arran'giare [arran'dʒare] *vt* to arrange; ~rsi *vr* to manage, do the best one can

arre'care *vt* to bring; (*causare*) to cause

arreda'mento *sm* (*studio*) interior design; (*mobili etc*) furnishings *pl*

arre'dare *vt* to furnish; arreda'tore, 'trice *sm/f* interior designer; ar'redo *sm* fittings *pl*, furnishings *pl*

ar'rendersi *vr* to surrender

arres'tare *vt* (*fermare*) to stop, halt; (*catturare*) to arrest; ~rsi *vr* (*fermarsi*) to stop; ar'resto *sm* (*cessazione*) stopping; (*fermata*) stop; (*cattura, MED*) arrest; subire un arresto to come to a stop *o* standstill; mettere agli arresti to place under arrest; arresti domiciliari house arrest *sg*

arre'trare *vt, vi* to withdraw; arre'trato, a *ag* (*lavoro*) behind schedule; (*paese, bambino*) backward; (*numero di giornale*) back *cpd*; arretrati *smpl* arrears

arric'chire [arrik'kire] *vt* to enrich; ~rsi *vr* to become rich

arricci'are [arrit't∫are] *vt* to curl; ~ il naso to turn up one's nose

ar'ringa, ghe *sf* harangue; (*DIR*) address

by counsel

arrischi'are [arris'kjare] *vt* to risk; **~rsi** *vr* to venture, dare; **arrischi'ato, a** *ag* risky; (*temerario*) reckless, rash

arri'vare *vi* to arrive; (*accadere*) to happen, occur; **~ a** (*livello, grado etc*) to reach; **lui arriva a Roma alle 7** he gets to *o* arrives at Rome at 7; **non ci arrivo** I can't reach it; (*fig: non capisco*) I can't understand it

arrive'derci [arrive'dertʃi] *escl* goodbye!

arrive'derla *escl* (*forma di cortesia*) goodbye!

arri'vista, i, e *sm/f* go-getter

ar'rivo *sm* arrival; (*SPORT*) finish, finishing line

arro'gante *ag* arrogant

arro'lare *vb* = **arruolare**

arros'sire *vi* (*per vergogna, timidezza*) to blush, flush; (*per gioia, rabbia*) to flush

arros'tire *vt* to roast; (*pane*) to toast; (*ai ferri*) to grill

ar'rosto *sm, ag inv* roast

arro'tare *vt* to sharpen; (*investire con un veicolo*) to run over

arroto'lare *vt* to roll up

arroton'dare *vt* (*forma, oggetto*) to round; (*stipendio*) to add to; (*somma*) to round off

arrovel'larsi *vr:* **~ (il cervello)** to rack one's brains

arruf'fare *vt* to ruffle; (*fili*) to tangle; (*fig: questione*) to confuse

arruggi'nire [arruddʒi'nire] *vt* to rust; **~rsi** *vr* to rust; (*fig*) to become rusty

arruo'lare *vt* (*MIL*) to enlist; **~rsi** *vr* to enlist, join up

arse'nale *sm* (*MIL*) arsenal; (*cantiere navale*) dockyard

'arso, a *pp di* **ardere** ♦ *ag* (*bruciato*) burnt; (*arido*) dry; **ar'sura** *sf* (*calore opprimente*) burning heat; (*siccità*) drought

'arte *sf* art; (*abilità*) skill

arte'fatto, a *ag* (*cibo*) adulterated; (*fig: modi*) artificial

ar'tefice [ar'tefitʃe] *sm/f* craftsman/woman; (*autore*) author

ar'teria *sf* artery

'artico, a, ci, che *ag* Arctic

artico'lare *ag* (*ANAT*) of the joints, articular ♦ *vt* to articulate; (*suddividere*) to divide, split up; **articolazi'one** *sf* articulation; (*ANAT, TECN*) joint

ar'ticolo *sm* article; **~ di fondo** (*STAMPA*) leader, leading article

'Artide *sm:* **l'~** the Arctic

artifici'ale [artifi'tʃale] *ag* artificial

arti'ficio [arti'fitʃo] *sm* (*espediente*) trick, artifice; (*ricerca di effetto*) artificiality

artigia'nato [artidʒa'nato] *sm* craftsmanship; craftsmen *pl*

artigi'ano, a [arti'dʒano] *sm/f* craftsman/woman

artiglie'ria [artiʎʎe'ria] *sf* artillery

ar'tiglio [ar'tiʎʎo] *sm* claw; (*di rapaci*) talon

ar'tista, i, e *sm/f* artist; **ar'tistico, a, ci, che** *ag* artistic

'arto *sm* (*ANAT*) limb

ar'trite *sf* (*MED*) arthritis

ar'trosi *sf* osteoarthritis

ar'zillo, a [ar'dzillo] *ag* lively, sprightly

a'scella [aʃ'ʃella] *sf* (*ANAT*) armpit

ascen'dente [aʃʃen'dente] *sm* ancestor; (*fig*) ascendancy; (*ASTR*) ascendant

ascensi'one [aʃʃen'sjone] *sf* (*ALPINISMO*) ascent; (*REL*): **l'A~** the Ascension

ascen'sore [aʃʃen'sore] *sm* lift

a'scesa [aʃ'ʃesa] *sf* ascent; (*al trono*) accession

a'scesso [aʃ'ʃesso] *sm* (*MED*) abscess

'ascia ['aʃʃa] (*pl* **'asce**) *sf* axe

asciugaca'pelli [aʃʃugaka'pelli] *sm* hair-drier

asciuga'mano [aʃʃuga'mano] *sm* towel

asciu'gare [aʃʃu'gare] *vt* to dry; **~rsi** *vr* to dry *o.s.*; (*diventare asciutto*) to dry

asci'utto, a [aʃ'ʃutto] *ag* dry; (*fig: magro*) lean; (: *burbero*) curt; **restare a bocca ~a** (*fig*) to be disappointed

ascol'tare *vt* to listen to; **ascolta'tore, 'trice** *sm/f* listener; **as'colto** *sm:* **essere** *o* **stare in ascolto** to be listening; **dare** *o* **prestare ascolto (a)** to pay attention (to)

as'falto *sm* asphalt

asfissi'are *vt* to suffocate, asphyxiate; (*fig*) to bore to tears

'**Asia** *sf*: l'~ Asia; **asi'atico, a, ci, che** *ag, sm/f* Asiatic, Asian

a'**silo** *sm* refuge, sanctuary; ~ **(d'infanzia)** nursery(-school); ~ **nido** crèche; ~ **politico** political asylum

'**asino** *sm* donkey, ass

'**asma** *sf* asthma

'**asola** *sf* buttonhole

as'**parago, gi** *sm* asparagus *no pl*

aspet'**tare** *vt* to wait for; (*anche COMM*) to await; (*aspettarsi*) to expect ♦ *vi* to wait; ~**rsi** *vr* to expect; ~ **un bambino** to be expecting (a baby); **questo non me l'aspettavo** I wasn't expecting this; **aspetta'tiva** *sf* wait; expectation; **inferiore all'aspettativa** worse than expected; **essere in aspettativa** (*AMM*) to be on leave of absence

as'**petto** *sm* (*apparenza*) aspect, appearance, look; (*punto di vista*) point of view; **di bell'~** good-looking

aspi'**rante** *ag* (*attore etc*) aspiring ♦ *sm/f* candidate, applicant

aspira'**polvere** *sm inv* vacuum cleaner

aspi'**rare** *vt* (*respirare*) to breathe in, inhale; (*sog: apparecchi*) to suck (up) ♦ *vi*: ~ **a** to aspire to; **aspira'tore** *sm* extractor fan

aspi'**rina** *sf* aspirin

aspor'**tare** *vt* (*anche MED*) to remove, take away

'**aspro, a** *ag* (*sapore*) sour, tart; (*odore*) acrid, pungent; (*voce, clima, fig*) harsh; (*superficie*) rough; (*paesaggio*) rugged

assaggi'**are** [assad'dʒare] *vt* to taste

assag'**gini** [assad'dʒini] *smpl* (*CUC*) *selection of first courses*

as'**sai** *av* (*molto*) a lot, much; (*: con ag*) very; (*a sufficienza*) enough ♦ *ag inv* (*quantità*) a lot of, much; (*numero*) a lot of, many; ~ **contento** very pleased

assa'**lire** *vt* to attack, assail

as'**salto** *sm* attack, assault

assapo'**rare** *vt* to savour

assassi'**nare** *vt* to murder; to assassinate; (*fig*) to ruin; **assas'sinio** *sm* murder; assassination; **assas'sino, a** *ag* murderous ♦ *sm/f* murderer; assassin

'**asse** *sm* (*TECN*) axle; (*MAT*) axis ♦ *sf* board;

~ *sf* **da stiro** ironing board

assedi'**are** *vt* to besiege; **as'sedio** *sm* siege

asse'**gnare** [assɛɲ'ɲare] *vt* to assign, allot; (*premio*) to award

as'**segno** [as'seɲɲo] *sm* allowance; (*anche*: ~ *bancario*) cheque (*BRIT*), check (*US*); **contro** ~ cash on delivery; ~ **circolare** bank draft; ~ **sbarrato** crossed cheque; ~ **di viaggio** traveller's cheque; ~ **a vuoto** dud cheque; ~**i familiari** ≈ child benefit *no pl*

assem'**blea** *sf* assembly

assen'**nato, a** *ag* sensible

as'**senso** *sm* assent, consent

as'**sente** *ag* absent; (*fig*) faraway, vacant; **as'senza** *sf* absence

asses'**sore** *sm* (*POL*) councillor

asses'**tare** *vt* (*mettere in ordine*) to put in order, arrange; ~**rsi** *vr* to settle in; ~ **un colpo a qn** to deal sb a blow

asse'**tato, a** *ag* thirsty, parched

as'**setto** *sm* order, arrangement; (*NAUT, AER*) trim; **in** ~ **di guerra** on a war footing

assicu'**rare** *vt* (*accertare*) to ensure; (*infondere certezza*) to assure; (*fermare, legare*) to make fast, secure; (*fare un contratto di assicurazione*) to insure; ~**rsi** *vr* (*accertarsi*): ~**rsi (di)** to make sure (of); (*contro il furto etc*): ~**rsi (contro)** to insure o.s. (against); **assicu'rata** *sf* (*anche*: *lettera assicurata*) registered letter; **assicu'rato, a** *ag* insured; **assicurazi'one** *sf* assurance; insurance

assidera'**mento** *sm* exposure

as'**siduo, a** *ag* (*costante*) assiduous; (*frequentatore etc*) regular

assi'**eme** *av* (*insieme*) together; ~ **a** (together) with

assil'**lare** *vt* to pester, torment

as'**sillo** *sm* (*fig*) worrying thought

as'**sise** *sfpl* (*DIR*) assizes; **Corte** *sf* **d'A~** Court of Assizes, ≈ Crown Court (*BRIT*)

assis'**tente** *sm/f* assistant; ~ **sociale** social worker; ~ **di volo** (*AER*) steward/ stewardess

assis'**tenza** [assis'tɛntsa] *sf* assistance; ~ **ospedaliera** free hospital treatment; ~

sanitaria health service; **~ sociale** welfare services *pl*

as'sistere *vt* (*aiutare*) to assist, help; (*curare*) to treat ♦ *vi*: **~ (a qc)** (*essere presente*) to be present (at sth), to attend (sth)

'asso *sm* ace; **piantare qn in ~** to leave sb in the lurch

associ'are [asso't∫are] *vt* to associate; (*rendere partecipe*): **~ qn a** (*affari*) to take sb into partnership in; (*partito*) to make sb a member of; **~rsi** *vr* to enter into partnership; **~rsi a** to become a member of, join; (*dolori, gioie*) to share in; **~ qn alle carceri** to take sb to prison

associazi'one [assot∫at'tsjone] *sf* association; (*COMM*) association, society; **~ a delinquere** (*DIR*) criminal association

asso'dato, a *ag* well-founded

assogget'tare [assoddʒet'tare] *vt* to subject, subjugate

asso'lato, a *ag* sunny

assol'dare *vt* to recruit

as'solto, a *pp di* **assolvere**

assoluta'mente *av* absolutely

asso'luto, a *ag* absolute

assoluzi'one [assolut'tsjone] *sf* (*DIR*) acquittal; (*REL*) absolution

as'solvere *vt* (*DIR*) to acquit; (*REL*) to absolve; (*adempiere*) to carry out, perform

assomigli'are [assomiʎ'ʎare] *vi*: **~ a** to resemble, look like

asson'nato, a *ag* sleepy

asso'pirsi *vr* to doze off

assor'bente *ag* absorbent ♦ *sm*: **~ igienico** sanitary towel; **~ interno** tampon

assor'bire *vt* to absorb; (*fig: far proprio*) to assimilate

assor'dare *vt* to deafen

assorti'mento *sm* assortment

assor'tito, a *ag* assorted; matched, matching

as'sorto, a *ag* absorbed, engrossed

assottigli'are [assotti ʎ'ʎare] *vt* to make thin, to thin; (*aguzzare*) to sharpen; (*ridurre*) to reduce; **~rsi** *vr* to grow thin; (*fig: ridursi*) to be reduced

assue'fare *vt* to accustom; **~rsi a** to get used to, accustom o.s. to

as'sumere *vt* (*impiegato*) to take on, engage; (*responsabilità*) to assume, take upon o.s.; (*contegno, espressione*) to assume, put on; (*droga*) to consume; **as'sunto, a** *pp di* **assumere** ♦ *sm* (*tesi*) proposition

assurdità *sf inv* absurdity; **dire delle ~** to talk nonsense

as'surdo, a *ag* absurd

'asta *sf* pole; (*modo di vendita*) auction

astante'ria *sf* casualty department

as'temio, a *ag* teetotal ♦ *sm/f* teetotaller

aste'nersi *vr*: **~ (da)** to abstain (from), refrain (from); (*POL*) to abstain (from)

aste'risco, schi *sm* asterisk

'astice ['astit∫e] *sm* lobster

asti'nenza [asti'nɛntsa] *sf* abstinence; **essere in crisi di ~** to suffer from withdrawal symptoms

'astio *sm* rancour, resentment

as'tratto, a *ag* abstract

'astro *sm* star

'astro... *prefisso*: **astrolo'gia** [astrolo'dʒia] *sf* astrology; **as'trologo, a, ghi, ghe** *sm/f* astrologer; **astro'nauta, i, e** *sm/f* astronaut; **astro'nave** *sf* space ship; **astrono'mia** *sf* astronomy; **astro'nomico, a, ci, che** *ag* astronomic(al)

as'tuccio [as'tuttʃo] *sm* case, box, holder

as'tuto, a *ag* astute, cunning, shrewd; **as'tuzia** *sf* astuteness, shrewdness; (*azione*) trick

A'tene *sf* Athens

ate'neo *sm* university

'ateo, a *ag*, *sm/f* atheist

at'lante *sm* atlas

at'lantico, a, ci, che *ag* Atlantic ♦ *sm*: **l'A~, l'Oceano A~** the Atlantic, the Atlantic Ocean

at'leta, i, e *sm/f* athlete; **at'letica** *sf* athletics *sg*; **atletica leggera** track and field events *pl*; **atletica pesante** weightlifting and wrestling

atmos'fera *sf* atmosphere

a'tomico, a, ci, che *ag* atomic; (*nucleare*) atomic, atom *cpd*, nuclear

'atomo *sm* atom

'atrio *sm* entrance hall, lobby

a'troce [a'trotʃe] *ag* (*che provoca orrore*) dreadful; (*terribile*) atrocious

attacca'mento *sm* (*fig*) attachment, affection

attacca'panni *sm* hook, peg; (*mobile*) hall stand

attac'care *vt* (*unire*) to attach; (*cucendo*) to sew on; (*far aderire*) to stick (on); (*appendere*) to hang (up); (*assalire: anche fig*) to attack; (*iniziare*) to begin, start; (*fig: contagiare*) to pass on ♦ *vi* to stick, adhere; ~rsi *vr* to stick, adhere; (*trasmettersi per contagio*) to be contagious; (*afferrarsi*): ~rsi (a) to cling (to); (*fig: affezionarsi*): ~rsi (a) to become attached (to); ~ discorso to start a conversation; at'tacco, chi *sm* (*azione offensiva: anche fig*) attack; (*MED*) attack, fit; (*SCI*) binding; (*ELETTR*) socket

atteggia'mento [atteddʒa'mento] *sm* attitude

atteggi'arsi [atted'dʒarsi] *vr*: ~ a to pose as

attem'pato, a *ag* elderly

at'tendere *vt* to wait for, await ♦ *vi*: ~ a to attend to

atten'dibile *ag* (*storia*) credible; (*testimone*) reliable

atte'nersi *vr*: ~ a to keep *o* stick to

atten'tare *vi*: ~ a to make an attempt on; atten'tato *sm* attack; attentato alla vita di qn attempt on sb's life

at'tento, a *ag* attentive; (*accurato*) careful, thorough; stare ~ a qc to pay attention to sth ♦ *escl* be careful!

attenu'ante *sf* (*DIR*) extenuating circumstance

attenu'are *vt* to attenuate; (*dolore, rumore*) to lessen, deaden; (*pena, tasse*) to alleviate; ~rsi *vr* to ease, abate

attenzi'one [atten'tsjone] *sf* attention ♦ *escl* watch out!, be careful!

atter'raggio [atter'raddʒo] *sm* landing

atter'rare *vt* to bring down ♦ *vi* to land

atter'rire *vt* to terrify

at'tesa *sf* waiting; (*tempo trascorso aspettando*) wait; essere in attesa di qc to be waiting for sth

at'teso, a *pp di* attendere

attes'tato *sm* certificate

'attico, ci *sm* attic

at'tiguo, a *ag* adjacent, adjoining

attil'lato, a *ag* (*vestito*) close-fitting, tight; (*persona*) dressed up

'attimo *sm* moment; in un ~ in a moment

atti'nente *ag*: ~ a relating to, concerning

atti'rare *vt* to attract

atti'tudine *sf* (*disposizione*) aptitude; (*atteggiamento*) attitude

atti'vare *vt* to activate; (*far funzionare*) to set going, start

attività *sf inv* activity; (*COMM*) assets *pl*

at'tivo, a *ag* active; (*COMM*) profit-making, credit *cpd* ♦ *sm* (*COMM*) assets *pl*; in ~ in credit

attiz'zare [attit'tsare] *vt* (*fuoco*) to poke

'atto *sm* act; (*azione, gesto*) action, act, deed; (*DIR: documento*) deed, document; ~i *smpl* (*di congressi ecc*) proceedings; mettere in ~ to put into action; fare ~ di fare qc to make as if to do sth

at'tonito, a *ag* dumbfounded, astonished

attorcigli'are [attortʃiʎ'ʎare] *vt* to twist; ~rsi *vr* to twist

at'tore, 'trice *sm/f* actor/actress

at'torno *av* round, around, about; ~ a round, around, about

at'tracco, chi *sm* (*NAUT*) docking *no pl*; berth

attra'ente *ag* attractive

at'trarre *vt* to attract; attrat'tiva *sf* (*fig: fascino*) attraction, charm; at'tratto, a *pp di* attrarre

attraversa'mento *sm*: ~ pedonale pedestrian crossing

attraver'sare *vt* to cross; (*città, bosco, fig: periodo*) to go through; (*sog: fiume*) to run through

attra'verso *prep* through; (*da una parte all'altra*) across

attrazi'one [attrat'tsjone] *sf* attraction

attrez'zare [attret'tsare] *vt* to equip; (*NAUT*) to rig; attrezza'tura *sf* equipment *no pl*; rigging; at'trezzo *sm* tool, instrument; (*SPORT*) piece of equipment

attribu'ire *vt*: ~ qc a qn (*assegnare*) to

give *o* award sth to sb; (*quadro etc*) to attribute sth to sb; **attri'buto**sm attribute

at'trice [at'tritʃe] *sf vedi* **attore**

at'tritosm (*anche fig*) friction

attu'aleag (*presente*) present; (*di attualità*) topical; (*che è in atto*) actual; **attualità**sf inv topicality; (*avvenimento*) current event; **attual'mente**av at the moment, at present

attu'arevt to carry out; ~**rsi** vr to be realized

attu'tirevt to deaden, reduce

au'dace [au'datʃe] ag audacious, daring, bold; (*provocante*) provocative; (*sfacciato*) impudent, bold; **au'dacia**sf audacity, daring; boldness; provocativeness; impudence

audiovi'sivo, aag audiovisual

audizi'one [audit'tsjone] *sf* hearing; (*MUS*) audition

'auge ['audʒe] *sf*: **in** ~ popular

augu'rarevt to wish; ~**rsi qc** to hope for sth

au'guriosm (*presagio*) omen; (*voto di benessere etc*) (good) wish; **essere di buon/cattivo** ~ to be of good omen/be ominous; **fare gli ~i a qn** to give sb one's best wishes; **tanti ~i!** all the best!

'aula *sf* (*scolastica*) classroom; (*universitaria*) lecture theatre; (*di edificio pubblico*) hall

aumen'tarevt, vi to increase; **au'mento** sm increase

au'reolasf halo

au'rora *sf* dawn

ausili'areag, sm, sm/f auxiliary

aus'picio [aus'pitʃo] sm omen; (*protezione*) patronage; **sotto gli ~i di** under the auspices of

aus'tero, aag austere

Aus'tralia *sf*: **l'~** Australia; **australi'ano, a** ag, sm/f Australian

'Austria *sf*: **l'~** Austria; **aus'triaco, a, ci, che** ag, sm/f Austrian

au'tentico, a, ci, che ag (*quadro, firma*) authentic, genuine; (*fatto*) true, genuine

au'tista, i sm driver

'autosf inv car

autoade'sivo, aag self-adhesive ♦ sm sticker

autobiogra'fiasf autobiography

auto'bottesf tanker

'autobussm inv bus

auto'carrosm lorry (*BRIT*), truck

autocorri'erasf coach, bus

au'tografo, aag, sm autograph

auto'lineasf bus company

au'toma, ism automaton

auto'matico, a, ci, cheag automatic ♦ sm (*bottone*) snap fastener; (*fucile*) automatic

automazi'one [automat'tsjone] *sf* automation

auto'mezzo [auto'mɛddzo] *sm* motor vehicle

auto'mobilesf (motor) car

autono'miasf autonomy; (*di volo*) range

au'tonomo, aag autonomous, independent

autop'siasf post-mortem (examination), autopsy

auto'radio *sf inv* (*apparecchio*) car radio; (*autoveicolo*) radio car

au'tore, 'tricesm/f author

auto'revoleag authoritative; (*persona*) influential

autori'messa *sf* garage

autorità *sf inv* authority

autoriz'zare [autorid'dzare] *vt* (*permettere*) to authorize; (*giustificare*) to allow, sanction; **autorizzazi'one**sf authorization

autoscu'olasf driving school

autos'topsm hitchhiking; **autostop'pista, i, e**sm/f hitchhiker

autos'tradasf motorway (*BRIT*), highway (*US*)

auto'treno sm articulated lorry (*BRIT*), semi (trailer) (*US*)

autove'icolosm motor vehicle

autovet'turasf (motor) car

au'tunnosm autumn

avam'braccio [avam'brattʃo] (*pl* (*f*) **-cia**) sm forearm

avangu'ardiasf vanguard

a'vantiav (*stato in luogo*) in front; (*moto:*

andare, venire) forward; (*tempo: prima*) before ♦ *prep* (*luogo*): ~ **a** before, in front of; (*tempo*): ~ **Cristo** before Christ ♦ *escl* (*entrate*) come (*o* go) in!; (*MIL*) forward!; (*coraggio*) come on! ♦ *sm inv* (*SPORT*) forward; ~ **e indietro** backwards and forwards; **andare** ~ to go forward; (*continuare*) to go on; (*precedere*) to go (on) ahead; (*orologio*) to be fast; **essere** ~ **negli studi** to be well advanced with one's studies

avanza'mento [avantsa'mento] *sm* progress; promotion

avan'zare [avan'tsare] *vt* (*spostare in avanti*) to move forward, advance; (*domanda*) to put forward; (*promuovere*) to promote; (*essere creditore*): ~ **qc da qn** to be owed sth by sb ♦ *vi* (*andare avanti*) to move forward, advance; (*fig: progredire*) to make progress; (*essere d'avanzo*) to be left, remain; **avan'zata** *sf* (*MIL*) advance; **a'vanzo** *sm* (*residuo*) remains *pl*, left-overs *pl*; (*MAT*) remainder; (*COMM*) surplus; **averne d'avanzo di qc** to have more than enough of sth; **avanzo di galera** (*fig*) jailbird

ava'ria *sf* (*guasto*) damage; (*: meccanico*) breakdown

a'varo, a *ag* avaricious, miserly ♦ *sm* miser

a'vena *sf* oats *pl*

PAROLA CHIAVE

a'vere *sm* (*COMM*) credit; **gli ~i** (*ricchezze*) wealth *sg*

♦ *vt* **1** (*possedere*) to have; **ha due bambini/una bella casa** she has (got) two children/a lovely house; **ha i capelli lunghi** he has (got) long hair; **non ho da mangiare/bere** I've (got) nothing to eat/ drink, I don't have anything to eat/drink

2 (*indossare*) to wear, have on; **aveva una maglietta rossa** he was wearing *o* he had on a red tee-shirt; **ha gli occhiali** he wears *o* has glasses

3 (*ricevere*) to get; **hai avuto l'assegno?** did you get *o* have you had the cheque?

4 (*età, dimensione*) to be; **ha 9 anni** he is 9 (years old); **la stanza ha 3 metri di**

lunghezza the room is 3 metres in length; *vedi* **fame; paura** *etc*

5 (*tempo*): **quanti ne abbiamo oggi?** what's the date today?; **ne hai per molto?** will you be long?

6 (*fraseologia*): **avercela con qn** to be angry with sb; **cos'hai?** what's wrong *o* what's the matter (with you)?; **non ha niente a che vedere** *o* **fare con me** it's got nothing to do with me

♦ *vb aus* **1** to have; **aver bevuto/ mangiato** to have drunk/eaten

2 (*+da +infinito*): ~ **da fare qc** to have to do sth; **non hai che da chiederlo** you only have to ask him

---

'avi *smpl* ancestors, forefathers

aviazi'one [avjat'tsjone] *sf* aviation; (*MIL*) air force

avidità *sf* eagerness; greed

'avido, a *ag* eager; (*peg*) greedy

avo'cado *sm* avocado

a'vorio *sm* ivory

Avv. *abbr* = **avvocato**

avvalla'mento *sm* sinking *no pl*; (*effetto*) depression

avvalo'rare *vt* to confirm

avvam'pare *vi* (*incendio*) to flare up

avvantaggi'are [avvantad'dʒare] *vt* to favour; ~**rsi** *vr*: ~**rsi negli affari/sui concorrenti** to get ahead in business/of one's competitors

avvele'nare *vt* to poison

avve'nente *ag* attractive, charming

avveni'mento *sm* event

avve'nire *vi, vb impers* to happen, occur ♦ *sm* future

avven'tarsi *vr*: ~ **su** *o* **contro qn/qc** to hurl o.s. *o* rush at sb/sth

avven'tato, a *ag* rash, reckless

avven'tizio, a [avven'tittsjo] *ag* (*impiegato*) temporary; (*guadagno*) casual

av'vento *sm* advent, coming; (*REL*) **l'A~** Advent

avven'tore *sm* (regular) customer

avven'tura *sf* adventure; (*amorosa*) affair

avventu'rarsi *vr* to venture

avventu'roso, a *ag* adventurous

avve'rarsi *vr* to come true

av'verbio *sm* adverb

avver'sario, a *ag* opposing ♦ *sm* opponent, adversary

av'verso, a *ag* (*contrario*) contrary; (*sfavorevole*) unfavourable

avver'tenza [avver'tɛntsa] *sf* (*ammonimento*) warning; (*cautela*) care; (*premessa*) foreword; **~e** *sfpl* (*istruzioni per l'uso*) instructions

avverti'mento *sm* warning

avver'tire *vt* (*avvisare*) to warn; (*rendere consapevole*) to inform, notify; (*percepire*) to feel

av'vezzo, a [av'vettso] *ag*: **~ a** used to

avvia'mento *sm* (*atto*) starting; (*effetto*) start; (*AUT*) starting; (*: dispositivo*) starter; (*COMM*) goodwill

avvi'are *vt* (*mettere sul cammino*) to direct; (*impresa, trattativa*) to begin, start; (*motore*) to start; **~rsi** *vr* to set off, set out

avvicen'darsi [avvitʃen'darsi] *vr* to alternate

avvici'nare [avvitʃi'nare] *vt* to bring near; (*trattare con: persona*) to approach; **~rsi** *vr*: **~rsi (a qn/qc)** to approach (sb/ sth), draw near (to sb/sth)

avvi'lire *vt* (*umiliare*) to humiliate; (*degradare*) to disgrace; (*scoraggiare*) to dishearten, discourage; **~rsi** *vr* (*abbattersi*) to lose heart

avvilup'pare *vt* (*avvolgere*) to wrap up; (*ingarbugliare*) to entangle

avvinaz'zato, a [avvinat'tsato] *ag* drunk

av'vincere [av'vintʃere] *vt* to charm, enthral; **avvin'cente** *ag* captivating

avvinghi'are [avvin'gjare] *vt* to clasp; **~rsi** *vr*: **~rsi a** to cling to

avvi'sare *vt* (*far sapere*) to inform; (*mettere in guardia*) to warn; **av'viso** *sm* warning; (*annuncio*) announcement; (*: affisso*) notice; (*inserzione pubblicitaria*) advertisement; **a mio avviso** in my opinion

avvis'tare *vt* to sight

avvi'tare *vt* to screw down (*o* in)

avviz'zire [avvit'tsire] *vi* to wither

avvo'cato, 'essa *sm/f* (*DIR*) barrister (*BRIT*), lawyer; (*fig*) defender, advocate

av'volgere [av'voldʒere] *vt* to roll up; (*avviluppare*) to wrap up; **~rsi** *vr* (*avvilupparsi*) to wrap o.s. up;

avvol'gibile *sm* roller blind (*BRIT*), blind

avvol'toio *sm* vulture

azi'enda [ad'dzjɛnda] *sf* business, firm, concern; **~ agricola** farm

azio'nare [attsjo'nare] *vt* to activate

azi'one [at'tsjone] *sf* action; (*COMM*) share; **azio'nista, i, e** *sm/f* (*COMM*) shareholder

a'zoto [ad'dzɔto] *sm* nitrogen

azzan'nare [attsan'nare] *vt* to sink one's teeth into

azzar'darsi [addzar'darsi] *vr*: **~ a fare** to dare (to) do; **azzar'dato, a** *ag* (*impresa*) risky; (*risposta*) rash

az'zardo [ad'dzardo] *sm* risk

azzec'care [attsek'kare] *vt* (*risposta etc*) to get right

azzuf'farsi [attsuf'farsi] *vr* to come to blows

az'zurro, a [ad'dzurro] *ag* blue ♦ *sm* (*colore*) blue; **gli ~i** (*SPORT*) the Italian national team

B

bab'beo *sm* simpleton

'babbo *sm* (*fam*) dad, daddy; **B~ natale** Father Christmas

bab'buccia, ce [bab'buttʃa] *sf* slipper; (*per neonati*) bootee

ba'bordo *sm* (*NAUT*) port side

ba'cato, a *ag* worm-eaten, rotten

'bacca, che *sf* berry

baccalà *sm* dried salted cod; (*fig: peg*) dummy

bac'cano *sm* din, clamour

bac'cello [bat'tʃɛllo] *sm* pod

bac'chetta [bak'ketta] *sf* (*verga*) stick, rod; (*di direttore d'orchestra*) baton; (*di tamburo*) drumstick; **~ magica** magic wand

baci'are [ba'tʃare] *vt* to kiss; **~rsi** *vr* to kiss (one another)

baci'nella [batʃi'nɛlla] *sf* basin

ba'cino [ba'tʃino] *sm* basin; (*MINERALOGIA*)

field, bed; (*ANAT*) pelvis; (*NAUT*) dock

'bacio ['batʃo] *sm* kiss

'baco, chi *sm* worm; ~ da seta silkworm

ba'dare *vi* (*fare attenzione*) to take care, be careful; (*occuparsi di*): ~ a to look after, take care of; (*dar ascolto*): ~ a to pay attention to; **bada ai fatti tuoi!** mind your own business!

ba'dia *sf* abbey

ba'dile *sm* shovel

'baffi *smpl* moustache *sg*; (*di animale*) whiskers; **ridere sotto i** ~ to laugh up one's sleeve; **leccarsi i** ~ to lick one's lips

ba'gagli [ba'gaʎʎi] *smpl* luggage *sg*

bagagli'aio [bagaʎ'ʎajo] *sm* luggage van (*BRIT*) *o* car (*US*); (*AUT*) boot (*BRIT*), trunk (*US*)

bagli'ore [baʎ'ʎore] *sm* flash, dazzling light; **un** ~ **di speranza** a ray of hope

ba'gnante [baɲ'ɲante] *sm/f* bather

ba'gnare [baɲ'ɲare] *vt* to wet; (*inzuppare*) to soak; (*innaffiare*) to water; (*sog: fiume*) to flow through; (*: mare*) to wash, bathe; ~**rsi** *vr* (*al mare*) to go swimming *o* bathing; (*in vasca*) to have a bath

ba'gnato, a [baɲ'ɲato] *ag* wet

ba'gnino [baɲ'ɲino] *sm* lifeguard

'bagno ['baɲɲo] *sm* bath; (*locale*) bathroom; ~**i** *smpl* (*stabilimento*) baths; **fare il** ~ to have a bath; (*nel mare*) to go swimming *o* bathing; **fare il** ~ **a qn** to give sb a bath; **mettere a** ~ to soak; ~ **schiuma** bubble bath

bagnoma'ria [baɲɲoma'ria] *sm*: **cuocere a** ~ to cook in a double saucepan

'baia *sf* bay

baio'netta *sf* bayonet

balbet'tare *vi* to stutter, stammer; (*bimbo*) to babble ♦ *vt* to stammer out

balbuzi'ente [balbut'tsjɛnte] *ag* stuttering, stammering

bal'cone *sm* balcony

baldac'chino [baldak'kino] *sm* canopy

bal'danza [bal'dantsa] *sf* self-confidence, boldness

'baldo, a *ag* bold, daring

bal'doria *sf*: **fare** ~ to have a riotous

time

ba'lena *sf* whale

bale'nare *vb impers*: **balena** there's lightning ♦ *vi* to flash; **mi balenò un'idea** an idea flashed through my mind; **ba'leno** *sm* flash of lightning; **in un baleno** in a flash

ba'lestra *sf* crossbow

ba'lia *sf*: **in** ~ **di** at the mercy of

'balla *sf* (*di merci*) bale; (*fandonia*) (tall) story

bal'lare *vt, vi* to dance; **bal'lata** *sf* ballad

balle'rina *sf* dancer; ballet dancer; (*scarpa*) ballet shoe

balle'rino *sm* dancer; ballet dancer

bal'letto *sm* ballet

'ballo *sm* dance; (*azione*) dancing *no pl*; **essere in** ~ (*fig: persona*) to be involved; (*: cosa*) to be at stake

ballot'taggio [ballot'taddʒo] *sm* (*POL*) second ballot

balne'are *ag* seaside *cpd*; (*stagione*) bathing

ba'locco, chi *sm* toy

ba'lordo, a *ag* stupid, senseless

'balsamo *sm* (*aroma*) balsam; (*lenimento, fig*) balm

balu'ardo *sm* bulwark

'balza ['baltsa] *sf* (*dirupo*) crag; (*di stoffa*) frill

bal'zare [bal'tsare] *vi* to bounce; (*lanciarsi*) to jump, leap; **'balzo** *sm* bounce; jump, leap; (*del terreno*) crag

bam'bagia [bam'badʒa] *sf* (*ovatta*) cotton wool (*BRIT*), absorbent cotton (*US*); (*cascame*) cotton waste

bam'bina *ag, sf vedi* **bambino**

bambi'naia *sf* nanny, nurse(maid)

bam'bino, a *sm/f* child

bam'boccio [bam'bottʃo] *sm* plump child; (*pupazzo*) rag doll

'bambola *sf* doll

bambù *sm* bamboo

ba'nale *ag* banal, commonplace

ba'nana *sf* banana; **ba'nano** *sm* banana tree

'banca, che *sf* bank; ~ **dei dati** data bank

banca'rella *sf* stall

ban'cario, a *ag* banking, bank *cpd* ♦ *sm* bank clerk

banca'rotta *sf* bankruptcy; **fare ~** to go bankrupt

ban'chetto [ban'ketto] *sm* banquet

banchi'ere [ban'kjɛre] *sm* banker

ban'china [ban'kina] *sf* (*di porto*) quay; (*per pedoni, ciclisti*) path; (*di stazione*) platform; **~ cedevole** (*AUT*) soft verge (*BRIT*) o shoulder (*US*)

'banco, chi *sm* bench; (*di negozio*) counter; (*di mercato*) stall; (*di officina*) (work-)bench; (*GEO, banca*) bank; **~ di corallo** coral reef; **~ degli imputati** dock; **~ dei pegni** pawnshop; **~ di nebbia** bank of fog; **~ di prova** (*fig*) testing ground; **~ dei testimoni** witness box

'Bancomat ® *sm inv* automated banking; (*tessera*) cash card

banco'nota *sf* banknote

'banda *sf* band; (*di stoffa*) band, stripe; (*lato, parte*) side; **~ perforata** punch tape

banderu'ola *sf* (*METEOR*) weathercock, weathervane

bandi'era *sf* flag, banner

ban'dire *vt* to proclaim; (*esiliare*) to exile; (*fig*) to dispense with

ban'dito *sm* outlaw, bandit

bandi'tore *sm* (*di aste*) auctioneer

'bando *sm* proclamation; (*esilio*) exile, banishment; **~ alle chiacchiere!** that's enough talk!

ban'dolo *sm*: **il ~ della matassa** (*fig*) the key to the problem

bar *sm inv* bar

'bara *sf* coffin

ba'racca, che *sf* shed, hut; (*peg*) hovel; **mandare avanti la ~** to keep things going

bara'onda *sf* hubbub, bustle

ba'rare *vi* to cheat

'baratro *sm* abyss

barat'tare *vt*: **~ qc con** to barter sth for, swap sth for; **ba'ratto** *sm* barter

ba'rattolo *sm* (*di latta*) tin; (*di vetro*) jar; (*di coccio*) pot

'barba *sf* beard; **farsi la ~** to shave; **farla in ~ a qn** (*fig*) to do sth to sb's face; **che ~!** what a bore!

barbabi'etola *sf* beetroot (*BRIT*), beet (*US*); **~ da zucchero** sugar beet

bar'barico, a, ci, che *ag* barbarian; barbaric

'barbaro, a *ag* barbarous; **~i** *smpl* barbarians

barbi'ere *sm* barber

bar'bone *sm* (*cane*) poodle; (*vagabondo*) tramp

bar'buto, a *ag* bearded

'barca, che *sf* boat; **~ a remi** rowing boat; **~ a vela** sail(ing) boat; **barcai'olo** *sm* boatman

barcol'lare *vi* to stagger

bar'cone *sm* (*per ponti di barche*) pontoon

ba'rella *sf* (*lettiga*) stretcher

ba'rile *sm* barrel, cask

ba'rista, i, e *sm/f* barman/maid; bar owner

ba'ritono *sm* baritone

bar'lume *sm* glimmer, gleam

ba'rocco, a, chi, che *ag, sm* baroque

ba'rometro *sm* barometer

ba'rone *sm* baron; **baro'nessa** *sf* baroness

'barra *sf* bar; (*NAUT*) helm; (*linea grafica*) line, stroke

barri'care *vt* to barricade; **barri'cata** *sf* barricade

barri'era *sf* barrier; (*GEO*) reef

ba'ruffa *sf* scuffle

barzel'letta [bardzel'letta] *sf* joke, funny story

ba'sare *vt* to base, found; **~rsi** *vr*: **~rsi su** (*sog: fatti, prove*) to be based o founded on; (: *persona*) to base one's arguments on

'basco, a, schi, sche *ag* Basque ♦ *sm* (*copricapo*) beret

'base *sf* base; (*fig: fondamento*) basis; (*POL*) rank and file; **di ~** basic; **in ~ a** on the basis of, according to; **a ~ di caffè** coffee-based

ba'setta *sf* sideburn

ba'silica, che *sf* basilica

ba'silico *sm* basil

bassi'fondi *smpl* (*fig*) dregs; **i ~ (della città)** the slums

'basso, a *ag* low; (*di statura*) short;

(*meridionale*) southern ♦ *sm* bottom, lower part; (*MUS*) bass; **la ~a Italia** southern Italy

bassorili'evo *sm* bas-relief

'basta *escl* (that's) enough!, that will do!

bas'tardo, a *ag* (*animale, pianta*) hybrid, crossbreed; (*persona*) illegitimate, bastard (*peg*) ♦ *sm/f* illegitimate child, bastard (*peg*)

bas'tare *vi, vb impers* to be enough, be sufficient; **~ a qn** to be enough for sb; **basta chiedere** *o* **che chieda a un vigile** you have only to *o* need only ask a policeman

basti'mento *sm* ship, vessel

basto'nare *vt* to beat, thrash

baston'cino [baston't∫ino] *sm* (*SCI*) ski pole

bas'tone *sm* stick; **~ da passeggio** walking stick

bat'taglia [bat'taʎʎa] *sf* battle; fight

bat'taglio [bat'taʎʎo] *sm* (*di campana*) clapper; (*di porta*) knocker

battagli'one [battaʎ'ʎone] *sm* battalion

bat'tello *sm* boat

bat'tente *sm* (*imposta: di porta*) wing, flap; (*: di finestra*) shutter; (*batacchio: di porta*) knocker; (*: di orologio*) hammer; **chiudere i ~i** (*fig*) to shut up shop

'battere *vt* to beat; (*grano*) to thresh; (*percorrere*) to scour ♦ *vi* (*bussare*) to knock; (*urtare*): **~ contro** to hit *o* strike against; (*pioggia, sole*) to beat down; (*cuore*) to beat; (*TENNIS*) to serve; **~rsi** *vr* to fight; **~ le mani** to clap; **~ i piedi** to stamp one's feet; **~ su un argomento** to hammer home an argument; **~ a macchina** to type; **~ bandiera italiana** to fly the Italian flag; **~ in testa** (*AUT*) to knock; **in un batter d'occhio** in the twinkling of an eye

bat'teri *smpl* bacteria

batte'ria *sf* battery; (*MUS*) drums *pl*

bat'tesimo *sm* baptism; christening

battez'zare [batted'dzare] *vt* to baptize; to christen

batticu'ore *sm* palpitations *pl*

batti'mano *sm* applause

batti'panni *sm inv* carpet-beater

battis'tero *sm* baptistry

battis'trada *sm inv* (*di pneumatico*) tread; (*di gara*) pacemaker

battitap'peto *sm* vacuum cleaner

'battito *sm* beat, throb; **~ cardiaco** heartbeat; **~ della pioggia/dell'orologio** beating of the rain/ticking of the clock

bat'tuta *sf* blow; (*di macchina da scrivere*) stroke; (*MUS*) bar; beat; (*TEATRO*) cue; (*frase spiritosa*) witty remark; (*di caccia*) beating; (*POLIZIA*) combing, scouring; (*TENNIS*) service

ba'ule *sm* trunk; (*AUT*) boot (*BRIT*), trunk (*US*)

'bava *sf* (*di animale*) slaver, slobber; (*di lumaca*) slime; (*di vento*) breath

bava'glino [bavaʎ'ʎino] *sm* bib

ba'vaglio [ba'vaʎʎo] *sm* gag

'bavero *sm* collar

ba'zar [bad'dzar] *sm inv* bazaar

baz'zecola [bad'dzekola] *sf* trifle

bazzi'care [battsi'kare] *vt* to frequent ♦ *vi*: **~ in/con** to frequent

be'ato, a *ag* blessed; (*fig*) happy; **~ te!** lucky you!

bec'caccia, ce [bek'katt∫a] *sf* woodcock

bec'care *vt* to peck; (*fig: raffreddore*) to pick up, catch; **~rsi** *vr* (*fig*) to squabble

beccheggi'are [bekked'dʒare] *vi* to pitch

bec'chino [bek'kino] *sm* gravedigger

'becco, chi *sm* beak, bill; (*di caffettiera etc*) spout; lip

Be'fana *sf* old woman who, according to legend, brings children their presents at the Epiphany; (*Epifania*) Epiphany; (*donna brutta*): **b~** hag, witch

'beffa *sf* practical joke; **farsi ~e di qn** to make a fool of sb; **bef'fardo, a** *ag* scornful, mocking; **bef'fare** *vt* (*anche*: *beffarsi di*) to make a fool of, mock

'bega, ghe *sf* quarrel

'begli ['beʎʎi] *ag vedi* **bello**

'bei *ag vedi* **bello**

bel *ag vedi* **bello**

be'lare *vi* to bleat

'belga, gi, ghe *ag, sm/f* Belgian

'Belgio ['bɛldʒo] *sm*: **il ~** Belgium

bel'lezza [bel'lettsa] *sf* beauty

'bella *sf* (*SPORT*) decider; *vedi anche* **bello**

'**bello, a** (*ag: dav sm* **bel** +*C*, **bell'** +*V*, **bello** +*s impura, gn, pn, ps, x, z, pl* **bei** +*C*, **begli** +*s impura etc o V*) *ag* **1** (*oggetto, donna, paesaggio*) beautiful, lovely; (*uomo*) handsome; (*tempo*) beautiful, fine, lovely; **le belle arti** fine arts

2 (*quantità*): **una ~a cifra** a considerable sum of money; **un bel niente** absolutely nothing

3 (*rafforzativo*): **è una truffa ~a e buona!** it's a real fraud!; **è bell'e finito** it's already finished

♦ *sm* **1** (*bellezza*) beauty; (*tempo*) fine weather

2: adesso viene il ~ now comes the best bit; **sul più ~** at the crucial point; **cosa fai di ~?** are you doing anything interesting?

♦ *av*: **fa ~** the weather is fine, it's fine

'**belva** *sf* wild animal
belve'dere *sm inv* panoramic viewpoint
benché [ben'ke] *cong* although
'**benda** *sf* bandage; (*per gli occhi*) blindfold; **ben'dare** *vt* to bandage; to blindfold
'**bene** *av* well; (*completamente, affatto*): **è ben difficile** it's very difficult ♦ *ag inv*: **gente ~** well-to-do people ♦ *sm* good; **~i** *smpl* (*averi*) property *sg*, estate *sg*; **io sto ~/poco ~** I'm well/not very well; **va ~** all right; **volere un ~ dell'anima a qn** to love sb very much; **un uomo per ~** a respectable man; **fare ~** to do the right thing; **fare ~ a** (*salute*) to be good for; **fare del ~ a qn** to do sb a good turn; **~i di consumo** consumer goods
bene'detto, a *pp di* **benedire** ♦ *ag* blessed, holy
bene'dire *vt* to bless; to consecrate; **benedizi'one** *sf* blessing
benedu'cato, a *ag* well-mannered
benefi'cenza [benefi't∫entsa] *sf* charity
bene'ficio [bene'fit∫o] *sm* benefit; **con ~ d'inventario** (*fig*) with reservations
be'nefico, a, ci, che *ag* beneficial; charitable

beneme'renza [beneme'rentsa] *sf* merit
bene'merito, a *ag* meritorious
be'nessere *sm* well-being
benes'tante *ag* well-to-do
benes'tare *sm* consent, approval
be'nevolo, a *ag* benevolent
be'nigno, a [be'niɲɲo] *ag* kind, kindly; (*critica etc*) favourable; (*MED*) benign
benin'teso *av* of course
bensì *cong* but (rather)
benve'nuto, a *ag, sm* welcome; **dare il ~ a qn** to welcome sb
ben'zina [ben'dzina] *sf* petrol (*BRIT*), gas (*US*); **fare ~** to get petrol (*BRIT*) *o* gas (*US*); **~ verde** unleaded (petrol); **benzi'naio** *sm* petrol (*BRIT*) *o* gas (*US*) pump attendant
'**bere** *vt* to drink; **darla a ~ a qn** (*fig*) to fool sb
ber'lina *sf* (*AUT*) saloon (car) (*BRIT*), sedan (*US*)
Ber'lino *sf* Berlin
ber'noccolo *sm* bump; (*inclinazione*) flair
ber'retto *sm* cap
bersagli'are [bersaʎ'ʎare] *vt* to shoot at; (*colpire ripetutamente, fig*) to bombard; **bersagliato dalla sfortuna** dogged by ill fortune
ber'saglio [ber'saʎʎo] *sm* target
bes'temmia *sf* curse; (*REL*) blasphemy
bestemmi'are *vi* to curse, swear; to blaspheme ♦ *vt* to curse, swear at; to blaspheme
'**bestia** *sf* animal; **andare in ~** (*fig*) to fly into a rage; **besti'ale** *ag* beastly; animal *cpd*; (*fam*): **fa un freddo bestiale** it's bitterly cold; **besti'ame** *sm* livestock; (*bovino*) cattle *pl*
'**bettola** (*peg*) *sf* dive
be'tulla *sf* birch
be'vanda *sf* drink, beverage
bevi'tore, 'trice *sm/f* drinker
be'vuta *sf* drink
be'vuto, a *pp di* **bere**
bi'ada *sf* fodder
bianche'ria [bjanke'ria] *sf* linen; **~ intima** underwear; **~ da donna** ladies' underwear, lingerie
bi'anco, a, chi, che *ag* white; (*non*

scritto) blank ♦ *sm* white; (*intonaco*)
whitewash ♦ *sm/f* white, white man/
woman; **in ~** (*foglio, assegno*) blank;
(*notte*) sleepless; **in ~ e nero** (*TV, FOT*)
black and white; **mangiare in ~** to follow
a bland diet; **pesce in ~** boiled fish;
andare in ~ (*non riuscire*) to fail; **~
dell'uovo** egg-white
biasi'mare *vt* to disapprove of, censure;
  bi'asimo *sm* disapproval, censure
'**bibbia** *sf* bible
bibe'ron *sm inv* feeding bottle
'**bibita** *sf* (soft) drink
biblio'teca, che *sf* library; (*mobile*)
bookcase; **bibliote'cario, a** *sm/f*
librarian
bicarbo'nato *sm*: **~ (di sodio)**
bicarbonate (of soda)
bicchi'ere [bik'kjɛre] *sm* glass
bici'cletta [bitʃi'kletta] *sf* bicycle;
andare in ~ to cycle
bidé *sm inv* bidet
bi'dello, a *sm/f* (*INS*) janitor
bi'done *sm* drum, can; (*anche*: **~
dell'immondizia**) (dust)bin; (*fam: truffa*)
swindle; **fare un ~ a qn** (*fam*) to let sb
down; to cheat sb
bien'nale *ag* biennial
bi'ennio *sm* period of two years
bi'etola *sf* beet
bifor'carsi *vr* to fork; **biforcazi'one** *sf*
fork
bighello'nare [bigello'nare] *vi* to loaf
(about)
bigiotte'ria [bidʒotte'ria] *sf* costume
jewellery; (*negozio*) jeweller's (*selling only
costume jewellery*)
bigli'ardo [biʎ'ʎardo] *sm* = **biliardo**
bigliette'ria [biʎʎette'ria] *sf* (*di stazione*)
ticket office; booking office; (*di teatro*) box
office
bigli'etto [biʎ'ʎetto] *sm* (*per viaggi,
spettacoli etc*) ticket; (*cartoncino*) card;
(*anche*: **~ di banca**) (bank)note; **~
d'auguri/da visita** greetings/visiting
card; **~ d'andata e ritorno** return
(ticket), round-trip ticket (*US*)
bignè [biɲ'ɲe] *sm inv* cream puff
bigo'dino *sm* roller, curler

bi'gotto, a *ag* over-pious ♦ *sm/f* church
fiend
bi'lancia, ce [bi'lantʃa] *sf* (*pesa*) scales
pl; (*: di precisione*) balance; (*dello
zodiaco*): **B~** Libra; **~ commerciale/dei
pagamenti** balance of trade/payments;
  bilanci'are *vt* (*pesare*) to weigh; (*: fig*) to
weigh up; (*pareggiare*) to balance
bi'lancio [bi'lantʃo] *sm* (*COMM*) balance
(-sheet); (*statale*) budget; **fare il ~ di** (*fig*)
to assess; **~ consuntivo** (final) balance; **~
preventivo** budget
'**bile** *sf* bile; (*fig*) rage, anger
bili'ardo *sm* billiards *sg*; billiard table
'**bilico, chi** *sm*: **essere in ~** to be
balanced; (*fig*) to be undecided; **tenere qn
in ~** to keep sb in suspense
bi'lingue *ag* bilingual
bili'one *sm* (*mille milioni*) thousand
million; (*milione di milioni*) billion (*BRIT*),
trillion (*US*)
'**bimbo, a** *sm/f* little boy/girl
bimen'sile *ag* fortnightly
bimes'trale *ag* two-monthly, bimonthly
bi'nario, a *ag* (*sistema*) binary ♦ *sm*
(railway) track *o* line; (*piattaforma*)
platform; **~ morto** dead-end track
bi'nocolo *sm* binoculars *pl*
bio... *prefisso*: **bio'chimica** [bio'kimika] *sf*
biochemistry; **biodegra'dabile** *ag*
biodegradable; **biogra'fia** *sf* biography;
biolo'gia *sf* biology; **bio'logico, a, ci,
che** *ag* biological
bi'ondo, a *ag* blond, fair
bir'bante *sm* rogue, rascal
biri'chino, a [biri'kino] *ag* mischievous
♦ *sm/f* scamp, little rascal
bi'rillo *sm* skittle (*BRIT*), pin (*US*); **~i** *smpl*
(*gioco*) skittles *sg* (*BRIT*), bowling (*US*)
'**biro** ® *sf inv* biro ®
'**birra** *sf* beer; **a tutta ~** (*fig*) at top speed;
birra chiara ≈ lager; **birra scura**
≈ stout; **birre'ria** *sf* ≈ bierkeller
bis *escl, sm inv* encore
bis'betico, a, ci, che *ag* ill-tempered,
crabby
bisbigli'are [bisbiʎ'ʎare] *vt, vi* to
whisper
'**bisca, sche** *sf* gambling-house

'biscia, sce ['biʃʃa] *sf* snake; ~ d'acqua grass snake

bis'cotto *sm* biscuit

bises'tile *ag*: anno ~ leap year

bis'lungo, a, ghi, ghe *ag* oblong

bis'nonno, a *sm/f* great grandfather/grandmother

biso'gnare [bizoɲ'ɲare] *vb impers*: bisogna che tu parta/lo faccia you'll have to go/do it; bisogna parlargli we'll (*o* I'll) have to talk to him

bi'sogno [bi'zoɲɲo] *sm* need; ~i *smpl*: fare i propri ~i to relieve o.s.; avere ~ di qc/di fare qc to need sth/to do sth; al ~, in caso di ~ if need be; biso'gnoso, a *ag* needy, poor; bisognoso di in need of, needing

bis'tecca, che *sf* steak, beefsteak

bisticci'are [bistit'tʃare] *vi* to quarrel, bicker; ~rsi *vr* to quarrel, bicker; bis'ticcio *sm* quarrel, squabble; (*gioco di parole*) pun

'bisturi *sm* scalpel

bi'sunto, a *ag* very greasy

'bitter *sm inv* bitters *pl*

bi'vacco, chi *sm* bivouac

'bivio *sm* fork; (*fig*) dilemma

'bizza ['biddza] *sf* tantrum; fare le ~e (*bambino*) to be naughty

biz'zarro, a [bid'dzarro] *ag* bizarre, strange

biz'zeffe [bid'dzeffe] *sf*: a ~ *av* in plenty, galore

blan'dire *vt* to soothe; to flatter

'blando, a *ag* mild, gentle

bla'sone *sm* coat of arms

blate'rare *vi* to chatter

blin'dato, a *ag* armoured

bloc'care *vt* to block; (*isolare*) to isolate, cut off; (*porto*) to blockade; (*prezzi, beni*) to freeze; (*meccanismo*) to jam; ~rsi *vr* (*motore*) to stall; (*freni, porta*) to jam, stick; (*ascensore*) to stop, get stuck

'blocco, chi *sm* block; (*MIL*) blockade; (*dei fitti*) restriction; (*quadernetto*) pad; (*fig: unione*) coalition; (*il bloccare*) blocking; isolating, cutting-off; blockading; freezing; jamming; in ~ (*nell'insieme*) as a whole; (*COMM*) in bulk; ~ cardiaco cardiac arrest

blu *ag inv*, *sm* dark blue

'blusa *sf* (*camiciotto*) smock; (*camicetta*) blouse

'boa *sm inv* (*ZOOL*) boa constrictor; (*sciarpa*) feather boa ♦ *sf* buoy

bo'ato *sm* rumble, roar

bo'bina *sf* reel, spool; (*di pellicola*) spool; (*di film*) reel; (*ELETTR*) coil

'bocca, che *sf* mouth; in ~ al lupo! good luck!

boc'caccia, ce [bok'kattʃa] *sf* (*malalingua*) gossip; fare le ~ce to pull faces

boc'cale *sm* jug; ~ da birra tankard

boc'cetta [bot'tʃetta] *sf* small bottle

boccheggi'are [bokked'dʒare] *vi* to gasp

boc'chino [bok'kino] *sm* (*di sigaretta, sigaro: cannella*) cigarette-holder; cigar-holder; (*di pipa, strumenti musicali*) mouthpiece

'boccia, ce ['bottʃa] *sf* bottle; (*da vino*) decanter, carafe; (*palla*) bowl; gioco delle ~ce bowls *sg*

bocci'are [bot'tʃare] *vt* (*proposta, progetto*) to reject; (*INS*) to fail; (*BOCCE*) to hit; boccia'tura *sf* failure

bocci'olo [bot'tʃɔlo] *sm* bud

boc'cone *sm* mouthful, morsel

boc'coni *av* face downwards

'boia *sm inv* executioner; hangman

boi'ata *sf* botch

boicot'tare *vt* to boycott

'bolide *sm* meteor; come un ~ like a flash, at top speed

'bolla *sf* bubble; (*MED*) blister; ~ papale papal bull; ~ di consegna (*COMM*) delivery note

bol'lare *vt* to stamp; (*fig*) to brand

bol'lente *ag* boiling; boiling hot

bol'letta *sf* bill; (*ricevuta*) receipt; essere in ~ to be hard up

bollet'tino *sm* bulletin; (*COMM*) note; ~ di spedizione consignment note

bol'lire *vt*, *vi* to boil; bol'lito *sm* (*CUC*) boiled meat

bolli'tore *sm* (*CUC*) kettle; (*per riscaldamento*) boiler

'bollo *sm* stamp; bollo per patente driving licence tax

'bomba *sf* bomb; tornare a ~ (*fig*) to get

back to the point; ~ **atomica** atom bomb

bombarda'mento *sm* bombardment; bombing

bombar'dare *vt* to bombard; (*da aereo*) to bomb

bombardi'ere *sm* bomber

bom'betta *sf* bowler (hat)

'bombola *sf* cylinder

bo'naccia, ce [bo'nattʃa] *sf* dead calm

bo'nario, a *ag* good-natured, kind

bo'nifica, che *sf* reclamation; reclaimed land

bo'nifico, ci *sm* (*riduzione, abbuono*) discount; (*versamento a terzi*) credit transfer

bontà *sf* goodness; (*cortesia*) kindness; **aver la ~ di fare qc** to be good *o* kind enough to do sth

borbot'tare *vi* to mumble; (*stomaco*) to rumble

'borchia ['borkja] *sf* stud

borda'tura *sf* (*SARTORIA*) border, trim

'bordo *sm* (*NAUT*) ship's side; (*orlo*) edge; (*striscia di guarnizione*) border, trim; **a ~ di** (*nave, aereo*) aboard, on board; (*macchina*) in

bor'gata *sf* hamlet

bor'ghese [bor'geze] *ag* (*spesso peg*) middle-class; bourgeois; **abito ~** civilian dress; **borghe'sia** *sf* middle classes *pl*; bourgeoisie

'borgo, ghi *sm* (*paesino*) village; (*quartiere*) district; (*sobborgo*) suburb

'boria *sf* self-conceit, arrogance

boro'talco *sm* talcum powder

bor'raccia, ce [bor'rattʃa] *sf* canteen, water-bottle

'borsa *sf* bag; (*anche: ~ da signora*) handbag; (*ECON*): **la B~ (valori)** the Stock Exchange; **la ~ nera** black market; **~ della spesa** shopping bag; **~ di studio** grant; **borsai'olo** *sm* pickpocket; **borsel'lino** *sm* purse; **bor'setta** *sf* handbag; **bor'sista, i, e** *sm/f* (*ECON*) speculator; (*INS*) grant-holder

bos'caglia [bos'kaʎʎa] *sf* woodlands *pl*

boscai'olo *sm* woodcutter; forester

'bosco, schi *sm* wood; **bos'coso, a** *ag* wooded

'bossolo *sm* cartridge-case

bo'tanica *sf* botany

bo'tanico, a, ci, che *ag* botanical ♦ *sm* botanist

'botola *sf* trap door

'botta *sf* blow; (*rumore*) bang

'botte *sf* barrel, cask

bot'tega, ghe *sf* shop; (*officina*) workshop; **botte'gaio, a** *sm/f* shopkeeper; **botte'ghino** *sm* ticket office; (*del lotto*) public lottery office

bot'tiglia [bot'tiʎʎa] *sf* bottle; **bottiglie'ria** *sf* wine shop

bot'tino *sm* (*di guerra*) booty; (*di rapina, furto*) loot

'botto *sm* bang; crash; **di ~** suddenly

bot'tone *sm* button; **attaccare ~ a qn** (*fig*) to buttonhole sb

bo'vino, a *ag* bovine; **~i** *smpl* cattle

boxe [bɔks] *sf* boxing

'bozza ['bɔttsa] *sf* draft; sketch; (*TIP*) proof; **boz'zetto** *sm* sketch

bozzolo ['bɔttsolo] *sm* cocoon

BR *sigla fpl* = **Brigate Rosse**

brac'care *vt* to hunt

brac'cetto [brat'tʃetto] *sm*: **a ~** arm in arm

bracci'ale [brat'tʃale] *sm* bracelet; (*distintivo*) armband; **braccia'letto** *sm* bracelet, bangle

bracci'ante [brat'tʃante] *sm* (*AGR*) day labourer

bracci'ata [brat'tʃata] *sf* (*nel nuoto*) stroke

'braccio ['brattʃo] (*pl(f)* **braccia**) *sm* (*ANAT*) arm; (*pl(m) braccio: di gru, fiume*) arm; (*: di edificio*) wing; **~ di mare** sound; **bracci'olo** *sm* (*appoggio*) arm

'bracco, chi *sm* hound

bracconi'ere *sm* poacher

'brace ['bratʃe] *sf* embers *pl*; **braci'ere** *sm* brazier

braci'ola [bra'tʃɔla] *sf* (*CUC*) chop

bra'mare *vt*: **~ qc/di fare** to long for sth/to do

'branca, che *sf* branch

'branchia ['brankja] *sf* (*ZOOL*) gill

'branco, chi *sm* (*di cani, lupi*) pack; (*di uccelli, pecore*) flock; (*peg: di persone*) gang, pack

branco'lare *vi* to grope, feel one's way

'branda *sf* camp bed

bran'dello *sm* scrap, shred; **a ~i** in tatters, in rags

bran'dire *vt* to brandish

'brano *sm* piece; (*di libro*) passage

bra'sato *sm* braised beef

Bra'sile *sm*: **il ~** Brazil; **brasili'ano, a** *ag, sm/f* Brazilian

'bravo, a *ag* (*abile*) clever, capable, skilful; (*buono*) good, honest; (: *bambino*) good; (*coraggioso*) brave; **~!** well done!; (*al teatro*) bravo!

bra'vura *sf* cleverness, skill

'breccia, ce ['brettʃa] *sf* breach

bre'tella *sf* (*AUT*) link; **~e** *sfpl* (*di calzoni*) braces

'breve *ag* brief, short; **in ~** in short

brevet'tare *vt* to patent

bre'vetto *sm* patent; **~ di pilotaggio** pilot's licence (*BRIT*) o license (*US*)

'brezza ['breddza] *sf* breeze

'bricco, chi *sm* jug; **~ del caffè** coffeepot

bric'cone, a *sm/f* rogue, rascal

'briciola ['britʃola] *sf* crumb

'briciolo ['britʃolo] *sm* (*specie fig*) bit

'briga, ghe *sf* (*fastidio*) trouble, bother; **pigliarsi la ~ di fare qc** to take the trouble to do sth

brigadi'ere *sm* (*dei carabinieri etc*) ≈ sergeant

bri'gante *sm* bandit

bri'gata *sf* (*MIL*) brigade; (*gruppo*) group, party

'briglia ['briʎʎa] *sf* rein; **a ~ sciolta** at full gallop; (*fig*) at full speed

bril'lante *ag* bright; (*anche fig*) brilliant; (*che luccica*) shining ♦ *sm* diamond

bril'lare *vi* to shine; (*mina*) to blow up ♦ *vt* (*mina*) to set off

'brillo, a *ag* merry, tipsy

'brina *sf* hoarfrost

brin'dare *vi*: **~ a qn/qc** to drink to o toast sb/sth

'brindisi *sm inv* toast

'brio *sm* liveliness, go; **bri'oso, a** *ag* lively

bri'tannico, a, ci, che *ag* British

'brivido *sm* shiver; (*di ribrezzo*) shudder; (*fig*) thrill

brizzo'lato, a [brittso'lato] *ag* (*persona*) going grey; (*barba, capelli*) greying

'brocca, che *sf* jug

broc'cato *sm* brocade

'broccolo *sm* broccoli *sg*

'brodo *sm* broth; (*per cucinare*) stock; **~ ristretto** consommé

brogli'accio [broʎ'ʎattʃo] *sm* scribbling pad

'broglio ['brɔʎʎo] *sm*: **~ elettorale** gerrymandering

bron'chite [bron'kite] *sf* (*MED*) bronchitis

'broncio ['brontʃo] *sm* sulky expression; **tenere il ~** to sulk

'bronco, chi *sm* bronchial tube

bronto'lare *vi* to grumble; (*tuono, stomaco*) to rumble

'bronzo ['brondzo] *sm* bronze

bru'care *vt* to browse on, nibble at

brucia'pelo [brutʃa'pelo] **a ~** *av* point-blank

bruci'are [bru'tʃare] *vt* to burn; (*scottare*) to scald ♦ *vi* to burn; **brucia'tore** *sm* burner; **brucia'tura** *sf* (*atto*) burning *no pl*; (*segno*) burn; (*scottatura*) scald;

bruci'ore *sm* burning o smarting sensation

'bruco, chi *sm* caterpillar; grub

brughi'era [bru'gjɛra] *sf* heath, moor

bruli'care *vi* to swarm

'brullo, a *ag* bare, bleak

'bruma *sf* mist

'bruno, a *ag* brown, dark; (*persona*) dark(-haired)

'brusco, a, schi, sche *ag* (*sapore*) sharp; (*modi, persona*) brusque, abrupt; (*movimento*) abrupt, sudden

bru'sio *sm* buzz, buzzing

bru'tale *ag* brutal

'bruto, a *ag* (*forza*) brute *cpd* ♦ *sm* brute

brut'tezza [brut'tettsa] *sf* ugliness

'brutto, a *ag* ugly; (*cattivo*) bad; (*malattia, strada, affare*) nasty, bad; **~ tempo** bad weather; **brut'tura** *sf* (*cosa brutta*) ugly thing; (*sudiciume*) filth; (*azione meschina*) mean action

Bru'xelles [bry'sɛl] *sf* Brussels

bub'bone *sm* swelling

'buca, che *sf* hole; (*avvallamento*) hollow; ~ **delle lettere** letterbox

buca'neve *sm inv* snowdrop

bu'care *vt (forare)* to make a hole (*o* holes) in; (*pungere*) to pierce; (*biglietto*) to punch; **~rsi** *vr* (*con eroina*) to mainline; ~ **una gomma** to have a puncture

bu'cato *sm* (*operazione*) washing; (*panni*) wash, washing

'buccia, ce ['buttʃa] *sf* skin, peel; (*corteccia*) bark

bucherel'lare [bukerel'lare] *vt* to riddle with holes

'buco, chi *sm* hole

bu'dello *sm* (*ANAT: pl(f)* ~a) bowel, gut; (*fig: tubo*) tube; (*vicolo*) alley

bu'dino *sm* pudding

'bue *sm* ox; (*anche: carne di* ~) beef

'bufalo *sm* buffalo

bu'fera *sf* storm

buf'fetto *sm:* **fare un** ~ **sulla guancia a qn** to give sb an affectionate pinch on the cheek

'buffo, a *ag* funny; (*TEATRO*) comic

buf'fone *sm* buffoon; (*peg*) clown

bu'gia, 'gie [bu'dʒia] *sf* lie; (*candeliere*) candleholder;**bugi'ardo, a** *ag* lying, deceitful ♦ *sm/f* liar

bugi'gattolo [budʒi'gattolo] *sm* poky little room

'buio, a *ag* dark ♦ *sm* dark, darkness; **fa** ~ **pesto** it's pitch-dark

'bulbo *sm (BOT)* bulb; ~ **oculare** eyeball

Bulga'ria *sf:* **la** ~ Bulgaria

bul'lone *sm* bolt

buona'notte *escl* good night! ♦ *sf:* **dare la** ~ **a** to say good night to

buona'sera *escl* good evening!

buongi'orno [bwon'dʒorno] *escl* good morning (*o* afternoon)!

buongus'taio, a *sm/f* gourmet

buon'gusto *sm* good taste

---PAROLA CHIAVE---

bu'ono, a (*ag: dav sm* **buon** *+C o V,* **buono** *+s impura, gn, pn, ps, x, z; dav sf* **buon'** *+V*) *ag***1** (*gen*) good; **un buon pranzo/ristorante** a good lunch/

restaurant; **(stai)** ~! behave!

2 (*benevolo*): ~ **(con)** good (to), kind (to)

3 (*giusto, valido*) right; **al momento** ~ at the right moment

4 (*adatto*): ~ **a/da** fit for/to; **essere** ~ **a nulla** to be no good *o* use at anything

5 (*auguri*): **buon compleanno!** happy birthday!; **buon divertimento!** have a nice time!; **~a fortuna!** good luck!; **buon riposo!** sleep well!; **buon viaggio!** bon voyage!, have a good trip!

6 : **a buon mercato** cheap; **di buon'ora** early; **buon senso** common sense; **alla ~a** *ag* simple ♦ *av* in a simple way, without any fuss

♦ *sm***1** (*bontà*) goodness, good

2 (*COMM*) voucher, coupon; ~ **di cassa** cash voucher; ~ **di consegna** delivery note; ~ **del Tesoro** Treasury bill

buontem'pone, a *sm/f* jovial person

burat'tino *sm* puppet

'burbero, a *ag* surly, gruff

'burla *sf* prank, trick;**bur'lare** *vt:* **burlare qc/qn, burlarsi di qc/qn** to make fun of sth/sb

burocra'zia [burokrat'tsia] *sf* bureaucracy

bur'rasca, sche *sf* storm

'burro *sm* butter

bur'rone *sm* ravine

bus'care *vt* (*anche: ~rsi: raffreddore*) to get, catch; **buscarle** (*fam*) to get a hiding

bus'sare *vi* to knock

'bussola *sf* compass; **perdere la** ~ (*fig*) to lose one's bearings

'busta *sf* (*da lettera*) envelope; (*astuccio*) case; **in** ~ **aperta/chiusa** in an unsealed/sealed envelope; ~ **paga** pay packet

busta'rella *sf* bribe, backhander

'busto *sm* bust; (*indumento*) corset, girdle; **a mezzo** ~ (*foto*) half-length

but'tare *vt* to throw; (*anche:* ~ *via*) to throw away; ~ **giù** (*scritto*) to scribble down; (*cibo*) to gulp down; (*edificio*) to pull down, demolish; (*pasta, verdura*) to put into boiling water

C

ca'bina *sf* (*di nave*) cabin; (*da spiaggia*) beach hut; (*di autocarro, treno*) cab; (*di aereo*) cockpit; (*di ascensore*) cage; ~ **telefonica** call *o* (tele)phone box

ca'cao *sm* cocoa

'caccia ['kattʃa] *sf* hunting; (*con fucile*) shooting; (*inseguimento*) chase; (*cacciagione*) game ♦ *sm inv* (*aereo*) fighter; (*nave*) destroyer; ~ **grossa** big-game hunting; ~ **all'uomo** manhunt

cacciabombardi'ere [kattʃabombar-'djere] *sm* fighter-bomber

cacciagi'one [kattʃa'dʒone] *sf* game

cacci'are [kat'tʃare] *vt* to hunt; (*mandar via*) to chase away; (*ficcare*) to shove, stick ♦ *vi* to hunt; ~**rsi** *vr* (*fam: mettersi*): ~**rsi tra la folla** to plunge into the crowd; **dove s'è cacciata la mia borsa?** where has my bag got to?; ~**rsi nei guai** to get into trouble; ~ **fuori qc** to whip *o* pull sth out; ~ **un urlo** to let out a yell; **caccia'tore** *sm* hunter; **cacciatore di frodo** poacher

caccia'vite [kattʃa'vite] *sm inv* screwdriver

'cactus *sm inv* cactus

ca'davere *sm* (dead) body, corpse

ca'dente *ag* falling; (*casa*) tumbledown

ca'denza [ka'dɛntsa] *sf* cadence; (*andamento ritmico*) rhythm; (*MUS*) cadenza

ca'dere *vi* to fall; (*denti, capelli*) to fall out; (*tetto*) to fall in; **questa gonna cade bene** this skirt hangs well; **lasciar** ~ (*anche fig*) to drop; ~ **dal sonno** to be falling asleep on one's feet; ~ **dalle nuvole** (*fig*) to be taken aback

ca'detto, a *ag* younger; (*squadra*) junior *cpd* ♦ *sm* cadet

ca'duta *sf* fall; **la** ~ **dei capelli** hair loss

caffè *sm inv* coffee; (*locale*) café; ~ **macchiato** coffee with a dash of milk; ~ **macinato** ground coffee

caffel'latte *sm inv* white coffee

caffetti'era *sf* coffeepot

cagio'nare [kadʒo'nare] *vt* to cause, be the cause of

cagio'nevole [kadʒo'nevole] *ag* delicate, weak

cagli'are [kaʎ'ʎare] *vi* to curdle

'cagna ['kaɲɲa] *sf* (*ZOOL, peg*) bitch

ca'gnesco, a, schi, sche [kaɲ'ɲesko] *ag* (*fig*): **guardare qn in** ~ to scowl at sb

cala'brone *sm* hornet

cala'maio *sm* inkpot; inkwell

cala'maro *sm* squid

cala'mita *sf* magnet

calamità *sf inv* calamity, disaster

ca'lare *vt* (*far discendere*) to lower; (*MAGLIA*) to decrease ♦ *vi* (*discendere*) to go (*o* come) down; (*tramontare*) to set, go down; ~ **di peso** to lose weight

'calca *sf* throng, press

cal'cagno [kal'kaɲɲo] *sm* heel

cal'care *sm* limestone ♦ *vt* (*premere coi piedi*) to tread, press down; (*premere con forza*) to press down; (*mettere in rilievo*) to stress; ~ **la mano** to overdo it, exaggerate

'calce ['kaltʃe] *sm*: **in** ~ at the foot of the page ♦ *sf* lime; ~ **viva** quicklime

calces'truzzo [kaltʃes'truttso] *sm* concrete

calci'are [kal'tʃare] *vt, vi* to kick; **calcia'tore** *sm* footballer

'calcio ['kaltʃo] *sm* (*pedata*) kick; (*sport*) football, soccer; (*di pistola, fucile*) butt; (*CHIM*) calcium; ~ **d'angolo** (*SPORT*) corner (kick); ~ **di punizione** (*SPORT*) free kick

'calco, chi *sm* (*ARTE*) casting, moulding; cast, mould

calco'lare *vt* to calculate, work out, reckon; (*ponderare*) to weigh (up)

calcola'tore, 'trice *ag* calculating ♦ *sm* calculator; (*fig*) calculating person; **calcolatore elettronico** computer; **calcola'trice** *sf* (*anche: macchina calcolatrice*) calculator

'calcolo *sm* (*anche MAT*) calculation; (*infinitesimale etc*) calculus; (*MED*) stone; **fare i propri ~i** (*fig*) to weigh the pros and cons; **per** ~ out of self-interest

cal'daia *sf* boiler

caldeggi'are [kalded'dʒare] *vt* to support

'**caldo, a** *ag* warm; (*molto ~*) hot; (*fig: appassionato*) keen; hearty ♦ *sm* heat; **ho ~** I'm warm; I'm hot; **fa ~** it's warm; it's hot

calen'dario *sm* calendar

'**calibro** *sm* (*di arma*) calibre, bore; (*TECN*) callipers *pl*; (*fig*) calibre; **di grosso ~** (*fig*) prominent

'**calice** ['kalitʃe] *sm* goblet; (*REL*) chalice

ca'ligine [ka'lidʒine] *sf* fog; (*mista con fumo*) smog

'**callo** *sm* callus; (*ai piedi*) corn

'**calma** *sf* calm

cal'mante *sm* sedative, tranquilliser

cal'mare *vt* to calm; (*lenire*) to soothe; **~rsi** *vr* to grow calm, calm down; (*vento*) to abate; (*dolori*) to ease

calmi'ere *sm* controlled price

'**calmo, a** *ag* calm, quiet

'**calo** *sm* (*COMM: di prezzi*) fall; (*: di volume*) shrinkage; (*: di peso*) loss

ca'lore *sm* warmth; heat; **in ~** (*ZOOL*) on heat

calo'ria *sf* calorie

calo'roso, a *ag* warm

calpes'tare *vt* to tread on, trample on; "**è vietato ~ l'erba**" "keep off the grass"

ca'lunnia *sf* slander; (*scritta*) libel

cal'vario *sm* (*fig*) affliction, cross

cal'vizie [kal'vittsje] *sf* baldness

'**calvo, a** *ag* bald

'**calza** ['kaltsa] *sf* (*da donna*) stocking; (*da uomo*) sock; **fare la ~** to knit; **~e di nailon** nylons, (nylon) stockings

cal'zare [kal'tsare] *vt* (*scarpe, guanti: mettersi*) to put on; (*: portare*) to wear ♦ *vi* to fit; **calza'tura** *sf* footwear

calzet'tone [kaltset'tone] *sm* heavy knee-length sock

cal'zino [kal'tsino] *sm* sock

calzo'laio [kaltso'lajo] *sm* shoemaker; (*che ripara scarpe*) cobbler; **calzole'ria** *sf* (*negozio*) shoe shop

calzon'cini [kaltson'tʃini] *smpl* shorts

cal'zone [kal'tsone] *sm* trouser leg; (*CUC*) savoury turnover made with pizza dough; **~i** *smpl* (*pantaloni*) trousers (*BRIT*), pants (*US*)

cambi'ale *sf* bill (of exchange); (*pagherò*

cambiario*) promissory note

cambia'mento *sm* change

cambi'are *vt* to change; (*modificare*) to alter, change; (*barattare*): **~ (qc con qn/ qc)** to exchange (sth with sb/for sth) ♦ *vi* to change, alter; **~rsi** *vr* (*variare abito*) to change; **~ casa** to move (house); **~ idea** to change one's mind; **~ treno** to change trains

'**cambio** *sm* change; (*modifica*) alteration, change; (*scambio, COMM*) exchange; (*corso dei cambi*) rate (of exchange); (*TECN, AUT*) gears *pl*; **in ~ di** in exchange for; **dare il ~ a qn** to take over from sb

'**camera** *sf* room; (*anche: ~ da letto*) bedroom; (*POL*) chamber, house; **~ ardente** mortuary chapel; **~ d'aria** inner tube; (*di pallone*) bladder; **C~ di Commercio** Chamber of Commerce; **C~ dei Deputati** Chamber of Deputies, ≈ House of Commons (*BRIT*), ≈ House of Representatives (*US*); **~ a gas** gas chamber; **~ a un letto/a due letti/ matrimoniale** single/twin-bedded/double room; **~ oscura** (*FOT*) dark room

came'rata, i, e *sm/f* companion, mate ♦ *sf* dormitory

cameri'era *sf* (*domestica*) maid; (*che serve a tavola*) waitress; (*che fa le camere*) chambermaid

cameri'ere *sm* (man)servant; (*di ristorante*) waiter

came'rino *sm* (*TEATRO*) dressing room

'**camice** ['kamitʃe] *sm* (*REL*) alb; (*per medici etc*) white coat

cami'cetta [kami'tʃetta] *sf* blouse

ca'micia, cie [ka'mitʃa] *sf* (*da uomo*) shirt; (*da donna*) blouse; **~ di forza** straitjacket; **camici'otto** *sm* casual shirt; (*per operai*) smock

cami'netto *sm* hearth, fireplace

ca'mino *sm* chimney; (*focolare*) fireplace, hearth

'**camion** *sm inv* lorry (*BRIT*), truck (*US*); **camion'cino** *sm* van

cam'mello *sm* (*ZOOL*) camel; (*tessuto*) camel hair

cammi'nare *vi* to walk; (*funzionare*) to work, go

cam'mino *sm* walk; (*sentiero*) path; (*itinerario, direzione, tragitto*) way; mettersi in ~ to set *o* start off

camo'milla *sf* camomile; (*infuso*) camomile tea

ca'morra *sf* camorra; racket

ca'moscio [ka'mɔʃʃo] *sm* chamois

cam'pagna [kam'paɲɲa] *sf* country, countryside; (*POL, COMM, MIL*) campaign; in ~ in the country; andare in ~ to go to the country; fare una ~ to campaign; campa'gnola *sf* (*AUT*) cross-country vehicle; campa'gnolo, a *ag* country *cpd*

cam'pale *ag* field *cpd*; (*fig*): una giornata ~ a hard day

cam'pana *sf* bell; (*anche:* ~ di vetro) bell jar; campa'nella *sf* small bell; (*di tenda*) curtain ring; campa'nello *sm* (*all'uscio, da tavola*) bell

campa'nile *sm* bell tower, belfry; campani'lismo *sm* parochialism

cam'pare *vi* to live; (*tirare avanti*) to get by, manage

cam'pato, a *ag*: ~ in aria unsound, unfounded

campeggi'are [kamped'dʒare] *vi* to camp; (*risaltare*) to stand out; campeggia'tore, 'trice *sm/f* camper; cam'peggio *sm* camping; (*terreno*) camp site; fare (del) campeggio to go camping

cam'pestre *ag* country *cpd*, rural

campio'nario, a *ag*: fiera ~a trade fair ♦ *sm* collection of samples

campio'nato *sm* championship

campi'one, 'essa *sm/f* (*SPORT*) champion ♦ *sm* (*COMM*) sample

'campo *sm* field; (*MIL*) field; (*: accampamento*) camp; (*spazio delimitato: sportivo etc*) ground; field; (*di quadro*) background; i ~i (*campagna*) the countryside; ~ da aviazione airfield; ~ di battaglia (*MIL, fig*) battlefield; ~ di concentramento concentration camp; ~ di golf golf course; ~ da tennis tennis court; ~ visivo field of vision

campo'santo (*pl* campisanti) *sm* cemetery

camuf'fare *vt* to disguise

'Canada *sm*: il ~ Canada; cana'dese *ag*,

sm/f Canadian ♦ *sf* (*anche:* tenda canadese) ridge tent

ca'naglia [ka'naʎʎa] *sf* rabble, mob; (*persona*) scoundrel, rogue

ca'nale *sm* (*anche fig*) channel; (*artificiale*) canal

'canapa *sf* hemp

cana'rino *sm* canary

cancel'lare [kantʃel'lare] *vt* (*con la gomma*) to rub out, erase; (*con la penna*) to strike out; (*annullare*) to annul, cancel; (*disdire*) to cancel

cancelle'ria [kantʃelle'ria] *sf* chancery; (*quanto necessario per scrivere*) stationery

cancelli'ere [kantʃel'ljere] *sm* chancellor; (*di tribunale*) clerk of the court

can'cello [kan'tʃello] *sm* gate

can'crena *sf* gangrene

'cancro *sm* (*MED*) cancer; (*dello zodiaco*): C~ Cancer

candeg'gina [kanded'dʒina] *sf* bleach

can'dela *sf* candle; ~ (di accensione) (*AUT*) spark(ing) plug

cande'labro *sm* candelabra

candeli'ere *sm* candlestick

candi'dato, a *sm/f* candidate; (*aspirante a una carica*) applicant

'candido, a *ag* white as snow; (*puro*) pure; (*sincero*) sincere, candid

can'dito, a *ag* candied

can'dore *sm* brilliant white; purity; sincerity, candour

'cane *sm* dog; (*di pistola, fucile*) cock; fa un freddo ~ it's bitterly cold; non c'era un ~ there wasn't a soul; ~ da caccia/ guardia hunting/guard dog; ~ lupo alsatian

ca'nestro *sm* basket

'canfora *sf* camphor

cangi'ante [kan'dʒante] *ag* iridescent

can'guro *sm* kangaroo

ca'nile *sm* kennel; (*di allevamento*) kennels *pl*; ~ municipale dog pound

ca'nino, a *ag*, *sm* canine

'canna *sf* (*pianta*) reed; (*: indica, da zucchero*) cane; (*bastone*) stick, cane; (*di fucile*) barrel; (*di organo*) pipe; ~ fumaria chimney flue; ~ da pesca (fishing) rod; ~ da zucchero sugar cane can'nella *sf* (*CUC*) cinnamon

cannel'loni *smpl* pasta tubes stuffed with sauce and baked

cannocchi'ale [kannok'kjale] *sm* telescope

can'none *sm* (*MIL*) gun; (: *STORIA*) cannon; (*tubo*) pipe, tube; (*piega*) box pleat; (*fig*) ace

can'nuccia, ce [kan'nuttʃa] *sf* (drinking) straw

ca'noa *sf* canoe

'canone *sm* canon, criterion; (*mensile, annuo*) rent; fee

ca'nonico, ci *sm* (*REL*) canon

ca'noro, a *ag* (*uccello*) singing, song *cpd*

canot'taggio [kanot'taddʒo] *sm* rowing

canotti'era *sf* vest

ca'notto *sm* small boat, dinghy; canoe

cano'vaccio [kano'vattʃo] *sm* (*tela*) canvas; (*strofinaccio*) duster; (*trama*) plot

can'tante *sm/f* singer

can'tare *vt, vi* to sing; cantau'tore, 'trice *sm/f* singer-composer

canti'ere *sm* (*EDIL*) (building) site; (*anche*: ~ *navale*) shipyard

canti'lena *sf* (*filastrocca*) lullaby; (*fig*) sing-song voice

can'tina *sf* (*locale*) cellar; (*bottega*) wine shop

'canto *sm* song; (*arte*) singing; (*REL*) chant; chanting; (*poesia*) poem, lyric; (*parte di una poesia*) canto; (*parte, lato*): da un ~ on the one hand; d'altro ~ on the other hand

canto'nata *sf* corner; prendere una ~ (*fig*) to blunder

can'tone *sm* (*in Svizzera*) canton

can'tuccio [kan'tuttʃo] *sm* corner, nook

canzo'nare [kantso'nare] *vt* to tease

can'zone [kan'tsone] *sf* song; (*POESIA*) canzone; canzoni'ere *sm* (*MUS*) songbook; (*LETTERATURA*) collection of poems

'caos *sm inv* chaos; ca'otico, a, ci, che *ag* chaotic

C.A.P. *sigla m* = codice di avviamento postale

ca'pace [ka'patʃe] *ag* able, capable; (*ampio, vasto*) large, capacious; sei ~ di farlo? can you *o* are you able to do it?;

capacità *sf inv* ability; (*DIR, di recipiente*) capacity; capaci'tarsi *vr*: capacitarsi di to make out, understand

ca'panna *sf* hut

capan'none *sm* (*AGR*) barn; (*fabbricato industriale*) (factory) shed

ca'parbio, a *ag* stubborn

ca'parra *sf* deposit, down payment

ca'pello *sm* hair; ~i *smpl* (*capigliatura*) hair *sg*

capez'zale [kapet'tsale] *sm* bolster; (*fig*) bedside

ca'pezzolo [ka'pettsolo] *sm* nipple

capi'enza [ka'pjɛntsa] *sf* capacity

capiglia'tura [kapiʎʎa'tura] *sf* hair

ca'pire *vt* to understand

capi'tale *ag* (*mortale*) capital; (*fondamentale*) main, chief ♦ *sf* (*città*) capital ♦ *sm* (*ECON*) capital; capita'lismo *sm* capitalism; capita'lista, i, e *ag*, *sm/f* capitalist

capi'tano *sm* captain

capi'tare *vi* (*giungere casualmente*) to happen to go, find o.s.; (*accadere*) to happen; (*presentarsi: cosa*) to turn up, present itself ♦ *vb impers* to happen; mi è capitato un guaio I've had a spot of trouble

capi'tello *sm* (*ARCHIT*) capital

ca'pitolo *sm* chapter

capi'tombolo *sm* headlong fall, tumble

'capo *sm* head; (*persona*) head, boss; (: *in ufficio*) head, boss; (: *in tribù*) chief; (*di oggetti*) head; top; end; (*GEO*) cape; andare a ~ to start a new paragraph; da ~ over again; ~ di bestiame head *inv* of cattle; ~ di vestiario item of clothing

'capo... *prefisso*: capocu'oco, chi *sm* head cook; Capo'danno *sm* New Year; capo'fitto a capofitto *av* headfirst, headlong; capo'giro *sm* dizziness *no pl*; capola'voro, i *sm* masterpiece; capo'linea (*pl* capi'linea) *sm* terminus; capo'lino *sm*: fare capolino to peep out (*o in etc*); capolu'ogo (*pl* -ghi *o* capilu'oghi) *sm* chief town, administrative centre

capo'rale *sm* (*MIL*) lance corporal (*BRIT*), private first class (*US*)

'capo... *prefisso*: capostazi'one (*pl* capistazi'one) *sm* station master; capo'treno (*pl* capi'treno *o* capo'treni) *sm* guard

capo'volgere [kapo'vɔldʒere] *vt* to overturn; (*fig*) to reverse; ~rsi *vr* to overturn; (*barca*) to capsize; (*fig*) to be reversed; capo'volto, a *pp di* capovolgere

'cappa *sf* (*mantello*) cape, cloak; (*del camino*) hood

cap'pella *sf* (*REL*) chapel; cappel'lano *sm* chaplain

cap'pello *sm* hat

'cappero *sm* caper

cap'pone *sm* capon

cap'potto *sm* (over)coat

cappuc'cino [kapput'tʃino] *sm* (*frate*) Capuchin monk; (*bevanda*) frothy white coffee

cap'puccio [kap'puttʃo] *sm* (*copricapo*) hood; (*della biro*) cap

'capra *sf* (she-)goat; ca'pretto *sm* kid

ca'priccio [ka'prittʃo] *sm* caprice, whim; (*bizza*) tantrum; fare i ~i to be very naughty; capricci'oso, a *ag* capricious, whimsical; naughty

Capri'corno *sm* Capricorn

capri'ola *sf* somersault

capri'olo *sm* roe deer

'capro *sm* billy-goat; ~ espiatorio (*fig*) scapegoat

'capsula *sf* capsule; (*di arma, per bottiglie*) cap

cap'tare *vt* (*RADIO, TV*) to pick up; (*cattivarsi*) to gain, win

cara'bina *sf* rifle

carabini'ere *sm* member of Italian military police force

ca'raffa *sf* carafe

cara'mella *sf* sweet

ca'rattere *sm* character; (*caratteristica*) characteristic, trait; avere un buon ~ to be good-natured; caratte'ristica, che *sf* characteristic, trait, peculiarity; caratte'ristico, a, ci, che *ag* characteristic; caratteriz'zare *vt* to characterize, distinguish

car'bone *sm* coal

carbu'rante *sm* (*motor*) fuel

carbura'tore *sm* carburettor

car'cassa *sf* carcass; (*fig: peg: macchina etc*) (old) wreck

carce'rato, a [kartʃe'rato] *sm/f* prisoner

'carcere ['kartʃere] *sm* prison; (*pena*) imprisonment

carci'ofo [kar'tʃɔfo] *sm* artichoke

car'diaco, a, ci, che *ag* cardiac, heart *cpd*

cardi'nale *ag, sm* cardinal

'cardine *sm* hinge

'cardo *sm* thistle

ca'renza [ka'rɛntsa] *sf* lack, scarcity; (*vitaminica*) deficiency

cares'tia *sf* famine; (*penuria*) scarcity, dearth

ca'rezza [ka'rettsa] *sf* caress; carez'zare *vt* to caress, stroke, fondle

'carica, che *sf* (*mansione ufficiale*) office, position; (*MIL, TECN, ELETTR*) charge; ha una forte ~ di simpatia he's very likeable; *vedi anche* carico

cari'care *vt* to load; (*aggravare: anche fig*) to weigh down; (*orologio*) to wind up; (*batteria, MIL*) to charge

'carico, a, chi, che *ag* (*che porta un peso*): ~ di loaded *o* laden with; (*fucile*) loaded; (*orologio*) wound up; (*batteria*) charged; (*colore*) deep; (*caffè, tè*) strong ♦ *sm* (*il caricare*) loading; (*ciò che si carica*) load; (*fig: peso*) burden, weight; persona a ~ dependent; essere a ~ di qn (*spese etc*) to be charged to sb

'carie *sf* (*dentaria*) decay

ca'rino, a *ag* lovely, pretty, nice; (*simpatico*) nice

carità *sf* charity; per ~! (*escl di rifiuto*) good heavens, no!

carnagi'one [karna'dʒone] *sf* complexion

car'nale *ag* (*amore*) carnal; (*fratello*) blood *cpd*

'carne *sf* flesh; (*bovina, ovina etc*) meat; ~ di manzo/maiale/pecora beef/pork/ mutton; ~ tritata mince (*BRIT*), hamburger meat (*US*), minced (*BRIT*) *o* ground (*US*) meat

car'nefice [kar'nefitʃe] *sm* executioner; hangman

carne'vale *sm* carnival

car'noso, a *ag* fleshy

'caro, a *ag* (*amato*) dear; (*costoso*) dear, expensive

ca'rogna [ka'roɲɲa] *sf* carrion; (*fig: fam*) swine

ca'rota *sf* carrot

caro'vana *sf* caravan

caro'vita *sm* high cost of living

carpenti'ere *sm* carpenter

car'pire *vt*: ~ qc a qn (*segreto etc*) to get sth out of sb

car'poni *av* on all fours

car'rabile *ag* suitable for vehicles; "**passo ~**" "keep clear"

car'raio, a *ag*: **passo ~** vehicle entrance

carreggi'ata [karred'dʒata] *sf* carriageway (*BRIT*), (road)way

car'rello *sm* trolley; (*AER*) undercarriage; (*CINEMA*) dolly; (*di macchina da scrivere*) carriage

carri'era *sf* career; **fare ~** to get on; **a gran ~** at full speed

carri'ola *sf* wheelbarrow

'carro *sm* cart, wagon; **~ armato** tank; **~ attrezzi** breakdown van

car'rozza [kar'rɔttsa] *sf* carriage, coach

carrozze'ria [karrottse'ria] *sf* body, coachwork (*BRIT*); (*officina*) coachbuilder's workshop (*BRIT*), body shop

carroz'zina [karrot'tsina] *sf* pram (*BRIT*), baby carriage (*US*)

'carta *sf* paper; (*al ristorante*) menu; (*GEO*) map; plan; (*documento, da gioco*) card; (*costituzione*) charter; **~e** *sfpl* (*documenti*) papers, documents; **alla ~** (*al ristorante*) à la carte; **~ assegni** bank card; **~ assorbente** blotting paper; **~ bollata** *o* **da bollo** official stamped paper; **~ di credito** credit card; **~ (geografica)** map; **~ d'identità** identity card; **~ igienica** toilet paper; **~ d'imbarco** (*AER, NAUT*) boarding card; **~ a lettere** writing paper; **~ libera** (*AMM*) unstamped paper; **~ da parati** wallpaper; **~ verde** (*AUT*) green card; **~ vetrata** sandpaper; **~ da visita** visiting card

cartacar'bone (*pl* **cartcar'bone**) *sf* carbon paper

car'taccia, ce [kar'tattʃa] *sf* waste paper

cartamo'neta *sf* paper money

carta'pecora *sf* parchment

carta'pesta *sf* papier-mâché

car'teggio [kar'teddʒo] *sm* correspondence

car'tella *sf* (*scheda*) card; (*custodia: di cartone*) folder; (*: di uomo d'affari etc*) briefcase; (*: di scolaro*) schoolbag, satchel; **~ clinica** (*MED*) case sheet

car'tello *sm* sign; (*pubblicitario*) poster; (*stradale*) sign, signpost; (*ECON*) cartel; (*in dimostrazioni*) placard; **cartel'lone** *sm* (*pubblicitario*) advertising poster; (*della tombola*) scoring frame; (*TEATRO*) playbill; **tenere il cartellone** (*spettacolo*) to have a long run

carti'era *sf* paper mill

car'tina *sf* (*AUT, GEO*) map

car'toccio [kar'tɔttʃo] *sm* paper bag

cartole'ria *sf* stationer's (shop)

carto'lina *sf* postcard; **~ postale** ready-stamped postcard

car'tone *sm* cardboard; (*ARTE*) cartoon; **~i animati** *smpl* (*CINEMA*) cartoons

car'tuccia, ce [kar'tuttʃa] *sf* cartridge

'casa *sf* house; (*specialmente la propria casa*) home; (*COMM*) firm, house; **essere a ~** to be at home; **vado a ~ mia/tua** I'm going home/to your house; **~ di cura** nursing home; **~ dello studente** student hostel; **~e popolari** ≈ council houses (*o* flats) (*BRIT*), ≈ public housing units (*US*)

ca'sacca, che *sf* military coat; (*di fantino*) blouse

casa'linga, ghe *sf* housewife

casa'lingo, a, ghi, ghe *ag* household, domestic; (*fatto a casa*) home-made; (*semplice*) homely; (*amante della casa*) home-loving; **~ghi** *smpl* household articles; **cucina ~a** plain home cooking

cas'care *vi* to fall; **cas'cata** *sf* fall; (*d'acqua*) cascade, waterfall

ca'scina [kaʃ'ʃina] *sf* farmstead

'casco, schi *sm* helmet; (*del parrucchiere*) hair-drier; (*di banane*) bunch

casei'ficio [kazei'fitʃo] *sm* creamery

ca'sella *sf* pigeon-hole; **~ postale** post

office box

casel'lario *sm* filing cabinet; ~ **giudiziale** court records *pl*

ca'sello *sm* (*di autostrada*) toll-house

ca'serma *sf* barracks *pl*

ca'sino *sm* (*confusione*) row, racket; (*casa di prostituzione*) brothel

casinò *sm inv* casino

'caso *sm* chance; (*fatto, vicenda*) event, incident; (*possibilità*) possibility; (*MED, LING*) case; **a** ~ at random; **per** ~ by chance, by accident; **in ogni** ~, **in tutti i** ~**i** in any case, at any rate; **al** ~ should the opportunity arise; **nel** ~ **che** in case; ~ **mai** if by chance; ~ **limite** borderline case

caso'lare *sm* cottage

'cassa *sf* case, crate, box; (*bara*) coffin; (*mobile*) chest; (*involucro: di orologio etc*) case; (*macchina*) cash register, till; (*luogo di pagamento*) checkout (counter); (*fondo*) fund; (*istituto bancario*) bank; ~ **automatica prelievi** automatic telling machine, cash dispenser; ~ **continua** night safe; ~ **integrazione: mettere in** ~ **integrazione** ≈ to lay off; ~ **mutua** *o* **malattia** health insurance scheme; ~ **di risparmio** savings bank; ~ **toracica** (*ANAT*)

cassa'forte (*pl* **casse'forti**) *sf* safe

cassa'panca (*pl* **cassa'panche** *o* **casse'panche**) *sf* settle

casse'rola *sf* = **casseruola**

casseru'ola *sf* saucepan

cas'setta *sf* box; (*per registratore*) cassette; (*CINEMA, TEATRO*) box-office takings *pl*; **film di** ~ box-office draw; ~ **di sicurezza** strongbox; ~ **delle lettere** letterbox

cas'setto *sm* drawer; **casset'tone** *sm* chest of drawers

cassi'ere, a *sm/f* cashier; (*di banca*) teller

'casta *sf* caste

cas'tagna [kas'taɲɲa] *sf* chestnut

cas'tagno [kas'taɲɲo] *sm* chestnut (tree)

cas'tano, a *ag* chestnut (brown)

cas'tello *sm* castle; (*TECN*) scaffolding

casti'gare *vt* to punish; **cas'tigo, ghi** *sm* punishment

castità *sf* chastity

cas'toro *sm* beaver

cas'trare *vt* to castrate; to geld; to doctor (*BRIT*), fix (*US*)

casu'ale *ag* chance *cpd*; (*INFORM*) random *cpd*

cata'comba *sf* catacomb

ca'talogo, ghi *sm* catalogue

catarifran'gente [catarifran'dʒɛnte] *sm* (*AUT*) reflector

ca'tarro *sm* catarrh

ca'tasta *sf* stack, pile

ca'tasto *sm* land register; land registry office

ca'tastrofe *sf* catastrophe, disaster

catego'ria *sf* category

ca'tena *sf* chain; ~ **di montaggio** assembly line; ~**e da neve** (*AUT*) snow chains; **cate'naccio** *sm* bolt

cate'ratta *sf* cataract; (*chiusa*) sluice-gate

cati'nella *sf*: **piovere a** ~**e** to pour, rain cats and dogs

ca'tino *sm* basin

ca'trame *sm* tar

'cattedra *sf* teacher's desk; (*di università*) chair

catte'drale *sf* cathedral

catti'veria *sf* malice, spite; naughtiness; (*atto*) spiteful act; (*parole*) malicious *o* spiteful remark

cattività *sf* captivity

cat'tivo, a *ag* bad; (*malvagio*) bad, wicked; (*turbolento: bambino*) bad, naughty; (*: mare*) rough; (*odore, sapore*) nasty, bad

cat'tolico, a, ci, che *ag*, *sm/f* (Roman) Catholic

cat'tura *sf* capture

cattu'rare *vt* to capture

caucciù [kaut't∫u] *sm* rubber

'causa *sf* cause; (*DIR*) lawsuit, case, action; **a** ~ **di, per** ~ **di** because of; **fare** *o* **muovere** ~ **a qn** to take legal action against sb

cau'sare *vt* to cause

cau'tela *sf* caution, prudence

caute'lare *vt* to protect; ~**rsi** *vr*: ~**rsi** (**da**) to take precautions (against)

'cauto, a *ag* cautious, prudent

cauzi'one [kaut'tsjone] *sf* security; *(DIR)* bail

cav. *abbr* = **cavaliere**

'cava *sf* quarry

caval'care *vt (cavallo)* to ride; *(muro)* to sit astride; *(sog: ponte)* to span; **caval-** **'cata** *sf* ride; *(gruppo di persone)* riding party

cavalca'via *sm inv* flyover

cavalci'oni [kaval't∫oni]: **a ~ di** *prep* astride

cavali'ere *sm* rider; *(feudale, titolo)* knight; *(soldato)* cavalryman; *(al ballo)* partner; **cavalle'resco, a, schi, sche** *ag* chivalrous; **cavalle'ria** *sf* chivalry; *(milizia a cavallo)* cavalry

cavalle'rizzo, a [kavalle'rittso] *sm/f* riding instructor; circus rider

caval'letta *sf* grasshopper

caval'letto *sm (FOT)* tripod; *(da pittore)* easel

ca'vallo *sm* horse; *(SCACCHI)* knight; *(AUT: anche:* ~ *vapore)* horsepower; *(dei pantaloni)* crotch; **a ~** on horseback; **a ~ di** astride, straddling; **~ di battaglia** *(fig)* hobby-horse; **~ da corsa** racehorse

ca'vare *vt (togliere)* to draw out, extract, take out; *(: giacca, scarpe)* to take off; *(: fame, sete, voglia)* to satisfy; **cavarsela** to get away with it; to manage, get on all right

cava'tappi *sm inv* corkscrew

ca'verna *sf* cave

'cavia *sf* guinea pig

cavi'ale *sm* caviar

ca'viglia [ka'viʎʎa] *sf* ankle

ca'villo *sm* quibble

'cavo, a *ag* hollow ♦ *sm (ANAT)* cavity; *(grossa corda)* rope, cable; *(ELETTR, TEL)* cable

cavolfi'ore *sm* cauliflower

'cavolo *sm* cabbage; *(fam):* **non m'importa un ~** I don't give a damn; **~ di Bruxelles** Brussels sprout

cazzu'ola [kat'tswɔla] *sf* trowel

c/c *abbr* = **conto corrente**

CD *sm inv* CD

CD-ROM [t∫idi'rɔm] *sm inv* CD-ROM

ce [t∫e] *pron, av vedi* **ci**

'cece [t∫et∫e] *sm* chickpea

cecità [t∫et∫i'ta] *sf* blindness

Cecoslo'vacchia [t∫ekoslo'vakkja] *sf:* **la ~** Czechoslovakia

'cedere [t∫edere] *vt (concedere: posto)* to give up; *(DIR)* to transfer, make over ♦ *vi (cadere)* to give way, subside; **~ (a)** to surrender (to), yield (to), give in (to); **ce'devole** *ag (terreno)* soft; *(fig)* yielding

'cedola [t∫edola] *sf (COMM)* coupon; voucher

'cedro [t∫edro] *sm* cedar; *(albero da frutto, frutto)* citron

C.E.E. [t∫e] *sigla f (= Comunità Economica Europea)* EEC

'ceffo [t∫effo] *(peg) sm* ugly mug

cef'fone [t∫ef'fone] *sm* slap, smack

ce'lare [t∫e'lare] *vt* to conceal; **~rsi** to hide

cele'brare [t∫ele'brare] *vt* to celebrate; **celebrazi'one** *sf* celebration

'celebre [t∫elebre] *ag* famous, celebrated; **celebrità** *sf inv* fame; *(persona)* celebrity

'celere [t∫elere] *ag* fast, swift; *(corso)* crash *cpd*

ce'leste [t∫e'lɛste] *ag* celestial; heavenly; *(colore)* sky-blue

'celibe [t∫elibe] *ag* single, unmarried ♦ *sm* bachelor

'cella [t∫ella] *sf* cell

'cellula [t∫ellula] *sf (BIOL, ELETTR, POL)* cell; **cellu'lare** *sm* cellphone

cellu'lite [t∫ellu'lite] *sf* cellulite

cemen'tare [t∫emen'tare] *vt (anche fig)* to cement

ce'mento [t∫e'mento] *sm* cement; **~ armato** reinforced concrete

'cena [t∫ena] *sf* dinner; *(leggera)* supper

ce'nare [t∫e'nare] *vi* to dine, have dinner

'cencio [t∫ent∫o] *sm* piece of cloth, rag; *(per spolverare)* duster

'cenere [t∫enere] *sf* ash

'cenno [t∫enno] *sm (segno)* sign, signal; *(gesto)* gesture; *(col capo)* nod; *(con la mano)* wave; *(allusione)* hint, mention; *(breve esposizione)* short account; **far ~ di si/no** to nod (one's head)/shake one's head

censi'mento [tʃensi'mento] *sm* census
cen'sore [tʃen'sore] *sm* censor
cen'sura [tʃen'sura] *sf* censorship; censor's office; (*fig*) censure
cente'nario, a [tʃente'narjo] *ag* (*che ha cento anni*) hundred-year-old; (*che ricorre ogni cento anni*) centennial, centenary *cpd* ♦ *sm/f* centenarian ♦ *sm* centenary
cen'tesimo, a [tʃen'tezimo] *ag, sm* hundredth
cen'tigrado, a [tʃen'tigrado] *ag* centigrade; **20 gradi ~i** 20 degrees centigrade
cen'timetro [tʃen'timetro] *sm* centimetre
centi'naio [tʃenti'najo] (*pl(f)* **-aia**) *sm*: **un ~ (di)** a hundred; about a hundred
'cento ['tʃento] *num* a hundred, one hundred
cen'trale [tʃen'trale] *ag* central ♦ *sf*: **~ telefonica** (telephone) exchange; **~ elettrica** electric power station; **centra-li'nista** *sm/f* operator; **centra'lino** *sm* (telephone) exchange; (*di albergo etc*) switchboard
cen'trare [tʃen'trare] *vt* to hit the centre of; (*TECN*) to centre
cen'trifuga [tʃen'trifuga] *sf* spin-drier
'centro ['tʃentro] *sm* centre; **~ civico** civic centre; **~ commerciale** shopping centre; (*città*) commercial centre
'ceppo ['tʃeppo] *sm* (*di albero*) stump; (*pezzo di legno*) log
'cera ['tʃera] *sf* wax; (*aspetto*) appearance, look
ce'ramica, che [tʃe'ramika] *sf* ceramic; (*ARTE*) ceramics *sg*
cerbi'atto [tʃer'bjatto] *sm* (*ZOOL*) fawn
'cerca ['tʃerka] *sf*: **in** *o* **alla ~ di** in search of
cer'care [tʃer'kare] *vt* to look for, search for ♦ *vi*: **~ di fare qc** to try to do sth
'cerchia ['tʃerkja] *sf* circle
'cerchio ['tʃerkjo] *sm* circle; (*giocattolo, di botte*) hoop
cere'ale [tʃere'ale] *sm* cereal
ceri'monia [tʃeri'monja] *sf* ceremony
ce'rino [tʃe'rino] *sm* wax match
'cernia ['tʃernja] *sf* (*ZOOL*) stone bass
cerni'era [tʃer'njera] *sf* hinge; **~ lampo**
zip (fastener) (*BRIT*), zipper (*US*)
'cernita ['tʃernita] *sf* selection
'cero ['tʃero] *sm* (church) candle
ce'rotto [tʃe'rɔtto] *sm* sticking plaster
certa'mente [tʃerta'mente] *av* certainly
cer'tezza [tʃer'tettsa] *sf* certainty
certifi'cato *sm* certificate; **~ medico/di nascita** medical/birth certificate

---

PAROLA CHIAVE

'certo, a ['tʃerto] *ag* (*sicuro*): **~ (di/che)** certain *o* sure (of/that)
♦ *det* **1** (*tale*) certain; **un ~ signor Smith** a (certain) Mr Smith
2 (*qualche; con valore intensivo*) some; **dopo un ~ tempo** after some time; **un fatto di una ~a importanza** a matter of some importance; **di una ~a età** past one's prime, not so young
♦ *pron*: **~i, e** *pl* some
♦ *av* (*certamente*) certainly; (*senz'altro*) of course; **di ~** certainly; **no (di) ~!**, **~ che no!** certainly not!; **sì ~** yes indeed, certainly

---

cer'vello, i [tʃer'vello] (*ANAT*: *pl(f)* **-a**) *sm* brain
'cervo, a ['tʃervo] *sm/f* stag/doe ♦ *sm* deer; **~ volante** stag beetle
ce'sello [tʃe'zɛllo] *sm* chisel
ce'soie [tʃe'zoje] *sfpl* shears
ces'puglio [tʃes'puʎʎo] *sm* bush
ces'sare [tʃes'sare] *vi, vt* to stop, cease; **~ di fare qc** to stop doing sth
'cesso ['tʃesso] (*fam*) *sm* (*gabinetto*) bog
'cesta ['tʃesta] *sf* (large) basket
ces'tino [tʃes'tino] *sm* basket; (*per la carta straccia*) wastepaper basket; **~ da viaggio** (*FERR*) packed lunch (*o* dinner)
'cesto ['tʃesto] *sm* basket
'ceto ['tʃeto] *sm* (social) class
cetrio'lino [tʃetrio'lino] *sm* gherkin
cetri'olo [tʃetri'ɔlo] *sm* cucumber
CFC *sm inv* (= *clorofluorocarburo*) CFC
cfr. *abbr* (= *confronta*) cf
CGIL *sigla f* (= *Confederazione Generale Italiana del Lavoro*) trades union organization

che [ke] *pron* **1** (*relativo: persona: soggetto*) who; (: *oggetto*) whom, that; (: *cosa, animale*) which, that; **il ragazzo ~ è venuto** the boy who came; **l'uomo ~ io vedo** the man (whom) I see; **il libro ~ è sul tavolo** the book which *o* that is on the table; **il libro ~ vedi** the book (which *o* that) you see; **la sera ~ ti ho visto** the evening I saw you
2 (*interrogativo, esclamativo*) what; ~ **(cosa) fai?** what are you doing?; **a ~ (cosa) pensi?** what are you thinking about?; **non sa ~ (cosa) fare** he doesn't know what to do; **ma ~ dici!** what are you saying!
3 (*indefinito*): **quell'uomo ha un ~ di losco** there's something suspicious about that man; **un certo non so ~** an indefinable something
♦ *det* **1** (*interrogativo: tra tanti*) what; (: *tra pochi*) which; ~ **tipo di film preferisci?** what sort of film do you prefer?; ~ **vestito ti vuoi mettere?** what (*o* which) dress do you want to put on?
2 (*esclamativo: seguito da aggettivo*) how; (: *seguito da sostantivo*) what; ~ **buono!** how delicious!; ~ **bel vestito!** what a lovely dress!
♦ *cong* **1** (*con proposizioni subordinate*) that; **credo ~ verrà** I think he'll come; **voglio ~ tu studi** I want you to study; **so ~ tu c'eri** I know (that) you were there; **non ~: non ~ sia sbagliato, ma ...** not that it's wrong, but ...
2 (*finale*) so that; **vieni qua, ~ ti veda** come here, so (that) I can see you
3 (*temporale*): **arrivai ~ eri già partito** you had already left when I arrived; **sono anni ~ non lo vedo** I haven't seen him for years
4 (*in frasi imperative, concessive*): ~ **venga pure!** let him come by all means!; ~ **tu sia benedetto!** may God bless you!
5 (*comparativo: con più, meno*) than; *vedi anche* **più; meno; così** *etc*

cheti'chella [keti'kɛlla]: **alla ~** *av*

stealthily, unobtrusively

chi [ki] *pron* **1** (*interrogativo: soggetto*) who; (: *oggetto*) who, whom; ~ **è?** who is it?; **di ~ è questo libro?** whose book is this?, whose is this book?; **con ~ parli?** who are you talking to?; **a ~ pensi?** who are you thinking about?; ~ **di voi?** which of you?; **non so a ~ rivolgermi** I don't know who to ask
2 (*relativo*) whoever, anyone who; **dillo a ~ vuoi** tell whoever you like
3 (*indefinito*): ~ ... ~ ... some ... others ...; ~ **dice una cosa, ~ dice un'altra** some say one thing, others say another

chiacchie'rare [kjakkje'rare] *vi* to chat; (*discorrere futilmente*) to chatter; (*far pettegolezzi*) to gossip; **chiacchie'rata** *sf* chat; **chi'acchiere** *sfpl*: **fare due** *o* **quattro chiacchiere** to have a chat; **chiacchie'rone, a** *ag* talkative, chatty; gossipy ♦ *sm/f* chatterbox; gossip
chia'mare [kja'mare] *vt* to call; (*rivolgersi a qn*) to call (in), send for; ~**rsi** *vr* (*aver nome*) to be called; **mi chiamo Paolo** my name is Paolo, I'm called Paolo; ~ **alle armi** to call up; ~ **in giudizio** to summon; **chia'mata** *sf* (*TEL*) call; (*MIL*) call-up
chia'rezza [kja'rettsa] *sf* clearness, clarity
chia'rire [kja'rire] *vt* to make clear; (*fig: spiegare*) to clear up, explain; ~**rsi** *vr* to become clear
chi'aro, a ['kjaro] *ag* clear; (*luminoso*) clear, bright; (*colore*) pale, light
chiaroveg'gente [kjaroved'dʒɛnte] *sm/f* clairvoyant
chi'asso ['kjasso] *sm* uproar, row; **chias'soso, a** *ag* noisy, rowdy; (*vistoso*) showy, gaudy
chi'ave ['kjave] *sf* key ♦ *ag inv* key *cpd*; ~ **d'accensione** (*AUT*) ignition key; ~ **inglese** monkey wrench; ~ **di volta** keystone; **chiavis'tello** *sm* bolt
chi'azza ['kjattsa] *sf* stain; splash
'chicco, chi ['kikko] *sm* grain; (*di caffè*)

bean; ~ **d'uva** grape

chi'edere ['kjɛdere] *vt* (*per sapere*) to ask; (*per avere*) to ask for ♦ *vi*: ~ **di qn** to ask after sb; (*al telefono*) to ask for *o* want sb; ~ **qc a qn** to ask sb sth; to ask sb for sth

chi'erico, ci ['kjɛriko] *sm* cleric; altar boy

chi'esa ['kjɛza] *sf* church

chi'esto, a *pp di* **chiedere**

'**chiglia** ['kiʎʎa] *sf* keel

'**chilo** ['kilo] *sm* kilo; **chilo'grammo** *sm* kilogram(me); **chi'lometro** *sm* kilometre

'**chimica** ['kimika] *sf* chemistry

'**chimico, a, ci, che** ['kimiko] *ag* chemical ♦ *sm/f* chemist

'**china** ['kina] *sf* (*pendio*) slope, descent; (*BOT*) cinchona

chi'nare [ki'nare] *vt* to lower, bend; ~**rsi** *vr* to stoop, bend

chi'nino [ki'nino] *sm* quinine

chi'occiola ['kjɔttʃola] *sf* snail; **scala a** ~ spiral staircase

chi'odo ['kjɔdo] *sm* nail; (*fig*) obsession

chi'oma ['kjɔma] *sf* (*capelli*) head of hair; (*di albero*) foliage

chi'osco, schi ['kjɔsko] *sm* kiosk, stall

chi'ostro ['kjɔstro] *sm* cloister

chiro'mante [kiro'mante] *sm/f* palmist

chirur'gia [kirur'dʒia] *sf* surgery; **estetica** cosmetic surgery; **chi'rurgo, ghi** *o* **gi** *sm* surgeon

chissà [kis'sa] *av* who knows, I wonder

chi'tarra [ki'tarra] *sf* guitar

chi'udere ['kjudere] *vt* to close, shut; (*luce, acqua*) to put off, turn off; (*definitivamente: fabbrica*) to close down, shut down; (*strada*) to close; (*recingere*) to enclose; (*porre termine*) to end ♦ *vi* to close, shut; to close down, shut down; to end; ~**rsi** *vr* to shut, close; (*ritirarsi: anche fig*) to shut o.s. away; (*ferita*) to close up

chi'unque [ki'unkwe] *pron* (*relativo*) whoever; (*indefinito*) anyone, anybody; ~ **sia** whoever it is

chi'uso, a [ki'juso] *pp di* **chiudere** ♦ *sf* (*di corso d'acqua*) sluice, lock; (*recinto*) enclosure; (*di discorso etc*) conclusion,

ending; **chiu'sura** *sf* closing; shutting; closing *o* shutting down; enclosing; putting *o* turning off; ending; (*dispositivo*) catch; fastening; fastener

---
PAROLA CHIAVE

ci [tʃi] (*dav lo, la, li, le, ne diventa* **ce**) *pron* **1** (*personale: complemento oggetto*) us; (*: a noi: complemento di termine*) (to) us; (*: riflessivo*) ourselves; (*: reciproco*) each other, one another; (*impersonale*): ~ **si veste** we get dressed; ~ **ha visti** he's seen us; **non** ~ **ha dato niente** he gave us nothing; ~ **vestiamo** we get dressed; ~ **amiamo** we love one another *o* each other

2 (*dimostrativo: di ciò, su ciò, in ciò etc*) about (*o* on *o* of) it; **non so cosa far**~ I don't know what to do about it; **che c'entro io?** what have I got to do with it? ♦ *av* (*qui*) here; (*lì*) there; (*moto attraverso luogo*): ~ **passa sopra un ponte** a bridge passes over it; **non** ~ **passa più nessuno** nobody comes this way any more; **esser**~ *vedi* **essere**

C.ia *abbr* (= *compagnia*) Co.

cia'batta [tʃa'batta] *sf* mule, slipper

ci'alda [tʃalda] *sf* (*CUC*) wafer

ciam'bella [tʃam'bella] *sf* (*CUC*) ring-shaped cake; (*salvagente*) rubber ring

ci'ao ['tʃao] *escl* (*all'arrivo*) hello!; (*alla partenza*) cheerio! (*BRIT*), bye!

ciarla'tano [tʃarla'tano] *sm* charlatan

cias'cuno, a [tʃas'kuno] (*det: dav sm:* ciascun +*C, V,* ciascuno +*s impura, gn, pn, ps, x, z; dav sf:* ciascuna +*C,* ciascun' +*V*) *det* every, each; (*ogni*) every ♦ *pron* each (one); (*tutti*) everyone, everybody

ci'barie [tʃi'barje] *sfpl* foodstuffs

'**cibo** ['tʃibo] *sm* food

ci'cala [tʃi'kala] *sf* cicada

cica'trice [tʃika'tritʃe] *sf* scar

'**cicca** ['tʃikka] *sf* cigarette end

'**ciccia** ['tʃittʃa] (*fam*) *sf* (*carne*) meat; (*grasso umano*) fat, flesh

cice'rone [tʃitʃe'rone] *sm* guide

ci'clismo [tʃi'klizmo] *sm* cycling;

ci'**clista, i, e** *sm/f* cyclist

'**ciclo** [ˈtʃiklo] *sm* cycle; *(di malattia)* course

ciclomo'tore [tʃiklomoˈtore] *sm* moped

ci'**clone** [tʃiˈklone] *sm* cyclone

ci'**cogna** [tʃiˈkoɲɲa] *sf* stork

ci'**coria** [tʃiˈkɔrja] *sf* chicory

ci'**eco, a, chi, che** [ˈtʃɛko] *ag* blind ♦ *sm/f* blind man/woman

ci'**elo** [ˈtʃɛlo] *sm* sky; *(REL)* heaven

'**cifra** [ˈtʃifra] *sf (numero)* figure; numeral; *(somma di denaro)* sum, figure; *(monogramma)* monogram, initials *pl*; *(codice)* code, cipher

'**ciglio, i** [ˈtʃiʎʎo] *(delle palpebre: pl(f)* **ciglia)** *sm (margine)* edge, verge; (eye)lash; (eye)lid; *(sopracciglio)* eyebrow

'**cigno** [ˈtʃiɲɲo] *sm* swan

cigo'**lare** [tʃigoˈlare] *vi* to squeak, creak

'**Cile** [ˈtʃile] *sm:* **il ~** Chile

ci'**lecca** [tʃiˈlekka] *sf:* **far ~** to fail

cili'**egia, gie** o **ge** [tʃiˈljedʒa] *sf* cherry; **cili'egio** *sm* cherry tree

cilin'**drata** [tʃilinˈdrata] *sf (AUT)* (cubic) capacity; **una macchina di grossa ~** a big-engined car

ci'**lindro** [tʃiˈlindro] *sm* cylinder; *(cappello)* top hat

'**cima** [ˈtʃima] *sf (sommità)* top; *(di monte)* top, summit; *(estremità)* end; **in ~ a** at the top of; **da ~ a fondo** from top to bottom; *(fig)* from beginning to end

'**cimice** [ˈtʃimitʃe] *sf (ZOOL)* bug; *(puntina)* drawing pin *(BRIT)*, thumbtack *(US)*

cimini'**era** [tʃimiˈnjera] *sf* chimney; *(di nave)* funnel

cimi'**tero** [tʃimiˈtɛro] *sm* cemetery

ci'**murro** [tʃiˈmurro] *sm (di cani)* distemper

'**Cina** [ˈtʃina] *sf:* **la ~** China

cin'**cin** [tʃinˈtʃin] *escl* cheers!

cin cin [tʃinˈtʃin] *escl* = **cincin**

'**cinema** [ˈtʃinema] *sm inv* cinema; **cine'presa** *sf* cine-camera

ci'**nese** [tʃiˈnese] *ag, sm/f, sm* Chinese *inv*

'**cingere** [ˈtʃindʒere] *vt (attorniare)* to surround, encircle; **~ la vita con una cintura** to put a belt round one's waist

'**cinghia** [ˈtʃiŋgja] *sf* strap; *(cintura, TECN)* belt

cinghi'ale [tʃinˈgjale] *sm* wild boar

cinguet'tare [tʃiŋgwetˈtare] *vi* to twitter

'**cinico, a, ci, che** [ˈtʃiniko] *ag* cynical ♦ *sm/f* cynic; **ci'nismo** *sm* cynicism

cin'**quanta** [tʃinˈkwanta] *num* fifty; **cinquan'tesimo, a** *num* fiftieth

cinquan'**tina** [tʃinkwanˈtina] *sf (serie):* **una ~ (di)** about fifty; *(età):* **essere sulla ~** to be about fifty

'**cinque** [ˈtʃinkwe] *num* five; **avere ~ anni** to be five (years old); **il ~ dicembre 1988** the fifth of December 1988; **alle ~** *(ora)* at five (o'clock)

cinque'**cento** [tʃinkweˈtʃento] *num* five hundred ♦ *sm:* **il C~** the sixteenth century

'**cinto, a** [ˈtʃinto] *pp di* **cingere**

cin'**tura** [tʃinˈtura] *sf* belt; **~ di salvataggio** lifebelt *(BRIT)*, life preserver *(US)*; **~ di sicurezza** *(AUT, AER)* safety o seat belt

ciò [tʃɔ] *pron* this; that; **~ che** what; **~ nonostante** o **nondimeno** nevertheless, in spite of that

ci'**occa, che** [ˈtʃɔkka] *sf (di capelli)* lock

ciocco'**lata** [tʃokkoˈlata] *sf* chocolate; *(bevanda)* (hot) chocolate; **ciocco'latino** *sm* chocolate; **ciocco'lato** *sm* chocolate

cioè [tʃoˈɛ] *av* that is (to say)

ciondo'**lare** [tʃondoˈlare] *vi* to dangle; *(fig)* to loaf (about); **ci'ondolo** *sm* pendant

ci'**otola** [ˈtʃɔtola] *sf* bowl

ci'**ottolo** [ˈtʃɔttolo] *sm* pebble; *(di strada)* cobble(stone)

ci'**polla** [tʃiˈpolla] *sf* onion; *(di tulipano etc)* bulb

ci'**presso** [tʃiˈprɛsso] *sm* cypress (tree)

'**cipria** [ˈtʃiprja] *sf* (face) powder

'**Cipro** [ˈtʃipro] *sm* Cyprus

'**circa** [ˈtʃirka] *av* about, roughly ♦ *prep* about, concerning; **a mezzogiorno ~** about midday

'**circo, chi** [ˈtʃirko] *sm* circus

circo'**lare** [tʃirkoˈlare] *vi* to circulate; *(AUT)* to drive (along), move (along) ♦ *ag* circular ♦ *sf (AMM)* circular; *(di autobus)* circle (line); **circolazi'one** *sf* circulation; (*AUT*): **la circolazione** (the) traffic

'circolo [tʃirkolo] *sm* circle

circon'dare [tʃirkon'dare] *vt* to surround

circonfe'renza [tʃirkonfe'rentsa] *sf* circumference

circonvallazi'one [tʃirkonvallat'tsjone] *sf* ring road (*BRIT*), beltway (*US*); (*per evitare una città*) by-pass

circos'critto, a [tʃirkos'kritto] *pp di* **circoscrivere**

circos'crivere [tʃirkos'krivere] *vt* to circumscribe; (*fig*) to limit, restrict; **circoscrizi'one** *sf* (*AMM*) district, area; **circoscrizione elettorale** constituency

circos'petto, a [tʃirkos'petto] *ag* circumspect, cautious

circos'tante [tʃirkos'tante] *ag* surrounding, neighbouring

circos'tanza [tʃirkos'tantsa] *sf* circumstance; (*occasione*) occasion

cir'cuito [tʃir'kuito] *sm* circuit

CISL *sigla f* (= *Confederazione Italiana Sindacati Lavoratori*) trades union organization

ciste ['tʃiste] *sf* = **cisti**

cis'terna [tʃis'tɛrna] *sf* tank, cistern

cisti ['tʃisti] *sf* cyst

C.I.T. [tʃit] *sigla f* = **Compagnia Italiana Turismo**

ci'tare [tʃi'tare] *vt* (*DIR*) to summon; (*autore*) to quote; (*a esempio, modello*) to cite; **citazi'one** *sf* summons *sg*; quotation; (*di persona*) mention

ci'tofono [tʃi'tɔfono] *sm* entry phone; (*in uffici*) intercom

città [tʃit'ta] *sf inv* town; (*importante*) city; ~ **universitaria** university campus

ittadi'nanza [tʃittadi'nantsa] *sf* citizens *pl*, inhabitants *pl* of a town (*o* city); (*DIR*) citizenship

itta'dino, a [tʃitta'dino] *ag* town *cpd*; city *cpd* ♦ *sm/f* (*di uno Stato*) citizen; (*abitante di città*) townsman, city dweller

** i'uco, a, chi, che** ['tʃuko] *sm/f* ass, donkey

i'uffo ['tʃuffo] *sm* tuft

i'vetta [tʃi'vetta] *sf* (*ZOOL*) owl; (*fig: donna*) coquette, flirt ♦ *ag inv*: **auto/**

nave ~ decoy car/ship

'civico, a, ci, che ['tʃivico] *ag* civic; (*museo*) municipal, town *cpd*; municipal, city *cpd*

ci'vile [tʃi'vile] *ag* civil; (*non militare*) civilian; (*nazione*) civilized ♦ *sm* civilian

civilizzazi'one [tʃiviliddzat'tsjone] *sf* civilization

civiltà [tʃivil'ta] *sf* civilization; (*cortesia*) civility

'clacson *sm inv* (*AUT*) horn

cla'more *sm* (*frastuono*) din, uproar, clamour; (*fig*) outcry; **clamo'roso, a** *ag* noisy; (*fig*) sensational

clandes'tino, a *ag* clandestine; (*POL*) underground, clandestine ♦ *sm/f* stowaway

clari'netto *sm* clarinet

'classe *sf* class; **di** ~ (*fig*) with class; of excellent quality

'classico, a, ci, che *ag* classical; (*tradizionale: moda*) classic(al) ♦ *sm* classic; classical author

clas'sifica *sf* classification; (*SPORT*) placings *pl*

classifi'care *vt* to classify; (*candidato, compito*) to grade; ~**rsi** *vr* to be placed

'clausola *sf* (*DIR*) clause

'clava *sf* club

clavi'cembalo [klavi'tʃembalo] *sm* harpsichord

cla'vicola *sf* (*ANAT*) collar bone

cle'mente *ag* merciful; (*clima*) mild; **cle'menza** *sf* mercy, clemency; mildness

'clero *sm* clergy

cli'ente *sm/f* customer, client; **clien'tela** *sf* customers *pl*, clientèle

'clima, i *sm* climate; **cli'matico, a, ci, che** *ag* climatic; **stazione climatica** health resort; **climatizzazi'one** *sf* (*TECN*) air conditioning

'clinica, che *sf* (*scienza*) clinical medicine; (*casa di cura*) clinic, nursing home; (*settore d'ospedale*) clinic

'clinico, a, ci, che *ag* clinical ♦ *sm* (*medico*) clinician

clo'aca, che *sf* sewer

'cloro *sm* chlorine

cloro'formio *sm* chloroform

club *sm inv* club

c.m. *abbr* = **corrente mese**

coabi'tare *vi* to live together, live under the same roof

coagu'lare *vt* to coagulate ♦ *vi* to coagulate; (*latte*) to curdle; **~rsi** *vr* to coagulate; to curdle

coalizi'one [koalit'tsjone] *sf* coalition

co'atto, a *ag* (*DIR*) compulsory, forced

'COBAS *sigla mpl* (= *Comitati di base*) *independent trades unions*

coca'ina *sf* cocaine

cocci'nella [kottʃi'nɛlla] *sf* ladybird (*BRIT*), ladybug (*US*)

'coccio ['kɔttʃo] *sm* earthenware; (*vaso*) earthenware pot; **~i** *smpl* (*frammenti*) fragments (of pottery)

cocci'uto, a [kot'tʃuto] *ag* stubborn, pigheaded

'cocco, chi *sm* (*pianta*) coconut palm; (*frutto*): **noce di ~** coconut ♦ *sm/f* (*fam*) darling

cocco'drillo *sm* crocodile

cocco'lare *vt* to cuddle, fondle

co'cente [ko'tʃɛnte] *ag* (*anche fig*) burning

co'comero *sm* watermelon

co'cuzzolo [ko'kuttsolo] *sm* top; (*di capo, cappello*) crown

'coda *sf* tail; (*fila di persone, auto*) queue (*BRIT*), line (*US*); (*di abiti*) train; **con la ~ dell'occhio** out of the corner of one's eye; **mettersi in ~** to queue (up) (*BRIT*), line up (*US*); to join the queue (*BRIT*) *o* line (*US*); **~ di cavallo** (*acconciatura*) ponytail

co'dardo, a *ag* cowardly ♦ *sm/f* coward

'codice ['koditʃe] *sm* code; **~ di avviamento postale** postcode (*BRIT*), zip code (*US*); **~ fiscale** tax code; **~ della strada** highway code

coe'rente *ag* coherent; **coe'renza** *sf* coherence

coe'taneo, a *ag, sm/f* contemporary

'cofano *sm* (*AUT*) bonnet (*BRIT*), hood (*US*); (*forziere*) chest

'cogli ['kɔʎʎi] *prep* + *det* = **con** + **gli**; *vedi* **con**

'cogliere ['kɔʎʎere] *vt* (*fiore, frutto*) to pick, gather; (*sorprendere*) to catch,

surprise; (*bersaglio*) to hit; (*fig: momento opportuno etc*) to grasp, seize, take; (: *capire*) to grasp; **~ qn in flagrante** *o* **in fallo** to catch sb red-handed

co'gnato, a [kon'nato] *sm/f* brother-/sister-in-law

cognizi'one [konnit'tsjone] *sf* knowledge

co'gnome [kon'nome] *sm* surname

'coi *prep* + *det* = **con** + **i**; *vedi* **con**

coinci'denza [kointʃi'dɛntsa] *sf* coincidence; (*FERR, AER, di autobus*) connection

coin'cidere [koin'tʃidere] *vi* to coincide; **coin'ciso, a** *pp di* **coincidere**

coin'volgere [koin'vɔldʒere] *vt*: **~ in** to involve in; **coin'volto, a** *pp di* **coinvolgere**

col *prep* + *det* = **con** + **il**; *vedi* **con**

cola'brodo *sm inv* strainer

cola'pasta *sm inv* colander

co'lare *vt* (*liquido*) to strain; (*pasta*) to drain; (*oro fuso*) to pour ♦ *vi* (*sudore*) to drip; (*botte*) to leak; (*cera*) to melt; **~ a picco** *vt, vi* (*nave*) to sink

co'lata *sf* (*di lava*) flow; (*FONDERIA*) casting

colazi'one [kolat'tsjone] *sf* (*anche: prima* **~**) breakfast; (*anche: seconda* **~**) lunch; **fare ~** to have breakfast (*o* lunch)

co'lei *pron vedi* **colui**

co'lera *sm* (*MED*) cholera

'colica *sf* (*MED*) colic

'colla *sf* glue; (*di farina*) paste

collabo'rare *vi* to collaborate; **~ a** to collaborate on; (*giornale*) to contribute to; **collabora'tore, 'trice** *sm/f* collaborator; contributor

col'lana *sf* necklace; (*collezione*) collection, series

col'lant [kɔ'lã] *sm inv* tights *pl*

col'lare *sm* collar

col'lasso *sm* (*MED*) collapse

collau'dare *vt* to test, try out; **col'laudo** *sm* testing *no pl*; test

'colle *sm* hill

col'lega, ghi, ghe *sm/f* colleague

collega'mento *sm* connection; (*MIL*) liaison

colle'gare *vt* to connect, join, link; **~rsi**

vr (RADIO, TV) to link up; ~**rsi con** (TEL) to get through to

col'legio [kol'lɛdʒo] sm college; (convitto) boarding school; ~ **elettorale** (POL) constituency

'collera sf anger

col'lerico, a, ci, che ag quick-tempered, irascible

col'letta sf collection

collettività sf community

collet'tivo, a ag collective; (interesse) general, everybody's; (biglietto, visita etc) group cpd ♦ sm (POL) (political) group

col'letto sm collar

collezio'nare [kollettsjo'nare] vt to collect

collezi'one [kollet'tsjone] sf collection

colli'mare vi to correspond, coincide

col'lina sf hill

col'lirio sm eyewash

collisi'one sf collision

'collo sm neck; (di abito) neck, collar; (pacco) parcel; ~ **del piede** instep

colloca'mento sm (impiego) employment; (disposizione) placing, arrangement

collo'care vt (libri, mobili) to place; (persona: trovare un lavoro per) to find a job for, place; (COMM: merce) to find a market for

col'loquio sm conversation, talk; (ufficiale, per un lavoro) interview; (INS) preliminary oral exam

col'mare vt: ~ **di** (anche fig) to fill with; (dare in abbondanza) to load o overwhelm with; 'colmo, a ag: colmo (di) full (of) ♦ sm summit, top; (fig) height; **al colmo della disperazione** in the depths of despair; **è il colmo!** it's the last straw!

co'lombo, a sm/f dove; pigeon

co'lonia sf colony; (per bambini) holiday camp; (acqua di) ~ (eau de) cologne; coloni'ale ag colonial ♦ sm/f colonist, settler

co'lonna sf column; ~ **vertebrale** spine, spinal column

colon'nello sm colonel

co'lono sm (coltivatore) tenant farmer

colo'rante sm colouring

colo'rare vt to colour; (disegno) to colour in

co'lore sm colour; **a ~i** in colour, colour cpd; **farne di tutti i ~i** to get up to all sorts of mischief

colo'rito, a ag coloured; (viso) rosy, pink; (linguaggio) colourful ♦ sm (tinta) colour; (carnagione) complexion

co'loro pron pl vedi colui

co'losso sm colossus

'colpa sf fault; (biasimo) blame; (colpevolezza) guilt; (azione colpevole) offence; (peccato) sin; **di chi è la ~?** whose fault is it?; **è ~ sua** it's his fault; **per ~ di** through, owing to; col'pevole ag guilty

col'pire vt to hit, strike; (fig) to strike; **rimanere colpito da qc** to be amazed o struck by sth

'colpo sm (urto) knock; (: affettivo) blow, shock; (: aggressivo) blow; (di pistola) shot; (MED) stroke; (rapina) raid; **di ~** suddenly; **fare ~** to make a strong impression; ~ **di grazia** coup de grâce; ~ **di scena** (TEATRO) coup de théâtre; (fig) dramatic turn of events; ~ **di sole** sunstroke; ~ **di Stato** coup d'état; ~ **di telefono** phone call; ~ **di testa** (sudden) impulse o whim; ~ **di vento** gust (of wind)

coltel'lata sf stab

col'tello sm knife; ~ **a serramanico** clasp knife

colti'vare vt to cultivate; (verdura) to grow, cultivate; coltiva'tore sm farmer; coltivazi'one sf cultivation; growing

'colto, a pp di cogliere ♦ ag (istruito) cultured, educated

'coltre sf blanket

col'tura sf cultivation

co'lui (f co'lei, pl co'loro) pron the one; ~ **che parla** the one o the man o the person who is speaking; **colei che amo** the one o the woman o the person (whom) I love

'coma sm inv coma

comanda'mento sm (REL) commandment

coman'dante sm (MIL) commander,

commandant; (*di reggimento*)
commanding officer; (*NAUT, AER*) captain
coman'dare *vi* to be in command ♦ *vt* to
command; (*imporre*) to order, command;
~ **a qn di fare** to order sb to do;
co'mando *sm* (*ingiunzione*) order, command; (*autorità*) command; (*TECN*) control
co'mare *sf* (*madrina*) godmother
combaci'are [komba't∫are] *vi* to meet;
(*fig: coincidere*) to coincide
com'battere *vt, vi* to fight;
combatti'mento *sm* fight; fighting *no pl*;
(*di pugilato*) match
combi'nare *vt* to combine; (*organizzare*)
to arrange; (*fam: fare*) to make, cause;
combinazi'one *sf* combination; (*caso
fortuito*) coincidence; **per combinazione**
by chance
combus'tibile *ag* combustible ♦ *sm* fuel
com'butta (*peg*) *sf*: **in** ~ in league

| *PAROLA CHIAVE* |

'come *av* **1** (*alla maniera di*) like; **ti
comporti** ~ **lui** you behave like him *o*
like he does; **bianco** ~ **la neve** (as) white
as snow; ~ **se** as if, as though
2 (*in qualità di*) as a; **lavora** ~ **autista**
he works as a driver
3 (*interrogativo*) how; ~ **ti chiami?**
what's your name?; ~ **sta?** how are you?;
com'è il tuo amico? what is your friend
like?; ~**?** (*prego?*) pardon?, sorry?; ~ **mai?**
how come?; ~ **mai non ci hai avvertiti?**
why on earth didn't you warn us?
4 (*esclamativo*): ~ **sei bravo!** how clever
you are!; ~ **mi dispiace!** I'm terribly
sorry!
♦ *cong* **1** (*in che modo*) how; **mi ha
spiegato** ~ **l'ha conosciuto** he told me
how he met him
2 (*correlativo*) as; (*con comparativi di
maggioranza*) than; **non è bravo** ~
pensavo he isn't as clever as I thought; **è
meglio di** ~ **pensassi** it's better than I
thought
3 (*appena che, quando*) as soon as; ~
arrivò, iniziò a lavorare as soon as he
arrived, he set to work; *vedi* **così**; **tanto**

'comico, a, ci, che *ag* (*TEATRO*) comic;
(*buffo*) comical ♦ *sm* (*attore*) comedian,
comic actor; (*comicità*) comic spirit,
comedy
co'mignolo [ko'mi∫∫olo] *sm* chimney
top
cominci'are [komin't∫are] *vt, vi* to begin,
start; ~ **a fare/col fare** to begin to do/by
doing
comi'tato *sm* committee
comi'tiva *sf* party, group
co'mizio [ko'mittsjo] *sm* (*POL*) meeting,
assembly
com'mando *sm inv* commando (squad)
com'media *sf* comedy; (*opera teatrale*)
play; (*: che fa ridere*) comedy; (*fig*)
playacting *no pl*; **commedi'ante** (*peg*)
sm/f third-rate actor/actress; (*fig*)
sham
commemo'rare *vt* to commemorate
commenda'tore *sm* official title
awarded for services to one's country
commen'tare *vt* to comment on; (*testo*)
to annotate; (*RADIO, TV*) to give a
commentary on; **commenta'tore, 'trice**
sm/f commentator; **com'mento** *sm*
comment; (*a un testo, RADIO, TV*)
commentary
commerci'ale [kommer't∫ale] *ag*
commercial, trading; (*peg*) commercial
commerci'ante [kommer't∫ante] *sm/f*
trader, dealer; (*negoziante*) shopkeeper
commerci'are [kommer't∫are] *vt, vi*: ~
in to deal *o* trade in
com'mercio [kom'mert∫o] *sm* trade,
commerce; **essere in** ~ (*prodotto*) to be on
the market *o* on sale; **essere nel** ~
(*persona*) to be in business; ~
all'ingrosso/al minuto wholesale/retail
trade
com'messa *sf* (*COMM*) order
com'messo, a *pp di* **commettere** ♦ *sm/
f* shop assistant (*BRIT*), sales clerk (*US*)
♦ *sm* (*impiegato*) clerk; ~ **viaggiatore**
commercial traveller
commes'tibile *ag* edible; ~**i** *smpl*
foodstuffs
com'mettere *vt* to commit
com'miato *sm* leave-taking

commi'nare *vt* (*DIR*) to threaten; to inflict

commissari'ato *sm* (*AMM*) commissionership; (*: sede*) commissioner's office; (*: di polizia*) police station

commis'sario *sm* commissioner; (*di pubblica sicurezza*) ≈ (police) superintendent (*BRIT*), (police) captain (*US*); (*SPORT*) steward; (*membro di commissione*) member of a committee *o* board

commissio'nario *sm* (*COMM*) agent, broker

commissi'one *sf* (*incarico*) errand; (*comitato, percentuale*) commission; (*COMM: ordinazione*) order; **~i** *sfpl* (*acquisti*) shopping *sg*

commit'tente *sm/f* (*COMM*) purchaser, customer

com'mosso, a *pp di* **commuovere**

commo'vente *ag* moving

commozi'one [kommot'tsjone] *sf* emotion, deep feeling; **~ cerebrale** (*MED*) concussion

commu'overe *vt* to move, affect; **~rsi** *vr* to be moved

commu'tare *vt* (*pena*) to commute; (*ELETTR*) to change *o* switch over

comò *sm inv* chest of drawers

como'dino *sm* bedside table

comodità *sf inv* comfort; convenience

'comodo, a *ag* comfortable; (*facile*) easy; (*conveniente*) convenient; (*utile*) useful, handy ♦ *sm* comfort; convenience; **con ~** at one's convenience *o* leisure; **fare il proprio ~** to do as one pleases; **far ~** to be useful *o* handy

compae'sano, a *sm/f* fellow countryman; person from the same town

com'pagine [kom'padʒine] *sf* (*squadra*) team

compa'gnia [kompaɲ'ɲia] *sf* company; (*gruppo*) gathering

com'pagno, a [kom'paɲɲo] *sm/f* (*di classe, gioco*) companion; (*POL*) comrade

compa'rare *vt* to compare

compara'tivo, a *ag, sm* comparative

compa'rire *vi* to appear; **com'parsa** *sf* appearance; (*TEATRO*) walk-on; (*CINEMA*) extra; **comparso, a** *pp di* **comparire**

compartecipazi'one [kompartetʃipat-'tsjone] *sf* sharing; (*quota*) share; **~ agli utili** profit-sharing

comparti'mento *sm* compartment; (*AMM*) district

compas'sato, a *ag* (*persona*) composed

compassi'one *sf* compassion, pity; **avere ~ di qn** to feel sorry for sb, to pity sb

com'passo *sm* (pair of) compasses *pl*; callipers *pl*

compa'tibile *ag* (*scusabile*) excusable; (*conciliabile, INFORM*) compatible

compa'tire *vt* (*aver compassione di*) to sympathize with, feel sorry for; (*scusare*) to make allowances for

com'patto, a *ag* compact; (*roccia*) solid; (*folla*) dense; (*fig: gruppo, partito*) united, close-knit

com'pendio *sm* summary; (*libro*) compendium

compen'sare *vt* (*equilibrare*) to compensate for, make up for; **~ qn di** (*rimunerare*) to pay *o* remunerate sb for; (*risarcire*) to pay compensation to sb for; (*fig: fatiche, dolori*) to reward sb for; **com'penso** *sm* compensation; payment, remuneration; reward; **in compenso** (*d'altra parte*) on the other hand

'compera *sf* (*acquisto*) purchase; **fare le ~e** to do the shopping

compe'rare *vt* = **comprare**

compe'tente *ag* competent; (*mancia*) apt, suitable; **compe'tenza** *sf* competence; **competenze** *sfpl* (*onorari*) fees

com'petere *vi* to compete, vie; (*DIR: spettare*): **~ a** to lie within the competence of; **competizi'one** *sf* competition

compia'cente [kompja'tʃɛnte] *ag* courteous, obliging; **compia'cenza** *sf* courtesy

compia'cere [kompja'tʃere] *vi*: **~ a** to gratify, please ♦ *vt* to please; **~rsi** *vr* (*provare soddisfazione*): **~rsi di** *o* **per qc** to be delighted at sth; (*rallegrarsi*): **~rsi con qn** to congratulate sb; (*degnarsi*): **~rsi di fare** to be so good as to do; **compiaci'uto, a** *pp di* **compiacere**

compi'angere [kom'pjandʒere] *vt* to sympathize with, feel sorry for; **compi'anto, a** *pp di* **compiangere**

'compiere *vt* (*concludere*) to finish, complete; (*adempiere*) to carry out, fulfil; ~**rsi** *vr* (*avverarsi*) to be fulfilled, come true; ~ **gli anni** to have one's birthday

compi'lare *vt* (*modulo*) to fill in; (*dizionario, elenco*) to compile

com'pire *vt* = **compiere**

compi'tare *vt* to spell out

'compito *sm* (*incarico*) task, duty; (*dovere*) duty; (*INS*) exercise; (*: a casa*) piece of homework; **fare i ~i** to do one's homework

com'pito, a *ag* well-mannered, polite

comple'anno *sm* birthday

complemen'tare *ag* complementary; (*INS: materia*) subsidiary

comple'mento *sm* complement; (*MIL*) reserve (troops); ~ **oggetto** (*LING*) direct object

complessità *sf* complexity

comples'sivo, a *ag* (*globale*) comprehensive, overall; (*totale: cifra*) total

com'plesso, a *ag* complex ♦ *sm* (*PSIC, EDIL*) complex; (*MUS: corale*) ensemble; (*: orchestrina*) band; (*: di musica pop*) group; **in o nel ~** on the whole

comple'tare *vt* to complete

com'pleto, a *ag* complete; (*teatro, autobus*) full ♦ *sm* suit; **al ~** full; (*tutti presenti*) all present

compli'care *vt* to complicate; ~**rsi** *vr* to become complicated; **complicazi'one** *sf* complication

'complice ['komplitʃe] *sm/f* accomplice

complimen'tarsi *vr*: ~ **con** to congratulate

compli'mento *sm* compliment; ~**i** *smpl* (*cortesia eccessiva*) ceremony *sg*; (*ossequi*) regards, compliments; ~**i!** congratulations!; **senza ~i!** don't stand on ceremony!; make yourself at home!; help yourself!

complot'tare *vi* to plot, conspire

com'plotto *sm* plot, conspiracy

compo'nente *sm/f* member ♦ *sm* component

componi'mento *sm* (*DIR*) settlement; (*INS*) composition; (*poetico, teatrale*) work

com'porre *vt* (*musica, testo*) to compose; (*mettere in ordine*) to arrange; (*DIR: lite*) to settle; (*TIP*) to set; (*TEL*) to dial

comporta'mento *sm* behaviour

compor'tare *vt* (*implicare*) to involve; (*consentire*) to permit, allow (of); ~**rsi** *vr* (*condursi*) to behave

composi'tore, 'trice *sm/f* composer; (*TIP*) compositor, typesetter

composizi'one [kompozit'tsjone] *sf* composition; (*DIR*) settlement

com'posta *sf* (*CUC*) stewed fruit *no pl*; (*AGR*) compost; *vedi anche* **composto**

compos'tezza [kompos'tettsa] *sf* composure; decorum

com'posto, a *pp di* **comporre** ♦ *ag* (*persona*) composed, self-possessed; (*: decoroso*) dignified; (*formato da più elementi*) compound *cpd* ♦ *sm* compound

com'prare *vt* to buy; **compra'tore, 'trice** *sm/f* buyer, purchaser

com'prendere *vt* (*contenere*) to comprise, consist of; (*capire*) to understand

comprensi'one *sf* understanding

compren'sivo, a *ag* (*prezzo*): ~ **di** inclusive of; (*indulgente*) understanding

com'preso, a *pp di* **comprendere** ♦ *ag* (*incluso*) included

com'pressa *sf* (*MED: garza*) compress; (*: pastiglia*) tablet; *vedi anche* **compresso**

compressi'one *sf* compression

com'presso, a *pp di* **comprimere** ♦ *ag* (*vedi comprimere*) pressed; compressed; repressed

com'primere *vt* (*premere*) to press; (*FISICA*) to compress; (*fig*) to repress

compro'messo, a *pp di* **compromettere** ♦ *sm* compromise

compro'mettere *vt* to compromise

compro'vare *vt* to confirm

com'punto, a *ag* contrite

compu'tare *vt* to calculate; (*addebitare*): ~ **qc a qn** to debit sb with sth

com'puter *sm inv* computer

computiste'ria *sf* accounting, bookkeeping

'**computo** *sm* calculation
comu'nale *ag* municipal, town *cpd*,
 ≈ borough *cpd*
co'mune *ag* common; (*consueto*) common,
 everyday; (*di livello medio*) average;
 (*ordinario*) ordinary ♦ *sm* (*AMM*) town
 council; (*: sede*) town hall ♦ *sf* (*di persone*)
 commune; **fuori del** ~ out of the
 ordinary; **avere in** ~ to have in common,
 share; **mettere in** ~ to share
comuni'care *vt* (*notizia*) to pass on,
 convey; (*malattia*) to pass on; (*ansia etc*)
 to communicate; (*trasmettere: calore etc*)
 to transmit, communicate; (*REL*) to
 administer communion to ♦ *vi* to
 communicate; ~**rsi** *vr* (*propagarsi*): ~**rsi a**
 to spread to; (*REL*) to receive communion
comuni'cato *sm* communiqué; ~ **stampa**
 press release
comunicazi'one [komunikat'tsjone] *sf*
 communication; (*annuncio*)
 announcement; (*TEL*): ~ (**telefonica**)
 (telephone) call; **dare la** ~ **a qn** to put sb
 through; **ottenere la** ~ to get through
comuni'one *sf* communion; ~ **di beni**
 (*DIR*) joint ownership of property
comu'nismo *sm* communism;
 comu'nista, i, e *ag, sm/f* communist
comunità *sf inv* community; **C~**
 Economica Europea European Economic
 Community
co'munque *cong* however, no matter
 how ♦ *av* (*in ogni modo*) in any case;
 (*tuttavia*) however, nevertheless
con *prep* with; **partire col treno** to leave
 by train; ~ **mio grande stupore** to my
 great astonishment; ~ **tutto ciò** for all
 that
co'nato *sm*: ~ **di vomito** retching
'**conca, che** *sf* (*GEO*) valley
con'cedere [kon'tʃɛdere] *vt* (*accordare*)
 to grant; (*ammettere*) to admit, concede;
 ~**rsi qc** to treat o.s. to sth, to allow o.s.
 sth
concentra'mento [kontʃentra'mento]
 sm concentration
concen'trare [kontʃen'trare] *vt* to
 concentrate; ~**rsi** *vr* to concentrate;
 concentrazi'one *sf* concentration

conce'pire [kontʃe'pire] *vt* (*bambino*) to
 conceive; (*progetto, idea*) to conceive (of);
 (*metodo, piano*) to devise
con'cernere [kon'tʃɛrnere] *vt* to concern
concer'tare [kontʃer'tare] *vt* (*MUS*) to
 harmonize; (*ordire*) to devise, plan; ~**rsi**
 vr to agree
con'certo [kon'tʃɛrto] *sm* (*MUS*) concert;
 (*: componimento*) concerto
concessio'nario [kontʃessjo'narjo] *sm*
 (*COMM*) agent, dealer
con'cesso, a [kon'tʃɛsso] *pp di*
 concedere
con'cetto [kon'tʃɛtto] *sm* (*pensiero, idea*)
 concept; (*opinione*) opinion
concezi'one [kontʃet'tsjone] *sf*
 conception
con'chiglia [kon'kiʎʎa] *sf* shell
'**concia** ['kontʃa] *sf* (*di pelle*) tanning; (*di
 tabacco*) curing; (*sostanza*) tannin
conci'are [kon'tʃare] *vt* (*pelli*) to tan;
 (*tabacco*) to cure; (*fig: ridurre in cattivo
 stato*) to beat up; ~**rsi** *vr* (*sporcarsi*) to get
 in a mess; (*vestirsi male*) to dress badly
concili'are [kontʃi'ljare] *vt* to reconcile;
 (*contravvenzione*) to pay on the spot;
 (*favorire: sonno*) to be conducive to,
 induce; (*procurare: simpatia*) to gain; ~**rsi**
 qc to gain *o* win sth (for o.s.); ~**rsi qn** to
 win sb over; ~**rsi con** to be reconciled
 with; **conciliazi'one** *sf* reconciliation;
 (*DIR*) settlement
con'cilio [kon'tʃiljo] *sm* (*REL*) council
con'cime [kon'tʃime] *sm* manure;
 (*chimico*) fertilizer
con'ciso, a [kon'tʃizo] *ag* concise,
 succinct
conci'tato, a [kontʃi'tato] *ag* excited,
 emotional
concitta'dino, a [kontʃitta'dino] *sm/f*
 fellow citizen
con'cludere *vt* to conclude; (*portare a
 compimento*) to conclude, finish, bring to
 an end; (*operare positivamente*) to achieve
 ♦ *vi* (*essere convincente*) to be conclusive;
 ~**rsi** *vr* to come to an end, close;
 conclusi'one *sf* conclusion; (*risultato*)
 result; **conclu'sivo, a** *ag* conclusive;
 (*finale*) final; **con'cluso, a** *pp di*

concludere

concor'danza [konkor'dantsa] *sf* (*anche* *LING*) agreement

concor'dare *vt* (*tregua, prezzo*) to agree on; (*LING*) to make agree ♦ *vi* to agree; **concor'dato** *sm* agreement; (*REL*) concordat

con'corde *ag* (*d'accordo*) in agreement; (*simultaneo*) simultaneous

concor'rente *sm/f* competitor; (*INS*) candidate; **concor'renza** *sf* competition

con'correre *vi*: ~ **(in)** (*MAT*) to converge *o* meet (in); ~ **(a)** (*competere*) to compete (for); (: *INS: a una cattedra*) to apply (for); (*partecipare: a un'impresa*) to take part (in), contribute (to); **con'corso, a** *pp di* **concorrere** ♦ *sm* competition; (*INS*) competitive examination; **concorso di colpa** (*DIR*) contributory negligence

con'creto, a *ag* concrete

concussi'one *sf* (*DIR*) extortion

con'danna *sf* sentence; conviction; condemnation

condan'nare *vt* (*DIR*): ~ **a** to sentence to; ~ **per** to convict of; (*disapprovare*) to condemn; **condan'nato, a** *sm/f* convict

conden'sare *vt* to condense; ~rsi *vr* to condense; **condensazi'one** *sf* condensation

condi'mento *sm* seasoning; dressing

con'dire *vt* to season; (*insalata*) to dress

condi'videre *vt* to share; **condi'viso, a** *pp di* **condividere**

condizio'nale [kondittsjo'nale] *ag* conditional ♦ *sm* (*LING*) conditional ♦ *sf* (*DIR*) suspended sentence

condizio'nare [kondittsjo'nare] *vt* to condition; **ad aria condizionata** air-conditioned

condizi'one [kondit'tsjone] *sf* condition; ~i *sfpl* (*di pagamento etc*) terms, conditions; **a** ~ **che** on condition that, provided that

condogli'anze [kondoʎ'ʎantse] *sfpl* condolences

condo'minio *sm* joint ownership; (*edificio*) jointly-owned building

condo'nare *vt* (*DIR*) to remit; **con'dono** *sm* remission; **condono fiscale**

conditional amnesty for people evading tax

con'dotta *sf* (*modo di comportarsi*) conduct, behaviour; (*di un affare etc*) handling; (*di acqua*) piping; (*incarico sanitario*) country medical practice controlled by a local authority

con'dotto, a *pp di* **condurre** ♦ *ag*: **medico** ~ local authority doctor (*in country district*) ♦ *sm* (*canale, tubo*) pipe, conduit; (*ANAT*) duct

condu'cente [kondu't ʃente] *sm* driver

con'durre *vt* to conduct; (*azienda*) to manage; (*accompagnare: bambino*) to take; (*automobile*) to drive; (*trasportare: acqua, gas*) to convey, conduct; (*fig*) to lead ♦ *vi* to lead; **condursi** *vr* to behave, conduct o.s.

condut'tore *ag*: **filo** ~ (*fig*) thread ♦ *sm* (*di mezzi pubblici*) driver; (*FISICA*) conductor

con'farsi *vr*: ~ **a** to suit, agree with

confederazi'one [konfederat'tsjone] *sf* confederation

confe'renza [konfe'rɛntsa] *sf* (*discorso*) lecture; (*riunione*) conference; ~ **stampa** press conference; **conferenzi'ere, a** *sm/f* lecturer

confe'rire *vt*: ~ **qc a qn** to give sth to sb, bestow sth on sb ♦ *vi* to confer

con'ferma *sf* confirmation

confer'mare *vt* to confirm

confes'sare *vt* to confess; ~rsi *vr* to confess; **andare a** ~rsi (*REL*) to go to confession; **confessio'nale** *ag, sm* confessional; **confessi'one** *sf* confession; (*setta religiosa*) denomination; **con-fes'sore** *sm* confessor

con'fetto *sm* sugared almond; (*MED*) pill

confezio'nare [konfettsjo'nare] *vt* (*vestito*) to make (up); (*merci, pacchi*) to package

confezi'one [konfet'tsjone] *sf* (*di abiti: da uomo*) tailoring; (: *da donna*) dressmaking; (*imballaggio*) packaging; ~ **regalo** gift pack; ~**i per signora** ladies' wear; ~**i da uomo** menswear

confic'care *vt*: ~ **qc in** to hammer *o* drive sth into; ~rsi *vr* to stick

confi'dare *vi*: ~ **in** to confide in, rely on ♦ *vt* to confide; **~rsi con qn** to confide in sb; **cofi'dente** *sm/f (persona amica)* confidant/confidante; *(informatore)* informer; **confi'denza** *sf (familiarità)* intimacy, familiarity; *(fiducia)* trust, confidence; *(rivelazione)* confidence; **confidenzi'ale** *ag* familiar, friendly; *(segreto)* confidential

configu'rarsi *vr*: ~ **a** to assume the shape *o* form of

confi'nare *vi*: ~ **con** to border on ♦ *vt (POL)* to intern; *(fig)* to confine; **~rsi** *vr (isolarsi)*: **~rsi in** to shut o.s. up in

Confin'dustria *sigla f (= Confederazione Generale dell'Industria Italiana) employers' association*, ≈ CBI *(BRIT)*

con'fine *sm* boundary; *(di paese)* border, frontier

con'fino *sm* internment

confis'care *vt* to confiscate

con'flitto *sm* conflict

conflu'enza [konflu'ɛntsa] *sf (di fiumi)* confluence; *(di strade)* junction

conflu'ire *vi (fiumi)* to flow into each other, meet; *(strade)* to meet

con'fondere *vt* to mix up, confuse; *(imbarazzare)* to embarrass; **~rsi** *vr (mescolarsi)* to mingle; *(turbarsi)* to be confused; *(sbagliare)* to get mixed up; ~ **le idee a qn** to mix sb up, confuse sb

confor'mare *vt (adeguare)*: ~ **a** to adapt *o* conform to; **~rsi** *vr*: **~rsi (a)** to conform (to)

confor'tare *vt* to comfort, console; **confor'tevole** *ag (consolante)* comforting; *(comodo)* comfortable; **con'forto** *sm* comfort, consolation

confron'tare *vt* to compare

con'fronto *sm* comparison; **in** *o* **a** ~ **di** in comparison with, compared to; **nei miei** *(o* **tuoi** *etc)* ~**i** towards me *(o* you *etc)*

confusi'one *sf* confusion; *(chiasso)* racket, noise; *(imbarazzo)* embarrassment

con'fuso, a *pp di* **confondere** ♦ *ag (vedi confondere)* confused; embarrassed

confu'tare *vt* to refute

conge'dare [kondʒe'dare] *vt* to dismiss; *(MIL)* to demobilize; **~rsi** *vr* to take one's leave; **con'gedo** *sm (anche MIL)* leave; **prendere congedo da qn** to take one's leave of sb; **congedo assoluto** *(MIL)* discharge

conge'gnare [kondʒeɲ'ɲare] *vt* to construct, put together; **con'gegno** *sm* device, mechanism

conge'lare [kondʒe'lare] *vt* to freeze; **~rsi** *vr* to freeze; **congela'tore** *sm* freezer

congestio'nare [kondʒestjo'nare] *vt* to congest

congesti'one [kondʒes'tjone] *sf* congestion

conget'tura [kondʒet'tura] *sf* conjecture, supposition

con'giungere [kon'dʒundʒere] *vt* to join (together); **~rsi** *vr* to join (together)

congiunti'vite [kondʒunti'vite] *sf* conjunctivitis

congiun'tivo [kondʒun'tivo] *sm (LING)* subjunctive

congi'unto, a [kon'dʒunto] *pp di* **congiungere** ♦ *ag (unito)* joined ♦ *sm/f* relative

congiun'tura [kondʒun'tura] *sf (giuntura)* junction, join; *(ANAT)* joint; *(circostanza)* juncture; *(ECON)* economic situation

congiunzi'one [kondʒun'tsjone] *sf (LING)* conjunction

congi'ura [kon'dʒura] *sf* conspiracy; **congiu'rare** *vi* to conspire

conglome'rato *sm (GEO)* conglomerate; *(fig)* conglomeration; *(EDIL)* concrete

congratu'larsi *vr*: ~ **con qn per qc** to congratulate sb on sth

congratulazi'oni [kongratulat'tsjoni] *sfpl* congratulations

con'grega, ghe *sf* band, bunch

con'gresso *sm* congress

congu'aglio [kon'gwaʎʎo] *sm* balancing, adjusting; *(somma di denaro)* balance

coni'are *vt* to mint, coin; *(fig)* to coin

co'niglio [ko'niʎʎo] *sm* rabbit

coniu'gare *vt (LING)* to conjugate; **~rsi** *vr* to get married; **coniu'gato, a** *ag (sposato)* married; **coniugazi'one** *sf*

(*LING*) conjugation
'**coniuge** ['kɔnjudʒe] *sm/f* spouse
connazio'nale [konnattsjo'nale] *sm/f*
fellow-countryman/woman
connessi'one *sf* connection
con'nesso, a *pp di* **connettere**
con'nettere *vt* to connect, join ♦ *vi* (*fig*)
to think straight
conni'vente *ag* conniving
conno'tati *smpl* distinguishing marks
'**cono** *sm* cone; ~ **gelato** ice-cream cone
cono'scente [konoʃ'ʃɛnte] *sm/f*
acquaintance
cono'scenza [konoʃ'ʃɛntsa] *sf* (*il sapere*)
knowledge *no pl*; (*persona*) acquaintance;
(*facoltà sensoriale*) consciousness *no pl*;
perdere ~ to lose consciousness
co'noscere [ko'noʃʃere] *vt* to know; **ci
siamo conosciuti a Firenze** we (first)
met in Florence; **conosci'tore, 'trice**
sm/f connoisseur; **conosci'uto, a** *pp di*
conoscere ♦ *ag* well-known
con'quista *sf* conquest
conquis'tare *vt* to conquer; (*fig*) to gain,
win
consa'crare *vt* (*REL*) to consecrate;
(*: sacerdote*) to ordain; (*dedicare*) to
dedicate; (*fig: uso etc*) to sanction; ~**rsi a**
to dedicate o.s. to
consangu'ineo, a *sm/f* blood relation
consa'pevole *ag*: ~ **di** aware *o*
conscious of; **consapevo'lezza** *sf*
awareness, consciousness
'**conscio, a, sci, sce** ['kɔnʃo] *ag*: ~ **di**
aware *o* conscious of
consecu'tivo, a *ag* consecutive;
(*successivo: giorno*) following, next
con'segna [kon'seɲɲa] *sf* delivery;
(*merce consegnata*) consignment;
(*custodia*) care, custody; (*MIL: ordine*)
orders *pl*; (*: punizione*) confinement to
barracks; **pagamento alla** ~ cash on
delivery; **dare qc in** ~ **a qn** to entrust
sth to sb
conse'gnare [konseɲ'ɲare] *vt* to deliver;
(*affidare*) to entrust, hand over; (*MIL*) to
confine to barracks
consegu'enza [konse'gwɛntsa] *sf*
consequence; **per** *o* **di** ~ consequently

consegu'ire *vt* to achieve ♦ *vi* to follow,
result
con'senso *sm* approval, consent
consen'tire *vi*: ~ **a** to consent *o* agree to
♦ *vt* to allow, permit
con'serva *sf* (*CUC*) preserve; ~ **di frutta**
jam; ~ **di pomodoro** tomato purée
conser'vare *vt* (*CUC*) to preserve;
(*custodire*) to keep; (*: dalla distruzione etc*)
to preserve, conserve; ~**rsi** *vr* to keep
conserva'tore, 'trice *sm/f* (*POL*)
conservative
conservazi'one [konservat'tsjone] *sf*
preservation; conservation
conside'rare *vt* to consider; (*reputare*) to
consider, regard; ~ **molto qn** to think
highly of sb; **considerazi'one** *sf*
consideration; (*stima*) regard, esteem;
prendere in considerazione to take into
consideration; **conside'revole** *ag*
considerable
consigli'are [konsiʎ'ʎare] *vt* (*persona*) to
advise; (*metodo, azione*) to recommend,
advise, suggest; ~**rsi** *vr*: ~**rsi con qn** to
ask sb for advice; **consigli'ere, a** *sm/f*
adviser ♦ *sm*: **consigliere d'amministrazione** board member; **consigliere
comunale** town councillor; **con'siglio** *sm*
(*suggerimento*) advice *no pl*, piece of
advice; (*assemblea*) council; **consiglio
d'amministrazione** board; **il Consiglio dei Ministri** (*POL*) ≈ the Cabinet
consis'tente *ag* thick; solid; (*fig*) sound,
valid; **consis'tenza** *sf* consistency,
thickness; solidity; validity
con'sistere *vi*: ~ **in** to consist of;
consis'tito, a *pp di* **consistere**
conso'lare *ag* consular ♦ *vt* (*confortare*)
to console, comfort; (*rallegrare*) to cheer
up; ~**rsi** *vr* to be comforted; to cheer up
conso'lato *sm* consulate
consolazi'one [konsolat'tsjone] *sf*
consolation, comfort
'**console**[1] *sm* consul
con'sole[2] [kon'sɔl] *sf* (*quadro di
comando*) console
conso'nante *sf* consonant
'**consono, a** *ag*: ~ **a** consistent with,

consonant with

con'sorte *sm/f* consort

con'sorzio [kon'sɔrtsjo] *sm* consortium

con'stare *vi*: ~ **di** to consist of ♦ *vb impers*: **mi consta che** it has come to my knowledge that, it appears that

consta'tare *vt* to establish, verify; **constatazi'one** *sf* observation; **constatazione amichevole** *jointly-agreed statement for insurance purposes*

consu'eto, a *ag* habitual, usual; **consue'tudine** *sf* habit, custom; (*usanza*) custom

consu'lente *sm/f* consultant; **consu'lenza** *sf* consultancy

consul'tare *vt* to consult; **~rsi** *vr*: **~rsi con qn** to seek the advice of sb; **consultazi'one** *sf* consultation; **consultazioni** *sfpl* (*POL*) talks, consultations

consul'torio *sm*: ~ **familiare** family planning clinic

consu'mare *vt* (*logorare: abiti, scarpe*) to wear out; (*usare*) to consume, use up; (*mangiare, bere*) to consume; (*DIR*) to consummate; **~rsi** *vr* to wear out; to be used up; (*anche fig*) to be consumed; (*combustibile*) to burn out; **consuma'tore** *sm* consumer; **consumazi'one** *sf* (*bibita*) drink, (*spuntino*) snack; (*DIR*) consummation; **consu'mismo** *sm* consumerism; **con'sumo** *sm* consumption; wear; use

consun'tivo *sm* (*ECON*) final balance

con'tabile *ag* accounts *cpd*, accounting ♦ *sm/f* accountant; **contabilità** *sf* (*attività, tecnica*) accounting, accountancy; (*insieme dei libri etc*) books *pl*, accounts *pl*; (*ufficio*) accounts department

conta'dino, a *sm/f* countryman/woman; farm worker; (*peg*) peasant

contagi'are [konta'dʒare] *vt* to infect

con'tagio [kon'tadʒo] *sm* infection; (*per contatto diretto*) contagion; (*epidemia*) epidemic; **contagi'oso, a** *ag* infectious; contagious

conta'gocce [konta'gottʃe] *sm inv* (*MED*) dropper

contami'nare *vt* to contaminate

con'tante *sm* cash; **pagare in ~i** to pay cash

con'tare *vt* to count; (*considerare*) to consider ♦ *vi* to count, be of importance; **~ su qn** to count *o* rely on sb; **~ di fare qc** to intend to do sth; **conta'tore** *sm* meter

contat'tare *vt* to contact

con'tatto *sm* contact

'conte *sm* count

conteggi'are [konted'dʒare] *vt* to charge, put on the bill; **con'teggio** *sm* calculation

con'tegno [kon'teɲɲo] *sm* (*comportamento*) behaviour; (*atteggiamento*) attitude; **darsi un ~** to act nonchalant; to pull o.s. together

contem'plare *vt* to contemplate, gaze at; (*DIR*) to make provision for

contemporanea'mente *av* simultaneously; at the same time

contempo'raneo, a *ag, sm/f* contemporary

conten'dente *sm/f* opponent, adversary

con'tendere *vi* (*competere*) to compete; (*litigare*) to quarrel ♦ *vt*: **~ qc a qn** to contend with *o* be in competition with sb for sth

conte'nere *vt* to contain; **conteni'tore** *sm* container

conten'tare *vt* to please, satisfy; **~rsi di** to be satisfied with, content o.s. with

conten'tezza [konten'tettsa] *sf* contentment

con'tento, a *ag* pleased, glad; ~ **di** pleased with

conte'nuto *sm* contents *pl*; (*argomento*) content

con'tesa *sf* dispute, argument

con'teso, a *pp di* **contendere**

con'tessa *sf* countess

contes'tare *vt* (*DIR*) to notify; (*fig*) to dispute; **contestazi'one** *sf* (*DIR*) notification; dispute; (*protesta*) protest

con'testo *sm* context

con'tiguo, a *ag*: ~ **(a)** adjacent (to)

continen'tale *ag, sm/f* continental

conti'nente *ag* continent ♦ *sm* (*GEO*) continent; (*: terra ferma*) mainland;

conti'nenza *sf* continence

contin'gente [kontin'dʒɛnte] *ag* contingent ♦ *sm* (*COMM*) quota; (*MIL*) contingent; **contin'genza** *sf* circumstance; (*ECON*): **(indennità di) contingenza** cost-of-living allowance

continu'are *vt* to continue (with), go on with ♦ *vi* to continue, go on; ~ **a fare qc** to go on *o* continue doing sth; **continuazi'one** *sf* continuation

continuità *sf* continuity

con'tinuo, a *ag* (*numerazione*) continuous; (*pioggia*) continual, constant; (*ELETTR*): **corrente ~a** direct current; **di ~** continually

'conto *sm* (*calcolo*) calculation; (*COMM, ECON*) account; (*di ristorante, albergo*) bill; (*fig: stima*) consideration, esteem; **fare i ~i con qn** to settle one's account with sb; **fare ~ su qn/qc** to count *o* rely on sb; **rendere ~ a qn di qc** to be accountable to sb for sth; **tener ~ di qn/qc** to take sb/sth into account; **per ~ di** on behalf of; **per ~ mio** as far as I'm concerned; **a ~i fatti, in fin dei ~i** all things considered; **~ corrente** current account; **~ alla rovescia** countdown

con'torcere [kon'tortʃere] *vt* to twist; (*panni*) to wring (out); **~rsi** *vr* to twist, writhe

contor'nare *vt* to surround

con'torno *sm* (*linea*) outline, contour; (*ornamento*) border; (*CUC*) vegetables *pl*

con'torto, a *pp di* **contorcere**

contrabbandi'ere, a *sm/f* smuggler

contrab'bando *sm* smuggling, contraband; **merce di ~** contraband, smuggled goods *pl*

contrab'basso *sm* (*MUS*) (double) bass

contraccambi'are *vt* (*favore etc*) to return

contraccet'tivo, a [kontrattʃet'tivo] *ag, sm* contraceptive

contrac'colpo *sm* rebound; (*di arma da fuoco*) recoil; (*fig*) repercussion

con'trada *sf* street; district

contrad'detto, a *pp di* **contraddire**

contrad'dire *vt* to contradict; **contraddit'torio, a** *ag* contradictory;

(*sentimenti*) conflicting ♦ *sm* (*DIR*) cross-examination; **contraddizi'one** *sf* contradiction

contraf'fare *vt* (*persona*) to mimic; (*alterare: voce*) to disguise; (*firma*) to forge, counterfeit; **contraf'fatto, a** *pp di* **contraffare** ♦ *ag* counterfeit; **contraffazi'one** *sf* mimicking *no pl*; disguising *no pl*; forging *no pl*; (*cosa contraffatta*) forgery

contrap'peso *sm* counterbalance, counterweight

contrap'porre *vt*: ~ **qc a qc** to counter sth with sth; (*paragonare*) to compare sth with sth; **contrap'posto, a** *pp di* **contrapporre**

contraria'mente *av*: ~ **a** contrary to

contrari'are *vt* (*contrastare*) to thwart, oppose; (*irritare*) to annoy, bother; **~rsi** *vr* to get annoyed

contrarietà *sf* adversity; (*fig*) aversion

con'trario, a *ag* opposite; (*sfavorevole*) unfavourable ♦ *sm* opposite; **essere ~ a qc** (*persona*) to be against sth; **in caso ~** otherwise; **avere qc in ~** to have some objection; **al ~** on the contrary

con'trarre *vt* to contract; **contrarsi** *vr* to contract

contrasse'gnare [kontrassɛɲ'ɲare] *vt* to mark; **contras'segno** *sm* (*distintivo*) distinguishing mark; **spedire in contrassegno** to send C.O.D.

contras'tare *vt* (*avversare*) to oppose; (*impedire*) to bar; (*negare: diritto*) to contest, dispute ♦ *vi*: ~ **(con)** (*essere in disaccordo*) to contrast (with); (*lottare*) to struggle (with); **con'trasto** *sm* contrast; (*conflitto*) conflict; (*litigio*) dispute

contrat'tacco *sm* counterattack

contrat'tare *vt, vi* to negotiate

contrat'tempo *sm* hitch

con'tratto, a *pp di* **contrarre** ♦ *sm* contract; **contrattu'ale** *ag* contractual

contravvenzi'one [contravven'tsjone] *sf* contravention; (*ammenda*) fine

contrazi'one [kontrat'tsjone] *sf* contraction; (*di prezzi etc*) reduction

contribu'ente *sm/f* taxpayer; ratepayer (*BRIT*), property tax payer (*US*)

contribu'ire *vi* to contribute;
contri'buto *sm* contribution; (*tassa*) tax
'**contro** *prep* against; ~ **di me/lui** against
me/him; **pastiglie ~ la tosse** throat
lozenges; ~ **pagamento** (*COMM*) on
payment ♦ *prefisso*: **contro'battere** *vt*
(*fig: a parole*) to answer back; (*: con-futare*) to refute; **controfi'gura** *sf*
(*CINEMA*) double; **controfir'mare** *vt* to
countersign
control'lare *vt* (*accertare*) to check;
(*sorvegliare*) to watch, control; (*tenere nel
proprio potere, fig: dominare*) to control;
con'trollo *sm* check; watch; control;
controllo delle nascite birth control;
control'lore *sm* (*FERR, AUTOBUS*) (ticket)
inspector
controprodu'cente [kontroprodu-
'tʃɛnte] *ag* counterproductive
contro'senso *sm* (*contraddizione*)
contradiction in terms; (*assurdità*)
nonsense
controspio'naggio [kontrospio'naddʒo]
sm counterespionage
contro'versia *sf* controversy; (*DIR*)
dispute
contro'verso, a *ag* controversial
contro'voglia [kontro'vɔʎʎa] *av*
unwillingly
contu'macia [kontu'matʃa] *sf* (*DIR*)
default
contusi'one *sf* (*MED*) bruise
convale'scente [konvaleʃ'ʃɛnte] *ag,
sm/f* convalescent; **convale'scenza** *sf*
convalescence
convali'dare *vt* (*AMM*) to validate; (*fig:
sospetto, dubbio*) to confirm
con'vegno [kon'veɲɲo] *sm* (*incontro*)
meeting; (*congresso*) convention, congress;
(*luogo*) meeting place
conve'nevoli *smpl* civilities
conveni'ente *ag* suitable; (*vantaggioso*)
profitable; (*: prezzo*) cheap; **conveni'enza**
sf suitability; advantage; cheapness; **le
convenienze** *sfpl* social conventions
conve'nire *vi* (*riunirsi*) to gather,
assemble; (*concordare*) to agree; (*tornare
utile*) to be worthwhile ♦ *vb impers*:
conviene fare questo it is advisable to

do this; **conviene andarsene** we should
go; **ne convengo** I agree
con'vento *sm* (*di frati*) monastery; (*di
suore*) convent
convenzio'nale [konventsjo'nale] *ag*
conventional
convenzi'one [konven'tsjone] *sf* (*DIR*)
agreement; (*nella società*) convention; **le
~i** *sfpl* social conventions
conver'sare *vi* to have a conversation,
converse
conversazi'one [konversat'tsjone] *sf*
conversation; **fare ~** to chat, have a chat
conversi'one *sf* conversion; ~ **ad U** (*AUT*)
U-turn
conver'tire *vt* (*trasformare*) to change;
(*POL, REL*) to convert; **~rsi** *vr*: **~rsi (a)** to
be converted (to); **conver'tito, a** *sm/f*
convert
con'vesso, a *ag* convex
con'vincere [kon'vintʃere] *vt* to
convince; ~ **qn di qc** to convince sb of
sth; ~ **qn a fare qc** to persuade sb to do
sth; **con'vinto, a** *pp di* **convincere**;
convinzi'one *sf* conviction, firm belief
convis'suto, a *pp di* **convivere**
con'vitto *sm* (*INS*) boarding school
con'vivere *vi* to live together
convo'care *vt* to call, convene; (*DIR*) to
summon; **convocazi'one** *sf* meeting;
summons *sg*
convogli'are [konvoʎ'ʎare] *vt* to convey;
(*dirigere*) to direct, send; **con'voglio** *sm*
(*di veicoli*) convoy; (*FERR*) train
convulsi'one *sf* convulsion; ~ **di riso**
fits of laughter
con'vulso, a *ag* (*pianto*) violent,
convulsive; (*attività*) feverish
coope'rare *vi*: ~ **(a)** to cooperate (in);
coopera'tiva *sf* cooperative;
cooperazi'one *sf* cooperation
coordi'nare *vt* to coordinate;
coordi'nate *sfpl* (*MAT, GEO*) coordinates;
coordi'nati *smpl* (*MODA*) coordinates
co'perchio [ko'perkjo] *sm* cover; (*di
pentola*) lid
co'perta *sf* cover; (*di lana*) blanket; (*da
viaggio*) rug; (*NAUT*) deck
coper'tina *sf* (*STAMPA*) cover, jacket

co'perto, a *pp di* coprire ♦ *ag* covered; (*cielo*) overcast ♦ *sm* place setting; (*posto a tavola*) place; (*al ristorante*) cover charge; ~ di covered in *o* with

coper'tone *sm* (*telo impermeabile*) tarpaulin; (*AUT*) rubber tyre

coper'tura *sf* (*anche ECON, MIL*) cover; (*di edificio*) roofing

'copia *sf* copy; brutta/bella ~ rough/ final copy

copi'are *vt* to copy; copia'trice *sf* copier, copying machine

copi'one *sm* (*CINEMA, TEATRO*) script

'coppa *sf* (*bicchiere*) goblet; (*per frutta, gelato*) dish; (*trofeo*) cup, trophy; ~ dell'olio oil sump (*BRIT*) *o* pan (*US*)

'coppia *sf* (*di persone*) couple; (*di animali, SPORT*) pair

coprifu'oco, chi *sm* curfew

copri'letto *sm* bedspread

co'prire *vt* to cover; (*occupare: carica, posto*) to hold; ~rsi *vr* (*cielo*) to cloud over; (*vestirsi*) to wrap up, cover up; (*ECON*) to cover o.s.; ~rsi di (*macchie, muffa*) to become covered in

co'raggio [ko'raddʒo] *sm* courage, bravery; ~! (*forza!*) come on!; (*animo!*) cheer up!; coraggi'oso, a *ag* courageous, brave

co'rallo *sm* coral

co'rano *sm* (*REL*) Koran

co'razza [ko'rattsa] *sf* armour; (*di animali*) carapace, shell; (*MIL*) armour(- plating); coraz'zata *sf* battleship

corbelle'ria *sf* stupid remark; ~e *sfpl* nonsense *no pl*

'corda *sf* cord; (*fune*) rope; (*spago, MUS*) string; dare ~ a qn to let sb have his (*o* her) way; tenere sulla ~ a qn to keep sb on tenterhooks; tagliare la ~ to slip away, sneak off; ~e vocali vocal cords

cordi'ale *ag* cordial, warm ♦ *sm* (*bevanda*) cordial

cor'doglio [kor'dɔʎʎo] *sm* grief; (*lutto*) mourning

cor'done *sm* cord, string; (*linea: di polizia*) cordon; ~ ombelicale umbilical cord

Co'rea *sf*: la ~ Korea

coreogra'fia *sf* choreography

cori'andolo *sm* (*BOT*) coriander; ~i *smpl* confetti *sg*

cori'care *vt* to put to bed; ~rsi *vr* to go to bed

'corna *sfpl vedi* corno

cor'nacchia [kor'nakkja] *sf* crow

corna'musa *sf* bagpipes *pl*

cor'netta *sf* (*MUS*) cornet; (*TEL*) receiver

cor'netto *sm* (*CUC*) croissant; ~ acustico ear trumpet

cor'nice [kor'nitʃe] *sf* frame; (*fig*) setting, background

cornici'one [korni'tʃone] *sm* (*di edificio*) ledge; (*ARCHIT*) cornice

'corno (*pl(f)* -a) *sm* (*ZOOL*) horn; (*pl(m)* -i: *MUS*) horn; fare le ~a a qn to be unfaithful to sb; cor'nuto, a *ag* (*con corna*) horned; (*fam!: marito*) cuckolded ♦ *sm* (*fam!*) cuckold; (*: insulto*) bastard (!)

Corno'vaglia [korno'vaʎʎa] *sf*: la ~ Cornwall

'coro *sm* chorus; (*REL*) choir

co'rona *sf* crown; (*di fiori*) wreath; coro'nare *vt* to crown

'corpo *sm* body; (*cadavere*) (dead) body; (*militare, diplomatico*) corps *inv*; (*di opere*) corpus; prendere ~ to take shape; a ~ a ~ hand-to-hand; ~ di ballo corps de ballet; ~ di guardia guardroom; ~ insegnante teaching staff

corpo'rale *ag* bodily; (*punizione*) corporal

corpora'tura *sf* build, physique

corporazi'one [korporat'tsjone] *sf* corporation

corpu'lento, a *ag* stout

corre'dare *vt*: ~ di to provide *o* furnish with; cor'redo *sm* equipment; (*di sposa*) trousseau

cor'reggere [kor'rɛddʒere] *vt* to correct; (*compiti*) to correct, mark

cor'rente *ag* (*fiume*) flowing; (*acqua del rubinetto*) running; (*moneta, prezzo*) current; (*comune*) everyday ♦ *sm*: essere al ~ (di) to be well-informed (about); mettere al ~ (di) to inform (of) ♦ *sf* (*movimento di liquido*) current, stream; (*spiffero*) draught; (*ELETTR, METEOR*) current; (*fig*) trend, tendency; **la vostra lettera del 5 ~ mese** (*COMM*) your letter of the 5th of this month;

corrente'mente *av* commonly; **parlare una lingua correntemente** to speak a language fluently

'**correre** *vi* to run; (*precipitarsi*) to rush; (*partecipare a una gara*) to race, run; (*fig: diffondersi*) to go round ♦ *vt* (*SPORT: gara*) to compete in; (*rischio*) to run; (*pericolo*) to face; **~ dietro a qn** to run after sb; **corre voce che ...** it is rumoured that ...

cor'retto, a *pp di* **correggere** ♦ *ag* (*comportamento*) correct, proper; **caffè ~ al cognac** coffee laced with brandy

correzi'one [korret'tsjone] *sf* correction; marking; **~ di bozze** proofreading

corri'doio *sm* corridor

corri'dore *sm* (*SPORT*) runner; (*: su veicolo*) racer

corri'era *sf* coach (*BRIT*), bus

corri'ere *sm* (*diplomatico, di guerra*) courier; (*posta*) mail, post; (*COMM*) carrier

corrispet'tivo *sm* (*somma*) amount due

corrispon'dente *ag* corresponding ♦ *sm/f* correspondent

corrispon'denza [korrispon'dɛntsa] *sf* correspondence

corris'pondere *vi* (*equivalere*): **~ (a)** to correspond (to); (*per lettera*): **~ con** to correspond with ♦ *vt* (*stipendio*) to pay; (*fig: amore*) to return; **corris'posto, a** *pp di* **corrispondere**

corrobo'rare *vt* to strengthen, fortify; (*fig*) to corroborate, bear out

cor'rodere *vt* to corrode; **~rsi** *vr* to corrode

cor'rompere *vt* to corrupt; (*comprare*) to bribe

corrosi'one *sf* corrosion

cor'roso, a *pp di* **corrodere**

cor'rotto, a *pp di* **corrompere** ♦ *ag* corrupt

corrucci'arsi [korrut'tʃarsi] *vr* to grow angry *o* vexed

corru'gare *vt* to wrinkle; **~ la fronte** to knit one's brows

corruzi'one [korrut'tsjone] *sf* corruption; bribery

'**corsa** *sf* running *no pl*; (*gara*) race; (*di autobus, taxi*) journey, trip; **fare una ~** to run, dash; (*SPORT*) to run a race

cor'sia *sf* (*AUT, SPORT*) lane; (*di ospedale*) ward

cor'sivo *sm* cursive (writing); (*TIP*) italics *pl*

'**corso, a** *pp di* **correre** ♦ *sm* course; (*strada cittadina*) main street; (*di unità monetaria*) circulation; (*di titoli, valori*) rate, price; **dar libero ~ a** to give free expression to; **in ~** in progress, under way; (*annata*) current; **~ d'acqua** river, stream; (*artificiale*) waterway; **~ d'aggiornamento** refresher course; **~ serale** evening class

'**corte** *sf* (court)yard; (*DIR, regale*) court; **fare la ~ a qn** to court sb; **~ marziale** court-martial

cor'teccia, ce [kor'tettʃa] *sf* bark

corteggi'are [korted'dʒare] *vt* to court

cor'teo *sm* procession

cor'tese *ag* courteous; **corte'sia** *sf* courtesy; **per cortesia ...** excuse me, please ...

cortigi'ana [korti'dʒana] *sf* courtesan

cortigi'ano, a [korti'dʒano] *sm/f* courtier

cor'tile *sm* (court)yard

cor'tina *sf* curtain; (*anche fig*) screen

'**corto, a** *ag* short; **essere a ~ di qc** to be short of sth; **~ circuito** short-circuit

'**corvo** *sm* raven

'**cosa** *sf* thing; (*faccenda*) affair, matter, business *no pl*; (*che*) **~?** what?; (*che*) **cos'è?** what is it?; **a ~ pensi?** what are you thinking about?

'**coscia, sce** [ˈkɔʃʃa] *sf* thigh; **~ di pollo** (*CUC*) chicken leg

cosci'ente [koʃˈʃɛnte] *ag* conscious; **~ di** conscious *o* aware of; **cosci'enza** *sf* conscience; (*consapevolezza*) consciousness; **coscienzi'oso, a** *ag* conscientious

cosci'otto [koʃˈʃɔtto] *sm* (*CUC*) leg

cos'critto *sm* (*MIL*) conscript

PAROLA CHIAVE
---

così *av* **1** (*in questo modo*) like this, (in)

this way; (*in tal modo*) so; **le cose stanno ~** this is the way things stand; **non ho detto ~!** I didn't say that!; **come stai? — (e) ~** how are you? — so-so; **e ~ via** and so on; **per ~ dire** so to speak **2** (*tanto*) so; **~ lontano** so far away; **un ragazzo ~ intelligente** such an intelligent boy
♦ *ag inv* (*tale*): **non ho mai visto un film ~** I've never seen such a film
♦ *cong* **1** (*perciò*) so, therefore
2: **~ ... come as ... as; non è ~ bravo come te** he's not as good as you; **~ ... che** so ... that

cosid'detto, a *ag* so-called
cos'metico, a, ci, che *ag, sm* cosmetic
cos'pargere [kos'pardʒere] *vt*: **~ di** to sprinkle with; **cos'parso, a** *pp di* **cospargere**
cos'petto *sm*: **al ~ di** in front of; in the presence of
cos'picuo, a *ag* considerable, large
cospi'rare *vi* to conspire; **cospirazi'one** *sf* conspiracy
'costa *sf* (*tra terra e mare*) coast(line); (*litorale*) shore; (ANAT) rib; **la C~ Azzurra** the French Riviera
costà *av* there
cos'tante *ag* constant; (*persona*) steadfast
♦ *sf* constant
cos'tare *vi, vt* to cost; **~ caro** to be expensive, cost a lot
cos'tata *sf* (CUC) large chop
cos'tato *sm* (ANAT) ribs *pl*
costeggi'are [kosted'dʒare] *vt* to be close to; to run alongside
cos'tei *pron vedi* **costui**
costi'era *sf* stretch of coast
costi'ero, a *ag* coastal, coast *cpd*
costitu'ire *vt* (*comitato, gruppo*) to set up, form; (*collezione*) to put together, build up; (*sog: elementi, parti: comporre*) to make up, constitute; (*rappresentare*) to constitute; (DIR) to appoint; **~rsi alla polizia** to give o.s. up to the police
costituzio'nale [kostituttsjo'nale] *ag* constitutional
costituzi'one [kostitut'tsjone] *sf* setting

up; building up; constitution
'costo *sm* cost; **a ogni o qualunque ~, a tutti i ~i** at all costs
'costola *sf* (ANAT) rib
costo'letta *sf* (CUC) cutlet
cos'toro *pron pl vedi* **costui**
cos'toso, a *ag* expensive, costly
cos'tretto, a *pp di* **costringere**
cos'tringere [kos'trindʒere] *vt*: **~ qn a fare qc** to force sb to do sth; **costrizi'one** *sf* coercion
costru'ire *vt* to construct, build; **costruzi'one** *sf* construction, building
cos'tui (*f* **cos'tei**, *pl* **cos'toro**) *pron* (*soggetto*) he/she; (*pl*) they; (*complemento*) him/her; (*pl*) them; **si può sapere chi è ~?** (*peg*) just who is that fellow?
cos'tume *sm* (*uso*) custom; (*foggia di vestire, indumento*) costume; **~i** *smpl* (*condotta morale*) morals, morality *sg*; **il buon ~** public morality; **~ da bagno** bathing o swimming costume (BRIT), swimsuit; (*da uomo*) bathing o swimming trunks *pl*
co'tenna *sf* bacon rind
co'togna [ko'toɲɲa] *sf* quince
coto'letta *sf* (*di maiale, montone*) chop; (*di vitello, agnello*) cutlet
co'tone *sm* cotton; **~ idrofilo** cotton wool (BRIT), absorbent cotton (US)
'cotta *sf* (*fam: innamoramento*) crush
'cottimo *sm*: **lavorare a ~** to do piecework
'cotto, a *pp di* **cuocere** ♦ *ag* cooked; (*fam: innamorato*) head-over-heels in love
cot'tura *sf* cooking; (*in forno*) baking; (*in umido*) stewing
co'vare *vt* to hatch; (*fig: malattia*) to be sickening for; (*: odio, rancore*) to nurse
♦ *vi* (*fuoco, fig*) to smoulder
'covo *sm* den
co'vone *sm* sheaf
'cozza ['kɔttsa] *sf* mussel
coz'zare [kot'tsare] *vi*: **~ contro** to bang into, collide with
C.P. *abbr* (= *casella postale*) P.O. Box
crack [kræk] *sm inv* (*droga*) crack
'crampo *sm* cramp
'cranio *sm* skull

cra'tere *sm* crater

cra'vatta *sf* tie

cre'anza [kre'antsa] *sf* manners *pl*

cre'are *vt* to create; **cre'ato** *sm* creation; **crea'tore, 'trice** *ag* creative ♦ *sm* creator; **crea'tura** *sf* creature; (*bimbo*) baby, infant; **creazi'one** *sf* creation; (*fondazione*) foundation, establishment

cre'dente *sm/f* (*REL*) believer

cre'denza [kre'dɛntsa] *sf* belief; (*armadio*) sideboard

credenzi'ali [kreden'tsjali] *sfpl* credentials

'credere *vt* to believe ♦ *vi*: ~ **in**, ~ **a** to believe in; ~ **qn onesto** to believe sb (to be) honest; ~ **che** to believe o think that; **~rsi furbo** to think one is clever

'credito *sm* (*anche COMM*) credit; (*reputazione*) esteem, repute; **comprare a** ~ to buy on credit

'credo *sm inv* creed

'crema *sf* cream; (*con uova, zucchero etc*) custard; **~ solare** sun cream

cre'mare *vt* to cremate

Crem'lino *sm*: **il** ~ the Kremlin

'crepa *sf* crack

cre'paccio [kre'pattʃo] *sm* large crack, fissure; (*di ghiacciaio*) crevasse

crepacu'ore *sm* broken heart

cre'pare *vi* (*fam: morire*) to snuff it, kick the bucket; ~ **dalle risa** to split one's sides laughing

crepi'tare *vi* (*fuoco*) to crackle; (*pioggia*) to patter

cre'puscolo *sm* twilight, dusk

'crescere ['kreʃʃere] *vi* to grow ♦ *vt* (*figli*) to raise; **'crescita** *sf* growth; **cresci'uto, a** *pp di* **crescere**

'cresima *sf* (*REL*) confirmation

'crespo, a *ag* (*capelli*) frizzy; (*tessuto*) puckered ♦ *sm* crêpe

'cresta *sf* crest; (*di polli, uccelli*) crest, comb

'creta *sf* chalk; clay

cre'tino, a *ag* stupid ♦ *sm/f* idiot, fool

cric *sm inv* (*TECN*) jack

'cricca, che *sf* clique

'cricco, chi *sm* = **cric**

crimi'nale *ag, sm/f* criminal

'crimine *sm* (*DIR*) crime

'crine *sm* horsehair; **crini'era** *sf* mane

crisan'temo *sm* chrysanthemum

'crisi *sf inv* crisis; (*MED*) attack, fit; ~ **di nervi** attack o fit of nerves

cristalliz'zare [kristalid'dzare] *vi* to crystallize; (*fig*) to become fossilized; **~rsi** *vr* to crystallize; to become fossilized

cris'tallo *sm* crystal

cristia'nesimo *sm* Christianity

cristi'ano, a *ag, sm/f* Christian

'Cristo *sm* Christ

cri'terio *sm* criterion; (*buon senso*) (common) sense

'critica, che *sf* criticism; **la** ~ (*attività*) criticism; (*persone*) the critics *pl*; *vedi anche* **critico**

criti'care *vt* to criticize

'critico, a, ci, che *ag* critical ♦ *sm* critic

Croa'zia [kroa'ttsja] *sf* Croatia

cri'vello *sm* riddle

'croce ['krotʃe] *sf* cross; **in** ~ (*di traverso*) crosswise; (*fig*) on tenterhooks; **la C~ Rossa** the Red Cross

croce'figgere *etc* [krotʃe'fiddʒere] = **crocifiggere** *etc*

croce'via [krotʃe'via] *sm inv* crossroads *sg*

croci'ata [kro'tʃata] *sf* crusade

cro'cicchio [kro'tʃikkjo] *sm* crossroads *sg*

croci'era [kro'tʃera] *sf* (*viaggio*) cruise; (*ARCHIT*) transept

croci'figgere [krotʃi'fiddʒere] *vt* to crucify; **crocifissi'one** *sf* crucifixion; **croci'fisso, a** *pp di* **crocifiggere**

crogi'olo [kro'dʒɔlo] *sm* (*fig*) melting pot

crol'lare *vi* to collapse; **'crollo** *sm* collapse; (*di prezzi*) slump, sudden fall

cro'mato, a *ag* chromium-plated

'cromo *sm* chrome, chromium

cromo'soma, i *sm* chromosome

'cronaca, che *sf* chronicle; (*STAMPA*) news *sg*; (*: rubrica*) column; (*TV, RADIO*) commentary; **fatto** o **episodio di** ~ news item; ~ **nera** crime news *sg*; crime column

'cronico, a, ci, che *ag* chronic

cro'nista, i *sm* (*STAMPA*) reporter
crono'logia [kronolo'dʒia] *sf* chronology
cro'nometro *sm* chronometer; (*a scatto*) stopwatch
'crosta *sf* crust
cros'tacei [kros'tatʃei] *smpl* shellfish
cros'tata *sf* (*CUC*) tart
cros'tino *sm* (*CUC*) croûton; (*: da antipasto*) canapé
'cruccio ['kruttʃo] *sm* worry, torment
cruci'verba *sm inv* crossword (puzzle)
cru'dele *ag* cruel; crudeltà *sf* cruelty
'crudo, a *ag* (*non cotto*) raw; (*aspro*) harsh, severe
cru'miro (*peg*) *sm* blackleg (*BRIT*), scab
'crusca *sf* bran
crus'cotto *sm* (*AUT*) dashboard
CSI *sigla f inv* (= *Comunità Stati Indipendenti*) CIS
'Cuba *sf* Cuba
'cubico, a, ci, che *ag* cubic
'cubo, a *ag* cubic ♦ *sm* cube; elevare al ~ (*MAT*) to cube
cuc'cagna [kuk'kaɲɲa] *sf*: paese della ~ land of plenty; albero della ~ greasy pole (*fig*)
cuc'cetta [kut'tʃetta] *sf* (*FERR*) couchette; (*NAUT*) berth
cucchiai'ata [kukja'jata] *sf* spoonful
cucchia'ino [kukkja'ino] *sm* teaspoon; coffee spoon
cucchi'aio [kuk'kjajo] *sm* spoon
'cuccia, ce ['kuttʃa] *sf* dog's bed; a ~! down!
'cucciolo ['kuttʃolo] *sm* cub; (*di cane*) puppy
cu'cina [ku'tʃina] *sf* (*locale*) kitchen; (*arte culinaria*) cooking, cookery; (*le vivande*) food, cooking; (*apparecchio*) cooker; ~ componibile fitted kitchen; cuci'nare *vt* to cook
cu'cire [ku'tʃire] *vt* to sew, stitch; cuci'trice *sf* stapler; cuci'tura *sf* sewing, stitching; (*costura*) seam
cucù *sm inv* = cuculo
cu'culo *sm* cuckoo
'cuffia *sf* bonnet, cap; (*da infermiera*) cap; (*da bagno*) (bathing) cap; (*per ascoltare*) headphones *pl*, headset

cu'gino, a [ku'dʒino] *sm/f* cousin

PAROLA CHIAVE

'cui *pron* 1 (*nei complementi indiretti: persona*) whom; (*: oggetto, animale*) which; la persona/le persone a ~ accennavi the person/people you were referring to *o* to whom you were referring; i libri di ~ parlavo the books I was talking about *o* about which I was talking; il quartiere in ~ abito the district where I live; la ragione per ~ the reason why
2 (*inserito tra articolo e sostantivo*) whose; la donna i ~ figli sono scomparsi the woman whose children have disappeared; il signore, dal ~ figlio ho avuto il libro the man from whose son I got the book

culi'naria *sf* cookery
'culla *sf* cradle
cul'lare *vt* to rock
culmi'nare *vi*: ~ con to culminate in
'culmine *sm* top, summit
'culo (*fam!*) *sm* arse (*Brit!*), ass (*US!*); (*fig: fortuna*): aver ~ to have the luck of the devil
'culto *sm* (*religione*) religion; (*adorazione*) worship, adoration; (*venerazione: anche fig*) cult
cul'tura *sf* culture; education, learning; cultu'rale *ag* cultural
cumula'tivo, a *ag* cumulative; (*prezzo*) inclusive; (*biglietto*) group *cpd*
'cumulo *sm* (*mucchio*) pile, heap; (*METEOR*) cumulus
'cuneo *sm* wedge
cu'oca *sf vedi* cuoco
cu'ocere ['kwɔtʃere] *vt* (*alimenti*) to cook; (*mattoni etc*) to fire ♦ *vi* to cook; ~ al forno (*pane*) to bake; (*arrosto*) to roast; cu'oco, a, chi, che *sm/f* cook; (*di ristorante*) chef
cu'oio *sm* leather; ~ capelluto scalp
cu'ore *sm* heart; ~i *smpl* (*CARTE*) hearts; avere buon ~ to be kind-hearted; stare a ~ a qn to be important to sb
cupi'digia [kupi'didʒa] *sf* greed, covetousness

'**cupo, a** *ag* dark; (*suono*) dull; (*fig*) gloomy, dismal

'**cupola** *sf* dome; cupola

'**cura** *sf* care; (*MED: trattamento*) (course of) treatment; **aver ~ di** (*occuparsi di*) to look after; **a ~ di** (*libro*) edited by; ~ **dimagrante** diet

cu'**rare** *vt* (*malato, malattia*) to treat; (*: guarire*) to cure; (*aver cura di*) to take care of; (*testo*) to edit; ~**rsi** *vr* to take care of o.s.; (*MED*) to follow a course of treatment; ~**rsi di** to pay attention to

cu'**rato** *sm* parish priest; (*protestante*) vicar, minister

cura'**tore, 'trice** *sm/f* (*DIR*) trustee; (*di antologia etc*) editor

curio'**sare** *vi* to look round, wander round; (*tra libri*) to browse; ~ **nei negozi** to look *o* wander round the shops

curiosità *sf inv* curiosity; (*cosa rara*) curio, curiosity

curi'**oso, a** *ag* curious; **essere ~ di** to be curious about

cur'**sore** *sm* (*INFORM*) cursor

'**curva** *sf* curve; (*stradale*) bend, curve

cur'**vare** *vt* to bend ♦ *vi* (*veicolo*) to take a bend; (*strada*) to bend, curve; ~**rsi** *vr* to bend; (*legno*) to warp

'**curvo, a** *ag* curved; (*piegato*) bent

cusci'**netto** [kuʃʃi'netto] *sm* pad, (*TECN*) bearing ♦ *ag inv*: **stato ~** buffer state; **~ a sfere** ball bearing

cu'**scino** [kuʃ'ʃino] *sm* cushion; (*guanciale*) pillow

'**cuspide** *sf* (*ARCHIT*) spire

cus'**tode** *sm/f* keeper, custodian

cus'**todia** *sf* care; (*DIR*) custody; (*astuccio*) case, holder

custo'**dire** *vt* (*conservare*) to keep; (*assistere*) to look after, take care of; (*fare la guardia*) to guard

'**cute** *sf* (*ANAT*) skin

C.V. *abbr* (= *cavallo vapore*) h.p.

D

PAROLA CHIAVE

da (*da+il* = **dal**, *da+lo* = **dallo**, *da+l'* = **dall'**, *da+la* = **dalla**, *da+i* = **dai**, *da+gli* = **dagli**, *da+le* = **dalle**) *prep* **1** (*agente*) by; **dipinto ~ un grande artista** painted by a great artist

2 (*causa*) with; **tremare dalla paura** to tremble with fear

3 (*stato in luogo*) at; **abito ~ lui** I'm living at his house *o* with him; **sono dal giornalaio/~ Francesco** I'm at the newsagent's/Francesco's (house)

4 (*moto a luogo*) to; (*moto per luogo*) through; **vado ~ Pietro/dal giornalaio** I'm going to Pietro's (house)/to the newsagent's; **sono passati dalla finestra** they came in through the window

5 (*provenienza, allontanamento*) from; **arrivare/partire ~ Milano** to arrive/depart from Milan; **scendere dal treno/dalla macchina** to get off the train/out of the car; **si trova a 5 km ~ qui** it's 5 km from here

6 (*tempo: durata*) for; (*: a partire da: nel passato*) since; (*: nel futuro*) from; **vivo qui ~ un anno** I've been living here for a year; **è dalle 3 che ti aspetto** I've been waiting for you since 3 (o'clock); **~ oggi in poi** from today onwards; **~ bambino** as a child, when I (*o* he *etc*) was a child

7 (*modo, maniera*) like; **comportarsi ~ uomo** to behave like a man; **l'ho fatto ~ me** I did it (by) myself

8 (*descrittivo*): **una macchina ~ corsa** a racing car; **una ragazza dai capelli biondi** a girl with blonde hair; **un vestito ~ 100.000 lire** a 100,000 lire dress

dab'**bene** *ag inv* honest, decent

da 'capo *av* = **daccapo**

dac'**capo** *av* (*di nuovo*) (once) again; (*dal principio*) all over again, from the beginning

dacché [dak'ke] *cong* since

'**dado** *sm* (*da gioco*) dice *o* die; (*CUC*) stock (*BRIT*) *o* bouillon (*US*) cube; (*TECN*) (screw)nut; **giocare a ~i** to play dice

da 'fare *sm* = **daffare**

daf'fare *sm* work, toil

dagli ['daʎʎi] *prep* + *det vedi* **da**

'**dai** *prep* + *det vedi* **da**

'**daino** *sm* (fallow) deer *inv*; (*pelle*) buckskin

dal *prep* + *det vedi* **da**

dall' *prep* + *det vedi* **da**

'**dalla** *prep* + *det vedi* **da**

'**dalle** *prep* + *det vedi* **da**

'**dallo** *prep* + *det vedi* **da**

dal'tonico, a, ci, che *ag* colour-blind

'**dama** *sf* lady; (*nei balli*) partner; (*gioco*) draughts *sg* (*BRIT*), checkers *sg* (*US*)

damigi'ana [dami'dʒana] *sf* demijohn

da'naro *sm* = **denaro**

da'nese *ag* Danish ♦ *sm/f* Dane ♦ *sm* (*LING*) Danish

Dani'marca *sf*: **la ~** Denmark

dan'nare *vt* (*REL*) to damn; **~rsi** *vr* (*fig: tormentarsi*) to be worried to death; **far ~ qn** to drive sb mad; **dannazi'one** *sf* damnation

danneggi'are [danned'dʒare] *vt* to damage; (*rovinare*) to spoil; (*nuocere*) to harm

'**danno** *sm* damage; (*a persona*) harm, injury; **~i** *smpl* (*DIR*) damages; **dan'noso, a** *ag*: **dannoso (a, per)** harmful (to), bad (for)

Da'nubio *sm*: **il ~** the Danube

'**danza** ['dantsa] *sf*: **la ~** dancing; **una ~** a dance

dan'zare [dan'tsare] *vt, vi* to dance

dapper'tutto *av* everywhere

dap'poco *ag inv* inept, worthless

dap'prima *av* at first

'**dardo** *sm* dart

'**dare** *sm* (*COMM*) debit ♦ *vt* to give; (*produrre: frutti, suono*) to produce ♦ *vi* (*guardare*): **~ su** to look (out) onto; **~rsi** *vr*: **~rsi a** to dedicate o.s. to; **~rsi al commercio** to go into business; **~rsi al bere** to take to drink; **~ da mangiare a qn** to give sb sth to eat; **~ per certo qc** to consider sth certain; **~ per morto qn** to give sb up for dead; **~rsi per vinto** to give in

'**darsena** *sf* dock; dockyard

'**data** *sf* date; **~ di nascita** date of birth

da'tare *vt* to date ♦ *vi*: **~ da** to date from

'**dato, a** *ag* (*stabilito*) given ♦ *sm* datum; **~i** *smpl* data *pl*; **~ che** given that; **un ~ di fatto** a fact

'**dattero** *sm* date

dattilogra'fare *vt* to type; **dattilogra'fia** *sf* typing; **datti'lografo, a** *sm/f* typist

da'vanti *av* in front; (*dirimpetto*) opposite ♦ *ag inv* front ♦ *sm* front; **~ a** in front of; facing, opposite; (*in presenza di*) before, in front of

davan'zale [davan'tsale] *sm* windowsill

d'a'vanzo [da'vantso] *av* = **davanzo**

da'vanzo [da'vantso] *av* more than enough

dav'vero *av* really, indeed

'**dazio** ['dattsjo] *sm* (*somma*) duty; (*luogo*) customs *pl*

DC *sigla f* = **Democrazia Cristiana**

d. C. *ad abbr* (= *dopo Cristo*) A.D.

'**dea** *sf* goddess

'**debito, a** *ag* due, proper ♦ *sm* debt; (*COMM: dare*) debit; **a tempo ~** at the right time; **debi'tore, 'trice** *sm/f* debtor

'**debole** *ag* weak, feeble; (*suono*) faint; (*luce*) dim ♦ *sm* weakness; **debo'lezza** *sf* weakness

debut'tare *vi* to make one's début; **de'butto** *sm* début

deca'denza [deka'dɛntsa] *sf* decline; (*DIR*) loss, forfeiture

decaffei'nato, a *ag* decaffeinated

decan'tare *vt* to praise, sing the praises of

decapi'tare *vt* to decapitate

decappot'tabile *ag, sf* convertible

dece'duto, a [detʃe'duto] *ag* deceased

de'cennio [de'tʃɛnnjo] *sm* decade

de'cente [de'tʃɛnte] *ag* decent, respectable, proper; (*accettabile*) satisfactory, decent

de'cesso [de'tʃɛsso] *sm* death; **atto di ~** death certificate

de'cidere [de'tʃidere] *vt*: **~ qc** to decide on sth; (*questione, lite*) to settle sth; **~ di**

fare/che to decide to do/that; ~ **di qc**
(*sog: cosa*) to determine sth; ~**rsi (a fare)**
to decide (to do), make up one's mind (to
do)

deci'frare [detʃi'frare] *vt* to decode; (*fig*)
to decipher, make out

deci'male [detʃi'male] *ag* decimal

'decimo, a ['detʃimo] *num* tenth

de'cina [de'tʃina] *sf* ten; (*circa dieci*): **una
~ (di)** about ten

decisi'one [detʃi'zjone] *sf* decision;
prendere una ~ to make a decision

de'ciso, a [de'tʃizo] *pp di* **decidere**

declas'sare *vt* to downgrade; to lower in
status

decli'nare *vi* (*pendio*) to slope down; (*fig:
diminuire*) to decline; (*tramontare*) to set,
go down ♦ *vt* to decline; **declinazi'one** *sf*
(*LING*) declension; **de'clino** *sm* decline

decodifica'tore *sm* (*TEL*) decoder

decol'lare *vi* (*AER*) to take off; **de'collo**
sm take-off

decolo'rare *vt* to bleach

decom'porre *vt* to decompose;
decomporsi *vr* to decompose;
decom'posto, a *pp di* **decomporre**

deconge'lare [dekondʒe'lare] *vt* to
defrost

deco'rare *vt* to decorate; **decora'tore,
'trice** *sm/f* (interior) decorator;
decorazi'one *sf* decoration

de'coro *sm* decorum; **deco'roso, a** *ag*
decorous, dignified

de'correre *vi* to pass, elapse; (*avere
effetto*) to run, have effect; **de'corso, a**
pp di **decorrere** ♦ *sm* (*evoluzione: anche
MED*) course

de'crepito, a *ag* decrepit

de'crescere [de'kreʃʃere] *vi* (*diminuire*)
to decrease, diminish; (*acque*) to subside,
go down; (*prezzi*) to go down;
decresci'uto, a *pp di* **decrescere**

de'creto *sm* decree; ~ **legge** *decree with
the force of law*

'dedalo *sm* maze, labyrinth

'dedica, che *sf* dedication

dedi'care *vt* to dedicate

'dedito, a *ag*: ~ **a** (*studio etc*) dedicated *o*
devoted to; (*vizio*) addicted to

de'dotto, a *pp di* **dedurre**

de'durre *vt* (*concludere*) to deduce;
(*defalcare*) to deduct; **deduzi'one** *sf*
deduction

defal'care *vt* to deduct

defe'rente *ag* respectful, deferential

defe'rire *vt*: ~ **a** (*DIR*) to refer to

defezi'one [defet'tsjone] *sf* defection,
desertion

defici'ente [defi'tʃɛnte] *ag* (*mancante*): ~
di deficient in; (*insufficiente*) insufficient
♦ *sm/f* mental defective; (*peg: cretino*)
idiot

'deficit ['dɛfitʃit] *sm inv* (*ECON*) deficit

defi'nire *vt* (*decidere*): (*risolvere*) to settle;
defini'tivo, a *ag* definitive, final;
definizi'one *sf* definition; settlement

deflet'tore *sm* (*AUT*) quarter-light

de'flusso *sm* (*della marea*) ebb

defor'mare *vt* (*alterare*) to put out of
shape; (*corpo*) to deform; (*pensiero, fatto*)
to distort; ~**rsi** *vr* to lose its shape

de'forme *ag* deformed; disfigured;
deformità *sf inv* deformity

defrau'dare *vt*: ~ **qn di qc** to defraud sb
of sth, cheat sb out of sth

de'funto, a *ag* late *cpd* ♦ *sm/f* deceased

degene'rare [dedʒene'rare] *vi* to
degenerate; **de'genere** *ag* degenerate

de'gente [de'dʒɛnte] *sm/f* bedridden
person; (*ricoverato in ospedale*) in-patient

'degli ['deʎʎi] *prep + det vedi* **di**

de'gnarsi [deɲ'ɲarsi] *vr*: ~ **di fare** to
deign *o* condescend to do

'degno, a [deɲo] *ag* dignified; ~ **di** worthy of; ~
di lode praiseworthy

degra'dare *vt* (*MIL*) to demote; (*privare
della dignità*) to degrade; ~**rsi** *vr* to
demean o.s.

degustazi'one [degustat'tsjone] *sf*
sampling, tasting

'dei *prep + det vedi* **di**

del *prep + det vedi* **di**

dela'tore, 'trice *sm/f* police informer

'delega, ghe *sf* (*procura*) proxy

dele'gare *vt* to delegate; **dele'gato** *sm*
delegate

dele'terio, a *ag* damaging; (*per salute
etc*) harmful

del'fino *sm* (ZOOL) dolphin; (STORIA) dauphin; (*fig*) probable successor

delibe'rare *vt* to come to a decision on ♦ *vi* (DIR): ~ **(su qc)** to rule (on sth)

delica'tezza [delika'tettsa] *sf* (*anche* CUC) delicacy; frailty; thoughtfulness; tactfulness

deli'cato, a *ag* delicate; (*salute*) delicate, frail; (*fig: gentile*) thoughtful, considerate; (: *che dimostra tatto*) tactful

deline'are *vt* to outline; ~**rsi** *vr* to be outlined; (*fig*) to emerge

delin'quente *sm/f* criminal, delinquent; ~ **abituale** regular offender, habitual offender; **delin'quenza** *sf* criminality, delinquency; **delinquenza minorile** juvenile delinquency

deli'rare *vi* to be delirious, rave; (*fig*) to rave

de'lirio *sm* delirium; (*ragionamento insensato*) raving; (*fig*): **andare/mandare in** ~ to go/send into a frenzy

de'litto *sm* crime

de'lizia [de'littsja] *sf* delight; **delizi'oso, a** *ag* delightful; (*cibi*) delicious

dell' *prep* + *det vedi* **di**

'della *prep* + *det vedi* **di**

'delle *prep* + *det vedi* **di**

'dello *prep* + *det vedi* **di**

delta'plano *sm* hang-glider; **volo col** ~ hang-gliding

de'ludere *vt* to disappoint; **delusi'one** *sf* disappointment; **de'luso, a** *pp di* **deludere**

de'manio *sm* state property

de'menza [de'mɛntsa] *sf* dementia; (*stupidità*) foolishness

demo'cratico, a, ci, che *ag* democratic

democra'zia [demokrat'tsia] *sf* democracy

democristi'ano, a *ag*, *sm/f* Christian Democrat

demo'lire *vt* to demolish

'demone *sm* demon

de'monio *sm* demon, devil; **il D~** the Devil

de'naro *sm* money

denomi'nare *vt* to name; ~**rsi** *vr* to be named *o* called; **denominazi'one** *sf*

name; denomination; **denominazione d'origine controllata** *label guaranteeing the quality and origin of a wine*

densità *sf inv* density

'denso, a *ag* thick, dense

den'tale *ag* dental

'dente *sm* tooth; (*di forchetta*) prong; (GEO: *cima*) jagged peak; **al** ~ (CUC: *pasta*) *cooked so as to be firm when eaten*; ~**i del giudizio** wisdom teeth; **denti'era** *sf* (set of) false teeth *pl*

denti'fricio [denti'fritʃo] *sm* toothpaste

den'tista, i, e *sm/f* dentist

'dentro *av* inside; (*in casa*) indoors; (*fig: nell'intimo*) inwardly ♦ *prep*: ~ **(a)** in; **piegato in** ~ folded over; **qui/là** ~ in here/there; ~ **di sé** (*pensare, brontolare*) to oneself

de'nuncia, ce *o* **cie** [de'nuntʃa] *sf* denunciation; declaration; ~ **dei redditi** (income) tax return

denunci'are [denun'tʃare] *vt* to denounce; (*dichiarare*) to declare

de'nunzia *etc* [de'nuntsja] = **denuncia** *etc*

denutrizi'one [denutrit'tsjone] *sf* malnutrition

deodo'rante *sm* deodorant

depe'rire *vi* to waste away

depila'torio, a *ag* hair-removing *cpd*, depilatory

dépli'ant [depli'ã] *sm inv* leaflet; (*opuscolo*) brochure

deplo'revole *ag* deplorable

de'porre *vt* (*depositare*) to put down; (*rimuovere: da una carica*) to remove; (: *re*) to depose; (DIR) to testify

depor'tare *vt* to deport

deposi'tare *vt* (*gen*, GEO, ECON) to deposit; (*lasciare*) to leave; (*merci*) to store

de'posito *sm* deposit; (*luogo*) warehouse; depot; (: MIL) depot; ~ **bagagli** left-luggage office

deposizi'one [depozit'tsjone] *sf* deposition; (*da una carica*) removal

de'posto, a *pp di* **deporre**

depra'vato, a *ag* depraved ♦ *sm/f* degenerate

depre'dare *vt* to rob, plunder

depressi'one *sf* depression

de'presso, a *pp di* **deprimere** ♦ *ag* depressed

deprez'zare [depret'tsare] *vt* (*ECON*) to depreciate

de'primere *vt* to depress

depu'rare *vt* to purify

depu'tato, a *o* **'essa** *sm/f* (*POL*) deputy, ≈ Member of Parliament (*BRIT*), ≈ Member of Congress (*US*);
   deputazi'one *sf* deputation; (*POL*) position of deputy, ≈ parliamentary seat (*BRIT*), ≈ seat in Congress (*US*)

deragli'are [deraʎ'ʎare] *vi* to be derailed; **far ~** to derail

dere'litto, a *ag* derelict

dere'tano (*fam*) *sm* bottom, buttocks *pl*

de'ridere *vt* to mock, deride; **de'riso, a** *pp di* **deridere**

de'riva *sf* (*NAUT, AER*) drift; **andare alla ~** (*anche fig*) to drift

deri'vare *vi*: **~ da** to derive from ♦ *vt* to derive; (*corso d'acqua*) to divert; **derivazi'one** *sf* derivation; diversion

derma'tologo, a, gi, ghe *sm/f* dermatologist

der'rate *sfpl* commodities; **~ alimentari** foodstuffs

deru'bare *vt* to rob

des'critto, a *pp di* **descrivere**

des'crivere *vt* to describe; **descrizi'one** *sf* description

de'serto, a *ag* deserted ♦ *sm* (*GEO*) desert; **isola ~a** desert island

deside'rare *vt* to want, wish for; (*sessualmente*) to desire; **~ fare/che qn faccia** to want *o* wish to do/sb to do; **desidera fare una passeggiata?** would you like to go for a walk?

desi'derio *sm* wish; (*più intenso, carnale*) desire

deside'roso, a *ag*: **~ di** longing *o* eager for

desi'nenza [dezi'nɛntsa] *sf* (*LING*) ending, inflexion

de'sistere *vi*: **~ da** to give up, desist from; **desis'tito, a** *pp di* **desistere**

deso'lato, a *ag* (*paesaggio*) desolate; (*persona: spiacente*) sorry

des'tare *vt* to wake (up); (*fig*) to awaken, arouse; **~rsi** *vr* to wake (up)

desti'nare *vt* to destine; (*assegnare*) to appoint, assign; (*indirizzare*) to address; **~ qc a qn** to intend to give sth to sb, intend sb to have sth; **destina'tario, a** *sm/f* (*di lettera*) addressee

destinazi'one [destinat'tsjone] *sf* destination; (*uso*) purpose

des'tino *sm* destiny, fate

destitu'ire *vt* to dismiss, remove

'desto, a *ag* (wide) awake

'destra *sf* (*mano*) right hand; (*parte*) right (side); (*POL*): **la ~** the Right; **a ~** (*essere*) on the right; (*andare*) to the right

destreggi'arsi [destred'dʒarsi] *vr* to manoeuvre (*BRIT*), maneuver (*US*)

des'trezza [des'trettsa] *sf* skill, dexterity

'destro, a *ag* right, right-hand; (*abile*) skilful, adroit

dete'nere *vt* (*incarico, primato*) to hold; (*proprietà*) to have, possess; (*in prigione*) to detain, hold; **dete'nuto, a** *sm/f* prisoner; **detenzi'one** *sf* holding; possession; detention

deter'gente [deter'dʒɛnte] *ag* detergent; (*crema, latte*) cleansing ♦ *sm* detergent

deterio'rare *vt* to damage; **~rsi** *vr* to deteriorate

determi'nare *vt* to determine; **determinazi'one** *sf* determination; (*decisione*) decision

deter'sivo *sm* detergent

detes'tare *vt* to detest, hate

de'trarre *vt*: **~ (da)** to deduct (from), take away (from); **de'tratto, a** *pp di* **detrarre**; **detrazi'one** *sf* deduction; **detrazione d'imposta** tax allowance

de'trito *sm* (*GEO*) detritus

'detta *sf*: **a ~ di** according to

dettagli'are [dettaʎ'ʎare] *vt* to detail, give full details of

det'taglio [det'taʎʎo] *sm* detail; (*COMM*): **il ~** retail; **al ~** (*COMM*) retail; separately

det'tare *vt* to dictate; **~ legge** (*fig*) to lay down the law; **det'tato** *sm* dictation; **detta'tura** *sf* dictation

'detto, a *pp di* **dire** ♦ *ag* (*soprannominato*) called, known as; (*già nominato*) above-mentioned ♦ *sm* saying; ~ **fatto** no sooner said than done

detur'pare *vt* to disfigure; *(moralmente)* to sully

devas'tare *vt* to devastate; *(fig)* to ravage

devi'are *vi*: ~ **(da)** to turn off (from) ♦ *vt* to divert; **deviazi'one** *sf (anche AUT)* diversion

devo'luto, a *pp di* **devolvere**

devoluzi'one [devolut'tsjone] *sf (DIR)* devolution, transfer

de'volvere *vt (DIR)* to transfer, devolve

de'voto, a *ag (REL)* devout, pious; *(affezionato)* devoted

devozi'one [devot'tsjone] *sf* devoutness; *(anche REL)* devotion

┌─────────────────┐
│ *PAROLA CHIAVE* │
└─────────────────┘

di (*di+il* = **del**, *di+lo* = **dello**, *di+l'* = **dell'**, *di+la* = **della**, *di+i* = **dei**, *di+gli* = **degli**, *di+le* = **delle**) *prep* **1** *(possesso, specificazione)* of; *(composto da, scritto da)* by; **la macchina ~ Paolo/mio fratello** Paolo's/my brother's car; **un amico ~ mio fratello** a friend of my brother's, one of my brother's friends; **un quadro ~ Botticelli** a painting by Botticelli

2 *(caratterizzazione, misura)* of; **una casa ~ mattoni** a brick house, a house made of bricks; **un orologio d'oro** a gold watch; **un bimbo ~ 3 anni** a child of 3, a 3-year-old child

3 *(causa, mezzo, modo)* with; **tremare ~ paura** to tremble with fear; **morire ~ cancro** to die of cancer; **spalmare ~ burro** to spread with butter

4 *(argomento)* about, of; **discutere ~ sport** to talk about sport

5 *(luogo: provenienza)* from; out of; **essere ~ Roma** to be from Rome; **uscire ~ casa** to come out of *o* leave the house

6 *(tempo)* in; **d'estate/d'inverno** in (the) summer/winter; **~ notte** by night, at night; **~ mattina/sera** in the morning/ evening; **~ lunedì** on Mondays

♦ *det (una certa quantità di)* some; *(: negativo)* any; *(: interrogativo)* any, some; **del pane** (some) bread; **delle caramelle**

(some) sweets; **degli amici miei** some friends of mine; **vuoi del vino?** do you want some *o* any wine?

dia'bete *sm* diabetes *sg*

di'acono *sm (REL)* deacon

dia'dema, i *sm* diadem; *(di donna)* tiara

dia'framma, i *sm (divisione)* screen; *(ANAT, FOT, contraccettivo)* diaphragm

di'agnosi [di'aɲɲozi] *sf* diagnosis *sg*

diago'nale *ag, sf* diagonal

dia'gramma, i *sm* diagram

dia'letto *sm* dialect

di'alogo, ghi *sm* dialogue

dia'mante *sm* diamond

di'ametro *sm* diameter

di'amine *escl*: **che ~ ...?** what on earth ...?

diaposi'tiva *sf* transparency, slide

di'ario *sm* diary; **~ degli esami** *(SCOL)* exam timetable

diar'rea *sf* diarrhoea

di'avolo *sm* devil

di'battere *vt* to debate, discuss; **~rsi** *vr* to struggle; **di'battito** *sm* debate, discussion

dicas'tero *sm* ministry

di'cembre [di't∫ɛmbre] *sm* December

dice'ria [dit∫e'ria] *sf* rumour, piece of gossip

dichia'rare [dikja'rare] *vt* to declare; **dichiarazi'one** *sf* declaration

dician'nove [dit∫an'nɔve] *num* nineteen

dicias'sette [dit∫as'sɛtte] *num* seventeen

dici'otto [di't∫ɔtto] *num* eighteen

dici'tura [dit∫i't∫i'tura] *sf* words *pl*, wording

di'eci ['djɛt∫i] *num* ten; **die'cina** *sf* = **decina**

'diesel ['dizəl] *sm inv* diesel engine

di'eta *sf* diet; **essere a ~** to be on a diet

di'etro *av* behind; *(in fondo)* at the back ♦ *prep* behind; *(tempo: dopo)* after ♦ *sm* back, rear; **~ ga** *inv* back *cpd*; **le zampe di ~** the hind legs; **~ richiesta** on demand; *(scritta)* on application

di'fatti *cong* in fact, as a matter of fact

di'fendere *vt* to defend; **difen'sivo, a** *ag* defensive ♦ *sf*: **stare sulla difensiva** *(anche fig)* to be on the defensive;

difen'sore, a *sm/f* defender; avvocato difensore counsel for the defence; di'fesa *sf* defence; di'feso, a *pp di* difendere

difet'tare *vi* to be defective; ~ di to be lacking in, lack; difet'tivo, a *ag* defective

di'fetto *sm* (*mancanza*): ~ di lack of; shortage of; (*di fabbricazione*) fault, flaw, defect; (*morale*) fault, failing, defect; (*fisico*) defect; far ~ to be lacking; in ~ at fault; in the wrong; difet'toso, a *ag* defective, faulty

diffa'mare *vt* to slander; to libel

diffe'rente *ag* different

diffe'renza [diffe'rɛntsa] *sf* difference; a ~ di unlike

differenzi'are [differen'tsjare] *vt* to differentiate; ~rsi da to differentiate o.s. from; to differ from

diffe'rire *vt* to postpone, defer ♦ *vi* to be different

dif'ficile [dif'fitʃile] *ag* difficult; (*persona*) hard to please, difficult (to please); (*poco probabile*): è ~ che sia libero it is unlikely that he'll be free ♦ *sm* difficult part; difficulty; difficoltà *sf inv* difficulty

dif'fida *sf* (*DIR*) warning, notice

diffi'dare *vi*: ~ di to be suspicious *o* distrustful of ♦ *vt* (*DIR*) to warn, ~ qn dal fare qc to warn sb not to do sth, caution sb against doing sth; diffi'dente *ag* suspicious, distrustful; diffi'denza *sf* suspicion, distrust

dif'fondere *vt* (*luce, calore*) to diffuse; (*notizie*) to spread, circulate; ~rsi di to spread; diffusi'one *sf* diffusion; spread; (*anche di giornale*) circulation; (*FISICA*) scattering; dif'fuso, a *pp di* diffondere ♦ *ag* (*malattia, fenomeno*) widespread

difi'lato *av* (*direttamente*) straight, directly; (*subito*) straight away

difte'rite *sf* (*MED*) diphtheria

'diga, ghe [diga] *sf* dam; (*portuale*) breakwater

dige'rente [didʒe'rɛnte] *ag* (*apparato*) digestive

dige'rire [didʒe'rire] *vt* to digest; digesti'one *sf* digestion; diges'tivo, a *ag* digestive ♦ *sm* (after-dinner) liqueur

digi'tale [didʒi'tale] *ag* digital; (*delle dita*) finger *cpd*, digital ♦ *sf* (*BOT*) foxglove

digi'tare [didʒi'tare] *vt, vi* (*INFORM*) to key (in)

digiu'nare [didʒu'nare] *vi* to starve o.s.; (*REL*) to fast; digi'uno, a *ag*: essere digiuno not to have eaten ♦ *sm* fast; a digiuno on an empty stomach

dignità [diɲɲi'ta] *sf inv* dignity; digni'toso, a *ag* dignified

'DIGOS ['digɔs] *sigla f* (= *Divisione Investigazioni Generali e Operazioni Speciali*) *police department dealing with political security*

digri'gnare [digriɲ'ɲare] *vt*: ~ i denti to grind one's teeth

dila'gare *vi* to flood; (*fig*) to spread

dilani'are *vt* (*preda*) to tear to pieces

dilapi'dare *vt* to squander, waste

dila'tare *vt* to dilate; (*gas*) to cause to expand; (*passaggio, cavità*) to open (up); ~rsi *vr* to dilate; (*FISICA*) to expand

dilazio'nare [dilattsjo'nare] *vt* to delay, defer; dilazi'one *sf* delay; (*COMM: di pagamento etc*) extension; (*rinvio*) postponement

dileggi'are [diled'dʒare] *vt* to mock, deride

dilegu'are *vi* to vanish, disappear; ~rsi *vr* to vanish, disappear

di'lemma, i *sm* dilemma

dilet'tante *sm/f* dilettante; (*anche SPORT*) amateur

dilet'tare *vt* to give pleasure to, delight; ~rsi *vr*: ~rsi di to take pleasure in, enjoy

di'letto, a *ag* dear, beloved ♦ *sm* pleasure, delight

dili'gente [dili'dʒɛnte] *ag* (*scrupoloso*) diligent; (*accurato*) careful, accurate; dili'genza *sf* diligence; care; (*carrozza*) stagecoach

dilu'ire *vt* to dilute

dilun'garsi *vr* (*fig*): ~ su to talk at length on *o* about

diluvi'are *vb impers* to pour (down)

di'luvio *sm* downpour; (*inondazione, fig*) flood

dima'grire *vi* to get thinner, lose weight

dime'nare *vt* to wave, shake; ~rsi *vr* to

toss and turn; (*fig*) to struggle; ~ **la coda** (*sog: cane*) to wag its tail

dimensi'one *sf* dimension; (*grandezza*) size

dimenti'canza [dimenti'kantsa] *sf* forgetfulness; (*errore*) oversight, slip; **per** ~ inadvertently

dimenti'care *vt* to forget; ~**rsi di qc** to forget sth

di'messo, a *pp di* **dimettere** ♦ *ag* (*voce*) subdued; (*uomo, abito*) modest, humble

dimesti'chezza [dimesti'kettsa] *sf* familiarity

di'mettere *vt*: ~ **qn da** to dismiss sb from; (*dall'ospedale*) to discharge sb from; ~**rsi (da)** to resign (from)

dimez'zare [dimed'dzare] *vt* to halve

diminu'ire *vt* to reduce, diminish; (*prezzi*) to bring down, reduce ♦ *vi* to decrease, diminish; (*rumore*) to die down, die away; (*prezzi*) to fall, go down;
diminuzi'one *sf* decreasing, diminishing

dimissi'oni *sfpl* resignation *sg*; **dare o presentare le** ~ to resign, hand in one's resignation

di'mora *sf* residence

dimo'rare *vi* to reside

dimos'trare *vt* to demonstrate, show; (*provare*) to prove, demonstrate; ~**rsi** *vr*: ~**rsi molto abile** to show o.s. *o* prove to be very clever; **dimostra 30 anni** he looks about 30 (years old);
dimostrazi'one *sf* demonstration; proof

di'namica *sf* dynamics *sg*

di'namico, a, ci, che *ag* dynamic

dina'mite *sf* dynamite

'dinamo *sf inv* dynamo

di'nanzi [di'nantsi]: ~ **a** *prep* in front of

dini'ego, ghi *sm* refusal; denial

dinocco'lato, a *ag* lanky; **camminare** ~ to walk with a slouch

din'torno *av* round, (round) about; ~**i** *smpl* outskirts; **nei** ~**i di** in the vicinity *o* neighbourhood of

'dio (*pl* **'dei**) *sm* god; **D**~ God; **gli dei** the gods; **D**~ **mio!** my goodness!, my God!

di'ocesi [di'ɔtʃezi] *sf inv* diocese

dipa'nare *vt* (*lana*) to wind into a ball; (*fig*) to disentangle, sort out

diparti'mento *sm* department

dipen'dente *ag* dependent ♦ *sm/f* employee; **dipen'denza** *sf* dependence; **essere alle dipendenze di qn** to be employed by sb *o* in sb's employ

di'pendere *vi*: ~ **da** to depend on; (*finanziariamente*) to be dependent on; (*derivare*) to come from, be due to; **di'peso, a** *pp di* **dipendere**

di'pingere [di'pindʒere] *vt* to paint; **di'pinto, a** *pp di* **dipingere** ♦ *sm* painting

di'ploma, i *sm* diploma

diplo'mare *vt* to award a diploma to, graduate (*US*) ♦ *vi* to obtain a diploma, graduate (*US*)

diplo'matico, a, ci, che *ag* diplomatic ♦ *sm* diplomat

diploma'zia [diplomat'tsia] *sf* diplomacy

di'porto: **imbarcazione da** ~ *sf* pleasure craft

dira'dare *vt* to thin (out); (*visite*) to reduce, make less frequent; ~**rsi** *vr* to disperse; (*nebbia*) to clear (up)

dira'mare *vt* to issue ♦ *vi* (*strade*) to branch; ~**rsi** *vr* to branch

'dire *vt* to say; (*segreto, fatto*) to tell; ~ **qc a qn** to tell sb sth; ~ **a qn di fare qc** to tell sb to do sth; ~ **di sì/no** to say yes/ no; **si dice che ...** they say that ...; **si direbbe che ...** it looks (*o* sounds) as though ...; **dica, signora?** (*in un negozio*) yes, Madam, can I help you?

diret'tissimo *sm* (*FERR*) fast (through) train

di'retto, a *pp di* **dirigere** ♦ *ag* direct ♦ *sm* (*FERR*) through train

diret'tore, 'trice *sm/f* (*di azienda*) director; manager/ess; (*di scuola elementare*) head (teacher) (*BRIT*), principal (*US*); ~ **d'orchestra** conductor; ~ **vendite** sales director *o* manager

direzi'one [diret'tsjone] *sf* board of directors; management; (*senso di movimento*) direction; **in** ~ **di** in the direction of, towards

diri'gente [diri'dʒɛnte] *sm/f* executive; (*POL*) leader ♦ *ag*: **classe** ~ ruling class

di'rigere [di'ridʒere] *vt* to direct;

(*impresa*) to run, manage; (*MUS*) to conduct; ~**rsi** *vr*: ~**rsi verso** *o* **a** to make *o* head for

dirim'petto *av* opposite; ~ **a** opposite, facing

di'ritto, a *ag* straight; (*onesto*) straight, upright ♦ *av* straight, directly; **andare** ~ to go straight on ♦ *sm* right side; (*TENNIS*) forehand; (*MAGLIA*) plain stitch; (*prerogativa*) right; (*leggi, scienza*): **il** ~ law; ~**i** *smpl* (*tasse*) duty *sg*; **stare** ~ to stand up straight; **aver** ~ **a qc** to be entitled to sth; ~**i d'autore** royalties

dirit'tura *sf* (*SPORT*) straight; (*fig*) rectitude

diroc'cato, a *ag* tumbledown, in ruins

dirot'tare *vt* (*nave, aereo*) to change the course of; (*aereo: sotto minaccia*) to hijack; (*traffico*) to divert ♦ *vi* (*nave, aereo*) to change course; **dirotta'tore, 'trice** *sm/f* hijacker

di'rotto, a *ag* (*pioggia*) torrential; (*pianto*) unrestrained; **piovere a** ~ to pour, rain cats and dogs; **piangere a** ~ to cry one's heart out

di'rupo *sm* crag, precipice

disabi'tato, a *ag* uninhabited

disabitu'arsi *vr*: ~ **a** to get out of the habit of

disac'cordo *sm* disagreement

disadat'tato, a *ag* (*PSIC*) maladjusted

disa'dorno, a *ag* plain, unadorned

disagi'ato, a [diza'dʒato] *ag* poor, needy; (*vita*) hard

di'sagio [di'zadʒo] *sm* discomfort; (*disturbo*) inconvenience; (*fig: imbarazzo*) embarrassment; **essere a** ~ to be ill at ease

disappro'vare *vt* to disapprove of; **disapprovazi'one** *sf* disapproval

disap'punto *sm* disappointment

disar'mare *vt, vi* to disarm; **di'sarmo** *sm* (*MIL*) disarmament

di'sastro *sm* disaster

disat'tento, a *ag* inattentive; **disattenzi'one** *sf* carelessness, lack of attention

disa'vanzo [diza'vantso] *sm* (*ECON*) deficit

disavven'tura *sf* misadventure, mishap

dis'brigo, ghi *sm* (prompt) clearing up *o* settlement

dis'capito *sm*: **a** ~ **di** to the detriment of

dis'carica, che *sf* (*di rifiuti*) rubbish tip *o* dump

discen'dente [diʃʃen'dɛnte] *ag* descending ♦ *sm/f* descendant

di'scendere [diʃ'ʃendere] *vt* to go (*o* come) down ♦ *vi* to go (*o* come) down; (*strada*) to go down; (*smontare*) to get off; ~ **da** (*famiglia*) to be descended from; ~ **dalla macchina/dal treno** to get out of the car/out of *o* off the train; ~ **da cavallo** to dismount, get off one's horse

di'scepolo, a [diʃ'ʃepolo] *sm/f* disciple

di'scernere [diʃ'ʃɛrnere] *vt* to discern

di'scesa [diʃ'ʃesa] *sf* descent; (*pendio*) slope; **in** ~ (*strada*) downhill *cpd*, sloping; ~ **libera** (*SCI*) downhill (race)

di'sceso, a [diʃ'ʃeso] *pp di* **discendere**

disci'ogliere [diʃ'ʃɔʎʎere] *vt* to dissolve; (*fondere*) to melt; ~**rsi** *vr* to dissolve; to melt; **disci'olto, a** *pp di* **disciogliere**

disci'plina [diʃʃi'plina] *sf* discipline; **discipli'nare** *ag* disciplinary ♦ *vt* to discipline

'disco, schi *sm* disc; (*SPORT*) discus; (*fonografico*) record; (*INFORM*) disk; ~ **orario** (*AUT*) parking disc; ~ **rigido** (*INFORM*) hard disk; ~ **volante** flying saucer

discol'pare *vt* to clear of blame

disco'noscere [disko'noʃʃere] *vt* (*figlio*) to disown; (*meriti*) to ignore, disregard; **disconosci'uto, a** *pp di* **disconoscere**

dis'corde *ag* conflicting, clashing; **dis'cordia** *sf* discord; (*dissidio*) disagreement, clash

dis'correre *vi*: ~ (**di**) to talk (about)

dis'corso, a *pp di* **discorrere** ♦ *sm* speech; (*conversazione*) conversation, talk

dis'costo, a *ag* faraway, distant ♦ *av* far away; ~ **da** far from

disco'teca, che *sf* (*raccolta*) record library; (*luogo di ballo*) disco(theque)

discre'panza [diskre'pantsa] *sf* disagreement

dis'creto, a *ag* discreet; (*abbastanza*

buono) reasonable, fair; **discrezi'one** *sf*
discretion; (*giudizio*) judgment,
discernment; **a discrezione di** at the
discretion of
discriminazi'one [diskriminat'tsjone] *sf*
discrimination
discussi'one *sf* discussion; (*litigio*)
argument
dis'cusso, a *pp di* **discutere**
dis'cutere *vt* to discuss, debate;
(*contestare*) to question ♦ *vi* (*conversare*):
~ **(di)** to discuss; (*litigare*) to argue
disde'gnare [disdeɲ'ɲare] *vt* to scorn
dis'detta *sf* (*di prenotazione etc*)
cancellation; (*sfortuna*) bad luck
dis'detto, a *pp di* **disdire**
dis'dire *vt* (*prenotazione*) to cancel; (*DIR*):
~ **un contratto d'affitto** to give notice
(to quit)
dise'gnare [diseɲ'ɲare] *vt* to draw;
(*progettare*) to design; (*fig*) to outline;
disegna'tore, 'trice *sm/f* designer
di'segno [di'seɲɲo] *sm* drawing; design;
outline; ~ **di legge** (*DIR*) bill
diser'bante *sm* weed-killer
diser'tare *vt, vi* to desert; **diser'tore** *sm*
(*MIL*) deserter
dis'fare *vt* to undo; (*valigie*) to unpack;
(*meccanismo*) to take to pieces; (*lavoro,
paese*) to destroy; (*neve*) to melt; **~rsi** *vr*
to come undone; (*neve*) to melt; ~ **il letto**
to strip the bed; **~rsi di qn** (*liberarsi*) to
get rid of sb; **dis'fatta** *sf* (*sconfitta*) rout;
dis'fatto, a *pp di* **disfare**
dis'gelo [diz'dʒelo] *sm* thaw
dis'grazia [diz'grattsja] *sf* (*sventura*)
misfortune; (*incidente*) accident, mishap;
disgrazi'ato, a *ag* unfortunate ♦ *sm/f*
wretch
disgre'gare *vt* to break up; **~rsi** *vr* to
break up
disgu'ido *sm*: ~ **postale** error in postal
delivery
disgus'tare *vt* to disgust; **~rsi** *vr*: **~rsi di**
to be disgusted by
dis'gusto *sm* disgust; **disgus'toso, a** *ag*
disgusting
disidra'tare *vt* to dehydrate
disil'ludere *vt* to disillusion, disenchant

disimpa'rare *vt* to forget
disimpe'gnare [dizimpeɲ'ɲare] *vt*
(*persona: da obblighi*): ~ **da** to release
from; (*oggetto dato in pegno*) to redeem,
get out of pawn; **~rsi** *vr*: **~rsi da**
(*obblighi*) to release o.s. from, free o.s.
from
disinfet'tante *ag, sm* disinfectant
disinfet'tare *vt* to disinfect
disini'bito, a *ag* uninhibited
disinte'grare *vt, vi* to disintegrate
disinteres'sarsi *vr*: ~ **di** to take no
interest in
disinte'resse *sm* indifference; (*generosità*) unselfishness
disintossi'care *vt* (*alcolizzato, drogato*)
to treat for alcoholism (*o* drug addiction);
~ **l'organismo** to clear out one's system
disin'volto, a *ag* casual, free and easy;
disinvol'tura *sf* casualness, ease
disles'sia *sf* dyslexia
dislo'care *vt* to station, position
dismi'sura *sf* excess; **a ~** to excess,
excessively
disobbe'dire *etc* = **disubbidire** *etc*
disoccu'pato, a *ag* unemployed ♦ *sm/f*
unemployed person; **disoccupazi'one** *sf*
unemployment
diso'nesto, a *ag* dishonest
diso'nore *sm* dishonour, disgrace
di'sopra *av* (*con contatto*) on top; (*senza
contatto*) above; (*al piano superiore*)
upstairs ♦ *ag inv* (*superiore*) upper ♦ *sm
inv* top, upper part
disordi'nato, a *ag* untidy; (*privo di
misura*) irregular, wild
di'sordine *sm* (*confusione*) disorder,
confusion; (*sregolatezza*) debauchery
disorien'tare *vt* to disorientate; **~rsi** *vr*
(*fig*) to get confused, lose one's bearings
di'sotto *av* below, underneath; (*in fondo*)
at the bottom; (*al piano inferiore*)
downstairs ♦ *ag inv* (*inferiore*) lower;
bottom *cpd* ♦ *sm inv* (*parte inferiore*)
lower part; bottom
dis'paccio [dis'pattʃo] *sm* dispatch
'dispari *ag inv* odd, uneven
dis'parte: **in ~** *av* (*da lato*) aside, apart;
tenersi *o* **starsene in ~** to keep to o.s.,

hold o.s. aloof

dispendi'oso, a *ag* expensive

dis'pensa *sf* pantry, larder; (*mobile*) sideboard; (*DIR*) exemption; (*REL*) dispensation; (*fascicolo*) number, issue

dispen'sare *vt* (*elemosine, favori*) to distribute; (*esonerare*) to exempt

dispe'rare *vi*: ~ **(di)** to despair (of); **~rsi** *vr* to despair; **dispe'rato, a** *ag* (*persona*) in despair; (*caso, tentativo*) desperate; **disperazi'one** *sf* despair

dis'perdere *vt* (*disseminare*) to disperse; (*MIL*) to scatter, rout; (*fig: consumare*) to waste, squander; **~rsi** *vr* to disperse; to scatter; **dis'perso, a** *pp di* **disperdere** ♦ *sm/f* missing person

dis'petto *sm* spite *no pl*, spitefulness *no pl*; **fare un** ~ **a qn** to play a (nasty) trick on sb; **a** ~ **di** in spite of; **dispet'toso, a** *ag* spiteful

dispia'cere [dispja't∫ere] *sm* (*rammarico*) regret, sorrow; (*dolore*) grief; **~i** *smpl* (*preoccupazioni*) troubles, worries ♦ *vi*: ~ **a** to displease ♦ *vb impers*: **mi dispiace (che)** I am sorry (that); **se non le dispiace, me ne vado adesso** if you don't mind, I'll go now; **dispiaci'uto, a** *pp di* **dispiacere** ♦ *ag* sorry

dispo'nibile *ag* available

dis'porre *vt* (*sistemare*) to arrange; (*preparare*) to prepare; (*DIR*) to order; (*persuadere*): ~ **qn a** to incline o dispose sb towards ♦ *vi* (*decidere*) to decide; (*usufruire*): ~ **di** to use, have at one's disposal; (*essere dotato*): ~ **di** to have; **disporsi** *vr* (*ordinarsi*) to place o.s., arrange o.s.; **disporsi a fare** to get ready to do

disposi'tivo *sm* (*meccanismo*) device

disposizi'one [dispozit'tsjone] *sf* arrangement, layout; (*stato d'animo*) mood; (*tendenza*) bent, inclination; (*comando*) order; (*DIR*) provision, regulation; **a** ~ **di qn** at sb's disposal

dis'posto, a *pp di* **disporre**

disprez'zare [dispret'tsare] *vt* to despise

dis'prezzo [dis'prettso] *sm* contempt

'disputa *sf* dispute, quarrel

dispu'tare *vt* (*contendere*) to dispute,

contest; (*gara*) to take part in ♦ *vi* to quarrel; ~ **di** to discuss; **~rsi qc** to fight for sth

dissan'guare *vt* (*fig: persona*) to bleed white; (*: patrimonio*) to suck dry; **~rsi** *vr* (*MED*) to lose blood; (*fig: rovinarsi*) to ruin o.s.

dissec'care *vt* to dry up; **~rsi** *vr* to dry up

dissemi'nare *vt* to scatter; (*fig: notizie*) to spread

dis'senso *sm* dissent; (*disapprovazione*) disapproval

dissente'ria *sf* dysentery

dissen'tire *vi*: ~ **(da)** to disagree (with)

dissertazi'one [dissertat'tsjone] *sf* dissertation

disser'vizio [disser'vittsjo] *sm* inefficiency

disses'tare *vt* (*ECON*) to ruin; **dis'sesto** *sm* (financial) ruin

disse'tante *ag* refreshing

dis'sidio *sm* disagreement

dis'simile *ag* different, dissimilar

dissimu'lare *vt* (*fingere*) to dissemble; (*nascondere*) to conceal

dissi'pare *vt* to dissipate; (*scialacquare*) to squander, waste

dis'solto, a *pp di* **dissolvere**

disso'lubile *ag* soluble

disso'luto, a *pp di* **dissolvere** ♦ *ag* dissolute, licentious

dis'solvere *vt* to dissolve; (*neve*) to melt; (*fumo*) to disperse; **~rsi** *vr* to dissolve; to melt; to disperse

dissu'adere *vt*: ~ **qn da** to dissuade sb from; **dissu'aso, a** *pp di* **dissuadere**

distac'care *vt* to detach, separate; (*SPORT*) to leave behind; **~rsi** *vr* to be detached; (*fig*) to stand out; **~rsi da** (*fig: allontanarsi*) to grow away from

dis'tacco, chi *sm* (*separazione*) separation; (*fig: indifferenza*) detachment; (*SPORT*): **vincere con un** ~ **di ...** to win by a distance of ...

dis'tante *av* far away ♦ *ag*: ~ **(da)** distant (from), far away (from)

dis'tanza [dis'tantsa] *sf* distance

distanzi'are [distan'tsjare] *vt* to space

out, place at intervals; (SPORT) to outdistance; (fig: superare) to outstrip, surpass

dis'tare vi: **distiamo pochi chilometri da Roma** we are only a few kilometres (away) from Rome

dis'tendere vt (coperta) to spread out; (gambe) to stretch (out); (mettere a giacere) to lay; (rilassare: muscoli, nervi) to relax; ~**rsi** vr (rilassarsi) to relax; (sdraiarsi) to lie down; **distensi'one** sf stretching; relaxation; (POL) détente

dis'tesa sf expanse, stretch

dis'teso, a pp di **distendere**

distil'lare vt to distil

distille'ria sf distillery

dis'tinguere vt to distinguish

dis'tinta sf (nota) note; (elenco) list

distin'tivo, a ag distinctive; distinguishing ♦ sm badge

dis'tinto, a pp di **distinguere** ♦ ag (dignitoso ed elegante) distinguished; ~**i saluti** (in lettera) yours faithfully

distinzi'one [distin'tsjone] sf distinction

dis'togliere [dis'tɔʎʎere] vt: ~ **da** to take away from; (fig) to dissuade from; **dis'tolto, a** pp di **distogliere**

distorsi'one sf (MED) sprain; (FISICA, OTTICA) distortion

dis'trarre vt to distract; (divertire) to entertain, amuse; **distrarsi** vr (non fare attenzione) to be distracted, let one's mind wander; (svagarsi) to amuse o enjoy o.s.; **dis'tratto, a** pp di **distrarre** ♦ ag absent-minded; (disattento) inattentive; **distrazi'one** sf absent-mindedness; inattention; (svago) distraction, entertainment

dis'tretto sm district

distribu'ire vt to distribute; (CARTE) to deal (out); (consegnare: posta) to deliver; (lavoro) to allocate, assign; (ripartire) to share out; **distribu'tore** sm (di benzina) petrol (BRIT) o gas (US) pump; (AUT, ELETTR) distributor; (automatico) vending machine; **distribuzi'one** sf distribution; delivery

distri'care vt to disentangle, unravel

dis'truggere [dis'truddʒere] vt to

destroy; **dis'trutto, a** pp di **distruggere**; **distruzi'one** sf destruction

distur'bare vt to disturb, trouble; (sonno, lezioni) to disturb, interrupt; ~**rsi** vr to put o.s. out

dis'turbo sm trouble, bother, inconvenience; (indisposizione) (slight) disorder, ailment; ~**i** smpl (RADIO, TV) static sg

disubbidi'ente ag disobedient; **disubbidi'enza** sf disobedience

disubbi'dire vi: ~ **(a qn)** to disobey (sb)

disugu'ale ag unequal; (diverso) different; (irregolare) uneven

disu'mano, a ag inhuman

di'suso sm: **andare** o **cadere in** ~ to fall into disuse

'dita fpl di **dito**

di'tale sm thimble

'dito (pl(f) **'dita**) sm finger; (misura) finger, finger's breadth; ~ **(del piede)** toe

'ditta sf firm, business

ditta'tore sm dictator

ditta'tura sf dictatorship

dit'tongo, ghi sm diphthong

di'urno, a ag day cpd, daytime cpd ♦ sm (anche: albergo ~) public toilets with washing and shaving facilities etc

'diva sf vedi **divo**

diva'gare vi to digress

divam'pare vi to flare up, blaze up

di'vano sm sofa; divan

divari'care vt to open wide

di'vario sm difference

dive'nire vi = **diventare**; **dive'nuto, a** pp di **divenire**

diven'tare vi to become; ~ **famoso/ professore** to become famous/a teacher

di'verbio sm altercation

di'vergere [di'vɛrdʒere] vi to diverge

diversifi'care vt to diversify, vary; to differentiate

diversi'one sf diversion

diversità sf inv difference, diversity; (varietà) variety

diver'sivo sm diversion, distraction

di'verso, a ag (differente): ~ **(da)** different (from); ~**i, e** det pl several, various; (COMM) sundry ♦ pron pl several (people), many (people)

diver'tente *ag* amusing

diverti'mento *sm* amusement, pleasure; (*passatempo*) pastime, recreation

diver'tire *vt* to amuse, entertain; **~rsi** *vr* to amuse *o* enjoy o.s.

divi'dendo *sm* dividend

di'videre *vt* (*anche MAT*) to divide; (*distribuire, ripartire*) to divide (up), split (up); **~rsi** *vr* (*separarsi*) to separate; (*strade*) to fork

divi'eto *sm* prohibition; "**~ di sosta**" (*AUT*) "no parking"

divinco'larsi *vr* to wriggle, writhe

divinità *sf inv* divinity

di'vino, a *ag* divine

di'visa *sf* (*MIL etc*) uniform; (*COMM*) foreign currency

divisi'one *sf* division

di'viso, a *pp di* **dividere**

'divo, a *sm/f* star

divo'rare *vt* to devour

divorzi'are [divor'tsjare] *vi*: **~ (da qn)** to divorce (sb); **divorzi'ato, a** *sm/f* divorcee

di'vorzio [di'vɔrtsjo] *sm* divorce

divul'gare *vt* to divulge, disclose; (*rendere comprensibile*) to popularize; **~rsi** *vr* to spread

dizio'nario [dittsjo'narjo] *sm* dictionary

dizi'one [dit'tsjone] *sf* diction; pronunciation

do *sm* (*MUS*) C; (*: solfeggiando la scala*) do(h)

DOC [dɔk] *abbr* (= *denominazione di origine controllata*) *label guaranteeing the quality of wine*

'doccia, ce ['dottʃa] *sf* (*bagno*) shower; (*condotto*) pipe; **fare la ~** to have a shower

do'cente [do'tʃɛnte] *ag* teaching ♦ *sm/f* teacher; (*di università*) lecturer; **do'cenza** *sf* university teaching *o* lecturing

'docile ['dɔtʃile] *ag* docile

documen'tare *vt* to document; **~rsi** *vr*: **~rsi (su)** to gather information *o* material (about)

documen'tario *sm* documentary

docu'mento *sm* document; **~i** *smpl*

(*d'identità etc*) papers

'dodici ['doditʃi] *num* twelve

do'gana *sf* (*ufficio*) customs *pl*; (*tassa*) (customs) duty; **passare la ~** to go through customs; **doga'nale** *ag* customs *cpd*; **dogani'ere** *sm* customs officer

'doglie ['dɔʎʎe] *sfpl* (*MED*) labour *sg*, labour pains

'dolce ['doltʃe] *ag* sweet; (*colore*) soft; (*carattere, persona*) gentle, mild; (*fig: mite: clima*) mild; (*non ripido: pendio*) gentle ♦ *sm* (*sapore dolce*) sweetness, sweet taste; (*CUC: portata*) sweet, dessert; (*: torta*) cake; **dol'cezza** *sf* sweetness; softness; mildness; gentleness; **dolci'umi** *smpl* sweets

do'lente *ag* sorrowful, sad

do'lere *vi* to be sore, hurt, ache; **~rsi** *vr* to complain; (*essere spiacente*): **~rsi di** to be sorry for; **mi duole la testa** my head aches, I've got a headache

'dollaro *sm* dollar

'dolo *sm* (*DIR*) malice

Dolo'miti *sfpl*: **le ~** the Dolomites

do'lore *sm* (*fisico*) pain; (*morale*) sorrow, grief; **dolo'roso, a** *ag* painful; sorrowful, sad

do'loso, a *ag* (*DIR*) malicious

do'manda *sf* (*interrogazione*) question; (*richiesta*) demand; (*: cortese*) request; (*DIR: richiesta scritta*) application; (*ECON*): **la ~** demand; **fare una ~ a qn** to ask sb a question; **fare ~ (per un lavoro)** to apply (for a job)

doman'dare *vt* (*per avere*) to ask for; (*per sapere*) to ask; (*esigere*) to demand; **~rsi** *vr* to wonder; to ask o.s.; **~ qc a qn** to ask sb for sth; to ask sb sth

do'mani *av* tomorrow ♦ *sm*: **il ~** (*il futuro*) the future; (*il giorno successivo*) the next day; **~ l'altro** the day after tomorrow

do'mare *vt* to tame

domat'tina *av* tomorrow morning

do'menica, che *sf* Sunday; **di** *o* **la ~** on Sundays; **domeni'cale** *ag* Sunday *cpd*

do'mestica, che *sf vedi* **domestico**

do'mestico, a, ci, che *ag* domestic ♦ *sm/f* servant, domestic

domi'cilio [domi't∫iljo] *sm* (*DIR*) domicile, place of residence

domi'nare *vt* to dominate; (*fig: sentimenti*) to control, master ♦ *vi* to be in the dominant position; **~rsi** *vr* (*controllarsi*) to control o.s.; **~ su** (*fig*) to surpass, outclass; **dominazi'one** *sf* domination

do'minio *sm* dominion; (*fig: campo*) field, domain

do'nare *vt* to give, present; (*per beneficenza etc*) to donate ♦ *vi* (*fig*): **~ a** to suit, become; **~ sangue** to give blood; **dona'tore, 'trice** *sm/f* donor; **donatore di sangue/di organi** blood/organ donor

dondo'lare *vt* (*cullare*) to rock; **~rsi** *vr* to swing, sway; **'dondolo** *sm*: **sedia/cavallo a dondolo** rocking chair/horse

'donna *sf* woman; **~ di casa** housewife; home-loving woman; **~ di servizio** maid

donnai'olo *sm* ladykiller

don'nesco, a, schi, sche *ag* women's, woman's

'donnola *sf* weasel

'dono *sm* gift

'dopo *av* (*tempo*) afterwards; (*: più tardi*) later; (*luogo*) after, next ♦ *prep* after ♦ *cong* (*temporale*): **~ aver studiato** after having studied; **~ mangiato va a dormire** after having eaten *o* after a meal he goes for a sleep ♦ *ag inv*: **il giorno ~** the following day; **un anno ~** a year later; **~ di me/lui** after me/him

dopo'barba *sm inv* after-shave

dopodo'mani *av* the day after tomorrow

dopogu'erra *sm* postwar years *pl*

dopo'pranzo [dopo'prandzo] *av* after lunch (*o* dinner)

dopo'sci [dopo∫'∫i] *sm inv* après-ski outfit

doposcu'ola *sm inv* school club offering extra tuition and recreational facilities

dopo'tutto *av* (*tutto considerato*) after all

doppi'aggio [dop'pjaddʒo] *sm* (*CINEMA*) dubbing

doppi'are *vt* (*NAUT*) to round; (*SPORT*) to lap; (*CINEMA*) to dub

'doppio, a *ag* double; (*fig: falso*) double-dealing, deceitful ♦ *sm* (*quantità*): **il ~ (di)** twice as much (*o* many), double the amount (*o* number) of; (*SPORT*) doubles *pl* ♦ *av* double

doppi'one *sm* duplicate (copy)

doppio'petto *sm* double-breasted jacket

do'rare *vt* to gild; (*CUC*) to brown; **do'rato, a** *ag* golden; (*ricoperto d'oro*) gilt, gilded; **dora'tura** *sf* gilding

dormicchi'are [dormik'kjare] *vi* to doze

dormigli'one, a [dormiʎ'ʎone] *sm/f* sleepyhead

dor'mire *vt, vi* to sleep; **dor'mita** *sf*: **farsi una dormita** to have a good sleep

dormi'torio *sm* dormitory

dormi'veglia [dormi've ʎʎa] *sm* drowsiness

'dorso *sm* back; (*di montagna*) ridge, crest; (*di libro*) spine; **a ~ di cavallo** on horseback

do'sare *vt* to measure out; (*MED*) to dose

'dose *sf* quantity, amount; (*MED*) dose

'dosso *sm* (*rilievo*) rise; (*di strada*) bump; (*dorso*): **levarsi di ~ i vestiti** to take one's clothes off

do'tare *vt*: **~ di** to provide *o* supply with; (*fig*) to endow with; **dotazi'one** *sf* (*insieme di beni*) endowment; (*di macchine etc*) equipment

'dote *sf* (*di sposa*) dowry; (*assegnata a un ente*) endowment; (*fig*) gift, talent

Dott. *abbr* (= *dottore*) Dr

'dotto, a *ag* (*colto*) learned ♦ *sm* (*sapiente*) scholar; (*ANAT*) duct

dotto'rato *sm* degree; **~ di ricerca** doctorate, doctor's degree

dot'tore, essa *sm/f* doctor

dot'trina *sf* doctrine

Dott.ssa *abbr* (= *dottoressa*) Dr.

'dove *av* (*gen*) where; (*in cui*) where, in which; (*dovunque*) wherever ♦ *cong* (*mentre, laddove*) whereas; **~ sei?/vai?** where are you?/are you going?; **dimmi dov'è** tell me where it is; **di ~ sei?** where are you from?; **per ~ si passa?** which way should we go?; **la città ~ abito** the town where *o* in which I live; **siediti ~ vuoi** sit wherever you like

do'vere *sm* (*obbligo*) duty ♦ *vt* (*essere debitore*): **~ qc (a qn)** to owe (sb) sth ♦ *vi* (*seguito dall'infinito: obbligo*) to have to;

rivolgersi a chi di ~ to apply to the appropriate authority *o* person; **lui deve farlo** he has to do it, he must do it; **è dovuto partire** he had to leave; **ha dovuto pagare** he had to pay; (*: intenzione*): **devo partire domani** I'm (due) to leave tomorrow; (*: probabilità*): **dev'essere tardi** it must be late; **come si deve** (*lavorare, comportarsi*) properly; **una persona come si deve** a respectable person

dove'roso, a *ag* (right and) proper

do'vunque *av* (*in qualunque luogo*) wherever; (*dappertutto*) everywhere; **~ io vada** wherever I go

do'vuto, a *ag* (*causato*): **~ a** due to

doz'zina [dod'dzina] *sf* dozen; **una ~ di uova** a dozen eggs

dozzi'nale [doddzi'nale] *ag* cheap, second-rate

dra'gare *vt* to dredge

'drago, ghi *sm* dragon

'dramma, i *sm* drama; **dram'matico a, ci, che** *ag* dramatic; **drammatiz'zare** *vt* to dramatize; **dramma'turgo, ghi** *sm* playwright, dramatist

drappeggi'are [draped'dʒare] *vt* to drape

drap'pello *sm* (*MIL*) squad; (*gruppo*) band, group

'drastico, a, ci, che *ag* drastic

dre'naggio [dre'naddʒo] *sm* drainage

dre'nare *vt* to drain

'dritto, a *ag, av* = **diritto**

driz'zare [drit'tsare] *vt* (*far tornare diritto*) to straighten; (*volgere: sguardo, occhi*) to turn, direct; (*innalzare: antenna, muro*) to erect; **~rsi** *vr*: **~rsi (in piedi)** to stand up; **~ le orecchie** to prick up one's ears

'droga, ghe *sf* (*sostanza aromatica*) spice; (*stupefacente*) drug; **dro'gare** *vt* to season, spice; to drug, dope; **drogarsi** *vr* to take drugs; **dro'gato, a** *sm/f* drug addict

droghe'ria [droge'ria] *sf* grocer's shop (*BRIT*), grocery (store) (*US*)

dubbio, a *ag* (*incerto*) doubtful, dubious; (*ambiguo*) dubious ♦ *sm* (*incertezza*) doubt; **avere il ~ che** to be afraid that, suspect that; **mettere in ~ qc** to question

sth; **dubbi'oso, a** *ag* doubtful, dubious

dubi'tare *vi*: **~ di** to doubt; (*risultato*) to be doubtful of

Dub'lino *sf* Dublin

'duca, chi *sm* duke

du'chessa [du'kessa] *sf* duchess

'due *num* two

due'cento [due'tʃɛnto] *num* two hundred ♦ *sm*: **il D~** the thirteenth century

due'pezzi [due'pɛttsi] *sm* (*costume da bagno*) two-piece swimsuit; (*abito femminile*) two-piece suit

du'etto *sm* duet

'dunque *cong* (*perciò*) so, therefore; (*riprendendo il discorso*) well (then) ♦ *sm inv*: **venire al ~** to come to the point

du'omo *sm* cathedral

'duplex *sm inv* (*TEL*) party line

dupli'cato *sm* duplicate

'duplice ['duplitʃe] *ag* double, twofold; **in ~ copia** in duplicate

du'rante *prep* during

du'rare *vi* to last; **~ fatica a** to have difficulty in; **du'rata** *sf* length (of time); duration; **dura'turo, a** *ag* lasting; **du'revole** *ag* lasting

du'rezza [du'rettsa] *sf* hardness; stubbornness; harshness; toughness

'duro, a *ag* (*pietra, lavoro, materasso, problema*) hard; (*persona: ostinato*) stubborn, obstinate; (*: severo*) harsh, hard; (*voce*) harsh; (*carne*) tough ♦ *sm* hardness; (*difficoltà*) hard part; (*persona*) tough guy; **tener ~** to stand firm, hold out; **~ d'orecchi** hard of hearing

du'rone *sm* hard skin

E

e (*dav V spesso* **ed**) *cong* and; **~ lui?** what about him?; **~ compralo!** well buy it then!

E. *abbr* (= *est*) E

è *vb vedi* **essere**

'ebano *sm* ebony

eb'bene *cong* well (then)

eb'brezza [eb'brettsa] *sf* intoxication

'ebbro, a *ag* drunk; **~ di** (*gioia etc*)

beside o.s. *o* wild with
'ebete *ag* stupid, idiotic
ebollizi'one [ebollit'tsjone] *sf* boiling;
punto di ~ boiling point
e'braico, a, ci, che *ag* Hebrew, Hebraic
♦ *sm* (LING) Hebrew
e'breo, a *ag* Jewish ♦ *sm/f* Jew/Jewess
'Ebridi *sfpl*: **le (isole) ~** the Hebrides
ecc *av abbr* (= *eccetera*) etc
ecce'denza [ettʃe'dɛntsa] *sf* excess,
surplus
ec'cedere [et'tʃedere] *vt* to exceed ♦ *vi*
to go too far; **~ nel bere/mangiare** to
indulge in drink/food to excess
eccel'lente [ettʃel'lɛnte] *ag* excellent;
eccel'lenza *sf* excellence; (*titolo*)
Excellency
ec'cellere [et'tʃɛllere] *vi*: **~ (in)** to excel
(at); **ec'celso, a** *pp di* **eccellere**
ec'centrico, a, ci, che [et'tʃɛntriko] *ag*
eccentric
ecces'sivo, a [ettʃes'sivo] *ag* excessive
ec'cesso [et'tʃɛsso] *sm* excess; **all'~**
(*gentile, generoso*) to excess, excessively; **~
di velocità** (AUT) speeding
ec'cetera [et'tʃetera] *av* et cetera, and so
on
ec'cetto [et'tʃɛtto] *prep* except, with the
exception of; **~ che** except, other than; **~
che (non)** unless
eccettu'are [ettʃettu'are] *vt* to except
eccezio'nale [ettʃetsjo'nale] *ag*
exceptional
eccezi'one [ettʃet'tsjone] *sf* exception;
(*DIR*) objection; **a ~ di** with the exception
of, except for; **d'~** exceptional
ec'cidio [et'tʃidjo] *sm* massacre
ecci'tare [ettʃi'tare] *vt* (*curiosità, interesse*) to excite, arouse; (*folla*) to incite;
~rsi *vr* to get excited; (*sessualmente*) to
become aroused; **eccitazi'one** *sf*
excitement
'ecco *av* (*per dimostrare*): **~ il treno!**
here's *o* here comes the train!; (*dav pron*)
~mi! here I am!; **~ne uno!** here's one (of
them)!; (*dav pp*): **~ fatto!** there, that's it
done!
echeggi'are [eked'dʒare] *vi* to echo
e'clissi *sf* eclipse

'eco (*pl(m)* **'echi**) *sm o f* echo
ecolo'gia [ekolo'dʒia] *sf* ecology
econo'mia *sf* economy; (*scienza*)
economics *sg*; (*risparmio: azione*) saving;
fare ~ to economize, make economies;
eco'nomico, a, ci, che *ag* economic;
(*poco costoso*) economical; **econo'mista, i**
sm economist; **economiz'zare** *vt, vi* to
save; **e'conomo, a** *ag* thrifty ♦ *sm/f* (INS)
bursar
E'CU [e'ku] *sm inv* (= *Unità monetaria
europea*) ECU *n*
ed *cong vedi* **e**
'edera *sf* ivy
e'dicola *sf* newspaper kiosk *o* stand (US)
edifi'care *vt* to build; (*fig: teoria, azienda*)
to establish; (*indurre al bene*) to edify
edi'ficio [edi'fitʃo] *sm* building; (*fig*)
structure
e'dile *ag* building *cpd*; **edi'lizia** *sf*
building, building trade; **edi'lizio, a** *ag*
building *cpd*
Edim'burgo *sf* Edinburgh
edi'tore, 'trice *ag* publishing *cpd* ♦ *sm/f*
publisher; (*curatore*) editor; **edito'ria** *sf*
publishing; **editori'ale** *ag* publishing *cpd*
♦ *sm* editorial, leader
edizi'one [edit'tsjone] *sf* edition;
(*tiratura*) printing; (*di manifestazioni,
feste etc*) production
edu'care *vt* to educate; (*gusto, mente*) to
train; **~ qn a fare** to train sb to do;
edu'cato, a *ag* polite, well-mannered;
educazi'one *sf* education; (*familiare*)
upbringing; (*comportamento*) (good)
manners *pl*; **educazione fisica** (INS)
physical training *o* education
effemi'nato, a *ag* effeminate
effet'tivo, a *ag* (*reale*) real, actual;
(*impiegato, professore*) permanent; (*MIL*)
regular ♦ *sm* (MIL) strength; (*di patrimonio etc*) sum total
ef'fetto *sm* effect; (*COMM: cambiale*) bill;
(*fig: impressione*) impression; **in ~i** in
fact, actually; **~ serra** greenhouse effect;
effettu'are *vt* to effect, carry out
effi'cace [effi'katʃe] *ag* effective
effici'ente [effi'tʃɛnte] *ag* efficient;
effici'enza *sf* efficiency

ef'fimero, a *ag* ephemeral

E'geo [e'dʒɛo] *sm:* **l'~, il mare ~** the Aegean (Sea)

E'gitto [e'dʒitto] *sm:* **l'~** Egypt

egizi'ano, a [edʒit'tsjano] *ag, sm/f* Egyptian

'egli ['eʎʎi] *pron* he; **~ stesso** he himself

ego'ismo *sm* selfishness, egoism; **ego'ista, i, e** *ag* selfish, egoistic ♦ *sm/f* egoist

egr. *abbr* = **egregio**

e'gregio, a, gi, gie [e'grɛdʒo] *ag* distinguished; (*nelle lettere*): **E~ Signore** Dear Sir

eguagli'anza *etc* [egwaʎ'ʎantsa] = **uguaglianza** *etc*

E.I. *abbr* = **Esercito Italiano**

elabo'rare *vt* (*progetto*) to work out, elaborate; (*dati*) to process; (*digerire*) to digest; **elabora'tore** *sm* (*INFORM*): **elaboratore elettronico** computer; **elaborazi'one** *sf* elaboration; digestion; **elaborazione dei dati** data processing

e'lastico, a, ci, che *ag* elastic; (*fig: andatura*) springy; (*: decisione, vedute*) flexible ♦ *sm* (*gommino*) rubber band; (*per il cucito*) elastic *no pl*

ele'fante *sm* elephant

ele'gante *ag* elegant

e'leggere [e'lɛddʒere] *vt* to elect

elemen'tare *ag* elementary; **le (scuole) ~i** *sfpl* primary (*BRIT*) *o* grade (*US*) school

ele'mento *sm* element; (*parte componente*) element, component, part; **~i** *smpl* (*della scienza etc*) elements, rudiments

ele'mosina *sf* charity, alms *pl*; **chiedere l'~** to beg

elen'care *vt* to list

e'lenco, chi *sm* list; **~ telefonico** telephone directory

e'letto, a *pp di* **eleggere** ♦ *sm/f* (*nominato*) elected member; **eletto'rale** *ag* electoral, election *cpd*; **eletto'rato** *sm* electorate; **elet'tore, 'trice** *sm/f* voter, elector

elet'trauto *sm inv* workshop for car electrical repairs; (*tecnico*) car electrician

elettri'cista, i [elettri'tʃista] *sm* electrician

elettricità [elettritʃi'ta] *sf* electricity

e'lettrico, a, ci, che *ag* electric(al)

elettriz'zare [elettrid'dzare] *vt* to electrify

e'lettro... *prefisso:* **elettrocardio-'gramma, i** *sm* electrocardiogram; **elettrodo'mestico, a, ci, che** *ag:* **apparecchi elettrodomestici** domestic (electrical) appliances; **elet'trone** *sm* electron; **elet'tronica** *sf* electronics *sg*; **elet'tronico, a, ci, che** *ag* electronic

ele'vare *vt* to raise; (*edificio*) to erect; (*multa*) to impose

elezi'one [elet'tsjone] *sf* election; **~i** (*POL*) election(s)

'elica, che *sf* propeller

eli'cottero *sm* helicopter

elimi'nare *vt* to eliminate; **elimina'toria** *sf* eliminating round

'elio *sm* helium

'ella *pron* she; (*forma di cortesia*) you; **~ stessa** she herself; you yourself

el'metto *sm* helmet

e'logio [e'lɔdʒo] *sm* (*discorso, scritto*) eulogy; (*lode*) praise (*di solito no pl*)

elo'quente *ag* eloquent

e'ludere *vt* to evade; **elu'sivo, a** *ag* evasive

ema'nare *vt* to send out, give off; (*fig: leggi, decreti*) to issue ♦ *vi:* **~ da** to come from

emanci'pare [emantʃi'pare] *vt* to emancipate; **~rsi** *vr* (*fig*) to become liberated *o* emancipated

embri'one *sm* embryo

emenda'mento *sm* amendment

emen'dare *vt* to amend

emer'genza [emer'dʒentsa] *sf* emergency; **in caso di ~** in an emergency

e'mergere [e'mɛrdʒere] *vi* to emerge; (*sommergibile*) to surface; (*fig: distinguersi*) to stand out; **e'merso, a** *pp di* **emergere**

e'messo, a *pp di* **emettere**

e'mettere *vt* (*suono, luce*) to give out, emit; (*onde radio*) to send out; (*assegno, francobollo, ordine*) to issue; (*fig: giudizio*) to express, voice

emi'crania *sf* migraine

emi'grare *vi* to emigrate; **emigrazi'one** *sf* emigration

emi'nente *ag* eminent, distinguished

emis'fero *sm* hemisphere; ~ **boreale/ australe** northern/southern hemisphere

emissi'one *sf* (*vedi emettere*) emission; sending out; issue; (*RADIO*) broadcast

emit'tente *ag* (*banca*) issuing; (*RADIO*) broadcasting, transmitting ♦ *sf* (*RADIO*) transmitter

emorra'gia, 'gie [emorra'dʒia] *sf* haemorrhage

emo'tivo, a *ag* emotional

emozio'nante [emottsjo'nante] *ag* exciting, thrilling

emozio'nare [emottsjo'nare] *vt* (*appassionare*) to thrill, excite; (*commuovere*) to move; (*innervosire*) to upset; **~rsi** *vr* to be excited; to be moved; to be upset

emozi'one [emot'tsjone] *sf* emotion; (*agitazione*) excitement

'empio, a *ag* (*sacrilego*) impious; (*spietato*) cruel, pitiless; (*malvagio*) wicked, evil

emulsi'one *sf* emulsion

enciclope'dia [entʃiklope'dia] *sf* encyclopaedia

endove'noso, a *ag* (*MED*) intravenous

'ENEL ['enel] *sigla m* (= *Ente Nazionale per l'Energia Elettrica*) ≈ C.E.G.B. (= *Central Electricity Generating Board*)

ener'gia, 'gie [ener'dʒia] *sf* (*FISICA*) energy; (*fig*) energy, strength, vigour; ~ **eolica** wind power; ~ **solare** solar energy, solar power; **e'nergico, a, ci, che** *ag* energetic, vigorous

'enfasi *sf* emphasis; (*peg*) bombast, pomposity; **en'fatico, a, ci, che** *ag* emphatic; pompous

'ENIT ['enit] *sigla m* = **Ente Nazionale Italiano per il Turismo**

en'nesimo, a *ag* (*MAT, fig*) nth; **per l'~a volta** for the umpteenth time

e'norme *ag* enormous, huge; **enormità** *sf inv* enormity, huge size; (*assurdità*) absurdity; **non dire enormità!** don't talk nonsense!

'ente *sm* (*istituzione*) body, board,

corporation; (*FILOSOFIA*) being

en'trambi, e *pron pl* both (of them) ♦ *ag pl*: ~ **i ragazzi** both boys, both of the boys

en'trare *vi* to enter, go (*o* come) in; ~ **in** (*luogo*) to enter, go (*o* come) into; (*trovar posto, poter stare*) to fit into; (*essere ammesso a: club etc*) to join, become a member of; ~ **in automobile** to get into the car; **far** ~ **qn** (*visitatore etc*) to show sb in; **questo non c'entra** (*fig*) that's got nothing to do with it; **en'trata** *sf* entrance, entry; **entrate** *sfpl* (*COMM*) receipts, takings; (*ECON*) income *sg*

'entro *prep* (*temporale*) within

entusias'mare *vt* to excite, fill with enthusiasm; **~rsi** (**per qc/qn**) to become enthusiastic (about sth/sb); **entusi'asmo** *sm* enthusiasm; **entusi'asta, i, e** *ag* enthusiastic ♦ *sm/f* enthusiast; **entusi'astico, a, ci, che** *ag* enthusiastic

enunci'are [enun'tʃare] *vt* (*teoria*) to enunciate, set out

'epico, a, ci, che *ag* epic

epide'mia *sf* epidemic

epi'dermide *sf* skin, epidermis

Epifa'nia *sf* Epiphany

epiles'sia *sf* epilepsy

e'pilogo, ghi *sm* conclusion

epi'sodio *sm* episode

e'piteto *sm* epithet

'epoca, che *sf* (*periodo storico*) age, era; (*tempo*) time; (*GEO*) age

ep'pure *cong* and yet, nevertheless

epu'rare *vt* (*POL*) to purge

equa'tore *sm* equator

equazi'one [ekwat'tsjone] *sf* (*MAT*) equation

e'questre *ag* equestrian

equi'latero, a *ag* equilateral

equili'brare *vt* to balance; **equi'librio** *sm* balance, equilibrium; **perdere l'~** to lose one's balance

e'quino, a *ag* horse *cpd*, equine

equipaggi'are [ekwipad'dʒare] *vt* (*di persone*) to man; (*di mezzi*) to equip; **equi'paggio** *sm* crew

equipa'rare *vt* to make equal

equità *sf* equity, fairness

equitazi'one [ekwitat'tsjone] *sf*
(horse-)riding

equiva'lente *ag, sm* equivalent;
equiva'lenza *sf* equivalence

equivo'care *vi* to misunderstand;
e'quivoco, a, ci, che *ag* equivocal,
ambiguous; (*sospetto*) dubious ♦ *sm*
misunderstanding; **a scanso di equivoci**
to avoid any misunderstanding; **giocare
sull'equivoco** to equivocate

'equo, a *ag* fair, just

'era *sf* era

'erba *sf* grass; (*aromatica, medicinale*)
herb; **in ~** (*fig*) budding; **er'baccia, ce** *sf*
weed

e'rede *sm/f* heir; **eredità** *sf* (*DIR*)
inheritance; (*BIOL*) heredity; **lasciare qc
in eredità a qn** to leave *o* bequeath sth
to sb; **eredi'tare** *vt* to inherit;
eredi'tario, a *ag* hereditary

ere'mita, i *sm* hermit

ere'sia *sf* heresy; **e'retico, a, ci, che** *ag*
heretical ♦ *sm/f* heretic

e'retto, a *pp di* **erigere** ♦ *ag* erect,
upright; **erezi'one** *sf* (*FISIOL*) erection

er'gastolo *sm* (*DIR: pena*) life
imprisonment

'erica *sf* heather

e'rigere [e'ridʒere] *vt* to erect, raise; (*fig:
fondare*) to found

ERM *sigla* (= *Meccanismo dei tassi di
cambio*) ERM *n*

ermel'lino *sm* ermine

er'metico, a, ci, che *ag* hermetic

'ernia *sf* (*MED*) hernia

e'roe *sm* hero

ero'gare *vt* (*somme*) to distribute; (*: per
beneficenza*) to donate; (*gas, servizi*) to
supply

e'roico, a, ci, che *ag* heroic

ero'ina *sf* heroine; (*droga*) heroin

ero'ismo *sm* heroism

erosi'one *sf* erosion

e'rotico, a, ci, che *ag* erotic

er'rare *vi* (*vagare*) to wander, roam;
(*sbagliare*) to be mistaken

er'rore *sm* error, mistake; (*morale*) error;
per ~ by mistake

'erta *sf* steep slope; **stare all'~** to be on

the alert

erut'tare *vt* (*sog: vulcano*) to throw out,
belch

eruzi'one [erut'tsjone] *sf* eruption

esacer'bare [ezatʃer'bare] *vt* to
exacerbate

esage'rare [ezadʒe'rare] *vt* to exaggerate
♦ *vi* to exaggerate; (*eccedere*) to go too far;
esagerazi'one *sf* exaggeration

e'sagono *sm* hexagon

esal'tare *vt* to exalt; (*entusiasmare*) to
excite, stir; **esal'tato, a** *sm/f* fanatic

e'same *sm* examination; (*INS*) exam,
examination; **fare** *o* **dare un ~** to sit *o*
take an exam; **~ del sangue** blood test

esami'nare *vt* to examine

e'sanime *ag* lifeless

esaspe'rare *vt* to exasperate; to
exacerbate; **~rsi** *vr* to become annoyed *o*
exasperated; **esasperazi'one** *sf*
exasperation

esatta'mente *av* exactly; accurately,
precisely

esat'tezza [ezat'tettsa] *sf* exactitude,
accuracy, precision

e'satto, a *pp di* **esigere** ♦ *ag* (*calcolo,
ora*) correct, right, exact; (*preciso*)
accurate, precise; (*puntuale*) punctual

esat'tore *sm* (*di imposte etc*) collector

esauri'ente *ag* exhaustive

esauri'mento *sm* exhaustion; **~ nervoso**
nervous breakdown

esau'rire *vt* (*stancare*) to exhaust, wear
out; (*provviste, miniera*) to exhaust; **~rsi**
vr to exhaust o.s., wear o.s. out;
(*provviste*) to run out; **esau'rito, a** *ag*
exhausted; (*merci*) sold out; (*libri*) out of
print; **registrare il tutto esaurito**
(*TEATRO*) to have a full house; **e'sausto, a**
ag exhausted

'esca (*pl* **'esche**) *sf* bait

escande'scenza [eskandeʃ'ʃentsa] *sf*:
dare in ~e to lose one's temper, fly into a
rage

'esce *etc* ['eʃe] *vb vedi* **uscire**

eschi'mese [eski'mese] *ag, sm/f* Eskimo

escla'mare *vi* to exclaim, cry out;
esclamazi'one *sf* exclamation

es'cludere *vt* to exclude
esclu'siva *sf* (*DIR, COMM*) exclusive *o* sole rights *pl*
esclu'sivo, a *ag* exclusive
es'cluso, a *pp di* **escludere**
'esco *etc vb vedi* **uscire**
escogi'tare [eskodʒi'tare] *vt* to devise, think up
escursi'one *sf* (*gita*) excursion, trip; (: *a piedi*) hike, walk; (*METEOR*) range
ese'crare *vt* to loathe, abhor
esecu'tivo, a *ag, sm* executive
esecu'tore, 'trice *sm/f* (*MUS*) performer; (*DIR*) executor
esecuzi'one [ezeku't sjone] *sf* execution, carrying out; (*MUS*) performance; ~ **capitale** execution
esegu'ire *vt* to carry out, execute; (*MUS*) to perform, execute
e'sempio *sm* example; **per** ~ for example, for instance; **fare un** ~ to give an example; **esem'plare** *ag* exemplary ♦ *sm* example; (*copia*) copy; **esemplifi'care** *vt* to exemplify
esen'tare *vt*: ~ **qn/qc da** to exempt sb/sth from
e'sente *ag*: ~ **da** (*dispensato da*) exempt from; (*privo di*) free from; **esenzi'one** *sf* exemption
e'sequie *sfpl* funeral rites; funeral service *sg*
eser'cente [ezer't ʃɛnte] *sm/f* trader, dealer; shopkeeper
eserci'tare [ezert ʃi'tare] *vt* (*professione*) to practise (*BRIT*), practice (*US*); (*allenare: corpo, mente*) to exercise, train; (*diritto*) to exercise; (*influenza, pressione*) to exert; ~**rsi** *vr* to practise; ~**rsi alla lotta** to practise fighting; **esercitazi'one** *sf* (*scolastica, militare*) exercise
e'sercito [e'zert ʃito] *sm* army
eser'cizio [ezer't ʃittsjo] *sm* practice; exercising; (*fisico, di matematica*) exercise; (*ECON*) financial year; (*azienda*) business, concern; **in** ~ (*medico etc*) practising
esi'bire *vt* to exhibit, display; (*documenti*) to produce, present; ~**rsi** *vr* (*attore*) to perform; (*fig*) to show off; **esibizi'one** *sf*

exhibition; (*di documento*) presentation; (*spettacolo*) show, performance
esi'gente [ezi'dʒɛnte] *ag* demanding; **esi'genza** *sf* demand, requirement
e'sigere [e'zidʒere] *vt* (*pretendere*) to demand; (*richiedere*) to demand, require; (*imposte*) to collect
e'siguo, a *ag* small, slight
'esile *ag* (*persona*) slender, slim; (*stelo*) thin; (*voce*) faint
esili'are *vt* to exile; **e'silio** *sm* exile
e'simere *vt*: ~ **qn/qc da** to exempt sb/sth from; ~**rsi** *vr*: ~**rsi da** to get out of
esis'tenza [ezis'tɛntsa] *sf* existence
e'sistere *vi* to exist
esis'tito, a *pp di* **esistere**
esi'tare *vi* to hesitate; **esitazi'one** *sf* hesitation
'esito *sm* result, outcome
'esodo *sm* exodus
esone'rare *vt* to exempt
e'sordio *sm* début
esor'tare *vt*: ~ **qn a fare** to urge sb to do
e'sotico, a, ci, che *ag* exotic
es'pandere *vt* to expand; (*confini*) to extend; (*influenza*) to extend, spread; ~**rsi** *vr* to expand; **espansi'one** *sf* expansion; **espan'sivo, a** *ag* expansive, communicative
espatri'are *vi* to leave one's country
espedi'ente *sm* expedient
es'pellere *vt* to expel
esperi'enza [espe'rjɛntsa] *sf* experience; (*SCIENZA: prova*) experiment
esperi'mento *sm* experiment
es'perto, a *ag, sm* expert
espi'are *vt* to atone for
espi'rare *vt, vi* to breathe out
espli'care *vt* (*attività*) to carry out, perform
es'plicito, a [es'plit ʃito] *ag* explicit
es'plodere *vi* (*anche fig*) to explode ♦ *vt* to fire
esplo'rare *vt* to explore; **esplora'tore** *sm* explorer; (*anche: giovane esploratore*) (boy) scout; (*NAUT*) scout (ship)
esplosi'one *sf* explosion; **esplo'sivo, a** *ag, sm* explosive; **es'ploso, a** *pp di* **esplodere**

espo'nente *sm/f* (*rappresentante*) representative

es'porre *vt* (*merci*) to display; (*quadro*) to exhibit, show; (*fatti, idee*) to explain, set out; (*porre in pericolo*, FOT) to expose

espor'tare *vt* to export; **esportazi'one** *sf* exportation; export

esposizi'one [espozit'tsjone] *sf* displaying; exhibiting; setting out; (*anche* FOT) exposure; (*mostra*) exhibition; (*narrazione*) explanation, exposition

es'posto, a *pp di* **esporre** ♦ *ag*: ~ **a nord** facing north ♦ *sm* (AMM) statement, account; (: *petizione*) petition

espressi'one *sf* expression

espres'sivo, a *ag* expressive

es'presso, a *pp di* **esprimere** ♦ *ag* express ♦ *sm* (*lettera*) express letter; (*anche: treno* ~) express train; (*anche: caffè* ~) espresso

es'primere *vt* to express

espulsi'one *sf* expulsion; **es'pulso, a** *pp di* **espellere**

'essa (*pl* **'esse**) *pron f vedi* **esso**

es'senza [es'sɛntsa] *sf* essence; **essenzi'ale** *ag* essential; **l'essenziale** the main *o* most important thing

<hr>
PAROLA CHIAVE
<hr>

'essere *sm* being; ~ **umano** human being ♦ *vb copulativo* **1** (*con attributo, sostantivo*) to be; **sei giovane/simpatico** you are *o* you're young/nice; **è medico** he is *o* he's a doctor

2 (+*di: appartenere*) to be; **di chi è la penna?** whose pen is it?; **è di Carla** it is *o* it's Carla's, it belongs to Carla

3 (+*di: provenire*) to be; **è di Venezia** he is *o* he's from Venice

4 (*data, ora*): **è il 15 agosto/lunedì** it is *o* it's the 15th of August/Monday; **che ora è?, che ore sono?** what time is it?; **è l'una** it is *o* it's one o'clock; **sono le due** it is *o* it's two o'clock

5 (*costare*): **quant'è?** how much is it?; **sono 20.000 lire** it's 20,000 lire ♦ *vb aus* **1** (*attivo*): ~ **arrivato/venuto** to have arrived/come; **è già partita** she has already left

2 (*passivo*) to be; ~ **fatto da** to be made by; **è stata uccisa** she has been killed

3 (*riflessivo*): **si sono lavati** they washed, they got washed

4 (+*da* +*infinito*): **è da farsi subito** it must be *o* is to be done immediately ♦ *vi* **1** (*esistere, trovarsi*) to be; **sono a casa** I'm at home; ~ **in piedi/seduto** to be standing/sitting

2: **esserci: c'è** there is; **ci sono** there are; **che c'è?** what's the matter?, what is it?; **ci sono!** I get it!; *vedi anche* **ci**

♦ *vb impers*: **è tardi/Pasqua** it's late/Easter; **è possibile che venga** he may come; **è così** that's the way it is

<hr>

'esso, a *pron* it; (*riferito a persona: soggetto*) he/she; (: *complemento*) him/her; ~**i, e** *pron pl* they; (*complemento*) them

est *sm* east

'estasi *sf* ecstasy

es'tate *sf* summer

es'tendere *vt* to extend; ~**rsi** *vr* (*diffondersi*) to spread; (*territorio, confini*) to extend; **estensi'one** *sf* extension; (*di superficie*) expanse; (*di voce*) range

esteri'ore *ag* outward, external

ester'nare *vt* to express

es'terno, a *ag* (*porta, muro*) outer, outside; (*scala*) outside; (*alunno, impressione*) external ♦ *sm* outside, exterior ♦ *sm/f* (*allievo*) day pupil; **per uso** ~ for external use only

'estero, a *ag* foreign ♦ *sm*: **all'**~ abroad

es'teso, a *pp di* **estendere** ♦ *ag* extensive, large; **scrivere per** ~ to write in full

es'tetico, a, ci, che *ag* aesthetic ♦ *sf* (*disciplina*) aesthetics *sg*; (*bellezza*) attractiveness; **este'tista, i, e** *sm/f* beautician

'estimo *sm* valuation; (*disciplina*) surveying

es'tinguere *vt* to extinguish, put out; (*debito*) to pay off; ~**rsi** *vr* to go out; (*specie*) to become extinct; **es'tinto, a** *pp di* **estinguere**; **estin'tore** *sm* (fire) extinguisher; **estinzi'one** *sf* putting out;

(*di specie*) extinction

estir'pare *vt* (*pianta*) to uproot, pull up; (*fig: vizio*) to eradicate

es'tivo, a *ag* summer *cpd*

es'torcere [es'tɔrtʃere] *vt*: ~ **qc (a qn)** to extort sth (from sb); **es'torto, a** *pp di* **estorcere**

estradizi'one [estradit'tsjone] *sf* extradition

es'traneo, a *ag* foreign; (*discorso*) extraneous, unrelated ♦ *sm/f* stranger; **rimanere ~ a qc** to take no part in sth

es'trarre *vt* to extract; (*minerali*) to mine; (*sorteggiare*) to draw; **es'tratto, a** *pp di* **estrarre** ♦ *sm* extract; (*di documento*) abstract; **estratto conto** statement of account; **estratto di carne** (*CUC*) meat extract; **estratto di nascita** birth certificate; **estrazi'one** *sf* extraction; mining; drawing *no pl*; draw

estremità *sf inv* extremity, end ♦ *sfpl* (*ANAT*) extremities

es'tremo, a *ag* extreme; (*ultimo: ora, tentativo*) final, last ♦ *sm* extreme; (*di pazienza, forze*) limit, end; ~**i** *smpl* (*AMM: dati essenziali*) details, particulars; **l'~ Oriente** the Far East

'estro *sm* (*capriccio*) whim, fancy; (*ispirazione creativa*) inspiration; **es'troso, a** *ag* whimsical, capricious; inspired

estro'verso, a *ag*, *sm* extrovert

'esule *sm/f* exile

età *sf inv* age; **all'~ di 8 anni** at the age of 8, at 8 years of age; **ha la mia ~** he (*o* she) is the same age as me *o* as I am; **raggiungere la maggiore ~** to come of age; **essere in ~ minore** to be under age

'etere *sm* ether; **e'tereo, a** *ag* ethereal

eternità *sf* eternity

e'terno, a *ag* eternal

etero'geneo, a [etero'dʒɛneo] *ag* heterogeneous

'etica *sf* ethics *sg*; *vedi anche* **etico**

eti'chetta [eti'ketta] *sf* label; (*cerimoniale*): **l'~** étiquette

'etico, a, ci, che *ag* ethical

etimolo'gia, 'gie [etimolo'dʒia] *sf* etymology

Eti'opia *sf*: **l'~** Ethiopia

'Etna *sm*: **l'~** Etna

'etnico, a, ci, che *ag* ethnic

e'trusco, a, schi, sche *ag*, *sm/f* Etruscan

'ettaro *sm* hectare (= *10,000 m²*)

'etto *sm abbr* = **ettogrammo**

etto'grammo *sm* hectogram(me) (= *100 grams*)

Eucaris'tia *sf*: **l'~** the Eucharist

Eu'ropa *sf*: **l'~** Europe; **euro'peo, a** *ag*, *sm/f* European

evacu'are *vt* to evacuate

e'vadere *vi* (*fuggire*): ~ **da** to escape from ♦ *vt* (*sbrigare*) to deal with, dispatch; (*tasse*) to evade

evan'gelico, a, ci, che [evan'dʒɛliko] *ag* evangelical

evapo'rare *vi* to evaporate; **evaporazi'one** *sf* evaporation

evasi'one *sf* (*vedi evadere*) escape; dispatch; ~ **fiscale** tax evasion

eva'sivo, a *ag* evasive

e'vaso, a *pp di* **evadere** ♦ *sm* escapee

eveni'enza [eve'njɛntsa] *sf*: **pronto(a) per ogni ~** ready for any eventuality

e'vento *sm* event

eventu'ale *ag* possible

evi'dente *ag* evident, obvious; **evi'denza** *sf* obviousness; **mettere in evidenza** to point out, highlight; **evidenzi'are** *vt* to emphasize; (*con evidenziatore*) to highlight; **evidenzia'tore** *sm* highlighter (pen)

evi'tare *vt* to avoid; ~ **di fare** to avoid doing; ~ **qc a qn** to spare sb sth

'evo *sm* age, epoch

evo'care *vt* to evoke

evo'luto, a *pp di* **evolvere** ♦ *ag* (*civiltà*) (highly) developed, advanced; (*persona*) independent

evoluzi'one [evolut'tsjone] *sf* evolution

e'volversi *vr* to evolve

ev'viva *escl* hurrah!; ~ **il re!** long live the king!, hurrah for the king!

ex *prefisso* ex, former

'extra *ag inv* first-rate; top-quality ♦ *sm inv* extra; **extracomuni'tario, a** *ag* from outside the EC ♦ *sm/f* non-EC citizen;

extraconiu'gale *ag* extramarital

F

fa *vb vedi* **fare** ♦ *sm inv* (*MUS*) F; (*: solfeggiando la scala*) fa ♦ *av*: **10 anni ~** 10 years ago

fabbi'sogno [fabbi'zoɲɲo] *sm* needs *pl*, requirements *pl*

'**fabbrica** *sf* factory; **fabbri'cante** *sm* manufacturer, maker; **fabbri'care** *vt* to build; (*produrre*) to manufacture, make; (*fig*) to fabricate, invent

'**fabbro** *sm* (black)smith

fac'cenda [fat'tʃɛnda] *sf* matter, affair; (*cosa da fare*) task, chore

fac'chino [fak'kino] *sm* porter

'**faccia** [fat'tʃa] *sf* face; (*di moneta, medaglia*) side; **~ a ~** face to face

facci'ata [fat'tʃata] *sf* façade; (*di pagina*) side

'**faccio** ['fattʃo] *vb vedi* **fare**

fa'ceto, a [fa'tʃeto] *ag* witty, humorous

'**facile** ['fatʃile] *ag* easy; (*affabile*) easy-going; (*disposto*): **~ a** inclined to, prone to; (*probabile*): **è ~ che piova** it's likely to rain; **facilità** *sf* easiness; (*disposizione, dono*) aptitude; **facili'tare** *vt* to make easier

facino'roso, a [fatʃino'roso] *ag* violent

facoltà *sf inv* faculty; (*CHIMICA*) property; (*autorità*) power

facolta'tivo, a *ag* optional; (*fermata d'autobus*) request *cpd*

fac'simile *sm* facsimile

'**faggio** ['faddʒo] *sm* beech

fagi'ano [fa'dʒano] *sm* pheasant

fagio'lino [fadʒo'lino] *sm* French (*BRIT*) o string bean

fagi'olo [fa'dʒɔlo] *sm* bean

fa'gotto *sm* bundle; (*MUS*) bassoon; **far ~** (*fig*) to pack up and go

'**fai** *vb vedi* **fare**

'**falce** ['faltʃe] *sf* scythe; **fal'cetto** *sm* sickle; **falci'are** *vt* to cut; (*fig*) to mow down

'**falco, chi** *sm* hawk

fal'cone *sm* falcon

'**falda** *sf* layer, stratum; (*di cappello*) brim; (*di cappotto*) tails *pl*; (*di monte*) lower slope; (*di tetto*) pitch; **nevica a larghe ~e** the snow is falling in large flakes; **abito a ~e** tails *pl*

fale'gname [faleɲ'ɲame] *sm* joiner

fal'lace [fal'latʃe] *ag* misleading

falli'mento *sm* failure; bankruptcy

fal'lire *vi* (*non riuscire*): **~ (in)** to fail (in); (*DIR*) to go bankrupt ♦ *vt* (*colpo, bersaglio*) to miss; **fal'lito, a** *ag* unsuccessful; bankrupt ♦ *sm/f* bankrupt

'**fallo** *sm* error, mistake; (*imperfezione*) defect, flaw; (*SPORT*) foul; fault; **senza ~** without fail

falò *sm inv* bonfire

fal'sare *vt* to distort, misrepresent; **fal'sario** *sm* forger; counterfeiter; **falsifi'care** *vt* to forge; (*monete*) to forge, counterfeit

'**falso, a** *ag* false; (*errato*) wrong; (*falsificato*) forged; fake; (*: oro, gioielli*) imitation *cpd* ♦ *sm* forgery; **giurare il ~** to commit perjury

'**fama** *sf* fame; (*reputazione*) reputation, name

'**fame** *sf* hunger; **aver ~** to be hungry; **fa'melico, a, ci, che** *ag* ravenous

fa'miglia [fa'miʎʎa] *sf* family

famili'are *ag* (*della famiglia*) family *cpd*; (*ben noto*) familiar; (*rapporti, atmosfera*) friendly; (*LING*) informal, colloquial ♦ *sm/f* relative, relation; **familiarità** *sf* familiarity; friendliness; informality

fa'moso, a *ag* famous, well-known

fa'nale *sm* (*AUT*) light, lamp (*BRIT*); (*luce stradale, NAUT*) light; (*di faro*) beacon

fa'natico, a, ci, che *ag* fanatical; (*del teatro, calcio etc*): **~ di** o **per** mad o crazy about ♦ *sm/f* fanatic; (*tifoso*) fan

fanci'ullo, a [fan'tʃullo] *sm/f* child

fan'donia *sf* tall story; **~e** *sfpl* (*assurdità*) nonsense *sg*

fan'fara *sf* brass band; (*musica*) fanfare

'**fango, ghi** *sm* mud; **fan'goso, a** *ag* muddy

'**fanno** *vb vedi* **fare**

fannul'lone, a *sm/f* idler, loafer

fantasci'enza [fantaʃ'ʃɛntsa] *sf* science

fiction

fanta'sia *sf* fantasy, imagination; (*capriccio*) whim, caprice ♦ *ag inv*: **vestito** ~ patterned dress

fan'tasma, i *sm* ghost, phantom

fan'tastico, a, ci, che *ag* fantastic; (*potenza, ingegno*) imaginative

'fante *sm* infantryman; (*CARTE*) jack, knave (*BRIT*); **fante'ria** *sf* infantry

fan'toccio [fan'tɔttʃo] *sm* puppet

fara'butto *sm* crook

far'dello *sm* bundle; (*fig*) burden

PAROLA CHIAVE

'fare *sm* **1** (*modo di fare*): **con** ~ **distratto** absent-mindedly; **ha un** ~ **simpatico** he has a pleasant manner

2: **sul far del giorno/della notte** at daybreak/nightfall

♦ *vt* **1** (*fabbricare, creare*) to make; (*: casa*) to build; (*: assegno*) to make out; ~ **un pasto/una promessa/un film** to make a meal/a promise/a film; ~ **rumore** to make a noise

2 (*effettuare: lavoro, attività, studi*) to do; (*: sport*) to play; **cosa fa?** (*adesso*) what are you doing?; (*di professione*) what do you do?; ~ **psicologia/italiano** (*INS*) to do psychology/Italian; ~ **un viaggio** to go on a trip *o* journey; ~ **una passeggiata** to go for a walk; ~ **la spesa** to do the shopping

3 (*funzione*) to be; (*TEATRO*) to play, be; ~ **il medico** to be a doctor; ~ **il malato** (*fingere*) to act the invalid

4 (*suscitare: sentimenti*): ~ **paura a qn** to frighten sb; **(non) fa niente** (*non importa*) it doesn't matter

5 (*ammontare*): **3 più 3 fa 6** 3 and 3 are *o* make 6; **fanno 6.000 lire** that's 6,000 lire; **Roma fa 2.000.000 di abitanti** Rome has 2,000,000 inhabitants; **che ora fai?** what time do you make it?

6 (+*infinito*): **far** ~ **qc a qn** (*obbligare*) to make sb do sth; (*permettere*) to let sb do sth; **fammi vedere** let me see; **far partire il motore** to start (up) the engine; **far riparare la macchina/costruire una casa** to get *o* have the car repaired/a house built

7: ~**rsi**: ~**rsi una gonna** to make o.s. a skirt; ~**rsi un nome** to make a name for o.s.; ~**rsi la permanente** to get a perm; ~**rsi tagliare i capelli** to get one's hair cut; ~**rsi operare** to have an operation

8 (*fraseologia*): **farcela** to succeed, manage; **non ce la faccio più** I can't go on; **ce la faremo** we'll make it; **me l'hanno fatta!** (*imbrogliare*) I've been done!; **lo facevo più giovane** I thought he was younger; **fare sì/no con la testa** to nod/shake one's head

♦ *vi* **1** (*agire*) to act, do; **fate come volete** do as you like; ~ **presto** to be quick; ~ **da** to act as; **non c'è niente da** ~ it's no use; **saperci** ~ **con qn/qc** to know how to deal with sb/sth; **faccia pure!** go ahead!

2 (*dire*) to say; **"davvero?" fece** "really?" he said

3: ~ **per** (*essere adatto*) to be suitable for; ~ **per** ~ **qc** to be about to do sth; **fece per andarsene** he made as if to leave

4: ~**rsi**: **si fa così** you do it like this, this is the way it's done; **non si fa così!** (*rimprovero*) that's no way to behave!; **la festa non si fa** the party is off

5: ~ **a gara con qn** to compete *o* vie with sb; ~ **a pugni** to come to blows; ~ **in tempo a** ~ to be in time to do

♦ *vb impers*: **fa bel tempo** the weather is fine; **fa caldo/freddo** it's hot/cold; **fa notte** it's getting dark

♦ *vr*: ~**rsi 1** (*diventare*) to become; ~**rsi prete** to become a priest; ~**rsi grande/vecchio** to grow tall/old

2 (*spostarsi*): ~**rsi avanti/indietro** to move forward/back

3 (*fam: drogarsi*) to be a junkie

---

far'falla *sf* butterfly

fa'rina *sf* flour

farma'cia, 'cie [farma'tʃia] *sf* pharmacy; (*negozio*) chemist's (shop) (*BRIT*), pharmacy; **farma'cista, i, e** *sm/f* chemist (*BRIT*), pharmacist

'farmaco, ci *o* **chi** *sm* drug, medicine

'faro *sm* (*NAUT*) lighthouse; (*AER*) beacon; (*AUT*) headlight

'farsa *sf* farce

'fascia, sce ['faʃʃa] *sf* band, strip; (*MED*) bandage; (*di sindaco, ufficiale*) sash; (*parte di territorio*) strip, belt; (*di contribuenti etc*) group, band; essere in ~sce (*anche fig*) to be in one's infancy; ~ oraria time band

fasci'are [faʃ'ʃare] *vt* to bind; (*MED*) to bandage; (*bambino*) to put a nappy (*BRIT*) *o* diaper (*US*) on

fa'scicolo [faʃ'ʃikolo] *sm* (*di documenti*) file, dossier; (*di rivista*) issue, number; (*opuscolo*) booklet, pamphlet

'fascino ['faʃʃino] *sm* charm, fascination

'fascio ['faʃʃo] *sm* bundle, sheaf; (*di fiori*) bunch; (*di luce*) beam; (*POL*): il F~ the Fascist Party

fa'scismo [faʃ'ʃizmo] *sm* fascism

'fase *sf* phase; (*TECN*) stroke; fuori ~ (*motore*) rough

fas'tidio *sm* bother, trouble; dare ~ a qn to bother *o* annoy sb; sento ~ allo stomaco my stomach's upset; avere ~i con la polizia to have trouble *o* bother with the police; fastidi'oso, a *ag* annoying, tiresome; (*schifiltoso*) fastidious

'fasto *sm* pomp, splendour

'fata *sf* fairy

fa'tale *ag* fatal; (*inevitabile*) inevitable; (*fig*) irresistible; fatalità *sf inv* inevitability; (*avversità*) misfortune; (*fato*) fate, destiny

fa'tica, che *sf* hard work, toil; (*sforzo*) effort; (*di metalli*) fatigue; a ~ with difficulty; fare ~ a fare qc to have a job doing sth; fati'care *vi* to toil; faticare a fare qc to have difficulty doing sth; fati'coso, a *ag* tiring, exhausting; (*lavoro*) laborious

'fato *sm* fate, destiny

'fatto, a *pp di* fare ♦ *ag*: un uomo ~ a grown man; ~ a mano/in casa hand-/home-made ♦ *sm* fact; (*azione*) deed; (*avvenimento*) event, occurrence; (*di romanzo, film*) action, story; cogliere qn sul ~ to catch sb red-handed; il ~ sta *o* è che the fact remains *o* is that; in ~ di as for, as far as ... is concerned

fat'tore *sm* (*AGR*) farm manager; (*MAT*, *elemento costitutivo*) factor

fatto'ria *sf* farm; farmhouse

fatto'rino *sm* errand-boy; (*di ufficio*) office-boy; (*d'albergo*) porter

fat'tura *sf* (*COMM*) invoice; (*di abito*) tailoring; (*malia*) spell

fattu'rare *vt* (*COMM*) to invoice; (*prodotto*) to produce; (*vino*) to adulterate

fattu'rato *sm* (*COMM*) turnover

'fatuo, a *ag* vain, fatuous

'fauna *sf* fauna

fau'tore, trice *sm/f* advocate, supporter

fa'vella *sf* speech

fa'villa *sf* spark

'favola *sf* (*fiaba*) fairy tale; (*d'intento morale*) fable; (*fandonia*) yarn; favo'loso, a *ag* fabulous; (*incredibile*) incredible

fa'vore *sm* favour; per ~ please; fare un ~ a qn to do sb a favour; favo'revole *ag* favourable

favo'rire *vt* to favour; (*il commercio, l'industria, le arti*) to promote, encourage; vuole ~? won't you help yourself?; favorisca in salotto please come into the sitting room; favo'rito, a *ag*, *sm/f* favourite

fazzo'letto [fattso'letto] *sm* handkerchief; (*per la testa*) (head)scarf

feb'braio *sm* February

'febbre *sf* fever; aver la ~ to have a high temperature; ~ da fieno hay fever; feb'brile *ag* (*anche fig*) feverish

'feccia, ce ['fettʃa] *sf* dregs *pl*

'fecola *sf* potato flour

fecondazi'one [fekondat'tsjone] *sf* fertilization; ~ artificiale artificial insemination

fe'condo, a *ag* fertile

'fede *sf* (*credenza*) belief, faith; (*REL*) faith; (*fiducia*) faith, trust; (*fedeltà*) loyalty; (*anello*) wedding ring; (*attestato*) certificate; aver ~ in qn to have faith in sb; in buona/cattiva ~ in good/bad faith; "in ~" (*DIR*) "in witness whereof"; fe'dele *ag*: fedele (a) faithful (to) ♦ *sm/f* follower; i fedeli (*REL*) the faithful; fedeltà *sf* faithfulness; (*coniugale*) fidelity; alta fedeltà (*RADIO*) high fidelity

'federa *sf* pillowslip, pillowcase

fede'rale *ag* federal

'fegato *sm* liver; (*fig*) guts *pl*, nerve

'felce ['feltʃe] *sf* fern

fe'lice [fe'litʃe] *ag* happy; (*fortunato*) lucky; **felicità** *sf* happiness

felici'tarsi [felitʃi'tarsi] *vr* (*congratularsi*): ~ **con qn per qc** to congratulate sb on sth

fe'lino, a *ag, sm* feline

'feltro *sm* felt

'femmina *sf* (*ZOOL, TECN*) female; (*figlia*) girl, daughter; (*spesso peg*) woman; **femmi'nile** *ag* feminine; (*sesso*) female; (*lavoro, giornale, moda*) woman's ♦ *sm* (*LING*) feminine; **femmi'nismo** *sm* feminism

'fendere *vt* to cut through; **fendi'nebbia** *sm inv* (*AUT*) fog lamp

fe'nomeno *sm* phenomenon

'feretro *sm* coffin

feri'ale *ag* working *cpd*, work *cpd*, week *cpd*; **giorno** ~ weekday

'ferie *sfpl* holidays (*BRIT*), vacation *sg* (*US*); **andare in** ~ to go on holiday *o* vacation

fe'rire *vt* to injure; (*deliberatamente: MIL etc*) to wound; (*colpire*) to hurt; **fe'rita** *sf* injury, wound; **fe'rito, a** *sm/f* wounded *o* injured man/woman

'ferma *sf* (*MIL*) (period of) service; (*CACCIA*): **cane da** ~ pointer

fer'maglio [fer'maʎʎo] *sm* clasp; (*gioiello*) brooch; (*per documenti*) clip

fer'mare *vt* to stop, halt; (*POLIZIA*) to detain, hold; (*bottone etc*) to fasten, fix ♦ *vi* to stop; **~rsi** *vr* to stop, halt; **~rsi a fare qc** to stop to do sth

fer'mata *sf* stop; ~ **dell'autobus** bus stop

fer'mento *sm* (*anche fig*) ferment; (*lievito*) yeast

fer'mezza [fer'mettsa] *sf* (*fig*) firmness, steadfastness

'fermo, a *ag* still, motionless; (*veicolo*) stationary; (*orologio*) not working; (*saldo: anche fig*) firm; (*voce, mano*) steady ♦ *escl* stop!; keep still! ♦ *sm* (*chiusura*) catch, lock; (*DIR*): ~ **di polizia** police detention

'fermo 'posta *av, sm inv* poste restante (*BRIT*), general delivery (*US*)

fe'roce [fe'rɔtʃe] *ag* (*animale*) wild, fierce, ferocious; (*persona*) cruel, fierce;

(*fame, dolore*) raging

ferra'gosto *sm* (*festa*) feast of the Assumption; (*periodo*) August holidays *pl*

ferra'menta *sfpl* ironmongery *sg* (*BRIT*), hardware *sg*; **negozio di** ~ ironmonger's (*BRIT*), hardware shop *o* store (*US*)

fer'rato, a *ag* (*FERR*): **strada** ~**a** railway (*BRIT*) *o* railroad (*US*) line; (*fig*): **essere** ~ **in** to be well up in

'ferreo, a *ag* iron *cpd*

'ferro *sm* iron; **una bistecca ai** ~**i** a grilled steak; ~ **battuto** wrought iron; ~ **da calza** knitting needle; ~ **di cavallo** horseshoe; ~ **da stiro** iron

ferro'via *sf* railway (*BRIT*), railroad (*US*); **ferrovi'ario, a** *ag* railway *cpd* (*BRIT*), railroad *cpd* (*US*); **ferrovi'ere** *sm* railwayman (*BRIT*), railroad man (*US*)

'fertile *ag* fertile; **fertiliz'zante** *sm* fertilizer

'fervido, a *ag* fervent

fer'vore *sm* fervour, ardour; (*punto culminante*) height

'fesso, a *pp di* **fendere** ♦ *ag* (*fam: sciocco*) crazy, cracked

fes'sura *sf* crack, split; (*per gettone, moneta*) slot

'festa *sf* (*religiosa*) feast; (*pubblica*) holiday; (*compleanno*) birthday; (*onomastico*) name day; (*ricevimento*) celebration, party; **far** ~ to have a holiday; to live it up; **far** ~ **a qn** to give sb a warm welcome

festeggi'are [fested'dʒare] *vt* to celebrate; (*persona*) to have a celebration for

fes'tino *sm* party; (*con balli*) ball

fes'tivo, a *ag* (*atmosfera*) festive; **giorno** ~ holiday

fes'toso, a *ag* merry, joyful

fe'ticcio [fe'tittʃo] *sm* fetish

'feto *sm* foetus (*BRIT*), fetus (*US*)

'fetta *sf* slice

fettuc'cine [fettut'tʃine] *sfpl* (*CUC*) ribbon-shaped pasta

FF.SS. *abbr* = **Ferrovie dello Stato**

fi'aba *sf* fairy tale

fi'acca *sf* weariness; (*svogliatezza*) listlessness

fiac'care *vt* to weaken

fi'acco, a, chi, che *ag* (*stanco*) tired, weary; (*svogliato*) listless; (*debole*) weak; (*mercato*) slack

fi'accola *sf* torch

fi'ala *sf* phial

fi'amma *sf* flame

fiam'mante *ag* (*colore*) flaming; nuovo ~ brand new

fiammeggi'are [fjammed'dʒare] *vi* to blaze

fiam'mifero *sm* match

fia'mingo, a, ghi, ghe *ag* Flemish ♦ *sm/f* Fleming ♦ *sm* (*LING*) Flemish; (*ZOOL*) flamingo; i F~ghi the Flemish

fiancheggi'are [fjanked'dʒare] *vt* to border; (*fig*) to support, back (up); (*MIL*) to flank

fi'anco, chi *sm* side; (*MIL*) flank; di ~ sideways, from the side; a ~ a ~ side by side

fi'asco, schi *sm* flask; (*fig*) fiasco; fare ~ to be a fiasco

fi'ato *sm* breath; (*resistenza*) stamina; avere il ~ grosso to be out of breath; prendere ~ to catch one's breath; ~i *smpl* (*MUS*) wind instruments; strumento a ~ wind instrument

'fibbia *sf* buckle

'fibra *sf* fibre; (*fig*) constitution

fic'care *vt* to push, thrust, drive; ~rsi *vr* (*andare a finire*) to get to

'fico, chi *sm* (*pianta*) fig tree; (*frutto*) fig; ~ d'India prickly pear; ~ secco dried fig

fidanza'mento [fidantsa'mento] *sm* engagement

fidan'zarsi [fidan'tsarsi] *vr* to get engaged; fidan'zato, a *sm/f* fiancé/fiancée

fi'darsi *vr*: ~ di to trust; fi'dato, a *ag* reliable, trustworthy

'fido, a *ag* faithful, loyal ♦ *sm* (*COMM*) credit

fi'ducia [fi'dutʃa] *sf* confidence, trust; incarico di ~ position of trust, responsible position; persona di ~ reliable person

fi'ele *sm* (*MED*) bile; (*fig*) bitterness

fie'nile *sm* barn; hayloft

fi'eno *sm* hay

fi'era *sf* fair

fie'rezza [fje'rettsa] *sf* pride

fi'ero, a *ag* proud; (*crudele*) fierce, cruel; (*audace*) bold

'fifa (*fam*) *sf*: aver ~ to have the jitters

'figlia ['fiʎʎa] *sf* daughter

figli'astro, a [fiʎ'ʎastro] *sm/f* stepson/daughter

'figlio ['fiʎʎo] *sm* son; (*senza distinzione di sesso*) child; ~ di papà spoilt, wealthy young man; ~ unico only child; figli'occio, a, ci, ce *sm/f* godchild, godson/daughter

fi'gura *sf* figure; (*forma, aspetto esterno*) form, shape; (*illustrazione*) picture, illustration; far ~ to look smart; fare una brutta ~ to make a bad impression

figu'rare *vi* to appear ♦ *vt*: ~rsi qc to imagine sth; ~rsi *vr*: figurati! imagine that!; ti do noia? — ma figurati! am I disturbing you? — not at all!

figura'tivo, a *ag* figurative

figu'rina *sf* figurine; (*cartoncino*) picture card

'fila *sf* row, line; (*coda*) queue; (*serie*) series, string; di ~ in succession; fare la ~ to queue; in ~ indiana in single file

filantro'pia *sf* philanthropy

fi'lare *vt* to spin ♦ *vi* (*baco, ragno*) to spin; (*formaggio fuso*) to go stringy; (*discorso*) to hang together; (*fam: amoreggiare*) to go steady; (*muoversi a forte velocità*) to go at full speed; (: *andarsene lentamente*) to make o.s. scarce; ~ diritto (*fig*) to toe the line

filas'trocca, che *sf* nursery rhyme

filate'lia *sf* philately, stamp collecting

fi'lato, a *ag* spun ♦ *sm* yarn; 3 giorni ~i 3 days running *o* on end; fila'tura *sf* spinning; (*luogo*) spinning mill

fi'letto *sm* (*di vite*) thread; (*di carne*) fillet

fili'ale *ag* filial ♦ *sf* (*di impresa*) branch

fili'grana *sf* (*in oreficeria*) filigree; (*su carta*) watermark

film *sm inv* film; fil'mare *vt* to film

'filo *sm* (*anche fig*) thread; (*filato*) yarn; (*metallico*) wire; (*di lama, rasoio*) edge; per ~ e per segno in detail; ~ d'erba blade of grass; ~ di perle string of pearls;

~ **spinato** barbed wire; **con un ~ di voce** in a whisper

'**filobus** *sm inv* trolley bus

filon'cino [filon'tʃino] *sm* ≈ French stick

fi'lone *sm* (*di minerali*) seam, vein; (*pane*) ≈ Vienna loaf; (*fig*) trend

filoso'fia *sf* philosophy; **fi'losofo, a** *sm/f* philosopher

fil'trare *vt, vi* to filter

'**filtro** *sm* filter; ~ **dell'olio** (*AUT*) oil filter

'**filza** ['filtsa] *sf* (*anche fig*) string

fin *av, prep* = **fino**

fi'nale *ag* final ♦ *sm* (*di opera*) end, ending; (: *MUS*) finale ♦ *sf* (*SPORT*) final; **finalità** *sf* (*scopo*) aim, purpose; **final'mente** *av* finally, at last

fi'nanza [fi'nantsa] *sf* finance; ~**e** *sfpl* (*di individuo, Stato*) finances; **finanzi'ario, a** *ag* financial; **finanzi'ere** *sm* financier; (*guardia di finanza: doganale*) customs officer; (: *tributaria*) inland revenue official

finché [fin'ke] *cong* (*per tutto il tempo che*) as long as; (*fino al momento in cui*) until; **aspetta ~ io (non) sia ritornato** wait until I get back

'**fine** *ag* (*lamina, carta*) thin; (*capelli, polvere*) fine; (*vista, udito*) keen, sharp; (*persona: raffinata*) refined, distinguished; (*osservazione*) subtle ♦ *sf* end ♦ *sm* aim, purpose; (*esito*) result, outcome; **secondo ~** ulterior motive; **in o alla ~** in the ehd, finally; ~ **settimana** *sm o f inv* weekend

fi'nestra *sf* window; **fines'trino** *sm* (*di treno, auto*) window

'**fingere** ['findʒere] *vt* to feign; (*supporre*) to imagine, suppose; ~**rsi** *vr*: ~**rsi ubriaco/pazzo** to pretend to be drunk/mad; ~ **di fare** to pretend to do

fini'mondo *sm* pandemonium

fi'nire *vt* to finish ♦ *vi* to finish, end; ~ **di fare** (*compiere*) to finish doing; (*smettere*) to stop doing; ~ **in galera** to end up *o* finish up in prison; **fini'tura** *sf* finish

finlan'dese *ag, sm* (*LING*) Finnish ♦ *sm/f* Finn

Fin'landia *sf*: **la ~** Finland

'**fino, a** *ag* (*capelli, seta*) fine; (*oro*) pure; (*fig: acuto*) shrewd ♦ *av* (*spesso troncato*

in fin: *pure, anche*) even ♦ *prep* (*spesso troncato in fin*: *tempo*): **fin quando?**: till when?; (: *luogo*): **fin qui** as far as here; ~ **a** (*tempo*) until, till; (*luogo*) as far as, (up) to; **fin da domani** from tomorrow onwards; **fin da ieri** since yesterday; **fin dalla nascita** from *o* since birth

fi'nocchio [fi'nɔkkjo] *sm* fennel; (*fam: peg: pederasta*) queer

fi'nora *av* up till now

'**finta** *sf* pretence, sham; (*SPORT*) feint; **far ~a (di fare)** to pretend (to do)

'**finto, a** *pp di* **fingere** ♦ *ag* false; artificial

finzi'one [fin'tsjone] *sf* pretence, sham

fi'occo, chi *sm* (*di nastro*) bow; (*di stoffa, lana*) flock; (*di neve*) flake; (*NAUT*) jib; **coi ~chi** (*fig*) first-rate; ~**chi di granoturco** cornflakes

fi'ocina ['fjɔtʃina] *sf* harpoon

fi'oco, a, chi, che *ag* faint, dim

fi'onda *sf* catapult

fio'raio, a *sm/f* florist

fi'ore *sm* flower; ~**i** *smpl* (*CARTE*) clubs; **a fior d'acqua** on the surface of the water; **avere i nervi a fior di pelle** to be on edge

fioren'tino, a *ag* Florentine

fio'retto *sm* (*SCHERMA*) foil

fio'rire *vi* (*rosa*) to flower; (*albero*) to blossom; (*fig*) to flourish

Fi'renze [fi'rɛntse] *sf* Florence

'**firma** *sf* signature; (*reputazione*) name

fir'mare *vt* to sign

fisar'monica, che *sf* accordion

fis'cale *ag* fiscal, tax *cpd*; **medico ~** *doctor employed by Social Security to verify cases of sick leave*

fischi'are [fis'kjare] *vi* to whistle ♦ *vt* to whistle; (*attore*) to boo, hiss

'**fischio** ['fiskjo] *sm* whistle

'**fisco** *sm* tax authorities *pl*, ≈ Inland Revenue (*BRIT*), ≈ Internal Revenue Service (*US*)

'**fisica** *sf* physics *sg*

'**fisico, a, ci, che** *ag* physical ♦ *sm/f* physicist ♦ *sm* physique

fisiolo'gia [fizjolo'dʒia] *sf* physiology

fisiono'mia *sf* face, physiognomy

fisiotera'pia *sf* physiotherapy

fis'sare *vt* to fix, fasten; (*guardare intensamente*) to stare at; (*data, condizioni*) to fix, establish, set; (*prenotare*) to book; **~rsi su** (*sog: sguardo, attenzione*) to focus on; (*fig: idea*) to become obsessed with; **fissazi'one** *sf* (*PSIC*) fixation

'fisso, a *ag* fixed; (*stipendio, impiego*) regular ♦ *av*: **guardare ~ qc/qn** to stare at sth/sb

'fitta *sf* sharp pain; *vedi anche* **fitto**

fit'tizio, a *ag* fictitious, imaginary

'fitto, a *ag* thick, dense; (*pioggia*) heavy ♦ *sm* depths *pl*, middle; (*affitto, pigione*) rent

fi'ume *sm* river

fiu'tare *vt* to smell, sniff; (*sog: animale*) to scent; (*fig: inganno*) to get wind of, smell; **~ tabacco/cocaina** to take snuff/cocaine; **fi'uto** *sm* (sense of) smell; (*fig*) nose

fla'gello [fla'dʒɛllo] *sm* scourge

fla'grante *ag* flagrant; **cogliere qn in ~** to catch sb red-handed

fla'nella *sf* flannel

flash [flaʃ] *sm inv* (*FOT*) flash; (*giornalistico*) newsflash

'flauto *sm* flute

'flebile *ag* faint, feeble

'flemma *sf* (*calma*) coolness, phlegm; (*MED*) phlegm

fles'sibile *ag* pliable; (*fig: che si adatta*) flexible

'flesso, a *pp di* **flettere**

flessu'oso, a *ag* supple, lithe; (*andatura*) flowing, graceful

'flettere *vt* to bend

F.lli *abbr* (= *fratelli*) Bros.

'flora *sf* flora

'florido, a *ag* flourishing; (*fig*) glowing with health

'floscio, a, sci, sce ['flɔʃʃo] *ag* (*cappello*) floppy, soft; (*muscoli*) flabby

'flotta *sf* fleet

'fluido, a *ag, sm* fluid

flu'ire *vi* to flow

flu'oro *sm* fluorine

fluo'ruro *sm* fluoride

'flusso *sm* flow; (*FISICA, MED*) flux; **~ e**

ri'flusso ebb and flow

fluttu'are *vi* to rise and fall; (*ECON*) to fluctuate

fluvi'ale *ag* river *cpd*, fluvial

'foca, che *sf* (*ZOOL*) seal

fo'caccia, ce [fo'kattʃa] *sf kind of pizza*; (*dolce*) bun

'foce ['fotʃe] *sf* (*GEO*) mouth

foco'laio *sm* (*MED*) centre of infection; (*fig*) hotbed

foco'lare *sm* hearth, fireside; (*TECN*) furnace

'fodera *sf* (*di vestito*) lining; (*di libro, poltrona*) cover; **fode'rare** *vt* to line; to cover

'fodero *sm* (*di spada*) scabbard; (*di pugnale*) sheath; (*di pistola*) holster

'foga *sf* enthusiasm, ardour

'foggia, ge ['fɔddʒa] *sf* (*maniera*) style; (*aspetto*) form, shape; (*moda*) fashion, style

'foglia ['fɔʎʎa] *sf* leaf; **~ d'argento/d'oro** silver/gold leaf; **fogli'ame** *sm* foliage, leaves *pl*

'foglio ['fɔʎʎo] *sm* (*di carta*) sheet (of paper); (*di metallo*) sheet; (*documento*) document; (*banconota*) (bank)note; **~ rosa** (*AUT*) provisional licence; **~ di via** (*DIR*) expulsion order; **~ volante** pamphlet

'fogna ['fɔɲɲa] *sf* drain, sewer; **fogna'tura** *sf* drainage, sewerage

föhn [føːn] *sm inv* hair dryer

folgo'rare *vt* (*sog: fulmine*) to strike down; (: *alta tensione*) to electrocute

'folla *sf* crowd, throng

'folle *ag* mad, insane; (*TECN*) idle; **in ~** (*AUT*) in neutral

fol'lia *sf* folly, foolishness; foolish act; (*pazzia*) madness, lunacy

'folto, a *ag* thick

fomen'tare *vt* to stir up, foment

fondamen'tale *ag* fundamental, basic

fonda'mento *sm* foundation; **~a** *sfpl* (*EDIL*) foundations

fon'dare *vt* to found; (*fig: dar base*): **~ qc su** to base sth on; **fondazi'one** *sf* foundation

'fondere *vt* (*neve*) to melt; (*metallo*) to fuse, melt; (*fig: colori*) to merge, blend;

(*: imprese, gruppi*) to merge ♦ *vi* to melt; **~rsi** *vr* to melt; (*fig: partiti, correnti*) to unite, merge; **fonde'ria** *sf* foundry

'**fondo, a** *ag* deep ♦ *sm* (*di recipiente, pozzo*) bottom; (*di stanza*) back; (*quantità di liquido che resta, deposito*) dregs *pl*; (*sfondo*) background; (*unità immobiliare*) property, estate; (*somma di denaro*) fund; (*SPORT*) long-distance race; **~i** *smpl* (*denaro*) funds; **a notte ~a** at dead of night; **in ~ a** at the bottom of; at the back of; (*strada*) at the end of; **andare a ~** (*nave*) to sink; **conoscere a ~** to know inside out; **dar ~ a** (*fig: provviste, soldi*) to use up; **in ~** (*fig*) after all, all things considered; **andare fino in ~ a** (*fig*) to examine thoroughly; **a ~ perduto** (*COMM*) without security; **~i di caffè** coffee grounds; **~i di magazzino** old *o* unsold stock *sg*

fo'netica *sf* phonetics *sg*

fon'tana *sf* fountain

'**fonte** *sf* spring, source; (*fig*) source ♦ *sm*: **~ battesimale** (*REL*) font

fon'tina *sm* *sweet full-fat hard cheese from Val d'Aosta*

fo'raggio [fo'raddʒo] *sm* fodder, forage

fo'rare *vt* to pierce, make a hole in; (*pallone*) to burst; (*biglietto*) to punch; **~ una gomma** to burst a tyre (*BRIT*) *o* tire (*US*)

'**forbici** ['fɔrbitʃi] *sfpl* scissors

'**forca, che** *sf* (*AGR*) fork, pitchfork; (*patibolo*) gallows *sg*

for'cella [for'tʃɛlla] *sf* (*TECN*) fork; (*di monte*) pass

for'chetta [for'ketta] *sf* fork

for'cina [for'tʃina] *sf* hairpin

'**forcipe** ['fɔrtʃipe] *sm* forceps *pl*

fo'resta *sf* forest

foresti'ero, a *ag* foreign ♦ *sm/f* foreigner

'**forfora** *sf* dandruff

'**forgia, ge** ['fɔrdʒa] *sf* forge; **forgi'are** *vt* to forge

'**forma** *sf* form; (*aspetto esteriore*) form, shape; (*DIR: procedura*) procedure; (*per calzature*) last; (*stampo da cucina*) mould; **~e** *sfpl* (*del corpo*) figure, shape; **le ~e**

(*convenzioni*) appearances; **essere in ~** to be in good shape

formag'gino [formad'dʒino] *sm* processed cheese

for'maggio [for'maddʒo] *sm* cheese

for'male *ag* formal; **formalità** *sf inv* formality

for'mare *vt* to form, shape, make; (*numero di telefono*) to dial; (*fig: carattere*) to form, mould; **~rsi** *vr* to form, take shape; **for'mato** *sm* format, size; **formazi'one** *sf* formation; (*fig: educazione*) training

for'mica, che *sf* ant; **formi'caio** *sm* anthill

formico'lare *vi* (*gamba, braccio*) to tingle; (*brulicare: anche fig*): **~ di** to be swarming with; **mi formicola la gamba** I've got pins and needles in my leg, my leg's tingling; **formico'lio** *sm* pins and needles *pl*; swarming

formi'dabile *ag* powerful, formidable; (*straordinario*) remarkable

'**formula** *sf* formula; **~ di cortesia** courtesy form

formu'lare *vt* to formulate; to express

for'nace [for'natʃe] *sf* (*per laterizi etc*) kiln; (*per metalli*) furnace

for'naio *sm* baker

for'nello *sm* (*elettrico, a gas*) ring; (*di pipa*) bowl

for'nire *vt*: **~ qn di qc, ~ qc a qn** to provide *o* supply sb with sth, to supply sth to sb

'**forno** *sm* (*di cucina*) oven; (*panetteria*) bakery; (*TECN: per calce etc*) kiln; (*: per metalli*) furnace

'**foro** *sm* (*buco*) hole; (*STORIA*) forum; (*tribunale*) (law) court

'**forse** *av* perhaps, maybe; (*circa*) about; **essere in ~** to be in doubt

forsen'nato, a *ag* mad, insane

'**forte** *ag* strong; (*suono*) loud; (*spesa*) considerable, great; (*passione, dolore*) great, deep ♦ *av* strongly; (*velocemente*) fast; (*a voce alta*) loud(ly); (*violentemente*) hard ♦ *sm* (*edificio*) fort; (*specialità*) forte, strong point; **essere ~ in qc** to be good at sth

for'tezza [for'tettsa] *sf* (*morale*) strength; (*luogo fortificato*) fortress

for'tuito, a *ag* fortuitous, chance

for'tuna *sf* (*destino*) fortune, luck; (*buona sorte*) success, fortune; (*eredità, averi*) fortune; **per ~** luckily, fortunately; **di ~** makeshift, improvised; **atterraggio di ~** emergency landing; **fortu'nato, a** *ag* lucky, fortunate; (*coronato da successo*) successful

forvi'are *vt, vi* = **fuorviare**

'forza ['fɔrtsa] *sf* strength; (*potere*) power; (*FISICA*) force; **~e** *sfpl* (*fisiche*) strength *sg*; (*MIL*) forces ♦ *escl* come on!; **per ~** against one's will; (*naturalmente*) of course; **a viva ~** by force; **a ~ di** by dint of; **~ maggiore** circumstances beyond one's control; **la ~ pubblica** the police *pl*; **le ~e armate** the armed forces; **~e dell'ordine** the forces of law and order

for'zare [for'tsare] *vt* to force; **~ qn a fare** to force sb to do; **for'zato, a** *ag* forced ♦ *sm* (*DIR*) prisoner sentenced to hard labour

fos'chia [fos'kia] *sf* mist, haze

'fosco, a, schi, sche *ag* dark, gloomy

'fosforo *sm* phosphorous

'fossa *sf* pit; (*di cimitero*) grave; **~ biologica** septic tank

fos'sato *sm* ditch; (*di fortezza*) moat

fos'setta *sf* dimple

'fossile *ag*, *sm* fossil

'fosso *sm* ditch; (*MIL*) trench

'foto *sf* photo ♦ *prefisso*: **foto'copia** *sf* photocopy; **fotocopi'are** *vt* to photocopy; **fotogra'fare** *vt* to photograph; **fotogra'fia** *sf* (*procedimento*) photography; (*immagine*) photograph; **fare una fotografia** to take a photograph; **una fotografia a colori/in bianco e nero** a colour/black and white photograph; **fo'tografo, a** *sm/f* photographer; **fotoro'manzo** *sm* romantic picture story

fra *prep* = **tra**

fracas'sare *vt* to shatter, smash; **~rsi** *vr* to shatter, smash; (*veicolo*) to crash; **fra'casso** *sm* smash; crash; (*baccano*) din, racket

'fradicio, a, ci, ce ['fraditʃo] *ag* (*molto bagnato*) soaking (wet); **ubriaco ~** blind drunk

'fragile ['fradʒile] *ag* fragile; (*fig: salute*) delicate

'fragola *sf* strawberry

fra'gore *sm* roar; (*di tuono*) rumble

frago'roso, a *ag* deafening

fra'grante *ag* fragrant

frain'tendere *vt* to misunderstand; **frain'teso, a** *pp di* **fraintendere**

fram'mento *sm* fragment

'frana *sf* landslide; (*fig: persona*): **essere una ~** to be useless; **fra'nare** *vi* to slip, slide down

fran'cese [fran'tʃeze] *ag* French ♦ *sm/f* Frenchman/woman ♦ *sm* (*LING*) French; **i F~i** the French

fran'chezza [fran'kettsa] *sf* frankness, openness

'Francia ['frantʃa] *sf*: **la ~** France

'franco, a, chi, che *ag* (*COMM*) free; (*sincero*) frank, open, sincere ♦ *sm* (*moneta*) franc; **farla ~a** (*fig*) to get off scot-free; **~ di dogana** duty-free; **~ a domicilio** delivered free of charge; **prezzo ~ fabbrica** ex-works price; **~ tiratore** *sm* sniper

franco'bollo *sm* (*postage*) stamp

fran'gente [fran'dʒɛnte] *sm* (*onda*) breaker; (*scoglio emergente*) reef; (*circostanza*) situation, circumstance

'frangia, ge ['frandʒa] *sf* fringe

frantu'mare *vt* to break into pieces, shatter; **~rsi** *vr* to break into pieces, shatter

frap'pé *sm* milk shake

'frasca, sche *sf* (leafy) branch

'frase *sf* (*LING*) sentence; (*locuzione, espressione, MUS*) phrase; **~ fatta** set phrase

'frassino *sm* ash (tree)

frastagli'ato, a [frastaʎ'ʎato] *ag* (*costa*) indented, jagged

frastor'nare *vt* to daze; to befuddle

frastu'ono *sm* hubbub, din

'frate *sm* friar, monk

fratel'lanza [fratel'lantsa] *sf* brotherhood; (*associazione*) fraternity

fratel'lastro *sm* stepbrother

fra'tello *sm* brother; **~i** *smpl* brothers; (*nel senso di fratelli e sorelle*) brothers and sisters

fra'terno, a *ag* fraternal, brotherly

frat'tanto *av* in the meantime, meanwhile

frat'tempo *sm*: **nel ~** in the meantime, meanwhile

frat'tura *sf* fracture; (*fig*) split, break

frazi'one [frat'tsjone] *sf* fraction; **~ di comune** small town

'freccia, ce ['frettʃa] *sf* arrow; **~ di direzione** (*AUT*) indicator

fred'dare *vt* to shoot dead

fred'dezza [fred'dettsa] *sf* coldness

'freddo, a *ag, sm* cold; **fa ~** it's cold; **aver ~** to be cold; **a ~** (*fig*) deliberately; **freddo'loso, a** *ag* sensitive to the cold

fred'dura *sf* pun

fre'gare *vt* to rub; (*fam: truffare*) to take in, cheat; (: *rubare*) to swipe, pinch; **fregarsene** (*fam!*): **chi se ne frega?** who gives a damn (about it)?

fre'gata *sf* rub; (*fam*) swindle; (*NAUT*) frigate

'fregio ['fredʒo] *sm* (*ARCHIT*) frieze; (*ornamento*) decoration

'fremere *vi*: **~ di** to tremble *o* quiver with; **'fremito** *sm* tremor, quiver

fre'nare *vt* (*veicolo*) to slow down; (*cavallo*) to rein in; (*lacrime*) to restrain, hold back ♦ *vi* to brake; **~rsi** *vr* (*fig*) to restrain o.s., control o.s.; **fre'nata** *sf*: **fare una frenata** to brake

frene'sia *sf* frenzy

'freno *sm* brake; (*morso*) bit; **~ a disco** disc brake; **~ a mano** handbrake; **tenere a ~** to restrain

frequen'tare *vt* (*scuola, corso*) to attend; (*locale, bar*) to go to, frequent; (*persone*) to see (often)

fre'quente *ag* frequent; **di ~** frequently; **fre'quenza** *sf* frequency; (*INS*) attendance

fres'chezza [fres'kettsa] *sf* freshness

'fresco, a, schi, sche *ag* fresh; (*temperatura*) cool; (*notizia*) recent, fresh ♦ *sm*: **godere il ~** to enjoy the cool air; **stare ~** (*fig*) to be in for it; **mettere al ~** to put in a cool place

'fretta *sf* hurry, haste; **in ~** in a hurry; **in ~ e furia** in a mad rush; **aver ~** to be in a hurry; **fretto'loso, a** *ag* (*persona*) in a hurry; (*lavoro etc*) hurried, rushed

fri'abile *ag* (*terreno*) friable; (*pasta*) crumbly

'friggere ['friddʒere] *vt* to fry ♦ *vi* (*olio etc*) to sizzle

'frigido, a ['fridʒido] *ag* (*MED*) frigid

'frigo *sm* fridge

frigo'rifero, a *ag* refrigerating ♦ *sm* refrigerator

fringu'ello *sm* chaffinch

frit'tata *sf* omelette; **fare una ~** (*fig*) to make a mess of things

frit'tella *sf* (*CUC*) pancake; (: *ripiena*) fritter

'fritto, a *pp di* **friggere** ♦ *ag* fried ♦ *sm* fried food; **~ misto** mixed fry

frit'tura *sf* (*CUC*): **~ di pesce** mixed fried fish

'frivolo, a *ag* frivolous

frizi'one [frit'tsjone] *sf* friction; (*di pelle*) rub, rub-down; (*AUT*) clutch

friz'zante [frid'dzante] *ag* (*anche fig*) sparkling

'frizzo ['friddzo] *sm* witticism

fro'dare *vt* to defraud, cheat

'frode *sf* fraud; **~ fiscale** tax evasion

'frollo, a *ag* (*carne*) tender; (: *di selvaggina*) high; (*fig: persona*) soft; **pasta ~a** short(crust) pastry

'fronda *sf* (leafy) branch; (*di partito politico*) internal opposition

fron'tale *ag* frontal; (*scontro*) head-on

'fronte *sf* (*ANAT*) forehead; (*di edificio*) front, façade ♦ *sm* (*MIL, POL, METEOR*) front; **a ~, di ~** facing, opposite; **di ~ a** (*posizione*) opposite, facing, in front of; (*a paragone di*) compared with

fronteggi'are [fronted'dʒare] *vt* (*avversari, difficoltà*) to face, stand up to; (*spese*) to cope with

fronti'era *sf* border, frontier

'fronzolo ['frondzolo] *sm* frill

'frottola *sf* fib; **~e** *sfpl* (*assurdità*) nonsense *sg*

fru'gare *vi* to rummage ♦ *vt* to search

frul'lare *vt* (*CUC*) to whisk ♦ *vi* (*uccelli*) to flutter; **frul'lato** *sm* milk shake; fruit drink; **frulla'tore** *sm* electric mixer; **frul'lino** *sm* whisk

fru'mento *sm* wheat

fru'scio [fruʃ'ʃio] *sm* rustle; rustling; (*di acque*) murmur

'frusta *sf* whip; (*CUC*) whisk

frus'tare *vt* to whip

frus'tino *sm* riding crop

frus'trare *vt* to frustrate

'frutta *sf* fruit; (*portata*) dessert; ~ **candita/secca** candied/dried fruit

frut'tare *vi* to bear dividends, give a return

frut'teto *sm* orchard

frutti'vendolo, a *sm/f* greengrocer (*BRIT*), produce dealer (*US*)

'frutto *sm* fruit; (*fig: risultato*) result(s); (*ECON: interesse*) interest; (: *reddito*) income; **~i di mare** seafood *sg*

FS *abbr* = **Ferrovie dello Stato**

fu *vb vedi* **essere** ♦ *ag inv*: **il ~ Paolo Bianchi** the late Paolo Bianchi

fuci'lare [futʃi'lare] *vt* to shoot; **fuci'lata** *sf* rifle shot

fu'cile [fu'tʃile] *sm* rifle, gun; (*da caccia*) shotgun, gun

fu'cina [fu'tʃina] *sf* forge

'fuga *sf* escape, flight; (*di gas, liquidi*) leak; (*MUS*) fugue; **~ di cervelli** brain drain

fu'gace [fu'gatʃe] *ag* fleeting, transient

fug'gevole [fud'dʒevole] *ag* fleeting

fuggi'asco, a, schi, sche [fud'dʒasko] *ag, sm/f* fugitive

fuggi'fuggi [fuddʒi'fuddʒi] *sm* scramble, stampede

fug'gire [fud'dʒire] *vi* to flee, run away; (*fig: passar veloce*) to fly ♦ *vt* to avoid; **fuggi'tivo, a** *sm/f* fugitive, runaway

ful'gore *sm* brilliance, splendour

fu'liggine [fu'liddʒine] *sf* soot

fulmi'nare *vt* (*sog: fulmine*) to strike; (: *elettricità*) to electrocute; (*con arma da fuoco*) to shoot dead; (*fig: con lo sguardo*) to look daggers at

'fulmine *sm* thunderbolt; lightning *no pl*

fumai'olo *sm* (*di nave*) funnel; (*di fabbrica*) chimney

fu'mare *vi* to smoke; (*emettere vapore*) to steam ♦ *vt* to smoke; **fu'mata** *sf* (*segnale*) smoke signal; **farsi una fumata** to have a smoke; **fuma'tore, 'trice** *sm/f* smoker

fu'metto *sm* comic strip; **giornale** *sm* a **~i** comic

'fumo *sm* smoke; (*vapore*) steam; (*il fumare tabacco*) smoking; **~i** *smpl* (*industriali etc*) fumes; **i ~i dell'alcool** the after-effects of drink; **vendere ~** to deceive, cheat; **~ passivo** passive smoking; **fu'moso, a** *ag* smoky; (*fig*) muddled

fu'nambolo, a *sm/f* tightrope walker

'fune *sf* rope, cord; (*più grossa*) cable

'funebre *ag* (*rito*) funeral; (*aspetto*) gloomy, funereal

fune'rale *sm* funeral

'fungere ['fundʒere] *vi*: **~ da** to act as

'fungo, ghi *sm* fungus; (*commestibile*) mushroom; **~ velenoso** toadstool

funico'lare *sf* funicular railway

funi'via *sf* cable railway

funzio'nare [funtsjo'nare] *vi* to work, function; (*fungere*): **~ da** to act as

funzio'nario [funtsjo'narjo] *sm* official

funzi'one [fun'tsjone] *sf* function; (*carica*) post, position; (*REL*) service; **in ~** (*meccanismo*) in operation; **in ~ di** (*come*) as; **fare la ~ di qn** (*farne le veci*) to take sb's place

fu'oco, chi *sm* fire; (*fornello*) ring; (*FOT, FISICA*) focus; **dare ~ a qc** to set fire to sth; **far ~** (*sparare*) to fire; **~ d'artificio** firework

fuorché [fwor'ke] *cong, prep* except

fu'ori *av* outside; (*all'aperto*) outdoors, outside; (*fuori di casa, SPORT*) out; (*esclamativo*) get out! ♦ *prep*: **~ (di)** out of, outside ♦ *sm* outside; **lasciar ~ qc/qn** to leave sth/sb out; **far ~ qn** (*fam*) to kill sb, do sb in; **essere ~ di sé** to be beside o.s.; **~ luogo** (*inopportuno*) out of place, uncalled for; **~ mano** out of the way, remote; **~ pericolo** out of danger; **~ uso** old-fashioned; obsolete

fu'ori... ** *prefisso*: **fuori'bordo *sm inv* speedboat (with outboard motor);

outboard motor; **fuori'classe** *sm/f inv* (undisputed) champion; **fuorigi'oco** *sm* offside; **fuori'legge** *sm/f inv* outlaw; **fuori'serie** *ag inv (auto etc)* custom-built ♦ *sf* custom-built car; **fuori'strada** *sm (AUT)* cross-country vehicle; **fuor(i)u-'scito, a** *sm/f* exile; **fuorvi'are** *vt* to mislead; *(fig)* to lead astray ♦ *vi* to go astray

'**furbo, a** *ag* clever, smart; *(peg)* cunning

fu'rente *ag*: ~ (contro) furious (with)

fur'fante *sm* rascal, scoundrel

fur'gone *sm* van

'**furia** *sf (ira)* fury, rage; *(fig: impeto)* fury, violence; *(fretta)* rush; **a ~ di** by dint of; **andare su tutte le ~e** to get into a towering rage; **furi'bondo, a** *ag* furious

furi'oso, a *ag* furious; *(mare, vento)* raging

fu'rore *sm* fury; *(esaltazione)* frenzy; **far ~** to be all the rage

fur'tivo, a *ag* furtive

'**furto** *sm* theft; ~ con scasso burglary

'**fusa** *sfpl*: **fare le ~** to purr

fu'sibile *sm (ELETTR)* fuse

fusi'one *sf (di metalli)* fusion, melting; *(colata)* casting; *(COMM)* merger; *(fig)* merging

'**fuso, a** *pp di* fondere ♦ *sm (FILATURA)* spindle; ~ orario time zone

fus'tagno [fus'taɲɲo] *sm* corduroy

fus'tino *sm (di detersivo)* tub

'**fusto** *sm (ANAT, di albero)* trunk; *(recipiente)* drum, can

fu'turo, a *ag, sm* future

G

gab'bare *vt* to take in, dupe; ~rsi *vr*: ~rsi di qn to make fun of sb

'**gabbia** *sf* cage; *(DIR)* dock; *(da imballaggio)* crate; ~ dell'ascensore lift *(BRIT)* o elevator *(US)* shaft; ~ toracica *(ANAT)* rib cage

gabbi'ano *sm* (sea)gull

gabi'netto *sm (MED etc)* consulting room; *(POL)* ministry; *(di decenza)* toilet, lavatory; *(INS: di fisica etc)* laboratory

'**gaffe** [gaf] *sf inv* blunder

gagli'ardo, a [gaʎ'ʎardo] *ag* strong, vigorous

'**gaio, a** *ag* cheerful, gay

'**gala** *sf (sfarzo)* pomp; *(festa)* gala

ga'lante *ag* gallant, courteous; *(avventura)* amorous; **galante'ria** *sf* gallantry

galantu'omo *(pl* galantu'omini) *sm* gentleman

ga'lassia *sf* galaxy

gala'teo *sm (good)* manners *pl*

gale'otto *sm (rematore)* galley slave; *(carcerato)* convict

ga'lera *sf (NAUT)* galley; *(prigione)* prison

'**galla** *sf*: **a ~** afloat; **venire a ~** to surface, come to the surface; *(fig: verità)* to come out

galleggi'ante [galled'dʒante] *ag* floating ♦ *sm (natante)* barge; *(di pescatore, lenza, TECN)* float

galleggi'are [galled'dʒare] *vi* to float

galle'ria *sf (traforo)* tunnel; *(ARCHIT, d'arte)* gallery; *(TEATRO)* circle; *(strada coperta con negozi)* arcade

'**Galles** *sm*: **il ~** Wales; **gal'lese** *ag, sm (LING)* Welsh ♦ *sm/f* Welshman/woman

gal'letta *sf* cracker

gal'lina *sf* hen

'**gallo** *sm* cock

gal'lone *sm* piece of braid; *(MIL)* stripe; *(unità di misura)* gallon

galop'pare *vi* to gallop

ga'loppo *sm* gallop; **al o di ~** at a gallop

'**gamba** *sf* leg; *(asta: di lettera)* stem; **in ~** *(in buona salute)* well; *(bravo, sveglio)* bright, smart; **prendere qc sotto ~** *(fig)* to treat sth too lightly

gambe'retto *sm* shrimp

'**gambero** *sm (di acqua dolce)* crayfish; *(di mare)* prawn

'**gambo** *sm* stem; *(di frutta)* stalk

'**gamma** *sf (MUS)* scale; *(di colori, fig)* range

ga'nascia, sce [ga'naʃʃa] *sf* jaw; ~sce del freno *(AUT)* brake shoes

'**gancio** ['gantʃo] *sm* hook

'**gangheri** ['gangeri] *smpl*: **uscire dai ~** *(fig)* to fly into a temper '**gara** *sf* competition; (*SPORT*) competition; contest; match; (: *corsa*) race; **fare a ~ to compete**, vie

ga'**rage** [ga'raʒ] *sm inv* garage

garan'**tire** *vt* to guarantee; (*debito*) to stand surety for; (*dare per certo*) to assure

garan'**zia** [garan'tsia] *sf* guarantee; (*pegno*) security

gar'**bato, a** *ag* courteous, polite

'**garbo** *sm* (*buone maniere*) politeness, courtesy; (*di vestito etc*) grace, style

gareggi'**are** [gared'dʒare] *vi* to compete

garga'**rismo** *sm* gargle; **fare i ~i to gargle**

ga'**rofano** *sm* carnation; **chiodo di ~ clove**

'**garza** ['gardza] *sf* (*per bende*) gauze

gar'**zone** [gar'dzone] *sm* (*di negozio*) boy

gas *sm inv* gas; **a tutto ~ at full speed; dare ~** (*AUT*) to accelerate

ga'**solio** *sm* diesel (oil)

ga's(s)**ato, a** *ag* (*bibita*) aerated, fizzy

gas'**sosa** *sf* fizzy drink

gas'**soso, a** *ag* gaseous; gassy

gastrono'**mia** *sf* gastronomy

gat'**tino** *sm* kitten

'**gatto, a** *sm/f* cat, tomcat/she-cat; **~ selvatico** wildcat; **~ delle nevi** (*AUT, SCI*) snowcat

gatto'**pardo** *sm*: **~ africano** serval; **~ americano** ocelot

'**gaudio** *sm* joy, happiness

ga'**vetta** *sf* (*MIL*) mess tin; **venire dalla ~** (*MIL, fig*) to rise from the ranks

'**gazza** ['gaddza] *sf* magpie

gaz'**zella** [gad'dzella] *sf* gazelle; (*dei carabinieri*) (high-speed) police car

gaz'**zetta** [gad'dzetta] *sf* news sheet; **G~ Ufficiale** *official publication containing details of new laws*

gel [dʒɛl] *sm inv* gel

ge'**lare** [dʒe'lare] *vt, vi, vb impers* to freeze; **ge'lata** *sf* frost

gelate'**ria** [dʒelate'ria] *sf* ice-cream shop

gela'**tina** [dʒela'tina] *sf* gelatine; **~ esplosiva** dynamite; **~ di frutta** fruit jelly

ge'**lato, a** [dʒe'lato] *ag* frozen ♦ *sm* ice cream

'**gelido, a** ['dʒɛlido] *ag* icy, ice-cold

'**gelo** ['dʒɛlo] *sm* (*temperatura*) intense cold; (*brina*) frost; (*fig*) chill; **ge'lone** *sm* chilblain

gelo'**sia** [dʒelo'sia] *sf* jealousy

ge'**loso, a** [dʒe'loso] *ag* jealous

'**gelso** ['dʒɛlso] *sm* mulberry (tree)

gelso'**mino** [dʒelso'mino] *sm* jasmine

ge'**mello, a** [dʒe'mɛllo] *ag, sm/f* twin; **~i** *smpl* (*di camicia*) cufflinks; (*dello zodiaco*): **G~i** Gemini *sg*

'**gemere** ['dʒɛmere] *vi* to moan, groan; (*cigolare*) to creak; (*gocciolare*) to drip, ooze; '**gemito** *sm* moan, groan

'**gemma** ['dʒɛmma] *sf* (*BOT*) bud; (*pietra preziosa*) gem

gene'**rale** [dʒene'rale] *ag, sm* general; **in ~** (*per sommi capi*) in general terms; (*di solito*) usually, in general; **a ~ richiesta** by popular request; **generalità** *sfpl* (*dati d'identità*) particulars; **generaliz'zare** *vt, vi* to generalize; **general'mente** *av* generally

gene'**rare** [dʒene'rare] *vt* (*dar vita*) to give birth to; (*produrre*) to produce; (*causare*) to arouse; (*TECN*) to produce, generate; **genera'tore** *sm* (*TECN*) generator; **generazi'one** *sf* generation

'**genere** ['dʒɛnere] *sm* kind, type, sort; (*BIOL*) genus; (*merce*) article, product; (*LING*) gender; (*ARTE, LETTERATURA*) genre; **in ~** generally, as a rule; **il ~ umano** mankind; **~i alimentari** foodstuffs

ge'**nerico, a, ci, che** [dʒe'nɛriko] *ag* generic; (*vago*) vague, imprecise

'**genero** ['dʒɛnero] *sm* son-in-law

generosità [dʒenerosi'ta] *sf* generosity

gene'**roso, a** [dʒene'roso] *ag* generous

ge'**netica** [dʒe'nɛtika] *sf* genetics *sg*

ge'**netico, a, ci, che** [dʒe'nɛtiko] *ag* genetic

gen'**giva** [dʒen'dʒiva] *sf* (*ANAT*) gum

geni'**ale** [dʒen'jale] *ag* (*persona*) of genius; (*idea*) ingenious, brilliant

'**genio** ['dʒɛnjo] *sm* genius; **andare a ~ a qn** to be to sb's liking, appeal to sb

geni'**tale** [dʒeni'tale] *ag* genital; **~i** *smpl* genitals

geni'**tore** [dʒeni'tore] *sm* parent, father *o*

mother; **i miei ~i** my parents, my father and mother

gen'naio [dʒen'najo] *sm* January

'Genova ['dʒenova] *sf* Genoa

gen'taglia [dʒen'taʎʎa] *(peg) sf* rabble

'gente ['dʒente] *sf* people *pl*

gen'tile [dʒen'tile] *ag (persona, atto)* kind; (: *garbato)* courteous, polite; *(nelle lettere)*: **G~ Signore** Dear Sir; (: *sulla busta)*: **G~ Signor Fernando Villa** Mr Fernando Villa; **genti'lezza** *sf* kindness; courtesy, politeness; **per gentilezza** *(per favore)* please

gentilu'omo [dʒenti'lwɔmo] *(pl* **gentilu'omini)** *sm* gentleman

genu'ino, a [dʒenu'ino] *ag (prodotto)* natural; *(persona, sentimento)* genuine, sincere

geogra'fia [dʒeogra'fia] *sf* geography

geolo'gia [dʒeolo'dʒia] *sf* geology

ge'ometra, i, e [dʒe'ɔmetra] *sm/f (professionista)* surveyor

geome'tria [dʒeome'tria] *sf* geometry; **geo'metrico, a, ci, che** *ag* geometric(al)

gerar'chia [dʒerar'kia] *sf* hierarchy

ge'rente [dʒe'rɛnte] *sm/f* manager/manageress

'gergo, ghi ['dʒergo] *sm* jargon; slang

geria'tria [dʒerja'tria] *sf* geriatrics *sg*

Ger'mania [dʒer'manja] *sf*: **la ~** Germany; **la ~ occidentale/orientale** West/East Germany

'germe ['dʒerme] *sm* germ; *(fig)* seed

germogli'are [dʒermoʎ'ʎare] *vi* to sprout; to germinate; **ger'moglio** *sm* shoot; bud

gero'glifico, ci [dʒero'glifiko] *sm* hieroglyphic

'gesso ['dʒesso] *sm* chalk; *(SCULTURA, MED, EDIL)* plaster; *(statua)* plaster figure; *(minerale)* gypsum

gesti'one [dʒes'tjone] *sf* management

ges'tire [dʒes'tire] *vt* to run, manage

'gesto ['dʒesto] *sm* gesture

ges'tore [dʒes'tore] *sm* manager

Gesù [dʒe'zu] *sm* Jesus

gesu'ita, i [dʒezu'ita] *sm* Jesuit

get'tare [dʒet'tare] *vt* to throw; *(anche:* **~ via)** to throw away *o* out; *(SCULTURA)* to cast; *(EDIL)* to lay; *(acqua)* to spout; *(grido)* to utter; **~rsi** *vr*: **~rsi in** *(sog: fiume)* to flow into; **~ uno sguardo su** to take a quick look at; **get'tata** *sf (di cemento, gesso, metalli)* cast; *(diga)* jetty

'getto ['dʒetto] *sm (di gas, liquido, AER)* jet; **a ~ continuo** uninterruptedly; **di ~** *(fig)* straight off, in one go

get'tone [dʒet'tone] *sm* token; *(per giochi)* counter; (: *roulette etc)* chip; **~ telefonico** telephone token

ghiacci'aio [gjat'tʃajo] *sm* glacier

ghiacci'are [gjat'tʃare] *vt* to freeze; *(fig)*: **~ qn** to make sb's blood run cold ♦ *vi* to freeze, ice over; **ghiacci'ato, a** *ag* frozen; *(bevanda)* ice-cold

ghi'accio ['gjattʃo] *sm* ice

ghiacci'olo [gjat'tʃɔlo] *sm* icicle; *(tipo di gelato)* ice lolly *(BRIT)*, popsicle *(US)*

ghi'aia ['gjaja] *sf* gravel

ghi'anda ['gjanda] *sf (BOT)* acorn

ghi'andola ['gjandola] *sf* gland

ghigliot'tina [giʎʎot'tina] *sf* guillotine

ghi'gnare [giɲ'ɲare] *vi* to sneer

ghi'otto, a ['gjotto] *ag* greedy; *(cibo)* delicious, appetizing; **ghiot'tone, a** *sm/f* glutton

ghiri'bizzo [giri'biddzo] *sm* whim

ghiri'goro [giri'gɔro] *sm* scribble, squiggle

ghir'landa [gir'landa] *sf* garland, wreath

'ghiro ['giro] *sm* dormouse

'ghisa ['giza] *sf* cast iron

già [dʒa] *av* already; *(ex, in precedenza)* formerly ♦ *escl* of course!, yes indeed!

gi'acca, che ['dʒakka] *sf* jacket; **~ a vento** windcheater *(BRIT)*, windbreaker *(US)*

giacché [dʒak'ke] *cong* since, as

giac'chetta [dʒak'ketta] *sf* (light) jacket

gia'cenza [dʒa'tʃentsa] *sf*: **merce in ~** goods in stock; **~e di magazzino** unsold stock

gia'cere [dʒa'tʃere] *vi* to lie; **giaci'mento** *sm* deposit

gia'cinto [dʒa'tʃinto] *sm* hyacinth

gi'ada ['dʒada] *sf* jade

giaggi'olo [dʒad'dʒɔlo] *sm* iris

giagu'aro [dʒa'gwaro] *sm* jaguar

gi'allo ['dʒallo] *ag* yellow; (*carnagione*) sallow ♦ *sm* yellow; (*anche: romanzo* ~) detective novel; (*anche: film* ~) detective film; ~ **dell'uovo** yolk

giam'mai [dʒam'mai] *av* never

Giap'pone [dʒap'pone] *sm* Japan; **giappo'nese** *ag, sm/f, sm* Japanese *inv*

gi'ara ['dʒara] *sf* jar

giardi'naggio [dʒardi'naddʒo] *sm* gardening

giardi'netta [dʒardi'netta] *sf* estate car (*BRIT*), station wagon (*US*)

giardini'era [dʒardi'njɛra] *sf* (*misto di sottaceti*) mixed pickles *pl*; (*automobile*) = **giardinetta**

giardini'ere, a [dʒardi'njɛre] *sm/f* gardener

giar'dino [dʒar'dino] *sm* garden; ~ **d'infanzia** nursery school; ~ **pubblico** public gardens *pl*, (public) park; ~ **zoologico** zoo

giarretti'era [dʒarret'tjɛra] *sf* garter

giavel'lotto [dʒavel'lɔtto] *sm* javelin

gi'gante, 'essa [dʒi'gante] *sm/f* giant ♦ *ag* giant, gigantic; (*COMM*) giant-size; **gigan'tesco, a, schi, sche** *ag* gigantic

'giglio ['dʒiʎʎo] *sm* lily

gilè [dʒi'lɛ] *sm inv* waistcoat

gin [dʒin] *sm inv* gin

gine'cologo, a, gi, ghe [dʒine'kɔlogo] *sm/f* gynaecologist

gi'nepro [dʒi'nepro] *sm* juniper

gi'nestra [dʒi'nestra] *sf* (*BOT*) broom

Gi'nevra [dʒi'nevra] *sf* Geneva

gingil'larsi [dʒindʒil'larsi] *vr* to fritter away one's time; (*giocare*): ~ **con** to fiddle with

gin'gillo [dʒin'dʒillo] *sm* plaything

gin'nasio [dʒin'nazjo] *sm* the 4th and 5th year of secondary school in Italy

gin'nasta, i, e [dʒin'nasta] *sm/f* gymnast; **gin'nastica** *sf* gymnastics *sg*; (*esercizio fisico*) keep-fit exercises; (*INS*) physical education

gi'nocchio [dʒi'nɔkkjo] (*pl(m)* **gi'nocchi** *o pl(f)* **gi'nocchia**) *sm* knee; **stare in** ~ to kneel, be on one's knees; **mettersi in** ~ to kneel (down); **ginocchi'oni** *av* on one's knees

gio'care [dʒo'kare] *vt* to play; (*scommettere*) to stake, wager, bet; (*ingannare*) to take in ♦ *vi* to play; (*a roulette etc*) to gamble; (*fig*) to play a part, be important; (*TECN: meccanismo*) to be loose; ~ **a** (*gioco, sport*) to play; (*cavalli*) to bet on; **~rsi la carriera** to put one's career at risk; **gioca'tore, 'trice** *sm/f* player; gambler

gio'cattolo [dʒo'kattolo] *sm* toy

gio'chetto [dʒo'ketto] *sm* (*tranello*) trick; (*fig*): **è un** ~ it's child's play

gi'oco, chi ['dʒɔko] *sm* game; (*divertimento, TECN*) play; (*al casinò*) gambling; (*CARTE*) hand; (*insieme di pezzi etc necessari per un gioco*) set; **per** ~ for fun; **fare il doppio** ~ **con qn** to double-cross sb; ~ **d'azzardo** game of chance; ~ **della palla** football; ~ **degli scacchi** chess set; **i Giochi Olimpici** the Olympic Games

giocoli'ere [dʒoko'ljɛre] *sm* juggler

gio'coso, a [dʒo'koso] *ag* playful, jesting

gi'ogo, ghi ['dʒɔgo] *sm* yoke

gi'oia ['dʒɔja] *sf* joy, delight; (*pietra preziosa*) jewel, precious stone

gioielle'ria [dʒojelle'ria] *sf* jeweller's craft; jeweller's (shop)

gioielli'ere, a [dʒojel'ljɛre] *sm/f* jeweller

gioi'ello [dʒo'jɛllo] *sm* jewel, piece of jewellery; **i ~i di una donna** a woman's jewels *o* jewellery

gioi'oso, a [dʒo'joso] *ag* joyful

Gior'dania [dʒor'danja] *sf*: **la** ~ Jordan

giorna'laio, a [dʒorna'lajo] *sm/f* newsagent (*BRIT*), newsdealer (*US*)

gior'nale [dʒor'nale] *sm* (news) paper; (*diario*) journal, diary; (*COMM*) journal; ~ **di bordo** log; ~ **radio** radio news *sg*

giornali'ero, a [dʒorna'ljero] *ag* daily; (*che varia: umore*) changeable ♦ *sm* day labourer

giorna'lismo [dʒorna'lizmo] *sm* journalism

giorna'lista, i, e [dʒorna'lista] *sm/f* journalist

gior'nata [dʒor'nata] *sf* day; ~ **lavorativa** working day

gi'orno ['dʒorno] *sm* day; (*opposto alla*

notte) day, daytime; (*luce del ~*) daylight; **al ~** per day; **di ~** by day; **al ~ d'oggi** nowadays

gi'ostra ['dʒɔstra] *sf* (*per bimbi*) merry-go-round; (*torneo storico*) joust

gi'ovane ['dʒɔvane] *ag* young; (*aspetto*) youthful ♦ *sm/f* youth/girl, young man/woman; **i ~i** young people; **giova'nile** *ag* youthful; (*scritti*) early; (*errore*) of youth; **giova'notto** *sm* young man

gio'vare [dʒo'vare] *vi*: **~ a** (*essere utile*) to be useful to; (*far bene*) to be good for ♦ *vb impers* (*essere bene, utile*) to be useful; **~rsi di qc** to make use of sth

giovedì [dʒove'di] *sm inv* Thursday; **di** *o* **il ~** on Thursdays

gioventù [dʒoven'tu] *sf* (*periodo*) youth; (*i giovani*) young people *pl*, youth

giovi'ale [dʒo'vjale] *ag* jovial, jolly

giovi'nezza [dʒovi'nettsa] *sf* youth

gira'dischi [dʒira'diski] *sm inv* record player

gi'raffa [dʒi'raffa] *sf* giraffe

gi'randola [dʒi'randola] *sf* (*fuoco d'artificio*) Catherine wheel; (*giocattolo*) toy windmill; (*banderuola*) weather vane, weathercock

gi'rare [dʒi'rare] *vt* (*far ruotare*) to turn; (*percorrere, visitare*) to go round; (*CINEMA*) to shoot; to make; (*COMM*) to endorse ♦ *vi* to turn; (*più veloce*) to spin; (*andare in giro*) to wander, go around; **~rsi** *vr* to turn; **~ attorno a** to go round; to revolve round; **far ~ la testa a qn** to make sb dizzy; (*fig*) to turn sb's head

girar'rosto [dʒirar'rɔsto] *sm* (*CUC*) spit

gira'sole [dʒira'sole] *sm* sunflower

gi'rata [dʒi'rata] *sf* (*passeggiata*) stroll; (*con veicolo*) drive; (*COMM*) endorsement

gira'volta [dʒira'vɔlta] *sf* twirl, turn; (*curva*) sharp bend; (*fig*) about-turn

gi'revole [dʒi'revole] *ag* revolving, turning

gi'rino [dʒi'rino] *sm* tadpole

'giro ['dʒiro] *sm* (*circuito, cerchio*) circle; (*di chiave, manovella*) turn; (*viaggio*) tour, excursion; (*passeggiata*) stroll, walk; (*in macchina*) drive; (*in bicicletta*) ride; (*SPORT: della pista*) lap; (*di denaro*)

circulation; (*CARTE*) hand; (*TECN*) revolution; **prendere in ~ qn** (*fig*) to pull sb's leg; **fare un ~** to go for a walk (*o a drive o a ride*); **andare in ~** to go about, walk around; **a stretto ~ di posta** by return of post; **nel ~ di un mese** in a month's time; **essere nel ~** (*fig*) to belong to a circle (of friends); **~ d'affari** (*COMM*) turnover; **~ di parole** circumlocution; **~ di prova** (*AUT*) test drive; **~ turistico** sightseeing tour; **giro'collo** *sm*: **a girocollo** crew-neck *cpd*

gironzo'lare [dʒirondzo'lare] *vi* to stroll about

'gita ['dʒita] *sf* excursion, trip; **fare una ~** to go for a trip, go on an outing

gi'tano, a [dʒi'tano] *sm/f* gipsy

giù [dʒu] *av* down; (*dabbasso*) downstairs; **in ~** downwards, down; **~ di lì** (*pressappoco*) thereabouts; **bambini dai 6 anni in ~** children aged 6 and under; **~ per**: **cadere ~ per le scale** to fall down the stairs; **essere ~** (*fig: di salute*) to be run down; (*: di spirito*) to be depressed

giub'botto [dʒub'bɔtto] *sm* jerkin; **~ antiproiettile** bulletproof vest

gi'ubilo ['dʒubilo] *sm* rejoicing

giudi'care [dʒudi'kare] *vt* to judge; (*accusato*) to try; (*lite*) to arbitrate in; **~ qn/qc bello** to consider sb/sth (to be) beautiful

gi'udice ['dʒuditʃe] *sm* judge; **~ conciliatore** justice of the peace; **~ istruttore** examining magistrate; **~ popolare** member of a jury

giu'dizio [dʒu'dittsjo] *sm* judgment; (*opinione*) opinion; (*DIR*) judgment, sentence; (*: processo*) trial; (*: verdetto*) verdict; **aver ~** to be wise *o* prudent; **citare in ~** to summons; **giudizi'oso, a** *ag* prudent, judicious

gi'ugno ['dʒuɲɲo] *sm* June

giul'lare [dʒul'lare] *sm* jester

giu'menta [dʒu'menta] *sf* mare

gi'unco, chi ['dʒunko] *sm* rush

gi'ungere ['dʒundʒere] *vi* to arrive ♦ *vt* (*mani etc*) to join; **~ a** to arrive at, reach

gi'ungla ['dʒungla] *sf* jungle

gi'unta ['dʒunta] *sf* addition; (*organo*

esecutivo, amministrativo) council, board; **per ~a** into the bargain, in addition; **~a militare** military junta

gi'unto, a ['dʒunto] *pp di* **giungere** ♦ *sm* (*TECN*) coupling, joint; **giun'tura** *sf* joint

giuo'care [dʒwo'kare] *vt, vi* = **giocare**; **giu'oco** *sm* = **gioco**

giura'mento [dʒura'mento] *sm* oath; **~ falso** perjury

giu'rare [dʒu'rare] *vt* to swear ♦ *vi* to swear, take an oath; **giu'rato, a** *ag*: **nemico giurato** sworn enemy ♦ *sm/f* juror, juryman/woman

giu'ria [dʒu'ria] *sf* jury

giu'ridico, a, ci, che [dʒu'ridiko] *ag* legal

giustifi'care [dʒustifi'kare] *vt* to justify; **giustificazi'one** *sf* justification; (*INS*) (note of) excuse

gius'tizia [dʒus'tittsja] *sf* justice; **giustizi'are** *vt* to execute, put to death; **giustizi'ere** *sm* executioner

gi'usto, a ['dʒusto] *ag* (*equo*) fair, just; (*vero*) true, correct; (*adatto*) right, suitable; (*preciso*) exact, correct ♦ *av* (*esattamente*) exactly, precisely; (*per l'appunto, appena*) just; **arrivare ~** to arrive just in time; **ho ~ bisogno di te** you're just the person I need

glaci'ale [gla'tʃale] *ag* glacial

'glandola *sf* = **ghiandola**

gli [ʎi] (*dav V, s impura, gn, pn, ps, x, z*) *det mpl* the ♦ *pron* (*a lui*) to him; (*a esso*) to it; (*in coppia con lo, la, li, le, ne: a lui, a lei, a loro etc*): **gliele do** I'm giving them to him (*o* her *o* them); *vedi anche* **il**

gli'ela ['ʎela] *etc vedi* **gli**

glo'bale *ag* overall

'globo *sm* globe

'globulo *sm* (*ANAT*): **~ rosso/bianco** red/white corpuscle

'gloria *sf* glory; **glori'oso, a** *ag* glorious

glos'sario *sm* glossary

'gnocchi ['ɲɔkki] *smpl* (*CUC*) small dumplings made of semolina pasta or potato

'gobba *sf* (*ANAT*) hump; (*protuberanza*) bump

'gobbo, a *ag* hunchbacked; (*ricurvo*)

round-shouldered ♦ *sm/f* hunchback

'goccia, ce ['gottʃa] *sf* drop; **goccio'lare** *vi, vt* to drip

go'dere *vi* (*compiacersi*): **~ (di)** to be delighted (at), rejoice (at); (*trarre vantaggio*): **~ di** to enjoy, benefit from ♦ *vt* to enjoy; **~rsi la vita** to enjoy life; **~sela** to have a good time, enjoy o.s.; **godi'mento** *sm* enjoyment

'goffo, a *ag* clumsy, awkward

'gola *sf* (*ANAT*) throat; (*golosità*) gluttony, greed; (*di camino*) flue; (*di monte*) gorge; **fare ~** (*anche fig*) to tempt

golf *sm inv* (*SPORT*) golf; (*maglia*) cardigan

'golfo *sm* gulf

go'loso, a *ag* greedy

'gomito *sm* elbow; (*di strada etc*) sharp bend

go'mitolo *sm* ball

'gomma *sf* rubber; (*colla*) gum; (*per cancellare*) rubber, eraser; (*di veicolo*) tyre (*BRIT*), tire (*US*); **~ americana** *o* **da masticare** chewing gum; **~ a terra** flat tyre (*BRIT*) *o* tire (*US*); **gommapi'uma** ® *sf* foam rubber

'gondola *sf* gondola; **gondoli'ere** *sm* gondolier

gonfa'lone *sm* banner

gonfi'are *vt* (*pallone*) to blow up, inflate; (*dilatare, ingrossare*) to swell; (*fig: notizia*) to exaggerate; **~rsi** *vr* to swell; (*fiume*) to rise; **'gonfio, a** *ag* swollen; (*stomaco*) bloated; (*vela*) full; **gonfi'ore** *sm* swelling

gongo'lare *vi* to look pleased with o.s.; **~ di gioia** to be overjoyed

'gonna *sf* skirt; **~ pantalone** culottes *pl*

'gonzo ['gondzo] *sm* simpleton, fool

gorgheggi'are [gorged'dʒare] *vi* to warble; to trill

'gorgo, ghi *sm* whirlpool

gorgogli'are [gorgoʎ'ʎare] *vi* to gurgle

go'rilla *sm inv* gorilla; (*guardia del corpo*) bodyguard

'gotta *sf* gout

gover'nante *sm/f* ruler ♦ *sf* (*di bambini*) governess; (*donna di servizio*) housekeeper

gover'nare *vt* (*stato*) to govern, rule; (*pilotare, guidare*) to steer; (*bestiame*) to tend, look after; **governa'tivo, a** *ag* government *cpd*; **governa'tore** *sm* governor

go'verno *sm* government

gozzovigli'are [gottsoviʎ'ʎare] *vi* to make merry, carouse

gracchi'are [grak'kjare] *vi* to caw

graci'dare [gratʃi'dare] *vi* to croak

'gracile ['gratʃile] *ag* frail, delicate

gra'dasso *sm* boaster

gradazi'one [gradat'tsjone] *sf* (*sfumatura*) gradation; ~ **alcolica** alcoholic content, strength

gra'devole *ag* pleasant, agreeable

gradi'mento *sm* pleasure, satisfaction; **è di suo ~?** is it to your liking?

gradi'nata *sf* flight of steps; (*in teatro, stadio*) tiers *pl*

gra'dino *sm* step; (*ALPINISMO*) foothold

gra'dire *vt* (*accettare con piacere*) to accept; (*desiderare*) to wish, like; **gradisce una tazza di tè?** would you like a cup of tea?; **gra'dito, a** *ag* pleasing; welcome

'grado *sm* (*MAT, FISICA etc*) degree; (*stadio*) degree, level; (*MIL, sociale*) rank; **essere in ~ di fare** to be in a position to do

gradu'ale *ag* gradual

gradu'are *vt* to grade; **gradu'ato, a** *ag* (*esercizi*) graded; (*scala, termometro*) graduated ♦ *sm* (*MIL*) non-commissioned officer

'graffa *sf* (*gancio*) clip; (*segno grafico*) brace

graffi'are *vt* to scratch

'graffio *sm* scratch

gra'fia *sf* spelling; (*scrittura*) handwriting

'grafica *sf* graphic arts *pl*

'grafico, a, ci, che *ag* graphic ♦ *sm* graph; (*persona*) graphic designer

gra'migna [gra'miɲɲa] *sf* weed; couch grass

gram'matica, che *sf* grammar; **grammati'cale** *ag* grammatical

'grammo *sm* gram(me)

gran *ag vedi* **grande**

'grana *sf* (*granello, di minerali, corpi spezzati*) grain; (*fam: seccatura*) trouble; (: *soldi*) cash ♦ *sm inv* Parmesan (cheese)

gra'naio *sm* granary, barn

gra'nata *sf* (*frutto*) pomegranate; (*pietra preziosa*) garnet; (*proiettile*) grenade

Gran Bre'tagna [-bre'taɲɲa] *sf*: **la ~** Great Britain

'granchio ['grankjo] *sm* crab; (*fig*) blunder; **prendere un ~** (*fig*) to blunder

grandango'lare *sm* wide-angle lens *sg*

'grande (*qualche volta* **gran** +*C*, **grand'** +*V*) *ag* (*grosso, largo, vasto*) big, large; (*alto*) tall; (*lungo*) long; (*in sensi astratti*) great ♦ *sm/f* (*persona adulta*) adult, grown-up; (*chi ha ingegno e potenza*) great man/woman; **fare le cose in ~** to do things in style; **una gran bella donna** a very beautiful woman; **non è una gran cosa** *o* **un gran che** it's nothing special; **non ne so gran che** I don't know very much about it

grandeggi'are [granded'dʒare] *vi* (*emergere per grandezza*): ~ **su** to tower over; (*darsi arie*) to put on airs

gran'dezza [gran'dettsa] *sf* (*dimensione*) size; magnitude; (*fig*) greatness; **in ~ naturale** lifesize

grandi'nare *vb impers* to hail

'grandine *sf* hail

gran'duca, chi *sm* grand duke

gra'nello *sm* (*di cereali, uva*) seed; (*di frutta*) pip; (*di sabbia, sale etc*) grain

gra'nita *sf* kind of water ice

gra'nito *sm* granite

'grano *sm* (*in quasi tutti i sensi*) grain; (*frumento*) wheat; (*di rosario, collana*) bead; ~ **di pepe** peppercorn

gran'turco *sm* maize

'granulo *sm* granule; (*MED*) pellet

'grappa *sf* rough, strong brandy

'grappolo *sm* bunch, cluster

gras'setto *sm* (*TIP*) bold (type)

'grasso, a *ag* fat; (*cibo*) fatty; (*pelle*) greasy; (*terreno*) rich; (*fig: guadagno, annata*) plentiful; (: *volgare*) coarse, lewd ♦ *sm* (*di persona, animale*) fat; (*sostanza che unge*) grease; **gras'soccio, a, ci, ce** *ag* plump

'grata *sf* grating

gra'ticola *sf* grill

gra'tifica, che *sf* bonus

'gratis *av* free, for nothing

grati'tudine *sf* gratitude

'**grato, a** *ag* grateful; (*gradito*) pleasant, agreeable

gratta'capo *sm* worry, headache

grattaci'elo [gratta'tʃɛlo] *sm* skyscraper

grat'tare *vt* (*pelle*) to scratch; (*raschiare*) to scrape; (*pane, formaggio, carote*) to grate; (*fam: rubare*) to pinch ♦ *vi* (*stridere*) to grate; (*AUT*) to grind; **~rsi** *vr* to scratch o.s

grat'tugia, gie [grat'tudʒa] *sf* grater; **grattugi'are** *vt* to grate; **pane grattugiato** breadcrumbs *pl*

gra'tuito, a *ag* free; (*fig*) gratuitous

gra'vare *vt* to burden ♦ *vi*: **~ su** to weigh on

'**grave** *ag* (*danno, pericolo, peccato etc*) grave, serious; (*responsabilità*) heavy, grave; (*contegno*) grave, solemn; (*voce, suono*) deep, low-pitched; (*LING*): **accento ~ grave** accent; **un malato ~** a person who is seriously ill

gravi'danza [gravi'dantsa] *sf* pregnancy

'**gravido, a** *ag* pregnant

gravità *sf* seriousness; (*anche FISICA*) gravity

gra'voso, a *ag* heavy, onerous

'**grazia** ['grattsja] *sf* grace; (*favore*) favour; (*DIR*) pardon; **grazi'are** *vt* (*DIR*) to pardon

'**grazie** ['grattsje] *escl* thank you!; **~ mille!** *o* **tante!** *o* **infinite!** thank you very much!; **~ a** thanks to

grazi'oso, a [grat'tsjoso] *ag* charming, delightful; (*gentile*) gracious

'**Grecia** ['grɛtʃa] *sf*: **la ~** Greece; '**greco, a, ci, che** *ag, sm/f, sm* Greek

'**gregge** ['greddʒe] (*pl(f)* **-i**) *sm* flock

'**greggio, a, gi, ge** ['greddʒo] *ag* raw, unrefined; (*diamante*) rough, uncut; (*tessuto*) unbleached ♦ *sm* (*anche: petrolio* **~**) crude (oil)

grembi'ule *sm* apron; (*sopravveste*) overall

'**grembo** *sm* lap; (*ventre della madre*) womb

gre'mito, a *ag*: **~ (di)** packed *o* crowded (with)

minded

'**greve** *ag* heavy

'**grezzo, a** ['greddzo] *ag* = **greggio**

gri'dare *vi* (*per chiamare*) to shout, cry (out); (*strillare*) to scream, yell ♦ *vt* to shout (out), yell (out); **~ aiuto** to cry *o* shout for help

'**grido** (*pl(m)* **-i** *o pl(f)* **-a**) *sm* shout, cry; scream, yell; (*di animale*) cry; **di ~** famous

'**grigio, a, gi, gie** ['gridʒo] *ag, sm* grey

'**griglia** ['griʎʎa] *sf* (*per arrostire*) grill; (*ELETTR*) grid; (*inferriata*) grating; **alla ~** (*CUC*) grilled; **grigli'ata** *sf* (*CUC*) grill

gril'letto *sm* trigger

'**grillo** *sm* (*ZOOL*) cricket; (*fig*) whim

grimal'dello *sm* picklock

'**grinta** *sf* grim expression; (*SPORT*) fighting spirit

'**grinza** ['grintsa] *sf* crease, wrinkle; (*ruga*) wrinkle; **non fare una ~** (*fig: ragionamento*) to be faultless; **grin'zoso, a** *ag* creased; wrinkled

grip'pare *vi* (*TECN*) to seize

gris'sino *sm* bread-stick

'**gronda** *sf* eaves *pl*

gron'daia *sf* gutter

gron'dare *vi* to pour; (*essere bagnato*): **~ di** to be dripping with ♦ *vt* to drip with

'**groppa** *sf* (*di animale*) back, rump; (*fam: dell'uomo*) back, shoulders *pl*

'**groppo** *sm* tangle; **avere un ~ alla gola** (*fig*) to have a lump in one's throat

gros'sezza [gros'settsa] *sf* size; thickness

gros'sista, i, e *sm/f* (*COMM*) wholesaler

'**grosso, a** *ag* big, large; (*di spessore*) thick; (*grossolano: anche fig*) coarse; (*grave, insopportabile*) serious, great; (*tempo, mare*) rough ♦ *sm*: **il ~ di** the bulk of; **un pezzo ~** (*fig*) a VIP, a bigwig; **farla ~a** to do something very stupid; **dirle ~e** to tell tall stories; **sbagliarsi di ~** to be completely wrong

grosso'lano, a *ag* rough, coarse; (*fig*) coarse, crude; (*: errore*) stupid

grosso'modo *av* roughly

'**grotta** *sf* cave; grotto

grot'tesco, a, schi, sche *ag* grotesque

grovi'era *sm o f* gruyère (cheese)

gro'viglio [groˈviʎʎo] *sm* tangle; *(fig)* muddle

gru *sf inv* crane

'gruccia, ce [ˈgruttʃa] *sf (per camminare)* crutch; *(per abiti)* coat-hanger

gru'gnire [grunˈɲire] *vi* to grunt; **gru'gnito** *sm* grunt

'grugno [ˈgruɲɲo] *sm* snout; *(fam: faccia)* mug

'grullo, a *ag* silly, stupid

'grumo *sm (di sangue)* clot; *(di farina etc)* lump

'gruppo *sm* group; ~ **sanguigno** blood group

gruvi'era *sm o f* = **groviera**

guada'gnare [gwadaɲˈɲare] *vt (ottenere)* to gain; *(soldi, stipendio)* to earn; *(vincere)* to win; *(raggiungere)* to reach

gua'dagno [gwaˈdaɲɲo] *sm* earnings *pl*; *(COMM)* profit; *(vantaggio, utile)* advantage, gain; ~ **lordo/netto** gross/net earnings *pl*

gu'ado *sm* ford; **passare a** ~ to ford

gu'ai *escl:* ~ **a te (o lui etc)!** woe betide you *(o him etc)!*

gua'ina *sf (fodero)* sheath; *(indumento per donna)* girdle

gu'aio *sm* trouble, mishap; *(inconveniente)* trouble, snag

gua'ire *vi* to whine, yelp

gu'ancia, ce [ˈgwantʃa] *sf* cheek

guanci'ale [gwanˈtʃale] *sm* pillow

gu'anto *sm* glove

gu'arda... *prefisso:* ~**'boschi** *sm inv* forester; ~**'caccia** *sm inv* gamekeeper; ~**'coste** *sm inv* coastguard; *(nave)* coastguard patrol vessel; ~**'linee** *sm inv (SPORT)* linesman

guar'dare *vt (con lo sguardo: osservare)* to look at; *(film, televisione)* to watch; *(custodire)* to look after, take care of ♦ *vi* to look; *(badare):* ~ **a** to pay attention to; *(luoghi: esser orientato):* ~ **a** to face; ~**rsi** *vr* to look at o.s.; ~**rsi da** *(astenersi)* to refrain from; *(stare in guardia)* to beware of; ~**rsi dal fare** to take care not to do; **guarda di non sbagliare** try not to make a mistake; ~ **a vista qn** to keep a close watch on sb

guarda'roba *sm inv* wardrobe; *(locale)* cloakroom; **guardarobi'ere, a** *sm/f* cloakroom attendant

gu'ardia *sf (individuo, corpo)* guard; *(sorveglianza)* watch; **fare la** ~ **a qc/qn** to guard sth/sb; **stare in** ~ *(fig)* to be on one's guard; **di** ~ *(medico)* on call; ~ **carceraria** (prison) warder; ~ **del corpo** bodyguard; ~ **di finanza** *(corpo)* customs *pl*; *(persona)* customs officer; ~ **medica** emergency doctor service

guardi'ano, a *sm/f (di carcere)* warder; *(di villa etc)* caretaker; *(di museo)* custodian; *(di zoo)* keeper; ~ **notturno** night watchman

guar'dingo, a, ghi, ghe *ag* wary, cautious

guardi'ola *sf* porter's lodge; *(MIL)* look-out tower

guarigi'one [gwariˈdʒone] *sf* recovery

gua'rire *vt (persona, malattia)* to cure; *(ferita)* to heal ♦ *vi* to recover, be cured; to heal (up)

guarnigi'one [gwarniˈdʒone] *sf* garrison

guar'nire *vt (ornare: abiti)* to trim; *(CUC)* to garnish; **guarnizi'one** *sf* trimming; garnish; *(TECN)* gasket

guasta'feste *sm/f inv* spoilsport

guas'tare *vt* to spoil, ruin; *(meccanismo)* to break; ~**rsi** *vr (cibo)* to go bad; *(meccanismo)* to break down; *(tempo)* to change for the worse; *(amici)* to quarrel, fall out

gu'asto, a *ag (non funzionante)* broken; (: *telefono etc)* out of order; *(andato a male)* bad, rotten; (: *dente)* decayed, bad; *(fig: corrotto)* depraved ♦ *sm* breakdown; *(avaria)* failure; ~ **al motore** engine failure

guazza'buglio [gwattsaˈbuʎʎo] *sm* muddle

gu'ercio, a, ci, ce [ˈgwertʃo] *ag* cross-eyed

gu'erra *sf* war; *(tecnica: atomica, chimica etc)* warfare; **fare la** ~ **(a)** to wage war (against); ~ **mondiale** world war; **guerreggi'are** *vi* to wage war; **guerri'ero, a** *ag* warlike ♦ *sm* warrior; **guer'riglia** *sf* guerrilla warfare; **guerrigli'ero** *sm* guerrilla

'**gufo** *sm* owl

gu'ida *sf* guidebook; (*comando, direzione*) guidance, direction; (*AUT*) driving; (: *sterzo*) steering; (*tappeto, di tenda, cassetto*) runner; ~ **a destra/sinistra** (*AUT*) right-/left-hand drive; ~ **telefonica** telephone directory; ~ **turistica** tourist guide

gui'dare *vt* to guide; (*condurre a capo*) to lead; (*auto*) to drive; (*aereo, nave*) to pilot; **sai ~?** can you drive?; **guida'tore, trice** *sm/f* (*conducente*) driver

guin'zaglio [gwin'tsaʎʎo] *sm* leash, lead

gu'isa *sf*: **a ~ di** like, in the manner of

guiz'zare [gwit'tsare] *vi* to dart; to flicker; to leap; ~ **via** (*fuggire*) to slip away

'**guscio** ['guʃʃo] *sm* shell

gus'tare *vt* (*cibi*) to taste; (: *assaporare con piacere*) to enjoy, savour; (*fig*) to enjoy, appreciate ♦ *vi*: ~ **a** to please; **non mi gusta affatto** I don't like it at all

'**gusto** *sm* taste; (*sapore*) flavour; (*godimento*) enjoyment; **al ~ di fragola** strawberry-flavoured; **mangiare di ~** to eat heartily; **prenderci ~: ci ha preso ~** he's acquired a taste for it, he's got to like it; **gus'toso, a** *ag* tasty; (*fig*) agreeable

H

h *abbr* = **ora**; **altezza**

ha *etc* [a] *vb vedi* **avere**

ha'cker [hæˈkəˈ] *sm inv* hacker

hall [hɔl] *sf inv* hall, foyer

'**handicap** ['handikap] *sm inv* handicap; **handicap'pato, a** *ag* handicapped ♦ *sm/f* handicapped person, disabled person

'**hanno** ['anno] *vb vedi* **avere**

'**hascisc** ['haʃiʃ] *sm* hashish

'**herpes** ['ɛrpes] *sm* (*MED*) herpes *sg*; ~ **zoster** shingles *sg*

ho [ɔ] *vb vedi* **avere**

'**hobby** ['hɔbi] *sm inv* hobby

'**hockey** ['hɔki] *sm* hockey; ~ **su ghiaccio** ice hockey

'**hostess** ['houstis] *sf inv* air hostess (*BRIT*) o stewardess

ho'tel *sm inv* hotel

I

i *det mpl* the

i'ato *sm* hiatus

ibernazi'one [ibernat'tsjone] *sf* hibernation

'**ibrido, a** *ag, sm* hybrid

Id'dio *sm* God

i'dea *sf* idea; (*opinione*) opinion, view; (*ideale*) ideal; **dare l'~ di** to seem, look like; ~ **fissa** obsession; **neanche** o **neppure per ~!** certainly not!

ide'ale *ag, sm* ideal

ide'are *vt* (*immaginare*) to think up, conceive; (*progettare*) to plan

i'dentico, a, ci, che *ag* identical

identifi'care *vt* to identify; **identificazi'one** *sf* identification

identità *sf inv* identity

ideolo'gia, 'gie [ideolo'dʒia] *sf* ideology

idi'oma, i *sm* idiom, language; **idio'matico, a, ci, che** *ag* idiomatic; **frase idiomatica** idiom

idi'ota, i, e *ag* idiotic ♦ *sm/f* idiot

idola'trare *vt* to worship; (*fig*) to idolize

'**idolo** *sm* idol

idoneità *sf* suitability

i'doneo, a *ag*: ~ **a** suitable for, fit for; (*MIL*) fit for; (*qualificato*) qualified for

i'drante *sm* hydrant

i'draulica *sf* hydraulics *sg*

i'draulico, a, ci, che *ag* hydraulic ♦ *sm* plumber

idroe'lettrico, a, ci, che *ag* hydro-electric

i'drofilo, a *ag vedi* **cotone**

i'drogeno [i'drɔdʒeno] *sm* hydrogen

idros'calo *sm* seaplane base

idrovo'lante *sm* seaplane

i'ena *sf* hyena

i'eri *av, sm* yesterday; **il giornale di** ~ yesterday's paper; ~ **l'altro** the day before yesterday; ~ **sera** yesterday evening

igi'ene [i'dʒɛne] *sf* hygiene; **~ pubblica** public health; **igi'enico, a, ci, che** *ag* hygienic; (*salubre*) healthy

i'gnaro, a [iɲ'ɲaro] *ag*: **~ di** unaware of, ignorant of

i'gnobile [iɲ'ɲɔbile] *ag* despicable, vile

igno'rante [iɲɲo'rante] *ag* ignorant

igno'rare [iɲɲo'rare] *vt* (*non sapere, conoscere*) to be ignorant *o* unaware of, not to know; (*fingere di non vedere, sentire*) to ignore

i'gnoto, a [iɲ'ɲɔto] *ag* unknown

PAROLA CHIAVE

il (*pl* (*m*) **i**; *diventa* **lo** (*pl* **gli**) *davanti a s impura, gn, pn, ps, x, z; f* **la** (*pl* **le**)) *det m*
1 the; **~ libro/lo studente/l'acqua** the book/the student/the water; **gli scolari** the pupils
2 (*astrazione*): **~ coraggio/l'amore/la giovinezza** courage/love/youth
3 (*tempo*): **~ mattino/la sera** in the morning/evening; **~ venerdì** *etc* (*abitualmente*) on Fridays *etc*; (*quel giorno*) on (the) Friday *etc*; **la settimana prossima** next week
4 (*distributivo*) a, an; **2.500 lire ~ chilo/paio** 2,500 lire a *o* per kilo/pair
5 (*partitivo*) some, any; **hai messo lo zucchero?** have you added sugar?; **hai comprato ~ latte?** did you buy (some *o* any) milk?
6 (*possesso*): **aprire gli occhi** to open one's eyes; **rompersi la gamba** to break one's leg; **avere i capelli neri/~ naso rosso** to have dark hair/a red nose
7 (*con nomi propri*): **~ Petrarca** Petrarch; **~ Presidente Clinton** President Clinton; **dov'è la Francesca?** where's Francesca?
8 (*con nomi geografici*): **~ Tevere** the Tiber; **l'Italia** Italy; **~ Regno Unito** the United Kingdom; **l'Everest** Everest

---

'ilare *ag* cheerful; **ilarità** *sf* hilarity, mirth

illangui'dire *vi* to grow weak *o* feeble

illazi'one [illat'tsjone] *sf* inference, deduction

ille'gale *ag* illegal

illeg'gibile [illed'dʒibile] *ag* illegible

ille'gittimo, a [ille'dʒittimo] *ag* illegitimate

il'leso, a *ag* unhurt, unharmed

illette'rato, a *ag* illiterate

illi'bato, a *ag*: **donna ~a** virgin

illimi'tato, a *ag* boundless; unlimited

ill.mo *abbr* = **illustrissimo**

il'ludere *vt* to deceive, delude; **~rsi** *vr* to deceive o.s., delude o.s.

illumi'nare *vt* to light up, illuminate; (*fig*) to enlighten; **~rsi** *vr* to light up; **~ a giorno** to floodlight; **illuminazi'one** *sf* lighting; illumination; floodlighting; (*fig*) flash of inspiration

illusi'one *sf* illusion; **farsi delle ~i** to delude o.s.

illusio'nismo *sm* conjuring

il'luso, a *pp di* **illudere**

illus'trare *vt* to illustrate; **illustra'tivo, a** *ag* illustrative; **illustrazi'one** *sf* illustration

il'lustre *ag* eminent, renowned; **illus'trissimo, a** *ag* (*negli indirizzi*) very revered

imbacuc'care *vt* to wrap up; **~rsi** *vr* to wrap up

imbal'laggio [imbal'laddʒo] *sm* packing *no pl*

imbal'lare *vt* to pack; (*AUT*) to race; **~rsi** *vr* (*AUT*) to race

imbalsa'mare *vt* to embalm

imbambo'lato, a *ag* (*sguardo*) vacant, blank

imban'dire *vt*: **~ un pranzo** to prepare a lavish meal

imbaraz'zare [imbarat'tsare] *vt* (*mettere a disagio*) to embarrass; (*ostacolare: movimenti*) to hamper; (: *stomaco*) to lie heavily on

imba'razzo [imba'rattso] *sm* (*disagio*) embarrassment; (*perplessità*) puzzlement, bewilderment; **~ di stomaco** indigestion

imbarca'dero *sm* landing stage

imbar'care *vt* (*passeggeri*) to embark; (*merci*) to load; **~rsi** *vr*: **~rsi su** to board; **~rsi per l'America** to sail for America; **~rsi in** (*fig: affare etc*) to embark on

imbarcazi'one [imbarkat'tsjone] *sf*

(small) boat, (small) craft *inv*; ~ **di salvataggio** lifeboat

im'barco, chi *sm* embarkation; loading; boarding; (*banchina*) landing stage

imbas'tire *vt* (*cucire*) to tack; (*fig*: *abbozzare*) to sketch, outline

im'battersi *vr*: ~ **in** (*incontrare*) to bump *o* run into

imbat'tibile *ag* unbeatable, invincible

imbavagli'are [imbavaʎ'ʎare] *vt* to gag

imbec'cata *sf* (TEATRO) prompt

imbe'cille [imbe'tʃille] *ag* idiotic ♦ *sm/f* idiot; (MED) imbecile

imbel'lire *vt* to adorn, embellish ♦ *vi* to grow more beautiful

im'berbe *ag* beardless

im'bevere *vt* to soak; ~**rsi** *vr*: ~**rsi di** to soak up, absorb

imbian'care *vt* to whiten; (*muro*) to whitewash ♦ *vi* to become *o* turn white

imbian'chino [imbjan'kino] *sm* (house) painter, painter and decorator

imboc'care *vt* (*bambino*) to feed; (*entrare*: *strada*) to enter, turn into ♦ *vi*: ~ **in** (*sog*: *strada*) to lead into; (: *fiume*) to flow into

imbocca'tura *sf* mouth; (*di strada, porto*) entrance; (MUS, *del morso*) mouthpiece

im'bocco, chi *sm* entrance

imbos'care *vt* to hide; ~**rsi** *vr* (MIL) to evade military service

imbos'cata *sf* ambush

imbottigli'are [imbottiʎ'ʎare] *vt* to bottle; (NAUT) to blockade; (MIL) to hem in; ~**rsi** *vr* to be stuck in a traffic jam

imbot'tire *vt* to stuff; (*giacca*) to pad; **imbot'tita** *sf* quilt; **imbotti'tura** *sf* stuffing; padding

imbrat'tare *vt* to dirty, smear, daub

imbrigli'are [imbriʎ'ʎare] *vt* to bridle

imbroc'care *vt* (*fig*) to guess correctly

imbrogli'are [imbroʎ'ʎare] *vt* to mix up; (*fig*: *raggirare*) to deceive, cheat; (: *confondere*) to confuse, mix up; ~**rsi** *vr* to get tangled; (*fig*) to become confused; **im'broglio** *sm* (*groviglio*) tangle; (*situazione confusa*) mess; (*truffa*) swindle, trick; **imbrogli'one, a** *sm/f* cheat, swindler

imbronci'are [imbron'tʃare] *vi* (*anche*: ~**rsi**) to sulk; **imbronci'ato, a** *ag* sulky

imbru'nire *vi, vb impers* to grow dark; **all'**~ at dusk

imbrut'tire *vt* to make ugly ♦ *vi* to become ugly

imbu'care *vt* to post

imbur'rare *vt* to butter

im'buto *sm* funnel

imi'tare *vt* to imitate; (*riprodurre*) to copy; (*assomigliare*) to look like; **imitazi'one** *sf* imitation

immaco'lato, a *ag* spotless; immaculate

immagazzi'nare [immagaddzi'nare] *vt* to store

immagi'nare [immadʒi'nare] *vt* to imagine; (*supporre*) to suppose; (*inventare*) to invent; **s'immagini!** don't mention it!, not at all!; **immagi'nario, a** *ag* imaginary; **immaginazi'one** *sf* imagination; (*cosa immaginata*) fancy

im'magine [im'madʒine] *sf* image; (*rappresentazione grafica, mentale*) picture

imman'cabile *ag* certain; unfailing

im'mane *ag* (*smisurato*) enormous; (*spaventoso*) terrible

immangi'abile [imman'dʒabile] *ag* inedible

immatrico'lare *vt* to register; ~**rsi** *vr* (INS) to matriculate, enrol; **immatricolazi'one** *sf* registration; matriculation, enrolment

imma'turo, a *ag* (*frutto*) unripe; (*persona*) immature; (*prematuro*) premature

immedesi'marsi *vr*: ~ **in** to identify with

immediata'mente *av* immediately, at once

immedi'ato, a *ag* immediate

im'memore *ag*: ~ **di** forgetful of

im'menso, a *ag* immense

im'mergere [im'mɛrdʒere] *vt* to immerse, plunge; ~**rsi** *vr* to plunge; (*sommergibile*) to dive, submerge; (*dedicarsi a*): ~**rsi in** to immerse o.s. in

immeri'tato, a *ag* undeserved

immeri'tevole *ag* undeserving, unworthy

immersi'one *sf* immersion; (*di sommergibile*) submersion, dive; (*di palombaro*) dive

im'merso, a *pp di* **immergere**

im'mettere *vt*: ~ **(in)** to introduce (into); ~ **dati in un computer** to enter data on a computer

immi'grato, a *sm/f* immigrant; **immigrazi'one** *sf* immigration

immi'nente *ag* imminent

immischi'are [immis'kjare] *vt*: ~ **qn in** to involve sb in; **~rsi in** to interfere *o* meddle in

immissi'one *sf* (*di aria, gas*) intake; ~ **di dati** (*INFORM*) data entry

im'mobile *ag* motionless, still; **~i** *smpl* (*anche: beni ~i*) real estate *sg*; **immobili'are** *ag* (*DIR*) property *cpd*; **immobilità** *sf* stillness; immobility

immo'desto, a *ag* immodest

immo'lare *vt* to sacrifice, immolate

immon'dizia [immon'dittsja] *sf* dirt, filth; (*spesso al pl: spazzatura, rifiuti*) rubbish *no pl*, refuse *no pl*

im'mondo, a *ag* filthy, foul

immo'rale *ag* immoral

immor'tale *ag* immortal

im'mune *ag* (*esente*) exempt; (*MED, DIR*) immune; **immunità** *sf* immunity; **immunità parlamentare** parliamentary privilege

immu'tabile *ag* immutable; unchanging

impacchet'tare [impakket'tare] *vt* to pack up

impacci'are [impat't∫are] *vt* to hinder, hamper; **impacci'ato, a** *ag* awkward, clumsy; (*imbarazzato*) embarrassed; **im'paccio** *sm* obstacle; (*imbarazzo*) embarrassment; (*situazione imbarazzante*) awkward situation

im'pacco, chi *sm* (*MED*) compress

impadro'nirsi *vr*: ~ **di** to seize, take possession of; (*fig: apprendere a fondo*) to master

impa'gabile *ag* priceless

impagi'nare [impadʒi'nare] *vt* (*TIP*) to paginate, page (up)

impagli'are [impaʎ'ʎare] *vt* to stuff (with straw)

impa'lato, a *ag* (*fig*) stiff as a board

impalca'tura *sf* scaffolding

impalli'dire *vi* to turn pale; (*fig*) to fade

impa'nare *vt* (*CUC*) to dip in breadcrumbs

impanta'narsi *vr* to sink (in the mud); (*fig*) to get bogged down

impappi'narsi *vr* to stammer, falter

impa'rare *vt* to learn

imparen'tarsi *vr*: ~ **con** to marry into

'impari *ag inv* (*disuguale*) unequal; (*dispari*) odd

impar'tire *vt* to bestow, give

imparzi'ale [impar'tsjale] *ag* impartial, unbiased

impas'sibile *ag* impassive

impas'tare *vt* (*pasta*) to knead; (*colori*) to mix

im'pasto *sm* (*l'impastare: di pane*) kneading; (: *di cemento*) mixing; (*pasta*) dough; (*anche fig*) mixture

im'patto *sm* impact

impau'rire *vt* to scare, frighten ♦ *vi* (*anche: ~rsi*) to become scared *o* frightened

im'pavido, a *ag* intrepid, fearless

impazi'ente [impat'tsjɛnte] *ag* impatient; **impazi'enza** *sf* impatience

impaz'zata [impat'tsata] *sf*: **all'~** (*precipitosamente*) at breakneck speed

impaz'zire [impat'tsire] *vi* to go mad; ~ **per qn/qc** to be crazy about sb/sth

impec'cabile *ag* impeccable

impedi'mento *sm* obstacle, hindrance

impe'dire *vt* (*vietare*): ~ **a qn di fare** to prevent sb from doing; (*ostruire*) to obstruct; (*impacciare*) to hamper, hinder

impe'gnare [impeɲ'ɲare] *vt* (*dare in pegno*) to pawn; (*onore etc*) to pledge; (*prenotare*) to book, reserve; (*obbligare*) to oblige; (*occupare*) to keep busy; (*MIL: nemico*) to engage; **~rsi** *vr* (*vincolarsi*): **~rsi a fare** to undertake to do; (*mettersi risolutamente*): **~rsi in qc** to devote o.s. to sth; **~rsi con qn** (*accordarsi*) to come to an agreement with sb; **impegna'tivo, a** *ag* binding; (*lavoro*) demanding, exacting; **impe'gnato, a** *ag* (*occupato*) busy; (*fig: romanzo, autore*) committed, engagé

im'pegno [im'peɲɲo] *sm* (*obbligo*) obligation; (*promessa*) promise, pledge; (*zelo*) diligence, zeal; (*compito, d'autore*) commitment

impel'lente *ag* pressing, urgent

impene'trabile *ag* impenetrable

impen'narsi *vr* (*cavallo*) to rear up; (*AER*) to nose up; (*fig*) to bridle

impen'sato, a *ag* unforeseen, unexpected

impensie'rire *vt* to worry; **~rsi** *vr* to worry

impe'rare *vi* (*anche fig*) to reign, rule

impera'tivo, a *ag, sm* imperative

impera'tore, 'trice *sm/f* emperor/empress

imperdo'nabile *ag* unforgivable, unpardonable

imper'fetto, a *ag* imperfect ♦ *sm* (*LING*) imperfect (tense); **imperfezi'one** *sf* imperfection

imperi'ale *ag* imperial

imperi'oso, a *ag* (*persona*) imperious; (*motivo, esigenza*) urgent, pressing

impe'rizia [impe'rittsja] *sf* lack of experience

imperma'lirsi *vr* to take offence

imperme'abile *ag* waterproof ♦ *sm* raincoat

imperni'are *vt*: ~ **qc su** to hinge sth on; (*fig*) to base sth on; **~rsi** *vr* (*fig*): **~rsi su** to be based on

im'pero *sm* empire; (*forza, autorità*) rule, control

imperscru'tabile *ag* inscrutable

imperso'nale *ag* impersonal

imperso'nare *vt* to personify; (*TEATRO*) to play, act (the part of)

imperter'rito, a *ag* fearless, undaunted; impassive

imperti'nente *ag* impertinent

imperver'sare *vi* to rage

im'peto *sm* (*moto, forza*) force, impetus; (*assalto*) onslaught; (*fig: impulso*) impulse; (*: slancio*) transport; **con ~** energetically; vehemently

impet'tito, a *ag* stiff, erect

impetu'oso, a *ag* (*vento*) strong, raging; (*persona*) impetuous

impian'tare *vt* (*motore*) to install; (*azienda, discussione*) to establish, start

impi'anto *sm* (*installazione*) installation; (*apparecchiature*) plant; (*sistema*) system; ~ **elettrico** wiring; ~ **sportivo** sports complex; **~i di risalita** (*SCI*) ski lifts

impiastricci'are [impjastrit't'ʃare] *vt* = **impiastrare**

impi'astro *sm* poultice

impic'care *vt* to hang; **~rsi** *vr* to hang o.s.

impicci'are [impit't'ʃare] *vt* to hinder, hamper; **~rsi** *vr* to meddle, interfere; **im'piccio** *sm* (*ostacolo*) hindrance; (*seccatura*) trouble, bother; (*affare imbrogliato*) mess; **essere d'impiccio** to be in the way

impie'gare *vt* (*usare*) to use, employ; (*assumere*) to employ, take on; (*spendere: denaro, tempo*) to spend; (*investire*) to invest; **~rsi** *vr* to get a job, obtain employment; **impie'gato, a** *sm/f* employee

impi'ego, ghi *sm* (*uso*) use; (*occupazione*) employment; (*posto di lavoro*) (regular) job, post; (*ECON*) investment

impieto'sire *vt* to move to pity; **~rsi** *vr* to be moved to pity

impie'trire *vt* (*fig*) to petrify

impigli'are [impiʎ'ʎare] *vt* to catch, entangle; **~rsi** *vr* to get caught up *o* entangled

impi'grire *vt* to make lazy ♦ *vi* (*anche*: **~rsi**) to grow lazy

impli'care *vt* to imply; (*coinvolgere*) to involve; **~rsi** *vr*: **~rsi (in)** to become involved (in); **implicazi'one** *sf* implication

im'plicito, a [im'plit'ʃito] *ag* implicit

implo'rare *vt* to implore; (*pietà etc*) to beg for

impolve'rare *vt* to cover with dust; **~rsi** *vr* to get dusty

impo'nente *ag* imposing, impressive

impo'nibile *ag* taxable ♦ *sm* taxable income

impopo'lare *ag* unpopular

im'porre *vt* to impose; (*costringere*) to force, make; (*far valere*) to impose,

enforce; **imporsi** *vr* (*persona*) to assert
o.s.; (*cosa: rendersi necessario*) to become
necessary; (*aver successo: moda, attore*) to
become popular; ~ **a qn di fare** to force
sb to do, make sb do

impor'tante *ag* important; **impor'tanza**
sf importance; **dare importanza a qc** to
attach importance to sth; **darsi importanza** to give o.s. airs

impor'tare *vt* (*introdurre dall'estero*) to
import ♦ *vi* to matter, be important ♦ *vb
impers* (*essere necessario*) to be necessary;
(*interessare*) to matter; **non importa!** it
doesn't matter!; **non me ne importa!** I
don't care!; **importazi'one** *sf* impor-
tation; (*merci importate*) imports *pl*

im'porto *sm* (total) amount

importu'nare *vt* to bother

impor'tuno, a *ag* irksome, annoying

imposizi'one [impozit'tsjone] *sf*
imposition; order, command; (*onere,
imposta*) tax

imposses'sarsi *vr*: ~ **di** to seize, take
possession of

impos'sibile *ag* impossible; **fare l'~** to
do one's utmost, do all one can;
impossibilità *sf* impossibility; **essere
nell'impossibilità di fare qc** to be
unable to do sth

im'posta *sf* (*di finestra*) shutter; (*tassa*)
tax; ~ **sul reddito** income tax; ~ **sul
valore aggiunto** value added tax (*BRIT*),
sales tax (*US*)

impos'tare *vt* (*imbucare*) to post;
(*preparare*) to plan, set out; (*avviare*) to
begin, start off; (*voce*) to pitch

im'posto, a *pp di* **imporre**

impo'tente *ag* weak, powerless; (*anche
MED*) impotent

impove'rire *vt* to impoverish ♦ *vi* (*anche:
~rsi*) to become poor

imprati'cabile *ag* (*strada*) impassable;
(*campo da gioco*) unplayable

imprati'chire [imprati'kire] *vt* to train;
~rsi in qc to practise (*BRIT*) *o* practice (*US*)
sth

impre'gnare [impreɲ'ɲare] *vt*: ~ **(di)**
(*imbevere*) to soak *o* impregnate (with);
(*riempire: anche fig*) to fill (with)

imprendi'tore *sm* (*industriale*)
entrepreneur; (*appaltatore*) contractor;
piccolo ~ small businessman

im'presa *sf* (*iniziativa*) enterprise;
(*azione*) exploit; (*azienda*) firm, concern

impre'sario *sm* (*TEATRO*) manager,
impresario; ~ **di pompe funebri** funeral
director

imprescin'dibile [impreʃʃin'dibile] *ag*
not to be ignored

impressio'nante *ag* impressive;
upsetting

impressio'nare *vt* to impress; (*turbare*)
to upset; (*FOT*) to expose; **~rsi** *vr* to be
easily upset

impressi'one *sf* impression; (*fig:
sensazione*) sensation, feeling; (*stampa*)
printing; **fare ~** (*colpire*) to impress;
(*turbare*) to frighten, upset; **fare buona/
cattiva ~ a** to make a good/bad
impression on

im'presso, a *pp di* **imprimere**

impres'tare *vt*: ~ **qc a qn** to lend sth to
sb

impreve'dibile *ag* unforeseeable;
(*persona*) unpredictable

imprevi'dente *ag* lacking in foresight

impre'visto, a *ag* unexpected,
unforeseen ♦ *sm* unforeseen event; **salvo
~i** unless anything unexpected happens

imprigio'nare [impridʒo'nare] *vt* to
imprison

im'primere *vt* (*anche fig*) to impress,
stamp; (*comunicare: movimento*) to
transmit, give

impro'babile *ag* improbable, unlikely

im'pronta *sf* imprint, impression, sign;
(*di piede, mano*) print; (*fig*) mark, stamp;
~ **digitale** fingerprint

impro'perio *sm* insult

im'proprio, a *ag* improper; **arma ~a**
offensive weapon

improvvisa'mente *av* suddenly;
unexpectedly

improvvi'sare *vt* to improvise; **~rsi** *vr*:
~rsi cuoco to (decide to) act as cook;
improvvi'sata *sf* (pleasant) surprise

improv'viso, a *ag* (*imprevisto*)
unexpected; (*subitaneo*) sudden; **all'~**

unexpectedly; suddenly

impru'dente *ag* unwise, rash

impu'dente *ag* impudent

impu'dico, a, chi, che *ag* immodest

impu'gnare [impuɲ'ɲare] *vt* to grasp, grip; (*DIR*) to contest

impul'sivo, a *ag* impulsive

im'pulso *sm* impulse

impun'tarsi *vr* to stop dead, refuse to budge; (*fig*) to be obstinate

impu'tare *vt* (*ascrivere*): ~ qc a to attribute sth to; (*DIR: accusare*): ~ qn di to charge sb with, accuse sb of; **impu'tato, a** *sm/f* (*DIR*) accused, defendant; **imputazi'one** *sf* (*DIR*) charge

imputri'dire *vi* to rot

PAROLA CHIAVE

in (*in+il* = **nel**, *in+lo* = **nello**, *in+l'* = **nell'**, *in+la* = **nella**, *in+i* = **nei**, *in+gli* = **negli**, *in+le* = **nelle**) *prep* **1** (*stato in luogo*) in; **vivere ~ Italia/città** to live in Italy/town; **essere ~ casa/ufficio** to be at home/the office; **se fossi ~ te** if I were you

2 (*moto a luogo*) to; (*: dentro*) into; **andare ~ Germania/città** to go to Germany/town; **andare ~ ufficio** to go to the office; **entrare ~ macchina/casa** to get into the car/go into the house

3 (*tempo*) in; **nel 1989** in 1989; ~ **giugno/estate** in June/summer

4 (*modo, maniera*) in; ~ **silenzio** in silence; ~ **abito da sera** in evening dress; ~ **guerra** at war; ~ **vacanza** on holiday; **Maria Bianchi ~ Rossi** Maria Rossi née Bianchi

5 (*mezzo*) by; **viaggiare ~ autobus/treno** to travel by bus/train

6 (*materia*) made of; ~ **marmo** made of marble, marble *cpd*; **una collana ~ oro** a gold necklace

7 (*misura*) in; **siamo ~ quattro** there are four of us; ~ **tutto** in all

8 (*fine*): **dare ~ dono** to give as a gift; **spende tutto ~ alcool** he spends all his money on drink; ~ **onore di** in honour of

---

inabi'tabile *ag* uninhabitable

inacces'sibile [inatt∫es'sibile] *ag* (*luogo*) inaccessible; (*persona*) unapproachable; (*mistero*) unfathomable

inaccet'tabile [inatt∫et'tabile] *ag* unacceptable

ina'datto, a *ag*: ~ (**a**) unsuitable *o* unfit (for)

inadegu'ato, a *ag* inadequate

inadempi'enza [inadem'pjentsa] *sf*: ~ (**a**) non-fulfilment (of)

inaffer'rabile *ag* elusive; (*concetto, senso*) difficult to grasp

ina'lare *vt* to inhale

inalbe'rare *vt* (*NAUT*) to hoist, raise; **~rsi** *vr* (*fig*) to flare up, fly off the handle

inalte'rabile *ag* unchangeable; (*colore*) fast, permanent; (*affetto*) constant

inalte'rato, a *ag* unchanged

inami'dato, a *ag* starched

inani'mato, a *ag* inanimate; (*senza vita: corpo*) lifeless

inappa'gabile *ag* insatiable

inappel'labile *ag* (*decisione*) final, irrevocable; (*DIR*) final, not open to appeal

inappe'tenza [inappe'tentsa] *sf* (*MED*) lack of appetite

inappun'tabile *ag* irreproachable

inar'care *vt* (*schiena*) to arch; (*sopracciglia*) to raise; **~rsi** *vr* to arch

inari'dire *vt* to make arid, dry up ♦ *vi* (*anche: ~rsi*) to dry up, become arid

inaspet'tato, a *ag* unexpected

inas'prire *vt* (*disciplina*) to tighten up, make harsher; (*carattere*) to embitter; **~rsi** *vr* to become harsher; to become bitter; to become worse

inattac'cabile *ag* (*anche fig*) unassailable; (*alibi*) cast-iron

inatten'dibile *ag* unreliable

inat'teso, a *ag* unexpected

inattu'abile *ag* impracticable

inau'dito, a *ag* unheard of

inaugu'rare *vt* to inaugurate, open; (*monumento*) to unveil

inavve'duto, a *ag* careless, inadvertent

inavver'tenza [inavver'tentsa] *sf* carelessness, inadvertence

incagli'are [inkaʎ'ʎare] *vi* (*NAUT: anche: ~rsi*) to run aground

incal'lito, a *ag* calloused; (*fig*) hardened, inveterate; (: *insensibile*) hard

incal'zare [inkal'tsare] *vt* to follow *o* pursue closely; (*fig*) to press ♦ *vi* (*urgere*) to be pressing; (*essere imminente*) to be imminent

incame'rare *vt* (*DIR*) to expropriate

incammi'nare *vt* (*fig: avviare*) to start up; ~**rsi** *vr* to set off

incande'scente [inkandeʃ'ʃɛnte] *ag* incandescent, white-hot

incan'tare *vt* to enchant, bewitch; ~**rsi** *vr* (*rimanere intontito*) to be spellbound; to be in a daze; (*meccanismo: bloccarsi*) to jam; **incanta'tore, 'trice** *ag* enchanting, bewitching ♦ *sm/f* enchanter/enchantress; **incan'tesimo** *sm* spell, charm; **incan'tevole** *ag* charming, enchanting

in'canto *sm* spell, charm, enchantment; (*asta*) auction; **come per ~** as if by magic; **mettere all'~** to put up for auction

incanu'tire *vi* to go white

inca'pace [inka'patʃe] *ag* incapable; **incapacità** *sf* inability; (*DIR*) incapacity

incapo'nirsi *vr* to be stubborn, be determined

incap'pare *vi*: ~ **in qc/qn** (*anche fig*) to run into sth/sb

incapricci'arsi [inkaprit'tʃarsi] *vr*: ~ **di** to take a fancy to *o* for

incapsu'lare *vt* (*dente*) to crown

incarce'rare [inkartʃe'rare] *vt* to imprison

incari'care *vt*: ~ **qn di fare** to give sb the responsibility of doing; ~**rsi di** to take care *o* charge of; **incari'cato, a** *ag*: **incaricato (di)** in charge (of), responsible (for) ♦ *sm/f* delegate, representative; **professore incaricato** *teacher with a temporary appointment*; **incaricato d'affari** (*POL*) chargé d'affaires

in'carico, chi *sm* task, job

incar'nare *vt* to embody; ~**rsi** *vr* to be embodied; (*REL*) to become incarnate

incarta'mento *sm* dossier, file

incar'tare *vt* to wrap (in paper)

incas'sare *vt* (*merce*) to pack (in cases); (*gemma: incastonare*) to set; (*ECON:*

riscuotere) to collect; (*PUGILATO: colpi*) to take, stand up to; **in'casso** *sm* cashing, encashment; (*introito*) takings *pl*

incasto'nare *vt* to set; **incastona'tura** *sf* setting

incas'trare *vt* to fit in, insert; (*fig: intrappolare*) to catch; ~**rsi** *vr* (*combaciare*) to fit together; (*restare bloccato*) to become stuck; **in'castro** *sm* slot, groove; (*punto di unione*) joint

incate'nare *vt* to chain up

incatra'mare *vt* to tar

incatti'vire *vt* to make wicked; ~**rsi** *vr* to turn nasty

in'cauto, a *ag* imprudent, rash

inca'vare *vt* to hollow out; **in'cavo** *sm* hollow; (*solco*) groove

incendi'are [intʃen'djare] *vt* to set fire to; ~**rsi** *vr* to catch fire, burst into flames

incendi'ario, a [intʃen'djarjo] *ag* incendiary ♦ *sm/f* arsonist

in'cendio [in'tʃendjo] *sm* fire

incene'rire [intʃene'rire] *vt* to burn to ashes, incinerate; (*cadavere*) to cremate; ~**rsi** *vr* to be burnt to ashes

in'censo [in'tʃenso] *sm* incense

incensu'rato, a [intʃensu'rato] *ag* (*DIR*): **essere ~** to have a clean record

incen'tivo [intʃen'tivo] *sm* incentive

incep'pare [intʃep'pare] *vt* to obstruct, hamper; ~**rsi** *vr* to jam

ince'rata [intʃe'rata] *sf* (*tela*) tarpaulin; (*impermeabile*) oilskins *pl*

incer'tezza [intʃer'tettsa] *sf* uncertainty

in'certo, a [in'tʃɛrto] *ag* uncertain; (*irresoluto*) undecided, hesitating ♦ *sm* uncertainty

in'cetta [in'tʃetta] *sf* buying up; **fare ~ di qc** to buy up sth

inchi'esta [in'kjɛsta] *sf* investigation, inquiry

inchi'nare [inki'nare] *vt* to bow; ~**rsi** *vr* to bend down; (*per riverenza*) to curtsy; (: *donna*) to curtsy; **in'chino** *sm* bow; curtsy

inchio'dare [inkjo'dare] *vt* to nail (down); ~ **la macchina** (*AUT*) to jam on the brakes

inchi'ostro [in'kjɔstro] *sm* ink; ~

simpatico invisible ink

inciam'pare [intʃam'pare] *vi* to trip, stumble

inci'ampo [in'tʃampo] *sm* obstacle; **essere d'~ a qn** (*fig*) to be in sb's way

inciden'tale [intʃiden'tale] *ag* incidental

inci'dente [intʃi'dɛnte] *sm* accident; **~ d'auto** car accident

inci'denza [intʃi'dɛntsa] *sf* incidence; **avere una forte ~ su qc** to affect sth greatly

in'cidere [in'tʃidere] *vi*: **~ su** to bear upon, affect ♦ *vt* (*tagliare incavando*) to cut into; (*ARTE*) to engrave; to etch; (*canzone*) to record

in'cinta [in'tʃinta] *ag f* pregnant

incipri'are [intʃi'prjare] *vt* to powder

in'circa [in'tʃirka] *av*: **all'~** more or less, very nearly

incisi'one [intʃi'zjone] *sf* cut; (*disegno*) engraving; etching; (*registrazione*) recording; (*MED*) incision

in'ciso, a [in'tʃizo] *pp di* **incidere** ♦ *sm*: **per ~** incidentally, by the way

inci'tare [intʃi'tare] *vt* to incite

inci'vile [intʃi'vile] *ag* uncivilized; (*villano*) impolite

incivi'lire [intʃivi'lire] *vt* to civilize

incl. *abbr* (= *incluso*) encl.

incli'nare *vt* to tilt ♦ *vi* (*fig*): **~ a qc/a fare** to incline towards sth/doing; to tend towards sth/to do; **~rsi** *vr* (*barca*) to list; (*aereo*) to bank; **incli'nato, a** *ag* sloping; **inclinazi'one** *sf* slope; (*fig*) inclination, tendency; **in'cline** *ag*: **incline a** inclined to

in'cludere *vt* to include; (*accludere*) to enclose; **in'cluso, a** *pp di* **includere** ♦ *ag* included; enclosed

incoe'rente *ag* incoherent; (*contraddittorio*) inconsistent

in'cognita [in'koɲɲita] *sf* (*MAT*, *fig*) unknown quantity

in'cognito, a [in'koɲɲito] *ag* unknown ♦ *sm*: **in ~** incognito

incol'lare *vt* to glue, gum; (*unire con colla*) to stick together

incolon'nare *vt* to draw up in columns

inco'lore *ag* colourless

incol'pare *vt*: **~ qn di** to charge sb with

in'colto, a *ag* (*terreno*) uncultivated; (*trascurato: capelli*) neglected; (*persona*) uneducated

in'colume *ag* safe and sound, unhurt

incom'benza [inkom'bɛntsa] *sf* duty, task

in'combere *vi* (*sovrastare minacciando*): **~ su** to threaten, hang over

incominci'are [inkomin'tʃare] *vi*, *vt* to begin, start

in'comodo, a *ag* uncomfortable; (*inopportuno*) inconvenient ♦ *sm* inconvenience, bother

incompe'tente *ag* incompetent

incompi'uto, a *ag* unfinished, incomplete

incom'pleto, a *ag* incomplete

incompren'sibile *ag* incomprehensible

incom'preso, a *ag* not understood; misunderstood

inconce'pibile [inkontʃe'pibile] *ag* inconceivable

inconcili'abile [inkontʃi'ljabile] *ag* irreconcilable

inconclu'dente *ag* inconclusive; (*persona*) ineffectual

incondizio'nato, a [inkondittsjo'nato] *ag* unconditional

inconfu'tabile *ag* irrefutable

incongru'ente *ag* inconsistent

inconsa'pevole *ag*: **~ di** unaware of, ignorant of

in'conscio, a, sci, sce [in'kɔnʃo] *ag* unconscious ♦ *sm* (*PSIC*): **l'~** the unconscious

inconsis'tente *ag* insubstantial; unfounded

inconsu'eto, a *ag* unusual

incon'sulto, a *ag* rash

incon'trare *vt* to meet; (*difficoltà*) to meet with; **~rsi** *vr* to meet

incontras'tabile *ag* incontrovertible, indisputable

in'contro *av*: **~ a** (*verso*) towards ♦ *sm* meeting; (*SPORT*) match; meeting; **~ di calcio** football match

inconveni'ente *sm* drawback, snag

incoraggia'mento [inkoraddʒa'mento]

sm encouragement

incoraggi'are [inkorad'dʒare] *vt* to encourage

incornici'are [inkorni't∫are] *vt* to frame

incoro'nare *vt* to crown; **incoronazi'one** *sf* coronation

incorpo'rare *vt* to incorporate; (*fig: annettere*) to annex

in'correre *vi*: ~ **in** to meet with, run into

incosci'ente [inko∫'∫ɛnte] *ag* (*inconscio*) unconscious; (*irresponsabile*) reckless, thoughtless; **incosci'enza** *sf* unconsciousness; recklessness, thoughtlessness

incre'dibile *ag* incredible, unbelievable

in'credulo, a *ag* incredulous, disbelieving

incremen'tare *vt* to increase; (*dar sviluppo a*) to promote

incre'mento *sm* (*sviluppo*) development; (*aumento numerico*) increase, growth

incresci'oso, a [inkre∫'∫oso] *ag* (*incidente etc*) regrettable

incres'parsi *vr* (*acqua*) to ripple; (*capelli*) to go frizzy; (*pelle, tessuto*) to wrinkle

incrimi'nare *vt* (*DIR*) to charge

incri'nare *vt* to crack; (*fig: rapporti, amicizia*) to cause to deteriorate; ~**rsi** *vr* to crack; to deteriorate; **incrina'tura** *sf* crack; (*fig*) rift

incroci'are [inkro't∫are] *vt* to cross; (*incontrare*) to meet ♦ *vi* (*NAUT, AER*) to cruise; ~**rsi** *vr* (*strade*) to cross, intersect; (*persone, veicoli*) to pass each other; ~ **le braccia/le gambe** to fold one's arms/cross one's legs; **incrocia'tore** *sm* cruiser

in'crocio [in'krot∫o] *sm* (*anche FERR*) crossing; (*di strade*) crossroads

incros'tare *vt* to encrust

incuba'trice [inkuba'trit∫e] *sf* incubator

'incubo *sm* nightmare

in'cudine *sf* anvil

incu'rante *ag*: ~ (**di**) heedless (of), careless (of)

incurio'sire *vt* to make curious; ~**rsi** *vr* to become curious

incursi'one *sf* raid

incur'vare *vt* to bend, curve; ~**rsi** *vr* to bend, curve

in'cusso, a *pp di* **incutere**

incusto'dito, a *ag* unguarded, unattended

in'cutere *vt* to arouse; ~ **timore/rispetto a qn** to strike fear into sb/command sb's respect

'indaco *sm* indigo

indaffa'rato, a *ag* busy

inda'gare *vt* to investigate

in'dagine [in'dadʒine] *sf* investigation, inquiry; (*ricerca*) research, study

indebi'tarsi *vr* to run *o* get into debt

in'debito, a *ag* undue; undeserved

indebo'lire *vt, vi* (*anche: ~rsi*) to weaken

inde'cente [inde't∫ɛnte] *ag* indecent; **inde'cenza** *sf* indecency

inde'ciso, a [inde't∫izo] *ag* indecisive; (*irrisoluto*) undecided

inde'fesso, a *ag* untiring, indefatigable

indefi'nito, a *ag* (*anche LING*) indefinite; (*impreciso, non determinato*) undefined

in'degno, a [in'deɲɲo] *ag* (*atto*) shameful; (*persona*) unworthy

indelica'tezza [indelika'tettsa] *sf* tactlessness

indemoni'ato, a *ag* possessed (by the devil)

in'denne *ag* unhurt, uninjured; **indennità** *sf inv* (*rimborso: di spese*) allowance; (*: di perdita*) compensation, indemnity; **indennità di contingenza** cost-of-living allowance; **indennità di trasferta** travel expenses *pl*

indenniz'zare [indennid'dzare] *vt* to compensate; **inden'nizzo** *sm* (*somma*) compensation, indemnity

indero'gabile *ag* binding

'India *sf*: **l'~** India; **indi'ano, a** *ag* Indian ♦ *sm/f* (*d'India*) Indian; (*d'America*) Native American, (*American*) Indian

indiavo'lato, a *ag* possessed (by the devil); (*vivace, violento*) wild

indi'care *vt* (*mostrare*) to show, indicate; (*: col dito*) to point to, point out; (*consigliare*) to suggest, recommend; **indica'tivo, a** *ag* indicative ♦ *sm* (*LING*) indicative (mood); **indica'tore** *sm* (*elenco*) guide; directory; (*TECN*) gauge; indicator; **cartello indicatore** sign; **indicatore di velocità** (*AUT*) speedometer; **indicatore**

della benzina fuel gauge; **indicazi'one** *sf* indication; (*informazione*) piece of information

'**indice** ['inditʃe] *sm* (ANAT: *dito*) index finger, forefinger; (*lancetta*) needle, pointer; (*fig: indizio*) sign; (TECN, MAT, *nei libri*) index; ~ **di gradimento** (RADIO, TV) popularity rating

indi'cibile [indi'tʃibile] *ag* inexpressible

indietreggi'are [indietred'dʒare] *vi* to draw back, retreat

indi'etro *av* back; (*guardare*) behind, back; (*andare, cadere: anche: all'~*) backwards; **rimanere** ~ to be left behind; **essere** ~ (*col lavoro*) to be behind; (*orologio*) to be slow; **rimandare qc** ~ to send sth back

indi'feso, a *ag* (*città etc*) undefended; (*persona*) defenceless

indiffe'rente *ag* indifferent; **indiffe'renza** *sf* indifference

in'digeno, a [in'didʒeno] *ag* indigenous, native ♦ *sm/f* native

indi'gente [indi'dʒente] *ag* poverty-stricken, destitute; **indi'genza** *sf* extreme poverty

indigesti'one [indidʒes'tjone] *sf* indigestion

indi'gesto, a [indi'dʒesto] *ag* indigestible

indi'gnare [indiɲ'ɲare] *vt* to fill with indignation; ~**rsi** *vr* to be (*o* get) indignant

indimenti'cabile *ag* unforgettable

indipen'dente *ag* independent; **indipen'denza** *sf* independence

in'dire *vt* (*concorso*) to announce; (*elezioni*) to call

indi'retto, a *ag* indirect

indiriz'zare [indirit'tsare] *vt* (*dirigere*) to direct; (*mandare*) to send; (*lettera*) to address

indi'rizzo [indi'rittso] *sm* address; (*direzione*) direction; (*avvio*) trend, course

indis'creto, a *ag* indiscreet

indis'cusso, a *ag* unquestioned

indispen'sabile *ag* indispensable, essential

indispet'tire *vt* to irritate, annoy ♦ *vi*

(*anche: ~rsi*) to get irritated *o* annoyed

in'divia *sf* endive

individu'ale *ag* individual; **individualità** *sf* individuality

individu'are *vt* (*dar forma distinta a*) to characterize; (*determinare*) to locate; (*riconoscere*) to single out

indi'viduo *sm* individual

indizi'are [indit'tsjare] *vt*: ~ **qn di qc** to cast suspicion on sb for sth; **indizi'ato, a** *ag* suspected ♦ *sm/f* suspect

in'dizio [in'dittsjo] *sm* (*segno*) sign, indication; (POLIZIA) clue; (DIR) piece of evidence

'**indole** *sf* nature, character

indolen'zito, a [indolen'tsito] *ag* stiff, aching; (*intorpidito*) numb

indo'lore *ag* painless

indo'mani *sm*: **l'**~ the next day, the following day

Indo'nesia *sf*: **l'**~ Indonesia

indos'sare *vt* (*mettere indosso*) to put on; (*avere indosso*) to have on; **indossa'tore, 'trice** *sm/f* model

in'dotto, a *pp di* **indurre**

indottri'nare *vt* to indoctrinate

indovi'nare *vt* (*scoprire*) to guess; (*immaginare*) to imagine, guess; (*il futuro*) to foretell; **indovi'nato, a** *ag* successful; (*scelta*) inspired; **indovi'nello** *sm* riddle; **indo'vino, a** *sm/f* fortuneteller

indubbia'mente *av* undoubtedly

in'dubbio, a *ag* certain, undoubted

indugi'are [indu'dʒare] *vi* to take one's time, delay

in'dugio [in'dudʒo] *sm* (*ritardo*) delay; **senza** ~ without delay

indul'gente [indul'dʒente] *ag* indulgent; (*giudice*) lenient; **indul'genza** *sf* indulgence; leniency

in'dulgere [in'duldʒere] *vi*: ~ **a** (*accondiscendere*) to comply with; (*abbandonarsi*) to indulge in; **in'dulto, a** *pp di* **indulgere** ♦ *sm* (DIR) pardon

indu'mento *sm* article of clothing, garment; ~**i** *smpl* (*vestiti*) clothes

indu'rire *vt* to harden ♦ *vi* (*anche: ~rsi*) to harden, become hard

in'durre *vt*: ~ **qn a fare qc** to induce *o* persuade sb to do sth; ~ **qn in errore** to mislead sb

in'dustria *sf* industry; **industri'ale** *ag* industrial ♦ *sm* industrialist

industri'arsi *vr* to do one's best, try hard

industri'oso, a *ag* industrious, hard-working

induzi'one [indut'tsjone] *sf* induction

inebe'tito, a *ag* dazed, stunned

inebri'are *vt* (*anche fig*) to intoxicate; ~rsi *vr* to become intoxicated

inecce'pibile [inettʃe'pibile] *ag* unexceptionable

i'nedia *sf* starvation

i'nedito, a *ag* unpublished

ineffi'cace [ineffi'katʃe] *ag* ineffective

ineffici'ente [ineffi'tʃɛnte] *ag* inefficient

inegu'ale *ag* unequal; (*irregolare*) uneven

ine'rente *ag*: ~ **a** concerning, regarding

i'nerme *ag* unarmed; defenceless

inerpi'carsi *vr*: ~ (**su**) to clamber (up)

i'nerte *ag* inert; (*inattivo*) indolent, sluggish; i'nerzia *sf* inertia; indolence, sluggishness

ine'satto, a *ag* (*impreciso*) inexact; (*erroneo*) incorrect; (*AMM: non riscosso*) uncollected

inesis'tente *ag* non-existent

inesperi'enza [inespe'rjɛntsa] *sf* inexperience

ines'perto, a *ag* inexperienced

i'netto, a *ag* (*incapace*) inept; (*che non ha attitudine*): ~ (**a**) unsuited (to)

ine'vaso, a *ag* (*ordine, corrispondenza*) outstanding

inevi'tabile *ag* inevitable

i'nezia [i'nɛttsja] *sf* trifle, thing of no importance

infagot'tare *vt* to bundle up, wrap up; ~rsi *vr* to wrap up

infal'libile *ag* infallible

infa'mare *vt* to defame

in'fame *ag* infamous; (*fig: cosa, compito*) awful, dreadful

infan'gare *vt* to cover with mud; (*fig: reputazione*) to sully

infan'tile *ag* child *cpd*; childlike; (*adulto, azione*) childish; **letteratura** ~ children's books *pl*

in'fanzia [in'fantsja] *sf* childhood; (*bambini*) children *pl*; **prima** ~ babyhood, infancy

infari'nare *vt* to cover with (*o* sprinkle with *o* dip in) flour; ~ **di zucchero** to sprinkle with sugar; **infarina'tura** *sf* (*fig*) smattering

in'farto *sm* (*MED*): ~ (**cardiaco**) coronary

infasti'dire *vt* to annoy, irritate; ~rsi *vr* to get annoyed *o* irritated

infati'cabile *ag* tireless, untiring

in'fatti *cong* as a matter of fact, in fact, actually

infatu'arsi *vr*: ~ **di** *o* **per** to become infatuated with, fall for; **infatuazi'one** *sf* infatuation

in'fausto, a *ag* unpropitious, unfavourable

infe'condo, a *ag* infertile

infe'dele *ag* unfaithful; **infedeltà** *sf* infidelity

infe'lice [infe'litʃe] *ag* unhappy; (*sfortunato*) unlucky, unfortunate; (*inopportuno*) inopportune, ill-timed; (*mal riuscito: lavoro*) bad, poor; **infelicità** *sf* unhappiness

inferi'ore *ag* lower; (*per intelligenza, qualità*) inferior ♦ *sm/f* inferior; ~ **a** (*numero, quantità*) less *o* smaller than; (*meno buono*) inferior to; ~ **alla media** below average; **inferiorità** *sf* inferiority

inferme'ria *sf* infirmary; (*di scuola, nave*) sick bay

infermi'ere, a *sm/f* nurse

infermità *sf inv* illness; infirmity

in'fermo, a *ag* (*ammalato*) ill; (*debole*) infirm

infer'nale *ag* infernal; (*proposito, complotto*) diabolical

in'ferno *sm* hell

inferri'ata *sf* grating

infervo'rare *vt* to arouse enthusiasm in; ~rsi *vr* to get excited, get carried away

infes'tare *vt* to infest

infet'tare *vt* to infect; ~rsi *vr* to become infected; infet'tivo, a *ag* infectious; in'fetto, a *ag* infected; (*acque*) polluted, contaminated; infezi'one *sf* infection

infiac'chire [infjak'kire] *vt* to weaken
♦ *vi* (*anche:* ~rsi) to grow weak
infiam'mabile *ag* inflammable
infiam'mare *vt* to set alight; (*fig, MED*) to inflame; ~**rsi** *vr* to catch fire; (*MED*) to become inflamed; (*fig*): ~**rsi di** to be fired with; **infiammazi'one** *sf* (*MED*) inflammation
in'fido, a *ag* unreliable, treacherous
infie'rire *vi*: ~ **su** (*fisicamente*) to attack furiously; (*verbalmente*) to rage at; (*epidemia*) to rage over
in'figgere [in'fidd3ere] *vt*: ~ **qc in** to thrust *o* drive sth into
infi'lare *vt* (*ago*) to thread; (*mettere: chiave*) to insert; (: *anello, vestito*) to slip *o* put on; (*strada*) to turn into, take; ~**rsi** *vr*: ~**rsi in** to slip into; (*indossare*) to slip on; ~ **l'uscio** to slip in; to slip out
infil'trarsi *vr* to penetrate, seep through; (*MIL*) to infiltrate; **infiltrazi'one** *sf* infiltration
infil'zare [infil'tsare] *vt* (*infilare*) to string together; (*trafiggere*) to pierce
'infimo, a *ag* lowest
in'fine *av* finally; (*insomma*) in short
infinità *sf* infinity; (*in quantità*): **un'~ di** an infinite number of
infi'nito, a *ag* infinite; (*LING*) infinitive
♦ *sm* infinity; (*LING*) infinitive; **all'~** (*senza fine*) endlessly
infinocchi'are [infinok'kjare] (*fam*) *vt* to hoodwink
infischi'arsi [infis'kjarsi] *vr*: ~ **di** not to care about
in'fisso, a *pp di* **infiggere** ♦ *sm* fixture; (*di porta, finestra*) frame
infit'tire *vt, vi* (*anche:* ~rsi) to thicken
inflazi'one [inflat'tsjone] *sf* inflation
in'fliggere [in'fliddʒere] *vt* to inflict; **in'flitto, a** *pp di* **infliggere**
influ'ente *ag* influential; **influ'enza** *sf* influence; (*MED*) influenza, flu
influ'ire *vi*: ~ **su** to influence
in'flusso *sm* influence
infol'tire *vt, vi* to thicken
infon'dato, a *ag* unfounded, groundless
in'fondere *vt*: ~ **qc in qn** to instill sth in sb

infor'care *vt* to fork (up); (*bicicletta, cavallo*) to get on; (*occhiali*) to put on
infor'mare *vt* to inform, tell; ~**rsi** *vr*: ~**rsi** (**di** *o* **su**) to inquire (about)
infor'matica *sf* computer science
informa'tivo, a *ag* informative
informa'tore *sm* informer
informazi'one [informat'tsjone] *sf* piece of information; **prendere ~i sul conto di qn** to get information about sb; **chiedere un'~** to ask for (some) information
in'forme *ag* shapeless
informico'larsi *vr* = **informicolirsi**
informico'lirsi *vr* to have pins and needles
infor'tunio *sm* accident; ~ **sul lavoro** industrial accident, accident at work
infos'sarsi *vr* (*terreno*) to sink; (*guance*) to become hollow; **infos'sato, a** *ag* hollow; (*occhi*) deep-set; (: *per malattia*) sunken
in'frangere [in'frandʒere] *vt* to smash; (*fig: legge, patti*) to break; ~**rsi** *vr* to smash, break; **infran'gibile** *ag* unbreakable; **in'franto, a** *pp di* **infrangere** ♦ *ag* broken
infrazi'one [infrat'tsjone] *sf*: ~ **a** breaking of, violation of
infredda'tura *sf* slight cold
infreddo'lito, a *ag* cold, chilled
infruttu'oso, a *ag* fruitless
infu'ori *av* out; **all'~** outwards; **all'~ di** (*eccetto*) except, with the exception of
infuri'are *vi* to rage; ~**rsi** *vr* to fly into a rage
infusi'one *sf* infusion
in'fuso, a *pp di* **infondere** ♦ *sm* infusion
Ing. *abbr* = **ingegnere**
ingabbi'are *vt* to cage
ingaggi'are [ingad'dʒare] *vt* (*assumere con compenso*) to take on, hire; (*SPORT*) to sign on; (*MIL*) to engage; **in'gaggio** *sm* hiring; signing on
ingan'nare *vt* to deceive; (*coniuge*) to be unfaithful to; (*fisco*) to cheat; (*eludere*) to dodge, elude; (*fig: tempo*) to while away ♦ *vi* (*apparenza*) to be deceptive; ~**rsi** *vr* to be mistaken, be wrong; **ingan'nevole** *ag* deceptive

in'ganno *sm* deceit, deception; (*azione*) trick; (*menzogna, frode*) cheat, swindle; (*illusione*) illusion

ingarbugli'are [ingarbuʎ'ʎare] *vt* to tangle; (*fig*) to confuse, muddle; ~rsi *vr* to become confused *o* muddled

inge'gnarsi [indʒeɲ'ɲarsi] *vr* to do one's best, try hard; ~ per vivere to live by one's wits

inge'gnere [indʒeɲ'ɲɛre] *sm* engineer; ~ civile/navale civil/naval engineer; ingegne'ria *sf* engineering; ~ genetica genetic engineering

in'gegno [in'dʒeɲɲo] *sm* (*intelligenza*) intelligence, brains *pl*; (*capacità creativa*) ingenuity; (*disposizione*) talent; inge'gnoso, a *ag* ingenious, clever

ingelo'sire [indʒelo'zire] *vt* to make jealous ♦ *vi* (*anche*: ~rsi) to become jealous

in'gente [in'dʒɛnte] *ag* huge, enormous

ingenuità [indʒenui'ta] *sf* ingenuousness

in'genuo, a [in'dʒɛnuo] *ag* ingenuous, naïve

inge'rire [indʒe'rire] *vt* to ingest

inges'sare [indʒes'sare] *vt* (*MED*) to put in plaster; ingessa'tura *sf* plaster

Inghil'terra [ingil'tɛrra] *sf*: l'~ England

inghiot'tire [ingjot'tire] *vt* to swallow

ingial'lire [indʒal'lire] *vi* to go yellow

ingigan'tire [indʒigan'tire] *vt* to enlarge, magnify ♦ *vi* to become gigantic *o* enormous

inginocchi'arsi [indʒinok'kjarsi] *vr* to kneel (down)

ingiù [in'dʒu] *av* down, downwards

ingiunzi'one [indʒun'tsjone] *sf* injunction

ingi'uria [in'dʒurja] *sf* insult; (*fig: danno*) damage; ingiuri'are *vt* to insult, abuse; ingiuri'oso, a *ag* insulting, abusive

ingius'tizia [indʒus'tittsja] *sf* injustice

ingi'usto, a [in'dʒusto] *ag* unjust, unfair

in'glese *ag* English ♦ *sm/f* Englishman/woman ♦ *sm* (*LING*) English; gli I~i the English; andarsene *o* filare all'~ to take French leave

ingoi'are *vt* to gulp (down); (*fig*) to swallow (up)

ingol'fare *vt* (*motore*) to flood; ~rsi *vr* to flood

ingom'brare *vt* (*strada*) to block; (*stanza*) to clutter up; in'gombro, a *ag* (*strada, passaggio*) blocked ♦ *sm* obstacle; essere d'ingombro to be in the way

in'gordo, a *ag*: ~ di greedy for; (*fig*) greedy *o* avid for

in'gorgo, ghi *sm* blockage, obstruction; (*anche*: ~ stradale) traffic jam

ingoz'zare [ingot'tsare] *vt* (*animali*) to fatten; (*fig: persona*) to stuff; ~rsi *vr*: ~rsi (di) to stuff o.s. (with)

ingra'naggio [ingra'naddʒo] *sm* (*TECN*) gear; (*di orologio*) mechanism; gli ~i della burocrazia the bureaucratic machinery

ingra'nare *vi* to mesh, engage ♦ *vt* to engage; ~ la marcia to get into gear

ingrandi'mento *sm* enlargement; extension

ingran'dire *vt* (*anche FOT*) to enlarge; (*estendere*) to extend; (*OTTICA, fig*) to magnify ♦ *vi* (*anche*: ~rsi) to become larger *o* bigger; (*aumentare*) to grow, increase; (*espandersi*) to expand

ingras'sare *vt* to make fat; (*animali*) to fatten; (*AGR: terreno*) to manure; (*lubrificare*) to oil, lubricate ♦ *vi* (*anche*: ~rsi) to get fat, put on weight

in'grato, a *ag* ungrateful; (*lavoro*) thankless, unrewarding

ingredi'ente *sm* ingredient

in'gresso *sm* (*porta*) entrance; (*atrio*) hall; (*l'entrare*) entrance, entry; (*facoltà di entrare*) admission; "~ libero" "admission free"

ingros'sare *vt* to increase; (*folla, livello*) to swell ♦ *vi* (*anche*: ~rsi) to increase; to swell

in'grosso *av*: all'~ (*COMM*) wholesale; (*all'incirca*) roughly, about

ingual'cibile [ingwal'tʃibile] *ag* crease-resistant

ingua'ribile *ag* incurable

'inguine *sm* (*ANAT*) groin

ini'bire *vt* to forbid, prohibit; (*PSIC*) to inhibit; inibizi'one *sf* prohibition; inhibition

iniet'tare *vt* to inject; ~**rsi** *vr*: ~**rsi di sangue** (*occhi*) to become bloodshot; **iniezi'one** *sf* injection

inimi'carsi *vr*: ~ **con qn** to fall out with sb

inimi'cizia [inimi'tʃittsja] *sf* animosity

ininter'rotto, a *ag* unbroken; uninterrupted

iniquità *sf inv* iniquity; (*atto*) wicked action

inizi'ale [init'tsjale] *ag, sf* initial

inizi'are [init'tsjare] *vi, vt* to begin, start; ~ **qn a** to initiate sb into; (*pittura etc*) to introduce sb to; ~ **a fare qc** to start doing sth

inizia'tiva [inittsja'tiva] *sf* initiative; ~ **privata** private enterprise

i'nizio [i'nittsjo] *sm* beginning; **all'**~ at the beginning, at the start; **dare** ~ **a qc** to start sth, get sth going

innaffi'are *etc* = **annaffiare** *etc*

innal'zare [innal'tsare] *vt* (*sollevare, alzare*) to raise; (*rizzare*) to erect; ~**rsi** *vr* to rise

innamo'rare *vt* to enchant, charm; ~**rsi** *vr*: ~**rsi (di qn)** to fall in love (with sb); **innamo'rato, a** *ag* (*che nutre amore*): **innamorato (di)** in love (with); (*appassionato*): **innamorato di** very fond of ♦ *sm/f* lover; sweetheart

in'nanzi [in'nantsi] *av* (*stato in luogo*) in front, ahead; (*moto a luogo*) forward, on; (*tempo: prima*) before ♦ *prep* (*prima*) before; ~ **a** in front of

in'nato, a *ag* innate

innatu'rale *ag* unnatural

inne'gabile *ag* undeniable

innervo'sire *vt*: ~ **qn** to get on sb's nerves; ~**rsi** *vr* to get irritated *o* upset

innes'care *vt* to prime; **in'nesco, schi** *sm* primer

innes'tare *vt* (*BOT, MED*) to graft; (*TECN*) to engage; (*inserire: presa*) to insert; **in'nesto** *sm* graft; grafting *no pl*; (*TECN*) clutch; (*ELETTR*) connection

'inno *sm* hymn; ~ **nazionale** national anthem

inno'cente [inno'tʃɛnte] *ag* innocent; **inno'cenza** *sf* innocence

in'nocuo, a *ag* innocuous, harmless

inno'vare *vt* to change, make innovations in

innume'revole *ag* innumerable

ino'doro, a *ag* odourless

inol'trare *vt* (*AMM*) to pass on, forward; ~**rsi** *vr* (*addentrarsi*) to advance, go forward

i'noltre *av* besides, moreover

inon'dare *vt* to flood; **inondazi'one** *sf* flooding *no pl*; flood

inope'roso, a *ag* inactive, idle

inoppor'tuno, a *ag* untimely, ill-timed; inappropriate; (*momento*) inopportune

inorgo'glire [inorgoʎ'ʎire] *vt* to make proud ♦ *vi* (*anche*: ~**rsi**) to become proud; ~**rsi di qc** to pride o.s. on sth

inorri'dire *vt* to horrify ♦ *vi* to be horrified

inospi'tale *ag* inhospitable

inosser'vato, a *ag* (*non notato*) unobserved; (*non rispettato*) not observed, not kept

inossi'dabile *ag* stainless

inqua'drare *vt* (*foto, immagine*) to frame; (*fig*) to situate, set

inquie'tare *vt* (*turbare*) to disturb, worry; ~**rsi** *vr* to worry, become anxious; (*impazientirsi*) to get upset

inqui'eto, a *ag* restless; (*preoccupato*) worried, anxious; **inquie'tudine** *sf* anxiety, worry

inqui'lino, a *sm/f* tenant

inquina'mento *sm* pollution

inqui'nare *vt* to pollute

inqui'sire *vt, vi* to investigate; **inquisi'tore, 'trice** *ag* (*sguardo*) inquiring; **inquisizi'one** *sf* (*STORIA*) inquisition

insabbi'are *vt* (*fig: pratica*) to shelve; ~**rsi** *vr* (*arenarsi: barca*) to run aground; (*fig: pratica*) to be shelved

insac'cati *smpl* (*CUC*) sausages

insa'lata *sf* salad; ~ **mista** mixed salad; **insalati'era** *sf* salad bowl

insa'lubre *ag* unhealthy

insa'nabile *ag* (*piaga*) which cannot be healed; (*situazione*) irremediable; (*odio*) implacable

insangui'nare *vt* to stain with blood

insa'puta *sf*: **all'~ di qn** without sb knowing

insce'nare [inʃe'nare] *vt* (*TEATRO*) to stage, put on; (*fig*) to stage

insedi'are *vt* to install; **~rsi** *vr* to take up office; (*popolo, colonia*) to settle

in'segna [in'seɲɲa] *sf* sign; (*emblema*) sign, emblem; (*bandiera*) flag, banner; **~e** *sfpl* (*decorazioni*) insignia *pl*

insegna'mento [inseɲɲa'mento] *sm* teaching

inse'gnante [inseɲ'ɲante] *ag* teaching ♦ *sm/f* teacher

inse'gnare [inseɲ'ɲare] *vt, vi* to teach; **~ a qn qc** to teach sb sth; **~ a qn a fare qc** to teach sb (how) to do sth

insegui'mento *sm* pursuit, chase

insegu'ire *vt* to pursue, chase

inselvati'chire [inselvati'kire] *vi* (*anche: ~rsi*) to grow wild

insena'tura *sf* inlet, creek

insen'sato, a *ag* senseless, stupid

insen'sibile *ag* (*nervo*) insensible; (*persona*) indifferent

inse'rire *vt* to insert; (*ELETTR*) to connect; (*allegare*) to enclose; (*annuncio*) to put in, place; **~rsi** *vr* (*fig*): **~rsi in** to become part of; **in'serto** *sm* (*pubblicazione*) insert

inservi'ente *sm/f* attendant

inserzi'one [inser'tsjone] *sf* insertion; (*avviso*) advertisement; **fare un'~ sul giornale** to put an advertisement in the paper

insetti'cida, i [insetti't ʃida] *sm* insecticide

in'setto *sm* insect

in'sidia *sf* snare, trap; (*pericolo*) hidden danger; **insidi'are** *vt*: **~ la vita di qn** to make an attempt on sb's life

insi'eme *av* together ♦ *prep*: **~ a o con** together with ♦ *sm* whole; (*MAT, servizio, assortimento*) set; (*MODA*) ensemble, outfit; **tutti ~** all together; **tutto ~** all together; (*in una volta*) at one go; **nell'~** on the whole; **d'~** (*veduta also*) overall

in'signe [in'siɲɲe] *ag* (*persona*) famous, distinguished; (*città, monumento*) notable

insignifi'cante [insiɲɲifi'kante] *ag* insignificant

insi'gnire [insiɲ'ɲire] *vt*: **~ qn di** to honour *o* decorate sb with

insin'cero, a [insin't ʃero] *ag* insincere

insinda'cabile *ag* unquestionable

insinu'are *vt* (*introdurre*): **~ qc in** to slip *o* slide sth into; (*fig*) to insinuate, imply; **~rsi** *vr*: **~rsi in** to seep into; (*fig*) to creep into; to worm one's way into

insis'tente *ag* insistent; persistent

in'sistere *vi*: **~ su qc** to insist on sth; **~ in qc/a fare** (*perseverare*) to persist in sth/in doing; **insis'tito, a** *pp di* **insistere**

insoddis'fatto, a *ag* dissatisfied

insoffe'rente *ag* intolerant

insolazi'one [insolat'tsjone] *sf* (*MED*) sunstroke

inso'lente *ag* insolent; **insolen'tire** *vi* to grow insolent ♦ *vt* to insult, be rude to

in'solito, a *ag* unusual, out of the ordinary

inso'luto, a *ag* (*non risolto*) unsolved; (*non pagato*) unpaid, outstanding

in'somma *av* (*in breve, in conclusione*) in short; (*dunque*) well ♦ *escl* for heaven's sake!

in'sonne *ag* sleepless; **in'sonnia** *sf* insomnia, sleeplessness

insonno'lito, a *ag* sleepy, drowsy

insoppor'tabile *ag* unbearable

in'sorgere [in'sordʒere] *vi* (*ribellarsi*) to rise up, rebel; (*apparire*) to come up, arise

in'sorto, a *pp di* **insorgere** ♦ *sm/f* rebel, insurgent

insospet'tire *vt* to make suspicious ♦ *vi* (*anche: ~rsi*) to become suspicious

inspi'rare *vt* to breathe in, inhale

in'stabile *ag* (*carico, indole*) unstable; (*tempo*) unsettled; (*equilibrio*) unsteady

instal'lare *vt* to install; **~rsi** *vr* (*sistemarsi*): **~rsi in** to settle in; **installazi'one** *sf* installation

instan'cabile *ag* untiring, indefatigable

instau'rare *vt* to introduce, institute

instra'dare *vt*: **~ (verso)** to direct (towards)

insuc'cesso [insut't ʃesso] *sm* failure, flop

insudici'are [insudi'tʃare] *vt* to dirty;
~**rsi** *vr* to get dirty
insuffici'ente [insuffi'tʃɛnte] *ag*
insufficient; (*compito, allievo*) inadequate;
insuffici'enza *sf* insufficiency;
inadequacy; (*INS*) fail
insu'lare *ag* insular
insu'lina *sf* insulin
in'sulso, a *ag* (*sciocco*) inane, silly;
(*persona*) dull, insipid
insul'tare *vt* to insult, affront
in'sulto *sm* insult, affront
insussis'tente *ag* non-existent
intac'care *vt* (*fare tacche*) to cut into;
(*corrodere*) to corrode; (*fig: cominciare ad
usare: risparmi*) to break into; (*: ledere*) to
damage
intagli'are [intaʎ'ʎare] *vt* to carve;
in'taglio *sm* carving
intan'gibile [intan'dʒibile] *ag*
untouchable; inviolable
in'tanto *av* (*nel frattempo*) meanwhile, in
the meantime; (*per cominciare*) just to
begin with; ~ **che** while
in'tarsio *sm* inlaying *no pl*, marquetry *no
pl*; inlay
inta'sare *vt* to choke (up), block (up);
(*AUT*) to obstruct, block; ~**rsi** *vr* to become
choked *o* blocked
intas'care *vt* to pocket
in'tatto, a *ag* intact; (*puro*) unsullied
intavo'lare *vt* to start, enter into
inte'grale *ag* complete; (*pane, farina*)
wholemeal (*BRIT*), whole-wheat (*US*); (*MAT*):
calcolo ~ integral calculus
inte'grante *ag*: **parte** ~ integral part
inte'grare *vt* to complete; (*MAT*) to
integrate; ~**rsi** *vr* (*persona*) to become
integrated
integrità *sf* integrity
'integro, a *ag* (*intatto, intero*) complete,
whole; (*retto*) upright
intelaia'tura *sf* frame; (*fig*) structure,
framework
intel'letto *sm* intellect; **intellettu'ale** *ag,
sm/f* intellectual
intelli'gente [intelli'dʒɛnte] *ag* intelligent; **intelli'genza** *sf* intelligence
intem'perie *sfpl* bad weather *sg*

intempes'tivo, a *ag* untimely
inten'dente *sm*: ~ **di Finanza** inland
(*BRIT*) *o* internal (*US*) revenue officer;
inten'denza *sf*: **intendenza di Finanza**
inland (*BRIT*) *o* internal (*US*) revenue office
in'tendere *vt* (*avere intenzione*): ~ **fare
qc** to intend *o* mean to do sth;
(*comprendere*) to understand; (*udire*) to
hear; (*significare*) to mean; ~**rsi** *vr*
(*conoscere*): ~**rsi di** to know a lot about,
be a connoisseur of; (*accordarsi*) to get on
(well); **intendersela con qn** (*avere una
relazione amorosa*) to have an affair with
sb; **intendi'mento** *sm* (*intelligenza*)
understanding; (*proposito*) intention;
intendi'tore, 'trice *sm/f* connoisseur,
expert
intene'rire *vt* (*fig*) to move (to pity); ~**rsi**
vr (*fig*) to be moved
inten'sivo, a *ag* intensive
in'tenso, a *ag* intense
in'tento, a *ag* (*teso, assorto*): ~ **(a)** intent
(on), absorbed (in) ♦ *sm* aim, purpose
intenzio'nale [intentsjo'nale] *ag*
intentional
intenzi'one [inten'tsjone] *sf* intention;
(*DIR*) intent; **avere** ~ **di fare qc** to intend
to do sth, have the intention of doing sth
interat'tivo, a *ag* interactive
interca'lare *sm* pet phrase, stock phrase
♦ *vt* to insert
interca'pedine *sf* gap, cavity
intercet'tare [intertʃet'tare] *vt* to
intercept
intercity [intəsi'ti] *sm inv* (*FERR*)
≈ intercity (train)
inter'detto, a *pp di* **interdire** ♦ *ag*
forbidden, prohibited; (*sconcertato*)
dumbfounded ♦ *sm* (*REL*) interdict
inter'dire *vt* to forbid, prohibit, ban; (*REL*)
to interdict; (*DIR*) to deprive of civil
rights; **interdizi'one** *sf* prohibition, ban
interessa'mento *sm* interest
interes'sante *ag* interesting; **essere in
stato** ~ to be expecting (a baby)
interes'sare *vt* to interest; (*concernere*) to
concern, be of interest to; (*far intervenire*): ~ **qn a** to draw sb's attention to
♦ *vi*: ~ **a** to interest, matter to; ~**rsi** *vr*

(*mostrare interesse*): ~**rsi a** to take an interest in, be interested in; (*occuparsi*): ~**rsi di** to take care of
inte'resse *sm* (*anche COMM*) interest
inter'faccia, ce [inter'fattʃa] *sf* (*INFORM*) interface
interfe'renza [interfe'rɛntsa] *sf* interference
interfe'rire *vi* to interfere
interiezi'one [interjet'tsjone] *sf* exclamation, interjection
interi'ora *sfpl* entrails
interi'ore *ag* interior, inner, inside, internal; (*fig*) inner
inter'ludio *sm* (*MUS*) interlude
inter'medio, a *ag* intermediate
inter'mezzo [inter'mɛddzo] *sm* (*intervallo*) interval; (*breve spettacolo*) intermezzo
inter'nare *vt* (*arrestare*) to intern; (*MED*) to commit (to a mental institution)
internazio'nale [internattsjo'nale] *ag* international
in'terno, a *ag* (*di dentro*) internal, interior, inner; (*: mare*) inland; (*nazionale*) domestic; (*allievo*) boarding ♦ *sm* inside, interior; (*di paese*) interior; (*fodera*) lining; (*di appartamento*) flat (number); (*TEL*) extension ♦ *sm/f* (*INS*) boarder; ~**i** *smpl* (*CINEMA*) interior shots; **all'~** inside; **Ministero degli I~i** Ministry of the Interior, ≈ Home Office (*BRIT*), Department of the Interior (*US*)
in'tero, a *ag* (*integro, intatto*) whole, entire; (*completo, totale*) complete; (*numero*) whole; (*non ridotto: biglietto*) full
interpel'lare *vt* to consult
inter'porre *vt* (*ostacolo*): ~ **qc a qc** to put sth in the way of sth; (*influenza*) to use; ~ **appello** (*DIR*) to appeal; **interporsi** *vr* to intervene; **interporsi fra** (*mettersi in mezzo*) to come between; **inter'posto, a** *pp di* **interporre**
interpre'tare *vt* to interpret; **in'terprete** *sm/f* interpreter; (*TEATRO*) actor/actress, performer; (*MUS*) performer
interro'gare *vt* to question; (*INS*) to test; **interroga'tivo, a** *ag* (*occhi, sguardo*)

questioning, inquiring; (*LING*) interrogative ♦ *sm* question; (*fig*) mystery; **interroga'torio, a** *ag* interrogatory, questioning ♦ *sm* (*DIR*) questioning *no pl*; **interrogazi'one** *sf* questioning *no pl*; (*INS*) oral test
inter'rompere *vt* to interrupt; (*studi, trattative*) to break off, interrupt; ~**rsi** *vr* to break off, stop; **inter'rotto, a** *pp di* **interrompere**
interrut'tore *sm* switch
interruzi'one [interrut'tsjone] *sf* interruption; break
interse'care *vt* to intersect; ~**rsi** *vr* to intersect
inter'stizio [inter'stittsjo] *sm* interstice, crack
interur'bana *sf* trunk call, long-distance call
interur'bano, a *ag* inter-city; (*TEL: chiamata*) trunk *cpd*, long-distance; (*: telefono*) long-distance
inter'vallo *sm* interval; (*spazio*) space, gap
interve'nire *vi* (*partecipare*): ~ **a** to take part in; (*intromettersi: anche POL*) to intervene; (*MED: operare*) to operate; **inter'vento** *sm* participation; (*intromissione*) intervention; (*MED*) operation; **fare un intervento nel corso di** (*dibattito, programma*) to take part in
inter'vista *sf* interview; **intervis'tare** *vt* to interview
in'tesa *sf* understanding; (*accordo*) agreement, understanding
in'teso, a *pp di* **intendere** ♦ *ag* agreed; **non darsi per ~ di qc** to take no notice of sth
intes'tare *vt* (*lettera*) to address; (*proprietà*): ~ **a** to register in the name of; ~ **un assegno a qn** to make out a cheque to sb; **intestazi'one** *sf* heading; (*su carta da lettere*) letterhead; (*registrazione*) registration
intes'tino, a *ag* (*lotte*) internal, civil ♦ *sm* (*ANAT*) intestine
inti'mare *vt* to order, command; **intimazi'one** *sf* order, command
intimidazi'one [intimidat'tsjone] *sf*

intimidation
intimi'dire *vt* to intimidate ♦ *vi (anche:* ~*rsi)* to grow shy
intimità *sf* intimacy; privacy; *(familiarità)* familiarity
'intimo, a *ag* intimate; *(affetti, vita)* private; *(fig: profondo)* inmost ♦ *sm (persona)* intimate *o* close friend; *(dell'animo)* bottom, depths *pl;* **parti** ~**e** *(ANAT)* private parts
intimo'rire *vt* to frighten; ~*rsi vr* to become frightened
in'tingolo *sm* sauce; *(pietanza)* stew
intiriz'zire [intirid'dzire] *vt* to numb ♦ *vi (anche:* ~*rsi)* to go numb
intito'lare *vt* to give a title to; *(dedicare)* to dedicate
intolle'rabile *ag* intolerable
intolle'rante *ag* intolerant
in'tonaco, ci *o* **chi** *sm* plaster
into'nare *vt (canto)* to start to sing; *(armonizzare)* to match; ~*rsi vr (colori)* to go together; ~*rsi a (carnagione)* to suit; *(abito)* to go with, match
inton'tire *vt* to stun, daze ♦ *vi* to be stunned *o* dazed; ~*rsi vr* to be stunned *o* dazed
in'toppo *sm* stumbling block, obstacle
in'torno *av* around; ~ **a** *(attorno a)* around; *(riguardo, circa)* about
intorpi'dire *vt* to numb; *(fig)* to make sluggish ♦ *vi (anche:* ~*rsi)* to grow numb; *(fig)* to become sluggish
intossi'care *vt* to poison; **intossicazi'one** *sf* poisoning
intralci'are [intral'tʃare] *vt* to hamper, hold up
intransi'tivo, a *ag, sm* intransitive
intrapren'dente *ag* enterprising, go-ahead
intra'prendere *vt* to undertake
intrat'tabile *ag* intractable
intrat'tenere *vt* to entertain; to engage in conversation; ~*rsi vr* to linger; ~*rsi su* **qc** to dwell on sth
intrave'dere *vt* to catch a glimpse of; *(fig)* to foresee
intrecci'are [intret'tʃare] *vt (capelli)* to plait, braid; *(intessere: anche fig)* to

weave, interweave, intertwine; ~*rsi vr* to intertwine, become interwoven; ~ **le mani** to clasp one's hands; **in'treccio** *sm (fig: trama)* plot, story
intri'gare *vi* to manoeuvre *(BRIT),* maneuver *(US),* scheme; **in'trigo, ghi** *sm* plot, intrigue
in'trinseco, a, ci, che *ag* intrinsic
in'triso, a *ag:* ~ **(di)** soaked (in)
intro'durre *vt* to introduce; *(chiave etc):* ~ **qc in** to insert sth into; *(persone: far entrare)* to show in; **introdursi** *vr (moda, tecniche)* to be introduced; **introdursi in** *(persona: penetrare)* to enter; *(: entrare furtivamente)* to steal *o* slip into; **introduzi'one** *sf* introduction
in'troito *sm* income, revenue
intro'mettersi *vr* to interfere, meddle; *(interporsi)* to intervene
in'truglio [in'truʎʎo] *sm* concoction
intrusi'one *sf* intrusion; interference
in'truso, a *sm/f* intruder
intu'ire *vt* to perceive by intuition; *(rendersi conto)* to realize; **in'tuito** *sm* intuition; *(perspicacia)* perspicacity; **intuizi'one** *sf* intuition
inu'mano, a *ag* inhuman
inumi'dire *vt* to dampen, moisten; ~*rsi vr* to become damp *o* wet
i'nutile *ag* useless; *(superfluo)* pointless, unnecessary; **inutilità** *sf* uselessness; pointlessness
inva'dente *ag (fig)* interfering, nosey
in'vadere *vt* to invade; *(affollare)* to swarm into, overrun; *(sog: acque)* to flood
inva'ghirsi [inva'girsi] *vr:* ~ **di** to take a fancy to
invalidità *sf* infirmity; disability; *(DIR)* invalidity
in'valido, a *ag (infermo)* infirm, invalid; *(al lavoro)* disabled; *(DIR: nullo)* invalid ♦ *sm/f* invalid; disabled person
in'vano *av* in vain
invasi'one *sf* invasion
in'vaso, a *pp di* **invadere**
inva'sore, invadi'trice [invadi'tritʃe] *ag* invading ♦ *sm* invader
invecchi'are [invek'kjare] *vi (persona)* to grow old; *(vino, popolazione)* to age;

(*moda*) to become dated ♦ *vt* to age; (*far apparire più vecchio*) to make look older
in'vece [in'vetʃe] *av* instead; (*al contrario*) on the contrary; ~ **di** instead of
inve'ire *vi*: ~ **contro** to rail against
inven'tare *vt* to invent; (*pericoli, pettegolezzi*) to make up, invent
inven'tario *sm* inventory; (*COMM*) stocktaking *no pl*
inven'tivo, a *ag* inventive ♦ *sf* inventiveness
inven'tore *sm* inventor
invenzi'one [inven'tsjone] *sf* invention; (*bugia*) lie, story
inver'nale *ag* winter *cpd*; (*simile all'inverno*) wintry
in'verno *sm* winter
invero'simile *ag* unlikely
inversi'one *sf* inversion; reversal; **"divieto d'~"** (*AUT*) "no U-turns"
in'verso, a *ag* opposite; (*MAT*) inverse ♦ *sm* contrary, opposite; **in senso** ~ in the opposite direction; **in ordine** ~ in reverse order
inver'tire *vt* to invert, reverse; ~ **la marcia** (*AUT*) to do a U-turn; **inver'tito, a** *sm/f* homosexual
investi'gare *vt, vi* to investigate; **investiga'tore, trice** *sm/f* investigator, detective; **investigazi'one** *sf* investigation, inquiry
investi'mento *sm* (*ECON*) investment; (*scontro, urto*) crash, collision; (*incidente stradale*) road accident
inves'tire *vt* (*denaro*) to invest; (*sog: veicolo: pedone*) to knock down; (: *altro veicolo*) to crash into; (*apostrofare*) to assail; (*incaricare*): ~ **qn di** to invest sb with
invi'are *vt* to send; **invi'ato, a** *sm/f* envoy; (*STAMPA*) correspondent
in'vidia *sf* envy; **invidi'are** *vt*: **invidiare qn (per qc)** to envy sb for sth; **invidiare qc a qn** to envy sb sth; **invidi'oso, a** *ag* envious
in'vio, 'vii *sm* sending; (*insieme di merci*) consignment
invipe'rito, a *ag* furious
invischi'are [invis'kjare] *vt* (*fig*): ~ **qn in**

to involve sb in; **~rsi** *vr*: **~rsi (con qn/in qc)** to get mixed up *o* involved (with sb/in sth)
invi'sibile *ag* invisible
invi'tare *vt* to invite; ~ **qn a fare** to invite sb to do; **invi'tato, a** *sm/f* guest; **in'vito** *sm* invitation
invo'care *vt* (*chiedere: aiuto, pace*) to cry out for; (*appellarsi: la legge, Dio*) to appeal to, invoke
invogli'are [invoʎ'ʎare] *vt*: ~ **qn a fare** to tempt sb to do, induce sb to do
involon'tario, a *ag* (*errore*) unintentional; (*gesto*) involuntary
invol'tino *sm* (*CUC*) roulade
in'volto *sm* (*pacco*) parcel; (*fagotto*) bundle
in'volucro *sm* cover, wrapping
involuzi'one [involut'tsjone] *sf* (*di stile*) convolutedness; (*regresso*): **subire un'~** to regress
inzacche'rare [intsakke'rare] *vt* to spatter with mud
inzup'pare [intsup'pare] *vt* to soak; **~rsi** *vr* to get soaked
'io *pron* I ♦ *sm inv*: **l'~** the ego, the self; ~ **stesso(a)** I myself
i'odio *sm* iodine
l'onio *sm*: **lo ~, il mar** ~ the Ionian (Sea)
ipermer'cato *sm* hypermarket
ipertensi'one *sf* high blood pressure, hypertension
ip'nosi *sf* hypnosis; **ipno'tismo** *sm* hypnotism; **ipnotiz'zare** *vt* to hypnotize
ipocri'sia *sf* hypocrisy
i'pocrita, i, e *ag* hypocritical ♦ *sm/f* hypocrite
ipo'teca, che *sf* mortgage; **ipote'care** *vt* to mortgage
i'potesi *sf inv* hypothesis; **ipo'tetico, a, ci, che** *ag* hypothetical
'ippica *sf* horseracing
'ippico, a, ci, che *ag* horse *cpd*
ippocas'tano *sm* horse chestnut
ip'podromo *sm* racecourse
ippo'potamo *sm* hippopotamus
'ira *sf* anger, wrath
l'ran *sm*: **l'~** Iran
l'raq *sm*: **l'~** Iraq

'**iride** *sf* (*arcobaleno*) rainbow; (*ANAT, BOT*) iris

Ir'landa *sf*: **l'~** Ireland; **l'~ del Nord** Northern Ireland, Ulster; **la Repubblica d'~** Eire, the Republic of Ireland; **irlan'dese** *ag* Irish ♦ *sm/f* Irishman/woman; **gli Irlandesi** the Irish

iro'nia *sf* irony; **i'ronico, a, ci, che** *ag* ironic(al)

irradi'are *vt* to radiate; (*sog: raggi di luce: illuminare*) to shine on ♦ *vi* (*diffondersi: anche: ~rsi*) to radiate; **irradiazi'one** *sf* radiation

irragio'nevole [irradʒo'nevole] *ag* irrational; unreasonable

irrazio'nale [irrattsjo'nale] *ag* irrational

irre'ale *ag* unreal

irrecupe'rabile *ag* irretrievable; (*fig: persona*) irredeemable

irrecu'sabile *ag* (*offerta*) not to be refused; (*prova*) irrefutable

irrego'lare *ag* irregular; (*terreno*) uneven

irremo'vibile *ag* (*fig*) unshakeable, unyielding

irrepa'rabile *ag* irreparable; (*fig*) inevitable

irrepe'ribile *ag* nowhere to be found

irrequi'eto, a *ag* restless

irresis'tibile *ag* irresistible

irrespon'sabile *ag* irresponsible

irridu'cibile [irridu't∫ibile] *ag* irreducible; (*fig*) indomitable

irri'gare *vt* (*annaffiare*) to irrigate; (*sog: fiume etc*) to flow through; **irrigazi'one** *sf* irrigation

irrigi'dire [irridʒi'dire] *vt* to stiffen; **~rsi** *vr* to stiffen

irri'sorio, a *ag* derisory

irri'tare *vt* (*mettere di malumore*) to irritate, annoy; (*MED*) to irritate; **~rsi** *vr* (*stizzirsi*) to become irritated *o* annoyed; (*MED*) to become irritated; **irritazi'one** *sf* irritation; annoyance

ir'rompere *vi*: **~ in** to burst into

irro'rare *vt* to sprinkle; (*AGR*) to spray

irru'ente *ag* (*fig*) impetuous, violent

irruzi'one [irrut'tsjone] *sf*: **fare ~ in** to burst into; (*sog: polizia*) to raid

'**irto, a** *ag* bristly; **~ di** bristling with

is'critto, a *pp di* **iscrivere** ♦ *sm/f* member; **per** *o* **in ~** in writing

is'crivere *vt* to register, enter; (*persona*): **~ (a)** to register (in), enrol (in); **~rsi** *vr*: **~rsi (a)** (*club, partito*) to join; (*università*) to register *o* enrol (at); (*esame, concorso*) to register *o* enter (for); **iscrizi'one** *sf* (*epigrafe etc*) inscription; (*a scuola, società*) enrolment, registration; (*registrazione*) registration

Is'lam *sm*: **l'~** Islam

Is'landa *sf*: **l'~** Iceland

'**isola** *sf* island; **~ pedonale** (*AUT*) pedestrian precinct

isola'mento *sm* isolation; (*TECN*) insulation

iso'lante *ag* insulating ♦ *sm* insulator

iso'lare *vt* to isolate; (*TECN*) to insulate; (*: acusticamente*) to soundproof; **iso'lato, a** *ag* isolated; insulated ♦ *sm* (*edificio*) block

ispetto'rato *sm* inspectorate

ispet'tore *sm* inspector

ispezio'nare [ispettsjo'nare] *vt* to inspect

ispezi'one [ispet'tsjone] *sf* inspection

'**ispido, a** *ag* bristly, shaggy

ispi'rare *vt* to inspire; **~rsi** *vr*: **~rsi a** to draw one's inspiration from

Isra'ele *sm*: **l'~** Israel; **israeli'ano, a** *ag, sm/f* Israeli

is'sare *vt* to hoist

istan'taneo, a *ag* instantaneous ♦ *sf* (*FOT*) snapshot

is'tante *sm* instant, moment; **all'~, sull'~** instantly, immediately

is'tanza [is'tantsa] *sf* petition, request

is'terico, a, ci, che *ag* hysterical

iste'rismo *sm* hysteria

isti'gare *vt* to incite; **istigazi'one** *sf* incitement; **istigazione a delinquere** (*DIR*) incitement to crime

is'tinto *sm* instinct

istitu'ire *vt* (*fondare*) to institute, found; (*porre: confronto*) to establish; (*intraprendere: inchiesta*) to set up

isti'tuto *sm* institute; (*di università*) department; (*ente, DIR*) institution; **~ di bellezza** beauty salon

istituzi'one [istitut'tsjone] *sf* institution
'istmo *sm* (GEO) isthmus
istra'dare *vt* = **instradare**
'istrice ['istritʃe] *sm* porcupine
istri'one (peg) *sm* ham actor
istru'ire *vt* (insegnare) to teach; (ammaestrare) to train; (informare) to instruct, inform; (DIR) to prepare;
  istrut'tore, 'trice *sm/f* instructor ♦ *ag*: **giudice istruttore** examining (BRIT) o committing (US) magistrate; **istrut'toria** *sf* (DIR) (preliminary) investigation and hearing; **istruzi'one** *sf* education; training; (direttiva) instruction; (DIR) = **istruttoria**
l'talia *sf*: **l'~** Italy
itali'ano, a *ag* Italian ♦ *sm/f* Italian ♦ *sm* (LING) Italian; **gli I~i** the Italians
itine'rario *sm* itinerary
itte'rizia [itte'rittsja] *sf* (MED) jaundice
'ittico, a, ci, che *ag* fish *cpd*; fishing *cpd*
lugos'lavia *sf* = **Jugoslavia**
iugos'lavo, a *ag, sm/f* = **jugoslavo, a**
i'uta *sf* jute
I.V.A. ['iva] *sigla f* (= imposta sul valore aggiunto) VAT

J

jazz [dʒaz] *sm* jazz
jeans [dʒinz] *smpl* jeans
Jugos'lavia [jugoz'lavja] *sf*: **la ~** Yugoslavia; **jugos'lavo, a** *ag, sm/f* Yugoslav(ian)
'juta ['juta] *sf* = **iuta**

K

K *abbr* (INFORM) K
k *abbr* (= kilo) k
karatè *sm* karate
Kg *abbr* (= chilogrammo) kg
'killer *sm inv* gunman, hired gun
km *abbr* (= chilometro) km
'krapfen *sm inv* (CUC) doughnut

L

l' *det vedi* **la**; **lo**; **il**
la¹ (dav V l') *det f* the ♦ *pron* (oggetto: persona) her; (: cosa) it; (: forma di cortesia) you; *vedi anche* **il**
la² *sm inv* (MUS) A; (: solfeggiando la scala) la
là *av* there; **di ~** (da quel luogo) from there; (in quel luogo) in there; (dall'altra parte) over there; **di ~ di** beyond; **per di ~** that way; **più in ~** further on; (tempo) later on; **fatti in ~** move up; **~ dentro/sopra/sotto** in/up (o on)/under there; *vedi* **quello**
'labbro (pl(f): **labbra**: solo nel senso ANAT) *sm* lip
labi'rinto *sm* labyrinth, maze
labora'torio *sm* (di ricerca) laboratory; (di arti, mestieri) workshop; **~ linguistico** language laboratory
labori'oso, a *ag* (faticoso) laborious; (attivo) hard-working
labu'rista, i, e *ag* Labour (BRIT) *cpd* ♦ *sm/f* Labour Party member (BRIT)
'lacca, che *sf* lacquer
'laccio ['lattʃo] *sm* noose; (legaccio, tirante) lasso; (di scarpa) lace; **~ emostatico** tourniquet
lace'rare [latʃe'rare] *vt* to tear to shreds, lacerate; **~rsi** *vr* to tear; **'lacero, a** *ag* (logoro) torn, tattered; (MED) lacerated
'lacrima *sf* tear; **in ~e** in tears; **lacri'mare** *vi* to water; **lacri'mogeno, a** *ag*: **gas lacrimogeno** tear gas
la'cuna *sf* (fig) gap
'ladro *sm* thief; **ladro'cinio** *sm* theft, larceny
laggiù [lad'dʒu] *av* down there; (di là) over there
la'gnarsi [laɲ'ɲarsi] *vr*: **~ (di)** to complain (about)
'lago, ghi *sm* lake
'lagrima *etc* = **lacrima** *etc*
la'guna *sf* lagoon
'laico, a, ci, che *ag* (apostolato) lay; (vita) secular; (scuola) non-

denominational ♦ *sm/f* layman/woman ♦ *sm* lay brother

'**lama** *sm inv* (*ZOOL*) llama; (*REL*) lama ♦ *sf* blade

lam'bire *vt* to lick; to lap

lamen'tare *vt* to lament; **~rsi** *vr* (*emettere lamenti*) to moan, groan; (*rammaricarsi*): **~rsi (di)** to complain (about); **lamen'tela** *sf* complaining *no pl*; **lamen'tevole** *ag* (*voce*) complaining, plaintive; (*destino*) pitiful; **la'mento** *sm* moan, groan; wail; **lamen'toso, a** *ag* plaintive

la'metta *sf* razor blade

lami'era *sf* sheet metal

'**lamina** *sf* (*lastra sottile*) thin sheet (*o* layer *o* plate); **~ d'oro** gold leaf; gold foil; **lami'nare** *vt* to laminate; **lami'nato, a** *ag* laminated; (*tessuto*) lamé ♦ *sm* laminate

'**lampada** *sf* lamp; **~ a gas** gas lamp; **~ a spirito** blow lamp (*BRIT*), blow torch (*US*); **~ da tavolo** table lamp

lampa'dario *sm* chandelier

lampa'dina *sf* light bulb; **~ tascabile** pocket torch (*BRIT*) *o* flashlight (*US*)

lam'pante *ag* (*fig: evidente*) crystal clear, evident

lampeggi'are [lamped'dʒare] *vi* (*luce, furi*) to flash ♦ *vb impers*: **lampeggia** there's lightning; **lampeggia'tore** *sm* (*AUT*) indicator

lampi'one *sm* street light *o* lamp (*BRIT*)

'**lampo** *sm* (*METEOR*) flash of lightning; (*di luce, fig*) flash; **~i** *smpl* lightning *no pl* ♦ *ag inv*: **cerniera ~** zip (fastener) (*BRIT*), zipper (*US*); **guerra ~** blitzkrieg

lam'pone *sm* raspberry

'**lana** *sf* wool; **~ d'acciaio** steel wool; **pura ~ vergine** pure new wool; **~ di vetro** glass wool

lan'cetta [lan'tʃetta] *sf* (*indice*) pointer, needle; (*di orologio*) hand

'**lancia** [ˈlantʃa] *sf* (*arma*) lance; (: *picca*) spear; (*di pompa antincendio*) nozzle; (*imbarcazione*) launch

lanciafi'amme [lantʃaˈfjamme] *sm inv* flamethrower

lanci'are [lanˈtʃare] *vt* to throw, hurl,

fling; (*SPORT*) to throw; (*far partire: automobile*) to get up to full speed; (*bombe*) to drop; (*razzo, prodotto, moda*) to launch; **~rsi** *vr*: **~rsi contro/su** to throw *o* hurl *o* fling o.s. against/on; **~rsi in** (*fig*) to embark on

lanci'nante [lantʃiˈnante] *ag* (*dolore*) shooting, throbbing; (*grido*) piercing

'**lancio** [ˈlantʃo] *sm* throwing *no pl*; throw; dropping *no pl*; drop; launching *no pl*; launch; **~ del peso** putting the shot

'**landa** *sf* (*GEO*) moor

'**languido, a** *ag* (*fiacco*) languid, weak; (*tenero, malinconico*) languishing

langu'ore *sm* weakness, languor

lani'ficio [laniˈfitʃo] *sm* woollen mill

la'noso, a *ag* woolly

lan'terna *sf* lantern; (*faro*) lighthouse

la'nugine [laˈnudʒine] *sf* down

lapi'dare *vt* to stone

lapi'dario, a *ag* (*fig*) terse

'**lapide** *sf* (*di sepolcro*) tombstone; (*commemorativa*) plaque

'**lapis** *sm inv* pencil

Lap'ponia *sf* Lapland

'**lapsus** *sm inv* slip

la'ptop [læˈptɔp] *sm inv* laptop (computer)

'**lardo** *sm* bacon fat, lard

lar'ghezza [larˈgettsa] *sf* width; breadth; looseness; generosity; **~ di vedute** broad-mindedness

'**largo, a, ghi, ghe** *ag* wide; broad; (*maniche*) wide; (*abito: troppo ampio*) loose; (*fig*) generous ♦ *sm* width; breadth; (*mare aperto*): **il ~** the open sea ♦ *sf*: **stare** *o* **tenersi alla ~a (da qn/qc)** to keep one's distance (from sb/sth), keep away (from sb/sth); **~ due metri** two metres wide; **~ di spalle** broad-shouldered; **di ~ghe vedute** broad-minded; **su ~a scala** on a large scale; **di manica ~a** generous, open-handed; **al ~ di Genova** off (the coast of) Genoa; **farsi ~ tra la folla** to push one's way through the crowd

'**larice** [ˈlaritʃe] *sm* (*BOT*) larch

larin'gite [larinˈdʒite] *sf* laryngitis

'**larva** *sf* larva; (*fig*) shadow

la'sagne [la'zaɲɲe] *sfpl* lasagna *sg*
lasci'are [laʃ'ʃare] *vt* to leave;
(*abbandonare*) to leave, abandon, give up;
(*cessare di tenere*) to let go of ♦ *vi*: ~
fare qn to let sb do ♦ *vi*: ~ di fare
(*smettere*) to stop doing; ~rsi andare/
truffare to let o.s. go/be cheated; ~
andare *o* correre *o* perdere to let things
go their own way; ~ stare qc/qn to leave
sth/sb alone
'lascito ['laʃʃito] *sm* (*DIR*) legacy
'laser ['lazer] *ag, sm inv*: (raggio) ~ laser
(beam)
lassa'tivo, a *ag, sm* laxative
'lasso *sm*: ~ di tempo interval, lapse of
time
lassù *av* up there
'lastra *sf* (*di pietra*) slab; (*di metallo, FOT*)
plate; (*di ghiaccio, vetro*) sheet;
(*radiografica*) X-ray (plate)
lastri'cato *sm*, 'lastrico, ci *o*chi *sm*
paving
late'rale *ag* lateral, side *cpd*; (*uscita,
ingresso etc*) side *cpd* ♦ *sm* (*CALCIO*) half-
back
late'rizio [late'rittsjo] *sm* (perforated)
brick
lati'fondo *sm* large estate
la'tino, a *ag* *sm* Latin; ~-ameri'cano, a
ag Latin-American
lati'tante *sm/f* fugitive (from justice)
lati'tudine *sf* latitude
'lato, a *ag* (*fig*) wide, broad ♦ *sm* side;
(*fig*) aspect, point of view; in senso ~
broadly speaking
la'trare *vi* to bark
la'trina *sf* public lavatory
'latta *sf* tin (plate); (*recipiente*) tin, can
lat'taio, a *sm/f* milkman/woman;
dairyman/woman
lat'tante *ag* unweaned
'latte *sm* milk; ~ detergente cleansing
milk *o* lotion; ~ in polvere dried *o*
powdered milk; ~ scremato skimmed
milk; latte'ria *sf* dairy; latti'cini *smpl*
dairy products
lat'tina *sf* (*di birra etc*) can
lat'tuga, ghe *sf* lettuce
'laurea *sf* degree; laure'are *vt* to confer a

degree on; laurearsi *vr* to graduate;
laure'ato, a *ag, sm/f* graduate
'lauro *sm* laurel
'lauto, a *ag* (*pranzo, mancia*) lavish
'lava *sf* lava
la'vabo *sm* washbasin
la'vaggio [la'vaddʒo] *sm* washing *no pl*;
~ del cervello brainwashing *no pl*
la'vagna [la'vaɲɲa] *sf* (*GEO*) slate; (*di
scuola*) blackboard
la'vanda *sf* (*anche MED*) wash; (*BOT*)
lavender; lavan'daia *sf* washerwoman;
lavande'ria *sf* laundry; lavanderia
automatica launderette; lavanderia a
secco dry-cleaner's; lavan'dino *sm* sink
lavapi'atti *sm/f* dishwasher
la'vare *vt* to wash; ~rsi *vr* to wash, have
a wash; ~ a secco to dry-clean; ~rsi le
mani/i denti to wash one's hands/clean
one's teeth
lava'secco *sm o f inv* drycleaner's
lavasto'viglie [lavasto'viλλe] *sm o f inv*
(*macchina*) dishwasher
lava'toio *sm* (public) washhouse
lava'trice [lava'tritʃe] *sf* washing
machine
lava'tura *sf* washing *no pl*; ~ di piatti
dishwater
lavo'rante *sm/f* worker
lavo'rare *vi* to work; (*fig: bar, studio etc*)
to do good business ♦ *vt* to work; ~rsi qn
(*persuaderlo*) to work on sb; ~ a to work
on; ~ a maglia to knit; lavora'tivo, a *ag*
working; lavora'tore, 'trice *sm/f* worker
♦ *ag* working; lavorazi'one *sf* (*gen*)
working; (*di legno, pietra*) carving; (*di
film*) making; (*di prodotto*) manufacture;
(*modo di esecuzione*) workmanship;
lavo'rio *sm* intense activity
la'voro *sm* work; (*occupazione*) job, work
no pl; (*opera*) piece of work, job; (*ECON*)
labour; ~i forzati hard labour *sg*; ~i
pubblici public works
le *det fpl* the ♦ *pron* (*oggetto*) them; (: *a
lei, a essa*) (to) her; (: *forma di cortesia*)
(to) you; *vedi anche* il
le'ale *ag* loyal; (*sincero*) sincere; (*onesto*)
fair; lealtà *sf* loyalty; sincerity; fairness
'lebbra *sf* leprosy

'lecca 'lecca *sm inv* lollipop
leccapi'edi *(peg) sm/f inv* toady, bootlicker
lec'care *vt* to lick; *(sog: gatto: latte etc)* to lick *o* lap up; *(fig)* to flatter; ~rsi i baffi to lick one's lips
'leccio ['lettʃo] *sm* holm oak, ilex
leccor'nia *sf* titbit, delicacy
'lecito, a ['lɛtʃito] *ag* permitted, allowed
'ledere *vt* to damage, injure
'lega, ghe *sf* league; *(di metalli)* alloy
le'gaccio ['gattʃo] *sm* string, lace
le'gale *ag* legal ♦ *sm* lawyer;
legaliz'zare *vt* to authenticate; *(regolarizzare)* to legalize
le'game *sm (corda, fig: affettivo)* tie, bond; *(nesso logico)* link, connection
le'gare *vt (prigioniero, capelli, cane)* to tie (up); *(libro)* to bind; *(CHIM)* to alloy; *(fig: collegare)* to bind, join ♦ *vi (far lega)* to unite; *(fig)* to get on well
lega'tario, a *sm/f (DIR)* legatee
le'gato *sm (REL)* legate; *(DIR)* legacy, bequest
lega'tura *sf (di libro)* binding; *(MUS)* ligature
le'genda [le'dʒɛnda] *sf (di carta geografica etc)* = leggenda
'legge ['leddʒe] *sf* law
leg'genda [led'dʒɛnda] *sf (narrazione)* legend; *(di carta geografica etc)* key, legend
'leggere ['lɛddʒere] *vt, vi* to read
legge'rezza [leddʒe'rettsa] *sf* lightness; thoughtlessness; fickleness
leg'gero, a [led'dʒɛro] *ag* light; *(agile, snello)* nimble, agile, light; *(tè, caffè)* weak; *(fig: non grave, piccolo)* slight; *(: spensierato)* thoughtless; *(: incostante)* fickle; free and easy; alla ~a thoughtlessly
leggi'adro, a [led'dʒadro] *ag* pretty, lovely; *(movimenti)* graceful
leg'gio, 'gii [led'dʒio] *sm* lectern; *(MUS)* music stand
legisla'tura [ledʒizla'tura] *sf* legislature
legislazi'one [ledʒizlat'tsjone] *sf* legislation
le'gittimo, a [le'dʒittimo] *ag* legitimate; *(fig: giustificato, lecito)* justified, legitimate; ~a difesa *(DIR)* self-defence
'legna ['leɲɲa] *sf* firewood; le'gname *sm* wood, timber
'legno ['leɲɲo] *sm* wood; *(pezzo di ~)* piece of wood; di ~ wooden; ~ compensato plywood; le'gnoso, a *ag* wooden; woody; *(carne)* tough
le'gumi *smpl (BOT)* pulses
'lei *pron (soggetto)* she; *(oggetto: per dare rilievo, con preposizione)* her; *(forma di cortesia: anche: L~)* you ♦ *sm:* dare del ~ a qn to address sb as "lei"; ~ stessa she herself; you yourself
'lembo *sm (di abito, strada)* edge; *(striscia sottile: di terra)* strip
'lemma, i *sm* headword
'lemme 'lemme *av* (very) very slowly
'lena *sf (fig)* energy, stamina
le'nire *vt* to soothe
'lente *sf (OTTICA)* lens *sg;* ~ d'ingrandimento magnifying glass; ~i a contatto *o* corneali contact lenses
len'tezza [len'tettsa] *sf* slowness
len'ticchia [len'tikkja] *sf (BOT)* lentil
len'tiggine [len'tiddʒine] *sf* freckle
'lento, a *ag* slow; *(molle: fune)* slack; *(non stretto: vite, abito)* loose ♦ *sm (ballo)* slow dance
'lenza ['lɛntsa] *sf* fishing-line
lenzu'olo [len'tswɔlo] *sm* sheet; ~a *sfpl* pair of sheets
le'one *sm* lion; *(dello zodiaco):* L~ Leo
lepo'rino, a *ag:* labbro ~ harelip
'lepre *sf* hare
'lercio, a, ci, cie ['lɛrtʃo] *ag* filthy
'lesbica, che *sf* lesbian
lesi'nare *vt* to be stingy with ♦ *vi:* ~ (su) to skimp (on), be stingy (with)
lesi'one *sf (MED)* lesion; *(DIR)* injury, damage; *(EDIL)* crack
'leso, a *pp di* ledere ♦ *ag (offeso)* injured; parte ~a *(DIR)* injured party
les'sare *vt (CUC)* to boil
'lessico, ci *sm* vocabulary; lexicon
'lesso, a *ag* boiled ♦ *sm* boiled meat
'lesto, a *ag* quick; *(agile)* nimble; ~ di mano *(per rubare)* light-fingered; *(per picchiare)* free with one's fists

le'tale *ag* lethal; fatal

leta'maio *sm* dunghill

le'tame *sm* manure, dung

le'targo, ghi *sm* lethargy; (*ZOOL*) hibernation

le'tizia [le'tittsja] *sf* joy, happiness

'lettera *sf* letter; ~e *sfpl* (*letteratura*) literature *sg*; (*studi umanistici*) arts (subjects); alla ~ literally; in ~e in words, in full; lette'rale *ag* literal

lette'rario, a *ag* literary

lette'rato, a *ag* well-read, scholarly

lettera'tura *sf* literature

let'tiga, ghe *sf* (*portantina*) litter; (*barella*) stretcher

let'tino *sm* cot (*BRIT*), crib (*US*)

'letto, a *pp di* leggere ♦ *sm* bed; andare a ~ to go to bed; ~ a castello bunk beds *pl*; ~ a una piazza/a due piazze *o* matrimoniale single/double bed

let'tore, 'trice *sm/f* reader; (*INS*) (foreign language) assistant (*BRIT*), (foreign) teaching assistant (*US*) ♦ *sm* (*TECN*): ~ ottico optical character reader

let'tura *sf* reading

leuce'mia [leutʃe'mia] *sf* leukaemia

'leva *sf* lever; (*MIL*) conscription; far ~ su qn to work on sb; ~ del cambio (*AUT*) gear lever

le'vante *sm* east; (*vento*) East wind; il L~ the Levant

le'vare *vt* (*occhi, braccio*) to raise; (*sollevare, togliere: tassa, divieto*) to lift; (*indumenti*) to take off, remove; (*rimuovere*) to take away; (: *dal di sopra*) to take off; (: *dal di dentro*) to take out; ~rsi *vr* to get up; (*sole*) to rise; le'vata *sf* (*di posta*) collection

leva'toio, a *ag*: ponte ~ drawbridge

leva'tura *sf* intelligence, mental capacity

levi'gare *vt* to smooth; (*con carta vetrata*) to sand

levri'ere *sm* greyhound

lezi'one [let'tsjone] *sf* lesson; (*all'università, sgridata*) lecture; fare ~ to teach; to lecture

lezi'oso, a [let'tsjoso] *ag* affected; simpering

'lezzo ['leddzo] *sm* stench, stink

li *pron pl* (*oggetto*) them

lì *av* there; di *o* da ~ from there; per di ~ that way; di ~ a pochi giorni a few days later; ~ per ~ there and then; at first; essere *o* (~) per fare to be on the point of doing, be about to do; ~ dentro in there; ~ sotto under there; ~ sopra on there; up there; *vedi* quello

liba'nese *ag*, *sm/f* Lebanese *inv*

Li'bano *sm*: il ~ the Lebanon

'libbra *sf* (*peso*) pound

li'beccio [li'bettʃo] *sm* south-west wind

li'bello *sm* libel

li'bellula *sf* dragonfly

libe'rale *ag*, *sm/f* liberal

liberaliz'zare [liberalid'dzare] *vt* to liberalize

libe'rare *vt* (*rendere libero: prigioniero*) to release; (: *popolo*) to free, liberate; (*sgombrare: passaggio*) to clear; (: *stanza*) to vacate; (*produrre: energia*) to release; ~rsi *vr*: ~rsi di qc/qn to get rid of sth/sb; libera'tore, 'trice *ag* liberating ♦ *sm/f* liberator; liberazi'one *sf* liberation, freeing; release; rescuing

'libero, a *ag* free; (*strada*) clear; (*non occupato: posto etc*) vacant; not taken; empty; not engaged; ~ di fare qc free to do sth; ~ da free from; ~ arbitrio free will; ~ professionista self-employed professional person; ~ scambio free trade; libertà *sf inv* freedom; (*tempo disponibile*) free time ♦ *sfpl* (*licenza*) liberties; in libertà provvisoria/vigilata released without bail/on probation

'Libia *sf*: la ~ Libya; 'libico, a, ci, che *ag*, *sm/f* Libyan

li'bidine *sf* lust

li'braio *sm* bookseller

li'brario, a *ag* book *cpd*

li'brarsi *vr* to hover

libre'ria *sf* (*bottega*) bookshop; (*stanza*) library; (*mobile*) bookcase

li'bretto *sm* booklet; (*taccuino*) notebook; (*MUS*) libretto; ~ degli assegni cheque book; ~ di circolazione (*AUT*) logbook; ~ di risparmio (*savings*) bank-book, passbook; ~ universitario student's report book '**libro** *sm* book; **~ bianco** (*POL*) white paper; **~ di cassa** cash book; **~ mastro** ledger; **~ paga** payroll

li'cenza [li'tʃɛntsa] *sf* (*permesso*) permission, leave; (*di pesca, caccia, circolazione*) permit, licence; (*MIL*) leave; (*INS*) school leaving certificate; (*libertà*) liberty; licence; licentiousness; **andare in ~** (*MIL*) to go on leave

licenzia'mento [litʃentsja'mento] *sm* dismissal

licenzi'are [litʃen'tsjare] *vt* (*impiegato*) to dismiss; (*INS*) to award a certificate to; **~rsi** *vr* (*impiegato*) to resign, hand in one's notice; (*INS*) to obtain one's school-leaving certificate

li'ceo [li'tʃɛo] *sm* (*INS*) secondary (*BRIT*) o high (*US*) school (*for 14- to 19-year-olds*)

'**lido** *sm* beach, shore

li'eto, a *ag* happy, glad; "**molto ~**" (*nelle presentazioni*) "pleased to meet you"

li'eve *ag* light; (*di poco conto*) slight; (*sommesso: voce*) faint, soft

lievi'tare *vi* (*anche fig*) to rise ♦ *vt* to leaven

li'evito *sm* yeast; **~ di birra** brewer's yeast

'**ligio, a, gi, gie** ['lidʒo] *ag* faithful, loyal

'**lilla** *sm inv* lilac

'**lillà** *sm inv* = **lilla**

'**lima** *sf* file

limacci'oso, a [limat'tʃoso] *ag* slimy; muddy

li'mare *vt* to file (down); (*fig*) to polish

'**limbo** *sm* (*REL*) limbo

li'metta *sf* nail file

limi'tare *vt* to limit, restrict; (*circoscrivere*) to bound, surround; **limita'tivo, a** *ag* limiting, restricting; **limi'tato, a** *ag* limited, restricted

'**limite** *sm* limit; (*confine*) border, boundary; **~ di velocità** speed limit

li'mitrofo, a *ag* neighbouring

limo'nata *sf* lemonade (*BRIT*), (lemon) soda (*US*); lemon squash (*BRIT*), lemonade (*US*)

li'mone *sm* (*pianta*) lemon tree; (*frutto*) lemon

'**limpido, a** *ag* clear; (*acqua*) limpid, clear

'**lince** ['lintʃe] *sf* lynx

linci'are *vt* to lynch

'**lindo, a** *ag* tidy, spick and span; (*biancheria*) clean

'**linea** *sf* line; (*di mezzi pubblici di trasporto: itinerario*) route; (*: servizio*) service; **a grandi ~e** in outline; **mantenere la ~** to look after one's figure; **aereo di ~** airliner; **nave di ~** liner; **volo di ~** scheduled flight; **~ aerea** airline; **~ di partenza/d'arrivo** (*SPORT*) starting/finishing line; **~ di tiro** line of fire

linea'menti *smpl* features; (*fig*) outlines

line'are *ag* linear; (*fig*) coherent, logical

line'etta *sf* (*trattino*) dash; (*d'unione*) hyphen

lin'gotto *sm* ingot, bar

'**lingua** *sf* (*ANAT, CUC*) tongue; (*idioma*) language; **mostrare la ~** to stick out one's tongue; **di ~ italiana** Italian-speaking; **~ madre** mother tongue; **una ~ di terra** a spit of land

lingu'aggio [lin'gwaddʒo] *sm* language

lingu'etta *sf* (*di strumento*) reed; (*di scarpa, TECN*) tongue; (*di busta*) flap

lingu'istica *sf* linguistics *sg*

'**lino** *sm* (*pianta*) flax; (*tessuto*) linen

li'noleum *sm inv* linoleum, lino

liposuzi'one [liposut'tsjone] *sf* liposuction

lique'fare *vt* (*render liquido*) to liquefy; (*fondere*) to melt; **~rsi** *vr* to liquefy; to melt

liqui'dare *vt* (*società, beni; persona: uccidere*) to liquidate; (*persona: sbarazzarsene*) to get rid of; (*conto, problema*) to settle; (*COMM: merce*) to sell off, clear; **liquidazi'one** *sf* liquidation; settlement; clearance sale

liquidità *sf* liquidity

'**liquido, a** *ag, sm* liquid; **~ per freni** brake fluid

liqui'rizia [likwi'rittsja] *sf* liquorice

li'quore *sm* liqueur

'**lira** *sf* (*unità monetaria*) lira; (*MUS*) lyre; **~ sterlina** pound sterling

'**lirica, che** *sf* (*poesia*) lyric poetry;

(*componimento poetico*) lyric; (*MUS*) opera

'lirico, a, ci, che *ag* lyric(al); (*MUS*) lyric; **cantante/teatro** ~ opera singer/house

'lisca, sche *sf* (*di pesce*) fishbone

lisci'are [liʃ'ʃare] *vt* to smooth; (*fig*) to flatter

'liscio, a, sci, sce ['liʃʃo] *ag* smooth; (*capelli*) straight; (*mobile*) plain; (*bevanda alcolica*) neat; (*fig*) straightforward, simple ♦ *av*: **andare** ~ to go smoothly; **passarla** ~**a** to get away with it

'liso, a *ag* worn out, threadbare

'lista *sf* (*striscia*) strip; (*elenco*) list; ~ **elettorale** electoral roll; ~ **delle vivande** menu

lis'tino *sm* list; ~ **dei cambi** (foreign) exchange rate; ~ **dei prezzi** price list

'lite *sf* quarrel, argument; (*DIR*) lawsuit

liti'gare *vi* to quarrel; (*DIR*) to litigate

li'tigio [li'tidʒo] *sm* quarrel; **litigi'oso, a** *ag* quarrelsome; (*DIR*) litigious

litogra'fia *sf* (*sistema*) lithography; (*stampa*) lithograph

lito'rale *ag* coastal, coast *cpd* ♦ *sm* coast

'litro *sm* litre

livel'lare *vt* to level, make level; ~**rsi** *vr* to become level; (*fig*) to level out, balance out

li'vello *sm* level; (*fig*) level, standard; **ad alto** ~ (*fig*) high-level; ~ **del mare** sea level

'livido, a *ag* livid; (*per percosse*) bruised, black and blue; (*cielo*) leaden ♦ *sm* bruise

li'vore *sm* malice, spite

Li'vorno *sf* Livorno, Leghorn

li'vrea *sf* livery

'lizza ['littsa] *sf* lists *pl*; **scendere in** ~ (*anche fig*) to enter the lists

lo (*dav s impura, gn, pn, ps, x, z; dav V l'*) *det m* the ♦ *pron* (*oggetto: persona*) him; (: *cosa*) it; ~ **sapevo** I knew it; ~ **so** I know; **sii buono, anche se lui non** ~ **è** be good, even if he isn't; *vedi anche* **il**

lo'cale *ag* local ♦ *sm* room; (*luogo pubblico*) premises *pl*; ~ **notturno** nightclub; **località** *sf inv* locality; **localiz'zare** *vt* (*circoscrivere*) to confine, localize; (*accertare*) to locate, place

lo'canda *sf* inn; **locandi'ere, a** *sm/f*

innkeeper

loca'tario, a *sm/f* tenant

loca'tore, 'trice *sm/f* landlord/lady

locazi'one [lokat'tsjone] *sf* (*da parte del locatario*) renting *no pl*; (*da parte del locatore*) renting out *no pl*, letting *no pl*; **(contratto di)** ~ lease; **(canone di)** ~ rent; **dare in** ~ to rent out, let

locomo'tiva *sf* locomotive

locomo'tore *sm* electric locomotive

locomozi'one [lokomot'tsjone] *sf* locomotion; **mezzi di** ~ vehicles, means of transport

lo'custa *sf* locust

locuzi'one [lokut'tsjone] *sf* phrase, expression

lo'dare *vt* to praise

'lode *sf* praise; (*INS*): **laurearsi con 110 e** ~ ≈ to graduate with a first-class honours degree (*BRIT*), graduate summa cum laude (*US*)

'loden *sm inv* (*stoffa*) loden; (*cappotto*) loden overcoat

lo'devole *ag* praiseworthy

loga'ritmo *sm* logarithm

'loggia, ge ['lɔddʒa] *sf* (*ARCHIT*) loggia; (*circolo massonico*) lodge; **loggi'one** *sm* (*di teatro*): **il loggione** the Gods *sg*

'logica *sf* logic

'logico, a, ci, che ['lɔdʒiko] *ag* logical

logo'rare *vt* to wear out; (*sciupare*) to waste; ~**rsi** *vr* to wear out; (*fig*) to wear o.s. out

logo'rio *sm* wear and tear; (*fig*) strain

'logoro, a *ag* (*stoffa*) worn out, threadbare; (*persona*) worn out

lom'baggine [lom'baddʒine] *sf* lumbago

Lombar'dia *sf*: **la** ~ Lombardy

lom'bata *sf* (*taglio di carne*) loin

'lombo *sm* (*ANAT*) loin

lom'brico, chi *sm* earthworm

londi'nese *ag* London *cpd* ♦ *sm/f* Londoner

'Londra *sf* London

lon'gevo, a [lon'dʒevo] *ag* long-lived

longi'tudine [londʒi'tudine] *sf* longitude

lonta'nanza [lonta'nantsa] *sf* distance; absence

lon'tano, a *ag* (*distante*) distant,

faraway; (*assente*) absent; (*vago: sospetto*) slight, remote; (*tempo: remoto*) far-off, distant; (*parente*) distant, remote ♦ *av* far; **è ~a la casa?** is it far to the house?, is the house far from here?; **è ~ un chilometro** it's a kilometre away o a kilometre from here; **più ~** farther; **da** o **di ~** from a distance; **~ da** a long way from; **alla ~a** slightly, vaguely

'lontra *sf* otter

lo'quace [lo'kwatʃe] *ag* talkative, loquacious; (*fig: gesto etc*) eloquent

'lordo, a *ag* dirty, filthy; (*peso, stipendio*) gross

'loro *pron pl* (*oggetto, con preposizione*) them; (*complemento di termine*) to them; (*soggetto*) they; (*forma di cortesia: anche: L~*) you; to you; **il(la) ~, i(le) ~** *det* their; (*forma di cortesia: anche: L~*) your ♦ *pron* theirs; (*forma di cortesia: anche: L~*) yours; **~ stessi(e)** they themselves; you yourselves

'losco, a, schi, sche *ag* (*fig*) shady, suspicious

'lotta *sf* struggle, fight; (*SPORT*) wrestling; **~ libera** all-in wrestling; **lot'tare** *vi* to fight, struggle; to wrestle; **lotta'tore, trice** *sm/f* wrestler

lotte'ria *sf* lottery; (*di gara ippica*) sweepstake

'lotto *sm* (*gioco*) (state) lottery; (*parte*) lot; (*EDIL*) site

lozi'one [lot'tsjone] *sf* lotion

lubrifi'cante *sm* lubricant

lubrifi'care *vt* to lubricate

luc'chetto [luk'ketto] *sm* padlock

lucci'care [luttʃi'kare] *vi* to sparkle, glitter, twinkle

'luccio [luttʃo] *sm* (*ZOOL*) pike

'lucciola ['luttʃola] *sf* (*ZOOL*) firefly; glowworm

'luce ['lutʃe] *sf* light; (*finestra*) window; **alla ~ di** by the light of; **fare ~ su qc** (*fig*) to shed o throw light on sth; **~ del sole/della luna** sun/moonlight; **lu'cente** *ag* shining

lu'cerna [lu'tʃɛrna] *sf* oil-lamp

lucer'nario [lutʃer'narjo] *sm* skylight

lu'certola [lu'tʃɛrtola] *sf* lizard

luci'dare [lutʃi'dare] *vt* to polish; (*ricalcare*) to trace

lucida'trice [lutʃida'tritʃe] *sf* floor polisher

'lucido, a ['lutʃido] *ag* shining, bright; (*lucidato*) polished; (*fig*) lucid ♦ *sm* shine, lustre; (*per scarpe etc*) polish; (*disegno*) tracing

'lucro *sm* profit, gain; **lu'croso, a** *ag* lucrative, profitable

lu'dibrio *sm* mockery *no pl*; (*oggetto di scherno*) laughing-stock

'luglio ['luʎʎo] *sm* July

'lugubre *ag* gloomy

'lui *pronome* (*soggetto*) he; (*oggetto: per dare rilievo, con preposizione*) him; **~ stesso** he himself

lu'maca, che *sf* slug; (*chiocciola*) snail

'lume *sm* light; (*lampada*) lamp; (*fig*): **chiedere ~i a qn** to ask sb for advice; **a ~ di naso** (*fig*) by rule of thumb

lumi'naria *sf* (*per feste*) illuminations *pl*

lumi'noso, a *ag* (*che emette luce*) luminous; (*cielo, colore, stanza*) bright; (*sorgente*) of light, light *cpd*; (*fig: sorriso*) bright, radiant

'luna *sf* moon; **~ nuova/piena** new/full moon; **~ di miele** honeymoon

'luna park *sm inv* amusement park, funfair

lu'nare *ag* lunar, moon *cpd*

lu'nario *sm* almanac; **sbarcare il ~** to make ends meet

lu'natico, a, ci, che *ag* whimsical, temperamental

lunedì *sm inv* Monday; **di** o **il ~** on Mondays

lun'gaggine [lun'gaddʒine] *sf* slowness; **~i della burocrazia** red tape

lun'ghezza [lun'gettsa] *sf* length; **~ d'onda** (*FISICA*) wavelength

'lungi ['lundʒi]: **~ da** *prep* far from

'lungo, a, ghi, ghe *ag* long; (*lento: persona*) slow; (*diluito: caffè, brodo*) weak, watery, thin ♦ *sm* length ♦ *prep* along; **~ 3 metri** 3 metres long; **a ~** for a long time; **a ~ andare** in the long run; **di gran ~a** (*molto*) by far; **andare in ~** o **per le lunghe** to drag on; **saperla ~a** to

know what's what; **in ~ e in largo** far
and wide, all over; **~ il corso dei secoli**
throughout the centuries

lungo'mare *sm* promenade

lu'notto *sm* (*AUT*) rear *o* back window; **~
termico** heated rear window

lu'ogo, ghi *sm* place; (*posto: di incidente
etc*) scene, site; (*punto, passo di libro*)
passage; **in ~ di** instead of; **in primo ~** in
the first place; **aver ~** to take place; **dar
~ a** to give rise to; **~ comune**
commonplace; **~ di nascita** birthplace;
(*AMM*) place of birth; **~ di provenienza**
place of origin

luogote'nente *sm* (*MIL*) lieutenant

lu'para *sf* sawn-off shotgun

'lupo, a *sm/f* wolf

'luppolo *sm* (*BOT*) hop

'lurido, a *ag* filthy

lu'singa, ghe *sf* (*spesso al pl*) flattery *no
pl*

lusin'gare *vt* to flatter; **lusinghi'ero, a**
ag flattering, gratifying

lus'sare *vt* (*MED*) to dislocate

Lussem'burgo *sm* (*stato*): **il ~**
Luxembourg ♦ *sf* (*città*) Luxembourg

'lusso *sm* luxury; **di ~** luxury *cpd*;
lussu'oso, a *ag* luxurious

lussureggi'are [lussured'dʒare] *vi* to be
luxuriant

lus'suria *sf* lust

lus'trare *vt* to polish, shine

lustras'carpe *sm/f inv* shoeshine

lus'trino *sm* sequin

'lustro, a *ag* shiny; (*pelliccia*) glossy
♦ *sm* shine, gloss; (*fig*) prestige,
glory; (*quinquennio*) five-year period

'lutto *sm* mourning; **essere in/portare il
~** to be in/wear mourning; **luttu'oso, a**
ag mournful, sad

M

ma *cong* but; **~ insomma!** for goodness
sake!; **~ no!** of course not!

'macabro, a *ag* gruesome, macabre

macché [mak'ke] *escl* not at all!,
certainly not!

macche'roni [makke'roni] *smpl* macaroni *sg*

'macchia ['makkja] *sf* stain, spot;
(*chiazza di diverso colore*) spot; splash,
patch; (*tipo di boscaglia*) scrub; **alla ~**
(*fig*) in hiding; **macchi'are** *vt* (*sporcare*)
to stain, mark; **macchiarsi** *vr* (*persona*)
to get o.s. dirty; (*stoffa*) to stain; to get
stained *o* marked

'macchina ['makkina] *sf* machine;
(*motore, locomotiva*) engine; (*automobile*)
car; (*fig: meccanismo*) machinery; **andare
in ~** (*AUT*) to go by car; (*STAMPA*) to go to
press; **~ da cucire** sewing machine; **~
fotografica** camera; **~ da presa** cine *o*
movie camera; **~ da scrivere** typewriter;
~ a vapore steam engine

macchi'nare [makki'nare] *vt* to plot

macchi'nario [makki'narjo] *sm*
machinery

macchi'netta [makki'netta] (*fam*) *sf*
(*caffettiera*) percolator; (*accendino*) lighter

macchi'nista, i [makki'nista] *sm* (*di
treno*) engine-driver; (*di nave*) engineer;
(*TEATRO, TV*) stagehand

macchi'noso, a [makki'noso] *ag*
complex, complicated

mace'donia [matʃe'dɔnja] *sf* fruit salad

macel'laio [matʃel'lajo] *sm* butcher

macel'lare [matʃel'lare] *vt* to slaughter,
butcher; **macelle'ria** *sf* butcher's (shop);
ma'cello *sm* (*mattatoio*) slaughterhouse,
abattoir (*BRIT*), (*fig*) slaughter, massacre;
(*: disastro*) shambles *sg*

mace'rare [matʃe'rare] *vt* to macerate;
(*CUC*) to marinate; **~rsi** *vr* (*fig*): **~rsi in** to
be consumed with

ma'cerie [ma'tʃɛrje] *sfpl* rubble *sg*,
debris *sg*

ma'cigno [ma'tʃinno] *sm* (*masso*) rock,
boulder

maci'lento, a [matʃi'lento] *ag* emaciated

'macina ['matʃina] *sf* (*pietra*) millstone;
(*macchina*) grinder; **macinacaffè** *sm inv*
coffee grinder; **macina'pepe** *sm inv*
peppermill

maci'nare [matʃi'nare] *vt* to grind;
(*carne*) to mince (*BRIT*), grind (*US*);
maci'nato *sm* meal, flour; (*carne*) minced

(*BRIT*) o ground (*US*) meat

maci'nino [matʃi'nino] *sm* coffee grinder; peppermill

'madido, a *ag*: ~ **(di)** wet o moist (with)

Ma'donna *sf* (*REL*) Our Lady

mador'nale *ag* enormous, huge

'madre *sf* mother; (*matrice di bolletta*) counterfoil ♦ *ag inv* mother *cpd*; **ragazza** ~ unmarried mother; **scena** ~ (*TEATRO*) principal scene; (*fig*) terrible scene

madre'lingua *sf* mother tongue, native language

madre'perla *sf* mother-of-pearl

ma'drina *sf* godmother

maestà *sf inv* majesty; **maes'toso, a** *ag* majestic

ma'estra *sf vedi* **maestro**

maes'trale *sm* north-west wind, mistral

maes'tranze [maes'trantse] *sfpl* workforce *sg*

maes'tria *sf* mastery, skill

ma'estro, a *sm/f* (*INS*: anche: ~ **di scuola** o **elementare**) primary (*BRIT*) o grade school (*US*) teacher; (*esperto*) expert ♦ *sm* (*artigiano, fig: guida*) master; (*MUS*) maestro ♦ *ag* (*principale*) main; (*di grande abilità*) masterly, skilful; **~a d'asilo** nursery teacher; ~ **di cerimonie** master of ceremonies

'mafia *sf* Mafia; **mafi'oso** *sm* member of the Mafia

'maga *sf* sorceress

ma'gagna [ma'gaɲɲa] *sf* defect, flaw, blemish; (*noia, guaio*) problem

ma'gari *escl* (*esprime desiderio*): ~ **fosse vero!** if only it were true!; **ti piacerebbe andare in Scozia?** — ~! would you like to go to Scotland? — and how! ♦ *av* (*anche*) even; (*forse*) perhaps

magaz'zino [magad'dzino] *sm* warehouse; **grande** ~ department store

'maggio ['maddʒo] *sm* May

maggio'rana [maddʒo'rana] *sf* (*BOT*) (sweet) marjoram

maggio'ranza [maddʒo'rantsa] *sf* majority

maggio'rare [maddʒo'rare] *vt* to increase, raise

maggior'domo [maddʒor'dɔmo] *sm* butler

maggi'ore [mad'dʒore] *ag* (*comparativo: più grande*) bigger, larger; taller; greater; (*: più vecchio: sorella, fratello*) older, elder; (*: di grado superiore*) senior; (*: più importante, MIL, MUS*) major; (*superlativo*) biggest, largest; tallest; greatest; oldest, eldest ♦ *sm/f* (*di grado*) superior; (*di età*) elder; (*MIL*) major; (*: AER*) squadron leader; **la maggior parte** the majority; **andare per la** ~ (*cantante etc*) to be very popular; **maggio'renne** *ag* of age ♦ *sm/f* person who has come of age; **maggior'mente** *av* much more; (*con senso superlativo*) most

ma'gia [ma'dʒia] *sf* magic; **'magico, a, ci, che** *ag* magic; (*fig*) fascinating, charming, magical

'magio ['madʒo] *sm* (*REL*): **i re Magi** the Magi, the Three Wise Men

magis'tero [madʒis'tero] *sm* teaching; (*fig: maestria*) skill; (*INS*): **facoltà di M~** ≈ teachers' training college; **magis'trale** *ag* primary (*BRIT*) o grade school (*US*) teachers', primary (*BRIT*) o grade school (*US*) teaching *cpd*; skilful

magis'trato [madʒis'trato] *sm* magistrate; **magistra'tura** *sf* magistrature; (*magistrati*): **la magistratura** the Bench

'maglia ['maʎʎa] *sf* stitch; (*lavoro ai ferri*) knitting *no pl*; (*tessuto, SPORT*) jersey; (*maglione*) jersey, sweater; (*di catena*) link; (*di rete*) mesh; ~ **diritta/rovescia** plain/purl; **maglie'ria** *sf* knitwear; (*negozio*) knitwear shop; **magli'etta** *sf* (*canottiera*) vest; (*tipo camicia*) T-shirt; **magli'ficio** *sm* knitwear factory

'maglio ['maʎʎo] *sm* mallet; (*macchina*) power hammer

ma'gnanimo, a [maɲ'ɲanimo, a] *ag* magnanimous

ma'gnete [maɲ'ɲete] *sm* magnet; **ma'gnetico, a, ci, che** *ag* magnetic

magne'tofono [maɲɲe'tɔfono] *sm* tape recorder

ma'gnifico, a, ci, che [maɲ'ɲifiko] *ag* magnificent, splendid; (*ospite*) generous

'**magno, a** ['maɲɲo] *ag*: **aula ~a** main hall

ma'gnolia [maɲ'nɔlja] *sf* magnolia

'**mago, ghi** *sm* (*stregone*) magician, wizard; (*illusionista*) magician

ma'grezza [ma'grettsa] *sf* thinness

'**magro, a** *ag* (very) thin, skinny; (*carne*) lean; (*formaggio*) low-fat; (*fig: scarso, misero*) meagre, meagre; (*: meschino: scusa*) poor, lame; **mangiare di ~** not to eat meat

'**mai** *av* (*nessuna volta*) never; (*talvolta*) ever; **non ... ~** never; **~ più** never again; **come ~?** why (*o* how) on earth?; **chi/dove/quando ~?** whoever/wherever/whenever?

mai'ale *sm* (*ZOOL*) pig; (*carne*) pork

maio'nese *sf* mayonnaise

'**mais** *sm inv* maize

mai'uscola *sf* capital letter

mai'uscolo, a *ag* (*lettera*) capital; (*fig*) enormous, huge

mal *av, sm vedi* **male**

malac'corto, a *ag* rash, careless

mala'fede *sf* bad faith

mala'lingua (*pl* **male'lingue**) *sf* gossip(monger)

mala'mente *av* badly; dangerously

malan'dato, a *ag* (*persona: di salute*) in poor health; (*: di condizioni finanziarie*) badly off; (*trascurato*) shabby

ma'lanno *sm* (*disgrazia*) misfortune; (*malattia*) ailment

mala'pena *sf*: **a ~** hardly, scarcely

ma'laria *sf* (*MED*) malaria

mala'sorte *sf* bad luck

mala'ticcio, a [mala'tittʃo] *ag* sickly

ma'lato, a *ag* ill, sick; (*gamba*) bad; (*pianta*) diseased ♦ *sm/f* sick person; (*in ospedale*) patient; **malat'tia** *sf* (*infettiva etc*) illness, disease; (*cattiva salute*) illness, sickness; (*di pianta*) disease

malau'gurio *sm* bad *o* ill omen

mala'vita *sf* underworld

mala'voglia [mala'vɔʎʎa] *sf*: **di ~** unwillingly, reluctantly

mal'concio, a, ci, ce [mal'kontʃo] *ag* in a sorry state

malcon'tento *sm* discontent

malcos'tume *sm* immorality

mal'destro, a *ag* (*inabile*) inexpert, inexperienced; (*goffo*) awkward

maldi'cenza [maldi'tʃɛntsa] *sf* malicious gossip

maldis'posto, a *ag*: **~ (verso)** ill-disposed (towards)

'**male** *av* badly ♦ *sm* (*ciò che è ingiusto, disonesto*) evil; (*danno, svantaggio*) harm; (*sventura*) misfortune; (*dolore fisico, morale*) pain, ache; **di ~ in peggio** from bad to worse; **sentirsi ~** to feel ill; **far ~** (*dolere*) to hurt; **far ~ alla salute** to be bad for one's health; **far del ~ a qn** to hurt *o* harm sb; **restare *o* rimanere ~** to be sorry; to be disappointed; to be hurt; **andare a ~** to go bad; **come va? — non c'è ~** how are you? — not bad; **mal di cuore** heart trouble; **~ di dente** toothache; **mal di mare** seasickness; **avere mal di gola/testa** to have a sore throat/a headache; **aver ~ ai piedi** to have sore feet

male'detto, a *pp di* **maledire** ♦ *ag* cursed, damned; (*fig: fam*) damned, blasted

male'dire *vt* to curse; **maledizi'one** *sf* curse; **maledizione!** damn it!

maledu'cato, a *ag* rude, ill-mannered

male'fatta *sf* misdeed

male'ficio [male'fitʃo] *sm* witchcraft

ma'lefico, a, ci, che *ag* (*aria, cibo*) harmful, bad; (*influsso, azione*) evil

ma'lessere *sm* indisposition, slight illness; (*fig*) uneasiness

ma'levolo, a *ag* malevolent

malfa'mato, a *ag* notorious

mal'fatto, a *ag* (*persona*) deformed; (*oggetto*) badly made; (*lavoro*) badly done

malfat'tore, 'trice *sm/f* wrongdoer

mal'fermo, a *ag* unsteady, shaky; (*salute*) poor, delicate

malformazi'one [malformat'tsjone] *sf* malformation

malgo'verno *sm* maladministration

mal'grado *prep* in spite of, despite ♦ *cong* although; **mio** (*o* **tuo** *etc*) **~** against my (*o* your *etc*) will

ma'lia *sf* spell; (*fig: fascino*) charm

mali'gnare [maliɲˈɲare] *vi:* ~ **su** to malign, speak ill of

ma'ligno, a [maˈliɲɲo] *ag* (*malvagio*) malicious, malignant; (*MED*) malignant

malinco'nia *sf* melancholy, gloom; **malin'conico, a, ci, che** *ag* melancholy

malincu'ore: a ~ *av* reluctantly, unwillingly

malintenzio'nato, a [malintentsjoˈnato] *ag* ill-intentioned

malin'teso, a *ag* misunderstood; (*riguardo, senso del dovere*) mistaken, wrong ♦ *sm* misunderstanding

ma'lizia [maˈlittsja] *sf* (*malignità*) malice; (*furbizia*) cunning; (*espediente*) trick; **malizi'oso, a** *ag* malicious; cunning; (*vivace, birichino*) mischievous

mal'loppo *sm* (*involto*) bundle; (*fam: refurtiva*) loot

malme'nare *vt* to beat up; (*fig*) to ill-treat

mal'messo, a *ag* shabby

malnu'trito, a *ag* undernourished

ma'locchio [maˈlɔkkjo] *sm* evil eye

ma'lora *sf:* **andare in** ~ to go to the dogs

ma'lore *sm* (sudden) illness

mal'sano, a *ag* unhealthy

malsi'curo, a *ag* unsafe

'Malta *sf:* **la** ~ Malta

'malta *sf* (*EDIL*) mortar

mal'tempo *sm* bad weather

'malto *sm* malt

maltrat'tare *vt* to ill-treat

malu'more *sm* bad mood; (*irritabilità*) bad temper; (*discordia*) ill feeling; **di** ~ **in** a bad mood

mal'vagio, a, gi, gie [malˈvadʒo] *ag* wicked, evil

malversazi'one [malversatˈtsjone] *sf* (*DIR*) embezzlement

mal'visto, a *ag:* ~ (**da**) disliked (by), unpopular (with)

malvi'vente *sm* criminal

malvolenti'eri *av* unwillingly, reluctantly

'mamma *sf* mummy, mum; ~ **mia!** my goodness!

mam'mella *sf* (*ANAT*) breast; (*di vacca, capra etc*) udder

mam'mifero *sm* mammal

'mammola *sf* (*BOT*) violet

ma'nata *sf* (*colpo*) slap; (*quantità*) handful

'manca *sf* left (hand); **a destra e a** ~ left, right and centre, on all sides

man'canza [manˈkantsa] *sf* lack; (*carenza*) shortage, scarcity; (*fallo*) fault; (*imperfezione*) failing, shortcoming; **per** ~ **di tempo** through lack of time; **in** ~ **di meglio** for lack of anything better

man'care *vi* (*essere insufficiente*) to be lacking; (*venir meno*) to fail; (*sbagliare*) to be wrong, make a mistake; (*non esserci*) to be missing, not to be there; (*essere lontano*): ~ (**da**) to be away (from) ♦ *vt* to miss; ~ **di** to lack; ~ **a** (*promessa*) to fail to keep; **tu mi manchi** I miss you; **mancò poco che morisse** he very nearly died; **mancano ancora 10 sterline** we're still £10 short; **manca un quarto alle 6** it's a quarter to 6; **man'cato, a** *ag* (*tentativo*) unsuccessful; (*artista*) failed

'mancia, ce [ˈmantʃa] *sf* tip; ~ **competente** reward

manci'ata [manˈtʃata] *sf* handful

man'cino, a [manˈtʃino] *ag* (*braccio*) left; (*persona*) left-handed; (*fig*) underhand

'manco *av* (*nemmeno*): ~ **per sogno** *o* **per idea!** not on your life!

man'dante *sm/f* (*di delitto*) instigator

man'dare *vt* to send; (*far funzionare: macchina*) to drive; (*emettere*) to send out; (: *grido*) to give, utter, let out; ~ **a chiamare qn** to send for sb; ~ **avanti** (*fig: famiglia*) to provide for; (: *fabbrica*) to run, look after; (: *giù*) to send down; (*anche fig*) to swallow; ~ **via** to send away; (*licenziare*) to fire

manda'rino *sm* mandarin (orange); (*cinese*) mandarin

man'data *sf* (*quantità*) lot, batch; (*di chiave*) turn; **chiudere a doppia** ~ to double-lock

manda'tario *sm* (*DIR*) representative, agent

man'dato *sm* (*incarico*) commission; (*DIR: provvedimento*) warrant; (*di deputato etc*) mandate; (*ordine di pagamento*) postal *o* money order; ~ **d'arresto** warrant for arrest

man'**dibola** *sf* mandible, jaw

'**mandorla** *sf* almond; '**mandorlo** *sm* almond tree

'**mandria** *sf* herd

maneggi'**are** [maned'dʒare] *vt* (*creta, cera*) to mould, work, fashion; (*arnesi, utensili*) to handle; (: *adoperare*) to use; (*fig: persone, denaro*) to handle, deal with; ma'**neggio** *sm* moulding; handling; use; (*intrigo*) plot, scheme; (*per cavalli*) riding school

ma'**nesco, a, schi, sche** *ag* free with one's fists

ma'**nette** *sfpl* handcuffs

manga'**nello** *sm* club

manga'**nese** *sm* manganese

mange'**reccio, a, ci, ce** [mandʒe-'rettʃo] *ag* edible

mangia'**dischi** [mandʒa'diski] *sm inv* record player

mangi'**are** [man'dʒare] *vt* to eat; (*intaccare*) to eat into *o* away; (*CARTE, SCACCHI etc*) to take ♦ *vi* to eat ♦ *sm* eating; (*cibo*) food; (*cucina*) cooking; ~**rsi le parole** to mumble; ~**rsi le unghie** to bite one's nails; **mangia'toia** *sf* feeding-trough

man'**gime** [man'dʒime] *sm* fodder

'**mango, ghi** *sm* mango

ma'**nia** *sf* (*PSIC*) mania; (*fig*) obsession, craze; ma'**niaco, a, ci, che** *ag* suffering from a mania; **maniaco (di)** obsessed (by), crazy (about)

'**manica** *sf* sleeve; (*fig: gruppo*) gang, bunch; (*GEO*): **la M~, il Canale della M~** the (English) Channel; **essere di ~ larga/stretta** to be easy-going/strict; ~ **a vento** (*AER*) wind sock

mani'**chino** [mani'kino] *sm* (*di sarto, vetrina*) dummy

'**manico, ci** *sm* handle; (*MUS*) neck

mani'**comio** *sm* mental hospital; (*fig*) madhouse

mani'**cotto** *sm* muff; (*TECN*) coupling; sleeve

mani'**cure** *sm o f inv* manicure ♦ *sf inv* manicurist

mani'**era** *sf* way, manner; (*stile*) style, manner; ~**e** *sfpl* (*comportamento*) manners; **in ~ che** so that; **in ~ da** so as to; **in tutte le ~e** at all costs

manie'**rato, a** *ag* affected

manifat'**tura** *sf* (*lavorazione*) manu-facture; (*stabilimento*) factory

manifes'**tare** *vt* to show, display; (*esprimere*) to express; (*rivelare*) to reveal, disclose ♦ *vi* to demonstrate; ~**rsi** *vr* to show o.s.; ~**rsi amico** to prove o.s. (to be) a friend; **manifestazi'one** *sf* show, display; expression; (*sintomo*) sign, symptom; (*dimostrazione pubblica*) demonstration; (*cerimonia*) event

mani'**festo, a** *ag* obvious, evident ♦ *sm* poster, bill; (*scritto ideologico*) manifesto

ma'**niglia** [ma'niʎʎa] *sf* handle; (*sostegno: negli autobus etc*) strap

manipo'**lare** *vt* to manipulate; (*alterare: vino*) to adulterate; **manipolazi'one** *sf* manipulation; adulteration

manis'**calco, chi** *sm* blacksmith

'**manna** *sf* (*REL*) manna

man'**naia** *sf* (*del boia*) (executioner's) axe; (*per carni*) cleaver

man'**naro: lupo ~** *sm* werewolf

'**mano, i** *sf* hand; (*strato: di vernice etc*) coat; **di prima ~** (*notizia*) first-hand; **di seconda ~** second-hand; **man ~** little by little, gradually; **man ~ che** as; **darsi** *o* **stringersi la ~** to shake hands; **mettere le ~i avanti** (*fig*) to safeguard o.s.; **restare a ~i vuote** to be left empty-handed; **venire alle ~i** to come to blows; **a ~** by hand; ~**i in alto!** hands up!

mano'**dopera** *sf* labour

mano'**messo, a** *pp di* **manomettere**

ma'**nometro** *sm* gauge, manometer

mano'**mettere** *vt* (*alterare*) to tamper with; (*aprire indebitamente*) to break open illegally

ma'**nopola** *sf* (*dell'armatura*) gauntlet; (*guanto*) mitt; (*di impugnatura*) hand-grip; (*pomello*) knob

manos'**critto, a** *ag* handwritten ♦ *sm* manuscript

mano'**vale** *sm* labourer

mano'**vella** *sf* handle; (*TECN*) crank

ma'novra *sf* manoeuvre (*BRIT*), maneuver (*US*); (*FERR*) shunting; mano'vrare *vt* (*veicolo*) to manoeuvre (*BRIT*), maneuver (*US*); (*macchina, congegno*) to operate; (*fig: persona*) to manipulate ♦ *vi* to manoeuvre

manro'vescio [manro'veʃʃo] *sm* slap (*with back of hand*)

man'sarda *sf* attic

mansi'one *sf* task, duty, job

mansu'eto, a *ag* gentle, docile

man'tello *sm* cloak; (*fig: di neve etc*) blanket, mantle; (*TECN: involucro*) casing, shell; (*ZOOL*) coat

mante'nere *vt* to maintain; (*adempiere: promesse*) to keep, abide by; (*provvedere a*) to support, maintain; ~rsi *vr*: ~rsi calmo/giovane to stay calm/young; manteni'mento *sm* maintenance

'mantice ['mantitʃe] *sm* bellows *pl*; (*di carrozza, automobile*) hood

'manto *sm* cloak; ~ stradale road surface

manu'ale *ag* manual ♦ *sm* (*testo*) manual, handbook

ma'nubrio *sm* handle; (*di bicicletta etc*) handlebars *pl*; (*SPORT*) dumbbell

manu'fatto *sm* manufactured article

manutenzi'one [manuten'tsjone] *sf* maintenance, upkeep; (*d'impianti*) maintenance, servicing

'manzo ['mandzo] *sm* (*ZOOL*) steer; (*carne*) beef

'mappa *sf* (*GEO*) map; mappa'mondo *sm* map of the world; (*globo girevole*) globe

ma'rasma, i *sm* (*fig*) decay, decline

mara'tona *sf* marathon

'marca, che *sf* mark; (*bollo*) stamp; (*COMM: di prodotti*) brand; (*contrassegno, scontrino*) ticket, check; prodotto di ~ (*di buona qualità*) high-class product; ~ da bollo official stamp

mar'care *vt* (*munire di contrassegno*) to mark; (*a fuoco*) to brand; (*SPORT: gol*) to score; (*: avversario*) to mark; (*accentuare*) to stress; ~ visita (*MIL*) to report sick

'Marche ['marke] *sfpl*: le ~ the Marches (*region of central Italy*)

mar'chese, a [mar'keze] *sm/f* marquis *o* marquess/marchioness

marchi'are [mar'kjare] *vt* to brand; 'marchio *sm* (*di bestiame*, *COMM*, *fig*) brand; marchio depositato registered trademark; marchio di fabbrica trademark

'marcia, ce ['martʃa] *sf* (*anche MUS, MIL*) march; (*funzionamento*) running; (*il camminare*) walking; (*AUT*) gear; mettere in ~ to start; mettersi in ~ to get moving; far ~ indietro (*AUT*) to reverse; (*fig*) to back-pedal

marciapi'ede [martʃa'pjɛde] *sm* (*di strada*) pavement (*BRIT*), sidewalk (*US*); (*FERR*) platform

marci'are [mar'tʃare] *vi* to march; (*andare: treno, macchina*) to go; (*funzionare*) to run, work

'marcio, a, ci, ce ['martʃo] *ag* (*frutta, legno*) rotten, bad; (*MED*) festering; (*fig*) corrupt, rotten

mar'cire [mar'tʃire] *vi* (*andare a male*) to go bad, rot; (*suppurare*) to fester; (*fig*) to rot, waste away

'marco, chi *sm* (*unità monetaria*) mark

'mare *sm* sea; in ~ at sea; andare al ~ (*in vacanza etc*) to go to the seaside; il M~ del Nord the North Sea

ma'rea *sf* tide; alta/bassa ~ high/low tide

mareggi'ata [mared'dʒata] *sf* heavy sea

ma'remma *sf* (*GEO*) maremma, swampy coastal area

mare'moto *sm* seaquake

maresci'allo [mareʃ'ʃallo] *sm* (*MIL*) marshal; (*: sottufficiale*) warrant officer

marga'rina *sf* margarine

marghe'rita [marge'rita] *sf* (ox-eye) daisy, marguerite; (*di stampante*) daisy wheel

'margine ['mardʒine] *sm* margin; (*di bosco, via*) edge, border

ma'rina *sf* navy; (*costa*) coast; (*quadro*) seascape; ~ militare/mercantile navy/ merchant navy (*BRIT*) *o* marine (*US*)

mari'naio *sm* sailor

mari'nare *vt* (*CUC*) to marinate; ~ la scuola to play truant; mari'nata *sf* marinade

ma'rino, a *ag* sea *cpd*, marine

mario'netta *sf* puppet
mari'tare *vt* to marry; **~rsi** *vr*: **~rsi a** *o* **con qn** to marry sb, get married to sb
ma'rito *sm* husband
ma'rittimo, a *ag* maritime, sea *cpd*
mar'maglia [mar'maʎʎa] *sf* mob, riff-raff
marmel'lata *sf* jam; (*di agrumi*) marmalade
mar'mitta *sf* (*recipiente*) pot; (*AUT*) silencer; **~ catalitica** catalytic convertor
'marmo *sm* marble
mar'mocchio [mar'mɔkkjo] (*fam*) *sm* tot, kid
mar'motta *sf* (*ZOOL*) marmot
Ma'rocco *sm*: **il ~** Morocco
ma'roso *sm* breaker
mar'rone *ag inv* brown ♦ *sm* (*BOT*) chestnut
mar'sala *sm inv* (*vino*) Marsala
mar'sina *sf* tails *pl*, tail coat
martedì *sm inv* Tuesday; **di** *o* **il ~** on Tuesdays; **~ grasso** Shrove Tuesday
martel'lare *vt* to hammer ♦ *vi* (*pulsare*) to throb; (: *cuore*) to thump
mar'tello *sm* hammer; (*di uscio*) knocker
marti'netto *sm* (*TECN*) jack
'martire *sm/f* martyr; **mar'tirio** *sm* martyrdom; (*fig*) agony, torture
'martora *sf* marten
martori'are *vt* to torment, torture
mar'xista, i, e *ag, sm/f* Marxist
marza'pane [martsa'pane] *sm* marzipan
'marzo ['martso] *sm* March
mascal'zone [maskal'tsone] *sm* rascal, scoundrel
ma'scella [maʃ'ʃɛlla] *sf* (*ANAT*) jaw
'maschera ['maskera] *sf* mask; (*travestimento*) disguise; (: *per un ballo etc*) fancy dress; (*TEATRO, CINEMA*) usher/usherette; (*personaggio del teatro*) stock character; **masche'rare** *vt* to mask; (*travestire*) to disguise; to dress up; (*fig: celare*) to hide, conceal; (*MIL*) to camouflage; **~rsi da** to disguise o.s. as; to dress up as; (*fig*) to masquerade as
mas'chile [mas'kile] *ag* masculine; (*sesso, popolazione*) male; (*abiti*) men's; (*per ragazzi: scuola*) boys'
'maschio, a ['maskjo] *ag* (*BIOL*) male;

(*virile*) manly ♦ *sm* (*anche ZOOL, TECN*) male; (*uomo*) man; (*ragazzo*) boy; (*figlio*) son
masco'lino, a *ag* masculine
'massa *sf* mass; (*di errori etc*): **una ~ di** heaps of, masses of; (*di gente*) mass, multitude; (*ELETTR*) earth; **in ~** (*COMM*) in bulk; (*tutti insieme*) en masse; **adunata in ~** mass meeting; **di ~** (*cultura, manifestazione*) mass *cpd*; **la ~ del popolo** the masses *pl*
mas'sacro *sm* massacre, slaughter; (*fig*) mess, disaster
mas'saggio [mas'saddʒo] *sm* massage
mas'saia *sf* housewife
masse'rizie [masse'rittsje] *sfpl* (household) furnishings
mas'siccio, a, ci, ce [mas'sittʃo] *ag* (*oro, legno*) solid; (*palazzo*) massive; (*corporatura*) stout ♦ *sm* (*GEO*) massif
'massima *sf* (*sentenza, regola*) maxim; (*METEOR*) maximum temperature; **in linea di ~** generally speaking; *vedi anche* **massimo**
massi'male *sm* maximum
'massimo, a *ag, sm* maximum; **al ~** at (the) most
'masso *sm* rock, boulder
mas'sone *sm* freemason; **massone'ria** *sf* freemasonry
mas'tello *sm* tub
masti'care *vt* to chew
'mastice ['mastitʃe] *sm* mastic; (*per vetri*) putty
mas'tino *sm* mastiff
ma'tassa *sf* skein
mate'matica *sf* mathematics *sg*
mate'matico, a, ci, che *ag* mathematical ♦ *sm/f* mathematician
mate'rasso *sm* mattress; **~ a molle** spring *o* interior-sprung mattress
ma'teria *sf* (*FISICA*) matter; (*TECN, COMM*) material, matter *no pl*; (*disciplina*) subject; (*argomento*) subject matter, material; **~e prime** raw materials; **in ~ di** (*per quanto concerne*) on the subject of; **materi'ale** *ag* material; (*fig: grossolano*) rough, rude ♦ *sm* material; (*insieme di strumenti etc*) equipment *no pl*, materials

pl

maternità *sf* motherhood, maternity; (*clinica*) maternity hospital

ma'terno, a *ag* (*amore, cura etc*) maternal, motherly; (*nonno*) maternal; (*lingua, terra*) mother *cpd*

ma'tita *sf* pencil

ma'trice [ma'tritʃe] *sf* matrix; (*COMM*) counterfoil; (*fig: origine*) background

ma'tricola *sf* (*registro*) register; (*numero*) registration number; (*nell'università*) freshman, fresher

ma'trigna [ma'triɲɲa] *sf* stepmother

matrimoni'ale *ag* matrimonial, marriage *cpd*

matri'monio *sm* marriage, matrimony; (*durata*) marriage, married life; (*cerimonia*) wedding

ma'trona *sf* (*fig*) matronly woman

mat'tina *sf* morning; **matti'nata** *sf* morning; (*spettacolo*) matinée, afternoon performance; **mattini'ero, a** *ag*: **essere mattiniero** to be an early riser; **mat'tino** *sm* morning

'matto, a *ag* mad, crazy; (*fig: falso*) false, imitation; (: *opaco*) matt, dull ♦ *sm/f* madman/woman; **avere una voglia ~a di qc** to be dying for sth

mat'tone *sm* brick; (*fig*): **questo libro/film è un ~** this book/film is heavy going

matto'nella *sf* tile

matu'rare *vi* (*anche: ~rsi*) (*frutta, grano*) to ripen; (*ascesso*) to come to a head; (*fig: persona, idea, ECON*) to mature ♦ *vt* to ripen; to (make) mature

maturità *sf* maturity; (*di frutta*) ripeness, maturity; (*INS*) school-leaving examination, ≈ GCE A-levels (*BRIT*)

ma'turo, a *ag* mature; (*frutto*) ripe, mature

'mazza ['mattsa] *sf* (*bastone*) club; (*martello*) sledge-hammer; (*SPORT: da golf*) club; (: *da baseball, cricket*) bat

maz'zata [mat'tsata] *sf* (*anche fig*) heavy blow

'mazzo ['mattso] *sm* (*di fiori, chiavi etc*) bunch; (*di carte da gioco*) pack

me *pron* me; **~ stesso(a)** myself; **sei bravo quanto ~** you are as clever as I

(am) *o* as me

me'andro *sm* meander

M.E.C. [mɛk] *sigla m* (= *Mercato Comune Europeo*) EEC

mec'canica, che *sf* mechanics *sg*; (*attività tecnologica*) mechanical engineering; (*meccanismo*) mechanism

mec'canico, a, ci, che *ag* mechanical ♦ *sm* mechanic

mecca'nismo *sm* mechanism

me'daglia [me'daʎʎa] *sf* medal; **medagli'one** *sm* (*ARCHIT*) medallion; (*gioiello*) locket

me'desimo, a *ag* same; (*in persona*): **io ~** I myself

'media *sf* average; (*MAT*) mean; (*INS: voto*) end-of-term average; **in ~** on average; *vedi anche* **medio**

medi'ano, a *ag* median; (*valore*) mean ♦ *sm* (*CALCIO*) half-back

medi'ante *prep* by means of

medi'are *vt* (*fare da mediatore*) to act as mediator in; (*MAT*) to average

media'tore, 'trice *sm/f* mediator; (*COMM*) middle man, agent

medica'mento *sm* medicine, drug

medi'care *vt* to treat; (*ferita*) to dress; **medicazi'one** *sf* treatment, medication; dressing

medi'cina [medi'tʃina] *sf* medicine; **~ legale** forensic medicine; **medici'nale** *ag* medicinal ♦ *sm* drug, medicine

'medico, a, ci, che *ag* medical ♦ *sm* doctor; **~ generico** general practitioner, GP

medie'vale *ag* medieval

'medio, a *ag* average; (*punto, ceto*) middle; (*altezza, statura*) medium ♦ *sm* (*dito*) middle finger; **licenza ~a** *leaving certificate awarded at the end of 3 years of secondary education*; **scuola ~a** *first 3 years of secondary school*

medi'ocre *ag* mediocre, poor

medioe'vale *ag* = **medievale**

medio'evo *sm* Middle Ages *pl*

medi'tare *vt* to ponder over, meditate on; (*progettare*) to plan, think out ♦ *vi* to meditate

mediter'raneo, a *ag* Mediterranean; **il**

(mare) M~ the Mediterranean (Sea)

me'dusa *sf* (*ZOOL*) jellyfish

me'gafono *sm* megaphone

'meglio ['mɛʎʎo] *av, ag inv* better; (*con senso superlativo*) best ♦ *sm* (*la cosa migliore*): **il ~** the best (thing); **faresti ~ ad andartene** you had better leave; **alla ~** as best one can; **andar di bene in ~** to get better and better; **fare del proprio ~** to do one's best; **per il ~** for the best; **aver la ~ su qn** to get the better of sb

'mela *sf* apple; **~ cotogna** quince

mela'grana *sf* pomegranate

melan'zana [melan'dzana] *sf* aubergine (*BRIT*), eggplant (*US*)

me'lenso, a *ag* dull, stupid

mel'lifluo, a (*peg*) *ag* sugary, honeyed

'melma *sf* mud, mire

'melo *sm* apple tree

melo'dia *sf* melody

me'lone *sm* (musk)melon

'membra *sfpl vedi* **membro**

'membro *sm* member; (*pl(f) ~a: arto*) limb

memo'randum *sm inv* memorandum

me'moria *sf* memory; **~e** *sfpl* (*opera autobiografica*) memoirs; **a ~** (*imparare, sapere*) by heart; **a ~ d'uomo** within living memory; **memori'ale** *sm* (*raccolta di memorie*) memoirs *pl*; (*DIR*) memorial

mena'dito: a ~ *av* perfectly, thoroughly; **sapere qc a ~** to have sth at one's fingertips

me'nare *vt* to lead; (*picchiare*) to hit, beat; (*dare: colpi*) to deal; **~ la coda** (*cane*) to wag its tail

mendi'cante *sm/f* beggar

mendi'care *vt* to beg for ♦ *vi* to beg

<u>*PAROLA CHIAVE*</u>

'meno *av* **1** (*in minore misura*) less; **dovresti mangiare ~** you should eat less, you shouldn't eat so much

2 (*comparativo*): **~ ... di** not as ... as, less ... than; **sono ~ alto di te** I'm not as tall as you (are), I'm less tall than you (are); **~ ... che** not as ... as, less ... than; **~ che mai** less than ever; **è ~ intelligente che ricco** he's more rich than intelligent; **~**

fumo più mangio the less I smoke the more I eat

3 (*superlativo*) least; **il ~ dotato degli studenti** the least gifted of the students; **è quello che compro ~ spesso** it's the one I buy least often

4 (*MAT*) minus; **8 ~ 5** 8 minus 5, 8 take away 5; **sono le 8 ~ un quarto** it's a quarter to 8; **~ 5 gradi** 5 degrees below zero, minus 5 degrees; **mille lire in ~** a thousand lire less

5 (*fraseologia*): **quanto ~ poteva telefonare** he could at least have phoned; **non so se accettare o ~** I don't know whether to accept or not; **fare a ~ di qc/qn** to do without sth/sb; **non potevo fare a ~ di ridere** I couldn't help laughing; **~ male!** thank goodness!; **~ male che sei arrivato** it's a good job that you've come ♦ *ag inv* (*tempo, denaro*) less; (*errori, persone*) fewer; **ha fatto ~ errori di tutti** he made fewer mistakes than anyone, he made the fewest mistakes of all ♦ *sm inv* **1**: **il ~** (*il minimo*) the least; **parlare del più e del ~** to talk about this and that

2 (*MAT*) minus ♦ *prep* (*eccetto*) except (for), apart from; **a ~ che, a ~ di** unless; **a ~ che non piova** unless it rains; **non posso, a ~ di prendere ferie** I can't, unless I take some leave

---

meno'mare *vt* (*danneggiare*) to maim, disable

meno'pausa *sf* menopause

'mensa *sf* (*locale*) canteen; (*: MIL*) mess; (*: nelle università*) refectory

men'sile *ag* monthly ♦ *sm* (*periodico*) monthly (magazine); (*stipendio*) monthly salary

'mensola *sf* bracket; (*ripiano*) shelf; (*ARCHIT*) corbel

'menta *sf* mint; (*anche: ~ piperita*) peppermint; (*bibita*) peppermint cordial; (*caramella*) mint, peppermint

men'tale *ag* mental; **mentalità** *sf inv* mentality

'mente *sf* mind; **imparare/sapere qc a ~**

to learn/know sth by heart; **avere in ~ qc** to have sth in mind; **passare di ~ a qn** to slip sb's mind

men'tire *vi* to lie

'mento *sm* chin

men'tolo *sm* menthol

'mentre *cong* (*temporale*) while; (*avversativo*) whereas

menù *sm inv* menu; **~ turistico** set menu

menzio'nare [mentsjo'nare] *vt* to mention

menzi'one [men'tsjone] *sf* mention; **fare ~ di** to mention

men'zogna [men'tsɔɲɲa] *sf* lie

mera'viglia [mera'viʎʎa] *sf* amazement, wonder; (*persona, cosa*) marvel, wonder; **a ~** perfectly, wonderfully; **meravigli'are** *vt* to amaze, astonish; **meravigliarsi (di)** to marvel (at); (*stupirsi*) to be amazed (at), be astonished (at); **meravigli'oso, a** *ag* wonderful, marvellous

mer'cante *sm* merchant; **~ d'arte** art dealer; **mercanteggi'are** *vt* (*onore, voto*) to sell ♦ *vi* to bargain, haggle; **mercan'tile** *ag* commercial, mercantile; (*nave, marina*) merchant *cpd* ♦ *sm* (*nave*) merchantman; **mercan'zia** *sf* merchandise, goods *pl*

mer'cato *sm* market; **~ dei cambi** exchange market; **M~ Comune (Europeo)** (European) Common Market; **~ nero** black market

'merce ['mɛrtʃe] *sf* goods *pl*, merchandise; **~ deperibile** perishable goods *pl*

mercé [mer'tʃe] *sf* mercy

merce'nario, a [mertʃe'narjo] *ag, sm* mercenary

merce'ria [mertʃe'ria] *sf* (*articoli*) haberdashery (*BRIT*); notions *pl* (*US*); (*bottega*) haberdasher's shop (*BRIT*); notions store (*US*)

mercoledì *sm inv* Wednesday; **di** *o* **il ~** on Wednesdays; **~ delle Ceneri** Ash Wednesday

mer'curio *sm* mercury

'merda (*fam!*) *sf* shit (*!*)

me'renda *sf* afternoon snack

meridi'ana *sf* (*orologio*) sundial

meridi'ano, a *ag* meridian; midday *cpd*, noonday ♦ *sm* meridian

meridio'nale *ag* southern ♦ *sm/f* southerner

meridi'one *sm* south

me'ringa, ghe *sf* (*CUC*) meringue

meri'tare *vt* to deserve, merit ♦ *vb impers*: **merita andare** it's worth going

meri'tevole *ag* worthy

'merito *sm* merit; (*valore*) worth; **in ~ a** as regards, with regard to; **dare ~ a qn di** to give sb credit for; **finire a pari ~** to finish joint first (*o second etc*); to tie; **meri'torio, a** *ag* praiseworthy

mer'letto *sm* lace

'merlo *sm* (*ZOOL*) blackbird; (*ARCHIT*) battlement

mer'luzzo [mer'luttso] *sm* (*ZOOL*) cod

mes'chino, a [mes'kino] *ag* wretched; (*scarso*) scanty, poor; (*persona: gretta*) mean; (: *limitata*) narrow-minded, petty

mesco'lanza [mesko'lantsa] *sf* mixture

mesco'lare *vt* to mix; (*vini, colori*) to blend; (*mettere in disordine*) to mix up, muddle up; (*carte*) to shuffle; **~rsi** *vr* to mix; to blend; to get mixed up; (*fig*): **~rsi in** to get mixed up in, meddle in

'mese *sm* month

'messa *sf* (*REL*) mass; (*il mettere*): **~ in moto** starting; **~ in piega** set; **~ a punto** (*TECN*) adjustment; (*AUT*) tuning; (*fig*) clarification; **~ in scena** = **messinscena**

messag'gero [messad'dʒɛro] *sm* messenger

mes'saggio [mes'saddʒo] *sm* message

mes'sale *sm* (*REL*) missal

'messe *sf* harvest

Mes'sia *sm inv* (*REL*): **il ~** the Messiah

'Messico *sm*: **il ~** Mexico

messin'scena [messin'ʃɛna] *sf* (*TEATRO*) production

'messo, a *pp di* **mettere** ♦ *sm* messenger

mesti'ere *sm* (*professione*) job; (: *manuale*) trade; (: *artigianale*) craft; (*fig: abilità nel lavoro*) skill, technique; **essere del ~** to know the tricks of the trade

'mesto, a *ag* sad, melancholy

'mestola *sf* (*CUC*) ladle; (*EDIL*) trowel

'**mestolo** *sm* (*CUC*) ladle

mestruazi'one [mestruat'tsjone] *sf* menstruation

'**meta** *sf* destination; (*fig*) aim, goal

metà *sf inv* half; (*punto di mezzo*) middle; **dividere qc a** *o* **per** ~ to divide sth in half, halve sth; **fare a** ~ (**di qc con qn**) to go halves (with sb in sth); **a** ~ **prezzo** at half price; **a** ~ **strada** halfway

me'tafora *sf* metaphor

me'tallico, a, ci, che *ag* (*di metallo*) metal *cpd*; (*splendore, rumore etc*) metallic

me'tallo *sm* metal

metalmec'canico, a, ci, che *ag* engineering *cpd* ♦ *sm* engineering worker

me'tano *sm* methane

meteorolo'gia [meteorolo'dʒia] *sf* meteorology; **meteoro'logico, a, ci, che** *ag* meteorological, weather *cpd*

me'ticcio, a, ci, ce [me'tittʃo] *sm/f* half-caste, half-breed

me'todico, a, ci, che *ag* methodical

'**metodo** *sm* method; (*manuale*) tutor (*BRIT*), manual

'**metrica** *sf* metrics *sg*

'**metrico, a, ci, che** *ag* metric; (*POESIA*) metrical

'**metro** *sm* metre; (*nastro*) tape measure; (*asta*) (metre) rule

metropoli'tana *sf* underground, subway

metropoli'tano, a *ag* metropolitan

'**mettere** *vt* to put; (*abito*) to put on; (: *portare*) to wear; (*installare*: *telefono*) to put in; (*fig: provocare*): ~ **fame/allegria a qn** to make sb hungry/happy; (*supporre*): **mettiamo che ...** let's suppose *o* say that ... ; ~**rsi** *vr* (*persona*) to put o.s.; (*oggetto*) to go; (*disporsi: faccenda*) to turn out; ~**rsi a sedere** to sit down; ~**rsi a letto** to get into bed; (*per malattia*) to take to one's bed; ~**rsi il cappello** to put on one's hat; ~**rsi a** (*cominciare*) to begin to, start to; ~**rsi al lavoro** to set to work; ~**rsi con qn** (*in società*) to team up with sb; (*in coppia*) to start going out with sb; ~**rci**: ~**rci molta cura/molto tempo** to take a lot of care/a lot of time; **ci ho messo 3 ore per venire** it's taken me 3 hours to get here; ~**rcela tutta** to do

one's best; ~ **a tacere qn/qc** to keep sb/ sth quiet; ~ **su casa** to set up house; ~ **su un negozio** to start a shop; ~ **via** to put away

'**mezza** ['mɛddza] *sf*: **la** ~ half-past twelve (*in the afternoon*); *vedi anche* **mezzo**

mez'zadro [med'dzadro] *sm* (*AGR*) sharecropper

mezza'luna [meddza'luna] *sf* half-moon; (*dell'islamismo*) crescent; (*coltello*) (semicircular) chopping knife

mezza'nino [meddza'nino] *sm* mezzanine (floor)

mez'zano, a [med'dzano] *ag* (*medio*) average, medium; (*figlio*) middle *cpd* ♦ *sm/f* (*intermediario*) go-between; (*ruffiano*) pimp

mezza'notte [meddza'nɔtte] *sf* midnight

'**mezzo, a** ['mɛddzo] *ag* half; **un** ~ **litro/panino** half a litre/roll ♦ *av* half-; ~ **morto** half-dead ♦ *sm* (*metà*) half; (*parte centrale: di strada etc*) middle; (*per raggiungere un fine*) means *sg*; (*veicolo*) vehicle; (*nell'indicare l'ora*): **le nove e** ~ half past nine; **mezzogiorno e** ~ half past twelve; ~**i** *smpl* (*possibilità economiche*) means; **di** ~**a età** middle-aged; **un soprabito di** ~**a stagione** a spring (*o* autumn) coat; **di** ~ middle, in the middle; **andarci di** ~ (*patir danno*) to suffer; **levarsi** *o* **togliersi di** ~ to get out of the way; **in** ~ **a** in the middle of; **per** *o* **a** ~ **di** by means of; ~**i di comunicazione di massa** mass media *pl*; ~**i pubblici** public transport *sg*; ~**i di trasporto** means of transport

mezzogi'orno [meddzo'dʒorno] *sm* midday, noon; (*GEO*) south; **a** ~ at 12 (o'clock) *o* midday *o* noon; **il** ~ **d'Italia** southern Italy

mez'z'ora [med'dzora] *sf* half-hour, half an hour

mez'zora [med'dzora] *sf* = **mezz'ora**

mi (*dav lo, la, li, le, ne diventa* **me**) *pron* (*oggetto*) me; (*complemento di termine*) to me; (*riflessivo*) myself ♦ *sm* (*MUS*) E; (: *solfeggiando la scala*) mi

'**mia** *vedi* **mio**

miago'lare *vi* to miaow, mew

'**mica** *sf* (*CHIM*) mica ♦ *av* (*fam*): **non ... ~** not ... at all; **non sono ~ stanco** I'm not a bit tired; **non sarà ~ partito?** he wouldn't have left, would he?; **~ male** not bad

'**miccia, ce** ['mittʃa] *sf* fuse

micidi'ale [mitʃi'djale] *ag* fatal; (*dannosissimo*) deadly

mi'crofono *sm* microphone

micros'copio *sm* microscope

mi'dollo (*pl(f)* ~**a**) *sm* (*ANAT*) marrow; **~ osseo** bone marrow

'**mie** *vedi* **mio**

mi'ele *sm* honey

mi'ei *vedi* **mio**

mi'etere *vt* (*AGR*) to reap, harvest; (*fig: vite*) to take, claim

'**miglia** ['miʎʎa] *sfpl di* **miglio**

migli'aio [miʎ'ʎajo] (*pl(f)* ~**a**) *sm* thousand; **un ~ (di)** about a thousand; **a ~a** by the thousand, in thousands

'**miglio** ['miʎʎo] *sm* (*BOT*) millet; (*pl(f)* ~**a**: *unità di misura*) mile; **~ marino** *o* **nautico** nautical mile

migliora'mento [miʎʎora'mento] *sm* improvement

miglio'rare [miʎʎo'rare] *vt, vi* to improve

migli'ore [miʎ'ʎore] *ag* (*comparativo*) better; (*superlativo*) best ♦ *sm*: **il ~** the best (thing) ♦ *sm/f*: **il(la) ~** the best (person); **il miglior vino di questa regione** the best wine in this area

'**mignolo** ['miɲɲolo] *sm* (*ANAT*) little finger, pinkie; (*: dito del piede*) little toe

mi'grare *vi* to migrate

'**mila** *pl di* **mille**

Mi'lano *sf* Milan

miliar'dario, a *sm/f* millionaire

mili'ardo *sm* thousand million, billion (*US*)

mili'are *ag*: **pietra ~** milestone

mili'one *sm* million; **un ~ di lire** a million lire

mili'tante *ag, sm/f* militant

mili'tare *vi* (*MIL*) to be a soldier, serve; (*fig: in un partito*) to be a militant ♦ *ag* military ♦ *sm* serviceman; **fare il ~** to do one's military service

'**milite** *sm* soldier

millanta'tore, 'trice *sm/f* boaster

'**mille** (*pl* **mila**) *num* a *o* one thousand; **dieci mila** ten thousand

mille'foglie [mille'fɔʎʎe] *sm inv* (*CUC*) cream *o* vanilla slice

mil'lennio *sm* millennium

millepi'edi *sm inv* centipede

mil'lesimo, a *ag, sm* thousandth

milli'grammo *sm* milligram(me)

mil'limetro *sm* millimetre

'**milza** ['miltsa] *sf* (*ANAT*) spleen

mimetiz'zare [mimetid'dzare] *vt* to camouflage; **~rsi** *vr* to camouflage o.s.

'**mimica** *sf* (*arte*) mime

'**mimo** *sm* (*attore, componimento*) mime

mi'mosa *sf* mimosa

'**mina** *sf* (*esplosiva*) mine; (*di matita*) lead

mi'naccia, ce [mi'nattʃa] *sf* threat; **minacci'are** *vt* to threaten; **minacciare qn di morte** to threaten to kill sb; **minacciare di fare qc** to threaten to do sth; **minacci'oso, a** *ag* threatening

mi'nare *vt* (*MIL*) to mine; (*fig*) to undermine

mina'tore *sm* miner

mina'torio, a *ag* threatening

mine'rale *ag, sm* mineral

mine'rario, a *ag* (*delle miniere*) mining; (*dei minerali*) ore *cpd*

mi'nestra *sf* soup; **~ in brodo/di verdure** noodle/vegetable soup; **mines'trone** *sm* thick vegetable and pasta soup

mingher'lino, a [minger'lino] *ag* thin, slender

'**mini** *ag inv* mini ♦ *sf inv* miniskirt

minia'tura *sf* miniature

mini'era *sf* mine

mini'gonna *sf* miniskirt

'**minimo, a** *ag* minimum, least, slightest; (*piccolissimo*) very small, slight; (*il più basso*) lowest, minimum ♦ *sm* minimum; **al ~** at least; **girare al ~** (*AUT*) to idle

minis'tero *sm* (*POL, REL*) ministry; (*governo*) government; **M~ delle Finanze** Ministry of Finance, ≈ Treasury

mi'nistro *sm* (*POL, REL*) minister; **M~ delle Finanze** Minister of Finance,

≈ Chancellor of the Exchequer

mino'ranza [mino'rantsa] *sf* minority

mino'rato, a *ag* handicapped ♦ *sm/f* physically (*o* mentally) handicapped person

mi'nore *ag* (*comparativo*) less; (*più piccolo*) smaller; (*numero*) lower; (*inferiore*) lower, inferior; (*meno importante*) minor; (*più giovane*) younger; (*superlativo*) least; smallest; lowest; youngest ♦ *sm/f* (*minorenne*) minor, person under age

mino'renne *ag* under age ♦ *sm/f* minor, person under age

mi'nuscolo, a *ag* (*scrittura, carattere*) small; (*piccolissimo*) tiny ♦ *sf* small letter

mi'nuta *sf* rough copy, draft

mi'nuto, a *ag* tiny, minute; (*pioggia*) fine; (*corporatura*) delicate, fine; (*lavoro*) detailed ♦ *sm* (*unità di misura*) minute; **al ~** (*COMM*) retail

'mio (*f* **'mia**, *pl* **mi'ei**, **'mie**) *det*: **il ~**, **la mia** *etc* my ♦ *pron*: **il ~**, **la mia** *etc* mine; **i miei** my family; **un ~ amico** a friend of mine

'miope *ag* short-sighted

'mira *sf* (*anche fig*) aim; **prendere la ~** to take aim; **prendere di ~ qn** (*fig*) to pick on sb

mi'rabile *ag* admirable, wonderful

mi'racolo *sm* miracle

mi'raggio [mi'raddʒo] *sm* mirage

mi'rare *vi*: **~ a** to aim at

mi'rino *sm* (*TECN*) sight; (*FOT*) viewer, viewfinder

mir'tillo *sm* bilberry (*BRIT*), blueberry (*US*), whortleberry

mi'scela [miʃ'ʃela] *sf* mixture; (*di caffè*) blend

miscel'lanea [miʃʃel'lanea] *sf* miscellany

'mischia ['miskja] *sf* scuffle; (*RUGBY*) scrum, scrummage

mischi'are [mis'kjare] *vt* to mix, blend; **~rsi** *vr* to mix, blend

mis'cuglio [mis'kuʎʎo] *sm* mixture, hotchpotch, jumble

mise'rabile *ag* (*infelice*) miserable, wretched; (*povero*) poverty-stricken; (*di scarso valore*) miserable

mi'seria *sf* extreme poverty; (*infelicità*) misery; **~e** *sfpl* (*del mondo etc*) misfortunes, troubles; **porca ~!** (*fam*) blast!, damn!

miseri'cordia *sf* mercy, pity

'misero, a *ag* miserable, wretched; (*povero*) poverty-stricken; (*insufficiente*) miserable

mis'fatto *sm* misdeed, crime

mi'sogino [mi'zodʒino] *sm* misogynist

'missile *sm* missile

missio'nario, a *ag*, *sm/f* missionary

missi'one *sf* mission

misteri'oso, a *ag* mysterious

mis'tero *sm* mystery

mistifi'care *vt* to fool, bamboozle

'misto, a *ag* mixed; (*scuola*) mixed, coeducational ♦ *sm* mixture

mis'tura *sf* mixture

mi'sura *sf* measure; (*misurazione, dimensione*) measurement; (*taglia*) size; (*provvedimento*) measure, step; (*moderazione*) moderation; (*MUS*) time; (: *divisione*) bar; (*fig: limite*) bounds *pl*, limit; **nella ~ in cui** inasmuch as, insofar as; **su ~** made to measure

misu'rare *vt* (*ambiente, stoffa*) to measure; (*terreno*) to survey; (*abito*) to try on; (*pesare*) to weigh; (*fig: parole etc*) to weigh up; (: *spese, cibo*) to limit ♦ *vi* to measure; **~rsi** *vr*: **~rsi con qn** to have a confrontation with sb; to compete with sb; **misu'rato, a** *ag* (*ponderato*) measured; (*prudente*) cautious; (*moderato*) moderate

'mite *ag* mild; (*prezzo*) moderate, reasonable

miti'gare *vt* to mitigate, lessen; (*lenire*) to soothe, relieve; **~rsi** *vr* (*odio*) to subside; (*tempo*) to become milder

'mito *sm* myth; **mitolo'gia**, **'gie** *sf* mythology

'mitra *sf* (*REL*) mitre ♦ *sm inv* (*arma*) submachine gun

mitraglia'trice [mitraʎʎa'tritʃe] *sf* machine gun

mit'tente *sm/f* sender

'mobile *ag* mobile; (*parte di macchina*) moving; (*DIR: bene*) movable, personal

♦ *sm* (*arredamento*) piece of furniture; **~i** *smpl* (*mobilia*) furniture *sg*

mo'bilia *sf* furniture

mobili'are *ag* (*DIR*) personal, movable

mo'bilio *sm* = **mobilia**

mobili'tare *vt* to mobilize

mocas'sino *sm* moccasin

mocci'oso, a [mot'tʃoso, a] *sm/f* (*peg*) snotty(-nosed) kid

'moccolo *sm* (*di candela*) candle-end; (*fam: bestemmia*) oath; (: *moccio*) snot; **reggere il ~** to play gooseberry (*BRIT*), act as chaperon

'moda *sf* fashion; **alla ~, di ~** fashionable, in fashion

modalità *sf inv* formality

mo'della *sf* model

model'lare *vt* (*creta*) to model, shape; **~rsi** *vr*: **~rsi su** to model o.s. on

mo'dello *sm* model; (*stampo*) mould ♦ *ag inv* model *cpd*

'modem *sm inv* modem

mode'rare *vt* to moderate; **~rsi** *vr* to restrain o.s.; **mode'rato, a** *ag* moderate

modera'tore, 'trice *sm/f* moderator

mo'derno, a *ag* modern

mo'destia *sf* modesty

mo'desto, a *ag* modest

'modico, a, ci, che *ag* reasonable, moderate

mo'difica, che *sf* modification

modifi'care *vt* to modify, alter; **~rsi** *vr* to alter, change

mo'dista *sf* milliner

'modo *sm* way, manner; (*mezzo*) means, way; (*occasione*) opportunity; (*LING*) mood; (*MUS*) mode; **~i** *smpl* (*comportamento*) manners; **a suo ~, a ~ suo** in his own way; **ad** *o* **in ogni ~** anyway; **di** *o* **in ~ che** so that; **in ~ da** so as to; **in tutti i ~i** at all costs; (*comunque sia*) anyway; (*in ogni caso*) in any case; **in qualche ~** somehow or other; **~ di dire** turn of phrase; **per ~ di dire** so to speak

modu'lare *vt* to modulate; **modulazi'one** *sf* modulation; **modulazione di frequenza** frequency modulation

'modulo *sm* (*modello*) form; (*ARCHIT*,

lunare, di comando) module

'mogano *sm* mahogany

'mogio, a, gi, gie ['mɔdʒo] *ag* down in the dumps, dejected

'moglie ['moʎʎe] *sf* wife

mo'ine *sfpl* cajolery *sg*; (*leziosità*) affectation *sg*

'mola *sf* (*di mulino*) millstone; (*utensile abrasivo*) grindstone

mo'lare *sm* (*dente*) molar

'mole *sf* mass; (*dimensioni*) size; (*edificio grandioso*) massive structure

moles'tare *vt* to bother, annoy; **mo'lestia** *sf* annoyance, bother; **recar molestia a qn** to bother sb; **mo'lesto, a** *ag* annoying

'molla *sf* spring; **~e** *sfpl* (*per camino*) tongs

mol'lare *vt* to release, let go; (*NAUT*) to ease; (*fig: ceffone*) to give ♦ *vi* (*cedere*) to give in

'molle *ag* soft; (*muscoli*) flabby; (*fig: debole*) weak, feeble

mol'letta *sf* (*per capelli*) hairgrip; (*per panni stesi*) clothes peg; **~e** *sfpl* (*per zucchero*) tongs

'mollica, che *sf* crumb, soft part

mol'lusco, schi *sm* mollusc

'molo *sm* mole, breakwater; jetty

mol'teplice [mol'teplitʃe] *ag* (*formato di più elementi*) complex; **~i** *pl* (*svariati: interessi, attività*) numerous, various

moltipli'care *vt* to multiply; **~rsi** *vr* to multiply; to increase in number; **moltiplicazi'one** *sf* multiplication

---

PAROLA CHIAVE

'molto, a *det* (*quantità*) a lot of, much; (*numero*) a lot of, many; **~ pane/carbone** a lot of bread/coal; **~a gente** a lot of people, many people; **~i libri** a lot of books, many books; **non ho ~ tempo** I haven't got much time; **per ~ (tempo)** for a long time

♦ *av* **1** a lot, (very) much; **viaggia ~** he travels a lot; **non viaggia ~** he doesn't travel much *o* a lot

2 (*intensivo: con aggettivi, avverbi*) very; (: *con participio passato*) (very) much; **~**

buono very good; ~ **migliore**, ~ **meglio** much *o* a lot better
♦ *pron* much, a lot; ~**i, e** *pron pl* many, a lot; ~**i pensano che ...** many (people) think ...

momen'taneo, a *ag* momentary, fleeting
mo'mento *sm* moment; **da un ~ all'altro** at any moment; (*all'improvviso*) suddenly; **al ~ di fare** just as I was (*o* you were *o* he was *etc*) doing; **per il ~** for the time being; **dal ~ che** ever since; (*dato che*) since; **a ~i** (*da un ~ all'altro*) any time *o* moment now; (*quasi*) nearly
'monaca, che *sf* nun
'Monaco *sf* Monaco; ~ **(di Baviera)** Munich
'monaco, ci *sm* monk
mo'narca, chi *sm* monarch; **monar'chia** *sf* monarchy
monas'tero *sm* (*di monaci*) monastery; (*di monache*) convent; **mo'nastico, a, ci, che** *ag* monastic
'monco, a, chi, che *ag* maimed; (*fig*) incomplete; ~ **d'un braccio** one-armed
mon'dana *sf* prostitute
mon'dano, a *ag* (*anche fig*) worldly; (*dell'alta società*) society *cpd*; fashionable
mon'dare *vt* (*frutta, patate*) to peel; (*piselli*) to shell; (*pulire*) to clean
mondi'ale *ag* (*campionato, popolazione*) world *cpd*; (*influenza*) world-wide
'mondo *sm* world; (*grande quantità*): **un ~ di** lots of, a host of; **il bel ~** high society
mo'nello, a *sm/f* street urchin; (*ragazzo vivace*) scamp, imp
mo'neta *sf* coin; (*ECON: valuta*) currency; (*denaro spicciolo*) (small) change; ~ **estera** foreign currency; ~ **legale** legal tender; **mone'tario, a** *ag* monetary
mongo'loide *ag, sm/f* (*MED*) mongol
'monito *sm* warning
'monitor *sm inv* (*TECN, TV*) monitor
monoco'lore *ag* (*POL*): **governo ~** one-party government
mono'polio *sm* monopoly
mo'notono, a *ag* monotonous

monsi'gnore [monsiɲˈɲore] *sm* (*REL: titolo*) Your (*o* His) Grace
mon'sone *sm* monsoon
monta'carichi [montaˈkariki] *sm inv* hoist, goods lift
mon'taggio [monˈtaddʒo] *sm* (*TECN*) assembly; (*CINEMA*) editing
mon'tagna [monˈtaɲɲa] *sf* mountain; (*zona montuosa*): **la ~** the mountains *pl*; **andare in ~** to go to the mountains; ~**e russe** roller coaster *sg*, big dipper *sg* (*BRIT*); **monta'gnoso, a** *ag* mountainous
monta'naro, a *ag* mountain *cpd* ♦ *sm/f* mountain dweller
mon'tano, a *ag* mountain *cpd*; alpine
mon'tare *vt* to go (*o* come) up; (*cavallo*) to ride; (*apparecchiatura*) to set up, assemble; (*CUC*) to whip; (*ZOOL*) to cover; (*incastonare*) to mount, set; (*CINEMA*) to edit; (*FOT*) to mount ♦ *vi* to go (*o* come) up; (*a cavallo*): ~ **bene/male** to ride well/badly; (*aumentare di livello, volume*) to rise; ~**rsi** *vr* to become big-headed; ~ **qc** to exaggerate sth; ~ **qn** *o* **la testa a qn** to turn sb's head; ~ **in bicicletta/macchina/treno** to get on a bicycle/into a car/on a train; ~ **a cavallo** to get on *o* mount a horse
monta'tura *sf* assembling *no pl*; (*di occhiali*) frames *pl*; (*di gioiello*) mounting, setting; (*fig*): ~ **pubblicitaria** publicity stunt
'monte *sm* mountain; **a ~** upstream; **mandare a ~ qc** to upset sth, cause sth to fail; **il M~ Bianco** Mont Blanc; ~ **di pietà** pawnshop
mon'tone *sm* (*ZOOL*) ram; **carne di ~** mutton
montu'oso, a *ag* mountainous
monu'mento *sm* monument
'mora *sf* (*del rovo*) blackberry; (*del gelso*) mulberry; (*DIR*) delay; (: *somma*) arrears *pl*
mo'rale *ag* moral ♦ *sf* (*scienza*) ethics *sg*, moral philosophy; (*complesso di norme*) moral standards *pl*, morality; (*condotta*) morals *pl*; (*insegnamento morale*) moral ♦ *sm* morale; **essere giù di ~** to be feeling down; **moralità** *sf* morality;

(*condotta*) morals *pl*

'**morbido, a** *ag* soft; (*pelle*) soft, smooth

mor'**billo** *sm* (*MED*) measles *sg*

'**morbo** *sm* disease

mor'**boso, a** *ag* (*fig*) morbid

mor'**dace** [mor'datʃe] *ag* biting, cutting

mor'**dente** *sm* (*fig: di satira, critica*) bite; (: *di persona*) drive

'**mordere** *vt* to bite; (*addentare*) to bite into; (*corrodere*) to eat into

mori'**bondo, a** *ag* dying, moribund

morige'**rato, a** [moridʒe'rato] *ag* of good morals

mo'**rire** *vi* to die; (*abitudine, civiltà*) to die out; ~ **di fame** to die of hunger; (*fig*) to be starving; ~ **di noia/paura** to be bored/scared to death; **fa un caldo da** ~ it's terribly hot

mormo'**rare** *vi* to murmur; (*brontolare*) to grumble

'**moro, a** *ag* dark(-haired); dark(-complexioned); **i M~i** *smpl* (*STORIA*) the Moors

mo'**roso, a** *ag* in arrears ♦ *sm/f* (*fam: innamorato*) sweetheart

'**morsa** *sf* (*TECN*) vice; (*fig: stretta*) grip

morsi'**care** *vt* to nibble (at), gnaw (at); (*sog: insetto*) to bite

'**morso, a** *pp di* **mordere** ♦ *sm* bite; (*di insetto*) sting; (*parte della briglia*) bit; ~**i della fame** pangs of hunger

mor'**taio** *sm* mortar

mor'**tale** *ag, sm* mortal; **mortalità** *sf* mortality, death rate

'**morte** *sf* death

mortifi'**care** *vt* to mortify

'**morto, a** *pp di* **morire** ♦ *ag* dead ♦ *sm/f* dead man/woman; **i ~i** the dead; **fare il** ~ (*nell'acqua*) to float on one's back; **il Mar M~** the Dead Sea

mor'**torio** *sm* (*anche fig*) funeral

mo'**saico, ci** *sm* mosaic

'**Mosca** *sf* Moscow

'**mosca, sche** *sf* fly; ~ **cieca** blind-man's-buff

mos'**cato** *sm* muscatel (wine)

mosce'**rino** [moʃʃe'rino] *sm* midge, gnat

mos'**chea** [mos'kɛa] *sf* mosque

mos'**chetto** [mos'ketto] *sm* musket

'**moscio, a, sci, sce** ['mɔʃʃo] *ag* (*fig*) lifeless

mos'**cone** *sm* (*ZOOL*) bluebottle; (*barca*) pedalo; (: *a remi*) *kind of pedalo with oars*

'**mossa** *sf* movement; (*nel gioco*) move

'**mosso, a** *pp di* **muovere** ♦ *ag* (*mare*) rough; (*capelli*) wavy; (*FOT*) blurred; (*ritmo, prosa*) animated

mos'**tarda** *sf* mustard

'**mostra** *sf* exhibition, show; (*ostentazione*) show; **in** ~ on show; **far** ~ **di** (*fingere*) to pretend; **far** ~ **di sé** to show off

mos'**trare** *vt* to show ♦ *vi*: ~ **di fare** to pretend to do; ~**rsi** *vr* to appear

'**mostro** *sm* monster; **mostru'oso, a** *ag* monstrous

mo'**tel** *sm inv* motel

moti'**vare** *vt* (*causare*) to cause; (*giustificare*) to justify, account for; **motivazi'one** *sf* justification; motive; (*PSIC*) motivation

mo'**tivo** *sm* (*causa*) reason, cause; (*movente*) motive; (*letterario*) (central) theme; (*disegno*) motif, design, pattern; (*MUS*) motif; **per quale** ~? why?, for what reason?

'**moto** *sm* (*anche FISICA*) motion; (*movimento, gesto*) movement; (*esercizio fisico*) exercise; (*sommossa*) rising, revolt; (*commozione*) feeling, impulse ♦ *sf inv* (*motocicletta*) motorbike; **mettere in** ~ to set in motion; (*AUT*) to start up

motoci'**cletta** [mototʃi'kletta] *sf* motorcycle; **motoci'clismo** *sm* motorcycling, motorcycle racing; **motoci'clista, i, e** *sm/f* motorcyclist

mo'**tore, 'trice** *ag* motor; (*TECN*) driving ♦ *sm* engine, motor; **a** ~ motor *cpd*, power-driven; ~ **a combustione interna/a reazione** internal combustion/jet engine; **moto'rino** *sm* moped; **motorino di avviamento** (*AUT*) starter; **motoriz'zato, a** *ag* (*truppe*) motorized; (*persona*) having a car *o* transport

motos'**cafo** *sm* motorboat

'**motto** *sm* (*battuta scherzosa*) witty remark; (*frase emblematica*) motto, maxim mo'vente *sm* motive

movimen'tare *vt* to liven up

movi'mento *sm* movement; (*fig*) activity, hustle and bustle; (*MUS*) tempo, movement

mozi'one [mot'tsjone] *sf* (*POL*) motion

moz'zare [mot'tsare] *vt* to cut off; (*coda*) to dock; ~ **il fiato** *o* **il respiro a qn** (*fig*) to take sb's breath away

mozza'rella [mottsa'rɛlla] *sf* mozzarella (*a moist Neapolitan curd cheese*)

mozzi'cone [mottsi'kone] *sm* stub, butt, end; (*anche*: ~ **di sigaretta**) cigarette end

'mozzo¹ ['mɔddzo] *sm* (*MECCANICA*) hub

'mozzo² ['mottso] *sm* (*NAUT*) ship's boy; ~ **di stalla** stable boy

'mucca, che *sf* cow

'mucchio ['mukkjo] *sm* pile, heap; (*fig*): **un** ~ **di** lots of, heaps of

'muco, chi *sm* mucus

'muffa *sf* mould, mildew

mug'gire [mud'dʒire] *vi* (*vacca*) to low, moo; (*toro*) to bellow; (*fig*) to roar; **mug'gito** *sm* low, moo; bellow; roar

mu'ghetto [mu'getto] *sm* lily of the valley

mu'gnaio, a [muɲ'najo] *sm/f* miller

mugo'lare *vi* (*cane*) to whimper, whine; (*fig: persona*) to moan

muli'nare *vi* to whirl, spin (round and round)

muli'nello *sm* (*moto vorticoso*) eddy, whirl; (*di canna da pesca*) reel; (*NAUT*) windlass

mu'lino *sm* mill; ~ **a vento** windmill

'mulo *sm* mule

'multa *sf* fine; mul'tare *vt* to fine

'multiplo, a *ag*, *sm* multiple

'mummia *sf* mummy

'mungere ['mundʒere] *vt* (*anche fig*) to milk

munici'pale [munitʃi'pale] *ag* municipal; town *cpd*

muni'cipio [muni'tʃipjo] *sm* town council, corporation; (*edificio*) town hall

mu'nire *vt*: ~ **qc/qn di** to equip sth/sb with

munizi'oni [munit'tsjoni] *sfpl* (*MIL*) ammunition *sg*

'munto, a *pp di* mungere

mu'overe *vt* to move; (*ruota, macchina*) to drive; (*sollevare: questione, obiezione*) to raise, bring up; (: *accusa*) to make, bring forward; ~**rsi** *vr* to move; **muoviti!** hurry up!, get a move on!

'mura *sfpl vedi* muro

mu'raglia [mu'raʎʎa] *sf* (high) wall

mu'rale *ag* wall *cpd*; mural

mu'rare *vt* (*persona, porta*) to wall up

mura'tore *sm* mason; bricklayer

'muro *sm* wall; ~**a** *sfpl* (*cinta cittadina*) walls; **a** ~ wall *cpd*; (*armadio etc*) built-in; ~ **del suono** sound barrier; **mettere al** ~ (*fucilare*) to shoot *o* execute (by firing squad)

'muschio ['muskjo] *sm* (*ZOOL*) musk; (*BOT*) moss

musco'lare *ag* muscular, muscle *cpd*

'muscolo *sm* (*ANAT*) muscle

mu'seo *sm* museum

museru'ola *sf* muzzle

'musica *sf* music; ~ **da ballo/camera** dance/chamber music; **musi'cale** *ag* musical; **musi'cista, i, e** *sm/f* musician

'muso *sm* muzzle; (*di auto, aereo*) nose; **tenere il** ~ to sulk; **mu'sone, a** *sm/f* sulky person

'muta *sf* (*di animali*) moulting; (*di serpenti*) sloughing; (*per immersioni subacquee*) diving suit; (*gruppo di cani*) pack

muta'mento *sm* change

mu'tande *sfpl* (*da uomo*) (under) pants; **mutan'dine** *sfpl* (*da donna, bambino*) pants (*BRIT*), briefs

mu'tare *vt*, *vi* to change, alter; **mutazi'one** *sf* change, alteration; (*BIOL*) mutation; **mu'tevole** *ag* changeable

muti'lare *vt* to mutilate, maim; (*fig*) to mutilate, deface; **muti'lato, a** *sm/f* disabled person (*through loss of limbs*)

mu'tismo *sm* (*MED*) mutism; (*atteggiamento*) (stubborn) silence

'muto, a *ag* (*MED*) dumb; (*emozione, dolore, CINEMA*) silent; (*LING*) silent, mute; (*carta geografica*) blank; ~ **per lo stupore** *etc* speechless with amazement *etc*

'mutua *sf* (*anche: cassa* ~) health insurance scheme

mutu'are *vt* (*fig*) to borrow
mutu'ato, a *sm/f* member of a health insurance scheme
'mutuo, a *ag* (*reciproco*) mutual ♦ *sm* (*ECON*) (long-term) loan

N

N. *abbr* (= *nord*) N
'nacchere ['nakkere] *sfpl* castanets
'nafta *sf* naphtha; (*per motori diesel*) diesel oil
nafta'lina *sf* (*CHIM*) naphthalene; (*tarmicida*) mothballs *pl*
'naia *sf* (*ZOOL*) cobra; (*MIL*) slang term for national service
'nailon *sm* nylon
'nanna *sf* (*linguaggio infantile*): **andare a ~** to go to beddy-byes
'nano, a *ag*, *sm/f* dwarf
napole'tano, a *ag*, *sm/f* Neapolitan
'Napoli *sf* Naples
'nappa *sf* tassel
nar'ciso [nar'tʃizo] *sm* narcissus
nar'cosi *sf* narcosis
nar'cotico, ci *sm* narcotic
na'rice [na'ritʃe] *sf* nostril
nar'rare *vt* to tell the story of, recount; **narra'tiva** *sf* (*branca letteraria*) fiction; **narra'tivo, a** *ag* narrative; **narra'tore, 'trice** *sm/f* narrator; **narrazi'one** *sf* narration; (*racconto*) story, tale
na'sale *ag* nasal
'nascere ['naʃʃere] *vi* (*bambino*) to be born; (*pianta*) to come *o* spring up; (*fiume*) to rise, have its source; (*sole*) to rise; (*dente*) to come through; (*fig: derivare, conseguire*): **~ da** to arise from, be born out of; **è nata nel 1952** she was born in 1952; **'nascita** *sf* birth
nas'condere *vt* to hide, conceal; **~rsi** *vr* to hide; **nascon'diglio** *sm* hiding place; **nascon'dino** *sm* (*gioco*) hide-and-seek; **nas'costo, a** *pp di* **nascondere** ♦ *ag* hidden; **di nascosto** secretly
na'sello *sm* (*ZOOL*) hake
'naso *sm* nose
'nastro *sm* ribbon; (*magnetico, isolante,*

SPORT) tape; **~ adesivo** adhesive tape; **~ trasportatore** conveyor belt
nas'turzio [nas'turtsjo] *sm* nasturtium
na'tale *ag* of one's birth ♦ *sm* (*REL*): **N~** Christmas; (*giorno della nascita*) birthday; **natalità** *sf* birth rate; **nata'lizio, a** *ag* (*del Natale*) Christmas *cpd*
na'tante *sm* craft *inv*, boat
'natica, che *sf* (*ANAT*) buttock
na'tio, a, 'tii, 'tie *ag* native
Nativ'ità *sf* (*REL*) Nativity
na'tivo, a *ag*, *sm/f* native
'nato, a *pp di* **nascere** ♦ *ag*: **un attore ~** a born actor; **~a Pieri** née Pieri
na'tura *sf* nature; **pagare in ~** to pay in kind; **~ morta** still life
natu'rale *ag* natural; **natura'lezza** *sf* naturalness; **natura'lista, i, e** *sm/f* naturalist
naturaliz'zare [naturalid'dzare] *vt* to naturalize
natural'mente *av* naturally; (*certamente, sì*) of course
naufra'gare *vi* (*nave*) to be wrecked; (*persona*) to be shipwrecked; (*fig*) to fall through; **nau'fragio** *sm* shipwreck; (*fig*) ruin, failure; **'naufrago, ghi** *sm* castaway, shipwreck victim
'nausea *sf* nausea; **nausea'bondo, a** *ag* nauseating, sickening; **nause'are** *vt* to nauseate, make (feel) sick
'nautica *sf* (art of) navigation
'nautico, a, ci, che *ag* nautical
na'vale *ag* naval
na'vata *sf* (*anche: ~ centrale*) nave; (*anche: ~ laterale*) aisle
'nave *sf* ship, vessel; **~ cisterna** tanker; **~ da guerra** warship; **~ passeggeri** passenger ship; **~ spaziale** spaceship
na'vetta *sf* shuttle; (*servizio di collegamento*) shuttle (service)
navi'cella [navi'tʃɛlla] *sf* (*di aerostato*) gondola
navi'gare *vi* to sail; **navigazi'one** *sf* navigation
na'viglio [na'viʎʎo] *sm* fleet, ships *pl*; (*canale artificiale*) canal; **~ da pesca** fishing fleet
nazio'nale [nattsjo'nale] *ag* national ♦ *sf*

(*SPORT*) national team;**naziona'lismo** *sm* nationalism;**nazionalità** *sf inv* nationality

nazi'one [nat'tsjone] *sf* nation

PAROLA CHIAVE
---

ne *pron* **1** (*di lui, lei, loro*) of him/her/ them; about him/her/them; ~ **riconosco la voce** I recognize his (*o* her) voice
2 (*di questa, quella cosa*) of it; about it; ~ **voglio ancora** I want some more (of it *o* them); **non parliamone più!** let's not talk about it any more!
3 (*con valore partitivo*): **hai dei libri?** — **sì,** ~ **ho** have you any books? — yes, I have (some); **hai del pane?** — **no, non** ~ **ho** have you any bread? — no, I haven't any; **quanti anni hai?** — ~ **ho 17** how old are you? — I'm 17
♦ *av* (*moto da luogo: da lì*) from there; ~ **vengo ora** I've just come from there

né *cong*: ~ ... ~ neither ... nor; ~ **l'uno** ~ **l'altro lo vuole** neither of them wants it; **non parla** ~ **l'italiano** ~ **il tedesco** he speaks neither Italian nor German, he doesn't speak either Italian or German; **non piove** ~ **nevica** it isn't raining or snowing

ne'anche [ne'anke] *av, cong* not even; **non ...** ~ not even; ~ **se volesse potrebbe venire** he couldn't come even if he wanted to; **non l'ho visto** — ~ **io I** didn't see him — neither did I *o* I didn't either; ~ **per idea** *o* **sogno!** not on your life!

'nebbia *sf* fog; (*foschia*) mist;**nebbi'oso, a** *ag* foggy; misty

nebu'loso, a *ag* (*atmosfera*) hazy; (*fig*) hazy, vague

necessaria'mente [netʃessarja'mente] *av* necessarily

neces'sario, a [netʃes'sarjo] *ag* necessary

necessità [netʃessi'ta] *sf inv* necessity; (*povertà*) need, poverty;**necessi'tare** *vt* to require ♦ *vi* (*aver bisogno*): **necessitare di** to need

necro'logio [nekro'lɔdʒo] *sm* obituary

notice; (*registro*) register of deaths

ne'fando, a *ag* infamous, wicked

ne'fasto, a *ag* inauspicious, ill-omened

ne'gare *vt* to deny; (*rifiutare*) to deny, refuse; ~ **di aver fatto/che** to deny having done/that;**nega'tivo, a** *ag, sf, sm* negative;**negazi'one** *sf* negation

ne'gletto, a *ag* (*trascurato*) neglected

'negli ['neʎʎi] *prep +det vedi* **in**

negli'gente [negli'dʒente] *ag* negligent, careless;**negli'genza** *sf* negligence, carelessness

negozi'ante [negot'tsjante] *sm/f* trader, dealer; (*bottegaio*) shopkeeper (*BRIT*), storekeeper (*US*)

negozi'are [negot'tsjare] *vt* to negotiate ♦ *vi*: ~ **in** to trade *o* deal in;**negozi'ato** *sm* negotiation

ne'gozio [ne'gɔttsjo] *sm* (*locale*) shop (*BRIT*), store (*US*); (*affare*) (piece of) business *no pl*

'negro, a *ag, sm/f* Negro

'nei *prep +det vedi* **in**

nel *prep +det vedi* **in**

nell' *prep +det vedi* **in**

'nella *prep +det vedi* **in**

'nelle *prep +det vedi* **in**

'nello *prep +det vedi* **in**

'nembo *sm* (*METEOR*) nimbus

ne'mico, a, ci, che *ag* hostile; (*MIL*) enemy *cpd* ♦ *sm/f* enemy; **essere** ~ **di** to be strongly averse *o* opposed to

nem'meno *av, cong* = **neanche**

'nenia *sf* dirge; (*motivo monotono*) monotonous tune

'neo *sm* mole; (*fig*) (slight) flaw

neo... *prefisso* neo...

'neon *sm* (*CHIM*) neon

neo'nato, a *ag* newborn ♦ *sm/f* newborn baby

neozelan'dese [neoddzelan'dese] *ag* New Zealand *cpd* ♦ *sm/f* New Zealander

nep'pure *av, cong* = **neanche**

'nerbo *sm* lash; (*fig*) strength, backbone; **nerbo'ruto, a** *ag* muscular; robust

ne'retto *sm* (*TIP*) bold type

'nero, a *ag* black; (*scuro*) dark ♦ *sm* black; **il Mar N~** the Black Sea

nerva'tura *sf* (*ANAT*) nervous system; (*BOT*)

veining; (*ARCHIT, TECN*) rib

'**nervo** *sm* (*ANAT*) nerve; (*BOT*) vein; **avere i ~i** to be on edge; **dare sui ~a qn** to get on sb's nerves; **ner'voso, a** *ag* nervous; (*irritabile*) irritable ♦ *sm* (*fam*): **far venire il nervoso a qn** to get on sb's nerves

'**nespola** *sf* (*BOT*) medlar; (*fig*) blow, punch; '**nespolo** *sm* medlar tree

'**nesso** *sm* connection, link

PAROLA CHIAVE
---

nes'suno, a (*det: dav sm* **nessun** +*C, V,* **nessuno** +*s impura, gn, pn, ps, x, z; dav sf* **nessuna** +*C,* **nessun'** +*V*) *det* **1** (*non uno*) no, *espressione negativa* +any; **non c'è nessun libro** there isn't any book, there is no book; **nessun altro** no one else, nobody else; **nessun'altra cosa** nothing else; **in nessun luogo** nowhere **2** (*qualche*) any; **hai ~a obiezione?** do you have any objections?
♦ *pron* **1** (*non uno*) no one, nobody, *espressione negativa* +any(one); (*: cosa*) none, *espressione negativa* +any; **~ è venuto**, **non è venuto ~** nobody came **2** (*qualcuno*) anyone, anybody; **ha telefonato ~?** did anyone phone?

---

net'tare¹ *vt* to clean

'**nettare²** *sm* nectar

net'tezza [net'tettsa] *sf* cleanness, cleanliness; **~ urbana** cleansing department

'**netto, a** *ag* (*pulito*) clean; (*chiaro*) clear, clear-cut; (*deciso*) definite; (*ECON*) net

nettur'bino *sm* dustman (*BRIT*), garbage collector (*US*)

neu'rosi *sf* = **nevrosi**

neu'trale *ag* neutral; **neutralità** *sf* neutrality; **neutraliz'zare** *vt* to neutralize

'**neutro, a** *ag* neutral; (*LING*) neuter ♦ *sm* (*LING*) neuter

ne'vaio *sm* snowfield

'**neve** *sf* snow; **nevi'care** *vb impers* to snow; **nevi'cata** *sf* snowfall

ne'vischio [ne'viskjo] *sm* sleet

ne'voso, a *ag* snowy; snow-covered

nevral'gia [nevral'dʒia] *sf* neuralgia

nevras'tenico, a, ci, che *ag* (*MED*) neurasthenic; (*fig*) hot-tempered

ne'vrosi *sf* neurosis

'**nibbio** *sm* (*ZOOL*) kite

'**nicchia** ['nikkja] *sf* niche; (*naturale*) cavity, hollow

nicchi'are [nik'kjare] *vi* to shilly-shally, hesitate

'**nichel** ['nikel] *sm* nickel

nico'tina *sf* nicotine

'**nido** *sm* nest; **a ~ d'ape** (*tessuto etc*) honeycomb *cpd*

PAROLA CHIAVE
---

ni'ente *pron* **1** (*nessuna cosa*) nothing; **~ può fermarlo** nothing can stop him; **~ di ~** absolutely nothing; **nient'altro** nothing else; **nient'altro che** nothing but, just, only; **~ affatto** not at all, not in the least; **come se ~ fosse** as if nothing had happened; **cose da ~** trivial matters; **per ~** (*gratis, invano*) for nothing **2** (*qualcosa*): **hai bisogno di ~?** do you need anything? **3 : non ... ~** nothing, *espressione negativa* + anything; **non ho visto ~** I saw nothing, I didn't see anything; **non ho ~ da dire** I have nothing *o* haven't anything to say
♦ *sm* nothing; **un bel ~** absolutely nothing; **basta un ~ per farla piangere** the slightest thing is enough to make her cry
♦ *av* (*in nessuna misura*): **non ... ~** not ... at all; **non è (per) ~ buono** it isn't good at all

---

nientedi'meno *av* actually, even ♦ *escl* really!, I say!

niente'meno *av, escl* = **nientedimeno**

'**Nilo** *sm*: **il ~** the Nile

'**ninfa** *sf* nymph

nin'fea *sf* water lily

ninna-'nanna *sf* lullaby

'**ninnolo** *sm* (*balocco*) plaything; (*gingillo*) knick-knack

ni'pote *sm/f* (*di zii*) nephew/niece; (*di nonni*) grandson/daughter, grandchild

'nitido, a *ag* clear; (*specchio*) bright

ni'trato *sm* nitrate

'nitrico, a, ci, che *ag* nitric

ni'trire *vi* to neigh

ni'trito *sm* (*di cavallo*) neighing *no pl*; neigh; (*CHIM*) nitrite

nitroglice'rina [nitrogliʃeˈrina] *sf* nitroglycerine

no (*risposta*) no; **vieni o ~?** are you coming or not?; **perché ~?** why not?; **lo conosciamo? — tu ~ ma io sì** do we know him? — you don't but I do; **verrai, ~?** you'll come, won't you?

'nobile *ag* noble ♦ *sm/f* noble, nobleman/woman; **nobili'are** *ag* noble; **nobiltà** *sf* nobility; (*di azione etc*) nobleness

'nocca, che *sf* (*ANAT*) knuckle

nocci'ola [notˈtʃɔla] *ag inv* (*colore*) hazel, light brown ♦ *sf* hazelnut

'nocciolo[1] [ˈnɔttʃolo] *sm* (*di frutto*) stone; (*fig*) heart, core

noc'ciolo[2] [notˈtʃɔlo] *sm* (*albero*) hazel

'noce [ˈnotʃe] *sm* (*albero*) walnut tree ♦ *sf* (*frutto*) walnut; **~ moscata** nutmeg

no'civo, a [noˈtʃivo] *ag* harmful, noxious

'nodo *sm* (*di cravatta, legname, NAUT*) knot; (*AUT, FERR*) junction; (*MED, ASTR, BOT*) node; (*fig: legame*) bond, tie; (*: punto centrale*) heart, crux; **avere un ~ alla gola** to have a lump in one's throat; **no'doso, a** *ag* (*tronco*) gnarled

'noi *pron* (*soggetto*) we; (*oggetto: per dare rilievo, con preposizione*) us; **~ stessi(e)** we ourselves; (*oggetto*) ourselves

'noia *sf* boredom; (*disturbo, impaccio*) bother *no pl*, trouble *no pl*; **avere qn/qc a ~** not to like sb/sth; **mi è venuto a ~** I'm tired of it; **dare ~ a** to annoy; **avere delle ~e con qn** to have trouble with sb

noi'altri *pron* we

noi'oso, a *ag* boring; (*fastidioso*) annoying, troublesome

noleggi'are [noledˈdʒare] *vt* (*prendere a noleggio*) to hire (*BRIT*), rent; (*dare a noleggio*) to hire out (*BRIT*), rent (out); (*aereo, nave*) to charter; **no'leggio** *sm* hire (*BRIT*), rental

'nolo *sm* hire (*BRIT*), rental; charter; (*per trasporto merci*) freight; **prendere/dare a ~ qc** to hire/hire out sth

'nomade *ag* nomadic ♦ *sm/f* nomad

'nome *sm* name; (*LING*) noun; **in/a ~ di** in the name of; **di o per ~** (*chiamato*) called, named; **conoscere qn di ~** to know sb by name; **~ d'arte** stage name; **~ di battesimo** Christian name; **~ di famiglia** surname

no'mea *sf* notoriety

no'mignolo [noˈmiɲɲolo] *sm* nickname

'nomina *sf* appointment

nomi'nale *ag* nominal; (*LING*) noun *cpd*

nomi'nare *vt* to name; (*eleggere*) to appoint; (*citare*) to mention

nomina'tivo, a *ag* (*LING*) nominative; (*ECON*) registered ♦ *sm* (*LING: anche: caso ~*) nominative (case); (*AMM*) name

non *av* not ♦ *prefisso* non-; *vedi* **affatto; appena** *etc*

nonché [nonˈke] *cong* (*tanto più, tanto meno*) let alone; (*e inoltre*) as well as

noncu'rante *ag*: **~ (di)** careless (of), indifferent (to); **noncu'ranza** *sf* carelessness, indifference

nondi'meno *cong* (*tuttavia*) however; (*nonostante*) nevertheless

'nonno, a *sm/f* grandfather/mother; (*in senso più familiare*) grandma/grandpa; **~i** *smpl* grandparents

non'nulla *sm inv*: **un ~** nothing, a trifle

'nono, a *ag, sm* ninth

nonos'tante *prep* in spite of, notwithstanding ♦ *cong* although, even though

nontiscordardimé *sm inv* (*BOT*) forget-me-not

nord *sm* North ♦ *ag inv* north; northern; **il Mare del N~** the North Sea; **nor'dest** *sm* north-east; **'nordico, a, ci, che** *ag* nordic, northern European; **nor'dovest** *sm* north-west

'norma *sf* (*principio*) norm; (*regola*) regulation, rule; (*consuetudine*) custom, rule; **a ~ di legge** according to law, as laid down by law

nor'male *ag* normal; standard *cpd*; **normalità** *sf* normality; **normaliz'zare** *vt* to normalize, bring back to normal

normal'mente *av* normally

norve'gese [norve'dʒese] *ag, sm/f, sm* Norwegian

Nor'vegia [nor'vedʒa] *sf*: la ~ Norway

nostal'gia [nostal'dʒia] *sf* (*di casa, paese*) homesickness; (*del passato*) nostalgia; nos'talgico, a, ci, che *ag* homesick; nostalgic

nos'trano, a *ag* local; national; home-produced

'nostro, a *det*: il(la) ~(a) *etc* our ♦ *pron*: il(la) ~(a) *etc* ours ♦ *sm*: il ~ our money; our belongings; i ~i our family; our own people; è dei ~i he's one of us

'nota *sf* (*segno*) mark; (*comunicazione scritta, MUS*) note; (*fattura*) bill; (*elenco*) list; degno di ~ noteworthy, worthy of note

no'tabile *ag* notable; (*persona*) important ♦ *sm* prominent citizen

no'taio *sm* notary

no'tare *vt* (*segnare: errori*) to mark; (*registrare*) to note (down), write down; (*rilevare, osservare*) to note, notice; farsi ~ to get o.s. noticed

notazi'one [notat'tsjone] *sf* (*MUS*) notation

no'tevole *ag* (*talento*) notable, remarkable; (*peso*) considerable

no'tifica, che *sf* notification

notifi'care *vt* (*DIR*): ~ qc a qn to notify sb of sth, give sb notice of sth

no'tizia [no'tittsja] *sf* (*piece of*) news *sg*; (*informazione*) piece of information; ~e *sfpl* (*informazioni*) news *sg*; information *sg*; notizi'ario *sm* (*RADIO, TV, STAMPA*) news *sg*

'noto, a *ag* (well-)known

notorietà *sf* fame; notoriety

no'torio, a *ag* well-known; (*peg*) notorious

not'tambulo, a *sm/f* night-bird (*fig*)

not'tata *sf* night

'notte *sf* night; di ~ at night; (*durante la notte*) in the night, during the night; peggio che andar di ~ worse than ever; ~ bianca sleepless night; notte'tempo *av* at night; during the night

not'turno, a *ag* nocturnal; (*servizio, guardiano*) night *cpd*

no'vanta *num* ninety; novan'tesimo, a *num* ninetieth; novan'tina *sf*: una novantina (di) about ninety

'nove *num* nine

nove'cento [nove'tʃɛnto] *num* nine hundred ♦ *sm*: il N~ the twentieth century

no'vella *sf* (*LETTERATURA*) short story

novel'lino, a *ag* (*pivello*) green, inexperienced

no'vello, a *ag* (*piante, patate*) new; (*insalata, verdura*) early; (*sposo*) newly-married

no'vembre *sm* November

novi'lunio *sm* new moon

novità *sf inv* novelty; (*innovazione*) innovation; (*cosa originale, insolita*) something new; (*notizia*) piece of news *sg*; le ~ della moda the latest fashions

novizi'ato [novit'tsjato] *sm* (*REL*) novitiate; (*tirocinio*) apprenticeship

no'vizio, a [no'vittsjo] *sm/f* (*REL*) novice; (*tirocinante*) beginner, apprentice

nozi'one [not'tsjone] *sf* notion, idea; ~i *sfpl* (*rudimenti*) basic knowledge *sg*, rudiments

'nozze ['nɔttse] *sfpl* wedding *sg*, marriage *sg*; ~ d'argento/d'oro silver/golden wedding *sg*

ns. *abbr* (*COMM*) = nostro

'nube *sf* cloud; nubi'fragio *sm* cloudburst

'nubile *ag* (*donna*) unmarried, single

'nuca *sf* nape of the neck

nucle'are *ag* nuclear

'nucleo *sm* nucleus; (*gruppo*) team, unit, group; (*MIL, POLIZIA*) squad; il ~ familiare the family unit

nu'dista, i, e *sm/f* nudist

'nudo, a *ag* (*persona*) bare, naked, nude; (*membra*) bare, naked; (*montagna*) bare ♦ *sm* (*ARTE*) nude

'nugolo *sm*: un ~ di a whole host of

'nulla *pron, av* = niente ♦ *sm*: il ~ nothing

nulla'osta *sm inv* authorization

nullità *sf inv* nullity; (*persona*) nonentity

'nullo, a *ag* useless, worthless; (*DIR*) null

(and void); (*SPORT*): **incontro** ~ draw
nume'rale *ag*, *sm* numeral
nume'rare *vt* to number; **numerazi'one**
sf numbering; (*araba, decimale*) notation
nu'merico, a, ci, che *ag* numerical
'numero *sm* number; (*romano, arabo*)
numeral; (*di spettacolo*) act, turn; ~ **civico**
house number; ~ **di telefono** telephone
number; **nume'roso, a** *ag* numerous,
many; (*con sostantivo sg: adunanza etc*)
large
'nunzio ['nuntsjo] *sm* (*REL*) nuncio
nu'ocere ['nwɔtʃere] *vi*: ~ **a** to harm,
damage; **nuoci'uto, a** *pp di* **nuocere**
nu'ora *sf* daughter-in-law
nuo'tare *vi* to swim; (*galleggiare: oggetti*)
to float; **nuota'tore, 'trice** *sm/f*
swimmer; **nu'oto** *sm* swimming
nu'ova *sf* (*notizia*) (piece of) news *sg*; *vedi
anche* **nuovo**
nuova'mente *av* again
Nu'ova Ze'landa [-dze'landa] *sf*: **la** ~
New Zealand
nu'ovo, a *ag* new; **di** ~ again; ~
fiammante *o* **di zecca** brand-new
nutri'ente *ag* nutritious, nourishing
nutri'mento *sm* food, nourishment
nu'trire *vt* to feed; (*fig: sentimenti*) to
harbour, nurse; **nutri'tivo, a** *ag*
nutritional; (*alimento*) nutritious;
nutrizi'one *sf* nutrition
'nuvola *sf* cloud; **'nuvolo, a** *ag*,
nuvo'loso, a *ag* cloudy
nuzi'ale [nut'tsjale] *ag* nuptial; wedding
cpd

O

o (*dav V spesso* **od**) *cong* or; ~ ... ~ either
... or; ~ **l'uno** ~ **l'altro** either (of them)
O. *abbr* (= *ovest*) W
'oasi *sf inv* oasis
obbedi'ente *etc* = **ubbidiente** *etc*
obbli'gare *vt* (*costringere*): ~ **qn a fare** to
force *o* compel sb to do; (*DIR*) to bind; **~rsi**
vr: **~rsi a fare** to undertake to do;
obbli'gato, a *ag* (*costretto, grato*)
obliged; (*percorso, tappa*) set, fixed;

obbliga'torio, a *ag* compulsory,
obligatory; **obbligazi'one** *sf* obligation;
(*COMM*) bond, debenture; **'obbligo, ghi**
sm obligation; (*dovere*) duty; **avere**
l'obbligo di fare, essere nell'obbligo di
fare to be obliged to do; **essere d'obbligo**
(*discorso, applauso*) to be called for
ob'brobrio *sm* disgrace; (*fig*) mess,
eyesore
o'beso, a *ag* obese
obiet'tare *vt*: ~ **che** to object that; ~ **su**
qc to object to sth, raise objections
concerning sth
obiet'tivo, a *ag* objective ♦ *sm* (*OTTICA,*
FOT) lens *sg*, objective; (*MIL, fig*) objective
obiet'tore *sm* objector; ~ **di coscienza**
conscientious objector
obiezi'one [objet'tsjone] *sf* objection
obi'torio *sm* morgue, mortuary
o'bliquo, a *ag* oblique; (*inclinato*)
slanting; (*fig*) devious, underhand;
sguardo ~ sidelong glance
oblite'rare *vt* (*biglietto*) to stamp;
(*francobollo*) to cancel
oblò *sm inv* porthole
o'blungo, a, ghi, ghe *ag* oblong
'oboe *sm* (*MUS*) oboe
'oca (*pl* **'oche**) *sf* goose
occasi'one *sf* (*caso favorevole*)
opportunity; (*causa, motivo, circostanza*)
occasion; (*COMM*) bargain; **d'**~ (*a buon*
prezzo) bargain *cpd*; (*usato*) secondhand
occhi'aia [ok'kjaja] *sf* eye socket; **avere**
le ~e to have shadows under one's eyes
occhi'ali [ok'kjali] *smpl* glasses,
spectacles; ~ **da sole** sunglasses; ~ **da**
vista (prescription) glasses
occhi'ata [ok'kjata] *sf* look, glance; **dare**
un'~ **a** to have a look at
occhieggi'are [okkjed'dʒare] *vi* (*appa-*
rire qua e là) to peep (out)
occhi'ello [ok'kjɛllo] *sm* buttonhole;
(*asola*) eyelet
'occhio ['ɔkkjo] *sm* eye; **~!** careful!,
watch out!; **a** ~ **nudo** with the naked eye;
a quattr'~**i** privately, tête-à-tête; **dare**
all'~ *o* **nell'**~ **a qn** to catch sb's eye; **fare**
l'~ **a qc** to get used to sth; **tenere d'**~ **qn**
to keep an eye on sb; **vedere di buon/**

mal ~ qc to look favourably/
unfavourably on sth

occhio'lino [okkjo'lino] *sm*: **fare l'~ a
qn** to wink at sb

occiden'tale [ottʃiden'tale] *ag* western
♦ *sm/f* Westerner

occi'dente [ottʃi'dɛnte] *sm* west; (*POL*):
l'O~ the West; **a ~** in the west

oc'cipite [ot'tʃipite] *sm* back of the head,
occiput

oc'cludere *vt* to block; **occlusi'one** *sf*
blockage, obstruction; **oc'cluso, a** *pp di*
occludere

occor'rente *ag* necessary ♦ *sm* all that is
necessary

occor'renza [okkor'rɛntsa] *sf* necessity,
need; **all'~** in case of need

oc'correre *vi* to be needed, be required
♦ *vb impers*: **occorre farlo** it must be
done; **occorre che tu parta** you must
leave, you'll have to leave; **mi occorrono
i soldi** I need the money; **oc'corso, a** *pp
di* **occorrere**

occul'tare *vt* to hide, conceal

oc'culto, a *ag* hidden, concealed;
(*scienze, forze*) occult

occu'pare *vt* to occupy; (*manodopera*) to
employ; (*ingombrare*) to occupy, take up;
~rsi *vr* to occupy o.s., keep o.s. busy;
(*impiegarsi*) to get a job; **~rsi di**
(*interessarsi*) to take an interest in;
(*prendersi cura di*) to look after, take care
of; **occu'pato, a** *ag* (*MIL, POL*) occupied;
(*persona: affaccendato*) busy; (*posto, sedia*)
taken; (*toilette, TEL*) engaged; **occupa-
zi'one** *sf* occupation; (*impiego, lavoro*)
job; (*ECON*) employment

o'ceano [o'tʃeano] *sm* ocean

'ocra *sf* ochre

ocu'lare *ag* ocular, eye *cpd*; **testimone ~**
eye witness

ocu'lato, a *ag* (*attento*) cautious,
prudent; (*accorto*) shrewd

ocu'lista, i, e *sm/f* eye specialist, oculist

'ode *sf* ode

odi'are *vt* to hate, detest

odi'erno, a *ag* today's, of today; (*attuale*)
present

'odio *sm* hatred; **avere in ~ qc/qn** to

hate *o* detest sth/sb; **odi'oso, a** *ag*
hateful, odious

odo'rare *vt* (*annusare*) to smell;
(*profumare*) to perfume, scent ♦ *vi*: **~ (di)**
to smell (of); **odo'rato** *sm* sense of smell

o'dore *sm* smell; **gli ~i** *smpl* (*CUC*)
(aromatic) herbs; **odo'roso, a** *ag* sweet-
smelling

of'fendere *vt* to offend; (*violare*) to
break, violate; (*insultare*) to insult; (*ferire*)
to hurt; **~rsi** *vr* (*con senso reciproco*) to
insult one another; (*risentirsi*): **~rsi (di)**
to take offence (at), be offended (by);
offen'sivo, a *ag*, *sf* offensive

offe'rente *sm* (*in aste*): **al maggior ~** to
the highest bidder

of'ferta *sf* offer; (*donazione, anche REL*)
offering; (*in gara d'appalto*) tender; (*in
aste*) bid; (*ECON*) supply; **"~e d'impiego"**
"situations vacant"; **fare un'~a** to make
an offer; to tender; to bid

of'ferto, a *pp di* **offrire**

of'fesa *sf* insult, affront; (*MIL*) attack; (*DIR*)
offence; *vedi anche* **offeso**

of'feso, a *pp di* **offendere** ♦ *ag* offended;
(*fisicamente*) hurt, injured ♦ *sm/f* offended
party; **essere ~ con qn** to be annoyed
with sb; **parte ~a** (*DIR*) plaintiff

offi'cina [offi'tʃina] *sf* workshop

of'frire *vt* to offer; **~rsi** *vr* (*proporsi*) to
offer (o.s.), volunteer; (*occasione*) to
present itself; (*esporsi*): **~rsi a** to expose
o.s. to; **ti offro da bere** I'll buy you a
drink

offus'care *vt* to obscure, darken; (*fig:
intelletto*) to dim, cloud; (: *fama*) to
obscure, overshadow; **~rsi** *vr* to grow
dark; to cloud, grow dim; to be obscured

ogget'tivo, a [oddʒet'tivo] *ag* objective

og'getto [od'dʒetto] *sm* object; (*materia,
argomento*) subject (matter); **~i smarriti**
lost property *sg*

'oggi ['oddʒi] *av*, *sm* today; **~ a otto** a
week today; **oggigi'orno** *av* nowadays

'ogni ['oɲɲi] *det* every, each; (*tutti*) all;
(*con valore distributivo*) every; **~ uomo è
mortale** all men are mortal; **viene ~ due
giorni** he comes every two days; **~ cosa**
everything; **ad ~ costo** at all costs, at any

price; **in ~ luogo** everywhere; **~ tanto**
every so often; **~ volta che** every time
that

Ognis'santi [oɲɲis'santi] *sm* All Saints'
Day

o'gnuno [oɲ'ɲuno] *pron* everyone,
everybody

'ohi *escl* oh!; (*esprimente dolore*) ow!

ohimè *escl* oh dear!

O'landa *sf*: **l'~** Holland; **olan'dese** *ag*
Dutch ♦ *sm* (*LING*) Dutch ♦ *sm/f*
Dutchman/woman; **gli Olandesi** the
Dutch

oleo'dotto *sm* oil pipeline

ole'oso, a *ag* oily; (*che contiene olio*) oil-
yielding

ol'fatto *sm* sense of smell

oli'are *vt* to oil

oli'era *sf* oil cruet

olim'piadi *sfpl* Olympic games;
o'limpico, a, ci, che *ag* Olympic

'olio *sm* oil; **sott'~** (*CUC*) in oil; **~ di
fegato di merluzzo** cod liver oil; **~
d'oliva** olive oil; **~ di semi** vegetable oil

o'liva *sf* olive; **oli'vastro, a** *ag* olive(-
coloured); (*carnagione*) sallow; **oli'veto**
sm olive grove; **o'livo** *sm* olive tree

'olmo *sm* elm

oltraggi'are [oltrad'dʒare] *vt* to outrage;
to offend gravely

ol'traggio [ol'traddʒo] *sm* outrage;
offence, insult; **~ a pubblico ufficiale**
(*DIR*) insulting a public official; **~ al
pudore** (*DIR*) indecent behaviour;
oltraggi'oso, a *ag* offensive

ol'tralpe *av* beyond the Alps

ol'tranza [ol'trantsa] *sf*: **a ~** to the last,
to the bitter end

'oltre *av* (*più in là*) further; (*di più:
aspettare*) longer, more ♦ *prep* (*di là da*)
beyond, over, on the other side of; (*più
di*) more than, over; (*in aggiunta a*)
besides; (*eccetto*): **~ a** except, apart from;
oltre'mare *av* overseas; **oltre'modo** *av*
extremely; **oltrepas'sare** *vt* to go
beyond, exceed

o'maggio [o'maddʒo] *sm* (*dono*) gift;
(*segno di rispetto*) homage, tribute; **~i**
smpl (*complimenti*) respects; **rendere ~ a**

to pay homage *o* tribute to; **in ~** (*copia,
biglietto*) complimentary

ombeli'cale *ag* umbilical

ombe'lico, chi *sm* navel

'ombra *sf* (*zona non assolata, fantasma*)
shade; (*sagoma scura*) shadow; **sedere
all'~** to sit in the shade; **restare nell'~**
(*fig*) to remain in obscurity

ombreggi'are [ombred'dʒare] *vt* to
shade

om'brello *sm* umbrella; **ombrel'lone** *sm*
beach umbrella

om'bretto *sm* eyeshadow

om'broso, a *ag* shady, shaded; (*cavallo*)
nervous, skittish; (*persona*) touchy, easily
offended

ome'lia *sf* (*REL*) homily, sermon

omeopa'tia *sf* homoeopathy

omertà *sf* conspiracy of silence

o'messo, a *pp di* omettere

o'mettere *vt* to omit, leave out; **~ di
fare** to omit *o* fail to do

omi'cida, i, e [omi'tʃida] *ag* homicidal,
murderous ♦ *sm/f* murderer/eress

omi'cidio [omi'tʃidjo] *sm* murder; **~
colposo** culpable homicide

omissi'one *sf* omission; **~ di soccorso**
(*DIR*) failure to stop and give assistance

omogeneiz'zato [omodʒeneid'dzato] *sm*
baby food

omo'geneo, a [omo'dʒɛneo] *ag*
homogeneous

omolo'gare *vt* to approve, recognize; to
ratify

o'monimo, a *sm/f* namesake ♦ *sm* (*LING*)
homonym

omosessu'ale *ag, sm/f* homosexual

'oncia, ce ['ontʃa] *sf* ounce

'onda *sf* wave; **mettere *o* mandare in ~**
(*RADIO, TV*) to broadcast; **andare in ~**
(*RADIO, TV*) to go on the air; **~e corte/
medie/lunghe** short/medium/long wave;
on'data *sf* wave, billow; (*fig*) wave,
surge; **a ondate** in waves; **ondata di
caldo** heatwave

'onde *cong* (*affinché: con il congiuntivo*)
so that, in order that; (*: con l'infinito*) so
as to, in order to

ondeggi'are [onded'dʒare] *vi* (*acqua*) to

ripple; (*muoversi sulle onde: barca*) to rock, roll; (*fig: muoversi come le onde, barcollare*) to sway; (: *essere incerto*) to waver

ondulazi'one [ondulat'tsjone] *sf* undulation; (*acconciatura*) wave

'**onere** *sm* burden; ~**i fiscali** taxes; **one'roso, a** *ag* (*fig*) heavy, onerous

onestà *sf* honesty

o'nesto, a *ag* (*probo, retto*) honest; (*giusto*) fair; (*casto*) chaste, virtuous

'**onice** ['ɔnitʃe] *sf* onyx

onnipo'tente *ag* omnipotent

onniveg'gente [onnived'dʒɛnte] *ag* all-seeing

ono'mastico, ci *sm* name-day

ono'ranze [ono'rantse] *sfpl* honours; ~ **funebri** funeral (service)

ono'rare *vt* to honour; (*far onore a*) to do credit to; ~**rsi** *vr*: ~**rsi di** to feel honoured at, be proud of

ono'rario, a *ag* honorary ♦ *sm* fee

o'nore *sm* honour; **in ~ di** in honour of; **fare gli ~i di casa** to play host (*o* hostess); **fare ~ a** to honour; (*pranzo*) to do justice to; (*famiglia*) to be a credit to; **farsi ~** to distinguish o.s.; **ono'revole** *ag* honourable ♦ *sm/f* (*POL*) ≈ Member of Parliament (*BRIT*), ≈ Congressman/woman (*US*); **onorifi'cenza** *sf* honour; decoration; **ono'rifico, a, ci, che** *ag* honorary

'**onta** *sf* shame, disgrace

on'tano *sm* (*BOT*) alder

'**O.N.U.** ['ɔnu] *sigla f* (= *Organizzazione delle Nazioni Unite*) UN, UNO

o'paco, a, chi, che *ag* (*vetro*) opaque; (*metallo*) dull, matt

o'pale *sm o f* opal

'**opera** *sf* work; (*azione rilevante*) action, deed, work; (*MUS*) work; opus; (: *melodramma*) opera; (: *teatro*) opera house; (*ente*) institution, organization; ~ **d'arte** work of art; ~ **lirica** (grand) opera; ~**e pubbliche** public works

ope'raio, a *ag* working-class; workers' ♦ *sm/f* worker; **classe ~a** working class

ope'rare *vt* to carry out, make; (*MED*) to operate on ♦ *vi* to operate, work; (*rimedio*) to act, work; (*MED*) to operate;

~**rsi** *vr* to occur, take place; (*MED*) to have an operation; ~**rsi d'appendicite** to have one's appendix out; **opera'tivo, a** *ag* operative, operating; **opera'tore, 'trice** *sm/f* operator; (*TV, CINEMA*) cameraman; **operatore economico** agent, broker; **operatore turistico** tour operator; **opera'torio, a** *ag* (*MED*) operating; **operazi'one** *sf* operation

ope'retta *sf* (*MUS*) operetta, light opera

ope'roso, a *ag* busy, active, hard-working

opi'ficio [opi'fitʃo] *sm* factory, works *pl*

opini'one *sf* opinion; ~ **pubblica** public opinion

'**oppio** *sm* opium

oppo'nente *ag* opposing ♦ *sm/f* opponent

op'porre *vt* to oppose; **opporsi** *vr*: **opporsi (a qc)** to oppose (sth); to object (to sth); ~ **resistenza/un rifiuto** to offer resistance/refuse

opportu'nista, i, e *sm/f* opportunist

opportunità *sf inv* opportunity; (*convenienza*) opportuneness, timeliness

oppor'tuno, a *ag* timely, opportune

opposi'tore, 'trice *sm/f* opposer, opponent

opposizi'one [oppozit'tsjone] *sf* opposition; (*DIR*) objection

op'posto, a *pp di* **opporre** ♦ *ag* opposite; (*opinioni*) conflicting ♦ *sm* opposite, contrary; **all'~** on the contrary

oppressi'one *sf* oppression

oppres'sivo, a *ag* oppressive

op'presso, a *pp di* **opprimere**

oppres'sore *sm* oppressor

op'primere *vt* (*premere, gravare*) to weigh down; (*estenuare: sog: caldo*) to suffocate, oppress; (*tiranneggiare: popolo*) to oppress

oppu'gnare [oppuɲ'ɲare] *vt* (*fig*) to refute

op'pure *cong* or (else)

op'tare *vi*: ~ **per** to opt for

o'puscolo *sm* booklet, pamphlet

opzi'one [op'tsjone] *sf* option

'**ora**[1] *sf* (*60 minuti*) hour; (*momento*) time; **che ~ è?, che ~e sono?** what time is it?;

non veder l'~ di fare to long to do, look forward to doing; **di buon'~** early; **alla buon'~!** at last!; **~ legale** *o* **estiva** summer time (*BRIT*), daylight saving time (*US*); **~ locale** local time; **~ di punta** (*AUT*) rush hour

ora² *av* (*adesso*) now; (*poco fa*): **è uscito proprio ~** he's just gone out; (*tra poco*) presently, in a minute; (*correlativo*): **~ ... ~** now ... now; **d'~ in avanti** *o* **poi** from now on; **or ~** just now, a moment ago; **5 anni or sono** 5 years ago; **~ come ~** right now, at present

o'racolo *sm* oracle

'orafo *sm* goldsmith

o'rale *ag, sm* oral

ora'mai *av* = **ormai**

o'rario, a *ag* hourly; (*fuso, segnale*) time *cpd*; (*velocità*) per hour ♦ *sm* timetable, schedule; (*di ufficio, visite etc*) hours *pl*, time(s *pl*)

o'rata *sf* (*ZOOL*) sea bream

ora'tore, 'trice *sm/f* speaker; orator

ora'toria *sf* (*arte*) oratory

ora'torio, a *ag* oratorical ♦ *sm* (*REL*) oratory; (*MUS*) oratorio

ora'zione [orat'tsjone] *sf* (*REL*) prayer; (*discorso*) speech, oration

or'bene *cong* so, well (then)

'orbita *sf* (*ASTR, FISICA*) orbit; (*ANAT*) (eye-)socket

or'chestra [or'kɛstra] *sf* orchestra; **orches'trare** *vt* to orchestrate; (*fig*) to mount, stage-manage

orchi'dea [orki'dɛa] *sf* orchid

'orco, chi *sm* ogre

'orda *sf* horde

or'digno [or'diɲɲo] *sm* (*esplosivo*) explosive device

ordi'nale *ag, sm* ordinal

ordina'mento *sm* order, arrangement; (*regolamento*) regulations *pl*, rules *pl*; **~ scolastico/giuridico** education/legal system

ordi'nanza [ordi'nantsa] *sf* (*DIR, MIL*) order; (*persona*: *MIL*) orderly, batman; **d'~** (*MIL*) regulation *cpd*

ordi'nare *vt* (*mettere in ordine*) to arrange, organize; (*COMM*) to order; (*prescrivere*: *medicina*) to prescribe; (*comandare*): **~ a qn di fare qc** to order *o* command sb to do sth; (*REL*) to ordain

ordi'nario, a *ag* (*comune*) ordinary; everyday; standard; (*grossolano*) coarse, common ♦ *sm* ordinary; (*INS*: *di università*) full professor

ordi'nato, a *ag* tidy, orderly

ordinazi'one [ordinat'tsjone] *sf* (*COMM*) order; (*REL*) ordination; **eseguire qc su ~** to make sth to order

'ordine *sm* order; (*carattere*): **d'~ pratico** of a practical nature; **all'~** (*COMM*: *assegno*) to order; **di prim'~** first-class; **fino a nuovo ~** until further notice; **essere in ~** (*documenti*) to be in order; (*stanza, persona*) to be tidy; **mettere in ~** to put in order, tidy (up); **~ del giorno** (*di seduta*) agenda; (*MIL*) order of the day; **~ di pagamento** (*COMM*) order for payment; **l'~ pubblico** law and order; **~i (sacri)** (*REL*) holy orders

or'dire *vt* (*fig*) to plot, scheme; **or'dito** *sm* (*di tessuto*) warp

orec'chino [orek'kino] *sm* earring

o'recchio [o'rekkjo] (*pl(f)* **o'recchie**) *sm* (*ANAT*) ear

orecchi'oni [orek'kjoni] *smpl* (*MED*) mumps *sg*

o'refice [o'rɛfitʃe] *sm* goldsmith; jeweller; **orefice'ria** *sf* (*arte*) goldsmith's art; (*negozio*) jeweller's (shop)

'orfano, a *ag* orphan(ed) ♦ *sm/f* orphan; **~ di padre/madre** fatherless/motherless; **orfano'trofio** *sm* orphanage

orga'netto *sm* barrel organ; (*fam*: *armonica a bocca*) mouth organ; (: *fisarmonica*) accordion

or'ganico, a, ci, che *ag* organic ♦ *sm* personnel, staff

organi'gramma, i *sm* organization chart

orga'nismo *sm* (*BIOL*) organism; (*corpo umano*) body; (*AMM*) body, organism

organiz'zare [organid'dzare] *vt* to organize; **~rsi** *vr* to get organized; **organizza'tore, 'trice** *ag* organizing ♦ *sm/f* organizer; **organizzazi'one** *sf* organization '**organo** *sm* organ; (*di congegno*) part; (*portavoce*) spokesman, mouthpiece

or'**gasmo** *sm* (*FISIOL*) orgasm; (*fig*) agitation, anxiety

'**orgia, ge** ['ɔrdʒa] *sf* orgy

or'**goglio** [or'ɡɔʎʎo] *sm* pride; **orgogli'oso, a** *ag* proud

orien'**tale** *ag* oriental; eastern; east

orienta'**mento** *sm* positioning; orientation; direction; **senso di ~** sense of direction; **perdere l'~** to lose one's bearings; **~ professionale** careers guidance

orien'**tare** *vt* (*situare*) to position; (*fig*) to direct, orientate; **~rsi** *vr* to find one's bearings; (*fig*: *tendere*) to tend, lean; (: *indirizzarsi*): **~rsi verso** to take up, go in for

ori'**ente** *sm* east; **l'O~** the East, the Orient; **a ~** in the east

o'**rigano** *sm* oregano

origi'**nale** [oridʒi'nale] *ag* original; (*bizzarro*) eccentric ♦ *sm* original; **originalità** *sf* originality; eccentricity

origi'**nare** [oridʒi'nare] *vt* to bring about, produce ♦ *vi*: **~ da** to arise *o* spring from

origi'**nario, a** [oridʒi'narjo] *ag* original; **essere ~ di** to be a native of; (*provenire da*) to originate from; to be native to

o'**rigine** [o'ridʒine] *sf* origin; **all'~** originally; **d'~ inglese** of English origin; **dare ~ a** to give rise to

origli'**are** [oriʎ'ʎare] *vi*: **~ (a)** to eavesdrop (on)

o'**rina** *sf* urine

ori'**nare** *vi* to urinate ♦ *vt* to pass; **orina'toio** *sm* (public) urinal

ori'**undo, a** *ag*: **essere ~ di Milano** *etc* to be of Milanese *etc* extraction *o* origin ♦ *sm/f* person of foreign extraction *o* origin

orizzon'**tale** [oriddzon'tale] *ag* horizontal

oriz'**zonte** [orid'dzonte] *sm* horizon

or'**lare** *vt* to hem

'**orlo** *sm* edge, border; (*di recipiente*) rim, brim; (*di vestito etc*) hem

'**orma** *sf* (*di persona*) footprint; (*di animale*) track; (*impronta, traccia*) mark, trace

or'**mai** *av* by now, by this time; (*adesso*) now; (*quasi*) almost, nearly

ormeggi'**are** [ormed'dʒare] *vt* (*NAUT*) to moor; **or'meggio** *sm* (*atto*) mooring *no pl*; (*luogo*) moorings *pl*

or'**mone** *sm* hormone

ornamen'**tale** *ag* ornamental, decorative

orna'**mento** *sm* ornament, decoration

or'**nare** *vt* to adorn, decorate; **~rsi** *vr*: **~rsi (di)** to deck o.s. (out) (with); **or'nato, a** *ag* ornate

ornitolo'**gia** [ornitolo'dʒia] *sf* ornithology

'**oro** *sm* gold; **d'~, in ~** gold *cpd*; **d'~** (*colore, occasione*) golden; (*persona*) marvellous

orologe'**ria** [orolodʒe'ria] *sf* watchmaking *no pl*; watchmaker's (shop); clockmaker's (shop); **bomba a ~** time bomb

orologi'**aio** [orolo'dʒajo] *sm* watchmaker; clockmaker

oro'**logio** [oro'lɔdʒo] *sm* clock; (*da tasca, da polso*) watch; **~ da polso** wristwatch; **~ al quarzo** quartz watch

o'**roscopo** *sm* horoscope

or'**rendo, a** *ag* (*spaventoso*) horrible, awful; (*bruttissimo*) hideous

or'**ribile** *ag* horrible

'**orrido, a** *ag* fearful, horrid

orripi'**lante** *ag* hair-raising, horrifying

or'**rore** *sm* horror; **avere in ~ qn/qc** to loathe *o* detest sb/sth; **mi fanno ~** I loathe *o* detest them

orsacchi'**otto** [orsak'kjɔtto] *sm* teddy bear

'**orso** *sm* bear; **~ bruno/bianco** brown/ polar bear

or'**taggio** [or'taddʒo] *sm* vegetable

or'**tensia** *sf* hydrangea

or'**tica, che** *sf* (*stinging*) nettle

orti'**caria** *sf* nettle rash

'**orto** *sm* vegetable garden, kitchen garden; (*AGR*) market garden (*BRIT*), truck farm (*US*)

orto'**dosso, a** *ag* orthodox

ortogra'**fia** *sf* spelling

orto'**lano, a** *sm/f* (*venditore*) greengrocer (*BRIT*), produce dealer (*US*)

ortope'dia *sf* orthopaedics *sg*; **orto'pedico, a, ci, che** *ag* orthopaedic ♦ *sm* orthopaedic specialist

orzai'olo [ordza'jɔlo] *sm* (MED) stye

or'zata [or'dzata] *sf* barley water

'orzo ['ordzo] *sm* barley

o'sare *vt, vi* to dare; ~ **fare** to dare (to) do

oscenità [oʃʃeni'ta] *sf inv* obscenity

o'sceno, a [oʃ'ʃɛno] *ag* obscene; (*ripugnante*) ghastly

oscil'lare [oʃʃil'lare] *vi* (*pendolo*) to swing; (*dondolare: al vento etc*) to rock; (*variare*) to fluctuate; (TECN) to oscillate; (*fig*): ~ **fra** to waver *o* hesitate between; **oscillazi'one** *sf* oscillation; (*di prezzi, temperatura*) fluctuation

oscura'mento *sm* darkening; obscuring; (*in tempo di guerra*) blackout

oscu'rare *vt* to darken, obscure; (*fig*) to obscure; ~**rsi** *vr* (*cielo*) to darken, cloud over; (*persona*): **si oscurò in volto** his face clouded over

os'curo, a *ag* dark; (*fig*) obscure; humble, lowly ♦ *sm*: **all'~** in the dark; **tenere qn all'~ di qc** to keep sb in the dark about sth

ospe'dale *sm* hospital; **ospedali'ero, a** *ag* hospital *cpd*

ospi'tale *ag* hospitable; **ospitalità** *sf* hospitality

ospi'tare *vt* to give hospitality to; (*sog: albergo*) to accommodate

'ospite *sm/f* (*persona che ospita*) host/hostess; (*persona ospitata*) guest

os'pizio [os'pittsjo] *sm* (*per vecchi etc*) home

'ossa *sfpl vedi* **osso**

ossa'tura *sf* (ANAT) skeletal structure, frame; (TECN, *fig*) framework

'osseo, a *ag* bony; (*tessuto etc*) bone *cpd*

os'sequio *sm* deference, respect; ~**i** *smpl* (*saluto*) respects, regards; **ossequi'oso, a** *ag* obsequious

osser'vanza [osser'vantsa] *sf* observance

osser'vare *vt* to observe, watch; (*esaminare*) to examine; (*notare, rilevare*) to notice, observe; (DIR: *la legge*) to observe, respect; (*mantenere: silenzio*) to keep, observe; **far** ~ **qc a qn** to point sth out to sb; **osserva'tore, 'trice** *ag* observant, perceptive ♦ *sm/f* observer; **osserva'torio** *sm* (ASTR) observatory; (MIL) observation post; **osservazi'one** *sf* observation; (*di legge etc*) observance; (*considerazione critica*) observation, remark; (*rimprovero*) reproof; **in osservazione** under observation

ossessio'nare *vt* to obsess, haunt; (*tormentare*) to torment, harass

ossessi'one *sf* obsession

os'sesso, a *ag* (*spiritato*) possessed

os'sia *cong* that is, to be precise

ossi'buchi [ossi'buki] *smpl di* **ossobuco**

ossi'dare *vt* to oxidize; ~**rsi** *vr* to oxidize

'ossido *sm* oxide; ~ **di carbonio** carbon monoxide

ossige'nare [ossidʒe'nare] *vt* to oxygenate; (*decolorare*) to bleach; **acqua ossigenata** hydrogen peroxide

os'sigeno *sm* oxygen

'osso (*pl(f)* **ossa** *nel senso* ANAT) *sm* bone; **d'~** (*bottone etc*) of bone, bone *cpd*

osso'buco (*pl* **ossi'buchi**) *sm* (CUC) marrowbone; (: *piatto*) stew made with knuckle of veal in tomato sauce

os'suto, a *ag* bony

ostaco'lare *vt* to block, obstruct

os'tacolo *sm* obstacle; (EQUITAZIONE) hurdle, jump

os'taggio [os'taddʒo] *sm* hostage

'oste, os'tessa *sm/f* innkeeper

osteggi'are [osted'dʒare] *vt* to oppose, be opposed to

os'tello *sm*: ~ **della gioventù** youth hostel

osten'tare *vt* to make a show of, flaunt; **ostentazi'one** *sf* ostentation, show

oste'ria *sf* inn

os'tessa *sf vedi* **oste**

os'tetrica *sf* midwife

os'tetrico, a, ci, che *ag* obstetric ♦ *sm* obstetrician

'ostia *sf* (REL) host; (*per medicinali*) wafer

'ostico, a, ci, che *ag* (*fig*) harsh; hard, difficult; unpleasant

os'tile *ag* hostile; **ostilità** *sf inv* hostility

♦ *sfpl* (*MIL*) hostilities

osti'narsi *vr* to insist, dig one's heels in; ~ a fare to persist (obstinately) in doing; osti'nato, a *ag* (*caparbio*) obstinate; (*tenace*) persistent, determined; ostinazi'one *sf* obstinacy; persistence

'ostrica, che *sf* oyster

ostru'ire *vt* to obstruct, block; ostruzi'one *sf* obstruction, blockage

'otre *sm* (*recipiente*) goatskin

ottago'nale *ag* octagonal

ot'tagono *sm* octagon

ot'tanta *num* eighty; ottan'tesimo, a *num* eightieth; ottan'tina *sf*: una ottantina (di) about eighty

ot'tava *sf* octave

ot'tavo, a *num* eighth

ottempe'rare *vi*: ~ a to comply with, obey

otte'nere *vt* to obtain, get; (*risultato*) to achieve, obtain

'ottica (*scienza*) optics *sg*; (*FOT: lenti, prismi etc*) optics *pl*

'ottico, a, ci, che *ag* (*della vista: nervo*) optic; (*dell'ottica*) optical ♦ *sm* optician

ottima'mente *av* excellently, very well

otti'mismo *sm* optimism; otti'mista, i, e *sm/f* optimist

'ottimo, a *ag* excellent, very good

'otto *num* eight

ot'tobre *sm* October

otto'cento [otto't∫ento] *num* eight hundred ♦ *sm*: l'O~ the nineteenth century

ot'tone *sm* brass; gli ~i (*MUS*) the brass

ottu'rare *vt* to close (up); (*dente*) to fill; ottura'tore *sm* (*FOT*) shutter; (*nelle armi*) breechblock; otturazi'one *sf* closing (up); (*dentaria*) filling

ot'tuso, a *ag* (*MAT, fig*) obtuse; (*suono*) dull

o'vaia *sf* (*ANAT*) ovary

o'vaio *sm* = ovaia

o'vale *ag, sm* oval

o'vatta *sf* cotton wool; (*per imbottire*) padding, wadding; ovat'tare *vt* (*fig: smorzare*) to muffle

ovazi'one [ovat'tsjone] *sf* ovation

'ovest *sm* west

o'vile *sm* pen, enclosure

o'vino, a *ag* sheep *cpd*, ovine

ovulazi'one [ovulat'tsjone] *sf* ovulation

'ovulo *sm* (*FISIOL*) ovum

o'vunque *av* = dovunque

ov'vero *cong* (*ossia*) that is, to be precise; (*oppure*) or (else)

ovvi'are *vi*: ~ a to obviate

'ovvio, a *ag* obvious

ozi'are [ot'tsjare] *vi* to laze, idle

'ozio ['ɔttsjo] *sm* idleness; (*tempo libero*) leisure; ore d'~ leisure time; stare in ~ to be idle; ozi'oso, a *ag* idle

o'zono [o'dzɔno] *sm* ozone

P

pa'cato, a *ag* quiet, calm

pac'chetto [pak'ketto] *sm* packet; ~ azionario (*COMM*) shareholding

pacchi'ano, a [pak'kjano, a] *ag* vulgar

'pacco, chi *sm* parcel; (*involto*) bundle

'pace ['pat∫e] *sf* peace; darsi ~ to resign o.s.

pacifi'care [pat∫ifi'kare] *vt* (*riconciliare*) to reconcile, make peace between; (*mettere in pace*) to pacify

pa'cifico, a, ci, che [pa't∫i:fiko] *ag* (*persona*) peaceable; (*vita*) peaceful; (*fig: indiscusso*) indisputable; (: *ovvio*) obvious, clear ♦ *sm*: il P~, l'Oceano P~ the Pacific (Ocean)

paci'fista, i, e [pat∫i'fista] *sm/f* pacifist

pa'della *sf* frying pan; (*per infermi*) bedpan

padigli'one [padiʎ'ʎone] *sm* pavilion; (*AUT*) roof

'Padova *sf* Padua

'padre *sm* father; ~i *smpl* (*antenati*) forefathers; pa'drino *sm* godfather

padro'nanza [padro'nantsa] *sf* command, mastery

pa'drone, a *sm/f* master/mistress; (*proprietario*) owner; (*datore di lavoro*) employer; essere ~ di sé to be in control of o.s.; ~ di casa (*ospite*) host/hostess; (*per gli inquilini*) landlord/lady; padroneggi'are *vt* (*fig: sentimenti*) to master, control; (: *materia*) to master, know thoroughly; **padroneggiarsi** *vr* to control o.s.

pae'saggio [pae'zaddʒo] *sm* landscape

pae'sano, a *ag* country *cpd* ♦ *sm/f* villager; countryman/woman

pa'ese *sm* (*nazione*) country, nation; (*terra*) country, land; (*villaggio*) village; (small) town; ~ **di provenienza** country of origin; **i P~i Bassi** the Netherlands

paf'futo, a *ag* chubby, plump

'paga, ghe *sf* pay, wages *pl*

paga'mento *sm* payment

pa'gano, a *ag, sm/f* pagan

pa'gare *vt* to pay; (*acquisto, fig: colpa*) to pay for; (*contraccambiare*) to repay, pay back ♦ *vi* to pay; **quanto l'hai pagato?** how much did you pay for it?; ~ **con carta di credito** to pay by credit card; ~ **in contanti** to pay cash

pa'gella [pa'dʒella] *sf* (*INS*) report card

'paggio [pa'ddʒo] *sm* page(boy)

paghe'rò [page'rɔ] *sm inv* acknowledgement of a debt, IOU

'pagina ['padʒina] *sf* page; **~e gialle** Yellow Pages

'paglia ['paʎʎa] *sf* straw

pagliac'cetto [paʎʎat't ʃetto] *sm* (*per bambini*) rompers *pl*

pagli'accio [paʎ'ʎattʃo] *sm* clown

pagli'etta [paʎ'ʎetta] *sf* (*cappello per uomo*) (straw) boater; (*per tegami etc*) steel wool

pa'gnotta [paɲ'ɲɔtta] *sf* round loaf

'paio (*pl(f)* '**paia**) *sm* pair; **un ~ di** (*alcuni*) a couple of

pai'olo *sm* (copper) pot

'pala *sf* shovel; (*di remo, ventilatore, elica*) blade; (*di ruota*) paddle

pa'lato *sm* palate

pa'lazzo [pa'lattso] *sm* (*reggia*) palace; (*edificio*) building; ~ **di giustizia** courthouse; ~ **dello sport** sports stadium

pal'chetto [pal'ketto] *sm* shelf

'palco, chi *sm* (*TEATRO*) box; (*tavolato*) platform, stand; (*ripiano*) layer

palco'scenico, ci [palkoʃ'ʃeniko] *sm* (*TEATRO*) stage

pale'sare *vt* to reveal, disclose; **~rsi** *vr* to

reveal *o* show o.s.

pa'lese *ag* clear, evident

Pales'tina *sf*: **la** ~ Palestine

pa'lestra *sf* gymnasium; (*esercizio atletico*) exercise, training; (*fig*) training ground, school

pa'letta *sf* spade; (*per il focolare*) shovel; (*del capostazione*) signalling disc

pa'letto *sm* stake, peg; (*spranga*) bolt

'palio *sm* (*gara*): **il P~** horserace run at *Siena*; **mettere qc in** ~ to offer sth as a prize

'palla *sf* ball; (*pallottola*) bullet; ~ **canestro** *sm* basketball; ~ **nuoto** *sm* water polo; ~ **ovale** rugby ball; ~ **volo** *sm* volleyball

palleggi'are [palled'dʒare] *vi* (*CALCIO*) to practise with the ball; (*TENNIS*) to knock up

pallia'tivo *sm* palliative; (*fig*) stopgap measure

'pallido, a *ag* pale

pal'lina *sf* (*bilia*) marble

pallon'cino [pallon'tʃino] *sm* balloon; (*lampioncino*) Chinese lantern

pal'lone *sm* (*palla*) ball; (*CALCIO*) football; (*aerostato*) balloon; **gioco del** ~ football

pal'lore *sm* pallor, paleness

pal'lottola *sf* pellet; (*proiettile*) bullet

'palma *sf* (*ANAT*) = **palmo**; (*BOT, simbolo*) palm; ~ **da datteri** date palm

'palmo *sm* (*ANAT*) palm; **restare con un** ~ **di naso** to be badly disappointed

'palo *sm* (*legno appuntito*) stake; (*sostegno*) pole; **fare da** *o* **il** ~ (*fig*) to act as look-out

palom'baro *sm* diver

pa'lombo *sm* (*pesce*) dogfish

pal'pare *vt* to feel, finger

'palpebra *sf* eyelid

palpi'tare *vi* (*cuore, polso*) to beat; (: *più forte*) to pound, throb; (*fremere*) to quiver; **'palpito** *sm* (*del cuore*) beat; (*fig: d'amore etc*) throb

paltò *sm inv* overcoat

pa'lude *sf* marsh, swamp; **palu'doso, a** *ag* marshy, swampy

pa'lustre *ag* marsh *cpd*, swamp *cpd*

'pampino *sm* vine leaf

pancarrè → paralisi

pancarrè *sm* sliced square bread (*used mainly for toasted sandwiches*)
'panca, che *sf* bench
pan'cetta [pan'tʃetta] *sf* (CUC) bacon
pan'chetto [pan'ketto] *sm* stool; footstool
pan'china [pan'kina] *sf* garden seat; (*di giardino pubblico*) (park) bench
'pancia, ce ['pantʃa] *sf* belly, stomach; **mettere** *o* **fare ~** to be getting a paunch; **avere mal di ~** to have stomachache *o* a sore stomach
panci'otto [pan'tʃɔtto] *sm* waistcoat
'pancreas *sm inv* pancreas
'panda *sm inv* panda
pande'monio *sm* pandemonium
'pane *sm* bread; (*pagnotta*) loaf (of bread); (*forma*): **un ~ di burro/cera** *etc* a pat of butter/bar of wax *etc*; **guadagnarsi il ~** to earn one's living; **~ a cassetta** sliced bread; **~ di Spagna** sponge cake; **~ integrale** wholemeal bread; **~ tostato** toast
panette'ria *sf* (*forno*) bakery; (*negozio*) baker's (shop), bakery
panetti'ere, a *sm/f* baker
panet'tone *sm* a kind of spiced brioche with sultanas, eaten at Christmas
'panfilo *sm* yacht
pangrat'tato *sm* breadcrumbs *pl*
'panico, a, ci, che *ag, sm* panic
pani'ere *sm* basket
pani'ficio [pani'fitʃo] *sm* (*forno*) bakery; (*negozio*) baker's (shop), bakery
pa'nino *sm* roll; **~ caldo** toasted sandwich; **~ imbottito** filled roll; sandwich; **panino'teca** *sf* sandwich bar
'panna *sf* (CUC) cream; (TECN) = **panne**; **~ da cucina** cooking cream; **~ montata** whipped cream
'panne *sf inv*: **essere in ~** (AUT) to have broken down
pan'nello *sm* panel; **~ solare** solar panel
'panno *sm* cloth; **~i** *smpl* (*abiti*) clothes; **mettiti nei miei ~i** (*fig*) put yourself in my shoes
pan'nocchia [pan'nɔkkja] *sf* (*di mais etc*) ear
panno'lino *sm* (*per bambini*) nappy (BRIT), diaper (US)

pano'rama, i *sm* panorama; **pano'ramico, a, ci, che** *ag* panoramic; **strada panoramica** scenic route
panta'loni *smpl* trousers (BRIT), pants (US), pair *sg* of trousers *o* pants
pan'tano *sm* bog
pan'tera *sf* panther
pan'tofola *sf* slipper
panto'mima *sf* pantomime
pan'zana [pan'tsana] *sf* fib, tall story
pao'nazzo, a [pao'nattso] *ag* purple
'papa, i *sm* pope
papà *sm inv* dad(dy)
pa'pale *ag* papal
pa'pato *sm* papacy
pa'pavero *sm* poppy
'papera *sf* (*fig*) slip of the tongue, blunder; *vedi anche* **papero**
'papero, a *sm/f* (ZOOL) gosling
pa'piro *sm* papyrus
'pappa *sf* baby cereal
pappa'gallo *sm* parrot; (*fig: uomo*) Romeo, wolf
pappa'gorgia, ge [pappa'gɔrdʒa] *sf* double chin
pap'pare *vt* (*fam: anche: ~rsi*) to gobble up
'para *sf*: **suole di ~** crepe soles
pa'rabola *sf* (MAT) parabola; (REL) parable
para'brezza [para'breddza] *sm inv* (AUT) windscreen (BRIT), windshield (US)
paraca'dute *sm inv* parachute
para'carro *sm* kerbstone (BRIT), curbstone (US)
para'diso *sm* paradise
parados'sale *ag* paradoxical
para'dosso *sm* paradox
para'fango, ghi *sm* mudguard
paraf'fina *sf* paraffin, paraffin wax
para'fulmine *sm* lightning conductor
pa'raggi [pa'raddʒi] *smpl*: **nei ~** in the vicinity, in the neighbourhood
parago'nare *vt*: **~ con/a** to compare with/to
para'gone *sm* comparison; (*esempio analogo*) analogy, parallel; **reggere al ~** to stand comparison
pa'ragrafo *sm* paragraph
pa'ralisi *sf* paralysis; **para'litico, a, ci,**

che *ag, sm/f* paralytic

paraliz'zare [paralid'dzare] *vt* to paralyze

paral'lela *sf* parallel (line); **~e** *sfpl* (*attrezzo ginnico*) parallel bars

paral'lelo, a *ag* parallel ♦ *sm* (GEO) parallel; (*comparazione*): **fare un ~ tra** to draw a parallel between

para'lume *sm* lampshade

pa'rametro *sm* parameter

para'noia *sf* paranoia; **para'noico, a, ci, che** *ag, sm/f* paranoid

para'occhi [para'ɔkki] *smpl* blinkers

para'petto *sm* balustrade

para'piglia [para'piʎʎa] *sm* commotion, uproar

pa'rare *vt* (*addobbare*) to adorn, deck; (*proteggere*) to shield, protect; (*scansare: colpo*) to parry; (CALCIO) to save ♦ *vi*: **dove vuole andare a ~?** what are you driving at?; **~rsi** *vr* (*presentarsi*) to appear, present o.s.

para'sole *sm inv* parasol, sunshade

paras'sita, i *sm* parasite

pa'rata *sf* (SPORT) save; (MIL) review, parade

para'tia *sf* (*di nave*) bulkhead

para'urti *sm inv* (AUT) bumper

para'vento *sm* folding screen; **fare da ~ a qn** (*fig*) to shield sb

par'cella [par'tʃɛlla] *sf* account, fee (*of lawyer etc*)

parcheggi'are [parked'dʒare] *vt* to park; **par'cheggio** *sm* parking *no pl*; (*luogo*) car park; (*singolo posto*) parking space

par'chimetro [par'kimetro] *sm* parking meter

'parco¹, chi *sm* park; (*spazio per deposito*) depot; (*complesso di veicoli*) fleet

'parco², a, chi, che *ag*: **~ (in)** (*sobrio*) moderate (in); (*avaro*) sparing (with)

pa'recchio, a [pa'rekkjo] *det* quite a lot of; (*tempo*) quite a lot of, a long; **~i, e** *det pl* quite a lot of, several ♦ *pron* quite a lot, quite a bit; (*tempo*) quite a while, a long time; **~i, e** *pron pl* quite a lot, several ♦ *av* (*con ag*) quite, rather; (*con vb*) quite a lot, quite a bit

pareggi'are [pared'dʒare] *vt* to make equal; (*terreno*) to level, make level;

(*bilancio, conti*) to balance ♦ *vi* (SPORT) to draw; **pa'reggio** *sm* (ECON) balance; (SPORT) draw

pa'rente *sm/f* relative, relation

paren'tela *sf* (*vincolo di sangue, fig*) relationship; (*insieme dei parenti*) relations *pl*, relatives *pl*

pa'rentesi *sf* (*segno grafico*) bracket, parenthesis; (*frase incisa*) parenthesis; (*digressione*) parenthesis, digression

pa'rere *sm* (*opinione*) opinion; (*consiglio*) advice, opinion; **a mio ~** in my opinion ♦ *vi* to seem, appear ♦ *vb impers*: **pare che** it seems o appears that, they say that; **mi pare che** it seems to me that; **mi pare di sì** I think so; **fai come ti pare** do as you like; **che ti pare del mio libro?** what do you think of my book?

pa'rete *sf* wall

'pari *ag inv* (*uguale*) equal, same; (*in giochi*) equal; drawn, tied; (MAT) even ♦ *sm inv* (POL: *di Gran Bretagna*) peer ♦ *sm/f inv* peer, equal; **copiato ~ ~** copied word for word; **alla ~** on the same level; **ragazza alla ~** au pair girl; **mettersi alla ~ con** to place o.s. on the same level as; **mettersi in ~ con** to catch up with; **andare di ~ passo con qn** to keep pace with sb

Pa'rigi [pa'ridʒi] *sf* Paris

pa'riglia [pa'riʎʎa] *sf* pair; **rendere la ~** to give tit for tat

parità *sf* parity, equality; (SPORT) draw, tie

parlamen'tare *ag* parliamentary ♦ *sm/f* ≈ Member of Parliament (BRIT), ≈ Congressman/woman (US) ♦ *vi* to negotiate, parley

parla'mento *sm* parliament

parlan'tina (*fam*) *sf* talkativeness; **avere una buona ~** to have the gift of the gab

par'lare *vi* to speak, talk; (*confidare cose segrete*) to talk ♦ *vt* to speak; **~ (a qn) di** to speak o talk (to sb) about; **parla'torio** *sm* (*di carcere etc*) visiting room; (REL) parlour

parmigi'ano [parmi'dʒano] *sm* (*grana*) Parmesan (cheese)

paro'dia *sf* parody

pa'rola *sf* word; (*facoltà*) speech; **~e** *sfpl*

(*chiacchiere*) talk *sg*; **chiedere la ~** to ask permission to speak; **prendere la ~** to take the floor; **~ d'onore** word of honour; **~ d'ordine** (*MIL*) password; **~e incrociate** crossword (puzzle) *sg*; **paro'laccia, ce** *sf* bad word, swearword

par'rocchia [par'rɔkkja] *sf* parish; parish church

'parroco, ci *sm* parish priest

par'rucca, che *sf* wig

parrucchi'ere, a [parruk'kjɛre] *sm/f* hairdresser ♦ *sm* barber

parsi'monia *sf* frugality, thrift

'parso, a *pp di* **parere**

'parte *sf* part; (*lato*) side; (*quota spettante a ciascuno*) share; (*direzione*) direction; (*POL*) party; faction; (*DIR*) party; **a ~** *ag* separate ♦ *av* separately; **scherzi a ~** joking aside; **a ~ ciò** apart from that; **da ~** (*in disparte*) to one side, aside; **d'altra ~** on the other hand; **da ~ di** (*per conto di*) on behalf of; **da ~ mia** as far as I'm concerned, as for me; **da ~ a ~** right through; **da ogni ~** on all sides, everywhere; (*moto da luogo*) from all sides; **da nessuna ~** nowhere; **da questa ~** (*in questa direzione*) this way; **prendere ~ a qc** to take part in sth; **mettere da ~** to put aside; **mettere qn a ~ di qc** to inform sb of sth

parteci'pare [partetʃi'pare] *vi*: **~ a** to take part in, participate in; (*utili etc*) to share in; (*spese etc*) to contribute to; (*dolore, successo di qn*) to share (in); **partecipazi'one** *sf* participation; sharing; (*ECON*) interest; **partecipazione agli utili** profit-sharing; **partecipazioni di nozze** *wedding announcement card*; **par'tecipe** *ag* participating; **essere partecipe di** to take part in, participate in; to share (in); (*consapevole*) to be aware of

parteggi'are [parted'dʒare] *vi*: **~ per** to side with, be on the side of

par'tenza [par'tɛntsa] *sf* departure; (*SPORT*) start; **essere in ~** to be about to leave, be leaving

parti'cella [parti'tʃella] *sf* particle

parti'cipio [parti'tʃipjo] *sm* participle

partico'lare *ag* (*specifico*) particular; (*proprio*) personal, private; (*speciale*) special, particular; (*caratteristico*) distinctive, characteristic; (*fuori dal comune*) peculiar ♦ *sm* detail, particular; **in ~** in particular, particularly;

particolarità *sf inv* particularity; detail; characteristic, feature

partigi'ano [parti'dʒano] *ag* partisan ♦ *sm* (*fautore*) supporter, champion; (*MIL*) partisan

par'tire *vi* to go, leave; (*allontanarsi*) to go (*o* drive *etc*) away *o* off; (*petardo, colpo*) to go off; (*fig: avere inizio, SPORT*) to start; **sono partita da Roma alle 7** I left Rome at 7; **il volo parte da Ciampino** the flight leaves from Ciampino; **a ~ da** from

par'tita *sf* (*COMM*) lot, consignment; (*ECON: registrazione*) entry, item; (*CARTE, SPORT: gioco*) game; (*: competizione*) match, game; **~ di caccia** hunting party; **~ IVA** VAT registration number

par'tito *sm* (*POL*) party; (*decisione*) decision, resolution; (*persona da maritare*) match

parti'tura *sf* (*MUS*) score

'parto *sm* (*MED*) delivery, (child)birth; labour; **parto'rire** *vt* to give birth to; (*fig*) to produce

parzi'ale [par'tsjale] *ag* (*limitato*) partial; (*non obiettivo*) biased, partial

'pascere ['paʃʃere] *vi* to graze ♦ *vt* (*brucare*) to graze on; (*far pascolare*) to graze, pasture; **pasci'uto, a** *pp di* **pascere**

pasco'lare *vt, vi* to graze

'pascolo *sm* pasture

'Pasqua *sf* Easter; **pas'quale** *ag* Easter *cpd*

pas'sabile *ag* fairly good, passable

pas'saggio [pas'saddʒo] *sm* passing *no pl*, passage; (*traversata*) crossing *no pl*, passage; (*luogo, prezzo della traversata, brano di libro etc*) passage; (*su veicolo altrui*) lift (*BRIT*), ride; (*SPORT*) pass; **di ~** (*persona*) passing through; **~ pedonale/a livello** pedestrian/level (*BRIT*) *o* grade (*US*) crossing

pas'sante *sm/f* passer-by ♦ *sm* loop

passa'porto *sm* passport

pas'sare *vi* (*andare*) to go; (*veicolo, pedone*) to pass (by), go by; (*fare una breve sosta: postino etc*) to come, call; (: *amico: per fare una visita*) to call o drop in; (*sole, aria, luce*) to get through; (*trascorrere: giorni, tempo*) to pass, go by; (*fig: proposta di legge*) to be passed; (: *dolore*) to pass, go away; (*CARTE*) to pass ♦ *vt* (*attraversare*) to cross; (*trasmettere: messaggio*): ~ **qc a qn** to pass sth on to sb; (*dare*): ~ **qc a qn** to pass sth to sb, give sb sth; (*trascorrere: tempo*) to spend; (*superare: esame*) to pass; (*triturare: verdura*) to strain; (*approvare*) to pass, approve; (*oltrepassare, sorpassare: anche fig*) to go beyond, pass; (*fig: subire*) to go through; ~ **da ... a** to pass from ... to; ~ **di padre in figlio** to be handed down o to pass from father to son; ~ **per** (*anche fig*) to go through; ~ **per stupido/un genio** to be taken for a fool/a genius; ~ **sopra** (*anche fig*) to pass over; ~ **attraverso** (*anche fig*) to go through; ~ **alla storia** to pass into history; ~ **a un esame** to pass (to the next class) after an exam; ~ **inosservato** to go unnoticed; ~ **di moda** to go out of fashion; **le passo il Signor X** (*al telefono*) here is Mr X; I'm putting you through to Mr X; **lasciar ~ qn/qc** to let sb/sth through; **passarsela: come te la passi?** how are you getting on o along?

pas'sata *sf*: **dare una ~ di vernice a qc** to give sth a coat of paint; **dare una ~ al giornale** to have a look at the paper, skim through the paper

passa'tempo *sm* pastime, hobby

pas'sato, a *ag* past; (*sfiorito*) faded ♦ *sm* past; (*LING*) past (tense); ~ **prossimo** (*LING*) present perfect; ~ **remoto** (*LING*) past historic; ~ **di verdura** (*CUC*) vegetable purée

passaver'dura *sm inv* vegetable mill

passeg'gero, a [passed'dʒero] *ag* passing ♦ *sm/f* passenger

passeggi'are [passed'dʒare] *vi* to go for a walk; (*in veicolo*) to go for a drive; **passeggi'ata** *sf* walk; drive; (*luogo*)

promenade; **fare una passeggiata** to go for a walk (o drive); **passeg'gino** *sm* pushchair (*BRIT*), stroller (*US*); **pas'seggio** *sm* walk, stroll; (*luogo*) promenade

passe'rella *sf* footbridge; (*di nave, aereo*) gangway; (*pedana*) catwalk

'passero *sm* sparrow

pas'sibile *ag*: ~ **di** liable to

passi'one *sf* passion

pas'sivo, a *ag* passive ♦ *sm* (*LING*) passive; (*ECON*) debit; (: *complesso dei debiti*) liabilities *pl*

'passo *sm* step; (*andatura*) pace; (*rumore*) (foot)step; (*orma*) footprint; (*passaggio, fig: brano*) passage; (*valico*) pass; **a ~ d'uomo** at walking pace; ~ **(a) ~** step by step; **fare due o quattro ~i** to go for a walk o a stroll; **di questo ~** at this rate; **"~ carraio"** "vehicle entrance — keep clear"

'pasta *sf* (*CUC*) dough; (: *impasto per dolce*) pastry; (: *anche*: ~ *alimentare*) pasta; (*massa molle di materia*) paste; (*fig: indole*) nature; ~**e** *sfpl* (*pasticcini*) pastries; ~ **in brodo** noodle soup

pastasci'utta [pastaʃ'ʃutta] *sf* pasta

pas'tella *sf* batter

pas'tello *sm* pastel

pas'ticca, che *sf* = **pastiglia**

pasticce'ria [pastittʃe'ria] *sf* (*pasticcini*) pastries *pl*, cakes *pl*; (*negozio*) cake shop; (*arte*) confectionery

pasticci'are [pastit'tʃare] *vt* to mess up, make a mess of ♦ *vi* to make a mess

pasticci'ere, a [pastit'tʃere] *sm/f* pastrycook; confectioner

pas'ticcio [pas'tittʃo] *sm* (*CUC*) pie; (*lavoro disordinato, imbroglio*) mess; **trovarsi nei ~i** to get into trouble

pasti'ficio [pasti'fitʃo] *sm* pasta factory

pas'tiglia [pas'tiʎʎa] *sf* pastille, lozenge

pas'tina *sf small pasta shapes used in soup*

'pasto *sm* meal

pas'tore *sm* shepherd; (*REL*) pastor, minister; (*anche: cane* ~) sheepdog; ~ **tedesco** (*ZOOL*) Alsatian, German shepherd

pastoriz'zare [pastorid'dzare] *vt* to

pasteurize

pas'toso, a *ag* doughy; pasty; (*fig: voce, colore*) mellow, soft

pas'trano *sm* greatcoat

pas'tura *sf* pasture

pa'tata *sf* potato; ~e **fritte** chips (*BRIT*), French fries; **pata'tine** *sfpl* (potato) crisps; ~ **fritte** chips

pata'trac *sm* (*crollo: anche fig*) crash

pa'tella *sf* (*ZOOL*) limpet

pa'tema, i *sm* anxiety, worry

pa'tente *sf* licence; (*anche:* ~ **di guida**) driving licence (*BRIT*), driver's license (*US*)

paternità *sf* paternity, fatherhood

pa'terno, a *ag* (*affetto, consigli*) fatherly; (*casa, autorità*) paternal

pa'tetico, a, ci, che *ag* pathetic; (*commovente*) moving, touching

pa'tibolo *sm* gallows *sg*, scaffold

'patina *sf* (*su rame etc*) patina; (*sulla lingua*) fur, coating

pa'tire *vt, vi* to suffer

pa'tito, a *sm/f* enthusiast, fan, lover

patolo'gia [patolo'dʒia] *sf* pathology; **pato'logico, a, ci, che** *ag* pathological

'patria *sf* homeland

patri'arca, chi *sm* patriarch

pa'trigno [pa'triɲɲo] *sm* stepfather

patri'monio *sm* estate, property; (*fig*) heritage

patri'ota, i, e *sm/f* patriot; **patri'ottico, a, ci, che** *ag* patriotic; **patriot'tismo** *sm* patriotism

patroci'nare [patrotʃi'nare] *vt* (*DIR: difendere*) to defend; (*sostenere*) to sponsor, support; **patro'cinio** *sm* defence; support, sponsorship

patro'nato *sm* patronage; (*istituzione benefica*) charitable institution *o* society

pa'trono *sm* (*REL*) patron saint; (*socio di patronato*) patron; (*DIR*) counsel

'patta *sf* flap; (*dei pantaloni*) fly

patteggia'mento [patteddʒa'mento] *sm* (*DIR*) plea bargaining

patteggi'are [patted'dʒare] *vt, vi* to negotiate

patti'naggio [patti'naddʒo] *sm* skating

patti'nare *vi* to skate; ~ **sul ghiaccio** to ice-skate; **pattina'tore, 'trice** *sm/f*

skater; **'pattino¹** *sm* skate; (*di slitta*) runner; (*AER*) skid; (*TECN*) sliding block; **pattini (da ghiaccio)** (ice) skates; **pattini a rotelle** roller skates; **pat'tino²** *sm* (*barca*) kind of pedalo with oars

'patto *sm* (*accordo*) pact, agreement; (*condizione*) term, condition; **a** ~ **che** on condition that

pat'tuglia [pat'tuʎʎa] *sf* (*MIL*) patrol

pattu'ire *vt* to reach an agreement on

pattumi'era *sf* (dust)bin (*BRIT*), ashcan (*US*)

pa'ura *sf* fear; **aver** ~ **di/di fare/che** to be frightened *o* afraid of/of doing/that; **far** ~ **a** to frighten; **per** ~ **di/che** for fear of/that; **pau'roso, a** *ag* (*che fa paura*) frightening; (*che ha paura*) fearful, timorous

'pausa *sf* (*sosta*) break; (*nel parlare, MUS*) pause

pavi'mento *sm* floor

pa'vone *sm* peacock; **pavoneggi'arsi** *vr* to strut about, show off

pazien'tare [pattsjen'tare] *vi* to be patient

pazi'ente [pat'tsjɛnte] *ag, sm/f* patient; **pazi'enza** *sf* patience

paz'zesco, a, schi, sche [pat'tsesko] *ag* mad, crazy

paz'zia [pat'tsia] *sf* (*MED*) madness, insanity; (*azione*) folly; (*di azione, decisione*) madness, folly

'pazzo, a ['pattso] *ag* (*MED*) mad, insane; (*strano*) wild, mad ♦ *sm/f* madman/woman; ~ **di** (*gioia, amore etc*) mad *o* crazy with; ~ **per** **qc/qn** mad *o* crazy about sth/sb

PCI *sigla m* = **Partito Comunista Italiano**

'pecca, che *sf* defect, flaw, fault

peccami'noso, a *ag* sinful

pec'care *vi* to sin; (*fig*) to err

pec'cato *sm* sin; **è un** ~ **che** it's a pity that; **che** ~! what a shame *o* pity!

pecca'tore, 'trice *sm/f* sinner

'pece ['petʃe] *sf* pitch

Pe'chino [pe'kino] *sf* Peking

'pecora *sf* sheep; **peco'raio** *sm* shepherd; **peco'rino** *sm* sheep's milk cheese

peculi'are *ag*: ~ **di** peculiar to

pe'daggio [pe'daddʒo] *sm* toll

pedago'gia [pedago'dʒia] *sf* pedagogy, educational methods *pl*

peda'lare *vi* to pedal; (*andare in bicicletta*) to cycle

pe'dale *sm* pedal

pe'dana *sf* footboard; (*SPORT: nel salto*) springboard; (: *nella scherma*) piste

pe'dante *ag* pedantic ♦ *sm/f* pedant

pe'data *sf* (*impronta*) footprint; (*colpo*) kick; **prendere a ~e** *qn/qc* to kick sb/sth

pede'rasta, i *sm* pederast; homosexual

pedi'atra, i, e *sm/f* paediatrician;
 pedia'tria *sf* paediatrics *sg*

pedi'cure *sm/f inv* chiropodist

pe'dina *sf* (*della dama*) draughtsman (*BRIT*), draftsman (*US*); (*fig*) pawn

pedi'nare *vt* to shadow, tail

pedo'nale *ag* pedestrian

pe'done, a *sm/f* pedestrian ♦ *sm* (*SCACCHI*) pawn

'peggio ['pɛddʒo] *av, ag inv* worse ♦ *sm o f*: **il o la ~** the worst; **alla ~** at worst, if the worst comes to the worst;
 peggiora'mento *sm* worsening;
 peggio'rare *vt* to make worse, worsen ♦ *vi* to grow worse, worsen;
 peggiora'tivo, a *ag* pejorative;
 peggi'ore *ag* (*comparativo*) worse; (*superlativo*) worst ♦ *sm/f*: **il(la) peggiore** the worst (person)

'pegno ['peɲɲo] *sm* (*DIR*) security, pledge; (*nei giochi di società*) forfeit; (*fig*) pledge, token; **dare in ~** *qc* to pawn sth

pe'lare *vt* (*spennare*) to pluck; (*spellare*) to skin; (*sbucciare*) to peel; (*fig*) to make pay through the nose; **~rsi** *vr* to go bald

pe'lato, a *ag*: **pomodori ~i** tinned tomatoes

pel'lame *sm* skins *pl*, hides *pl*

'pelle *sf* skin; (*di animale*) skin, hide; (*cuoio*) leather; **avere la ~ d'oca** to have goose pimples *o* goose flesh

pellegri'naggio [pellegri'naddʒo] *sm* pilgrimage

pelle'grino, a *sm/f* pilgrim

pelle'rossa (*pl* **pelli'rosse**) *sm/f* Red Indian

pelli'rossa *sm/f* = **pellerossa**

pellette'ria *sf* leather goods *pl*; (*negozio*) leather goods shop

pelli'cano *sm* pelican

pellicce'ria [pellittʃe'ria] *sf* (*negozio*) furrier's (shop); (*quantità di pellicce*) furs *pl*

pel'liccia, ce [pel'littʃa] *sf* (*mantello di animale*) coat, fur; (*indumento*) fur coat

pel'licola *sf* (*membrana sottile*) film, layer; (*FOT, CINEMA*) film

'pelo *sm* hair; (*pelame*) coat, hair; (*pelliccia*) fur; (*di tappeto*) pile; (*di liquido*) surface; **per un ~: per un ~ non ho perduto il treno** I very nearly missed the train; **c'è mancato un ~ che affogasse** he escaped drowning by the skin of his teeth; **pe'loso, a** *ag* hairy

'peltro *sm* pewter

pe'luria *sf* down

'pena *sf* (*DIR*) sentence; (*punizione*) punishment; (*sofferenza*) sadness *no pl*, sorrow; (*fatica*) trouble *no pl*, effort; (*difficoltà*) difficulty; **far ~** to be pitiful; **mi fai ~** I feel sorry for you; **prendersi** *o* **darsi la ~ di fare** to go to the trouble of doing; **~ di morte** death sentence; **~ pecuniaria** fine; **pe'nale** *ag* penal; **penalità** *sf inv* penalty; **penaliz'zare** *vt* (*SPORT*) to penalize

pe'nare *vi* (*patire*) to suffer; (*faticare*) to struggle

pen'dente *ag* hanging; leaning ♦ *sm* (*ciondolo*) pendant; (*orecchino*) drop earring; **pen'denza** *sf* slope, slant; (*grado d'inclinazione*) gradient; (*ECON*) outstanding account

'pendere *vi* (*essere appeso*): **~ da** to hang from; (*essere inclinato*) to lean; (*fig: incombere*): **~ su** to hang over

pen'dice [pen'ditʃe] *sf*: **alle ~i del monte** at the foot of the mountain

pen'dio, 'dii *sm* slope, slant; (*luogo in pendenza*) slope

'pendola *sf* pendulum clock

pendo'lare *sm/f* commuter

'pendolo *sm* (*peso*) pendulum; (*anche: orologio a ~*) pendulum clock

'pene *sm* penis

pene'trante *ag* piercing, penetrating
pene'trare *vi* to come *o* get in ♦ *vt* to penetrate; ~ **in** to enter; (*sog: proiettile*) to penetrate; (: *acqua, aria*) to go *o* come into
penicil'lina [penitʃil'lina] *sf* penicillin
pe'nisola *sf* peninsula
peni'tenza [peni'tɛntsa] *sf* penitence; (*punizione*) penance
penitenzi'ario [peniten'tsjarjo] *sm* prison
'penna *sf* (*di uccello*) feather; (*per scrivere*) pen; **~e** *sfpl* (CUC) quills (*type of pasta*); ~ **a feltro/stilografica/a sfera** felt-tip/fountain/ballpoint pen
penna'rello *sm* felt(-tip) pen
pennel'lare *vi* to paint
pen'nello *sm* brush; (*per dipingere*) (paint)brush; **a** ~ (*perfettamente*) to perfection, perfectly; ~ **per la barba** shaving brush
pen'nino *sm* nib
pen'none *sm* (NAUT) yard; (*stendardo*) banner, standard
pe'nombra *sf* half-light, dim light
pe'noso, a *ag* painful, distressing; (*faticoso*) tiring, laborious
pen'sare *vi* to think ♦ *vt* to think; (*inventare, escogitare*) to think out; ~ **a** to think of; (*amico, vacanze*) to think of *o* about; (*problema*) to think about; ~ **di fare qc** to think of doing sth; **ci penso io** I'll see to *o* take care of it
pensi'ero *sm* thought; (*modo di pensare, dottrina*) thinking *no pl*; (*preoccupazione*) worry, care, trouble; **stare in** *o* **per qn** to be worried about sb; **pensie'roso, a** *ag* thoughtful
'pensile *ag* hanging
pensio'nante *sm/f* (*presso una famiglia*) lodger; (*di albergo*) guest
pensio'nato, a *sm/f* pensioner
pensi'one *sf* (*al prestatore di lavoro*) pension; (*vitto e alloggio*) board and lodging; (*albergo*) boarding house; **andare in** ~ to retire; **mezza** ~ half board; ~ **completa** full board
pen'soso, a *ag* thoughtful, pensive, lost in thought

pentapar'tito *sm* five-party government
Pente'coste *sf* Pentecost, Whit Sunday (BRIT)
penti'mento *sm* repentance, contrition
pen'tirsi *vr*: ~ **di** to repent of; (*rammaricarsi*) to regret, be sorry for
'pentola *sf* pot; ~ **a pressione** pressure cooker
pe'nultimo, a *ag* last but one (BRIT), next to last, penultimate
pe'nuria *sf* shortage
penzo'lare [pendzo'lare] *vi* to dangle, hang loosely; **penzo'loni** *av* dangling, hanging down; **stare penzoloni** to dangle, hang down
'pepe *sm* pepper; ~ **macinato/in grani** ground/whole pepper
pepero'nata *sf* (CUC) stewed peppers, tomatoes and onions
pepe'rone *sm* pepper, capsicum; (*piccante*) chili
pe'pita *sf* nugget

PAROLA CHIAVE

per *prep* **1** (*moto attraverso luogo*) through; **i ladri sono passati ~ la finestra** the thieves got in (*o* out) through the window; **l'ho cercato ~ tutta la casa** I've searched the whole house *o* all over the house for it
2 (*moto a luogo*) for, to; **partire ~ la Germania/il mare** to leave for Germany/the sea; **il treno ~ Roma** the Rome train, the train for *o* to Rome
3 (*stato in luogo*): **seduto/sdraiato ~ terra** sitting/lying on the ground
4 (*tempo*) for; ~ **anni/lungo tempo** for years/a long time; ~ **tutta l'estate** throughout the summer, all summer long; **lo rividi ~ Natale** I saw him again at Christmas; **lo faccio ~ lunedì** I'll do it for Monday
5 (*mezzo, maniera*) by; ~ **lettera/via aerea/ferrovia** by letter/airmail/rail; **prendere qn ~ un braccio** to take sb by the arm
6 (*causa, scopo*) for; **assente ~ malattia** absent because of *o* through *o* owing to illness; **ottimo ~ il mal di gola** excellent

for sore throats

7 (*limitazione*) for; **è troppo difficile ~ lui** it's too difficult for him; **~ quel che mi riguarda** as far as I'm concerned; **~ poco che sia** however little it may be; **~ questa volta ti perdono** I'll forgive you this time

8 (*prezzo, misura*) for; (*distributivo*) a, per; **venduto ~ 3 milioni** sold for 3 million; **1000 lire ~ persona** 1000 lire a *o* per person; **uno ~ volta** one at a time; **uno ~ uno** one by one; **5 ~ cento** 5 per cent; **3 ~ 4 fa 12** 3 times 4 equals 12; **dividere/moltiplicare 12 ~ 4** to divide/~ multiply 12 by 4

9 (*in qualità di*) as; (*al posto di*) for; **avere qn ~ professore** to have sb as a teacher; **ti ho preso ~ Mario** I mistook you for Mario, I thought you were Mario; **dare ~ morto qn** to give sb up for dead

10 (*seguito da vb: finale*): **~ fare qc** (so as) to do sth, in order to do sth; (*: causale*): **~ aver fatto qc** for having done sth; (*: consecutivo*): **è abbastanza grande ~ andarci da solo** he's big enough to go on his own

'pera *sf* pear

pe'raltro *av* moreover, what's more

per'bene *ag inv* respectable, decent ♦ *av* (*con cura*) properly, well

percentu'ale [pertʃentu'ale] *sf* percentage

perce'pire [pertʃe'pire] *vt* (*sentire*) to perceive; (*ricevere*) to receive; **percezi'one** *sf* perception

perché [per'ke] *av* why; **~ no?** why not?; **~ non vuoi andarci?** why don't you want to go?; **spiegami ~ l'hai fatto** tell me why you did it
♦ *cong* **1** (*causale*) because; **non posso uscire ~ ho da fare** I can't go out because *o* as I've a lot to do
2 (*finale*) in order that, so that; **te lo do ~ tu lo legga** I'm giving it to you so (that) you can read it
3 (*consecutivo*): **è troppo forte ~ si possa**

batterlo he's too strong to be beaten
♦ *sm inv* reason; **il ~ di** the reason for

perciò [per'tʃɔ] *cong* so, for this (*o* that) reason

per'correre *vt* (*luogo*) to go all over; (*: paese*) to travel up and down, go all over; (*distanza*) to cover

per'corso, a *pp di* **percorrere** ♦ *sm* (*tragitto*) journey; (*tratto*) route

per'cossa *sf* blow

per'cosso, a *pp di* **percuotere**

percu'otere *vt* to hit, strike

percussi'one *sf* percussion; **strumenti a ~** (*MUS*) percussion instruments

'perdere *vt* to lose; (*lasciarsi sfuggire*) to miss; (*sprecare: tempo, denaro*) to waste; (*mandare in rovina: persona*) to ruin ♦ *vi* to lose; (*serbatoio etc*) to leak; **~rsi** *vr* (*smarrirsi*) to get lost; (*svanire*) to disappear, vanish; **saper ~** to be a good loser; **lascia ~!** forget it!, never mind!

perdigi'orno [perdi'dʒorno] *sm/f inv* idler, waster

'perdita *sf* loss; (*spreco*) waste; (*fuoriuscita*) leak; **siamo in ~** (*COMM*) we are running at a loss; **a ~ d'occhio** as far as the eye can see

perdo'nare *vt* to pardon, forgive; (*scusare*) to excuse, pardon

per'dono *sm* forgiveness; (*DIR*) pardon

perdu'rare *vi* to go on, last; (*perseverare*) to persist

perduta'mente *av* desperately, passionately

per'duto, a *pp di* **perdere**

peregri'nare *vi* to wander, roam

pe'renne *ag* eternal, perpetual, perennial; (*BOT*) perennial

peren'torio, a *ag* peremptory; (*definitivo*) final

per'fetto, a *ag* perfect ♦ *sm* (*LING*) perfect (tense)

perfezio'nare [perfettsjo'nare] *vt* to improve, perfect; **~rsi** *vr* to improve

perfezi'one [perfet'tsjone] *sf* perfection

'perfido, a *ag* perfidious, treacherous

per'fino *av* even

perfo'rare *vt* to perforate; to punch a

hole (*o* holes) in; (*banda, schede*) to punch; (*trivellare*) to drill; **perfora'tore, 'trice** *sm/f* punch-card operator ♦ *sm* (*utensile*) punch; (*INFORM*): **perforatore di schede** card punch; **perfora'trice** *sf* (*TECN*) boring *o* drilling machine; (*INFORM*) card punch; *vedi anche* **perforatore; perforazi'one** *sf* perforation; punching; drilling; (*INFORM*) punch; (*MED*) perforation

perga'mena *sf* parchment

'pergola *sf* (*per rampicanti*) pergola

perico'lante *ag* precarious

pe'ricolo *sm* danger; **mettere in** ~ **to** endanger, put in danger; **perico'loso, a** *ag* dangerous

perife'ria *sf* periphery; (*di città*) outskirts *pl*

pe'rifrasi *sf* circumlocution

pe'rimetro *sm* perimeter

peri'odico, a, ci, che *ag* periodic(al); (*MAT*) recurring ♦ *sm* periodical

pe'riodo *sm* period

peripe'zie [peripet'tsie] *sfpl* ups and downs, vicissitudes

pe'rire *vi* to perish, die

pe'rito, a *ag* expert, skilled ♦ *sm/f* expert; (*agronomo, navale*) surveyor; **un** ~ **chimico** a qualified chemist

pe'rizia [pe'rittsja] *sf* (*abilità*) ability; (*giudizio tecnico*) expert opinion; expert's report

'perla *sf* pearl; **per'lina** *sf* bead

perlus'trare *vt* to patrol

perma'loso, a *ag* touchy

perma'nente *ag* permanent ♦ *sf* permanent wave, perm; **perma'nenza** *sf* permanence; (*soggiorno*) stay

perma'nere *vi* to remain

perme'are *vt* to permeate

per'messo, a *pp di* **permettere** ♦ *sm* (*autorizzazione*) permission, leave; (*dato a militare, impiegato*) leave; (*licenza*) licence, permit; (*MIL: foglio*) pass; **~?, è ~?** (*posso entrare?*) may I come in?; (*posso passare?*) excuse me; **~ di lavoro/pesca** work/fishing permit; **~ di soggiorno** residence permit

per'mettere *vt* to allow, permit; **~ a qn qc/di fare** to allow sb sth/to do; **~rsi**

qc/di fare to allow o.s. sth/to do; (*avere la possibilità*) to afford sth/to do

per'nacchia [per'nakkja] (*fam*) *sf*: **fare una** ~ to blow a raspberry

per'nice [per'nitʃe] *sf* partridge

'perno *sm* pivot

pernot'tare *vi* to spend the night, stay overnight

'pero *sm* pear tree

però *cong* (*ma*) but; (*tuttavia*) however, nevertheless

pero'rare *vt* (*DIR, fig*): ~ **la causa di qn** to plead sb's case

perpendico'lare *ag, sf* perpendicular

perpe'trare *vt* to perpetrate

perpetu'are *vt* to perpetuate

per'petuo, a *ag* perpetual

per'plesso, a *ag* perplexed; uncertain, undecided

perqui'sire *vt* to search; **perquisizi'one** *sf* (police) search

persecu'tore *sm* persecutor

persecuzi'one [persekut'tsjone] *sf* persecution

persegu'ire *vt* to pursue

persegui'tare *vt* to persecute

perseve'rante *ag* persevering

perseve'rare *vi* to persevere

'Persia *sf*: **la** ~ Persia

persi'ana *sf* shutter; ~ **avvolgibile** Venetian blind

persi'ano, a *ag, sm/f* Persian

'persico, a, ci, che *ag*: **il golfo P~** the Persian Gulf

per'sino *av* = **perfino**

persis'tente *ag* persistent

per'sistere *vi* to persist; ~ **a fare** to persist in doing; **persis'tito, a** *pp di* **persistere**

'perso, a *pp di* **perdere**

per'sona *sf* person; (*qualcuno*): **una** ~ someone, somebody, *espressione interrogativa* +anyone *o* anybody; ~**e** *sfpl* people; **non c'è** ~ **che ...** there's nobody who ..., there isn't anybody who ...

perso'naggio [perso'naddʒo] *sm* (*persona ragguardevole*) personality, figure; (*tipo*) character, individual; (*LETTERATURA*) character

perso'nale *ag* personal ♦ *sm* staff;
personnel; *(figura fisica)* build
personalità *sf inv* personality
personifi'care *vt* to personify; to embody
perspi'cace [perspi'katʃe] *ag* shrewd,
discerning
persu'adere *vt*: ~ qn (di qc/a fare) to
persuade sb (of sth/to do); **persuasi'one**
sf persuasion; **persua'sivo, a** *ag*
persuasive; **persu'aso, a** *pp di*
persuadere
per'tanto *cong* (*quindi*) so, therefore
'pertica, che *sf* pole
perti'nente *ag*: ~ (a) relevant (to),
pertinent (to)
per'tosse *sf* whooping cough
per'tugio [per'tudʒo] *sm* hole, opening
perturbazi'one [perturbat'tsjone] *sf*
disruption; perturbation; ~ **atmosferica**
atmospheric disturbance
per'vadere *vt* to pervade; **per'vaso, a**
pp di **pervadere**
perve'nire *vi*: ~ a to reach, arrive at,
come to; *(venire in possesso)*: **gli
pervenne una fortuna** he inherited a
fortune; **far ~ qc a** to have sth sent to;
perve'nuto, a *pp di* **pervenire**
per'verso, a *ag* depraved; perverse
p. es. *abbr* (= *per esempio*) e.g.
'pesa *sf* weighing *no pl*; weighbridge
pe'sante *ag* heavy; *(fig: noioso)* dull,
boring
pe'sare *vt* to weigh ♦ *vi* (*avere un peso*)
to weigh; *(essere pesante)* to be heavy; *(fig)*
to carry weight; ~ **su** *(fig)* to lie heavy
on; to influence; to hang over; **mi pesa
sgridarlo** I find it hard to scold him
'pesca (*pl* **pesche:** *frutto*) *sf* peach; (*il
pescare*) fishing; **andare a ~** to go fishing;
~ **di beneficenza** *(lotteria)* lucky dip; ~
con la lenza angling
pes'care *vt* *(pesce)* to fish for; to catch;
(qc nell'acqua) to fish out; *(fig: trovare)* to
get hold of, find
pesca'tore *sm* fisherman; angler
'pesce [*'peʃʃe*] *sm* fish *gen inv*; **P~i** (*dello
zodiaco*) Pisces; ~ **d'aprile!** April Fool!; ~
spada swordfish; **pesce'cane** *sm* shark
pesche'reccio [peske'rettʃo] *sm* fishing

boat
pesche'ria [peske'ria] *sf* fishmonger's
(shop) *(BRIT)*, fish store *(US)*
pesci'vendolo, a [peʃʃi'vendolo] *sm/f*
fishmonger *(BRIT)*, fish merchant *(US)*
'pesco, schi *sm* peach tree
pes'coso, a *ag* abounding in fish
'peso *sm* weight; *(SPORT)* shot; **rubare sul
~** to give short weight; **essere di ~ a** qn
(fig) to be a burden to sb; ~ **lordo/netto**
gross/net weight; ~ **piuma/mosca/
gallo/medio/massimo** *(PUGILATO)* feath-
er/fly/bantam/middle/heavyweight
pessi'mismo *sm* pessimism;
pessi'mista, i, e *ag* pessimistic ♦ *sm/f*
pessimist
'pessimo, a *ag* very bad, awful
pes'tare *vt* to tread on, trample on; *(sale,
pepe)* to grind; *(uva, aglio)* to crush; *(fig:
picchiare)*: ~ **qn** to beat sb up
'peste *sf* plague; *(persona)* nuisance, pest
pes'tello *sm* pestle
pesti'lenza [pesti'lentsa] *sf* pestilence;
(fetore) stench
'pesto, a *ag*: **c'è buio ~** it's pitch-dark;
occhio ~ black eye ♦ *sm* *(CUC)* sauce made
with basil, garlic, cheese and oil
'petalo *sm* *(BOT)* petal
pe'tardo *sm* firecracker, banger *(BRIT)*
petizi'one [petit'tsjone] *sf* petition
'peto *(fam!)* *sm* fart (!)
petrol'chimica [petrol'kimika] *sf* pet-
rochemical industry
petroli'era *sf* *(nave)* oil tanker
petro'lifero, a *ag* oil-bearing; oil *cpd*
pe'trolio *sm* oil, petroleum; *(per
lampada, fornello)* paraffin
pettego'lare *vi* to gossip
pettego'lezzo [pettego'leddzo] *sm*
gossip *no pl*; **fare ~i** to gossip
pet'tegolo, a *ag* gossipy ♦ *sm/f* gossip
petti'nare *vt* to comb (the hair of); **~rsi**
vr to comb one's hair; **pettina'tura** *sf*
(acconciatura) hairstyle
'pettine *sm* comb; *(ZOOL)* scallop
petti'rosso *sm* robin
'petto *sm* chest; *(seno)* breast, bust; *(CUC:
di carne bovina)* brisket; (: *di pollo etc*)
breast; **a doppio ~** *(abito)* double-

breasted; **petto'ruto, a** *ag* broad-chested; full-breasted

petu'lante *ag* insolent

pe'tunia *sf* (*BOT*) petunia

'pezza ['pɛttsa] *sf* piece of cloth; (*toppa*) patch; (*cencio*) rag, cloth

pez'zato, a [pet'tsato] *ag* piebald

pez'zente [pet'tsɛnte] *sm/f* beggar

'pezzo ['pɛttso] *sm* (*gen*) piece; (*brandello, frammento*) piece, bit; (*di macchina, arnese etc*) part; (*STAMPA*) article; (*di tempo*): **aspettare un ~** to wait quite a while *o* some time; **in** *o* **a ~i** in pieces; **andare in ~i** to break into pieces; **un bel ~ d'uomo** a fine figure of a man; **abito a due ~i** two-piece suit; **~ di cronaca** (*STAMPA*) report; **~ grosso** (*fig*) bigwig; **~ di ricambio** spare part

pia'cente [pja'tʃɛnte] *ag* attractive, pleasant

pia'cere [pja'tʃere] *vi* to please; **una ragazza che piace** a likeable girl; an attractive girl; **~ a: mi piace** I like it; **quei ragazzi non mi piacciono** I don't like those boys; **gli piacerebbe andare al cinema** he would like to go to the cinema ♦ *sm* pleasure; (*favore*) favour; **"~!"** (*nelle presentazioni*) "pleased to meet you!"; **con ~** certainly, with pleasure; **per ~!** please; **fare un ~ a qn** to do sb a favour; **pia'cevole** *ag* pleasant, agreeable; **piaci'uto, a** *pp di* **piacere**

pi'aga, ghe *sf* (*lesione*) sore; (*ferita: anche fig*) wound; (*fig: flagello*) scourge, curse; (: *persona*) pest, nuisance

piagnis'teo [pjanɲis'tɛo] *sm* whining, whimpering

piagnuco'lare [pjanɲuko'lare] *vi* to whimper

pi'alla *sf* (*arnese*) plane; **pial'lare** *vt* to plane

pi'ana *sf* stretch of-level ground; (*più esteso*) plain

pianeggi'ante [pjaned'dʒante] *ag* flat, level

piane'rottolo *sm* landing

pia'neta *sm* (*ASTR*) planet

pi'angere ['pjandʒere] *vi* to cry, weep; (*occhi*) to water ♦ *vt* to cry, weep; (*lamentare*) to bewail, lament; **~ la morte di qn** to mourn sb's death

pianifi'care *vt* to plan; **pianificazi'one** *sf* planning

pia'nista, i, e *sm/f* pianist

pi'ano, a *ag* (*piatto*) flat, level; (*MAT*) plane; (*facile*) straightforward, simple; (*chiaro*) clear, plain ♦ *av* (*adagio*) slowly; (*a bassa voce*) softly; (*con cautela*) slowly, carefully ♦ *sm* (*MAT*) plane; (*GEO*) plain; (*livello*) level, plane; (*di edificio*) floor; (*programma*) plan; (*MUS*) piano; **pian ~** very slowly; (*poco a poco*) little by little; **in primo/secondo ~** in the foreground/background; **di primo ~** (*fig*) prominent, high-ranking

piano'forte *sm* piano, pianoforte

pi'anta *sf* (*BOT*) plant; (*ANAT: anche: ~ del piede*) sole (of the foot); (*grafico*) plan; (*topografica*) map; **in ~ stabile** on the permanent staff; **piantagi'one** *sf* plantation; **pian'tare** *vt* to plant; (*conficcare*) to drive *o* hammer in; (*tenda*) to put up, pitch; (*fig: lasciare*) to leave, desert; **~rsi** *vr*: **~rsi davanti a qn** to plant o.s. in front of sb; **piantala!** (*fam*) cut it out!

pianter'reno *sm* ground floor

pi'anto, a *pp di* **piangere** ♦ *sm* tears *pl*, crying

pian'tone *sm* (*vigilante*) sentry, guard; (*soldato*) orderly; (*AUT*) steering column

pia'nura *sf* plain

pi'astra *sf* plate; (*di pietra*) slab; (*di fornello*) hotplate; **~ di registrazione** tape deck; **panino alla ~** ≈ toasted sandwich

pias'trella *sf* tile

pias'trina *sf* (*MIL*) identity disc

piatta'forma *sf* (*anche fig*) platform

piat'tino *sm* saucer

pi'atto, a *ag* flat; (*fig: scialbo*) dull ♦ *sm* (*recipiente, vivanda*) dish; (*portata*) course; (*parte piana*) flat (part); **~i** *smpl* (*MUS*) cymbals; **~ fondo** soup dish; **~ forte** main course; **~ del giorno** dish of the day, plat du jour; **~ del giradischi** turntable

pi'azza ['pjattsa] *sf* square; (*COMM*) market; **far ~ pulita** to make a clean

sweep; ~ **d'armi** (*MIL*) parade ground;
piaz'zale *sm* (large) square
piaz'zare [pjat'tsare] *vt* to place; (*COMM*)
to market, sell; **~rsi** *vr* (*SPORT*) to be
placed
piaz'zista, i [pjat'tsista] *sm* (*COMM*)
commercial traveller
piaz'zola [pjat'tsɔla] *sf* (*AUT*) lay-by
'picca, che *sf* pike; **~che** *sfpl* (*CARTE*)
spades
pic'cante *ag* hot, pungent; (*fig*) racy;
biting
pic'carsi *vr*: ~ **di fare** to pride o.s. on
one's ability to do; ~ **per qc** to take
offence at sth
pic'chetto [pik'ketto] *sm* (*MIL*, *di
scioperanti*) picket
picchi'are [pik'kjare] *vt* (*persona: colpire*)
to hit, strike; (: *prendere a botte*) to beat
(up); (*battere*) to beat; (*sbattere*) to bang
♦ *vi* (*bussare*) to knock; (: *con forza*) to
bang; (*colpire*) to hit, strike; (*sole*) to beat
down; **picchi'ata** *sf* (*percosse*) beating,
thrashing; (*AER*) dive
picchiet'tare [pikkjet'tare] *vt* (*pun-
teggiare*) to spot, dot; (*colpire*) to tap
'picchio ['pikkjo] *sm* woodpecker
pic'cino, a [pit'tʃino] *ag* tiny, very small
piccio'naia [pittʃo'naja] *sf* pigeon-loft;
(*TEATRO*): **la** ~ the gods *sg*
picci'one [pit'tʃone] *sm* pigeon
'picco, chi *sm* peak; **a** ~ vertically
'piccolo, a *ag* small; (*oggetto, mano, di
età: bambino*) small, little (*dav sostantivo*);
(*di breve durata: viaggio*) short; (*fig*)
mean, petty ♦ *sm/f* child, little one; **~i**
smpl (*di animale*) young *pl*; **in** ~ in miniature
pic'cone *sm* pick(-axe)
pic'cozza [pik'kɔttsa] *sf* ice-axe
pic'nic *sm inv* picnic
pi'docchio [pi'dɔkkjo] *sm* louse
pi'ede *sm* foot; (*di mobile*) leg; **in ~i**
standing; **a ~i** on foot; **a ~i nudi** barefoot;
su due ~i (*fig*) at once; **prendere** ~ (*fig*)
to gain ground, catch on; **sul** ~ **di guerra**
(*MIL*) ready for action; ~ **di porco**
crowbar
piedes'tallo *sm* = **piedistallo**

piedipi'atti *sm inv* (*peg*) cop
piedis'tallo *sm* pedestal
pi'ega, ghe *sf* (*piegatura*, *GEO*) fold; (*di
gonna*) pleat; (*di pantaloni*) crease;
(*grinza*) wrinkle, crease; **prendere una
brutta** ~ (*avvenimento*) to take a turn for
the worse
pie'gare *vt* to fold; (*braccia, gambe, testa*)
to bend ♦ *vi* to bend; **~rsi** *vr* to bend;
(*fig*): **~rsi (a)** to yield (to), submit (to);
pieghet'tare *vt* to pleat; **pie'ghevole** *ag*
pliable, flexible; (*porta*) folding; (*fig*)
yielding, docile
Pie'monte *sm*: **il** ~ Piedmont
pi'ena *sf* (*di fiume*) flood, spate; (*gran
folla*) crowd, throng
pi'eno, a *ag* full; (*muro, mattone*) solid
♦ *sm* (*colmo*) height, peak; (*carico*) full
load; ~ **di** full of; **in** ~ **giorno** in broad
daylight; **fare il** ~ **(di benzina)** to fill up
(with petrol)
pietà *sf* pity; (*REL*) piety; **senza** ~ pitiless,
merciless; **avere** ~ **di** (*compassione*) to
pity, feel sorry for; (*misericordia*) to have
pity *o* mercy on
pie'tanza [pje'tantsa] *sf* dish; (main)
course
pie'toso, a *ag* (*compassionevole*) pitying,
compassionate; (*che desta pietà*) pitiful
pi'etra *sf* stone; ~ **preziosa** precious
stone, gem; **pie'traia** *sf* (*terreno*) stony
ground; **pietrifi'care** *vt* to petrify; (*fig*) to
transfix, paralyze
'piffero *sm* (*MUS*) pipe
pigi'ama, i [pi'dʒama] *sm* pyjamas *pl*
'pigia 'pigia ['pidʒa'pidʒa] *sm* crowd,
press
pigi'are [pi'dʒare] *vt* to press
pigi'one [pi'dʒone] *sf* rent
pigli'are [piʎ'ʎare] *vt* to take, grab;
(*afferrare*) to catch
'piglio ['piʎʎo] *sm* look, expression
pig'meo, a *sm/f* pygmy
'pigna ['piɲɲa] *sf* pine cone
pi'gnolo, a [piɲ'ɲɔlo] *ag* pernickety
pigo'lare *vi* to cheep, chirp
pigno'rare [piɲɲo'rare] *vt* to distrain
pi'grizia [pi'grittsja] *sf* laziness
'pigro, a *ag* lazy

'pila *sf* (*catasta, di ponte*) pile; (*ELETTR*) battery; (*fam: torcia*) torch (*BRIT*), flashlight

pi'lastro *sm* pillar

'pillola *sf* pill; **prendere la** ~ to be on the pill

pi'lone *sm* (*di ponte*) pier; (*di linea elettrica*) pylon

pi'lota, i, e *sm/f* pilot; (*AUT*) driver ♦ *ag inv* pilot *cpd*; ~ **automatico** automatic pilot; **pilo'tare** *vt* to pilot; to drive

pi'mento *sm* pimento, allspice

pinaco'teca, che *sf* art gallery

pi'neta *sf* pinewood

ping-'pong [piŋ'pɔŋ] *sm* table tennis

'pingue *ag* fat, corpulent

pingu'ino *sm* (*ZOOL*) penguin

'pinna *sf* fin; (*di pinguino, spatola di gomma*) flipper

'pino *sm* pine (tree); **pi'nolo** *sm* pine kernel

'pinza ['pintsa] *sf* pliers *pl*; (*MED*) forceps *pl*; (*ZOOL*) pincer

pinzette [pin'tsette] *sfpl* tweezers

'pio, a, 'pii, 'pie *ag* pious; (*opere, istituzione*) charitable, charity *cpd*

pi'oggia, ge ['pjɔddʒa] *sf* rain; ~ **acida** acid rain

pi'olo *sm* peg; (*di scala*) rung

piom'bare *vi* to fall heavily; (*gettarsi con impeto*): ~ **su** to fall upon, assail ♦ *vt* (*dente*) to fill; **piomba'tura** *sf* (*di dente*) filling

piom'bino *sm* (*sigillo*) (lead) seal; (*del filo a piombo*) plummet; (*PESCA*) sinker

pi'ombo *sm* (*CHIM*) lead; (*sigillo*) (lead) seal; (*proiettile*) (lead) shot; **a** ~ (*cadere*) straight down; **senza** ~ (*benzina*) unleaded

pioni'ere, a *sm/f* pioneer

pi'oppo *sm* poplar

pi'overe *vb impers* to rain ♦ *vi* (*fig: scendere dall'alto*) to rain down; (: *affluire in gran numero*): ~ **in** to pour into; **pioviggi'nare** *vb impers* to drizzle; **pio'voso, a** *ag* rainy

pi'ovra *sf* octopus

'pipa *sf* pipe

pipì (*fam*) *sf*: **fare** ~ to have a wee (wee)

pipis'trello *sm* (*ZOOL*) bat

pi'ramide *sf* pyramid

pi'rata, i *sm* pirate; ~ **della strada** hit-and-run driver

Pire'nei *smpl*: **i** ~ the Pyrenees

'pirico, a, ci, che *ag*: **polvere** ~**a** gunpowder

pi'rite *sf* pyrite

pi'rofilo, a *ag* heat-resistant; **pi'rofila** *sf* heat-resistant dish

pi'roga, ghe *sf* dug-out canoe

pi'romane *sm/f* pyromaniac; arsonist

pi'roscafo *sm* steamer, steamship

pisci'are [piʃ'ʃare] (*fam!*) *vi* to piss (*!*), pee (*!*)

pi'scina [piʃ'ʃina] *sf* (swimming) pool; (*stabilimento*) (swimming) baths *pl*

pi'sello *sm* pea

piso'lino *sm* nap

'pista *sf* (*traccia*) track, trail; (*di stadio*) track; (*di pattinaggio*) rink; (*da sci*) run; (*AER*) runway; (*di circo*) ring; ~ **da ballo** dance floor

pis'tacchio [pis'takkjo] *sm* pistachio (tree); pistachio (nut)

pis'tola *sf* pistol, gun

pis'tone *sm* piston

pi'tone *sm* python

pit'tore, 'trice *sm/f* painter; **pitto'resco, a, schi, sche** *ag* picturesque

pit'tura *sf* painting; **pittu'rare** *vt* to paint

PAROLA CHIAVE

più *av* **1** (*in maggiore quantità*) more; ~ **del solito** more than usual; **in** ~, **di** ~ more; **ne voglio di** ~ I want some more; **ci sono 3 persone in** *o* **di** ~ there are 3 more *o* extra people; ~ **o meno** more or less; **per di** ~ (*inoltre*) what's more, moreover

2 (*comparativo*) more, *aggettivo corto* +...er; ~ **... di/che** more ... than; **lavoro** ~ **di te/Paola** I work harder than you/ Paola; **è** ~ **intelligente che ricco** he's more intelligent than rich

3 (*superlativo*) most, *aggettivo corto* +...est; **il** ~ **grande/intelligente** the biggest/most intelligent; **è quello che**

compro ~ spesso that's the one I buy most often; **al ~ presto** as soon as possible; **al ~ tardi** at the latest
4 (*negazione*): **non ... ~** no more, no longer; **non ho ~ soldi** I've got no more money, I don't have any more money; **non lavoro ~** I'm no longer working, I don't work any more; **a ~ non posso** (*gridare*) at the top of one's voice; (*correre*) as fast as one can
5 (*MAT*) plus; **4 ~ 5 fa 9** 4 plus 5 equals 9; **~ 5 gradi** 5 degrees above freezing, plus 5
♦ *prep* plus
♦ *ag inv* **1**: **~ ... (di)** more ... (than); **~ denaro/tempo** more money/time; **~ persone di quante ci aspettassimo** more people than we expected
2 (*numerosi, diversi*) several; **l'aspettai per ~ giorni** I waited for it for several days
♦ *sm* **1** (*la maggior parte*): **il ~ è fatto** most of it is done
2 (*MAT*) plus (sign)
3: **i ~** the majority

piucchepper'fetto [pjukkepper'fetto] *sm* (*LING*) pluperfect, past perfect
pi'uma *sf* feather; **piu'maggio** *sm* plumage, feathers *pl*; **piu'mino** *sm* (eider)down; (*per letto*) eiderdown; (: *tipo danese*) duvet, continental quilt; (*giacca*) quilted jacket (*with goose-feather padding*); (*per cipria*) powder puff; (*per spolverare*) feather duster
piut'tosto *av* rather; **~ che** (*anziché*) rather than
pi'vello, a *sm/f* greenhorn
'pizza ['pittsa] *sf* pizza; **pizze'ria** *sf* place where pizzas are made, sold or eaten
pizzi'cagnolo, a [pittsi'kaɲɲolo] *sm/f* specialist grocer
pizzi'care [pittsi'kare] *vt* (*stringere*) to nip, pinch; (*pungere*) to sting; to bite; (*MUS*) to pluck ♦ *vi* (*prudere*) to itch, be itchy; (*cibo*) to be hot o spicy
pizziche'ria [pittsike'ria] *sf* delicatessen (shop)
'pizzico, chi ['pittsiko] *sm* (*pizzicotto*) pinch, nip; (*piccola quantità*) pinch, dash;

(*d'insetto*) sting; bite
pizzi'cotto [pittsi'kɔtto] *sm* pinch, nip
'pizzo ['pittso] *sm* (*merletto*) lace; (*barbetta*) goatee beard
pla'care *vt* to placate, soothe; **~rsi** *vr* to calm down
'placca, che *sf* plate; (*con iscrizione*) plaque; (*anche:* **~ dentaria**) (dental) plaque; **plac'care** *vt* to plate; **placcato in oro/argento** gold-/silver-plated
'placido, a ['platʃido] *ag* placid, calm
plagi'are [pla'dʒare] *vt* (*copiare*) to plagiarize; **'plagio** *sm* plagiarism
pla'nare *vi* (*AER*) to glide
'plancia, ce ['plantʃa] *sf* (*NAUT*) bridge
plane'tario, a *ag* planetary ♦ *sm* (*locale*) planetarium
'plasma *sm* plasma
plas'mare *vt* to mould, shape
'plastica, che *sf* (*arte*) plastic arts *pl*; (*MED*) plastic surgery; (*sostanza*) plastic
'plastico, a, ci, che *ag* plastic ♦ *sm* (*rappresentazione*) relief model; (*esplosivo*): **bomba al ~** plastic bomb
plasti'lina ® *sf* plasticine ®
'platano *sm* plane tree
pla'tea *sf* (*TEATRO*) stalls *pl*
'platino *sm* platinum
pla'tonico, a, ci, che *ag* platonic
plau'sibile *ag* plausible
'plauso *sm* (*fig*) approval
ple'baglia [ple'baʎʎa] (*peg*) *sf* rabble, mob
'plebe *sf* common people; **ple'beo, a** *ag* plebeian; (*volgare*) coarse, common
ple'nario, a *ag* plenary
pleni'lunio *sm* full moon
'plettro *sm* plectrum
pleu'rite *sf* pleurisy
'plico, chi *sm* (*pacco*) parcel; **in ~ a parte** (*COMM*) under separate cover
plo'tone *sm* (*MIL*) platoon; **~ d'esecuzione** firing squad
'plumbeo, a *ag* leaden
plu'rale *ag, sm* plural; **pluralità** *sf* plurality; (*maggioranza*) majority
plusva'lore *sm* (*ECON*) surplus
pneu'matico, a, ci, che *ag* inflatable; pneumatic ♦ *sm* (*AUT*) tyre (*BRIT*), tire (*US*)

po' *av, sm vedi* **poco**

PAROLA CHIAVE

'**poco, a, chi, che** *ag* (*quantità*) little, not much; (*numero*) few, not many; ~ **pane/denaro/spazio** little *o* not much bread/money/space; ~**che persone/idee** few *o* not many people/ideas; **ci vediamo tra** ~ (*sottinteso: tempo*) see you soon
♦ *av* **1** (*in piccola quantità*) little, not much; (*numero limitato*) few, not many; **guadagna** ~ he doesn't earn much, he earns little
2 (*con ag, av*) (a) little, not very; **sta ~ bene** he isn't very well; **è ~ più vecchia di lui** she's a little *o* slightly older than him
3 (*tempo*): ~ **dopo/prima** shortly afterwards/before; **il film dura** ~ the film doesn't last very long; **ci vediamo molto** ~ we don't see each other very often, we hardly ever see each other
4: **un po'** a little, a bit; **è un po' corto** it's a little *o* a bit short; **arriverà fra un po'** he'll arrive shortly *o* in a little while
5: **a dir** ~ to say the least; **a ~ a ~** little by little; **per** ~ **non cadevo** I nearly fell; **è una cosa da** ~ it's nothing, it's of no importance; **una persona da** ~ a worthless person
♦ *pron* (a) little; ~**chi, che** *pron pl* (*persone*) few (people); (*cose*) few
♦ *sm* **1** little; **vive del** ~ **che ha** he lives on the little he has
2: **un po'** a little; **un po' di zucchero** a little sugar; **un bel po' di denaro** quite a lot of money; **un po' per ciascuno** a bit each

po'dere *sm* (*AGR*) farm
pode'roso, a *ag* powerful
podestà *sm inv* (*nel fascismo*) podesta, mayor
'**podio** *sm* dais, platform; (*MUS*) podium
po'dismo *sm* (*SPORT*) track events *pl*
po'ema, i *sm* poem
poe'sia *sf* (*arte*) poetry; (*componimento*) poem
po'eta, '**essa** *sm/f* poet/poetess;

po'etico, a, ci, che *ag* poetic(al)
poggi'are [pod'dʒare] *vt* to lean, rest; (*posare*) to lay, place; **poggia'testa** *sm inv* (*AUT*) headrest
'**poggio** ['pɔddʒo] *sm* hillock, knoll
poggi'olo [pod'dʒɔlo] *sm* balcony
'**poi** *av* then; (*alla fine*) finally, at last; **e ~** (*inoltre*) and besides; **questa ~ (è bella)!** (*ironico*) that's a good one!
poiché [poi'ke] *cong* since, as
'**poker** *sm* poker
po'lacco, a, chi, che *ag* Polish ♦ *sm/f* Pole
po'lare *ag* polar
po'lemica, che *sf* controversy
po'lemico, a, ci, che *ag* polemic(al), controversial
po'lenta *sf* (*CUC*) sort of thick porridge *made with maize flour*
poli'clinico, ci *sm* general hospital, polyclinic
poli'estere *sm* polyester
'**polio(mie'lite)** *sf* polio(myelitis)
'**polipo** *sm* polyp
polisti'rolo *sm* polystyrene
poli'tecnico, ci *sm* postgraduate technical college
po'litica, che *sf* politics *sg*; (*linea di condotta*) policy; *vedi anche* **politico**
politiciz'zare [politit∫id'dzare] *vt* to politicize
po'litico, a, ci, che *ag* political ♦ *sm/f* politician
poli'zia [polit'tsia] *sf* police; ~ **giudiziaria** ≈ Criminal Investigation Department (*BRIT*), ≈ Federal Bureau of Investigation (*US*); ~ **stradale** traffic police; **polizi'esco, a, schi, sche** *ag* police *cpd*; (*film, romanzo*) detective *cpd*; **polizi'otto** *sm* policeman; **cane poliziotto** police dog; **donna poliziotto** policewoman
'**polizza** ['pɔlittsa] *sf* (*COMM*) bill; ~ **di assicurazione** insurance policy; ~ **di carico** bill of lading
pol'laio *sm* henhouse
pol'lame *sm* poultry
pol'lastro *sm* (*ZOOL*) cockerel
'**pollice** ['pɔllit∫e] *sm* thumb

'polline *sm* pollen

'pollo *sm* chicken

pol'mone *sm* lung; **~ d'acciaio** (*MED*) iron lung; polmo'nite *sf* pneumonia

'polo *sm* (*GEO, FISICA*) pole; (*gioco*) polo; il **~ sud/nord** the South/North Pole

Po'lonia *sf*: **la ~** Poland

'polpa *sf* flesh, pulp; (*carne*) lean meat

pol'paccio [pol'pattʃo] *sm* (*ANAT*) calf

polpas'trello *sm* fingertip

pol'petta *sf* (*CUC*) meatball; polpet'tone *sm* (*CUC*) meatloaf

'polpo *sm* octopus

pol'poso, a *ag* fleshy

pol'sino *sm* cuff

'polso *sm* (*ANAT*) wrist; (*pulsazione*) pulse; (*fig: forza*) drive, vigour

pol'tiglia [pol'tiʎʎa] *sf* (*composto*) mash, mush; (*di fango e neve*) slush

pol'trire *vi* to laze about

pol'trona *sf* armchair; (*TEATRO: posto*) seat in the front stalls (*BRIT*) o orchestra (*US*)

pol'trone *ag* lazy, slothful

'polvere *sf* dust; (*anche:* **~ da sparo**) (gun)powder; (*sostanza ridotta minutissima*) powder, dust; **latte in ~** dried o powdered milk; **caffè in ~** instant coffee; **sapone in ~** soap powder; polveri'era *sf* powder magazine; polveriz'zare *vt* to pulverize; (*nebulizzare*) to atomize; (*fig*) to crush, pulverize; to smash; polve'rone *sm* thick cloud of dust; polve'roso, a *ag* dusty

po'mata *sf* ointment, cream

po'mello *sm* knob

pomeridi'ano, a *ag* afternoon *cpd*; **nelle ore ~e** in the afternoon

pome'riggio [pome'riddʒo] *sm* afternoon

'pomice ['pomitʃe] *sf* pumice

'pomo *sm* (*mela*) apple; (*ornamentale*) knob; (*di sella*) pommel; **~ d'Adamo** (*ANAT*) Adam's apple

pomo'doro *sm* tomato

'pompa *sf* pump; (*sfarzo*) pomp (and ceremony); **~e funebri** funeral parlour *sg* (*BRIT*), undertaker's *sg*; pom'pare *vt* to pump; (*trarre*) to pump out; (*gonfiare d'aria*) to pump up

pom'pelmo *sm* grapefruit

pompi'ere *sm* fireman

pom'poso, a *ag* pompous

ponde'rare *vt* to ponder over, consider carefully

ponde'roso, a *ag* (*anche fig*) weighty

po'nente *sm* west

'ponte *sm* bridge; (*di nave*) deck; (*: anche:* **~ di comando**) bridge; (*impalcatura*) scaffold; **fare il ~** (*fig*) to take the extra day off (*between 2 public holidays*); **governo ~** interim government; **~ aereo** airlift; **~ sospeso** suspension bridge

pon'tefice [pon'tefitʃe] *sm* (*REL*) pontiff

pontifi'care *vi* (*anche fig*) to pontificate

ponti'ficio, a, ci, cie [ponti'fitʃo] *ag* papal

popo'lano, a *ag* popular, of the people

popo'lare *ag* popular; (*quartiere, clientela*) working-class ♦ *vt* (*rendere abitato*) to populate; **~rsi** *vr* to fill with people, get crowded; popolarità *sf* popularity; popolazi'one *sf* population

'popolo *sm* people; popo'loso, a *ag* densely populated

po'pone *sm* melon

'poppa *sf* (*di nave*) stern; (*mammella*) breast

pop'pare *vt* to suck

poppa'toio *sm* (feeding) bottle

porcel'lana [portʃel'lana] *sf* porcelain, china; piece of china

porcel'lino, a [portʃel'lino] *sm/f* piglet

porche'ria [porke'ria] *sf* filth, muck; (*fig: oscenità*) obscenity; (*: azione disonesta*) dirty trick; (*: cosa mal fatta*) rubbish

por'cile [por'tʃile] *sm* pigsty

por'cino, a [por'tʃino] *ag* of pigs, pork *cpd* ♦ *sm* (*fungo*) type of edible mushroom

'porco, ci *sm* pig; (*carne*) pork

porcos'pino *sm* porcupine

'porgere ['pɔrdʒere] *vt* to hand, give; (*tendere*) to hold out

pornogra'fia *sf* pornography; porno'grafico, a, ci, che *ag* pornographic

'poro *sm* pore; po'roso, a *ag* porous

'porpora *sf* purple

'porre *vt* (*mettere*) to put; (*collocare*) to place; (*posare*) to lay (down), put (down);

(*fig: supporre*): **poniamo (il caso) che ...** let's suppose that ...; **porsi** *vr* (*mettersi*): **porsi a sedere/in cammino** to sit down/set off; **~ una domanda a qn** to ask sb a question, put a question to sb

'**porro** *sm* (*BOT*) leek; (*MED*) wart

'**porta** *sf* door; (*SPORT*) goal; **~e** *sfpl* (*di città*) gates; **a ~e chiuse** (*DIR*) in camera

'**porta...** *prefisso*: **portaba'gagli** *sm inv* (*facchino*) porter; (*AUT, FERR*) luggage rack; **porta'cenere** *sm inv* ashtray; **portachi'avi** *sm inv* keyring; **porta'cipria** *sm inv* powder compact; **porta'erei** *sf inv* (*nave*) aircraft carrier ♦ *sm inv* (*aereo*) aircraft transporter; **portafi'nestra** (*pl* **portefi'nestre**) *sf* French window; **porta'foglio** *sm* (*busta*) wallet; (*cartella*) briefcase; (*POL, BORSA*) portfolio; **portafor'tuna** *sm inv* lucky charm; mascot; **portagi'oie** *sm inv* jewellery box; **portagioi'elli** *sm inv* = **portagioie**

porta'lettere *sm/f inv* postman/woman (*BRIT*), mailman/woman (*US*)

porta'mento *sm* carriage, bearing

portamo'nete *sm inv* purse

por'tante *ag* (*muro etc*) supporting, load-bearing

portan'tina *sf* sedan chair; (*per ammalati*) stretcher

por'tare *vt* (*sostenere, sorreggere: peso, bambino, pacco*) to carry; (*indossare: abito, occhiali*) to wear; (: *capelli lunghi*) to have; (*avere: nome, titolo*) to have, bear; (*recare*): **~ qc a qn** to take (*o* bring) sth to sb; (*fig: sentimenti*) to bear; **~rsi** *vr* (*recarsi*) to go; **~ avanti** (*discorso, idea*) to pursue; **~ via** to take away; (*rubare*) to take; **~ i bambini a spasso** to take the children for a walk; **~ fortuna** to bring good luck

portasiga'rette *sm inv* cigarette case

por'tata *sf* (*vivanda*) course; (*AUT*) carrying (*o* loading) capacity; (*di arma*) range; (*volume d'acqua*) (rate of) flow; (*fig: limite*) scope, capability; (: *importanza*) impact, import; **alla ~ di tutti** (*conoscenza*) within everybody's capabilities; (*prezzo*) within everybody's

means; **a/fuori ~ (di)** within/out of reach (of); **a ~ di mano** within (arm's) reach

por'tatile *ag* portable

por'tato, a *ag* (*incline*): **~ a** inclined *o* apt to

porta'tore, 'trice *sm/f* (*anche COMM*) bearer; (*MED*) carrier

portau'ovo *sm inv* eggcup

porta'voce [porta'votʃe] *sm/f inv* spokesman/woman

por'tento *sm* wonder, marvel

'**portico, ci** *sm* portico

porti'era *sf* (*AUT*) door

porti'ere *sm* (*portinaio*) concierge, caretaker; (*di hotel*) porter; (*nel calcio*) goalkeeper

porti'naio, a *sm/f* concierge, caretaker

portine'ria *sf* caretaker's lodge

'**porto, a** *pp di* **porgere** ♦ *sm* (*NAUT*) harbour, port; (*spesa di trasporto*) carriage ♦ *sm inv* port (wine); **~ d'armi** (*documento*) gun licence

Porto'gallo *sm*: **il ~** Portugal; **porto'ghese** *ag, sm/f, sm* Portuguese *inv*

por'tone *sm* main entrance, main door

portu'ale *ag* harbour *cpd*, port *cpd* ♦ *sm* dock worker

porzi'one [por'tsjone] *sf* portion, share; (*di cibo*) portion, helping

'**posa** *sf* (*FOT*) exposure; (*atteggiamento, di modello*) pose

posa'cenere [posa'tʃenere] *sm inv* ashtray

po'sare *vt* to put (down), lay (down) ♦ *vi* (*ponte, edificio, teoria*): **~ su** to rest on; (*FOT, atteggiarsi*) to pose; **~rsi** *vr* (*aereo*) to land; (*uccello*) to alight; (*sguardo*) to settle

po'sata *sf* piece of cutlery; **~e** *sfpl* (*servizio*) cutlery *sg*

po'sato, a *ag* serious

pos'critto *sm* postscript

posi'tivo, a *ag* positive

posizi'one [pozit'tsjone] *sf* position; **prendere ~** (*fig*) to take a stand; **luci di ~** (*AUT*) sidelights

posolo'gia, 'gie [pozolo'dʒia] *sf* dosage, directions *pl* for use

pos'porre *vt* to place after; (*differire*) to

postpone, defer; **pos'posto, a** *pp di* **posporre**

posse'dere *vt* to own, possess; *(qualità, virtù)* to have, possess; *(conoscere a fondo: lingua etc)* to have a thorough knowledge of; *(sog: ira etc)* to possess; **possedi-'mento** *sm* possession

posses'sivo, a *ag* possessive

pos'sesso *sm* ownership *no pl*; possession

posses'sore *sm* owner

pos'sibile *ag* possible ♦ *sm*: **fare tutto il** ~ to do everything possible; **nei limiti del** ~ as far as possible; **al più tardi** ~ as late as possible; **possibilità** *sf inv* possibility ♦ *sfpl (mezzi)* means; **aver la possibilità di fare** to be in a position to do; to have the opportunity to do

possi'dente *sm/f* landowner

'posta *sf (servizio)* post, postal service; *(corrispondenza)* post, mail; *(ufficio postale)* post office; *(nei giochi d'azzardo)* stake; ~**e** *sfpl (amministrazione)* post office; ~ **aerea** airmail; **ministro delle P~e e Telecomunicazioni** Postmaster General; **posta'giro** *sm* post office cheque, postal giro *(BRIT)*; **pos'tale** *ag* postal, post office *cpd*

post'bellico, a, ci, che *ag* postwar

posteggi'are [posted'dʒare] *vt, vi* to park; **pos'teggio** *sm* car park *(BRIT)*, parking lot *(US)*; *(di taxi)* rank *(BRIT)*, stand *(US)*

postelegra'fonico, a, ci, che *ag* postal and telecommunications *cpd*

posteri'ore *ag (dietro)* back; *(dopo)* later ♦ *sm (fam: sedere)* behind

pos'ticcio, a, ci, ce [pos'tittʃo] *ag* false ♦ *sm* hairpiece

postici'pare [postitʃi'pare] *vt* to defer, postpone

pos'tilla *sf* marginal note

pos'tino *sm* postman *(BRIT)*, mailman *(US)*

'posto, a *pp di* **porre** ♦ *sm (sito, posizione)* place; *(impiego)* job; *(spazio libero)* room, space; *(di parcheggio)* space; *(sedile: al teatro, in treno etc)* seat; *(MIL)* post; **a** ~ *(in ordine)* in place, tidy; *(fig)* settled; *(: persona)* reliable; **al** ~ **di** in

place of; **sul** ~ on the spot; **mettere a** ~ to tidy (up), put in order; *(faccende)* straighten out; ~ **di blocco** roadblock; ~ **di polizia** police station

pos'tribolo *sm* brothel

'postumo, a *ag* posthumous; *(tardivo)* belated; ~**i** *smpl (conseguenze)* after-effects, consequences

po'tabile *ag* drinkable; **acqua** ~ drinking water

po'tare *vt* to prune

po'tassio *sm* potassium

po'tente *ag (nazione)* strong, powerful; *(veleno, farmaco)* potent, strong; **po'tenza** *sf (forza)* strength

potenzi'ale [poten'tsjale] *ag, sm* potential

PAROLA CHIAVE

po'tere *sm* power; **al** ~ *(partito etc)* in power; ~ **d'acquisto** purchasing power ♦ *vb aus* **1** *(essere in grado di)* can, be able to; **non ha potuto ripararlo** he couldn't *o* he wasn't able to repair it; **non è potuto venire** he couldn't *o* he wasn't able to come; **spiacente di non poter aiutare** sorry not to be able to help

2 *(avere il permesso)* can, may, be allowed to; ~ **posso entrare?** can *o* may I come in?; **si può sapere dove sei stato?** where on earth have you been?

3 *(eventualità)* may, might, could; **potrebbe essere vero** it might *o* could be true; **può aver avuto un incidente** he may *o* might *o* could have had an accident; **può darsi** perhaps; **può darsi** *o* **essere che non venga** he may *o* might not come

4 *(augurio)*: **potessi almeno parlargli!** if only I could speak to him!

5 *(suggerimento)*: **potresti almeno scusarti!** you could at least apologize!

♦ *vt* can, be able to; **può molto per noi** he can do a lot for us; **non ne posso più** *(per stanchezza)* I'm exhausted; *(per rabbia)* I can't take any more

---

potestà *sf (potere)* power; *(DIR)* authority

'povero, a *ag* poor; *(disadorno)* plain,

bare ♦ *sm/f* poor man/woman; **i ~i** the poor; **~ di** lacking in, having little; **povertà** *sf* poverty

'pozza ['pottsa] *sf* pool

poz'zanghera [pot'tsangera] *sf* puddle

'pozzo ['pottso] *sm* well; (*cava: di carbone*) pit; (*di miniera*) shaft; **~ petrolifero** oil well

pran'zare [pran'dzare] *vi* to dine, have dinner; to lunch, have lunch

'pranzo ['prandzo] *sm* dinner; (*a mezzogiorno*) lunch

'prassi *sf* usual procedure

'pratica, che *sf* practice; (*esperienza*) experience; (*conoscenza*) knowledge, familiarity; (*tirocinio*) training, practice; (*AMM: affare*) matter, case; (: *incartamento*) file, dossier; **in ~** (*praticamente*) in practice; **mettere in ~** to put into practice

prati'cabile *ag* (*progetto*) practicable, feasible; (*luogo*) passable, practicable

prati'cante *sm/f* apprentice, trainee; (*REL*) (regular) churchgoer

prati'care *vt* to practise; (*SPORT: tennis etc*) to play; (: *nuoto, scherma etc*) to go in for; (*eseguire: apertura, buco*) to make; **~ uno sconto** to give a discount

'pratico, a, ci, che *ag* practical; **~ di** (*esperto*) experienced o skilled in; (*familiare*) familiar with

'prato *sm* meadow; (*di giardino*) lawn

preav'viso *sm* notice; **telefonata con ~** personal o person to person call

pre'cario, a *ag* precarious; (*INS*) temporary

precauzi'one [prekaut'tsjone] *sf* caution, care; (*misura*) precaution

prece'dente [pretʃe'dɛnte] *ag* previous ♦ *sm* precedent; **il discorso/film ~** the previous o preceding speech/film; **senza ~i** unprecedented; **~i penali** criminal record *sg*; **prece'denza** *sf* priority, precedence; (*AUT*) right of way

pre'cedere [pre'tʃedere] *vt* to precede, go (o come) before

pre'cetto [pre'tʃetto] *sm* precept; (*MIL*) call-up notice

precet'tore [pretʃet'tore] *sm* (private)

tutor

precipi'tare [pretʃipi'tare] *vi* (*cadere*) to fall headlong; (*fig: situazione*) to get out of control ♦ *vt* (*gettare dall'alto in basso*) to hurl, fling; (*fig: affrettare*) to rush; **~rsi** *vr* (*gettarsi*) to hurl o fling o.s.; (*affrettarsi*) to rush; **precipitazi'one** *sf* (*METEOR*) precipitation; (*fig*) haste; **precipi'toso, a** *ag* (*caduta, fuga*) headlong; (*fig: avventato*) rash, reckless; (: *affrettato*) hasty, rushed

preci'pizio [pretʃi'pittsjo] *sm* precipice; **a ~** (*fig: correre*) headlong

preci'sare [pretʃi'zare] *vt* to state, specify; (*spiegare*) to explain (in detail)

precisi'one [pretʃi'zjone] *sf* precision; accuracy

pre'ciso, a [pre'tʃizo] *ag* (*esatto*) precise; (*accurato*) accurate, precise; (*deciso: idee*) precise, definite; (*uguale*): **2 vestiti ~i** 2 dresses exactly the same; **sono le 9 ~e** it's exactly 9 o'clock

pre'cludere *vt* to block, obstruct; **pre'cluso, a** *pp di* **precludere**

pre'coce [pre'kɔtʃe] *ag* early; (*bambino*) precocious; (*vecchiaia*) premature

precon'cetto [prekon'tʃetto] *sm* preconceived idea, prejudice

precur'sore *sm* forerunner, precursor

'preda *sf* (*bottino*) booty; (*animale, fig*) prey; **essere ~ di** to fall prey to; **essere in ~ a** to be prey to; **preda'tore** *sm* predator

predeces'sore, a [predetʃes'sore] *sm/f* predecessor

predesti'nare *vt* to predestine

pre'detto, a *pp di* **predire**

'predica, che *sf* sermon; (*fig*) lecture, talking-to

predi'care *vt, vi* to preach

predi'cato *sm* (*LING*) predicate

predi'letto, a *pp di* **prediligere** ♦ *ag*, *sm/f* favourite

predilezi'one [predilet'tsjone] *sf* fondness, partiality; **avere una ~ per qc/qn** to be partial to sth/fond of sb

predi'ligere [predi'lidʒere] *vt* to prefer, have a preference for

pre'dire *vt* to foretell, predict

predis'porre *vt* to get ready, prepare; ~ **qn a qc** to predispose sb to sth; **predis'posto, a** *pp di* **predisporre**

predizi'one [predit'tsjone] *sf* prediction

predomi'nare *vi* to predominate; **predo'minio** *sm* predominance; supremacy

prefabbri'cato, a *ag* (*EDIL*) prefabricated

prefazi'one [prefat'tsjone] *sf* preface, foreword

prefe'renza [prefe'rɛntsa] *sf* preference; **preferenzi'ale** *ag* preferential; **corsia ~** bus and taxi lane

prefe'rire *vt* to prefer, like better; ~ **il caffè al tè** to prefer coffee to tea, like coffee better than tea

pre'fetto *sm* prefect; **prefet'tura** *sf* prefecture

pre'figgersi [pre'fiddʒersi] *vr*: ~**rsi uno scopo** to set o.s. a goal

pre'fisso, a *pp di* **prefiggere** ♦ *sm* (*LING*) prefix; (*TEL*) dialling (*BRIT*) o dial (*US*) code

pre'gare *vi* to pray ♦ *vt* (*REL*) to pray to; (*implorare*) to beg; (*chiedere*): ~ **qn di fare** to ask sb to do; **farsi ~** to need coaxing o persuading

pre'gevole [pre'dʒevole] *ag* valuable

preghi'era [pre'gjɛra] *sf* (*REL*) prayer; (*domanda*) request

pregi'ato, a [pre'dʒato] *ag* (*di valore*) valuable; **vino ~** vintage wine

'pregio ['prɛdʒo] *sm* (*stima*) esteem, regard; (*qualità*) (good) quality, merit; (*valore*) value, worth

pregiudi'care [predʒudi'kare] *vt* to prejudice, harm, be detrimental to; **pregiudi'cato, a** *sm/f* (*DIR*) previous offender

pregiu'dizio [predʒu'dittsjo] *sm* (*idea errata*) prejudice; (*danno*) harm *no pl*

'pregno, a ['preɲɲo] *ag* (*gravido*) pregnant; (*saturo*): ~ **di** full of, saturated with

'prego *escl* (*a chi ringrazia*) don't mention it!; (*invitando qn ad accomodarsi*) please sit down!; (*invitando qn ad andare prima*) after you!

pregus'tare *vt* to look forward to

preis'torico, a, ci, che *ag* prehistoric

pre'lato *sm* prelate

prele'vare *vt* (*denaro*) to withdraw; (*campione*) to take; (*sog: polizia*) to take, capture

preli'evo *sm* (*MED*): **fare un ~ (di)** to take a sample (of)

prelimi'nare *ag* preliminary; ~**i** *smpl* preliminary talks; preliminaries

pre'ludio *sm* prelude

pré-ma'man [prema'mã] *sm inv* maternity dress

prema'turo, a *ag* premature

premeditazi'one [premeditat'tsjone] *sf* (*DIR*) premeditation; **con ~** *ag* premeditated ♦ *av* with intent

'premere *vt* to press ♦ *vi*: ~ **su** to press down on; (*fig*) to put pressure on; ~ **a** (*fig: importare*) to matter to

pre'messa *sf* introductory statement, introduction

pre'messo, a *pp di* **premettere**

pre'mettere *vt* to put before; (*dire prima*) to start by saying, state first

premi'are *vt* to give a prize to; (*fig: merito, onestà*) to reward

'premio *sm* prize; (*ricompensa*) reward; (*COMM*) premium; (*AMM: indennità*) bonus

premu'nirsi *vr*: ~ **di** to provide o.s. with; ~ **contro** to protect o.s. from, guard o.s. against

pre'mura *sf* (*fretta*) haste, hurry; (*riguardo*) attention, care; **premu'roso, a** *ag* thoughtful, considerate

prena'tale *ag* antenatal

'prendere *vt* to take; (*andare a prendere*) to get, fetch; (*ottenere*) to get; (*guadagnare*) to get, earn; (*catturare: ladro, pesce*) to catch; (*collaboratore, dipendente*) to take on; (*passeggero*) to pick up; (*chiedere: somma, prezzo*) to charge, ask; (*trattare: persona*) to handle ♦ *vi* (*colla, cemento*) to set; (*pianta*) to take; (*fuoco: nel camino*) to catch; (*voltare*): ~ **a destra** to turn (to the) right; ~**rsi** *vr* (*azzuffarsi*): ~**rsi a pugni** to come to blows; **prendi qualcosa?** (*da bere, da mangiare*) would you like something to eat (*o* drink)?; **prendo un caffè** I'll have a coffee; ~ **a fare qc** to start doing sth; ~

qn/qc per (*scambiare*) to take sb/sth for; ~ **fuoco** to catch fire; ~ **parte a** to take part in; ~**rsi cura di qn/qc** to look after sb/sth; **prendersela** (*adirarsi*) to get annoyed; (*preoccuparsi*) to get upset, worry

prendi'sole *sm inv* sundress

preno'tare *vt* to book, reserve; **prenotazi'one** *sf* booking, reservation

preoccu'pare *vt* to worry; to preoccupy; ~**rsi** *vr*: ~**rsi di qn/qc** to worry about sb/sth; ~**rsi per qn** to be anxious for sb; **preoccupazi'one** *sf* worry, anxiety

prepa'rare *vt* to prepare; (*esame, concorso*) to prepare for; ~**rsi** *vr* (*vestirsi*) to get ready; ~**rsi a qc/a fare** to get ready *o* prepare (o.s.) for sth/to do; ~ **da mangiare** to prepare a meal; **prepara'tivi** *smpl* preparations; **prepa'rato** *sm* (*prodotto*) preparation; **preparazi'one** *sf* preparation

preposizi'one [prepozit'tsjone] *sf* (*LING*) preposition

prepo'tente *ag* (*persona*) domineering, arrogant; (*bisogno, desiderio*) overwhelming, pressing ♦ *sm/f* bully; **prepo'tenza** *sf* arrogance; arrogant behaviour

'presa *sf* taking *no pl*; catching *no pl*; (*di città*) capture; (*indurimento: di cemento*) setting; (*appiglio, SPORT*) hold; (*di acqua, gas*) (supply) point; (*ELETTR*): ~ (**di corrente**) socket; (: *al muro*) point; (*piccola quantità: di sale etc*) pinch; (*CARTE*) trick; **far** ~ (*colla*) to set; **far** ~ **sul pubblico** to catch the public's imagination; ~ **d'aria** air inlet; **essere alle** ~**e con qc** (*fig*) to be struggling with sth

pre'sagio [pre'zadʒo] *sm* omen

presa'gire [preza'dʒire] *vt* to foresee

'presbite *ag* long-sighted

presbi'terio *sm* presbytery

pre'scindere [preʃ'ʃindere] *vi*: ~ **da** to leave out of consideration; **a** ~ **da** apart from

pres'critto, a *pp di* **prescrivere**

pres'crivere *vt* to prescribe; **prescrizi'one** *sf* (*MED, DIR*) prescription;

(*norma*) rule, regulation

presen'tare *vt* to present; (*far conoscere*): ~ **qn (a)** to introduce sb (to); (*AMM: inoltrare*) to submit; ~**rsi** *vr* (*recarsi, farsi vedere*) to present o.s., appear; (*farsi conoscere*) to introduce o.s.; (*occasione*) to arise; ~**rsi come candidato** (*POL*) to stand as a candidate; ~**rsi bene/male** to have a good/poor appearance; **presentazi'one** *sf* presentation; introduction

pre'sente *ag* present; (*questo*) this ♦ *sm* present; **i** ~**i** those present; **aver** ~ **qc/qn** to remember sth/sb

presenti'mento *sm* premonition

pre'senza [pre'zɛntsa] *sf* presence; (*aspetto esteriore*) appearance; ~ **di spirito** presence of mind

pre'sepe *sm* = **presepio**

pre'sepio *sm* crib

preser'vare *vt* to protect; to save; **preserva'tivo** *sm* sheath, condom

'preside *sm/f* (*INS*) head (teacher) (*BRIT*), principal (*US*); (*di facoltà universitaria*) dean

presi'dente *sm* (*POL*) president; (*di assemblea, COMM*) chairman; ~ **del consiglio** prime minister; **presiden'tessa** *sf* president; president's wife; chairwoman; **presi'denza** *sf* presidency; office of president; chairmanship

presidi'are *vt* to garrison; **pre'sidio** *sm* garrison

presi'edere *vt* to preside over ♦ *vi*: ~ **a** to direct, be in charge of

'preso, a *pp di* **prendere**

'pressa *sf* (*TECN*) press

pressap'poco *av* about, roughly

pres'sare *vt* to press

pressi'one *sf* pressure; **far** ~ **su qn** to put pressure on sb; ~ **sanguigna** blood pressure

'presso *av* (*vicino*) nearby, close at hand ♦ *prep* (*vicino a*) near; (*accanto a*) beside, next to; (*in casa di*): ~ **qn** at sb's home; (*nelle lettere*) care of, c/o; (*alle dipendenze di*): **lavora** ~ **di noi** he works for *o* with us ♦ *smpl*: **nei** ~**i di** near, in the vicinity of

pressuriz'zare [pressurid'dzare] *vt* to

pressurize

presta'nome *(peg) sm/f inv* figurehead

pres'tante *ag* good-looking

pres'tare *vt*: ~ (qc a qn) to lend (sb sth *o* sth to sb); **~rsi** *vr (offrirsi)*: **~rsi a fare** to offer to do; *(essere adatto)*: **~rsi a** to lend itself to, be suitable for; ~ **aiuto** to lend a hand; ~ **attenzione** to pay attention; ~ **fede a qc/qn** to give credence to sth/sb; ~ **orecchio** to listen; **prestazi'one** *sf* (TECN, SPORT) performance; **prestazioni** *sfpl (di persona: servizi)* services

prestigia'tore, 'trice [prestidʒa'tore] *sm/f* conjurer

pres'tigio [pres'tidʒo] *sm (potere)* prestige; *(illusione)*: **gioco di** ~ conjuring trick

'prestito *sm* lending *no pl*; loan; **dar in** ~ to lend; **prendere in** ~ to borrow

'presto *av (tra poco)* soon; *(in fretta)* quickly; *(di buon'ora)* early; **a** ~ see you soon; **fare** ~ **a fare qc** to hurry up and do sth; *(non costare fatica)* to have no trouble doing sth; **si fa** ~ **a criticare** it's easy to criticize

pre'sumere *vt* to presume, assume; **pre'sunto, a** *pp di* **presumere**

presuntu'oso, a *ag* presumptuous

presunzi'one [prezun'tsjone] *sf* presumption

presup'porre *vt* to suppose; to presuppose

'prete *sm* priest

preten'dente *sm/f* pretender ♦ *sm (corteggiatore)* suitor

pre'tendere *vt (esigere)* to demand, require; *(sostenere)*: ~ **che** to claim that; **pretende di aver sempre ragione** he thinks he's always right

pretenzi'oso, a [preten'tsjoso] *ag* pretentious

pre'tesa *sf (esigenza)* claim, demand; *(presunzione, sfarzo)* pretentiousness; **senza ~e** unpretentious; *vedi anche* **preteso**

pre'teso, a *pp di* **pretendere**

pre'testo *sm* pretext, excuse

pre'tore *sm* magistrate

pre'tura *sf* magistracy; *(sede)* magistrate's

court

preva'lente *ag* prevailing; **preva'lenza** *sf* predominance

preva'lere *vi* to prevail; **pre'valso, a** *pp di* **prevalere**

preve'dere *vt (indovinare)* to foresee; *(presagire)* to foretell; *(considerare)* to make provision for

preve'nire *vt (anticipare)* to forestall; to anticipate; *(evitare)* to avoid, prevent; *(avvertire)*: ~ **qn (di)** to warn sb (of); to inform sb (of)

preven'tivo, a *ag* preventive ♦ *sm* (COMM) estimate

prevenzi'one [preven'tsjone] *sf* prevention; *(preconcetto)* prejudice

previ'dente *ag* showing foresight; prudent; **previ'denza** *sf* foresight; **istituto di previdenza** provident institution; **previdenza sociale** social security (BRIT), welfare (US)

previsi'one *sf* forecast, prediction; **~i meteorologiche** *o* **del tempo** weather forecast *sg*

pre'visto, a *pp di* **prevedere** ♦ *sm*: **più/ meno del** ~ more/less than expected

prezi'oso, a [pret'tsjoso] *ag* precious; invaluable ♦ *sm* jewel; valuable

prez'zemolo [pret'tsemolo] *sm* parsley

'prezzo ['prettso] *sm* price; ~ **d'acquisto/di vendita** buying/selling price

prigi'one [pri'dʒone] *sf* prison; **prigio'nia** *sf* imprisonment; **prigioni'ero, a** *ag* captive ♦ *sm/f* prisoner

'prima *sf* (TEATRO) first night; *(CINEMA)* première; *(AUT)* first gear; *vedi anche* **primo** ♦ *av* before; *(in anticipo)* in advance, beforehand; *(per l'addietro)* at one time, formerly; *(più presto)* sooner, earlier; *(in primo luogo)* first ♦ *cong*: ~ **di fare/che parta** before doing/he leaves; ~ **di** before; ~ **o poi** sooner or later

pri'mario, a *ag* primary; *(principale)* chief, leading, primary ♦ *sm* (MED) chief physician

pri'mato *sm* supremacy; *(SPORT)* record

prima'vera *sf* spring; **primave'rile** *ag*

spring *cpd*

primeggi'are [primed'dʒare] *vi* to excel, be one of the best

primi'tivo, a *ag* primitive; original

pri'mizie [pri'mittsje] *sfpl* early produce *sg*

'primo, a *ag* first; *(fig)* initial; basic; prime ♦ *sm/f* first (one) ♦ *sm (CUC)* first course; *(in date)*: **il ~ luglio** the first of July; **le ~e ore del mattino** the early hours of the morning; **ai ~i di maggio** at the beginning of May; **viaggiare in ~a** to travel first-class; **in ~ luogo** first of all, in the first place; **di prim'ordine** *o* **~a qualità** first-class, first-rate; **in un ~ tempo** at first; **~a donna** leading lady; *(di opera lirica)* prima donna

primo'genito, a [primo'dʒɛnito] *ag*, *sm/f* firstborn

primordi'ale *ag* primordial

'primula *sf* primrose

princi'pale [printʃi'pale] *ag* main, principal ♦ *sm* manager, boss

princi'pato [printʃi'pato] *sm* principality

'principe ['printʃipe] *sm* prince; **~ ereditario** crown prince; **princi'pessa** *sf* princess

principi'ante [printʃi'pjante] *sm/f* beginner

prin'cipio [prin'tʃipjo] *sm (inizio)* beginning, start; *(origine)* origin, cause; *(concetto, norma)* principle; **al** *o* **in ~** at first; **per ~** on principle

pri'ore *sm (REL)* prior

priorità *sf* priority

'prisma, i *sm* prism

pri'vare *vt*: **~ qn di** to deprive sb of; **~rsi di** to go *o* do without

pri'vato, a *ag* private ♦ *sm/f* private citizen; **in ~** in private

privazi'one [privat'tsjone] *sf* privation, hardship

privilegi'are [privile'dʒare] *vt* to grant a privilege to

privi'legio [privi'lɛdʒo] *sm* privilege

'privo, a *ag*: **~ di** without, lacking

pro *prep* for, on behalf of ♦ *sm inv (utilità)* advantage, benefit; **a che ~?** what's the use?; **il ~ e il contro** the pros and cons

pro'babile *ag* probable, likely; **probabilità** *sf inv* probability

pro'blema, i *sm* problem

pro'boscide [pro'bɔʃʃide] *sf (di elefante)* trunk

procacci'are [prokat'tʃare] *vt* to get, obtain

pro'cedere [pro'tʃedere] *vi* to proceed; *(comportarsi)* to behave; *(iniziare)*: **~ a** to start; **~ contro** *(DIR)* to start legal proceedings against; **procedi'mento** *sm (modo di condurre)* procedure; *(di avvenimenti)* course; *(TECN)* process; **procedimento penale** *(DIR)* criminal proceedings; **proce'dura** *sf (DIR)* procedure

proces'sare [protʃes'sare] *vt (DIR)* to try

processi'one [protʃes'sjone] *sf* procession

pro'cesso [pro'tʃɛsso] *sm (DIR)* trial; **proceedings** *pl*; *(metodo)* process

pro'cinto [pro'tʃinto] *sm*: **in ~ di fare** about to do, on the point of doing

pro'clama, i *sm* proclamation

procla'mare *vt* to proclaim

procre'are *vt* to procreate

pro'cura *sf (DIR)* proxy; power of attorney; *(ufficio)* attorney's office

procu'rare *vt*: **~ qc a qn** *(fornire)* to get *o* obtain sth for sb; *(causare: noie etc)* to bring *o* give sb sth

procura'tore, 'trice *sm/f (DIR)* ≈ solicitor; *(: chi ha la procura)* attorney; proxy; **~ generale** *(in corte d'appello)* public prosecutor; *(in corte di cassazione)* Attorney General; **~ della Repubblica** *(in corte d'assise, tribunale)* public prosecutor

prodi'gare *vt* to be lavish with; **~rsi per qn** to do all one can for sb

pro'digio [pro'didʒo] *sm* marvel, wonder; *(persona)* prodigy; **prodigi'oso, a** *ag* prodigious; phenomenal

'prodigo, a, ghi, ghe *ag* lavish, extravagant

pro'dotto, a *pp di* **produrre** ♦ *sm* product; **~i agricoli** farm produce *sg*

pro'durre *vt* to produce; **produttività** *sf* productivity; **produt'tivo, a** *ag*

productive; **produt'tore, 'trice** *sm/f*
producer; **produzi'one** *sf* production;
(*rendimento*) output
pro'emio *sm* introduction, preface
Prof. *abbr* (= *professore*) Prof
profa'nare *vt* to desecrate
pro'fano, a *ag* (*mondano*) secular;
profane; (*sacrilego*) profane
profe'rire *vt* to utter
profes'sare *vt* to profess; (*medicina etc*)
to practise
professio'nale *ag* professional
professi'one *sf* profession;
professio'nista, i, e *sm/f* professional
profes'sore, 'essa *sm/f* (*INS*) teacher;
(*: di università*) lecturer; (*: titolare di
cattedra*) professor
pro'feta, i *sm* prophet; **profe'zia** *sf*
prophecy
pro'ficuo, a *ag* useful, profitable
profi'larsi *vr* to stand out, be silhouetted;
to loom up
profi'lattico *sm* condom
pro'filo *sm* profile; (*breve descrizione*)
sketch, outline; **di** ~ in profile
profit'tare *vi*: ~ **di** (*trarre profitto*) to
profit by; (*approfittare*) to take advantage
of
pro'fitto *sm* advantage, profit, benefit;
(*fig: progresso*) progress; (*COMM*) profit
profondità *sf inv* depth
pro'fondo, a *ag* deep; (*rancore,
meditazione*) profound ♦ *sm* depth(s *pl*),
bottom; ~ **8 metri** 8 metres deep
'profugo, a, ghi, ghe *sm/f* refugee
profu'mare *vt* to perfume ♦ *vi* to be
fragrant; ~**rsi** *vr* to put on perfume *o*
scent
profume'ria *sf* perfumery; (*negozio*)
perfume shop
pro'fumo *sm* (*prodotto*) perfume, scent;
(*fragranza*) scent, fragrance
profusi'one *sf* profusion; **a** ~ in plenty
proget'tare [prodʒet'tare] *vt* to plan;
(*TECN: edificio*) to plan, design; **pro'getto**
sm plan; (*idea*) plan, project; **progetto di
legge** bill
pro'gramma, i *sm* programme; (*TV,
RADIO*) programmes *pl*; (*INS*) syllabus,

curriculum; (*INFORM*) program;
program'mare *vt* (*TV, RADIO*) to put on;
(*INFORM*) to program; (*ECON*) to plan;
programma'tore, 'trice *sm/f* (*INFORM*)
computer programmer
progre'dire *vi* to progress, make
progress
progres'sivo, a *ag* progressive
pro'gresso *sm* progress *no pl*; **fare ~i** to
make progress
proi'bire *vt* to forbid, prohibit;
proibi'tivo, a *ag* prohibitive;
proibizi'one *sf* prohibition
proiet'tare *vt* (*gen, GEOM, CINEMA*) to
project; (*: presentare*) to show, screen;
(*luce, ombra*) to throw, cast, project;
proi'ettile *sm* projectile, bullet (*o* shell
etc); **proiet'tore** *sm* (*CINEMA*) projector;
(*AUT*) headlamp; (*MIL*) searchlight;
proiezi'one *sf* (*CINEMA*) projection;
showing
'prole *sf* children *pl*, offspring
prole'tario, a *ag, sm* proletarian
prolife'rare *vi* (*fig*) to proliferate
pro'lisso, a *ag* verbose
'prologo, ghi *sm* prologue
pro'lunga, ghe *sf* (*di cavo elettrico etc*)
extension
prolun'gare *vt* (*discorso, attesa*) to
prolong; (*linea, termine*) to extend
prome'moria *sm inv* memorandum
pro'messa *sf* promise
pro'messo, a *pp di* **promettere**
pro'mettere *vt* to promise ♦ *vi* to be *o*
look promising; ~ **a qn di fare** to
promise sb that one will do
promi'nente *ag* prominent
promiscuità *sf* promiscuousness
promon'torio *sm* promontory, headland
pro'mosso, a *pp di* **promuovere**
promo'tore, trice *sm/f* promoter,
organizer
promozi'one [promot'tsjone] *sf*
promotion
promul'gare *vt* to promulgate
promu'overe *vt* to promote
proni'pote *sm/f* (*di nonni*) great-
grandchild, great-grandson/grand-
daughter; (*di zii*) great-nephew/niece; ~**i**

smpl *(discendenti)* descendants

pro'nome *sm (LING)* pronoun

pro'nostico, ci *sm* forecast, prediction

pron'tezza [pron'tettsa] *sf* readiness; quickness, promptness

'pronto, a *ag* ready; *(rapido)* fast, quick, prompt; ~! *(TEL)* hello!; ~ **all'ira** quick-tempered; ~ **soccorso** first aid

prontu'ario *sm* manual, handbook

pro'nuncia [pro'nuntʃa] *sf* pronunciation

pronunci'are [pronun'tʃare] *vt (parola, sentenza)* to pronounce; *(dire)* to utter; *(discorso)* to deliver; ~**rsi** *vr* to declare one's opinion; **pronunci'ato, a** *ag (spiccato)* pronounced, marked; *(sporgente)* prominent

pro'nunzia *etc* [pro'nuntsja] = **pronuncia** *etc*

propa'ganda *sf* propaganda

propa'gare *vt (notizia, malattia)* to spread; *(REL, BIOL)* to propagate; ~**rsi** *vr* to spread; *(BIOL)* to propagate; *(FISICA)* to be propagated

pro'pendere *vi:* ~ **per** to favour, lean towards; **propensi'one** *sf* inclination, propensity; **pro'penso, a** *pp di* **propendere**

propi'nare *vt* to administer

pro'pizio, a [pro'pittsjo] *ag* favourable

pro'porre *vt (suggerire):* ~ **qc (a qn)** to suggest sth (to sb); *(candidato)* to put forward; *(legge, brindisi)* to propose; ~ **di fare** to suggest o propose doing; **proporsi di fare** to propose o intend to do; **proporsi una meta** to set o.s. a goal

proporzio'nale [proportsjo'nale] *ag* proportional

proporzio'nare [proportsjo'nare] *vt:* ~ **qc a** to proportion o adjust sth to

proporzi'one [propor'tsjone] *sf* proportion; **in** ~ **a** in proportion to

pro'posito *sm (intenzione)* intention, aim; *(argomento)* subject, matter; **a** ~ **di** regarding, with regard to; **di** ~ *(apposta)* deliberately, on purpose; **a** ~ by the way; **capitare a** ~ *(cosa, persona)* to turn up at the right time

proposizi'one [propozit'tsjone] *sf (LING)* clause; *(: periodo)* sentence

pro'posta *sf* proposal; *(suggerimento)* suggestion; ~ **di legge** bill

pro'posto, a *pp di* **proporre**

proprietà *sf inv (ciò che si possiede)* property *gen no pl*, estate; *(caratteristica)* property; *(correttezza)* correctness; **proprie'tario, a** *sm/f* owner; *(di albergo etc)* proprietor, owner; *(per l'inquilino)* landlord/lady

'proprio, a *ag (possessivo)* own; *(: impersonale)* one's; *(esatto)* exact, correct, proper; *(senso, significato)* literal; *(LING: nome)* proper; *(particolare):* ~ **di** characteristic of, peculiar to ♦ *av (precisamente)* just, exactly; *(davvero)* really; *(affatto):* **non ...** ~ not ... at all; **l'ha visto con i (suoi)** ~**i occhi** he saw it with his own eyes

'prora *sf (NAUT)* bow(s *pl*), prow

proroga, ghe *sf* extension; postponement; **proro'gare** *vt* to extend; *(differire)* to postpone, defer

pro'rompere *vi* to burst out; **pro'rotto, a** *pp di* **prorompere**

'prosa *sf* prose; **pro'saico, a, ci, che** *ag (fig)* prosaic, mundane

pro'sciogliere [proʃ'ʃɔλλere] *vt* to release; *(DIR)* to acquit; **prosci'olto, a** *pp di* **prosciogliere**

prosciu'gare [proʃʃu'gare] *vt (terreni)* to drain, reclaim; ~**rsi** *vr* to dry up

prosci'utto [proʃ'ʃutto] *sm* ham; ~ **cotto/crudo** cooked/cured ham

prosegui'mento *sm* continuation; **buon** ~! all the best!; *(a chi viaggia)* enjoy the rest of your journey!

prosegu'ire *vt* to carry on with, continue ♦ *vi* to carry on, go on

prospe'rare *vi* to thrive; **prosperità** *sf* prosperity; **'prospero, a** *ag (fiorente)* flourishing, thriving, prosperous; **prospe'roso, a** *ag (robusto)* hale and hearty; *(: ragazza)* buxom

prospet'tare *vt (esporre)* to point out, show; ~**rsi** *vr* to look, appear

prospet'tiva *sf (ARTE)* perspective; *(veduta)* view; *(fig: previsione, possibilità)* prospect

pros'petto *sm (DISEGNO)* elevation;

(*veduta*) view, prospect; (*facciata*) façade, front; (*tabella*) table; (*sommario*) summary

prospici'ente [prospi't∫ɛnte] *ag*: ~ **qc** facing *o* overlooking sth

prossimità *sf* nearness, proximity; **in ~ di** near (to), close to

'**prossimo, a** (*vicino*): ~ **a** near (to), close to; (*che viene subito dopo*) next; (*parente*) close ♦ *sm* neighbour, fellow man

prosti'tuta *sf* prostitute; **prostituzi'one** *sf* prostitution

pros'trare *vt* (*fig*) to exhaust, wear out; ~**rsi** *vr* (*fig*) to humble o.s

protago'nista, i, e *sm/f* protagonist

pro'teggere [pro'tɛddʒere] *vt* to protect

prote'ina *sf* protein

pro'tendere *vt* to stretch out; **pro'teso, a** *pp di* **protendere**

pro'testa *sf* protest

protes'tante *ag, sm/f* Protestant

protes'tare *vt, vi* to protest; ~**rsi** *vr*: ~**rsi innocente** *etc* to protest one's innocence *o* that one is innocent *etc*

protet'tivo, a *ag* protective

pro'tetto, a *pp di* **proteggere**

protet'tore, 'trice *sm/f* protector; (*sostenitore*) patron

protezi'one [protet'tsjone] *sf* protection; (*patrocinio*) patronage

protocol'lare *vt* to register ♦ *ag* formal; of protocol

proto'collo *sm* protocol; (*registro*) register of documents

pro'totipo *sm* prototype

pro'trarre *vt* (*prolungare*) to prolong; **pro'tratto, a** *pp di* **protrarre**

protube'ranza [protube'rantsa] *sf* protuberance, bulge

'**prova** *sf* (*esperimento, cimento*) test, trial; (*tentativo*) attempt, try; (*MAT, testimonianza, documento etc*) proof; (*DIR*) evidence *no pl*, proof; (*INS*) exam, test; (*TEATRO*) rehearsal; (*di abito*) fitting; **a ~ di** (*in testimonianza di*) as proof of; **a ~ di fuoco** fireproof; **fino a ~ contraria** until it is proved otherwise; **mettere alla ~** to put to the test; **giro di ~** test *o* trial run;

~ **generale** (*TEATRO*) dress rehearsal

pro'vare *vt* (*sperimentare*) to test; (*tentare*) to try, attempt; (*assaggiare*) to try, taste; (*sperimentare in sé*) to experience; (*sentire*) to feel; (*cimentare*) to put to the test; (*dimostrare*) to prove; (*abito*) to try on; ~ **a fare** to try *o* attempt to do

proveni'enza [prove'njɛntsa] *sf* origin, source

prove'nire *vi*: ~ **da** to come from

pro'venti *smpl* revenue *sg*

prove'nuto, a *pp di* **provenire**

pro'verbio *sm* proverb

pro'vetta *sf* test tube; **bambino in ~** test-tube baby

pro'vetto, a *ag* skilled, experienced

pro'vincia, ce *o* **cie** [pro'vint∫a] *sf* province; **provinci'ale** *ag* provincial; (**strada**) **provinciale** main road (*BRIT*), highway (*US*)

pro'vino *sm* (*CINEMA*) screen test; (*campione*) specimen

provo'cante *ag* (*attraente*) provocative

provo'care *vt* (*causare*) to cause, bring about; (*eccitare: riso, pietà*) to arouse; (*irritare, sfidare*) to provoke; **provoca'torio, a** *ag* provocative; **provocazi'one** *sf* provocation

provve'dere *vi* (*disporre*): ~ (**a**) to provide (for); (*prendere un provvedimento*) to take steps, act ♦ *vt*: ~ **qc a qn** to supply sth to sb; ~**rsi** *vr*: ~**rsi di** to provide o.s. with; **provvedi'mento** *sm* measure; (*di previdenza*) precaution

provvi'denza [provvi'dɛntsa] *sf*: **la ~** providence; **provvidenzi'ale** *ag* providential

provvigi'one [provvi'dʒone] *sf* (*COMM*) commission

provvi'sorio, a *ag* temporary

prov'vista *sf* provision, supply

'**prua** *sf* (*NAUT*) = **prora**

pru'dente *ag* cautious, prudent; (*assennato*) sensible, wise; **pru'denza** *sf* prudence, caution; wisdom

'**prudere** *vi* to itch, be itchy

'**prugna** ['pruɲɲa] *sf* plum; ~ **secca** prune

prurigi'noso, a [pruridʒi'noso] *ag* itchy
pru'rito *sm* itchiness *no pl*; itch
P.S. *abbr* (= *postscriptum*) P.S.; (*POLIZIA*) = **Pubblica Sicurezza**
pseu'donimo *sm* pseudonym
PSI *sigla m* = **Partito Socialista Italiano**
psicana'lista, i, e *sm/f* psychoanalyst
'**psiche** ['psike] *sf* (*PSIC*) psyche
psichi'atra, i, e [psi'kjatra] *sm/f* psychiatrist; **psichi'atrico, a, ci, che** *ag* psychiatric
'**psichico, a, ci, che** ['psikiko] *ag* psychological
psicolo'gia [psikolo'dʒia] *sf* psychology; **psico'logico, a, ci, che** *ag* psychological; **psi'cologo, a, gi, ghe** *sm/f* psychologist
psico'patico, a, ci, che *ag* psychopathic ♦ *sm/f* psychopath
P.T. *abbr* = **Posta e Telegrafi**
pubbli'care *vt* to publish
pubblicazi'one [pubblikat'tsjone] *sf* publication; **~i (matrimoniali)** *sfpl* (marriage) banns
pubbli'cista, i, e [pubbli'tʃista] *sm/f* (*STAMPA*) occasional contributor
pubblicità [pubblitʃi'ta] *sf* (*diffusione*) publicity; (*attività*) advertising; (*annunci nei giornali*) advertisements *pl*; **pubblici'tario, a** *ag* advertising *cpd*; (*trovata, film*) publicity *cpd*
'**pubblico, a, ci, che** *ag* public; (*statale*: *scuola etc*) state *cpd* ♦ *sm* public; (*spettatori*) audience; **in ~** in public; **~ funzionario** civil servant; **P~ Ministero** Public Prosecutor's Office; **la P~a Sicurezza** the police
'**pube** *sm* (*ANAT*) pubis
pubertà *sf* puberty
'**pudico, a, ci, che** *ag* modest
pu'dore *sm* modesty
puericul'tura *sf* paediatric nursing; infant care
pue'rile *ag* childish
pugi'lato [pudʒi'lato] *sm* boxing
'**pugile** ['pudʒile] *sm* boxer
pugna'lare [puɲɲa'lare] *vt* to stab
pu'gnale [puɲ'ɲale] *sm* dagger
'**pugno** ['puɲɲo] *sm* fist; (*colpo*) punch;

(*quantità*) fistful
'**pulce** ['pultʃe] *sf* flea
pul'cino [pul'tʃino] *sm* chick
pu'ledro, a *sm/f* colt/filly
pu'leggia, ge [pu'leddʒa] *sf* pulley
pu'lire *vt* to clean; (*lucidare*) to polish; **pu'lita** *sf* quick clean; **pu'lito, a** *ag* (*anche fig*) clean; (*ordinato*) neat, tidy; **puli'tura** *sf* cleaning; **pulitura a secco** dry cleaning; **pu'lizia** *sf* cleaning; cleanness; **fare le pulizie** to do the cleaning, do the housework
'**pullman** *sm inv* coach
pul'lover *sm inv* pullover, jumper
pullu'lare *vi* to swarm, teem
pul'mino *sm* minibus
'**pulpito** *sm* pulpit
pul'sante *sm* (push-)button
pul'sare *vi* to pulsate, beat; **pulsazi'one** *sf* beat
pul'viscolo *sm* fine dust
'**puma** *sm inv* puma
pun'gente [pun'dʒente] *ag* prickly; stinging; (*anche fig*) biting
'**pungere** ['pundʒere] *vt* to prick; (*sog*: *insetto, ortica*) to sting; (: *freddo*) to bite
pungigli'one [pundʒiʎ'ʎone] *sm* sting
pu'nire *vt* to punish; **punizi'one** *sf* punishment; (*SPORT*) penalty
'**punta** *sf* point; (*parte terminale*) tip, end; (*di monte*) peak; (*di costa*) promontory; (*minima parte*) touch, trace; **in ~ di piedi** on tip-toe; **ore di ~** peak hours; **uomo di ~ front-rank** *o* leading man
pun'tare *vt* (*piedi a terra, gomiti sul tavolo*) to plant; (*dirigere*: *pistola*) to point; (*scommettere*) to bet ♦ *vi* (*mirare*): **~ a** to aim at; (*avviarsi*): **~ su** to head *o* make for; (*fig*: *contare*): **~ su** to count *o* rely on
pun'tata *sf* (*gita*) short trip; (*scommessa*) bet; (*parte di opera*) instalment; **romanzo a ~e** serial
punteggia'tura [puntedʒa'tura] *sf* (*LING*) punctuation
pun'teggio [pun'teddʒo] *sm* score
puntel'lare *vt* to support
pun'tello *sm* prop, support
puntigli'oso, a [puntiʎ'ʎoso] *ag*

punctilious

pun'tina *sf*: ~ **da disegno** drawing pin

pun'tino *sm* dot; **fare qc a** ~ to do sth properly

'punto, a *pp di* **pungere** ♦ *sm* (*segno, macchiolina*) dot; (*LING*) full stop; (*MAT, momento, di punteggio, fig: argomento*) point; (*posto*) spot; (*a scuola*) mark; (*nel cucire, nella maglia, MED*) stitch ♦ *av*: **non ... ~** not at all; **due ~i** *sm* (*LING*) colon; **sul ~ di fare** (just) about to do; **fare il ~** (*NAUT*) to take a bearing; (*fig*) **fare il ~ della situazione** to take stock of the situation; to sum up the situation; **alle 6 in ~** at 6 o'clock sharp o on the dot; **essere a buon ~** to have reached a satisfactory stage; **mettere a ~** to adjust; (*motore*) to tune; (*cannocchiale*) to focus; (*fig*) to settle; **di ~ in bianco** point-blank; **~ cardinale** point of the compass, cardinal point; **~ debole** weak point; **~ esclamativo/interrogativo** exclamation/question mark; **~ di riferimento** landmark; (*fig*) point of reference; **~ di vendita** retail outlet; **~ e virgola** semicolon; **~ di vista** point of view; **~i di sospensione** suspension points

puntu'ale *ag* punctual; **puntualità** *sf* punctuality

pun'tura *sf* (*di ago*) prick; (*di insetto*) sting, bite; (*MED*) puncture; (*: iniezione*) injection; (*dolore*) sharp pain

punzecchi'are [puntsek'kjare] *vt* to prick; (*fig*) to tease

pun'zone [pun'tsone] *sm* (*per metalli*) stamp, die

'pupa *sf* doll

pu'pazzo [pu'pattso] *sm* puppet

pu'pilla *sf* (*ANAT*) pupil; *vedi anche* **pupillo**

pu'pillo, a *sm/f* (*DIR*) ward; (*prediletto*) favourite, pet

purché [pur'ke] *cong* provided that, on condition that

'pure *cong* (*tuttavia*) and yet, nevertheless; (*anche se*) even if ♦ *av* (*anche*) too, also; **pur di** (*al fine di*) just to; **faccia ~!** go ahead!, please do!

purè *sm* (*CUC*) purée; (*: di patate*) mashed

potatoes

pu'rea *sf* = **purè**

pu'rezza [pu'rettsa] *sf* purity

'purga, ghe *sf* (*MED*) purging *no pl*; purge; (*POL*) purge

pur'gante *sm* (*MED*) purgative, purge

pur'gare *vt* (*MED, POL*) to purge; (*pulire*) to clean

purga'torio *sm* purgatory

purifi'care *vt* to purify; (*metallo*) to refine

puri'tano, a *ag, sm/f* puritan

'puro, a *ag* pure; (*acqua*) clear, limpid; (*vino*) undiluted; **puro'sangue** *sm/f inv* thoroughbred

pur'troppo *av* unfortunately

'pustola *sf* pimple

puti'ferio *sm* rumpus, row

putre'fare *vi* to putrefy, rot; **putre'fatto, a** *pp di* **putrefare**

'putrido, a *ag* putrid, rotten

put'tana (*fam!*) *sf* whore (!)

'puzza ['puttsa] *sf* = **puzzo**

puz'zare [put'tsare] *vi* to stink

'puzzo ['puttso] *sm* stink, foul smell

'puzzola ['puttsola] *sf* polecat

puzzo'lente [puttso'lɛnte] *ag* stinking

Q

qua *av* here; **in ~** (*verso questa parte*) this way; **da un anno in ~** for a year now; **da quando in ~?** since when?; **per di ~** (*passare*) this way; **al di ~ di** (*fiume, strada*) on this side of; **~ dentro/fuori** *etc* in/out here *etc*; *vedi* **questo**

qua'derno *sm* notebook; (*per scuola*) exercise book

qua'drante *sm* quadrant; (*di orologio*) face

qua'drare *vi* (*bilancio*) to balance, tally; (*descrizione*) to correspond; (*fig*): **~ a** to please, be to one's liking ♦ *vt* (*MAT*) to square; **non mi quadra** I don't like it; **qua'drato, a** *ag* square; (*fig: equilibrato*) level-headed, sensible; (*: peg*) square ♦ *sm* (*MAT*) square; (*PUGILATO*) ring; **5 al quadrato** 5 squared

qua'dretto *sm*: **a ~i** (*tessuto*) checked;

(*foglio*) squared

quadri'foglio [kwadri'fɔʎʎo] *sm* four-leaf clover

'**quadro** *sm* (*pittura*) painting, picture; (*quadrato*) square; (*tabella*) table, chart; (*TECN*) board, panel; (*TEATRO*) scene; (*fig: scena, spettacolo*) sight; (: *descrizione*) outline, description; ~**i** *smpl* (*POL*) party organizers; (*MIL*) cadres; (*COMM*) managerial staff; (*CARTE*) diamonds

'**quadruplo, a** *ag, sm* quadruple

quaggiù [kwad'dʒu] *av* down here

'**quaglia** ['kwaʎʎa] *sf* quail

PAROLA CHIAVE

'**qualche** ['kwalke] *det* **1** some, a few; (*in interrogative*) any; **ho comprato ~ libro** I've bought some *o* a few books; **~ volta** sometimes; **hai ~ sigaretta?** have you any cigarettes?

2 (*uno*): **c'è ~ medico?** is there a doctor?; **in ~ modo** somehow

3 (*un certo, parecchio*) some; **un personaggio di ~ rilievo** a figure of some importance

4: **~ cosa = qualcosa**

qualche'duno [kwalke'duno] *pron* = **qualcuno**

qual'cosa *pron* something; (*in espressioni interrogative*) anything; **qualcos'altro** something else; anything else; **~ di nuovo** something new; anything new; **~ da mangiare** something to eat; anything to eat; **c'è ~ che non va?** is there something *o* anything wrong?

qual'cuno *pron* (*persona*) someone, somebody; (: *in espressioni interrogative*) anyone, anybody; (*alcuni*) some; **~ è favorevole a noi** some are on our side; **qualcun altro** someone *o* somebody else; anyone *o* anybody else

PAROLA CHIAVE

'**quale** (*spesso troncato in* **qual**) *det* **1** (*interrogativo*) what; (: *scegliendo tra due o più cose o persone*) which; **~ uomo/denaro?** what man/money?; which man/money?; **~i sono i tuoi programmi?**

what are your plans?; **~ stanza preferisci?** which room do you prefer?

2 (*relativo: come*): **il risultato fu ~ ci si aspettava** the result was as expected

3 (*esclamativo*) what; **~ disgrazia!** what bad luck!

♦ *pron* **1** (*interrogativo*) which; **~ dei due scegli?** which of the two do you want?

2 (*relativo*): **il(la) ~** (*persona: soggetto*) who; (: *oggetto, con preposizione*) whom; (*cosa*) which; (*possessivo*) whose; **suo padre, il ~ è avvocato, ...** his father, who is a lawyer, ...; **il signore con il ~ parlavo** the gentleman to whom I was speaking; **l'albergo al ~ ci siamo fermati** the hotel where we stayed *o* which we stayed at; **la signora della ~ ammiriamo la bellezza** the lady whose beauty we admire

3 (*relativo: in elenchi*) such as, like; **piante ~i l'edera** plants like *o* such as ivy; **~ sindaco di questa città** as mayor of this town

qua'lifica, che *sf* qualification; (*titolo*) title

qualifi'care *vt* to qualify; (*definire*): **~ qn/qc come** to describe sb/sth as; **~rsi** *vr* (*anche SPORT*) to qualify;

qualifica'tivo, a *ag* qualifying; **gara di qualificazione** (*SPORT*) qualifying event

qualità *sf inv* quality; **in ~ di** in one's capacity as

qua'lora *cong* in case, if

qual'siasi *det inv* = **qualunque**

qua'lunque *det inv* any; (*quale che sia*) whatever; (*discriminativo*) whichever; (*posposto: mediocre*) poor, indifferent; ordinary; **mettiti un vestito ~** put on any old dress; **~ cosa** anything; **~ cosa accada** whatever happens; **a ~ costo** at any cost, whatever the cost; **l'uomo ~** the man in the street; **~ persona** anyone, anybody

'**quando** *cong, av* when; **~ sarò ricco** when I'm rich; **da ~** (*dacché*) since; (*interrogativo*): **da ~ sei qui?** how long have you been here?; **quand'anche** even if

quantità *sf inv* quantity; (*gran numero*): **una ~ di** a great deal of; a lot of; **in grande ~** in large quantities; **quantita'tivo** *sm* (*COMM*) amount, quantity

'**quanto, a** *det* **1** (*interrogativo: quantità*) how much; (: *numero*) how many; **~ pane/denaro?** how much bread/money?; **~i libri/ragazzi?** how many books/boys?; **~ tempo?** how long?; **~i anni hai?** how old are you?
2 (*esclamativo*): **~e storie!** what a lot of nonsense!; **~ tempo sprecato!** what a waste of time!
3 (*relativo: quantità*) as much ... as; (: *numero*) as many ... as; **ho ~ denaro mi occorre** I have as much money as I need; **prendi ~i libri vuoi** take as many books as you like
♦ *pron* **1** (*interrogativo: quantità*) how much; (: *numero*) how many; (: *tempo*) how long; **~ mi dai?** how much will you give me?; **~i me ne hai portati?** how many did you bring me?; **da ~ sei qui?** how long have you been here?; **~i ne abbiamo oggi?** what's the date today?
2 (*relativo: quantità*) as much as; (: *numero*) as many as; **farò ~ posso** I'll do as much as I can; **possono venire ~i sono stati invitati** all those who have been invited can come
♦ *av* **1** (*interrogativo: con ag, av*) how; (: *con vb*) how much; **~ stanco ti sembrava?** how tired did he seem to you?; **~ corre la tua moto?** how fast can your motorbike go?; **~ costa?** how much does it cost?; **quant'è?** how much is it?
2 (*esclamativo: con ag, av*) how; (: *con vb*) how much; **~ sono felice!** how happy I am!; **sapessi ~ abbiamo camminato!** if you knew how far we've walked!; **studierò ~ posso** I'll study as much as I can; **~ prima** as soon as possible
3: **in ~** (*in qualità di*) as; (*perché, per il fatto che*) as, since; **(in) ~ a** (*per ciò che riguarda*) as for, as regards
4: **per ~** (*nonostante, anche se*) however;

per ~ si sforzi, non ce la farà try as he may, he won't manage it; **per ~ sia brava, fa degli errori** however good she may be, she makes mistakes; **per ~ io sappia** as far as I know

quan'tunque *cong* although, though
qua'ranta *num* forty
quaran'tena *sf* quarantine
quaran'tesimo, a *num* fortieth
quaran'tina *sf*: **una ~ (di)** about forty
qua'resima *sf*: **la ~** Lent
'**quarta** *sf* (*AUT*) fourth (gear); *vedi anche* **quarto**
quar'tetto *sm* quartet(te)
quarti'ere *sm* district, area; (*MIL*) quarters *pl*; **~ generale** headquarters *pl*, HQ
'**quarto, a** *ag* fourth ♦ *sm* fourth; (*quarta parte*) quarter; **le 6 e un ~** a quarter past six; **~ d'ora** quarter of an hour; **~i di finale** quarter final
'**quarzo** ['kwartso] *sm* quartz
'**quasi** *av* almost, nearly ♦ *cong* (*anche: ~ che*) as if; **(non) ... ~ mai** hardly ever; **~ ~ me ne andrei** I've half a mind to leave
quas'sù *av* up here
'**quatto, a** *ag* crouched, squatting; (*silenzioso*) silent; **~ ~** very quietly; stealthily
quat'tordici [kwat'torditʃi] *num* fourteen
quat'trini *smpl* money *sg*, cash *sg*
'**quattro** *num* four; **in ~ e quattr'otto** in less than no time; **quattro'cento** *num* four hundred ♦ *sm*: **il Quattrocento** the fifteenth century; **quattro'mila** *num* four thousand

'**quello, a** (*dav sm* **quel** +C, **quell'** +V, **quello** +*s impura, gn, pn, ps, x, z; pl* **quei** +C, **quegli** +V *o s impura, gn, pn, ps, x, z; dav sf* **quella** +C, **quell'** +V; *pl* **quelle**) *det* that; those *pl*; **~a casa** that house; **quegli uomini** those men; **voglio ~a camicia (lì o là)** I want that shirt
♦ *pron* **1** (*dimostrativo*) that (one); those (ones) *pl*; (*ciò*) that; **conosci ~a?** do you know that woman?; **prendo ~ bianco** I'll

take the white one; **chi è ~?** who's that?; **prendiamo ~ (lì o là)** let's take that one (there)
2 (*relativo*): **~(a) che** (*persona*) the one (who); (*cosa*) the one (which), the one (that); **~i(e) che** (*persone*) those who; (*cose*) those which; **è lui ~ che non voleva venire** he's the one who didn't want to come; **ho fatto ~ che potevo** I did what I could

'**quercia, ce** ['kwɛrtʃa] *sf* oak (tree); (*legno*) oak
que'rela *sf* (*DIR*) (legal) action;
quere'lare *vt* to bring an action against
que'sito *sm* question, query; problem
questio'nario *sm* questionnaire
questi'one *sf* problem, question; (*controversia*) issue; (*litigio*) quarrel; **in ~** in question; **fuor di ~** out of the question; **è ~ di tempo** it's a matter o question of time

PAROLA CHIAVE

'**questo, a** *det* **1** (*dimostrativo*) this; these *pl*; **~ libro (qui o qua)** this book; **io prendo ~ cappotto, tu quello** I'll take this coat, you take that one; **quest'oggi** today; **~a sera** this evening
2 (*enfatico*): **non fatemi più prendere di ~e paure** don't frighten me like that again
♦ *pron* (*dimostrativo*) this (one); these (ones) *pl*; (*ciò*) this; **prendo ~ (qui o qua)** I'll take this one; **preferisci ~i o quelli?** do you prefer these (ones) or those (ones)?; **~ intendevo io** this is what I meant; **vengono Paolo e Luca: ~ da Roma, quello da Palermo** Paolo and Luca are coming: the former from Palermo, the latter from Rome

ques'tore *sm* ≈ chief constable (*BRIT*), ≈ police commissioner (*US*)
'**questua** *sf* collection (of alms)
ques'tura *sf* police headquarters *pl*
qui *av* here; **da o di ~** from here; **di ~ in avanti** from now on; **di ~ a poco/una settimana** in a little while/a week's time;

~ dentro/sopra/vicino in/up/near here; *vedi* **questo**
quie'tanza [kwje'tantsa] *sf* receipt
quie'tare *vt* to calm, soothe
qui'ete *sf* quiet, quietness; calmness; stillness; peace
qui'eto, a *ag* quiet; (*notte*) calm, still; (*mare*) calm
'**quindi** *av* then ♦ *cong* therefore, so
'**quindici** ['kwinditʃi] *num* fifteen; **~ giorni** a fortnight (*BRIT*), two weeks
quindi'cina [kwindi'tʃina] *sf* (*serie*): **una ~ (di)** about fifteen; **fra una ~ di giorni** in a fortnight
quin'quennio *sm* period of five years
quin'tale *sm* quintal (*100 kg*)
'**quinte** *sfpl* (*TEATRO*) wings
'**quinto, a** *num* fifth
'**quota** *sf* (*parte*) quota, share; (*AER*) height, altitude; (*IPPICA*) odds *pl*; **prendere/perdere ~** (*AER*) to gain/lose height o altitude; **~ d'iscrizione** enrolment fee; (*ad un club*) membership fee
quo'tare *vt* (*BORSA*) to quote;
quotazi'one *sf* quotation
quotidi'ano, a *ag* daily; (*banale*) everyday ♦ *sm* (*giornale*) daily (paper)
quozi'ente [kwot'tsjɛnte] *sm* (*MAT*) quotient; **~ d'intelligenza** intelligence quotient, IQ

R

ra'barbaro *sm* rhubarb
'**rabbia** *sf* (*ira*) anger, rage; (*accanimento, furia*) fury; (*MED: idrofobia*) rabies *sg*
rab'bino *sm* rabbi
rabbi'oso, a *ag* angry, furious; (*facile all'ira*) quick-tempered; (*forze, acqua etc*) furious, raging; (*MED*) rabid, mad
rabbo'nire *vt* to calm down; **~rsi** *vr* to calm down
rabbrivi'dire *vi* to shudder, shiver
rabbui'arsi *vr* to grow dark
raccapez'zarsi [rakkapet'tsarsi] *vr*: **non ~** to be at a loss
raccapricci'ante [rakkaprit'tʃante] *ag*

horrifying

raccatta'palle *sm inv* (SPORT) ballboy

raccat'tare *vt* to pick up

rac'chetta [rak'ketta] *sf* (per tennis) racket; (per ping-pong) bat; ~ **da neve** snowshoe; ~ **da sci** ski stick

racchi'udere [rak'kjudere] *vt* to contain; **racchi'uso, a** *pp di* **racchiudere**

rac'cogliere [rak'kɔʎʎere] *vt* to collect; (raccattare) to pick up; (frutti, fiori) to pick, pluck; (AGR) to harvest; (approvazione, voti) to win; (profughi) to take in; ~**rsi** *vr* to gather; (fig) to gather one's thoughts; to meditate; **raccogli'mento** *sm* meditation; **raccogli'tore** *sm* (cartella) folder, binder; **raccoglitore a fogli mobili** loose-leaf binder

rac'colta *sf* collecting *no pl*; collection; (AGR) harvesting *no pl*, gathering *no pl*; harvest, crop; (adunata) gathering

rac'colto, a *pp di* **raccogliere** ♦ *ag* (persona: pensoso) thoughtful; (luogo: appartato) secluded, quiet ♦ *sm* (AGR) crop, harvest

raccoman'dare *vt* to recommend; (affidare) to entrust; (esortare): ~ **a qn di non fare** to tell *o* warn sb not to do; ~**rsi** *vr*: ~**rsi a qn** to commend o.s. to sb; **mi raccomando!** don't forget!; **racco-man'data** *sf* (anche: lettera racco-mandata) recorded-delivery letter; **racco-mandazi'one** *sf* recommendation

raccon'tare *vt*: ~ **(a qn)** (dire) to tell (sb); (narrare) to relate (to sb), tell (sb) about; **rac'conto** *sm* telling *no pl*, relating *no pl*; (fatto raccontato) story, tale

raccorci'are [rakkor'tʃare] *vt* to shorten

rac'cordo *sm* (TECN: giunzione) connection, joint; (AUT: di autostrada) slip road (BRIT), entrance (*o* exit) ramp (US); ~ **anulare** (AUT) ring road (BRIT), beltway (US)

ra'chitico, a, ci, che [ra'kitiko] *ag* suffering from rickets; (fig) scraggy, scrawny

racimo'lare [ratʃimo'lare] *vt* (fig) to scrape together, glean

'rada *sf* (natural) harbour

'radar *sm* radar

raddol'cire [raddol'tʃire] *vt* (persona, carattere) to soften; ~**rsi** *vr* (tempo) to grow milder; (persona) to soften, mellow

raddoppi'are *vt, vi* to double

raddriz'zare [raddrit'tsare] *vt* to straighten; (fig: correggere) to put straight, correct

'radere *vt* (barba) to shave off; (mento) to shave; (fig: rasentare) to graze; to skim; ~**rsi** *vr* to shave (o.s.); ~ **al suolo** to raze to the ground

radi'are *vt* to strike off

radia'tore *sm* radiator

radiazi'one [radjat'tsjone] *sf* (FISICA) radiation; (cancellazione) striking off

radi'cale *ag* radical ♦ *sm* (LING) root

ra'dicchio [ra'dikkjo] *sm* chicory

ra'dice [ra'ditʃe] *sf* root

'radio *sf inv* radio ♦ *sm* (CHIM) radium; **radioat'tivo, a** *ag* radioactive; **radiodiffusi'one** *sf* (radio) broadcasting; **radiogra'fare** *vt* to X-ray; **radiogra'fia** *sf* radiography; (foto) X-ray photograph

radi'oso, a *ag* radiant

radiostazi'one [radjostat'tsjone] *sf* radio station

'rado, a *ag* (capelli) sparse, thin; (visite) infrequent; **di** ~ rarely

radu'nare *vt*, to gather, assemble; ~**rsi** *vr* to gather, assemble

ra'dura *sf* clearing

raffazzo'nare [raffattso'nare] *vt* to patch up

raf'fermo, a *ag* stale

'raffica, che *sf* (METEOR) gust (of wind); (di colpi: scarica) burst of gunfire

raffigu'rare *vt* to represent

raffi'nare *vt* to refine; **raffina'tezza** *sf* refinement; **raffi'nato, a** *ag* refined; **raffine'ria** *sf* refinery

raffor'zare [raffor'tsare] *vt* to reinforce

raffredda'mento *sm* cooling

raffred'dare *vt* to cool; (fig) to dampen, have a cooling effect on; ~**rsi** *vr* to grow cool *o* cold; (prendere un raffreddore) to catch a cold; (fig) to cool (off)

raffred'dato, a *ag* (MED): **essere** ~ to have a cold

raffred'dore *sm* (*MED*) cold
raf'fronto *sm* comparison
'rafia *sf* (*fibra*) raffia
ra'gazzo, a [ra'gattso] *sm/f* boy/girl;
(*fam*: *fidanzato*) boyfriend/girlfriend
raggi'ante [rad'dʒante] *ag* radiant,
shining
'raggio ['raddʒo] *sm* (*di sole etc*) ray;
(*MAT*, *distanza*) radius; (*di ruota etc*)
spoke; ~ **d'azione** range; ~**i X** X-rays
raggi'rare [raddʒi'rare] *vt* to take in,
trick; rag'giro *sm* trick
raggi'ungere [rad'dʒundʒere] *vt* to
reach; (*persona*: *riprendere*) to catch up
(with); (*bersaglio*) to hit; (*fig*: *meta*) to
achieve; raggi'unto, a *pp di*
raggiungere
raggomito'larsi *vr* to curl up
raggranel'lare *vt* to scrape together
raggrup'pare *vt* to group (together)
raggu'aglio [rag'gwaʎʎo] *sm* comparison; (*informazione, relazione*) piece of
information
ragguar'devole *ag* (*degno di riguardo*)
distinguished, notable; (*notevole*: *somma*)
considerable
ragiona'mento [radʒona'mento] *sm*
reasoning *no pl*; arguing *no pl*; argument
ragio'nare [radʒo'nare] *vi* (*usare la
ragione*) to reason; (*discorrere*): ~ (**di**) to
argue (about)
ragi'one [ra'dʒone] *sf* reason;
(*dimostrazione, prova*) argument, reason;
(*diritto*) right; **aver** ~ to be right; **aver** ~
di qn to get the better of sb; **dare** ~ **a qn**
to agree with sb; to prove sb right;
perdere la ~ to become insane; (*fig*) to
take leave of one's senses; **in** ~ **di** at the
rate of; to the amount of; according to; **a**
o **con** ~ rightly, justly; ~ **sociale** (*COMM*)
corporate name; **a ragion veduta** after
due consideration
ragione'ria [radʒone'ria] *sf* accountancy;
accounts department
ragio'nevole [radʒo'nevole] *ag*
reasonable
ragioni'ere, a [radʒo'njere] *sm/f*
accountant
ragli'are [raʎ'ʎare] *vi* to bray

ragna'tela [raɲɲa'tela] *sf* cobweb,
spider's web
'ragno ['raɲɲo] *sm* spider
ragù *sm inv* (*CUC*) meat sauce; stew
RAI-TV [raiti'vu] *sigla f* = **Radio
televisione italiana**
rallegra'menti *smpl* congratulations
ralle'grare *vt* to cheer up; ~**rsi** *vr* to
cheer up; (*provare allegrezza*) to rejoice;
~**rsi con qn** to congratulate sb
rallen'tare *vt* to slow down; (*fig*) to
lessen, slacken ♦ *vi* to slow down
raman'zina [raman'dzina] *sf* lecture,
telling-off
'rame *sm* (*CHIM*) copper
rammari'carsi *vr*: ~ (**di**) (*rincrescersi*) to
be sorry (about), regret; (*lamentarsi*) to
complain (about); ram'marico, chi *sm*
regret
rammen'dare *vt* to mend; (*calza*) to
darn; ram'mendo *sm* mending *no pl*;
darning *no pl*; mend; darn
rammen'tare *vt* to remember, recall;
(*richiamare alla memoria*): ~ **qc a qn** to
remind sb of sth; ~**rsi** *vr*: ~**rsi (di qc)** to
remember (sth)
rammol'lire *vt* to soften ♦ *vi* (*anche*:
~**rsi**) to go soft
'ramo *sm* branch
ramo'scello [ramoʃ'ʃello] *sm* twig
'rampa *sf* flight (of stairs); ~ **di lancio**
launching pad
rampi'cante *ag* (*BOT*) climbing
ram'pone *sm* harpoon; (*ALPINISMO*)
crampon
'rana *sf* frog
'rancido, a ['rantʃido] *ag* rancid
ran'core *sm* rancour, resentment
ran'dagio, a, gi, gie *o* ge [ran'dadʒo]
ag (*gatto, cane*) stray
ran'dello *sm* club, cudgel
'rango, ghi *sm* (*condizione sociale, MIL*:
riga) rank
rannicchi'arsi [rannik'kjarsi] *vr* to
crouch, huddle
rannuvo'larsi *vr* to cloud over, become
overcast
ra'nocchio [ra'nɔkkjo] *sm* (*edible*) frog
'rantolo *sm* wheeze; (*di agonizzanti*)

death rattle

'**rapa** *sf* (*BOT*) turnip

ra'**pace** [ra'patʃe] *ag* (*animale*) predatory; (*fig*) rapacious, grasping ♦ *sm* bird of prey

ra'**pare** *vt* (*capelli*) to crop, cut very short

'**rapida** *sf* (*di fiume*) rapid; *vedi anche* **rapido**

rapida'**mente** *av* quickly, rapidly

rapidità *sf* speed

'**rapido, a** *ag* fast; (*esame, occhiata*) quick, rapid ♦ *sm* (*FERR*) express (train)

rapi'**mento** *sm* kidnapping; (*fig*) rapture

ra'**pina** *sf* robbery; ~ **a mano armata** armed robbery; **rapi'nare** *vt* to rob; **rapina'tore, 'trice** *sm/f* robber

ra'**pire** *vt* (*cose*) to steal; (*persone*) to kidnap; (*fig*) to enrapture, delight; **rapi'tore, 'trice** *sm/f* kidnapper

rappor'**tare** *vt* (*confrontare*) to compare; (*riprodurre*) to reproduce

rap'**porto** *sm* (*resoconto*) report; (*legame*) relationship; (*MAT, TECN*) ratio; ~**i** *smpl* (*fra persone, paesi*) relations; ~**i sessuali** sexual intercourse *sg*

rap'**prendersi** *vr* to coagulate, clot; (*latte*) to curdle

rappre'**saglia** [rappre'saʎʎa] *sf* reprisal, retaliation

rappresen'**tante** *sm/f* representative; **rappresen'tanza** *sf* delegation, deputation; (*COMM: ufficio, sede*) agency

rappresen'**tare** *vt* to represent; (*TEATRO*) to perform; **rappresentazi'one** *sf* representation; performing *no pl*; (*spettacolo*) performance

rap'**preso, a** *pp di* **rapprendere**

rapso'**dia** *sf* rhapsody

rara'**mente** *av* seldom, rarely

rare'**fatto, a** *ag* rarefied

'**raro, a** *ag* rare

ra'**sare** *vt* (*barba etc*) to shave off; (*siepi, erba*) to trim, cut; ~**rsi** *vr* to shave (o.s.)

raschi'**are** [ras'kjare] *vt* to scrape; (*macchia, fango*) to scrape off ♦ *vi* to clear one's throat

rasen'**tare** *vt* (*andar rasente*) to keep close to; (*sfiorare*) to skim along (*o* over); (*fig*) to border on

ra'**sente** *prep*: ~ (**a**) close to, very near

'**raso, a** *pp di* **radere** ♦ *ag* (*barba*) shaved; (*capelli*) cropped; (*con misure di capacità*) level; (*pieno: bicchiere*) full to the brim ♦ *sm* (*tessuto*) satin; ~ **terra** close to the ground; **un cucchiaio** ~ a level spoonful

ra'**soio** *sm* razor; ~ **elettrico** electric shaver *o* razor

ras'**segna** [ras'seɲɲa] *sf* (*MIL*) inspection, review; (*esame*) inspection; (*resoconto*) review, survey; (*pubblicazione letteraria etc*) review; (*mostra*) exhibition, show; **passare in** ~ (*MIL, fig*) to review

rasse'**gnare** [rasseɲ'ɲare] *vt*: ~ **le dimissioni** to resign, hand in one's resignation; ~**rsi** *vr* (*accettare*): ~**rsi (a qc/a fare**) to resign o.s. (to sth/to doing); **rassegnazi'one** *sf* resignation

rassere'**narsi** *vr* (*tempo*) to clear up

rasset'**tare** *vt* to tidy, put in order; (*aggiustare*) to repair, mend

rassicu'**rare** *vt* to reassure

rasso'**dare** *vt* to harden, stiffen

rassomigli'**anza** [rassomiʎ'ʎantsa] *sf* resemblance

rassomigli'**are** [rassomiʎ'ʎare] *vi*: ~ **a** to resemble, look like

rastrel'**lare** *vt* to rake; (*fig: perlustrare*) to comb

rastrelli'**era** *sf* rack; (*per piatti*) dish rack

ras'**trello** *sm* rake

'**rata** *sf* (*quota*) instalment; **pagare a ~e** to pay by instalments *o* on hire purchase (*BRIT*)

ratifi'**care** *vt* (*DIR*) to ratify

'**ratto** *sm* (*DIR*) abduction; (*ZOOL*) rat

rattop'**pare** *vt* to patch; **rat'toppo** *sm* patching *no pl*; patch

rattrap'**pire** *vt* to make stiff; ~**rsi** *vr* to be stiff

rattris'**tare** *vt* to sadden; ~**rsi** *vr* to become sad

'**rauco, a, chi, che** *ag* hoarse

rava'**nello** *sm* radish

ravi'**oli** *smpl* ravioli *sg*

ravve'**dersi** *vr* to mend one's ways

ravvici'**nare** [ravvitʃi'nare] *vt* (*avvicinare*): ~ **qc a** to bring sth nearer to; (: *due tubi*) to bring closer together; (*riconciliare*) to reconcile, bring together

ravvi'sare *vt* to recognize

ravvi'vare *vt* to revive; (*fig*) to brighten up, enliven; **~rsi** *vr* to revive; to brighten up

razio'cinio [ratsjo't∫injo] *sm* reasoning *no pl*; reason; (*buon senso*) common sense

razio'nale [rattsjo'nale] *ag* rational

razio'nare [rattsjo'nare] *vt* to ration

razi'one [rat'tsjone] *sf* ration; (*porzione*) portion, share

'razza ['rattsa] *sf* race; (*ZOOL*) breed; (*discendenza, stirpe*) stock, race; (*sorta*) sort, kind

raz'zia [rat'tsia] *sf* raid, foray

razzi'ale [rat'tsjale] *ag* racial

raz'zismo [rat'tsizmo] *sm* racism, racialism

raz'zista, i, e [rat'tsista] *ag, sm/f* racist, racialist

'razzo ['raddzo] *sm* rocket

razzo'lare [rattso'lare] *vi* (*galline*) to scratch about

re *sm inv* king; (*MUS*) D; (: *solfeggiando la scala*) re

rea'gire [rea'dʒire] *vi* to react

re'ale *ag* real; (*di, da re*) royal ♦ *sm*: **il ~** reality; **rea'lismo** *sm* realism; **rea'lista, i, e** *sm/f* realist; (*POL*) royalist

realiz'zare [realid'dzare] *vt* (*progetto etc*) to realize, carry out; (*sogno, desiderio*) to realize, fulfil; (*scopo*) to achieve; (*COMM: titoli etc*) to realize; (*CALCIO etc*) to score; **~rsi** *vr* to be realized; **realizzazi'one** *sf* realization; fulfilment; achievement

real'mente *av* really, actually

realtà *sf inv* reality

re'ato *sm* offence

reat'tore *sm* (*FISICA*) reactor; (*AER: aereo*) jet; (: *motore*) jet engine

reazio'nario, a [reattsjo'narjo] *ag* (*POL*) reactionary

reazi'one [reat'tsjone] *sf* reaction

recapi'tare *vt* to deliver

re'capito *sm* (*indirizzo*) address; (*consegna*) delivery

re'care *vt* (*portare*) to bring; (*avere su di sé*) to carry, bear; (*cagionare*) to cause,

bring; **~rsi** *vr* to go

re'cedere [re't∫edere] *vi* to withdraw

recensi'one [ret∫en'sjone] *sf* review; **recen'sire** *vt* to review

re'cente [re't∫ente] *ag* recent; **di ~** recently; **recente'mente** *av* recently

recessi'one [ret∫es'sjone] *sf* (*ECON*) recession

re'cidere [re't∫idere] *vt* to cut off, chop off

reci'divo, a [ret∫i'divo] *sm/f* (*DIR*) second (*o* habitual) offender, recidivist

re'cinto [re't∫into] *sm* enclosure; (*ciò che recinge*) fence; surrounding wall

recipi'ente [ret∫i'pjente] *sm* container

re'ciproco, a, ci, che [re't∫iproko] *ag* reciprocal

re'ciso, a [re't∫izo] *pp di* **recidere**

'recita ['ret∫ita] *sf* performance

reci'tare [ret∫i'tare] *vt* (*poesia, lezione*) to recite; (*dramma*) to perform; (*ruolo*) to play *o* act (the part of); **recitazi'one** *sf* recitation; (*di attore*) acting

recla'mare *vi* to complain ♦ *vt* (*richiedere*) to demand

ré'clame [re'klam] *sf inv* advertising *no pl*; advertisement, advert (*BRIT*), ad (*fam*)

re'clamo *sm* complaint

reclusi'one *sf* (*DIR*) imprisonment

'recluta *sf* recruit; **reclu'tare** *vt* to recruit

re'condito, a *ag* secluded; (*fig*) secret, hidden

recriminazi'one [rekriminat'tsjone] *sf* recrimination

recrude'scenza [rekrudeʃ'ʃentsa] *sf* fresh outbreak

recupe'rare *vt* = **ricuperare**

redargu'ire *vt* to rebuke

re'datto, a *pp di* **redigere**; **redat'tore, 'trice** *sm/f* (*STAMPA*) editor; (: *di articolo*) writer; (*di dizionario etc*) compiler; **redattore capo** chief editor; **redazi'one** *sf* editing; writing; (*sede*) editorial office(s); (*personale*) editorial staff; (*versione*) version

reddi'tizio, a [reddi'tittsjo] *ag* profitable

'reddito *sm* income; (*dello Stato*) revenue; (*di un capitale*) yield

re'dento, a *pp di* redimere

redenzi'one [reden'tsjone] *sf* redemption

re'digere [re'didʒere] *vt* to write; (*contratto*) to draw up

re'dimere *vt* to deliver; (*REL*) to redeem

'redini *sfpl* reins

'reduce ['rɛdutʃe] *ag*: ~ da returning from, back from ♦ *sm/f* survivor

refe'rendum *sm inv* referendum

refe'renza [refe'rɛntsa] *sf* reference

re'ferto *sm* medical report

refet'torio *sm* refectory

refrat'tario, a *ag* refractory

refrige'rare [refridʒe'rare] *vt* to refrigerate; (*rinfrescare*) to cool, refresh

rega'lare *vt* to give (as a present), make a present of

re'gale *ag* regal

re'galo *sm* gift, present

re'gata *sf* regatta

reg'gente [red'dʒɛnte] *sm/f* regent

'reggere ['rɛddʒere] *vt* (*tenere*) to hold; (*sostenere*) to support, bear, hold up; (*portare*) to carry, bear; (*resistere*) to withstand; (*dirigere: impresa*) to manage, run; (*governare*) to rule, govern; (*LING*) to take, be followed by ♦ *vi* (*resistere*): ~ a to stand up to, hold out against; (*sopportare*): ~ a to stand; (*durare*) to last; (*fig: teoria etc*) to hold water; ~rsi *vr* (*stare ritto*) to stand; (*fig: dominarsi*) to control o.s.; ~rsi sulle gambe *o* in piedi to stand up

'reggia, ge ['rɛddʒa] *sf* royal palace

reggi'calze [reddʒi'kaltse] *sm inv* suspender belt

reggi'mento [reddʒi'mento] *sm* (*MIL*) regiment

reggi'petto [reddʒi'pɛtto] *sm* = reggiseno

reggi'seno [reddʒi'seno] *sm* bra

re'gia, 'gie [re'dʒia] *sf* (*TV, CINEMA etc*) direction

re'gime [re'dʒime] *sm* (*POL*) regime; (*DIR: aureo, patrimoniale etc*) system; (*MED*) diet; (*TECN*) (engine) speed

re'gina [re'dʒina] *sf* queen

'regio, a, gi, gie ['rɛdʒo] *ag* royal

regio'nale [redʒo'nale] *ag* regional

regi'one [re'dʒone] *sf* region; (*territorio*) region, district, area

re'gista, i, e [re'dʒista] *sm/f* (*TV, CINEMA etc*) director

regis'trare [redʒis'trare] *vt* (*AMM*) to register; (*COMM*) to enter; (*notare*) to note, take note of; (*canzone, conversazione, sog: strumento di misura*) to record; (*mettere a punto*) to adjust, regulate; (*bagagli*) to check in; **registra'tore** *sm* (*strumento*) recorder, register; (*magnetofono*) tape recorder; **registratore di cassa** cash register; **registrazi'one** *sf* recording; (*AMM*) registration; (*COMM*) entry; (*di bagagli*) check-in

re'gistro [re'dʒistro] *sm* (*libro*) register; ledger; logbook; (*DIR*) registry; (*MUS, TECN*) register

re'gnare [reɲ'ɲare] *vi* to reign, rule; (*fig*) to reign

'regno ['reɲɲo] *sm* kingdom; (*periodo*) reign; (*fig*) realm; il ~ animale/vegetale the animal/vegetable kingdom; il R~ Unito the United Kingdom

'regola *sf* rule; a ~ d'arte duly; perfectly; in ~ in order

regola'mento *sm* (*complesso di norme*) regulations *pl*; (*di debito*) settlement; ~ di conti (*fig*) settling of scores

rego'lare *ag* regular; (*in regola: domanda*) in order, lawful ♦ *vt* to regulate, control; (*apparecchio*) to adjust, regulate; (*questione, conto, debito*) to settle; ~rsi *vr* (*moderarsi*): ~rsi nel bere/nello spendere to control one's drinking/spending; (*comportarsi*) to behave, act; **regolarità** *sf inv* regularity

'regolo *sm* ruler; ~ calcolatore slide rule

reinte'grare *vt* (*energie*) to recover; (*in una carica*) to reinstate

rela'tivo, a *ag* relative

relazi'one [relat'tsjone] *sf* (*fra cose, persone*) relation(ship); (*resoconto*) report, account; ~i *sfpl* (*conoscenze*) connections

rele'gare *vt* to banish; (*fig*) to relegate

religi'one [reli'dʒone] *sf* religion; **religi'oso, a** *ag* religious ♦ *sm/f* monk/nun

re'liquia *sf* relic

re'litto *sm* wreck; *(fig)* down-and-out
re'mare *vi* to row
remini'scenze [reminiʃˈʃentse] *sfpl*
reminiscences
remissi'one *sf* remission
remis'sivo, a *ag* submissive, compliant
'remo *sm* oar
re'moto, a *ag* remote
'rendere *vt (ridare)* to return, give back;
(: saluto etc) to return; *(produrre)* to yield,
bring in; *(esprimere, tradurre)* to render;
(far diventare): ~ **qc possibile** to make
sth possible; ~ **grazie a qn** to thank sb;
~rsi utile to make o.s. useful; **~rsi conto**
di qc to realize sth
rendi'conto *sm (rapporto)* report,
account; *(AMM, COMM)* statement of account
rendi'mento *sm (reddito)* yield; *(di*
manodopera, TECN) efficiency; *(capacità di*
produrre) output; *(di studenti)* performance
'rendita *sf (di individuo)* private *o*
unearned income; *(COMM)* revenue; ~
annua annuity
'rene *sm* kidney
'reni *sfpl* back *sg*
reni'tente *ag* reluctant, unwilling; ~ **ai**
consigli di qn unwilling to follow sb's
advice; **essere ~ alla leva** *(MIL)* to fail to
report for military service
'renna *sf* reindeer *inv*
'Reno *sm*: **il ~** the Rhine
'reo, a *sm/f (DIR)* offender
re'parto *sm* department, section; *(MIL)*
detachment
repel'lente *ag* repulsive
repen'taglio [repenˈtaʎʎo] *sm*: **mettere**
a ~ to jeopardize, risk
repen'tino, a *ag* sudden, unexpected
repe'rire *vt* to find, trace
re'perto *sm (ARCHEOLOGIA)* find; *(MED)*
report; *(DIR: anche: ~ giudiziario)* exhibit
reper'torio *sm (TEATRO)* repertory; *(elenco)*
index, (alphabetical) list
'replica, che *sf* repetition; reply, answer;
(obiezione) objection; *(TEATRO, CINEMA)*
repeat performance; *(copia)* replica
repli'care *vt (ripetere)* to repeat;
(rispondere) to answer, reply

repressi'one *sf* repression
re'presso, a *pp di* **reprimere**
re'primere *vt* to suppress, repress
re'pubblica, che *sf* republic;
repubbli'cano, a *ag, sm/f* republican
repu'tare *vt* to consider, judge
reputazi'one [reputatˈtsjone] *sf* reputation
'requie *sf*: **senza ~** unceasingly
requi'sire *vt* to requisition
requi'sito *sm* requirement
requisizi'one [rekwizitˈtsjone] *sf*
requisition
'resa *sf (l'arrendersi)* surrender; *(resti-*
tuzione, rendimento) return; ~ **dei conti**
rendering of accounts; *(fig)* day of
reckoning
resi'dente *ag* resident; **resi'denza** *sf*
residence; **residenzi'ale** *ag* residential
re'siduo, a *ag* residual, remaining ♦ *sm*
remainder; *(CHIM)* residue
'resina *sf* resin
resis'tente *ag (che resiste)*: ~ **a** resistant
to; *(forte)* strong; *(duraturo)* long-lasting,
durable; ~ **al caldo** heat-resistant;
resis'tenza *sf* resistance; *(di persona:*
fisica) stamina, endurance; *(: mentale)*
endurance, resistance
re'sistere *vi* to resist; ~ **a** *(assalto,*
tentazioni) to resist; *(dolore, sog: pianta)*
to withstand; *(non patir danno)* to be
resistant to; **resis'tito, a** *pp di* **resistere**
'reso, a *pp di* **rendere**
reso'conto *sm* report, account
res'pingere [resˈpindʒere] *vt* to drive
back, repel; *(rifiutare)* to reject; *(INS:*
bocciare) to fail; **res'pinto, a** *pp di*
respingere
respi'rare *vi* to breathe; *(fig)* to get one's
breath; to breathe again ♦ *vt* to breathe
(in), inhale; **respira'tore** *sm* respirator;
respirazi'one *sf* breathing; **respirazione**
artificiale artificial respiration; **res'piro**
sm breathing *no pl*; *(singolo atto)* breath;
(fig) respite, rest; **mandare un respiro di**
sollievo to give a sigh of relief
respon'sabile *ag* responsible ♦ *sm/f*
person responsible; *(capo)* person in
charge; ~ **di** responsible for; *(DIR)* liable

for; **responsabilità** *sf inv* responsibility; (*legale*) liability

res'ponso *sm* answer

'ressa *sf* crowd, throng

res'tare *vi* (*rimanere*) to remain, stay; (*diventare*): ~ **orfano/cieco** to become *o* be left an orphan/become blind; (*trovarsi*): ~ **sorpreso** to be surprised; (*avanzare*) to be left, remain; ~ **d'accordo** to agree; **non resta più niente** there's nothing left; **restano pochi giorni** there are only a few days left

restau'rare *vt* to restore; **restaurazi'one** *sf* (*POL*) restoration; **res'tauro** *sm* (*di edifici etc*) restoration

res'tio, a, 'tii, 'tie *ag* restive; (*persona*): ~ **a** reluctant to

restitu'ire *vt* to return, give back; (*energie, forze*) to restore

'resto *sm* remainder, rest; (*denaro*) change; (*MAT*) remainder; ~**i** *smpl* (*di cibo*) leftovers; (*di città*) remains; **del** ~ moreover, besides; ~**i mortali** (*mortal*) remains

res'tringere [res'trindʒere] *vt* to reduce; (*vestito*) to take in; (*stoffa*) to shrink; (*fig*) to restrict, limit; ~**rsi** *vr* (*strada*) to narrow; (*stoffa*) to shrink; **restrizi'one** *sf* restriction

'rete *sf* net; (*fig*) trap, snare; (*di recinzione*) wire netting; (*AUT, FERR, di spionaggio etc*) network; **segnare una** ~ (*CALCIO*) to score a goal; ~ **del letto** (sprung) bed base

reti'cente [reti'tʃɛnte] *ag* reticent

retico'lato *sm* grid; (*rete metallica*) wire netting; (*di filo spinato*) barbed wire (fence)

'retina *sf* (*ANAT*) retina

re'torica *sf* rhetoric

re'torico, a, ci, che *ag* rhetorical

retribu'ire *vt* to pay; (*premiare*) to reward; **retribuzi'one** *sf* payment; reward

'retro *sm inv* back ♦ *av* (*dietro*): **vedi** ~ see over(leaf)

retro'cedere [retro'tʃɛdere] *vi* to withdraw ♦ *vt* (*CALCIO*) to relegate; (*MIL*) to degrade

re'trogrado, a *ag* (*fig*) reactionary, backward-looking

retro'marcia [retro'martʃa] *sf* (*AUT*) reverse; (: *dispositivo*) reverse gear

retro'scena [retro'ʃɛna] *sm inv* (*TEATRO*) backstage; **i** ~ (*fig*) the behind-the-scenes activities

retrospet'tivo, a *ag* retrospective

retrovi'sore *sm* (*AUT*) (rear-view) mirror

'retta *sf* (*MAT*) straight line; (*di convitto*) charge for bed and board; (*fig*: *ascolto*): **dar** ~ **a** to listen to, pay attention to

rettango'lare *ag* rectangular

ret'tangolo, a *ag* right-angled ♦ *sm* rectangle

ret'tifica, che *sf* rectification, correction

rettifi'care *vt* (*curva*) to straighten; (*fig*) to rectify, correct

'rettile *sm* reptile

retti'lineo, a *ag* rectilinear

retti'tudine *sf* rectitude, uprightness

'retto, a *pp di* **reggere** ♦ *ag* straight; (*MAT*): **angolo** ~ right angle; (*onesto*) honest, upright; (*giusto, esatto*) correct, proper, right

ret'tore *sm* (*REL*) rector; (*di università*) ≈ chancellor

reuma'tismo *sm* rheumatism

reve'rendo, a *ag*: **il** ~ **padre Belli** the Reverend Father Belli

rever'sibile *ag* reversible

revisio'nare *vt* (*conti*) to audit; (*TECN*) to overhaul, service; (*DIR*: *processo*) to review; (*componimento*) to revise

revisi'one *sf* auditing *no pl*; audit; servicing *no pl*; overhaul; review; revision

revi'sore *sm*: ~ **di conti/bozze** auditor/proofreader

'revoca *sf* revocation

revo'care *vt* to revoke

re'volver *sm inv* revolver

riabili'tare *vt* to rehabilitate; (*fig*) to restore to favour

rial'zare [rial'tsare] *vt* to raise, lift; (*alzare di più*) to heighten, raise; (*aumentare*: *prezzi*) to increase, raise ♦ *vi* (*prezzi*) to rise, increase; **ri'alzo** *sm* (*di prezzi*) increase, rise; (*sporgenza*) rise

rianimazi'one [rianimat'tsjone] *sf* (*MED*) resuscitation; **centro di** ~ intensive care unit

riap'pendere *vt* to rehang; (*TEL*) to hang up

ria'prire *vt* to reopen, open again; **~rsi** *vr* to reopen, open again

ri'armo *sm* (*MIL*) rearmament

riasset'tare *vt* (*stanza*) to tidy (up)

rias'setto *sm* (*di stanza etc*) rearrangement; (*ordinamento*) reorganization

rias'sumere *vt* (*riprendere*) to resume; (*impiegare di nuovo*) to re-employ; (*sintetizzare*) to summarize; **rias'sunto, a** *pp di* **riassumere ♦** *sm* summary

ria'vere *vt* to have again; (*avere indietro*) to get back; (*riacquistare*) to recover; **~rsi** *vr* to recover

riba'dire *vt* (*fig*) to confirm

ri'balta *sf* flap; (*TEATRO: proscenio*) front of the stage; (: *apparecchio d'illuminazione*) footlights *pl*; (*fig*) limelight

ribal'tabile *ag* (*sedile*) tip-up

ribal'tare *vt, vi* (*anche:* ~*rsi*) to turn over, tip over

ribas'sare *vt* to lower, bring down ♦ *vi* to come down, fall; **ri'basso** *sm* reduction, fall

ri'battere *vt* to return, hit back; (*confutare*) to refute; ~ **che** to retort that

ribel'larsi *vr* to rebel (against); **ri'belle** *ag* (*soldati*) rebel; (*ragazzo*) rebellious ♦ *sm/f* rebel; **ribelli'one** *sf* rebellion

'ribes *sm inv* currant; ~ **nero** blackcurrant; ~ **rosso** redcurrant

ribol'lire *vi* (*fermentare*) to ferment; (*fare bolle*) to bubble, boil; (*fig*) to seethe

ri'brezzo [ri'breddzo] *sm* disgust, loathing; **far** ~ **a** to disgust

ribut'tante *ag* disgusting, revolting

rica'dere *vi* to fall again; (*scendere a terra, fig: nel peccato etc*) to fall back; (*vestiti, capelli etc*) to hang (down); (*riversarsi: fatiche, colpe*): ~ **su** to fall on; **rica'duta** *sf* (*MED*) relapse

rical'care *vt* (*disegni*) to trace; (*fig*) to follow faithfully

rica'mare *vt* to embroider

ricambi'are *vt* to change again; (*contraccambiare*) to repay, return; **ri'cambio** *sm* exchange, return; (*FISIOL*) metabolism; **ricambi** *smpl* (*TECN*) spare parts

ri'camo *sm* embroidery

ricapito'lare *vt* to recapitulate, sum up

ricari'care *vt* (*arma, macchina fotografica*) to reload; (*pipa*) to refill; (*orologio*) to rewind; (*batteria*) to recharge

ricat'tare *vt* to blackmail; **ricatta'tore, 'trice** *sm/f* blackmailer; **ri'catto** *sm* blackmail

rica'vare *vt* (*estrarre*) to draw out, extract; (*ottenere*) to obtain, gain; **ri'cavo** *sm* proceeds *pl*

ric'chezza [rik'kettsa] *sf* wealth; (*fig*) richness; **~e** *sfpl* (*beni*) wealth *sg*, riches

'riccio, a ['rittʃo] *ag* curly ♦ *sm* (*ZOOL*) hedgehog; (: *anche*: ~ **di mare**) sea urchin; **'ricciolo** *sm* curl; **ricci'uto, a** *ag* curly

'ricco, a, chi, che *ag* rich; (*persona, paese*) rich, wealthy ♦ *sm/f* rich man/ woman; **i ~chi** the rich; ~ **di** full of; rich in

ri'cerca, che [ri'tʃerka] *sf* search; (*indagine*) investigation, inquiry; (*studio*): **la** ~ research; **una** ~ piece of research

ricer'care [ritʃer'kare] *vt* (*motivi, cause*) to look for, try to determine; (*successo, piacere*) to pursue; (*onore, gloria*) to seek; **ricer'cato, a** *ag* (*apprezzato*) much sought-after; (*affettato*) studied, affected ♦ *sm/f* (*POLIZIA*) wanted man/woman

ri'cetta [ri'tʃetta] *sf* (*MED*) prescription; (*CUC*) recipe

ricettazi'one [ritʃettat'tsjone] *sf* (*DIR*) receiving (stolen goods)

ri'cevere [ri'tʃevere] *vt* to receive; (*stipendio, lettera*) to get, receive; (*accogliere: ospite*) to welcome; (*vedere: cliente, rappresentante etc*) to see; **ricevi'mento** *sm* receiving *no pl*; (*trattenimento*) reception; **ricevi'tore** *sm* (*TECN*) receiver; **ricevito'ria** *sf* lottery *o* pools office; **rice'vuta** *sf* receipt; **ricevuta fiscale** receipt for tax purposes; **ricezi'one** *sf* (*RADIO, TV*) reception

richia'mare [rikja'mare] *vt (chiamare indietro, ritelefonare)* to call back; *(ambasciatore, truppe)* to recall; *(rimproverare)* to reprimand; *(attirare)* to attract, draw; **~rsi a** *(riferirsi a)* to refer to; **richi'amo** *sm* call; recall; reprimand; attraction

richi'edere [ri'kjɛdere] *vt* to ask again for; *(chiedere indietro)*: **~ qc** to ask for sth back; *(chiedere: per sapere)* to ask; (: *per avere*) to ask for; *(AMM: documenti)* to apply for; *(esigere)* to need, require; **richi'esta** *sf (domanda)* request; *(AMM)* application, request; *(esigenza)* demand, request; **a richiesta** on request; **richi'esto, a** *pp di* **richiedere**

rici'clare [ritʃi'klare] *vt* to recycle

'ricino ['ritʃino] *sm*: **olio di ~** castor oil

ricogni'one [rikoɲɲi'tsjone] *sf (MIL)* reconnaissance; *(DIR)* recognition, acknowledgement

ricominci'are [rikomin'tʃare] *vt, vi* to start again, begin again

ricom'pensa *sf* reward

ricompen'sare *vt* to reward

riconcili'are [rikontʃi'ljare] *vt* to reconcile; **~rsi** *vr* to be reconciled; **riconciliazi'one** *sf* reconciliation

ricono'scente [rikonoʃ'ʃɛnte] *ag* grateful; **ricono'scenza** *sf* gratitude

rico'noscere [riko'noʃʃere] *vt* to recognize; *(DIR: figlio, debito)* to acknowledge; *(ammettere: errore)* to admit, acknowledge; **riconosci'mento** *sm* recognition; acknowledgement; *(identificazione)* identification; **riconosci'uto, a** *pp di* **riconoscere**

ricopi'are *vt* to copy

rico'prire *vt (coprire)* to cover; *(occupare: carica)* to hold

ricor'dare *vt* to remember, recall; *(richiamare alla memoria)*: **~ qc a qn** to remind sb of sth; **~rsi** *vr*: **~rsi (di)** to remember; **~rsi di qc/di aver fatto** to remember sth/having done

ri'cordo *sm* memory; *(regalo)* keepsake, souvenir; *(di viaggio)* souvenir; **~i** *smpl (memorie)* memoirs

ricor'rente *ag* recurrent, recurring;

ricor'renza *sf* recurrence; *(festività)* anniversary

ri'correre *vi (ripetersi)* to recur; **~ a** *(rivolgersi)* to turn to; (: *DIR*) to appeal to; *(servirsi di)* to have recourse to; **ri'corso, a** *pp di* **ricorrere ♦** *sm* recurrence; *(DIR)* appeal; **far ricorso a** = **ricorrere a**

ricostitu'ente *ag (MED)*: **cura ~** tonic

ricostru'ire *vt (casa)* to rebuild; *(fatti)* to reconstruct; **ricostruzi'one** *sf* rebuilding *no pl*; reconstruction

ri'cotta *sf soft white unsalted cheese made from sheep's milk*

ricove'rare *vt* to give shelter to; **~ qn in ospedale** to admit sb to hospital

ri'covero *sm* shelter, refuge; *(MIL)* shelter; *(MED)* admission (to hospital)

ricre'are *vt* to recreate; *(rinvigorire)* to restore; *(fig: distrarre)* to amuse

ricreazi'one [rikreat'tsjone] *sf* recreation, entertainment; *(INS)* break

ri'credersi *vr* to change one's mind

ricupe'rare *vt (rientrare in possesso di)* to recover, get back; *(tempo perduto)* to make up for; *(NAUT)* to salvage; (: *naufraghi)* to rescue; *(delinquente)* to rehabilitate; **~ lo svantaggio** *(SPORT)* to close the gap

ridacchi'are [ridak'kjare] *vi* to snigger

ri'dare *vt* to return, give back

'ridere *vi* to laugh; *(deridere, beffare)*: **~ di** to laugh at, make fun of

ri'detto, a *pp di* **ridire**

ri'dicolo, a *ag* ridiculous, absurd

ridimensio'nare *vt* to reorganize; *(fig)* to see in the right perspective

ri'dire *vt* to repeat; *(criticare)* to find fault with; to object to; **trova sempre qualcosa da ~** he always manages to find fault

ridon'dante *ag* redundant

ri'dotto, a *pp di* **ridurre**

ri'durre *vt (anche CHIM, MAT)* to reduce; *(prezzo, spese)* to cut, reduce; *(accorciare: opera letteraria)* to abridge; (: *RADIO, TV)* to adapt; **ridursi** *vr (diminuirsi)* to be reduced, shrink; **ridursi a** to be reduced to; **ridursi pelle e ossa** to be reduced to skin and bone; **riduzi'one** *sf* reduction;

abridgement; adaptation

riem'pire *vt* to fill (up); (*modulo*) to fill in *o* out; ~**rsi** *vr* to fill (up); (*mangiare troppo*) to stuff o.s.; ~ **qc di** to fill sth (up) with

rien'tranza [rien'trantsa] *sf* recess; indentation

rien'trare *vi* (*entrare di nuovo*) to go (*o* come) back in; (*tornare*) to return; (*fare una rientranza*) to go in, curve inwards; to be indented; (*riguardare*): ~ **in** to be included among, form part of; **ri'entro** *sm* (*ritorno*) return; (*di astronave*) re-entry

riepilo'gare *vt* to summarize ♦ *vi* to recapitulate

ri'fare *vt* to do again; (*ricostruire*) to make again; (*nodo*) to tie again, do up again; (*imitare*) to imitate, copy; ~**rsi** *vr* (*risarcirsi*) to make up for; (*vendicarsi*): ~**rsi di qc su qn** to get one's own back on sb for sth; (*riferirsi*): ~**rsi a** to go back to; to follow; ~ **il letto** to make the bed; ~**rsi una vita** to make a new life for o.s.; **ri'fatto, a** *pp di* rifare

riferi'mento *sm* reference; **in** *o* **con** ~ **a** with reference to

rife'rire *vt* (*riportare*) to report; (*ascrivere*): ~ **qc a** to attribute sth to ♦ *vi* to do a report; ~**rsi** *vr*: ~**rsi a** to refer to

rifi'nire *vt* to finish off, put the finishing touches to; **rifini'tura** *sf* finishing touch; **rifiniture** *sfpl* (*di mobile, auto*) finish *sg*

rifiu'tare *vt* to refuse; ~ **di fare** to refuse to do; **rifi'uto** *sm* refusal; **rifiuti** *smpl* (*spazzatura*) rubbish *sg*, refuse *sg*

riflessi'one *sf* (*FISICA, meditazione*) reflection; (*il pensare*) thought, reflection; (*osservazione*) remark

ri'flessivo, a *ag* (*persona*) thoughtful, reflective; (*LING*) reflexive

ri'flesso, a *pp di* riflettere ♦ *sm* (*di luce, rispecchiamento*) reflection; (*FISIOL*) reflex; **di** *o* **per** ~ indirectly

ri'flettere *vt* to reflect ♦ *vi* to think; ~**rsi** *vr* to be reflected; ~ **su** to think over

riflet'tore *sm* reflector; (*proiettore*) floodlight; searchlight

ri'flusso *sm* flowing back; (*della marea*)

ebb; **un'epoca di** ~ an era of nostalgia

ri'fondere *vt* (*rimborsare*) to refund, repay

ri'forma *sf* reform; **la R~** (*REL*) the Reformation

rifor'mare *vt* to re-form; (*cambiare, innovare*) to reform; (*MIL: recluta*) to declare unfit for service; (: *soldato*) to invalid out, discharge; **riforma'torio** *sm* (*DIR*) community home (*BRIT*), reformatory (*US*)

riforni'mento *sm* supplying, providing; restocking; ~**i** *smpl* (*provviste*) supplies, provisions

rifor'nire *vt* (*provvedere*): ~ **di** to supply *o* provide with; (*fornire di nuovo: casa etc*) to restock

rifrazi'one [rifrat'tsjone] *sf* refraction

rifug'gire [rifud'dʒire] *vi* to escape again; (*fig*): ~ **da** to shun

rifugi'arsi [rifu'dʒarsi] *vr* to take refuge; **rifugi'ato, a** *sm/f* refugee

ri'fugio [ri'fudʒo] *sm* refuge, shelter; (*in montagna*) shelter; ~ **antiaereo** air-raid shelter

'riga, ghe *sf* line; (*striscia*) stripe; (*di persone, cose*) line, row; (*regolo*) ruler; (*scriminatura*) parting; **mettersi in** ~ to line up; **a** ~**ghe** (*foglio*) lined; (*vestito*) striped

ri'gagnolo [ri'gaɲɲolo] *sm* rivulet

ri'gare *vt* (*foglio*) to rule ♦ *vi*: ~ **diritto** (*fig*) to toe the line

rigatti'ere *sm* junk dealer

riget'tare [ridʒet'tare] *vt* (*gettare indietro*) to throw back; (*fig: respingere*) to reject; (*vomitare*) to bring *o* throw up; **ri'getto** *sm* (*anche MED*) rejection

rigidità [ridʒidi'ta] *sf* rigidity; stiffness; severity, rigours *pl*; strictness

'rigido, a [ridʒido] *ag* rigid, stiff; (*membra etc: indurite*) stiff; (*METEOR*) harsh, severe; (*fig*) strict

rigi'rare [ridʒi'rare] *vt* to turn; ~**rsi** *vr* to turn round; (*nel letto*) to turn over; ~ **qc tra le mani** to turn sth over in one's hands; ~ **il discorso** to change the subject

'rigo, ghi *sm* line; (*MUS*) staff, stave

rigogli'oso, a [rigoʎ'ʎoso] *ag (pianta)* luxuriant; *(fig: commercio, sviluppo)* thriving

ri'gonfio, a *ag* swollen

ri'gore *sm (METEOR)* harshness, rigours *pl*; *(fig)* severity, strictness; *(anche: calcio di ~)* penalty; **di ~** compulsory; **a rigor di termini** strictly speaking; **rigo'roso, a** *ag (severo: persona, ordine)* strict; *(preciso)* rigorous

rigover'nare *vt* to wash (up)

riguar'dare *vt* to look at again; *(considerare)* to regard, consider; *(concernere)* to regard, concern; **~rsi** *vr (aver cura di sé)* to look after o.s.

rigu'ardo *sm (attenzione)* care; *(considerazione)* regard, respect; **~ a** concerning, with regard to; **non aver ~i nell'agire/nel parlare** to act/speak freely

rilasci'are [rilaʃ'ʃare] *vt (rimettere in libertà)* to release; *(AMM: documenti)* to issue; **ri'lascio** *sm* release; issue

rilas'sare *vt* to relax; **~rsi** *vr* to relax; *(fig: disciplina)* to become slack

rile'gare *vt (libro)* to bind; **rilega'tura** *sf* binding

ri'leggere [ri'lɛddʒere] *vt* to reread, read again; *(rivedere)* to read over

ri'lento: a ~ *av* slowly

rileva'mento *sm (topografico, statistico)* survey; *(NAUT)* bearing

rile'vante *ag* considerable; important

rile'vare *vt (ricavare)* to find; *(notare)* to notice; *(mettere in evidenza)* to point out; *(venire a conoscere: notizia)* to learn; *(raccogliere: dati)* to gather, collect; *(TOPOGRAFIA)* to survey; *(MIL)* to relieve; *(COMM)* to take over

rili'evo *sm (ARTE, GEO)* relief; *(fig: rilevanza)* importance; *(osservazione)* point, remark; *(TOPOGRAFIA)* survey; **dar ~ a** *o* **mettere in ~ qc** *(fig)* to bring sth out, highlight sth

rilut'tante *ag* reluctant; **rilut'tanza** *sf* reluctance

'rima *sf* rhyme; *(verso)* verse

riman'dare *vt* to send again; *(restituire, rinviare)* to send back, return; *(differire):* ~ qc (a) to postpone sth *o* put sth off (till); *(fare riferimento):* ~ qn a to refer sb to; **essere rimandato** *(INS)* to have to repeat one's exams; **ri'mando** *sm (rinvio)* return; *(dilazione)* postponement; *(riferimento)* cross-reference

rima'nente *ag* remaining ♦ *sm* rest, remainder; **i ~i** *(persone)* the rest of them, the others; **rima'nenza** *sf* rest, remainder; **rimanenze** *sfpl (COMM)* unsold stock *sg*

rima'nere *vi (restare)* to remain, stay; *(avanzare)* to be left, remain; *(restare stupito)* to be amazed; *(restare, mancare):* **rimangono poche settimane a Pasqua** there are only a few weeks left till Easter; **rimane da vedere se** it remains to be seen whether; *(diventare):* **~ vedovo** to be left a widower; *(trovarsi):* **~ confuso/sorpreso** to be confused/ surprised

ri'mare *vt, vi* to rhyme

rimargi'nare [rimardʒi'nare] *vt, vi (anche: ~rsi)* to heal

ri'masto, a *pp di* **rimanere**

rima'sugli [rima'suʎʎi] *smpl* leftovers

rimbal'zare [rimbal'tsare] *vi* to bounce back, rebound; *(proiettile)* to ricochet; **rim'balzo** *sm* rebound; ricochet

rimbam'bito, a *ag* senile, in one's dotage

rimboc'care *vt (orlo)* to turn up; *(coperta)* to tuck in; *(maniche, pantaloni)* to turn *o* roll up

rimbom'bare *vi* to resound

rimbor'sare *vt* to pay back, repay; **rim'borso** *sm* repayment

rimedi'are *vi:* **~ a** to remedy ♦ *vt (fam: procurarsi)* to get *o* scrape together

ri'medio *sm (medicina)* medicine; *(cura, fig)* remedy, cure

rimesco'lare *vt* to mix well, stir well; *(carte)* to shuffle; **sentirsi ~ il sangue** *(per paura)* to feel one's blood run cold; *(per rabbia)* to feel one's blood boil

ri'messa *sf (locale: per veicoli)* garage; *(: per aerei)* hangar; *(COMM: di merce)* consignment; *(: di denaro)* remittance; *(TENNIS)* return; *(CALCIO: anche: ~ in gioco)* throw-in

ri'messo, a *pp di* **rimettere**

ri'mettere *vt* (*mettere di nuovo*) to put back; (*indossare di nuovo*): ~ **qc** to put sth back on, put sth on again; (*restituire*) to return, give back; (*affidare*) to entrust; (: *decisione*) to refer; (*condonare*) to remit; (*COMM: merci*) to deliver; (: *denaro*) to remit; (*vomitare*) to bring up; (*perdere: anche: rimetterci*) to lose; **~rsi al bello** (*tempo*) to clear up; **~rsi in salute** to get better, recover one's health

'rimmel ® *sm inv* mascara

rimoder'nare *vt* to modernize

rimon'tare *vt* (*meccanismo*) to reassemble; (: *tenda*) to put up again ♦ *vi* (*salire di nuovo*): ~ **in** (*macchina, treno*) to get back into; (*SPORT*) to close the gap

rimorchi'are [rimor'kjare] *vt* to tow; (*fig: ragazza*) to pick up; **rimorchia'tore** *sm* (*NAUT*) tug(boat)

ri'morchio [ri'mɔrkjo] *sm* tow; (*veicolo*) trailer

ri'morso *sm* remorse

rimozi'one [rimot'tsjone] *sf* removal; (*da un impiego*) dismissal; (*PSIC*) repression

rim'pasto *sm* (*POL*) reshuffle

rimpatri'are *vi* to return home ♦ *vt* to repatriate; **rim'patrio** *sm* repatriation

rimpi'angere [rim'pjandʒere] *vt* to regret; (*persona*) to miss; **rimpi'anto, a** *pp di* **rimpiangere** ♦ *sm* regret

rimpiat'tino *sm* hide-and-seek

rimpiaz'zare [rimpjat'tsare] *vt* to replace

rimpiccio'lire [rimpittʃo'lire] *vt* to make smaller ♦ *vi* (*anche: ~rsi*) to become smaller

rimpin'zare [rimpin'tsare] *vt*: ~ **di** to cram *o* stuff with

rimprove'rare *vt* to rebuke, reprimand; **rim'provero** *sm* rebuke, reprimand

rimugi'nare [rimudʒi'nare] *vt* (*fig*) to turn over in one's mind

rimunerazi'one [rimunerat'tsjone] *sf* remuneration; (*premio*) reward

rimu'overe *vt* to remove; (*destituire*) to dismiss

Rinasci'mento [rinaʃʃi'mento] *sm*: **il ~** the Renaissance

ri'nascita [ri'naʃʃita] *sf* rebirth, revival

rincal'zare [rinkal'tsare] *vt* (*palo, albero*) to support, prop up; (*lenzuola*) to tuck in

rinca'rare *vt* to increase the price of ♦ *vi* to go up, become more expensive

rinca'sare *vi* to go home

rinchi'udere [rin'kjudere] *vt* to shut (*o* lock) up; **~rsi** *vr*: **~rsi in** to shut o.s. up in; **~rsi in se stesso** to withdraw into o.s.; **rinchi'uso, a** *pp di* **rinchiudere**

rin'correre *vt* to chase, run after; **rin'corsa** *sf* short run; **rin'corso, a** *pp di* **rincorrere**

rin'crescere [rin'kreʃʃere] *vb impers*: **mi rincresce che/di non poter fare** I'm sorry that/I can't do, I regret that/being unable to do; **rincresci'mento** *sm* regret; **rincresci'uto, a** *pp di* **rincrescere**

rincu'lare *vi* to draw back; (*arma*) to recoil

rinfacci'are [rinfat'tʃare] *vt* (*fig*): ~ **qc qn** to throw sth in sb's face

rinfor'zare [rinfor'tsare] *vt* to reinforce, strengthen ♦ *vi* (*anche: ~rsi*) to grow stronger; **rin'forzo** *sm*: **mettere un rinforzo a** to strengthen; **di rinforzo** (*asse, sbarra*) strengthening; (*esercito*) supporting; (*personale*) extra, additional; **rinforzi** *smpl* (*MIL*) reinforcements

rinfran'care *vt* to encourage, reassure

rinfres'care *vt* (*atmosfera, temperatura*) to cool (down); (*abito, pareti*) to freshen up ♦ *vi* (*tempo*) to grow cooler; **~rsi** *vr* (*ristorarsi*) to refresh o.s.; (*lavarsi*) to freshen up; **rin'fresco, schi** *sm* (*festa*) party; **rinfreschi** *smpl* refreshments

rin'fusa *sf*: **alla ~** in confusion, higgledy-piggledy

ringhi'are [rin'gjare] *vi* to growl, snarl

ringhi'era [rin'gjɛra] *sf* railing; (*delle scale*) banister(s *pl*)

ringiova'nire [rindʒova'nire] *vt* (*sog: vestito, acconciatura etc*): ~ **qn** to make sb look younger; (: *vacanze etc*) to rejuvenate ♦ *vi* (*anche: ~rsi*) to become (*o* look) younger

ringrazia'mento [ringrattsja'mento] *sm* thanks *pl*

ringrazi'are [ringrat'tsjare] *vt* to thank;

~ **qn di qc** to thank sb for sth
rinne'gare *vt (fede)* to renounce; *(figlio)* to disown, repudiate; **rinne'gato, a** *sm/f* renegade
rinnova'mento *sm* renewal; *(economico)* revival
rinno'vare *vt* to renew; *(ripetere)* to repeat, renew; **rin'novo** *sm (di contratto)* renewal; **"chiuso per rinnovo dei locali"** "closed for alterations"
rinoce'ronte [rinotʃe'ronte] *sm* rhinoceros
rino'mato, a *ag* renowned, celebrated
rinsal'dare *vt* to strengthen
rintoc'care *vi (campana)* to toll; *(orologio)* to strike
rintracci'are [rintrat'tʃare] *vt* to track down
rintro'nare *vi* to boom, roar ♦ *vt (assordare)* to deafen; *(stordire)* to stun
ri'nuncia [ri'nuntʃa] *etc* = **rinunzia** *etc*
ri'nunzia [ri'nuntsja] *sf* renunciation
rinunzi'are [rinun'tsjare] *vi*: ~ **a** to give up, renounce
rinve'nire *vt* to find, recover; *(scoprire)* to discover, find out ♦ *vi (riprendere i sensi)* to come round; *(riprendere l'aspetto naturale)* to revive
rinvi'are *vt (rimandare indietro)* to send back, return; *(differire)*: ~ **qc (a)** to postpone sth *o* put sth off (till); to adjourn sth (till); *(fare un rimando)*: ~ **qn a** to refer sb to
rinvigo'rire *vt* to strengthen
rin'vio, 'vii *sm (rimando)* return; *(differimento)* postponement; *(: di seduta)* adjournment; *(in un testo)* cross-reference
ri'one *sm* district, quarter
riordi'nare *vt (rimettere in ordine)* to tidy; *(riorganizzare)* to reorganize
riorganiz'zare [riorganid'dzare] *vt* to reorganize
ripa'gare *vt* to repay
ripa'rare *vt (proteggere)* to protect, defend; *(correggere: male, torto)* to make up for; *(: errore)* to put right; *(aggiustare)* to repair ♦ *vi (mettere rimedio)*: ~ **a** to make up for; **~rsi** *vr (rifugiarsi)* to take refuge *o* shelter; **riparazi'one** *sf (di un*

torto) reparation; *(di guasto, scarpe)* repairing *no pl*; repair; *(risarcimento)* compensation
ri'paro *sm (protezione)* shelter, protection; *(rimedio)* remedy
ripar'tire *vt (dividere)* to divide up; *(distribuire)* to share out ♦ *vi* to set off again; to leave again
ripas'sare *vi* to come *(o* go) back ♦ *vt (scritto, lezione)* to go over (again)
ripen'sare *vi* to think; *(cambiare pensiero)* to change one's mind; *(tornare col pensiero)*: ~ **a** to recall
ripercu'otersi *vr*: ~ **su** *(fig)* to have repercussions on
ripercussi'one *sf (fig)*: **avere una** ~ *o* **delle ~i su** to have repercussions on
ripes'care *vt (pesce)* to catch again; *(persona, cosa)* to fish out; *(fig: ritrovare)* to dig out
ri'petere *vt* to repeat; *(ripassare)* to go over; **ripetizi'one** *sf* repetition; *(di lezione)* revision; **ripetizioni** *sfpl (INS)* private tutoring *o* coaching *sg*
ripi'ano *sm (GEO)* terrace; *(di mobile)* shelf
ri'picca *sf*: **per** ~ out of spite
'ripido, a *ag* steep
ripie'gare *vt* to refold; *(piegare più volte)* to fold (up) ♦ *vi (MIL)* to retreat, fall back; *(fig: accontentarsi)*: ~ **su** to make do with; **~rsi** *vr* to bend; **ripi'ego, ghi** *sm* expedient
ripi'eno, a *ag* full; *(CUC)* stuffed; *(: panino)* filled ♦ *sm (CUC)* stuffing
ri'porre *vt (porre al suo posto)* to put back, replace; *(mettere via)* to put away; *(fiducia, speranza)*: ~ **qc in qn** to place *o* put sth in sb
ripor'tare *vt (portare indietro)* to bring *(o* take) back; *(riferire)* to report; *(citare)* to quote; *(ricevere)* to receive, get; *(vittoria)* to gain; *(successo)* to have; *(MAT)* to carry; **~rsi a** *(anche fig)* to go back to; *(riferirsi a)* to refer to; ~ **danni** to suffer damage
ripo'sare *vt (bicchiere, valigia)* to put down; *(dare sollievo)* to rest ♦ *vi* to rest; **~rsi** *vr* to rest; **ri'poso** *sm* rest; *(MIL)*: **riposo!** at ease!; **a riposo** *(in pensione)*

retired; **giorno di riposo** day off
ripos'tiglio [ripos'tiʎʎo] *sm* lumber-room
ri'posto, a *pp di* **riporre**
ri'prendere *vt* (*prigioniero, fortezza*) to
recapture; (*prendere indietro*) to take
back; (*ricominciare: lavoro*) to resume;
(*andare a prendere*) to fetch, come back
for; (*assumere di nuovo: impiegati*) to take
on again, re-employ; (*rimproverare*) to tell
off; (*restringere: abito*) to take in; (CINEMA)
to shoot; **~rsi** *vr* to recover; (*correggersi*)
to correct o.s.; **ri'presa** *sf* recapture;
resumption; (*economica, da malattia,
emozione*) recovery; (AUT) acceleration *no
pl*; (TEATRO, CINEMA) rerun; (CINEMA: *presa*)
shooting *no pl*; shot; (SPORT) second half;
(: PUGILATO) round; **a più riprese** on
several occasions, several times; **ripreso,
a** *pp di* **riprendere**
ripristi'nare *vt* to restore
ripro'durre *vt* to reproduce; **riprodursi**
vr (BIOL) to reproduce; (*riformarsi*) to
form again; **riproduzi'one** *sf* reproduction; **riproduzione vietata** all rights
reserved
ripudi'are *vt* to repudiate, disown
ripu'gnante [ripuɲ'ɲante] *ag* disgusting,
repulsive
ripu'gnare [ripuɲ'ɲare] *vi*: **~ a qn** to
repel *o* disgust sb
ripu'lire *vt* to clean up; (*sog: ladri*) to
clean out; (*perfezionare*) to polish, refine
ri'quadro *sm* square; (ARCHIT) panel
ri'saia *sf* paddy field
risa'lire *vi* (*ritornare in su*) to go back up;
~ a (*ritornare con la mente*) to go back to;
(*datare da*) to date back to, go back to
risal'tare *vi* (*fig: distinguersi*) to stand
out; (ARCHIT) to project, jut out; **ri'salto**
sm prominence; (*sporgenza*) projection;
mettere *o* **porre in risalto qc** to make
sth stand out
risa'nare *vt* (*guarire*) to heal, cure;
(*palude*) to reclaim; (*economia*) to
improve; (*bilancio*) to reorganize
risa'puto, a *ag*: **è ~ che ...** everyone
knows that ..., it is common knowledge
that ...
risarci'mento [risartʃi'mento] *sm*: **~ (di)**

compensation (for)
risar'cire [risar'tʃire] *vt* (*cose*) to pay
compensation for; (*persona*): **~ qn di qc**
to compensate sb for sth
ri'sata *sf* laugh
riscalda'mento *sm* heating; **~ centrale**
central heating
riscal'dare *vt* (*scaldare*) to heat; (: *mani,
persona*) to warm; (*minestra*) to reheat;
~rsi *vr* to warm up
riscat'tare *vt* (*prigioniero*) to ransom, pay
a ransom for; (DIR) to redeem; **~rsi** *vr* (*da
disonore*) to redeem o.s.; **ris'catto** *sm*
ransom; redemption
rischia'rare [riskja'rare] *vt* (*illuminare*)
to light up; (*colore*) to make lighter; **~rsi**
vr (*tempo*) to clear up; (*cielo*) to clear; (*fig:
volto*) to brighten up; **~rsi la voce** to
clear one's throat
rischi'are [ris'kjare] *vt* to risk ♦ *vi*: **~ di
fare qc** to risk *o* run the risk of doing
sth
'rischio ['riskjo] *sm* risk; **rischi'oso, a**
ag risky, dangerous
riscia'cquare [riʃʃa'kware] *vt* to rinse
riscon'trare *vt* (*confrontare: due cose*) to
compare; (*esaminare*) to check, verify;
(*rilevare*) to find; **ris'contro** *sm*
comparison; check, verification; (AMM:
lettera di risposta) reply
ris'cossa *sf* (*riconquista*) recovery,
reconquest; *vedi anche* **riscosso**
riscossi'one *sf* collection
ris'cosso, a *pp di* **riscuotere**
ris'cuotere *vt* (*ritirare una somma
dovuta*) to collect; (: *stipendio*) to draw,
collect; (*assegno*) to cash; (*fig: successo etc*)
to win, earn; **~rsi** *vr*: **~rsi (da)** to shake
o.s. (out of), rouse o.s. (from)
risenti'mento *sm* resentment
risen'tire *vt* to hear again; (*provare*) to
feel ♦ *vi*: **~ di** to feel (*o* show) the effects
of; **~rsi** *vr*: **~rsi di** *o* **per** to take offence
at, resent; **risen'tito, a** *ag* resentful
ri'serbo *sm* reserve
ri'serva *sf* reserve; (*di caccia, pesca*)
preserve; (*restrizione, di indigeni*)
reservation; **di ~** (*provviste etc*) in reserve
riser'vare *vt* (*tenere in serbo*) to keep, put

aside; (*prenotare*) to book, reserve; **~rsi**
vr: **~rsi di fare qc** to intend to do sth;
riser'vato, a *ag* (*prenotato, fig: persona*)
reserved; (*confidenziale*) confidential;
riserva'tezza *sf* reserve
risi'edere *vi*: **~ a o in** to reside in
'**risma** *sf* (*di carta*) ream; (*fig*) kind, sort
'**riso** (*pl(f)* **~a**: *il ridere*) *sm*: **un ~** a laugh;
il ~ laughter; (*pianta*) rice ♦ *pp di* **ridere**
riso'lino *sm* snigger
ri'solto, a *pp di* **risolvere**
risolu'tezza [risolu'tettsa] *sf* determination
riso'luto, a *ag* determined, resolute
risoluzi'one [risolut'tsjone] *sf* solving *no
pl*; (*MAT*) solution; (*decisione, di immagine*)
resolution
ri'solvere *vt* (*difficoltà, controversia*) to
resolve; (*problema*) to solve; (*decidere*): **~
di fare** to resolve to do; **~rsi** *vr*
(*decidersi*): **~rsi a fare** to make up one's
mind to do; (*andare a finire*): **~rsi in** to
end up, turn out; **~rsi in nulla** to come
to nothing
riso'nanza [riso'nantsa] *sf* resonance;
aver vasta ~ (*fig: fatto etc*) to be known
far and wide
riso'nare *vt, vi* = **risuonare**
ri'sorgere [ri'sordʒere] *vi* to rise again;
risorgi'mento *sm* revival; **il Risorgimento** (*STORIA*) the Risorgimento
ri'sorsa *sf* expedient, resort; **~e** *sfpl*
(*naturali, finanziarie etc*) resources;
persona piena di ~e resourceful person
ri'sorto, a *pp di* **risorgere**
ri'sotto *sm* (*CUC*) risotto
risparmi'are *vt* to save; (*non uccidere*) to
spare ♦ *vi* to save; **~ qc a qn** to spare sb
sth
ris'parmio *sm* saving *no pl*; (*denaro*)
savings *pl*
rispec'chiare [rispek'kjare] *vt* to reflect
rispet'tabile *ag* respectable
rispet'tare *vt* to respect; **farsi ~** to
command respect
rispet'tivo, a *ag* respective
ris'petto *sm* respect; **~i** *smpl* (*saluti*)
respects, regards; **~ a** (*in paragone a*)
compared to; (*in relazione a*) as regards,

as for; **rispet'toso, a** *ag* respectful
ris'plendere *vi* to shine
ris'pondere *vi* to answer, reply; (*freni*) to
respond; **~ a** (*domanda*) to answer, reply
to; (*persona*) to answer; (*invito*) to reply
to; (*provocazione, sog: veicolo, apparecchio*) to respond to; (*corrispondere a*) to
correspond to; (: *speranze, bisogno*) to
answer; **~ di** to answer for; **ris'posta** *sf*
answer, reply; **in risposta a** in reply to;
risposto, a *pp di* **rispondere**
'**rissa** *sf* brawl
ristabi'lire *vt* to re-establish, restore;
(*persona: sog: riposo etc*) to restore to
health; (*persona*) **~rsi** *vr* to recover
rista'gnare [rista ɲ'ɲare] *vi* (*acqua*) to
become stagnant; (*sangue*) to cease
flowing; (*fig: industria*) to stagnate;
ris'tagno *sm* stagnation
ris'tampa *sf* reprinting *no pl*; reprint
risto'rante *sm* restaurant
risto'rarsi *vr* to have something to eat
and drink; (*riposarsi*) to rest, have a rest;
ris'toro *sm* (*bevanda, cibo*) refreshment;
servizio di ristoro (*FERR*) refreshments *pl*
ristret'tezza [ristret'tettsa] *sf* (*strettezza*)
narrowness; (*fig: scarsezza*) scarcity, lack;
(: *meschinità*) meanness; **~e** *sfpl* (*povertà*)
financial straits
ris'tretto, a *pp di* **restringere** ♦ *ag*
(*racchiuso*) enclosed, hemmed in;
(*angusto*) narrow; (*limitato*): **~ (a)**
restricted *o* limited (to); (*CUC: brodo*)
thick; (: *caffè*) extra strong
risucchi'are [risuk'kjare] *vt* to suck in
risul'tare *vi* (*dimostrarsi*) to prove (to be),
turn out (to be); (*riuscire*): **~ vincitore** to
emerge as the winner; **~ da** (*provenire*) to
result from, be the result of; **mi risulta
che ...** I understand that ...; **non mi
risulta** not as far as I know; **risul'tato** *sm*
result
risuo'nare *vi* (*rimbombare*) to resound
risurrezi'one [risurret'tsjone] *sf* (*REL*)
resurrection
risusci'tare [risuʃʃi'tare] *vt* to
resuscitate, restore to life; (*fig*) to revive,
bring back ♦ *vi* to rise (from the dead)
ris'veglio [riz've ʎʎo] *sm* waking up; (*fig*)

revival

ris'volto *sm* (*di giacca*) lapel; (*di pantaloni*) turn-up; (*di manica*) cuff; (*di tasca*) flap; (*di libro*) inside flap; (*fig*) implication

ritagli'are [ritaʎ'ʎare] *vt* (*tagliar via*) to cut out; **ri'taglio** *sm* (*di giornale*) cutting, clipping; (*di stoffa etc*) scrap; **nei ritagli di tempo** in one's spare time

ritar'dare *vi* (*persona, treno*) to be late; (*orologio*) to be slow ♦ *vt* (*rallentare*) to slow down; (*impedire*) to delay, hold up; (*differire*) to postpone, delay; **ritarda'tario, a** *sm/f* latecomer

ri'tardo *sm* delay; (*di persona aspettata*) lateness *no pl*; (*fig: mentale*) backwardness; **in ~** late

ri'tegno [ri'teɲɲo] *sm* restraint

rite'nere *vt* (*trattenere*) to hold back; (: *somma*) to deduct; (*giudicare*) to consider, believe; **rite'nuta** *sf* (*sul salario*) deduction

riti'rare *vt* to withdraw; (*POL: richiamare*) to recall; (*andare a prendere: pacco etc*) to collect, pick up; **~rsi** *vr* to withdraw; (*da un'attività*) to retire; (*stoffa*) to shrink; (*marea*) to recede; **riti'rata** *sf* (*MIL*) retreat; (*latrina*) lavatory; **ri'tiro** *sm* withdrawal; recall; collection; (*luogo appartato*) retreat

'ritmo *sm* rhythm; (*fig*) rate; (: *della vita*) pace, tempo

'rito *sm* rite; **di ~** usual, customary

ritoc'care *vt* (*disegno, fotografia*) to touch up; (*testo*) to alter; **ri'tocco, chi** *sm* touching up *no pl*; alteration

ritor'nare *vi* to return, go (o come) back; (*ripresentarsi*) to recur; (*ridiventare*): **~ ricco** to become rich again ♦ *vt* (*restituire*) to return, give back

ritor'nello *sm* refrain

ri'torno *sm* return; **essere di ~** to be back; **avere un ~ di fiamma** (*AUT*) to backfire; (*fig: persona*) to be back in love again

ritorsi'one *sf* retaliation

ri'trarre *vt* (*trarre indietro, via*) to withdraw; (*distogliere: sguardo*) to turn away; (*rappresentare*) to portray, depict;

(*ricavare*) to get, obtain

ritrat'tare *vt* (*disdire*) to retract, take back; (*trattare nuovamente*) to deal with again

ri'tratto, a *pp di* **ritrarre** ♦ *sm* portrait

ri'troso, a *ag* (*restio*): **~ (a)** reluctant (to); (*schivo*) shy; **andare a ~** to go backwards

ritro'vare *vt* to find; (*salute*) to regain; (*persona*) to find; to meet again; **~rsi** *vr* (*essere, capitare*) to find o.s.; (*raccapezzarsi*) to find one's way; (*con senso reciproco*) to meet (again); **ri'trovo** *sm* meeting place; **ritrovo notturno** night club

'ritto, a *ag* (*in piedi*) standing, on one's feet; (*levato in alto*) erect, raised; (: *capelli*) standing on end; (*posto verticalmente*) upright

ritu'ale *ag, sm* ritual

riuni'one *sf* (*adunanza*) meeting; (*riconciliazione*) reunion

riu'nire *vt* (*ricongiungere*) to join (together); (*riconciliare*) to reunite, bring together (again); **~rsi** *vr* (*adunarsi*) to meet; (*tornare a stare insieme*) to be reunited

riu'scire [riuʃ'ʃire] *vi* (*uscire di nuovo*) to go out again, go back out; (*aver esito: fatti, azioni*) to go, turn out; (*aver successo*) to succeed, be successful; (*essere, apparire*) to be, prove; (*raggiungere il fine*) to manage, succeed; **~ a fare qc** to manage to do *o* succeed in doing *o* be able to do sth; **questo mi riesce nuovo** this is new to me; **riu'scita** *sf* (*esito*) result, outcome; (*buon esito*) success

'riva *sf* (*di fiume*) bank; (*di lago, mare*) shore

ri'vale *sm/f* rival; **rivalità** *sf* rivalry

ri'valsa *sf* (*rivincita*) revenge; (*risarcimento*) compensation

rivalu'tare *vt* (*ECON*) to revalue

rivan'gare *vt* (*ricordi etc*) to dig up (again)

rive'dere *vt* to see again; (*ripassare*) to revise; (*verificare*) to check

rive'lare *vt* to reveal; (*divulgare*) to reveal, disclose; (*dare indizio*) to reveal, show; **~rsi** *vr* (*manifestarsi*) to be revealed; **~rsi onesto** *etc* to prove to be honest *etc*; **rivela'tore** *sm* (*TECN*) detector; (*FOT*) developer; **rivelazi'one** *sf* revelation

rivendi'care *vt* to claim, demand

ri'vendita *sf* (*bottega*) retailer's (shop)

rivendi'tore, 'trice *sm/f* retailer; **~ autorizzato** (*COMM*) authorized dealer

ri'verbero *sm* (*di luce, calore*) reflection; (*di suono*) reverberation

rive'renza [rive'rɛntsa] *sf* reverence; (*inchino*) bow; curtsey

rive'rire *vt* (*rispettare*) to revere; (*salutare*) to pay one's respects to

river'sare *vt* (*anche fig*) to pour; **~rsi** *vr* (*fig: persone*) to pour out

rivesti'mento *sm* covering; coating

rives'tire *vt* to dress again; (*ricoprire*) to cover; to coat; (*fig: carica*) to hold; **~rsi** *vr* to get dressed again; to change (one's clothes)

rivi'era *sf* coast; **la ~ italiana** the Italian Riviera

ri'vincita [ri'vintʃita] *sf* (*SPORT*) return match; (*fig*) revenge

rivis'suto, a *pp di* **rivivere**

ri'vista *sf* review; (*periodico*) magazine, review; (*TEATRO*) revue; variety show

ri'vivere *vi* (*riacquistare forza*) to come alive again; (*tornare in uso*) to be revived ♦ *vt* to relive

ri'volgere [ri'vɔldʒere] *vt* (*attenzione, sguardo*) to turn, direct; (*parole*) to address; **~rsi** *vr* to turn round; (*fig: dirigersi per informazioni*): **~rsi a** to go and see, go and speak to; (: *ufficio*) to enquire at

ri'volta *sf* revolt, rebellion

rivol'tare *vt* to turn over; (*con l'interno all'esterno*) to turn inside out; (*disgustare: stomaco*) to upset, turn; **~rsi** *vr* (*ribellarsi*): **~rsi (a)** to rebel (against)

rivol'tella *sf* revolver

ri'volto, a *pp di* **rivolgere**

rivoluzio'nare [rivoluttsjo'nare] *vt* to revolutionize

rivoluzio'nario, a [rivoluttsjo'narjo] *ag, sm/f* revolutionary

rivoluzi'one [rivolut'tsjone] *sf* revolution

riz'zare [rit'tsare] *vt* to raise, erect; **~rsi**

vr to stand up; (*capelli*) to stand on end

'roba *sf* stuff, things *pl*; (*possessi, beni*) belongings *pl*, things *pl*, possessions *pl*; **~ da mangiare** things *pl* to eat, food; **~ da matti** sheer madness *o* lunacy

'robot *sm inv* robot

ro'busto, a *ag* robust, sturdy; (*solido: catena*) strong

'rocca, che *sf* fortress

rocca'forte *sf* stronghold

roc'chetto [rok'ketto] *sm* reel, spool

'roccia, ce [rɔttʃa] *sf* rock; **fare ~** (*SPORT*) to go rock climbing; **roc'cioso, a** *ag* rocky

ro'daggio [ro'daddʒo] *sm* running (*BRIT*) *o* breaking (*US*) in; **in ~** running (*BRIT*) *o* breaking (*US*) in

'Rodano *sm*: **il ~** the Rhone

'rodere *vt* to gnaw (at); (*distruggere poco a poco*) to eat into

rodi'tore *sm* (*ZOOL*) rodent

rodo'dendro *sm* rhododendron

'rogna [ˈrɔɲɲa] *sf* (*MED*) scabies *sg*; (*fig*) bother, nuisance

ro'gnone [roɲˈɲone] *sm* (*CUC*) kidney

'rogo, ghi *sm* (*per cadaveri*) (funeral) pyre; (*supplizio*): **il ~** the stake

rol'lio *sm* roll(ing)

'Roma *sf* Rome

Roma'nia *sf*: **la ~** Romania

ro'manico, a, ci, che *ag* Romanesque

ro'mano, a *ag, sm/f* Roman

romanti'cismo [romanti'tʃizmo] *sm* romanticism

ro'mantico, a, ci, che *ag* romantic

ro'manza [ro'mandza] *sf* (*MUS, LETTERATURA*) romance

roman'zesco, a, schi, sche [roman'dzesko] *ag* (*stile, personaggi*) fictional; (*fig*) storybook *cpd*

romanzi'ere [roman'dzjere] *sm* novelist

ro'manzo, a [ro'mandzo] *ag* (*LING*) romance *cpd* ♦ *sm* (*medievale*) romance; (*moderno*) novel; **~ d'appendice** serial (story)

rom'bare *vi* to rumble, thunder, roar

'rombo *sm* rumble, thunder, roar; (*MAT*) rhombus; (*ZOOL*) turbot; brill

ro'meno, a *ag, sm/f, sm* = **rumeno, a**

'rompere *vt* to break; (*conversazione, fidanzamento*) to break off ♦ *vi* to break; ~rsi *vr* to break; **mi rompe le scatole** (*fam*) he (*o* she) is a pain in the neck; ~rsi un braccio to break an arm; rompi'capo *sm* worry, headache; (*indovinello*) puzzle; (*in enigmistica*) brainteaser; rompighi'accio *sm* (*NAUT*) icebreaker; rompis'catole (*fam*) *sm/f inv* pest, pain in the neck

'ronda *sf* (*MIL*) rounds *pl*, patrol

ron'della *sf* (*TECN*) washer

'rondine *sf* (*ZOOL*) swallow

ron'done *sm* (*ZOOL*) swift

ron'zare [ron'dzare] *vi* to buzz, hum

ron'zino [ron'dzino] *sm* (*peg: cavallo*) nag

'rosa *sf* rose ♦ *ag inv*, *sm* pink; ro'saio *sm* (*pianta*) rosebush, rose tree; (*giardino*) rose garden; ro'sario *sm* (*REL*) rosary; ro'sato, a *ag* pink, rosy ♦ *sm* (*vino*) rosé (wine); ro'seo, a *ag* (*anche fig*) rosy

rosicchi'are [rosik'kjare] *vt* to gnaw (at); (*mangiucchiare*) to nibble (at)

rosma'rino *sm* rosemary

'roso, a *pp di* rodere

roso'lare *vt* (*CUC*) to brown

roso'lia *sf* (*MED*) German measles *sg*, rubella

ro'sone *sm* rosette; (*vetrata*) rose window

'rospo *sm* (*ZOOL*) toad

ros'setto *sm* (*per labbra*) lipstick; (*per guance*) rouge

'rosso, a *ag*, *sm*, *sm/f* red; **il mar R**~ the Red Sea; ~ **d'uovo** egg yolk; ros'sore *sm* flush, blush

rosticce'ria [rostittʃe'ria] *sf* shop selling roast meat and other cooked food

ro'tabile *ag* (*percorribile*): **strada** ~ roadway; (*FERR*): **materiale** ~ rolling stock

ro'taia *sf* rut, track; (*FERR*) rail

ro'tare *vt*, *vi* to rotate; rotazi'one *sf* rotation

rote'are *vt*, *vi* to whirl; ~ **gli occhi** to roll one's eyes

ro'tella *sf* small wheel; (*di mobile*) castor

roto'lare *vt*, *vi* to roll; ~rsi *vr* to roll (about)

'rotolo *sm* roll; **andare a** ~**i** (*fig*) to go to

rack and ruin

ro'tonda *sf* rotunda

ro'tondo, a *ag* round

ro'tore *sm* rotor

'rotta *sf* (*AER*, *NAUT*) course, route; (*MIL*) rout; **a** ~ **di collo** at breakneck speed; **essere in** ~ **con qn** to be on bad terms with sb

rot'tame *sm* fragment, scrap, broken bit; ~**i** *smpl* (*di nave, aereo etc*) wreckage *sg*

'rotto, a *pp di* rompere ♦ *ag* broken; (*calzoni*) torn, split; (*persona: pratico, resistente*): ~ **a** accustomed *o* inured to; **per il** ~ **della cuffia** by the skin of one's teeth

rot'tura *sf* breaking *no pl*; break; breaking off; (*MED*) fracture, break

rou'lotte [ru'lɔt] *sf* caravan

ro'vente *ag* red-hot

'rovere *sm* oak

rovesci'are [roveʃ'ʃare] *vt* (*versare in giù*) to pour; (*: accidentalmente*) to spill; (*capovolgere*) to turn upside down; (*gettare a terra*) to knock down; (*: fig: governo*) to overthrow; (*piegare all'indietro: testa*) to throw back; ~rsi *vr* (*sedia, macchina*) to overturn; (*barca*) to capsize; (*liquido*) to spill; (*fig: situazione*) to be reversed

ro'vescio, sci [ro'veʃʃo] *sm* other side, wrong side; (*della mano*) back; (*di moneta*) reverse; (*pioggia*) sudden downpour; (*fig*) setback; (*MAGLIA: anche: punto* ~) purl (stitch); (*TENNIS*) backhand (stroke); **a** ~ upside-down; inside-out; **capire qc a** ~ to misunderstand sth

ro'vina *sf* ruin; **andare in** ~ (*andare a pezzi*) to collapse; (*fig*) to go to rack and ruin

rovi'nare *vi* to collapse, fall down ♦ *vt* (*far cadere giù: casa*) to demolish; (*danneggiare, fig*) to ruin; rovi'noso, a *ag* disastrous; damaging; violent

rovis'tare *vt* (*casa*) to ransack; (*tasche*) to rummage in (*o* through)

'rovo *sm* (*BOT*) blackberry bush, bramble bush

'rozzo, a ['roddzo] *ag* rough, coarse

'ruba *sf*: **andare a** ~ to sell like hot cakes

ru'bare *vt* to steal; ~ qc a qn to steal sth from sb

rubi'netto *sm* tap, faucet (*US*)

ru'bino *sm* ruby

ru'brica, che *sf* (*STAMPA*) column; (*quadernetto*) index book; address book

'rude *ag* tough, rough

'rudere *sm* (*rovina*) ruins *pl*

rudimen'tale *ag* rudimentary, basic

rudi'menti *smpl* rudiments; basic principles; basic knowledge *sg*

ruffi'ano *sm* pimp

'ruga, ghe *sf* wrinkle

'ruggine ['ruddʒine] *sf* rust

rug'gire [rud'dʒire] *vi* to roar

rugi'ada [ru'dʒada] *sf* dew

ru'goso, a *ag* wrinkled

rul'lare *vi* (*tamburo, nave*) to roll; (*aereo*) to taxi

rul'lino *sm* (*FOT*) spool; (: *pellicola*) film

'rullo *sm* (*di tamburi*) roll; (*arnese cilindrico, TIP*) roller; ~ compressore steam roller; ~ di pellicola roll of film

rum *sm* rum

ru'meno, a *ag*, *sm/f*, *sm* Romanian

rumi'nare *vt* (*ZOOL*) to ruminate

ru'more *sm*: un ~ a noise, a sound; (*fig*) a rumour; il ~ noise; rumo'roso, a *ag* noisy

ru'olo *sm* (*TEATRO, fig*) role, part; (*elenco*) roll, register, list; di ~ permanent, on the permanent staff

ru'ota *sf* wheel; a ~ (*forma*) circular; ~ anteriore/posteriore front/back wheel; ~ di scorta spare wheel

ruo'tare *vt*, *vi* = rotare

'rupe *sf* cliff

ru'rale *ag* rural, country *cpd*

ru'scello [ruʃ'ʃɛllo] *sm* stream

'ruspa *sf* excavator

rus'sare *vi* to snore

'Russia *sf*: la ~ Russia; 'russo, a *ag*, *sm/f*, *sm* Russian

'rustico, a, ci, che *ag* rustic; (*fig*) rough, unrefined

rut'tare *vi* to belch; 'rutto *sm* belch

'ruvido, a *ag* rough, coarse

ruzzo'lare [ruttso'lare] *vi* to tumble down; ruzzo'loni *av*: cadere ruzzoloni

to tumble down; fare le scale ruzzoloni to tumble down the stairs

S

S. *abbr* (= *sud*) S

sa *vb vedi* sapere

'sabato *sm* Saturday; di *o* il ~ on Saturdays

'sabbia *sf* sand; ~e mobili quicksand(s); sabbi'oso, a *ag* sandy

sabo'taggio [sabo'taddʒo] *sm* sabotage

sabo'tare *vt* to sabotage

'sacca, che *sf* bag; (*bisaccia*) haversack; (*insenatura*) inlet; ~ da viaggio travelling bag

sacca'rina *sf* saccharin(e)

sac'cente [sat'tʃɛnte] *sm/f* know-all (*BRIT*), know-it-all (*US*)

sacchegi'are [sakked'dʒare] *vt* to sack, plunder; sac'cheggio *sm* sack(ing)

sac'chetto [sak'ketto] *sm* (small) bag; (small) sack

'sacco, chi *sm* bag; (*per carbone etc*) sack; (*ANAT, BIOL*) sac; (*tela*) sacking; (*saccheggio*) sack(ing); (*fig: grande quantità*): un ~ di lots of, heaps of; ~ a pelo sleeping bag; ~ per i rifiuti bin bag

sacer'dote [satʃer'dɔte] *sm* priest; sacer'dozio *sm* priesthood

sacra'mento *sm* sacrament

sacrifi'care *vt* to sacrifice; ~rsi *vr* to sacrifice o.s.; (*privarsi di qc*) to make sacrifices

sacri'ficio [sakri'fitʃo] *sm* sacrifice

sacri'legio [sacri'lɛdʒo] *sm* sacrilege

'sacro, a *ag* sacred

'sadico, a, ci, che *ag* sadistic ♦ *sm/f* sadist

sa'etta *sf* arrow; (*fulmine: anche fig*) thunderbolt; flash of lightning

sa'fari *sm inv* safari

sa'gace [sa'gatʃe] *ag* shrewd, sagacious

sag'gezza [sad'dʒettsa] *sf* wisdom

saggi'are [sad'dʒare] *vt* (*metalli*) to assay; (*fig*) to test

'saggio, a, gi, ge ['saddʒo] *ag* wise ♦ *sm* (*persona*) sage; (*operazione speri-*

mentale) test; (: *dell'oro*) assay; (*fig: prova*) proof; (*campione indicativo*) sample; (*ricerca, esame critico*) essay

Sagit'tario [sadʒit'tarjo] *sm* Sagittarius

'sagoma *sf* (*profilo*) outline, profile; (*forma*) form, shape; (*TECN*) template; (*bersaglio*) target; (*fig: persona*) character

'sagra *sf* festival

sagres'tano *sm* sacristan; sexton

sagres'tia *sf* sacristy; (*culto protestante*) vestry

Sa'hara [sa'ara] *sm*: **il (deserto del) ~** the Sahara (Desert)

'sai *vb vedi* **sapere**

'sala *sf* hall; (*stanza*) room; **~ d'aspetto** waiting room; **~ da ballo** ballroom; **~ per concerti** concert hall; **~ da gioco** gaming room; **~ operatoria** operating theatre; **~ da pranzo** dining room

sa'lame *sm* salami *no pl*, salami sausage

sala'moia *sf* (*CUC*) brine

sa'lare *vt* to salt

salari'ato, a *sm/f* wage-earner

sa'lario *sm* pay, wages *pl*

sa'lato, a *ag* (*sapore*) salty; (*CUC*) salted, salt *cpd*; (*fig: discorso etc*) biting, sharp; (: *prezzi*) steep, stiff

sal'dare *vt* (*congiungere*) to join, bind; (*parti metalliche*) to solder; (: *con saldatura autogena*) to weld; (*conto*) to settle, pay; **salda'tura** *sf* soldering; welding; (*punto saldato*) soldered joint; weld

sal'dezza [sal'dettsa] *sf* firmness; strength

'saldo, a *ag* (*resistente, forte*) strong, firm; (*fermo*) firm, steady, stable; (*fig*) firm, steadfast ♦ *sm* (*svendita*) sale; (*di conto*) settlement; (*ECON*) balance

'sale *sm* salt; (*fig*): **ha poco ~ in zucca** he doesn't have much sense; **~ fino/grosso** table/cooking salt

'salice ['salitʃe] *sm* willow; **~ piangente** weeping willow

sali'ente *ag* (*fig*) salient, main

sali'era *sf* salt cellar

sa'lina *sf* saltworks *sg*

sa'lino, a *ag* saline

sa'lire *vi* to go (*o come*) up; (*aereo etc*) to climb, go up; (*passeggero*) to get on; (*sentiero, prezzi, livello*) to go up, rise ♦ *vt* (*scale, gradini*) to go (*o come*) up; **~ su** to climb (up); **~ sul treno/sull'autobus** to board the train/the bus; **~ in macchina** to get into the car; **sa'lita** *sf* climb, ascent; (*erta*) hill, slope; **in salita** *ag, av* uphill

sa'liva *sf* saliva

'salma *sf* corpse

'salmo *sm* psalm

sal'mone *sm* salmon

sa'lone *sm* (*stanza*) sitting room, lounge; (*in albergo*) lounge; (*su nave*) lounge, saloon; (*mostra*) show, exhibition; **~ di bellezza** beauty salon

sa'lotto *sm* lounge, sitting room; (*mobilio*) lounge suite

sal'pare *vi* (*NAUT*) to set sail; (*anche*: **~ l'ancora**) to weigh anchor

'salsa *sf* (*CUC*) sauce; **~ di pomodoro** tomato sauce

sal'siccia, ce [sal'sittʃa] *sf* pork sausage

sal'tare *vi* to jump, leap; (*esplodere*) to blow up, explode; (: *valvola*) to blow; (*venir via*) to pop off; (*non aver luogo: corso etc*) to be cancelled ♦ *vt* to jump (over), leap (over); (*fig: pranzo, capitolo*) to skip, miss (out); (*CUC*) to sauté; **far ~** to blow up; to burst open; **~ fuori** (*fig: apparire all'improvviso*) to turn up

saltel'lare *vi* to skip; to hop

saltim'banco *sm* acrobat

'salto *sm* jump; (*SPORT*) jumping; **fare un ~** to jump, leap; **fare un ~ da qn** to pop over to sb's (place); **~ in alto/lungo** high/long jump; **~ con l'asta** pole vaulting; **~ mortale** somersault

saltu'ario, a *ag* occasional, irregular

sa'lubre *ag* healthy, salubrious

salume'ria *sf* delicatessen

sa'lumi *smpl* salted pork meats

salu'tare *ag* healthy; (*fig*) salutary, beneficial ♦ *vt* (*per dire buon giorno, fig*) to greet; (*per dire addio*) to say goodbye to; (*MIL*) to salute

sa'lute *sf* health; **~!** (*a chi starnutisce*) bless you!; (*nei brindisi*) cheers!; **bere alla ~ di qn** to drink (to) sb's health

sa'luto *sm* (*gesto*) wave; (*parola*) greeting; (*MIL*) salute; ~i *smpl* (*formula di cortesia*) greetings; cari ~i best regards; vogliate gradire i nostri più distinti ~i Yours faithfully

salvacon'dotto *sm* (*MIL*) safe-conduct

salva'gente [salva'dʒɛnte] *sm* (*NAUT*) lifebuoy; (*stradale*) traffic island; ~ a ciambella life belt; ~ a giubbotto lifejacket

salvaguar'dare *vt* to safeguard

sal'vare *vt* to save; (*trarre da un pericolo*) to rescue; (*proteggere*) to protect; ~rsi *vr* to save o.s.; to escape; salva'taggio *sm* rescue; salva'tore, 'trice *sm/f* saviour

'salve (*fam*) *escl* hi!

sal'vezza [sal'vettsa] *sf* salvation; (*sicurezza*) safety

'salvia *sf* (*BOT*) sage

'salvo, a *ag* safe, unhurt, unharmed; (*fuori pericolo*) safe, out of danger ♦ *sm*: in ~ safe ♦ *prep* (*eccetto*) except; mettere qc in ~ to put sth in a safe place; ~ che (*a meno che*) unless; (*eccetto che*) except (that); ~ imprevisti barring accidents

sam'buco *sm* elder (tree)

san *ag vedi* santo

sa'nare *vt* to heal, cure; (*economia*) to put right

san'cire [san'tʃire] *vt* to sanction

'sandalo *sm* (*BOT*) sandalwood; (*calzatura*) sandal

'sangue *sm* blood; farsi cattivo ~ to fret, get in a state; ~ freddo (*fig*) sang-froid, calm; a ~ freddo in cold blood; sangu'igno, a *ag* blood *cpd*; (*colore*) blood-red; sangui'nare *vi* to bleed; sangui'noso, a *ag* bloody; sangui'suga *sf* leech

sanità *sf* health; (*salubrità*) healthiness; Ministero della S~ Department of Health; ~ mentale sanity

sani'tario, a *ag* health *cpd*; (*condizioni*) sanitary ♦ *sm* (*AMM*) doctor; (*impianti*) ~i *smpl* bathroom *o* sanitary fittings

'sanno *vb vedi* sapere

'sano, a *ag* healthy; (*denti, costituzione*) healthy, sound; (*integro*) whole, unbroken; (*fig: politica, consigli*) sound; ~ di mente

sane; di ~a pianta completely, entirely; ~ e salvo safe and sound

sant' *ag vedi* santo

santifi'care *vt* to sanctify; (*feste*) to observe

santità *sf* sanctity; holiness; Sua/Vostra ~ (*titolo di Papa*) His/Your Holiness

'santo, a *ag* holy; (*fig*) saintly; (*seguito da nome proprio*) saint ♦ *sm/f* saint; la S~a Sede the Holy See

santu'ario *sm* sanctuary

sanzio'nare [santsjo'nare] *vt* to sanction

sanzi'one [san'tsjone] *sf* sanction; (*penale, civile*) sanction, penalty

sa'pere *vt* to know; (*essere capace di*): so nuotare I know how to swim, I can swim ♦ *vi*: ~ di (*aver sapore*) to taste of; (*aver odore*) to smell of ♦ *sm* knowledge; far ~ qc a qn to inform sb about sth, let sb know sth; mi sa che non sia vero I don't think that's true

sapi'enza [sa'pjentsa] *sf* wisdom

sa'pone *sm* soap; ~ da bucato washing soap; sapo'netta *sf* cake *o* bar *o* tablet of soap

sa'pore *sm* taste, flavour; sapo'rito, a *ag* tasty

sappi'amo *vb vedi* sapere

saraci'nesca [saratʃi'neska] *sf* (*serranda*) rolling shutter

sar'casmo *sm* sarcasm *no pl*; sarcastic remark

Sar'degna [sar'deɲɲa] *sf*: la ~ Sardinia

sar'dina *sf* sardine

'sardo, a *ag, sm/f* Sardinian

'sarto, a *sm/f* tailor/dressmaker; sarto'ria *sf* tailor's (shop); dressmaker's (shop); (*casa di moda*) fashion house; (*arte*) couture

'sasso *sm* stone; (*ciottolo*) pebble; (*masso*) rock

sas'sofono *sm* saxophone

sas'soso, a *ag* stony; pebbly

'Satana *sm* Satan; sa'tanico, a, ci, che *ag* satanic, fiendish

sa'tellite *sm, ag* satellite

'satira *sf* satire

'saturo, a *ag* saturated; (*fig*): ~ di full of

'S.A.U.B. ['saub] *sigla f* (= *Struttura*

Amministrativa Unificata di Base) state welfare system

'sauna *sf* sauna

Sa'voia *sf:* **la ~** Savoy

savoi'ardo, a *ag* of Savoy, Savoyard ♦ *sm (biscotto)* sponge finger

sazi'are [sat'tsjare] *vt* to satisfy, satiate; **~rsi** *vr (riempirsi di cibo):* **~rsi (di)** to eat one's fill (of); *(fig):* **~rsi di** to grow tired *o* weary of

'sazio, a ['sattsjo] *ag:* **~ (di)** sated (with), full (of); *(fig: stufo)* fed up (with), sick (of)

sba'dato, a *ag* careless, inattentive

sbadigli'are [zbadiʎ'ʎare] *vi* to yawn; **sba'diglio** *sm* yawn

sbagli'are [zbaʎ'ʎare] *vt* to make a mistake in, get wrong ♦ *vi* to make a mistake, be mistaken, be wrong; *(operare in modo non giusto)* to err; **~rsi** *vr* to make a mistake, be mistaken, be wrong; **~ la mira/strada** to miss one's aim/take the wrong road; **'sbaglio** *sm* mistake, error; *(morale)* error; **fare uno sbaglio** to make a mistake

sbal'lare *vt (merce)* to unpack ♦ *vi (nel fare un conto)* to overestimate; *(fam: gergo della droga)* to get high

sballot'tare *vt* to toss (about)

sbalor'dire *vt* to stun, amaze ♦ *vi* to be stunned, be amazed; **sbalordi'tivo, a** *ag* amazing; *(prezzo)* incredible, absurd

sbal'zare [zbal'tsare] *vt* to throw, hurl ♦ *vi (balzare)* to bounce; *(saltare)* to leap, bound; **'sbalzo** *sm (spostamento improvviso)* jolt, jerk; **a sbalzi** jerkily; *(fig)* in fits and starts; **uno sbalzo di temperatura** a sudden change in temperature

sban'dare *vi (NAUT)* to list; *(AER)* to bank; *(AUT)* to skid; **~rsi** *vr (folla)* to disperse; *(fig: famiglia)* to break up

sbandie'rare *vt (bandiera)* to wave; *(fig)* to parade, show off

sbaragli'are [zbaraʎ'ʎare] *vt (MIL)* to rout; *(in gare sportive etc)* to beat, defeat

sba'raglio [zba'raʎʎo] *sm* rout; defeat; **gettarsi allo ~** to risk everything

sbaraz'zarsi [zbarat'tsarsi] *vr:* **~ di** to get rid of, rid o.s. of

sbar'care *vt (passeggeri)* to disembark; *(merci)* to unload ♦ *vi* to disembark; **'sbarco** *sm* disembarkation; unloading; *(MIL)* landing

'sbarra *sf* bar; *(di passaggio a livello)* barrier; *(DIR):* **presentarsi alla ~** to appear before the court

sbarra'mento *sm (stradale)* barrier; *(diga)* dam, barrage; *(MIL)* barrage

sbar'rare *vt (strada etc)* to block, bar; *(assegno)* to cross; **~ il passo** to bar the way; **~ gli occhi** to open one's eyes wide

'sbattere *vt (porta)* to slam, bang; *(tappeti, ali, CUC)* to beat; *(urtare)* to knock, hit ♦ *vi (porta, finestra)* to bang; *(agitarsi: ali, vele etc)* to flap; **me ne sbatto!** *(fam)* I don't give a damn!; **sbat'tuto, a** *ag (viso, aria)* dejected, worn out; *(uovo)* beaten

sba'vare *vi* to dribble; *(colore)* to smear, smudge

sbia'dire *vi, vt* to fade; **~rsi** *vr* to fade, **sbia'dito, a** *ag* faded; *(fig)* colourless, dull

sbian'care *vt* to whiten; *(tessuto)* to bleach ♦ *vi (impallidire)* to grow pale *o* white

sbi'eco, a, chi, che *ag (storto)* squint, askew; **di ~: guardare qn di ~** *(fig)* to look askance at sb; **tagliare una stoffa di ~** to cut a material on the bias

sbigot'tire *vt* to dismay, stun ♦ *vi (anche: ~rsi)* to be dismayed

sbilanci'are [zbilan'tʃare] *vt* to throw off balance; **~rsi** *vr (perdere l'equilibrio)* to overbalance, lose one's balance; *(fig: compromettersi)* to compromise o.s.

sbirci'are [zbir'tʃare] *vt* to cast sidelong glances at, eye

'sbirro *(peg)* *sm* cop

sbizzar'rirsi [zbiddzar'rirsi] *vr* to indulge one's whims

sbloc'care *vt* to unblock, free; *(freno)* to release; *(prezzi, affitti)* to decontrol

sboc'care *vi:* **~ in** *(fiume)* to flow into; *(strada)* to lead into; *(persona)* to come (out) into; *(fig: concludersi)* to end (up) in

sboc'cato, a *ag (persona)* foul-mouthed; *(linguaggio)* foul

sbocci'are [zbot'tʃare] *vi* (*fiore*) to bloom, open (out)

'sbocco, chi *sm* (*di fiume*) mouth; (*di strada*) end; (*di tubazione, COMM*) outlet; (*uscita: anche fig*) way out; **siamo in una situazione senza ~chi** there's no way out of this for us

sbol'lire *vi* (*fig*) to cool down, calm down

'sbornia (*fam*) *sf*: **prendersi una ~** to get plastered

sbor'sare *vt* (*denaro*) to pay out

sbot'tare *vi*: **~ in una risata/per la collera** to burst out laughing/explode with anger

sbotto'nare *vt* to unbutton, undo

sbracci'ato, a [zbrat'tʃato] *ag* (*camicia*) sleeveless; (*persona*) bare-armed

sbrai'tare *vi* to yell, bawl

sbra'nare *vt* to tear to pieces

sbricio'lare [zbritʃo'lare] *vt* to crumble; **~rsi** *vr* to crumble

sbri'gare *vt* to deal with, get through; (*cliente*) to attend to, deal with; **~rsi** *vr* to hurry (up); **sbriga'tivo, a** *ag* (*persona, modo*) quick, expeditious; (*giudizio*) hasty

sbrindel'lato, a *ag* tattered, in tatters

sbrodo'lare *vt* to stain, dirty

'sbronza ['zbrontsa] (*fam*) *sf* (*ubriaco*): **prendersi una ~** to get tight *o* plastered

'sbronzo, a ['zbrontso] (*fam*) *ag* (*ubriaco*) tight

sbruf'fone, a *sm/f* boaster

sbu'care *vi* to come out, emerge; (*apparire improvvisamente*) to pop out (*o* up)

sbucci'are [zbut'tʃare] *vt* (*arancia, patata*) to peel; (*piselli*) to shell; **~rsi un ginocchio** to graze one's knee

sbudel'larsi *vr*: **~ dalle risa** to split one's sides laughing

sbuf'fare *vi* (*persona, cavallo*) to snort; (: *ansimare*) to puff, pant; (*treno*) to puff; **'sbuffo** *sm* (*di aria, fumo, vapore*) puff; **maniche a sbuffo** puff(ed) sleeves

'scabbia *sf* (*MED*) scabies *sg*

sca'broso, a *ag* (*fig: difficile*) difficult, thorny; (: *imbarazzante*) embarrassing; (: *sconcio*) indecent

scacchi'era [skak'kjɛra] *sf* chessboard

scacci'are [skat'tʃare] *vt* to chase away *o* out, drive away *o* out

'scacco, chi *sm* (*pezzo del gioco*) chessman; (*quadretto di scacchiera*) square; (*fig*) setback, reverse; **~chi** *smpl* (*gioco*) chess *sg*; **a ~chi** (*tessuto*) check(ed); **scacco'matto** *sm* checkmate

sca'dente *ag* shoddy, of poor quality

sca'denza [ska'dɛntsa] *sf* (*di cambiale, contratto*) maturity; (*di passaporto*) expiry date; **a breve/lunga ~** short-/long-term; **data di ~** expiry date

sca'dere *vi* (*contratto etc*) to expire; (*debito*) to fall due; (*valore, forze, peso*) to decline, go down

sca'fandro *sm* (*di palombaro*) diving suit; (*di astronauta*) space-suit

scaf'fale *sm* shelf; (*mobile*) set of shelves

'scafo *sm* (*NAUT, AER*) hull

scagio'nare [skadʒo'nare] *vt* to exonerate, free from blame

'scaglia ['skaʎʎa] *sf* (*ZOOL*) scale; (*scheggia*) chip, flake

scagli'are [skaʎ'ʎare] *vt* (*lanciare: anche fig*) to hurl, fling; **~rsi** *vr*: **~rsi su** *o* **contro** to hurl *o* fling o.s. at; (*fig*) to rail at

scaglio'nare [skaʎʎo'nare] *vt* (*pagamenti*) to space out, spread out; (*MIL*) to echelon; **scagli'one** *sm* echelon; (*GEO*) terrace; **a scaglioni** in groups

'scala *sf* (*a gradini etc*) staircase, stairs *pl*; (*a pioli, di corda*) ladder; (*MUS, GEO, di colori, valori, fig*) scale; **~e** *sfpl* (*scalinata*) stairs; **su vasta ~/~ ridotta** on a large/small scale; **~ a libretto** stepladder; **~ mobile** escalator; (*ECON*) sliding scale; **~ mobile (dei salari)** index-linked pay scale

sca'lare *vt* (*ALPINISMO, muro*) to climb, scale; (*debito*) to scale down, reduce; **sca'lata** *sf* scaling *no pl*, climbing *no pl*; (*arrampicata, fig*) climb; **scala'tore, 'trice** *sm/f* climber

scalda'bagno [skalda'baɲɲo] *sm* waterheater

scal'dare *vt* to heat; **~rsi** *vr* to warm up, heat up; (*al fuoco, al sole*) to warm o.s.; (*fig*) to get excited

scal'fire *vt* to scratch

scali'nata *sf* staircase

sca'lino *sm* (*anche fig*) step; (*di scala a pioli*) rung

'scalo *sm* (*NAUT*) slipway; (: *porto d'approdo*) port of call; (*AER*) stopover; **fare ~ (a)** (*NAUT*) to call (at), put in (at); (*AER*) to land (at), make a stop (at); **~ merci** (*FERR*) goods (*BRIT*) *o* freight yard

scalop'pina *sf* (*CUC*) escalope

scal'pello *sm* chisel

scal'pore *sm* noise, row; **far ~** (*notizia*) to cause a sensation *o* a stir

'scaltro, a *ag* cunning, shrewd

scal'zare [skal'tsare] *vt* (*albero*) to bare the roots of; (*muro, fig: autorità*) to undermine

'scalzo, a ['skaltso] *ag* barefoot

scambi'are *vt* to exchange; (*confondere*): **~ qn/qc per** to take *o* mistake sb/sth for; **mi hanno scambiato il cappello** they've given me the wrong hat

scambi'evole *ag* mutual, reciprocal

'scambio *sm* exchange; (*FERR*) points *pl*; **fare (uno) ~** to make a swap

scampa'gnata [skampaɲ'ɲata] *sf* trip to the country

scam'pare *vt* (*salvare*) to rescue, save; (*evitare: morte, prigione*) to escape ♦ *vi*: **~ (a qc)** to survive (sth), escape (sth); **scamparla bella** to have a narrow escape

'scampo *sm* (*salvezza*) escape; (*ZOOL*) prawn; **cercare ~ nella fuga** to seek safety in flight

'scampolo *sm* remnant

scanala'tura *sf* (*incavo*) channel, groove

scandagli'are [skanda'ʎʎare] *vt* (*NAUT*) to sound; (*fig*) to sound out; to probe

scandaliz'zare [skandalid'dzare] *vt* to shock, scandalize; **~rsi** *vr* to be shocked

'scandalo *sm* scandal

Scandi'navia *sf*: **la ~** Scandinavia; **scandi'navo, a** *ag, sm/f* Scandinavian

scan'dire *vt* (*versi*) to scan; (*parole*) to articulate, pronounce distinctly; **~ il tempo** (*MUS*) to beat time

scan'nare *vt* (*animale*) to butcher, slaughter; (*persona*) to cut *o* slit the throat of

'scanno *sm* seat, bench

scansa'fatiche [skansafa'tike] *sm/f inv* idler, loafer

scan'sare *vt* (*rimuovere*) to move (aside), shift; (*schivare: schiaffo*) to dodge; (*sfuggire*) to avoid; **~rsi** *vr* to move aside

scan'sia *sf* shelves *pl*; (*per libri*) bookcase

'scanso *sm*: **a ~ di** in order to avoid, as a precaution against

scanti'nato *sm* basement

scanto'nare *vi* to turn the corner; (*svignarsela*) to sneak off

scapacci'one [skapat'tʃone] *sm* clout

scapes'trato, a *ag* dissolute

'scapito *sm* (*perdita*) loss; (*danno*) damage, detriment; **a ~ di** to the detriment of

'scapola *sf* shoulder blade

'scapolo *sm* bachelor

scappa'mento *sm* (*AUT*) exhaust

scap'pare *vi* (*fuggire*) to escape; (*andare via in fretta*) to rush off; **lasciarsi ~ un'occasione** to let an opportunity go by; **~ di prigione** to escape from prison; **~ di mano** (*oggetto*) to slip out of one's hands; **~ di mente a qn** to slip sb's mind; **mi scappò detto** I let it slip; **scap'pata** *sf* quick visit *o* call; **scappa'tella** *sf* escapade; **scappa'toia** *sf* way out

scara'beo *sm* beetle

scarabocchi'are [skarabok'kjare] *vt* to scribble, scrawl; **scara'bocchio** *sm* scribble, scrawl

scara'faggio [skara'faddʒo] *sm* cockroach

scaraven'tare *vt* to fling, hurl

scardi'nare *vt*: **~ una porta** to take a door off its hinges

scarce'rare [skartʃe'rare] *vt* to release (from prison)

'scarica, che *sf* (*di più armi*) volley of shots; (*di sassi, pugni*) hail, shower; (*ELETTR*) discharge; **~ di mitra** burst of machine-gun fire

scari'care *vt* (*merci, camion etc*) to unload; (*passeggeri*) to set down, put off; (*arma*) to unload; (: *sparare, ELETTR*) to discharge; (*sog: corso d'acqua*) to empty, pour; (*fig: liberare da un peso*) to unburden, relieve; ~**rsi** *vr* (*orologio*) to run *o* wind down; (*batteria, accumulatore*) to go flat *o* dead; (*fig: rilassarsi*) to unwind; (: *sfogarsi*) to let off steam; **il fulmine si scaricò su un albero** the lightning struck a tree; **scarica'tore** *sm* loader; (*di porto*) docker

'**scarico, a, chi, che** *ag* unloaded; (*orologio*) run down; (*accumulatore*) dead, flat ♦ *sm* (*di merci, materiali*) unloading; (*di immondizie*) dumping, tipping (*BRIT*); (: *luogo*) rubbish dump; (*TECN: deflusso*) draining; (: *dispositivo*) drain; (*AUT*) exhaust

scarlat'tina *sf* scarlet fever

scar'latto, a *ag* scarlet

'**scarno, a** *ag* thin, bony

'**scarpa** *sf* shoe; ~**e da ginnastica/tennis** gym/tennis shoes

scar'pata *sf* escarpment

scarseggi'are [skarsed'dʒare] *vi* to be scarce; ~ **di** to be short of, lack

scar'sezza [skar'settsa] *sf* scarcity, lack

'**scarso, a** *ag* (*insufficiente*) insufficient, meagre; (*povero: annata*) poor, lean; (*INS: voto*) poor; ~ **di** lacking in; **3 chili** ~**i** just under 3 kilos, barely 3 kilos

scarta'mento *sm* (*FERR*) gauge; ~ **normale/ridotto** standard/narrow gauge

scar'tare *vt* (*pacco*) to unwrap; (*idea*) to reject; (*MIL*) to declare unfit for military service; (*carte da gioco*) to discard; (*CALCIO*) to dodge (past) ♦ *vi* to swerve

'**scarto** *sm* (*cosa scartata, anche COMM*) reject; (*di veicolo*) swerve; (*differenza*) gap, difference

scassi'nare *vt* to break, force

'**scasso** *sm vedi* **furto**

scate'nare *vt* (*fig*) to incite, stir up; ~**rsi** *vr* (*temporale*) to break; (*rivolta*) to break out; (*persona: infuriarsi*) to rage

'**scatola** *sf* box; (*di latta*) tin (*BRIT*), can; **cibi in** ~ tinned (*BRIT*) *o* canned foods; ~ **cranica** cranium

scat'tare *vt* (*fotografia*) to take ♦ *vi* (*congegno, molla etc*) to be released; (*balzare*) to spring up; (*SPORT*) to put on a spurt; (*fig: per l'ira*) to fly into a rage; ~ **in piedi** to spring to one's feet

'**scatto** *sm* (*dispositivo*) release; (: *di arma da fuoco*) trigger mechanism; (*rumore*) click; (*balzo*) jump, start; (*SPORT*) spurt; (*fig: di ira etc*) fit; (: *di stipendio*) increment; **di** ~ suddenly

scatu'rire *vi* to gush, spring

scaval'care *vt* (*ostacolo*) to pass (*o* climb) over; (*fig*) to get ahead of, overtake

sca'vare *vt* (*terreno*) to dig; (*legno*) to hollow out; (*pozzo, galleria*) to bore; (*città sepolta etc*) to excavate

'**scavo** *sm* excavating *no pl*; excavation

'**scegliere** ['ʃeʎʎere] *vt* to choose, select

sce'icco, chi [ʃe'ikko] *sm* sheik

scelle'rato, a [ʃelle'rato] *ag* wicked, evil

scel'lino [ʃel'lino] *sm* shilling

'**scelta** ['ʃelta] *sf* choice; selection; **di prima** ~ top grade *o* quality; **frutta** *o* **formaggi a** ~ choice of fruit or cheese

'**scelto, a** ['ʃelto] *pp di* **scegliere** ♦ *ag* (*gruppo*) carefully selected; (*frutta, verdura*) choice, top quality; (*MIL: specializzato*) crack *cpd*, highly skilled

sce'mare [ʃe'mare] *vt, vi* to diminish

'**scemo, a** ['ʃemo] *ag* stupid, silly

'**scempio** ['ʃempjo] *sm* slaughter, massacre; (*fig*) ruin; **far** ~ **di** (*fig*) to play havoc with, ruin

'**scena** ['ʃena] *sf* (*gen*) scene; (*palcoscenico*) stage; **le** ~**e** (*fig: teatro*) the stage; **fare una** ~ to make a scene; **andare in** ~ to be staged *o* put on *o* performed; **mettere in** ~ to stage

sce'nario [ʃe'narjo] *sm* scenery; (*di film*) scenario

sce'nata [ʃe'nata] *sf* row, scene

'**scendere** ['ʃendere] *vi* to go (*o* come) down; (*strada, sole*) to go down; (*notte*) to fall; (*passeggero: fermarsi*) to get out, alight; (*fig: temperatura, prezzi*) to go *o* come down, fall, drop ♦ *vt* (*scale, pendio*) to go (*o* come) down; ~ **dalle scale** to go (*o* come) down the stairs; ~ **dal treno** to get off *o* out of the train; ~ **dalla macchina** to get out of the car; ~ **da cavallo** to dismount, get off one's horse

'**scenico, a, ci, che** ['ʃeniko] *ag* stage *cpd*, scenic

scervel'lato, a [ʃervel'lato] *ag* featherbrained, scatterbrained

'**sceso, a** ['ʃeso] *pp di* **scendere**

'**scettico, a, ci, che** ['ʃettiko] *ag* sceptical

'**scettro** ['ʃettro] *sm* sceptre

'**scheda** ['skɛda] *sf* (index) card; **~ elettorale** ballot paper; **~ perforata** punch card; **~ telefonica** phone card; **sche'dare** *vt* (*dati*) to file; (*libri*) to catalogue; (*registrare: anche POLIZIA*) to put on one's files; **sche'dario** *sm* file; (*mobile*) filing cabinet

'**scheggia, ge** ['skeddʒa] *sf* splinter, sliver

'**scheletro** ['skɛletro] *sm* skeleton

'**schema, i** ['skɛma] *sm* (*diagramma*) diagram, sketch; (*progetto, abbozzo*) outline, plan

'**scherma** ['skerma] *sf* fencing

scher'maglia [sker'maʎʎa] *sf* (*fig*) skirmish

'**schermo** ['skermo] *sm* shield, screen; (*CINEMA, TV*) screen

scher'nire [sker'nire] *vt* to mock, sneer at; '**scherno** *sm* mockery, derision

scher'zare [sker'tsare] *vi* to joke

'**scherzo** ['skertso] *sm* joke; (*tiro*) trick; (*MUS*) scherzo; **è uno ~!** (*una cosa facile*) it's child's play!, it's easy!; **per ~** in jest; **for a joke** *o* a laugh; **fare un brutto ~ a qn** to play a nasty trick on sb; **scher'zoso, a** *ag* (*tono, gesto*) playful; (*osservazione*) facetious; **è un tipo scherzoso** he likes a joke

schiaccia'noci [skjattʃa'notʃi] *sm inv* nutcracker

schiacci'are [skjat'tʃare] *vt* (*dito*) to crush; (*noci*) to crack; **~ un pisolino** to have a nap

schiaffeggi'are [skjaffed'dʒare] *vt* to slap

schi'affo ['skjaffo] *sm* slap

schiamaz'zare [skjamat'tsare] *vi* to squawk, cackle

schian'tare [skjan'tare] *vt* to break, tear apart; **~rsi** *vr* to break (up), shatter; **schi'anto** *sm* (*rumore*) crash; tearing sound; **è uno schianto!** (*fam*) it's (*o* he's *o* she's) terrific!; **di schianto** all of a

sudden

schia'rire [skja'rire] *vt* to lighten, make lighter ♦ *vi* (*anche: ~rsi*) to grow lighter; (*tornar sereno*) to clear, brighten up; **~rsi la voce** to clear one's throat

schiavitù [skjavi'tu] *sf* slavery

schi'avo, a ['skjavo] *sm/f* slave

schi'ena ['skjɛna] *sf* (*ANAT*) back; **schie'nale** *sm* (*di sedia*) back

schi'era ['skjɛra] *sf* (*MIL*) rank; (*gruppo*) group, band

schiera'mento [skjera'mento] *sm* (*MIL, SPORT*) formation; (*fig*) alliance

schie'rare [skje'rare] *vt* (*esercito*) to line up, draw up, marshal; **~rsi** *vr* to line up; (*fig*): **~rsi con** *o* **dalla parte di/contro qn** to side with/oppose sb

schi'etto, a ['skjɛtto] *ag* (*puro*) pure; (*fig*) frank, straightforward; sincere

'**schifo** ['skifo] *sm* disgust; **fare ~** (*essere fatto male, dare pessimi risultati*) to be awful; **mi fa ~** it makes me sick, it's disgusting; **quel libro è uno ~** that book's rotten; **schi'foso, a** *ag* disgusting, revolting; (*molto scadente*) rotten, lousy

schioc'care [skjok'kare] *vt* (*frusta*) to crack; (*dita*) to snap; (*lingua*) to click; **~ le labbra** to smack one's lips

schi'udere ['skjudere] *vt* to open; **~rsi** *vr* to open

schi'uma ['skjuma] *sf* foam; (*di sapone*) lather; (*di latte*) froth; (*fig: feccia*) scum; **schiu'mare** *vt* to skim ♦ *vi* to foam

schi'uso, a ['skjuso] *pp di* **schiudere**

schi'vare [ski'vare] *vt* to dodge, avoid

'**schivo, a** ['skivo] *ag* (*ritroso*) stand-offish, reserved; (*timido*) shy

schiz'zare [skit'tsare] *vt* (*spruzzare*) to spurt, squirt; (*sporcare*) to splash, spatter; (*fig: abbozzare*) to sketch ♦ *vi* to spurt, squirt; (*saltar fuori*) to dart up (*o* off *etc*)

schizzi'noso, a [skittsi'noso] *ag* fussy, finicky

'**schizzo** ['skittso] *sm* (*di liquido*) spurt; splash, spatter; (*abbozzo*) sketch

sci [ʃi] *sm* (*attrezzo*) ski; (*attività*) skiing; **~ nautico** water-skiing

'**scia** ['ʃia] (*pl* **scie**) *sf* (*di imbarcazione*) wake; (*di profumo*) trail

scià [ʃa] *sm inv* shah
sci'abola ['ʃabola] *sf* sabre
scia'callo [ʃa'kallo] *sm* jackal
sciac'quare [ʃak'kware] *vt* to rinse
scia'gura [ʃa'gura] *sf* disaster, calamity; misfortune; **sciagu'rato, a** *ag* unfortunate; (*malvagio*) wicked
scialac'quare [ʃalak'kware] *vt* to squander
scia'lare [ʃa'lare] *vi* to lead a life of luxury
sci'albo, a ['ʃalbo] *ag* pale, dull; (*fig*) dull, colourless
sci'alle ['ʃalle] *sm* shawl
scia'luppa [ʃa'luppa] *sf* (*NAUT*) sloop; (*anche*: ~ *di salvataggio*) lifeboat
sci'ame ['ʃame] *sm* swarm
scian'cato, a [ʃan'kato] *ag* lame; (*mobile*) rickety
sci'are [ʃi'are] *vi* to ski
sci'arpa ['ʃarpa] *sf* scarf; (*fascia*) sash
scia'tore, 'trice [ʃia'tore] *sm/f* skier
sci'atto, a [ʃ'ʃatto] *ag* (*persona: nell'aspetto*) slovenly, unkempt; (: *nel lavoro*) sloppy, careless
scien'tifico, a, ci, che [ʃen'tifiko] *ag* scientific
sci'enza ['ʃɛntsa] *sf* science; (*sapere*) knowledge; ~**e** *sfpl* (*INS*) science *sg*; ~**e naturali** natural sciences; **scienzi'ato, a** *sm/f* scientist
'scimmia ['ʃimmja] *sf* monkey; **scimmiot'tare** *vt* to ape, mimic
scimpanzé [ʃimpan'tse] *sm inv* chimpanzee
scimu'nito, a [ʃimu'nito] *ag* silly, idiotic
'scindere ['ʃindere] *vt* to split (up); ~**rsi** *vr* to split (up)
scin'tilla [ʃin'tilla] *sf* spark; **scintil'lare** *vi* to spark; (*acqua, occhi*) to sparkle
scioc'chezza [ʃok'kettsa] *sf* stupidity *no pl*; stupid *o* foolish thing; **dire ~e** to talk nonsense
sci'occo, a, chi, che [ʃ'ʃokko] *ag* stupid, foolish
sci'ogliere [ʃ'ʃɔʎʎere] *vt* (*nodo*) to untie; (*capelli*) to loosen; (*persona, animale*) to untie, release; (*fig: persona*): ~ **da** to release from; (*neve*) to melt; (*nell'acqua*:

zucchero etc) to dissolve; (*fig: mistero*) to solve; (*porre fine a: contratto*) to cancel; (: *società, matrimonio*) to dissolve; (: *riunione*) to bring to an end; ~**rsi** *vr* to loosen, come untied; to melt; to dissolve; (*assemblea etc*) to break up; ~ **i muscoli** to limber up
sciol'tezza [ʃol'tettsa] *sf* agility; suppleness; ease
sci'olto, a ['ʃɔlto] *pp di* **sciogliere** ♦ *ag* loose; (*agile*) agile, nimble; supple; (*disinvolto*) free and easy; **versi ~i** (*POESIA*) blank verse
sciope'rante [ʃope'rante] *sm/f* striker
sciope'rare [ʃope'rare] *vi* to strike, go on strike
sci'opero ['ʃɔpero] *sm* strike; **fare ~** to strike; ~ **bianco** work-to-rule (*BRIT*), slowdown (*US*); ~ **selvaggio** wildcat strike; ~ **a singhiozzo** on-off strike
sci'rocco [ʃi'rɔkko] *sm* sirocco
sci'roppo [ʃi'rɔppo] *sm* syrup
'scisma, i ['ʃizma] *sm* (*REL*) schism
scissi'one [ʃis'sjone] *sf* (*anche fig*) split, division; (*FISICA*) fission
'scisso, a ['ʃisso] *pp di* **scindere**
sciu'pare [ʃu'pare] *vt* (*abito, libro, appetito*) to spoil, ruin; (*tempo, denaro*) to waste; ~**rsi** *vr* to get spoilt *o* ruined; (*rovinarsi la salute*) to ruin one's health
scivo'lare [ʃivo'lare] *vi* to slide *o* glide along; (*involontariamente*) to slip, slide; **'scivolo** *sm* slide; (*TECN*) chute
scle'rosi [skle'rɔzi] *sf* sclerosis
scoc'care *vt* (*freccia*) to shoot ♦ *vi* (*guizzare*) to shoot up; (*battere: ora*) to strike
scocci'are [skot'tʃare] (*fam*) *vt* to bother, annoy; ~**rsi** *vr* to be bothered *o* annoyed
sco'della *sf* bowl
scodinzo'lare [skodintso'lare] *vi* to wag its tail
scogli'era [skoʎ'ʎɛra] *sf* reef; cliff
'scoglio ['skɔʎʎo] *sm* (*al mare*) rock
scoi'attolo *sm* squirrel
sco'lare *ag*: **età ~** school age ♦ *vt* to drain ♦ *vi* to drip
scola'resca *sf* schoolchildren *pl*, pupils *pl*

sco'laro, a *sm/f* pupil, schoolboy/girl
sco'lastico, a, ci, che *ag* school *cpd*; scholastic
scol'lare *vt* (*staccare*) to unstick; ~**rsi** *vr* to come unstuck
scolla'tura *sf* neckline
'scolo *sm* drainage
scolo'rire *vt* to fade; to discolour ♦ *vi* (*anche*: ~**rsi**) to fade; to become discoloured; (*impallidire*) to turn pale
scol'pire *vt* to carve, sculpt
scombi'nare *vt* to mess up, upset
scombusso'lare *vt* to upset
scom'messa *sf* bet, wager
scom'messo, a *pp di* **scommettere**
scom'mettere *vt*, *vi* to bet
scomo'dare *vt* to trouble, bother; to disturb; ~**rsi** *vr* to put o.s. out; ~**rsi a fare** to go to the bother *o* trouble of doing
'scomodo, a *ag* uncomfortable; (*sistemazione, posto*) awkward, inconvenient
scompa'rire *vi* (*sparire*) to disappear, vanish; (*fig*) to be insignificant; **scom'parsa** *sf* disappearance; **scom'parso, a** *pp di* **scomparire**
scomparti'mento *sm* (*FERR*) compartment
scom'parto *sm* compartment, division
scompigli'are [skompiʎˈʎare] *vt* (*cassetto, capelli*) to mess up, disarrange; (*fig*: *piani*) to upset; **scom'piglio** *sm* mess, confusion
scom'porre *vt* (*parola, numero*) to break up; (*CHIM*) to decompose; **scomporsi** *vr* (*fig*) to get upset, lose one's composure; **scom'posto, a** *pp di* **scomporre** ♦ *ag* (*gesto*) unseemly; (*capelli*) ruffled, dishevelled
sco'munica *sf* excommunication
scomuni'care *vt* to excommunicate
sconcer'tare [skontʃerˈtare] *vt* to disconcert, bewilder
'sconcio, a, ci, ce [ˈskontʃo] *ag* (*osceno*) indecent, obscene ♦ *sm* (*cosa riprovevole, mal fatta*) disgrace
sconfes'sare *vt* to renounce, disavow; to repudiate

scon'figgere [skonˈfiddʒere] *vt* to defeat, overcome
sconfi'nare *vi* to cross the border; (*in proprietà privata*) to trespass; (*fig*): ~ **da** to stray *o* digress from; **sconfi'nato, a** *ag* boundless, unlimited
scon'fitta *sf* defeat
scon'fitto, a *pp di* **sconfiggere**
scon'forto *sm* despondency
scongiu'rare [skondʒuˈrare] *vt* (*implorare*) to entreat, beseech, implore; (*eludere: pericolo*) to ward off, avert; **scongi'uro** *sm* entreaty; (*esorcismo*) exorcism; **fare gli scongiuri** to touch wood (*BRIT*), knock on wood (*US*)
scon'nesso, a *ag* (*fig: discorso*) incoherent, rambling
sconosci'uto, a [skonoʃˈʃuto] *ag* unknown; new, strange ♦ *sm/f* stranger; unknown person
sconquas'sare *vt* to shatter, smash
sconside'rato, a *ag* thoughtless, rash
sconsigli'are [skonsiʎˈʎare] *vt*: ~ **qc a qn** to advise sb against sth; ~ **qn dal fare qc** to advise sb not to do *o* against doing sth
sconso'lato, a *ag* inconsolable; desolate
scon'tare *vt* (*COMM: detrarre*) to deduct; (*: debito*) to pay off; (*: cambiale*) to discount; (*pena*) to serve; (*colpa, errori*) to pay for, suffer for
scon'tato, a *ag* (*previsto*) foreseen, taken for granted; **dare per ~ che** to take it for granted that
scon'tento, a *ag*: ~ **(di)** discontented *o* dissatisfied (with) ♦ *sm* discontent, dissatisfaction
'sconto *sm* discount; **fare uno ~** to give a discount
scon'trarsi *vr* (*treni etc*) to crash, collide; (*venire ad uno scontro, fig*) to clash; ~ **con** to crash into, collide with
scon'trino *sm* ticket
'scontro *sm* clash, encounter; crash, collision
scon'troso, a *ag* sullen, surly; (*permaloso*) touchy
sconveni'ente *ag* unseemly, improper
scon'volgere [skonˈvoldʒere] *vt* to throw

into confusion, upset; (*turbare*) to shake, disturb, upset; **scon'volto, a** *pp di* **sconvolgere**

'**scopa** *sf* broom; (*CARTE*) Italian card game; **sco'pare** *vt* to sweep

sco'perta *sf* discovery

sco'perto, a *pp di* **scoprire** ♦ *ag* uncovered; (*capo*) uncovered, bare; (*macchina*) open; (*MIL*) exposed, without cover; (*conto*) overdrawn

'**scopo** *sm* aim, purpose; **a che ~?** what for?

scoppi'are *vi* (*spaccarsi*) to burst; (*esplodere*) to explode; (*fig*) to break out; **~ in pianto** *o* **a piangere** to burst out crying; **~ dalle risa** *o* **dal ridere** to split one's sides laughing

scoppiet'tare *vi* to crackle

'**scoppio** *sm* explosion; (*di tuono, arma etc*) crash, bang; (*fig: di risa, ira*) fit, outburst; (: *di guerra*) outbreak; **a ~ ritardato** delayed-action

sco'prire *vt* to discover; (*liberare da ciò che copre*) to uncover; (: *monumento*) to unveil; **~rsi** *vr* to put on lighter clothes; (*fig*) to give o.s. away

scoraggi'are [skorad'dʒare] *vt* to discourage; **~rsi** *vr* to become discouraged, lose heart

scorcia'toia [skortʃa'toja] *sf* short cut

'**scorcio** ['skortʃo] *sm* (*ARTE*) foreshortening; (*di secolo, periodo*) end, close

scor'dare *vt* to forget; **~rsi** *vr*: **~rsi di qc/di fare** to forget sth/to do

'**scorgere** ['skordʒere] *vt* to make out, distinguish, see

sco'ria *sf* (*di metalli*) slag; (*vulcanica*) scoria; **~e radioattive** (*FISICA*) radioactive waste *sg*

'**scorno** *sm* ignominy, disgrace

scorpacci'ata [skorpat'tʃata] *sf*: **fare una ~ (di)** to stuff o.s. (with), eat one's fill (of)

scorpi'one *sm* scorpion; (*dello zodiaco*): **S~** Scorpio

scorraz'zare [skorrat'tsare] *vi* to run about

'**scorrere** *vt* (*giornale, lettera*) to run *o*

skim through ♦ *vi* (*liquido, fiume*) to run, flow; (*fune*) to run; (*cassetto, porta*) to slide easily; (*tempo*) to pass (by)

scor'retto, a *ag* incorrect; (*sgarbato*) impolite; (*sconveniente*) improper

scor'revole *ag* (*porta*) sliding; (*fig: stile*) fluent, flowing

scorri'banda *sf* (*MIL*) raid; (*escursione*) trip, excursion

'**scorsa** *sf* quick look, glance

'**scorso, a** *pp di* **scorrere** ♦ *ag* last

scor'soio, a *ag*: **nodo ~** noose

'**scorta** *sf* (*di personalità, convoglio*) escort; (*provvista*) supply, stock; **scor'tare** *vt* to escort

scor'tese *ag* discourteous, rude; **scorte'sia** *sf* discourtesy, rudeness; (*azione*) discourtesy

scorti'care *vt* to skin

'**scorto, a** *pp di* **scorgere**

'**scorza** ['skordza] *sf* (*di albero*) bark; (*di agrumi*) peel, skin

sco'sceso, a [skoʃ'ʃeso] *ag* steep

'**scossa** *sf* jerk, jolt, shake; (*ELETTR, fig*) shock

'**scosso, a** *pp di* **scuotere** ♦ *ag* (*turbato*) shaken, upset

scos'tante *ag* (*fig*) off-putting (*BRIT*), unpleasant

scos'tare *vt* to move (away), shift; **~rsi** *vr* to move away

scostu'mato, a *ag* immoral, dissolute

scot'tare *vt* (*ustionare*) to burn; (: *con liquido bollente*) to scald ♦ *vi* to burn; (*caffè*) to be too hot; **scotta'tura** *sf* burn; scald

'**scotto, a** *ag* overcooked ♦ *sm* (*fig*): **pagare lo ~ (di)** to pay the penalty (for)

sco'vare *vt* to drive out, flush out; (*fig*) to discover

'**Scozia** ['skɔttsja] *sf*: **la ~** Scotland; **scoz'zese** *ag* Scottish ♦ *sm/f* Scot

scredi'tare *vt* to discredit

screpo'lare *vt* to crack; **~rsi** *vr* to crack; **screpola'tura** *sf* cracking *no pl*; crack

screzi'ato, a [skret'tsjato] *ag* streaked

'**screzio** ['skrɛttsjo] *sm* disagreement

scricchio'lare [skrikkjo'lare] *vi* to creak, squeak

'scric'ciolo ['skrittʃolo] *sm* wren

'scrigno ['skriɲno] *sm* casket

scrimina'tura *sf* parting

'scritta *sf* inscription

'scritto, a *pp di* scrivere ♦ *ag* written
♦ *sm* writing; (*lettera*) letter, note; ~i *smpl*
(*letterari etc*) writing *sg*; per *o* in ~ in
writing

scrit'toio *sm* writing desk

scrit'tore, 'trice *sm/f* writer

scrit'tura *sf* writing; (*COMM*) entry;
(*contratto*) contract; (*REL*): la Sacra S~ the
Scriptures *pl*; ~e *sfpl* (*COMM*) accounts,
books

scrittu'rare *vt* (*TEATRO, CINEMA*) to sign up,
engage; (*COMM*) to enter

scriva'nia *sf* desk

scri'vente *sm/f* writer

'scrivere *vt* to write; come si scrive?
how is it spelt?, how do you write it?

scroc'cone, a *sm/f* scrounger

'scrofa *sf* (*ZOOL*) sow

scrol'lare *vt* to shake; ~rsi *vr* (*anche fig*)
to give o.s. a shake; ~ le spalle/il capo
to shrug one's shoulders/shake one's
head

scrosci'are [skroʃ'ʃare] *vi* (*pioggia*) to
pour down, pelt down; (*torrente, fig*:
applausi) to thunder, roar; 'scroscio *sm*
pelting; thunder, roar; (*di applausi*) burst

scros'tare *vt* (*intonaco*) to scrape off,
strip; ~rsi *vr* to peel off, flake off

'scrupolo *sm* scruple; (*meticolosità*) care,
conscientiousness

scru'tare *vt* to scrutinize; (*intenzioni,
causa*) to examine, scrutinize

scruti'nare *vt* (*voti*) to count; scru'tinio
sm (*votazione*) ballot; (*insieme delle
operazioni*) poll; (*INS*) (*meeting for*)
*assignment of marks at end of a term or
year*

scu'cire [sku'tʃire] *vt* (*orlo etc*) to unpick,
undo

scude'ria *sf* stable

scu'detto *sm* (*SPORT*) (championship)
shield; (*distintivo*) badge

'scudo *sm* shield

scul'tore, 'trice *sm/f* sculptor

scul'tura *sf* sculpture

scu'ola *sf* school; ~ elementare/
materna/media primary (*BRIT*) *o* grade
(*US*)/nursery/secondary (*BRIT*) *o* high (*US*)
school; ~ guida driving school; ~
dell'obbligo compulsory education; ~e
serali evening classes, night school *sg*; ~
tecnica technical college

scu'otere *vt* to shake; ~rsi *vr* to jump,
be startled; (*fig: muoversi*) to rouse o.s.,
stir o.s.; (: *turbarsi*) to be shaken

'scure *sf* axe

'scuro, a *ag* dark; (*fig: espressione*) grim
♦ *sm* darkness; dark colour; (*imposta*)
(window) shutter; verde/rosso *etc* ~ dark
green/red *etc*

scur'rile *ag* scurrilous

'scusa *sf* apology; (*pretesto*) excuse;
chiedere ~ a qn (per) to apologize to sb
(for); chiedo ~ I'm sorry; (*disturbando
etc*) excuse me

scu'sare *vt* to excuse; ~rsi *vr*: ~rsi (di)
to apologize (for); (mi) scusi I'm sorry;
(*per richiamare l'attenzione*) excuse me

sde'gnato, a [zdeɲ'ɲato] *ag* indignant,
angry

'sdegno ['zdeɲɲo] *sm* scorn, disdain;
sde'gnoso, a *ag* scornful, disdainful

sdoga'nare *vt* (*merci*) to clear through
customs

sdolci'nato, a [zdoltʃi'nato] *ag*
mawkish, oversentimental

sdoppi'are *vt* (*dividere*) to divide *o* split
in two

sdrai'arsi *vr* to stretch out, lie down

'sdraio *sm*: sedia a ~ deck chair

sdruccio'levole [zdruttʃo'levole] *ag*
slippery

PAROLA CHIAVE

se *pron vedi* si
♦ *cong* 1 (*condizionale, ipotetica*) if; ~
nevica non vengo I won't come if it
snows; sarei rimasto ~ me l'avessero
chiesto I would have stayed if they'd
asked me; non puoi fare altro ~ non
telefonare all you can do is phone; ~
mai if, if ever; siamo noi ~ mai che te
siamo grati it is we who should be
grateful to you; ~ no (*altrimenti*) or (else),

otherwise
2 (*in frasi dubitative, interrogative indirette*) if, whether; **non so ~ scrivere o telefonare** I don't know whether o if I should write or phone

sé *pron* (*gen*) oneself; (*esso, essa, lui, lei, loro*) itself; himself; herself; themselves; **~ stesso(a)** *pron* oneself; itself; himself; herself; **~ stessi(e)** *pron pl* themselves
seb'bene *cong* although, though
sec. *abbr* (= *secolo*) c
'secca *sf* (*del mare*) shallows *pl*; *vedi anche* **secco**
sec'care *vt* to dry; (*prosciugare*) to dry up; (*fig: importunare*) to annoy, bother ♦ *vi* to dry; to dry up; **~rsi** *vr* to dry; to dry up; (*fig*) to grow annoyed; **secca'tura** *sf* (*fig*) bother *no pl*, trouble *no pl*
'secchia ['sekkja] *sf* bucket, pail
'secco, a, chi, che *ag* dry; (*fichi, pesce*) dried; (*foglie, ramo*) withered; (*magro: persona*) thin, skinny; (*fig: risposta, modo di fare*) curt, abrupt; (: *colpo*) clean, sharp ♦ *sm* (*siccità*) drought; **restarci ~** (*fig: morire sul colpo*) to drop dead; **mettere in ~** (*barca*) to beach; **rimanere in** o **a ~** (*NAUT*) to run aground; (*fig*) to be left in the lurch
seco'lare *ag* age-old, centuries-old; (*laico, mondano*) secular
'secolo *sm* century; (*epoca*) age
se'conda *sf* (*AUT*) second (gear); **viaggiare in ~** to travel second-class; *vedi anche* **secondo**
secon'dario, a *ag* secondary
se'condo, a *ag* second ♦ *sm* second; (*di pranzo*) main course ♦ *prep* according to; (*nel modo prescritto*) in accordance with; **~ me** in my opinion, to my mind; **di ~a classe** second-class; **di ~a mano** second-hand; **a ~a di** according to; in accordance with
'sedano *sm* celery
seda'tivo, a *ag, sm* sedative
'sede *sf* seat; (*di ditta*) head office; (*di organizzazione*) headquarters *pl*; **in ~ di** (*in occasione di*) during; **~ sociale** registered office

seden'tario, a *ag* sedentary
se'dere *vi* to sit, be seated; **~rsi** *vr* to sit down ♦ *sm* (*deretano*) behind, bottom
'sedia *sf* chair
sedi'cente [sedi'tʃɛnte] *ag* self-styled
'sedici ['seditʃi] *num* sixteen
se'dile *sm* seat; (*panchina*) bench
se'dotto, a *pp di* **sedurre**
sedu'cente [sedu'tʃɛnte] *ag* seductive; (*proposta*) very attractive
se'durre *vt* to seduce
se'duta *sf* session, sitting; (*riunione*) meeting; **~ spiritica** séance; **~ stante** (*fig*) immediately
seduzi'one [sedut'tsjone] *sf* seduction; (*fascino*) charm, appeal
'sega, ghe *sf* saw
'segale *sf* rye
se'gare *vt* to saw; (*recidere*) to saw off; **sega'tura** *sf* (*residuo*) sawdust
'seggio ['sɛddʒo] *sm* seat; **~ elettorale** polling station
'seggiola ['sɛddʒola] *sf* chair; **seggio'lino** *sm* seat; (*per bambini*) child's chair; **seggio'lone** *sm* (*per bambini*) highchair
seggio'via [sɛddʒo'via] *sf* chairlift
seghe'ria [sege'ria] *sf* sawmill
segna'lare [seɲɲa'lare] *vt* (*manovra etc*) to signal; to indicate; (*annunciare*) to announce; to report; (*fig: far conoscere*) to point out; (: *persona*) to single out; **~rsi** *vr* (*distinguersi*) to distinguish o.s.
se'gnale [seɲ'ɲale] *sm* signal; (*cartello*): **~ stradale** road sign; **~ d'allarme** alarm; (*FERR*) communication cord; **~ orario** (*RADIO*) time signal; **segna'letica** *sf* signalling, signposting; **segnaletica stradale** road signs *pl*
se'gnare [seɲ'ɲare] *vt* to mark; (*prendere nota*) to note; (*indicare*) to indicate, mark; (*SPORT: goal*) to score; **~rsi** *vr* (*REL*) to make the sign of the cross, cross o.s.
'segno ['seɲɲo] *sm* sign; (*impronta, contrassegno*) mark; (*limite*) limit, bounds *pl*; (*bersaglio*) target; **fare ~ di sì/no** to nod (one's head)/shake one's head; **fare ~ a qn di fermarsi** to motion (to) sb to stop; **cogliere** o **colpire nel ~** (*fig*) to hit

the mark

segre'gare *vt* to segregate, isolate; **segregazi'one** *sf* segregation

segre'tario, a *sm/f* secretary; ~ **comunale** town clerk; **S~ di Stato** Secretary of State

segrete'ria *sf* (*di ditta, scuola*) (secretary's) office; (*d'organizzazione internazionale*) secretariat; (*POL etc: carica*) office of Secretary; ~ **telefonica** answering service

segre'tezza [segre'tettsa] *sf* secrecy

se'greto, a *ag* secret ♦ *sm* secret; secrecy *no pl*; **in ~** in secret, secretly

segu'ace [se'gwatʃe] *sm/f* follower, disciple

segu'ente *ag* following, next

segu'ire *vt* to follow; (*frequentare: corso*) to attend ♦ *vi* to follow; (*continuare: testo*) to continue

segui'tare *vt* to continue, carry on with ♦ *vi* to continue, carry on

'seguito *sm* (*scorta*) suite, retinue; (*discepoli*) followers *pl*; (*favore*) following; (*serie*) sequence, series *sg*; (*continuazione*) continuation; (*conseguenza*) result; **di ~** at a stretch, on end; **in ~** later on; **in ~ a, a ~ di** following; (*a causa di*) as a result of, owing to

'sei *vb vedi* **essere** ♦ *num* six

sei'cento [sei'tʃɛnto] *num* six hundred ♦ *sm*: **il S~** the seventeenth century

selci'ato [sel'tʃato] *sm* cobbled surface

selezio'nare [selettsjo'nare] *vt* to select

selezi'one [selet'tsjone] *sf* selection

'sella *sf* saddle; **sel'lare** *vt* to saddle

selvag'gina [selvad'dʒina] *sf* (*animali*) game

sel'vaggio, a, gi, ge [sel'vaddʒo] *ag* wild; (*tribù*) savage, uncivilized; (*fig*) savage, brutal ♦ *sm/f* savage

sel'vatico, a, ci, che *ag* wild

se'maforo *sm* (*AUT*) traffic lights *pl*

sem'brare *vi* to seem ♦ *vb impers*: **sembra che** it seems that; **mi sembra che** it seems to me that; I think (that); ~ **di essere** to seem to be

'seme *sm* seed; (*sperma*) semen; (*CARTE*) suit

se'mestre *sm* half-year, six-month period

'semi... *prefisso* semi...; **semi'cerchio** *sm* semicircle; **semifi'nale** *sf* semifinal; **semi'freddo, a** *ag* (*CUC*) chilled ♦ *sm* ice-cream cake

'semina *sf* (*AGR*) sowing

semi'nare *vt* to sow

semi'nario *sm* seminar; (*REL*) seminary

seminter'rato *sm* basement; (*appartamento*) basement flat

se'mitico, a, ci, che *ag* semitic

sem'mai = **se mai**; *vedi* **se**

'semola *sf* bran; ~ **di grano duro** durum wheat

semo'lino *sm* semolina

'semplice ['semplitʃe] *ag* simple; (*di un solo elemento*) single; **semplice'mente** *av* simply; **semplicità** *sf* simplicity

'sempre *av* always; (*ancora*) still; **posso ~ tentare** I can always *o* still try; **da ~** always; **per ~** forever; **una volta per ~** once and for all; ~ **che** provided (that); ~ **più** more and more; ~ **meno** less and less

sempre'verde *ag*, *sm o f* (*BOT*) evergreen

'senape *sf* (*CUC*) mustard

se'nato *sm* senate; **sena'tore, 'trice** *sm/f* senator

'senno *sm* judgment, (common) sense; **col ~ di poi** with hindsight

sennò *av* = **se no**; *vedi* **se**

'seno *sm* (*ANAT: petto, mammella*) breast; (: *grembo, fig*) womb; (: *cavità*) sinus; (*GEO*) inlet, creek; (*MAT*) sine

sen'sato, a *ag* sensible

sensazio'nale [sensattsjo'nale] *ag* sensational

sensazi'one [sensat'tsjone] *sf* feeling, sensation; **avere la ~ che** to have a feeling that; **fare ~** to cause a sensation, create a stir

sen'sibile *ag* sensitive; (*ai sensi*) perceptible; (*rilevante, notevole*) appreciable, noticeable; ~ **a** sensitive to; **sensibilità** *sf* sensitivity

'senso *sm* (*FISIOL, istinto*) sense; (*impressione, sensazione*) feeling, sensation; (*significato*) meaning, sense; (*direzione*) direction; ~**i** *smpl* (*coscienza*) consciousness *sg*; (*sensualità*) senses; **ciò**

non ha ~ that doesn't make sense; **fare** ~ **a** (*ripugnare*) to disgust, repel; ~ **comune** common sense; **in** ~ **orario/antiorario** clockwise/anticlockwise; **a** ~ **unico** (*strada*) one-way; "~ **vietato**" (*AUT*) "no entry"

sensu'ale *ag* sensual; sensuous; **sensualità** *sf* sensuality; sensuousness

sen'tenza [sen'tɛntsa] *sf* (*DIR*) sentence; (*massima*) maxim; **sentenzi'are** *vi* (*DIR*) to pass judgment

senti'ero *sm* path

sentimen'tale *ag* sentimental; (*vita, avventura*) love *cpd*

senti'mento *sm* feeling

senti'nella *sf* sentry

sen'tire *vt* (*percepire al tatto, fig*) to feel; (*udire*) to hear; (*ascoltare*) to listen to; (*odore*) to smell; (*avvertire con il gusto, assaggiare*) to taste ♦ *vi*: ~ **di** (*avere sapore*) to taste of; (*avere odore*) to smell of; ~**rsi** *vr* (*uso reciproco*) to be in touch; ~**rsi bene/male** to feel well/unwell *o* ill; ~**rsi di fare qc** (*essere disposto*) to feel like doing sth

sen'tito, a *ag* (*sincero*) sincere, warm; **per** ~ **dire** by hearsay

'senza ['sɛntsa] *prep, cong* without; ~ **dir nulla** without saying a word; **fare** ~ **qc** to do without sth; ~ **di me** without me; ~ **che io lo sapessi** without me *o* my knowing; **senz'altro** of course, certainly; ~ **dubbio** no doubt; ~ **scrupoli** unscrupulous; ~ **amici** friendless; ~ **piombo** unleaded

sepa'rare *vt* to separate; (*dividere*) to divide; (*tenere distinto*) to distinguish; ~**rsi** *vr* (*coniugi*) to separate, part; (*amici*) to part, leave each other; ~**rsi da** (*coniuge*) to separate *o* part from; (*amico, socio*) to part company with; (*oggetto*) to part with; **sepa'rato, a** *ag* (*letti, conto etc*) separate; (*coniugi*) separated; **separazi'one** *sf* separation

se'polcro *sm* sepulchre

se'polto, a *pp di* **seppellire**

seppel'lire *vt* to bury

'seppia *sf* cuttlefish ♦ *ag inv* sepia

se'quenza [se'kwɛntsa] *sf* sequence

seques'trare *vt* (*DIR*) to impound; (*rapire*) to kidnap; (*costringere in un luogo*) to keep, confine; **se'questro** *sm* (*DIR*) impoundment; **sequestro di persona** kidnapping

'sera *sf* evening; **di** ~ in the evening; **domani** ~ tomorrow evening, tomorrow night; **se'rale** *ag* evening *cpd*; **se'rata** *sf* evening; (*ricevimento*) party

ser'bare *vt* to keep; (*mettere da parte*) to put aside; ~ **rancore/odio verso qn** to bear sb a grudge/hate sb

serba'toio *sm* tank; (*cisterna*) cistern

'serbo *sm*: **mettere/tenere** *o* **avere in** ~ **qc** to put/keep sth aside

se'reno, a *ag* (*tempo, cielo*) clear; (*fig*) serene, calm

ser'gente [ser'dʒɛnte] *sm* (*MIL*) sergeant

'serie *sf inv* (*successione*) series *inv*; (*gruppo, collezione: di chiavi etc*) set; (*SPORT*) division; league; (*COMM*): **modello di** ~/**fuori** ~ standard/custom-built model; **in** ~ in quick succession; (*COMM*) mass *cpd*

serietà *sf* seriousness; reliability

'serio, a *ag* serious; (*impiegato*) responsible, reliable; (*ditta, cliente*) reliable, dependable; **sul** ~ (*davvero*) really, truly; (*seriamente*) seriously, in earnest

ser'mone *sm* sermon

serpeggi'are [serped'dʒare] *vi* to wind; (*fig*) to spread

ser'pente *sm* snake; ~ **a sonagli** rattlesnake

'serra *sf* greenhouse; hothouse

ser'randa *sf* roller shutter

ser'rare *vt* to close, shut; (*a chiave*) to lock; (*stringere*) to squeeze; (*premere: nemico*) to close in on; ~ **i pugni/i denti** to clench one's fists/teeth; ~ **le file** to close ranks

serra'tura *sf* lock

'serva *sf vedi* **servo**

ser'vire *vt* to serve; (*clienti: al ristorante*) to wait on; (*: al negozio*) to serve, attend to; (*fig: giovare*) to aid, help; (*CARTE*) to deal ♦ *vi* (*TENNIS*) to serve; (*essere utile*): ~ **a qn** to be of use to sb; ~ **a qc/a fare**

(*utensile etc*) to be used for sth/for doing; ~ **(a qn) da** to serve as (for sb); **~rsi** *vr* (*usare*): **~rsi di** to use; (*prendere: cibo*): **~rsi (di)** to help o.s. (to); (*essere cliente abituale*): **~rsi da** to be a regular customer at, to go to

servitù *sf* servitude; slavery; (*personale di servizio*) servants *pl*, domestic staff

servizi'evole [servit'tsjevole] *ag* obliging, willing to help

ser'vizio [ser'vittsjo] *sm* service; (*al ristorante: sul conto*) service (charge); (*STAMPA, TV, RADIO*) report; (*da tè, caffè etc*) set, service; **~i** *smpl* (*di casa*) kitchen and bathroom; (*ECON*) services; **essere di ~** to be on duty; **fuori ~** (*telefono etc*) out of order; **~ compreso** service included; **~ militare** military service; **~i segreti** secret service sg

'**servo, a** *sm/f* servant

ses'santa *num* sixty; **sessan'tesimo, a** *num* sixtieth

sessan'tina *sf:* **una ~ (di)** about sixty

sessi'one *sf* session

'**sesso** *sm* sex; **sessu'ale** *ag* sexual, sex *cpd*

ses'tante *sm* sextant

'**sesto, a** *ag, sm* sixth

'**seta** *sf* silk

'**sete** *sf* thirst; **avere ~** to be thirsty

'**setola** *sf* bristle

'**setta** *sf* sect

set'tanta *num* seventy; **settan'tesimo, a** *num* seventieth

settan'tina *sf:* **una ~ (di)** about seventy

'**sette** *num* seven

sette'cento [sette'tʃɛnto] *num* seven hundred ♦ *sm:* **il S~** the eighteenth century

set'tembre *sm* September

settentrio'nale *ag* northern

settentri'one *sm* north

setti'mana *sf* week; **settima'nale** *ag, sm* weekly

'**settimo, a** *ag, sm* seventh

set'tore *sm* sector

severità *sf* severity

se'vero, a *ag* severe

sevizi'are [sevit'tsjare] *vt* to torture

se'vizie [se'vittsje] *sfpl* torture *sg*

sezio'nare [settsjo'nare] *vt* to divide into sections; (*MED*) to dissect

sezi'one [set'tsjone] *sf* section; (*MED*) dissection

sfaccen'dato, a [sfattʃen'dato] *ag* idle

sfacci'ato, a [sfat'tʃato] *ag* (*maleducato*) cheeky, impudent; (*vistoso*) gaudy

sfa'celo [sfa'tʃɛlo] *sm* (*fig*) ruin, collapse

sfal'darsi *vr* to flake (off)

sfa'mare *vt* to feed; (*sog: cibo*) to fill

'**sfarzo** ['sfartso] *sm* pomp, splendour

sfasci'are [sfaʃ'ʃare] *vt* (*ferita*) to unbandage; (*distruggere: porta*) to smash, shatter; **~rsi** *vr* (*rompersi*) to smash, shatter

sfa'tare *vt* (*leggenda*) to explode

sfavil'lare *vi* to spark, send out sparks; (*risplendere*) to sparkle

sfavo'revole *ag* unfavourable

'**sfera** *sf* sphere; '**sferico, a, ci, che** *ag* spherical

sfer'rare *vt* (*fig: colpo*) to land, deal; (*: attacco*) to launch

sfer'zare [sfer'tsare] *vt* to whip; (*fig*) to lash out at

sfi'brare *vt* (*indebolire*) to exhaust, enervate

'**sfida** *sf* challenge; **sfi'dare** *vt* to challenge; (*fig*) to defy, brave

sfi'ducia [sfi'dutʃa] *sf* distrust, mistrust

sfigu'rare *vt* (*persona*) to disfigure; (*quadro, statua*) to deface ♦ *vi* (*far cattiva figura*) to make a bad impression

sfi'lare *vt* (*ago*) to unthread; (*abito, scarpe*) to slip off ♦ *vi* (*truppe*) to march past; (*atleti*) to parade; **~rsi** *vr* (*perle etc*) to come unstrung; (*orlo, tessuto*) to fray; (*calza*) to run, ladder; **sfi'lata** *sf* march past; parade; **sfilata di moda** fashion show

'**sfinge** ['sfindʒe] *sf* sphinx

sfi'nito, a *ag* exhausted

sfio'rare *vt* to brush (against); (*argomento*) to touch upon

sfio'rire *vi* to wither, fade

sfo'cato, a *ag* (*FOT*) out of focus

sfoci'are [sfo'tʃare] *vi:* **~ in** to flow into; (*fig: malcontento*) to develop into

sfo'gare *vt* to vent, pour out; **~rsi** *vr* (*sfogare la propria rabbia*) to give vent to one's anger; (*confidarsi*): **~rsi (con)** to pour out one's feelings (to); **non sfogarti su di me!** don't take your bad temper out on me!

sfoggi'are [sfod'dʒare] *vt, vi* to show off

'sfoglia ['sfoʎʎa] *sf* sheet of pasta dough; **pasta ~** (*CUC*) puff pastry

sfogli'are [sfoʎ'ʎare] *vt* (*libro*) to leaf through

'sfogo, ghi *sm* outlet; (*eruzione cutanea*) rash; (*fig*) outburst; **dare ~ a** (*fig*) to give vent to

sfolgo'rante *ag* (*luce*) blazing; (*fig: vittoria*) brilliant

sfol'lare *vt* to empty, clear ♦ *vi* to disperse; **~ da** (*città*) to evacuate

sfon'dare *vt* (*porta*) to break down; (*scarpe*) to wear a hole in; (*cesto, scatola*) to burst, knock the bottom out of; (*MIL*) to break through ♦ *vi* (*riuscire*) to make a name for o.s.

'sfondo *sm* background

sfor'mato *sm* (*CUC*) type of soufflé

sfor'nare *vt* (*pane etc*) to take out of the oven; (*fig*) to churn out

sfor'nito, a *ag*: **~ di** lacking in, without; (*negozio*) out of

sfor'tuna *sf* misfortune, ill luck *no pl*; **avere ~** to be unlucky; **sfortu'nato, a** *ag* unlucky; (*impresa, azione*) unsuccessful

sfor'zare [sfor'tsare] *vt* to force; (*voce, occhi*) to strain; **~rsi** *vr*: **~rsi di o a o per fare** to try hard to do

'sforzo ['sfortso] *sm* effort; (*tensione eccessiva, TECN*) strain; **fare uno ~** to make an effort

sfrat'tare *vt* to evict; **'sfratto** *sm* eviction

sfrecci'are [sfret'tʃare] *vi* to shoot *o* flash past

sfregi'are [sfre'dʒare] *vt* to slash, gash; (*persona*) to disfigure; (*quadro*) to deface; **'sfregio** *sm* gash; scar; (*fig*) insult

sfre'nato, a *ag* (*fig*) unrestrained, unbridled

sfron'tato, a *ag* shameless

sfrutta'mento *sm* exploitation

sfrut'tare *vt* (*terreno*) to overwork, exhaust; (*miniera*) to exploit, work; (*fig: operai, occasione, potere*) to exploit

sfug'gire [sfud'dʒire] *vi* to escape; **~ a** (*custode*) to escape (from); (*morte*) to escape; **~ a qn** (*dettaglio, nome*) to escape sb; **~ di mano a qn** to slip out of sb's hand (*o* hands); **sfug'gita: di sfuggita** *ad* (*rapidamente, in fretta*) in passing

sfu'mare *vt* (*colori, contorni*) to soften, shade off ♦ *vi* to shade (off), fade; (*fig: svanire*) to vanish, disappear; (: *speranze*) to come to nothing; **sfuma'tura** *sf* shading off *no pl*; (*tonalità*) shade, tone; (*fig*) touch, hint

sfuri'ata *sf* (*scatto di collera*) fit of anger; (*rimprovero*) sharp rebuke

sga'bello *sm* stool

sgabuz'zino [sgabud'dzino] *sm* lumber room

sgambet'tare *vi* to kick one's legs about

sgam'betto *sm*: **far lo ~ a qn** to trip sb up; (*fig*) to oust sb

sganasci'arsi [zganaʃ'ʃarsi] *vr*: **~ dalle risa** to roar with laughter

sganci'are [zgan'tʃare] *vt* to unhook; (*FERR*) to uncouple; (*bombe: da aereo*) to release, drop; (*fig: fam: soldi*) to fork out; **~rsi** *vr* (*fig*): **~rsi (da)** to get away (from)

sganghe'rato, a [zgange'rato] *ag* (*porta*) off its hinges; (*auto*) ramshackle; (*risata*) wild, boisterous

sgar'bato, a *ag* rude, impolite

'sgarbo *sm*: **fare uno ~ a qn** to be rude to sb

sgattaio'lare *vi* to sneak away *o* off

sge'lare [zdʒe'lare] *vi, vt* to thaw

'sghembo, a ['zgembo] *ag* (*obliquo*) slanting; (*storto*) crooked

sghignaz'zare [zginnat'tsare] *vi* to laugh scornfully

sgob'bare (*fam*) *vi* (*scolaro*) to swot; (*operaio*) to slog

sgoccio'lare [zgottʃo'lare] *vt* (*vuotare*) to drain (to the last drop) ♦ *vi* (*acqua*) to drip; (*recipiente*) to drain; **'sgoccioli** *smpl*: **essere agli ~** (*provviste*) to be nearly finished; (*periodo*) to be nearly over

sgo'larsi *vr* to talk (*o* shout *o* sing) o.s. hoarse

sgomb(e)'rare *vt* to clear; (*andarsene da: stanza*) to vacate; (*evacuare*) to evacuate

'sgombro, a *ag:* ~ (**di**) clear (of), free (from) ♦ *sm* (ZOOL) mackerel; (*anche: sgombero*) clearing; vacating; evacuation; (: *trasloco*) removal

sgomen'tare *vt* to dismay; **sgo'mento, a** *ag* dismayed ♦ *sm* dismay, consternation

sgonfi'are *vt* to let down, deflate; ~**rsi** *vr* to go down

'sgorbio *sm* blot; scribble

sgor'gare *vi* to gush (out)

sgoz'zare [zgot'tsare] *vt* to cut the throat of

sgra'devole *ag* unpleasant, disagreeable

sgra'dito, a *ag* unpleasant, unwelcome

sgra'nare *vt* (*piselli*) to shell; ~ **gli occhi** to open one's eyes wide

sgran'chirsi [zgran'kirsi] *vr* to stretch; ~ **le gambe** to stretch one's legs

sgranocchi'are [zgranok'kjare] *vt* to munch

'sgravio *sm:* ~ **fiscale** tax relief

sgrazi'ato, a [zgrat'tsjato] *ag* clumsy, ungainly

sgreto'lare *vt* to cause to crumble; ~**rsi** *vr* to crumble

sgri'dare *vt* to scold; **sgri'data** *sf* scolding

sguai'ato, a *ag* coarse, vulgar

sgual'cire [zgwal'tʃire] *vt* to crumple (up), crease

sgual'drina (*peg*) *sf* slut

sgu'ardo *sm* (*occhiata*) look, glance; (*espressione*) look (in one's eye)

'sguattero, a *sm/f* dishwasher (*person*)

sguaz'zare [zgwat'tsare] *vi* (*nell'acqua*) to splash about; (*nella melma*) to wallow; ~ **nell'oro** to be rolling in money

sguinzagli'are [zgwintsaʎ'ʎare] *vt* to let off the leash; (*fig: persona*): ~ **qn dietro a qn** to set sb on sb

sgusci'are [zguʃ'ʃare] *vt* to shell ♦ *vi* (*sfuggire di mano*) to slip; ~ **via** to slip *o* slink away

'shampoo ['ʃampo] *sm inv* shampoo

shock [ʃɔk] *sm inv* shock

PAROLA CHIAVE

si¹ (*dav lo, la, li, le, ne diventa* **se**) *pron* **1** (*riflessivo: maschile*) himself; (: *femminile*) herself; (: *neutro*) itself; (: *impersonale*) oneself; (: *pl*) themselves; **lavarsi** to wash (oneself); ~ **è tagliato** he has cut himself; ~ **credono importanti** they think a lot of themselves

2 (*riflessivo: con complemento oggetto*): **lavarsi le mani** to wash one's hands; ~ **sta lavando i capelli** he (*o* she) is washing his (*o* her) hair

3 (*reciproco*) one another, each other; **si amano** they love one another *o* each other

4 (*passivo*): ~ **ripara facilmente** it is easily repaired

5 (*impersonale*): ~ **dice che ...** they *o* people say that ...; ~ **vede che è vecchio** one *o* you can see that it's old

6 (*noi*) we; **tra poco** ~ **parte** we're leaving soon

si² *sm* (MUS) B; (*solfeggiando la scala*) ti

sì *av* yes; **un giorno** ~ **e uno no** every other day

'sia *cong:* ~ ... ~ (*o* ... *o*): ~ **che lavori**, ~ **che non lavori** whether he works or not; (*tanto ... quanto*): **verranno** ~ **Luigi** ~ **suo fratello** both Luigi and his brother will be coming

si'amo *vb vedi* **essere**

sibi'lare *vi* to hiss; (*fischiare*) to whistle; **'sibilo** *sm* hiss; whistle

si'cario *sm* hired killer

sicché [sik'ke] *cong* (*perciò*) so (that), therefore; (*e quindi*) (and) so

siccità [sittʃi'ta] *sf* drought

sic'come *cong* since, as

Si'cilia [si'tʃilja] *sf:* **la** ~ Sicily; **sicili'ano, a** *ag, sm/f* Sicilian

sicu'rezza [siku'rettsa] *sf* safety; security; (*fiducia*) confidence; (*certezza*) certainty; **di** ~ safety *cpd*; **la** ~ **stradale** road safety

si'curo, a *ag* safe; (*ben difeso*) secure;

(*fiducioso*) confident; (*certo*) sure, certain; (*notizia, amico*) reliable; (*esperto*) skilled ♦ *av* (*anche: di* ~) certainly; **essere/ mettere al** ~ to be safe/put in a safe place; ~ **di sé** self-confident, sure of o.s.; **sentirsi** ~ to feel safe *o* secure

siderur'gia [siderur'dʒia] *sf* iron and steel industry

'sidro *sm* cider

si'epe *sf* hedge

si'ero *sm* (*MED*) serum; **sieronega'tivo, a** *ag* HIV-negative; **sieroposi'tivo, a** *ag* HIV-positive

si'esta *sf* siesta, (afternoon) nap

si'ete *vb vedi* **essere**

si'filide *sf* syphilis

si'fone *sm* siphon

Sig. *abbr* (= *signore*) Mr

siga'retta *sf* cigarette

'sigaro *sm* cigar

Sigg. *abbr* (= *signori*) Messrs

sigil'lare [sidʒil'lare] *vt* to seal

si'gillo [si'dʒillo] *sm* seal

'sigla *sf* initials *pl*; acronym, abbreviation; ~ **automobilistica** *abbreviation of province on vehicle number plate*; ~ **musicale** signature tune

si'glare *vt* to initial

Sig.na *abbr* (= *signorina*) Miss

signifi'care [siɲɲifi'kare] *vt* to mean; **significa'tivo, a** *ag* significant; **signifi'cato** *sm* meaning

si'gnora [siɲ'ɲora] *sf* lady; **la** ~ **X** Mrs X; **buon giorno S~/Signore/Signorina** good morning; (*deferente*) good morning Madam/Sir/Madam; (*quando si conosce il nome*) good morning Mrs/Mr/Miss X; **Gentile S~/Signore/Signorina** (*in una lettera*) Dear Madam/Sir/Madam; **il signor Rossi e** ~ Mr Rossi and his wife; ~**e e signori** ladies and gentlemen

si'gnore [siɲ'ɲore] *sm* gentleman; (*padrone*) lord, master; (*REL*) **il S~** the Lord; **il signor X** Mr X; **i** ~**i Bianchi** (*coniugi*) Mr and Mrs Bianchi; *vedi anche* **signora**

signo'rile [siɲɲo'rile] *ag* refined

signo'rina [siɲɲo'rina] *sf* young lady; **la** ~ **X** Miss X; *vedi anche* **signora**

Sig.ra *abbr* (= *signora*) Mrs

silenzia'tore [silentsja'tore] *sm* silencer

si'lenzio [si'lentsjo] *sm* silence; **fare** ~ to be quiet, stop talking; **silenzi'oso, a** *ag* silent, quiet

si'licio [si'litʃo] *sm* silicon; **piastrina di** ~ silicon chip

'sillaba *sf* syllable

silu'rare *vt* to torpedo; (*fig: privare del comando*) to oust

si'luro *sm* torpedo

simboleggi'are [simboled'dʒare] *vt* to symbolize

'simbolo *sm* symbol

'simile *ag* (*analogo*) similar; (*di questo tipo*): **un uomo** ~ such a man, a man like this; **libri** ~**i** such books; ~ **a** similar to; **i suoi** ~**i** one's fellow men; one's peers

simme'tria *sf* symmetry

simpa'tia *sf* (*qualità*) pleasantness; (*inclinazione*) liking; **avere** ~ **per qn** to like sb, have a liking for sb; **sim'patico, a, ci, che** *ag* (*persona*) nice, pleasant, likeable; (*casa, albergo etc*) nice, pleasant

simpatiz'zare [simpatid'dzare] *vi*: ~ **con** to take a liking to

sim'posio *sm* symposium

simu'lare *vt* to sham, simulate; (*TECN*) to simulate; **simulazi'one** *sf* shamming; simulation

simul'taneo, a *ag* simultaneous

sina'goga, ghe *sf* synagogue

since'rità [sintʃeri'ta] *sf* sincerity

sin'cero, a [sin'tʃero] *ag* sincere; genuine; heartfelt

'sincope *sf* syncopation; (*MED*) blackout

sinda'cale *ag* (trade-)union *cpd*; **sindaca'lista, i, e** *sm/f* trade unionist

sinda'cato *sm* (*di lavoratori*) (trade) union; (*AMM, ECON, DIR*) syndicate, trust, pool

'sindaco, ci *sm* mayor

sinfo'nia *sf* (*MUS*) symphony

singhioz'zare [singjot'tsare] *vi* to sob; to hiccup

singhi'ozzo [sin'gjottso] *sm* sob; (*MED*) hiccup; **avere il** ~ to have the hiccups; **a** ~ (*fig*) by fits and starts

singo'lare *ag* (*insolito*) remarkable,

singular; (*LING*) singular ♦ *sm* (*LING*)
singular; (*TENNIS*): ~ **maschile/femminile**
men's/women's singles

'**singolo, a** *ag* single, individual ♦ *sm*
(*persona*) individual; (*TENNIS*) = **singolare**

si'**nistra** *sf* (*POL*) left (wing); **a** ~ on the
left; (*direzione*) to the left

si'**nistro, a** *ag* left, left-hand; (*fig*)
sinister ♦ *sm* (*incidente*) accident

'**sino** *prep* = **fino**

si'**nonimo, a** *ag* synonymous ♦ *sm*
synonym; ~ **di** synonymous with

sin'**tassi** *sf* syntax

'**sintesi** *sf* synthesis; (*riassunto*)
summary, résumé

sin'**tetico, a, ci, che** *ag* synthetic

sintetiz'**zare** [sintetid'dzare] *vt* to
synthesize; (*riassumere*) to summarize

sinto'**matico, a, ci, che** *ag*
symptomatic

'**sintomo** *sm* symptom

sinu'**oso, a** *ag* (*strada*) winding

S.I.P. *sigla f* (= *Società italiana per
l'esercizio telefonico*) *Italian telephone
company*

si'**pario** *sm* (*TEATRO*) curtain

si'**rena** *sf* (*apparecchio*) siren; (*nella
mitologia, fig*) siren, mermaid

'**Siria** *sf*: **la** ~ Syria

si'**ringa, ghe** *sf* syringe

'**sismico, a, ci, che** *ag* seismic

sis'**mografo** *sm* seismograph

sis'**tema, i** *sm* system; method, way; ~ **di
vita** way of life

siste'**mare** *vt* (*mettere a posto*) to tidy,
put in order; (*risolvere: questione*) to sort
out, settle; (*procurare un lavoro a*) to find
a job for; (*dare un alloggio a*) to settle,
find accommodation for; ~**rsi** *vr*
(*problema*) to be settled; (*persona: trovare
alloggio*) to find accommodation (*BRIT*) *o*
accommodations (*US*); (: *trovarsi un
lavoro*) to get fixed up with a job; **ti
sistemo io!** I'll soon sort you out!

siste'**matico, a, ci, che** *ag* systematic

sistemazi'**one** [sistemat'tsjone] *sf*
arrangement, order; settlement;
employment; accommodation (*BRIT*),
accommodations (*US*)

'**sito** *sm* (*letterario*) place

situ'**are** *vt* to site, situate; **situ'ato, a** *ag*:
situato a/su situated at/on

situazi'**one** [situat'tsjone] *sf* situation

ski-lift ['ski:lift] *sm inv* ski-lift

slacci'**are** [zlat'tʃare] *vt* to undo,
unfasten

slanci'**arsi** [zlan'tʃarsi] *vr* to dash, fling
o.s.; **slanci'ato, a** *ag* slender; '**slancio**
sm dash, leap; (*fig*) surge; **di slancio**
impetuously

sla'**vato, a** *ag* faded, washed out; (*fig:
viso, occhi*) pale, colourless

'**slavo, a** *ag* Slav(onic), Slavic

sle'**ale** *ag* disloyal; (*concorrenza etc*)
unfair

sle'**gare** *vt* to untie

slip [zlip] *sm inv* briefs *pl*

'**slitta** *sf* sledge; (*trainata*) sleigh

slit'**tare** *vi* to slip, slide; (*AUT*) to skid

slo'**gare** *vt* (*MED*) to dislocate

sloggi'**are** [zlod'dʒare] *vt* (*inquilino*) to
turn out; (*nemico*) to drive out, dislodge
♦ *vi* to move out

Slovenia [zlo'vɛnja] *sf* Slovenia

smacchi'**are** [zmak'kjare] *vt* to remove
stains from

'**smacco, chi** *sm* humiliating defeat

smagli'**ante** [zmaʎ'ʎante] *ag* brilliant,
dazzling

smaglia'**tura** [zmaʎʎa'tura] *sf* (*su
maglia, calza*) ladder; (*della pelle*) stretch
mark

smalizi'**ato, a** [smalit'tsjato] *ag* shrewd,
cunning

smal'**tare** *vt* to enamel; (*ceramica*) to
glaze; (*unghie*) to varnish

smal'**tire** *vt* (*merce*) to sell off; (*rifiuti*) to
dispose of; (*cibo*) to digest; (*peso*) to lose;
(*rabbia*) to get over; ~ **la sbornia** to
sober up

'**smalto** *sm* (*anche: di denti*) enamel; (*per
ceramica*) glaze; ~ **per unghie** nail
varnish

'**smania** *sf* agitation, restlessness; (*fig*): ~
di thirst for, craving for; **avere la** ~
addosso to have the fidgets; **avere la** ~
di fare to be desperate to do

smantel'**lare** *vt* to dismantle

smarri'mento *sm* loss; (*fig*) bewilderment; dismay

smar'rire *vt* to lose; (*non riuscire a trovare*) to mislay; **~rsi** *vr* (*perdersi*) to lose one's way, get lost; (: *oggetto*) to go astray; **smar'rito, a** *ag* (*sbigottito*) bewildered

smasche'rare [zmaske'rare] *vt* to unmask

smemo'rato, a *ag* forgetful

smen'tire *vt* (*negare*) to deny; (*testimonianza*) to refute; (*reputazione*) to give the lie to; **~rsi** *vr* to be inconsistent; **smen'tita** *sf* denial; retraction

sme'raldo *sm* emerald

smerci'are [zmer'tʃare] *vt* (COMM) to sell; (: *svendere*) to sell off

sme'riglio [zme'riʎʎo] *sm* emery

'smesso, a *pp di* **smettere**

'smettere *vt* to stop; (*vestiti*) to stop wearing ♦ *vi* to stop, cease; **~ di fare** to stop doing

'smilzo, a ['zmiltso] *ag* thin, lean

sminu'ire *vt* to diminish, lessen; (*fig*) to belittle

sminuz'zare [zminut'tsare] *vt* to break into small pieces; to crumble

smis'tare *vt* (*pacchi etc*) to sort; (FERR) to shunt

smisu'rato, a *ag* boundless, immeasurable; (*grandissimo*) immense, enormous

smobili'tare *vt* to demobilize

smo'dato, a *ag* immoderate

smoking ['sməukiŋ] *sm inv* dinner jacket

smon'tare *vt* (*mobile, macchina etc*) to take to pieces, dismantle; (*fig: scoraggiare*) to dishearten ♦ *vi* (*scendere: da cavallo*) to dismount; (: *da treno*) to get off; (*terminare il lavoro*) to stop (work); **~rsi** *vr* to lose heart; to lose one's enthusiasm

'smorfia *sf* grimace; (*atteggiamento lezioso*) simpering; **fare ~e** to make faces; to simper; **smorfi'oso, a** *ag* simpering

'smorto, a *ag* (*viso*) pale, wan; (*colore*) dull

smor'zare [zmor'tsare] *vt* (*suoni*) to deaden; (*colori*) to tone down; (*luce*) to dim; (*sete*) to quench; (*entusiasmo*) to dampen; **~rsi** *vr* (*suono, luce*) to fade; (*entusiasmo*) to dampen

'smosso, a *pp di* **smuovere**

smotta'mento *sm* landslide

'smunto, a *ag* haggard, pinched

smu'overe *vt* to move, shift; (*fig: commuovere*) to move; (: *dall'inerzia*) to rouse, stir; **~rsi** *vr* to move, shift

smus'sare *vt* (*angolo*) to round off, smooth; (*lama etc*) to blunt; **~rsi** *vr* to become blunt

snatu'rato, a *ag* inhuman, heartless

'snello, a *ag* (*agile*) agile; (*svelto*) slender, slim

sner'vare *vt* to enervate, wear out; **~rsi** *vr* to become enervated

sni'dare *vt* to drive out, flush out

snob'bare *vt* to snub

sno'bismo *sm* snobbery

snoccio'lare [znottʃo'lare] *vt* (*frutta*) to stone; (*fig: orazioni*) to rattle off; (: *verità*) to blab

sno'dare *vt* (*rendere agile, mobile*) to loosen; **~rsi** *vr* to come loose; (*articolarsi*) to bend; (*strada, fiume*) to wind

so *vb vedi* **sapere**

so'ave *ag* sweet, gentle, soft

sobbal'zare [sobbal'tsare] *vi* to jolt, jerk; (*trasalire*) to jump, start; **sob'balzo** *sm* jerk, jolt; jump, start

sobbar'carsi *vr*: **~ a** to take on, undertake

sob'borgo, ghi *sm* suburb

sobil'lare *vt* to stir up, incite

'sobrio, a *ag* sober

socchi'udere [sok'kjudere] *vt* (*porta*) to leave ajar; (*occhi*) to half-close; **socchi'uso, a** *pp di* **socchiudere**

soc'correre *vt* to help, assist; **soc'corso, a** *pp di* **soccorrere** ♦ *sm* help, aid, assistance; **soccorsi** *smpl* relief *sg*, aid *sg*; **soccorso stradale** breakdown service

socialdemo'cratico, a, ci, che [sotʃaldemo'kratiko] *sm/f* Social Democrat

soci'ale [so'tʃale] *ag* social; (*di associazione*) club *cpd*, association *cpd*

socia'lismo [sotʃa'lizmo] *sm* socialism;

socia'lista, i, e *ag, sm/f* socialist
società [sot∫e'ta] *sf inv* society; *(sportiva)* club; *(COMM)* company; ~ **per azioni** limited *(BRIT)* o incorporated *(US)* company; ~ **a responsabilità limitata** *type of limited liability company*
soci'evole [so't∫evole] *ag* sociable
'socio ['sɔt∫o] *sm (DIR, COMM)* partner; *(membro di associazione)* member
'soda *sf (CHIM)* soda; *(acqua gassata)* soda (water)
soda'lizio [soda'littsjo] *sm* association, society
soddisfa'cente [soddisfa't∫ɛnte] *ag* satisfactory
soddis'fare *vt, vi:* ~ **a** to satisfy; *(impegno)* to fulfil; *(debito)* to pay off; *(richiesta)* to meet, comply with; *(offesa)* to make amends for; **soddis'fatto, a** *pp di* **soddisfare ♦** *ag* satisfied; **soddisfatto di** happy o satisfied with; pleased with; **soddisfazi'one** *sf* satisfaction
'sodo, a *ag (picchiare, lavorare)* firm, hard ♦ *av (picchiare, lavorare)* hard; **dormire** ~ to sleep soundly
sofà *sm inv* sofa
soffe'renza [soffe'rɛntsa] *sf* suffering
sof'ferto, a *pp di* **soffrire**
soffi'are *vt* to blow; *(notizia, segreto)* to whisper ♦ *vi* to blow; *(sbuffare)* to puff (and blow); ~**rsi il naso** to blow one's nose; ~ **qc/qn a qn** *(fig)* to pinch o steal sth/sb from sb; ~ **via qc** to blow sth away
'soffice ['sɔffit∫e] *ag* soft
'soffio *sm (di vento)* breath; *(di fumo)* puff; *(MED)* murmur
sof'fitta *sf* attic
sof'fitto *sm* ceiling
soffo'care *vi (anche:* ~**rsi)** to suffocate, choke ♦ *vt* to suffocate, choke; *(fig)* to stifle, suppress
sof'friggere [sof'friddʒere] *vt* to fry lightly
sof'frire *vt* to suffer, endure; *(sopportare)* to bear, stand ♦ *vi* to suffer; to be in pain; ~ **(di) qc** *(MED)* to suffer from sth
sof'fritto, a *pp di* **soffriggere** ♦ *sm (CUC) fried mixture of herbs, bacon and onions*

sofisti'cato, a *ag* sophisticated; *(vino)* adulterated
sogget'tivo, a [soddʒet'tivo] *ag* subjective
sog'getto, a [sod'dʒetto] *ag:* ~ **a** *(sottomesso)* subject to; *(esposto: a variazioni, danni etc)* subject o liable to ♦ *sm* subject
soggezi'one [soddʒet'tsjone] *sf* subjection; *(timidezza)* awe; **avere** ~ **di qn** to stand in awe of sb; to be ill at ease in sb's presence
sogghi'gnare [soggin'nare] *vi* to sneer
soggior'nare [soddʒor'nare] *vi* to stay; **soggi'orno** *sm (invernale, marino)* stay; *(stanza)* living room
sog'giungere [sod'dʒundʒere] *vt* to add
'soglia ['sɔʎʎa] *sf* doorstep; *(anche fig)* threshold
sogli'ola ['sɔʎʎola] *sf (ZOOL)* sole
so'gnare [son'nare] *vt, vi* to dream; ~ **a occhi aperti** to daydream; **sogna'tore, 'trice** *sm/f* dreamer
'sogno ['sonno] *sm* dream
'soia *sf (BOT)* soya
sol *sm (MUS)* G; *(: solfeggiando la scala)* so(h)
so'laio *sm (soffitta)* attic
sola'mente *av* only, just
so'lare *ag* solar, sun *cpd*
'solco, chi *sm (scavo, fig: ruga)* furrow; *(incavo)* rut, track; *(di disco)* groove; *(scia)* wake
sol'dato *sm* soldier; ~ **semplice** private
'soldo *sm (fig):* **non avere un** ~ to be penniless; **non vale un** ~ it's not worth a penny; ~**i** *smpl (denaro)* money *sg*
'sole *sm* sun; *(luce)* sun(light); *(tempo assolato)* sun(shine); **prendere il** ~ to sunbathe
soleggi'ato, a [soled'dʒato] *ag* sunny
so'lenne *ag* solemn; **solennità** *sf* solemnity; *(festività)* holiday, feast day
sol'fato *sm (CHIM)* sulphate
soli'dale *ag:* **essere** ~ **(con)** to be in agreement (with)
solidarietà *sf* solidarity
'solido, a *ag* solid; *(forte, robusto)* sturdy, solid; *(fig: ditta)* sound, solid ♦ *sm (MAT)*

solid
soli'loquio *sm* soliloquy
so'lista, i, e *ag* solo ♦ *sm/f* soloist
solita'mente *av* usually, as a rule
soli'tario, a *ag* (*senza compagnia*)
solitary, lonely; (*solo, isolato*) solitary,
lone; (*deserto*) lonely ♦ *sm* (*gioiello, gioco*)
solitaire
'solito, a *ag* usual; **essere ~ fare** to be
in the habit of doing; **di ~** usually; **più
tardi del ~** later than usual; **come al ~**
as usual
soli'tudine *sf* solitude
solleci'tare [solletʃi'tare] *vt* (*lavoro*) to
speed up; (*persona*) to urge on; (*chiedere
con insistenza*) to press for, request
urgently; (*stimolare*): **~ qn a fare** to urge
sb to do; (*TECN*) to stress; **sollecitazi'one**
sf entreaty, request; (*fig*) incentive; (*TECN*)
stress
sol'lecito, a [sol'letʃito] *ag* prompt,
quick ♦ *sm* (*lettera*) reminder;
solleci'tudine *sf* promptness, speed
solleti'care *vt* to tickle
sol'letico *sm* tickling; **soffrire il ~** to be
ticklish
solleva'mento *sm* raising; lifting; revolt;
~ pesi (*SPORT*) weight-lifting
solle'vare *vt* to lift, raise; (*fig: persona:
alleggerire*): **~ (da)** to relieve (of); (: *dar
conforto*) to comfort, relieve; (: *questione*)
to raise; (: *far insorgere*) to stir (to
revolt); **~rsi** *vr* to rise; (*fig: riprendersi*) to
recover; (: *ribellarsi*) to rise up
solli'evo *sm* relief; (*conforto*) comfort
'solo, a *ag* alone; (*in senso spirituale:
isolato*) lonely; (*unico*): **un ~ libro** only
one book, a single book; (*con ag
numerale*): **veniamo noi tre ~i** just *o*
only the three of us are coming ♦ *av*
(*soltanto*) only, just; **non ~ ... ma anche**
not only ... but also; **fare qc da ~** to do
sth (all) by oneself; **da me ~** single-
handed, on my own
sol'tanto *av* only
so'lubile *ag* (*sostanza*) soluble
soluzi'one [solut'tsjone] *sf* solution
sol'vente *ag, sm* solvent
'soma *sf*: **bestia da ~** beast of burden

so'maro *sm* ass, donkey
somigli'anza [somiʎ'ʎantsa] *sf*
resemblance
somigli'are [somiʎ'ʎare] *vi*: **~ a** to be
like, resemble; (*nell'aspetto fisico*) to look
like; **~rsi** *vr* to (o look) alike
'somma *sf* (*MAT*) sum; (*di denaro*) sum (of
money); (*complesso di varie cose*) whole
amount, sum total
som'mare *vt* to add up; (*aggiungere*) to
add; **tutto sommato** all things considered
som'mario, a *ag* (*racconto, indagine*)
brief; (*giustizia*) summary ♦ *sm* summary
som'mergere [som'mɛrdʒere] *vt* to
submerge
sommer'gibile [sommer'dʒibile] *sm*
submarine
som'merso, a *pp di* **sommergere**
som'messo, a *ag* (*voce*) soft, subdued
somminis'trare *vt* to give, administer
sommità *sf inv* summit, top; (*fig*) height
'sommo, a *ag* highest; (*rispetto etc*)
highest, greatest; (*poeta, artista*) great,
outstanding ♦ *sm* (*fig*) height; **per ~i capi**
briefly, covering the main points
som'mossa *sf* uprising
so'nare *etc* = **suonare** *etc*
son'daggio [son'daddʒo] *sm* sounding;
probe; boring, drilling; (*indagine*) survey;
~ d'opinioni opinion poll
son'dare *vt* (*NAUT*) to sound; (*atmosfera,
piaga*) to probe; (*MINERALOGIA*) to bore,
drill; (*fig: opinione etc*) to survey, poll
so'netto *sm* sonnet
son'nambulo, a *sm/f* sleepwalker
sonnecchi'are [sonnek'kjare] *vi* to doze,
nod
son'nifero *sm* sleeping drug (*o* pill)
'sonno *sm* sleep; **prendere ~** to fall
asleep; **aver ~** to be sleepy
'sono *vb vedi* **essere**
so'noro, a *ag* (*ambiente*) resonant; (*voce*)
sonorous, ringing; (*onde, film*) sound *cpd*
sontu'oso, a *ag* sumptuous; lavish
sopo'rifero, a *ag* soporific
soppe'sare *vt* to weigh in one's hand(s),
feel the weight of; (*fig*) to weigh up
soppi'atto: di ~ *av* secretly; furtively
soppor'tare *vt* (*reggere*) to support;

(*subire: perdita, spese*) to bear, sustain; (*soffrire: dolore*) to bear, endure; (*sog: cosa: freddo*) to withstand; (*sog: persona: freddo, vino*) to take; (*tollerare*) to put up with, tolerate

sop'presso, a *pp di* sopprimere

sop'primere *vt* (*carica, privilegi, testimone*) to do away with; (*pubblicazione*) to suppress; (*parola, frase*) to delete

'sopra *prep* (*gen*) on; (*al di sopra di, più in alto di*) above; over; (*riguardo a*) on, about ♦ *av* on top; (*attaccato, scritto*) on it; (*al di sopra*) above; (*al piano superiore*) upstairs; **donne ~ i 30 anni** women over 30 (years of age); **abito di ~** I live upstairs; **dormirci ~** (*fig*) to sleep on it

so'prabito *sm* overcoat

soprac'ciglio [soprat'tʃiʎʎo] (*pl(f)* soprac'ciglia) *sm* eyebrow

sopracco'perta *sf* (*di letto*) bedspread; (*di libro*) jacket

soprad'detto, a *ag* aforesaid

sopraf'fare *vt* to overcome, overwhelm; sopraf'fatto, a *pp di* sopraffare

sopraf'fino, a *ag* (*pranzo, vino*) excellent

sopraggi'ungere [soprad'dʒundʒere] *vi* (*giungere all'improvviso*) to arrive (unexpectedly); (*accadere*) to occur (unexpectedly)

sopral'luogo, ghi *sm* (*di esperti*) inspection; (*di polizia*) on-the-spot investigation

sopram'mobile *sm* ornament

soprannatu'rale *ag* supernatural

sopran'nome *sm* nickname

so'prano, a *sm/f* (*persona*) soprano ♦ *sm* (*voce*) soprano

soprappensi'ero *av* lost in thought

sopras'salto *sm*: **di ~** with a start; suddenly

soprasse'dere *vi*: **~ a** to delay, put off

soprat'tutto *av* (*anzitutto*) above all; (*specialmente*) especially

soprav'vento *sm*: **avere/prendere il ~ su** to have/get the upper hand over

sopravvis'suto, a *pp di* sopravvivere

soprav'vivere *vi* to survive; (*continuare a vivere*): **~ (in)** to live on (in); **~ a**

(*incidente etc*) to survive; (*persona*) to outlive

soprele'vata *sf* (*strada*) flyover; (*ferrovia*) elevated railway

soprinten'dente *sm/f* supervisor; (*statale: di belle arti etc*) keeper; soprinten'denza *sf* supervision; (*ente*): **soprintendenza alle Belle Arti** *government department responsible for monuments and artistic treasures*

so'pruso *sm* abuse of power; **subire un ~** to be abused

soq'quadro *sm*: **mettere a ~** to turn upside-down

sor'betto *sm* sorbet, water ice

sor'bire *vt* to sip; (*fig*) to put up with

'sorcio, ci ['sortʃo] *sm* mouse

'sordido, a *ag* sordid; (*fig: gretto*) stingy

sor'dina *sf*: **in ~** softly; (*fig*) on the sly

sordità *sf* deafness

'sordo, a *ag* deaf; (*rumore*) muffled; (*dolore*) dull; (*odio, rancore*) veiled ♦ *sm/f* deaf person; sordo'muto, a *ag* deaf-and-dumb ♦ *sm/f* deaf-mute

so'rella *sf* sister; sorel'lastra *sf* stepsister

sor'gente [sor'dʒɛnte] *sf* (*acqua che sgorga*) spring; (*di fiume*, FISICA, *fig*) source

'sorgere ['sordʒere] *vi* to rise; (*scaturire*) to spring, rise; (*fig: difficoltà*) to arise

sormon'tare *vt* (*fig*) to overcome, surmount

sorni'one, a *ag* sly

sorpas'sare *vt* (AUT) to overtake; (*fig*) to surpass; (*: eccedere*) to exceed, go beyond; **~ in altezza** to be higher than; (*persona*) to be taller than

sorpren'dente *ag* surprising

sor'prendere *vt* (*cogliere: in flagrante etc*) to catch; (*stupire*) to surprise; **~rsi** *vr*: **~rsi (di)** to be surprised (at); **sor'presa** *sf* surprise; **fare una sorpresa a qn** to give sb a surprise; **sor'preso, a** *pp di* sorprendere

sor'reggere [sor'reddʒere] *vt* to support, hold up; (*fig*) to sustain; **sor'retto, a** *pp di* sorreggere

sor'ridere *vi* to smile; **sor'riso, a** *pp di*

sorridere ♦ *sm* smile

'sorso *sm* sip

'sorta *sf* sort, kind; **di ~** whatever, of any kind, at all

'sorte *sf* (*fato*) fate, destiny; (*evento fortuito*) chance; **tirare a ~** to draw lots

sor'teggio [sor'teddʒo] *sm* draw

sorti'legio [sorti'lɛdʒo] *sm* witchcraft *no pl*; (*incantesimo*) spell; **fare un ~ a qn** to cast a spell on sb

sor'tita *sf* (MIL) sortie

'sorto, a *pp di* **sorgere**

sorvegli'anza [sorveʎ'ʎantsa] *sf* watch; supervision; (POLIZIA, MIL) surveillance

sorvegli'are [sorveʎ'ʎare] *vt* (*bambino, bagagli, prigioniero*) to watch, keep an eye on; (*malato*) to watch over; (*territorio, casa*) to watch *o* keep watch over; (*lavori*) to supervise

sorvo'lare *vt* (*territorio*) to fly over ♦ *vi*: **~ su** (*fig*) to skim over

'sosia *sm inv* double

sos'pendere *vt* (*appendere*) to hang (up); (*interrompere, privare di una carica*) to suspend; (*rimandare*) to defer; **~ un quadro al muro/un lampadario al soffitto** to hang a picture on the wall/a chandelier from the ceiling; **sospensi'one** *sf* (*anche* CHIM, AUT) suspension; deferment; **sos'peso, a** *pp di* **sospendere** ♦ *ag* (*appeso*): **sospeso a** hanging on (*o* from); (*treno, autobus*) cancelled; **in sospeso** in abeyance; (*conto*) outstanding; **tenere in sospeso** (*fig*) to keep in suspense

sospet'tare *vt* to suspect ♦ *vi*: **~ di** to suspect; (*diffidare*) to be suspicious of

sos'petto, a *ag* suspicious ♦ *sm* suspicion; **sospet'toso, a** *ag* suspicious

sos'pingere [sos'pindʒere] *vt* to drive, push; **sos'pinto, a** *pp di* **sospingere**

sospi'rare *vi* to sigh ♦ *vt* to long for, yearn for; **sos'piro** *sm* sigh

'sosta *sf* (*fermata*) stop, halt; (*pausa*) pause, break; **senza ~** non-stop, without a break

sostan'tivo *sm* noun, substantive

sos'tanza [sos'tantsa] *sf* substance; **~e** *sfpl* (*ricchezze*) wealth *sg*, possessions; **in**

~ in short, to sum up; **sostanzi'oso, a** *ag* (*cibo*) nourishing, substantial

sos'tare *vi* (*fermarsi*) to stop (for a while), stay; (*fare una pausa*) to take a break

sos'tegno [sos'teɲɲo] *sm* support

soste'nere *vt* to support; (*prendere su di sé*) to take on, bear; (*resistere*) to withstand, stand up to; (*affermare*): **~ che** to maintain that; **~rsi** *vr* to hold o.s. up, support o.s.; (*fig*) to keep up one's strength; **~ gli esami** to sit exams; **sosteni'tore, 'trice** *sm/f* supporter

sostenta'mento *sm* maintenance, support

soste'nuto, a *ag* (*stile*) elevated; (*velocità, ritmo*) sustained; (*prezzo*) high ♦ *sm/f*: **fare il(la) ~(a)** to be standoffish, keep one's distance

sostitu'ire *vt* (*mettere al posto di*): **~ qn/qc a** to substitute sb/sth for; (*prendere il posto di: persona*) to substitute for; (: *cosa*) to take the place of

sosti'tuto, a *sm/f* substitute

sostituzi'one [sostitut'tsjone] *sf* substitution; **in ~ di** as a substitute for, in place of

sotta'ceti [sotta'tʃeti] *smpl* pickles

sot'tana *sf* (*sottoveste*) underskirt; (*gonna*) skirt; (REL) soutane, cassock

sotter'fugio [sotter'fudʒo] *sm* subterfuge

sotter'raneo, a *ag* underground ♦ *sm* cellar

sotter'rare *vt* to bury

sottigli'ezza [sottiʎ'ʎettsa] *sf* thinness; slimness; (*fig: acutezza*) subtlety; shrewdness; **~e** *sfpl* (*pedanteria*) quibbles

sot'tile *ag* thin; (*figura, caviglia*) thin, slim, slender; (*fine: polvere, capelli*) fine; (*fig: leggero*) light; (: *vista*) sharp, keen; (: *olfatto*) fine, discriminating; (: *mente*) subtle; shrewd ♦ *sm*: **non andare per il ~** not to mince matters

sottin'tendere *vt* (*intendere qc non espresso*) to understand; (*implicare*) to imply; **sottin'teso, a** *pp di* **sottintendere** ♦ *sm* allusion; **parlare senza sottintesi** to speak plainly

'sotto *prep* (*gen*) under; (*più in basso di*)

below ♦ *av* underneath, beneath; below; (*al piano inferiore*): **(al piano) di ~** downstairs; **~ forma di** in the form of; **~ il monte** at the foot of the mountain; **siamo ~ Natale** it's nearly Christmas; **~ la pioggia/il sole** in the rain/sun(shine); **~ terra** underground; **~ voce** in a low voice; **chiuso ~ vuoto** vacuum-packed

sottoline'are *vt* to underline; (*fig*) to emphasize, stress

sottoma'rino, a *ag* (*flora*) submarine; (*cavo, navigazione*) underwater ♦ *sm* (*NAUT*) submarine

sotto'messo, a *pp di* **sottomettere**

sotto'mettere *vt* to subdue, subjugate; **~rsi** *vr* to submit

sottopas'saggio [sottopas'saddʒo] *sm* (*AUT*) underpass; (*pedonale*) subway, underpass

sotto'porre *vt* (*costringere*) to subject; (*fig: presentare*) to submit; **sottoporsi** *vr* to submit; **sottoporsi a** (*subire*) to undergo; **sotto'posto, a** *pp di* **sottoporre**

sottos'critto, a *pp di* **sottoscrivere**

sottos'crivere *vt* to sign ♦ *vi*: **~ a** to subscribe to; **sottoscrizi'one** *sf* signing; subscription

sottosegre'tario *sm*: **~ di Stato** Under-Secretary of State (*BRIT*), Assistant Secretary of State (*US*)

sotto'sopra *av* upside-down

sotto'terra *av* underground

sotto'titolo *sm* subtitle

sotto'veste *sf* underskirt

sotto'voce [sotto'votʃe] *av* in a low voice

sot'trarre *vt* (*MAT*) to subtract, take away; **~ qn/qc a** (*togliere*) to remove sb/sth from; (*salvare*) to save o rescue sb/sth from; **~ qc a qn** (*rubare*) to steal sth from sb; **sottrarsi** *vr*: **sottrarsi a** (*sfuggire*) to escape; (*evitare*) to avoid; **sot'tratto, a** *pp di* **sottrarre**; **sottrazi'one** *sf* subtraction; removal

sovi'etico, a, ci, che *ag* Soviet ♦ *sm/f* Soviet citizen

sovraccari'care *vt* to overload

sovrannatu'rale *ag* = **soprannaturale**

so'vrano, a *ag* sovereign; (*fig: sommo*) supreme ♦ *sm/f* sovereign, monarch

sovrap'porre *vt* to place on top of, put on top of

sovras'tare *vi*: **~ a** (*vallata, fiume*) to overhang; (*fig*) to hang over, threaten ♦ *vt* to overhang; to hang over, threaten

sovrinten'dente *sm/f* = **soprintendente**; **sovrinten'denza** *sf* = **soprintendenza**

sovru'mano, a *ag* superhuman

sovvenzi'one [sovven'tsjone] *sf* subsidy, grant

sovver'sivo, a *ag* subversive

'sozzo, a ['sottso] *ag* filthy, dirty

S.p.A. *abbr* = **società per azioni**

spac'care *vt* to split, break; (*legna*) to chop; **~rsi** *vr* to split, break; **spacca'tura** *sf* split

spacci'are [spat'tʃare] *vt* (*vendere*) to sell (off); (*mettere in circolazione*) to circulate; (*droga*) to peddle, push; **~rsi** *vr*: **~rsi per** (*farsi credere*) to pass o.s. off as, pretend to be; **spaccia'tore, 'trice** *sm/f* (*di droga*) pusher; (*di denaro falso*) dealer; **'spaccio** *sm* (*di merce rubata, droga*): **spaccio (di)** trafficking (in); (*in denaro falso*): **spaccio (di)** passing (of); (*vendita*) sale; (*bottega*) shop

'spacco, chi *sm* (*fenditura*) split, crack; (*strappo*) tear; (*di gonna*) slit

spac'cone *sm/f* boaster, braggart

'spada *sf* sword

spae'sato, a *ag* disorientated, lost

spa'ghetti [spa'getti] *smpl* (*CUC*) spaghetti *sg*

'Spagna ['spaɲɲa] *sf*: **la ~** Spain; **spa'gnolo, a** *ag* Spanish ♦ *sm/f* Spaniard ♦ *sm* (*LING*) Spanish; **gli Spagnoli** the Spanish

'spago, ghi *sm* string, twine

spai'ato, a *ag* (*calza, guanto*) odd

spalan'care *vt* to open wide; **~rsi** *vr* to open wide

spa'lare *vt* to shovel

'spalla *sf* shoulder; (*fig: TEATRO*) stooge; **~e** *sfpl* (*dorso*) back; **spalleggi'are** *vt* to back up, support

spalli'era *sf* (*di sedia etc*) back; (*di letto*:

da capo) head(board); (: *da piedi)* foot(board); (GINNASTICA) wall bars *pl*
spal'mare *vt* to spread
'spalti *smpl* (*di stadio)* terracing
'spandere *vt* to spread; (*versare)* to pour (out); ~rsi *vr* to spread; spanto, a *pp di* spandere
spa'rare *vt* to fire ♦ *vi* (*far fuoco)* to fire; (*tirare)* to shoot; spara'tore *sm* gunman; spara'toria *sf* exchange of shots
sparecchi'are [sparek'kjare] *vt*: ~ (la tavola) to clear the table
spa'reggio [spa'reddʒo] *sm* (SPORT) play-off
'spargere ['spardʒere] *vt* (*sparpagliare)* to scatter; (*versare: vino)* to spill; (: *lacrime, sangue)* to shed; (*diffondere)* to spread; (*emanare)* to give off (*o* out); ~rsi *vr* to spread; spargi'mento *sm* scattering, strewing; spilling; shedding; spargimento di sangue bloodshed
spa'rire *vi* to disappear, vanish
spar'lare *vi*: ~ di to run down, speak ill of
'sparo *sm* shot
sparpagli'are [sparpaʎ'ʎare] *vt* to scatter; ~rsi *vr* to scatter
'sparso, a *pp di* spargere ♦ *ag* scattered; (*sciolto)* loose
spar'tire *vt* (*eredità, bottino)* to share out; (*avversari)* to separate
spar'tito *sm* (MUS) score
sparti'traffico *sm inv* (AUT) central reservation (BRIT), median (strip) (US)
spa'ruto, a *ag* (*viso etc)* haggard
sparvi'ero *sm* (ZOOL) sparrowhawk
spasi'mante *sm* suitor
spasi'mare *vi* to be in agony; ~ di fare (*fig)* to yearn to do; ~ per qn to be madly in love with sb
'spasimo *sm* pang; 'spasmo *sm* (MED) spasm; spas'modico, a, ci, che *ag* (*angoscioso)* agonizing; (MED) spasmodic
spassio'nato, a *ag* dispassionate, impartial
'spasso *sm* (*divertimento)* amusement, enjoyment; andare a ~ to go out for a walk; essere a ~ (*fig)* to be out of work; mandare qn a ~ (*fig)* to give sb the sack

'spatola *sf* spatula; (*di muratore)* trowel
spau'racchio [spau'rakkjo] *sm* scarecrow
spau'rire *vt* to frighten, terrify
spa'valdo, a *ag* arrogant
spaventa'passeri *sm inv* scarecrow
spaven'tare *vt* to frighten, scare; ~rsi *vr* to be frightened, be scared; to get a fright; spa'vento *sm* fear, fright; far spavento a qn to give sb a fright; spaven'toso, a *ag* frightening, terrible; (*fig: fam)* tremendous, fantastic
spazien'tire [spattsjen'tire] *vi* (*anche:* ~rsi) to lose one's patience
'spazio ['spattsjo] *sm* space; ~ aereo airspace; spazi'oso, a *ag* spacious
spazzaca'mino [spattsaka'mino] *sm* chimney sweep
spaz'zare [spat'tsare] *vt* to sweep; (*foglie etc)* to sweep up; (*cacciare)* to sweep away; spazza'tura *sf* sweepings *pl*; (*immondizia)* rubbish; spaz'zino *sm* street sweeper
'spazzola ['spattsola] *sf* brush; ~ per abiti clothesbrush; ~ da capelli hairbrush; spazzo'lare *vt* to brush; spazzo'lino *sm* (small) brush; spazzolino da denti toothbrush
specchi'arsi [spek'kjarsi] *vr* to look at o.s. in a mirror; (*riflettersi)* to be mirrored, be reflected
'specchio ['spekkjo] *sm* mirror
speci'ale [spe't ʃale] *ag* special; specia'lista, i, e *sm/f* specialist; specialità *sf inv* speciality; (*branca di studio)* special field, speciality; specializ'zarsi *vr*: specializzarsi (in) to specialize (in); special'mente *av* especially, particularly
'specie ['spetʃe] *sf inv* (BIOL, BOT, ZOOL) species *inv*; (*tipo)* kind, sort ♦ *av* especially, particularly; una ~ di a kind of; fare ~ a qn to surprise sb; la ~ umana mankind
specifi'care [spetʃifi'kare] *vt* to specify, state
spe'cifico, a, ci, che [spe'tʃifiko] *ag* specific
specu'lare *vi*: ~ su (COMM) to speculate

in; (*sfruttare*) to exploit; (*meditare*) to speculate on; **speculazi'one** *sf* speculation

spe'dire *vt* to send; **spedizi'one** *sf* sending; (*collo*) consignment; (*scientifica etc*) expedition

'spegnere ['spɛɲɲere] *vt* (*fuoco, sigaretta*) to put out, extinguish; (*apparecchio elettrico*) to turn o switch off; (*gas*) to turn off; (*fig: suoni, passioni*) to stifle; (*debito*) to extinguish; **~rsi** *vr* to go out; to go off; (*morire*) to pass away

spel'lare *vt* (*scuoiare*) to skin; (*scorticare*) to graze; **~rsi** *vr* to peel

'spendere *vt* to spend

spen'nare *vt* to pluck

spensie'rato, a *ag* carefree

'spento, a *pp di* **spegnere** ♦ *ag* (*suono*) muffled; (*colore*) dull; (*sigaretta*) out; (*civiltà, vulcano*) extinct

spe'ranza [spe'rantsa] *sf* hope

spe'rare *vt* to hope for ♦ *vi*: **~ in** to trust in; **~ che/di fare** to hope that/to do; **lo spero, spero di sì** I hope so

sper'duto, a *ag* (*isolato*) out-of-the-way; (*persona: smarrita, a disagio*) lost

spergi'uro, a [sper'dʒuro] *sm/f* perjurer ♦ *sm* perjury

sperimen'tale *ag* experimental

sperimen'tare *vt* to experiment with, test; (*fig*) to test, put to the test

'sperma, i *sm* (*BIOL*) sperm

spe'rone *sm* spur

sperpe'rare *vt* to squander

'spesa *sf* (*somma di denaro*) expense; (*costo*) cost; (*acquisto*) purchase; (*fam: acquisto del cibo quotidiano*) shopping; **~e** *sfpl* (*soldi spesi*) expenses; (*COMM*) costs; charges; **fare la ~** to do the shopping; **a ~e di** (*a carico di*) at the expense of; **~e generali** overheads; **~e postali** postage *sg*; **~e di viaggio** travelling expenses

'speso, a *pp di* **spendere**

'spesso, a *ag* (*fitto*) thick; (*frequente*) frequent ♦ *av* often; **~e volte** frequently, often

spes'sore *sm* thickness

spet'tabile (*abbr*: **Spett.**: *in lettere*) *ag*: **~ ditta X** Messrs X and Co.

spet'tacolo *sm* (*rappresentazione*) performance, show; (*vista, scena*) sight; **dare ~ di sé** to make an exhibition o a spectacle of o.s.; **spettaco'loso, a** *ag* spectacular

spet'tare *vi*: **~ a** (*decisione*) to be up to; (*stipendio*) to be due to; **spetta a te decidere** it's up to you to decide

spetta'tore, 'trice *sm/f* (*CINEMA, TEATRO*) member of the audience; (*di avvenimento*) onlooker, witness

spetti'nare *vt*: **~ qn** to ruffle sb's hair; **~rsi** *vr* to get one's hair in a mess

'spettro *sm* (*fantasma*) spectre; (*FISICA*) spectrum

'spezie ['spɛttsje] *sfpl* (*CUC*) spices

spez'zare [spet'tsare] *vt* (*rompere*) to break; (*fig: interrompere*) to break up; **~rsi** *vr* to break

spezza'tino [spettsa'tino] *sm* (*CUC*) stew

spezzet'tare [spettset'tare] *vt* to break up (o chop) into small pieces

'spia *sf* spy; (*confidente della polizia*) informer; (*ELETTR*) indicating light; warning light; (*fessura*) peep-hole; (*fig: sintomo*) sign, indication

spia'cente [spja'tʃɛnte] *ag* sorry; **essere ~ di qc/di fare qc** to be sorry about sth/ for doing sth

spia'cevole [spja'tʃevole] *ag* unpleasant, disagreeable

spi'aggia, ge ['spjaddʒa] *sf* beach; **~ libera** public beach

spia'nare *vt* (*terreno*) to level, make level; (*edificio*) to raze to the ground; (*pasta*) to roll out; (*rendere liscio*) to smooth (out)

spi'ano *sm*: **a tutto ~** (*lavorare*) non-stop, without a break; (*spendere*) lavishly

spian'tato, a *ag* penniless, ruined

spi'are *vt* to spy on; (*occasione etc*) to watch o wait for

spi'azzo ['spjattso] *sm* open space; (*radura*) clearing

spic'care *vt* (*assegno, mandato di cattura*) to issue ♦ *vi* (*risaltare*) to stand out; **~ il volo** to fly off; (*fig*) to spread one's wings; **~ un balzo** to leap; **spic'cato, a** *ag* (*marcato*) marked, strong; (*notevole*) remarkable 'spicchio ['spikkjo] *sm* (*di agrumi*) segment; (*di aglio*) clove; (*parte*) piece, slice

spicci'are [spit't∫are] *vt* to finish off quickly; ~rsi *vr* to hurry up

'spicciolo, a ['spitt∫olo] *ag*: moneta ~a, ~i *smpl* (small) change

'spicco, chi *sm*: di ~ outstanding; (*tema*) main, principal; fare ~ to stand out

spi'edo *sm* (*CUC*) spit

spie'gare *vt* (*far capire*) to explain; (*tovaglia*) to unfold; (*vele*) to unfurl; ~rsi *vr* to explain o.s., make o.s. clear; ~ qc a qn to explain sth to sb; il problema si spiega one can understand the problem; spiegazi'one *sf* explanation

spiegaz'zare [spjegat'tsare] *vt* to crease, crumple

spie'tato, a *ag* ruthless, pitiless

spiffe'rare (*fam*) *vt* to blurt out, blab

'spiga, ghe *sf* (*BOT*) ear

spigli'ato, a [spiʎ'ʎato] *ag* self-possessed, self-confident

'spigolo *sm* corner; (*MAT*) edge

'spilla *sf* brooch; (*da cravatta, cappello*) pin

spil'lare *vt* (*vino, fig*) to tap; ~ denaro/notizie a qn to tap sb for money/information

'spillo *sm* pin; (*spilla*) brooch; ~ di sicurezza *o* da balia safety pin

spi'lorcio, a, ci, ce [spi'lort∫o] *ag* mean, stingy

'spina *sf* (*BOT*) thorn; (*ZOOL*) spine, prickle; (*di pesce*) bone; (*ELETTR*) plug; (*di botte*) bunghole; birra alla ~ draught beer; ~ dorsale (*ANAT*) backbone

spi'nacio [spi'nat∫o] *sm* spinach; (*CUC*): ~i spinach *sg*

'spingere ['spindʒere] *vt* to push; (*condurre: anche fig*) to drive; (*stimolare*): ~ qn a fare to urge *o* press sb to do; ~rsi *vr* (*inoltrarsi*) to push on, carry on; ~rsi troppo lontano (*anche fig*) to go too far

spi'noso, a *ag* thorny, prickly

'spinta *sf* (*urto*) push; (*FISICA*) thrust; (*fig: stimolo*) incentive, spur; (*: appoggio*) string-pulling *no pl*; dare una ~a a qn (*fig*) to pull strings for sb

'spinto, a *pp di* spingere

spio'naggio [spio'naddʒo] *sm* espionage, spying

spi'overe *vi* (*scorrere*) to flow down; (*ricadere*) to hang down, fall

'spira *sf* coil

spi'raglio [spi'raʎʎo] *sm* (*fessura*) chink, narrow opening; (*raggio di luce, fig*) glimmer, gleam

spi'rale *sf* spiral; (*contraccettivo*) coil; a ~ spiral(-shaped)

spi'rare *vi* (*vento*) to blow; (*morire*) to expire, pass away

spiri'tato, a *ag* possessed; (*fig: persona, espressione*) wild

spiri'tismo *sm* spiritualism

'spirito *sm* (*REL, CHIM, disposizione d'animo, di legge etc, fantasma*) spirit; (*pensieri, intelletto*) mind; (*arguzia*) wit; (*umorismo*) humour, wit; lo S~ Santo the Holy Spirit *o* Ghost

spirito'saggine [spirito'saddʒine] *sf* witticism; (*peg*) wisecrack

spiri'toso, a *ag* witty

spiritu'ale *ag* spiritual

'splendere *vi* to shine

'splendido, a *ag* splendid; (*splendente*) shining; (*sfarzoso*) magnificent, splendid

splen'dore *sm* splendour; (*luce intensa*) brilliance, brightness

spodes'tare *vt* to deprive of power; (*sovrano*) to depose

'spoglia ['spoʎʎa] *sf* (*ZOOL*) skin, hide; (*: di rettile*) slough; ~e *sfpl* (*salma*) remains; (*preda*) spoils, booty *sg*; vedi anche spoglio

spogli'are [spoʎ'ʎare] *vt* (*svestire*) to undress; (*privare, fig: depredare*): ~ qn di qc to deprive sb of sth; (*togliere ornamenti: anche fig*): ~ qn/qc di to strip sb/sth of; ~rsi *vr* to undress, strip; ~rsi di (*ricchezze etc*) to deprive o.s. of, give up; (*pregiudizi*) to rid o.s. of;

spoglia'toio *sm* dressing room; (*di scuola etc*) cloakroom; (*SPORT*) changing room; 'spoglio, a *ag* (*pianta, terreno*) bare; (*privo*): spoglio di stripped of; lacking in, without ♦ *sm* (*di voti*) counting

'spola sf shuttle; (bobina di filo) cop; fare la ~ (fra) to go to and fro o shuttle (between)

spol'pare vt to strip the flesh off

spolve'rare vt (anche CUC) to dust; (con spazzola) to brush; (con battipanni) to beat; (fig) to polish off ♦ vi to dust

'sponda sf (di fiume) bank; (di mare, lago) shore; (bordo) edge

spon'taneo, a ag spontaneous; (persona) unaffected, natural

spopo'lare vt to depopulate ♦ vi (attirare folla) to draw the crowds; ~rsi vr to become depopulated

spor'care vt to dirty, make dirty; (fig) to sully, soil; ~rsi vr to get dirty

spor'cizia [spor'tʃittsja] sf (stato) dirtiness; (sudiciume) dirt, filth; (cosa sporca) dirt no pl, something dirty; (fig: cosa oscena) obscenity

'sporco, a, chi, che ag dirty, filthy

spor'genza [spor'dʒɛntsa] sf projection

'sporgere ['spɔrdʒere] vt to put out, stretch out ♦ vi (venire in fuori) to stick out; ~rsi vr to lean out; ~ querela contro qn (DIR) to take legal action against sb

sport sm inv sport

'sporta sf shopping bag

spor'tello sm (di treno, auto etc) door; (di banca, ufficio) window, counter; ~ automatico (BANCA) cash dispenser, automated telling machine

spor'tivo, a ag (gara, giornale) sports cpd; (persona) sporty; (abito) casual; (spirito, atteggiamento) sporting

'sporto, a pp di sporgere

'sposa sf bride; (moglie) wife

sposa'lizio [spoza'littsjo] sm wedding

spo'sare vt to marry; (fig: idea, fede) to espouse; ~rsi vr to get married, marry; ~rsi con qn to marry sb, get married to sb; spo'sato, a ag married

'sposo sm (bride)groom; (marito) husband; gli ~i smpl the newlyweds

spos'sato, a ag exhausted, weary

spos'tare vt to move, shift; (cambiare: orario) to change; ~rsi vr to move

'spranga, ghe sf (sbarra) bar

'sprazzo ['sprattso] sm (di sole etc) flash; (fig: di gioia etc) burst

spre'care vt to waste; ~rsi vr (persona) to waste one's energy; 'spreco sm waste

spre'gevole [spre'dʒevole] ag contemptible, despicable

spregiudi'cato, a [spredʒudi'kato] ag unprejudiced, unbiased; (peg) unscrupulous

'spremere vt to squeeze

spre'muta sf fresh juice; ~ d'arancia fresh orange juice

sprez'zante [spret'tsante] ag scornful, contemptuous

sprigio'nare [spridʒo'nare] vt to give off, emit; ~rsi vr to emanate; (uscire con impeto) to burst out

spriz'zare [sprit'tsare] vt, vi to spurt; ~ gioia/salute to be bursting with joy/health

sprofon'dare vi to sink; (casa) to collapse; (suolo) to give way, subside; ~rsi vr: ~rsi in (poltrona) to sink into; (fig) to become immersed o absorbed in

spro'nare vt to spur (on)

sprone sm (sperone, fig) spur

sproporzio'nato, a [sproportsjo'nato] ag disproportionate, out of all proportion

sproporzi'one [spropor'tsjone] sf disproportion

s.proposi'tato, a ag (lettera, discorso) full of mistakes; (fig: costo) excessive, enormous

spro'posito sm blunder; a ~ at the wrong time; (rispondere, parlare) irrelevantly

sprovve'duto, a ag inexperienced, naïve

sprov'visto, a ag (mancante): ~ di lacking in, without; alla ~a unawares

spruz'zare [sprut'tsare] vt (a nebulizzazione) to spray; (aspergere) to sprinkle; (inzaccherare) to splash; 'spruzzo sm spray; splash

'spugna ['spuɲɲa] sf (ZOOL) sponge; (tessuto) towelling; spu'gnoso, a ag spongy

'spuma sf (schiuma) foam; (bibita) mineral water

spu'mante *sm* sparkling wine
spumeggi'ante [spumed'dʒante] *ag*
(*birra*) foaming; (*vino, fig*) sparkling
spu'mone *sm* (*CUC*) mousse
spun'tare *vt* (*coltello*) to break the point
of; (*capelli*) to trim ♦ *vi* (*uscire: germogli*)
to sprout; (: *capelli*) to begin to grow;
(: *denti*) to come through; (*apparire*) to
appear (suddenly); **~rsi** *vr* to become
blunt, lose its point; **spuntarla** (*fig*) to
make it, win through
spun'tino *sm* snack
'spunto *sm* (*TEATRO, MUS*) cue; (*fig*)
starting point; **dare lo ~ a** (*fig*) to give
rise to
spur'gare *vt* (*fogna*) to clean, clear
spu'tare *vt* to spit out; (*fig*) to belch (out)
♦ *vi* to spit; **'sputo** *sm* spittle *no pl*, spit
no pl
'squadra *sf* (*strumento*) (set) square;
(*gruppo*) team, squad; (*di operai*) gang,
squad; (*MIL*) squad; (: *AER, NAUT*) squadron;
(*SPORT*) team; **lavoro a ~e** teamwork
squa'drare *vt* to square, make square;
(*osservare*) to look at closely
squa'driglia [skwa'driʎʎa] *sf* (*AER*) flight;
(*NAUT*) squadron
squa'drone *sm* squadron
squagli'arsi [skwaʎ'ʎarsi] *vr* to melt;
(*fig*) to sneak off
squa'lifica *sf* disqualification
squalifi'care *vt* to disqualify
'squallido, a *ag* wretched, bleak
squal'lore *sm* wretchedness, bleakness
'squalo *sm* shark
'squama *sf* scale; **squa'mare** *vt* to scale;
squamarsi *vr* to flake *o* peel (off)
squarcia'gola [skwartʃa'gola]: **a ~** *av* at
the top of one's voice
squarci'are [skwar'tʃare] *vt* to rip (open);
(*fig*) to pierce
squar'tare *vt* to quarter, cut up
squattri'nato, a *ag* penniless
squili'brato, a *ag* (*PSIC*) unbalanced;
squi'librio *sm* (*differenza, sbilancio*)
imbalance; (*PSIC*) unbalance
squil'lante *ag* shrill, sharp
squil'lare *vi* (*campanello, telefono*) to ring
(out); (*tromba*) to blare; **'squillo** *sm* ring,

ringing *no pl*; blare; **ragazza** *f* **squillo**
inv call girl
squi'sito, a *ag* exquisite; (*cibo*) delicious;
(*persona*) delightful
squit'tire *vi* (*uccello*) to squawk; (*topo*) to
squeak
sradi'care *vt* to uproot; (*fig*) to eradicate
sragio'nare [zradʒo'nare] *vi* to talk
nonsense, rave
srego'lato, a *ag* (*senza ordine: vita*)
disorderly; (*smodato*) immoderate;
(*dissoluto*) dissolute
S.r.l. *abbr* = **società a responsabilità
limitata**
'stabile *ag* stable, steady; (*tempo: non
variabile*) settled; (*TEATRO: compagnia*)
resident ♦ *sm* (*edificio*) building
stabili'mento *sm* (*edificio*)
establishment; (*fabbrica*) plant, factory
stabi'lire *vt* to establish; (*fissare: prezzi,
data*) to fix; (*decidere*) to decide; **~rsi** *vr*
(*prendere dimora*) to settle
stac'care *vt* (*levare*) to detach, remove;
(*separare: anche fig*) to separate, divide;
(*strappare*) to tear off (*o* out); (*scandire:
parole*) to pronounce clearly; (*SPORT*) to
leave behind; **~rsi** *vr* (*bottone etc*) to come
off; (*scostarsi*): **~rsi (da)** to move away
(from); (*fig: separarsi*): **~rsi da** to leave;
non ~ gli occhi da qn not to take one's
eyes off sb
'stadio *sm* (*SPORT*) stadium; (*periodo, fase*)
phase, stage
'staffa *sf* (*di sella, TECN*) stirrup; **perdere
le ~e** (*fig*) to fly off the handle
staf'fetta *sf* (*messo*) dispatch rider;
(*SPORT*) relay race
stagio'nale [stadʒo'nale] *ag* seasonal
stagio'nare [stadʒo'nare] *vt* (*legno*) to
season; (*formaggi, vino*) to mature
stagi'one [sta'dʒone] *sf* season; **alta/
bassa ~** high/low season
stagli'arsi [staʎ'ʎarsi] *vr* to stand out, be
silhouetted
sta'gnare [stan'nare] *vt* (*vaso, tegame*) to
tin-plate; (*barca, botte*) to make
watertight; (*sangue*) to stop ♦ *vi* to
stagnate
'stagno, a ['stanno] *ag* watertight; (*a*

tenuta d'aria) airtight ♦ *sm* (*acquitrino*) pond; (*CHIM*) tin

sta'gnola [staɲˈɲɔla] *sf* tinfoil

'stalla *sf* (*per bovini*) cowshed; (*per cavalli*) stable

stal'lone *sm* stallion

sta'mani *av* = stamattina

stamat'tina *av* this morning

stam'becco, chi *sm* ibex

'stampa *sf* (*TIP, FOT: tecnica*) printing; (*impressione, copia fotografica*) print; (*insieme di quotidiani, giornalisti etc*) press; "~e" *sfpl* "printed matter"

stam'pante *sf* (*INFORM*) printer

stam'pare *vt* to print; (*pubblicare*) to publish; (*coniare*) to strike, coin; (*imprimere: anche fig*) to impress

stampa'tello *sm* block letters *pl*

stam'pella *sf* crutch

'stampo *sm* mould; (*fig: indole*) type, kind, sort

sta'nare *vt* to drive out

stan'care *vt* to tire, make tired; (*annoiare*) to bore; (*infastidire*) to annoy; ~rsi *vr* to get tired, tire o.s. out; ~rsi (di) to grow weary (of), grow tired (of)

stan'chezza [stanˈkettsa] *sf* tiredness, fatigue

'stanco, a, chi, che *ag* tired; ~ di tired of, fed up with

'stanga, ghe *sm* bar; (*di carro*) shaft

stan'gata *sf* (*colpo: anche fig*) blow; (*cattivo risultato*) poor result; (*CALCIO*) shot

sta'notte *av* tonight; (*notte passata*) last night

'stante *prep*: a sé ~ (*appartamento, casa*) independent, separate

stan'tio, a, 'tii, 'tie *ag* stale; (*burro*) rancid; (*fig*) old

stan'tuffo *sm* piston

'stanza ['stantsa] *sf* room; (*POESIA*) stanza; ~ da letto bedroom

stanzi'are [stanˈtsjare] *vt* to allocate

stap'pare *vt* to uncork; to uncap

'stare *vi* (*restare in un luogo*) to stay, remain; (*abitare*) to stay, live; (*essere situato*) to be, be situated; (*anche: ~ in piedi*) to be, stand; (*essere, trovarsi*) to be; (*dipendere*): se stesse in me if it were up

to me, if it depended on me; (*seguito da gerundio*): sta studiando he's studying; starci (*esserci spazio*): nel baule non ci sta più niente there's no more room in the boot; (*accettare*) to accept; ci stai? is that okay with you?; ~ a (*attenersi a*) to follow, stick to; (*seguito dall'infinito*): stiamo a discutere we're talking; (*toccare a*): sta a te giocare it's your turn to play; ~ per fare qc to be about to do sth; come sta? how are you?; io sto bene/male I'm very well/not very well; ~ a qn (*abiti etc*) to fit sb; queste scarpe mi stanno strette these shoes are tight for me; il rosso ti sta bene red suits you

starnu'tire *vi* to sneeze; star'nuto *sm* sneeze

sta'sera *av* this evening, tonight

sta'tale *ag* state *cpd*; government *cpd* ♦ *sm/f* state employee, local authority employee; (*nell'amministrazione*) ≈ civil servant

sta'tista, i *sm* statesman

sta'tistica *sf* statistics *sg*

'stato, a *pp di* essere; stare ♦ *sm* (*condizione*) state, condition; (*POL*) state; (*DIR*) status; essere in ~ d'accusa (*DIR*) to be committed for trial; ~ d'assedio/d'emergenza state of siege/emergency; ~ civile (*AMM*) marital status; ~ maggiore (*MIL*) staff; gli S~i Uniti (d'America) the United States (of America)

'statua *sf* statue

statuni'tense *ag* United States *cpd*, of the United States

sta'tura *sf* (*ANAT*) height, stature; (*fig*) stature

sta'tuto *sm* (*DIR*) statute; constitution

sta'volta *av* this time

stazio'nario, a [stattsjoˈnarjo] *ag* stationary; (*fig*) unchanged

stazi'one [statˈtsjone] *sf* station; (*balneare, termale*) resort; ~ degli autobus bus station; ~ balneare seaside resort; ~ ferroviaria railway (*BRIT*) *o* railroad (*US*) station; ~ invernale winter sports resort; ~ di polizia police station (*in small town*); ~ di servizio service *o* petrol (*BRIT*) *o* filling station

'**stecca, che** *sf* stick; (*di ombrello*) rib; (*di sigarette*) carton; (*MED*) splint; (*stonatura*): **fare una ~** to sing (*o* play) a wrong note

stec'cato *sm* fence

stec'chito, a [stek'kito] *ag* dried up; (*persona*) skinny; **lasciar ~ qn** (*fig*) to leave sb flabbergasted; **morto ~** stone dead

'**stella** *sf* star; **~ alpina** (*BOT*) edelweiss; **~ di mare** (*ZOOL*) starfish

'**stelo** *sm* stem; (*asta*) rod; **lampada a ~** standard lamp

'**stemma, i** *sm* coat of arms

stempe'rare *vt* to dilute; to dissolve; (*colori*) to mix

sten'dardo *sm* standard

'**stendere** *vt* (*braccia, gambe*) to stretch (out); (*tovaglia*) to spread (out); (*bucato*) to hang out; (*mettere a giacere*) to lay (down); (*spalmare: colore*) to spread; (*mettere per iscritto*) to draw up; **~rsi** *vr* (*coricarsi*) to stretch out, lie down; (*estendersi*) to extend, stretch

stenodatti'lografo, a *sm/f* shorthand typist (*BRIT*), stenographer (*US*)

stenogra'fare *vt* to take down in shorthand; **stenogra'fia** *sf* shorthand

sten'tare *vi*: **~ a fare** to find it hard to do, have difficulty doing

'**stento** *sm* (*fatica*) difficulty; **~i** *smpl* (*privazioni*) hardship *sg*, privation *sg*; **a ~** with difficulty, barely

'**sterco** *sm* dung

'**stereo('fonico, a, ci, che**) *ag* stereo(phonic)

'**sterile** *ag* sterile; (*terra*) barren; (*fig*) futile, fruitless; **sterilità** *sf* sterility

steriliz'zare [sterilid'dzare] *vt* to sterilize; **sterilizzazi'one** *sf* sterilization

ster'lina *sf* pound (sterling)

stermi'nare *vt* to exterminate, wipe out

stermi'nato, a *ag* immense; endless

ster'minio *sm* extermination, destruction

'**sterno** *sm* (*ANAT*) breastbone

'**sterpo** *sm* dry twig; **~i** *smpl* brushwood *sg*

ster'zare [ster'tsare] *vt, vi* (*AUT*) to steer; '**sterzo** *sm* steering; (*volante*) steering

wheel

'**steso, a** *pp di* **stendere**

'**stesso, a** *ag* same; (*rafforzativo: in persona, proprio*): **il re ~** the king himself *o* in person ♦ *pron*: **lo(la) ~(a)** the same (one); **i suoi ~i avversari lo ammirano** even his enemies admire him; **fa lo ~** it doesn't matter; **per me è lo ~** it's all the same to me, it doesn't matter to me; *vedi* **io; tu** *etc*

ste'sura *sf* drafting *no pl*, drawing up *no pl*; draft

'**stigma, i** *sm* stigma

'**stigmate** *sfpl* (*REL*) stigmata

sti'lare *vt* to draw up, draft

'**stile** *sm* style; **sti'lista, i** *sm* designer

stil'lare *vi* (*trasudare*) to ooze; (*gocciolare*) to drip; **stilli'cidio** *sm* (*fig*) continual pestering (*o* moaning *etc*)

stilo'grafica, che *sf* (*anche: penna ~*) fountain pen

'**stima** *sf* esteem; valuation; assessment, estimate

sti'mare *vt* (*persona*) to esteem, hold in high regard; (*terreno, casa etc*) to value; (*stabilire in misura approssimativa*) to estimate, assess; (*ritenere*): **~ che** to consider that; **~rsi fortunato** to consider o.s. (to be) lucky

stimo'lare *vt* to stimulate; (*incitare*): **~ qn (a fare)** to spur sb on (to do)

'**stimolo** *sm* (*anche fig*) stimulus

'**stinco, chi** *sm* shin; shinbone

'**stingere** ['stindʒere] *vt, vi* (*anche: ~rsi*) to fade; '**stinto, a** *pp di* **stingere**

sti'pare *vt* to cram, pack; **~rsi** *vr* (*accalcarsi*) to crowd, throng

sti'pendio *sm* salary

'**stipite** *sm* (*di porta, finestra*) jamb

stipu'lare *vt* (*redigere*) to draw up

sti'rare *vt* (*abito*) to iron; (*distendere*) to stretch; (*strappare: muscolo*) to strain; **~rsi** *vr* to stretch (o.s.); **stira'tura** *sf* ironing

'**stirpe** *sf* birth, stock; descendants *pl*

stiti'chezza [stiti'kettsa] *sf* constipation

'**stitico, a, ci, che** *ag* constipated

'**stiva** *sf* (*di nave*) hold

sti'vale *sm* boot

'**stizza** ['stittsa] *sf* anger, vexation; **stiz'zirsi** *vr* to lose one's temper; **stiz'zoso, a** *ag (persona)* quick-tempered, irascible; *(risposta)* angry

stocca'fisso *sm* stockfish, dried cod

stoc'cata *sf (colpo)* stab, thrust; *(fig)* gibe, cutting remark

'**stoffa** *sf* material, fabric; *(fig)*: **aver la ~ di** to have the makings of

'**stola** *sf* stole

'**stolto, a** *ag* stupid, foolish

'**stomaco, chi** *sm* stomach; **dare di ~** to vomit, be sick

sto'nare *vt* to sing *(o* play) out of tune ♦ *vi* to be out of tune, sing *(o* play) out of tune; *(fig)* to be out of place, jar; *(: colori)* to clash; **stona'tura** *sf (suono)* false note

stop *sm inv (TEL)* stop; *(AUT: cartello)* stop sign; *(: fanalino d'arresto)* brake-light

'**stoppa** *sf* tow

'**stoppia** *sf (AGR)* stubble

stop'pino *sm* wick; *(miccia)* fuse

'**storcere** ['stɔrtʃere] *vt* to twist; ~**rsi** *vr* to writhe, twist; ~ **il naso** *(fig)* to turn up one's nose; ~**rsi la caviglia** to twist one's ankle

stor'dire *vt (intontire)* to stun, daze; ~**rsi** *vr*: ~**rsi col bere** to dull one's senses with drink; **stor'dito, a** *ag* stunned, *(sventato)* scatterbrained, heedless

'**storia** *sf (scienza, avvenimenti)* history; *(racconto, bugia)* story; *(faccenda, questione)* business *no pl*; *(pretesto)* excuse, pretext; ~**e** *sfpl (smancerie)* fuss *sg*; '**storico, a, ci, che** *ag* historic(al) ♦ *sm* historian

stori'one *sm (ZOOL)* sturgeon

stor'mire *vi* to rustle

'**stormo** *sm (di uccelli)* flock

stor'nare *vt (COMM)* to transfer

'**storno** *sm* starling

storpi'are *vt* to cripple, maim; *(fig: parole)* to mangle; *(: significato)* to twist

'**storpio, a** *ag* crippled, maimed

'**storta** *sf (distorsione)* sprain, twist; *(recipiente)* retort

'**storto, a** *pp di* **storcere** ♦ *ag (chiodo)* twisted, bent; *(gamba, quadro)* crooked; *(fig: ragionamento)* false, wrong

sto'viglie [sto'viʎʎe] *sfpl* dishes *pl*, crockery

stra'bico, a, ci, che *ag* squint-eyed; *(occhi)* squint

stra'bismo *sm* squinting

stra'carico, a, chi, che *ag* overloaded

strac'chino [strak'kino] *sm type of soft cheese*

stracci'are [strat'tʃare] *vt* to tear

'**straccio, a, ci, ce** ['strattʃo] *ag*: **carta ~a** waste paper ♦ *sm* rag; *(per pulire)* cloth, duster; **stracci'vendolo** *sm* ragman

stra'cotto, a *ag* overcooked ♦ *sm (CUC)* beef stew

'**strada** *sf* road; *(di città)* street; *(cammino, via, fig)* way; **farsi ~** *(fig)* to do well for o.s.; **essere fuori ~** *(fig)* to be on the wrong track; ~ **facendo** on the way; ~ **senza uscita** dead end; **stra'dale** *ag* road *cpd*

strafalci'one [strafal'tʃone] *sm* blunder, howler

stra'fare *vi* to overdo it; **stra'fatto, a** *pp di* **strafare**

strafot'tente *ag*: **è ~** he doesn't give a damn, he couldn't care less

'**strage** ['stradʒe] *sf* massacre, slaughter

stralu'nato, a *ag (occhi)* rolling; *(persona)* beside o.s., very upset

stramaz'zare [stramat'tsare] *vi* to fall heavily

'**strambo, a** *ag* strange, queer

strampa'lato, a *ag* odd, eccentric

stra'nezza [stra'nettsa] *sf* strangeness

strango'lare *vt* to strangle; ~**rsi** *vr* to choke

strani'ero, a *ag* foreign ♦ *sm/f* foreigner

'**strano, a** *ag* strange, odd

straordi'nario, a *ag* extraordinary; *(treno etc)* special ♦ *sm (lavoro)* overtime

strapaz'zare [strapat'tsare] *vt* to ill-treat; ~**rsi** *vr* to tire o.s. out, overdo things; **stra'pazzo** *sm* strain, fatigue; **da strapazzo** *(fig)* third-rate

strapi'ombo *sm* overhanging rock; **a ~** overhanging

strapo'tere *sm* excessive power

strap'pare *vt (gen)* to tear, rip; *(pagina*

etc) to tear off, tear out; (*sradicare*) to pull up; (*togliere*): ~ **qc a qn** to snatch sth from sb; (*fig*) to wrest sth from sb; **~rsi** *vr* (*lacerarsi*) to rip, tear; (*rompersi*) to break; **~rsi un muscolo** to tear a muscle; '**strappo** *sm* pull, tug; tear, rip; **fare uno strappo alla regola** to make an exception to the rule; **strappo muscolare** torn muscle

strari'pare *vi* to overflow

strasci'care [straʃʃi'kare] *vt* to trail; (*piedi*) to drag; **~rsi** *vr* to drawl

'**strascico, chi** ['straʃʃiko] *sm* (*di abito*) train; (*conseguenza*) after-effect

strata'gemma, i [strata'dʒɛmma] *sm* stratagem

strate'gia, 'gie [strate'dʒia] *sf* strategy; **stra'tegico, a, ci, che** *ag* strategic

'**strato** *sm* layer; (*rivestimento*) coat, coating; (*GEO, fig*) stratum; (*METEOR*) stratus; ~ **di ozono** ozone layer

strava'gante *ag* odd, eccentric; **strava'ganza** *sf* eccentricity

stra'vecchio, a [stra'vekkjo] *ag* very old

stra'vizio [stra'vittsjo] *sm* excess

stra'volgere [stra'vɔldʒere] *vt* (*volto*) to contort; (*fig: animo*) to trouble deeply; (: *verità*) to twist, distort; **stra'volto, a** *pp di* **stravolgere**

strazi'are [strat'tsjare] *vt* to torture, torment; '**strazio** *sm* torture; (*fig: cosa fatta male*): **essere uno** ~ to be appalling

'**strega, ghe** *sf* witch

stre'gare *vt* to bewitch

stre'gone *sm* (*mago*) wizard; (*di tribù*) witch doctor

'**stregua** *sf*: **alla** ~ **di** by the same standard as

stre'mare *vt* to exhaust

'**stremo** *sm* very end; **essere allo** ~ to be at the end of one's tether

'**strenna** *sf* Christmas present

'**strenuo, a** *ag* brave, courageous

strepi'toso, a *ag* clamorous, deafening; (*fig: successo*) resounding

stres'sante *ag* stressful

'**stretta** *sf* (*di mano*) grasp; (*finanziaria*) squeeze; (*fig: dolore, turbamento*) pang; **una ~a di mano** a handshake; **essere**

alle ~e to have one's back to the wall; *vedi anche* **stretto**

stretta'mente *av* tightly; (*rigorosamente*) strictly

stret'tezza [stret'tettsa] *sf* narrowness

'**stretto, a** *pp di* **stringere** ♦ *ag* (*corridoio, limiti*) narrow; (*gonna, scarpe, nodo, curva*) tight; (*intimo: parente, amico*) close; (*rigoroso: osservanza*) strict; (*preciso: significato*) precise, exact ♦ *sm* (*braccio di mare*) strait; **a denti ~i** with clenched teeth; **lo ~ necessario** the bare minimum; **stret'toia** *sf* bottleneck; (*fig*) tricky situation

stri'ato, a *ag* streaked

stri'dere *vi* (*porta*) to squeak; (*animale*) to screech, shriek; (*colori*) to clash; '**strido** (*pl*(*f*) **strida**) *sm* screech, shriek; **stri'dore** *sm* screeching, shrieking; '**stridulo, a** *ag* shrill

stril'lare *vt, vi* to scream, shriek; '**strillo** *sm* scream, shriek

stril'lone *sm* newspaper seller

strimin'zito, a [strimin'tsito] *ag* (*misero*) shabby; (*molto magro*) skinny

strimpel'lare *vt* (*MUS*) to strum

'**stringa, ghe** *sf* lace

strin'gato, a *ag* (*fig*) concise

'**stringere** ['strindʒere] *vt* (*avvicinare due cose*) to press (together), squeeze (together); (*tenere stretto*) to hold tight, clasp, clutch; (*pugno, mascella, denti*) to clench; (*labbra*) to compress; (*avvitare*) to tighten; (*abito*) to take in; (*sog: scarpe*) to pinch, be tight for; (*fig: concludere: patto*) to make; (: *accelerare: passo, tempo*) to quicken ♦ *vi* (*essere stretto*) to be tight; (*tempo: incalzare*) to be pressing; **~rsi** *vr* (*accostarsi*): **~rsi a** to press o.s. up against; ~ **la mano a qn** to shake sb's hand; ~ **gli occhi** to screw up one's eyes

'**striscia, sce** ['striʃʃa] *sf* (*di carta, tessuto etc*) strip; (*riga*) stripe; **~sce (pedonali)** zebra crossing *sg*

strisci'are [striʃ'ʃare] *vt* (*piedi*) to drag; (*muro, macchina*) to graze ♦ *vi* to crawl, creep

'**striscio** ['striʃʃo] *sm* graze; (*MED*) smear; **colpire di** ~ to graze

strito'lare *vt* to grind

striz'zare [strit'tsare] *vt* (*arancia*) to squeeze; (*panni*) to wring (out); ~ l'occhio to wink

'strofa *sf* = strofe

'strofe *sf inv* strophe

strofi'naccio [strofi'nattʃo] *sm* duster, cloth; (*per piatti*) dishcloth; (*per pavimenti*) floorcloth

strofi'nare *vt* to rub

stron'care *vt* to break off; (*fig: ribellione*) to suppress, put down; (*: film, libro*) to tear to pieces

stropicci'are [stropit'tʃare] *vt* to rub

stroz'zare [strot'tsare] *vt* (*soffocare*) to choke, strangle; ~rsi *vr* to choke; strozza'tura *sf* (*restringimento*) narrowing; (*di strada etc*) bottleneck

'struggersi ['struddʒersi] *vr* (*fig*): ~ di to be consumed with

strumen'tale *ag* (*MUS*) instrumental

strumentaliz'zare [strumentalid'dzare] *vt* to exploit, use to one's own ends

stru'mento *sm* (*arnese, fig*) instrument, tool; (*MUS*) instrument; ~ a corda o ad arco/a fiato stringed/wind instrument

'strutto *sm* lard

strut'tura *sf* structure; struttu'rare *vt* to structure

'struzzo ['struttso] *sm* ostrich

stuc'care *vt* (*muro*) to plaster; (*vetro*) to putty; (*decorare con stucchi*) to stucco

stuc'chevole [stuk'kevole] *ag* nauseating; (*fig*) tedious, boring

'stucco, chi *sm* plaster; (*da vetri*) putty; (*ornamentale*) stucco; rimanere di ~ (*fig*) to be dumbfounded

stu'dente, 'essa *sm/f* student; (*scolaro*) pupil, schoolboy/girl; studen'tesco, a, schi, sche *ag* student *cpd*; school *cpd*

studi'are *vt* to study

'studio *sm* studying; (*ricerca, saggio, stanza*) study; (*di professionista*) office; (*di artista, CINEMA, TV, RADIO*) studio; ~i *smpl* (*INS*) studies; ~ medico doctor's surgery (*BRIT*) o office (*US*)

studi'oso, a *ag* studious, hard-working ♦ *sm/f* scholar

'stufa *sf* stove; ~ elettrica electric fire o heater

stu'fare *vt* (*CUC*) to stew; (*fig: fam*) to bore; stu'fato *sm* (*CUC*) stew; 'stufo, a (*fam*) *ag*: essere stufo di to be fed up with, be sick and tired of

stu'oia *sf* mat

stupefa'cente [stupefa'tʃɛnte] *ag* stunning, astounding ♦ *sm* drug, narcotic

stu'pendo, a *ag* marvellous, wonderful

stupi'daggine [stupi'daddʒine] *sf* stupid thing (to do o say)

stupidità *sf* stupidity

'stupido, a *ag* stupid

stu'pire *vt* to amaze, stun ♦ *vi* (*anche: ~rsi*): ~ (di) to be amazed (at), be stunned (by)

stu'pore *sm* amazement, astonishment

'stupro *sm* rape

stu'rare *vt* (*lavandino*) to clear

stuzzica'denti [stuttsika'dɛnti] *sm* toothpick

stuzzi'care [stuttsi'kare] *vt* (*ferita etc*) to poke (at), prod (at); (*fig*) to tease; (*: appetito*) to whet; (*: curiosità*) to stimulate; ~ i denti to pick one's teeth

---
PAROLA CHIAVE
---

su (*su +il* = sul, *su +lo* = sullo, *su +l'* = sull', *su +la* = sulla, *su +i* = sui, *su +gli* = sugli, *su +le* = sulle) *prep* 1 (*gen*) on; (*moto*) on(to); (*in cima a*) on (top of); mettilo sul tavolo put it on the table; un paesino sul mare a village by the sea

2 (*argomento*) about, on; un libro ~ Cesare a book on o about Caesar

3 (*circa*) about; costerà sui 3 milioni it will cost about 3 million; una ragazza sui 17 anni a girl of about 17 (years of age)

4: ~ misura made to measure; ~ richiesta on request; 3 casi ~ dieci 3 cases out of 10

♦ *av* 1 (*in alto, verso l'alto*) up; vieni ~ come on up; guarda ~ look up; ~ le mani! hands up!; in ~ (*verso l'alto*) up(wards); (*in poi*) onwards; dai 20 anni in ~ from the age of 20 onwards

2 (*addosso*) on; cos'hai ~? what have you

got on?
♦ *escl* come on!; ~ **coraggio!** come on,
cheer up!

'**sua** *vedi* **suo**
su'**bacqueo, a** *ag* underwater ♦ *sm*
skindiver
sub'**buglio** [sub'buʎʎo] *sm* confusion,
turmoil
subcosci'**ente** [subkoʃ'ʃɛnte] *ag*, *sm*
subconscious
'**subdolo, a** *ag* underhand, sneaky
suben'**trare** *vi*: ~ **a qn in qc** to take
over sth from sb
su'**bire** *vt* to suffer, endure
subis'**sare** *vt* (*fig*): ~ **di** to overwhelm
with, load with
subi'**taneo, a** *ag* sudden
'**subito** *av* immediately, at once, straight
away
subodo'**rare** *vt* (*insidia etc*) to smell,
suspect
subordi'**nato, a** *ag* subordinate;
(*dipendente*): ~ **a** dependent on, subject to
subur'**bano, a** *ag* suburban
succe'**daneo** [suttʃe'daneo] *sm*
substitute
suc'**cedere** [sut'tʃedere] *vi* (*prendere il
posto di qn*): ~ **a** to succeed; (*venire dopo*):
~ **a** to follow; (*accadere*) to happen; ~**rsi**
vr to follow each other; ~ **al trono** to
succeed to the throne; **successi'one** *sf*
succession; **succes'sivo, a** *ag* successive;
suc'**cesso, a** *pp di* **succedere** ♦ *sm* (*esito*) outcome; (*buona riuscita*) success; **di
successo** (*libro, personaggio*) successful
succhi'**are** [suk'kjare] *vt* to suck (up)
suc'**cinto, a** [sut'tʃinto] *ag* (*discorso*)
succinct; (*abito*) brief
'**succo, chi** *sm* juice; (*fig*) essence, gist; ~
di frutta fruit juice; **suc'coso, a** *ag*
juicy; (*fig*) pithy
succur'**sale** *sf* branch (office)
sud *sm* south ♦ *ag inv* south; (*lato*) south,
southern
Su'**dafrica** *sm*: **il** ~ South Africa;
sudafri'cano, a *ag*, *sm/f* South African
Suda'**merica** *sm*: **il** ~ South America;
sudameri'cano, a *ag*, *sm/f* South

American
su'**dare** *vi* to perspire, sweat; ~ **freddo** to
come out in a cold sweat; **su'data** *sf*
sweat; **ho fatto una bella sudata per
finirlo in tempo** it was a real sweat to
get it finished in time
sud'**detto, a** *ag* above-mentioned
sud'**dito, a** *sm/f* subject
suddi'**videre** *vt* to subdivide
su'**dest** *sm* south-east
'**sudicio, a, ci, ce** ['suditʃo] *ag* dirty,
filthy; **sudici'ume** *sm* dirt, filth
su'**dore** *sm* perspiration, sweat
su'**dovest** *sm* south-west
'**sue** *vedi* **suo**
suffici'**ente** [suffi'tʃɛnte] *ag* enough,
sufficient; (*borioso*) self-important; (*INS*)
satisfactory; **suffici'enza** *sf* self-
importance; pass mark; **a sufficienza**
enough; **ne ho avuto a sufficienza!** I've
had enough of this!
suf'**fisso** *sm* (*LING*) suffix
suf'**fragio** [suf'fradʒo] *sm* (*voto*) vote; ~
universale universal suffrage
suggel'**lare** [suddʒel'lare] *vt* (*fig*) to seal
suggeri'**mento** [suddʒeri'mento] *sm*
suggestion; (*consiglio*) piece of advice,
advice *no pl*
sugge'**rire** [suddʒe'rire] *vt* (*risposta*) to
tell; (*consigliare*) to advise; (*proporre*) to
suggest; (*TEATRO*) to prompt;
suggeri'tore, 'trice *sm/f* (*TEATRO*)
prompter
suggestio'**nare** [suddʒestjo'nare] *vt* to
influence
suggesti'**one** [suddʒes'tjone] *sf* (*PSIC*)
suggestion; (*istigazione*) instigation
sugges'**tivo, a** [suddʒes'tivo] *ag*
(*paesaggio*) evocative; (*teoria*) interesting,
attractive
'**sughero** ['sugero] *sm* cork
'**sugli** ['suʎʎi] *prep +det vedi* **su**
'**sugo, ghi** *sm* (*succo*) juice; (*di carne*)
gravy; (*condimento*) sauce; (*fig*) gist,
essence
'**sui** *prep +det vedi* **su**
sui'**cida, i, e** [sui'tʃida] *ag* suicidal
♦ *sm/f* suicide
suici'**darsi** [suitʃi'darsi] *vr* to commit

suicide
sui'cidio [sui'tʃidjo] *sm* suicide
su'ino, a *ag*: **carne ~a** pork ♦ *sm* pig; **~i** *smpl* swine *pl*
sul *prep* + *det vedi* **su**
sull' *prep* + *det vedi* **su**
'sulla *prep* + *det vedi* **su**
'sulle *prep* + *det vedi* **su**
'sullo *prep* + *det vedi* **su**
sulta'nina *ag f*: **(uva) ~** sultana
sul'tano, a *sm/f* sultan/sultana
'sunto *sm* summary
'suo (*f* **'sua**, *pl* **'sue, su'oi**) *det*: **il ~, la sua** *etc* (*di lui*) his; (*di lei*) her; (*di esso*) its; (*con valore indefinito*) one's, his/her; (*forma di cortesia: anche: S~*) your ♦ *pron*: **il ~, la sua** *etc* his; hers; yours; **i suoi** his (*o* her *o* one's *o* your) family
su'ocero, a ['swɔtʃero] *sm/f* father/mother-in-law; **i ~i** *smpl* father-and mother-in-law
su'oi *vedi* **suo**
su'ola (*di scarpa*) sole
su'olo *sm* (*terreno*) ground; (*terra*) soil
suo'nare *vt* (*MUS*) to play; (*campana*) to ring; (*ore*) to strike; (*clacson, allarme*) to sound ♦ *vi* to play; (*telefono, campana*) to ring; (*ore*) to strike; (*clacson, fig: parole*) to sound
suone'ria *sf* alarm
su'ono *sm* sound
su'ora *sf* (*REL*) sister
'super *sf* (*anche: benzina ~*) ≈ four-star (petrol) (*BRIT*), premium (*US*)
supe'rare *vt* (*oltrepassare: limite*) to exceed, surpass; (*percorrere*) to cross; (*sorpassare: veicolo*) to overtake; (*fig: essere più bravo di*) to surpass, outdo; (*: difficoltà*) to overcome; (*: esame*) to get through; **~ qn in altezza/peso** to be taller/heavier than sb; **ha superato la cinquantina** he's over fifty (years of age)
su'perbia *sf* pride
su'perbo, a *ag* proud; (*fig*) magnificent, superb
superfici'ale [superfi'tʃale] *ag* superficial
super'ficie, ci [super'fitʃe] *sf* surface
su'perfluo, a *ag* superfluous

superi'ore *ag* (*piano, arto, classi*) upper; (*più elevato: temperatura, livello*): **~ (a)** higher (than); (*migliore*): **~ (a)** superior (to); **~, a** *sm/f* (*anche REL*) superior; **superiorità** *sf* superiority
superla'tivo, a *ag, sm* superlative
supermer'cato *sm* supermarket
su'perstite *ag* surviving ♦ *sm/f* survivor
superstizi'one [superstit'tsjone] *sf* superstition; **superstizi'oso, a** *ag* superstitious
su'pino, a *ag* supine
suppel'lettile *sf* furnishings *pl*
suppergiù [supper'dʒu] *av* more or less, roughly
supplemen'tare *ag* extra; (*treno*) relief *cpd*; (*entrate*) additional
supple'mento *sm* supplement
sup'plente *ag* temporary; (*insegnante*) supply *cpd* (*BRIT*), substitute *cpd* (*US*) ♦ *sm/f* temporary member of staff; supply (*o* substitute) teacher
'supplica, che *sf* (*preghiera*) plea; (*domanda scritta*) petition, request
suppli'care *vt* to implore, beseech
sup'plire *vi*: **~ a** to make up for, compensate for
sup'plizio [sup'plittsjo] *sm* torture
sup'porre *vt* to suppose
sup'porto *sm* (*sostegno*) support
sup'posta *sf* (*MED*) suppository
sup'posto, a *pp di* **supporre**
su'premo, a *ag* supreme
surge'lare [surdʒe'lare] *vt* to (deep-)freeze; **surge'lati** *smpl* frozen food *sg*
sur'plus *sm inv* (*ECON*) surplus
surriscal'dare *vt* to overheat
surro'gato *sm* substitute
suscet'tibile [suʃʃet'tibile] *ag* (*sensibile*) touchy, sensitive; (*soggetto*): **~ di miglioramento** that can be improved, open to improvement
susci'tare [suʃʃi'tare] *vt* to provoke, arouse
su'sina *sf* plum; **su'sino** *sm* plum (tree)
sussegu'ire *vt* to follow; **~rsi** *vr* to follow one another
sussidi'ario, a *ag* subsidiary; auxiliary
sus'sidio *sm* subsidy

sus'sistere *vi* to exist; *(essere fondato)* to be valid *o* sound

sussul'tare *vi* to shudder

sussur'rare *vt, vi* to whisper, murmur; **sus'surro** *sm* whisper, murmur

sutu'rare *vt (MED)* to stitch up, suture

sva'gare *vt (distrarre)* to distract; *(divertire)* to amuse; **~rsi** *vr* to amuse o.s.; to enjoy o.s.

'svago, ghi *sm (riposo)* relaxation; *(ricreazione)* amusement; *(passatempo)* pastime

svaligi'are [zvali'dʒare] *vt* to rob, burgle *(BRIT)*, burglarize *(US)*

svalu'tare *vt (ECON)* to devalue; *(fig)* to belittle; **~rsi** *vr (ECON)* to be devalued; **svalutazi'one** *sf* devaluation

sva'nire *vi* to disappear, vanish

svan'taggio [zvan'taddʒo] *sm* disadvantage; *(inconveniente)* drawback, disadvantage

svapo'rare *vi* to evaporate

svari'ato, a *ag* varied; various

'svastica *sf* swastika

sve'dese *ag* Swedish ♦ *sm/f* Swede ♦ *sm (LING)* Swedish

'sveglia ['zveʎʎa] *sf* waking up; *(orologio)* alarm (clock); **suonare la ~** *(MIL)* to sound the reveille; **~ telefonica** alarm call

svegli'are [zveʎ'ʎare] *vt* to wake up; *(fig)* to awaken, arouse; **~rsi** *vr* to wake up; *(fig)* to be revived, reawaken

'sveglio, a ['zveʎʎo] *ag* awake; *(fig)* quick-witted

sve'lare *vt* to reveal

'svelto, a *ag (passo)* quick; *(mente)* quick, alert; *(linea)* slim, slender; **alla ~a** quickly

'svendita *sf (COMM)* (clearance) sale

sveni'mento *sm* fainting fit, faint

sve'nire *vi* to faint

sven'tare *vt* to foil, thwart

sven'tato, a *ag (distratto)* scatterbrained; *(imprudente)* rash

svento'lare *vt, vi* to wave, flutter

sven'trare *vt* to disembowel

sven'tura *sf* misfortune; **sventu'rato, a** *ag* unlucky, unfortunate

sve'nuto, a *pp di* **svenire**

svergo'gnato, a [zvergoɲ'ɲato] *ag* shameless

sver'nare *vi* to spend the winter

sves'tire *vt* to undress; **~rsi** *vr* to get undressed

'Svezia ['zvɛttsja] *sf*: **la ~** Sweden

svez'zare [zvet'tsare] *vt* to wean

svi'are *vt* to divert; *(fig)* to lead astray; **~rsi** *vr* to go astray

svi'gnarsela [zviɲ'ɲarsela] *vr* to slip away, sneak off

svilup'pare *vt* to develop; **~rsi** *vr* to develop

svi'luppo *sm* development

'svincolo *sm (COMM)* clearance; *(stradale)* motorway *(BRIT) o* expressway *(US)* intersection

svisce'rare [zviʃʃe'rare] *vt (fig: argomento)* to examine in depth; **svisce'rato, a** *ag (amore)* passionate; *(lodi)* obsequious

'svista *sf* oversight

svi'tare *vt* to unscrew

'Svizzera ['zvittsera] *sf*: **la ~** Switzerland

'svizzero, a ['zvittsero] *ag, sm/f* Swiss

svogli'ato, a [zvoʎ'ʎato] *ag* listless; *(pigro)* lazy

svolaz'zare [zvolat'tsare] *vi* to flutter

'svolgere ['zvɔldʒere] *vt* to unwind; *(srotolare)* to unroll; *(fig: argomento)* to develop; *(: piano, programma)* to carry out; **~rsi** *vr* to unwind; to unroll; *(fig: aver luogo)* to take place; *(: procedere)* to go on; **svolgi'mento** *sm* development; carrying out; *(andamento)* course

'svolta *sf (atto)* turning *no pl*; *(curva)* turn, bend; *(fig)* turning-point

svol'tare *vi* to turn

'svolto, a *pp di* **svolgere**

svuo'tare *vt* to empty (out)

T

tabac'caio, a *sm/f* tobacconist

tabacche'ria [tabakke'ria] *sf* tobacconist's (shop)

ta'bacco, chi *sm* tobacco

ta'bella *sf* (*tavola*) table; (*elenco*) list

taber'nacolo *sm* tabernacle

tabu'lato *sm* (*INFORM*) printout

'tacca, che *sf* notch, nick; di mezza ~ (*fig*) mediocre

tac'cagno, a [tak'kaɲɲo] *ag* mean, stingy

tac'cheggio [tak'keddʒo] *sm* shoplifting

tac'chino [tak'kino] *sm* turkey

tacci'are [tat'tʃare] *vt*: ~ qn di to accuse sb of

'tacco, chi *sm* heel; ~chi a spillo stiletto heels

taccu'ino *sm* notebook

ta'cere [ta'tʃere] *vi* to be silent *o* quiet; (*smettere di parlare*) to fall silent ♦ *vt* to keep to oneself, say nothing about; far ~ qn to make sb be quiet; (*fig*) to silence sb

ta'chimetro [ta'kimetro] *sm* speedometer

'tacito, a ['tatʃito] *ag* silent; (*sottinteso*) tacit, unspoken

ta'fano *sm* horsefly

taffe'ruglio [taffe'ruʎʎo] *sm* brawl, scuffle

taffettà *sm* taffeta

'taglia ['taʎʎa] *sf* (*statura*) height; (*misura*) size; (*riscatto*) ransom; (*ricompensa*) reward; ~ forte (*di abito*) large size

taglia'carte [taʎʎa'karte] *sm inv* paperknife

tagli'ando [taʎ'ʎando] *sm* coupon

tagli'are [taʎ'ʎare] *vt* to cut; (*recidere, interrompere*) to cut off; (*intersecare*) to cut across, intersect; (*carne*) to carve; (*vini*) to blend ♦ *vi* to cut; (*prendere una scorciatoia*) to take a short-cut; ~ corto (*fig*) to cut short

taglia'telle [taʎʎa'tɛlle] *sfpl* tagliatelle *pl*

tagli'ente [taʎ'ʎɛnte] *ag* sharp

'taglio ['taʎʎo] *sm* cutting *no pl*; cut; (*parte tagliente*) cutting edge; (*di abito*) cut, style; (*di stoffa: lunghezza*) length; (*di vini*) blending; di ~ on edge, edgeways; banconote di piccolo/grosso ~ notes of small/large denomination

tagli'ola [taʎ'ʎola] *sf* trap, snare

tagliuz'zare [taʎʎut'tsare] *vt* to cut into small pieces

'talco *sm* talcum powder

'tale *det* 1 (*simile, così grande*) such; un(a) ~ ... such (a) ...; non accetto ~i discorsi I won't allow such talk; è di una ~ arroganza he is so arrogant; fa una ~ confusione! he makes such a mess!

2 (*persona o cosa indeterminata*) such-and-such; il giorno ~ all'ora ~ on such-and-such a day at such-and-such a time; la tal persona that person; ha telefonato una ~ Giovanna somebody called Giovanna phoned

3 (*nelle similitudini*): ~ ... ~ like ... like; ~ padre ~ figlio like father, like son; hai il vestito ~ quale il mio your dress is just *o* exactly like mine

♦ *pron* (*indefinito: persona*): un(a) ~ someone; quel (*o* quella) ~ that person, that man (*o* woman); il tal dei ~i what's-his-name

ta'lento *sm* talent

talis'mano *sm* talisman

tallon'cino [tallon'tʃino] *sf* counterfoil

tal'lone *sm* heel

tal'mente *av* so

ta'lora *av* = talvolta

'talpa *sf* (*ZOOL*) mole

tal'volta *av* sometimes, at times

tambu'rello *sm* tambourine

tam'buro *sm* drum

Ta'migi [ta'midʒi] *sm*: il ~ the Thames

tampo'nare *vt* (*otturare*) to plug; (*urtare: macchina*) to crash *o* ram into

tam'pone *sm* (*MED*) wad, pad; (*per timbri*) ink-pad; (*respingente*) buffer; ~ assorbente tampon

'tana *sf* lair, den

'tanfo *sm* stench; musty smell

tan'gente [tan'dʒɛnte] *ag* (*MAT*): ~ a tangential to ♦ *sf* tangent; (*quota*) share

tan'tino: un ~ *av* a little, a bit

'tanto, a *det* 1 (*molto: quantità*) a lot of, much; (: *numero*) a lot of, many; (*così* ~: *quantità*) so much, such a lot of;

(: *numero*) so many, such a lot of; ~**e volte** so many times, so often; ~**i auguri!** all the best!; ~**e grazie** many thanks; ~ **tempo** so long, such a long time; **ogni** ~**i chilometri** every so many kilometres

2: ~ **... quanto** (*quantità*) as much ... as; (*numero*) as many ... as; **ho** ~**a pazienza quanta ne hai tu** I have as much patience as you have *o* as you; **ha** ~**i amici quanti nemici** he has as many friends as he has enemies

3 (*rafforzativo*) such; **ho aspettato per** ~ **tempo** I waited so long *o* for such a long time

♦ *pron* **1** (*molto*) much, a lot; (*così* ~) so much, such a lot; ~**i, e** many, a lot; so many, such a lot; **credevo ce ne fosse** ~ I thought there was (such) a lot, I thought there was plenty

2: ~ **quanto** (*denaro*) as much as; (*cioccolatini*) as many as; **ne ho** ~ **quanto basta** I have as much as I need; **due volte** ~ twice as much

3 (*indeterminato*) so much; ~ **per l'affitto,** ~ **per il gas** so much for the rent, so much for the gas; **costa un** ~ **al metro** it costs so much per metre; **di** ~ **in** ~, **ogni** ~ every so often; ~ **vale che ... I** (*o* **we** *etc*) may as well ...; ~ **meglio!** so much the better!; ~ **peggio per lui!** so much the worse for him!

♦ *av* **1** (*molto*) very; **vengo** ~ **volentieri** I'd be very glad to come; **non ci vuole** ~ **a capirlo** it doesn't take much to understand it

2 (*così* ~: *con ag, av*) so; (: *con vb*) so much, such a lot; **è** ~ **bella!** she's so beautiful!; **non urlare** ~ don't shout so much; **sto** ~ **meglio adesso** I'm so much better now; ~ **... che** so ... (that); ~ **... da** so ... as

3: ~ **... quanto** as ... as; **conosco** ~ **Carlo quanto suo padre** I know both Carlo and his father; **non è poi** ~ **complicato quanto sembri** it's not as difficult as it seems; ~ **più insisti,** ~ **più non mollerà** the more you insist, the more stubborn he'll be; **quanto più ...** ~ **meno** the more ... the less

4 (*solamente*) just; ~ **per cambiare/ scherzare** just for a change/a joke; **una volta** ~ for once

5 (*a lungo*) (for) long

♦ *cong* after all

'**tappa** *sf* (*luogo di sosta, fermata*) stop, halt; (*parte di un percorso*) stage, leg; (*SPORT*) lap; **a** ~**e** in stages

tap'pare *vt* to plug, stop up; (*bottiglia*) to cork

tap'peto *sm* carpet; (*anche: tappetino*) rug; (*di tavolo*) cloth; (*SPORT*): **andare al** ~ to go down for the count; **mettere sul** ~ (*fig*) to bring up for discussion

tappez'zare [tappet'tsare] *vt* (*con carta*) to paper; (*rivestire*): ~ **qc (di)** to cover sth (with); **tappezze'ria** *sf* (*tessuto*) tapestry; (*carta da parato*) wallpaper; (*arte*) upholstery; **far da tappezzeria** (*fig*) to be a wallflower; **tappezzi'ere** *sm* upholsterer

'**tappo** *sm* stopper; (*in sughero*) cork

tarchi'ato, a [tar'kjato] *ag* stocky, thickset

tar'dare *vi* to be late ♦ *vt* to delay; ~ **a fare** to delay doing

'**tardi** *av* late; **più** ~ later (on); **al più** ~ at the latest; **sul** ~ (*verso sera*) late in the day; **far** ~ to be late; (*restare alzato*) to stay up late

tar'divo, a *ag* (*primavera*) late; (*rimedio*) belated, tardy; (*fig: bambino*) retarded

'**tardo, a** *ag* (*lento, fig: ottuso*) slow; (*tempo: avanzato*) late

'**targa, ghe** *sf* plate; (*AUT*) number (*BRIT*) *o* license (*US*) plate

ta'riffa *sf* (*gen*) rate, tariff; (*di trasporti*) fare; (*elenco*) price list; tariff

'**tarlo** *sm* woodworm

'**tarma** *sf* moth

ta'rocco, chi *sm* tarot card; ~**chi** *smpl* (*gioco*) tarot *sg*

tartagli'are [tartaʎ'ʎare] *vi* to stutter, stammer

'**tartaro, a** *ag, sm* (*in tutti i sensi*) tartar

tarta'ruga, ghe *sf* tortoise; (*di mare*) turtle; (*materiale*) tortoiseshell

tar'tina *sf* canapé

tar'tufo *sm* (*BOT*) truffle

'tasca, sche *sf* pocket; tas'cabile *ag* (*libro*) pocket *cpd*; tasca'pane *sm* haversack; tas'chino *sm* breast pocket

'tassa *sf* (*imposta*) tax; (*doganale*) duty; (*per iscrizione: a scuola etc*) fee; ~ di circolazione/di soggiorno road/tourist tax

tas'sametro *sm* taximeter

tas'sare *vt* to tax; to levy a duty on

tassa'tivo, a *ag* peremptory

tassazi'one [tassat'tsjone] *sf* taxation

tas'sello *sm* plug; wedge

tassì *sm inv* = taxi; tas'sista, i, e *sm/f* taxi driver

'tasso *sm* (*di natalità, d'interesse etc*) rate; (*BOT*) yew; (*ZOOL*) badger; ~ di cambio/d'interesse rate of exchange/interest

tas'tare *vt* to feel; ~ il terreno (*fig*) to see how the land lies

tasti'era *sf* keyboard

'tasto *sm* key; (*tatto*) touch, feel

tas'toni *av*: procedere (a) ~ to grope one's way forward

'tattica *sf* tactics *pl*

'tattico, a, ci, che *ag* tactical

'tatto *sm* (*senso*) touch; (*fig*) tact; duro al ~ hard to the touch; aver ~ to be tactful, have tact

tatu'agglo [tatu'addʒo] *sm* tattooing; (*disegno*) tattoo

tatu'are *vt* to tattoo

'tavola *sf* table; (*asse*) plank, board; (*lastra*) tablet; (*quadro*) panel (painting); (*illustrazione*) plate; ~ calda snack bar

tavo'lato *sm* boarding; (*pavimento*) wooden floor

tavo'letta *sf* tablet, bar; a ~ (*AUT*) flat out

tavo'lino *sm* small table; (*scrivania*) desk

'tavolo *sm* table

tavo'lozza [tavo'lɔttsa] *sf* (*ARTE*) palette

'taxi *sm inv* taxi

'tazza ['tattsa] *sf* cup; ~ da caffè/tè coffee/tea cup; una ~ di caffè/tè a cup of coffee/tea

te *pron* (*soggetto: in forme comparative, oggetto*) you

tè *sm inv* tea; (*trattenimento*) tea party

tea'trale *ag* theatrical

te'atro *sm* theatre

'tecnica, che *sf* technique; (*tecnologia*) technology

'tecnico, a, ci, che *ag* technical ♦ *sm/f* technician

tecnolo'gia [teknolo'dʒia] *sf* technology

te'desco, a, schi, sche *ag, sm/f, sm* German

'tedio *sm* tedium, boredom

te'game *sm* (*CUC*) pan

'teglia ['teʎʎa] *sf* (*per dolci*) (baking) tin; (*per arrosti*) (roasting) tin

'tegola *sf* tile

tei'era *sf* teapot

'tela *sf* (*tessuto*) cloth; (*per vele, quadri*) canvas; (*dipinto*) canvas, painting; di ~ (*calzoni*) (heavy) cotton *cpd*; (*scarpe, borsa*) canvas *cpd*; ~ cerata oilcloth; (*copertone*) tarpaulin

te'laio *sm* (*apparecchio*) loom; (*struttura*) frame

tele'camera *sf* television camera

tele'copia *sf* fax (document)

telecopia'trice *sf* fax (machine)

tele'cronaca *sf* television report

tele'ferica, che *sf* cableway

telefo'nare *vi* to telephone, ring; to make a phone call ♦ *vt* to telephone; ~ a to phone up, ring up, call up

telefo'nata *sf* (telephone) call; ~ a carico del destinatario reverse charge (*BRIT*) *o* collect (*US*) call

tele'fonico, a, ci, che *ag* (tele)phone *cpd*

telefon'ino [telefon'ino] *sm* mobile phone

tele'fonista, i, e *sm/f* telephonist; (*d'impresa*) switchboard operator

te'lefono *sm* telephone; ~ a gettoni ≈ pay phone

telegior'nale [teledʒor'nale] *sm* television news (programme)

te'legrafo *sm* telegraph; (*ufficio*) telegraph office

tele'gramma, i *sm* telegram

tele'matica *sf* data transmission; telematics *sg*

telepa'tia *sf* telepathy

teles'copio *sm* telescope

teleselezi'one [teleselet'tsjone] *sf* direct dialling

telespetta'tore, 'trice *sm/f* (television) viewer

televisi'one *sf* television

televi'sore *sm* television set

'telex *sm inv* telex

'tema, i *sm* theme; (*INS*) essay, composition

teme'rario, a *ag* rash, reckless

te'mere *vt* to fear, be afraid of; (*essere sensibile a: freddo, calore*) to be sensitive to ♦ *vi* to be afraid; (*essere preoccupato*): ~ **per** to worry about, fear for; ~ **di/che** to be afraid of/that

temperama'tite *sm inv* pencil sharpener

tempera'mento *sm* temperament

tempe'rare *vt* (*aguzzare*) to sharpen; (*fig*) to moderate, control, temper

tempe'rato, a *ag* moderate, temperate; (*clima*) temperate

tempera'tura *sf* temperature

tempe'rino *sm* penknife

tem'pesta *sf* storm; ~ **di sabbia/neve** sand/snowstorm

tempes'tare *vt*: ~ **qn di domande** to bombard sb with questions; ~ **qn di colpi** to rain blows on sb

tempes'tivo, a *ag* timely

tempes'toso, a *ag* stormy

'tempia *sf* (*ANAT*) temple

'tempio *sm* (*edificio*) temple

'tempo *sm* (*METEOR*) weather; (*cronologico*) time; (*epoca*) time, times *pl*; (*di film, gioco: parte*) part; (*MUS*) time; (: *battuta*) beat; (*LING*) tense; **un** ~ once; ~ **fa** some time ago; **al** ~ **stesso** *o* **a un** ~ at the same time; **per** ~ early; **aver fatto il suo** ~ to have had its (*o* his *etc*) day; **primo/secondo** ~ (*TEATRO*) first/second part; (*SPORT*) first/second half; **in** ~ **utile** in due time *o* course

tempo'rale *ag* temporal ♦ *sm* (*METEOR*) (thunder)storm

tempo'raneo, a *ag* temporary

temporeggi'are [tempored'dʒare] *vi* to play for time, temporize

tem'prare *vt* to temper

te'nace [te'natʃe] *ag* strong, tough; (*fig*) tenacious; **te'nacia** *sf* tenacity

te'naglie [te'naʎʎe] *sfpl* pincers *pl*

'tenda *sf* (*riparo*) awning; (*di finestra*) curtain; (*per campeggio etc*) tent

ten'denza [ten'dɛntsa] *sf* tendency; (*orientamento*) trend; **avere** ~ **a** *o* **per qc** to have a bent for sth

'tendere *vt* (*allungare al massimo*) to stretch, draw tight; (*porgere: mano*) to hold out; (*fig: trappola*) to lay, set ♦ *vi*: ~ **a qc/a fare** to tend towards sth/to do; ~ **l'orecchio** to prick up one's ears; **il tempo tende al caldo** the weather is getting hot; **un blu che tende al verde** a greenish blue

ten'dina *sf* curtain

'tendine *sm* tendon, sinew

ten'done *sm* (*da circo*) tent

'tenebre *sfpl* darkness *sg*; **tene'broso, a** *ag* dark, gloomy

te'nente *sm* lieutenant

te'nere *vt* to hold; (*conservare, mantenere*) to keep; (*ritenere, considerare*) to consider; (*spazio: occupare*) to take up, occupy; (*seguire: strada*) to keep to *o* to hold; (*colori*) to be fast; (*dare importanza*): ~ **a** to care about; ~ **a fare** to want to do, be keen to do; ~**rsi** *vr* (*stare in una determinata posizione*) to stand; (*stimarsi*) to consider o.s.; (*aggrapparsi*): ~**rsi a** to hold on to; (*attenersi*): ~**rsi a** to stick to; ~ **una conferenza** to give a lecture; ~ **conto di qc** to take sth into consideration; ~ **presente qc** to bear sth in mind

'tenero, a *ag* tender; (*pietra, cera, colore*) soft; (*fig*) tender, loving

'tenia *sf* tapeworm

'tennis *sm* tennis

te'nore *sm* (*tono*) tone; (*MUS*) tenor; ~ **di vita** way of life; (*livello*) standard of living

tensi'one *sf* tension

ten'tare *vt* (*indurre*) to tempt; (*provare*): ~ **qc/di fare** to attempt *o* try sth/to do; **tenta'tivo** *sm* attempt; **tentazi'one** *sf* temptation

tenten'nare *vi* to shake, be unsteady;

(*fig*) to hesitate, waver ♦ *vt*: ~ **il capo** to shake one's head

ten'toni *av*: **andare a** ~ (*anche fig*) to grope one's way

'tenue *ag* (*sottile*) fine; (*colore*) soft; (*fig*) slender, slight

te'nuta *sf* (*capacità*) capacity; (*divisa*) uniform; (*àbito*) dress; (*AGR*) estate; **a** ~ **d'aria** airtight; ~ **di strada** roadholding power

teolo'gia [teolo'dʒia] *sf* theology; **te'ologo, gi** *sm* theologian

teo'rema, i *sm* theorem

teo'ria *sf* theory; **te'orico, a, ci, che** *ag* theoretic(al)

'tepido, a *ag* = **tiepido**

te'pore *sm* warmth

'teppa *sf* mob, hooligans *pl*; **tep'pismo** *sm* hooliganism; **tep'pista, i** *sm* hooligan

tera'pia *sf* therapy

tergicris'tallo [terdʒikris'tallo] *sm* windscreen (*BRIT*) o windshield (*US*) wiper

tergiver'sare [terdʒiver'sare] *vi* to shilly-shally

'tergo *sm*: **a** ~ behind; **vedi a** ~ please turn over

ter'male *ag* thermal; **stazione** *sf* ~ spa

'terme *sfpl* thermal baths

'termico, a, ci, che *ag* thermic; (*unità*) thermal

termi'nale *ag, sm* terminal

termi'nare *vt* to end; (*lavoro*) to finish ♦ *vi* to end

'termine *sm* term; (*fine, estremità*) end; (*di territorio*) boundary, limit; **contratto a** ~ (*COMM*) forward contract; **a breve/lungo** ~ short-/long-term; **parlare senza mezzi** ~**i** to talk frankly, not to mince one's words

ter'mometro *sm* thermometer

termonucle'are *ag* thermonuclear

'termos *sm inv* = **thermos**

termosi'fone *sm* radiator; (**riscaldamento a**) ~ central heating

ter'mostato *sm* thermostat

'terra *sf* (*gen, ELETTR*) earth; (*sostanza*) soil, earth; (*opposto al mare*) land *no pl*; (*regione, paese*) land; (*argilla*) clay; ~**e** *sfpl* (*possedimento*) lands, land *sg*; **a o per** ~

(*stato*) on the ground (*o* floor); (*moto*) to the ground, down; **mettere a** ~ (*ELETTR*) to earth

terra'cotta *sf* terracotta; **vasellame** *sm* **di** ~ earthenware

terra'ferma *sf* dry land, terra firma; (*continente*) mainland

terrapi'eno *sm* embankment, bank

ter'razza [ter'rattsa] *sf* terrace

ter'razzo [ter'rattso] *sm* = **terrazza**

terre'moto *sm* earthquake

ter'reno, a *ag* (*vita, beni*) earthly ♦ *sm* (*suolo, fig*) ground; (*COMM*) land *no pl*, plot (of land); site; (*SPORT, MIL*) field

ter'restre *ag* (*superficie*) of the earth, earth's; (*di terra: battaglia, animale*) land *cpd*; (*REL*) earthly, worldly

ter'ribile *ag* terrible, dreadful

terrifi'cante *ag* terrifying

ter'rina *sf* tureen

territori'ale *ag* territorial

terri'torio *sm* territory

ter'rore *sm* terror; **terro'rismo** *sm* terrorism; **terro'rista, i, e** *sm/f* terrorist

'terso, a *ag* clear

'terzo, a [ter'tso] *ag* third ♦ *sm* (*frazione*) third; (*DIR*) third party; ~**i** *smpl* (*altri*) others, other people; **la** ~**a pagina** (*STAMPA*) the Arts page

'tesa *sf* brim

'teschio ['teskjo] *sm* skull

'tesi *sf* thesis

'teso, a *pp di* **tendere** ♦ *ag* (*tirato*) taut, tight; (*fig*) tense

tesore'ria *sf* treasury

tesori'ere *sm* treasurer

te'soro *sm* treasure; **il Ministero del T~** the Treasury

'tessera *sf* (*documento*) card

'tessere *vt* to weave; **'tessile** *ag, sm* textile; **tessi'tore, 'trice** *sm/f* weaver; **tessi'tura** *sf* weaving

tes'suto *sm* fabric, material; (*BIOL*) tissue; (*fig*) web

'testa *sf* head; (*di cose: estremità, parte anteriore*) head, front; **di** ~ (*vettura etc*) front; **tenere** ~ **a qn** (*nemico etc*) to stand up to sb; **fare di** ~ **propria** to go one's own way; **in** ~ (*SPORT*) in the lead; ~ **o**

croce? heads or tails?; **avere la ~ dura**
to be stubborn; **~ di serie** (*TENNIS*) seed,
seeded player

testa'mento *sm* (*atto*) will; **l'Antico/il
Nuovo T~** (*REL*) the Old/New Testament

tes'tardo, a *ag* stubborn, pig-headed

tes'tata *sf* (*parte anteriore*) head;
(*intestazione*) heading

'teste *sm/f* witness

tes'ticolo *sm* testicle

testi'mone *sm/f* (*DIR*) witness

testimoni'anza [testimo'njantsa] *sf*
testimony

testimoni'are *vt* to testify; (*fig*) to bear
witness to, testify to ♦ *vi* to give
evidence, testify

tes'tina *sf* (*TECN*) head

'testo *sm* text; **fare ~** (*opera, autore*) to
be authoritative; **questo libro non fa ~**
this book is not essential reading;
testu'ale *ag* textual; literal, word for
word

tes'tuggine [tes'tuddʒine] *sf* tortoise; (*di
mare*) turtle

'tetano *sm* (*MED*) tetanus

'tetro, a *ag* gloomy

'tetto *sm* roof; **tet'toia** *sf* roofing; canopy

'Tevere *sm*: **il ~** the Tiber

Tg. *abbr* = **telegiornale**

'thermos ['tɛrmos] ® *sm inv* vacuum o
Thermos ® flask

ti *pron* (*dav lo, la, li, le, ne diventa* te)
pron (*oggetto*) you; (*complemento di
termine*) (to) you; (*riflessivo*) yourself

ti'ara *sf* (*REL*) tiara

'tibia *sf* tibia, shinbone

tic *sm inv* tic, (*nervous*) twitch; (*fig*)
mannerism

ticchet'tio [tikket'tio] *sm* (*di macchina
da scrivere*) clatter; (*di orologio*) ticking;
(*della pioggia*) patter

'ticchio ['tikkjo] *sm* (*ghiribizzo*) whim;
(*tic*) tic, (*nervous*) twitch

ti'epido, a *ag* lukewarm, tepid

ti'fare *vi*: **~ per** to be a fan of;
(*parteggiare*) to side with

'tifo *sm* (*MED*) typhus; (*fig*): **fare il ~ per**
to be a fan of

tifoi'dea *sf* typhoid

ti'fone *sm* typhoon

ti'foso, a *sm/f* (*SPORT etc*) fan

'tiglio ['tiʎʎo] *sm* lime (tree), linden (tree)

'tigre *sf* tiger

tim'ballo *sm* (*strumento*) kettledrum;
(*CUC*) timbale

'timbro *sm* stamp; (*MUS*) timbre, tone

'timido, a *ag* shy; timid

'timo *sm* thyme

ti'mone *sm* (*NAUT*) rudder; **timoni'ere** *sm*
helmsman

ti'more *sm* (*paura*) fear; (*rispetto*) awe;
timo'roso, a *ag* timid, timorous

'timpano *sm* (*ANAT*) eardrum; (*MUS*): **~i**
smpl kettledrums, timpani

ti'nello *sm* small dining room

'tingere ['tindʒere] *vt* to dye

'tino *sm* vat

ti'nozza [ti'nɔttsa] *sf* tub

'tinta *sf* (*materia colorante*) dye; (*colore*)
colour, shade; **tinta'rella** (*fam*) *sf*
(sun)tan

tintin'nare *vi* to tinkle

'tinto, a *pp di* **tingere**

tinto'ria *sf* (*officina*) dyeworks *sg*;
(*lavasecco*) dry cleaner's (shop)

tin'tura *sf* (*operazione*) dyeing; (*colorante*)
dye; **~ di iodio** tincture of iodine

'tipico, a, ci, che *ag* typical

'tipo *sm* type; (*genere*) kind, type; (*fam*)
chap, fellow

tipogra'fia *sf* typography; (*procedimento*)
letterpress (printing); (*officina*) printing
house; **tipo'grafico, a, ci, che** *ag*
typographic(al); letterpress *cpd*; **ti'pogra-
fo** *sm* typographer

ti'ranno, a *ag* tyrannical ♦ *sm* tyrant

ti'rante *sm* (*per tenda*) guy

ti'rare *vt* (*gen*) to pull; (*estrarre*): **~ qc da**
to take o pull sth out of; to get sth out of;
to extract sth from; (*chiudere: tenda etc*)
to draw, pull; (*tracciare, disegnare*) to
draw, trace; (*lanciare: sasso, palla*) to
throw; (*stampare*) to print; (*pistola,
freccia*) to fire ♦ *vi* (*pipa, camino*) to
draw; (*vento*) to blow; (*abito*) to be tight;
(*fare fuoco*) to fire; (*fare del tiro, CALCIO*) to
shoot; **~ avanti** *vi* to struggle on ♦ *vt* to
keep going; **~ fuori** (*estrarre*) to take out,

pull out; ~ **giù** (*abbassare*) to bring down; ~ **su** to pull up; (*capelli*) to put up; (*fig: bambino*) to bring up; ~**rsi indietro** to move back

tira'tore *sm* gunman; **un buon** ~ a good shot; ~ **scelto** marksman

tira'tura *sf* (*azione*) printing; (*di libro*) (print) run; (*di giornale*) circulation

'**tirchio, a** ['tirkjo] *ag* mean, stingy

'**tiro** *sm* shooting *no pl*, firing *no pl*; (*colpo, sparo*) shot; (*di palla: lancio*) throwing *no pl*; throw; (*fig*) trick; **cavallo da** ~ draught (*BRIT*) o draft (*US*) horse; ~ **a segno** target shooting; (*luogo*) shooting range

tiro'cinio [tiro't∫injo] *sm* apprenticeship; (*professionale*) training

ti'roide *sf* thyroid (gland)

Tir'reno *sm*: **il (mar)** ~ the Tyrrhenian Sea

ti'sana *sf* herb tea

tito'lare *ag* appointed; (*sovrano*) titular ♦ *sm/f* incumbent; (*proprietario*) owner; (*CALCIO*) regular player

'**titolo** *sm* title; (*di giornale*) headline; (*diploma*) qualification; (*COMM*) security; (*: azione*) share; **a che** ~? for what reason?; **a** ~ **di amicizia** out of friendship; **a** ~ **di premio** as a prize; ~ **di credito** share

titu'bante *ag* hesitant, irresolute

'**tizio, a** ['tittsjo] *sm/f* fellow, chap

tiz'zone [tit'tsone] *sm* brand

toc'cante *ag* touching

toc'care *vt* to touch; (*tastare*) to feel; (*fig: riguardare*) to concern; (*: commuovere*) to touch, move; (*: pungere*) to hurt, wound; (*: far cenno a: argomento*) to touch on, mention ♦ *vi*: ~ **a** (*accadere*) to happen to; (*spettare*) to be up to; ~ **(il fondo)** (*in acqua*) to touch the bottom; **tocca a te difenderci** it's up to you to defend us; **a chi tocca?** whose turn is it?; **mi toccò pagare** I had to pay

'**tocco, chi** *sm* touch; (*ARTE*) stroke, touch

'**toga, ghe** *sf* toga; (*di magistrato, professore*) gown

'**togliere** ['tɔʎʎere] *vt* (*rimuovere*) to take away (*o* off), remove; (*riprendere, non*

concedere più) to take away, remove; (*MAT*) to take away, subtract; (*liberare*) to free; ~ **qc a qn** to take sth (away) from sb; **ciò non toglie che** nevertheless, be that as it may; ~**rsi il cappello** to take off one's hat

toi'lette [twa'lɛt] *sf inv* toilet; (*mobile*) dressing table

to'letta *sf* = **toilette**

tolle'ranza [tolle'rantsa] *sf* tolerance

tolle'rare *vt* to tolerate

'**tolto, a** *pp di* **togliere**

to'maia *sf* (*di scarpa*) upper

'**tomba** *sf* tomb

tom'bino *sm* manhole cover

'**tombola** *sf* (*gioco*) tombola; (*ruzzolone*) tumble

'**tomo** *sm* volume

'**tonaca, che** *sf* (*REL*) habit

to'nare *vi* = **tuonare**

'**tondo, a** *ag* round

'**tonfo** *sm* splash; (*rumore sordo*) thud; (*caduta*): **fare un** ~ to take a tumble

'**tonico, a, ci, che** *ag, sm* tonic

tonifi'care *vt* (*muscoli, pelle*) to tone up; (*irrobustire*) to invigorate, brace

tonnel'laggio [tonnel'laddʒo] *sm* (*NAUT*) tonnage

tonnel'lata *sf* ton

'**tonno** *sm* tuna (fish)

'**tono** *sm* (*gen*) tone; (*MUS: di pezzo*) key; (*di colore*) shade, tone

ton'silla *sf* tonsil; **tonsil'lite** *sf* tonsillitis

'**tonto, a** *ag* dull, stupid

to'pazio [to'pattsjo] *sm* topaz

'**topo** *sm* mouse

topogra'fia *sf* topography

'**toppa** *sf* (*serratura*) keyhole; (*pezza*) patch

to'race [to'rat∫e] *sm* chest

'**torba** *sf* peat

'**torbido, a** *ag* (*liquido*) cloudy; (*: fiume*) muddy; (*fig*) dark; troubled ♦ *sm*: **pescare nel** ~ (*fig*) to fish in troubled water

'**torcere** ['tort∫ere] *vt* to twist; (*biancheria*) to wring (out); ~**rsi** *vr* to twist, writhe

torchi'are [tor'kjare] *vt* to press;

'**torchio** *sm* press

'torcia, ce ['tɔrtʃa] *sf* torch; ~ elettrica torch (*BRIT*), flashlight (*US*)

torci'collo [tortʃi'kɔllo] *sm* stiff neck

'tordo *sm* thrush

To'rino *sf* Turin

tor'menta *sf* snowstorm

tormen'tare *vt* to torment; ~rsi *vr* to fret, worry o.s.; tor'mento *sm* torment

torna'conto *sm* advantage, benefit

tor'nado *sm* tornado

tor'nante *sm* hairpin bend

tor'nare *vi* to return, go (*o* come) back; (*ridiventare: anche fig*) to become (again); (*riuscire giusto, esatto: conto*) to work out; (*risultare*) to turn out (to be), prove (to be); ~ **utile** to prove *o* turn out (to be) useful; ~ **a casa** to go (*o* come) home

torna'sole *sm inv* litmus

tor'neo *sm* tournament

'tornio *sm* lathe

'toro *sm* bull; (*dello zodiaco*): T~ Taurus

tor'pedine *sf* torpedo; torpedini'era *sf* torpedo boat

'torre *sf* tower; (*SCACCHI*) rook, castle; ~ **di controllo** (*AER*) control tower

torrefazi'one [torrefat'tsjone] *sf* roasting

tor'rente *sm* torrent

tor'retta *sf* turret

torri'one *sm* keep

tor'rone *sm* nougat

torsi'one *sf* twisting; torsion

'torso *sm* torso, trunk; (*ARTE*) torso

'torsolo *sm* (*di cavolo etc*) stump; (*di frutta*) core

'torta *sf* cake

'torto, a *pp di* torcere ♦ *ag* (*ritorto*) twisted; (*storto*) twisted, crooked ♦ *sm* (*ingiustizia*) wrong; (*colpa*) fault; a ~ wrongly; aver ~ to be wrong

'tortora *sf* turtle dove

tortu'oso, a *ag* (*strada*) twisting; (*fig*) tortuous

tor'tura *sf* torture; tortu'rare *vt* to torture

'torvo, a *ag* menacing, grim

tosa'erba *sm o f inv* (lawn)mower

to'sare *vt* (*pecora*) to shear; (*siepe*) to clip, trim

Tos'cana *sf*: la ~ Tuscany; tos'cano, a *ag*, *sm/f* Tuscan ♦ *sm* (*sigaro*) strong Italian cigar

'tosse *sf* cough

'tossico, a, ci, che *ag* toxic

tossicodipen'dente *sm/f* drug addict

tossi'comane *sm/f* drug addict

tos'sire *vi* to cough

tosta'pane *sm inv* toaster

tos'tare *vt* to toast; (*caffè*) to roast

'tosto, a *ag*: faccia ~a cheek

to'tale *ag*, *sm* total; totalità *sf*: la totalità di all of, the total amount (*o* number) of; the whole +*sg*; totaliz'zare *vt* to total; (*SPORT*: *punti*) to score

toto'calcio [toto'kaltʃo] *sm* gambling pool betting on football results, ≈ (football) pools *pl* (*BRIT*)

to'vaglia [to'vaʎʎa] *sf* tablecloth; tovagli'olo *sm* napkin

'tozzo, a ['tɔttso] *ag* squat ♦ *sm*: ~ di pane crust of bread

tra *prep* (*di due persone, cose*) between; (*di più persone, cose*) among(st); (*tempo: entro*) within, in; ~ **5 giorni** in 5 days' time; sia detto ~ noi ... between you and me ...; litigano ~ (di) loro they're fighting amongst themselves; ~ breve soon; ~ sé e sé (*parlare etc*) to oneself

trabal'lare *vi* to stagger, totter

traboc'care *vi* to overflow

traboc'chetto [trabok'ketto] *sm* (*fig*) trap

tracan'nare *vt* to gulp down

'traccia, ce ['trattʃa] *sf* (*segno, striscia*) trail, track; (*orma*) tracks *pl*; (*residuo, testimonianza*) trace, sign; (*abbozzo*) outline

tracci'are [trat'tʃare] *vt* to trace, mark (out); (*disegnare*) to draw; (*fig: abbozzare*) to outline; tracci'ato *sm* (*grafico*) layout, plan

tra'chea [tra'kɛa] *sf* windpipe, trachea

tra'colla *sf* shoulder strap; borsa a ~ shoulder bag

tra'collo *sm* (*fig*) collapse, crash

traco'tante *ag* overbearing, arrogant

tradi'mento *sm* betrayal; (*DIR*, *MIL*) treason

tra'dire *vt* to betray; (*coniuge*) to be unfaithful to; (*doveri: mancare*) to fail in; (*rivelare*) to give away, reveal; **tradi'tore**, **'trice** *sm/f* traitor

tradizio'nale [tradittsjo'nale] *ag* traditional

tradizi'one [tradit'tsjone] *sf* tradition

tra'dotto, a *pp di* **tradurre**

tra'durre *vt* to translate; (*spiegare*) to render, convey; **tradut'tore**, **'trice** *sm/f* translator; **traduzi'one** *sf* translation

tra'ente *sm/f* (*ECON*) drawer

trafe'lato, a *ag* out of breath

traffi'cante *sm/f* dealer; (*peg*) trafficker

traffi'care *vi* (*commerciare*): ~ **(in)** to trade (in), deal (in); (*affaccendarsi*) to busy o.s. ♦ *vt* (*peg*) to traffic in

'traffico, ci *sm* traffic; (*commercio*) trade, traffic

tra'figgere [tra'fiddʒere] *vt* to run through, stab; (*fig*) to pierce; **tra'fitto, a** *pp di* **trafiggere**

trafo'rare *vt* to bore, drill; **tra'foro** *sm* (*azione*) boring, drilling; (*galleria*) tunnel

tra'gedia [tra'dʒedja] *sf* tragedy

tra'ghetto [tra'getto] *sm* crossing; (*barca*) ferry(boat)

'tragico, a, ci, che ['tradʒiko] *ag* tragic

tra'gitto [tra'dʒitto] *sm* (*passaggio*) crossing; (*viaggio*) journey

tragu'ardo *sm* (*SPORT*) finishing line; (*fig*) goal, aim

traiet'toria *sf* trajectory

trai'nare *vt* to drag, haul; (*rimorchiare*) to tow; **'traino** *sm* (*carro*) wagon; (*slitta*) sledge; (*carico*) load

tralasci'are [tralaʃ'ʃare] *vt* (*studi*) to neglect; (*dettagli*) to leave out, omit

'tralcio ['traltʃo] *sm* (*BOT*) shoot

tra'liccio [tra'littʃo] *sm* (*tela*) ticking; (*struttura*) trellis; (*ELETTR*) pylon

tram *sm inv* tram

'trama *sf* (*filo*) weft, woof; (*fig: argomento, maneggio*) plot

traman'dare *vt* to pass on, hand down

tra'mare *vt* (*fig*) to scheme, plot

tram'busto *sm* turmoil

trames'tio *sm* bustle

tramez'zino [tramed'dzino] *sm* sandwich

tra'mezzo [tra'meddzo] *sm* (*EDIL*) partition

'tramite *prep* through

tramon'tare *vi* to set, go down; **tra'monto** *sm* setting; (*del sole*) sunset

tramor'tire *vi* to faint ♦ *vt* to stun

trampo'lino *sm* (*per tuffi*) springboard, diving board; (*per lo sci*) ski-jump

'trampolo *sm* stilt

tramu'tare *vt*: ~ **in** to change into, turn into

tra'nello *sm* trap

trangugi'are [trangu'dʒare] *vt* to gulp down

'tranne *prep* except (for), but (for); ~ **che** unless

tranquil'lante *sm* (*MED*) tranquillizer

tranquillità *sf* calm, stillness; quietness; peace of mind

tranquilliz'zare [trankwillid'dzare] *vt* to reassure

tran'quillo, a *ag* calm, quiet; (*bambino, scolaro*) quiet; (*sereno*) with one's mind at rest; **sta' ~** don't worry

transat'lantico, a, ci, che *ag* transatlantic ♦ *sm* transatlantic liner

tran'satto, a *pp di* **transigere**

transazi'one [transat'tsjone] *sf* compromise; (*DIR*) settlement; (*COMM*) transaction, deal

tran'senna *sf* barrier

tran'sigere [tran'sidʒere] *vi* (*DIR*) to reach a settlement; (*venire a patti*) to compromise, come to an agreement

tran'sistor *sm inv* transistor

transi'tabile *ag* passable

transi'tare *vi* to pass

transi'tivo, a *ag* transitive

'transito *sm* transit; **di ~** (*merci*) in transit; (*stazione*) transit *cpd*; **"divieto di ~"** "no entry"

transi'torio, a *ag* transitory, transient; (*provvisorio*) provisional

tran'via *sf* tramway (*BRIT*), streetcar line (*US*)

'trapano *sm* (*utensile*) drill; (: *MED*) trepan

trapas'sare *vt* to pierce

tra'passo *sm* passage

trape'lare *vi* to leak, drip; (*fig*) to leak

out

tra'pezio [tra'pɛttsjo] *sm* (*MAT*) trapezium; (*attrezzo ginnico*) trapeze

trapian'tare *vt* to transplant; trapi'anto *sm* transplanting; (*MED*) transplant

'trappola *sf* trap

tra'punta *sf* quilt

'trarre *vt* to draw, pull; (*portare*) to take; (*prendere, tirare fuori*) to take (out), draw; (*derivare*) to obtain; ~ origine da qc to have its origins *o* originate in sth

trasa'lire *vi* to start, jump

trasan'dato, a *ag* shabby

trasbor'dare *vt* to transfer; (*NAUT*) to tran(s)ship ♦ *vi* (*NAUT*) to change ship; (*AER*) to change plane; (*FERR*) to change (trains)

trasci'nare [traʃʃi'nare] *vt* to drag; ~rsi *vr* to drag o.s. along; (*fig*) to drag on

tras'correre *vt* (*tempo*) to spend, pass ♦ *vi* to pass; tras'corso, a *pp di* trascorrere

tras'critto, a *pp di* trascrivere

tras'crivere *vt* to transcribe

trascu'rare *vt* to neglect; (*non considerare*) to disregard; trascura'tezza *sf* carelessness, negligence; trascu'rato, a *ag* (*casa*) neglected; (*persona*) careless, negligent

traseco'lato, a *ag* astounded, amazed

trasferi'mento *sm* transfer; (*trasloco*) removal, move

trasfe'rire *vt* to transfer; ~rsi *vr* to move; tras'ferta *sf* transfer; (*indennità*) travelling expenses *pl*; (*SPORT*) away game

trasfigu'rare *vt* to transfigure

trasfor'mare *vt* to transform, change

trasfusi'one *sf* (*MED*) transfusion

trasgre'dire *vt* to disobey, contravene

tras'lato, a *ag* metaphorical, figurative

traslo'care *vt* to move, transfer; ~rsi *vr* to move; tras'loco, chi *sm* removal

tras'messo, a *pp di* trasmettere

tras'mettere *vt* (*passare*): ~ qc a qn to pass sth on to sb; (*mandare*) to send; (*TECN, TEL, MED*) to transmit; (*TV, RADIO*) to broadcast; trasmetti'tore *sm* transmitter; trasmissi'one *sf* (*gen, FISICA, TECN*) transmission; (*passaggio*) transmission,

passing on; (*TV, RADIO*) broadcast; trasmit'tente *sf* transmitting *o* broadcasting station

traso'gnato, a [traso'ɲato] *ag* dreamy

traspa'rente *ag* transparent

traspa'rire *vi* to show (through)

traspi'rare *vi* to perspire; (*fig*) to come to light, leak out; traspirazi'one *sf* perspiration

traspor'tare *vt* to carry, move; (*merce*) to transport, convey; lasciarsi ~ (da qc) (*fig*) to let o.s. be carried away (by sth); tras'porto *sm* transport

trastul'lare *vt* to amuse; ~rsi *vr* to amuse o.s.

trasu'dare *vi* (*filtrare*) to ooze; (*sudare*) to sweat ♦ *vt* to ooze with

trasver'sale *ag* transverse, cross(-); running at right angles

trasvo'lare *vt* to fly over

'tratta *sf* (*ECON*) draft; (*di persone*): la ~ delle bianche the white slave trade

tratta'mento *sm* treatment; (*servizio*) service

trat'tare *vt* (*gen*) to treat; (*commerciare*) to deal in; (*svolgere: argomento*) to discuss, deal with; (*negoziare*) to negotiate ♦ *vi*: ~ di to deal with; ~ con (*persona*) to deal with; si tratta di ... it's about ...; tratta'tive *sfpl* negotiations; trat'tato *sm* (*testo*) treatise; (*accordo*) treaty; trattazi'one *sf* treatment

tratteggi'are [tratted'dʒare] *vt* (*disegnare: a tratti*) to sketch, outline; (*: col tratteggio*) to hatch

trat'tenere *vt* (*far rimanere: persona*) to detain; (*intrattenere: ospiti*) to entertain; (*tenere, frenare, reprimere*) to hold back, keep back; (*astenersi dal consegnare*) to hold, keep; (*detrarre: somma*) to deduct; ~rsi *vr* (*astenersi*) to restrain o.s., stop o.s.; (*soffermarsi*) to stay, remain

tratteni'mento *sm* entertainment; (*festa*) party

tratte'nuta *sf* deduction

trat'tino *sm* dash; (*in parole composte*) hyphen

'tratto, a *pp di* trarre ♦ *sm* (*di penna, matita*) stroke; (*parte*) part, piece; (*di *strada*) stretch; (*di mare, cielo*) expanse; (*di tempo*) period (of time); **~i** *smpl* (*caratteristiche*) features; (*modo di fare*) ways, manners; **a un ~, d'un ~** suddenly

trat'tore *sm* tractor

tratto'ria *sf* restaurant

'trauma, i *sm* trauma; **trau'matico, a, ci, che** *ag* traumatic

tra'vaglio [tra'vaʎʎo] *sm* (*angoscia*) pain, suffering; (*MED*) pains *pl*

trava'sare *vt* to decant

'trave *sf* beam

tra'versa *sf* (*trave*) crosspiece; (*via*) sidestreet; (*FERR*) sleeper (*BRIT*), (railroad) tie (*US*); (*CALCIO*) crossbar

traver'sare *vt* to cross; **traver'sata** *sf* crossing; (*AER*) flight, trip

traver'sie *sfpl* mishaps, misfortunes

traver'sina *sf* (*FERR*) sleeper (*BRIT*), (railroad) tie (*US*)

tra'verso, a *ag* oblique; **di ~** *ag* askew ♦ *av* sideways; **andare di ~** (*cibo*) to go down the wrong way; **guardare di ~** to look askance at

travesti'mento *sm* disguise

traves'tire *vt* to disguise; **~rsi** *vr* to disguise o.s.

travi'are *vt* (*fig*) to lead astray

travi'sare *vt* (*fig*) to distort, misrepresent

tra'volgere [tra'vɔldʒere] *vt* to sweep away, carry away; (*fig*) to overwhelm; **tra'volto, a** *pp di* **travolgere**

tre *num* three

trebbi'are *vt* to thresh

'treccia, ce ['trettʃa] *sf* plait, braid

tre'cento [tre'tʃɛnto] *num* three hundred ♦ *sm*: **il T~** the fourteenth century

'tredici ['treditʃi] *num* thirteen

'tregua *sf* truce; (*fig*) respite

tre'mare *vi*: **~ di** (*freddo etc*) to shiver o tremble with; (*paura, rabbia*) to shake o tremble with

tre'mendo, a *ag* terrible, awful

tre'mila *num* three thousand

'tremito *sm* trembling *no pl*; shaking *no pl*; shivering *no pl*

tremo'lare *vi* to tremble; (*luce*) to flicker; (*foglie*) to quiver

tre'more *sm* tremor

'treno *sm* train; **~ di gomme** set of tyres (*BRIT*) o tires (*US*); **~ merci** goods (*BRIT*) o freight train; **~ viaggiatori** passenger train

'trenta *num* thirty; **tren'tesimo, a** *num* thirtieth; **tren'tina** *sf*: **una trentina (di)** thirty or so, about thirty

'trepido, a *ag* anxious

treppi'ede *sm* tripod; (*CUC*) trivet

'tresca, sche *sf* (*fig*) intrigue; (: *relazione amorosa*) affair

'trespolo *sm* trestle

tri'angolo *sm* triangle

tri'bù *sf inv* tribe

tri'buna *sf* (*podio*) platform; (*in aule etc*) gallery; (*di stadio*) stand

tribu'nale *sm* court

tribu'tare *vt* to bestow

tri'buto *sm* tax; (*fig*) tribute

tri'checo, chi [tri'kɛko] *sm* (*ZOOL*) walrus

tri'ciclo [tri'tʃiklo] *sm* tricycle

trico'lore *ag* three-coloured ♦ *sm* tricolour; (*bandiera italiana*) Italian flag

tri'dente *sm* trident

tri'foglio [tri'fɔʎʎo] *sm* clover

'triglia ['triʎʎa] *sf* red mullet

tril'lare *vi* (*MUS*) to trill

tri'mestre *sm* period of three months; (*INS*) term, quarter (*US*); (*COMM*) quarter

'trina *sf* lace

trin'cea [trin'tʃea] *sf* trench; **trince'rare** *vt* to entrench

trinci'are [trin'tʃare] *vt* to cut up

trion'fare *vi* to triumph, win; **~ su** to triumph over, overcome; **tri'onfo** *sm* triumph

tripli'care *vt* to triple

'triplice ['triplitʃe] *ag* triple; **in ~ copia** in triplicate

'triplo, a *ag* triple; treble ♦ *sm*: **il ~ (di)** three times as much (as); **la spesa è ~a** it costs three times as much

'tripode *sm* tripod

'trippa *sf* (*CUC*) tripe

'triste *ag* sad; (*luogo*) dreary, gloomy; **tris'tezza** *sf* sadness; gloominess

trita'carne *sm inv* mincer, grinder (*US*)

tri'tare *vt* to mince, grind (*US*)

'trito, a *ag* (*tritato*) minced, ground (*US*);

~ **e ritrito** (*fig*) trite, hackneyed

'**trittico, ci** *sm* (*ARTE*) triptych

trivel'lare *vt* to drill

trivi'ale *ag* vulgar, low

tro'feo *sm* trophy

'trogolo *sm* (*per maiali*) trough

'tromba *sf* (*MUS*) trumpet; (*AUT*) horn; ~ **d'aria** whirlwind; ~ **delle scale** stairwell

trom'bone *sm* trombone

trom'bosi *sf* thrombosis

tron'care *vt* to cut off; (*spezzare*) to break off

'tronco, a, chi, che *ag* cut off; broken off; (*LING*) truncated; (*fig*) cut short ♦ *sm* (*BOT*, *ANAT*) trunk; (*fig*: *tratto*) section; (: *pezzo*: *di lancia*) stump; **licenziare qn in** ~ to fire sb on the spot

troneggi'are [troned'dʒare] *vi*: ~ **(su)** to tower (over)

'tronfio, a *ag* conceited

'trono *sm* throne

tropi'cale *ag* tropical

'tropico, ci *sm* tropic; ~ci *smpl* (*GEO*) tropics

'**troppo, a** *det* (*in eccesso*: *quantità*) too much; (: *numero*) too many; **c'era ~a gente** there were too many people; **fa ~ caldo** it's too hot

♦ *pron* (*in eccesso*: *quantità*) too much; (: *numero*) too many; **ne hai messo** ~ you've put in too much; **meglio ~i che pochi** better too many than too few

♦ *av* (*eccessivamente*: *con ag*, *av*) too; (: *con vb*) too much; ~ **amaro/tardi** too bitter/late; **lavora** ~ he works too much; **di** ~ too much; too many; **qualche tazza di** ~ a few cups too many; **3000 lire di** ~ 3000 lire too much; **essere di** ~ to be in the way

'trota *sf* trout

trot'tare *vi* to trot; trotterel'lare *vi* to trot along; (*bambino*) to toddle; '**trotto** *sm* trot

'trottola *sf* spinning top

tro'vare *vt* to find; (*giudicare*): **trovo che** I find *o* think that; ~**rsi** *vr* (*reciproco*:

incontrarsi) to meet; (*essere, stare*) to be; (*arrivare, capitare*) to find o.s.; **andare a** ~ **qn** to go and see sb; ~ **qn colpevole** to find sb guilty; ~**rsi bene** (*in un luogo, con qn*) to get on well; **tro'vata** *sf* good idea

truc'care *vt* (*falsare*) to fake; (*attore etc*) to make up; (*travestire*) to disguise; (*SPORT*) to fix; (*AUT*) to soup up; ~**rsi** *vr* to make up (one's face); **trucca'tore, 'trice** *sm/f* (*CINEMA, TEATRO*) make-up artist

'**trucco, chi** *sm* trick; (*cosmesi*) make-up

'truce ['trutʃe] *ag* fierce

truci'dare [trutʃi'dare] *vt* to slaughter

'truciolo ['trutʃolo] *sm* shaving

'truffa *sf* fraud, swindle; **truf'fare** *vt* to swindle, cheat

'truppa *sf* troop

tu *pron* you; ~ **stesso(a)** you yourself; **dare del** ~ **a qn** to address sb as "tu"

'tua *vedi* tuo

'tuba *sf* (*MUS*) tuba; (*cappello*) top hat

tu'bare *vi* to coo

tuba'tura *sf* piping *no pl*, pipes *pl*

tubazi'one [tubat'tsjone] *sf* = tubatura

tu'betto *sm* tube

'tubo *sm* tube; pipe; ~ **digerente** (*ANAT*) alimentary canal, digestive tract; ~ **di scappamento** (*AUT*) exhaust pipe

'tue *vedi* tuo

tuf'fare *vt* to plunge, dip; ~**rsi** *vr* to plunge, dive; '**tuffo** *sm* dive; (*breve bagno*) dip

tu'gurio *sm* hovel

tuli'pano *sm* tulip

tume'farsi *vr* (*MED*) to swell

'tumido, a *ag* swollen

tu'more *sm* (*MED*) tumour

tu'multo *sm* uproar, commotion; (*sommossa*) riot; (*fig*) turmoil; **tumultu'oso, a** *ag* rowdy, unruly; (*fig*) turbulent, stormy

'tunica, che *sf* tunic

Tuni'sia *sf*: **la** ~ Tunisia

'tuo (*f* '**tua**, *pl* **tu'oi**, '**tue**) *det*: **il** ~, **la tua** *etc* your ♦ *pron*: **il** ~, **la tua** *etc* yours

tuo'nare *vi* to thunder; **tuona** it is thundering, there's some thunder

tu'ono *sm* thunder

tu'orlo *sm* yolk

tu'racciolo [tu'rattʃolo] *sm* cap, top; (*di sughero*) cork

tu'rare *vt* to stop, plug; (*con sughero*) to cork; **~rsi il naso** to hold one's nose

turba'mento *sm* disturbance; (*di animo*) anxiety, agitation

tur'bante *sm* turban

tur'bare *vt* to disturb, trouble

'turbine *sm* whirlwind

turbo'lento, a *ag* turbulent; (*ragazzo*) boisterous, unruly

turbo'lenza [turbo'lɛntsa] *sf* turbulence

tur'chese [tur'kese] *sf* turquoise

Tur'chia [tur'kia] *sf*: **la ~** Turkey

tur'chino, a [tur'kino] *ag* deep blue

'turco, a, chi, che *ag* Turkish ♦ *sm/f* Turk/Turkish woman ♦ *sm* (*LING*) Turkish; **parlare ~** (*fig*) to talk double-dutch

tu'rismo *sm* tourism; tourist industry; **tu'rista, i, e** *sm/f* tourist; **tu'ristico, a, ci, che** *ag* tourist *cpd*

'turno *sm* turn; (*di lavoro*) shift; **di ~** (*soldato, medico, custode*) on duty; **a ~** (*rispondere*) in turn; (*lavorare*) in shifts; **fare a ~ a fare qc** to take turns to do sth; **è il suo ~** it's your (*o* his *etc*) turn

'turpe *ag* filthy, vile; **turpi'loquio** *sm* obscene language

'tuta *sf* overalls *pl*; (*SPORT*) tracksuit

tu'tela *sf* (*DIR: di minore*) guardianship; (*: protezione*) protection; (*difesa*) defence; **tute'lare** *vt* to protect, defend

tu'tore, 'trice *sm/f* (*DIR*) guardian

tutta'via *cong* nevertheless, yet

─── PAROLA CHIAVE ───

'tutto, a *det* **1** (*intero*) all; **~ il latte** all the milk; **~a la notte** all night, the whole night; **~ il libro** the whole book; **~a una bottiglia** a whole bottle

2 (*pl, collettivo*) all; every; **~i i libri** all the books; **~e le notti** every night; **~i venerdì** every Friday; **~i gli uomini** all the men; (*collettivo*) all men; **~i e due** both *o* each of us (*o* them *o* you); **~i e cinque** all five of us (*o* them *o* you)

3 (*completamente*): **era ~a sporca** she was all dirty; **tremava ~** he was

trembling all over; **è ~a sua madre** she's just *o* exactly like her mother

4: **a tutt'oggi** so far, up till now; **a ~a velocità** at full *o* top speed

♦ *pron* **1** (*ogni cosa*) everything, all; (*qualsiasi cosa*) anything; **ha mangiato ~** he's eaten everything; **~ considerato** all things considered; **in ~: 10,000 lire in ~** 10.000 lire in all; **in ~ eravamo 50** there were 50 of us in all

2: **~i, e** (*ognuno*) all, everybody; **vengono ~i** they are all coming, everybody's coming; **~i quanti** all and sundry

♦ *av* (*completamente*) entirely, quite; **è ~ il contrario** it's quite *o* exactly the opposite; **tutt'al più: saranno stati tutt'al più una cinquantina** there were about fifty of them at (the very) most; **tutt'al più possiamo prendere un treno** if the worst comes to the worst we can take a train; **tutt'altro** on the contrary; **è tutt'altro che felice** he's anything but happy; **tutt'a un tratto** suddenly

♦ *sm*: **il ~** the whole lot, all of it

─────────────

tutto'fare *ag inv*: **domestica ~** general maid; **ragazzo ~** office boy ♦ *sm/f inv* handyman/woman

tut'tora *av* still

U

ubbidi'ente *ag* obedient; **ubbidi'enza** *sf* obedience

ubbi'dire *vi* to obey; **~ a** to obey; (*sog: veicolo, macchina*) to respond to

ubria'care *vt*: **~ qn** to get sb drunk; (*sog: alcool*) to make sb drunk; (*fig*) to make sb's head spin *o* reel; **~rsi** *vr* to get drunk; **~rsi di** (*fig*) to become intoxicated with

ubri'aco, a, chi, che *ag, sm/f* drunk

uccelli'era [uttʃel'ljera] *sf* aviary

uccel'lino [uttʃel'lino] *sm* baby bird, chick

uc'cello [ut'tʃello] *sm* bird

uc'cidere [ut'tʃidere] *vt* to kill; **~rsi** *vr* (*suicidarsi*) to kill o.s.; (*perdere la vita*) to be killed; **uccisi'one** *sf* killing; **uc'ciso, a** *pp di* **uccidere**; **ucci'sore** *sm* killer

udi'enza [u'djɛntsa] *sf* audience; (*DIR*) hearing; **dare ~ (a)** to grant an audience (to)

u'dire *vt* to hear; **udi'tivo, a** *ag* auditory; **u'dito** *sm* (sense of) hearing; **udi'tore, 'trice** *sm/f* listener; (*INS*) unregistered student (*attending lectures*); **udi'torio** *sm* (*persone*) audience

'uffa *escl* tut!

uffici'ale [uffi'tʃale] *ag* official ♦ *sm* (*AMM*) official, officer; (*MIL*) officer; **~ di stato civile** registrar

uf'ficio [uf'fitʃo] *sm* (*gen*) office; (*dovere*) duty; (*mansione*) task, function, job; (*agenzia*) agency, bureau; (*REL*) service; **d'~** *ag* office *cpd*; official ♦ *av* officially; **~ di collocamento** employment office; **~ informazioni** information bureau; **~ oggetti smarriti** lost property office (*BRIT*), lost and found (*US*); **~ postale** post office

uffici'oso, a [uffi'tʃoso] *ag* unofficial

'ufo: a ~ *av* free, for nothing

uggi'oso, a [ud'dʒoso] *ag* tiresome; (*tempo*) dull

uguagli'anza [ugwaʎ'ʎantsa] *sf* equality

uguagli'are [ugwaʎ'ʎare] *vt* to make equal; (*essere uguale*) to equal, be equal to; (*livellare*) to level; **~rsi a** *o* **con qn** (*paragonarsi*) to compare o.s. to sb

ugu'ale *ag* equal; (*identico*) identical, the same; (*uniforme*) level, even ♦ *av*: **costano ~** they cost the same; **sono bravi ~** they're equally good; **ugual'mente** *av* equally; (*lo stesso*) all the same

'ulcera ['ultʃera] *sf* ulcer

u'liva *etc* = **oliva** *etc*

ulteri'ore *ag* further

ulti'mare *vt* to finish, complete

'ultimo, a *ag* (*finale*) last; (*estremo*) farthest, utmost; (*recente: notizia, moda*) latest; (*fig: sommo, fondamentale*) ultimate ♦ *sm/f* last (one); **fino all'~** to the last, until the end; **da ~, in ~** in the end; **abitare all'~ piano** to live on the top floor; **per ~** (*entrare, arrivare*) last

ulu'lare *vi* to howl; **ulu'lato** *sm* howling *no pl*; howl

umanità *sf* humanity; **umani'tario, a** *ag* humanitarian

u'mano, a *ag* human; (*comprensivo*) humane

umbi'lico *sm* = **ombelico**

umet'tare *vt* to dampen, moisten

umidità *sf* dampness; humidity

'umido, a *ag* damp; (*mano, occhi*) moist; (*clima*) humid ♦ *sm* dampness, damp; **carne in ~** stew

'umile *ag* humble

umili'are *vt* to humiliate; **~rsi** *vr* to humble o.s.; **umiliazi'one** *sf* humiliation

umiltà *sf* humility, humbleness

u'more *sm* (*disposizione d'animo*) mood; (*carattere*) temper; **di buon/cattivo ~** in a good/bad mood

umo'rismo *sm* humour; **avere il senso dell'~** to have a sense of humour; **umo'rista, i, e** *sm/f* humorist; **umo'ristico, a, ci, che** *ag* humorous, funny

un *vedi* **uno**

un' *vedi* **uno**

una *vedi* **uno**

u'nanime *ag* unanimous; **unanimità** *sf* unanimity; **all'unanimità** unanimously

unci'netto [untʃi'netto] *sm* crochet hook

un'cino [un'tʃino] *sm* hook

'undici ['unditʃi] *num* eleven

'ungere ['undʒere] *vt* to grease, oil; (*REL*) to anoint; (*fig*) to flatter, butter up; **~rsi** *vr* (*sporcarsi*) to get covered in grease; **~rsi con la crema** to put on cream

unghe'rese [unge'rese] *ag, sm/f, sm* Hungarian

Unghe'ria [unge'ria] *sf*: **l'~** Hungary

'unghia ['ungja] *sf* (*ANAT*) nail; (*di animale*) claw; (*di rapace*) talon; (*di cavallo*) hoof; **unghi'ata** *sf* (*graffio*) scratch

ungu'ento *sm* ointment

'unico, a, ci, che *ag* (*solo*) only; (*ineguagliabile*) unique; (*singolo: binario*) single; **figlio(a) ~(a)** only son/daughter, only child

unifi'care *vt* to unite, unify; (*sistemi*) to standardize; **unificazi'one** *sf* uniting;

unification; standardization

uni'forme *ag* uniform; (*superficie*) even
♦ *sf* (*divisa*) uniform

unilate'rale *ag* one-sided; (*DIR*) unilateral

uni'one *sf* union; (*fig: concordia*) unity,
harmony.

u'nire *vt* to unite; (*congiungere*) to join,
connect; (*: ingredienti, colori*) to combine;
(*in matrimonio*) to unite, join together;
~rsi *vr* to unite; (*in matrimonio*) to be
joined together; ~ **qc a** to unite sth with;
to join *o* connect sth with; to combine sth
with; ~rsi **a** (*gruppo, società*) to join

unità *sf inv* (*unione, concordia*) unity;
(*MAT*, *MIL*, *COMM*, *di misura*) unit;
uni'tario, **a** *ag* unitary; **prezzo unitario**
price per unit

u'nito, **a** *ag* (*paese*) united; (*amici,
famiglia*) close; **in tinta** ~**a** plain, self-
coloured

univer'sale *ag* universal; general

università *sf inv* university;
universi'tario, **a** *ag* university *cpd*
♦ *sm/f* (*studente*) university student;
(*insegnante*) academic, university lecturer

uni'verso *sm* universe

'uno, **a** (*dav sm* **un** +*C*, *V*, **uno** +*s
impura*, *gn*, *pn*, *ps*, *x*, *z*; *dav sf* **un'** + *V*,
una +*C*) *art indef* **1** a; (*dav vocale*) an;
un bambino a child; ~**a strada** a street;
~ **zingaro** a gypsy

2 (*intensivo*): **ho avuto** ~**a paura!** I got
such a fright!

♦ *pron* **1** one; **prendine** ~ take one (of
them); **l'**~ **o l'altro** either (of them); **l'**~ **e
l'altro** both (of them); **aiutarsi l'un
l'altro** to help one another *o* each other;
sono entrati l'~ **dopo l'altro** they came
in one after the other

2 (*un tale*) someone, somebody

3 (*con valore impersonale*) one; **se** ~
vuole if one wants, if you want

♦ *num* one; ~**a mela e due pere** one
apple and two pears; ~ **più** ~ **fa due** one
plus one equals two, one and one are two
♦ *sf*: **è l'**~**a** it's one (o'clock)

'unto, **a** *pp di* **ungere** ♦ *ag* greasy, oily
♦ *sm* grease; untu'oso, **a** *ag* greasy,
oily

u'omo (*pl* u'omini) *sm* man; **da** ~ (*abito,
scarpe*) men's, for men; ~ **d'affari**
businessman; ~ **di paglia** stooge; ~ **rana**
frogman

u'opo *sm*: **all'**~ if necessary

u'ovo (*pl(f)* u'ova) *sm* egg; ~ **affogato**
poached egg; ~ **al tegame** fried egg; ~
alla coque boiled egg; ~ **bazzotto/sodo**
soft-/hard-boiled egg; ~ **di Pasqua** Easter
egg; ~ **in camicia** poached egg; ~**a
strapazzate** scrambled eggs

ura'gano *sm* hurricane

urba'nistica *sf* town planning

ur'bano, **a** *ag* urban, city *cpd*, town *cpd*;
(*TEL: chiamata*) local; (*fig*) urbane

ur'gente [ur'dʒɛnte] *ag* urgent; ur'genza
sf urgency; **in caso d'urgenza** in (case
of) an emergency; **d'urgenza** *ag*
emergency ♦ *av* urgently, as a matter of
urgency

'urgere ['urdʒere] *vi* to be urgent; to be
needed urgently

u'rina *sf* = **orina**

ur'lare *vi* (*persona*) to scream, yell;
(*animale, vento*) to howl ♦ *vt* to scream,
yell

'urlo (*pl(m)* 'urli, *pl(f)* 'urla) *sm* scream,
yell; howl

'urna *sf* urn; (*elettorale*) ballot-box;
andare alle ~**e** to go to the polls

urrà *escl* hurrah!

U.R.S.S. *abbr f*: **l'**~ the USSR

ur'tare *vt* to bump into, knock against;
(*fig: irritare*) to annoy ♦ *vi*: ~ **contro** *o* **in**
to bump into, knock against, crash into;
(*fig: imbattersi*) to come up against; ~**rsi**
vr (*reciproco: scontrarsi*) to collide; (*: fig*)
to clash; (*irritarsi*) to get annoyed; 'urto
sm (*colpo*) knock, bump; (*scontro*) crash,
collision; (*fig*) clash

'U.S.A. ['uza] *smpl*: **gli** ~ the USA

u'sanza [u'zantsa] *sf* custom; (*moda*)
fashion

u'sare *vt* to use, employ ♦ *vi* (*servirsi*): ~
di to use; (*: diritto*) to exercise; (*essere di
moda*) to be fashionable; (*essere solito*): ~

fare to be in the habit of doing, be accustomed to doing ♦ *vb impers*: **qui usa così** it's the custom round here; **u'sato, a** *ag* used; (*consumato*) worn; (*di seconda mano*) used, second-hand ♦ *sm* second-hand goods *pl*

usci'ere [uʃˈʃɛre] *sm* usher

'uscio [ˈuʃʃo] *sm* door

u'scire [uʃˈʃire] *vi* (*gen*) to come out; (*partire, andare a passeggio, a uno spettacolo etc*) to go out; (*essere sorteggiato: numero*) to come up; ~ **da** (*gen*) to leave; (*posto*) to go (o come) out of, leave; (*solco, vasca etc*) to come out of; (*muro*) to stick out of; (*competenza etc*) to be outside; (*infanzia, adolescenza*) to leave behind; (*famiglia nobile etc*) to come from; ~ **da** *o* **di casa** to go out; (*fig*) to leave home; ~ **in automobile** to go out in the car, go for a drive; ~ **di strada** (*AUT*) to go off *o* leave the road

u'scita [uʃˈʃita] *sf* (*passaggio, varco*) exit, way out; (*per divertimento*) outing; (*ECON: somma*) expenditure; (*TEATRO*) entrance; (*fig: battuta*) witty remark; ~ **di sicurezza** emergency exit

usi'gnolo [uziɲˈɲɔlo] *sm* nightingale

U.S.L. [uzl] *sigla f* (= *unità sanitaria locale*) local health centre

'uso *sm* (*utilizzazione*) use; (*esercizio*) practice; (*abitudine*) custom; **a ~ di** for (the use of); **d'~** (*corrente*) in use; **fuori ~** out of use

usti'one *sf* burn

usu'ale *ag* common, everyday

u'sura *sf* usury; (*logoramento*) wear (and tear)

uten'sile *sm* tool, implement; ~**i da cucina** kitchen utensils

u'tente *sm/f* user

'utero *sm* uterus

'utile *ag* useful ♦ *sm* (*vantaggio*) advantage, benefit; (*ECON: profitto*) profit; **utilità** *sf* usefulness *no pl*; use; (*vantaggio*) benefit; **utili'taria** *sf* (*AUT*) economy car; **utili'tario, a** *ag* utilitarian

utiliz'zare [utilidˈdzare] *vt* to use, make use of, utilize

'uva *sf* grapes *pl*; ~ **passa** raisins *pl*; ~

spina gooseberry

V

v. *abbr* (= *vedi*) v

va *vb vedi* **andare**

va'cante *ag* vacant

va'canza [vaˈkantsa] *sf* (*l'essere vacante*) vacancy; (*riposo, ferie*) holiday(s *pl*) (*BRIT*), vacation (*US*); (*giorno di permesso*) day off, holiday; ~**e** *sfpl* (*periodo di ferie*) holidays (*BRIT*), vacation *sg* (*US*); **essere/andare in** ~ to be/go on holiday *o* vacation; ~**e estive** summer holiday(s) *o* vacation

'vacca, che *sf* cow

vacci'nare [vattʃiˈnare] *vt* to vaccinate

vac'cino [vatˈtʃino] *sm* (*MED*) vaccine

vacil'lare [vatʃilˈlare] *vi* to sway, wobble; (*luce*) to flicker; (*fig: memoria, coraggio*) to be failing, falter

'vacuo, a *ag* (*fig*) empty, vacuous ♦ *sm* vacuum

'vado *vb vedi* **andare**

vaga'bondo, a *sm/f* tramp, vagrant; (*fannullone*) idler, loafer

vagheggi'are [vagedˈdʒare] *vt* to long for, dream of

va'gina [vaˈdʒina] *sf* vagina

va'gire [vaˈdʒire] *vi* to whimper

va'gito [vaˈdʒito] *sm* cry

'vaglia [ˈvaʎʎa] *sm inv* money order; ~ **postale** postal order

vagli'are [vaʎˈʎare] *vt* to sift; (*fig*) to weigh up; **'vaglio** *sm* sieve

'vago, a, ghi, ghe *ag* vague

va'gone *sm* (*FERR: per passeggeri*) coach; (: *per merci*) truck, wagon; ~ **letto** sleeper, sleeping car; ~ **ristorante** dining *o* restaurant car

'vai *vb vedi* **andare**

vai'olo *sm* smallpox

va'langa, ghe *sf* avalanche

va'lente *ag* able, talented

va'lere *vi* (*avere forza, potenza*) to have influence; (*essere valido*) to be valid; (*avere vigore, autorità*) to hold, apply; (*essere capace: poeta, studente*) to be good, be able ♦ *vt* (*prezzo, sforzo*) to be worth; (*corrispondere*) to correspond to; (*procurare*): ~ **qc a qn** to earn sb sth; **~rsi di** to make use of, take advantage of; **far ~** (*autorità etc*) to assert; **vale a dire** that is to say; ~ **la pena** to be worth the effort *o* worth it

va'levole *ag* valid

vali'care *vt* to cross

'valico, chi *sm* (*passo*) pass

'valido, a *ag* valid; (*rimedio*) effective; (*aiuto*) real; (*persona*) worthwhile

valige'ria [validʒe'ria] *sf* leather goods *pl*; leather goods factory; leather goods shop

va'ligia, gie *o* **ge** [va'lidʒa] *sf* (suit)case; **fare le ~gie** to pack (up); ~ **diplomatica** diplomatic bag

val'lata *sf* valley

'valle *sf* valley; **a ~** (*di fiume*) downstream; **scendere a ~** to go downhill

val'letto *sm* valet

va'lore *sm* (*gen*) value; (*merito*) merit, worth; (*coraggio*) valour, courage; (*COMM: titolo*) security; **~i** *smpl* (*oggetti preziosi*) valuables

valoriz'zare [valorid'dzare] *vt* (*terreno*) to develop; (*fig*) to make the most of

'valso, a *pp di* **valere**

va'luta *sf* currency, money; (*BANCA*): ~ **15 gennaio** interest to run from January 15th

valu'tare *vt* (*casa, gioiello, fig*) to value; (*stabilire: peso, entrate, fig*) to estimate; **valutazi'one** *sf* valuation; estimate

'valvola *sf* (*TECN, ANAT*) valve; (*ELETTR*) fuse

'valzer ['valtser] *sm inv* waltz

vam'pata *sf* (*di fiamma*) blaze; (*di calore*) blast; (*: al viso*) flush

vam'piro *sm* vampire

vanda'lismo *sm* vandalism

'vandalo *sm* vandal

vaneggi'are [vaned'dʒare] *vi* to rave

'vanga, ghe *sf* spade; **van'gare** *vt* to dig

van'gelo [van'dʒɛlo] *sm* gospel

va'niglia [va'niʎʎa] *sf* vanilla

vanità *sf* vanity; (*di promessa*) emptiness; (*di sforzo*) futility; **vani'toso, a** *ag* vain, conceited

'vanno *vb vedi* **andare**

'vano, a *ag* vain ♦ *sm* (*spazio*) space; (*apertura*) opening; (*stanza*) room

van'taggio [van'taddʒo] *sm* advantage; **essere/portarsi in ~** (*SPORT*) to be in/take the lead; **vantaggi'oso, a** *ag* advantageous; favourable

van'tare *vt* to praise, speak highly of; **~rsi** *vr*: **~rsi (di/di aver fatto)** to boast *o* brag (about/about having done); **vante'ria** *sf* boasting; **'vanto** *sm* boasting; (*merito*) virtue, merit; (*gloria*) pride

'vanvera *sf*: **a ~** haphazardly; **parlare a ~** to talk nonsense

va'pore *sm* vapour; (*anche*: ~ **acqueo**) steam; (*nave*) steamer; **a ~** (*turbina etc*) steam *cpd*; **al ~** (*CUC*) steamed; **vapo'retto** *sm* steamer; **vapori'era** *sf* (*FERR*) steam engine; **vaporiz'zare** *vt* to vaporize; **vapo'roso, a** *ag* (*tessuto*) filmy; (*capelli*) soft and full

va'rare *vt* (*NAUT, fig*) to launch; (*DIR*) to pass

var'care *vt* to cross

'varco, chi *sm* passage; **aprirsi un ~ tra la folla** to push one's way through the crowd

vari'abile *ag* variable; (*tempo, umore*) changeable, variable ♦ *sf* (*MAT*) variable

vari'are *vt, vi* to vary; ~ **di opinione** to change one's mind; **variazi'one** *sf* variation; change

va'rice [va'ritʃe] *sf* varicose vein

vari'cella [vari'tʃɛlla] *sf* chickenpox

vari'coso, a *ag* varicose

varie'gato, a *ag* variegated

varietà *sf inv* variety ♦ *sm inv* variety show

'vario, a *ag* varied; (*parecchi: col sostantivo al pl*) various; (*mutevole: umore*) changeable; **vario'pinto, a** *ag* multicoloured

'varo *sm* (*NAUT, fig*) launch; (*di leggi*) passing

va'saio *sm* potter

'vasca, sche *sf* basin; (*anche*: ~ **da bagno**) bathtub, bath

va'scello [vaʃ'ʃɛllo] *sm* (*NAUT*) vessel, ship

vase'lina *sf* vaseline

vasel'lame *sm* (*stoviglie*) crockery; (: *di porcellana*) china; ~ **d'oro/d'argento** gold/silver plate

'vaso *sm* (*recipiente*) pot; (: *barattolo*) jar; (: *decorativo*) vase; (*ANAT*) vessel; ~ **da fiori** vase; (*per piante*) flowerpot

vas'soio *sm* tray

'vasto, a *ag* vast, immense

Vati'cano *sm*: **il** ~ the Vatican

ve *pron, av* vedi **vi**

vecchi'aia [vek'kjaja] *sf* old age

'vecchio, a ['vekkjo] *ag* old ♦ *sm/f* old man/woman; **i ~i** the old

'vece ['vetʃe] *sf*: **in** ~ **di** in the place of, for; **fare le ~i di qn** to take sb's place

ve'dere *vt, vi* to see; **~rsi** *vr* to meet, see one another; **avere a che** ~ **con** to have something to do with; **far** ~ **qc a qn** to show sb sth; **farsi** ~ to show o.s.; (*farsi vivo*) to show one's face; **vedi di non farlo** make sure *o* see you don't do it; **non (ci) si vede** (*è buio etc*) you can't see a thing; **non lo posso** ~ (*fig*) I can't stand him

ve'detta *sf* (*sentinella, posto*) look-out; (*NAUT*) patrol boat

'vedovo, a *sm/f* widower/widow

ve'duta *sf* view

vee'mente *ag* vehement; violent

vege'tale [vedʒe'tale] *ag, sm* vegetable

vegetari'ano, a [vedʒeta'rjano] *ag, sm/f* vegetarian

'vegeto, a ['vɛdʒeto] *ag* (*pianta*) thriving; (*persona*) strong, vigorous

'veglia ['veʎʎa] *sf* wakefulness; (*sorveglianza*) watch; (*trattenimento*) evening gathering; **fare la** ~ **a un malato** to watch over a sick person

vegli'are [veʎ'ʎare] *vi* to be awake; to stay *o* sit up; (*stare vigile*) to watch; to keep watch ♦ *vt* (*malato, morto*) to watch over, sit up with

ve'icolo *sm* vehicle; ~ **spaziale** spacecraft *inv*

'vela *sf* (*NAUT: tela*) sail; (*sport*) sailing

ve'lare *vt* to veil; **~rsi** *vr* (*occhi, luna*) to mist over; (*voce*) to become husky; **~rsi il viso** to cover one's face (with a veil);

ve'lato, a *ag* veiled

veleggi'are [veled'dʒare] *vi* to sail; (*AER*) to glide

ve'leno *sm* poison; **vele'noso, a** *ag* poisonous

veli'ero *sm* sailing ship

ve'lina *sf* (*anche: carta* ~: *per imballare*) tissue paper; (: *per copie*) flimsy paper; (*copia*) carbon copy

ve'livolo *sm* aircraft

velleità *sf inv* vain ambition, vain desire

'vello *sm* fleece

vel'luto *sm* velvet; ~ **a coste** cord

'velo *sm* veil; (*tessuto*) voile

ve'loce [ve'lotʃe] *ag* fast, quick ♦ *av* fast, quickly; **velo'cista, i, e** *sm/f* (*SPORT*) sprinter; **velocità** *sf* speed; **a forte velocità** at high speed; **velocità di crociera** cruising speed

ve'lodromo *sm* velodrome

'vena *sf* (*gen*) vein; (*filone*) vein, seam; (*fig: ispirazione*) inspiration; (: *umore*) mood; **essere in** ~ **di qc** to be in the mood for sth

ve'nale *ag* (*prezzo, valore*) market *cpd*; (*fig*) venal; mercenary

ven'demmia *sf* (*raccolta*) grape harvest; (*quantità d'uva*) grape crop, grapes *pl*; (*vino ottenuto*) vintage; **vendemmi'are** *vt* to harvest ♦ *vi* to harvest the grapes

'vendere *vt* to sell; **"vendesi"** "for sale"

ven'detta *sf* revenge

vendi'care *vt* to avenge; **~rsi** *vr*: **~rsi (di)** to avenge o.s. (for); (*per rancore*) to take one's revenge (for); **~rsi su qn** to revenge o.s. on sb; **vendica'tivo, a** *ag* vindictive

'vendita *sf* sale; **la** ~ (*attività*) selling; (*smercio*) sales *pl*; **in** ~ on sale; ~ **all'asta** sale by auction; **vendi'tore** *sm* seller, vendor; (*gestore di negozio*) trader, dealer

ve'nefico, a, ci, che *ag* poisonous

vene'rabile *ag* venerable

venerando, a *ag* = **venerabile**

vene'rare *vt* to venerate

venerdì *sm inv* Friday; **di** *o* **il** ~ on Fridays; **V~ Santo** Good Friday

ve'nereo, a *ag* venereal

'veneto, a *ag, sm/f* Venetian

Ve'nezia [ve'nɛttsja] *sf* Venice;
venezi'ano, a *ag*, *sm/f* Venetian
veni'ale *ag* venial
ve'nire *vi* to come; (*riuscire: dolce,
fotografia*) to turn out; (*come ausiliare:
essere*): **viene ammirato da tutti** he is
admired by everyone; ~ **da** to come from;
quanto viene? how much does it cost?;
far ~ (*mandare a chiamare*) to send for;
~ **giù** to come down; ~ **meno** (*svenire*) to
faint; ~ **meno a qc** not to fulfil sth; ~ **su**
to come up; ~ **a trovare qn** to come and
see sb; ~ **via** to come away
ven'taglio [ven'taʎʎo] *sm* fan
ven'tata *sf* gust (of wind)
ven'tenne *ag*: **una ragazza** ~ a twenty-
year-old girl, a girl of twenty
ven'tesimo, a *num* twentieth
'venti *num* twenty
venti'lare *vt* (*stanza*) to air, ventilate;
(*fig: idea, proposta*) to air; **ventila'tore**
sm ventilator, fan
ven'tina *sf*: **una** ~ (**di**) around twenty,
twenty or so
venti'sette *num* twenty-seven; **il** ~
(*giorno di paga*) (monthly) pay day
'vento *sm* wind
'ventola *sf* (*AUT, TECN*) fan
ven'tosa *sf* (*ZOOL*) sucker; (*di gomma*)
suction pad
ven'toso, a *ag* windy
'ventre *sm* stomach
ven'tura *sf*: **andare alla** ~ to trust to
luck; **soldato di** ~ mercenary
ven'turo, a *ag* next, coming
ve'nuta *sf* coming, arrival
ve'nuto, a *pp di* **venire**
vera'mente *av* really
ver'bale *ag* verbal ♦ *sm* (*di riunione*)
minutes *pl*
'verbo *sm* (*LING*) verb; (*parola*) word;
(*REL*): **il V~** the Word
'verde *ag*, *sm* green; **essere al** ~ to be
broke; ~ **bottiglia/oliva** bottle/olive
green
verde'rame *sm* verdigris
ver'detto *sm* verdict
ver'dura *sf* vegetables *pl*
vere'condo, a *ag* modest

'verga, ghe *sf* rod
ver'gato, a *ag* (*foglio*) ruled
'vergine ['verdʒine] *sf* virgin; (*dello
zodiaco*): **V~** Virgo ♦ *ag* virgin; (*ragazza*):
essere ~ to be a virgin
ver'gogna [ver'ɡoɲɲa] *sf* shame;
(*timidezza*) shyness, embarrassment;
vergo'gnarsi *vr*: **vergognarsi (di)** to be
o feel ashamed (of); to be shy (about), be
embarrassed (about); **vergo'gnoso, a** *ag*
ashamed; (*timido*) shy, embarrassed;
(*causa di vergogna: azione*) shameful
ve'rifica, che *sf* checking *no pl*, check
verifi'care *vt* (*controllare*) to check;
(*confermare*) to confirm, bear out
verità *sf inv* truth
veriti'ero, a *ag* (*che dice la verità*)
truthful; (*conforme a verità*) true
'verme *sm* worm
vermi'celli [vermi'tʃɛlli] *smpl* vermicelli
sg
ver'miglio [ver'miʎʎo] *sm* vermilion,
scarlet
'vermut *sm inv* vermouth
ver'nice [ver'nitʃe] *sf* (*colorazione*) paint;
(*trasparente*) varnish; (*pelle*) patent
leather; **"~ fresca"** "wet paint";
vernici'are *vt* to paint; to varnish
'vero, a *ag* (*veridico: fatti, testimonianza*)
true; (*autentico*) real ♦ *sm* (*verità*) truth;
(*realtà*) (real) life; **un** ~ **e proprio
delinquente** a real criminal, an out-and-
out criminal
vero'simile *ag* likely, probable
ver'ruca, che *sf* wart
versa'mento *sm* (*pagamento*) payment;
(*deposito di denaro*) deposit
ver'sante *sm* slopes *pl*, side
ver'sare *vt* (*fare uscire: vino, farina*) to
pour (out); (*spargere: lacrime, sangue*) to
shed; (*rovesciare*) to spill; (*ECON*) to pay;
(*: depositare*) to deposit, pay in; ~**rsi** *vr*
(*rovesciarsi*) to spill; (*fiume, folla*): ~**rsi
(in)** to pour (into)
versa'tile *ag* versatile
ver'setto *sm* (*REL*) verse
versi'one *sf* version; (*traduzione*)
translation
'verso *sm* (*di poesia*) verse, line; (*di*

animale, uccello, venditore ambulante) cry; (*direzione*) direction; (*modo*) way; (*di foglio di carta*) verso; (*di moneta*) reverse; ~**i** *smpl* (*poesia*) verse *sg*; **non c'è ~ di persuaderlo** there's no way of persuading him, he can't be persuaded ♦ *prep* (*in direzione di*) toward(s); (*nei pressi di*) near, around (about); (*in senso temporale*) about, around; (*nei confronti di*) for; ~ **di me** towards me; ~ **sera** towards evening

'vertebra *sf* vertebra

verti'cale *ag, sf* vertical

'vertice ['vertitʃe] *sm* summit, top; (*MAT*) vertex; **conferenza al ~** (*POL*) summit conference

ver'tigine [ver'tidʒine] *sf* dizziness *no pl*; dizzy spell; (*MED*) vertigo; **avere le ~i** to feel dizzy; **vertigi'noso, a** *ag* (*altezza*) dizzy; (*fig*) breathtakingly high (*o deep etc*)

ve'scica, che [veʃ'ʃika] *sf* (*ANAT*) bladder; (*MED*) blister

'vescovo *sm* bishop

'vespa *sf* wasp

'vespro *sm* (*REL*) vespers *pl*

ves'sillo *sm* standard; (*bandiera*) flag

ves'taglia [ves'taʎʎa] *sf* dressing gown

'veste *sf* garment; (*rivestimento*) covering; (*qualità, facoltà*) capacity; **in ~ ufficiale** (*fig*) in an official capacity; **in ~ di** in the guise of, as; **vesti'ario** *sm* wardrobe, clothes *pl*

ves'tibolo *sm* (entrance) hall

ves'tire *vt* (*bambino, malato*) to dress; (*avere indosso*) to have on, wear; ~**rsi** *vr* to dress, get dressed; **ves'tito, a** *ag* dressed ♦ *sm* garment; (*da donna*) dress; (*da uomo*) suit; **vestiti** *smpl* (*indumenti*) clothes; **vestito di bianco** dressed in white

Ve'suvio *sm*: **il ~** Vesuvius

vete'rano, a *ag, sm/f* veteran

veteri'naria *sf* veterinary medicine

veteri'nario, a *ag* veterinary ♦ *sm* veterinary surgeon (*BRIT*), veterinarian (*US*), vet

'veto *sm inv* veto

ve'traio *sm* glassmaker; glazier

ve'trata *sf* glass door (*o* window); (*di*

chiesa) stained glass window

ve'trato, a *ag* (*porta, finestra*) glazed; (*che contiene vetro*) glass *cpd*

vetre'ria *sf* (*stabilimento*) glassworks *sg*; (*oggetti di vetro*) glassware

ve'trina *sf* (*di negozio*) (shop) window; (*armadio*) display cabinet; **vetri'nista, i, e** *sm/f* window dresser

vetri'olo *sm* vitriol

'vetro *sm* glass; (*per finestra, porta*) pane (of glass)

'vetta *sf* peak, summit, top

vet'tore *sm* (*MAT, FISICA*) vector; (*chi trasporta*) carrier

vetto'vaglie [vetto'vaʎʎe] *sfpl* supplies

vet'tura *sf* (*carrozza*) carriage; (*FERR*) carriage (*BRIT*), car (*US*); (*auto*) car (*BRIT*), automobile (*US*)

vezzeggi'are [vettsed'dʒare] *vt* to fondle, caress; **vezzeggia'tivo** *sm* (*LING*) term of endearment

'vezzo ['vettso] *sm* habit; ~**i** *smpl* (*smancerie*) affected ways; (*leggiadria*) charms; **vez'zoso, a** *ag* (*grazioso*) charming, pretty; (*lezioso*) affected

vi (*dav lo, la, li, le, ne diventa ve*) *pron* (*oggetto*) you; (*complemento di termine*) (to) you; (*riflessivo*) yourselves; (*reciproco*) each other ♦ *av* (*lì*) there; (*qui*) here; (*per questo/quel luogo*) through here/there; ~ **è/sono** there is/are

'via *sf* (*gen*) way; (*strada*) street; (*sentiero, pista*) path, track; (*AMM: procedimento*) channels *pl* ♦ *prep* (*passando per*) via, by way of ♦ *av* away ♦ *escl* go away!; (*suvvia*) come on!; (*SPORT*) go! ♦ *sm* (*SPORT*) starting signal; **in ~ di guarigione** on the road to recovery; **per ~ di** (*a causa di*) because of, on account of; **in** *o* **per ~** on the way; **per ~ aerea** by air; (*lettere*) by airmail; **andare/essere ~** to go/be away; ~ ~ **che** (*a mano a mano*) as; **dare il ~** (*SPORT*) to give the starting signal; **dare il ~ a** (*fig*) to start; **V~ lattea** (*ASTR*) Milky Way; ~ **di mezzo** middle course; **in ~ provvisoria** provisionally

viabilità *sf* (*di strada*) practicability; (*rete stradale*) roads *pl*, road network

via'dotto *sm* viaduct

viaggi'are [viad'dʒare] *vi* to travel; **viaggia'tore, 'trice** *ag* travelling ♦ *sm* traveller; (*passeggero*) passenger

vi'aggio ['vjaddʒo] *sm* travel(ling); (*tragitto*) journey, trip; **buon ~!** have a good trip!; **~ di nozze** honeymoon

vi'ale *sm* avenue

via'vai *sm* coming and going, bustle

vi'brare *vi* to vibrate; (*agitarsi*): **~ (di)** to quiver (with)

vi'cario *sm* (*apostolico etc*) vicar

'vice ['vitʃe] *sm/f* deputy ♦ *prefisso*: **~'console** *sm* vice-consul; **~diret'tore** *sm* assistant manager

vi'cenda [vi'tʃɛnda] *sf* event; **a ~** in turn; **vicen'devole** *ag* mutual, reciprocal

vice'versa [vitʃe'vɛrsa] *av* vice versa; **da Roma a Pisa e ~** from Rome to Pisa and back

vici'nanza [vitʃi'nantsa] *sf* nearness, closeness; **~e** *sfpl* (*paraggi*) neighbourhood, vicinity

vici'nato [vitʃi'nato] *sm* neighbourhood; (*vicini*) neighbours *pl*

vi'cino, a [vi'tʃino] *ag* (*gen*) near; (*nello spazio*) near, nearby; (*accanto*) next; (*nel tempo*) near, close at hand ♦ *sm/f* neighbour ♦ *av* near, close; **da ~** (*guardare*) close up; (*esaminare, seguire*) closely; (*conoscere*) well, intimately; **~ a** near (to), close to; (*accanto a*) beside; **~ di casa** neighbour

'vicolo *sm* alley; **~ cieco** blind alley

'video *sm inv* (*TV: schermo*) screen; **~'camera** *sf* camcorder; **~cas'setta** *sf* videocassette; **~registra'tore** *sm* video (recorder)

vie'tare *vt* to forbid; (*AMM*) to prohibit; **~ a qn di fare** to forbid sb to do; to prohibit sb from doing; **"vietato fumare/l'ingresso"** "no smoking/admittance"

Viet'nam *sm*: **il ~** Vietnam; **vietna'mita, i, e** *ag, sm/f, sm* Vietnamese *inv*

vi'gente [vi'dʒɛnte] *ag* in force

vigi'lante [vidʒi'lante] *ag* vigilant, watchful

vigi'lare [vidʒi'lare] *vt* to watch over, keep an eye on; **~ che** to make sure that, see to it that

'vigile ['vidʒile] *ag* watchful ♦ *sm* (*anche*: **~ urbano**) policeman (*in towns*); **~ del fuoco** fireman

vi'gilia [vi'dʒilja] *sf* (*giorno antecedente*) eve; **la ~ di Natale** Christmas Eve

vigli'acco, a, chi, che [viʎ'ʎakko] *ag* cowardly ♦ *sm/f* coward

'vigna ['viɲɲa] *sf* = **vi'gneto**

vi'gneto [viɲ'ɲeto] *sm* vineyard

vi'gnetta [viɲ'ɲetta] *sf* cartoon

vi'gore *sm* vigour; (*DIR*): **essere/entrare in ~** to be in/come into force; **vigo'roso, a** *ag* vigorous

'vile *ag* (*spregevole*) low, mean, base; (*codardo*) cowardly

vili'pendio *sm* contempt, scorn; public insult

'villa *sf* villa

vil'laggio [vil'laddʒo] *sm* village

villa'nia *sf* rudeness, lack of manners; **fare (o dire) una ~ a qn** to be rude to sb

vil'lano, a *ag* rude, ill-mannered ♦ *sm* boor

villeggia'tura [villeddʒa'tura] *sf* holiday(s *pl*) (*BRIT*), vacation (*US*)

vil'lino *sm* small house (with a garden), cottage

vil'loso, a *ag* hairy

viltà *sf* cowardice *no pl*; cowardly act

'vimine *sm* wicker; **mobili di ~i** wicker furniture *sg*

'vincere ['vintʃere] *vt* (*in guerra, al gioco, a una gara*) to defeat, beat; (*premio, guerra, partita*) to win; (*fig*) to overcome, conquer ♦ *vi* to win; **~ qn in bellezza** to be better-looking than sb; **'vincita** *sf* win; (*denaro vinto*) winnings *pl*; **vinci'tore** *sm* winner; (*MIL*) victor

vinco'lare *vt* to bind; (*COMM: denaro*) to tie up; **'vincolo** *sm* (*fig*) bond, tie; (*DIR: servitù*) obligation

vi'nicolo, a *ag* wine *cpd*

'vino *sm* wine; **~ bianco/rosso** white/red wine; **~ da pasto** table wine

'vinto, a *pp di* **vincere**

vi'ola *sf* (*BOT*) violet; (*MUS*) viola ♦ *ag, sm inv* (*colore*) purple

vio'lare *vt* (*chiesa*) to desecrate, violate; (*giuramento, legge*) to violate

violen'tare *vt* to use violence on; (*donna*) to rape

vio'lento, a *ag* violent; **vio'lenza** *sf* violence; **violenza carnale** rape

vio'letta *sf* (*BOT*) violet

vio'letto, a *ag, sm* (*colore*) violet

violi'nista, i, e *sm/f* violinist

vio'lino *sm* violin

violon'cello [violon'tʃɛllo] *sm* cello

vi'ottolo *sm* path, track

'vipera *sf* viper, adder

vi'rare *vt* (*NAUT*) to haul (in), heave (in) ♦ *vi* (*NAUT, AER*) to turn; (*FOT*) to tone; ~ **di bordo** (*NAUT*) to tack

'virgola *sf* (*LING*) comma; (*MAT*) point; **virgo'lette** *sfpl* inverted commas, quotation marks

vi'rile *ag* (*proprio dell'uomo*) masculine; (*non puerile, da uomo*) manly, virile

virtù *sf inv* virtue; **in** *o* **per ~ di** by virtue of, by

virtu'ale *ag* virtual

virtu'oso, a *ag* virtuous ♦ *sm/f* (*MUS etc*) virtuoso

'virus *sm inv* (*anche COMPUT*) virus

'viscere ['viʃʃere] *sm* (*ANAT*) internal organ ♦ *sfpl* (*di animale*) entrails *pl*; (*fig*) bowels *pl*

'vischio ['viskjo] *sm* (*BOT*) mistletoe; (*pania*) birdlime; **vischi'oso, a** *ag* sticky

'viscido, a ['viʃʃido] *ag* slimy

vi'sibile *ag* visible

visi'bilio *sm:* **andare in ~** to go into raptures

visibilità *sf* visibility

visi'era *sf* (*di elmo*) visor; (*di berretto*) peak

visi'one *sf* vision; **prendere ~ di qc** to examine sth, look sth over; **prima/ seconda ~** (*CINEMA*) first/second showing

'visita *sf* visit; (*MED*) visit, call; (*: esame*) examination; **visi'tare** *vt* to visit; (*MED*) to visit, call on; (*: esaminare*) to examine; **visita'tore, 'trice** *sm/f* visitor

vi'sivo, a *ag* visual

'viso *sm* face

vi'sone *sm* mink

'vispo, a *ag* quick, lively

vis'suto, a *pp di* **vivere** ♦ *ag* (*aria, modo di fare*) experienced

'vista *sf* (*facoltà*) (eye)sight; (*fatto di vedere*): **la ~ di** the sight of; (*veduta*) view; **sparare a ~** to shoot on sight; **in ~** in sight; **perdere qn di ~** to lose sight of sb; (*fig*) to lose touch with sb; **a ~ d'occhio** as far as the eye can see; (*fig*) before one's very eyes; **far ~ di fare** to pretend to

'visto, a *pp di* **vedere** ♦ *sm* visa; ~ **che** seeing (that)

vis'toso, a *ag* gaudy, garish; (*ingente*) considerable

visu'ale *ag* visual; **visualizza'tore** *sm* (*INFORM*) visual display unit, VDU

'vita *sf* life; (*ANAT*) waist; **a ~ for life**

vi'tale *ag* vital; **vita'lizio, a** *ag* life *cpd* ♦ *sm* life annuity

vita'mina *sf* vitamin

'vite *sf* (*BOT*) vine; (*TECN*) screw

vi'tello *sm* (*ZOOL*) calf; (*carne*) veal; (*pelle*) calfskin

vi'ticcio [vi'tittʃo] *sm* (*BOT*) tendril

viticol'tore *sm* wine grower; **viticol'tura** *sf* wine growing

'vitreo, a *ag* vitreous; (*occhio, sguardo*) glassy

'vittima *sf* victim

'vitto *sm* food; (*in un albergo etc*) board; ~ **e alloggio** board and lodging

vit'toria *sf* victory

'viva *escl:* ~ **il re!** long live the king!

vi'vace [vi'vatʃe] *ag* (*vivo, animato*) lively; (*: mente*) lively, sharp; (*colore*) bright; **vivacità** *sf* vivacity; liveliness; brightness

vi'vaio *sm* (*di pesci*) hatchery; (*AGR*) nursery

vi'vanda *sf* food; (*piatto*) dish

vi'vente *ag* living, alive; **i ~i** the living

'vivere *vi* to live ♦ *vt* to live; (*passare: brutto momento*) to live through, go through; (*sentire: gioie, pene di qn*) to share ♦ *sm* life; (*anche: modo di ~*) way of life; ~**i** *smpl* (*cibo*) food *sg*, provisions; ~ **di** to live on

'vivido, a *ag* (*colore*) vivid, bright

'vivo, a *ag* (*vivente*) alive, living; (*: animale*) live; (*fig*) lively; (*: colore*) bright, brilliant; **i ~i** the living; **~ e vegeto** hale and hearty; **farsi ~** to show one's face; to be heard from; **ritrarre dal ~** to paint from life; **pungere qn nel ~** (*fig*) to cut sb to the quick

vizi'are [vit'tsjare] *vt* (*bambino*) to spoil; (*corrompere moralmente*) to corrupt; **vizi'ato, a** *ag* spoilt; (*aria, acqua*) polluted

'vizio ['vittsjo] *sm* (*morale*) vice; (*cattiva abitudine*) bad habit; (*imperfezione*) flaw, defect; (*errore*) fault, mistake; **vizi'oso, a** *ag* depraved; defective; (*inesatto*) incorrect, wrong

vocabo'lario *sm* (*dizionario*) dictionary; (*lessico*) vocabulary

vo'cabolo *sm* word

vo'cale *ag* vocal ♦ *sf* vowel

vocazi'one [vokat'tsjone] *sf* vocation; (*fig*) natural bent

'voce ['votʃe] *sf* voice; (*diceria*) rumour; (*di un elenco, in bilancio*) item; **aver ~ in capitolo** (*fig*) to have a say in the matter

voci'are [vo'tʃare] *vi* to shout, yell

'voga *sf* (*NAUT*) rowing; (*usanza*): **essere in ~** to be in fashion *o* in vogue

vo'gare *vi* to row

'voglia ['vɔʎʎa] *sf* desire, wish; (*macchia*) birthmark; **aver ~ di qc/di fare** to feel like sth/like doing; (*più forte*) to want sth/to do

'voi *pron* you; **voi'altri** *pron* you

vo'lano *sm* (*SPORT*) shuttlecock; (*TECN*) flywheel

vo'lante *ag* flying ♦ *sm* (steering) wheel

volan'tino *sm* leaflet

vo'lare *vi* (*uccello, aereo, fig*) to fly; (*cappello*) to blow away *o* off, fly away *o* off; **~ via** to fly away *o* off

vo'latile *ag* (*CHIM*) volatile ♦ *sm* (*ZOOL*) bird

volente'roso, a *ag* willing

volenti'eri *av* willingly; **"~"** "with pleasure", "I'd be glad to"

vo'lere *sm* will, wish(es); **contro il ~ di** against the wishes of; **per ~ di qn** in obedience to sb's will *o* wishes

♦ *vt* **1** (*esigere, desiderare*) to want; **voler fare/che qn faccia** to want to do/sb to do; **volete del caffè?** would you like *o* do you want some coffee?; **vorrei questo/ fare** I would *o* I'd like this/to do; **come vuoi** as you like; **senza ~** (*inavvertitamente*) without meaning to, unintentionally

2 (*consentire*): **vogliate attendere, per piacere** please wait; **vogliamo andare?** shall we go?; **vuole essere così gentile da ...?** would you be so kind as to ...?; **non ha voluto ricevermi** he wouldn't see me

3: **volerci** (*essere necessario: materiale, attenzione*) to need; (*: tempo*) to take; **quanta farina ci vuole per questa torta?** how much flour do you need for this cake?; **ci vuole un'ora per arrivare a Venezia** it takes an hour to get to Venice

4: **voler bene a qn** (*amore*) to love sb; (*affetto*) to be fond of sb, like sb very much; **voler male a qn** to dislike sb; **volerne a qn** to bear sb a grudge; **voler dire** to mean

vol'gare *ag* vulgar; **volgariz'zare** *vt* to popularize

'volgere ['vɔldʒere] *vt* to turn ♦ *vi* to turn; (*tendere*): **~ a: il tempo volge al brutto** the weather is breaking; **un rosso che volge al viola** a red verging on purple; **~rsi** *vr* to turn; **~ al peggio** to take a turn for the worse; **~ al termine** to draw to an end

'volgo *sm* common people

voli'era *sf* aviary

voli'tivo, a *ag* strong-willed

'volo *sm* flight; **al ~: colpire qc al ~** to hit sth as it flies past; **capire al ~** to understand straight away

volontà *sf* will; **a ~** (*mangiare, bere*) as much as one likes; **buona/cattiva ~** goodwill/lack of goodwill

volon'tario, a *ag* voluntary ♦ *sm* (*MIL*) volunteer

'volpe *sf* fox

'volta *sf* (*momento, circostanza*) time; (*turno, giro*) turn; (*curva*) turn, bend; (*ARCHIT*) vault; (*direzione*): partire alla ~ di to set off for; a mia (*o* tua *etc*) ~ in turn; una ~ once; una ~ sola only once; due ~e twice; una cosa per ~ one thing at a time; una ~ per tutte once and for all; a ~e at times, sometimes; una ~ che (*temporale*) once; (*causale*) since; 3 ~e 4 3 times 4

volta'faccia [volta'fattʃa] *sm inv* (*fig*) volte-face

vol'taggio [vol'taddʒo] *sm* (*ELETTR*) voltage

vol'tare *vt* to turn; (*girare: moneta*) to turn over; (*rigirare*) to turn round ♦ *vi* to turn; ~rsi *vr* to turn; to turn over; to turn round

volteggi'are [volted'dʒare] *vi* (*volare*) to circle; (*in equitazione*) to do trick riding; (*in ginnastica*) to vault; to perform acrobatics

'volto, a *pp di* volgere ♦ *sm* face

vo'lubile *ag* changeable, fickle

vo'lume *sm* volume; volumi'noso, a *ag* voluminous, bulky

voluttà *sf* sensual pleasure *o* delight; voluttu'oso, a *ag* voluptuous

vomi'tare *vt, vi* to vomit; 'vomito *sm* vomiting *no pl*; vomit

'vongola *sf* clam

vo'race [vo'ratʃe] *ag* voracious, greedy

vo'ragine [vo'radʒine] *sf* abyss, chasm

'vortice ['vɔrtitʃe] *sm* whirlwind; whirlpool; (*fig*) whirl

'vostro, a *det*: il(la) ~(a) *etc* your ♦ *pron*: il(la) ~(a) *etc* yours

vo'tante *sm/f* voter

vo'tare *vi* to vote ♦ *vt* (*sottoporre a votazione*) to take a vote on; (*approvare*) to vote for; (*REL*): ~ qc a to dedicate sth to; votazi'one *sf* vote, voting; votazi'oni *sfpl* (*POL*) votes; (*INS*) marks

'voto *sm* (*POL*) vote; (*INS*) mark; (*REL*) vow; (*: offerta*) votive offering; aver ~i belli/ brutti (*INS*) to get good/bad marks

vs. *abbr* (*COMM*) = vostro

vul'cano *sm* volcano

vulne'rabile *ag* vulnerable

vuo'tare *vt* to empty; ~rsi *vr* to empty

vu'oto, a *ag* empty; (*fig: privo*): ~ di (*senso etc*) devoid of ♦ *sm* empty space, gap; (*spazio in bianco*) blank; (*FISICA*) vacuum; (*fig: mancanza*) gap, void; a mani ~e empty-handed; ~ d'aria air pocket; ~ a rendere returnable bottle

W X Y

watt [vat] *sm inv* watt

'weekend ['wiːkend] *sm inv* weekend

'whisky ['wiski] *sm inv* whisky

'xeres ['kseres] *sm inv* sherry

xero'copia [ksero'kɔpja] *sf* xerox ®, photocopy

xi'lofono [ksi'lɔfono] *sm* xylophone

yacht [jɔt] *sm inv* yacht

'yoghurt ['jɔgurt] *sm inv* yoghurt

Z

zabai'one [dzaba'jone] *sm dessert made of egg yolks, sugar and marsala*

zaf'fata [tsaf'fata] *sf* (*tanfo*) stench

zaffe'rano [dzaffe'rano] *sm* saffron

zaf'firo [dzaf'firo] *sm* sapphire

'zaino ['dzaino] *sm* rucksack

'zampa ['tsampa] *sf* (*di animale: gamba*) leg; (*: piede*) paw; a quattro ~e on all fours

zampil'lare [tsampil'lare] *vi* to gush, spurt; zam'pillo *sm* gush, spurt

zam'pogna [tsam'pɔɲɲa] *sf instrument similar to bagpipes*

'zanna ['tsanna] *sf* (*di elefante*) tusk; (*di carnivori*) fang

zan'zara [dzan'dzara] *sf* mosquito; zanzari'era *sf* mosquito net

'zappa ['tsappa] *sf* hoe; zap'pare *vt* to hoe

zar, za'rina [tsar, tsa'rina] *sm/f* tsar/ tsarina

'zattera ['dzattera] *sf* raft

za'vorra [dza'vɔrra] *sf* ballast

'zazzera ['tsattsera] *sf* shock of hair

'**zebra** [ˈdzɛbra] *sf* zebra; **~e** *sfpl* (*AUT*) zebra crossing *sg* (*BRIT*), crosswalk *sg* (*US*)

'**zecca, che** [ˈtsekka] *sf* (*ZOOL*) tick; (*officina di monete*) mint

'**zelo** [ˈdzɛlo] *sm* zeal

'**zenit** [ˈdzɛnit] *sm* zenith

'**zenzero** [ˈdzendzero] *sm* ginger

'**zeppa** [ˈtseppa] *sf* wedge

'**zeppo, a** [ˈtseppo] *ag:* **~ di** crammed *o* packed with

zer'bino [dzerˈbino] *sm* doormat

'**zero** [ˈdzɛro] *sm* zero, nought; **vincere per tre a ~** (*SPORT*) to win three-nil

'**zeta** [ˈdzɛta] *sm o f* zed, (the letter) z

'**zia** [ˈtsia] *sf* aunt

zibel'lino [dzibelˈlino] *sm* sable

'**zigomo** [ˈdzigomo] *sm* cheekbone

zig'zag [dzigˈdzag] *sm inv* zigzag; **andare a ~** to zigzag

zim'bello [dzimˈbɛllo] *sm* (*oggetto di burle*) laughing-stock

'**zinco** [ˈdzinko] *sm* zinc

'**zingaro, a** [ˈdzingaro] *sm/f* gipsy

'**zio** [ˈtsio] (*pl* '**zii**) *sm* uncle; **zii** *smpl* (*zio e zia*) uncle and aunt

zi'tella [dziˈtɛlla] *sf* spinster; (*peg*) old maid

'**zitto, a** [ˈtsitto] *ag* quiet, silent; **sta' ~!** be quiet!

ziz'zania [dzidˈdzanja] *sf* (*fig*): **gettare** *o* **seminare ~** to sow discord

'**zoccolo** [ˈtsɔkkolo] *sm* (*calzatura*) clog; (*di cavallo etc*) hoof; (*basamento*) base; plinth

zo'diaco [dzoˈdiako] *sm* zodiac

'**zolfo** [ˈtsolfo] *sm* sulphur

'**zolla** [ˈdzɔlla] *sf* clod (of earth)

zol'letta [dzolˈletta] *sf* sugar lump

'**zona** [ˈdzɔna] *sf* zone, area; **~ di depressione** (*METEOR*) trough of low pressure; **~ disco** (*AUT*) ≈ meter zone; **~ pedonale** pedestrian precinct; **~ verde** (*di abitato*) green area

'**zonzo** [ˈdzondzo]: **a ~** *av:* **andare a ~** to wander about, stroll about

zoo [ˈdzɔo] *sm inv* zoo

zoolo'gia [dzooloˈdʒia] *sf* zoology

zoppi'care [tsoppiˈkare] *vi* to limp; to be shaky, rickety

'**zoppo, a** [ˈtsɔppo] *ag* lame; (*fig: mobile*) shaky, rickety

zoti'cone [dzotiˈkone] *sm* lout

'**zucca, che** [ˈtsukka] *sf* (*BOT*) marrow; pumpkin

zucche'rare [tsukkeˈrare] *vt* to put sugar in; **zucche'rato, a** *ag* sweet, sweetened

zuccheri'era [tsukkeˈrjɛra] *sf* sugar bowl

zuccheri'ficio [tsukkeriˈfitʃo] *sm* sugar refinery

zucche'rino, a [tsukkeˈrino] *ag* sugary, sweet

'**zucchero** [ˈtsukkero] *sm* sugar

zuc'china [tsukˈkina] *sf* courgette (*BRIT*), zucchini (*US*)

zuc'chino [tsukˈkino] *sm* = **zucchina**

'**zuffa** [ˈtsuffa] *sf* brawl

'**zuppa** [ˈtsuppa] *sf* soup; (*fig*) mixture, muddle; **~ inglese** (*CUC*) dessert made with sponge cake, custard and chocolate, ≈ trifle (*BRIT*); **zuppi'era** *sf* soup tureen

'**zuppo, a** [ˈtsuppo] *ag:* **~ (di)** drenched (with), soaked (with)

PUZZLES AND WORDGAMES

Introduction

We are delighted that you have decided to invest in this Collins Pocket Dictionary! Whether you intend to use it in school, at home, on holiday or at work, we are sure that you will find it very useful.

In the pages which follow you will find explanations and wordgames (not too difficult!) designed to give you practice in exploring the dictionary's contents and in retrieving information for a variety of purposes. Answers are provided at the end. If you spend a little time on these pages you should be able to use your dictionary more efficiently and effectively. Have fun!

Supplement by
Roy Simon
reproduced by kind permission of
Tayside Region Education Department

USING YOUR COLLINS POCKET DICTIONARY

Introduction

We are delighted that you have decided to invest in this Collins Pocket Dictionary! Whether you intend to use it in school, at home, on holiday or at work, we are sure that you will find it very useful.

The purpose of this supplement is to help you become aware of the wealth of vocabulary and grammatical information your dictionary contains, to explain how this information is presented and also to point out some of the traps one can fall into when using an Italian-English English-Italian dictionary.

In the pages which follow you will find explanations and wordgames (not too difficult!) designed to give you practice in exploring the dictionary's contents and in retrieving information for a variety of purposes. Answers are provided at the end. If you spend a little time on these pages you should be able to use your dictionary more efficiently and effectively. Have fun!

Contents

1

HOW INFORMATION IS PRESENTED IN YOUR DICTIONARY

A great deal of information is packed into your Collins Pocket Dictionary using colour, various typefaces, sizes of type, symbols, abbreviations and brackets. The purpose of this section is to acquaint you with the conventions used in presenting information.

Headwords

A headword is the word you look up in a dictionary. Headwords are listed in alphabetical order throughout the dictionary. They are printed in colour so that they stand out clearly from all the other words on the dictionary page.

Note that at the top of each page two headwords appear. These tell you which is the first and last word dealt with on the page in question. They are there to help you scan through the dictionary more quickly.

The Italian alphabet consists in practice of the same 26 letters as the English alphabet but j, k, w, x and y are found only in words of foreign origin. Where words are distinguished only by an accent, the unaccented form precedes the accented — e.g. te, tè.

A dictionary entry

An entry is made up of a headword and all the information about that headword. Entries will be short or long depending on how frequently a word is used in either English or Italian and how many meanings it has. Inevitably, the fuller the dictionary entry the more care is needed in sifting through it to find the information you require.

Meanings

The translations of a headword are given in ordinary type. Where there is more than one meaning or usage, a semi-colon separates one from the other.

cannocchi'ale [kannok'kjale] *sm* telescope.

can'none *sm* (*MIL*) gun; (: *STORIA*) cannon; (*tubo*) pipe, tube; (*piega*) box pleat; (*fig*) ace.

can'nuccia, ce [kan'nuttʃa] *sf* (drinking) straw.

ca'noa *sf* canoe.

profes'sare *vt* to profess; (*medicina etc*) to practise.

te *pron* (*soggetto: in forme comparative, oggetto*) you.

tè *sm inv* tea; (*trattenimento*) tea party.

fragola *sf* strawberry.

'grande (*qualche volta* **gran** +*C*, **grand'** +*V*) *ag* (*grosso, largo, vasto*) big, large; (*alto*) tall; (*lungo*) long; (*in sensi astratti*) great ♦ *sm/f* (*persona adulta*) adult, grown-up; (*chi ha ingegno e potenza*) great man/woman; **fare le cose in ~** to do things in style; **una gran bella donna** a very beautiful woman; **non è una gran cosa** *o* **un gran che** it's nothing special; **non ne so gran che** I don't know very much about it.

pro'gresso *sm* progress *no pl*; **fare ~i** to make progress.

fu'ori *av* outside; (*all'aperto*) outdoors, outside; (*fuori di casa, SPORT*) out; (*esclamativo*) get out! ♦ *prep*: **~ (di)** out of, outside ♦ *sm* outside; **lasciar ~ qc/qn** to leave sth/sb out; **far ~ qn** (*fam*) to kill sb, do sb in; **essere ~ di sé** to be beside o.s.; **~ luogo** (*inopportuno*) out of place, uncalled for; **~ mano** out of the way, remote; **~ pericolo** out of danger; **~ uso** old-fashioned; obsolete.

3

In addition, you will often find other words appearing in *italics* in brackets before the translations. These either give some notion of the contexts in which the headword might appear (as with 'alto' opposite — 'una persona alta', 'un suono alto', etc.) or else they provide synonyms (as with 'reggere' opposite — 'tenere', 'sostenere', etc.).

Phonetic spellings

Where an Italian word contains a sound which is difficult for the English-speaker, the phonetic spelling of the word — i.e. its pronunciation — is given in square brackets immediately after it. The phonetic transcription of Italian and English vowels and consonants is given on pages vii to viii at the front of your dictionary.

Additional information about headwords

Information about the form or usage of certain headwords is given in brackets between the headword and the translation or translations. Have a look at the entries for 'A.C.I.', 'camerino', 'materia' and 'leccapiedi' opposite. This information is usually given in abbreviated form. A helpful list of abbreviations is given on pages xi to xiii at the front of your dictionary.

You should be particularly careful with colloquial words or phrases. Words labelled (*fam*) would not normally be used in formal speech, while those labelled (*fam!*) would be considered offensive. Careful consideration of such style labels will help you avoid many an embarrassing situation when using Italian!

Expressions in which the headword appears

An entry will often feature certain common expressions in which the head-word appears. These expressions are in **bold** type but in black as opposed to colour. A swung dash (~) is used instead of repeating a headword in an entry. 'Freno' and 'idea' opposite illustrate this point. Sometimes the swung dash is used with the appropriate ending shown after it; e.g. 'mano', where '~i' is used to indicate the plural form, 'mani'.

Related words

In the Pocket Dictionary words related to certain headwords are sometimes given at the end of an entry, as with 'finestra' and 'accept' opposite. These are easily picked out as they are also in colour. These words are placed in alphabetical order after the headword to which they belong: cf. 'acceptable', 'acceptance' opposite.

4

'alto, a *ag* high; *(persona)* tall; *(tessuto)* wide, broad; *(sonno, acque)* deep; *(suono)* high(-pitched); *(GEO)* upper; *(: settentrionale)* northern ♦ *sm* top (part) ♦ *av* high; *(parlare)* aloud, loudly; **il palazzo è ~ 20 metri** the building is 20 metres high;

pron'tezza [pron'tettsa] *sf* readiness; quickness, promptness.

A.C.I. ['atʃi] *sigla m (= Automobile Club d'Italia)* ≈ A.A.

came'rino *sm (TEATRO)* dressing room.

scocci'are [skot'tʃare] *(fam)* *vt* to bother, annoy; **~rsi** *vr* to be bothered *o* annoyed.

fre'gare *vt* to rub; *(fam: truffare)* to take in, cheat; *(: rubare)* to swipe, pinch; **fregarsene** *(fam!)*: **chi se ne frega?** who gives a damn (about it)?

'freno *sm* brake; *(morso)* bit; **~ a disco** disc brake; **~ a mano** handbrake; **tenere a ~** to restrain.

i'dea *sf* idea; *(opinione)* opinion, view; *(ideale)* ideal; **dare l'~ di** to seem, look like; **~ fissa** obsession; **neanche o neppure per ~!** certainly not!

fi'nestra *sf* window; **fines'trino** *sm (di*

accept [ək'sɛpt] *vt* accettare; **~able** *adj* accettabile; **~ance** *n* accettazione *f*.

'reggere ['rɛddʒere] *vt (tenere)* to hold; *(sostenere)* to support, bear, hold up; *(portare)* to carry, bear; *(resistere)* to withstand; *(dirigere: impresa)* to manage, run; *(governare)* to rule,

reci'tare [retʃi'tare] *vt (poesia, lezione)* to recite; *(dramma)* to perform; *(ruolo)* to play *o* act (the part of); **recitazi'one** *sf* recitation; *(di attore)* acting.

ma'teria *sf (FISICA)* matter; *(TECN, COMM)* material, matter *no pl*; *(disciplina)* subject; *(argomento)* subject

leccapi'edi *(peg)* *sm/f inv* toady, bootlicker.

'rompere *vt* to break; *(conversazione, fidanzamento)* to break off ♦ *vi* to break; **~rsi** *vr* to break; **mi rompe le scatole** *(fam)* he *(o* she) is a pain in the neck; **~rsi un braccio** to break an arm;

mano, i *sf* hand; *(strato: di vernice etc)* coat; **di prima ~** *(notizia)* first-hand; **di seconda ~** second-hand; **man ~ little by little, gradually; **man ~ che** as; **darsi** *o* **stringersi la ~** to shake hands; **mettere le ~i avanti** *(fig)* to safeguard o.s.; **restare a ~i vuote** to be left empty-handed; **venire alle ~i** to come to blows; **a ~ by hand; **~i in alto!** hands up!

'Key' words

Your Collins Pocket Dictionary gives special status to certain Italian and English words which can be looked on as 'key' words in each language. These are words which have many different usages. 'Molto', 'volere' and 'così' opposite are typical examples in Italian. You are likely to become familiar with them in your day-to-day language studies.

There will be occasions, however, when you want to check on a particular usage. Your dictionary can be very helpful here. Note how with 'volere', for example, different parts of speech and different usages are clearly indicated by a combination of lozenges - ♦ - and numbers. Additionally, further guides to usage are given in the language of the user who needs them. These are bracketed and in italics.

vo'lere *sm* will, wish(es); **contro il ~ di** against the wishes of; **per ~ di qn** in obedience to sb's will *o* wishes

♦ *vt* **1** (*esigere, desiderare*) to want; **voler fare/che qn faccia** to want to do/sb to do; **volete del caffè?** would you like *o* do you want some coffee?; **vorrei questo/fare** I would *o* I'd like this/to do; **come vuoi** as you like; **senza ~** (*inavvertitamente*) without meaning to, unintentionally

2 (*consentire*): **vogliate attendere, per piacere** please wait; **vogliamo andare?** shall we go?; **vuole essere così gentile da ...?** would you be so kind as to ...?; **non ha voluto ricevermi** he wouldn't see me

3: **volerci** (*essere necessario: materiale, attenzione*) to need; (: *tempo*) to take; **quanta farina ci vuole per questa torta?** how much flour do you need for this cake?; **ci vuole un'ora per arrivare a Venezia** it takes an hour to get to Venice

4: **voler bene a qn** (*amore*) to love sb; (*affetto*) to be fond of sb, like sb very much; **voler male a qn** to dislike sb; **volerne a qn** to bear sb a grudge; **voler dire** to mean.

'molto, a *det* (*quantità*) a lot of, much; (*numero*) a lot of, many; **~ pane/carbone** a lot of bread/coal; **~a gente** a lot of people, many people; **~i libri** a lot of books, many books; **non ho ~ tempo** I haven't got much time; **per ~ (tempo)** for a long time

♦ *av* **1** a lot, (very) much; **viaggia ~** he travels a lot; **non viaggia ~** he doesn't travel much *o* a lot

2 (*intensivo: con aggettivi, avverbi*) very; (: *con participio passato*) (very) much; **~ buono** very good; **~ migliore, ~ meglio** much *o* a lot better

♦ *pron* much, a lot; **~i, e** *pron pl* many, a lot; **~i pensano che ...** many (people) think ....

così *av* **1** (*in questo modo*) like this, (in) this way; (*in tal modo*) so; **le cose stanno ~** this is the way things stand; **non ho detto ~!** I didn't say that!; **come stai? — (e) ~ how** are you? — so-so; **e ~ via** and so on; **per ~ dire** so to speak

2 (*tanto*) so; **~ lontano** so far away; **un ragazzo ~ intelligente** such an intelligent boy

♦ *ag inv* (*tale*): **non ho mai visto un film ~** I've never seen such a film

♦ *cong* **1** (*perciò*) so, therefore

2: **~ ... come** as ... as; **non è ~ bravo come te** he's not as good as you; **~ ... che** so ... that.

WORDGAME 1

HEADWORDS

Study the following sentences. In each sentence a wrong word spelt very similarly to the correct word has deliberately been put in and the sentence doesn't make sense. This word is shaded each time. Write out each sentence again, putting in the <u>correct</u> word which you will find in your dictionary near the wrong word.

Example   Vietato l'ingrosso agli estranei

['ingrosso' ('all 'ingrosso' = 'wholesale') is the wrong word and should be replaced by 'ingresso' (= 'entry')]

1. Ha agito contro il volare della maggioranza.
2. Inserire la moneta e pigliare il pulsante.
3. Non dobbiamo molare proprio adesso.
4. Ho dovuto impanare la lezione a memoria.
5. Il prato era circondato da uno stecchito.
6. Vorrei sentire il tuo parare.
7. Vorrei un po' di panno sulle fragole.
8. Qual'è l'oratorio d'apertura dell'ufficio?
9. Quel negoziante mi ha imbrigliato!
10. Sedevano fiasco a fiasco.

WORDGAME 2
DICTIONARY ENTRIES

Complete the crossword below by looking up the English words in the list and finding the correct Italian translations. There is a slight catch, however! All the English words can be translated several ways into Italian, but only one translation will fit correctly into each part of the crossword.

1. THREAD
2. PERMIT
3. PRESENT
4. WANT
5. JOURNEY
6. FREE

7. COLD
8. WAIT
9. NOTICE
10. RETURN
11. CUT
12. REST

WORDGAME 3
FINDING MEANINGS

In this list there are eight pairs of words that have some sort of connection with each other. For example, **'laurea'** (= 'degree') and **'studente'** (= 'student') are linked. Find the other pairs.

1. vestaglia
2. nido
3. pelletteria
4. pantofola
5. campanile
6. studente
7. libro
8. borsetta
9. passerella
10. pinna
11. laurea
12. scaffale
13. gazza
14. nave
15. campana
16. squalo

WORDGAME 4
SYNONYMS

Complete the crossword by supplying SYNONYMS of the words below. You will sometimes find the synonym you are looking for in italics and bracketed at the entries for the words listed below. Sometimes you will have to turn to the English-Italian section for help.

1. RIGUARDO
2. GALA
3. GALLERIA
4. CANCELLARE
5. GALERA

6. BUFFO
7. GIOCARE
8. RAPIDO
9. PAURA
10. MARRONE

WORDGAME 5

SPELLING

You will often use your dictionary to check spellings. The person who has compiled this list of ten Italian words has made <u>three</u> spelling mistakes. Find the three words which have been misspelt and write them out correctly.

1. uccello
2. docia
3. unghia
4. opportuno
5. temporale
6. ortica
7. ovest
8. arabiato
9. folio
10. ossigeno

WORDGAME 6
ANTONYMS

Complete the crossword by supplying ANTONYMS (i.e. opposites) in Italian of the words below. Use your dictionary to help you.

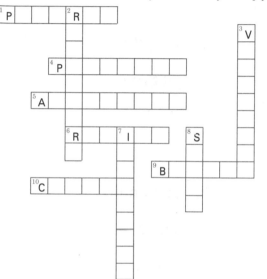

1. ricchezza
2. accettare
3. coraggioso
4. ridere
5. difendere
6. liscio
7. colpevole
8. chiaro
9. bello
10. aperto

WORDGAME 7
PHONETIC SPELLINGS

The phonetic transcriptions of ten Italian words are given below. If you study pages xiv to xv near the front of your dictionary you should be able to work out what the words are.

1. 'ridʒido

2. pit'tʃone

3. 'dʒɛlo

4. 'mattso

5. de'tʃennjo

6. 'kjave

7. 'fɔʎʎa

8. 'soɲɲo

9. 'aʃʃa

10. 'gjanda

WORDGAME 8

EXPRESSIONS IN WHICH THE HEADWORD APPEARS

If you look up the headword 'colpo' in the Italian-English section of your dictionary you will find that the word can have many meanings. Study the entry carefully and translate the following sentences into English.

1. La sua sconfitta è stata un duro colpo per tutti.

2. Ha preso un brutto colpo in testa.

3. Dammi un colpo di telefono domani mattina.

4. Sparò quattro colpi di pistola.

5. Il rumore cessò di colpo.

6. La sua fuga è stata un colpo di testa.

7. Un colpo di vento fece sbattere le persiane.

8. Gli è preso un colpo ed è morto.

9. Hai fatto colpo col tuo discorso, ieri.

10. Gli ho dato un colpo senza volere ed è caduto.

11. Con questo caldo è facile prendere un colpo di sole.

12. Hanno arrestato gli autori del fallito colpo di Stato.

WORDGAME 9
RELATED WORDS

Fill in the blanks in the pairs of sentences below. The missing words are related to the words on the left. Choose the correct 'relative' each time. You will find it in your dictionary near the headword provided.

HEADWORD	RELATED WORDS
impiegare	1. Fa l'_____ di banca. 2. Ha appena lasciato il suo _____.
studiare	3. Ha vissuto a Firenze quand'era _____. 4. Ha uno _____ in centro.
usare	5. Si raccomanda l'_____ delle cinture di sicurezza. 6. La tua macchina è nuova o _____?
unità	7. È una famiglia molto _____. 8. Vi potete _____ a noi, se volete.
rifiuto	9. È un'offerta che non potrete _____. 10. Dov'è il bidone dei _____?
festeggiare	11. Il negozio è chiuso nei giorni _____. 12. Ha organizzato una _____ di compleanno.

WORDGAME 10
'KEY' WORDS

Study carefully the entry **'fare'** in your dictionary and find translations for the following:

1.   the weather is fine

2.   to do psychology

3.   go ahead!

4.   let me see

5.   to get one's hair cut

6.   this is the way it's done

7.   to do the shopping

8.   to be quick

9.   to start up the engine

10. he made as if to leave

THE DICTIONARY AND GRAMMAR

While it is true that a dictionary can never be a substitute for a detailed grammar reference book, the dictionary nevertheless provides a great deal of grammatical information. If you know how to extract this information you will be able to use Italian more accurately both in speech and in writing.

The Collins Pocket Dictionary presents grammatical information as follows.

Parts of speech

Parts of speech are given in italics immediately after the phonetic spellings of headwords. Abbreviated forms are used. Abbreviations can be checked on pages xi to xiii.

Changes in parts of speech within an entry — for example, from adjective to adverb to noun — are indicated by means of lozenges - ♦ - as with the Italian 'forte' and the English 'act' opposite.

Genders of Italian nouns

The gender of each noun in the Italian-English section of the dictionary is indicated in the following way:

$$sm\ =\ \text{sostantivo maschile}$$

$$sf\ =\ \text{sostantivo femminile}$$

You will occasionally see *'sm/f'* beside an entry. This indicates that a noun — 'insegnante', for example — can be either masculine or feminine.

Feminine and *irregular* plural forms of nouns are shown, as with 'bambino', 'autore' and 'bruco' opposite.

So many things depend on your knowing the correct gender of an Italian noun — whether you use 'il' or 'la' etc. to translate 'the'; the way you spell and pronounce certain adjectives; the changes you make to past participles, etc. If you are in any doubt as to the gender of a noun, it is always best to check it in your dictionary.

18

ono'rare *vt* to honour; (*far onore a*) to do credit to; **~rsi** *vr*: **~rsi di** to feel honoured at, be proud of.

quassù *av* up here.

perciò [per'tʃɔ] *cong* so, for this (*o* that) reason.

'pranzo ['prandzo] *sm* dinner; (*a mezzogiorno*) lunch.

'cena ['tʃena] *sf* dinner; (*leggera*) supper.

bam'bino, a *sm/f* child.

au'tore, 'trice *sm/f* author.

'bruco, chi *sm* caterpillar; grub.

'forte *ag* strong; (*suono*) loud; (*spesa*) considerable, great; (*passione, dolore*) great, deep ♦ *av* strongly; (*velocemente*) fast; (*a voce alta*) loud(ly); (*violentemente*) hard ♦ *sm* (*edificio*) fort; (*specialità*) forte, strong point; **essere ~ in qc** to be good at sth.

act [ækt] *n* atto; (*in music-hall etc*) numero; (*LAW*) decreto ♦ *vi* agire; (*THEATRE*) recitare; (*pretend*) fingere ♦ *vt* (*part*) recitare; **to ~ as** agire da; **~ing** *adj* che fa le funzioni di ♦ *n* (*of actor*) recitazione *f*; (*activity*): **to do some ~ing** fare del teatro (*or* del cinema).

inse'gnante [insen'nante] *ag* teaching ♦ *sm/f* teacher.

19

Adjectives

Adjectives are given in both their masculine and feminine forms, where these are different. The usual rule is to drop the 'o' of the masculine form and add an 'a' to make an adjective feminine, as with 'nero' opposite.

Some adjectives have identical masculine and feminine forms, as with 'verde' opposite.

Many Italian adjectives, however, do not follow the regular pattern. Where an adjective has irregular plural forms, this information is clearly provided in your dictionary, usually with the irregular endings, being given. Consider the entries for 'bianco' and 'lungo' opposite.

Adverbs

Adverbs are not always listed in your dictionary. The normal rule for forming adverbs in Italian is to add '-mente' to the feminine form of the adjective. Thus:

    vero > vera > veramente

The '-mente' ending is often the equivalent of the English '-ly':

    veramente   — really
    certamente   — certainly

Adjectives ending in '-e' and '-le' are slightly different:

    recente > recentemente
    reale   > realmente

Where an adverb is very common in Italian, or where its translation(s) cannot be derived from translations for the adjective, it will be listed in alphabetical order, either as a headword or as a subentry. Compare 'solamente' and 'attualmente' opposite.

In many cases, however, Italian adverbs are not given, since the English translation can easily be derived from the relevant translation of the adjective headword: e.g. 'cortese' opposite.

Information about verbs

A major problem facing language learners is that the form of a verb will change according to the subject and/or the tense being used. A typical Italian verb can take on many different forms — too many to list in a dictionary entry.

20

'nero, a *ag* black; (*scuro*) dark ♦ *sm* black; **il Mar N~** the Black Sea.

'verde *ag, sm* green; **essere al ~** to be broke; **~ bottiglia/oliva** bottle/olive green.

bi'anco, a, chi, che *ag* white; (*non scritto*) blank ♦ *sm* white; (*intonaco*) whitewash ♦ *sm/f* white, white man/woman; **in ~** (*foglio, assegno*) blank; (*notte*) sleepless; **in ~ e nero** (*TV, FOT*) black and white; **mangiare in ~** to follow a bland diet; **pesce in ~** boiled fish; **andare in ~** (*non riuscire*) to fail; **~ dell'uovo** egg-white.

'lungo, a, ghi, ghe *ag* long; (*lento: persona*) slow; (*diluito: caffè, brodo*) weak, watery, thin ♦ *sm* length ♦ *prep* along; **~ 3 metri** 3 metres long; **a ~** for a long time; **a ~ andare** in the long run; **di gran ~a** (*molto*) by far; **andare in ~ o per le lunghe** to drag on; **saperla ~a** to know what's what; **in ~ e in largo** far and wide, all over; **~ il corso dei secoli** throughout the centuries.

vera'mente *av* really.

certa'mente [tʃerta'mente] *av* certainly.

re'cente [re'tʃɛnte] *ag* recent; **di ~** recently; **recente'mente** *av* recently.

sola'mente *av* only, just.

'solo, a *ag* alone; (*in senso spirituale: isolato*) lonely; (*unico*): **un ~ libro** only one book, a single book; (*con ag numerale*): **veniamo noi tre ~i** just *o* only the three of us are coming ♦ *av* (*soltanto*) only, just; **non ~ ... ma anche** not only ... but also; **fare qc da ~** to do sth (all) by oneself; **da me ~** single-handed, on my own.

cor'tese *ag* courteous; **corte'sia** *sf* courtesy; **per cortesia ...** excuse me, please ....

attu'ale *ag* (*presente*) present; (*di attualità*) topical; (*che è in atto*) actual; **attualità** *sf inv* topicality; (*avvenimento*) current event; **attual'mente** *av* at the moment, at present.

Yet, although verbs are listed in your dictionary in their infinitive forms only, this does not mean that the dictionary is of limited value when it comes to handling the verb system of the Italian language. On the contrary, it contains much valuable information.

First of all, your dictionary will help you with the meanings of unfamiliar verbs. If you came across the word 'riempie' in a text and looked it up in your dictionary you wouldn't find it. You must deduce that it is part of a verb and look for the infinitive form. Thus you will see that 'riempie' is a form of the verb 'riempire'. You now have the basic meaning of the word you are concerned with — something to do with the English verb 'fill' — and this should be enough to help you understand the text you are reading.

It is usually an easy task to make the connection between the form of a verb and the infinitive. For example, 'riempiono', 'riempirò', 'riempissero' and 'riempii' are all recognisable as parts of the infinitive 'riempire'. However, sometimes it is less obvious — for example, 'vengo', 'vieni' and 'verrò' are all parts of 'venire'. The only real solution to this problem is to learn the various forms of the main Italian regular and irregular verbs.

And this is the second source of help offered by your dictionary. The verb tables on pages 1 to 2 at the back of the Collins Pocket Dictionary provide a summary of some of the main forms of the main tenses of regular and irregular verbs. Consider the verb 'venire' below where the following information is given:

2	venuto	— Past Participle
3	vengo, vieni, viene, vengono	— Present Tense forms
5	venni, venisti	— Past Tense forms
6	verrò *etc.*	— 1st Person Singular of the Future Tense
8	venga	— 1st, 2nd, 3rd Person of Present Subjunctive

The regular '-are' verb 'parlare' is presented in greater detail, as are the regular '-ire' and '-ere' verbs. The main tenses and the different endings are given in full. This information can be transferred and applied to all verbs in the list. In addition, the main parts of the most common irregular verbs are listed in the body of the dictionary.

PARLARE
1 parlando
2 parlato
3 parlo, parli, parla, parliamo, parlate, parlano
4 parlavo, parlavi, parlava, parlavamo, parlavate, parlavano
5 parlai, parlasti, parlò, parlammo, parlaste, parlarono
6 parlerò, parlerai, parlerà, parleremo, parlerete, parleranno
7 parlerei, parleresti, parlerebbe, parleremmo, parlereste, parlerebbero
8 parli, parli, parli, parliamo, parliate, parlino
9 parlassi, parlassi, parlasse, parlassimo, parlaste, parlassero
10 parla!, parli!, parlate!, parlino!

In order to make maximum use of the information contained in these pages, a good working knowledge of the various rules affecting Italian verbs is required. You will acquire this in the course of your Italian studies and your Collins dictionary will serve as a useful reminder. If you happen to forget how to form the second person singular form of the Future Tense of 'venire' there will be no need to panic — your dictionary contains the information!

WORDGAME 11
PARTS OF SPEECH

In each sentence below a word has been shaded. Put a tick in the appropriate box to indicate the **part of speech** each time. Remember, different parts of speech are indicated by lozenges within entries.

SENTENCE	Noun	Adj	Adv	Verb
1. Studia diritto a Roma.				
2. Parla più piano! Il bambino dorme.				
3. Ho già versato la minestra nel piatto.				
4. Ho spento il televisore prima della fine del film.				
5. Ha finto di andarsene ed è rimasto ad ascoltare.				
6. Non gli ho permesso di venire.				
7. Vuoi una fetta di dolce?				
8. Abbassi il volume, per favore? Così è troppo forte.				
9. Dopo la notizia sembrava molto scossa.				
10. Hanno assunto un capo del personale per la nostra sezione.				

WORDGAME 12

NOUNS

This list contains the feminine form of some Italian nouns. Use your dictionary to find the **masculine** form.

MASCULINE	FEMININE
	amica
	cantante
	direttrice
	straniera
	regista
	studentessa
	cugina
	lettrice
	professoressa
	collaboratrice

WORDGAME 13
MEANING CHANGES WITH GENDER

There are some pairs of Italian nouns which are distinguished only by their ending and gender, e.g. 'il partito' and 'la partita'. Fill in the blanks below with the appropriate member of each pair and the correct article — **'il, la, un'** etc — where an article is required.

1. L'ho scritto su _____ da qualche parte   foglio *or*
   Guarda! Sulla pianta è spuntata _____   foglia?

2. Non è questo _____ di fare le cose!   moda *or*
   È un colore che non va più di _____   modo?

3. È arrivato di _____   corso *or*
   Credo che mi iscriverò ad _____   corsa?
   di spagnolo

4. In questa zona ci sono tanti _____   castagne *or*
   Ho comprato un sacchetto di _____   castagni?

5. Fammi vedere _____ della mano!   palma *or*
   Sedevano sulla spiaggia all'ombra   palmo?
   di _____

6. Ti va di fare _____ a tennis?   partito *or*
   _____ si sta preparando alle elezioni   partita?

7. Devo mettere _____ su questi pantaloni   pezzo *or*
   Vuoi _____ di torta?   pezza?

8. Per oggi basta lavorare! Vado a _____   caso *or*
   Ci siamo conosciuti per _____   casa?

WORDGAME 14
NOUN AND ADJECTIVE FORMS

Use your dictionary to find the following forms of these words.

MASCULINE	FEMININE
1. bianco	
2. fresco	
3. largo	
4. verde	
5. grave	

SINGULAR	PLURAL
6. poca	
7. giovane	
8. grande	
9. veloce	
10. poeta	
11. diadema	
12. triste	
13. tronco	
14. tromba	
15. dialogo	

WORDGAME 15

ADVERBS

Translate the following Italian adverbs into English. Put an asterisk next to those that don't appear in the Italian-English section of the Collins dictionary.

1. recentemente

2. redditiziamente

3. costantemente

4. gentilmente

5. mensilmente

6. naturalmente

7. aggressivamente

8. semplicemente

9. tenacemente

10. esattamente

WORDGAME 16
VERB TENSES

Use your dictionary to help you fill in the blanks in the table below. (Remember the important pages at the front of your dictionary.)

INFINITIVE	PRESENT TENSE	PAST PARTICIPLE	FUTURE
venire			io
rimanere			
vedere			io
avere	io		
offrire			
muovere			
finire	io		
uscire	io		
dovere			io
dormire			io
vivere			
potere	io		

29

WORDGAME 17
PAST PARTICIPLES

Use the verb tables at the front of your dictionary to work out the past participle of these verbs. Check that you have found the correct form by looking in the main text.

INFINITIVE	PAST PARTICIPLE
venire	
contrarre	
coprire	
vivere	
offrire	
sorridere	
prendere	
mettere	
sorprendere	
percorrere	
accogliere	
dipingere	
condurre	
scendere	

WORDGAME 18
IDENTIFYING INFINITIVES

In the sentences below you will see various Italian verbs shaded. Use your dictionary to help you find the **infinitive** form of each verb.

1. Quand'ero a Londra dividevo un'appartamento con degli amici.

2. I miei amici mi raggiunsero in discoteca.

3. Sua madre lo accompagnava a scuola in macchina.

4. Domani mi alzerò alle nove.

5. Questo fine settimana andremo tutti in campagna.

6. Hanno già venduto la casa.

7. Entrò e si mise a sedere.

8. È nato in Germania.

9. Gli piacerebbe vivere negli Stati Uniti.

10. Faranno una partita a tennis.

11. Ha ricominciato a piovere.

12. Non so cosa gli sia successo.

13. Vorremmo visitare il castello.

14. I bambini avevano freddo.

15. Non so cosa sia meglio fare.

MORE ABOUT MEANING

In this section we will consider some of the problems associated with using a bilingual dictionary.

Overdependence on your dictionary

That the dictionary is an invaluable tool for the language learner is beyond dispute. Nevertheless, it is possible to become overdependent on your dictionary, turning to it in an almost automatic fashion every time you come up against a new Italian word or phrase. Tackling an unfamiliar text in this way will turn reading in Italian into an extremely tedious activity. If you stop to look up every new word you may actually be *hindering* your ability to read in Italian — you are so concerned with the individual words that you pay no attention to the text as a whole and to the context which gives them meaning. It is therefore important to develop appropriate reading skills — using clues such as titles, headlines, illustrations, etc, understanding relations within a sentence, etc to predict or infer what a text is about.

A detailed study of the development of reading skills is not within the scope of this supplement; we are concerned with knowing how to use a dictionary, which is only one of several important skills involved in reading. Nevertheless, it may be instructive to look at one example. You see the following text in an Italian newspaper and are interested in working out what it is about.

Contextual clues here include the words in large type which you would probably recognise as an Italian name, something that looks like a date in the middle, and the name and address in the bottom right-hand corner. The Italian words 'annunciare' and 'clinica' resemble closely the words 'announce' and 'clinic' in English, so you would not

> Siamo lieti di annunciare
> la nascita di
>
> # Mario, Francesco
>
> il 29 marzo 1988
>
> Monica e Franco ROSSI
> Clinica   corso Italia n° 18
> del Sole   34142 Padova

have to look them up in your dictionary. Other 'form' words such as 'siamo', 'la', 'il', and 'di' will be familiar to you from your general studies in Italian. Given that we are dealing with a newspaper, you will probably have worked out by now that this could be an announcement placed in the 'Personal Column'.

So you have used a series of cultural, contextual and word-formation clues to get you to the point where you have understood that Monica and Franco Rossi have placed this notice in the 'Personal Column' of the newspaper and that something happened to Francesco on 29 March 1988, something connected with a hospital. And you have reached this point *without* opening your dictionary once. Common sense and your knowledge of newspaper contents in this country might suggest that this must be an announcement of someone's birth or death. Thus 'lieti' ('happy') and 'nascita' ('birth') become the only words that you might have to look up in order to confirm that this is indeed a birth announcement.

When learning Italian we are helped considerably by the fact that many Italian and English words look and sound alike and have exactly the same meaning. Such words are called 'COGNATES'. Many words which look similar in Italian and English come from a common Latin root. Other words are the same or nearly the same in both languages because Italian has borrowed a word from English or vice versa. The dictionary will often not be necessary where cognates are concerned — provided you know the English word that the Italian word resembles!

Words with more than one meaning

The need to examine with care *all* the information contained in a dictionary entry must be stressed. This is particularly important with the many Italian words which have more than one meaning. For example, the Italian 'giornale' can mean 'personal diary' as well as 'newspaper'. How you translated the word would depend on the context in which you found it.

Similarly, if you were trying to translate a phrase such as 'era in corso . . .', you would have to look through the whole entry for 'corso' to get the right translation. If you restricted your search to the first lines of the entry and saw that the meanings given are 'course' and 'main street', you might be tempted to assume that the phrase meant 'it was in the main street'. But if you examined the entry closely you would see that 'in corso' means 'in progress, under way'. So 'era in corso' means 'it was in progress', as in the phrase 'lavori in corso'.

The same need for care applies when you are using the English-Italian section of your dictionary to translate a word from English into Italian. Watch out in particular for the lozenges indicating changes in parts of speech.

The noun 'sink' is 'lavandino, acquaio', while the verb is 'affondare'. If you don't watch what you are doing, you could end up with ridiculous non-Italian e.g. 'Ha messo i piatti sporchi nell'affondare.'

Phrasal verbs

Another potential source of difficulty is English phrasal verbs. These consist of a common verb ('go', 'make', etc.) plus an adverb and/or a preposition to give English expressions such as 'to make out', 'to take after', etc. Entries for such verbs tend to be fairly full, so close examination of the contents is required. Note how these verbs appear in colour within the entry.

False friends

make [meɪk] (*pt, pp* **made**) *vt* fare; (*manufacture*) fare, fabbricare; (*cause to be*): **to ~ sb sad** *etc* rendere qn triste *etc*; (*force*): **to ~ sb do sth** costringere qn a fare qc, far fare qc a qn; (*equal*): **2 and 2 ~ 4** 2 più 2 fa 4 ♦ *n* fabbricazione *f*; (*brand*) marca; **to ~ a fool of sb** far fare a qn la figura dello scemo; **to ~ a profit** realizzare un profitto; **to ~ a loss** subire una perdita; **~ for** *vt fus* (*place*) avviarsi verso; **~ out** *vt* (*write out*) scrivere; (: *cheque*) emettere; (*understand*) capire; (*see*) distinguere; (: *numbers*) decifrare; **~ up** *vt* (*constitute*) formare; (*invent*) inventare; (*parcel*) fare ♦ *vi* conciliarsi; (*with cosmetics*) truccarsi; **~ up for** *vt fus* compensare; ricuperare; **~-believe** *n*: **a world of ~-**

Many Italian and English words have similar forms *and* meanings. Many Italian words, however, *look* like English words but have a completely *different* meaning. For example, 'attualmente' means 'at present'; 'eventuale' means 'possible'. This can easily lead to serious mistranslations.

Sometimes the meaning of the Italian word is *close* to the English. For example, 'la moneta' means 'small change' rather than 'money'; 'il soprannome' means 'nickname' not 'surname'. But some Italian words have two meanings, one the same as the English, the other completely different! 'L'editore' can mean 'publisher' as well as 'editor'; 'la marcia' can mean 'march/running/walking' but also 'the gear (of a car)'.

Such words are often referred to as 'false friends'. You will have to look at the context in which they appear to arrive at the correct meaning. If they seem to fit with the sense of the passage as a whole, you will probably not need to look them up. If they don't make sense, however, you may be dealing with 'false friends'.

WORDGAME 19
WORDS IN CONTEXT

Study the sentences below. Translations of the shaded words are given at the bottom. Match the number of the sentence and the letter of the translation correctly each time.

1. In questa zona è proibito cacciare.
2. L'ho visto cacciare i soldi in tasca.
3. È il ritratto di una dama del Settecento.
4. Facciamo una partita a dama?
5. Ha versato il vino nei bicchieri.
6. Hanno versato tutti i soldi sul loro conto.
7. Ti presento il mio fratello maggiore.
8. Aveva il grado di maggiore nell'esercito.
9. Ho finito i dadi per brodo.
10. In un angolo due uomini giocavano a dadi.
11. Sua madre è già partita per il mare.
12. Ti va di fare una partita a carte?
13. Il ladro è stato visto da un passante.
14. Devi infilare la cintura nel passante.
15. È corso verso di me.
16. Leggete ad alta voce il primo verso della poesia.

a. poured	e. loop	i. dice	m. passer-by
b. hunt	f. towards	j. major	n. draughts
c. left	g. paid	k. stock cubes	o. older
d. game	h. line	l. stick	p. lady

35

WORDGAME 20

WORDS WITH MORE THAN ONE MEANING

Look at the advertisements below. The words which are shaded can have more than one meaning. Use your dictionary to help you work out the correct translation in the context.

1
Desidero ricevere maggiori informazioni per un soggiorno al Lago di Garda

Nome e cognome: _____

Indirizzo: _____

2
Con il patrocinio della

REGIONE TOSCANA e CAMERA DI

COMMERCIO DELLA TOSCANA

3
TRILLO
LA SVEGLIA ELETTRONICA
CHE NON TI TRADISCE
4 funzioni: ore, minuti, secondi,
sveglia
Funzionamento a pile

4
**ECONOMIA E
FINANZA
BORSA E FONDI**

5
Albergo Ristorante

"La Cantina"

cucina casalinga

a 500 metri dalla piazza

SI PREGA DI RITIRARE LO SCONTRINO ALLA CASSA

7

Visite guidate al paese
di Alassio

8

CASSA
rurale ed artigiana
Via Basovizza 2
Trieste

9

Una casa in riva al mare
"CALA DEI TEMPLARI"

Soggiorno, una camera da letto,
bagno, balcone

10

PRATOLINI
la cucina su misura per te
Pratolini S.p.A. — 57480 Frascati — Roma
(0733) 5581 (10 linee) —
Telex 478192 PRATO I

WORDGAME 21
FALSE FRIENDS

Look at the advertisements below. The words which are shaded resemble English words but have different meanings here. Find a correct translation for each word in the context.

1

Boutique "La Moda"
Liquidazione di tutti gli articoli

2

Pensione Miramonti

camere con bagno/doccia
parcheggio privato
bar, ristorante

3

ACCENDERE LE LUCI IN GALLERIA

4

LIBRERIA
Il Gabbiano

Libri — Giornali — Articoli
spiaggia — Guide turistiche
— Cartoline

SASSARI
Via Mazzini 46

5

ITALMODA CRAVATTE
LE GRANDI FIRME
Divisione della BST,
Bergamo S.p.A

La direzione di questo albergo declina ogni responsabilità per lo smarrimento di oggetti lasciati incustoditi

6

7

Questo esercizio resterà chiuso nei giorni festivi e il lunedì

8

"Le bollicine"
Locale notturno
— pianobar
— discoteca

9

**Lago di Garda
campeggi, sport acquatici, gite in battello**

10

**Attenzione: per l'uso leggere attentamente l'istruzione interna.
Da vendersi dietro presentazione di ricetta medica.**

HAVE FUN WITH YOUR DICTIONARY

Here are some word games for you to try. You will find your dictionary helpful as you attempt the activities.

WORDGAME 22

In the boxes below, the letters of eight Italian words have been replaced by numbers. A number represents the same letter each time.

Try to crack the code and find the eight words. If you need help, use your dictionary.

Here is a clue: all the words you are looking for have something to do with TRANSPORT.

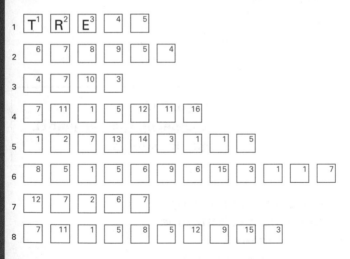

1. | T¹ | R² | E³ | 4 | 5 |

2. | 6 | 7 | 8 | 9 | 5 | 4 |

3. | 4 | 7 | 10 | 3 |

4. | 7 | 11 | 1 | 5 | 12 | 11 | 16 |

5. | 1 | 2 | 7 | 13 | 14 | 3 | 1 | 1 | 5 |

6. | 8 | 5 | 1 | 5 | 6 | 9 | 6 | 15 | 3 | 1 | 1 | 7 |

7. | 12 | 7 | 2 | 6 | 7 |

8. | 7 | 11 | 1 | 5 | 8 | 5 | 12 | 9 | 15 | 3 |

WORDGAME 23
PAROLE DECAPITATE

If you 'behead' certain Italian words, i.e. take away their first letter, you are left with another Italian word. For example, if you behead **'maglio'** (= 'mallet'), you get **'aglio'** (= 'garlic').

The following words have their heads chopped off, i.e. the first letter has been removed. Use your dictionary to help you form a new Italian word by adding one letter to the start of each word below. Write down the new Italian word and its meaning. There may be more than one new word you can form.

1. arto (= limb)
2. alto (= high)
3. esca (= bait)
4. unto (= greasy)
5. ora (= hour)
6. acca (= letter H)
7. orale (= oral)
8. otto (= eight)
9. orda (= horde)
10. alone (= halo)
11. oca (= goose)
12. anca (= hip)
13. ascia (= axe)
14. anno (= year)
15. rete (= net)

WORDGAME 24

PAROLE INCROCIATE

Complete this crossword by looking up the words listed below in the English-Italian section of your dictionary. Remember to read through the entry carefully to find the word that will fit.

1 (a piece of) news	5 story	10 rough	15 adder
2 to dirty	6 relationship	11 swarm	16 harbour
3 to admire	7 porthole	12 air	17 ebony
4 to reassure	8 deposit	13 employ	18 to take off
	9 strip	14 sad	19 night

WORDGAME 25
PAROLE TAGLIATE

There are twelve Italian words hidden in the grid below. Each word is made up of five letters but has been split into two parts.

Find the Italian words. Each group of letters can only be used once.

Use your dictionary to help you.

fer	ba	por	sce	za	che
an	mo	to	gam	se	duo
pri	ta	co	ro	fuo	na
fal	sen	men	so	for	mo

WORDGAME 26

TERMINI DI CUCINA

Here is a list of Italian words for things you will find in the kitchen. Unfortunately, the letters have all been jumbled up. Try to work out what each word is and put the word in the boxes on the right. You will see that there are six shaded boxes below. With the six letters in the shaded boxes make up <u>another</u> Italian word for an object you can find in the kitchen.

1. zazta   Vuoi una ____ di caffé?

2. grifo   Metti il burro nel ____ !

3. vatloa   A ____ ! È pronto!

4. norfo   Cuocere in ____ per 20 minuti.

5. chiocciau   Assaggia la minestra col ____.

6. polacasta   Usa il ____ per gli spaghetti.

The word you are looking for is:

44

WORDGAME 27
PAROLE IN CROCE

Take the four letters given each time and put them in the four empty boxes in the centre of each grid. Arrange them in such a way that you form four six-letter words. Use your dictionary to check the words.

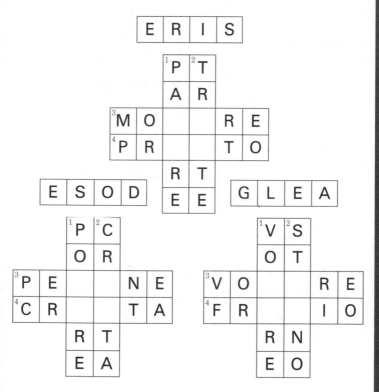

E	R	I	S

ANSWERS

WORDGAME 1

1 volere
2 pigiare
3 mollare
4 imparare
5 steccato
6 parere
7 panna
8 orario
9 imbrogliato
10 fianco

WORDGAME 2

1 filo
2 permettere
3 regalo
4 volere
5 tragitto
6 liberare
7 raffreddore
8 attendere
9 notare
10 ritorno
11 ridurre
12 riposo

WORDGAME 3

vestaglia + pantofola
nido + gazza
pelletteria + borsetta
campanile + campana
studente + laurea
libro + scaffale
passerella + nave
pinna + squalo

WORDGAME 4

1 attenzione
2 sfarzo
3 traforo
4 annullare
5 prigione
6 divertente
7 ingannare
8 veloce
9 timore
10 bruno

WORDGAME 5

1 doccia 2 arrabbiato 3 foglio

WORDGAME 6

1 povertà
2 rifiutare
3 vigliacco
4 piangere
5 attaccare
6 ruvido
7 innocente
8 scuro
9 brutto
10 chiuso

WORDGAME 7

1 rigido
2 piccione
3 gelo
4 mazzo
5 decennio
6 chiave
7 foglia
8 sogno
9 ascia
10 ghianda

WORDGAME 8

1 shock
2 blow
3 ring
4 shot
5 suddenly
6 whim
7 gust of wind
8 stroke
9 strong impression
10 knock
11 sunstroke
12 coup d'état

46

WORDGAME 9

1	impiegato	7	unita
2	impiego	8	unire
3	studente	9	rifiutare
4	studio	10	rifiuti
5	uso	11	festivi
6	usata	12	festa

WORDGAME 10

1 fa bel tempo
2 fare psicologia
3 faccia pure
4 fammi vedere
5 farsi tagliare i capelli
6 si fa così
7 fare la spesa
8 fare presto
9 far partire il motore
10 fece per andarsene

WORDGAME 11

1	n	5	v	8	adj
2	adv	6	v	9	adj
3	n	7	n	10	n
4	n				

WORDGAME 12

1	amico	6	studente
2	cantante	7	cugino
3	direttore	8	lettore
4	straniero	9	professore
5	regista	10	collaboratore

WORDGAME 13

1 un foglio
  una foglia
2 il modo
  moda
3 corsa
  un corso
4 castagni
  castagne
5 il palmo
  una palma
6 una partita
  il partito
7 una pezza
  un pezzo
8 casa
  caso

WORDGAME 14

1	bianca	6	poche	11	diademi
2	fresca	7	giovani	12	tristi
3	larga	8	grandi	13	tronchi
4	verde	9	veloci	14	trombe
5	grave	10	poeti	15	dialoghi

WORDGAME 16

1	io verrò	5	offerto	9	io dovrò
2	rimasto	6	mosso	10	io dormirò
3	io vedrò	7	io finisco	11	vissuto
4	io ho	8	io esco	12	io posso

WORDGAME 17

1	venuto	8	messo
2	contratto	9	sorpreso
3	coperto	10	percorso
4	vissuto	11	accolto
5	offerto	12	dipinto
6	sorriso	13	condotto
7	preso	14	sceso

WORDGAME 18

1	essere	9	piacere
2	raggiungere	10	fare
3	accompagnare	11	ricominciare
4	alzarsi	12	succedere
5	andare	13	volere
6	vendere	14	avere
7	mettersi	15	essere
8	nascere		

WORDGAME 19

1	b	5	a	9	k	13	m
2	l	6	g	10	i	14	e
3	p	7	o	11	c	15	f
4	n	8	j	12	d	16	h

47

WORDGAME 20

1. stay
2. chamber
3. alarm clock
4. stock exchange; funds
5. cooking
6. checkout (here; till)
7. village (here; town)
8. savings bank
9. living room
10. kitchen

WORDGAME 21

1. clearance sale
2. boarding house
3. tunnel
4. newspapers
5. ties
6. management
7. business
8. night club
9. campsite
10. prescription

WORDGAME 22

1. treno
2. camion
3. nave
4. autobus
5. traghetto
6. motocicletta
7. barca
8. automobile

WORDGAME 23

1. sarto (= tailor)
2. salto (= jump)
3. pesca (= peach)
4. punto (= point)
5. mora (= blackberry)
6. vacca (= cow)
7. morale (= moral)
8. rotto (= broken)
9. corda (= cord)
10. salone (= lounge)
11. foca (= seal)
12. panca (= bench)
13. fascia (= band)
14. danno (= damage)
15. prete (= priest)

WORDGAME 24

1. notizia
2. sporcare
3. ammirare
4. rassicurare
5. favola
6. rapporto
7. oblò
8. acconto
9. striscia
10. rozzo
11. sciame
12. aria
13. impiegare
14. triste
15. vipera
16. porto
17. ebano
18. togliere
19. sera

WORDGAME 25

ferro	senza	duomo
gamba	anche	fuoco
porta	primo	falso
scena	mento	forse

WORDGAME 26

1. tazza
2. frigo
3. tavola
4. forno
5. cucchiaio
6. colapasta

Missing word — FRUSTA

WORDGAME 27

1 parere	1 podere	1 volere
2 triste	2 crosta	2 stagno
3 morire	3 pedone	3 volare
4 presto	4 cresta	4 fregio

48

ENGLISH - ITALIAN
INGLESE - ITALIANO

A a

A [eɪ] *n* (*MUS*) la *m*

a [ə] (*before vowel or silent h*: **an**) *indef art*
1 un (uno +*s impure, gn, pn, ps, x, z*), *f*
una (un' +*vowel*); ~ **book** un libro; ~
mirror uno specchio; **an apple** una mela;
she's ~ doctor è medico
2 (*instead of the number "one"*) un(o), *f*
una; ~ **year ago** un anno fa; ~
hundred/thousand *etc* **pounds** cento/
mille *etc* sterline
3 (*in expressing ratios, prices etc*) a, per; **3**
~ **day/week** 3 al giorno/alla settimana;
10 km an hour 10 km all'ora; **£5** ~
person 5 sterline a persona *or* per
persona

A.A. *n abbr* (= *Alcoholics Anonymous*)
AA; (*BRIT*: = *Automobile Association*)
≈ A.C.I.
A.A.A. (*US*) *n abbr* (= *American
Automobile Association*) ≈ A.C.I. *m*
aback [ə'bæk] *adv*: **to be taken** ~ essere
sbalordito(a)
abandon [ə'bændən] *vt* abbandonare ♦ *n*:
with ~ sfrenatamente, spensieratamente
abashed [ə'bæʃt] *adj* imbarazzato(a)
abate [ə'beɪt] *vi* calmarsi
abattoir ['æbətwɑː*] (*BRIT*) *n* mattatoio
abbey ['æbɪ] *n* abbazia, badia
abbot ['æbət] *n* abate *m*
abbreviation [əbriːvɪ'eɪʃən] *n*
abbreviazione *f*
abdicate ['æbdɪkeɪt] *vt* abdicare a ♦ *vi*
abdicare
abdomen ['æbdəmən] *n* addome *m*
abduct [æb'dʌkt] *vt* rapire
aberration [æbə'reɪʃən] *n* aberrazione *f*
abet [ə'bet] *vt see* **aid**
abeyance [ə'beɪəns] *n*: **in** ~ (*law*) in

disuso; (*matter*) in sospeso
abide [ə'baɪd] *vt*: **I can't** ~ **it/him** non lo
posso soffrire *or* sopportare; ~ **by** *vt fus*
conformarsi a
ability [ə'bɪlɪtɪ] *n* abilità *f inv*
abject ['æbdʒekt] *adj* (*poverty*) abietto(a);
(*apology*) umiliante
ablaze [ə'bleɪz] *adj* in fiamme
able ['eɪbl] *adj* capace; **to be** ~ **to do sth**
essere capace di fare qc, poter fare qc; ~-
bodied *adj* robusto(a); **ably** *adv*
abilmente
abnormal [æb'nɔːməl] *adj* anormale
aboard [ə'bɔːd] *adv* a bordo ♦ *prep* a
bordo di
abode [ə'bəud] *n*: **of no fixed** ~ senza
fissa dimora
abolish [ə'bɔlɪʃ] *vt* abolire
abominable [ə'bɔmɪnəbl] *adj*
abominevole
aborigine [æbə'rɪdʒɪnɪ] *n* aborigeno/a
abort [ə'bɔːt] *vt* abortire; ~**ion** [ə'bɔːʃən]
n aborto; **to have an** ~**ion** abortire; ~**ive**
adj abortivo(a)
abound [ə'baund] *vi* abbondare; **to** ~ **in**
or **with** abbondare di

about [ə'baut] *adv* **1** (*approximately*)
circa, quasi; ~ **a hundred/thousand** *etc*
un centinaio/migliaio *etc*, circa cento/
mille *etc*; **it takes** ~ **10 hours** ci vogliono
circa 10 ore; **at** ~ **2 o'clock** verso le 2;
I've just ~ **finished** ho quasi finito
2 (*referring to place*) qua e là, in giro; **to
leave things lying** ~ lasciare delle cose
in giro; **to run** ~ correre qua e là; **to
walk** ~ camminare
3: **to be** ~ **to do sth** stare per fare qc
♦ *prep* **1** (*relating to*) su, di; **a book** ~
London un libro su Londra; **what is it**

~? di che si tratta?; (*book, film etc*) di cosa tratta?; **we talked ~ it** ne abbiamo parlato; **what** *or* **how ~ doing this?** che ne dici di fare questo?

2 (*referring to place*): **to walk ~ the town** camminare per la città; **her clothes were scattered ~ the room** i suoi vestiti erano sparsi *or* in giro per tutta la stanza

about-face *n* dietro front *m inv*
about-turn *n* dietro front *m inv*
above [ə'bʌv] *adv, prep* sopra; ~ **mentioned** ~ suddetto; ~ **all** soprattutto; **~board** *adj* aperto(a); onesto(a)
abrasive [ə'breɪzɪv] *adj* abrasivo(a); (*fig*) caustico(a)
abreast [ə'brɛst] *adv* di fianco; **to keep ~ of** tenersi aggiornato su
abridge [ə'brɪdʒ] *vt* ridurre
abroad [ə'brɔːd] *adv* all'estero
abrupt [ə'brʌpt] *adj* (*sudden*) improvviso(a); (*gruff, blunt*) brusco(a)
abscess ['æbsɪs] *n* ascesso
abscond [əb'skɔnd] *vi* scappare
absence ['æbsəns] *n* assenza
absent ['æbsənt] *adj* assente; **~ee** [-'tiː] *n* assente *m/f*; **~-minded** *adj* distratto(a)
absolute ['æbsəluːt] *adj* assoluto(a); **~ly** [-'luːtlɪ] *adv* assolutamente
absolve [əb'zɔlv] *vt*: **to ~ sb (from)** (*sin*) assolvere qn (da); (*oath*) sciogliere qn (da)
absorb [əb'zɔːb] *vt* assorbire; **to be ~ed in a book** essere immerso in un libro; **~ent cotton** (*US*) *n* cotone *m* idrofilo; **~ing** *adj* avvincente
absorption [əb'sɔːpʃən] *n* assorbimento
abstain [əb'steɪn] *vi*: **to ~ (from)** astenersi (da)
abstemious [əb'stiːmɪəs] *adj* astemio(a)
abstract ['æbstrækt] *adj* astratto(a)
absurd [əb'sɜːd] *adj* assurdo(a)
abuse [*n* ə'bjuːs, *vb* ə'bjuːz] *n* abuso; (*insults*) ingiurie *fpl* ♦ *vt* abusare di; **abusive** *adj* ingiurioso(a)
abysmal [ə'bɪzməl] *adj* spaventoso(a)
abyss [ə'bɪs] *n* abisso
AC *abbr* (= *alternating current*) c.a.
academic [ækə'dɛmɪk] *adj* accade-

mico(a); (*pej: issue*) puramente formale ♦ *n* universitario/a
academy [ə'kædəmɪ] *n* (*learned body*) accademia; (*school*) scuola privata; ~ **of music** conservatorio
accelerate [æk'sɛləreɪt] *vt, vi* accelerare; **accelerator** *n* acceleratore *m*
accent ['æksɛnt] *n* accento
accept [ək'sɛpt] *vt* accettare; **~able** *adj* accettabile; **~ance** *n* accettazione *f*
access ['æksɛs] *n* accesso; **~ible** [æk'sɛsəbl] *adj* accessibile
accessory [æk'sɛsərɪ] *n* accessorio; (*LAW*): ~ **to** complice *m/f* di
accident ['æksɪdənt] *n* incidente *m*; (*chance*) caso; **by ~** per caso; **~al** [-'dɛntl] *adj* accidentale; **~ally** [-'dɛntəlɪ] *adv* per caso; **~-prone** *adj*: **he's very ~-prone** è un vero passaguai
acclaim [ə'kleɪm] *n* acclamazione *f*
accolade ['ækəleɪd] *n* encomio
accommodate [ə'kɔmədeɪt] *vt* alloggiare; (*oblige, help*) favorire
accommodating [ə'kɔmədeɪtɪŋ] *adj* compiacente
accommodation [əkɔmə'deɪʃən] *n* alloggio; **~s** (*US*) *npl* alloggio
accompany [ə'kʌmpənɪ] *vt* accompagnare
accomplice [ə'kʌmplɪs] *n* complice *m/f*
accomplish [ə'kʌmplɪʃ] *vt* compiere; (*goal*) raggiungere; **~ed** *adj* esperto(a); **~ment** *n* compimento; realizzazione *f*; **~ments** *npl* (*skills*) doti *fpl*
accord [ə'kɔːd] *n* accordo ♦ *vt* accordare; **of his own ~** di propria iniziativa; **~ance** *n*: **in ~ance with** in conformità con; **~ing**: **~ing to** *prep* secondo; **~ingly** *adv* in conformità
accordion [ə'kɔːdɪən] *n* fisarmonica
accost [ə'kɔst] *vt* avvicinare
account [ə'kaʊnt] *n* (*COMM*) conto; (*report*) descrizione *f*; **~s** *npl* (*COMM*) conti *mpl*; **of no ~** di nessuna importanza; **on ~** in acconto; **on no ~** per nessun motivo; **on ~ of** a causa di; **to take into ~, take ~ of** tener conto di; ~ **for** *vt fus* spiegare; giustificare; **~able** *adj*: **~able (to)** responsabile (verso)

accountancy [ə'kauntənsı] n ragioneria
accountant [ə'kauntənt] n ragioniere/a
account number n numero di conto
accrued interest [ə'kru:d-] n interesse m maturato
accumulate [ə'kju:mjuleıt] vt accumulare ♦ vi accumularsi
accuracy ['ækjurəsı] n precisione f
accurate ['ækjurıt] adj preciso(a); **~ly** adv precisamente
accusation [ækju'zeıʃən] n accusa
accuse [ə'kju:z] vt accusare; **~d** n accusato/a
accustom [ə'kʌstəm] vt abituare; **~ed** adj: **~ed** to abituato(a) a
ace [eıs] n asso
ache [eık] n male m, dolore m ♦ vi (be sore) far male, dolere; **my head ~s** mi fa male la testa
achieve [ə'tʃi:v] vt (aim) raggiungere; (victory, success) ottenere; **~ment** n compimento; successo
acid ['æsıd] adj acido(a) ♦ n acido; **~ rain** n pioggia acida
acknowledge [ək'nɔlıdʒ] vt (letter: also: **~ receipt of**) confermare la ricevuta di; (fact) riconoscere; **~ment** n conferma; riconoscimento
acne ['æknı] n acne f
acorn ['eıkɔ:n] n ghianda
acoustic [ə'ku:stık] adj acustico(a); **~s** n, npl acustica
acquaint [ə'kweınt] vt: **to ~ sb with sth** far sapere qc a qn; **to be ~ed with** (person) conoscere; **~ance** n conoscenza; (person) conoscente m/f
acquiesce [ækwı'es] vi: **to ~ (to)** acconsentire (a)
acquire [ə'kwaıə*] vt acquistare
acquisition [ækwı'zıʃən] n acquisto
acquit [ə'kwıt] vt assolvere; **to ~ o.s. well** comportarsi bene; **~tal** n assoluzione f
acre ['eıkə*] n acro (= 4047 m²)
acrid ['ækrıd] adj acre; pungente
acrimonious [ækrı'məunıəs] adj astioso(a)
acrobat ['ækrəbæt] n acrobata m/f
across [ə'krɔs] prep (on the other side)

dall'altra parte di; (crosswise) attraverso ♦ adv dall'altra parte; in larghezza; **to run/swim ~** attraversare di corsa/a nuoto; **~ from** di fronte a
acrylic [ə'krılık] adj acrilico(a)
act [ækt] n atto; (in music-hall etc) numero; (LAW) decreto ♦ vi agire; (THEATRE) recitare; (pretend) fingere ♦ vt (part) recitare; **to ~ as** agire da; **~ing** adj che fa le funzioni di ♦ n (of actor) recitazione f; (activity): **to do some ~ing** fare del teatro (or del cinema)
action ['ækʃən] n azione f; (MIL) combattimento; (LAW) processo; **out of ~** fuori combattimento; fuori servizio; **to take ~** agire; **~ replay** n (TV) replay m inv
activate ['æktıveıt] vt (mechanism) attivare
active ['æktıv] adj attivo(a); **~ly** adv (participate) attivamente; (discourage, dislike) vivamente
activity [æk'tıvıtı] n attività f inv
actor ['æktə*] n attore m
actress ['æktrıs] n attrice f
actual ['æktjuəl] adj reale, vero(a); **~ly** adv veramente; (even) addirittura
acumen ['ækjumən] n acume m
acute [ə'kju:t] adj acuto(a); (mind, person) perspicace
ad [æd] n abbr = **advertisement**
A.D. adv abbr (= Anno Domini) d.C.
adamant ['ædəmənt] adj irremovibile
adapt [ə'dæpt] vt adattare ♦ vi: **to ~ (to)** adattarsi (a); **~able** adj (device) adattabile; (person) che sa adattarsi; **~er** or **~or** n (ELEC) adattatore m
add [æd] vt aggiungere; (figures: also: **~ up**) addizionare ♦ vi: **to ~ to** (increase) aumentare; **it doesn't ~ up** (fig) non quadra, non ha senso
adder ['ædə*] n vipera
addict ['ædıkt] n tossicomane m/f; (fig) fanatico/a; **~ed** [ə'dıktıd] adj: **to be ~ed to** (drink etc) essere dedito(a) a; (fig: football etc) essere tifoso(a) di; **~ion** [ə'dıkʃən] n (MED) tossicodipendenza; **~ive** [ə'dıktıv] adj che dà assuefazione
addition [ə'dıʃən] n addizione f; (thing

added) aggiunta; **in** ~ inoltre; **in** ~ **to**
oltre; **~al** *adj* supplementare
additive ['ædɪtɪv] *n* additivo
address [ə'drɛs] *n* indirizzo; *(talk)*
discorso ♦ *vt* indirizzare; *(speak to)* fare
un discorso a; *(issue)* affrontare
adept ['ædɛpt] *adj*: ~ **at** esperto(a) in
adequate ['ædɪkwɪt] *adj* adeguato(a);
sufficiente
adhere [əd'hɪə*] *vi*: **to** ~ **to** aderire a;
(fig: rule, decision) seguire
adhesive [əd'hiːzɪv] *n* adesivo; ~ **tape** *n*
(BRIT: for parcels etc) nastro adesivo; *(US:
MED)* cerotto adesivo
adjective ['ædʒɛktɪv] *n* aggettivo
adjoining [ə'dʒɔɪnɪŋ] *adj* accanto *inv*,
adiacente
adjourn [ə'dʒəːn] *vt* rimandare ♦ *vi*
essere aggiornato(a)
adjudicate [ə'dʒuːdɪkeɪt] *vt* *(contest)*
giudicare; *(claim)* decidere su
adjust [ə'dʒʌst] *vt* aggiustare; *(change)*
rettificare ♦ *vi*: **to** ~ **(to)** adattarsi (a);
~able *adj* regolabile; **~ment** *n* *(PSYCH)*
adattamento; *(of machine)* regolazione *f*;
(of prices, wages) modifica
ad-lib [æd'lɪb] *vi* improvvisare ♦ *adv*: **ad
lib** a piacere, a volontà
administer [əd'mɪnɪstə*] *vt*
amministrare; *(justice, drug)*
somministrare
administration [ədmɪnɪs'treɪʃən] *n*
amministrazione *f*
administrative [əd'mɪnɪstrətɪv] *adj*
amministrativo(a)
admiral ['ædmərəl] *n* ammiraglio; **A~ty**
(BRIT) *n* Ministero della Marina
admiration [ædmə'reɪʃən] *n*
ammirazione *f*
admire [əd'maɪə*] *vt* ammirare
admission [əd'mɪʃən] *n* ammissione *f*;
(to exhibition, night club etc) ingresso;
(confession) confessione *f*
admit [əd'mɪt] *vt* ammettere; far entrare;
(agree) riconoscere; **to** ~ **to** riconoscere;
~tance *n* ingresso; **~tedly** *adv* bisogna
pur riconoscere (che)
admonish [əd'mɔnɪʃ] *vt* ammonire
ad nauseam [æd'nɔːsɪæm] *adv* fino alla

nausea, a non finire
ado [ə'duː] *n*: **without (any) more** ~
senza più indugi
adolescence [ædəu'lɛsns] *n* adolescenza
adolescent [ædəu'lɛsnt] *adj, n*
adolescente *m/f*
adopt [ə'dɔpt] *vt* adottare; **~ed** *adj*
adottivo(a); **~ion** [ə'dɔpʃən] *n* adozione *f*
adore [ə'dɔː*] *vt* adorare
Adriatic [eɪdrɪ'ætɪk] *n*: **the** ~ **(Sea)** il
mare Adriatico, l'Adriatico
adrift [ə'drɪft] *adv* alla deriva
adult ['ædʌlt] *adj* adulto(a); *(work,
education)* per adulti ♦ *n* adulto/a
adultery [ə'dʌltərɪ] *n* adulterio
advance [əd'vɑːns] *n* avanzamento;
(money) anticipo ♦ *adj* *(booking etc)* in
anticipo ♦ *vt* *(money)* anticipare ♦ *vi*
avanzare; **in** ~ in anticipo; **~d** *adj*
avanzato(a); *(SCOL: studies)* superiore
advantage [əd'vɑːntɪdʒ] *n* *(also: TENNIS)*
vantaggio; **to take** ~ **of** approfittarsi di
advent ['ædvənt] *n* avvento; *(REL)*: **A~**
Avvento
adventure [əd'vɛntʃə*] *n* avventura
adverb ['ædvəːb] *n* avverbio
adverse ['ædvəːs] *adj* avverso(a)
advert ['ædvəːt] *(BRIT)* *n abbr*
= **advertisement**
advertise ['ædvətaɪz] *vi* *(vt)* fare
pubblicità *or* réclame (a); fare
un'inserzione *(per vendere)*; **to** ~ **for**
(staff) mettere un annuncio sul giornale
per trovare
advertisement [əd'vəːtɪsmənt] *n* *(COMM)*
réclame *f inv*, pubblicità *f inv*; *(in
classified ads)* inserzione *f*
advertiser ['ædvətaɪzə*] *n* *(in newspaper
etc)* inserzionista *m/f*
advertising ['ædvətaɪzɪŋ] *n* pubblicità
advice [əd'vaɪs] *n* consigli *mpl*;
(notification) avviso; **piece of** ~ consiglio;
to take legal ~ consultare un avvocato
advisable [əd'vaɪzəbl] *adj* consigliabile
advise [əd'vaɪz] *vt* consigliare; **to** ~ **sb of
sth** informare qn di qc; **to** ~ **sb against
sth/doing sth** sconsigliare qc a qn/a qn
di fare qc; **~dly** [-dlɪ] *adv* *(deliberately)*
di proposito; **~r** *or* **advisor** *n*

consigliere/a; **advisory** [-ərɪ] *adj* consultivo(a)

advocate [*n* 'ædvəkɪt, *vb* 'ædvəkeɪt] *n* (*upholder*) sostenitore/trice; (*LAW*) avvocato (difensore) ♦ *vt* propugnare

Aegean [ɪ'dʒiːən] *n*: **the ~ (Sea)** il mar Egeo, l'Egeo

aerial ['ɛərɪəl] *n* antenna ♦ *adj* aereo(a)

aerobics [ɛə'rəubɪks] *n* aerobica

aeroplane ['ɛərəpleɪn] (*BRIT*) *n* aeroplano

aerosol ['ɛərəsɔl] (*BRIT*) *n* aerosol *m inv*

aesthetic [ɪs'θetɪk] *adj* estetico(a)

afar [ə'fɑ:*] *adv*: **from ~** da lontano

affair [ə'fɛə*] *n* affare *m*; (*also: love ~*) relazione *f* amorosa

affect [ə'fɛkt] *vt* toccare; (*influence*) influire su, incidere su; (*feign*) fingere; **~ed** *adj* affettato(a)

affection [ə'fɛkʃən] *n* affezione *f*; **~ate** *adj* affettuoso(a)

affix [ə'fɪks] *vt* apporre; attaccare

afflict [ə'flɪkt] *vt* affliggere

affluence ['æfluəns] *n* abbondanza; opulenza

affluent ['æfluənt] *adj* ricco(a); **the ~ society** la società del benessere

afford [ə'fɔːd] *vt* permettersi; (*provide*) fornire

afield [ə'fiːld] *adv*: **far ~** lontano

afloat [ə'fləut] *adv* a galla

afoot [ə'fut] *adv*: **there is something ~** si sta preparando qualcosa

afraid [ə'freɪd] *adj* impaurito(a); **to be ~ of** *or* **to/that** aver paura di/che; **I am ~ so/not** ho paura di sì/no

afresh [ə'frɛʃ] *adv* di nuovo

Africa ['æfrɪkə] *n* Africa; **~n** *adj, n* africano(a)

aft [ɑ:ft] *adv* a poppa, verso poppa

after ['ɑ:ftə*] *prep, adv* dopo ♦ *conj* dopo che; **what/who are you ~?** che/chi cerca?; **~ he left/having done** dopo che se ne fu andato/dopo aver fatto; **to name sb ~ sb** dare a qn il nome di qn; **it's twenty ~ eight** (*US*) sono le otto e venti; **to ask ~ sb** chiedere di qn; **~ all** dopo tutto; **~ you!** dopo di lei!; **~effects** *npl* conseguenze *fpl*; (*of illness*) postumi *mpl*; **~math** *n* conseguenze *fpl*; **in the ~math**

of nel periodo dopo; **~noon** *n* pomeriggio; **~s** *n* (*inf: dessert*) dessert *m inv*; **~-sales service** (*BRIT*) *n* servizio assistenza clienti; **~-shave (lotion)** *n* dopobarba *m inv*; **~thought** *n*: **as an ~thought** come aggiunta; **~wards** (*US* **~ward**) *adv* dopo

again [ə'gen] *adv* di nuovo; **to begin/see ~** ricominciare/rivedere; **not ... ~** non ... più; **~ and ~** ripetutamente

against [ə'genst] *prep* contro

age [eɪdʒ] *n* età *f inv* ♦ *vt, vi* invecchiare; **it's been ~s since** sono secoli che; **he is 20 years of ~** ha 20 anni; **to come of ~** diventare maggiorenne; **~d 10** di 10 anni; **the ~d** ['eɪdʒɪd] gli anziani; **~ group** *n* generazione *f*; **~ limit** *n* limite *m* d'età

agency ['eɪdʒənsɪ] *n* agenzia

agenda [ə'dʒɛndə] *n* ordine *m* del giorno

agent ['eɪdʒənt] *n* agente *m*

aggravate ['ægrəveɪt] *vt* aggravare; (*person*) irritare

aggregate ['ægrɪgeɪt] *n* aggregato

aggressive [ə'grɛsɪv] *adj* aggressivo(a)

aggrieved [ə'griːvd] *adj* addolorato(a)

aghast [ə'gɑːst] *adj* sbigottito(a)

agitate ['ædʒɪteɪt] *vt* turbare; agitare ♦ *vi*: **to ~ for** agitarsi per

AGM *n abbr* = **annual general meeting**

ago [ə'gəu] *adv*: **2 days ~** 2 giorni fa; **not long ~** poco tempo fa; **how long ~?** quanto tempo fa?

agog [ə'gɔg] *adj* ansioso(a), emozionato(a)

agonizing ['ægənaɪzɪŋ] *adj* straziante

agony ['ægənɪ] *n* dolore *m* atroce; **to be in ~** avere dolori atroci

agree [ə'griː] *vt* (*price*) pattuire ♦ *vi*: **to ~ (with)** essere d'accordo (con); (*LING*) concordare (con); **to ~ to sth/to do sth** accettare qc/di fare qc; **to ~ that** (*admit*) ammettere che; **to ~ on sth** accordarsi su qc; **garlic doesn't ~ with me** l'aglio non mi va; **~able** *adj* gradevole; (*willing*) disposto(a); **~d** *adj* (*time, place*) stabilito(a); **~ment** *n* accordo; **in ~ment** d'accordo

agricultural [ægrɪ'kʌltʃərəl] *adj* agricolo(a)

agriculture [ˈægrɪkʌltʃə*] *n* agricoltura
aground [əˈgraʊnd] *adv*: **to run ~** arenarsi
ahead [əˈhed] *adv* avanti; davanti; **~ of** davanti a; *(fig: schedule etc)* in anticipo su; **~ of time** in anticipo; **go right** *or* **straight ~** tiri diritto
aid [eɪd] *n* aiuto ♦ *vt* aiutare; **in ~ of** a favore di; **to ~ and abet** *(LAW)* essere complice di
aide [eɪd] *n (person)* aiutante *m*
AIDS [eɪdz] *n abbr* (= *acquired immune deficiency syndrome*) AIDS *f*
ailing [ˈeɪlɪŋ] *adj* sofferente
ailment [ˈeɪlmənt] *n* indisposizione *f*
aim [eɪm] *vt*: **to ~ sth at** *(such as gun)* mirare qc a, puntare qc a; *(camera)* rivolgere qc a; *(missile)* lanciare qc contro ♦ *vi (also: to take ~)* prendere la mira ♦ *n* mira; **to ~ at** mirare; **to ~ to do** aver l'intenzione di fare; **~less** *adj* senza scopo
ain't [eɪnt] *(inf)* = **am not; aren't; isn't**
air [ɛə*] *n* aria ♦ *vt (room)* arieggiare; *(clothes*) far prendere aria a; *(grievances, ideas)* esprimere pubblicamente ♦ *cpd (currents)* d'aria; *(attack)* aereo(a); **to throw sth into the ~** lanciare qc in aria; **by ~** *(travel)* in aereo; **on the ~** *(RADIO, TV)* in onda; **~bed** *(BRIT) n* materassino; **~borne** *adj* in volo; aerotrasportato(a); **~ conditioning** *n* condizionamento d'aria; **~craft** *n inv* apparecchio; **~craft carrier** *n* portaerei *f inv*; **~field** *n* campo d'aviazione; **A~ Force** *n* aviazione *f* militare; **~ freshener** *n* deodorante *m* per ambienti; **~gun** *n* fucile *m* ad aria compressa; **~ hostess** *(BRIT) n* hostess *f inv*; **~ letter** *(BRIT) n* aerogramma *m*; **~lift** *n* ponte *m* aereo; **~line** *n* linea aerea; **~liner** *n* aereo di linea; **~mail** *n*: **by ~mail** per via aerea; **~plane** *(US) n* aeroplano; **~port** *n* aeroporto; **~ raid** *n* incursione *f* aerea; **~sick** *adj*: **to be ~sick** soffrire di mal d'aria; **~ terminal** *n* air-terminal *m inv*; **~tight** *adj* ermetico(a); **~ traffic controller** *n* controllore *m* del traffico aereo; **~y** *adj* arioso(a); *(manners)* noncurante
aisle [aɪl] *n (of church)* navata laterale;

navata centrale; *(of plane)* corridoio
ajar [əˈdʒɑː*] *adj* socchiuso(a)
akin [əˈkɪn] *adj*: **~ to** simile a
alacrity [əˈlækrɪtɪ] *n*: **with ~** con prontezza
alarm [əˈlɑːm] *n* allarme *m* ♦ *vt* allarmare; **~ call** *n (in hotel etc)* sveglia; **~ clock** *n* sveglia
alas [əˈlæs] *excl* ohimè!, ahimè!
albeit [ɔːlˈbiːɪt] *conj* sebbene +*sub*, benché +*sub*
album [ˈælbəm] *n* album *m inv*
alcohol [ˈælkəhɔl] *n* alcool *m*; **~ic** [-ˈhɔlɪk] *adj* alcolico(a) ♦ *n* alcolizzato/a
ale [eɪl] *n* birra
alert [əˈlɜːt] *adj* vigile ♦ *n* allarme *m* ♦ *vt* avvertire; mettere in guardia; **on the ~** all'erta
algebra [ˈældʒɪbrə] *n* algebra
alias [ˈeɪlɪəs] *adv* alias ♦ *n* pseudonimo, falso nome *m*
alibi [ˈælɪbaɪ] *n* alibi *m inv*
alien [ˈeɪlɪən] *n* straniero/a; *(extraterrestrial)* alieno/a ♦ *adj*: **~ (to)** estraneo(a) (a); **~ate** *vt* alienare
alight [əˈlaɪt] *adj* acceso(a) ♦ *vi* scendere; *(bird)* posarsi
align [əˈlaɪn] *vt* allineare
alike [əˈlaɪk] *adj* simile ♦ *adv* sia ... sia; **to look ~** assomigliarsi
alimony [ˈælɪmənɪ] *n (payment)* alimenti *mpl*
alive [əˈlaɪv] *adj* vivo(a); *(lively)* vivace

━━━ *KEYWORD* ━━━

all [ɔːl] *adj* tutto(a); **~ day** tutto il giorno; **~ night** tutta la notte; **~ men** tutti gli uomini; **~ five came** sono venuti tutti e cinque; **~ the books** tutti i libri; **~ the food** tutto il cibo; **~ the time** sempre; tutto il tempo; **~ his life** tutta la vita
♦ *pron* **1** tutto(a); **I ate it ~, I ate ~ of it** l'ho mangiato tutto; **~ of us went** tutti noi siamo andati; **~ of the boys went** tutti i ragazzi sono andati
2 *(in phrases)*: **above ~** soprattutto; **after ~** dopotutto; **at ~**: **not at ~** *(in answer to question)* niente affatto; *(in answer to thanks)* prego!, di niente!, s'immagini!;

I'm not at ~ **tired** non sono affatto stanco(a); **anything at ~ will do** andrà bene qualsiasi cosa; ~ **in** ~ tutto sommato ♦ *adv:* ~ **alone** tutto(a) solo(a); **it's not as hard as ~ that** non è poi così difficile; ~ **the more/the better** tanto più/meglio; ~ **but** quasi; **the score is two** ~ il punteggio è di due a due

allay [ə'leɪ] *vt (fears)* dissipare

all clear *n (also fig)* segnale *m* di cessato allarme

allegation [ælɪ'geɪʃən] *n* asserzione *f*

allege [ə'ledʒ] *vt* asserire; ~**dly** [ə'ledʒɪdlɪ] *adv* secondo quanto si asserisce

allegiance [ə'liːdʒəns] *n* fedeltà

allergic [ə'ləːdʒɪk] *adj:* ~ **to** allergico(a) a

allergy ['ælədʒɪ] *n* allergia

alleviate [ə'liːvɪeɪt] *vt* sollevare

alley ['ælɪ] *n* vicolo

alliance [ə'laɪəns] *n* alleanza

allied ['ælaɪd] *adj* alleato(a)

all-in *adj (BRIT: also adv: charge)* tutto compreso; ~ **wrestling** *n* lotta americana

all-night *adj* aperto(a) *(or* che dura) tutta la notte

allocate ['æləkeɪt] *vt* assegnare

allot [ə'lɔt] *vt* assegnare; ~**ment** *n* assegnazione *f; (garden)* lotto di terra

all-out *adj (effort etc)* totale ♦ *adv:* **to go all out for** mettercela tutta per

allow [ə'laʊ] *vt (practice, behaviour)* permettere; *(sum to spend etc)* accordare; *(sum, time estimated)* dare; *(concede):* **to** ~ **that** ammettere che; **to** ~ **sb to do** permettere a qn di fare; **he is** ~**ed to** lo può fare; ~ **for** *vt fus* tener conto di; ~**ance** *n (money received)* assegno; indennità *f inv; (TAX)* detrazione *f* di imposta; **to make** ~**ances for** tener conto di

alloy ['ælɔɪ] *n* lega

all right *adv (feel, work)* bene; *(as answer)* va bene

all-round *adj* completo(a)

all-time *adj (record)* assoluto(a)

allude [ə'luːd] *vi:* **to** ~ **to** alludere a

alluring [ə'ljʊərɪŋ] *adj* seducente

ally ['ælaɪ] *n* alleato

almighty [ɔːl'maɪtɪ] *adj* onnipotente; *(row etc)* colossale

almond ['ɑːmənd] *n* mandorla

almost ['ɔːlməʊst] *adv* quasi

alms [ɑːmz] *npl* elemosina *sg*

aloft [ə'lɔft] *adv* in alto

alone [ə'ləʊn] *adj, adv* solo(a); **to leave sb** ~ lasciare qn in pace; **to leave sth** ~ lasciare stare qc; **let** ~ ... figuriamoci poi ..., tanto meno ....

along [ə'lɔŋ] *prep* lungo ♦ *adv:* **is he coming** ~? viene con noi?; **he was limping** ~ veniva zoppicando; ~ **with** insieme con; **all** ~ *(all the time)* sempre, fin dall'inizio; lungo ♦ *adv* accanto

aloof [ə'luːf] *adj* distaccato(a) ♦ *adv:* **to stand** ~ tenersi a distanza *or* in disparte

aloud [ə'laʊd] *adv* ad alta voce

alphabet ['ælfəbet] *n* alfabeto

alpine ['ælpaɪn] *adj* alpino(a)

Alps [ælps] *npl:* **the** ~ le Alpi

already [ɔːl'redɪ] *adv* già

alright ['ɔːl'raɪt] *(BRIT) adv* = **all right**

Alsatian [æl'seɪʃən] *(BRIT) n (dog)* pastore *m* tedesco, *(cane m)* lupo

also ['ɔːlsəʊ] *adv* anche

altar ['ɔltə*] *n* altare *m*

alter ['ɔltə*] *vt, vi* alterare

alternate [*adj* ɔl'təːnɪt, *vb* 'ɔltəːneɪt] *adj* alterno(a); *(US: plan etc)* alternativo(a) ♦ *vi:* **to** ~ **(with)** alternarsi (a); **on** ~ **days** ogni due giorni; **alternating** *adj (current)* alternato(a)

alternative [ɔl'təːnətɪv] *adj* alternativo(a) ♦ *n (choice)* alternativa; ~**ly** *adv:* ~**ly one could** ... come alternativa si potrebbe ...; ~ **medicine** *n* medicina alternativa

alternator ['ɔltəːneɪtə*] *n (AUT)* alternatore *m*

although [ɔːl'ðəʊ] *conj* benché +*sub*, sebbene +*sub*

altitude ['æltɪtjuːd] *n* altitudine *f*

alto ['æltəʊ] *n* contralto; *(male)* contraltino

altogether [ɔːltə'geðə*] *adv* del tutto, completamente; *(on the whole)* tutto considerato; (*in all*) in tutto

aluminium [ælju'mɪnɪəm] *n* alluminio

aluminum [ə'luːmɪnəm] (*US*) *n*
= **aluminium**

always ['ɔːlweɪz] *adv* sempre

Alzheimer's (disease) ['æltshaɪməz-] *n*
(malattia di) Alzheimer

am [æm] *vb see* **be**

a.m. *adv abbr* (= *ante meridiem*) della
mattina

amalgamate [ə'mælgəmeɪt] *vt*
amalgamare ♦ *vi* amalgamarsi

amateur ['æmətə*] *n* dilettante *m/f* ♦ *adj*
(*SPORT*) dilettante; **~ish** (*pej*) *adj* da
dilettante

amaze [ə'meɪz] *vt* stupire; **to be ~d** (**at**)
essere sbalordito (da); **~ment** *n* stupore
m; **amazing** *adj* sorprendente,
sbalorditivo(a)

ambassador [æm'bæsədə*] *n*
ambasciatore/trice

amber ['æmbə*] *n* ambra; **at ~** (*BRIT: AUT*)
giallo

ambiguous [æm'bɪgjuəs] *adj* ambiguo(a)

ambition [æm'bɪʃən] *n* ambizione *f*

ambitious [æm'bɪʃəs] *adj* ambizioso(a)

amble ['æmbl] *vi* (*gen: to ~ along*)
camminare tranquillamente

ambulance ['æmbjuləns] *n* ambulanza

ambush ['æmbuʃ] *n* imboscata ♦ *vt* fare
un'imboscata a

amenable [ə'miːnəbl] *adj*: **~ to** (*advice
etc*) ben disposto(a) a

amend [ə'mend] *vt* (*law*) emendare; (*text*)
correggere; **to make ~s** fare ammenda

amenities [ə'miːnɪtɪz] *npl* attrezzature
fpl ricreative e culturali

America [ə'merɪkə] *n* America; **~n** *adj, n*
americano(a)

amiable ['eɪmɪəbl] *adj* amabile, gentile

amicable ['æmɪkəbl] *adj* amichevole

amid(st) [ə'mɪd(st)] *prep* fra, tra, in
mezzo a

amiss [ə'mɪs] *adj, adv*: **there's
something ~** c'è qualcosa che non va
bene; **don't take it ~** non prendertela (a
male)

ammonia [ə'məunɪə] *n* ammoniaca

ammunition [æmju'nɪʃən] *n*

munizioni *fpl*

amok [ə'mɒk] *adv*: **to run ~** diventare
pazzo(a) furioso(a)

among(st) [ə'mʌŋ(st)] *prep* fra, tra, in
mezzo a

amorous ['æmərəs] *adj* amoroso(a)

amount [ə'maunt] *n* somma; ammontare
m; quantità *f inv* ♦ *vi*: **to ~ to** (*total*)
ammontare a; (*be same as*) essere come

amp(ère) ['æmp(eə*)] *n* ampère *m inv*

ample ['æmpl] *adj* ampio(a); spazioso(a);
(*enough*): **this is ~** questo è più che
sufficiente

amplifier ['æmplɪfaɪə*] *n* amplificatore *m*

amuck [ə'mʌk] *adv* = **amok**

amuse [ə'mjuːz] *vt* divertire; **~ment** *n*
divertimento; **~ment arcade** *n* sala
giochi

an [æn] *indef art see* **a**

anaemic [ə'niːmɪk] *adj* anemico(a)

anaesthetic [ænɪs'θetɪk] *adj*
anestetico(a) ♦ *n* anestetico

analog(ue) ['ænəlɒg] *adj* (*watch,
computer*) analogico(a)

analyse ['ænəlaɪz] (*BRIT*) *vt* analizzare

analyses [ə'næləsiːz] *npl of* **analysis**

analysis [ə'næləsɪs] (*pl* **analyses**) *n*
analisi *f inv*

analyst ['ænəlɪst] *n* (*POL etc*) analista *m/f*;
(*US*) (psic)analista *m/f*

analyze ['ænəlaɪz] (*US*) *vt* = **analyse**

anarchist ['ænəkɪst] *n* anarchico/a

anarchy ['ænəkɪ] *n* anarchia

anathema [ə'næθɪmə] *n*: **that is ~ to
him** non vuole nemmeno sentirne parlare

anatomy [ə'nætəmɪ] *n* anatomia

ancestor ['ænsɪstə*] *n* antenato/a

anchor ['æŋkə*] *n* ancora ♦ *vi* (*also: to
drop ~*) gettare l'ancora ♦ *vt* ancorare; **to
weigh ~** salpare *or* levare l'ancora

anchovy ['æntʃəvɪ] *n* acciuga

ancient ['eɪnʃənt] *adj* antico(a); (*person,
car*) vecchissimo(a)

ancillary [æn'sɪlərɪ] *adj* ausiliario(a)

and [ænd] *conj* e (*often* ed *before vowel*); **~
so on** e così via; **try ~ come** cerca di
venire; **he talked ~ talked** non la finiva
di parlare; **better ~ better** sempre meglio

anemic [ə'niːmɪk] (*US*) *adj* = **anaemic**

anesthetic [ænɪs'θetɪk] (*US*) *adj, n*
= **anaesthetic**
anew [ə'njuː] *adv* di nuovo
angel ['eɪndʒəl] *n* angelo
anger ['æŋgə*] *n* rabbia
angina [æn'dʒaɪnə] *n* angina pectoris
angle ['æŋgl] *n* angolo; **from their ~** dal
loro punto di vista
Anglican ['æŋglɪkən] *adj, n* anglicano(a)
angling ['æŋglɪŋ] *n* pesca con la lenza
Anglo- ['æŋgləʊ] *prefix* anglo....
angrily ['æŋgrɪlɪ] *adv* con rabbia
angry ['æŋgrɪ] *adj* arrabbiato(a),
furioso(a); (*wound*) infiammato(a); **to be ~
with sb/at sth** essere in collera con qn/
per qc; **to get ~** arrabbiarsi; **to make sb
~** fare arrabbiare qn
anguish ['æŋgwɪʃ] *n* angoscia
animal ['ænɪməl] *adj* animale ♦ *n*
animale *m*
animate ['ænɪmɪt] *adj* animato(a)
animated ['ænɪmeɪtɪd] *adj* animato(a)
aniseed ['ænɪsiːd] *n* semi *mpl* di anice
ankle ['æŋkl] *n* caviglia; **~ sock** *n* calzino
annex [*n* 'æneks, *vb* ə'neks] *n* (*also*: *BRIT*:
annexe) (edificio) annesso ♦ *vt* annettere
annihilate [ə'naɪəleɪt] *vt* annientare
anniversary [ænɪ'vəːsərɪ] *n* anniversario
announce [ə'naʊns] *vt* annunciare;
~ment *n* annuncio; (*letter, card*)
partecipazione *f*; **~r** *n* (*RADIO, TV*: *between
programmes*) annunciatore/ trice; (: *in a
programme*) presentatore/trice
annoy [ə'nɔɪ] *vt* dare fastidio a; **don't get
~ed!** non irritarti!; **~ance** *n* fastidio;
(*cause of ~ance*) noia; **~ing** *adj* noioso(a)
annual ['ænjuəl] *adj* annuale ♦ *n* (*BOT*)
pianta annua; (*book*) annuario
annul [ə'nʌl] *vt* annullare
annum ['ænəm] *n see* **per**
anonymous [ə'nɒnɪməs] *adj* anonimo(a)
anorak ['ænəræk] *n* giacca a vento
another [ə'nʌðə*] *adj*: **~ book** (*one more*)
un altro libro, ancora un libro; (*a
different one*) un altro libro ♦ *pron* un
altro(un'altra), ancora uno(a); *see also*
one
answer ['ɑːnsə*] *n* risposta; soluzione *f*
♦ *vi* rispondere ♦ *vt* (*reply to*) rispondere

a; (*problem*) risolvere; (*prayer*) esaudire;
in ~ to your letter in risposta alla sua
lettera; **to ~ the phone** rispondere (al
telefono); **to ~ the bell** rispondere al
campanello; **to ~ the door** aprire la
porta; **~ back** *vi* ribattere; **~ for** *vt fus*
essere responsabile di; **~ to** *vt fus*
(*description*) corrispondere a; **~able** *adj*:
~able (to sb/for sth) responsabile (verso
qn/di qc); **~ing machine** *n* segreteria
(telefonica) automatica
ant [ænt] *n* formica
antagonism [æn'tægənɪzəm] *n*
antagonismo
antagonize [æn'tægənaɪz] *vt* provocare
l'ostilità di
Antarctic [ænt'ɑːktɪk] *n*: **the ~**
l'Antartide *f*
antenatal ['æntɪ'neɪtl] *adj* prenatale; **~
clinic** *n* assistenza medica preparto
anthem ['ænθəm] *n*: **national ~** inno
nazionale
anthology [æn'θɒlədʒɪ] *n* antologia
antibiotic ['æntɪbaɪ'ɒtɪk] *n* antibiotico
antibody ['æntɪbɒdɪ] *n* anticorpo
anticipate [æn'tɪsɪpeɪt] *vt* prevedere;
pregustare; (*wishes, request*) prevenire
anticipation [æntɪsɪ'peɪʃən] *n*
anticipazione *f*; (*expectation*) aspettative
fpl
anticlimax ['æntɪ'klaɪmæks] *n*: **it was an
~** fu una completa delusione
anticlockwise ['æntɪ'klɒkwaɪz] *adj, adv*
in senso antiorario
antics ['æntɪks] *npl* buffonerie *fpl*
antifreeze ['æntɪ'friːz] *n* anticongelante
m
antihistamine [æntɪ'hɪstəmɪn] *n*
antistaminico
antiquated ['æntɪkweɪtɪd] *adj*
antiquato(a)
antique [æn'tiːk] *n* antichità *f inv* ♦ *adj*
antico(a); **~ dealer** *n* antiquario/a; **~
shop** *n* negozio d'antichità
antiquity [æn'tɪkwɪtɪ] *n* antichità *f inv*
anti-Semitism ['æntɪ'semɪtɪzəm] *n*
antisemitismo
antiseptic [æntɪ'septɪk] *n* antisettico
antisocial ['æntɪ'səʊʃəl] *adj* asociale

antlers ['æntləz] *npl* palchi *mpl*
anvil ['ænvɪl] *n* incudine *f*
anxiety [æŋ'zaɪətɪ] *n* ansia; *(keenness):* ~ **to do** smania di fare
anxious ['æŋkʃəs] *adj* ansioso(a), inquieto(a); *(worrying)* angosciante; *(keen):* ~ **to do/that** impaziente di fare/che +*sub*

KEYWORD

any ['ɛnɪ] *adj* **1** *(in questions etc):* **have you** ~ **butter?** hai del burro?, hai un po' di burro?; **have you** ~ **children?** hai bambini?; **if there are** ~ **tickets left** se ci sono ancora (dei) biglietti, se c'è ancora qualche biglietto
2 *(with negative):* **I haven't** ~ **money/books** non ho soldi/libri
3 *(no matter which)* qualsiasi, qualunque; **choose** ~ **book you like** scegli un libro qualsiasi
4 *(in phrases):* **in** ~ **case** in ogni caso; ~ **day now** da un giorno all'altro; **at** ~ **moment** in qualsiasi momento, da un momento all'altro; **at** ~ **rate** ad ogni modo
♦ *pron* **1** *(in questions, with negative):* **have you got** ~? ne hai?; **can** ~ **of you sing?** qualcuno di voi sa cantare?; **I haven't** ~ **(of them)** non ne ho
2 *(no matter which one(s)):* **take** ~ **of those books (you like)** prendi uno qualsiasi di quei libri
♦ *adv* **1** *(in questions etc):* **do you want** ~ **more soup/sandwiches?** vuoi ancora un po' di minestra/degli altri panini?; **are you feeling** ~ **better?** ti senti meglio?
2 *(with negative):* **I can't hear him** ~ **more** non lo sento più; **don't wait** ~ **longer** non aspettare più

anybody ['ɛnɪbɔdɪ] *pron (in questions etc)* qualcuno, nessuno; *(with negative)* nessuno; *(no matter who)* chiunque; **can you see** ~? vedi qualcuno *or* nessuno?; **if** ~ **should phone ...** se telefona qualcuno ...; **I can't see** ~ non vedo nessuno; ~ **could do it** chiunque potrebbe farlo
anyhow ['ɛnɪhaʊ] *adv (at any rate)* ad ogni modo, comunque; *(haphazard):* **do it** ~ **you like** fallo come ti pare; **I shall go** ~ ci andrò lo stesso *or* comunque; **she leaves things just** ~ lascia tutto come capita
anyone ['ɛnɪwʌn] *pron* = **anybody**
anything ['ɛnɪθɪŋ] *pron (in question etc)* qualcosa, niente; *(with negative)* niente; *(no matter what):* **you can say** ~ **you like** puoi dire quello che ti pare; **can you see** ~? vedi niente *or* qualcosa?; **if** ~ **happens to me ...** se mi dovesse succedere qualcosa ...; **I can't see** ~ non vedo niente; ~ **will do** va bene qualsiasi cosa *or* tutto
anyway ['ɛnɪweɪ] *adv (at any rate)* ad ogni modo, comunque; *(besides)* ad ogni modo
anywhere ['ɛnɪwɛə*] *adv (in questions etc)* da qualche parte; *(with negative)* da nessuna parte; *(no matter where)* da qualsiasi *or* qualunque parte, dovunque; **can you see him** ~? lo vedi da qualche parte?; **I can't see him** ~ non lo vedo da nessuna parte; ~ **in the world** dovunque nel mondo
apart [ə'pɑːt] *adv (to one side)* a parte; *(separately)* separatamente; **with one's legs** ~ con le gambe divaricate; **10 miles** ~ a 10 miglia di distanza (l'uno dall'altro); **to take** ~ smontare; ~ **from** a parte, eccetto
apartheid [ə'pɑːteɪt] *n* apartheid *f*
apartment [ə'pɑːtmənt] *n (US)* appartamento; *(room)* locale *m*; ~ **building** *(US)* n stabile *m*, caseggiato
apathetic [æpə'θɛtɪk] *adj* apatico(a)
ape [eɪp] *n* scimmia ♦ *vt* scimmiottare
apéritif [ə'pɛrɪtɪv] *n* aperitivo
aperture ['æpətjuə*] *n* apertura
apex ['eɪpɛks] *n* apice *m*
apiece [ə'piːs] *adv* ciascuno(a)
aplomb [ə'plɔm] *n* disinvoltura
apologetic [əpɔlə'dʒɛtɪk] *adj (tone, letter)* di scusa
apologize [ə'pɔlədʒaɪz] *vi:* **to** ~ **(for sth to sb)** scusarsi (di qc a qn), chiedere scusa (a qn per qc)
apology [ə'pɔlədʒɪ] *n* scuse *fpl*

apostle [əˈpɔsl] *n* apostolo
apostrophe [əˈpɔstrəfɪ] *n* (*sign*) apostrofo
appal [əˈpɔːl] *vt* scioccare; **~ling** *adj* spaventoso(a)
apparatus [æpəˈreɪtəs] *n* apparato; (*in gymnasium*) attrezzatura
apparel [əˈpærl] (*US*) *n* abbigliamento, confezioni *fpl*
apparent [əˈpærənt] *adj* evidente; **~ly** *adv* evidentemente
apparition [æpəˈrɪʃən] *n* apparizione *f*
appeal [əˈpiːl] *vi* (*LAW*) appellarsi alla legge ♦ *n* (*LAW*) appello; (*request*) richiesta; (*charm*) attrattiva; **to ~ for** chiedere (con insistenza); **to ~ to** (*subj: person*) appellarsi a; (*subj: thing*) piacere a; **it doesn't ~ to me** mi dice poco; **~ing** *adj* (*nice*) attraente
appear [əˈpɪə*] *vi* apparire; (*LAW*) comparire; (*publication*) essere pubblicato(a); (*seem*) sembrare; **it would ~ that** sembra che; **~ance** *n* apparizione *f*; apparenza; (*look, aspect*) aspetto
appease [əˈpiːz] *vt* calmare, appagare
appendices [əˈpɛndɪsiːz] *npl of* **appendix**
appendicitis [əpɛndɪˈsaɪtɪs] *n* appendicite *f*
appendix [əˈpɛndɪks] (*pl* **appendices**) *n* appendice *f*
appetite [ˈæpɪtaɪt] *n* appetito
appetizer [ˈæpɪtaɪzə*] *n* stuzzichino
applaud [əˈplɔːd] *vt, vi* applaudire
applause [əˈplɔːz] *n* applauso
apple [ˈæpl] *n* mela; **~ tree** *n* melo
appliance [əˈplaɪəns] *n* apparecchio
applicant [ˈæplɪkənt] *n* candidato/a
application [æplɪˈkeɪʃən] *n* applicazione *f*; (*for a job, a grant etc*) domanda; **~ form** *n* modulo per la domanda
applied [əˈplaɪd] *adj* applicato(a)
apply [əˈplaɪ] *vt*: **to ~ (to)** (*paint, ointment*) dare (a); (*theory, technique*) applicare (a) ♦ *vi*: **to ~ to** (*ask*) rivolgersi a; (*be suitable for, relevant to*) riguardare, riferirsi a; **to ~ (for)** (*permit, grant, job*) fare domanda (per); **to ~ o.s.** to dedicarsi a

appoint [əˈpɔɪnt] *vt* nominare; **~ed** *adj*: **at the ~ed time** all'ora stabilita; **~ment** *n* nomina; (*arrangement to meet*) appuntamento; **to make an ~ment (with)** prendere un appuntamento (con)
appraisal [əˈpreɪzl] *n* valutazione *f*
appreciate [əˈpriːʃɪeɪt] *vt* (*like*) apprezzare; (*be grateful for*) essere riconoscente di; (*be aware of*) rendersi conto di ♦ *vi* (*FINANCE*) aumentare
appreciation [əpriːʃɪˈeɪʃən] *n* apprezzamento; (*FINANCE*) aumento del valore
appreciative [əˈpriːʃɪətɪv] *adj* (*person*) sensibile; (*comment*) elogiativo(a)
apprehend [æprɪˈhɛnd] *vt* (*arrest*) arrestare
apprehension [æprɪˈhɛnʃən] *n* (*fear*) inquietudine *f*
apprehensive [æprɪˈhɛnsɪv] *adj* apprensivo(a)
apprentice [əˈprɛntɪs] *n* apprendista *m/f*; **~ship** *n* apprendistato
approach [əˈprəʊtʃ] *vi* avvicinarsi ♦ *vt* (*come near*) avvicinarsi a; (*ask, apply to*) rivolgersi a; (*subject, passer-by*) avvicinare ♦ *n* approccio; accesso; (*to problem*) modo di affrontare; **~able** *adj* accessibile
appropriate [*adj* əˈprəʊprɪɪt, *vb* əˈprəʊprɪeɪt] *adj* appropriato(a); adatto(a) ♦ *vt* (*take*) appropriarsi
approval [əˈpruːvəl] *n* approvazione *f*; **on ~** (*COMM*) in prova, in esame
approve [əˈpruːv] *vt, vi* approvare; **~ of** *vt fus* approvare
approximate [əˈprɔksɪmɪt] *adj* approssimativo(a); **~ly** *adv* circa
apricot [ˈeɪprɪkɔt] *n* albicocca
April [ˈeɪprəl] *n* aprile *m*; **~ fool!** pesce d'aprile!
apron [ˈeɪprən] *n* grembiule *m*
apt [æpt] *adj* (*suitable*) adatto(a); (*able*) capace; (*likely*): **to be ~ to do** avere tendenza a fare
aptitude [ˈæptɪtjuːd] *n* abilità *f inv*
aquarium [əˈkwɛərɪəm] *n* acquario
Aquarius [əˈkwɛərɪəs] *n* Acquario
Arab [ˈærəb] *adj, n* arabo(a)

Arabian [əˈreɪbɪən] *adj* arabo(a)

Arabic [ˈærəbɪk] *adj* arabico/a, arabo(a)
♦ *n* arabo; **~ numerals** numeri *mpl*
arabi, numerazione *f* araba

arbitrary [ˈɑːbɪtrərɪ] *adj* arbitrario(a)

arbitration [ɑːbɪˈtreɪʃən] *n* (*LAW*)
arbitrato; (*INDUSTRY*) arbitraggio

arcade [ɑːˈkeɪd] *n* portico; (*passage with shops*) galleria

arch [ɑːtʃ] *n* arco; (*of foot*) arco plantare
♦ *vt* inarcare

archaeologist [ɑːkɪˈɔlədʒɪst] *n*
archeologo/a

archaeology [ɑːkɪˈɔlədʒɪ] *n* archeologia

archbishop [ɑːtʃˈbɪʃəp] *n* arcivescovo

arch-enemy *n* arcinemico/a

archeology [ɑːkɪˈɔlədʒɪ] *etc* (*US*)
= **archaeology** *etc*

archery [ˈɑːtʃərɪ] *n* tiro all'arco

architect [ˈɑːkɪtekt] *n* architetto; **~ure**
[ˈɑːkɪtektʃə*] *n* architettura

archives [ˈɑːkaɪvz] *npl* archivi *mpl*

Arctic [ˈɑːktɪk] *adj* artico(a) ♦ *n*: **the ~**
l'Artico

ardent [ˈɑːdənt] *adj* ardente

are [ɑː*] *vb see* **be**

area [ˈɛərɪə] *n* (*GEOM*) area; (*zone*) zona;
(: *smaller*) settore *m*

aren't [ɑːnt] = **are not**

Argentina [ɑːdʒənˈtiːnə] *n* Argentina;
Argentinian [-ˈtɪnɪən] *adj*, *n* argentino(a)

arguably [ˈɑːgjuəblɪ] *adv*: **it is ~ ...** si
può sostenere che sia ....

argue [ˈɑːgjuː] *vi* (*quarrel*) litigare;
(*reason*) ragionare; **to ~ that** sostenere
che

argument [ˈɑːgjumənt] *n* (*reasons*)
argomento; (*quarrel*) lite *f*; **~ative**
[ɑːgjuˈmentətɪv] *adj* litigioso(a)

Aries [ˈɛərɪz] *n* Ariete *m*

arise [əˈraɪz] (*pt* **arose**, *pp* **arisen**) *vi*
(*opportunity, problem*) presentarsi; **arisen**
[əˈrɪzn] *pp of* **arise**

aristocrat [ˈærɪstəkræt] *n* aristocratico/a

arithmetic [əˈrɪθmətɪk] *n* aritmetica

ark [ɑːk] *n*: **Noah's A~** l'arca di Noè

arm [ɑːm] *n* braccio ♦ *vt* armare; **~s** *npl*
(*weapons*) armi *fpl*; **~ in ~** a braccetto

armaments [ˈɑːməmənts] *npl* armamenti

mpl

arm: **~chair** *n* poltrona; **~ed** *adj*
armato(a); **~ed robbery** *n* rapina a mano
armata

armour [ˈɑːmə*] (*US* **armor**) *n* armatura;
(*MIL*: *tanks*) mezzi *mpl* blindati; **~ed car** *n*
autoblinda *f inv*

armpit [ˈɑːmpɪt] *n* ascella

armrest [ˈɑːmrest] *n* bracciolo

army [ˈɑːmɪ] *n* esercito

aroma [əˈrəumə] *n* aroma; **~therapy** *n*
aromaterapia

arose [əˈrəuz] *pt of* **arise**

around [əˈraund] *adv* attorno, intorno
♦ *prep* intorno a; (*fig*: *about*): ~ **£5/3
o'clock** circa 5 sterline/le 3; **is he ~?** è in
giro?

arouse [əˈrauz] *vt* (*sleeper*) svegliare;
(*curiosity, passions*) suscitare

arrange [əˈreɪndʒ] *vt* sistemare;
(*programme*) preparare; **to ~ to do sth**
mettersi d'accordo per fare qc; **~ment** *n*
sistemazione *f*; (*agreement*) accordo;
~ments *npl* (*plans*) progetti *mpl*, piani
mpl

array [əˈreɪ] *n*: ~ **of** fila di

arrears [əˈrɪəz] *npl* arretrati *mpl*; **to be
in ~ with one's rent** essere in arretrato
con l'affitto

arrest [əˈrest] *vt* arrestare; (*sb's attention*)
attirare ♦ *n* arresto; **under ~** in arresto

arrival [əˈraɪvəl] *n* arrivo; (*person*)
arrivato/a; **a new ~** un nuovo venuto;
(*baby*) un neonato

arrive [əˈraɪv] *vi* arrivare

arrogant [ˈærəgənt] *adj* arrogante

arrow [ˈærəu] *n* freccia

arse [ɑːs] (*inf!*) *n* culo (!)

arson [ˈɑːsn] *n* incendio doloso

art [ɑːt] *n* arte *f*; (*craft*) mestiere *m*; **A~s**
npl (*SCOL*) Lettere *fpl*

artefact [ˈɑːtɪfækt] *n* manufatto

artery [ˈɑːtərɪ] *n* arteria

artful [ˈɑːtful] *adj* abile

art gallery *n* galleria d'arte

arthritis [ɑːˈθraɪtɪs] *n* artrite *f*

artichoke [ˈɑːtɪtʃəuk] *n* carciofo;
Jerusalem ~ topinambur *m inv*

article [ˈɑːtɪkl] *n* articolo; **~s** *npl* (*BRIT*:

LAW: *training*) contratto di tirocinio; ~ **of clothing** capo di vestiario

articulate [*adj* ɑ:'tɪkjulɪt, *vb* ɑ:'tɪkjuleɪt] *adj* (*person*) che si esprime forbitamente; (*speech*) articolato(a) ♦ *vi* articolare; **~d lorry** (*BRIT*) *n* autotreno

artificial [ɑ:tɪ'fɪʃəl] *adj* artificiale; **~ respiration** *n* respirazione *f* artificiale

artillery [ɑ:'tɪlərɪ] *n* artiglieria

artisan ['ɑ:tɪzæn] *n* artigiano/a

artist ['ɑ:tɪst] *n* artista *m/f*; **~ic** [ɑ:'tɪstɪk] *adj* artistico(a); **~ry** *n* arte *f*

artless ['ɑ:tlɪs] *adj* semplice, ingenuo(a)

art school *n* scuola d'arte

KEYWORD

as [æz] *conj* 1 (*referring to time*) mentre; ~ **the years went by** col passare degli anni; **he came in** ~ **I was leaving** arrivò mentre stavo uscendo; ~ **from tomorrow** da domani

2 (*in comparisons*): ~ **big** ~ grande come; **twice** ~ **big** ~ due volte più grande di; ~ **much/many** ~ tanto quanto/tanti quanti; ~ **soon** ~ **possible** prima possibile

3 (*since, because*) dal momento che, siccome

4 (*referring to manner, way*) come; **do** ~ **you wish** fa' come vuoi; ~ **she said** come ha detto lei

5 (*concerning*): ~ **for** *or* **to that** per quanto riguarda *or* quanto a quello

6: ~ **if** *or* **though** come se; **he looked** ~ **if he was ill** sembrava stare male; *see also* **long; such; well**

♦ *prep*: **he works** ~ **a driver** fa l'autista; ~ **chairman of the company, he** ... come presidente della compagnia, lui ...; **he gave me it** ~ **a present** me lo ha regalato

---

a.s.a.p. *abbr* = **as soon as possible**

ascend [ə'sɛnd] *vt* salire; **~ancy** *n* ascendente *m*

ascent [ə'sɛnt] *n* salita; (*of mountain*) ascensione *f*

ascertain [æsə'teɪn] *vt* accertare

ascribe [ə'skraɪb] *vt*: **to** ~ **sth to** attribuire qc a

ash [æʃ] *n* (*dust*) cenere *f*; (*wood, tree*) frassino

ashamed [ə'ʃeɪmd] *adj* vergognoso(a); **to be** ~ **of** vergognarsi di

ashen ['æʃn] *adj* (*pale*) livido(a)

ashore [ə'ʃɔ:*] *adv* a terra

ashtray ['æʃtreɪ] *n* portacenere *m*

Ash Wednesday *n* mercoledì *m inv* delle Ceneri

Asia ['eɪʃə] *n* Asia; **~n** *adj, n* asiatico(a)

aside [ə'saɪd] *adv* da parte ♦ *n* a parte *m*

ask [ɑ:sk] *vt* (*question*) domandare; (*invite*) invitare; **to** ~ **sb sth/sb to do sth** chiedere qc a qn/a qn di fare qc; **to** ~ **sb about sth** chiedere a qn di qc; **to** ~ **(sb) a question** fare una domanda (a qn); **to** ~ **sb out to dinner** invitare qn a mangiare fuori; ~ **after** *vt fus* chiedere di; ~ **for** *vt fus* chiedere; (*trouble etc*) cercare

askance [ə'skɑ:ns] *adv*: **to look** ~ **at sb** guardare qn di traverso

askew [ə'skju:] *adv* di traverso, storto

asleep [ə'sli:p] *adj* addormentato(a); **to be** ~ dormire; **to fall** ~ addormentarsi

asparagus [əs'pærəgəs] *n* asparagi *mpl*

aspect ['æspɛkt] *n* aspetto

aspersions [əs'pə:ʃənz] *npl*: **to cast** ~ **on** diffamare

asphyxiation [æsfɪksɪ'eɪʃən] *n* asfissia

aspire [əs'paɪə*] *vi*: **to** ~ **to** aspirare a

aspirin ['æsprɪn] *n* aspirina

ass [æs] *n* asino; (*inf*) scemo/a; (*US: inf!*) culo (*!*)

assailant [ə'seɪlənt] *n* assalitore *m*

assassinate [ə'sæsɪneɪt] *vt* assassinare; **assassination** [əsæsɪ'neɪʃən] *n* assassinio

assault [ə'sɔ:lt] *n* (*MIL*) assalto; (*gen: attack*) aggressione *f* ♦ *vt* assaltare; aggredire; (*sexually*) violentare

assemble [ə'sɛmbl] *vt* riunire; (*TECH*) montare ♦ *vi* riunirsi

assembly [ə'sɛmblɪ] *n* (*meeting*) assemblea; (*construction*) montaggio; ~ **line** *n* catena di montaggio

assent [ə'sɛnt] *n* assenso, consenso

assert [ə'sə:t] *vt* asserire; (*insist on*) far valere

assess [ə'sɛs] *vt* valutare; **~ment** *n*

valutazione *f*

asset ['æset] *n* vantaggio; ~s *npl* (FINANCE: *of individual*) beni *mpl*; (: *of company*) attivo

assign [ə'saɪn] *vt:* **to ~ (to)** (*task*) assegnare (a); (*resources*) riservare (a); (*cause, meaning*) attribuire (a); **to ~ a date to sth** fissare la data di qc; ~**ment** *n* compito

assist [ə'sɪst] *vt* assistere, aiutare; ~**ance** *n* assistenza, aiuto; ~**ant** *n* assistente *m/f*; (BRIT: *also: shop* ~*ant*) commesso/a

associate [*adj, n* ə'səʊʃɪɪt, *vb* ə'səʊʃɪeɪt] *adj* associato(a); (*member*) aggiunto(a) ♦ *n* collega *m/f* ♦ *vt* associare ♦ *vi:* **to ~ with sb** frequentare qn

association [əsəʊsɪ'eɪʃən] *n* associazione *f*

assorted [ə'sɔːtɪd] *adj* assortito(a)

assortment [ə'sɔːtmənt] *n* assortimento

assume [ə'sjuːm] *vt* supporre; (*responsibilities etc*) assumere; (*attitude, name*) prendere; ~**d name** *n* nome *m* falso

assumption [ə'sʌmpʃən] *n* supposizione *f*, ipotesi *f inv*; (*of power*) assunzione *f*

assurance [ə'ʃʊərəns] *n* assicurazione *f*; (*self-confidence*) fiducia in se stesso

assure [ə'ʃʊə*] *vt* assicurare

asthma ['æsmə] *n* asma

astonish [ə'stɒnɪʃ] *vt* stupire; ~**ment** *n* stupore *m*

astound [ə'staʊnd] *vt* sbalordire

astray [ə'streɪ] *adv:* **to go ~** smarrirsi; **to lead ~** portare sulla cattiva strada

astride [ə'straɪd] *prep* a cavalcioni di

astrology [əs'trɒlədʒɪ] *n* astrologia

astronaut ['æstrənɔːt] *n* astronauta *m/f*

astronomy [əs'trɒnəmɪ] *n* astronomia

astute [əs'tjuːt] *adj* astuto(a)

asylum [ə'saɪləm] *n* asilo; (*building*) manicomio

KEYWORD

---

at [æt] *prep* **1** (*referring to position, direction*) a; ~ **the top** in cima; ~ **the desk** al banco, alla scrivania; ~ **home/ school** a casa/scuola; ~ **the baker's** dal panettiere; **to look ~ sth** guardare qc; **to**

throw sth ~ sb lanciare qc a qn

2 (*referring to time*) a; ~ **4 o'clock** alle 4; ~ **night** di notte; ~ **Christmas** a Natale; ~ **times** a volte

3 (*referring to rates, speed etc*) a; ~ **£1 a kilo** a 1 sterlina al chilo; **two ~ a time** due alla volta, due per volta; ~ **50 km/h** a 50 km/h

4 (*referring to manner*): ~ **a stroke** d'un solo colpo; ~ **peace** in pace

5 (*referring to activity*): **to be ~ work** essere al lavoro; **to play ~ cowboys** giocare ai cowboy; **to be good ~ sth/ doing sth** essere bravo in qc/a fare qc

6 (*referring to cause*): **shocked/ surprised/annoyed ~ sth** colpito da/ sorpreso da/arrabbiato per qc; **I went ~ his suggestion** ci sono andato dietro suo consiglio

---

ate [eɪt] *pt of* eat

atheist ['eɪθɪɪst] *n* ateo/a

Athens ['æθɪnz] *n* Atene *f*

athlete ['æθliːt] *n* atleta *m/f*

athletic [æθ'letɪk] *adj* atletico(a); ~**s** *n* atletica

Atlantic [ət'læntɪk] *adj* atlantico(a) ♦ *n:* **the ~ (Ocean)** l'Atlantico, l'Oceano Atlantico

atlas ['ætləs] *n* atlante *m*

atmosphere ['ætməsfɪə*] *n* atmosfera

atom ['ætəm] *n* atomo; ~**ic** [ə'tɒmɪk] *adj* atomico(a); ~**(ic) bomb** *n* bomba atomica; ~**izer** ['ætəmaɪzə*] *n* atomizzatore *m*

atone [ə'təʊn] *vi:* **to ~ for** espiare

atrocious [ə'trəʊʃəs] *adj* pessimo(a), atroce

attach [ə'tætʃ] *vt* attaccare; (*document, letter*) allegare; (*importance etc*) attribuire; **to be ~ed to sb/sth** (*to like*) essere affezionato(a) a qn/qc

attaché case [ə'tæʃeɪ-] *n* valigetta per documenti

attachment [ə'tætʃmənt] *n* (*tool*) accessorio; (*love*): ~ **(to)** affetto (per)

attack [ə'tæk] *vt* attaccare; (*person*) aggredire; (*task etc*) iniziare; (*problem*) affrontare ♦ *n* attacco; **heart ~** infarto;

~er *n* aggressore *m*

attain [ə'teɪn] *vt* (*also: to ~ to*) arrivare a, raggiungere; ~ments *npl* cognizioni *fpl*

attempt [ə'tɛmpt] *n* tentativo ♦ *vt* tentare; **to make an ~ on sb's life** attentare alla vita di qn

attend [ə'tɛnd] *vt* frequentare; (*meeting, talk*) andare a; (*patient*) assistere; ~ **to** *vt fus* (*needs, affairs etc*) prendersi cura di; (*customer*) occuparsi di; ~ance *n* (*being present*) presenza; (*people present*) gente *f* presente; ~ant *n* custode *m/f*; persona di servizio ♦ *adj* concomitante

attention [ə'tɛnʃən] *n* attenzione *f* ♦ *excl* (*MIL*) attenti!; **for the ~ of** (*ADMIN*) per l'attenzione di

attentive [ə'tɛntɪv] *adj* attento(a); (*kind*) premuroso(a)

attic ['ætɪk] *n* soffitta

attitude ['ætɪtjuːd] *n* atteggiamento; posa

attorney [ə'təːnɪ] *n* (*lawyer*) avvocato; (*having proxy*) mandatario; **A~ General** *n* (*BRIT*) Procuratore *m* Generale; (*US*) Ministro della Giustizia

attract [ə'trækt] *vt* attirare; ~ion [ə'trækʃən] *n* (*gen pl: pleasant things*) attrattiva; (*PHYSICS, fig: towards sth*) attrazione *f*; ~ive *adj* attraente

attribute [*n* 'ætrɪbjuːt, *vb* ə'trɪbjuːt] *n* attributo ♦ *vt*: **to ~ sth to** attribuire qc a

attrition [ə'trɪʃən] *n*: **war of ~** guerra di logoramento

aubergine ['əʊbəʒiːn] *n* melanzana

auburn ['ɔːbən] *adj* tizianesco(a)

auction ['ɔːkʃən] *n* (*also: sale by ~*) asta ♦ *vt* (*also: to sell by ~*) vendere all'asta; (*also: to put up for ~*) mettere all'asta; ~eer [-'nɪə*] *n* banditore *m*

audible ['ɔːdɪbl] *adj* udibile

audience ['ɔːdɪəns] *n* (*people*) pubblico *m*; spettatori *mpl*; ascoltatori *mpl*; (*interview*) udienza

audio-typist ['ɔːdɪəʊ'taɪpɪst] *n* dattilografo/a che trascrive da nastro

audio-visual [ɔːdɪəʊ'vɪzjuəl] *adj* audiovisivo(a); ~ **aid** *n* sussidio audiovisivo

audit ['ɔːdɪt] *vt* rivedere, verificare

audition [ɔː'dɪʃən] *n* audizione *f*

auditor ['ɔːdɪtə*] *n* revisore *m*

augment [ɔːg'mɛnt] *vt, vi* aumentare

augur ['ɔːgə*] *vi*: **it ~s well** promette bene

August ['ɔːgəst] *n* agosto

aunt [ɑːnt] *n* zia; ~ie *n* zietta; ~y *n* zietta

au pair ['əʊ'pɛə*] *n* (*also: ~ girl*) (ragazza *f*) alla pari *inv*

aura ['ɔːrə] *n* aura

auspicious [ɔːs'pɪʃəs] *adj* propizio(a)

austerity [ɔs'tɛrɪtɪ] *n* austerità

Australia [ɔs'treɪlɪə] *n* Australia; ~n *adj*, *n* australiano(a)

Austria ['ɒstrɪə] *n* Austria; ~n *adj*, *n* austriaco(a)

authentic [ɔː'θɛntɪk] *adj* autentico(a)

author ['ɔːθə*] *n* autore/trice

authoritarian [ɔːθɔrɪ'tɛərɪən] *adj* autoritario(a)

authoritative [ɔː'θɔrɪtətɪv] *adj* (*account etc*) autorevole; (*manner*) autoritario(a)

authority [ɔː'θɔrɪtɪ] *n* autorità *f inv*; (*permission*) autorizzazione *f*; **the authorities** *npl* (*government etc*) le autorità

authorize ['ɔːθəraɪz] *vt* autorizzare

auto ['ɔːtəʊ] (*US*) *n* auto *f inv*

autobiography [ɔːtəbaɪ'ɔgrəfɪ] *n* autobiografia

autograph ['ɔːtəgrɑːf] *n* autografo ♦ *vt* firmare

automata [ɔː'tɔmətə] *npl of* **automaton**

automatic [ɔːtə'mætɪk] *adj* automatico(a) ♦ *n* (*gun*) arma automatica; (*washing machine*) lavatrice *f* automatica; (*car*) automobile *f* con cambio automatico; ~ally *adv* automaticamente

automation [ɔːtə'meɪʃən] *n* automazione *f*

automaton [ɔː'tɔmətən] (*pl* **automata**) *n* automa *m*

automobile ['ɔːtəməbiːl] (*US*) *n* automobile *f*

autonomy [ɔː'tɔnəmɪ] *n* autonomia

autumn ['ɔːtəm] *n* autunno

auxiliary [ɔːg'zɪlɪərɪ] *adj* ausiliario(a) ♦ *n* ausiliare *m/f*

Av. *abbr* = **avenue**

avail [ə'veɪl] *vt*: **to ~ o.s. of** servirsi di;

approfittarsi di ♦ *n*: **to no** ~ inutilmente
available [ə'veɪləbl] *adj* disponibile
avalanche ['ævəlɑːnʃ] *n* valanga
avant-garde ['ævãŋ'gɑːd] *adj* d'avanguardia
Ave. *abbr* = **avenue**
avenge [ə'vɛndʒ] *vt* vendicare
avenue ['ævənjuː] *n* viale *m*; (*fig*) strada, via
average ['ævərɪdʒ] *n* media ♦ *adj* medio(a) ♦ *vt* (*a certain figure*) fare di *or* in media; **on** ~ in media; ~ **out** *vi*: **to** ~ **out at** aggirarsi in media su, essere in media di
averse [ə'vɜːs] *adj*: **to be** ~ **to sth/doing** essere contrario a qc/a fare
avert [ə'vɜːt] *vt* evitare, prevenire; (*one's eyes*) distogliere
aviary ['eɪvɪərɪ] *n* voliera, uccelliera
avid ['ævɪd] *adj* (*supporter etc*) accanito(a)
avocado [ævə'kɑːdəʊ] *n* (*also: BRIT:* ~ *pear*) avocado *m inv*
avoid [ə'vɔɪd] *vt* evitare
avuncular [ə'vʌŋkjʊlə*] *adj* paterno(a)
await [ə'weɪt] *vt* aspettare
awake [ə'weɪk] (*pt* **awoke**, *pp* **awoken**, **awaked**) *adj* sveglio(a) ♦ *vt* svegliare ♦ *vi* svegliarsi; ~**ning** [ə'weɪknɪŋ] *n* risveglio
award [ə'wɔːd] *n* premio; (*LAW*) risarcimento ♦ *vt* assegnare; (*LAW: damages*) accordare
aware [ə'weə*] *adj*: ~ **of** (*conscious*) conscio(a) di; (*informed*) informato(a) di; **to become** ~ **of** accorgersi di; ~**ness** *n* consapevolezza
awash [ə'wɔʃ] *adj*: ~ (**with**) inondato(a) (da)
away [ə'weɪ] *adj*, *adv* via; lontano(a); **two kilometres** ~ a due chilometri di distanza; **two hours** ~ **by car** a due ore di distanza in macchina; **the holiday was two weeks** ~ mancavano due settimane alle vacanze; **he's** ~ **for a week** è andato via per una settimana; **to take** ~ togliere; **he was working/ pedalling** *etc* ~ *la particella indica la continuità e l'energia dell'azione*: lavorava/pedalava *etc* più che poteva; **to fade/wither** *etc* ~ *la particella rinforza*

l'idea della diminuzione; ~ **game** *n* (*SPORT*) partita fuori casa
awe [ɔː] *n* timore *m*; ~**-inspiring** imponente; ~**some** *adj* imponente
awful ['ɔːfəl] *adj* terribile; **an** ~ **lot of** un mucchio di; ~**ly** *adv* (*very*) terribilmente
awhile [ə'waɪl] *adv* (per) un po'
awkward ['ɔːkwəd] *adj* (*clumsy*) goffo(a); (*inconvenient*) scomodo(a); (*embarrassing*) imbarazzante
awning ['ɔːnɪŋ] *n* (*of shop, hotel etc*) tenda
awoke [ə'wəʊk] *pt of* **awake**
awoken [ə'wəʊkn] *pp of* **awake**
awry [ə'raɪ] *adv* di traverso; **to go** ~ andare a monte
axe [æks] (*US* **ax**) *n* scure *f* ♦ *vt* (*project etc*) abolire; (*jobs*) sopprimere
axes ['æksiːz] *npl of* **axis**
axis ['æksɪs] (*pl* **axes**) *n* asse *m*
axle ['æksl] *n* (*also:* ~-*tree*) asse *m*
ay(e) [aɪ] *excl* (*yes*) sì

B

B [biː] *n* (*MUS*) si *m*
B.A. *n abbr* = **Bachelor of Arts**
babble ['bæbl] *vi* (*person, voices*) farfugliare; (*brook*) gorgogliare
baby ['beɪbɪ] *n* bambino/a; ~ **carriage** (*US*) *n* carrozzina; ~-**sit** *vi* fare il (*or* la) babysitter; ~-**sitter** *n* baby-sitter *m/f inv*
bachelor ['bætʃələ*] *n* scapolo; **B~ of Arts/Science** ≈ laureato/a in lettere/ scienze
back [bæk] *n* (*of person, horse*) dorso, schiena; (*as opposed to front*) dietro; (*of hand*) dorso; (*of train*) coda; (*of chair*) schienale *m*; (*of page*) rovescio; (*of book*) retro; (*FOOTBALL*) difensore *m* ♦ *vt* (*candidate: also:* ~ *up*) appoggiare; (*horse: at races*) puntare su; (*car*) guidare a marcia indietro ♦ *vi* indietreggiare; (*car etc*) fare marcia indietro ♦ *cpd* posteriore, di dietro; (*AUT: seat, wheels*) posteriore ♦ *adv* (*not forward*) indietro; (*returned*): **he's** ~ è tornato; **he ran** ~ tornò indietro di corsa; (*restitution*): **throw the ball** ~

ritira la palla; **can I have it ~?** posso riaverlo?; *(again)*: **he called** = ha richiamato; **~ down** *vi* fare marcia indietro; **~ out** *vi (of promise)* tirarsi indietro; **~ up** *vt (support)* appoggiare, sostenere; *(COMPUT)* fare una copia di riserva di; **~bencher** *(BRIT) n membro del Parlamento senza potere amministrativo*; **~bone** *n* spina dorsale; **~cloth** *n* scena di sfondo; **~date** *vt (letter)* retrodatare; **~dated pay rise** aumento retroattivo; **~drop** *n* = **~cloth**; **~fire** *vi (AUT)* dar ritorni di fiamma; *(plans)* fallire; **~ground** *n* sfondo; *(of events)* background *m inv*; *(basic knowledge)* base *f*; *(experience)* esperienza; **family ~ground** ambiente *m* familiare; **~hand** *n (TENNIS: also: ~hand stroke)* rovescio; **~handed** *adj (fig)* ambiguo(a); **~hander** *(BRIT) n (bribe)* bustarella; **~ing** *n (fig)* appoggio; **~lash** *n* contraccolpo, ripercussione *f*; **~log** *n:* **~log of work** lavoro arretrato; **~ number** *n (of magazine etc)* numero arretrato; **~pack** *n* zaino; **~ pay** *n* arretrato di paga; **~ payments** *npl* arretrati *mpl*; **~side** *(inf) n* sedere *m*; **~stage** *adv* nel retroscena; **~stroke** *n* nuoto sul dorso; **~up** *adj (train, plane)* supplementare; *(COMPUT)* di riserva ♦ *n (support)* appoggio, sostegno; *(also: ~up file)* file *m inv* di riserva; **~ward** *adj (movement)* indietro *inv*; *(person)* tardivo(a); *(country)* arretrato(a); **~wards** *adv* indietro; *(fall, walk)* all'indietro; **~water** *n (fig)* posto morto; **~yard** *n* cortile *m* dietro la casa

bacon ['beɪkən] *n* pancetta
bad [bæd] *adj* cattivo(a); *(accident, injury)* brutto(a); *(meat, food)* andato(a) a male; **his ~ leg** la sua gamba malata; **to go ~** andare a male
bade [bæd] *pt of* **bid**
badge [bædʒ] *n* insegna; *(of policeman)* stemma *m*
badger ['bædʒə*] *n* tasso
badly ['bædlɪ] *adv (work, dress etc)* male; **~ wounded** gravemente ferito; **he needs it ~** ne ha un gran bisogno; **~ off** *adj* povero(a)

badminton ['bædmɪntən] *n* badminton *m*
bad-tempered ['bæd'tempəd] *adj* irritabile; di malumore
baffle ['bæfl] *vt (puzzle)* confondere
bag [bæg] *n* sacco; *(handbag etc)* borsa; **~s of** *(inf: lots of)* un sacco di; **~gage** *n* bagagli *mpl*; **~gy** *adj* largo(a), sformato(a); **~pipes** *npl* cornamusa
bail [beɪl] *n* cauzione *f* ♦ *vt (prisoner: also: grant ~ to)* concedere la libertà provvisoria su cauzione a; *(boat: also: ~ out)* aggottare; **on ~** in libertà provvisoria su cauzione; **~ out** *vt (prisoner)* ottenere la libertà provvisoria su cauzione di; *see also* **bale**
bailiff ['beɪlɪf] *n (LAW: BRIT)* ufficiale *m* giudiziario; *(: US)* usciere *m*
bait [beɪt] *n* esca ♦ *vt (hook)* innescare; *(trap)* munire di esca; *(fig)* tormentare
bake [beɪk] *vt* cuocere al forno ♦ *vi* cuocersi al forno; **~d beans** *npl* fagioli *mpl* in salsa di pomodoro; **~r** *n* fornaio/a, panettiere/a; **~ry** *n* panetteria; **baking** *n* cottura (al forno); **baking powder** *n* lievito in polvere
balance ['bæləns] *n* equilibrio; *(COMM: sum)* bilancio; *(remainder)* resto; *(scales)* bilancia ♦ *vt* tenere in equilibrio; *(budget)* far quadrare; *(account)* pareggiare; *(compensate)* contrappesare; **~ of trade/ payments** bilancia commerciale/dei pagamenti; **~d** *adj (personality, diet)* equilibrato(a); **~ sheet** *n* bilancio
balcony ['bælkənɪ] *n* balcone *m*; *(in theatre)* balconata
bald [bɔːld] *adj* calvo(a); *(tyre)* liscio(a)
bale [beɪl] *n* balla; **~ out** *vi (of a plane)* gettarsi col paracadute
baleful ['beɪlful] *adj* funesto(a)
ball [bɔːl] *n* palla; *(football)* pallone *m*; *(for golf)* pallina; *(of wool, string)* gomitolo; *(dance)* ballo; **to play ~** *(fig)* stare al gioco
ballast ['bæləst] *n* zavorra
ball bearings *npl* cuscinetti a sfere
ballerina [bælə'riːnə] *n* ballerina
ballet ['bæleɪ] *n* balletto; **~ dancer** *n* ballerino(a) classico(a)
balloon [bə'luːn] *n* pallone *m*

ballot paper ['bælət-] *n* scheda
ball-point pen *n* penna a sfera
ballroom ['bɔːlrum] *n* sala da ballo
balm [baːm] *n* balsamo
ban [bæn] *n* interdizione *f* ♦ *vt* interdire
banana [bə'naːnə] *n* banana
band [bænd] *n* banda; (*at a dance*) orchestra; (*MIL*) fanfara; ~ **together** *vi* collegarsi
bandage ['bændɪdʒ] *n* benda, fascia
bandaid ['bændeɪd] ® (*US*) *n* cerotto
bandwagon ['bændwægən] *n*: **to jump on the** ~ (*fig*) seguire la corrente
bandy ['bændɪ] *vt* (*jokes, insults*) scambiare
bandy-legged [-'lɛgɪd] *adj* dalle gambe storte
bang [bæŋ] *n* (*of door*) lo sbattere; (*of gun, blow*) colpo ♦ *vt* battere (violentemente); (*door*) sbattere ♦ *vi* scoppiare; sbattere
Bangladesh [baːŋglə'dɛʃ] *n* Bangladesh *m*
bangle ['bæŋgl] *n* braccialetto
bangs [bæŋz] (*US*) *npl* (*fringe*) frangia, frangetta
banish ['bænɪʃ] *vt* bandire
banister(s) ['bænɪstə(z)] *n(pl)* ringhiera
bank [bæŋk] *n* banca, banco; (*of river, lake*) riva, sponda; (*of earth*) banco ♦ *vi* (*AVIAT*) inclinarsi in virata; ~ **on** *vt fus* contare su; ~ **account** *n* conto in banca; ~ **card** *n* carta *f* assegni *inv*; ~**er** *n* banchiere *m*; ~**er's card** (*BRIT*) *n* = ~ **card**; **B**~ **holiday** (*BRIT*) *n* giorno di festa (*in cui le banche sono chiuse*); ~**ing** *n* attività bancaria; professione *f* di banchiere; ~**note** *n* banconota; ~ **rate** *n* tasso bancario
bankrupt ['bæŋkrʌpt] *adj* fallito(a); **to go** ~ fallire; ~**cy** *n* fallimento
bank statement *n* estratto conto
banner ['bænə*] *n* striscione *m*
banns [bænz] *npl* pubblicazioni *fpl* di matrimonio
baptism ['bæptɪzəm] *n* battesimo
bar [baː*] *n* (*place*) bar *m inv*; (*counter*) banco; (*rod*) barra; (*of window etc*) sbarra; (*of chocolate*) tavoletta; (*fig*) ostacolo;

restrizione *f*; (*MUS*) battuta ♦ *vt* (*road, window*) sbarrare; (*person*) escludere; (*activity*) interdire; ~ **of soap** saponetta; **the B**~ (*LAW*) l'Ordine *m* degli avvocati; **behind** ~**s** (*prisoner*) dietro le sbarre; ~ **none** senza eccezione
barbaric [baː'bærɪk] *adj* barbarico(a)
barbecue ['baːbɪkjuː] *n* barbecue *m inv*
barbed wire ['baːbd-] *n* filo spinato
barber ['baːbə*] *n* barbiere *m*
bar code *n* (*on goods*) codice *m* a barre
bare [bɛə*] *adj* nudo(a) ♦ *vt* scoprire, denudare; (*teeth*) mostrare; **the** ~ **necessities** lo stretto necessario; ~**back** *adv* senza sella; ~**faced** *adj* sfacciato(a); ~**foot** *adj*, *adv* scalzo(a); ~**ly** *adv* appena
bargain ['baːgɪn] *n* (*transaction*) contratto; (*good buy*) affare *m* ♦ *vi* trattare; **into the** ~ per giunta; ~ **for** *vt fus*: **he got more than he** ~**ed for** gli è andata peggio di quel che si aspettasse
barge [baːdʒ] *n* chiatta; ~ **in** *vi* (*walk in*) piombare dentro; (*interrupt talk*) intromettersi a sproposito
bark [baːk] *n* (*of tree*) corteccia; (*of dog*) abbaio ♦ *vi* abbaiare
barley ['baːlɪ] *n* orzo
barmaid ['baːmeɪd] *n* cameriera al banco
barman ['baːmən] *n* barista *m*
barn [baːn] *n* granaio
barometer [bə'rɔmɪtə*] *n* barometro
baron ['bærən] *n* barone *m*; ~**ess** *n* baronessa
barracks ['bærəks] *npl* caserma
barrage ['bæraːʒ] *n* (*MIL, dam*) sbarramento; (*fig*) fiume *m*
barrel ['bærəl] *n* barile *m*; (*of gun*) canna
barren ['bærən] *adj* sterile; (*soil*) arido(a)
barricade [bærɪ'keɪd] *n* barricata
barrier ['bærɪə*] *n* barriera
barring ['baːrɪŋ] *prep* salvo
barrister ['bærɪstə*] (*BRIT*) *n* avvocato/essa (*con diritto di parlare davanti a tutte le corti*)
barrow ['bærəu] *n* (*cart*) carriola
bartender ['baːtɛndə*] (*US*) *n* barista *m*
barter ['baːtə*] *vt*: **to** ~ **sth for** barattare qc con
base [beɪs] *n* base *f* ♦ *vt*: **to** ~ **sth on**

basare qc su ♦ *adj* vile

baseball ['beɪsbɔːl] *n* baseball *m*

basement ['beɪsmənt] *n* seminterrato; (*of shop*) interrato

bases[1] ['beɪsiːz] *npl of* **basis**

bases[2] ['beɪsiz] *npl of* **base**

bash [bæʃ] (*inf*) *vt* picchiare

bashful ['bæʃful] *adj* timido(a)

basic ['beɪsɪk] *adj* rudimentale; essenziale; **~ally** [-lɪ] *adv* fondamentalmente; sostanzialmente; **~s** *npl*: **the ~s** l'essenziale *m*

basil ['bæzl] *n* basilico

basin ['beɪsn] *n* (*vessel, also GEO*) bacino; (*also: wash~*) lavabo

basis ['beɪsis] *n* (*pl* **bases**) *n* base *f*; **on a part-time ~** part-time; **on a trial ~** in prova

bask [bɑːsk] *vi*: **to ~ in the sun** crogiolarsi al sole

basket ['bɑːskɪt] *n* cesta; (*smaller*) cestino; (*with handle*) paniere *m*; **~ball** *n* pallacanestro *f*

bass [beɪs] *n* (*MUS*) basso

bassoon [bə'suːn] *n* fagotto

bastard ['bɑːstəd] *n* bastardo/a; (*inf!*) stronzo (!)

bat [bæt] *n* pipistrello; (*for baseball etc*) mazza; (*BRIT: for table tennis*) racchetta ♦ *vt*: **he didn't ~ an eyelid** non battè ciglio

batch [bætʃ] *n* (*of bread*) infornata; (*of papers*) cumulo

bated ['beɪtɪd] *adj*: **with ~ breath** col fiato sospeso

bath [bɑːθ] *n* bagno; (*bathtub*) vasca da bagno ♦ *vt* far fare il bagno a; **to have a ~** fare un bagno; *see also* **baths**

bathe [beɪð] *vi* fare il bagno ♦ *vt* (*wound*) lavare; **~r** *n* bagnante *m/f*

bathing ['beɪðɪŋ] *n* bagni *mpl*; **~ cap** *n* cuffia da bagno; **~ costume** (*US* = **suit**) *n* costume *m* da bagno

bathrobe ['bɑːθrəub] *n* accappatoio

bathroom ['bɑːθrum] *n* stanza da bagno

baths [bɑːðz] *npl* bagni *mpl* pubblici

bath towel *n* asciugamano da bagno

baton ['bætən] *n* (*MUS*) bacchetta; (*ATHLETICS*) testimone *m*; (*club*) manganello

batter ['bætə*] *vt* battere ♦ *n* pastetta; **~ed** *adj* (*hat*) sformato(a); (*pan*) ammaccato(a)

battery ['bætəri] *n* batteria; (*of torch*) pila

battle ['bætl] *n* battaglia ♦ *vi* battagliare, lottare; **~field** *n* campo di battaglia; **~ship** *n* nave *f* da guerra

bawdy ['bɔːdɪ] *adj* piccante

bawl [bɔːl] *vi* urlare

bay [beɪ] *n* (*of sea*) baia; **to hold sb at ~** tenere qn a bada; **~ leaf** *n* foglia d'alloro; **~ window** *n* bovindo

bazaar [bə'zɑː*] *n* bazar *m inv*; vendita di beneficenza

B. & B. *abbr* = **bed and breakfast**

BBC *n abbr* (= *British Broadcasting Corporation*) rete nazionale di radiotelevisione in Gran Bretagna

B.C. *adv abbr* (= *before Christ*) a.C

KEYWORD

---

be [biː] (*pt* **was, were**, *pp* **been**) *aux vb* **1** (*with present participle: forming continuous tenses*): **what are you doing?** che fa?, che sta facendo?; **they're coming tomorrow** vengono domani; **I've been waiting for her for hours** sono ore che l'aspetto

2 (*with pp: forming passives*) essere; **to ~ killed** essere *or* venire ucciso(a); **the box had been opened** la scatola era stata aperta; **the thief was nowhere to ~ seen** il ladro non si trovava da nessuna parte

3 (*in tag questions*): **it was fun, wasn't it?** è stato divertente, no?; **he's good-looking, isn't he?** è un bell'uomo, vero?; **she's back, is she?** così è tornata, eh?

4 (**+ to + infinitive**): **the house is to ~ sold** abbiamo (*or* hanno *etc*) intenzione di vendere casa; **you're to ~ congratulated for all your work** dovremo farvi i complimenti per tutto il vostro lavoro; **he's not to open it** non deve aprirlo

♦ *vb* **+ complement 1** (*gen*) essere; **I'm English** sono inglese; **I'm tired** sono stanco(a); **I'm hot/cold** ho caldo/freddo; **he's a doctor** è medico; **2 and 2 are 4** 2 più 2 fa 4; **~ careful!** sta attento(a)!; **~**

good sii buono(a)
2 (*of health*) stare; **how are you?** come sta?; **he's very ill** sta molto male
3 (*of age*): **how old are you?** quanti anni hai?; **I'm sixteen (years old)** ho sedici anni
4 (*cost*) costare; **how much was the meal?** quant'era *or* quanto costava il pranzo?; **that'll = £5, please** (fa) 5 sterline, per favore
♦ *vi* 1 (*exist, occur etc*) essere, esistere; **the best singer that ever was** il migliore cantante mai esistito *or* di tutti tempi; ~ **that as it may** comunque sia, sia come sia; **so** ~ **it** sia pure, e sia
2 (*referring to place*) essere, trovarsi; **I won't** ~ **here tomorrow** non ci sarò domani; **Edinburgh is in Scotland** Edimburgo si trova in Scozia
3 (*referring to movement*): **where have you been?** dov'è stato?; **I've been to China** sono stato in Cina
♦ *impers vb* 1 (*referring to time, distance*) essere; **it's 5 o'clock** sono le 5; **it's the 28th of April** è il 28 aprile; **it's 10 km to the village** di qui al paese sono 10 km
2 (*referring to the weather*) fare; **it's too hot/cold** fa troppo caldo/freddo; **it's windy** c'è vento
3 (*emphatic*): **it's me** sono io; **it was Maria who paid the bill** è stata Maria che ha pagato il conto

beach [bi:tʃ] *n* spiaggia ♦ *vt* tirare in secco
beacon ['bi:kən] *n* (*lighthouse*) faro; (*marker*) segnale *m*
bead [bi:d] *n* perlina
beak [bi:k] *n* becco
beaker ['bi:kə*] *n* coppa
beam [bi:m] *n* trave *f*; (*of light*) raggio ♦ *vi* brillare
bean [bi:n] *n* fagiolo; (*of coffee*) chicco; **runner** ~ fagiolino; **broad** ~ fava; **~sprouts** *npl* germogli *mpl* di soia
bear [beə*] *n* (*pt* **bore**, *pp* **borne**) *n* orso ♦ *vt* portare; (*endure*) sopportare; (*produce*) generare ♦ *vi*: **to** ~ **right/left** piegare a destra/sinistra; ~ **out** *vt*

(*suspicions*) confermare, convalidare; (*person*) dare il proprio appoggio a; ~ **up** *vi* (*person*) fare buon viso a cattiva sorte
beard [biəd] *n* barba
bearer ['beərə*] *n* portatore *m*
bearing ['beəriŋ] *n* portamento; (*connection*) rapporto; ~**s** *npl* (*also*: **ball** ~**s**) cuscinetti *mpl* a sfere; **to take a** ~ fare un rilevamento; **to find one's** ~**s** orientarsi
beast [bi:st] *n* bestia; ~**ly** *adj* meschino(a); (*weather*) da cani
beat [bi:t] *n* (*pt* **beat**, *pp* **beaten**) *n* colpo; (*of heart*) battito; (*MUS*) tempo; battuta; (*of policeman*) giro ♦ *vt* battere; (*eggs, cream*) sbattere ♦ *vi* battere; **off the** ~**en track** fuori mano; ~ **it!** (*inf*) fila!, fuori dai piedi!; ~ **off** *vt* respingere; ~ **up** *vt* (*person*) picchiare; (*eggs*) sbattere; **beaten** *pp* *of* **beat**; ~**ing** *n* bastonata
beautiful ['bju:tɪful] *adj* bello(a); ~**ly** *adv* splendidamente
beauty ['bju:tɪ] *n* bellezza; ~ **salon** *n* istituto di bellezza; ~ **spot** (*BRIT*) *n* (*TOURISM*) luogo pittoresco
beaver ['bi:və*] *n* castoro
became [bɪ'keɪm] *pt* *of* **become**
because [bɪ'kɒz] *conj* perché; ~ **of** a causa di
beck [bɛk] *n*: **to be at sb's** ~ **and call** essere a completa disposizione di qn
beckon ['bɛkən] *vt* (*also*: ~ **to**) chiamare con un cenno
become [bɪ'kʌm] (*irreg*: *like* **come**) *vt* diventare; **to** ~ **fat/thin** ingrassarsi/ dimagrire
becoming [bɪ'kʌmɪŋ] *adj* (*behaviour*) che si conviene; (*clothes*) grazioso(a)
bed [bɛd] *n* letto; (*of flowers*) aiuola; (*of coal, clay*) strato; **single/double** ~ letto a una piazza/a due piazze *or* matrimoniale; ~ **and breakfast** *n* (*place*) ≈ pensione *f* familiare; (*terms*) camera con colazione; ~**clothes** *npl* biancheria e coperte *fpl* da letto; ~**ding** *n* coperte e lenzuola *fpl*
bedlam ['bɛdləm] *n* baraonda
bedraggled [bɪ'drægld] *adj* fradicio(a)
bed: ~**ridden** *adj* costretto(a) a letto; ~**room** *n* camera da letto; ~**side** *n*: **at**

bee → *bend*

sb's ~**side** al capezzale di qn; ~**sit(ter)** (*BRIT*) *n* monolocale *m*; ~**time** *n*: **it's ~time** è ora di andare a letto

bee [biː] *n* ape *f*

beech [biːtʃ] *n* faggio

beef [biːf] *n* manzo; **roast ~** arrosto di manzo; ~**burger** *n* hamburger *m inv*; **B~eater** *n* guardia della Torre di Londra

beehive ['biːhaɪv] *n* alveare *m*

beeline ['biːlaɪn] *n*: **to make a ~ for** buttarsi a capo fitto verso

been [biːn] *pp of* **be**

beer [bɪə*] *n* birra

beetle ['biːtl] *n* scarafaggio; coleottero

beetroot ['biːtruːt] (*BRIT*) *n* barbabietola

before [bɪ'fɔː*] *prep* (*in time*) prima di; (*in space*) davanti a ♦ *conj* prima che + *sub*; prima di ♦ *adv* prima; ~ **going** prima di andare; ~ **she goes** prima che vada; **the week ~** la settimana prima; **I've seen it ~** l'ho già visto; **I've never seen it ~** è la prima volta che lo vedo; ~**hand** *adv* in anticipo

beg [bɛg] *vi* chiedere l'elemosina ♦ *vt* (*also: ~ for*) chiedere in elemosina; (: *favour*) chiedere; **to ~ sb to do** pregare qn di fare

began [bɪ'gæn] *pt of* **begin**

beggar ['bɛgə*] *n* mendicante *m/f*

begin [bɪ'gɪn] (*pt* **began**, *pp* **begun**) *vt, vi* cominciare; **to ~ doing** *or* **to do sth** incominciare *or* iniziare a fare qc; ~**ner** *n* principiante *m/f*; ~**ning** *n* inizio, principio

begun [bɪ'gʌn] *pp of* **begin**

behalf [bɪ'hɑːf] *n*: **on ~ of** per conto di; a nome di

behave [bɪ'heɪv] *vi* comportarsi; (*well*: *also:* ~ *o.s.*) comportarsi bene

behaviour [bɪ'heɪvjə*] (*US* **behavior**) *n* comportamento, condotta

behead [bɪ'hɛd] *vt* decapitare

beheld [bɪ'hɛld] *pt, pp of* **behold**

behind [bɪ'haɪnd] *prep* dietro; (*followed by pronoun*) dietro di; (*time*) indietro con ♦ *adv* dietro; (*leave, stay*) indietro ♦ *n* didietro; **to be ~ (schedule)** essere in ritardo rispetto al programma; ~ **the**

scenes (*fig*) dietro le quinte

behold [bɪ'həuld] (*irreg*: *like* **hold**) *vt* vedere, scorgere

beige [beɪʒ] *adj* beige *inv*

Beijing ['beɪ'dʒɪŋ] *n* Pechino *f*

being ['biːɪŋ] *n* essere *m*

belated [bɪ'leɪtɪd] *adj* tardo(a)

belch [bɛltʃ] *vi* ruttare ♦ *vt* (*gen*: ~ *out*: *smoke etc*) eruttare

belfry ['bɛlfrɪ] *n* campanile *m*

Belgian ['bɛldʒən] *adj, n* belga *m/f*

Belgium ['bɛldʒəm] *n* Belgio

belie [bɪ'laɪ] *vt* smentire

belief [bɪ'liːf] *n* (*opinion*) opinione *f*, convinzione *f*; (*trust, faith*) fede *f*

believe [bɪ'liːv] *vt, vi* credere; **to ~ in** (*God*) credere in; (*ghosts*) credere a; (*method*) avere fiducia in; ~**r** *n* (*REL*) credente *m/f*; (*in idea, activity*): **to be a ~r in** credere in

belittle [bɪ'lɪtl] *vt* sminuire

bell [bɛl] *n* campana; (*small, on door, electric*) campanello

belligerent [bɪ'lɪdʒərənt] *adj* bellicoso(a)

bellow ['bɛləu] *vi* muggire

bellows ['bɛləuz] *npl* soffietto

belly ['bɛlɪ] *n* pancia

belong [bɪ'lɒŋ] *vi*: **to ~ to** appartenere a; (*club etc*) essere socio di; **this book ~s here** questo libro va qui; ~**ings** *npl* cose *fpl*, roba

beloved [bɪ'lʌvɪd] *adj* adorato(a)

below [bɪ'ləu] *prep* sotto, al di sotto di ♦ *adv* sotto, di sotto; giù; **see ~** vedi sotto *or* oltre

belt [bɛlt] *n* cintura; (*TECH*) cinghia ♦ *vt* (*thrash*) picchiare ♦ *vi* (*inf*) filarsela; ~**way** (*US*) *n* (*AUT*: *ring road*) circonvallazione *f*; (: *motorway*) autostrada

bemused [bɪ'mjuːzd] *adj* perplesso(a), stupito(a)

bench [bɛntʃ] *n* panca; (*in workshop, POL*) banco; **the B~** (*LAW*) la Corte

bend [bɛnd] (*pt, pp* **bent**) *vt* curvare; (*leg, arm*) piegare ♦ *vi* curvarsi; piegarsi ♦ *n* (*BRIT*: *in road*) curva; (*in pipe, river*) gomito; ~ **down** *vi* chinarsi; ~ **over** *vi* piegarsi

beneath [bɪˈniːθ] *prep* sotto, al di sotto di; (*unworthy of*) indegno(a) di ♦ *adv* sotto, di sotto

benefactor [ˈbɛnɪfæktə*] *n* benefattore *m*

beneficial [bɛnɪˈfɪʃəl] *adj* che fa bene; vantaggioso(a)

benefit [ˈbɛnɪfɪt] *n* beneficio, vantaggio; (*allowance of money*) indennità *f inv* ♦ *vt* far bene a ♦ *vi*: **he'll ~ from it** ne trarrà beneficio or profitto

benevolent [bɪˈnɛvələnt] *adj* benevolo(a)

benign [bɪˈnaɪn] *adj* (*person, smile*) benevolo(a); (*MED*) benigno(a)

bent [bɛnt] *pt, pp of* **bend** ♦ *n* inclinazione *f* ♦ *adj* (*inf: dishonest*) losco(a); **to be ~ on** essere deciso(a) a

bequest [bɪˈkwɛst] *n* lascito

bereaved [bɪˈriːvd] *n*: **the ~** i familiari in lutto

beret [ˈbɛreɪ] *n* berretto

berm [bəːm] (*US*) *n* (*AUT*) corsia d'emergenza

berry [ˈbɛrɪ] *n* bacca

berserk [bəˈsəːk] *adj*: **to go ~** montare su tutte le furie

berth [bəːθ] *n* (*bed*) cuccetta; (*for ship*) ormeggio ♦ *vi* (*in harbour*) entrare in porto; (*at anchor*) gettare l'ancora

beseech [bɪˈsiːtʃ] (*pt, pp* **besought**) *vt* implorare

beset [bɪˈsɛt] (*pt, pp* **beset**) *vt* assalire

beside [bɪˈsaɪd] *prep* accanto a; **to be ~ o.s. (with anger)** essere fuori di sé (dalla rabbia); **that's ~ the point** non c'entra

besides [bɪˈsaɪdz] *adv* inoltre, per di più ♦ *prep* oltre a; a parte

besiege [bɪˈsiːdʒ] *vt* (*town*) assediare; (*fig*) tempestare

besought [bɪˈsɔːt] *pt, pp of* **beseech**

best [bɛst] *adj* migliore ♦ *adv* meglio; **the ~ part of** (*quantity*) la maggior parte di; **at ~** tutt'al più; **to make the ~ of sth** cavare il meglio possibile da qc; **to do one's ~** fare del proprio meglio; **to the ~ of my knowledge** per quel che ne so; **to the ~ of my ability** al massimo delle mie capacità; **~ man** *n* testimone *m* dello sposo

bestow [bɪˈstəu] *vt* accordare; (*title*) conferire

bet [bɛt] (*pt, pp* **bet** *or* **betted**) *n* scommessa ♦ *vt, vi* scommettere; **to ~ sb sth** scommettere qc con qn

betray [bɪˈtreɪ] *vt* tradire; **~al** *n* tradimento

better [ˈbɛtə*] *adj* migliore ♦ *adv* meglio ♦ *vt* migliorare ♦ *n*: **to get the ~ of** avere la meglio su; **you had ~ do it** è meglio che lo faccia; **he thought ~ of it** cambiò idea; **to get ~** migliorare; **~ off** *adj* più ricco(a); (*fig*) **you'd be ~ off this way** starebbe meglio così

betting [ˈbɛtɪŋ] *n* scommesse *fpl*; **~ shop** (*BRIT*) *n* ufficio dell'allibratore

between [bɪˈtwiːn] *prep* tra ♦ *adv* in mezzo, nel mezzo

beverage [ˈbɛvərɪdʒ] *n* bevanda

beware [bɪˈwɛə*] *vt, vi*: **to ~ (of)** stare attento(a) (a); **"~ of the dog"** "attenti al cane"

bewildered [bɪˈwɪldəd] *adj* sconcertato(a), confuso(a)

bewitching [bɪˈwɪtʃɪŋ] *adj* affascinante

beyond [bɪˈjɒnd] *prep* (*in space*) oltre; (*exceeding*) al di sopra di ♦ *adv* di là; **~ doubt** senza dubbio; **~ repair** irreparabile

bias [ˈbaɪəs] *n* (*prejudice*) pregiudizio; (*preference*) preferenza; **~(s)ed** *adj* parziale

bib [bɪb] *n* bavaglino

Bible [ˈbaɪbl] *n* Bibbia

bicarbonate of soda [baɪˈkɑːbənɪt-] *n* bicarbonato (di sodio)

bicker [ˈbɪkə*] *vi* bisticciare

bicycle [ˈbaɪsɪkl] *n* bicicletta

bid [bɪd] (*pt* **bade** *or* **bid**, *pp* **bidden** *or* **bid**) *n* offerta; (*attempt*) tentativo ♦ *vi* fare un'offerta ♦ *vt* fare un'offerta di; **to ~ sb good day** dire buon giorno a qn; **bidden** *pp of* **bid**; **~der** *n*: **the highest ~der** il maggior offerente; **~ding** *n* offerte *fpl*

bide [baɪd] *vt*: **to ~ one's time** aspettare il momento giusto

bifocals [baɪˈfəuklz] *npl* occhiali *mpl* bifocali

big [bɪg] *adj* grande; grosso(a)

big dipper [-'dɪpə*] *n* montagne *fpl* russe, otto *m inv* volante

bigheaded ['bɪg'hɛdɪd] *adj* presuntuoso(a)

bigot ['bɪgət] *n* persona gretta; **~ed** *adj* gretto(a); **~ry** *n* grettezza

big top *n* tendone *m* del circo

bike [baɪk] *n* bici *f inv*

bikini [bɪ'ki:nɪ] *n* bikini *m inv*

bilingual [baɪ'lɪŋgwəl] *adj* bilingue

bill [bɪl] *n* conto; (*POL*) atto; (*US: banknote*) banconota; (*of bird*) becco; (*of show*) locandina; **"post no ~s"** "divieto di affissione"; **to fit** *or* **fill the ~** (*fig*) fare al caso; **~board** *n* tabellone *m*

billet ['bɪlɪt] *n* alloggio

billfold ['bɪlfəuld] (*US*) *n* portafoglio

billiards ['bɪljədz] *n* biliardo

billion ['bɪljən] *n* (*BRIT*) bilione *m*; (*US*) miliardo

bimbo ['bɪmbəu] *n* (*pej, col*) pollastrella, svampitella

bin [bɪn] *n* (*for coal, rubbish*) bidone *m*; (*for bread*) cassetta; (*dust~*) pattumiera; (*litter ~*) cestino

bind [baɪnd] (*pt, pp* **bound**) *vt* legare; (*oblige*) obbligare ♦ *n* (*inf*) scocciatura; **~ing** *adj* (*contract*) vincolante

binge [bɪndʒ] (*inf*) *n*: **to go on a ~** fare baldoria

bingo ['bɪŋgəu] *n* gioco simile alla tombola

binoculars [bɪ'nɔkjuləz] *npl* binocolo

bio... [baɪə'...] *prefix*: **~chemistry** *n* biochimica; **~graphy** [baɪ'ɔgrəfɪ] *n* biografia; **~logical** *adj* biologico(a); **~logy** [baɪ'ɔlədʒɪ] *n* biologia

birch [bə:tʃ] *n* betulla

bird [bə:d] *n* uccello; (*BRIT: inf: girl*) bambola; **~'s eye view** *n* vista panoramica; **~ watcher** *n* ornitologo/a dilettante

Biro ['baɪrəu] ® *n* biro *f inv* ®

birth [bə:θ] *n* nascita; **to give ~ to** partorire; **~ certificate** *n* certificato di nascita; **~ control** *n* controllo delle nascite; contraccezione *f*; **~day** *n* compleanno ♦ *cpd* di compleanno; **~ rate** *n* indice *m* di natalità

biscuit ['bɪskɪt] (*BRIT*) *n* biscotto

bisect [baɪ'sɛkt] *vt* tagliare in due (parti)

bishop ['bɪʃəp] *n* vescovo

bit [bɪt] *pt of* **bite** ♦ *n* pezzo; (*COMPUT*) bit *m inv*; (*of horse*) morso; **a ~ of** un po' di; **a ~ mad** un po' matto; **~ by ~** a poco a poco

bitch [bɪtʃ] *n* (*dog*) cagna; (*inf!*) vacca

bite [baɪt] (*pt* **bit**, *pp* **bitten**) *vt, vi* mordere; (*subj: insect*) pungere ♦ *n* morso; (*insect ~*) puntura; (*mouthful*) boccone *m*; **let's have a ~ (to eat)** mangiamo un boccone; **to ~ one's nails** mangiarsi le unghie; **bitten** ['bɪtn] *pp of* **bite**

bitter ['bɪtə*] *adj* amaro(a); (*wind, criticism*) pungente ♦ *n* (*BRIT: beer*) birra amara; **~ness** *n* amarezza; gusto amaro

blab [blæb] *vi* parlare troppo

black [blæk] *adj* nero(a) ♦ *n* nero; (*person*): **B~** negro/a ♦ *vt* (*BRIT: INDUSTRY*) boicottare; **to give sb a ~ eye** fare un occhio nero a qn; **in the ~** (*bank account*) in attivo; **~ and blue** *adj* tutto(a) pesto(a); **~berry** *n* mora; **~bird** *n* merlo; **~board** *n* lavagna; **~currant** *n* ribes *m inv*; **~en** *vt* annerire; **~ ice** *n* strato trasparente di ghiaccio; **~leg** (*BRIT*) *n* crumiro; **~list** *n* lista nera; **~mail** *n* ricatto ♦ *vt* ricattare; **~ market** *n* mercato nero; **~out** *n* oscuramento; (*TV, RADIO*) interruzione *f* delle trasmissioni; (*fainting*) svenimento; **B~ Sea** *n*: **the B~ Sea** il Mar Nero; **~ sheep** *n* pecora nera; **~smith** *n* fabbro ferraio; **~ spot** *n* (*AUT*) luogo famigerato per gli incidenti; (*for unemployment etc*) zona critica

bladder ['blædə*] *n* vescica

blade [bleɪd] *n* lama; (*of oar*) pala; **~ of grass** filo d'erba

blame [bleɪm] *n* colpa ♦ *vt*: **to ~ sb/sth for sth** dare la colpa di qc a qn/qc; **who's to ~?** chi è colpevole?

bland [blænd] *adj* mite; (*taste*) blando(a)

blank [blæŋk] *adj* bianco(a); (*look*) distratto(a) ♦ *n* spazio vuoto; (*cartridge*) cartuccia a salve; **~ cheque** *n* assegno in bianco

blanket ['blæŋkɪt] *n* coperta

blare [blɛə*] *vi* strombettare

blasphemy ['blæsfɪmɪ] *n* bestemmia
blast [blɑːst] *n* (*of wind*) raffica; (*of bomb etc*) esplosione *f* ♦ *vt* far saltare; **~-off** *n* (*SPACE*) lancio
blatant ['bleɪtənt] *adj* flagrante
blaze [bleɪz] *n* (*fire*) incendio; (*fig*) vampata; splendore *m* ♦ *vi* (*fire*) ardere, fiammeggiare; (*guns*) sparare senza sosta; (*fig: eyes*) ardere ♦ *vt*: **to ~ a trail** (*fig*) tracciare una via nuova; **in a ~ of publicity** circondato da grande pubblicità
blazer ['bleɪzə*] *n* blazer *m inv*
bleach [bliːtʃ] *n* (*also: household ~*) varechina ♦ *vt* (*material*) candeggiare; **~ed** *adj* (*hair*) decolorato(a); **~ers** (*US*) *npl* (*SPORT*) posti *mpl* di gradinata
bleak [bliːk] *adj* tetro(a)
bleary-eyed ['blɪərɪ'aɪd] *adj* dagli occhi offuscati
bleat [bliːt] *vi* belare
bled [blɛd] *pt, pp of* **bleed**
bleed [bliːd] (*pt, pp* **bled**) *vi* sanguinare; **my nose is ~ing** mi viene fuori sangue dal naso
bleeper ['bliːpə*] *n* (*device*) cicalino
blemish ['blɛmɪʃ] *n* macchia
blend [blɛnd] *n* miscela ♦ *vt* mescolare ♦ *vi* (*colours etc: also: ~ in*) armonizzare
bless [blɛs] (*pt, pp* **blessed** *or* **blest**) *vt* benedire; **~ you!** (*after sneeze*) salute!; **~ing** *n* benedizione *f*; fortuna; **blest** [blɛst] *pt, pp of* **bless**
blew [bluː] *pt of* **blow**
blight [blaɪt] *vt* (*hopes etc*) deludere; (*life*) rovinare
blimey ['blaɪmɪ] (*BRIT: inf*) *excl* accidenti!
blind [blaɪnd] *adj* cieco(a) ♦ *n* (*for window*) avvolgibile *m*; (*Venetian ~*) veneziana ♦ *vt* accecare; **the ~** *npl* i ciechi; **~ alley** *n* vicolo cieco; **~ corner** (*BRIT*) *n* svolta cieca; **~fold** *n* benda ♦ *adj, adv* bendato(a) ♦ *vt* bendare gli occhi a; **~ly** *adv* ciecamente; **~ness** *n* cecità; **~ spot** *n* (*AUT etc*) punto cieco; (*fig*) punto debole
blink [blɪŋk] *vi* battere gli occhi; (*light*) lampeggiare; **~ers** *npl* paraocchi *mpl*
bliss [blɪs] *n* estasi *f*
blister ['blɪstə*] *n* (*on skin*) vescica; (*on*

paintwork) bolla ♦ *vi* (*paint*) coprirsi di bolle
blithely ['blaɪðlɪ] *adv* allegramente
blizzard ['blɪzəd] *n* bufera di neve
bloated ['bləʊtɪd] *adj* gonfio(a)
blob [blɔb] *n* (*drop*) goccia; (*stain, spot*) macchia
bloc [blɔk] *n* (*POL*) blocco
block [blɔk] *n* blocco; (*in pipes*) ingombro; (*toy*) cubo; (*of buildings*) isolato ♦ *vt* bloccare; **~ade** [-'keɪd] *n* blocco; **~age** *n* ostacolo; **~buster** *n* (*film, book*) grande successo; **~ letters** *npl* stampatello; **~ of flats** (*BRIT*) *n* caseggiato.
bloke [bləʊk] (*BRIT: inf*) *n* tizio
blonde [blɔnd] *adj, n* biondo(a)
blood [blʌd] *n* sangue *m*; **~ donor** *n* donatore/trice di sangue; **~ group** *n* gruppo sanguigno; **~hound** *n* segugio; **~ poisoning** *n* setticemia; **~ pressure** *n* pressione *f* sanguigna; **~shed** *n* spargimento di sangue; **~shot** *adj*: **~shot eyes** occhi iniettati di sangue; **~stream** *n* flusso del sangue; **~ test** *n* analisi *f inv* del sangue; **~thirsty** *adj* assetato(a) di sangue; **~y** *adj* (*fight*) sanguinoso(a); (*nose*) sanguinante; (*BRIT: inf!*): **this ~y ...** questo maledetto ...; **~y awful/good** (*inf!*) veramente terribile/forte; **~y-minded** (*BRIT: inf*) *adj* indisponente
bloom [bluːm] *n* fiore *m* ♦ *vi* (*tree*) essere in fiore; (*flower*) aprirsi
blossom ['blɔsəm] *n* fiore *m*; (*with pl sense*) fiori *mpl* ♦ *vi* essere in fiore
blot [blɔt] *n* macchia ♦ *vt* macchiare; **~ out** (*memories*) cancellare; (*view*) nascondere
blotchy ['blɔtʃɪ] *adj* (*complexion*) coperto(a) di macchie
blotting paper ['blɔtɪŋ-] *n* carta assorbente
blouse [blauz] *n* (*feminine garment*) camicetta
blow [bləʊ] (*pt* **blew**, *pp* **blown**) *n* colpo ♦ *vi* soffiare ♦ *vt* (*fuse*) far saltare; (*subj: wind*) spingere; (*instrument*) suonare; **to ~ one's nose** soffiarsi il naso; **to ~ a whistle** fischiare; **~ away** *vt* portare via; **~ down** *vt* abbattere; **~ off** *vt* far volare

via; ~ **out** *vi* scoppiare; ~ **over** *vi* calmarsi; ~ **up** *vi* saltare in aria ♦ *vt* far saltare in aria; (*tyre*) gonfiare; (*PHOT*) ingrandire; ~~**dry** *n* messa in piega a föhn; ~**lamp** (*BRIT*) *n* lampada a benzina per saldare; **blown** *pp* of **blow**; ~**out** *n* (*of tyre*) scoppio; ~**torch** *n* = ~**lamp**

blue [blu:] *adj* azzurro(a); (*depressed*) giù *inv*; ~ **film/joke** film/ barzelletta pornografico(a); **out of the** ~ (*fig*) all'improvviso; ~**bell** *n* giacinto dei boschi; ~**bottle** *n* moscone *m*; ~**print** *n* (*fig*): ~**print (for)** formula (di)

bluff [blʌf] *vi* bluffare ♦ *n* bluff *m inv* ♦ *adj* (*person*) brusco(a); **to call sb's** ~ mettere alla prova il bluff di qn

blunder ['blʌndə*] *n* abbaglio ♦ *vi* prendere un abbaglio

blunt [blʌnt] *adj* smussato(a); spuntato(a); (*person*) brusco(a)

blur [blə:*] *n* forma indistinta ♦ *vt* offuscare

blurb [blə:b] *n* trafiletto pubblicitario

blurt out [blə:t-] *vt* lasciarsi sfuggire

blush [blʌʃ] *vi* arrossire ♦ *n* rossore *m*

blustering ['blʌstərɪŋ] *adj* infuriato(a)

blustery ['blʌstərɪ] *adj* (*weather*) burrascoso(a)

boar [bɔ:*] *n* cinghiale *m*

board [bɔ:d] *n* tavola; (*on wall*) tabellone *m*; (*committee*) consiglio, comitato; (*in firm*) consiglio d'amministrazione; (*NAUT, AVIAT*): **on** ~ a bordo ♦ *vt* (*ship*) salire a bordo di; (*train*) salire su; **full** ~ (*BRIT*) pensione completa; **half** ~ (*BRIT*) mezza pensione; ~ **and lodging** vitto e alloggio; **which goes by the** ~ (*fig*) che viene abbandonato; ~ **up** *vt* (*door*) chiudere con assi; ~**er** *n* (*SCOL*) convittore/trice; ~**ing card** *n* = ~**ing pass**; ~**ing house** *n* pensione *f*; ~**ing pass** *n* (*AVIAT, NAUT*) carta d'imbarco; ~**ing school** *n* collegio; ~ **room** *n* sala del consiglio

boast [bəust] *vi*: **to** ~ (**about** *or* **of**) vantarsi (di)

boat [bəut] *n* nave *f*; (*small*) barca; ~**er** *n* (*hat*) paglietta; ~**swain** ['bəusn] *n* nostromo

bob [bɔb] *vi* (*boat, cork on water: also*: ~

up and down) andare su e giù; ~ **up** *vi* saltare fuori

bobby ['bɔbɪ] (*BRIT: inf*) *n* poliziotto

bobsleigh ['bɔbsleɪ] *n* bob *m inv*

bode [bəud] *vi*: **to** ~ **well/ill (for)** essere di buon/cattivo auspicio (per)

bodily ['bɔdɪlɪ] *adj* fisico(a), corporale ♦ *adv* corporalmente; interamente; in persona

body ['bɔdɪ] *n* corpo; (*of car*) carrozzeria; (*of plane*) fusoliera; (*fig: group*) gruppo; (: *organization*) organizzazione *f*; (: *quantity*) quantità *f inv*; ~**building** *n* culturismo; ~**guard** *n* guardia del corpo; ~**work** *n* carrozzeria

bog [bɔg] *n* palude *f* ♦ *vt*: **to get** ~**ged down** (*fig*) impantanarsi

boggle ['bɔgl] *vi*: **the mind** ~**s** è incredibile

bogus ['bəugəs] *adj* falso(a); finto(a)

boil [bɔɪl] *vt, vi* bollire ♦ *n* (*MED*) foruncolo; **to come to the** (*BRIT*) *or* **a** (*US*) ~ raggiungere l'ebollizione; ~ **down to** *vt fus* (*fig*) ridursi a; ~ **over** *vi* traboccare (bollendo); ~**ed egg** *n* uovo alla coque; ~**ed potatoes** *npl* patate *fpl* bollite *or* lesse; ~**er** *n* caldaia; ~**er suit** (*BRIT*) *n* tuta; ~**ing point** *n* punto di ebollizione

boisterous ['bɔɪstərəs] *adj* chiassoso(a)

bold [bəuld] *adj* audace; (*child*) impudente; (*colour*) deciso(a)

bollard ['bɔləd] (*BRIT*) *n* (*AUT*) colonnina luminosa

bolster ['bəulstə*] *vt*: ~ **up** sostenere

bolt [bəult] *n* chiavistello; (*with nut*) bullone *m* ♦ *adv*: ~ **upright** diritto(a) come un fuso ♦ *vt* serrare; (*also*: ~ *together*) imbullonare; (*food*) mangiare in fretta ♦ *vi* scappare via

bomb [bɔm] *n* bomba ♦ *vt* bombardare

bombastic [bɔm'bæstɪk] *adj* magniloquente

bomb: ~ **disposal unit** *n* corpo degli artificieri; ~**er** *n* (*AVIAT*) bombardiere *m*; ~**shell** *n* (*fig*) notizia bomba

bona fide ['bəunə'faɪdɪ] *adj* sincero(a); (*offer*) onesto(a)

bond [bɔnd] *n* legame *m*; (*binding promise, FINANCE*) obbligazione *f*; (*COMM*):

in ~ in attesa di sdoganamento

bondage ['bɔndɪdʒ] *n* schiavitù *f*

bone [bəun] *n* osso; (*of fish*) spina, lisca
♦ *vt* disossare; togliere le spine a; ~ **idle**
adj pigrissimo(a); ~ **marrow** *n* midollo
osseo

bonfire ['bɔnfaɪə*] *n* falò *m inv*

bonnet ['bɔnɪt] *n* cuffia; (*BRIT: of car*)
cofano

bonus ['bəunəs] *n* premio; (*fig*) sovrappiù
m inv

bony ['bəunɪ] *adj* (*MED: tissue*) osseo(a); (*arm, face*) ossuto(a); (*meat*) pieno(a) di
ossi; (*fish*) pieno(a) di spine

boo [bu:] *excl* ba! ♦ *vt* fischiare

booby trap ['bu:bɪ-] *n* trappola

book [buk] *n* libro; (*of stamps etc*)
blocchetto ♦ *vt* (*ticket, seat, room*)
prenotare; (*driver*) multare; (*football
player*) ammonire; ~**s** *npl* (*COMM*) conti
mpl; ~**case** *n* scaffale *m*; ~**ing office**
(*BRIT*) *n* (*RAIL*) biglietteria; (*THEATRE*)
botteghino; ~-**keeping** *n* contabilità; ~**let**
n libricino; ~**maker** *n* allibratore *m*;
~**seller** *n* libraio; ~**shop**, ~**store** *n*
libreria

boom [bu:m] *n* (*noise*) rimbombo; (*in
prices etc*) boom *m inv* ♦ *vi* rimbombare;
andare a gonfie vele

boon [bu:n] *n* vantaggio

boost [bu:st] *n* spinta ♦ *vt* spingere; ~**er**
n (*MED*) richiamo

boot [bu:t] *n* stivale *m*; (*for hiking*)
scarpone *m* da montagna; (*for football etc*)
scarpa; (*BRIT: of car*) portabagagli *m inv*
♦ *vt* (*COMPUT*) inizializzare; **to** ~ (*in
addition*) per giunta, in più

booth [bu:ð] *n* cabina; (*at fair*) baraccone
m

booty ['bu:tɪ] *n* bottino

booze [bu:z] (*inf*) *n* alcool *m*

border ['bɔːdə*] *n* orlo; margine *m*; (*of a
country*) frontiera; (*for flowers*) aiuola
(laterale) ♦ *vt* (*road*) costeggiare; (*another
country: also:* ~ **on**) confinare con; **the
B~s** *la zona di confine tra l'Inghilterra e
la Scozia*; ~ **on** *vt fus* (*fig: insanity etc*)
sfiorare; ~**line** *n* (*fig*): **on the** ~**line**
incerto(a); ~**line case** *n* caso incerto

bore [bɔ:*] *pt of* **bear** ♦ *vt* (*hole etc*)
scavare; (*person*) annoiare ♦ *n* (*person*)
seccatore/trice; (*of gun*) calibro; **to be** ~**d**
annoiarsi; ~**dom** *n* noia; **boring** *adj*
noioso(a)

born [bɔ:n] *adj*: **to be** ~ nascere; **I was** ~
in 1960 sono nato nel 1960

borne [bɔ:n] *pp of* **bear**

borough ['bʌrə] *n* comune *m*

borrow ['bɔrəu] *vt*: **to** ~ **sth (from sb)**
prendere in prestito qc (da qn)

bosom ['buzəm] *n* petto; ~ **friend** *n*
amico/a del cuore

boss [bɔs] *n* capo ♦ *vt* comandare; ~**y** *adj*
prepotente

bosun ['bəusn] *n* nostromo

botany ['bɔtənɪ] *n* botanica

botch [bɔtʃ] *vt* (*also:* ~ **up**) fare un
pasticcio di

both [bəuθ] *adj* entrambi(e), tutt'e due
♦ *pron*: ~ (**of them**) entrambi(e); ~ **of us
went, we** ~ **went** ci siamo andati tutt'e
due ♦ *adv*: **they sell** ~ **meat and poultry**
vendono insieme la carne ed il pollame

bother ['bɔðə*] *vt* (*worry*) preoccupare;
(*annoy*) infastidire ♦ *vi* (*also:* ~ *o.s.*)
preoccuparsi ♦ *n*: **it is a** ~ **to have to do**
è una seccatura dover fare; **it was no** ~
non c'era problema; **to** ~ **doing sth** darsi
la pena di fare qc

bottle ['bɔtl] *n* bottiglia; (*baby's*) biberon
m inv ♦ *vt* imbottigliare; ~ **up** *vt*
contenere; ~ **bank** *n* contenitore *m* per la
raccolta del vetro; ~**neck** *n*
imbottigliamento; ~-**opener** *n*
apribottiglie *m inv*

bottom ['bɔtəm] *n* fondo; (*buttocks*)
sedere *m* ♦ *adj* più basso(a); ultimo(a); **at
the** ~ **of** in fondo a

bough [bau] *n* ramo

bought [bɔ:t] *pt, pp of* **buy**

boulder ['bəuldə*] *n* masso
(tondeggiante)

bounce [bauns] *vi* (*ball*) rimbalzare;
(*cheque*) essere restituito(a) ♦ *vt* far
rimbalzare ♦ *n* (*rebound*) rimbalzo; ~**r**
(*inf*) *n* buttafuori *m inv*

bound [baund] *pt, pp of* **bind** ♦ *n* (*gen pl*)
limite *m*; (*leap*) salto ♦ *vi* saltare ♦ *vt*

(limit) delimitare ♦ *adj*: ~ **by law** obbligato(a) per legge; **to be** ~ **to do sth** *(obliged)* essere costretto(a) a fare qc; **he's** ~ **to fail** *(likely)* fallirà di certo; ~ **for** diretto(a) a; **out of** ~**s** il cui accesso è vietato

boundary ['baundrɪ] *n* confine *m*

boundless ['baundlɪs] *adj* senza limiti

bourgeois ['buəʒwaː] *adj* borghese

bout [baut] *n* periodo; *(of malaria etc)* attacco; *(BOXING etc)* incontro

bow¹ [bəu] *n* nodo; *(weapon)* arco; *(MUS)* archetto

bow² [bau] *n* *(with body)* inchino; *(NAUT: also:* ~**s)** prua ♦ *vi* inchinarsi; *(yield):* **to** ~ **to** *or* **before** sottomettersi a

bowels ['bauəlz] *npl* intestini *mpl*; *(fig)* viscere *fpl*

bowl [bəul] *n* *(for eating)* scodella; *(for washing)* bacino; *(ball)* boccia ♦ *vi* *(CRICKET)* servire (la palla)

bow-legged ['bəu'lɛgɪd] *adj* dalle gambe storte

bowler ['bəulə*] *n* *(CRICKET, BASEBALL)* lanciatore *m*; *(BRIT: also:* ~ **hat)** bombetta

bowling ['bəulɪŋ] *n* *(game)* gioco delle bocce; ~ **alley** *n* pista da bowling; ~ **green** *n* campo di bocce

bowls [bəulz] *n* gioco delle bocce

bow tie *n* cravatta a farfalla

box [bɔks] *n* scatola; *(also: cardboard* ~) cartone *m*; *(THEATRE)* palco ♦ *vt* inscatolare ♦ *vi* fare del pugilato; ~**er** *n* *(person)* pugile *m*; ~**ing** *n* *(SPORT)* pugilato; **B**~**ing Day** *(BRIT)* *n* Santo Stefano; ~**ing gloves** *npl* guantoni *mpl* da pugile; ~**ing ring** *n* ring *m inv*; ~ **office** *n* biglietteria; ~ **room** *n* ripostiglio

boy [bɔɪ] *n* ragazzo

boycott ['bɔɪkɔt] *n* boicottaggio ♦ *vt* boicottare

boyfriend ['bɔɪfrɛnd] *n* ragazzo

boyish ['bɔɪɪʃ] *adj* da ragazzo

B.R. *abbr* = **British Rail**

bra [braː] *n* reggipetto, reggiseno

brace [breɪs] *n* *(on teeth)* apparecchio correttore; *(tool)* trapano ♦ *vt* rinforzare, sostenere; ~**s** *(BRIT)* *npl* *(DRESS)* bretelle *fpl*; **to** ~ **o.s.** *(also fig)* tenersi forte

bracelet ['breɪslɪt] *n* braccialetto

bracing ['breɪsɪŋ] *adj* invigorante

bracken ['brækən] *n* felce *f*

bracket ['brækɪt] *n* *(TECH)* mensola; *(group)* gruppo; *(TYP)* parentesi *f inv* ♦ *vt* mettere fra parentesi

brag [bræg] *vi* vantarsi

braid [breɪd] *n* *(trimming)* passamano; *(of hair)* treccia

brain [breɪn] *n* cervello; ~**s** *npl* *(intelligence)* cervella *fpl*; **he's got** ~**s** è intelligente; ~**child** *n* creatura, creazione *f*; ~**wash** *vt* fare un lavaggio di cervello a; ~**wave** *n* lampo di genio; ~**y** *adj* intelligente

braise [breɪz] *vt* brasare

brake [breɪk] *n* *(on vehicle)* freno ♦ *vi* frenare; ~ **fluid** *n* liquido dei freni; ~ **light** *n* (fanalino dello) stop *m inv*

bramble ['bræmbl] *n* rovo

bran [bræn] *n* crusca

branch [braːntʃ] *n* ramo; *(COMM)* succursale *f*; ~ **out** *vi* *(fig)* intraprendere una nuova attività

brand [brænd] *n* *(also:* ~ **name)** marca; *(fig)* tipo ♦ *vt* *(cattle)* marcare (a ferro rovente)

brand-new *adj* nuovo(a) di zecca

brandy ['brændɪ] *n* brandy *m inv*

brash [bræʃ] *adj* sfacciato(a)

brass [braːs] *n* ottone *m*; **the** ~ *(MUS)* gli ottoni; ~ **band** *n* fanfara

brassière ['bræsɪə*] *n* reggipetto, reggiseno

brat [bræt] *(pej)* *n* marmocchio, monello/a

bravado [brə'vaːdəu] *n* spavalderia

brave [breɪv] *adj* coraggioso(a) ♦ *vt* affrontare; ~**ry** *n* coraggio

brawl [brɔːl] *n* rissa

brawny ['brɔːnɪ] *adj* muscoloso(a)

bray [breɪ] *vi* ragliare

brazen ['breɪzn] *adj* sfacciato(a) ♦ *vt*: **to** ~ **it out** fare lo sfacciato

brazier ['breɪzɪə*] *n* braciere *m*

Brazil [brə'zɪl] *n* Brasile *m*

breach [briːtʃ] *vt* aprire una breccia in ♦ *n* *(gap)* breccia, varco; *(breaking):* ~ **of contract** rottura di contratto; ~ **of the peace** violazione *f* dell'ordine pubblico

bread [brɛd] *n* pane *m*; ~ **and butter** *n* pane e burro; (*fig*) mezzi *mpl* di sussistenza; **~bin** (*US* **~box**) *n* cassetta *f* portapane *inv*; **~crumbs** *npl* briciole *fpl*; (*CULIN*) pangrattato; **~line** *n*: **to be on the ~line** avere appena il denaro per vivere

breadth [brɛtθ] *n* larghezza; (*fig: of knowledge etc*) ampiezza

breadwinner ['brɛdwɪnə*] *n* chi guadagna il pane per tutta la famiglia

break [breɪk] (*pt* **broke**, *pp* **broken**) *vt* rompere; (*law*) violare; (*record*) battere ♦ *vi* rompersi; (*storm*) scoppiare; (*weather*) cambiare; (*dawn*) spuntare; (*news*) saltare fuori ♦ *n* (*gap*) breccia; (*fracture*) rottura; (*rest, also SCOL*) intervallo; (*: short*) pausa; (*chance*) possibilità *f inv*; **to ~ one's leg** *etc* rompersi la gamba *etc*; **to ~ the news to sb** comunicare per primo la notizia a qn; **to ~ even** coprire le spese; **to ~ free** *or* **loose** spezzare i legami; **to ~ open** (*door etc*) sfondare; ~ **down** *vt* (*figures, data*) analizzare ♦ *vi* (*person*) avere un esaurimento (nervoso); (*AUT*) guastarsi; ~ **in** *vt* (*horse etc*) domare ♦ *vi* (*burglar*) fare irruzione; (*interrupt*) interrompere; ~ **into** *vt fus* (*house*) fare irruzione in; ~ **off** *vi* (*speaker*) interrompersi; (*branch*) troncarsi; ~ **out** *vi* evadere; (*war, fight*) scoppiare; **to ~ out in spots** coprirsi di macchie; ~ **up** *vi* (*ship*) sfondarsi; (*meeting*) sciogliersi; (*crowd*) disperdersi; (*marriage*) andare a pezzi; (*SCOL*) chiudere ♦ *vt* fare a pezzi, spaccare; (*fight etc*) interrompere, far cessare; **~age** *n* rottura; (*object broken*) cosa rotta; **~down** *n* (*AUT*) guasto; (*in communications*) interruzione *f*; (*of marriage*) rottura; (*MED: also: nervous ~down*) esaurimento nervoso; (*of statistics*) resoconto; **~down van** (*BRIT*) *n* carro m attrezzi *inv*; **~er** *n* frangente *m*

breakfast ['brɛkfəst] *n* colazione *f*

break: **~-in** *n* irruzione *f*; **~ing and entering** *n* (*LAW*) violazione *f* del diritto con scasso; **~through** *n* (*fig*) passo avanti; **~water** *n* frangiflutti *m inv*

breast [brɛst] *n* (*of woman*) seno; (*chest,*

CULIN) petto; **~-feed** (*irreg: like* **feed**) *vt, vi* allattare (al seno); **~-stroke** *n* nuoto a rana

breath [brɛθ] *n* respiro; **out of ~** senza fiato

Breathalyser ['brɛθəlaɪzə*] ® (*BRIT*) *n* alcoltest *m inv*

breathe [bri:ð] *vt, vi* respirare; ~ **in** *vt* respirare ♦ *vi* inspirare; ~ **out** *vt, vi* espirare; **~r** *n* attimo di respiro; **breathing** *n* respiro, respirazione *f*

breathless ['brɛθlɪs] *adj* senza fiato

breathtaking ['brɛθteɪkɪŋ] *adj* mozzafiato *inv*

bred [brɛd] *pt, pp of* **breed**

breed [bri:d] (*pt, pp* **bred**) *vt* allevare ♦ *vi* riprodursi ♦ *n* razza; (*type, class*) varietà *f inv*; **~ing** *n* riproduzione *f*; allevamento; (*upbringing*) educazione *f*

breeze [bri:z] *n* brezza

breezy ['bri:zɪ] *adj* allegro(a); ventilato(a)

brew [bru:] *vt* (*tea*) fare un infuso di; (*beer*) fare ♦ *vi* (*storm, fig: trouble etc*) prepararsi; **~er** *n* birraio; **~ery** *n* fabbrica di birra

bribe [braɪb] *n* bustarella ♦ *vt* comprare; **~ry** *n* corruzione *f*

brick [brɪk] *n* mattone *m*; **~layer** *n* muratore *m*

bridal ['braɪdl] *adj* nuziale

bride [braɪd] *n* sposa; **~groom** *n* sposo; **~smaid** *n* damigella d'onore

bridge [brɪdʒ] *n* ponte *m*; (*NAUT*) ponte di comando; (*of nose*) dorso; (*CARDS*) bridge *m inv* ♦ *vt* (*fig: gap*) colmare

bridle ['braɪdl] *n* briglia; ~ **path** *n* sentiero (per cavalli)

brief [bri:f] *adj* breve ♦ *n* (*LAW*) comparsa; (*gen*) istruzioni *fpl* ♦ *vt* mettere al corrente; **~s** *npl* (*underwear*) mutande *fpl*; **~case** *n* cartella; **~ing** *n* briefing *m inv*; **~ly** *adv* (*glance*) di sfuggita; (*explain, say*) brevemente

bright [braɪt] *adj* luminoso(a); (*clever*) sveglio(a); (*lively*) vivace; **~en** (*also: ~en up*) *vt* (*room*) rendere luminoso(a) ♦ *vi* schiarirsi; (*person*) rallegrarsi

brilliance ['brɪljəns] *n* splendore *m*

brilliant ['brɪljənt] *adj* brillante; (*light,*

smile) radioso(a); (*inf*) splendido(a)
brim [brim] *n* orlo
brine [brain] *n* (*CULIN*) salamoia
bring [briŋ] (*pt, pp* **brought**) *vt* portare; ~ **about** *vt* causare; ~ **back** *vt* riportare; ~ **down** *vt* portare giù; abbattere; ~ **forward** *vt* (*proposal*) avanzare; (*meeting*) anticipare; ~ **off** *vt* (*task, plan*) portare a compimento; ~ **out** *vt* tirar fuori; (*meaning*) mettere in evidenza; (*book, album*) far uscire; ~ **round** *vt* (*unconscious person*) far rinvenire; ~ **up** *vt* (*carry up*) portare su; (*child*) allevare; (*question*) introdurre; (*food: vomit*) rimettere, rigurgitare
brink [briŋk] *n* orlo
brisk [brisk] *adj* (*manner*) spiccio(a); (*trade*) vivace; (*pace*) svelto(a)
bristle ['brisl] *n* setola ♦ *vi* rizzarsi; **bristling with** irto(a) di
Britain ['britən] *n* (*also*: **Great** ~) Gran Bretagna
British ['britiʃ] *adj* britannico(a); **the** ~ *npl* i Britannici; **the** ~ **Isles** *npl* le Isole Britanniche; ~ **Rail** *n* compagnia ferroviaria britannica, ≈ Ferrovie *fpl* dello Stato
Briton ['britən] *n* britannico/a
brittle ['britl] *adj* fragile
broach [brəutʃ] *vt* (*subject*) affrontare
broad [brɔːd] *adj* largo(a); (*distinction*) generale; (*accent*) spiccato(a); **in** ~ **daylight** in pieno giorno; ~**cast** (*pt, pp* ~**cast**) *n* trasmissione *f* ♦ *vt* trasmettere per radio (*or* per televisione) ♦ *vi* fare una trasmissione; ~**en** *vt* allargare ♦ *vi* allargarsi; ~**ly** *adv* (*fig*) in generale; ~-**minded** *adj* di mente aperta
broccoli ['brɔkəli] *n* broccoli *mpl*
brochure ['brəuʃjuə*] *n* dépliant *m inv*
broil [brɔil] *vt* cuocere a fuoco vivo
broke [brəuk] *pt of* **break** ♦ *adj* (*inf*) squattrinato(a)
broken ['brəukn] *pp of* **break** ♦ *adj* rotto(a); **a** ~ **leg** una gamba rotta; **in** ~ **English** in un inglese stentato; ~-**hearted** *adj*: **to be** ~**hearted** avere il cuore spezzato
broker ['brəukə*] *n* agente *m*

brolly ['brɔli] (*BRIT*: *inf*) *n* ombrello
bronchitis [brɔŋ'kaitis] *n* bronchite *f*
bronze [brɔnz] *n* bronzo
brooch [brəutʃ] *n* spilla
brood [bruːd] *n* covata ♦ *vi* (*person*) rimuginare
brook [bruk] *n* ruscello
broom [brum] *n* scopa; (*BOT*) ginestra; ~**stick** *n* manico da scopa
Bros. *abbr* (= **Brothers**) F.lli
broth [brɔθ] *n* brodo
brothel ['brɔθl] *n* bordello
brother ['brʌðə*] *n* fratello; ~-**in-law** *n* cognato
brought [brɔːt] *pt, pp of* **bring**
brow [brau] *n* fronte *f*; (*rare, gen: eye*~) sopracciglio; (*of hill*) cima
brown [braun] *adj* bruno(a), marrone; (*tanned*) abbronzato(a) ♦ *n* (*colour*) colore *m* bruno *or* marrone ♦ *vt* (*CULIN*) rosolare; ~ **bread** *n* pane *m* integrale, pane nero
brownie ['brauni] *n* giovane esploratrice *f*; (*US*: *cake*) dolce al cioccolato e nocciole
brown paper *n* carta da pacchi *or* da imballaggio
brown sugar *n* zucchero greggio
browse [brauz] *vi* (*among books*) curiosare fra i libri; **to** ~ **through a book** sfogliare un libro
bruise [bruːz] *n* (*on person*) livido ♦ *vt* farsi un livido a
brunette [bruː'nɛt] *n* bruna
brunt [brʌnt] *n*: **the** ~ **of** (*attack, criticism etc*) il peso maggiore di
brush [brʌʃ] *n* spazzola; (*for painting, shaving*) pennello; (*quarrel*) schermaglia ♦ *vt* spazzolare; (*also*: ~ **against**) sfiorare; ~ **aside** *vt* scostare; ~ **up** *vt* (*knowledge*) rinfrescare; ~**wood** *n* macchia
Brussels ['brʌslz] *n* Bruxelles *f*; ~ **sprout** *n* cavolo di Bruxelles
brutal ['bruːtl] *adj* brutale
brute [bruːt] *n* bestia ♦ *adj*: **by** ~ **force** con la forza, a viva forza
B.Sc. *n abbr* = **Bachelor of Science**
BSE *n abbr* (= **bovine spongiform encephalopathy**) encefalite *f* bovina, spongiforme
bubble ['bʌbl] *n* bolla ♦ *vi* ribollire;

(*sparkle*, *fig*) essere effervescente; ~ **bath** *n* bagnoschiuma *m inv*; ~ **gum** *n* gomma americana

buck [bʌk] *n* maschio (*di camoscio*, *caprone*, *coniglio etc*); (*US*: *inf*) dollaro ♦ *vi* sgroppare; **to pass the ~ (to sb)** scaricare (su di qn) la propria responsabilità; ~ **up** *vi* (*cheer up*) rianimarsi

bucket ['bʌkɪt] *n* secchio

buckle ['bʌkl] *n* fibbia ♦ *vt* allacciare ♦ *vi* (*wheel etc*) piegarsi

bud [bʌd] *n* gemma; (*of flower*) bocciolo ♦ *vi* germogliare; (*flower*) sbocciare

Buddhism ['budɪzəm] *n* buddismo

budding ['bʌdɪŋ] *adj* (*poet etc*) in erba

buddy ['bʌdɪ] (*US*) *n* compagno

budge [bʌdʒ] *vt* scostare; (*fig*) smuovere ♦ *vi* spostarsi; smuoversi

budgerigar ['bʌdʒərɪgɑː*] *n* pappagallino

budget ['bʌdʒɪt] *n* bilancio preventivo ♦ *vi*: **to ~ for sth** fare il bilancio per qc

budgie ['bʌdʒɪ] *n* = **budgerigar**

buff [bʌf] *adj* color camoscio ♦ *n* (*inf*: *enthusiast*) appassionato/a

buffalo ['bʌfələu] (*pl* ~ *or* ~**es**) *n* bufalo; (*US*) bisonte *m*

buffer ['bʌfə*] *n* respingente *m*; (*COMPUT*) memoria tampone, buffer *m inv*

buffet[1] ['bufeɪ] *n* (*food*, *BRIT*: *bar*) buffet *m inv*; ~ **car** (*BRIT*) (*in RAIL*) ≈ servizio ristoro

buffet[2] ['bʌfɪt] *vt* sferzare

bug [bʌg] *n* (*esp US*: *insect*) insetto; (*COMPUT*, *fig*: *germ*) virus *m inv*; (*spy device*) microfono spia ♦ *vt* mettere sotto controllo; (*inf*: *annoy*) scocciare

buggy ['bʌgɪ] *n* (*baby* ~) passeggino

bugle ['bjuːgl] *n* tromba

build [bɪld] (*pt*, *pp* **built**) *n* (*of person*) corporatura ♦ *vt* costruire; ~ **up** *vt* accumulare; aumentare; ~**er** *n* costruttore *m*; ~**ing** *n* costruzione *f*; edificio; (*industry*) edilizia; ~**ing society** (*BRIT*) *n* società *f inv* immobiliare

built [bɪlt] *pt*, *pp of* **build** ♦ *adj*: ~-**in** (*cupboard*) a muro; (*device*) incorporato(a); ~-**up area** *n* abitato

bulb [bʌlb] *n* (*BOT*) bulbo; (*ELEC*) lampadina

bulge [bʌldʒ] *n* rigonfiamento ♦ *vi* essere protuberante *or* rigonfio(a); **to be bulging with** essere pieno(a) *or* zeppo(a) di

bulk [bʌlk] *n* massa, volume *m*; **in ~ a** pacchi (*or* cassette *etc*); (*COMM*) all'ingrosso; **the ~ of** il grosso di; ~**y** *adj* grosso(a); voluminoso(a)

bull [bul] *n* toro; (*male elephant*, *whale*) maschio; ~**dog** *n* bulldog *m inv*

bulldozer ['buldəuzə*] *n* bulldozer *m inv*

bullet ['bulɪt] *n* pallottola

bulletin ['bulɪtɪn] *n* bollettino

bulletproof ['bulɪtpruːf] *adj* (*car*) blindato(a); (*vest etc*) antiproiettile *inv*

bullfight ['bulfaɪt] *n* corrida; ~**er** *n* torero; ~**ing** *n* tauromachia

bullion ['buljən] *n* oro *or* argento in lingotti

bullock ['bulək] *n* manzo

bullring ['bulrɪŋ] *n* arena (per corride)

bull's-eye ['bulzaɪ] *n* centro del bersaglio

bully ['bulɪ] *n* prepotente *m* ♦ *vt* angariare; (*frighten*) intimidire

bum [bʌm] (*inf*) *n* (*backside*) culo; (*tramp*) vagabondo/a

bumblebee ['bʌmblbiː] *n* bombo

bump [bʌmp] *n* (*in car*) piccolo tamponamento; (*jolt*) scossa; (*on road etc*) protuberanza; (*on head*) bernoccolo ♦ *vt* battere; ~ **into** *vt fus* scontrarsi con; (*person*) imbattersi in; ~**er** *n* paraurti *m inv* ♦ *adj*: ~**er harvest** raccolto eccezionale; ~**er cars** *npl* autoscontri *mpl*

bumptious ['bʌmpʃəs] *adj* presuntuoso(a)

bumpy ['bʌmpɪ] *adj* (*road*) dissestato(a)

bun [bʌn] *n* focaccia; (*of hair*) crocchia

bunch [bʌntʃ] *n* (*of flowers*, *keys*) mazzo; (*of bananas*) casco; (*of people*) gruppo; ~ **of grapes** grappolo d'uva; ~**es** *npl* (*in hair*) codine *fpl*

bundle ['bʌndl] *n* fascio ♦ *vt* (*also*: ~ **up**) legare in un fascio; (*put*): **to ~ sth/sb into** spingere qc/qn in

bungalow ['bʌngələu] *n* bungalow *m inv*

bungle ['bʌngl] *vt* fare un pasticcio di

bunion ['bʌnjən] *n* callo (al piede)

bunk [bʌŋk] *n* cuccetta; ~ **beds** *npl* letti *mpl* a castello

bunker ['bʌŋkə*] n (coal store) ripostiglio per il carbone; (MIL, GOLF) bunker m inv

bunny ['bʌnɪ] n (also: ~ rabbit) coniglietto

bunting ['bʌntɪŋ] n pavesi mpl, bandierine fpl

buoy [bɔɪ] n boa; ~ up vt (fig) sostenere; ~ant adj galleggiante; (fig) vivace

burden ['bə:dn] n carico, fardello ♦ vt: to ~ sb with caricare di

bureau [bjuə'rəu] (pl **bureaux**) n (BRIT: writing desk) scrivania; (US: chest of drawers) cassettone m; (office) ufficio, agenzia

bureaucracy [bjuə'rɔkrəsɪ] n burocrazia

bureaux [bjuə'rəuz] npl of **bureau**

burglar ['bə:glə*] n scassinatore m; ~ alarm n campanello antifurto; ~y n furto con scasso

burial ['berɪəl] n sepoltura

burly ['bə:lɪ] adj robusto(a)

Burma ['bə:mə] n Birmania

burn [bə:n] (pt, pp **burned** or **burnt**) vt, vi bruciare ♦ n bruciatura, scottatura; ~ down vt distruggere col fuoco; ~er n (on cooker) fornello; (TECH) bruciatore m, becco (a gas); ~ing adj in fiamme; (sand) che scotta; (ambition) bruciante; **burnt** pt, pp of **burn**

burrow ['bʌrəu] n tana ♦ vt scavare

bursary ['bə:sərɪ] (BRIT) n (SCOL) borsa di studio

burst [bə:st] (pt, pp **burst**) vt far scoppiare ♦ vi esplodere; (tyre) scoppiare ♦ n scoppio; (also: ~ pipe) rottura nel tubo, perdita; a ~ of speed uno scatto di velocità; to ~ into flames/tears scoppiare in fiamme/lacrime; to ~ out laughing scoppiare a ridere; to be ~ing with scoppiare di; ~ into vt fus (room etc) irrompere in

bury ['berɪ] vt seppellire

bus [bʌs] (pl ~es) n autobus m inv

buses ['bʌsɪz] npl of **bus**

bush [buʃ] n cespuglio; (scrub land) macchia; to beat about the ~ menare il cane per l'aia

bushy ['buʃɪ] adj cespuglioso(a)

busily ['bɪzɪlɪ] adv con impegno, alacremente

business ['bɪznɪs] n (matter) affare m; (trading) affari mpl; (firm) azienda; (job, duty) lavoro; to be away on ~ essere andato via per affari; it's none of my ~ questo non mi riguarda; he means ~ non scherza; ~like adj serio(a); efficiente; ~man/woman n uomo/donna d'affari; ~ trip n viaggio d'affari

busker ['bʌskə*] (BRIT) n suonatore/trice ambulante

bus-stop n fermata d'autobus

bust [bʌst] n busto; (ANAT) seno ♦ adj (inf: broken) rotto(a); to go ~ fallire

bustle ['bʌsl] n movimento, attività ♦ vi darsi da fare; **bustling** adj movimentato(a)

busy ['bɪzɪ] adj occupato(a); (shop, street) molto frequentato(a) ♦ vt: to ~ o.s. darsi da fare; ~body n ficcanaso m/f inv; ~ signal (US) n (TEL) segnale m di occupato

---

KEYWORD

but [bʌt] conj ma; **I'd love to come, ~ I'm busy** vorrei tanto venire, ma ho da fare

♦ prep (apart from, except) eccetto, tranne, meno; **he was nothing ~ trouble** non dava altro che guai; **it's none of my ~ this** è solo un bambino; **no-one ~ him can do it** nessuno può farlo tranne lui; ~ **for you/your help** se non fosse per te/per il tuo aiuto; **anything ~ that** tutto ma non questo

♦ adv (just, only) solo, soltanto; **she's ~ a child** è solo una bambina; **had I ~ known** se solo avessi saputo; **I can ~ try** tentar non nuoce; **all ~ finished** quasi finito

---

butcher ['butʃə*] n macellaio ♦ vt macellare; ~'s (shop) n macelleria

butler ['bʌtlə*] n maggiordomo

butt [bʌt] n (cask) grossa botte f; (of gun) calcio; (of cigarette) mozzicone m; (BRIT: fig: target) oggetto ♦ vt cozzare; ~ in vi (interrupt) interrompere

butter ['bʌtə*] n burro ♦ vt imburrare; ~cup n ranuncolo

butterfly ['bʌtəflaɪ] n farfalla; (SWIMMING:

also: ~ *stroke*) (nuoto a) farfalla

buttocks ['bʌtəks] *npl* natiche *fpl*

button ['bʌtn] *n* bottone *m*; (*US: badge*) distintivo ♦ *vt* (*also*: ~ *up*) abbottonare ♦ *vi* abbottonarsi

buttress ['bʌtrɪs] *n* contrafforte *f*

buxom ['bʌksəm] *adj* formoso(a)

buy [baɪ] (*pt, pp* **bought**) *vt* comprare ♦ *n* acquisto; **to** ~ **sb sth/sth from sb** comprare qc per qn/qc da qn; **to** ~ **sb a drink** offrire da bere a qn; ~**er** *n* compratore/trice

buzz [bʌz] *n* ronzio; (*inf: phone call*) colpo di telefono ♦ *vi* ronzare

buzzer ['bʌzə*] *n* cicalino

buzz word (*inf*) *n* termine *m* di gran moda

by [baɪ] *prep* **1** (*referring to cause, agent*) da; **killed** ~ **lightning** ucciso da un fulmine; **surrounded** ~ **a fence** circondato da uno steccato; **a painting** ~ **Picasso** un quadro di Picasso

2 (*referring to method, manner, means*): ~ **bus/car/train** in autobus/macchina/treno, con l'autobus/la macchina/il treno; **to pay** ~ **cheque** pagare con (un) assegno; ~ **moonlight** al chiaro di luna; ~ **saving hard, he ...** risparmiando molto, lui ...

3 (*via, through*) per; **we came** ~ **Dover** siamo venuti via Dover

4 (*close to, past*) accanto a; **the house** ~ **the river** la casa sul fiume; **a holiday** ~ **the sea** una vacanza al mare; **she sat** ~ **his bed** si sedette accanto al suo letto; **she rushed** ~ **me** mi è passata accanto correndo; **I go** ~ **the post office every day** passo davanti all'ufficio postale ogni giorno

5 (*not later than*) per, entro; ~ **4 o'clock** per *or* entro le 4; ~ **this time tomorrow** domani a quest'ora; ~ **the time I got here it was too late** quando sono arrivato era ormai troppo tardi

6 (*during*): ~ **day/night** di giorno/notte

7 (*amount*) a; ~ **the kilo/metre** a chili/metri; **paid** ~ **the hour** pagato all'ora;

one ~ **one** uno per uno; **little** ~ **little** a poco a poco

8 (*MATH, measure*): **to divide/multiply** ~ **3** dividere/moltiplicare per 3; **it's broader** ~ **a metre** è un metro più largo, è più largo di un metro

9 (*according to*) per; **to play** ~ **the rules** attenersi alle regole; **it's all right** ~ **me** per me va bene

10: (**all**) ~ **oneself** *etc* (tutto(a)) solo(a); **he did it (all)** ~ **himself** lo ha fatto (tutto) da solo

11: ~ **the way** a proposito; **this wasn't my idea** ~ **the way** tra l'altro l'idea non è stata mia

♦ *adv* **1** *see* **go**; **pass** *etc*

2: ~ **and** ~ (*in past*) poco dopo; (*in future*) fra breve; ~ **and large** nel complesso

bye(-bye) ['baɪ('baɪ)] *excl* ciao!, arrivederci!

by(e)-law *n* legge *f* locale

by-election (*BRIT*) *n* elezione *f* straordinaria

bygone ['baɪgɒn] *adj* passato(a) ♦ *n*: **let** ~**s be** ~**s** mettiamoci una pietra sopra

bypass ['baɪpɑːs] *n* circonvallazione *f*; (*MED*) by-pass *m inv* ♦ *vt* fare una deviazione intorno a

by-product *n* sottoprodotto; (*fig*) conseguenza secondaria

bystander ['baɪstændə*] *n* spettatore/trice

byte [baɪt] *n* (*COMPUT*) byte *m inv*, bicarattere *m*

byword ['baɪwəːd] *n*: **to be a** ~ **for** essere sinonimo di

by-your-leave *n*: **without so much as a** ~ senza nemmeno chiedere il permesso

C

C [siː] *n* (*MUS*) do

C.A. *n abbr* = **chartered accountant**

cab [kæb] *n* taxi *m inv*; (*of train, truck*) cabina

cabaret ['kæbəreɪ] *n* cabaret *m inv*

cabbage ['kæbɪdʒ] *n* cavolo

cabin ['kæbɪn] n capanna; (on ship) cabina; ~ cruiser n cabinato
cabinet ['kæbɪnɪt] n (POL) consiglio dei ministri; (furniture) armadietto; (also: display ~) vetrinetta
cable ['keɪbl] n cavo; fune f; (TEL) cablogramma m ♦ vt telegrafare; ~-car n funivia; ~ television n televisione f via cavo
cache [kæʃ] n deposito segreto
cackle ['kækl] vi schiamazzare
cacti ['kæktaɪ] npl of cactus
cactus ['kæktəs] (pl cacti) n cactus m inv
cadet [kə'dɛt] n (MIL) cadetto
cadge [kædʒ] (inf) vt scroccare
café ['kæfeɪ] n caffè m inv
cafeteria [kæfɪ'tɪərɪə] n self-service m inv
cage [keɪdʒ] n gabbia
cagey ['keɪdʒɪ] (inf) adj chiuso(a); guardingo(a)
cagoule [kə'guːl] n K-way m inv ®
cajole [kə'dʒəul] vt allettare
cake [keɪk] n (large) torta; (small) pasticcino; ~ of soap saponetta; ~d adj: ~d with incrostato(a) di
calculate ['kælkjuleɪt] vt calcolare; calculation n [-'leɪʃən] n calcolo; calculator n calcolatrice f
calendar ['kæləndə*] n calendario; ~ year n anno civile
calf [kɑːf] n (pl calves) n (of cow) vitello; (of other animals) piccolo; (also: ~skin) (pelle f di) vitello; (ANAT) polpaccio
calibre ['kælɪbə*] (US caliber) n calibro
call [kɔːl] vt (gen, also TEL) chiamare; (meeting) indire ♦ vi chiamare; (visit: also: ~ in, ~ round) passare ♦ n (shout) grido, urlo; (TEL) telefonato; to be ~ed (person, object) chiamarsi; to be on ~ essere a disposizione; ~ back vi (return) ritornare; (TEL) ritelefonare, richiamare; ~ for vt fus richiedere; (fetch) passare a prendere; ~ off vt disdire; ~ on vt fus (visit) passare da; (appeal to) chiedere a; ~ out vi (in pain) urlare; ~ up vt (MIL) chiamare; (TEL) telefonare a; ~box n (BRIT) cabina telefonica; ~er n persona che chiama;

visitatore/trice; ~ girl n ragazza f squillo inv; ~-in (US) n (phone-in) trasmissione f a filo diretto con gli ascoltatori; ~ing n vocazione f; ~ing card (US) n biglietto da visita
callous ['kæləs] adj indurito(a), insensibile
calm [kɑːm] adj calmo(a) ♦ n calma ♦ vt calmare; ~ down vi calmarsi ♦ vt calmare
Calor gas ['kælə*-] ® n butano
calorie ['kælərɪ] n caloria
calves [kɑːvz] npl of calf
camber ['kæmbə*] n (of road) bombatura
Cambodia [kæm'bəudjə] n Cambogia
camcorder ['kæmkɔːdə*] n camcorder f inv
came [keɪm] pt of come
camel ['kæməl] n cammello
camera ['kæmərə] n macchina fotografica; (CINEMA, TV) cinepresa; in ~ a porte chiuse; ~man n cameraman m inv
camouflage ['kæməflɑːʒ] n (MIL, ZOOL) mimetizzazione f ♦ vt mimetizzare
camp [kæmp] n campeggio; (MIL) campo ♦ vi accamparsi ♦ adj effeminato(a)
campaign [kæm'peɪn] n (MIL, POL etc) campagna ♦ vi (also fig) fare una campagna
camp bed (BRIT) n brandina
camper ['kæmpə*] n campeggiatore/trice; (vehicle) camper m inv
camping ['kæmpɪŋ] n campeggio; to go ~ andare in campeggio
campsite ['kæmpsaɪt] n campeggio
campus ['kæmpəs] n campus m inv
can[1] [kæn] n (of milk) scatola; (of oil) bidone m; (of water) tanica; (tin) scatola ♦ vt mettere in scatola

---
KEYWORD
---

can[2] [kæn] (negative cannot, can't; conditional and pt could) aux vb 1 (be able to) potere; I ~'t go any further non posso andare oltre; you ~ do it if you try sei in grado di farlo — basta provarci; I'll help you all I ~ ti aiuterò come potrò; I ~'t see you non ti vedo 2 (know how to) sapere, essere capace di;

I ~ **swim** so nuotare; ~ **you speak French?** parla francese? **3** (*may*) potere; **could I have a word with you?** posso parlarle un momento? **4** (*expressing disbelief, puzzlement etc*): **it ~'t be true!** non può essere vero!; **what** CAN **he want?** cosa può mai volere? **5** (*expressing possibility, suggestion etc*): **he could be in the library** può darsi che sia in biblioteca; **she could have been delayed** può aver avuto un contrattempo

Canada ['kænədə] *n* Canada *m*
Canadian [kə'neɪdɪən] *adj, n* canadese *m/f*
canal [kə'næl] *n* canale *m*
canary [kə'nɛərɪ] *n* canarino
cancel ['kænsəl] *vt* annullare; (*train*) sopprimere; (*cross out*) cancellare; **~lation** [-'leɪʃən] *n* annullamento; soppressione *f*; cancellazione *f*; (*TOURISM*) prenotazione *f* annullata
cancer ['kænsə*] *n* cancro; **C~** (*sign*) Cancro
candid ['kændɪd] *adj* onesto(a)
candidate ['kændɪdeɪt] *n* candidato/a
candle ['kændl] *n* candela; (*in church*) cero; **~light** *n*: **by ~light** a lume di candela; **~stick** *n* bugia; (*bigger, ornate*) candeliere *m*
candour ['kændə*] (*US* **candor**) *n* sincerità
candy ['kændɪ] *n* zucchero candito; (*US*) caramella; caramelle *fpl*; **~-floss** (*BRIT*) *n* zucchero filato
cane [keɪn] *n* canna; (*for furniture*) bambù *m*; (*stick*) verga ♦ *vt* (*BRIT: SCOL*) punire a colpi di verga
canister ['kænɪstə*] *n* scatola metallica
cannabis ['kænəbɪs] *n* canapa indiana
canned ['kænd] *adj* (*food*) in scatola
cannon ['kænən] (*pl* ~ *or* ~**s**) *n* (*gun*) cannone *m*
cannot ['kænɔt] = **can not**
canny ['kænɪ] *adj* furbo(a)
canoe [kə'nuː] *n* canoa
canon ['kænən] *n* (*clergyman*) canonico; (*standard*) canone *m*
can opener [-'əʊpnə*] *n* apriscatole

m inv
canopy ['kænəpɪ] *n* baldacchino
can't [kɑːnt] = **can not**
cantankerous [kæn'tæŋkərəs] *adj* stizzoso(a)
canteen [kæn'tiːn] *n* mensa; (*BRIT: of cutlery*) portaposate *m inv*
canter ['kæntə*] *vi* andare al piccolo galoppo
canvas ['kænvəs] *n* tela
canvass ['kænvəs] *vi* (*POL*): **to ~ for** raccogliere voti per ♦ *vt* fare un sondaggio di
canyon ['kænjən] *n* canyon *m inv*
cap [kæp] *n* (*hat*) berretto; (*of pen*) coperchio; (*of bottle, toy gun*) tappo; (*contraceptive*) diaframma *m* ♦ *vt* (*outdo*) superare; (*limit*) fissare un tetto a
capability [keɪpə'bɪlɪtɪ] *n* capacità *f inv*, abilità *f inv*
capable ['keɪpəbl] *adj* capace
capacity [kə'pæsɪtɪ] *n* capacità *f inv*; (*of lift etc*) capienza
cape [keɪp] *n* (*garment*) cappa; (*GEO*) capo
caper ['keɪpə*] *n* (*CULIN*) cappero; (*prank*) scherzetto
capital ['kæpɪtl] *n* (*also*: ~ **city**) capitale *f*; (*money*) capitale *m*; (*also*: ~ **letter**) (*lettera*) maiuscola; **~ gains tax** *n* imposta sulla plusvalenza; **~ism** *n* capitalismo; **~ist** *adj, n* capitalista (*m/f*); **~ize**: **to ~ize on** *vt fus* trarre vantaggio da; **~ punishment** *n* pena capitale
Capricorn ['kæprɪkɔːn] *n* Capricorno
capsize [kæp'saɪz] *vt* capovolgere ♦ *vi* capovolgersi
capsule ['kæpsjuːl] *n* capsula
captain ['kæptɪn] *n* capitano
caption ['kæpʃən] *n* leggenda
captivate ['kæptɪveɪt] *vt* avvincere
captive ['kæptɪv] *adj, n* prigioniero(a)
captivity [kæp'tɪvɪtɪ] *n* cattività
capture ['kæptʃə*] *vt* catturare; (*COMPUT*) registrare ♦ *n* cattura; (*data* ~) registrazione *f* or rilevazione *f* di dati
car [kɑː*] *n* (*AUT*) macchina, automobile *f*; (*RAIL*) vagone *m*
carafe [kə'ræf] *n* caraffa
caramel ['kærəməl] *n* caramello

caravan ['kærəvæn] *n (BRIT)* roulotte *f inv*; *(of camels)* carovana; **~ site** *(BRIT) n* campeggio per roulotte

carbohydrates [kɑːbəʊ'haɪdreɪts] *npl (foods)* carboidrati *mpl*

carbon ['kɑːbən] *n* carbonio; **~ paper** *n* carta carbone

carburettor [kɑːbju'rɛtə*] *(US* **carburetor**) *n* carburatore *m*

card [kɑːd] *n* carta; *(visiting ~ etc)* biglietto; *(Christmas ~ etc)* cartolina; **~board** *n* cartone *m*; **~ game** *n* gioco di carte

cardiac ['kɑːdɪæk] *adj* cardiaco(a)

cardigan ['kɑːdɪgən] *n* cardigan *m inv*

cardinal ['kɑːdɪnl] *adj* cardinale ♦ *n* cardinale *m*

card index *n* schedario

care [kɛə*] *n* cura, attenzione *f*; *(worry)* preoccupazione *f* ♦ *vi*: **to ~ about** curarsi di; *(thing, idea)* interessarsi di; **~ of** presso; **in sb's ~** alle cure di qn; **to take ~ (to do)** fare attenzione (a fare); **to take ~ of** curarsi di; *(bill, problem)* occuparsi di; **I don't ~** non me ne importa; **I couldn't ~ less** non m'interessa affatto; **~ for** *vt fus* aver cura di; *(like)* volere bene a

career [kə'rɪə*] *n* carriera ♦ *vi (also: ~ along)* andare di (gran) carriera

carefree ['kɛəfriː] *adj* sgombro(a) di preoccupazioni

careful ['kɛəful] *adj* attento(a); *(cautious)* cauto(a); **(be) ~!** attenzione!; **~ly** *adv* con cura; cautamente

careless ['kɛəlɪs] *adj* negligente; *(heedless)* spensierato(a)

carer ['kɛərə*] *n* assistente *m/f (di persone malata o handicappata)*

caress [kə'rɛs] *n* carezza ♦ *vt* accarezzare

caretaker ['kɛəteɪkə*] *n* custode *m*

car-ferry *n* traghetto

cargo ['kɑːgəʊ] *(pl* **~es**) *n* carico

car hire *n* autonoleggio

Caribbean [kærɪ'biːən] *adj*: **the ~ (Sea)** il Mar dei Caraibi

caring ['kɛərɪŋ] *adj (person)* premuroso(a); *(society, organization)* umanitario(a)

carnage ['kɑːnɪdʒ] *n* carneficina

carnation [kɑː'neɪʃən] *n* garofano

carnival ['kɑːnɪvəl] *n (public celebration)* carnevale *m*; *(US: funfair)* luna park *m inv*

carol ['kærəl] *n*: **(Christmas) ~** canto di Natale

carp [kɑːp] *n (fish)* carpa; **~ at** *vt fus* trovare a ridire su

car park *(BRIT) n* parcheggio

carpenter ['kɑːpɪntə*] *n* carpentiere *m*

carpentry ['kɑːpɪntrɪ] *n* carpenteria

carpet ['kɑːpɪt] *n* tappeto ♦ *vt* coprire con tappeto; **~ bombing** *n* bombardamento a tappeto; **~ slippers** *npl* pantofole *fpl*; **~ sweeper** *n* scopatappeti *m inv*

car phone *n* telefonino per auto, cellulare *m* per auto

carriage ['kærɪdʒ] *n* vettura; *(of goods)* trasporto; **~ return** *n (on typewriter etc)* leva *(or* tasto) del ritorno a capo; **~way** *(BRIT) n (part of road)* carreggiata

carrier ['kærɪə*] *n (of disease)* portatore/trice; *(COMM)* impresa di trasporti; **~ bag** *(BRIT) n* sacchetto

carrot ['kærət] *n* carota

carry ['kærɪ] *vt (subj: person)* portare; *(: vehicle)* trasportare; *(involve: responsibilities etc)*; *(MED)* essere portatore/trice di ♦ *vi (sound)* farsi sentire; **to be** *or* **get carried away** *(fig)* entusiasmarsi; **~ on** *vi*: **to ~ on with sth/doing** continuare qc/a fare ♦ *vt* mandare avanti; **~ out** *vt (orders)* eseguire; *(investigation)* svolgere; **~cot** *(BRIT) n* culla portabile; **~-on** *(inf) n (fuss)* casino, confusione *f*

cart [kɑːt] *n* carro ♦ *vt (inf)* trascinare

carton ['kɑːtən] *n (box)* scatola di cartone; *(of yogurt)* cartone *m*; *(of cigarettes)* stecca

cartoon [kɑː'tuːn] *n (PRESS)* disegno umoristico; *(comic strip)* fumetto; *(CINEMA)* disegno animato

cartridge ['kɑːtrɪdʒ] *n (for gun, pen)* cartuccia; *(music tape)* cassetta

carve [kɑːv] *vt (meat)* trinciare; *(wood, stone)* intagliare; **~ up** *vt (fig: country)* suddividere; **carving** *n (in wood etc)*

scultura; **carving knife** *n* trinciante *m*
car wash *n* lavaggio auto
cascade [kæs'keɪd] *n* cascata
case [keɪs] *n* caso; (LAW) causa, processo;
(*box*) scatola; (BRIT: *also*: suit~) valigia; **in
~ of** in caso di; **in ~ he** caso mai lui; **in
any ~** in ogni caso; **just in ~** in caso di
bisogno
cash [kæʃ] *n* denaro; (*coins, notes*) denaro
liquido ♦ *vt* incassare; **to pay (in) ~**
pagare in contanti; **~ on delivery**
pagamento alla consegna; **~-book** *n*
giornale *m* di cassa; **~ card** (BRIT) *n*
tesserino di prelievo; **~ desk** (BRIT) *n*
cassa; **~ dispenser** (BRIT) *n* sportello
automatico
cashew [kæ'ʃu:] *n* (*also*: ~ **nut**) anacardio
cashier [kæ'ʃɪə*] *n* cassiere/a
cashmere ['kæʃmɪə*] *n* cachemire *m*
cash register *n* registratore *m* di cassa
casing ['keɪsɪŋ] *n* rivestimento
casino [kə'si:nəʊ] *n* casinò *m* *inv*
cask [kɑ:sk] *n* botte *f*
casket ['kɑ:skɪt] *n* cofanetto; (US: *coffin*)
bara
casserole ['kæsərəʊl] *n* casseruola;
(*food*): **chicken ~** pollo in casseruola
cassette [kæ'set] *n* cassetta; **~ player** *n*
riproduttore *m* a cassette; **~ recorder** *n*
registratore *m* a cassette
cast [kɑ:st] (*pt, pp* **cast**) *vt* (*throw*)
gettare; (*metal*) gettare, fondere; (THEATRE):
to ~ sb as Hamlet scegliere qn per la
parte di Amleto ♦ *n* (THEATRE) cast *m* *inv*;
(*also*: *plaster* ~) ingessatura; **to ~ one's
vote** votare, dare il voto; **~ off** *vi* (NAUT)
salpare; (KNITTING) calare; **~ on** *vi*
(KNITTING) avviare le maglie
castaway ['kɑ:stəwəɪ] *n* naufrago/a
caster sugar ['kɑ:stə*-] (BRIT) *n* zucchero
semolato
casting vote ['kɑ:stɪŋ-] (BRIT) *n* voto
decisivo
cast iron *n* ghisa
castle ['kɑ:sl] *n* castello
castor ['kɑ:stə*] *n* (*wheel*) rotella; **~ oil** *n*
olio di ricino
castrate [kæs'treɪt] *vt* castrare
casual ['kæʒjul] *adj* (*by chance*) casuale;

fortuito(a); (*irregular*: *work etc*)
avventizio(a); (*unconcerned*) noncurante,
indifferente; **~ wear** casual *m*; **~ly** *adv*
(*in a relaxed way*) con noncuranza; (*dress*)
casual
casualty ['kæʒjultɪ] *n* ferito/a; (*dead*)
morto/a, vittima; (MED: *department*)
pronto soccorso
cat [kæt] *n* gatto
catalogue ['kætəlɔg] (US **catalog**) *n*
catalogo ♦ *vt* catalogare
catalyst ['kætəlɪst] *n* catalizzatore *m*
catalytic convertor [kætəlɪtɪk-] *n*
marmitta catalitica, catalizzatore *m*
catapult ['kætəpʌlt] *n* catapulta; fionda
cataract ['kætərækt] *n* (*also* MED)
cateratta
catarrh [kə'tɑ:*] *n* catarro
catastrophe [kə'tæstrəfɪ] *n* catastrofe *f*
catch [kætʃ] (*pt, pp* **caught**) *vt* prendere;
(*ball*) afferrare; (*surprise*: *person*)
sorprendere; (*attention*) attirare;
(*comment, whisper*) cogliere; (*person*: *also*:
~ **up**) raggiungere ♦ *vi* (*fire*) prendere ♦ *n*
(*fish etc caught*) retata; (*of ball*) presa;
(*trick*) inganno; (TECH) gancio; (*game*)
catch *m* *inv*; **to ~ fire** prendere fuoco; **to
~ sight of** scorgere; **~ on** *vi* capire;
(*become popular*) affermarsi, far presa; **~
up** *vi* mettersi in pari ♦ *vt* (*also*: ~ *up
with*) raggiungere
catching ['kætʃɪŋ] *adj* (MED) contagioso(a)
catchment area ['kætʃmənt-] (BRIT) *n*
(SCOL) circoscrizione *f* scolare
catch phrase *n* slogan *m* *inv*; frase *f*
fatta
catchy ['kætʃɪ] *adj* orecchiabile
category ['kætɪgərɪ] *n* categoria
cater ['keɪtə*] *vi*: **~ for** (BRIT: *needs*)
provvedere a; (: *readers, consumers*)
incontrare i gusti di; (COMM: *provide food*)
provvedere alla ristorazione di; **~er** *n*
fornitore *m*; **~ing** *n* approvvigionamento
caterpillar ['kætəpɪlə*] *n* bruco; **~ track**
n catena a cingoli
cathedral [kə'θi:drəl] *n* cattedrale *f*,
duomo
catholic ['kæθəlɪk] *adj* universale;
aperto(a); eclettico(a); **C~** *adj*, *n* (REL)

cattolico(a)

Catseye ['kæts'aɪ] (®: *BRIT*) *n* (*AUT*) catarifrangente *m*

cattle ['kætl] *npl* bestiame *m*, bestie *fpl*

catty ['kætɪ] *adj* maligno(a), dispettoso(a)

caucus ['kɔːkəs] *n* (*POL: group*) comitato di dirigenti; (: *US*) (riunione *f* del) comitato elettorale

caught [kɔːt] *pt, pp of* **catch**

cauliflower ['kɔlɪflauə*] *n* cavolfiore *m*

cause [kɔːz] *n* causa ♦ *vt* causare

caution ['kɔːʃən] *n* prudenza; (*warning*) avvertimento ♦ *vt* avvertire; ammonire

cautious ['kɔːʃəs] *adj* cauto(a), prudente

cavalier [kævə'lɪə*] *adj* brusco(a)

cavalry ['kævəlrɪ] *n* cavalleria

cave [keɪv] *n* caverna, grotta; ~ **in** *vi* (*roof etc*) crollare; ~**man** *n* uomo delle caverne

caviar(e) ['kævɪɑː*] *n* caviale *m*

cavort [kə'vɔːt] *vi* far capriole

CB *n abbr* (= *Citizens' Band (Radio)*): ~ **radio (set)** baracchino

CBI *n abbr* (= *Confederation of British Industries*) ≈ Confindustria

cc *abbr* = **cubic centimetres; carbon copy**

CD *abbr* (*disc*) CD *m inv*; (*player*) lettore *m* CD *inv*

CD-ROM [-rɔm] *n abbr* CD-ROM *m inv*

cease [siːs] *vt, vi* cessare; ~**fire** *n* cessate il fuoco *m inv*; ~**less** *adj* incessante, continuo(a)

cedar ['siːdə*] *n* cedro

ceiling ['siːlɪŋ] *n* soffitto; (*on wages etc*) tetto

celebrate ['sɛlɪbreɪt] *vt, vi* celebrare; ~**d** *adj* celebre; **celebration** [-'breɪʃən] *n* celebrazione *f*

celery ['sɛlərɪ] *n* sedano

cell [sɛl] *n* cella; (*of revolutionaries, BIOL*) cellula; (*ELEC*) elemento (di batteria)

cellar ['sɛlə*] *n* sottosuolo; cantina

'cello ['tʃɛləu] *n* violoncello

cellphone ['sɛl,fəun] *n* cellulare *m*

Celt [kɛlt, sɛlt] *n* celta *m/f*

Celtic ['kɛltɪk, 'sɛltɪk] *adj* celtico(a)

cement [sə'mɛnt] *n* cemento; ~ **mixer** *n* betoniera

cemetery ['sɛmɪtrɪ] *n* cimitero

censor ['sɛnsə*] *n* censore *m* ♦ *vt* censurare; ~**ship** *n* censura

censure ['sɛnʃə*] *vt* riprovare, censurare

census ['sɛnsəs] *n* censimento

cent [sɛnt] *n* (*US: coin*) centesimo (= *1:100 di un dollaro*); *see also* **per**

centenary [sɛn'tiːnərɪ] *n* centenario

center ['sɛntə*] (*US*) *n, vt* = **centre**

centigrade ['sɛntɪgreɪd] *adj* centigrado(a)

centimetre ['sɛntɪmiːtə*] (*US* **centimeter**) *n* centimetro

centipede ['sɛntɪpiːd] *n* centopiedi *m inv*

central ['sɛntrəl] *adj* centrale; **C~ America** *n* America centrale; ~ **heating** *n* riscaldamento centrale; ~**ize** *vt* accentrare

centre ['sɛntə*] (*US* **center**) *n* centro ♦ *vt* centrare; ~**-forward** *n* (*SPORT*) centroavanti *m inv*; ~**-half** *n* (*SPORT*) centromediano

century ['sɛntjurɪ] *n* secolo; **20th** ~ ventesimo secolo

ceramic [sɪ'ræmɪk] *adj* ceramico(a); ~**s** *npl* ceramica

cereal ['siːrɪəl] *n* cereale *m*

ceremony ['sɛrɪmənɪ] *n* cerimonia; **to stand on** ~ fare complimenti

certain ['səːtən] *adj* corto(a); **to make** ~ **of** assicurarsi di; **for** ~ per certo, di sicuro; ~**ly** *adv* certamente, certo; ~**ty** *n* certezza

certificate [sə'tɪfɪkɪt] *n* certificato; diploma *m*

certified ['səːtɪfaɪd]: ~ **mail** (*US*) *n* posta raccomandata con ricevuta di ritorno; ~ **public accountant** (*US*) *n* ≈ commercialista *m/f*

certify ['səːtɪfaɪ] *vt* certificare; (*award diploma to*) conferire un diploma a; (*declare insane*) dichiarare pazzo(a)

cervical ['səːvɪkl] *adj*: ~ **cancer** cancro della cervice; ~ **smear** Pap-test *m inv*

cervix ['səːvɪks] *n* cervice *f*

cesspit ['sɛspɪt] *n* pozzo nero

cf. *abbr* (= *compare*) cfr

CFC *n* (= *chlorofluorocarbon*) CFC *m inv*

ch. *abbr* (= *chapter*) cap

chafe [tʃeɪf] *vt* fregare, irritare

chagrin ['ʃægrɪn] *n* disappunto

chain [tʃeɪn] *n* catena ♦ *vt* (*also*: ~ *up*) incatenare; ~ **reaction** *n* reazione *f* a catena; ~-**smoke** *vi* fumare una sigaretta dopo l'altra; ~ **store** *n* negozio a catena

chair [tʃɛə*] *n* sedia; (*armchair*) poltrona; (*of university*) cattedra; (*of meeting*) presidenza ♦ *vt* (*meeting*) presiedere; ~**lift** *n* seggiovia; ~**man** *n* presidente *m*

chalice ['tʃælɪs] *n* calice *m*

chalk [tʃɔːk] *n* gesso

challenge ['tʃælɪndʒ] *n* sfida ♦ *vt* sfidare; (*statement, right*) mettere in dubbio; **to ~ sb to do** sfidare qn a fare; **challenging** *adj* (*task*) impegnativo(a); (*look*) di sfida

chamber ['tʃeɪmbə*] *n* camera; ~ **of commerce** *n* camera di commercio; ~**maid** *n* cameriera; ~ **music** *n* musica da camera

chamois ['ʃæmwɑː] *n* camoscio; (*also: leather*) panno in pelle di camoscio

champagne [ʃæm'peɪn] *n* champagne *m inv*

champion ['tʃæmpɪən] *n* campione/essa; ~**ship** *n* campionato

chance [tʃɑːns] *n* caso; (*opportunity*) occasione *f*; (*likelihood*) possibilità *f inv* ♦ *vt*: **to ~ it** rischiare, provarci ♦ *adj* fortuito(a); **to take a ~** rischiare; **by ~** per caso

chancellor ['tʃɑːnsələ*] *n* cancelliere *m*; **C~ of the Exchequer** (*BRIT*) *n* Cancelliere dello Scacchiere

chandelier [ʃændə'lɪə*] *n* lampadario

change [tʃeɪndʒ] *vt* cambiare; (*transform*): **to ~ sb into** trasformare qn in ♦ *vi* cambiare; (~ *one's clothes*) cambiarsi; (*be transformed*): **to ~ into** trasformarsi in ♦ *n* cambiamento; (*of clothes*) cambio; (*money*) resto; **to ~ one's mind** cambiare idea; **for a ~** tanto per cambiare; ~**able** *adj* (*weather*) variabile; ~ **machine** *n* distributore automatico di monete; ~**over** *n* cambiamento, passaggio

changing ['tʃeɪndʒɪŋ] *adj* che cambia; (*colours*) cangiante; ~ **room** *n* (*BRIT*: *in shop*) camerino; (: *SPORT*) spogliatoio

channel ['tʃænl] *n* canale *m*; (*of river,*

sea) alveo ♦ *vt* canalizzare; **the (English) C~** la Manica; **the C~ Islands** *npl* le Isole Normanne; **the C~ Tunnel** *n* il tunnel sotto la Manica

chant [tʃɑːnt] *n* canto; salmodia ♦ *vt* cantare; salmodiare

chaos ['keɪɔs] *n* caos *m*

chap [tʃæp] (*BRIT*: *inf*) *n* (*man*) tipo

chapel ['tʃæpəl] *n* cappella

chaperone ['ʃæpərəun] *n* accompagnatrice *f* ♦ *vt* accompagnare

chaplain ['tʃæplɪn] *n* cappellano

chapped [tʃæpt] *adj* (*skin, lips*) screpolato(a)

chapter ['tʃæptə*] *n* capitolo

char [tʃɑː*] *vt* (*burn*) carbonizzare ♦ *n* (*BRIT*) = **charlady**

character ['kærɪktə*] *n* carattere *m*; (*in novel, film*) personaggio; ~**istic** [-'rɪstɪk] *adj* caratteristico(a) ♦ *n* caratteristica

charade [ʃə'rɑːd] *n* sciarada

charcoal ['tʃɑːkəul] *n* carbone *m* di legna

charge [tʃɑːdʒ] *n* accusa; (*cost*) prezzo; (*responsibility*) responsabilità ♦ *vt* (*gun, battery, MIL*: *enemy*) caricare; (*customer*) fare pagare a; (*sum*) fare pagare; (*LAW*): **to ~ sb (with)** accusare qn (di) ♦ *vi* (*gen with*: *up, along etc*) lanciarsi; ~**s** *npl* (*bank ~s etc*) tariffe *fpl*; **to reverse the ~s** (*TEL*) fare una telefonata a carico del destinatario; **to take ~ of** incaricarsi di; **to be in ~ of** essere responsabile per; **how much do you ~?** quanto chiedete?; **to ~ an expense (up) to sb** addebitare una spesa a qn; ~ **card** *n* carta *f* clienti *inv*

charitable ['tʃærɪtəbl] *adj* caritatevole

charity ['tʃærɪtɪ] *n* carità; (*organization*) opera pia

charlady ['tʃɑːleɪdɪ] (*BRIT*) *n* domestica a ore

charlatan ['ʃɑːlətən] *n* ciarlatano

charm [tʃɑːm] *n* fascino; (*on bracelet*) ciondolo ♦ *vt* affascinare, incantare; ~**ing** *adj* affascinante

chart [tʃɑːt] *n* tabella; grafico; (*map*) carta nautica ♦ *vt* fare una carta nautica di; ~**s** *npl* (*MUS*) hit parade *f*

charter ['tʃɑːtə*] *vt* (*plane*) noleggiare

♦ n (*document*) carta; ~ed accountant (*BRIT*) n ragioniere/a professionista; ~ flight n volo m charter *inv*

charwoman ['tʃɑːwumən] n = charlady

chase [tʃeɪs] vt inseguire; (*also*: ~ *away*) cacciare ♦ n caccia

chasm ['kæzəm] n abisso

chassis ['ʃæsɪ] n telaio

chastity ['tʃæstɪtɪ] n castità

chat [tʃæt] vi (*also*: have a ~) chiacchierare ♦ n chiacchierata; ~ show (*BRIT*) n talk show m *inv*

chatter ['tʃætə*] vi (*person*) ciarlare; (*bird*) cinguettare; (*teeth*) battere ♦ n ciarle *fpl*; cinguettio; ~box (*inf*) n chiacchierone/a

chatty ['tʃætɪ] adj (*style*) familiare; (*person*) chiacchierino(a)

chauffeur ['ʃəufə*] n autista m

chauvinist ['ʃəuvɪnɪst] n (*male* ~) maschilista m; (*nationalist*) sciovinista m/f

cheap [tʃiːp] adj a buon mercato; (*joke*) grossolano(a); (*poor quality*) di cattiva qualità ♦ adv a buon mercato; ~er adj meno caro(a); ~ly adv a buon prezzo, a buon mercato

cheat [tʃiːt] vi imbrogliare; (*at school*) copiare ♦ vt ingannare ♦ n imbroglione m; to ~ sb out of sth defraudare qn di qc

check [tʃek] vt verificare; (*passport, ticket*) controllare; (*halt*) fermare; (*restrain*) contenere ♦ n verifica, controllo; (*curb*) freno; (*US: bill*) conto; (*pattern: gen pl*) quadretti *mpl*; (*US*) = cheque ♦ adj (*pattern, cloth*) a quadretti; ~ in vi (*in hotel*) registrare; (*at airport*) presentarsi all'accettazione ♦ vt (*luggage*) depositare; ~ out vi (*in hotel*) saldare il conto; ~ up vi: to ~ up (on sth) investigare (qc); to ~ up on sb informarsi sul conto di qn; ~ered (*US*) adj = chequered; ~ers (*US*) n dama; ~-in (desk) n check-in m *inv*, accettazione f (bagagli *inv*); ~ing account (*US*) n conto corrente; ~mate n scaccomatto; ~out n (*in supermarket*) cassa; ~point n posto di blocco; ~room (*US*) n deposito m bagagli *inv*; ~up (*MED*) n controllo medico

cheek [tʃiːk] n guancia; (*impudence*) faccia tosta; ~bone n zigomo; ~y adj sfacciato(a)

cheep [tʃiːp] vi pigolare

cheer [tʃɪə*] vt applaudire; (*gladden*) rallegrare ♦ vi applaudire ♦ n grido (di incoraggiamento); ~s npl (*of approval, encouragement*) applausi *mpl*; evviva *mpl*; ~s! salute!; ~ up vi rallegrarsi, farsi animo ♦ vt rallegrare; ~ful adj allegro(a)

cheerio ['tʃɪərɪ'əu] (*BRIT*) excl ciao!

cheese [tʃiːz] n formaggio; ~board n piatto del (*or* per il) formaggio

cheetah ['tʃiːtə] n ghepardo

chef [ʃef] n capocuoco

chemical ['kemɪkəl] adj chimico(a) ♦ n prodotto chimico

chemist ['kemɪst] n (*BRIT: pharmacist*) farmacista m/f; (*scientist*) chimico/a; ~ry n chimica; ~'s (shop) (*BRIT*) n farmacia

cheque [tʃek] (*BRIT*) n assegno; ~book n libretto degli assegni; ~ card n carta f assegni *inv*

chequered ['tʃekəd] (*US* checkered) adj (*fig*) movimentato(a)

cherish ['tʃerɪʃ] vt aver caro

cherry ['tʃerɪ] n ciliegia; (*also*: ~ *tree*) ciliegio

chess [tʃes] n scacchi *mpl*; ~board n scacchiera

chest [tʃest] n petto; (*box*) cassa; ~ of drawers n cassettone m

chestnut ['tʃesnʌt] n castagna; (*also*: ~ *tree*) castagno

chew [tʃuː] vt masticare; ~ing gum n chewing gum m

chic [ʃiːk] adj elegante

chick [tʃɪk] n pulcino; (*inf*) pollastrella

chicken ['tʃɪkɪn] n pollo; (*inf: coward*) coniglio; ~ out (*inf*) vi avere fifa; ~pox n varicella

chicory ['tʃɪkərɪ] n cicoria

chief [tʃiːf] n capo ♦ adj principale; ~ executive n direttore m generale; ~ly adv per lo più, soprattutto

chilblain ['tʃɪlbleɪn] n gelone m

child [tʃaɪld] (*pl* ~ren) n bambino/a; ~birth n parto; ~hood n infanzia; ~ish adj puerile; ~like adj fanciullesco(a); ~

minder (*BRIT*) *n* bambinaia
children ['tʃɪldrən] *npl of* **child**
Chile ['tʃɪlɪ] *n* Cile *m*
chill [tʃɪl] *n* freddo; (*MED*) infreddatura
♦ *vt* raffreddare
chill(i)i ['tʃɪlɪ] *n* peperoncino
chilly ['tʃɪlɪ] *adj* freddo(a), fresco(a); **to
feel ~** sentirsi infreddolito(a)
chime [tʃaɪm] *n* carillon *m inv* ♦ *vi*
suonare, scampanare
chimney ['tʃɪmnɪ] *n* camino; **~ sweep** *n*
spazzacamino
chimpanzee [tʃɪmpæn'ziː] *n* scimpanzé
m inv
chin [tʃɪn] *n* mento
China ['tʃaɪnə] *n* Cina
china ['tʃaɪnə] *n* porcellana
Chinese [tʃaɪ'niːz] *adj* cinese ♦ *n inv*
cinese *m/f*; (*LING*) cinese *m*
chink [tʃɪŋk] *n* (*opening*) fessura; (*noise*)
tintinnio
chip [tʃɪp] *n* (*gen pl*: *CULIN*) patatina fritta;
(: *US*: *also*: *potato ~*) patatina; (*of wood,
glass, stone*) scheggia; (*also*: *micro~*) chip
m inv ♦ *vt* (*cup, plate*) scheggiare; **~ in**
(*inf*) *vi* (*contribute*) contribuire; (*interrupt*)
intromettersi
chiropodist [kɪ'rɔpədɪst] (*BRIT*) *n*
pedicure *m/f inv*
chirp [tʃɜːp] *vi* cinguettare; fare cri cri
chisel ['tʃɪzl] *n* cesello
chit [tʃɪt] *n* biglietto
chitchat ['tʃɪttʃæt] *n* chiacchiere *fpl*
chivalry ['ʃɪvəlrɪ] *n* cavalleria; cortesia
chives [tʃaɪvz] *npl* erba cipollina
chock-a-block ['tʃɔk-] *adj* pieno(a)
zeppo(a)
chock-full ['tʃɔk-] *adj* = **chock-a-block**
chocolate ['tʃɔklɪt] *n* (*substance*)
cioccolato, cioccolata; (*drink*) cioccolata;
(*a sweet*) cioccolatino
choice [tʃɔɪs] *n* scelta ♦ *adj* scelto(a)
choir ['kwaɪə*] *n* coro; **~boy** *n* corista *m*
fanciullo
choke [tʃəuk] *vi* soffocare ♦ *vt* soffocare;
(*block*): **to be ~d with** essere intasato(a)
di ♦ *n* (*AUT*) valvola dell'aria
cholera ['kɔlərə] *n* colera *m*
cholesterol [kə'lɛstərɔl] *n* colesterolo

choose [tʃuːz] (*pt* **chose**, *pp* **chosen**) *vt*
scegliere; **to ~ to do** decidere di fare;
preferire fare
choosy ['tʃuːzɪ] *adj* schizzinoso(a)
chop [tʃɔp] *vt* (*wood*) spaccare; (*CULIN*:
also: *~ up*) tritare ♦ *n* (*CULIN*) costoletta;
~s *npl* (*jaws*) mascelle *fpl*
chopper ['tʃɔpə*] *n* (*helicopter*) elicottero
choppy ['tʃɔpɪ] *adj* (*sea*) mosso(a)
chopsticks ['tʃɔpstɪks] *npl* bastoncini
mpl cinesi
choral ['kɔːrəl] *adj* corale
chord [kɔːd] *n* (*MUS*) accordo
chore [tʃɔː*] *n* faccenda; **household ~s**
faccende *fpl* domestiche
choreographer [kɔrɪ'ɔɡrəfə*] *n*
coreografo/a
chortle ['tʃɔːtl] *vi* ridacchiare
chorus ['kɔːrəs] *n* coro; (*repeated part of
song, also fig*) ritornello
chose [tʃəuz] *pt of* **choose**
chosen ['tʃəuzn] *pp of* **choose**
Christ [kraɪst] *n* Cristo
christen ['krɪsn] *vt* battezzare
Christian ['krɪstɪən] *adj, n* cristiano(a);
~ity [-'ænɪtɪ] *n* cristianesimo; **~ name** *n*
nome *m* (di battesimo)
Christmas ['krɪsməs] *n* Natale *m*; **Merry
~!** Buon Natale!; **~ card** *n* cartolina di
Natale; **~ Day** *n* il giorno di Natale; **~
Eve** *n* la vigilia di Natale; **~ tree** *n*
albero di Natale
chrome [krəum] *n* cromo
chromium ['krəumɪəm] *n* cromo
chronic ['krɔnɪk] *adj* cronico(a)
chronicle ['krɔnɪkl] *n* cronaca
chronological [krɔnə'lɔdʒɪkəl] *adj*
cronologico(a)
chrysanthemum [krɪ'sænθəməm] *n*
crisantemo
chubby ['tʃʌbɪ] *adj* paffuto(a)
chuck [tʃʌk] (*inf*) *vt* buttare, gettare;
(*BRIT*: *also*: *~ up*) piantare; **~ out** *vt* buttar
fuori
chuckle ['tʃʌkl] *vi* ridere sommessamente
chug [tʃʌɡ] *vi* fare ciuf ciuf
chum [tʃʌm] *n* compagno/a
chunk [tʃʌŋk] *n* pezzo
church [tʃɜːtʃ] *n* chiesa; **~yard** *n* sagrato

churlish ['tʃəːlɪʃ] *adj* rozzo(a), sgarbato(a)

churn [tʃəːn] *n (for butter)* zangola; *(for milk)* bidone *m*; **~ out** *vt* sfornare

chute [ʃuːt] *n (also: rubbish ~)* canale *m* di scarico; *(BRIT: children's slide)* scivolo

chutney ['tʃʌtnɪ] *n* salsa piccante *(di frutta, zucchero e spezie)*

CIA *(US) n abbr (= Central Intelligence Agency)* CIA *f*

CID *(BRIT) n abbr (= Criminal Investigation Department)* ≈ polizia giudiziaria

cider ['saɪdə*] *n* sidro

cigar [sɪ'gɑː*] *n* sigaro

cigarette [sɪgə'rɛt] *n* sigaretta; **~ case** *n* portasigarette *m inv*; **~ end** *n* mozzicone *m*

Cinderella [sɪndə'rɛlə] *n* Cenerentola

cinders ['sɪndəz] *npl* ceneri *fpl*

cine camera ['sɪnɪ-] *(BRIT) n* cinepresa

cine-film ['sɪnɪ-] *(BRIT) n* pellicola

cinema ['sɪnəmə] *n* cinema *m inv*

cinnamon ['sɪnəmən] *n* cannella

cipher ['saɪfə*] *n* cifra

circle ['səːkl] *n* cerchio; *(of friends etc)* circolo; *(in cinema)* galleria ♦ *vi* girare in circolo ♦ *vt (surround)* circondare; *(move round)* girare intorno a

circuit ['səːkɪt] *n* circuito; **~ous** [səː'kjuɪtəs] *adj* indiretto(a)

circular ['səːkjulə*] *adj* circolare ♦ *n* circolare *f*

circulate ['səːkjuleɪt] *vi* circolare ♦ *vt* far circolare; **circulation** [-'leɪʃən] *n* circolazione *f*; *(of newspaper)* tiratura

circumstances ['səːkəmstənsɪz] *npl* circostanze *fpl*; *(financial condition)* condizioni *fpl* finanziarie

circumvent [səːkəm'vɛnt] *vt* aggirare

circus ['səːkəs] *n* circo

CIS *n abbr (= Commonwealth of Independent States)* CSI *f*

cistern ['sɪstən] *n* cisterna; *(in toilet)* serbatoio d'acqua

citizen ['sɪtɪzn] *n (of country)* cittadino/a; *(of town)* abitante *m/f*; **~ship** *n* cittadinanza

citrus fruit ['sɪtrəs-] *n* agrume *m*

city ['sɪtɪ] *n* città *f inv*; **the C~** la Città di Londra *(centro commerciale)*

civic ['sɪvɪk] *adj* civico(a); **~ centre** *(BRIT) n* centro civico

civil ['sɪvɪl] *adj* civile; **~ engineer** *n* ingegnere *m* civile; **~ian** [sɪ'vɪlɪən] *adj, n* borghese *m/f*

civilization [sɪvɪlaɪ'zeɪʃən] *n* civiltà *f inv*

civilized ['sɪvɪlaɪzd] *adj* civilizzato(a); *(fig)* cortese

civil: **~ law** *n* codice *m* civile; *(study)* diritto civile; **~ servant** *n* impiegato/a statale; **C~ Service** *n* amministrazione *f* statale; **~ war** *n* guerra civile

clad [klæd] *adj:* **~ (in)** vestito(a) (di)

claim [kleɪm] *vt (assert):* **to ~ (that)/to be** sostenere (che)/di essere; *(credit, rights etc)* rivendicare; *(damages)* richiedere ♦ *vi (for insurance)* fare una domanda d'indennizzo ♦ *n* pretesa; rivendicazione *f*; richiesta; **~ant** *n (ADMIN, LAW)* richiedente *m/f*

clairvoyant [klɛə'vɔɪənt] *n* chiaroveggente *m/f*

clam [klæm] *n* vongola

clamber ['klæmbə*] *vi* arrampicarsi

clammy ['klæmɪ] *adj (weather)* caldo(a) umido(a); *(hands)* viscido(a)

clamour ['klæmə*] *(US* **clamor)** *vi:* **to ~ for** chiedere a gran voce

clamp [klæmp] *n* pinza, morsa ♦ *vt* stringere con una morsa; **~ down on** *vt fus* dare un giro di vite a

clan [klæn] *n* clan *m inv*

clang [klæŋ] *vi* emettere un suono metallico

clap [klæp] *vi* applaudire; **~ping** *n* applausi *mpl*

claret ['klærət] *n* vino di Bordeaux

clarify ['klærɪfaɪ] *vt* chiarificare, chiarire

clarinet [klærɪ'nɛt] *n* clarinetto

clarity ['klærɪtɪ] *n* clarità

clash [klæʃ] *n* frastuono; *(fig)* scontro ♦ *vi* scontrarsi; cozzare

clasp [klɑːsp] *n (hold)* stretta; *(of necklace, bag)* fermaglio, fibbia ♦ *vt* stringere

class [klɑːs] *n* classe *f* ♦ *vt* classificare

classic ['klæsɪk] *adj* classico(a) ♦ *n* classico; **~al** *adj* classico(a)

classified ['klæsɪfaɪd] *adj (information)*

segreto(a), riservato(a); **~ advertisement** *n* annuncio economico

classmate ['klɑːsmeɪt] *n* compagno/a di classe

classroom ['klɑːsrum] *n* aula

clatter ['klætə*] *n* tintinnio; scalpitio ♦ *vi* tintinnare; scalpitare

clause [klɔːz] *n* clausola; (*LING*) proposizione *f*

claw [klɔː] *n* (*of bird of prey*) artiglio; (*of lobster*) pinza; **~ at** *vt fus* graffiare; afferrare

clay [kleɪ] *n* argilla

clean [kliːn] *adj* pulito(a); (*clear, smooth*) liscio(a) ♦ *vt* pulire; **~ out** *vt* ripulire; **~ up** *vt* (*also fig*) ripulire; **~-cut** *adj* (*man*) curato(a); **~er** *n* (*person*) donna delle pulizie; **~er's** *n* (*also: dry ~er's*) tintoria; **~ing** *n* pulizia; **~liness** ['klɛnlɪnɪs] *n* pulizia

cleanse [klɛnz] *vt* pulire; purificare; **~r** *n* detergente *m*

clean-shaven [-'ʃeɪvn] *adj* sbarbato(a)

cleansing department ['klɛnzɪŋ-] (*BRIT*) *n* nettezza urbana

clear [klɪə*] *adj* chiaro(a); (*glass etc*) trasparente*; (*road, way*) libero(a); (*conscience*) pulito(a) ♦ *vt* sgombrare; liberare; (*table*) sparecchiare; (*cheque*) fare la compensazione di; (*LAW: suspect*) discolpare; (*obstacle*) superare ♦ *vi* (*weather*) rasserenarsi; (*fog*) andarsene ♦ *adv*: **~ of** distante da; **~ up** *vt* mettere in ordine; (*mystery*) risolvere; **~ance** *n* (*removal*) sgombro; (*permission*) autorizzazione *f*, permesso; **~-cut** *adj* ben delineato(a), distinto(a); **~ing** *n* radura; **~ing bank** (*BRIT*) *n* banca (che fa uso della camera di compensazione); **~ly** *adv* chiaramente; **~way** (*BRIT*) *n* strada con divieto di sosta

cleaver ['kliːvə*] *n* mannaia

clef [klɛf] *n* (*MUS*) chiave *f*

cleft [klɛft] *n* (*in rock*) crepa, fenditura

clench [klɛntʃ] *vt* stringere

clergy ['kləːdʒɪ] *n* clero; **~man** *n* ecclesiastico

clerical ['klɛrɪkəl] *adj* d'impiegato, (*REL*) clericale

clerk [klɑːk, (*US*) kləːrk] *n* (*BRIT*) impiegato/a; (*US*) commesso/a

clever ['klɛvə*] *adj* (*mentally*) intelligente; (*deft, skilful*) abile; (*device, arrangement*) ingegnoso(a)

click [klɪk] *vi* scattare ♦ *vt* (*heels etc*) battere; (*tongue*) far schioccare

client ['klaɪənt] *n* cliente *m/f*

cliff [klɪf] *n* scogliera scoscesa, rupe *f*

climate ['klaɪmɪt] *n* clima *m*

climax ['klaɪmæks] *n* culmine *m*; (*sexual*) orgasmo

climb [klaɪm] *vi* salire; (*clamber*) arrampicarsi ♦ *vt* salire; (*CLIMBING*) scalare ♦ *n* salita; arrampicata; scalata; **~-down** *n* marcia indietro; **~er** *n* rocciatore/trice; alpinista *m/f*; **~ing** *n* alpinismo

clinch [klɪntʃ] *vt* (*deal*) concludere

cling [klɪŋ] (*pt, pp* clung) *vi*: **to ~ (to)** aggrapparsi (a); (*of clothes*) aderire strettamente (a)

clinic ['klɪnɪk] *n* clinica; **~al** *adj* clinico(a); (*fig*) distaccato(a); (: *room*) freddo(a)

clink [klɪŋk] *vi* tintinnare

clip [klɪp] *n* (*for hair*) forcina; (*also: paper ~*) graffetta; (*TV, CINEMA*) sequenza ♦ *vt* attaccare insieme; (*hair, nails*) tagliare; (*hedge*) tosare; **~pers** *npl* (*for gardening*) cesoie *fpl*; (*also: nail ~pers*) forbicine *fpl* per le unghie; **~ping** *n* (*from newspaper*) ritaglio

clique [kliːk] *n* cricca

cloak [kləuk] *n* mantello ♦ *vt* avvolgere; **~room** *n* (*for coats etc*) guardaroba *m inv*; (*BRIT: W.C.*) gabinetti *mpl*

clock [klɔk] *n* orologio; **~ in** *or* **on** *vi* timbrare il cartellino (all'entrata); **~ off** *or* **out** *vi* timbrare il cartellino (all'uscita); **~wise** *adv* in senso orario; **~work** *n* movimento *or* meccanismo a orologeria ♦ *adj* a molla

clog [klɔg] *n* zoccolo ♦ *vt* intasare ♦ *vi* (*also*: **~ up**) intasarsi, bloccarsi

cloister ['klɔɪstə*] *n* chiostro

clone [kləun] *n* clone *m*

close[1] [kləus] *adj*: **~ (to)** vicino(a) (a); (*watch, link, relative*) stretto(a);

(*examination*) attento(a); (*contest*) combattuto(a); (*weather*) afoso(a) ♦ *adv* vicino, dappresso; ~ **to** vicino a; ~ **by**, ~ **at hand** a portata di mano; **a** ~ **friend** un amico intimo; **to have a** ~ **shave** (*fig*) scamparla bella

close² [kləuz] *vt* chiudere ♦ *vi* (*shop etc*) chiudere; (*lid, door etc*) chiudersi; (*end*) finire ♦ *vi* (*end*) fine *f*; ~ **down** *vi* cessare (definitivamente); ~**d** *adj* chiuso(a); ~**d shop** *n* azienda o fabbrica che impiega solo aderenti ai sindacati

close-knit [kləus'nɪt] *adj* (*family, community*) molto unito(a)

closely ['kləuslɪ] *adv* (*examine, watch*) da vicino; (*related*) strettamente

closet ['klɔzɪt] *n* (*cupboard*) armadio

close-up ['kləusʌp] *n* primo piano

closure ['kləuʒə*] *n* chiusura

clot [klɔt] *n* (*also: blood* ~) coagulo; (*inf: idiot*) scemo/a ♦ *vi* coagularsi

cloth [klɔθ] *n* (*material*) tessuto, stoffa; (*rag*) strofinaccio

clothe [kləuð] *vt* vestire; ~**s** *npl* abiti *mpl*, vestiti *mpl*; ~**s brush** *n* spazzola per abiti; ~**s line** *n* corda (per stendere il bucato); ~**s peg** (*US* ~**s pin**) *n* molletta

clothing ['kləuðɪŋ] *n* = **clothes**

cloud [klaut] *n* nuvola; ~**burst** *n* acquazzone *m*; ~**y** *adj* nuvoloso(a); (*liquid*) torbido(a)

clout [klaut] *vt* dare un colpo a

clove [kləuv] *n* chiodo di garofano; ~ **of garlic** spicchio d'aglio

clover ['kləuvə*] *n* trifoglio

clown [klaun] *n* pagliaccio ♦ *vi* (*also:* ~ *about*, ~ *around*) fare il pagliaccio

cloying ['klɔɪɪŋ] *adj* (*taste, smell*) nauseabondo(a)

club [klʌb] *n* (*society*) club *m inv*, circolo; (*weapon, GOLF*) mazza ♦ *vt* bastonare ♦ *vi*: **to** ~ **together** associarsi; ~**s** *npl* (*CARDS*) fiori *mpl*; ~ **car** (*US*) (*RAIL*) vagone *m* ristorante; ~ **class** *n* (*AVIAT*) classe *f* club *inv*; ~**house** *n* sede *f* del circolo

cluck [klʌk] *vi* chiocciare

clue [klu:] *n* indizio; (*in crosswords*) definizione *f*; **I haven't a** ~ non ho la minima idea

clump [klʌmp] *n* (*of flowers, trees*) gruppo; (*of grass*) ciuffo

clumsy ['klʌmzɪ] *adj* goffo(a)

clung [klʌŋ] *pt, pp of* **cling**

cluster ['klʌstə*] *n* gruppo ♦ *vi* raggrupparsi

clutch [klʌtʃ] *n* (*grip, grasp*) presa, stretta; (*AUT*) frizione *f* ♦ *vt* afferrare, stringere forte

clutter ['klʌtə*] *vt* ingombrare

CND *n abbr* = **Campaign for Nuclear Disarmament**

Co. *abbr* = **county**; **company**

c/o *abbr* (= *care of*) presso

coach [kəutʃ] *n* (*bus*) pullman *m inv*; (*horse-drawn, of train*) carrozza; (*SPORT*) allenatore/trice; (*tutor*) chi dà ripetizioni ♦ *vt* allenare; dare ripetizioni a; ~ **trip** *n* viaggio in pullman

coal [kəul] *n* carbone *m*; ~ **face** *n* fronte *f*; ~**field** *n* bacino carbonifero

coalition [kəuə'lɪʃən] *n* coalizione *f*

coal: ~**man** *n* negoziante *m* di carbone; ~ **merchant** *n* = ~**man**; ~**mine** *n* miniera di carbone

coarse [kɔ:s] *adj* (*salt, sand etc*) grosso(a); (*cloth, person*) rozzo(a)

coast [kəust] *n* costa ♦ *vi* (*with cycle etc*) scendere a ruota libera; ~**al** *adj* costiero(a); ~**guard** *n* guardia costiera; ~**line** *n* linea costiera

coat [kəut] *n* cappotto; (*of animal*) pelo; (*of paint*) mano *f* ♦ *vt* coprire; ~ **of arms** *n* stemma *m*; ~ **hanger** *n* attaccapanni *m inv*; ~**ing** *n* rivestimento

coax [kəuks] *vt* indurre (con moine)

cob [kɔb] *n see* **corn**

cobbler ['kɔblə*] *n* calzolaio

cobbles ['kɔblz] *npl* ciottoli *mpl*

cobblestones ['kɔblstəunz] *npl* ciottoli *mpl*

cobweb ['kɔbwɛb] *n* ragnatela

cocaine [kə'keɪn] *n* cocaina

cock [kɔk] *n* (*rooster*) gallo; (*male bird*) maschio ♦ *vt* (*gun*) armare; ~**erel** *n* galletto; ~**-eyed** *adj* (*fig*) storto(a); strampalato(a)

cockle ['kɔkl] *n* cardio

cockney ['kɔknɪ] *n* cockney *m/f inv*

(*abitante dei quartieri popolari dell'East End di Londra*)

cockpit ['kɔkpɪt] *n* abitacolo

cockroach ['kɔkrəutʃ] *n* blatta

cocktail ['kɔkteɪl] *n* cocktail *m inv*; ~ **cabinet** *n* mobile *m* bar *inv*; ~ **party** *n* cocktail *m inv*

cocoa ['kəukəu] *n* cacao

coconut ['kəukənʌt] *n* noce *f* di cocco

cocoon [kə'ku:n] *n* bozzolo

cod [kɔd] *n* merluzzo

C.O.D. *abbr* = **cash on delivery**

code [kəud] *n* codice *m*

cod-liver oil *n* olio di fegato di merluzzo

coercion [kəu'ə:ʃən] *n* coercizione *f*

coffee ['kɔfɪ] *n* caffè *m inv*; ~ **bar** (*BRIT*) *n* caffè *m inv*; ~ **break** *n* pausa per il caffè; **~pot** *n* caffettiera; ~ **table** *n* tavolino

coffin ['kɔfɪn] *n* bara

cog [kɔg] *n* dente *m*

cogent ['kəudʒənt] *adj* convincente

coherent [kəu'hɪərənt] *adj* coerente

coil [kɔɪl] *n* rotolo; (*ELEC*) bobina; (*contraceptive*) spirale *f* ♦ *vt* avvolgere

coin [kɔɪn] *n* moneta ♦ *vt* (*word*) coniare; **~age** *n* sistema *m* monetario; **~-box** (*BRIT*) *n* telefono a gettoni

coincide [kəuɪn'saɪd] *vi* coincidere; **~nce** [kəu'ɪnsɪdəns] *n* combinazione *f*

Coke [kəuk] ® *n* coca

coke [kəuk] *n* coke *m*

colander ['kɔləndə*] *n* colino

cold [kəuld] *adj* freddo(a) ♦ *n* freddo; (*MED*) raffreddore *m*; **it's** ~ fa freddo; **to be** ~ (*person*) aver freddo; (*object*) essere freddo(a); **to catch** ~ prendere freddo; **to catch a** ~ prendere un raffreddore; **in** ~ **blood** a sangue freddo; **~-shoulder** *vt* trattare con freddezza; ~ **sore** *n* erpete *m*

coleslaw ['kəulslɔ:] *n* insalata di cavolo bianco

colic ['kɔlɪk] *n* colica

collapse [kə'læps] *vi* crollare ♦ *n* crollo; (*MED*) collasso

collapsible [kə'læpsəbl] *adj* pieghevole

collar ['kɔlə*] *n* (*of coat, shirt*) colletto; (*of dog, cat*) collare *m*; **~bone** *n* clavicola

collateral [kə'lætərl] *n* garanzia

colleague ['kɔli:g] *n* collega *m/f*

collect [kə'lɛkt] *vt* (*gen*) raccogliere; (*as a hobby*) fare collezione di; (*BRIT: call and pick up*) prendere; (*money owed, pension*) riscuotere; (*donations, subscriptions*) fare una colletta di ♦ *vi* adunarsi, riunirsi; ammucchiarsi; **to call** ~ (*US: TEL*) fare una chiamata a carico del destinatario; **~ion** [kə'lɛkʃən] *n* raccolta; collezione *f*; (*for money*) colletta

collector [kə'lɛktə*] *n* collezionista *m/f*

college ['kɔlɪdʒ] *n* college *m inv*; (*of technology etc*) istituto superiore

collide [kə'laɪd] *vi*: **to** ~ (**with**) scontrarsi (con)

collie ['kɔlɪ] *n* (*dog*) collie *m inv*

colliery ['kɔlɪərɪ] (*BRIT*) *n* miniera di carbone

collision [kə'lɪʒən] *n* collisione *f*, scontro

colloquial [kə'ləukwɪəl] *adj* familiare

colon ['kəulən] *n* (*sign*) due punti *mpl*; (*MED*) colon *m inv*

colonel ['kə:nl] *n* colonnello

colonial [kə'ləunɪəl] *adj* coloniale

colony ['kɔlənɪ] *n* colonia

colour ['kʌlə*] (*US* **color**) *n* colore *m* ♦ *vt* colorare; (*tint, dye*) tingere; (*fig: affect*) influenzare ♦ *vi* (*blush*) arrossire; **~s** *npl* (*of party, club*) colori *mpl*; **in** ~ a colori; ~ **in** *vt* colorare; **~ bar** *n* discriminazione *f* razziale (*in locali etc*); **~-blind** *adj* daltonico(a); **~ed** *adj* (*photo*) a colori; (*person*) di colore; ~ **film** *n* (*for camera*) pellicola a colori; **~ful** *adj* pieno(a) di colore, a vivaci colori; (*personality*) colorato(a); **~ing** *n* (*substance*) colorante *m*; (*complexion*) colorito; ~ **scheme** *n* combinazione *f* di colori; ~ **television** *n* televisione *f* a colori

colt [kəult] *n* puledro

column ['kɔləm] *n* colonna; **~ist** ['kɔləmnɪst] *n* articolista *m/f*

coma ['kəumə] *n* coma *m inv*

comb [kəum] *n* pettine *m* ♦ *vt* (*hair*) pettinare; (*area*) battere a tappeto

combat ['kɔmbæt] *n* combattimento ♦ *vt* combattere, lottare contro

combination [kɔmbɪ'neɪʃən] *n* combinazione *f*

combine [*vb* kəm'baɪn, *n* 'kɔmbaɪn] *vt*: **to**

~ **(with)** combinare (con); (*one quality with another*) unire (a) ♦ *vi* unirsi; (*CHEM*) combinarsi ♦ *n* (*ECON*) associazione *f*; ~ **(harvester)** *n* mietitrebbia

come [kʌm] (*pt* **came**, *pp* **come**) *vi* venire; arrivare; **to ~ to** (*decision etc*) raggiungere; **I've ~ to like him** ha cominciato a piacermi; **to ~ undone** slacciarsi; **to ~ loose** allentarsi; ~ **about** *vi* succedere; ~ **across** *vt fus* trovare per caso; ~ **away** *vi* venire via; staccarsi; ~ **back** *vi* ritornare; ~ **by** *vt fus* (*acquire*) ottenere; procurarsi; ~ **down** *vi* scendere; (*prices*) calare; (*buildings*) essere demolito(a); ~ **forward** *vi* farsi avanti; presentarsi; ~ **from** *vt fus* venire da; provenire da; ~ **in** *vi* entrare; ~ **in for** *vt fus* (*criticism etc*) ricevere; ~ **into** *vt fus* (*money*) ereditare; ~ **off** *vi* (*button*) staccarsi; (*stain*) andar via; (*attempt*) riuscire; ~ **on** *vi* (*pupil, work, project*) fare progressi; (*lights*) accendersi; (*electricity*) entrare in funzione; ~ **on!** avanti!, andiamo!, forza!; ~ **out** *vi* uscire; (*stain*) andare via; ~ **round** *vi* (*after faint, operation*) riprendere conoscenza, rinvenire; ~ **to** *vi* rinvenire; ~ **up** *vi* (*sun*) salire; (*problem*) sorgere; (*event*) essere in arrivo; (*in conversation*) saltar fuori; ~ **up against** *vt fus* (*resistance, difficulties*) urtare contro; ~ **up with** *vt fus*: **he came up with an idea** venne fuori con un'idea; ~ **upon** *vt fus* trovare per caso; ~**back** *n* (*THEATRE etc*) ritorno

comedian [kə'miːdɪən] *n* comico

comedienne [kəmiːdɪ'ɛn] *n* attrice *f* comica

comedy ['kɔmɪdɪ] *n* commedia

comeuppance [kʌm'ʌpəns] *n*: **to get one's ~** ricevere ciò che si merita

comfort ['kʌmfət] *n* comodità *f inv*, benessere *m*; (*relief*) consolazione *f*, conforto ♦ *vt* consolare, confortare; ~**s** *npl* comodità *fpl*; ~**able** *adj* comodo(a); (*financially*) agiato(a); ~**ably** *adv* (*sit etc*) comodamente; (*live*) bene; ~ **station** (*US*) *n* gabinetti *mpl*

comic ['kɔmɪk] *adj* (*also*: ~**al**) comico(a) ♦ *n* comico; (*BRIT: magazine*) giornaletto;

~ **strip** *n* fumetto

coming ['kʌmɪŋ] *n* arrivo ♦ *adj* (*next*) prossimo(a); (*future*) futuro(a); ~**(s) and going(s)** *n*(*pl*) andirivieni *m inv*

comma ['kɔmə] *n* virgola

command [kə'mɑːnd] *n* ordine *m*, comando; (*MIL: authority*) comando; (*mastery*) padronanza ♦ *vt* comandare; **to ~ sb to do** ordinare a qn di fare; ~**eer** [kɔmən'dɪə*] *vt* requisire; ~**er** *n* capo; (*MIL*) comandante *m*

commando [kə'mɑːndəu] *n* commando *m inv*; membro di un commando

commence [kə'mɛns] *vt, vi* cominciare

commend [kə'mɛnd] *vt* lodare; raccomandare

commensurate [kə'mɛnʃərɪt] *adj*: ~ **with** proporzionato(a) a

comment ['kɔmɛnt] *n* commento ♦ *vi*: **to ~ (on)** fare commenti (su); ~**ary** ['kɔmɛntərɪ] *n* commentario; (*SPORT*) radiocronaca; telecronaca; ~**ator** ['kɔmɛnteɪtə*] *n* commentatore/trice; radiocronista *m/f*; telecronista *m/f*

commerce ['kɔmɔːs] *n* commercio

commercial [kə'məːʃəl] *adj* commerciale ♦ *n* (*TV, RADIO: advertisement*) pubblicità *f inv*; ~ **radio/television** *n* radio *f inv*/ televisione *f* privata

commiserate [kə'mɪzəreɪt] *vi*: **to ~ with** partecipare al dolore di

commission [kə'mɪʃən] *n* commissione *f* ♦ *vt* (*work of art*) commissionare; **out of ~** (*NAUT*) in disarmo; ~**aire** [kəmɪʃə'nɛə*] (*BRIT*) *n* (*at shop, cinema etc*) portiere *m* in livrea; ~**er** *n* (*POLICE*) questore *m*

commit [kə'mɪt] *vt* (*act*) commettere; (*to sb's care*) affidare; **to ~ o.s. (to do)** impegnarsi (a fare); **to ~ suicide** suicidarsi; ~**ment** *n* impegno; promessa

committee [kə'mɪtɪ] *n* comitato

commodity [kə'mɔdɪtɪ] *n* prodotto, articolo

common ['kɔmən] *adj* comune; (*pej*) volgare; (*usual*) normale ♦ *n* terreno comune; **the C~s** (*BRIT*) *npl* la Camera dei Comuni; **in ~** in comune; ~**er** *n* cittadino/a (non nobile); ~ **law** *n* diritto consuetudinario; ~**ly** *adv* comunemente, usualmente; **C~ Market** *n* Mercato Comune; **~place** *adj* banale, ordinario(a); **~room** *n* sala di riunione; (*SCOL*) sala dei professori; **~ sense** *n* buon senso; **the C~wealth** [kə'mju:n] *n* il Commonwealth

commotion [kə'məuʃən] *n* confusione *f*, tumulto

communal ['kɔmju:nl] *adj* (*for common use*) pubblico(a)

commune [*n* 'kɔmju:n, *vb* kə'mju:n] *n* (*group*) comune *f* ♦ *vi*: **to ~ with** mettersi in comunione con

communicate [kə'mju:nɪkeɪt] *vt* comunicare, trasmettere ♦ *vi*: **to ~ (with)** comunicare (con)

communication [kəmju:nɪ'keɪʃən] *n* comunicazione *f*; **~ cord** (*BRIT*) *n* segnale *m* d'allarme

communion [kə'mju:nɪən] *n* (*also: Holy C~*) comunione *f*

communiqué [kə'mju:nɪkeɪ] *n* comunicato

communism ['kɔmjunɪzəm] *n* comunismo; **communist** *adj*, *n* comunista *m/f*

community [kə'mju:nɪtɪ] *n* comunità *f* *inv*; **~ centre** *n* circolo ricreativo; **~ chest** (*US*) *n* fondo di beneficenza; **~ home** (*BRIT*) *n* riformatorio

commutation ticket [kɔmju'teɪʃən-] (*US*) *n* biglietto di abbonamento

commute [kə'mju:t] *vi* fare il pendolare ♦ *vt* (*LAW*) commutare; **~r** *n* pendolare *m/f*

compact [*adj* kəm'pækt, *n* 'kɔmpækt] *adj* compatto(a) ♦ *n* (*also: powder ~*) portacipria *m inv*; **~ disc** *n* compact disc *m inv*; **~ disc player** *n* lettore *m* CD *inv*

companion [kəm'pænɪən] *n* compagno/a; **~ship** *n* compagnia

company ['kʌmpənɪ] *n* (*also COMM, MIL, THEATRE*) compagnia; **to keep sb ~** tenere compagnia a qn; **~ secretary** (*BRIT*) *n* segretario/a generale

comparable ['kɔmpərəbl] *adj* simile

comparative [kəm'pærətɪv] *adj* relativo(a); (*adjective etc*) comparativo(a); **~ly** *adv* relativamente

compare [kəm'pɛə*] *vt*: **to ~ sth/sb with/to** confrontare qc/qn con/a ♦ *vi*: **to**

~ (with) reggere il confronto (con); **comparison** [-'pærɪsn] *n* confronto; **in comparison (with)** in confronto (a)

compartment [kəm'pɑ:tmənt] *n* compartimento; (*RAIL*) scompartimento

compass ['kʌmpəs] *n* bussola; **~es** *npl* (*MATH*) compasso

compassion [kəm'pæʃən] *n* compassione *f*

compatible [kəm'pætɪbl] *adj* compatibile

compel [kəm'pɛl] *vt* costringere, obbligare; **~ling** *adj* (*fig: argument*) irresistibile

compensate ['kɔmpənseɪt] *vt* risarcire ♦ *vi*: **to ~ for** compensare; **compensation** [-'seɪʃən] *n* compensazione *f*; (*money*) risarcimento

compère ['kɔmpɛə*] *n* presentatore/trice

compete [kəm'pi:t] *vi* (*take part*) concorrere; (*vie*): **to ~ (with)** fare concorrenza (a)

competent ['kɔmpɪtənt] *adj* competente

competition [kɔmpɪ'tɪʃən] *n* gara; concorso; (*ECON*) concorrenza

competitive [kəm'pɛtɪtɪv] *adj* (*ECON*) concorrenziale; (*sport*) agonistico(a); (*person*) che ha spirito di competizione; che ha spirito agonistico

competitor [kəm'pɛtɪtə*] *n* concorrente *m/f*

complacency [kəm'pleɪsnsɪ] *n* compiacenza di sé

complain [kəm'pleɪn] *vi* lagnarsi, lamentarsi; **~t** *n* lamento; (*in shop etc*) reclamo; (*MED*) malattia

complement [*n* 'kɔmplɪmənt, *vb* 'kɔmplɪment] *n* complemento; (*especially of ship's crew etc*) effettivo ♦ *vt* (*enhance*) accompagnarsi bene a; **~ary** [kɔmplɪ'mentərɪ] *adj* complementare

complete [kəm'pli:t] *adj* completo(a) ♦ *vt* completare; (*a form*) riempire; **~ly** *adv* completamente; **completion** *n* completamento

complex ['kɔmplɛks] *adj* complesso(a) ♦ *n* (*PSYCH, buildings etc*) complesso

complexion [kəm'plɛkʃən] *n* (*of face*) carnagione *f*

compliance [kəm'plaɪəns] *n*

acquiescenza; **in ~ with** (*orders, wishes etc*) in conformità con

complicate ['kɔmplɪkeɪt] *vt* complicare; **~d** *adj* complicato(a); **complication** [-'keɪʃən] *n* complicazione *f*

compliment [*n* 'kɔmplɪmənt, *vb* 'kɔmplɪment] *n* complimento ♦ *vt* fare un complimento a; **~s** *npl* (*greetings*) complimenti *mpl*; rispetti *mpl*; **to pay sb a ~** fare un complimento a qn; **~ary** [-'mentərɪ] *adj* complimentoso(a), elogiativo(a); (*free*) in omaggio; **~ary ticket** *n* biglietto omaggio

comply [kəm'plaɪ] *vi*: **to ~ with** assentire a; conformarsi a

component [kəm'pəunənt] *a* componente ♦ *n* componente *m*

compose [kəm'pəuz] *vt* (*form*): **to be ~d of** essere composto di; (*music, poem etc*) comporre; **to ~ o.s.** ricomporsi; **~d** *adj* calmo(a); **~r** *n* (MUS) compositore/trice

composition [kɔmpə'zɪʃən] *n* composizione *f*

composure [kəm'pəuʒə*] *n* calma

compound ['kɔmpaund] *n* (CHEM, LING) composto; (*enclosure*) recinto ♦ *adj* composto(a); **~ fracture** *n* frattura esposta

comprehend [kɔmprɪ'hend] *vt* comprendere, capire; **comprehension** [-'henʃən] *n* comprensione *f*

comprehensive [kɔmprɪ'hensɪv] *adj* comprensivo(a); **~ policy** *n* (INSURANCE) polizza che copre tutti i rischi; **~ (school)** (BRIT) *n* scuola secondaria aperta a tutti

compress [*vb* kəm'pres, *n* 'kɔmpres] *vt* comprimere ♦ *n* (MED) compressa

comprise [kəm'praɪz] *vt* (*also:* **be ~d of**) comprendere

compromise ['kɔmprəmaɪz] *n* compromesso ♦ *vt* compromettere ♦ *vi* venire a un compromesso

compulsion [kəm'pʌlʃən] *n* costrizione *f*

compulsive [kəm'pʌlsɪv] *adj* (*liar, gambler*) che non riesce a controllarsi; (*viewing, reading*) cui non si può fare a meno

compulsory [kəm'pʌlsərɪ] *adj*

obbligatorio(a)

computer [kəm'pju:tə*] *n* computer *m inv*, elaboratore *m* elettronico; **~ game** *n* gioco per computer; **~ize** *vt* computerizzare; **~ programmer** *n* programmatore/trice; **~ programming** *n* programmazione *f* di computer; **~ science** *n* informatica; **computing** *n* informatica

comrade ['kɔmrɪd] *n* compagno/a; **~ship** *n* cameratismo

con [kɔn] (*inf*) *vt* truffare ♦ *n* truffa

conceal [kən'si:l] *vt* nascondere

concede [kən'si:d] *vt* ammettere

conceit [kən'si:t] *n* presunzione *f*, vanità; **~ed** *adj* presuntuoso(a), vanitoso(a)

conceive [kən'si:v] *vt* concepire ♦ *vi* concepire un bambino

concentrate ['kɔnsəntreɪt] *vi* concentrarsi ♦ *vt* concentrare

concentration [kɔnsən'treɪʃən] *n* concentrazione *f*; **~ camp** *n* campo di concentramento

concept ['kɔnsept] *n* concetto

concern [kən'sə:n] *n* affare *m*; (COMM) azienda, ditta; (*anxiety*) preoccupazione *f* ♦ *vt* riguardare; **to be ~ed (about)** preoccuparsi (di); **~ing** *prep* riguardo a, circa

concert ['kɔnsət] *n* concerto; **~ed** [kən'sə:tɪd] *adj* concertato(a); **~ hall** *n* sala da concerti

concertina [kɔnsə'ti:nə] *n* piccola fisarmonica

concerto [kən'tʃə:təu] *n* concerto

conclude [kən'klu:d] *vt* concludere; **conclusion** [-'klu:ʒən] *n* conclusione *f*; **conclusive** [-'klu:sɪv] *adj* conclusivo(a)

concoct [kən'kɔkt] *vt* inventare; **~ion** [-'kɔkʃən] *n* miscuglio

concourse ['kɔŋkɔ:s] *n* (*hall*) atrio

concrete ['kɔŋkri:t] *n* calcestruzzo ♦ *adj* concreto(a); di calcestruzzo

concur [kən'kə:*] *vi* concordare

concurrently [kən'kʌrntlɪ] *adv* simultaneamente

concussion [kən'kʌʃən] *n* commozione *f* cerebrale

condemn [kən'dem] *vt* condannare;

(*building*) dichiarare pericoloso(a)

condensation [kɔndɛn'seɪʃən] *n*
condensazione *f*

condense [kən'dɛns] *vi* condensarsi ♦ *vt*
condensare; **~d milk** *n* latte *m*
condensato

condescending [kɔndɪ'sɛndɪŋ] *adj*
(*person*) che ha un'aria di superiorità

condition [kən'dɪʃən] *n* condizione *f*;
(*MED*) malattia ♦ *vt* condizionare; **on ~
that** a condizione che + *sub*, a condizione
di; **~al** *adj* condizionale; **~er** *n* (*for hair*)
balsamo; (*for fabrics*) ammorbidente *m*

condolences [kən'dəʊlənsɪz] *npl*
condoglianze *fpl*

condom ['kɔndəm] *n* preservativo

condominium [kɔndə'mɪnɪəm] (*US*) *n*
condominio

conducive [kən'djuːsɪv] *adj*: **~ to**
favorevole a

conduct [*n* 'kɔndʌkt, *vb* kən'dʌkt] *n*
condotta ♦ *vt* condurre; (*manage*)
dirigere; amministrare; (*MUS*) dirigere; **to
~ o.s.** comportarsi; **~ed tour** *n* gita
accompagnata; **~or** *n* (*of orchestra*)
direttore *m* d'orchestra; (*on bus*)
bigliettaio; (*US: on train*) controllore *m*;
(*ELEC*) conduttore *m*; **~ress** *n* (*on bus*)
bigliettaia

cone [kəʊn] *n* cono; (*BOT*) pigna; (*traffic ~*)
birillo

confectioner [kən'fɛkʃənə*] *n*
pasticciere *m*; **~'s (shop)** *n*
≈ pasticceria; **~y** *n* dolciumi *mpl*

confer [kən'fəː*] *vt*: **to ~ sth on** conferire
qc a ♦ *vi* conferire

conference ['kɔnfərns] *n* congresso

confess [kən'fɛs] *vt* confessare,
ammettere ♦ *vi* confessare; **~ion** [-'fɛʃən]
n confessione *f*

confetti [kən'fɛtɪ] *n* coriandoli *mpl*

confide [kən'faɪd] *vi*: **to ~ in** confidarsi
con

confidence ['kɔnfɪdns] *n* confidenza;
(*trust*) fiducia; (*self-assurance*) sicurezza di
sé; **in ~** (*speak, write*) in confidenza,
confidenzialmente; **~ trick** *n* truffa;
confident *adj* sicuro(a); sicuro(a) di sé;
confidential [kɔnfɪ'dɛnʃəl] *adj*

riservato(a), confidenziale

confine [kən'faɪn] *vt* limitare; (*shut up*)
rinchiudere; **~d** *adj* (*space*) ristretto(a);
~ment *n* prigionia; **~s** ['kɔnfaɪnz] *npl*
confini *mpl*

confirm [kən'fəːm] *vt* confermare;
~ation [kɔnfə'meɪʃən] *n* conferma; (*REL*)
cresima; **~ed** *adj* inveterato(a)

confiscate ['kɔnfɪskeɪt] *vt* confiscare

conflict [*n* 'kɔnflɪkt, *vb* kən'flɪkt] *n*
conflitto ♦ *vi* essere in conflitto; **~ing** *adj*
contrastante

conform [kən'fɔːm] *vi*: **to ~ (to)**
conformarsi (a)

confound [kən'faund] *vt* confondere

confront [kən'frʌnt] *vt* (*enemy, danger*)
affrontare; **~ation** [kɔnfrən'teɪʃən] *n*
scontro

confuse [kən'fjuːz] *vt* (*one thing with
another*) confondere; **~d** *adj* confuso(a);
confusing *adj* che fa confondere;
confusion [-'fjuːʒən] *n* confusione *f*

congeal [kən'dʒiːl] *vi* (*blood*) congelarsi

congenial [kən'dʒiːnɪəl] *adj* (*person*)
simpatico(a); (*thing*) congeniale

congested [kən'dʒɛstɪd] *adj*
congestionato(a)

congestion [kən'dʒɛstʃən] *n* congestione
f

congratulate [kən'grætjuleɪt] *vt*: **to ~ sb
(on)** congratularsi con qn (per *or* di);
congratulations [-'leɪʃənz] *npl* auguri
mpl; (*on success*) complimenti *mpl*,
congratulazioni *fpl*

congregate ['kɔngrɪgeɪt] *vi* congregarsi,
riunirsi

congress ['kɔngrɛs] *n* congresso; **C~man**
(*US*) *n* membro del Congresso

conjecture [kən'dʒɛktʃə*] *n* congettura

conjunction [kən'dʒʌŋkʃən] *n*
congiunzione *f*

conjunctivitis [kəndʒʌŋktɪ'vaɪtɪs] *n*
congiuntivite *f*

conjure ['kʌndʒə*] *vi* fare giochi di
prestigio; **~ up** *vt* (*ghost, spirit*) evocare;
(*memories*) rievocare; **~r** *n*
prestidigitatore/trice, prestigiatore/trice

conk out [kɔŋk-] (*inf*) *vi* andare in panne

con man *n* truffatore *m*

connect [kə'nɛkt] *vt* connettere, collegare; (*ELEC, TEL*) collegare; (*fig*) associare ♦ *vi* (*train*): **to ~ with** essere in coincidenza con; **to be ~ed with** (*associated*) aver rapporti con; **~ion** [-ʃən] *n* relazione *f*, rapporto; (*ELEC*) connessione *f*; (*train, plane*) coincidenza; (*TEL*) collegamento

connive [kə'naɪv] *vi*: **to ~ at** essere connivente in

connoisseur [kɔnɪ'sə*] *n* conoscitore/trice

conquer ['kɔŋkə*] *vt* conquistare; (*feelings*) vincere

conquest ['kɔŋkwɛst] *n* conquista

cons [kɔnz] *npl see* **convenience; pro**

conscience ['kɔnʃəns] *n* coscienza

conscientious [kɔnʃɪ'ɛnʃəs] *adj* coscienzioso(a)

conscious ['kɔnʃəs] *adj* consapevole; (*MED*) cosciente; **~ness** *n* consapevolezza; coscienza

conscript ['kɔnskrɪpt] *n* coscritto; **~ion** [-'skrɪpʃən] *n* arruolamento (obbligatorio)

consent [kən'sɛnt] *n* consenso ♦ *vi*: **to ~ (to)** acconsentire a

consequence ['kɔnsɪkwəns] *n* conseguenza, risultato; importanza

consequently ['kɔnsɪkwəntlɪ] *adv* di conseguenza, dunque

conservation [kɔnsə'veɪʃən] *n* conservazione *f*

conservative [kən'sə:vətɪv] *adj* conservatore(trice); (*cautious*) cauto(a); **C~** (*BRIT*) *adj, n* (*POL*) conservatore(trice)

conservatory [kən'sə:vətrɪ] *n* (*greenhouse*) serra; (*MUS*) conservatorio

conserve [kən'sə:v] *vt* conservare ♦ *n* conserva

consider [kən'sɪdə*] *vt* considerare; (*take into account*) tener conto di; **to ~ doing sth** considerare la possibilità di fare qc

considerable [kən'sɪdərəbl] *adj* considerevole, notevole; **considerably** *adv* notevolmente, decisamente

considerate [kən'sɪdərɪt] *adj* premuroso(a)

consideration [kənsɪdə'reɪʃən] *n* considerazione *f*

considering [kən'sɪdərɪŋ] *prep* in considerazione di

consign [kən'saɪn] *vt*: **to ~ to** (*sth unwanted*) relegare in; (*person: to sb's care*) consegnare a; (: *to poverty*) condannare a; **~ment** *n* (*of goods*) consegna; spedizione *f*

consist [kən'sɪst] *vi*: **to ~ of** constare di, essere composto(a) di

consistency [kən'sɪstənsɪ] *n* consistenza; (*fig*) coerenza

consistent [kən'sɪstənt] *adj* coerente

consolation [kɔnsə'leɪʃən] *n* consolazione *f*

console¹ [kən'səul] *vt* consolare

console² ['kɔnsəul] *n* quadro di comando

consonant ['kɔnsənənt] *n* consonante *f*

consortium [kən'sɔ:tɪəm] *n* consorzio

conspicuous [kən'spɪkjuəs] *adj* cospicuo(a)

conspiracy [kən'spɪrəsɪ] *n* congiura, cospirazione *f*

constable ['kʌnstəbl] (*BRIT*) *n* ≈ poliziotto, agente *m* di polizia; **chief ~** ≈ questore *m*

constabulary [kən'stæbjulərɪ] *n* forze *fpl* dell'ordine

constant ['kɔnstənt] *adj* costante; continuo(a); **~ly** *adv* costantemente; continuamente

constipated ['kɔnstɪpeɪtɪd] *adj* stitico(a)

constipation [kɔnstɪ'peɪʃən] *n* stitichezza

constituency [kən'stɪtjuənsɪ] *n* collegio elettorale

constituent [kən'stɪtjuənt] *n* elettore/trice; (*part*) elemento componente

constitution [kɔnstɪ'tju:ʃən] *n* costituzione *f*; **~al** *adj* costituzionale

constraint [kən'streɪnt] *n* costrizione *f*

construct [kən'strʌkt] *vt* costruire; **~ion** [-ʃən] *n* costruzione *f*; **~ive** *adj* costruttivo(a)

construe [kən'stru:] *vt* interpretare

consul ['kɔnsl] *n* console *m*; **~ate** ['kɔnsjulɪt] *n* consolato

consult [kən'sʌlt] *vt* consultare; **~ant** *n* (*MED*) consulente *m* medico; (*other specialist*) consulente; **~ation** [-'teɪʃən] *n*

(*MED*) consulto; (*discussion*) consultazione
f; **~ing room** (*BRIT*) *n* ambulatorio
consume [kən'sju:m] *vt* consumare; **~r** *n*
consumatore/trice; **~r goods** *npl* beni
mpl di consumo; **~r society** *n* società dei
consumi
consumption [kən'sʌmpʃən] *n* consumo
cont. *abbr* = **continued**
contact ['kɔntækt] *n* contatto; (*person*)
conoscenza ♦ *vt* mettersi in contatto con;
~ lenses *npl* lenti *fpl* a contatto
contagious [kən'teɪdʒəs] *adj* (*also fig*)
contagioso(a)
contain [kən'teɪn] *vt* contenere; **to ~ o.s.**
contenersi; **~er** *n* recipiente *m*; (*for
shipping etc*) container *m inv*
contaminate [kən'tæmɪneɪt] *vt*
contaminare
cont'd *abbr* = **continued**
contemplate ['kɔntəmpleɪt] *vt*
contemplare; (*consider*) pensare a (*or* di)
contemporary [kən'tempərərɪ] *adj, n*
contemporaneo(a)
contempt [kən'tempt] *n* disprezzo; **~ of
court** (*LAW*) oltraggio alla Corte; **~ible** *adj*
deprecabile; **~uous** *adj* sdegnoso(a)
contend [kən'tend] *vt*: **to ~ that**
sostenere che ♦ *vi*: **to ~ with** lottare
contro; **~er** *n* contendente *m/f*;
concorrente *m/f*
content¹ ['kɔntent] *n* contenuto; **~s** *npl*
(*of box, case etc*) contenuto; (**table of**) **~s**
indice *m*
content² [kən'tent] *adj* contento(a),
soddisfatto/a ♦ *vt* contentare, soddisfare;
~ed *adj* contento(a), soddisfatto(a)
contention [kən'tenʃən] *n* contesa;
(*assertion*) tesi *f inv*
contentment [kən'tentmənt] *n*
contentezza
contest [*n* 'kɔntest, *vb* kən'test] *n* lotta;
(*competition*) gara, concorso ♦ *vt*
contestare; impugnare; (*compete for*)
essere in lizza per; **~ant** [kən'testənt] *n*
concorrente *m/f*; (*in fight*) avversario/a
context ['kɔntekst] *n* contesto
continent ['kɔntɪnənt] *n* continente *m*;
the C~ (*BRIT*) l'Europa continentale; **~al**
[-'nentl] *adj* continentale; **~al quilt** (*BRIT*)

n piumino
contingency [kən'tɪndʒənsɪ] *n*
eventualità *f inv*
continual [kən'tɪnjuəl] *adj* continuo(a)
continuation [kəntɪnju'eɪʃən] *n*
continuazione *f*; (*after interruption*)
ripresa; (*of story*) seguito
continue [kən'tɪnju:] *vi* continuare ♦ *vt*
continuare; (*start again*) riprendere
continuity [kɔntɪ'nju:ɪtɪ] *n* continuità;
(*TV, CINEMA*) (ordine *m* della) sceneggiatura
continuous [kən'tɪnjuəs] *adj*
continuo(a); ininterrotto(a); **~ stationery**
n carta a moduli continui
contort [kən'tɔ:t] *vt* contorcere
contour ['kɔntuə*] *n* contorno, profilo;
(*also*: **~ line**) curva di livello
contraband ['kɔntrəbænd] *n*
contrabbando
contraceptive [kɔntrə'septɪv] *adj*
contraccettivo(a) ♦ *n* contraccettivo
contract [*n* 'kɔntrækt, *vb* kən'trækt] *n*
contratto ♦ *vi* (*become smaller*) contrarsi;
(*COMM*): **to ~ to do sth** fare un contratto
per fare qc ♦ *vt* (*illness*) contrarre; **~ion**
[-ʃən] *n* contrazione *f*; **~or** *n* imprenditore
m
contradict [kɔntrə'dɪkt] *vt* contraddire
contraption [kən'træpʃən] (*pej*) *n*
aggeggio
contrary¹ ['kɔntrərɪ] *adj* contrario(a);
(*unfavourable*) avverso(a), contrario(a)
♦ *n* contrario; **on the ~** al contrario;
unless you hear to the ~ salvo
contrordine
contrary² [kən'treərɪ] *adj* (*perverse*)
bisbetico(a)
contrast [*n* 'kɔntrɑ:st, *vb* kən'trɑ:st] *n*
contrasto ♦ *vt* mettere in contrasto; **in ~
to** contrariamente a
contribute [kən'trɪbju:t] *vi* contribuire
♦ *vt*: **to ~ £10/an article to** dare 10
sterline/un articolo a; **to ~ to** contribuire
a; (*newspaper*) scrivere per; **contribution**
[kɔntrɪ'bju:ʃən] *n* contributo;
contributor *n* (*to newspaper*)
collaboratore/trice
contrivance [kən'traɪvəns] *n* congegno;
espediente *m*

contrive [kən'traɪv] *vi*: **to ~ to do** fare in modo di fare

control [kən'trəʊl] *vt* controllare; (*firm, operation etc*) dirigere ♦ *n* controllo; **~s** *npl* (*of vehicle etc*) comandi *mpl*; (*governmental*) controlli *mpl*; **under ~** sotto controllo; **to be in ~ of** avere il controllo di; **to go out of ~** (*car*) non rispondere ai comandi; (*situation*) sfuggire di mano; **~ panel** *n* quadro dei comandi; **~ room** *n* (*NAUT, MIL*) sala di comando; (*RADIO, TV*) sala di regia; **~ tower** *n* (*AVIAT*) torre *f* di controllo

controversial [kɒntrə'vəːʃl] *adj* controverso(a), polemico(a)

controversy ['kɒntrəvəːsɪ] *n* controversia, polemica

convalesce [kɒnvə'lɛs] *vi* rimettersi in salute

convene [kən'viːn] *vt* convocare ♦ *vi* convenire, adunarsi

convenience [kən'viːnɪəns] *n* comodità *f inv*; **at your ~** a suo comodo; **all modern ~s**, (*BRIT*) **all mod cons** tutte le comodità moderne

convenient [kən'viːnɪənt] *adj* conveniente, comodo(a)

convent ['kɒnvənt] *n* convento

convention [kən'vɛnʃən] *n* convenzione *f*, (*meeting*) convegno; **~al** *adj* convenzionale

conversant [kən'vəːsnt] *adj*: **to be ~ with** essere al corrente di; essere pratico(a) di

conversation [kɒnvə'seɪʃən] *n* conversazione *f*; **~al** *adj* non formale

converse¹ [kən'vəːs] *vi* conversare

converse² ['kɒnvəːs] *n* contrario, opposto; **~ly** [-'vəːslɪ] *adv* al contrario, per contro

convert [*vb* kən'vəːt, *n* 'kɒnvəːt] *vt* (*COMM, REL*) convertire; (*alter*) trasformare ♦ *n* convertito/a; **~ible** *n* macchina decappottabile

convex ['kɒnvɛks] *adj* convesso(a)

convey [kən'veɪ] *vt* trasportare; (*thanks*) comunicare; (*idea*) dare; **~or belt** *n* nastro trasportatore

convict [*vb* kən'vɪkt, *n* 'kɒnvɪkt] *vt*

dichiarare colpevole ♦ *n* carcerato/a; **~ion** [-ʃən] *n* condanna; (*belief*) convinzione *f*

convince [kən'vɪns] *vt* convincere, persuadere; **convincing** *adj* convincente

convoluted [kɒnvə'luːtɪd] *adj* (*argument etc*) involuto(a)

convoy ['kɒnvɔɪ] *n* convoglio

convulse [kən'vʌls] *vt*: **to be ~d with laughter** contorcersi dalle risa

coo [kuː] *vi* tubare

cook [kʊk] *vt* cucinare, cuocere ♦ *vi* cuocere; (*person*) cucinare ♦ *n* cuoco/a; **~book** *n* libro di cucina; **~er** *n* fornello, cucina; **~ery** *n* cucina; **~ery book** (*BRIT*) *n* = **~book**; **~ie** (*US*) *n* biscotto; **~ing** *n* cucina

cool [kuːl] *adj* fresco(a); (*not afraid, calm*) calmo(a); (*unfriendly*) freddo(a) ♦ *vt* raffreddare; (*room*) rinfrescare ♦ *vi* (*water*) raffreddarsi; (*air*) rinfrescarsi

coop [kuːp] *n* stia ♦ *vt*: **to ~ up** (*fig*) rinchiudere

cooperate [kəʊ'ɒpəreɪt] *vi* cooperare, collaborare; **cooperation** [-'reɪʃən] *n* cooperazione *f*, collaborazione *f*

cooperative [kəʊ'ɒpərətɪv] *adj* cooperativo(a) ♦ *n* cooperativa

coordinate [*vb* kəʊ'ɔːdɪneɪt, *n* kəʊ'ɔːdɪnət] *vt* coordinare ♦ *n* (*MATH*) coordinata; **~s** *npl* (*clothes*) coordinati *mpl*

co-ownership [kəʊ'əʊnəʃɪp] *n* comproprietà

cop [kɒp] (*inf*) *n* sbirro

cope [kəʊp] *vi*: **to ~ with** (*problems*) far fronte a

copper ['kɒpə*] *n* rame *m*; (*inf: policeman*) sbirro; **~s** *npl* (*coins*) spiccioli *mpl*

coppice ['kɒpɪs] *n* bosco ceduo

copse [kɒps] *n* bosco ceduo

copulate ['kɒpjʊleɪt] *vi* accoppiarsi

copy ['kɒpɪ] *n* copia ♦ *vt* copiare; **~right** *n* diritto d'autore

coral ['kɒrəl] *n* corallo; **~ reef** *n* barriera corallina

cord [kɔːd] *n* corda; (*ELEC*) filo; (*fabric*) velluto a coste

cordial ['kɔːdɪəl] *adj* cordiale ♦ *n* (*BRIT*)

cordiale *m*

cordon ['kɔ:dn] *n* cordone *m*; ~ **off** *vt* fare cordone a

corduroy ['kɔ:dərɔɪ] *n* fustagno

core [kɔ:*] *n* (*of fruit*) torsolo; (*of organization etc*) cuore *m* ♦ *vt* estrarre il torsolo da

cork [kɔ:k] *n* sughero; (*of bottle*) tappo; ~**screw** *n* cavatappi *m inv*

corn [kɔ:n] *n* (*BRIT: wheat*) grano; (*US: maize*) granturco; (*on foot*) callo; ~ **on the cob** (*CULIN*) pannocchia cotta

corned beef ['kɔ:nd-] *n* carne *f* di manzo in scatola

corner ['kɔ:nə*] *n* angolo; (*AUT*) curva ♦ *vt* intrappolare; mettere con le spalle al muro; (*COMM: market*) accaparrare ♦ *vi* prendere una curva; ~**stone** *n* pietra angolare

cornet ['kɔ:nɪt] *n* (*MUS*) cornetta; (*BRIT: of ice-cream*) cono

cornflakes ['kɔ:nfleɪks] *npl* fiocchi *mpl* di granturco

cornflour ['kɔ:nflauə*] (*BRIT*) *n* farina finissima di granturco

cornstarch ['kɔ:nstɑ:tʃ] (*US*) *n* = cornflour

Cornwall ['kɔ:nwəl] *n* Cornovaglia

corny ['kɔ:nɪ] (*inf*) *adj* trito(a)

coronary ['kɔrənərɪ] *n*: ~ (**thrombosis**) trombosi *f* coronaria

coronation [kɔrə'neɪʃən] *n* incoronazione *f*

coroner ['kɔrənə*] *n* magistrato incaricato di indagare la causa di morte in circostanze sospette

coronet ['kɔrənɪt] *n* diadema *m*

corporal ['kɔ:pərl] *n* caporalmaggiore *m* ♦ *adj*: ~ **punishment** pena corporale

corporate ['kɔ:pərɪt] *adj* costituito(a) (in corporazione); comune

corporation [kɔ:pə'reɪʃən] *n* (*of town*) consiglio comunale; (*COMM*) ente *m*

corps [kɔ:*, *pl* kɔ:z] *n inv* corpo

corpse [kɔ:ps] *n* cadavere *m*

corral [kə'rɑ:l] *n* recinto

correct [kə'rɛkt] *adj* (*accurate*) corretto(a), esatto(a); (*proper*) corretto(a) ♦ *vt* correggere; ~**ion** [-ʃən] *n* correzione

f

correspond [kɔrɪs'pɔnd] *vi* corrispondere; ~**ence** *n* corrispondenza; ~**ence course** *n* corso per corrispondenza; ~**ent** *n* corrispondente *m/f*

corridor ['kɔrɪdɔ:*] *n* corridoio

corrode [kə'rəud] *vt* corrodere ♦ *vi* corrodersi

corrugated ['kɔrəgeɪtɪd] *adj* increspato(a); ondulato(a); ~ **iron** *n* lamiera di ferro ondulata

corrupt [kə'rʌpt] *adj* corrotto(a); (*COMPUT*) alterato(a) ♦ *vt* corrompere; ~**ion** [-ʃən] *n* corruzione *f*

corset ['kɔ:sɪt] *n* busto

Corsica ['kɔ:sɪkə] *n* Corsica

cosh [kɔʃ] (*BRIT*) *n* randello (corto)

cosmetic [kɔz'mɛtɪk] *n* cosmetico ♦ *adj* (*fig: measure etc*) superficiale

cosset ['kɔsɪt] *vt* vezzeggiare

cost [kɔst] (*pt, pp* cost) *n* costo ♦ *vt* costare; (*find out the ~ of*) stabilire il prezzo di; ~**s** *npl* (*COMM, LAW*) spese *fpl*; **how much does it ~?** quanto costa?; **at all ~s** a ogni costo

co-star ['kəu-] *n* attore/trice della stessa importanza del protagonista

cost-effective *adj* conveniente

costly ['kɔstlɪ] *adj* costoso(a), caro(a)

cost-of-living *adj*: ~ **allowance** indennità *f inv* di contingenza

cost price (*BRIT*) *n* prezzo all'ingrosso

costume ['kɔstju:m] *n* costume *m*; (*lady's suit*) tailleur *m inv*; (*BRIT: also: swimming* ~) costume da bagno; ~ **jewellery** *n* bigiotteria

cosy ['kəuzɪ] (*US* **cozy**) *adj* intimo(a); **I'm very** ~ **here** sto proprio bene qui

cot [kɔt] *n* (*BRIT: child's*) lettino; (*US: campbed*) brandina

cottage ['kɔtɪdʒ] *n* cottage *m inv*; ~ **cheese** *n* fiocchi *mpl* di latte magro

cotton ['kɔtn] *n* cotone *m*; ~ **on to** (*inf*) *vt fus* afferrare; ~ **candy** (*US*) *n* zucchero filato; ~ **wool** (*BRIT*) *n* cotone idrofilo

couch [kautʃ] *n* sofà *m inv*

couchette [ku:'ʃɛt] *n* (*on train, boat*) cuccetta

cough [kɔf] *vi* tossire ♦ *n* tosse *f*; ~ **drop** *n* pasticca per la tosse

could [kud] *pt of* **can**; **~n't** = **could not**

council ['kaunsl] *n* consiglio; **city** *or* **town ~** consiglio comunale; ~ **estate** (*BRIT*) *n* quartiere *m* di case popolari; ~ **house** (*BRIT*) *n* casa popolare; **~lor** *n* consigliere/a

counsel ['kaunsl] *n* avvocato; consultazione *f* ♦ *vt* consigliare; **~lor** *n* consigliere/a; (*US*) avvocato

count [kaunt] *vt*, *vi* contare ♦ *n* (*of votes etc*) conteggio; (*of pollen etc*) livello; (*nobleman*) conte *m*; ~ **on** *vt fus* contare su; **~down** *n* conto alla rovescia

countenance ['kauntɪnəns] *n* volto, aspetto ♦ *vt* approvare

counter ['kauntə*] *n* banco ♦ *vt* opporsi a ♦ *adv*: ~ **to** contro; in opposizione a; **~act** *vt* agire in opposizione a; (*poison etc*) annullare gli effetti di; **~-espionage** *n* controspionaggio

counterfeit ['kauntəfɪt] *n* contraffazione *f*, falso ♦ *vt* contraffare, falsificare ♦ *adj* falso(a)

counterfoil ['kauntəfɔɪl] *n* matrice *f*

countermand [kauntə'mɑːnd] *vt* annullare

counterpart ['kauntəpɑːt] *n* (*of document etc*) copia; (*of person*) corrispondente *m/f*

counter-productive [-prə'dʌktɪv] *adj* controproducente

countersign ['kauntəsaɪn] *vt* controfirmare

countess ['kauntɪs] *n* contessa

countless ['kauntlɪs] *adj* innumerevole

country ['kʌntrɪ] *n* paese *m*; (*native land*) patria; (*as opposed to town*) campagna; (*region*) regione *f*; ~ **dancing** (*BRIT*) *n* danza popolare; ~ **house** *n* villa in campagna; **~man** *n* (*national*) compatriota *m*; (*rural*) contadino *m*; **~side** *n* campagna

county ['kauntɪ] *n* contea

coup [kuː] (*pl* **coups**) *n* colpo; (*also*: ~ **d'état**) colpo di Stato

couple ['kʌpl] *n* coppia; **a ~ of** un paio di

coupon ['kuːpɔn] *n* buono; (*detachable form*) coupon *m inv*

courage ['kʌrɪdʒ] *n* coraggio

courgette [kuə'ʒet] (*BRIT*) *n* zucchina

courier ['kurɪə*] *n* corriere *m*; (*for tourists*) guida

course [kɔːs] *n* corso; (*of ship*) rotta; (*for golf*) campo; (*part of meal*) piatto; **of ~** senz'altro, naturalmente; ~ **of action** modo d'agire; **a ~ of treatment** (*MED*) una cura

court [kɔːt] *n* corte *f*; (*TENNIS*) campo ♦ *vt* (*woman*) fare la corte a; **to take to ~** citare in tribunale

courteous ['kəːtɪəs] *adj* cortese

courtesan [kɔːtɪ'zæn] *n* cortigiana

courtesy ['kəːtəsɪ] *n* cortesia; **(by) ~ of** per gentile concessione di

court-house (*US*) *n* palazzo di giustizia

courtier ['kɔːtɪə*] *n* cortigiano/a

court-martial [-'mɑːʃəl] (*pl* **courts-martial**) *n* corte *f* marziale

courtroom ['kɔːtrum] *n* tribunale *m*

courtyard ['kɔːtjɑːd] *n* cortile *m*

cousin ['kʌzn] *n* cugino/a; **first ~** cugino di primo grado

cove [kəuv] *n* piccola baia

covenant ['kʌvənənt] *n* accordo

cover ['kʌvə*] *vt* coprire; (*book, table*) rivestire; (*include*) comprendere; (*PRESS*) fare un servizio su ♦ *n* (*of pan*) coperchio; (*over furniture*) fodera; (*of bed*) copriletto; (*of book*) copertina; (*shelter*) riparo; (*COMM, INSURANCE, of spy*) copertura; **to take ~** (*shelter*) ripararsi; **under ~** al riparo; **under ~ of darkness** protetto dall'oscurità; **under separate ~** (*COMM*) a parte, in plico separato; ~ **up** *vi*: **to ~ up for sb** coprire qn; **~age** *n* (*PRESS, RADIO, TV*): **to give full ~age to sth** fare un ampio servizio su qc; ~ **charge** *n* coperto; **~ing** *n* copertura; **~ing letter** (*US* ~ **letter**) *n* lettera d'accompagnamento; ~ **note** *n* (*INSURANCE*) polizza (di assicurazione) provvisoria

cover-up *n* occultamento (di informazioni)

covet ['kʌvɪt] *vt* bramare

cow [kau] *n* vacca ♦ *vt* (*person*)

intimidire

coward ['kauəd] *n* vigliacco/a; **~ice** [-ɪs] *n* vigliaccheria; **~ly** *adj* vigliacco(a)

cowboy ['kaubɔɪ] *n* cow-boy *m inv*

cower ['kauə*] *vi* acquattarsi

coxswain ['kɔksn] (*abbr*: **cox**) *n* timoniere *m*

coy [kɔɪ] *adj* falsamente timido(a)

cozy ['kəuzɪ] (*US*) *adj* = **cosy**

CPA (*US*) *n abbr* = **certified public accountant**

crab [kræb] *n* granchio; **~ apple** *n* mela selvatica

crack [kræk] *n* fessura, crepa; incrinatura; (*noise*) schiocco; (: *of gun*) scoppio; (*drug*) crack *m inv* ♦ *vt* spaccare; incrinare; (*whip*) schioccare; (*nut*) schiacciare; (*problem*) risolvere; (*code*) decifrare ♦ *adj* (*troops*) fuori classe; **to ~ a joke** fare una battuta; **~ down on** *vt fus* porre freno a; **~ up** *vi* crollare; **~er** *n* cracker *m inv*; petardo

crackle ['krækl] *vi* crepitare

cradle ['kreɪdl] *n* culla

craft [krɑ:ft] *n* mestiere *m*; (*cunning*) astuzia; (*boat*) naviglio; **~sman** *n* artigiano; **~smanship** *n* abilità; **~y** *adj* furbo(a), astuto(a)

crag [kræg] *n* roccia

cram [kræm] *vt* (*fill*): **to ~ sth with** riempire qc di; (*put*): **to ~ sth into** stipare qc in ♦ *vi* (*for exams*) prepararsi (in gran fretta)

cramp [kræmp] *n* crampo; **~ed** *adj* ristretto(a)

crampon ['kræmpən] *n* (*CLIMBING*) rampone *m*

cranberry ['krænbərɪ] *n* mirtillo

crane [kreɪn] *n* gru *f inv*

crank [kræŋk] *n* manovella; (*person*) persona stramba; **~shaft** *n* albero a gomiti

cranny ['krænɪ] *n* see **nook**

crash [kræʃ] *n* fragore *m*; (*of car*) incidente *m*; (*of plane*) caduta; (*of business etc*) crollo ♦ *vt* fracassare ♦ *vi* (*plane*) fracassarsi; (*car*) avere un incidente; (*two cars*) scontrarsi; (*business etc*) fallire, andare in rovina; **~ course** *n*

corso intensivo; **~ helmet** *n* casco; **~ landing** *n* atterraggio di fortuna

crate [kreɪt] *n* cassa

cravat(e) [krə'væt] *n* fazzoletto da collo

crave [kreɪv] *vt, vi*: **to ~ (for)** desiderare ardentemente

crawl [krɔ:l] *vi* strisciare carponi; (*vehicle*) avanzare lentamente ♦ *n* (*SWIMMING*) crawl *m*

crayfish ['kreɪfɪʃ] *n inv* (*freshwater*) gambero (d'acqua dolce); (*saltwater*) gambero

crayon ['kreɪən] *n* matita colorata

craze [kreɪz] *n* mania

crazy ['kreɪzɪ] *adj* matto(a); (*inf: keen*): **~ about sb** pazzo(a) di qn; **~ about sth** matto(a) per qc; **~ paving** (*BRIT*) *n* lastricato a mosaico irregolare

creak [kri:k] *vi* cigolare, scricchiolare

cream [kri:m] *n* crema; (*fresh*) panna ♦ *adj* (*colour*) color crema *inv*; **~ cake** *n* torta alla panna; **~ cheese** *n* formaggio fresco; **~y** *adj* cremoso(a)

crease [kri:s] *n* grinza; (*deliberate*) piega ♦ *vt* sgualcire ♦ *vi* sgualcirsi

create [kri:'eɪt] *vt* creare; **creation** [-ʃən] *n* creazione *f*; **creative** *adj* creativo(a)

creature ['kri:tʃə*] *n* creatura

crèche [krɛʃ] *n* asilo infantile

credence ['kri:dns] *n*: **to lend** *or* **give ~ to** prestar fede a

credentials [krɪ'dɛnʃlz] *npl* credenziali *fpl*

credit ['krɛdɪt] *n* credito; onore *m* ♦ *vt* (*COMM*) accreditare; (*believe: also: give ~ to*) credere, prestar fede a; **~s** *npl* (*CINEMA*) titoli *mpl*; **to ~ sb with** (*fig*) attribuire a qn; **to be in ~** (*person*) essere creditore (trice); (*bank account*) essere coperto(a); **~ card** *n* carta di credito; **~or** *n* creditore/trice

creed [kri:d] *n* credo; dottrina

creek [kri:k] *n* insenatura; (*US*) piccolo fiume *m*

creep [kri:p] (*pt, pp* **crept**) *vi* avanzare furtivamente (*or* pian piano); **~er** *n* pianta rampicante; **~y** *adj* (*frightening*) che fa accapponare la pelle

crematoria [krɛmə'tɔ:rɪə] *npl of*

crematorium

crematorium [krɛmə'tɔːrɪəm] (*pl* **crematoria**) *n* forno crematorio

crêpe [kreɪp] *n* crespo; ~ **bandage** (*BRIT*) *n* fascia elastica

crept [krɛpt] *pt, pp of* **creep**

crescent ['krɛsnt] *n* (*shape*) mezzaluna; (*street*) strada semicircolare

cress [krɛs] *n* crescione *m*

crest [krɛst] *n* cresta; (*of coat of arms*) cimiero; **~fallen** *adj* mortificato(a)

Crete [kriːt] *n* Creta

crevasse [krɪ'væs] *n* crepaccio

crevice ['krɛvɪs] *n* fessura, crepa

crew [kruː] *n* equipaggio; **to have a ~-cut** avere i capelli a spazzola; **~-neck** *n* girocollo

crib [krɪb] *n* culla ♦ *vt* (*inf*) copiare

crick [krɪk] *n* crampo

cricket ['krɪkɪt] *n* (*insect*) grillo; (*game*) cricket *m*

crime [kraɪm] *n* crimine *m*; **criminal** ['krɪmɪnl] *adj, n* criminale *m/f*

crimson ['krɪmzn] *adj* color cremisi *inv*

cringe [krɪndʒ] *vi* acquattarsi; (*in embarrassment*) sentirsi sprofondare

crinkle ['krɪŋkl] *vt* arricciare, increspare

cripple ['krɪpl] *n* zoppo/a ♦ *vt* azzoppare

crises ['kraɪsiːz] *npl of* **crisis**

crisis ['kraɪsɪs] (*pl* **crises**) *n* crisi *f inv*

crisp [krɪsp] *adj* croccante; (*fig*) frizzante; vivace; deciso(a); **~s** (*BRIT*) *npl* patatine *fpl*

criss-cross ['krɪs-] *adj* incrociato(a)

criteria [kraɪ'tɪərɪə] *npl of* **criterion**

criterion [kraɪ'tɪərɪən] (*pl* **criteria**) *n* criterio

critic ['krɪtɪk] *n* critico; **~al** *adj* critico(a); **~ally** *adv* (*speak etc*) criticamente; **~ally ill** gravemente malato; **~ism** ['krɪtɪsɪzm] *n* critica; **~ize** ['krɪtɪsaɪz] *vt* criticare

croak [krəuk] *vi* gracchiare; (*frog*) gracidare

Croatia [krəu'eɪʃə] *n* Croazia

crochet ['krəuʃeɪ] *n* lavoro all'uncinetto

crockery ['krɔkərɪ] *n* vasellame *m*

crocodile ['krɔkədaɪl] *n* coccodrillo

crocus ['krəukəs] *n* croco

croft [krɔft] (*BRIT*) *n* piccolo podere *m*

crony ['krəunɪ] (*inf: pej*) *n* compare *m*

crook [kruk] *n* truffatore *m*; (*of shepherd*) bastone *m*; **~ed** ['krukɪd] *adj* curvo(a), storto(a); (*action*) disonesto(a)

crop [krɔp] *n* (*produce*) coltivazione *f*; (*amount produced*) raccolto; (*riding* ~) frustino ♦ *vt* (*hair*) rapare; **~ up** *vi* presentarsi

croquette [krə'kɛt] *n* crocchetta

cross [krɔs] *n* croce *f*; (*BIOL*) incrocio ♦ *vt* (*street etc*) attraversare; (*arms, legs, BIOL*) incrociare; (*cheque*) sbarrare ♦ *adj* di cattivo umore; **~ out** *vt* cancellare; **~ over** *vi* attraversare; **~bar** *n* traversa; **~country (race)** *n* cross-country *m inv*; **~-examine** *vt* (*LAW*) interrogare in contraddittorio; **~-eyed** *adj* strabico(a); **~fire** *n* fuoco incrociato; **~ing** *n* incrocio; (*sea passage*) traversata; (*also: pedestrian ~ing*) passaggio pedonale; **~ing guard** (*US*) *n dipendente comunale che aiuta i bambini ad attraversare la strada*; **~ purposes** *npl*: **to be at ~ purposes** non parlare della stessa cosa; **~-reference** *n* rinvio, rimando; **~roads** *n* incrocio; **~section** *n* sezione *f* trasversale; (*in population*) settore *m* rappresentativo; **~walk** (*US*) *n* strisce *fpl* pedonali, passaggio pedonale; **~wind** *n* vento di traverso; **~word** *n* cruciverba *m inv*

crotch [krɔtʃ] *n* (*ANAT*) inforcatura; (*of garment*) pattina

crotchet ['krɔtʃɪt] *n* (*MUS*) semiminima

crotchety ['krɔtʃɪtɪ] *adj* (*person*) burbero(a)

crouch [krautʃ] *vi* acquattarsi; rannicchiarsi

crow [krəu] *n* (*bird*) cornacchia; (*of cock*) canto del gallo ♦ *vi* (*cock*) cantare

crowbar ['krəubaː*] *n* piede *m* di porco

crowd [kraud] *n* folla ♦ *vt* affollare, stipare ♦ *vi*: **to ~ round/in** affollarsi intorno a/in; **~ed** *adj* affollato(a); **~ed with** stipato(a) di

crown [kraun] *n* corona; (*of head*) calotta cranica; (*of hat*) cocuzzolo; (*of hill*) cima ♦ *vt* incoronare; (*fig: career*) coronare; **~ jewels** *npl* gioielli *mpl* della Corona; **~ prince** *n* principe *m* ereditario

crow's feet *npl* zampe *fpl* di gallina

crucial ['kru:ʃl] *adj* cruciale, decisivo(a)
crucifix ['kru:sɪfɪks] *n* crocifisso; **~ion** [-'fɪkʃən] *n* crocifissione *f*
crude [kru:d] *adj* (*materials*) greggio(a); non raffinato(a); (*fig: basic*) crudo(a), primitivo(a); (: *vulgar*) rozzo(a), grossolano(a); **~ (oil)** *n* (petrolio) greggio *m*
cruel ['kruəl] *adj* crudele; **~ty** *n* crudeltà *f inv*
cruise [kru:z] *n* crociera ♦ *vi* andare a velocità di crociera; (*taxi*) circolare; **~r** *n* incrociatore *m*
crumb [krʌm] *n* briciola
crumble ['krʌmbl] *vt* sbriciolare ♦ *vi* sbriciolarsi; (*plaster etc*) sgretolarsi; (*land, earth*) franare; (*building, fig*) crollare; **crumbly** *adj* friabile
crumpet ['krʌmpɪt] *n* specie di frittella
crumple ['krʌmpl] *vt* raggrinzare, spiegazzare
crunch [krʌntʃ] *vt* sgranocchiare; (*underfoot*) scricchiolare ♦ *n* (*fig*) punto *or* momento cruciale; **~y** *adj* croccante
crusade [kru:'seɪd] *n* crociata
crush [krʌʃ] *n* folla; (*love*): **to have a ~ on sb** avere una cotta per qn; (*drink*): **lemon ~** spremuta di limone ♦ *vt* schiacciare; (*crumple*) sgualcire
crust [krʌst] *n* crosta
crutch [krʌtʃ] *n* gruccia
crux [krʌks] *n* nodo
cry [kraɪ] *vi* piangere; (*shout: also: ~ out*) urlare ♦ *n* urlo, grido; **~ off** *vi* ritirarsi
cryptic ['krɪptɪk] *adj* ermetico(a)
crystal ['krɪstl] *n* cristallo; **~-clear** *adj* cristallino(a)
cub [kʌb] *n* cucciolo; (*also: ~ scout*) lupetto
Cuba ['kju:bə] *n* Cuba
cubbyhole ['kʌbɪhəʊl] *n* angolino
cube [kju:b] *n* cubo ♦ *vt* (*MATH*) elevare al cubo; **cubic** *adj* cubico(a); (*metre, foot*) cubo(a); **cubic capacity** *n* cilindrata
cubicle ['kju:bɪkl] *n* scompartimento separato; cabina
cuckoo ['kuku:] *n* cucù *m inv*; **~ clock** *n* orologio a cucù
cucumber ['kju:kʌmbə*] *n* cetriolo
cuddle ['kʌdl] *vt* abbracciare, coccolare

♦ *vi* abbracciarsi
cue [kju:] *n* (*snooker ~*) stecca; (*THEATRE etc*) segnale *m*
cuff [kʌf] *n* (*BRIT: of shirt, coat etc*) polsino; (*US: of trousers*) risvolto; **off the ~** improvvisando; **~link** *n* gemello
cuisine [kwɪ'zi:n] *n* cucina
cul-de-sac ['kʌldəsæk] *n* vicolo cieco
cull [kʌl] *vt* (*ideas etc*) scegliere ♦ *n* (*of animals*) abbattimento selettivo
culminate ['kʌlmɪneɪt] *vi*: **to ~ in** culminare con; **culmination** [-'neɪʃən] *n* culmine *m*
culottes [kju:'lɔts] *npl* gonna *f* pantalone *inv*
culpable ['kʌlpəbl] *adj* colpevole
culprit ['kʌlprɪt] *n* colpevole *m/f*
cult [kʌlt] *n* culto
cultivate ['kʌltɪveɪt] *vt* (*also fig*) coltivare; **cultivation** [-'veɪʃən] *n* coltivazione *f*
cultural ['kʌltʃərəl] *adj* culturale
culture ['kʌltʃə*] *n* (*also fig*) cultura; **~d** *adj* colto(a)
cumbersome ['kʌmbəsəm] *adj* ingombrante
cunning ['kʌnɪŋ] *n* astuzia, furberia ♦ *adj* astuto(a), furbo(a)
cup [kʌp] *n* tazza; (*prize, of bra*) coppa
cupboard ['kʌbəd] *n* armadio
cup-tie (*BRIT*) *n* partita di coppa
curate ['kjuərɪt] *n* cappellano
curator [kjuə'reɪtə*] *n* direttore *m* (*di museo etc*)
curb [kə:b] *vt* tenere a freno ♦ *n* freno; (*US*) bordo del marciapiede
curdle ['kə:dl] *vi* cagliare
cure [kjuə*] *vt* guarire; (*CULIN*) trattare; affumicare; essiccare ♦ *n* rimedio
curfew ['kə:fju:] *n* coprifuoco
curio ['kjuərɪəʊ] *n* curiosità *f inv*
curiosity [kjuərɪ'ɔsɪtɪ] *n* curiosità
curious ['kjuərɪəs] *adj* curioso(a)
curl [kə:l] *n* riccio ♦ *vt* ondulare; (*tightly*) arricciare ♦ *vi* arricciarsi; **~ up** *vi* rannicchiarsi; **~er** *n* bigodino
curly ['kə:lɪ] *adj* ricciuto(a)
currant ['kʌrnt] *n* (*dried*) sultanina; (*bush, fruit*) ribes *m inv*

currency ['kʌrnsɪ] *n* moneta; **to gain ~** (*fig*) acquistare larga diffusione

current ['kʌrnt] *adj* corrente ♦ *n* corrente *f*; **~ account** (*BRIT*) *n* conto corrente; **~ affairs** *npl* attualità *fpl* (*freedom etc*); **~ly** *adv* attualmente

curricula [kə'rɪkjulə] *npl of* **curriculum**

curriculum [kə'rɪkjuləm] (*pl* ~**s** *or* **curricula**) *n* curriculum *m inv*; **~ vitae** *n* curriculum vitae *m inv*

curry ['kʌrɪ] *n* curry *m inv* ♦ *vt*: **to ~ favour with** cercare di attirarsi i favori di; **~ powder** *n* curry *m*

curse [kə:s] *vt* maledire ♦ *vi* bestemmiare ♦ *n* maledizione *f*; bestemmia

cursor ['kə:sə*] *n* (*COMPUT*) cursore *m*

cursory ['kə:sərɪ] *adj* superficiale

curt [kə:t] *adj* secco(a)

curtail [kə:'teɪl] *vt* (*freedom etc*) limitare; (*visit etc*) accorciare; (*expenses etc*) ridurre, decurtare

curtain ['kə:tn] *n* tenda; (*THEATRE*) sipario

curts(e)y ['kə:tsɪ] *vi* fare un inchino *or* una riverenza

curve [kə:v] *n* curva ♦ *vi* curvarsi

cushion ['kuʃən] *n* cuscino ♦ *vt* (*shock*) fare da cuscinetto a

custard ['kʌstəd] *n* (*for pouring*) crema

custodian [kʌs'təudɪən] *n* custode *m/f*

custody ['kʌstədɪ] *n* (*of child*) tutela; **to take into ~** (*suspect*) mettere in detenzione preventiva

custom ['kʌstəm] *n* costume *m*, consuetudine *f*; (*COMM*) clientela; **~ary** *adj* consueto(a)

customer ['kʌstəmə*] *n* cliente *m/f*

customized ['kʌstəmaɪzd] *adj* (*car etc*) fuoriserie *inv*

custom-made *adj* (*clothes*) fatto(a) su misura; (*other goods*) fatto(a) su ordinazione

customs ['kʌstəmz] *npl* dogana; **~ duty** *n* tassa doganale; **~ officer** *n* doganiere *m*

cut [kʌt] (*pt, pp* **cut**) *vt* tagliare; (*shape, make*) ridurre ♦ *vi* tagliare ♦ *n* taglio; (*in salary etc*) riduzione *f*; **to ~ a tooth** mettere un dente; **~ down** *vt* (*tree etc*) abbattere ♦ *vt*

fus (*also*: **~ down on**) ridurre; **~ off** *vt* tagliare; (*fig*) isolare; **~ out** *vt* tagliare fuori; eliminare; ritagliare; **~ up** *vt* (*paper, meat*) tagliare a pezzi; **~back** *n* riduzione *f*

cute [kju:t] *adj* (*sweet*) carino(a)

cuticle ['kju:tɪkl] *n* (*on nail*) pellicina, cuticola

cutlery ['kʌtlərɪ] *n* posate *fpl*

cutlet ['kʌtlɪt] *n* costoletta; (*nut etc ~*) cotoletta vegetariana

cut: **~out** *n* interruttore *m*; (*cardboard ~out*) ritaglio; **~-price** (*US* **~-rate**) *adj* a prezzo ridotto; **~throat** *n* assassino ♦ *adj* (*competition*) spietato(a)

cutting ['kʌtɪŋ] *adj* tagliente ♦ *n* (*from newspaper*) ritaglio (di giornale); (*from plant*) talea

CV *n abbr* = **curriculum vitae**

cwt *abbr* = **hundredweight(s)**

cyanide ['saɪənaɪd] *n* cianuro

cycle ['saɪkl] *n* ciclo; (*bicycle*) bicicletta ♦ *vi* andare in bicicletta

cycling ['saɪklɪŋ] *n* ciclismo

cyclist ['saɪklɪst] *n* ciclista *m/f*

cygnet ['sɪgnɪt] *n* cigno giovane

cylinder ['sɪlɪndə*] *n* cilindro; **~-head gasket** *n* guarnizione *f* della testata del cilindro

cymbals ['sɪmblz] *npl* cembali *mpl*

cynic ['sɪnɪk] *n* cinico/a; **~al** *adj* cinico(a); **~ism** ['sɪnɪsɪzəm] *n* cinismo

Cyprus ['saɪprəs] *n* Cipro

cyst [sɪst] *n* cisti *f inv*

cystitis [sɪs'taɪtɪs] *n* cistite *f*

czar [zɑ:*] *n* zar *m inv*

Czech [tʃɛk] *adj* ceco(a) ♦ *n* ceco/a; (*LING*) ceco

Czechoslovakia [tʃɛkəslə'vækɪə] *n* Cecoslovacchia; **~n** *adj*, *n* cecoslovacco(a)

D

D [di:] *n* (*MUS*) re *m*

dab [dæb] *vt* (*eyes, wound*) tamponare; (*paint, cream*) applicare (con leggeri colpetti)

dabble ['dæbl] *vi*: **to ~ in** occuparsi (da

dilettante) di
dad(dy) [dæd(ɪ)] (*inf*) *n* babbo, papà *m*
inv
daffodil ['dæfədɪl] *n* trombone *m*,
giunchiglia
daft [dɑːft] *adj* sciocco(a)
dagger ['dægə*] *n* pugnale *m*
daily ['deɪlɪ] *adj* quotidiano(a),
giornaliero(a) ♦ *n* quotidiano ♦ *adv* tutti i
giorni
dainty ['deɪntɪ] *adj* delicato(a),
grazioso(a)
dairy ['dɛərɪ] *n* (*BRIT*: *shop*) latteria; (*on
farm*) caseificio ♦ *adj* caseario(a); ~ **farm**
n caseificio; ~ **products** *npl* latticini
mpl; ~ **store** (*US*) *n* latteria
dais ['deɪɪs] *n* pedana, palco
daisy ['deɪzɪ] *n* margherita; ~ **wheel** *n*
(*on printer*) margherita
dale [deɪl] (*BRIT*) *n* valle *f*
dam [dæm] *n* diga ♦ *vt* sbarrare;
costruire dighe su
damage ['dæmɪdʒ] *n* danno, danni *mpl*;
(*fig*) danno ♦ *vt* danneggiare; ~**s** *npl* (*LAW*)
danni
damn [dæm] *vt* condannare; (*curse*)
maledire ♦ *n* (*inf*): **I don't give a** ~ non
me ne frega niente ♦ *adj* (*inf*: *also*: ~*ed*):
this ~ ... questo maledetto ...; ~ **(it)!**
accidenti!; ~**ing** *adj* (*evidence*)
schiacciante
damp [dæmp] *adj* umido(a) ♦ *n* umidità,
umido ♦ *vt* (*also*: ~*en*: *cloth, rag*)
inumidire, bagnare; (: *enthusiasm etc*)
spegnere
damson ['dæmzən] *n* susina damaschina
dance [dɑːns] *n* danza, ballo; (*ball*) ballo
♦ *vi* ballare; ~ **hall** *n* dancing *m inv*, sala
da ballo; ~**r** *n* danzatore/trice;
(*professional*) ballerino/a
dancing ['dɑːnsɪŋ] *n* danza, ballo
dandelion ['dændɪlaɪən] *n* dente *m* di
leone
dandruff ['dændrəf] *n* forfora
Dane [deɪn] *n* danese *m/f*
danger ['deɪndʒə*] *n* pericolo; **there is a**
~ **of fire** c'è pericolo di incendio; **in** ~ in
pericolo; **he was in** ~ **of falling**
rischiava di cadere; ~**ous** *adj*

pericoloso(a)
dangle ['dæŋgl] *vt* dondolare; (*fig*) far
balenare ♦ *vi* pendolare
Danish ['deɪnɪʃ] *adj* danese ♦ *n* (*LING*)
danese *m*
dapper ['dæpə*] *adj* lindo(a)
dare [dɛə*] *vt*: **to** ~ **sb to do** sfidare qn a
fare ♦ *vi*: **to** ~ **(to) do sth** osare fare qc; **I**
~ **say** (*I suppose*) immagino (che); ~**devil**
n scavezzacollo *m/f*; **daring** *adj* audace,
ardito(a) ♦ *n* audacia
dark [dɑːk] *adj* (*night, room*) buio(a),
scuro(a); (*colour, complexion*) scuro(a);
(*fig*) cupo(a), tetro(a), nero(a) ♦ *n*: **in the**
~ al buio; **in the** ~ **about** (*fig*) all'oscuro
di; **after** ~ a notte fatta; ~**en** *vt* (*colour*)
scurire ♦ *vi* (*sky, room*) oscurarsi; ~
glasses *npl* occhiali *mpl* scuri; ~**ness** *n*
oscurità, buio; ~ **room** *n* camera oscura
darling ['dɑːlɪŋ] *adj* caro(a) ♦ *n* tesoro
darn [dɑːn] *vt* rammendare
dart [dɑːt] *n* freccetta; (*SEWING*) pince *f inv*
♦ *vi*: **to** ~ **towards** precipitarsi verso; **to**
~ **away/along** sfrecciare via/lungo;
~**board** *n* bersaglio (per freccette); ~**s** *n*
tiro al bersaglio (con freccette)
dash [dæʃ] *n* (*sign*) lineetta; (*small
quantity*) punta ♦ *vt* (*missile*) gettare;
(*hopes*) infrangere ♦ *vi*: **to** ~ **towards**
precipitarsi verso; ~ **away** *or* **off** *vi*
scappare via
dashboard ['dæʃbɔːd] *n* (*AUT*) cruscotto
dashing ['dæʃɪŋ] *adj* ardito(a)
data ['deɪtə] *npl* dati *mpl*; ~**base** *n* base *f*
di dati, data base *m inv*; ~ **processing** *n*
elaborazione *f* (elettronica) dei dati
date [deɪt] *n* data; appuntamento; (*fruit*)
dattero ♦ *vt* datare; (*person*) uscire con; ~
of birth data di nascita; **to** ~ (*until now*)
fino a oggi; ~**d** *adj* passato(a) di moda; ~
rape *n* stupro perpetrato da persona
conosciuta
daub [dɔːb] *vt* imbrattare
daughter ['dɔːtə*] *n* figlia; ~**-in-law** *n*
nuora
daunting ['dɔːntɪŋ] *adj* non invidiabile
dawdle ['dɔːdl] *vi* bighellonare
dawn [dɔːn] *n* alba ♦ *vi* (*day*) spuntare;
(*fig*): **it** ~**ed on him that** ... gli è venuto

in mente che ....

day [deɪ] *n* giorno; (*as duration*) giornata; (*period of time, age*) tempo, epoca; **the ~ before** il giorno avanti *or* prima; **the ~ after, the following** ~ il giorno dopo *or* seguente; **the ~ after tomorrow** dopodomani; **the ~ before yesterday** l'altroieri; **by** ~ di giorno; **~break** *n* spuntar *m* del giorno; **~dream** *vi* sognare a occhi aperti; **~light** *n* luce *f* del giorno; **~ return** (*BRIT*) *n* biglietto giornaliero di andata e ritorno; **~time** *n* giorno; **~-to-~** *adj* (*life, organization*) quotidiano(a)

daze [deɪz] *vt* (*subject: drug*) inebetire; (: *blow*) stordire ♦ *n*: **in a ~** inebetito(a); stordito(a)

dazzle ['dæzl] *vt* abbagliare

DC *abbr* (= *direct current*) c.c

D-day *n* giorno dello sbarco alleato in Normandia

dead [dɛd] *adj* morto(a); (*numb*) intirizzito(a); (*telephone*) muto(a); (*battery*) scarico(a) ♦ *adv* assolutamente, perfettamente ♦ *npl*: **the** ~ i morti; **he was shot** ~ fu colpito a morte; **~ tired** stanco(a) morto(a); **to stop** ~ fermarsi di colpo; **~en** *vt* (*blow, sound*) ammortire; **~ end** *n* vicolo cieco; **~ heat** *n* (*SPORT*): **to finish in a ~ heat** finire alla pari; **~line** *n* scadenza; **~lock** *n* punto morto; **~ loss** *n*: **to be a ~ loss** (*inf*: *person, thing*) non valere niente; **~ly** *adj* mortale; (*weapon, poison*) micidiale; **~pan** *adj* a faccia impassibile

deaf [dɛf] *adj* sordo(a); **~en** *vt* assordare; **~ness** *n* sordità

deal [di:l] (*pt, pp* dealt) *n* accordo; (*business* ~) affare *m* ♦ *vt* (*blow, cards*) dare; **a great ~ (of)** molto(a); **~ in** *vt fus* occuparsi di; **~ with** *vt fus* (*COMM*) fare affari con, trattare con; (*handle*) occuparsi di; (*be about: book etc*) trattare di; **~er** *n* commerciante *m/f*; **~ings** *npl* (*COMM*) relazioni *fpl*; (*relations*) rapporti *mpl*; **dealt** [dɛlt] *pt, pp of* **deal**

dean [di:n] *n* (*REL*) decano; (*SCOL*) preside *m* di facoltà (*or* di collegio)

dear [dɪə*] *adj* caro(a) ♦ *n*: **my ~** caro mio/cara mia ♦ *excl*: **~ me!** Dio mio!; **D~**

Sir/Madam (*in letter*) Egregio Signore/ Egregia Signora; **D~ Mr/Mrs X** Gentile Signor/Signora X; **~ly** *adv* (*love*) moltissimo; (*pay*) a caro prezzo

death [dɛθ] *n* morte *f*; (*ADMIN*) decesso; **~ certificate** *n* atto di decesso; **~ly** *adj* di morte; **~ penalty** *n* pena di morte; **~ rate** *n* indice *m* di mortalità; **~ toll** *n* vittime *fpl*

debacle [dɪ'bækl] *n* fiasco

debar [dɪ'bɑ:*] *vt*: **to ~ sb from doing** impedire a qn di fare

debase [dɪ'beɪs] *vt* (*currency*) adulterare; (*person*) degradare

debatable [dɪ'beɪtəbl] *adj* discutibile

debate [dɪ'beɪt] *n* dibattito ♦ *vt* dibattere; discutere

debauchery [dɪ'bɔ:tʃərɪ] *n* dissolutezza

debit ['dɛbɪt] *n* debito ♦ *vt*: **to ~ a sum to sb** *or* **to sb's account** addebitare una somma a qn

debris ['dɛbri:] *n* detriti *mpl*

debt [dɛt] *n* debito; **to be in ~** essere indebitato(a); **~or** *n* debitore/trice

debunk [di:'bʌŋk] *vt* (*theory, claim*) smentire

début ['deɪbju:] *n* debutto

decade ['dɛkeɪd] *n* decennio

decadence ['dɛkədəns] *n* decadenza

decaffeinated [dɪ'kæfɪneɪtɪd] *adj* decaffeinato(a)

decanter [dɪ'kæntə*] *n* caraffa

decay [dɪ'keɪ] *n* decadimento; (*also: tooth ~*) carie *f* ♦ *vi* (*rot*) imputridire

deceased [dɪ'si:st] *n* defunto/a

deceit [dɪ'si:t] *n* inganno; **~ful** *adj* ingannevole, perfido(a)

deceive [dɪ'si:v] *vt* ingannare

December [dɪ'sɛmbə*] *n* dicembre *m*

decent ['di:sənt] *adj* decente; (*respectable*) per bene; (*kind*) gentile

deception [dɪ'sɛpʃən] *n* inganno

deceptive [dɪ'sɛptɪv] *adj* ingannevole

decide [dɪ'saɪd] *vt* (*person*) far prendere una decisione a; (*question, argument*) risolvere, decidere ♦ *vi* decidere, decidersi; **to ~ to do/that** decidere di fare/che; **to ~ on** decidere per; **~d** *adj* (*resolute*) deciso(a); (*clear, definite*) netto(a), chiaro(a); **~dly** [-dɪdlɪ] *adv* indubbiamente; decisamente

decimal ['dɛsɪməl] *adj* decimale ♦ *n* decimale *m*; **~ point** *n* ≈ virgola

decipher [dɪ'saɪfə*] *vt* decifrare

decision [dɪ'sɪʒən] *n* decisione *f*

decisive [dɪ'saɪsɪv] *adj* decisivo(a); (*person*) deciso(a)

deck [dɛk] *n* (NAUT) ponte *m*; (*of bus*): **top ~** imperiale *m*; (*record* ~) piatto; (*of cards*) mazzo; **~chair** *n* sedia a sdraio

declaration [dɛklə'reɪʃən] *n* dichiarazione *f*

declare [dɪ'klɛə*] *vt* dichiarare

decline [dɪ'klaɪn] *n* (*decay*) declino; (*lessening*) ribasso ♦ *vt* declinare; rifiutare ♦ *vi* declinare; diminuire

decode [di:'kəʊd] *vt* decifrare

decoder [di:'kəʊdə*] *n* (TV) decodificatore *m*

decompose [di:kəm'pəʊz] *vi* decomporre

décor ['deɪkɔ:*] *n* decorazione *f*

decorate ['dɛkəreɪt] *vt* (*adorn, give a medal to*) decorare; (*paint and paper*) tinteggiare e tappezzare; **decoration** [-'reɪʃən] *n* (*medal etc, adornment*) decorazione *f*; **decorator** *n* decoratore *m*

decorum [dɪ'kɔ:rəm] *n* decoro

decoy ['di:kɔɪ] *n* zimbello

decrease [*n* 'di:kri:s, *vb* di:'kri:s] *n* diminuzione *f* ♦ *vt, vi* diminuire

decree [dɪ'kri:] *n* decreto; **~ nisi** [-'naɪsaɪ] *n* sentenza provvisoria di divorzio

dedicate ['dɛdɪkeɪt] *vt* consacrare; (*book etc*) dedicare

dedication [dɛdɪ'keɪʃən] *n* (*devotion*) dedizione *f*; (*in book etc*) dedica

deduce [dɪ'dju:s] *vt* dedurre

deduct [dɪ'dʌkt] *vt*: **to ~ sth (from)** dedurre qc (da); **~ion** [dɪ'dʌkʃən] *n* deduzione *f*

deed [di:d] *n* azione *f*, atto; (LAW) atto

deem [di:m] *vt* giudicare, ritenere

deep [di:p] *adj* profondo(a); **4 metres ~** profondo(a) 4 metri ♦ *adv*: **spectators stood 20 ~** c'erano 20 file di spettatori; **~en** *vt* (*hole*) approfondire ♦ *vi* approfondirsi; (*darkness*) farsi più buio; **~-freeze** *n* congelatore *m*; **~-fry** *vt*

friggere in olio abbondante; **~ly** *adv* profondamente; **~-sea diving** *n* immersione *f* in alto mare; **~-seated** *adj* radicato(a)

deer [dɪə*] *n inv*: **the ~** i cervidi; **(red) ~** cervo; **(fallow) ~** daino; **(roe) ~** capriolo; **~skin** *n* pelle *f* di daino

deface [dɪ'feɪs] *vt* imbrattare

default [dɪ'fɔ:lt] *n* (COMPUT: *also*: ~ *value*) default *m inv*; **by ~** (SPORT) per abbandono

defeat [dɪ'fi:t] *n* sconfitta ♦ *vt* (*team, opponents*) sconfiggere; **~ist** *adj, n* disfattista *m/f*

defect [*n* 'di:fɛkt, *vb* dɪ'fɛkt] *n* difetto ♦ *vi*: **to ~ to the enemy** passare al nemico; **~ive** [dɪ'fɛktɪv] *adj* difettoso(a)

defence [dɪ'fɛns] (US **defense**) *n* difesa; **~less** *adj* senza difesa

defend [dɪ'fɛnd] *vt* difendere; **~ant** *n* imputato/a; **~er** *n* difensore/a

defense [dɪ'fɛns] (US) *n* = **defence**

defensive [dɪ'fɛnsɪv] *adj* difensivo(a) ♦ *n*: **on the ~** sulla difensiva

defer [dɪ'fə:*] *vt* (*postpone*) differire, rinviare

defiance [dɪ'faɪəns] *n* sfida; **in ~ of** a dispetto di

defiant [dɪ'faɪənt] *adj* (*attitude*) di sfida; (*person*) ribelle

deficiency [dɪ'fɪʃənsɪ] *n* deficienza; carenza

deficit ['dɛfɪsɪt] *n* deficit *m inv*

defile [dɪ'faɪl] *vt* deturpare

define [dɪ'faɪn] *vt* definire

definite ['dɛfɪnɪt] *adj* (*fixed*) definito(a), preciso(a); (*clear, obvious*) ben definito(a), esatto(a); (LING) determinativo(a); **he was ~ about it** ne era sicuro; **~ly** *adv* indubbiamente

definition [dɛfɪ'nɪʃən] *n* definizione *f*

deflate [di:'fleɪt] *vt* sgonfiare

deflect [dɪ'flɛkt] *vt* deflettere, deviare

deformed [dɪ'fɔ:md] *adj* deforme

defraud [dɪ'frɔ:d] *vt* defraudare

defrost [di:'frɔst] *vt* (*fridge*) disgelare; **~er** (US) *n* (*demister*) sbrinatore *m*

deft [dɛft] *adj* svelto(a), destro(a)

defunct [dɪ'fʌŋkt] *adj* che non esiste più

defuse [di:'fju:z] *vt* disinnescare; (*fig*)

distendere

defy [dɪ'faɪ] *vt* sfidare; (*efforts etc*) resistere a; **it defies description** supera ogni descrizione

degenerate [*vb* dɪ'dʒɛnəreɪt, *adj* dɪ'dʒɛnərɪt] *vi* degenerare ♦ *adj* degenere

degree [dɪ'griː] *n* grado; (*SCOL*) laurea (universitaria); **a (first) ~ in maths** una laurea in matematica; **by ~s** (*gradually*) gradualmente, a poco a poco; **to some ~** fino a un certo punto, in certa misura

dehydrated [diːhaɪ'dreɪtɪd] *adj* disidratato(a); (*milk, eggs*) in polvere

de-ice [diː'aɪs] *vt* (*windscreen*) disgelare

deign [deɪn] *vi*: **to ~ to do** degnarsi di fare

deity ['diːɪtɪ] *n* divinità *f inv*

dejected [dɪ'dʒɛktɪd] *adj* abbattuto(a), avvilito(a)

delay [dɪ'leɪ] *vt* ritardare ♦ *vi*: **to ~ (in doing sth)** ritardare (a fare qc) ♦ *n* ritardo; **to be ~ed** subire un ritardo; (*person*) essere trattenuto(a)

delectable [dɪ'lɛktəbl] *adj* (*person, food*) delizioso(a)

delegate [*n* 'dɛlɪgɪt, *vb* 'dɛlɪgeɪt] *n* delegato/a ♦ *vt* delegare; **delegation** [-'geɪʃən] *n* (*group*) delegazione *f*; (*by manager*) delega

delete [dɪ'liːt] *vt* cancellare

deliberate [*adj* dɪ'lɪbərɪt, *vb* dɪ'lɪbəreɪt] *adj* (*intentional*) intenzionale; (*slow*) misurato(a) ♦ *vi* deliberare, riflettere; **~ly** *adv* (*on purpose*) deliberatamente

delicacy ['dɛlɪkəsɪ] *n* delicatezza

delicate ['dɛlɪkɪt] *adj* delicato(a)

delicatessen [dɛlɪkə'tɛsn] *n* ≈ salumeria

delicious [dɪ'lɪʃəs] *adj* delizioso(a), squisito(a)

delight [dɪ'laɪt] *n* delizia, gran piacere *m* ♦ *vt* dilettare; **to take (a) ~ in** dilettarsi in; **~ed** *adj*: **~ed (at** *or* **with)** contentissimo/a (di), felice (di); **~ed to do** felice di fare; **~ful** *adj* delizioso(a); incantevole

delinquent [dɪ'lɪŋkwənt] *adj, n* delinquente *m/f*

delirious [dɪ'lɪrɪəs] *adj*: **to be ~** delirare

deliver [dɪ'lɪvə*] *vt* (*mail*) distribuire;

(*goods*) consegnare; (*speech*) pronunciare; (*MED*) far partorire; **~y** *n* distribuzione *f*; consegna; (*of speaker*) dizione *f*; (*MED*) parto

delude [dɪ'luːd] *vt* illudere

deluge ['dɛljuːdʒ] *n* diluvio

delusion [dɪ'luːʒən] *n* illusione *f*

delve [dɛlv] *vi*: **to ~ into** frugare in; (*subject*) far ricerche in

demand [dɪ'mɑːnd] *vt* richiedere; (*rights*) rivendicare ♦ *n* domanda; (*claim*) rivendicazione *f*; **in ~** ricercato(a), richiesto(a); **on ~** a richiesta; **~ing** *adj* (*boss*) esigente; (*work*) impegnativo(a)

demean [dɪ'miːn] *vt*: **to ~ o.s.** umiliarsi

demeanour [dɪ'miːnə*] (*US* **demeanor**) *n* comportamento; contegno

demented [dɪ'mɛntɪd] *adj* demente, impazzito(a)

demise [dɪ'maɪz] *n* decesso

demister [diː'mɪstə*] (*BRIT*) *n* (*AUT*) sbrinatore *m*

demo ['dɛməu] (*inf*) *n abbr* (= *demonstration*) manifestazione *f*

democracy [dɪ'mɔkrəsɪ] *n* democrazia

democrat ['dɛməkræt] *n* democratico/a; **~ic** [dɛmə'krætɪk] *adj* democratico(a)

demolish [dɪ'mɔlɪʃ] *vt* demolire

demonstrate ['dɛmənstreɪt] *vt* dimostrare, provare ♦ *vi* dimostrare, manifestare; **demonstration** [-'streɪʃən] *n* dimostrazione *f*; (*POL*) dimostrazione, manifestazione *f*; **demonstrator** *n* (*POL*) dimostrante *m/f*; (*COMM*) dimostratore/trice

demote [dɪ'məut] *vt* far retrocedere

demure [dɪ'mjuə*] *adj* contegnoso(a)

den [dɛn] *n* tana, covo; (*room*) buco

denatured alcohol [diː'neɪtʃəd-] (*US*) *n* alcool *m inv* denaturato

denial [dɪ'naɪəl] *n* diniego; rifiuto

denim ['dɛnɪm] *n* tessuto di cotone ritorto; **~s** *npl* (*jeans*) blue jeans *mpl*

Denmark ['dɛnmɑːk] *n* Danimarca

denomination [dɪnɔmɪ'neɪʃən] *n* (*money*) valore *m*; (*REL*) confessione *f*

denounce [dɪ'nauns] *vt* denunciare

dense [dɛns] *adj* fitto(a); (*smoke*) denso(a); (*inf: person*) ottuso(a), duro(a)

density ['dɛnsɪtɪ] *n* densità *f inv*

dent [dɛnt] *n* ammaccatura ♦ *vt* (*also*: **make a ~ in**) ammaccare

dental ['dɛntl] *adj* dentale; **~ surgeon** *n* medico/a dentista

dentist ['dɛntɪst] *n* dentista *m/f*; **~ry** *n* odontoiatria

dentures ['dɛntʃəz] *npl* dentiera

deny [dɪ'naɪ] *vt* negare; (*refuse*) rifiutare

deodorant [di:'əudərənt] *n* deodorante *m*

depart [dɪ'pɑ:t] *vi* partire; **to ~ from** (*fig*) deviare da

department [dɪ'pɑ:tmənt] *n* (*COMM*) reparto; (*SCOL*) sezione *f*, dipartimento; (*POL*) ministero; **~ store** *n* grande magazzino

departure [dɪ'pɑ:tʃə*] *n* partenza; (*fig*): **~ from** deviazione *f* da; **a new ~** una svolta (decisiva); **~ lounge** *n* (*at airport*) sala d'attesa

depend [dɪ'pɛnd] *vi*: **to ~ on** dipendere da; (*rely on*) contare su; **it ~s** dipende; **~ing on the result ...** a seconda del risultato ...; **~able** *adj* fidato(a); (*car etc*) affidabile; **~ant** *n* persona a carico; **~ent** *adj*: **to be ~ent on** dipendere da; (*child, relative*) essere a carico di ♦ *n* = **~ant**

depict [dɪ'pɪkt] *vt* (*in picture*) dipingere; (*in words*) descrivere

depleted [dɪ'pli:tɪd] *adj* diminuito(a)

deploy [dɪ'plɔɪ] *vt* dispiegare

depopulation ['di:pɔpju'leɪʃən] *n* spopolamento

deport [dɪ'pɔ:t] *vt* deportare; espellere

deportment [dɪ'pɔ:tmənt] *n* portamento

depose [dɪ'pəuz] *vt* deporre

deposit [dɪ'pɔzɪt] *n* (*COMM, GEO*) deposito; (*of ore, oil*) giacimento; (*CHEM*) sedimento; (*part payment*) acconto; (*for hired goods etc*) cauzione *f* ♦ *vt* depositare; dare in acconto; mettere *or* lasciare in deposito; **~ account** *n* conto vincolato

depot ['dɛpəu] *n* deposito; (*US*) stazione *f* ferroviaria

depreciate [dɪ'pri:ʃɪeɪt] *vi* svalutarsi

depress [dɪ'prɛs] *vt* deprimere; (*price, wages*) abbassare; (*press down*) premere; **~ed** *adj* (*person*) depresso(a), abbattuto(a); (*price*) in ribasso; (*industry*) in crisi; **~ing**

adj deprimente; **~ion** [dɪ'prɛʃən] *n* depressione *f*

deprivation [dɛprɪ'veɪʃən] *n* privazione *f*

deprive [dɪ'praɪv] *vt*: **to ~ sb of** privare qn di; **~d** *adj* disgraziato(a)

depth [dɛpθ] *n* profondità *f inv*; **in the ~s of** nel profondo di; nel cuore di; **out of one's ~** (*in water*) dove non si tocca; (*fig*) a disagio

deputize ['dɛpjutaɪz] *vi*: **to ~ for** svolgere le funzioni di

deputy ['dɛpjutɪ] *adj*: **~ head** (*BRIT: SCOL*) vicepreside *m/f* ♦ *n* (*assistant*) vice *m/f inv*; (*US: also*: **~ sheriff**) vice-sceriffo

derail [dɪ'reɪl] *vt*: **to be ~ed** deragliare

deranged [dɪ'reɪndʒd] *adj*: **to be (mentally) ~** essere pazzo(a)

derby ['də:bɪ] (*US*) *n* (*bowler hat*) bombetta

derelict ['dɛrɪlɪkt] *adj* abbandonato(a)

derisory [dɪ'raɪsərɪ] *adj* (*sum*) irrisorio(a); (*laughter, person*) beffardo(a)

derive [dɪ'raɪv] *vt*: **to ~ sth from** derivare qc da; trarre qc da ♦ *vi*: **to ~ from** derivare da

derogatory [dɪ'rɔgətərɪ] *adj* denigratorio(a)

derv [də:v] (*BRIT*) *n* gasolio

descend [dɪ'sɛnd] *vt, vi* discendere, scendere; **to ~ from** discendere da; **to ~ to** (*lying, begging*) abbassarsi a; **~ant** *n* discendente *m/f*

descent [dɪ'sɛnt] *n* discesa; (*origin*) discendenza, famiglia

describe [dɪs'kraɪb] *vt* descrivere; **description** [-'krɪpʃən] *n* descrizione *f*; (*sort*) genere *m*, specie *f*

desecrate ['dɛsɪkreɪt] *vt* profanare

desert [*n* 'dɛzət, *vb* dɪ'zə:t] *n* deserto ♦ *vt* lasciare, abbandonare ♦ *vi* (*MIL*) disertare; **~er** *n* disertore *m*; **~ion** [dɪ'zə:ʃən] *n* (*MIL*) diserzione *f*; (*LAW*) abbandono del tetto coniugale; **~ island** *n* isola deserta; **~s** [dɪ'zə:ts] *npl*: **to get one's just ~s** avere ciò che si merita

deserve [dɪ'zə:v] *vt* meritare; **deserving** *adj* (*person*) meritevole, degno(a); (*cause*) meritorio(a)

design [dɪ'zaɪn] *n* (*art, sketch*) disegno;

(*layout, shape*) linea; (*pattern*) fantasia; (*intention*) intenzione *f* ♦ *vt* disegnare; progettare

designer [dɪ'zaɪnə*] *n* (*ART, TECH*) disegnatore/trice; (*of fashion*) modellista *m/f*

desire [dɪ'zaɪə*] *n* desiderio, voglia ♦ *vt* desiderare, volere

desk [dɛsk] *n* (*in office*) scrivania; (*for pupil*) banco; (*BRIT: in shop, restaurant*) cassa; (*in hotel*) ricevimento; (*at airport*) accettazione *f*

desolate ['dɛsəlɪt] *adj* desolato(a)

despair [dɪs'pɛə*] *n* disperazione *f* ♦ *vi*: **to ~ of** disperare di

despatch [dɪs'pætʃ] *n, vt* = **dispatch**

desperate ['dɛspərɪt] *adj* disperato(a); (*fugitive*) capace di tutto; **to be ~ for sth/to do** volere disperatamente qc/fare; **~ly** *adv* disperatamente; (*very*) terribilmente, estremamente

desperation [dɛspə'reɪʃən] *n* disperazione *f*

despicable [dɪs'pɪkəbl] *adj* disprezzabile

despise [dɪs'paɪz] *vt* disprezzare, sdegnare

despite [dɪs'paɪt] *prep* malgrado, a dispetto di, nonostante

despondent [dɪs'pɒndənt] *adj* abbattuto(a), scoraggiato(a)

dessert [dɪ'zə:t] *n* dolce *m*; frutta; **~spoon** *n* cucchiaio da dolci

destination [dɛstɪ'neɪʃən] *n* destinazione *f*

destined ['dɛstɪnd] *adj*: **to be ~ to do/ for** essere destinato(a) a fare/per

destiny ['dɛstɪnɪ] *n* destino

destitute ['dɛstɪtjuːt] *adj* indigente, bisognoso(a)

destroy [dɪs'trɔɪ] *vt* distruggere; **~er** *n* (*NAUT*) cacciatorpediniere *m*

destruction [dɪs'trʌkʃən] *n* distruzione *f*

detach [dɪ'tætʃ] *vt* staccare, distaccare; **~ed** *adj* (*attitude*) distante; **~ed house** *n* villa; **~ment** *n* (*MIL*) distaccamento; (*fig*) distacco

detail ['diːteɪl] *n* particolare *m*, dettaglio ♦ *vt* dettagliare, particolareggiare; **in ~** nei particolari; **~ed** *adj* particola-

reggiato(a)

detain [dɪ'teɪn] *vt* trattenere; (*in captivity*) detenere

detect [dɪ'tɛkt] *vt* scoprire, scorgere; (*MED, POLICE, RADAR etc*) individuare; **~ion** [dɪ'tɛkʃən] *n* scoperta; individuazione *f*; **~ive** *n* investigatore/trice; **~ive story** *n* giallo

détente [deɪ'tɑːnt] *n* (*POL*) distensione *f*

detention [dɪ'tɛnʃən] *n* detenzione *f*; (*SCOL*) permanenza forzata per punizione

deter [dɪ'tə:*] *vt* dissuadere

detergent [dɪ'tə:dʒənt] *n* detersivo

deteriorate [dɪ'tɪərɪəreɪt] *vi* deteriorarsi

determine [dɪ'tə:mɪn] *vt* determinare; **~d** *adj* (*person*) risoluto(a), deciso(a); **~d to do** deciso(a) a fare

detour ['diːtuə*] *n* deviazione *f*

detract [dɪ'trækt] *vi*: **to ~ from** detrarre da

detriment ['dɛtrɪmənt] *n*: **to the ~ of** a detrimento di; **~al** [dɛtrɪ'mɛntl] *adj*: **~al to** dannoso(a) a, nocivo(a) a

devaluation [dɪvælju'eɪʃən] *n* svalutazione *f*

devastate ['dɛvəsteɪt] *vt* devastare; (*fig*): **~d by** sconvolto(a) da; **devastating** *adj* devastatore(trice); sconvolgente

develop [dɪ'vɛləp] *vt* sviluppare; (*habit*) prendere (gradualmente) ♦ *vi* svilupparsi; (*facts, symptoms: appear*) manifestarsi, rivelarsi; **~er** *n* (*also: property ~er*) costruttore *m* edile; **~ing country** *n* paese *m* in via di sviluppo; **~ment** *n* sviluppo

device [dɪ'vaɪs] *n* (*apparatus*) congegno

devil ['dɛvl] *n* diavolo; demonio

devious ['diːvɪəs] *adj* (*person*) subdolo(a)

devise [dɪ'vaɪz] *vt* escogitare, concepire

devoid [dɪ'vɔɪd] *adj*: **~ of** privo(a) di

devolution [diːvə'luːʃən] *n* (*POL*) decentramento

devote [dɪ'vəʊt] *vt*: **to ~ sth to** dedicare qc a; **~d** *adj* devoto(a); **to be ~d to sb** essere molto affezionato(a) a qn; **~e** [dɛvəʊ'tiː] *n* (*MUS, SPORT*) appassionato/a

devotion [dɪ'vəʊʃən] *n* devozione *f*, attaccamento; (*REL*) atto di devozione, preghiera

devour [dɪ'vauə*] *vt* divorare

devout [dɪ'vaut] *adj* pio(a), devoto(a)

dew [djuː] *n* rugiada

dexterity [dɛks'tɛrɪtɪ] *n* destrezza

diabetes [daɪə'biːtiːz] *n* diabete *m*; **diabetic** [-'bɛtɪk] *adj*, *n* diabetico(a)

diabolical [daɪə'bɒlɪkl] (*inf*) *adj* (*weather*, *behaviour*) orribile

diagnoses [daɪəg'nəusiːz] *npl of* **diagnosis**

diagnosis [daɪəg'nəusɪs] (*pl* **diagnoses**) *n* diagnosi *f inv*

diagonal [daɪ'ægənl] *adj* diagonale ♦ *n* diagonale *f*

diagram ['daɪəgræm] *n* diagramma *m*

dial ['daɪəl] *n* quadrante *m*; (*on radio*) lancetta; (*on telephone*) disco combinatore ♦ *vt* (*number*) fare

dialect ['daɪəlɛkt] *n* dialetto

dialling code ['daɪəlɪŋ-] *n* prefisso

dialling tone ['daɪəlɪŋ-] (*US* **dial tone**) *n* segnale *m* di linea libera

dialogue ['daɪəlɒg] (*US* **dialog**) *n* dialogo

diameter [daɪ'æmɪtə*] *n* diametro

diamond ['daɪəmənd] *n* diamante *m*; (*shape*) rombo; **~s** *npl* (*CARDS*) quadri *mpl*

diaper ['daɪəpə*] (*US*) *n* pannolino

diaphragm ['daɪəfræm] *n* diaframma *m*

diarrhoea [daɪə'riːə] (*US* **diarrhea**) *n* diarrea

diary ['daɪərɪ] *n* (*daily account*) diario; (*book*) agenda

dice [daɪs] *n inv* dado ♦ *vt* (*CULIN*) tagliare a dadini

Dictaphone ['dɪktəfəun] ® *n* dittafono ®

dictate [dɪk'teɪt] *vt* dettare

dictation [dɪk'teɪʃən] *n* dettatura; (*SCOL*) dettato

dictator [dɪk'teɪtə*] *n* dittatore *m*; **~ship** *n* dittatura

dictionary ['dɪkʃənrɪ] *n* dizionario

did [dɪd] *pt of* **do**

didn't = **did not**

die [daɪ] *vi* morire; **to be dying for sth/ to do sth** morire dalla voglia di qc/di fare qc; **~ away** *vi* spegnersi a poco a poco; **~ down** *vi* abbassarsi; **~ out** *vi* estinguersi

diehard ['daɪhɑːd] *n* reazionario/a

diesel ['diːzəl] *n* (*vehicle*) diesel *m inv*; **~ engine** *n* motore *m* diesel *inv*; **~ (oil)** *n* gasolio (per motori diesel), diesel *m inv*

diet ['daɪət] *n* alimentazione *f*; (*restricted food*) dieta ♦ *vi* (*also:* **be on a ~**) stare a dieta

differ ['dɪfə*] *vi*: **to ~ from sth** differire da qc; essere diverso(a) da qc; **to ~ from sb over sth** essere in disaccordo con qn su qc; **~ence** *n* differenza; (*disagreement*) screzio; **~ent** *adj* diverso(a); **~entiate** [-'rɛnʃɪeɪt] *vi*: **to ~entiate between** discriminare *or* fare differenza fra

difficult ['dɪfɪkəlt] *adj* difficile; **~y** *n* difficoltà *f inv*

diffident ['dɪfɪdənt] *adj* sfiduciato(a)

diffuse [*adj* dɪ'fjuːs, *vb* dɪ'fjuːz] *adj* diffuso(a) ♦ *vt* diffondere

dig [dɪg] (*pt, pp* **dug**) *vt* (*hole*) scavare; (*garden*) vangare ♦ *n* (*prod*) gomitata; (*archaeological*) scavo; (*fig*) frecciata; **~ into** *vt fus* (*savings*) scavare in; **to ~ one's nails into** conficcare le unghie in; **~ up** *vt* (*tree etc*) sradicare; (*information*) scavare fuori

digest [*vb* daɪ'dʒɛst, *n* 'daɪdʒɛst] *vt* digerire ♦ *n* compendio; **~ion** [dɪ'dʒɛstʃən] *n* digestione *f*; **~ive** *adj* (*juices, system*) digerente

digit ['dɪdʒɪt] *n* cifra; (*finger*) dito; **~al** *adj* digitale

dignified ['dɪgnɪfaɪd] *adj* dignitoso(a)

dignity ['dɪgnɪtɪ] *n* dignità

digress [daɪ'grɛs] *vi*: **to ~ from** divagare da

digs [dɪgz] (*BRIT: inf*) *npl* camera ammobiliata

dike [daɪk] *n* = **dyke**

dilapidated [dɪ'læpɪdeɪtɪd] *adj* cadente

dilemma [daɪ'lɛmə] *n* dilemma *m*

diligent ['dɪlɪdʒənt] *adj* diligente

dilute [daɪ'luːt] *vt* diluire; (*with water*) annacquare

dim [dɪm] *adj* (*light*) debole; (*outline, figure*) vago(a); (*room*) in penombra; (*inf: person*) tonto(a) ♦ *vt* (*light*) abbassare

dime [daɪm] (*US*) *n* = **10 cents**

dimension [daɪ'mɛnʃən] *n* dimensione *f*

diminish [dɪˈmɪnɪʃ] *vt, vi* diminuire
diminutive [dɪˈmɪnjʊtɪv] *adj*
minuscolo(a) ♦ *n* (*LING*) diminutivo
dimmers [ˈdɪməz] (*US*) *npl* (*AUT*)
anabbaglianti *mpl*; luci *fpl* di posizione
dimple [ˈdɪmpl] *n* fossetta
din [dɪn] *n* chiasso, fracasso
dine [daɪn] *vi* pranzare; **~r** *n* (*person*)
cliente *m/f*; (*US: place*) tavola calda
dinghy [ˈdɪŋgɪ] *n* battello pneumatico;
(*also: rubber* ~) gommone *m*
dingy [ˈdɪndʒɪ] *adj* grigio(a)
dining car [ˈdaɪnɪŋ-] (*BRIT*) *n* vagone *m*
ristorante
dining room [ˈdaɪnɪŋ-] *n* sala da pranzo
dinner [ˈdɪnə*] *n* (*lunch*) pranzo; (*evening
meal*) cena; (*public*) banchetto; ~ **jacket** *n*
smoking *m inv*; ~ **party** *n* cena; ~ **time**
n ora di pranzo (*or* cena)
dint [dɪnt] *n*: **by** ~ **of** a forza di
dip [dɪp] *n* discesa; (*in sea*) bagno; (*CULIN*)
salsetta ♦ *vt* immergere; bagnare; (*BRIT:
AUT: lights*) abbassare ♦ *vi* abbassarsi
diphthong [ˈdɪfθɒŋ] *n* dittongo
diploma [dɪˈpləʊmə] *n* diploma *m*
diplomacy [dɪˈpləʊməsɪ] *n* diplomazia
diplomat [ˈdɪpləmæt] *n* diplomatico; **~ic**
[dɪpləˈmætɪk] *adj* diplomatico(a)
diprod [ˈdɪprɒd] (*US*) *n* = **dipstick**
dipstick [ˈdɪpstɪk] *n* (*AUT*) indicatore *m* di
livello dell'olio
dipswitch [ˈdɪpswɪtʃ] (*BRIT*) *n* (*AUT*)
levetta dei fari
dire [daɪə*] *adj* terribile; estremo(a)
direct [daɪˈrɛkt] *adj* diretto(a) ♦ *vt*
dirigere; (*order*): **to** ~ **sb to do sth** dare
direttive a qn di fare qc ♦ *adv*
direttamente; **can you** ~ **me to ...?** mi
può indicare la strada per ...?
direction [dɪˈrɛkʃən] *n* direzione *f*; ~**s** *npl*
(*advice*) chiarimenti *mpl*; **sense of** ~
senso dell'orientamento; ~**s for use**
istruzioni *fpl*
directly [dɪˈrɛktlɪ] *adv* (*in straight line*)
direttamente; (*at once*) subito
director [dɪˈrɛktə*] *n* direttore/trice;
amministratore/trice; (*THEATRE, CINEMA*)
regista *m/f*
directory [dɪˈrɛktərɪ] *n* elenco

dirt [dɜːt] *n* sporcizia; immondizia; (*earth*)
terra; **~-cheap** *adj* da due soldi; **~y** *adj*
sporco(a) ♦ *vt* sporcare; **~y trick** *n* brutto
scherzo
disability [dɪsəˈbɪlɪtɪ] *n* invalidità *f inv*;
(*LAW*) incapacità *f inv*
disabled [dɪsˈeɪbld] *adj* invalido(a);
(*mentally*) ritardato(a) ♦ *npl*: **the** ~ gli
invalidi
disadvantage [dɪsədˈvɑːntɪdʒ] *n*
svantaggio
disaffection [dɪsəˈfɛkʃən] *n*: ~ **(with)**
allontanamento (da)
disagree [dɪsəˈgriː] *vi* (*differ*) discordare;
(*be against, think otherwise*): **to** ~ **(with)**
essere in disaccordo (con), dissentire (da);
~able *adj* sgradevole; (*person*)
antipatico(a); **~ment** *n* disaccordo;
(*argument*) dissapore *m*
disallow [dɪsəˈlaʊ] *vt* (*appeal*) respingere
disappear [dɪsəˈpɪə*] *vi* scomparire;
~ance *n* scomparsa
disappoint [dɪsəˈpɔɪnt] *vt* deludere; **~ed**
adj deluso(a); **~ing** *adj* deludente; **~ment**
n delusione *f*
disapproval [dɪsəˈpruːvəl] *n*
disapprovazione *f*
disapprove [dɪsəˈpruːv] *vi*: **to** ~ **of**
disapprovare
disarm [dɪsˈɑːm] *vt* disarmare; **~ament**
n disarmo
disarray [dɪsəˈreɪ] *n*: **in** ~ (*army*) in rotta;
(*organization*) in uno stato di confusione;
(*clothes, hair*) in disordine
disaster [dɪˈzɑːstə*] *n* disastro
disband [dɪsˈbænd] *vt* sbandare; (*MIL*)
congedare ♦ *vi* sciogliersi
disbelief [ˈdɪsbəˈliːf] *n* incredulità
disc [dɪsk] *n* disco; (*COMPUT*) = **disk**
discard [dɪsˈkɑːd] *vt* (*old things*) scartare;
(*fig*) abbandonare
discern [dɪˈsɜːn] *vt* discernere,
distinguere; **~ing** *adj* perspicace
discharge [*vb* dɪsˈtʃɑːdʒ, *n* ˈdɪstʃɑːdʒ] *vt*
(*duties*) compiere; (*ELEC, waste etc*)
scaricare; (*MED*) emettere; (*patient*)
dimettere; (*employee*) licenziare; (*soldier*)
congedare; (*defendant*) liberare ♦ *n* (*ELEC*)
scarica; (*MED*) emissione *f*; (*dismissal*)

licenziamento; congedo; liberazione *f*

disciple [dɪ'saɪpl] *n* discepolo

discipline ['dɪsɪplɪn] *n* disciplina ♦ *vt* disciplinare; (*punish*) punire

disc jockey *n* disc jockey *m inv*

disclaim [dɪs'kleɪm] *vt* negare, smentire

disclose [dɪs'kləʊz] *vt* rivelare, svelare; **disclosure** [-'kləʊʒə*] *n* rivelazione *f*

disco ['dɪskəʊ] *n abbr* = **discotheque**

discoloured [dɪs'kʌləd] (*US* **discolored**) *adj* scolorito(a); ingiallito(a)

discomfort [dɪs'kʌmfət] *n* disagio; (*lack of comfort*) scomodità *f inv*

disconcert [dɪskən'sɜːt] *vt* sconcertare

disconnect [dɪskə'nɛkt] *vt* sconnettere, staccare; (*ELEC, RADIO*) staccare; (*gas, water*) chiudere

discontent [dɪskən'tɛnt] *n* scontentezza; **~ed** *adj* scontento(a)

discontinue [dɪskən'tɪnjuː] *vt* smettere, cessare; **"~d"** (*COMM*) "fuori produzione"

discord ['dɪskɔːd] *n* disaccordo; (*MUS*) dissonanza

discotheque ['dɪskəʊtɛk] *n* discoteca

discount [*n* 'dɪskaʊnt, *vb* dɪs'kaʊnt] *n* sconto ♦ *vt* scontare; (*idea*) non badare a

discourage [dɪs'kʌrɪdʒ] *vt* scoraggiare

discourteous [dɪs'kɜːtɪəs] *adj* scortese

discover [dɪs'kʌvə*] *vt* scoprire; **~y** *n* scoperta

discredit [dɪs'krɛdɪt] *vt* screditare; mettere in dubbio

discreet [dɪ'skriːt] *adj* discreto(a)

discrepancy [dɪ'skrepənsɪ] *n* discrepanza

discriminate [dɪ'skrɪmɪneɪt] *vi*: **to ~ between** distinguere tra; **to ~ against** discriminare contro; **discriminating** *adj* fine, giudizioso(a); **discrimination** [-'neɪʃən] *n* discriminazione *f*; (*judgment*) discernimento

discuss [dɪ'skʌs] *vt* discutere; (*debate*) dibattere; **~ion** [dɪ'skʌʃən] *n* discussione *f*

disdain [dɪs'deɪn] *n* disdegno

disease [dɪ'ziːz] *n* malattia

disembark [dɪsɪm'bɑːk] *vt, vi* sbarcare

disengage [dɪsɪn'geɪdʒ] *vt* (*AUT: clutch*) disinnestare

disentangle [dɪsɪn'tæŋgl] *vt* liberare; (*wool etc*) sbrogliare

disfigure [dɪs'fɪgə*] *vt* sfigurare

disgrace [dɪs'greɪs] *n* vergogna; (*disfavour*) disgrazia ♦ *vt* disonorare, far cadere in disgrazia; **~ful** *adj* scandaloso(a), vergognoso(a)

disgruntled [dɪs'grʌntld] *adj* scontento(a), di cattivo umore

disguise [dɪs'gaɪz] *n* travestimento ♦ *vt*: **to ~ (as)** travestire (da); **in ~** travestito(a)

disgust [dɪs'gʌst] *n* disgusto, nausea ♦ *vt* disgustare, far schifo a; **~ing** *adj* disgustoso(a); ripugnante

dish [dɪʃ] *n* piatto; **to do** *or* **wash the ~es** fare i piatti; **~ out** *vt* distribuire; **~ up** *vt* servire; **~cloth** *n* strofinaccio

dishearten [dɪs'hɑːtn] *vt* scoraggiare

dishevelled [dɪ'ʃevəld] *adj* arruffato(a); scapigliato(a)

dishonest [dɪs'ɔnɪst] *adj* disonesto(a)

dishonour [dɪs'ɔnə*] (*US* **dishonor**) *n* disonore *m*; **~able** *adj* disonorevole

dishtowel ['dɪʃtaʊəl] (*US*) *n* strofinaccio dei piatti

dishwasher ['dɪʃwɔʃə*] *n* lavastoviglie *f inv*

disillusion [dɪsɪ'luːʒən] *vt* disilludere, disingannare

disincentive [dɪsɪn'sɛntɪv] *n*: **to be a ~** non essere un incentivo

disinfect [dɪsɪn'fɛkt] *vt* disinfettare; **~ant** *n* disinfettante *m*

disintegrate [dɪs'ɪntɪgreɪt] *vi* disintegrarsi

disinterested [dɪs'ɪntrəstɪd] *adj* disinteressato(a)

disjointed [dɪs'dʒɔɪntɪd] *adj* sconnesso(a)

disk [dɪsk] *n* (*COMPUT*) disco; **single-/double-sided ~** disco a facciata singola/doppia; **~ drive** *n* lettore *m*; **~ette** (*US*) *n* = **disk**

dislike [dɪs'laɪk] *n* antipatia, avversione *f*; (*gen pl*) cosa che non piace ♦ *vt*: **he ~s it** non gli piace

dislocate ['dɪsləkeɪt] *vt* slogare

dislodge [dɪs'lɔdʒ] *vt* rimuovere

disloyal [dɪs'lɔɪəl] *adj* sleale

dismal ['dɪzml] *adj* triste, cupo(a)

dismantle [dɪs'mæntl] *vt* (*machine*)

smontare

dismay [dɪs'meɪ] n costernazione f ♦ vt
sgomentare

dismiss [dɪs'mɪs] vt congedare; (*employee*)
licenziare; (*idea*) scacciare; (*LAW*)
respingere; **~al** n congedo; licenziamento

dismount [dɪs'maunt] vi scendere

disobedience [dɪsə'biːdɪəns] n
disubbidienza

disobedient [dɪsə'biːdɪənt] adj
disubbidiente

disobey [dɪsə'beɪ] vt disubbidire a

disorder [dɪs'ɔːdə*] n disordine m;
(*rioting*) tumulto m; (*MED*) disturbo; **~ly** adj
disordinato(a); tumultuoso(a)

disorientated [dɪs'ɔːrɪənteɪtɪd] adj
disorientato(a)

disown [dɪs'əun] vt rinnegare

disparaging [dɪs'pærɪdʒɪŋ] adj
spregiativo(a), sprezzante

dispassionate [dɪs'pæʃənət] adj
calmo(a), freddo(a); imparziale

dispatch [dɪs'pætʃ] vt spedire, inviare ♦ n
spedizione f, invio; (*MIL, PRESS*) dispaccio

dispel [dɪs'pɛl] vt dissipare, scacciare

dispense [dɪs'pɛns] vt distribuire,
amministrare; **~ with** vt fus fare a meno
di; **~r** n (*container*) distributore m;
dispensing chemist (*BRIT*) n farmacista
m/f

disperse [dɪs'pəːs] vt disperdere;
(*knowledge*) disseminare ♦ vi disperdersi

dispirited [dɪs'pɪrɪtɪd] adj scoraggiato(a),
abbattuto(a)

displace [dɪs'pleɪs] vt spostare; **~d
person** n (*POL*) profugo/a

display [dɪs'pleɪ] n esposizione f; (*of
feeling etc*) manifestazione f; (*screen*)
schermo ♦ vt mostrare; (*goods*) esporre;
(*pej*) ostentare

displease [dɪs'pliːz] vt dispiacere a,
scontentare; **~d with** scontento di;
displeasure [-'plɛʒə*] n dispiacere m

disposable [dɪs'pəuzəbl] adj (*pack etc*) a
perdere; (*income*) disponibile; **~ nappy** n
pannolino di carta

disposal [dɪs'pəuzl] n eliminazione f; (*of
property*) cessione f; **at one's ~** alla sua
disposizione

dispose [dɪs'pəuz] vi: **~ of** sbarazzarsi di;
~d adj: **~d to do** disposto(a) a fare;
disposition [-'zɪʃən] n disposizione f;
(*temperament*) carattere m

disproportionate [dɪsprə'pɔːʃənət] adj
sproporzionato(a)

disprove [dɪs'pruːv] vt confutare

dispute [dɪs'pjuːt] n disputa; (*also:
industrial ~*) controversia (sindacale) ♦ vt
contestare; (*matter*) discutere; (*victory*)
disputare

disqualify [dɪs'kwɔlɪfaɪ] vt (*SPORT*)
squalificare; **to ~ sb from sth/from
doing** rendere qn incapace a qc/a fare;
squalificare qn da qc/da fare; **to ~ sb
from driving** ritirare la patente a qn

disquiet [dɪs'kwaɪət] n inquietudine f

disregard [dɪsrɪ'gɑːd] vt non far caso a,
non badare a

disrepair [dɪsrɪ'pɛə*] n: **to fall into ~**
(*building*) andare in rovina; (*machine*)
deteriorarsi

disreputable [dɪs'rɛpjutəbl] adj poco
raccomandabile; indecente

disrupt [dɪs'rʌpt] vt disturbare; creare
scompiglio in

dissatisfaction [dɪssætɪs'fækʃən] n
scontentezza, insoddisfazione f

dissect [dɪ'sɛkt] vt sezionare

dissent [dɪ'sɛnt] n dissenso

dissertation [dɪsə'teɪʃən] n tesi f inv,
dissertazione f

disservice [dɪs'səːvɪs] n: **to do sb a ~**
fare un cattivo servizio a qn

dissimilar [dɪ'sɪmɪlə*] adj: **~ (to)**
dissimile or diverso(a) (da)

dissipate ['dɪsɪpeɪt] vt dissipare

dissolute ['dɪsəluːt] adj dissoluto(a),
licenzioso(a)

dissolution [dɪsə'luːʃən] n (*of
organization, marriage, POL*) scioglimento

dissolve [dɪ'zɔlv] vt dissolvere,
sciogliere; (*POL, marriage etc*) sciogliere
♦ vi dissolversi, sciogliersi

distance ['dɪstns] n distanza; **in the ~** in
lontananza

distant ['dɪstnt] adj lontano(a), distante;
(*manner*) riservato(a), freddo(a)

distaste [dɪs'teɪst] n ripugnanza; **~ful**

adj ripugnante, sgradevole

distended [dɪsˈtɛndɪd] *adj* (*stomach*) dilatato(a)

distil [dɪsˈtɪl] (*US* **distill**) *vt* distillare; **~lery** *n* distilleria

distinct [dɪsˈtɪŋkt] *adj* distinto(a); **as ~ from** a differenza di; **~ion** [dɪsˈtɪŋkʃən] *n* distinzione *f*; (*in exam*) lode *f*; **~ive** *adj* distintivo(a)

distinguish [dɪsˈtɪŋgwɪʃ] *vt* distinguere; discernere; **~ed** *adj* (*eminent*) eminente; **~ing** *adj* (*feature*) distinto(a), caratteristico(a)

distort [dɪsˈtɔːt] *vt* distorcere; (*TECH*) deformare

distract [dɪsˈtrækt] *vt* distrarre; **~ed** *adj* distratto(a); **~ion** [dɪsˈtrækʃən] *n* distrazione *f*

distraught [dɪsˈtrɔːt] *adj* stravolto(a)

distress [dɪsˈtrɛs] *n* angoscia ♦ *vt* affliggere; **~ing** *adj* doloroso(a); **~ signal** *n* segnale *m* di soccorso

distribute [dɪsˈtrɪbjuːt] *vt* distribuire; **distribution** [-ˈbjuːʃən] *n* distribuzione *f*; **distributor** *n* distributore *m*

district [ˈdɪstrɪkt] *n* (*of country*) regione *f*; (*of town*) quartiere *m*; (*ADMIN*) distretto; **~ attorney** (*US*) *n* ≈ sostituto procuratore *m* della Repubblica; **~ nurse** (*BRIT*) *n* infermiera di quartiere

distrust [dɪsˈtrʌst] *n* diffidenza, sfiducia ♦ *vt* non aver fiducia in

disturb [dɪsˈtɔːb] *vt* disturbare; **~ance** *n* disturbo; (*political etc*) disordini *mpl*; **~ed** *adj* (*worried, upset*) turbato(a); **emotionally ~ed** con turbe emotive; **~ing** *adj* sconvolgente

disuse [dɪsˈjuːs] *n*: **to fall into ~** cadere in disuso

disused [dɪsˈjuːzd] *adj* abbandonato(a)

ditch [dɪtʃ] *n* fossa ♦ *vt* (*inf*) piantare in asso

dither [ˈdɪðə*] (*pej*) *vi* vacillare

ditto [ˈdɪtəu] *adv* idem

dive [daɪv] *n* tuffo; (*of submarine*) immersione *f* ♦ *vi* tuffarsi; immergersi; **~r** *n* tuffatore/trice; palombaro

diverse [daɪˈvɔːs] *adj* vario(a)

diversion [daɪˈvɔːʃən] *n* (*BRIT: AUT*)

deviazione *f*; (*distraction*) divertimento

divert [daɪˈvɔːt] *vt* deviare

divide [dɪˈvaɪd] *vt* dividere; (*separate*) separare ♦ *vi* dividersi; **~d highway** (*US*) *n* strada a doppia carreggiata

dividend [ˈdɪvɪdɛnd] *n* dividendo; (*fig*): **to pay ~s** dare dei frutti

divine [dɪˈvaɪn] *adj* divino(a)

diving [ˈdaɪvɪŋ] *n* tuffo; **~ board** *n* trampolino

divinity [dɪˈvɪnɪtɪ] *n* divinità *f inv*; teologia

division [dɪˈvɪʒən] *n* divisione *f*; separazione *f*; (*esp FOOTBALL*) serie *f*

divorce [dɪˈvɔːs] *n* divorzio ♦ *vt* divorziare da; (*dissociate*) separare; **~d** *adj* divorziato(a); **~e** [-ˈsiː] *n* divorziato/a

D.I.Y. (*BRIT*) *n abbr* = **do-it-yourself**

dizzy [ˈdɪzɪ] *adj*: **to feel ~** avere il capogiro

DJ *n abbr* = **disc jockey**

KEYWORD

do [duː] (*pt* **did**, *pp* **done**) *n* (*inf: party etc*) festa; **it was rather a grand ~** è stato un ricevimento piuttosto importante

♦ *vb* 1 (*in negative constructions*) non tradotto; **I don't understand** non capisco

2 (*to form questions*) non tradotto; **didn't you know?** non lo sapevi?; **why didn't you come?** perché non sei venuto?

3 (*for emphasis, in polite expressions*): **she does seem rather late** sembra essere piuttosto in ritardo; **~ sit down** si accomodi la prego, prego si sieda; **~ take care!** mi raccomando, sta attento!

4 (*used to avoid repeating vb*): **she swims better than I ~** lei nuota meglio di me; **~ you agree? — yes, I ~/no, I don't** sei d'accordo? — si/no; **she lives in Glasgow — so ~ I** lei vive a Glasgow — anch'io; **he asked me to help him and I did** mi ha chiesto di aiutarlo ed io l'ho fatto

5 (*in question tags*): **you like him, don't you?** ti piace, vero?; **I don't know him, ~ I?** non lo conosco, vero?

♦ *vt* (*gen, carry out, perform etc*) fare; **what are you ~ing tonight?** che fa

stasera?; **to ~ the cooking** cucinare; **to ~ the washing-up** fare i piatti; **to ~ one's teeth** lavarsi i denti; **to ~ one's hair/nails** farsi i capelli/le unghie; **the car was ~ing 100** la macchina faceva i 100 all'ora
♦ *vi* **1** (*act, behave*) fare; **~ as I ~** faccia come me, faccia come faccio io
2 (*get on, fare*) andare; **he's ~ing well/badly at school** va bene/male a scuola; **how ~ you ~?** piacere!
3 (*suit*) andare bene; **this room will ~** questa stanza va bene
4 (*be sufficient*) bastare; **will £10 ~?** basteranno 10 sterline?; **that'll ~** basta così; **that'll ~!** (*in annoyance*) ora basta!; **to make ~ (with)** arrangiarsi (con)
do away with *vt fus* (*kill*) far fuori; (*abolish*) abolire
do up *vt* (*laces*) allacciare; (*dress, buttons*) abbottonare; (*renovate: room, house*) rimettere a nuovo, rifare
do with *vt fus* (*need*) aver bisogno di; (*be connected*): **what has it got to ~ with you?** e tu che c'entri?; **I won't have anything to ~ with it** non voglio avere niente a che farci; **it has to ~ with money** si tratta di soldi
do without *vi* fare senza ♦ *vt fus* fare a meno di

dock [dɔk] *n* (*NAUT*) bacino; (*LAW*) banco degli imputati ♦ *vi* entrare in bacino; (*SPACE*) agganciarsi; **~s** *npl* (*NAUT*) dock *m inv*; **~er** *n* scaricatore *m*; **~yard** *n* cantiere *m* (navale)
doctor ['dɔktə*] *n* medico/a; (*Ph.D. etc*) dottore/essa ♦ *vt* (*drink etc*) adulterare; **D~ of Philosophy** *n* dottorato di ricerca; (*person*) titolare *m/f* di un dottorato di ricerca
doctrine ['dɔktrɪn] *n* dottrina
document ['dɔkjumənt] *n* documento; **~ary** [-'mɛntəri] *adj* (*evidence*) documentato(a) ♦ *n* documentario
dodge [dɔdʒ] *n* trucco; schivata ♦ *vt* schivare, eludere
dodgems ['dɔdʒəmz] (*BRIT*) *npl* autoscontri *mpl*

doe [dəu] *n* (*deer*) femmina di daino; (*rabbit*) coniglia
does [dʌz] *vb see* **do**; **doesn't** = **does not**
dog [dɔg] *n* cane *m* ♦ *vt* (*follow closely*) pedinare; (*fig: memory etc*) perseguitare; **~ collar** *n* collare *m* di cane; (*fig*) collarino; **~-eared** *adj* (*book*) con orecchie
dogged ['dɔgɪd] *adj* ostinato(a), tenace
dogsbody ['dɔgzbɔdɪ] (*BRIT: inf*) *n* factotum *m inv*
doings ['duɪŋz] *npl* attività *fpl*
do-it-yourself *n* il far da sé
doldrums ['dɔldrəmz] *npl* (*fig*): **to be in the ~** avere un brutto periodo
dole [dəul] (*BRIT*) *n* sussidio di disoccupazione; **to be on the ~** vivere del sussidio; **~ out** *vt* distribuire
doleful ['dəulful] *adj* triste
doll [dɔl] *n* bambola; **~ed up** (*inf*) *adj* in ghingheri
dollar ['dɔlə*] *n* dollaro
dolphin ['dɔlfɪn] *n* delfino
domain [də'meɪn] *n* dominio
dome [dəum] *n* cupola
domestic [də'mɛstɪk] *adj* (*duty, happiness, animal*) domestico(a); (*policy, affairs, flights*) nazionale; **~ated** *adj* addomesticato(a)
dominate ['dɔmɪneɪt] *vt* dominare
domineering [dɔmɪ'nɪərɪŋ] *adj* dispotico(a), autoritario(a)
dominion [də'mɪnɪən] *n* dominio; sovranità; dominion *m inv*
domino ['dɔmɪnəu] (*pl* **~es**) *n* domino; **~es** *n* (*game*) gioco del domino
don [dɔn] (*BRIT*) *n* docente *m/f* universitario(a)
donate [də'neɪt] *vt* donare
done [dʌn] *pp of* **do**
donkey ['dɔŋkɪ] *n* asino
donor ['dəunə*] *n* donatore/trice
don't [dəunt] = **do not**
doodle ['du:dl] *vi* scarabocchiare
doom [du:m] *n* destino; rovina ♦ *vt*: **to be ~ed (to failure)** essere predestinato(a) (a fallire); **~sday** *n* il giorno del Giudizio
door [dɔ:*] *n* porta; **~bell** *n* campanello; **~ handle** *n* maniglia; **~man** *n* (*in hotel*)

portiere *m* in livrea; **~mat** *n* stuoia della porta; **~step** *n* gradino della porta; **~way** *n* porta

dope [dəup] *n* (*inf*: *drugs*) roba ♦ *vt* (*horse etc*) drogare

dopey ['dəupɪ] (*inf*) *adj* inebetito(a)

dormant ['dɔ:mənt] *adj* inattivo(a)

dormice ['dɔ:maɪs] *npl of* **dormouse**

dormitory ['dɔ:mɪtrɪ] *n* dormitorio; (*US*) casa dello studente

dormouse ['dɔ:maus] (*pl* **dormice**) *n* ghiro

dosage ['dəusɪdʒ] *n* posologia

dose [dəus] *n* dose *f*; (*bout*) attacco

doss house ['dɔs-] (*BRIT*) *n* asilo notturno

dot [dɔt] *n* punto; macchiolina ♦ *vt*: **~ted with** punteggiato(a) di; **on the ~** in punto

dote [dəut]: **~ on** *vt fus* essere infatuato(a) di

dot-matrix printer [dɔt'meɪtrɪks-] *n* stampante *f* a matrice a punti

dotted line ['dɔtɪd-] *n* linea punteggiata

double ['dʌbl] *adj* doppio(a) ♦ *adv* (*twice*): **to cost ~** (**sth**) costare il doppio (di qc) ♦ *n* sosia *m inv* ♦ *vt* raddoppiare; (*fold*) piegare doppio *or* in due ♦ *vi* raddoppiarsi; **at the ~** (*BRIT*), **on the ~** a passo di corsa; **~ bass** *n* contrabbasso; **~ bed** *n* letto matrimoniale; **~-breasted** *adj* a doppio petto; **~cross** *vt* fare il doppio gioco con; **~decker** *n* autobus *m inv* a due piani; **~ glazing** (*BRIT*) *n* doppi vetri *mpl*; **~ room** *n* camera per due; **~s** *n* (*TENNIS*) doppio; **doubly** *adv* doppiamente

doubt [daut] *n* dubbio ♦ *vt* dubitare di; **to ~ that** dubitare che + *sub*; **~ful** *adj* dubbioso(a), incerto(a); (*person*) equivoco(a); **~less** *adv* indubbiamente

dough [dəu] *n* pasta, impasto; **~nut** *n* bombolone *m*

douse [dauz] *vt* (*drench*) inzuppare; (*extinguish*) spegnere

dove [dʌv] *n* colombo/a

dovetail ['dʌvteɪl] *vi* (*fig*) combaciare

dowdy ['daudɪ] *adj* trasandato(a); malvestito(a)

down [daun] *n* piume *fpl* ♦ *adv* giù, di

sotto ♦ *prep* giù per ♦ *vt* (*inf*: *drink*) scolarsi; **~ with X!** abbasso X!; **~-and-out** *n* barbone *m*; **~-at-heel** *adj* scalcagnato(a); **~cast** *adj* abbattuto(a); **~fall** *n* caduta; rovina; **~hearted** *adj* scoraggiato(a); **~hill** *adv*: **to go ~hill** andare in discesa; (*fig*) lasciarsi andare; andare a rotoli; **~ payment** *n* acconto; **~pour** *n* scroscio di pioggia; **~right** *adj* franco(a); (*refusal*) assoluto(a); **~stairs** *adv* di sotto; al piano inferiore; **~stream** *adv* a valle; **~-to-earth** *adj* pratico(a); **~town** *adv* in città; **~ under** *adv* (*Australia etc*) agli antipodi; **~ward** ['daunwəd] *adj*, *adv* in giù, in discesa; **~wards** ['daunwədz] *adv* = **~ward**

dowry ['dauri] *n* dote *f*

doz. *abbr* = **dozen**

doze [dəuz] *vi* sonnecchiare; **~ off** *vi* appisolarsi

dozen ['dʌzn] *n* dozzina; **a ~ books** una dozzina di libri; **~s of** decine *fpl* di

Dr. *abbr* (= *doctor*) dott.; (*in street names*) = **drive** *n*

drab [dræb] *adj* tetro(a), grigio(a)

draft [drɑ:ft] *n* abbozzo; (*POL*) bozza; (*COMM*) tratta; (*US*: *call-up*) leva ♦ *vt* abbozzare; *see also* **draught**

draftsman ['drɑ:ftsmən] (*US*) *n* = **draughtsman**

drag [dræg] *vt* trascinare; (*river*) dragare ♦ *vi* trascinarsi ♦ *n* (*inf*) noioso/a; noia, fatica; (*women's clothing*): **in ~** travestito (da donna); **~ on** *vi* tirar avanti lentamente

dragon ['drægən] *n* drago

dragonfly ['drægənflaɪ] *n* libellula

drain [dreɪn] *n* (*for sewage*) fogna; (*on resources*) salasso ♦ *vt* (*land, marshes*) prosciugare; (*vegetables*) scolare ♦ *vi* (*water*) defluire (via); **~age** *n* prosciugamento; fognatura; **~ing board** (*US* **~board**) *n* piano del lavello; **~pipe** *n* tubo di scarico

drama ['drɑ:mə] *n* (*art*) dramma *m*, teatro; (*play*) commedia; (*event*) dramma; **~tic** [drə'mætɪk] *adj* drammatico(a); **~tist** ['dræmətɪst] *n* drammaturgo/a; **~tize** *vt* (*events*) drammatizzare; (*adapt*: *for TV/*

cinema) ridurre or adattare per la televisione/lo schermo

drank [dræŋk] pt of **drink**

drape [dreip] vt drappeggiare; **~r** (BRIT) n negoziante m/f di stoffe; **~s** (US) npl (curtains) tende fpl

drastic ['dræstɪk] adj drastico(a)

draught [drɑːft] (US **draft**) n corrente f d'aria; (NAUT) pescaggio; **on ~** (beer) alla spina; **~board** (BRIT) n scacchiera; **~s** (BRIT) n (gioco della) dama

draughtsman ['drɑːftsmən] (US **draftsman**) n disegnatore m

draw [drɔː] (pt **drew**, pp **drawn**) vt tirare; (take out) estrarre; (attract) attirare; (picture) disegnare; (line, circle) tracciare; (money) ritirare ♦ vi (SPORT) pareggiare ♦ n pareggio; (in lottery) estrazione f; **to ~ near** avvicinarsi; **~ out** vi (lengthen) allungarsi ♦ vt (money) ritirare; **~ up** vi (stop) arrestarsi, fermarsi ♦ vt (chair) avvicinare; (document) compilare; **~back** n svantaggio, inconveniente m; **~bridge** n ponte m levatoio

drawer [drɔː*] n cassetto

drawing ['drɔːɪŋ] n disegno; **~ board** n tavola da disegno; **~ pin** (BRIT) n puntina da disegno; **~ room** n salotto

drawl [drɔːl] n pronuncia strascicata

drawn [drɔːn] pp of **draw**

dread [drɛd] n terrore m ♦ vt tremare all'idea di; **~ful** adj terribile

dream [driːm] (pt, pp **dreamed** or **dreamt**) n sogno ♦ vt, vi sognare; **dreamt** [drɛmt] pt, pp of **dream**; **~y** adj sognante

dreary ['drɪərɪ] adj tetro(a); monotono(a)

dredge [drɛdʒ] vt dragare

dregs [drɛgz] npl feccia

drench [drɛntʃ] vt inzuppare

dress [drɛs] n vestito; (no pl: clothing) abbigliamento ♦ vt vestire; (wound) fasciare ♦ vi vestirsi; **to get ~ed** vestirsi; **~ up** vi vestirsi a festa; (in fancy dress) vestirsi in costume; **~ circle** (BRIT) n prima galleria; **~er** n (BRIT: cupboard) credenza; (US) cassettone m; **~ing** n (MED) benda; (CULIN) condimento; **~ing gown**

(BRIT) n vestaglia; **~ing room** n (THEATRE) camerino; (SPORT) spogliatoio; **~ing table** n toilette f inv; **~maker** n sarta; **~ rehearsal** n prova generale; **~y** (inf) adj elegante

drew [druː] pt of **draw**

dribble ['drɪbl] vi (baby) sbavare ♦ vt (ball) dribblare

dried [draɪd] adj (fruit, beans) secco(a); (eggs, milk) in polvere

drier ['draɪə*] n = **dryer**

drift [drɪft] n (of current etc) direzione f; forza; (of snow) cumulo; turbine m; (general meaning) senso ♦ vi (boat) essere trasportato(a) dalla corrente; (sand, snow) ammucchiarsi; **~wood** n resti mpl della mareggiata

drill [drɪl] n trapano; (MIL) esercitazione f ♦ vt trapanare; (troops) addestrare ♦ vi (for oil) fare trivellazioni

drink [drɪŋk] (pt **drank**, pp **drunk**) n bevanda, bibita; (alcoholic ~) bicchierino; (sip) sorso ♦ vt, vi bere; **to have a ~** bere qualcosa; **a ~ of water** un po' d'acqua; **~er** n bevitore/trice; **~ing water** n acqua potabile

drip [drɪp] n goccia; gocciolamento; (MED) fleboclisi f inv ♦ vi gocciolare; (tap) sgocciolare; **~-dry** adj (shirt) che non si stira; **~ping** n grasso d'arrosto

drive [draɪv] (pt **drove**, pp **driven**) n passeggiata or giro in macchina; (also: **~way**) viale m d'accesso; (energy) energia; (campaign) campagna; (also: disk **~**) lettore m ♦ vt guidare; (nail) piantare; (push) cacciare, spingere; (TECH: motor) azionare; far funzionare ♦ vi (AUT: at controls) guidare; (: travel) andare in macchina; **left-/right-hand ~** guida a sinistra/destra; **to ~ sb mad** far impazzire qn

drivel ['drɪvl] (inf) n idiozie fpl

driven ['drɪvn] pp of **drive**

driver ['draɪvə*] n conducente m/f; (of taxi) tassista m; (chauffeur, of bus) autista m/f; **~'s license** (US) n patente f di guida

driveway ['draɪvweɪ] n viale m d'accesso

driving ['draɪvɪŋ] n guida; **~ instructor** n istruttore/trice di scuola guida; **~**

lesson *n* lezione *f* di guida; ~ **licence** (*BRIT*) *n* patente *f* di guida; ~ **mirror** *n* specchietto retrovisore; ~ **school** *n* scuola *f* guida *inv*; ~ **test** *n* esame *m* di guida

drizzle ['drɪzl] *n* pioggerella

drone [drəun] *n* ronzio; (*male bee*) fuco

drool [dru:l] *vi* sbavare

droop [dru:p] *vi* (*flower*) appassire; (*head, shoulders*) chinarsi

drop [drɔp] *n* (*of water*) goccia; (*lessening*) diminuzione *f*; (*fall*) caduta ♦ *vt* lasciare cadere; (*voice, eyes, price*) abbassare; (*set down from car*) far scendere; (*name from list*) lasciare fuori ♦ *vi* cascare; (*wind*) abbassarsi; ~**s** *npl* (*MED*) gocce *fpl*; ~ **off** *vi* (*sleep*) addormentarsi ♦ *vt* (*passenger*) far scendere; ~ **out** *vi* (*withdraw*) ritirarsi; (*student etc*) smettere di studiare; ~**-out** *n* (*from society/from university*) chi ha abbandonato (la società/gli studi); ~**per** *n* contagocce *m inv*; ~**pings** *npl* sterco

drought [draut] *n* siccità *f inv*

drove [drəuv] *pt of* **drive**

drown [draun] *vt* affogare; (*fig: noise*) soffocare ♦ *vi* affogare

drowsy ['drauzɪ] *adj* sonnolento(a), assonnato(a)

drudgery ['drʌdʒərɪ] *n* lavoro faticoso

drug [drʌg] *n* farmaco; (*narcotic*) droga ♦ *vt* drogare; **to be on** ~**s** drogarsi; (*MED*) prendere medicinali; **hard/soft** ~**s** droghe pesanti/leggere; ~ **addict** *n* tossicomane *m/f*; ~**gist** (*US*) *n* persona che gestisce un *drugstore*; ~**store** (*US*) *n* drugstore *m inv*

drum [drʌm] *n* tamburo; (*for oil, petrol*) fusto ♦ *vi* tamburellare; ~**s** *npl* (*set of* ~**s**) batteria; ~**mer** *n* batterista *m/f*

drunk [drʌŋk] *pp of* **drink** ♦ *adj* ubriaco(a); ebbro(a) ♦ *n* (*also:* ~**ard**) ubriacone/a; ~**en** *adj* ubriaco(a); da ubriaco

dry [draɪ] *adj* secco(a); (*day, clothes*) asciutto(a) ♦ *vt* seccare; (*clothes, hair, hands*) asciugare ♦ *vi* asciugarsi; ~ **up** *vi* seccarsi; ~**-cleaner's** *n* lavasecco *m inv*; ~**-cleaning** *n* pulitura a secco; ~**er** *n* (*for hair*) föhn *m inv*, asciugacapelli *m inv*;

(*for clothes*) asciugabiancheria; (*US: spin-dryer*) centrifuga; ~ **goods store** (*US*) *n* negozio di stoffe; ~ **rot** *n* fungo del legno

DSS *n abbr* (= *Department of Social Security*) *ministero della Previdenza sociale*

dual ['djuəl] *adj* doppio(a); ~ **carriageway** (*BRIT*) *n* strada a doppia carreggiata; ~**-purpose** *adj* a doppio uso

dubbed [dʌbd] *adj* (*CINEMA*) doppiato(a)

dubious ['dju:bɪəs] *adj* dubbio(a)

Dublin ['dʌblɪn] *n* Dublino *f*

duchess ['dʌtʃɪs] *n* duchessa

duck [dʌk] *n* anatra ♦ *vi* abbassare la testa; ~**ling** *n* anatroccolo

duct [dʌkt] *n* condotto; (*ANAT*) canale *m*

dud [dʌd] *n* (*object, tool*): **it's a ~** è inutile, non funziona ♦ *adj*: ~ **cheque** (*BRIT*) assegno a vuoto

due [dju:] *adj* dovuto(a); (*expected*) atteso(a); (*fitting*) giusto(a) ♦ *n* dovuto ♦ *adv*: ~ **north** diritto verso nord; ~**s** *npl* (*for club, union*) quota; (*in harbour*) diritti *mpl* di porto; **in** ~ **course** a tempo debito; finalmente; ~ **to** dovuto a; a causa di; **to be** ~ **to do** dover fare

duet [dju:'ɛt] *n* duetto

duffel bag ['dʌfl-] *n* sacca da viaggio di tela

duffel coat ['dʌfl-] *n* montgomery *m inv*

dug [dʌg] *pt, pp of* **dig**

duke [dju:k] *n* duca *m*

dull [dʌl] *adj* (*light*) debole; (*boring*) noioso(a); (*slow-witted*) ottuso(a); (*sound, pain*) sordo(a); (*weather, day*) fosco(a), scuro(a) ♦ *vt* (*pain, grief*) attutire; (*mind, senses*) intorpidire

duly ['dju:lɪ] *adv* (*on time*) a tempo debito; (*as expected*) debitamente

dumb [dʌm] *adj* muto(a); (*pej*) stupido(a); ~**founded** [dʌm'faundɪd] *adj* stupito(a), stordito(a)

dummy ['dʌmɪ] *n* (*tailor's model*) manichino; (*TECH, COMM*) riproduzione *f*; (*BRIT: for baby*) tettarella ♦ *adj* falso(a), finto(a)

dump [dʌmp] *n* (*also: rubbish* ~) discarica di rifiuti; (*inf: place*) buco ♦ *vt* (*put down*) scaricare; mettere giù; (*get rid* *of)* buttar via

dumpling ['dʌmplɪŋ] *n* specie di gnocco

dumpy ['dʌmpɪ] *adj* tracagnotto(a)

dunce [dʌns] *n* (*SCOL*) somaro/a

dung [dʌŋ] *n* concime *m*

dungarees [dʌŋɡə'ri:z] *npl* tuta

dungeon ['dʌndʒən] *n* prigione *f* sotterranea

dupe [dju:p] *n* zimbello ♦ *vt* gabbare, ingannare

duplex ['dju:plɛks] (*US*) *n* (*house*) casa con muro divisorio in comune con un'altra; (*apartment*) appartamento su due piani

duplicate [*n* 'dju:plɪkət, *vb* 'dju:plɪkeɪt] *n* doppio ♦ *vt* duplicare; **in ~** in doppia copia

durable ['djuərəbl] *adj* durevole; (*clothes, metal*) resistente

duration [djuə'reɪʃən] *n* durata

duress [djuə'rɛs] *n*: **under ~** sotto costrizione

during ['djuərɪŋ] *prep* durante, nel corso di

dusk [dʌsk] *n* crepuscolo

dust [dʌst] *n* polvere *f* ♦ *vt* (*furniture*) spolverare; (*cake etc*) **to ~ with** cospargere con; **~bin** (*BRIT*) *n* pattumiera; **~er** *n* straccio per la polvere; **~man** (*BRIT*) *n* netturbino; **~y** *adj* polveroso(a)

Dutch [dʌtʃ] *adj* olandese ♦ *n* (*LING*) olandese *m*; **the ~** *npl* gli Olandesi; **to go ~** (*inf*) fare alla romana; **~man/woman** *n* olandese *m/f*

dutiful ['dju:tɪful] *adj* (*child*) rispettoso(a)

duty ['dju:tɪ] *n* dovere *m*; (*tax*) dazio, tassa; **on ~** di servizio; **off ~** libero(a), fuori servizio; **~-free** *adj* esente da dazio

duvet ['du:veɪ] (*BRIT*) *n* piumino, piumone *m*

dwarf [dwɔ:f] *n* nano/a ♦ *vt* far apparire piccolo

dwell [dwɛl] (*pt, pp* **dwelt**) *vi* dimorare; **~ on** *vt fus* indugiare su; **~ing** *n* dimora; **dwelt** *pt, pp of* **dwell**

dwindle ['dwɪndl] *vi* diminuire, decrescere

dye [daɪ] *n* tinta ♦ *vt* tingere

dying ['daɪɪŋ] *adj* morente, moribondo(a)

dyke [daɪk] (*BRIT*) *n* diga

dynamic [daɪ'næmɪk] *adj* dinamico(a)

dynamite ['daɪnəmaɪt] *n* dinamite *f*

dynamo ['daɪnəməu] *n* dinamo *f inv*

dyslexia [dɪs'lɛksɪə] *n* dislessia

E

E [i:] *n* (*MUS*) mi *m*

each [i:tʃ] *adj* ogni, ciascuno(a) ♦ *pron* ciascuno(a), ognuno(a); **~ one** ognuno(a); **~ other** si (*or* ci *etc*); **they hate ~ other** si odiano (l'un l'altro); **you are jealous of ~ other** siete gelosi l'uno dell'altro; **they have 2 books ~** hanno 2 libri ciascuno

eager ['i:ɡə*] *adj* impaziente; desideroso(a); ardente; **to be ~ for** essere desideroso di, aver gran voglia di

eagle ['i:ɡl] *n* aquila

ear [ɪə*] *n* orecchio; (*of corn*) pannocchia; **~ache** *n* mal *m* d'orecchi; **~drum** *n* timpano

earl [ə:l] (*BRIT*) *n* conte *m*

earlier ['ə:lɪə*] *adj* precedente ♦ *adv* prima

early ['ə:lɪ] *adv* presto, di buon'ora; (*ahead of time*) in anticipo ♦ *adj* (*near the beginning*) primo(a); (*sooner than expected*) prematuro(a); (*quick: reply*) veloce; **at an ~ hour** di buon'ora; **to have an ~ night** andare a letto presto; **in the ~** *or* **~ in the spring/19th century** all'inizio della primavera/dell'Ottocento; **~ retirement** *n* ritiro anticipato

earmark ['ɪəmɑ:k] *vt*: **to ~ sth for** destinare qc a

earn [ə:n] *vt* guadagnare; (*rest, reward*) meritare

earnest ['ə:nɪst] *adj* serio(a); **in ~** sul serio

earnings ['ə:nɪŋz] *npl* guadagni *mpl*; (*salary*) stipendio

earphones ['ɪəfəunz] *npl* cuffia

earring ['ɪərɪŋ] *n* orecchino

earshot ['ɪəʃɔt] *n*: **within ~** a portata d'orecchio

earth [ə:θ] *n* terra ♦ *vt* (*BRIT: ELEC*) mettere a terra; **~enware** *n* terracotta;

stoviglie *fpl* di terracotta; **~quake** *n* terremoto; **~y** *adj* (*fig*) grossolano(a)

ease [i:z] *n* agio, comodo ♦ *vt* (*soothe*) calmare; (*loosen*) allentare; **to ~ sth out/in** tirare fuori/infilare qc con delicatezza; facilitare l'uscita/l'entrata di qc; **at ~** a proprio agio; (*MIL*) a riposo; **~ off** *or* **up** *vi* diminuire; (*slow down*) rallentare

easel ['i:zl] *n* cavalletto

easily ['i:zılı] *adv* facilmente

east [i:st] *n* est *m* ♦ *adj* dell'est ♦ *adv* a oriente; **the E~** l'Oriente *m*; (*POL*) l'Est

Easter ['i:stə*] *n* Pasqua; **~ egg** *n* uovo di Pasqua

easterly ['i:stəlı] *adj* dall'est, d'oriente

eastern ['i:stən] *adj* orientale, d'oriente; dell'est

East Germany *n* Germania dell'Est

eastward(s) ['i:stwəd(z)] *adv* verso est, verso levante

easy ['i:zı] *adj* facile; (*manner*) disinvolto(a) ♦ *adv*: **to take it** *or* **things ~** prendersela con calma; **~ chair** *n* poltrona; **~-going** *adj* accomodante

eat [i:t] (*pt* **ate**, *pp* **eaten**) *vt*, *vi* mangiare; **~ away** *vt fus* rodere; **~ into** *vt fus* rodere; **~en** ['i:tn] *pp of* **eat**

eaves [i:vz] *npl* gronda

eavesdrop ['i:vzdrɔp] *vi*: **to ~ (on a conversation)** origliare (una conversazione)

ebb [εb] *n* riflusso ♦ *vi* rifluire; (*fig: also*: **~ away**) declinare

ebony ['εbənı] *n* ebano

EC *n abbr* (= *European Community*) CEE *f*

eccentric [ık'sεntrık] *adj, n* eccentrico(a)

echo ['εkəu] (*pl* **~es**) *n* eco *m or f* ♦ *vt* ripetere; fare eco a ♦ *vi* echeggiare; dare un eco

éclair [eı'klεə*] *n* ≈ bignè *m inv*

eclipse [ı'klıps] *n* eclissi *f inv*

ecology [ı'kɔlədʒı] *n* ecologia

economic [i:kə'nɔmık] *adj* economico(a); **~al** *adj* economico(a); (*person*) economo(a); **~s** *n* economia ♦ *npl* lato finanziario

economize [ı'kɔnəmaız] *vi* risparmiare, fare economia

economy [ı'kɔnəmı] *n* economia; **~ class** *n* (*AVIAT*) classe *f* turistica; **~ size** *n* (*COMM*) confezione *f* economica

ecstasy ['εkstəsı] *n* estasi *f inv*

ECU ['eıkju:] *n abbr* (= *European Currency Unit*) ECU *m inv*

eczema ['εksımə] *n* eczema *m*

edge [εdʒ] *n* margine *m*; (*of table, plate, cup*) orlo; (*of knife etc*) taglio ♦ *vt* bordare; **on ~** (*fig*) = **edgy**; **to ~ away from** sgattaiolare da; **~ways** *adv*: **he couldn't get a word in ~ways** non riuscì a dire una parola; **edgy** *adj* nervoso(a)

edible ['εdıbl] *adj* commestibile; (*meal*) mangiabile

edict ['i:dıkt] *n* editto

Edinburgh ['εdınbərə] *n* Edimburgo *f*

edit ['εdıt] *vt* curare; **~ion** [ı'dıʃən] *n* edizione *f*; **~or** *n* (*in newspaper*) redattore/trice; redattore/trice capo; (*of sb's work*) curatore/trice; **~orial** [-'tɔ:rıəl] *adj* redazionale, editoriale ♦ *n* editoriale *m*

educate ['εdjukeıt] *vt* istruire; educare

education [εdju'keıʃən] *n* educazione *f*; (*schooling*) istruzione *f*; **~al** *adj* pedagogico(a); scolastico(a); istruttivo(a)

EEC *n abbr* = **EC**

eel [i:l] *n* anguilla

eerie ['ıərı] *adj* che fa accapponare la pelle

effect [ı'fεkt] *n* effetto ♦ *vt* effettuare; **to take ~** (*law*) entrare in vigore; (*drug*) fare effetto; **in ~** effettivamente; **~ive** *adj* efficace; (*actual*) effettivo(a); **~ively** *adv* efficacemente; effettivamente; **~iveness** *n* efficacia

effeminate [ı'fεmınıt] *adj* effeminato(a)

efficiency [ı'fıʃənsı] *n* efficienza; rendimento effettivo

efficient [ı'fıʃənt] *adj* efficiente

effort ['εfət] *n* sforzo

effrontery [ı'frʌntərı] *n* sfrontatezza

effusive [ı'fju:sıv] *adj* (*handshake, welcome*) caloroso(a)

e.g. *adv abbr* (= *exempli gratia*) per esempio, p.es

egg [εg] *n* uovo; **hard-boiled/soft-boiled ~** uovo sodo/alla coque; **~ on** *vt* incitare;

~cup *n* portauovo *m inv*; **~plant** *n*
(*especially US*) melanzana; **~shell** *n* guscio
d'uovo

ego ['i:gəu] *n* ego *m inv*

egotism ['egəutizəm] *n* egotismo

Egypt ['i:dʒɪpt] *n* Egitto; **~ian** [ɪ'dʒɪpʃən]
adj, n egiziano(a)

eiderdown ['aɪdədaun] *n* piumino

eight [eɪt] *num* otto; **~een** *num* diciotto;
eighth [eɪtθ] *num* ottavo(a); **~y** *num*
ottanta

Eire ['ɛərə] *n* Repubblica d'Irlanda

either ['aɪðə*] *adj* l'uno(a) o l'altro(a);
(*both, each*) ciascuno(a) ♦ *pron:* ~ (**of**
them) o l'uno(a) o l'altro(a) ♦ *adv*
neanche ♦ *conj:* ~ **good or bad** o buono o
cattivo; **on** ~ **side** su ciascun lato; **I don't**
like ~ non mi piace ne l'uno ne l'altro;
no, I don't ~ no, neanch'io

eject [ɪ'dʒɛkt] *vt* espellere; lanciare

eke [i:k]: **to** ~ **out** *vt* far durare;
aumentare

elaborate [*adj* ɪ'læbərɪt, *vb* ɪ'læbəreɪt] *adj*
elaborato(a), minuzioso(a) ♦ *vt* elaborare
♦ *vi* fornire i particolari

elapse [ɪ'læps] *vi* trascorrere, passare

elastic [ɪ'læstɪk] *adj* elastico(a) ♦ *n*
elastico; ~ **band** (*BRIT*) *n* elastico

elated [ɪ'leɪtɪd] *adj* pieno(a) di gioia

elbow ['ɛlbəu] *n* gomito

elder ['ɛldə*] *adj* maggiore, più
vecchio(a) ♦ *n* (*tree*) sambuco; **one's ~s** è
più anziani; **~ly** *adj* anziano(a) ♦ *npl:* **the**
~ly gli anziani

eldest ['ɛldɪst] *adj, n:* **the** ~ (**child**) il(la)
maggiore (dei bambini)

elect [ɪ'lɛkt] *vt* eleggere ♦ *adj:* **the**
president ~ il presidente designato; **to** ~
to do decidere di fare; **~ion** [ɪ'lɛkʃən] *n*
elezione *f*; **~ioneering** [ɪlɛkʃə'nɪərɪŋ] *n*
propaganda elettorale; **~or** *n* elettore/
trice; **~orate** *n* elettorato

electric [ɪ'lɛktrɪk] *adj* elettrico(a); **~al** *adj*
elettrico(a); ~ **blanket** *n* coperta
elettrica; ~ **fire** *n* stufa elettrica

electrician [ɪlɛk'trɪʃən] *n* elettricista *m*

electricity [ɪlɛk'trɪsɪtɪ] *n* elettricità

electrify [ɪ'lɛktrɪfaɪ] *vt* (*RAIL*) elettrificare;
(*audience*) elettrizzare

electrocute [ɪ'lɛktrəukju:t] *vt* fulminare

electronic [ɪlɛk'trɒnɪk] *adj* elettronico(a);
~ **mail** *n* posta elettronica; **~s** *n*
elettronica

elegant ['ɛlɪgənt] *adj* elegante

element ['ɛlɪmənt] *n* elemento; (*of heater,*
kettle etc) resistenza; **~ary** [-'mɛntərɪ] *adj*
elementare

elephant ['ɛlɪfənt] *n* elefante/essa

elevation [ɛlɪ'veɪʃən] *n* elevazione *f*

elevator ['ɛlɪveɪtə*] *n* elevatore *m*; (*US:*
lift) ascensore *m*

eleven [ɪ'lɛvn] *num* undici; **~ses** (*BRIT*) *n*
caffè *m* a metà mattina; **~th** *adj*
undicesimo(a)

elicit [ɪ'lɪsɪt] *vt:* **to** ~ (**from**) trarre (da),
cavare fuori (da)

eligible ['ɛlɪdʒəbl] *adj* eleggibile; (*for*
membership) che ha i requisiti

elm [ɛlm] *n* olmo

elocution [ɛlə'kju:ʃən] *n* dizione *f*

elongated ['i:lɒŋgeɪtɪd] *adj* allungato(a)

elope [ɪ'ləup] *vi* (*lovers*) scappare; **~ment**
n fuga

eloquent ['ɛləkwənt] *adj* eloquente

else [ɛls] *adv* altro; **something** ~
qualcos'altro; **somewhere** ~ altrove;
everywhere ~ in qualsiasi altro luogo;
nobody ~ nessun altro; **where** ~? in
quale altro luogo?; **little** ~ poco altro;
~where *adv* altrove

elucidate [ɪ'lu:sɪdeɪt] *vt* delucidare

elude [ɪ'lu:d] *vt* eludere

elusive [ɪ'lu:sɪv] *adj* elusivo(a)

emaciated [ɪ'meɪsɪeɪtɪd] *adj* emaciato(a)

emanate ['ɛməneɪt] *vi:* **to** ~ **from**
provenire da

emancipate [ɪ'mænsɪpeɪt] *vt* emancipare

embankment [ɪm'bæŋkmənt] *n* (*of road,*
railway) terrapieno

embark [ɪm'bɑ:k] *vi:* **to** ~ (**on**)
imbarcarsi (su) ♦ *vt* imbarcare; **to** ~ **on**
(*fig*) imbarcarsi in; **~ation** [ɛmbɑ:'keɪʃən]
n imbarco

embarrass [ɪm'bærəs] *vt* imbarazzare;
~ed *adj* imbarazzato(a); **~ing** *adj*
imbarazzante; **~ment** *n* imbarazzo

embassy ['ɛmbəsɪ] *n* ambasciata

embedded [ɪm'bɛdɪd] *adj* incastrato(a)

embellish [ɪmˈbɛlɪʃ] *vt* abbellire

embers [ˈɛmbəz] *npl* braci *fpl*

embezzle [ɪmˈbɛzl] *vt* appropriarsi indebitamente di

embitter [ɪmˈbɪtə*] *vt* amareggiare; inasprire

embody [ɪmˈbɔdɪ] *vt* (*features*) racchiudere, comprendere; (*ideas*) dar forma concreta a, esprimere

embossed [ɪmˈbɔst] *adj* in rilievo; goffrato(a)

embrace [ɪmˈbreɪs] *vt* abbracciare ♦ *vi* abbracciarsi ♦ *n* abbraccio

embroider [ɪmˈbrɔɪdə*] *vt* ricamare; **~y** *n* ricamo

embryo [ˈɛmbrɪəu] *n* embrione *m*

emerald [ˈɛmərəld] *n* smeraldo

emerge [ɪˈmɔːdʒ] *vi* emergere

emergency [ɪˈmɔːdʒənsɪ] *n* emergenza; **in an ~** in caso di emergenza; **~ cord** (*US*) *n* segnale *m* d'allarme; **~ exit** *n* uscita di sicurezza; **~ landing** *n* atterraggio forzato; **~ services** *npl* (*fire, police, ambulance*) servizi *mpl* di pronto intervento

emery board [ˈɛmərɪ-] *n* limetta di carta smerigliata

emigrate [ˈɛmɪgreɪt] *vi* emigrare

eminent [ˈɛmɪnənt] *adj* eminente

emissions [ɪˈmɪʃənz] *npl* emissioni *fpl*

emit [ɪˈmɪt] *vt* emettere

emotion [ɪˈməuʃən] *n* emozione *f*; **~al** *adj* (*person*) emotivo(a); (*scene*) commovente; (*tone, speech*) carico(a) d'emozione

emperor [ˈɛmpərə*] *n* imperatore *m*

emphases [ˈɛmfəsiːz] *npl of* **emphasis**

emphasis [ˈɛmfəsɪs] (*pl* **-ases**) *n* enfasi *f inv*

emphasize [ˈɛmfəsaɪz] *vt* (*word, point*) sottolineare; (*feature*) mettere in evidenza

emphatic [ɛmˈfætɪk] *adj* (*strong*) vigoroso(a); (*unambiguous, clear*) netto(a); **~ally** *adv* vigorosamente; nettamente

empire [ˈɛmpaɪə*] *n* impero

employ [ɪmˈplɔɪ] *vt* impiegare; **~ee** [-ˈiː] *n* impiegato/a; **~er** *n* principale *m/f*, datore *m* di lavoro; **~ment** *n* impiego; **~ment agency** *n* agenzia di

collocamento

empower [ɪmˈpauə*] *vt*: **to ~ sb to do** concedere autorità a qn di fare

empress [ˈɛmprɪs] *n* imperatrice *f*

emptiness [ˈɛmptɪnɪs] *n* vuoto

empty [ˈɛmptɪ] *adj* vuoto(a); (*threat, promise*) vano(a) ♦ *vt* vuotare ♦ *vi* vuotarsi; (*liquid*) scaricarsi; **~-handed** *adj* a mani vuote

emulate [ˈɛmjuleɪt] *vt* emulare

emulsion [ɪˈmʌlʃən] *n* emulsione *f*; **~ (paint)** *n* colore *m* a tempera

enable [ɪˈneɪbl] *vt*: **to ~ sb to do** permettere a qn di fare

enact [ɪnˈækt] *vt* (*law*) emanare; (*play, scene*) rappresentare

enamel [ɪˈnæməl] *n* smalto; (*also: ~ paint*) vernice *f* a smalto

encased [ɪnˈkeɪst] *adj*: **~ in** racchiuso(a) in; rivestito(a) di

enchant [ɪnˈtʃɑːnt] *vt* incantare; (*subj: magic spell*) catturare; **~ing** *adj* incantevole, affascinante

encircle [ɪnˈsɜːkl] *vt* accerchiare

encl. *abbr* (= *enclosed*) all

enclave [ˈɛnkleɪv] *n* enclave *f*

enclose [ɪnˈkləuz] *vt* (*land*) circondare, recingere; (*letter etc*) allegare (con); **please find ~d** trovi qui accluso

enclosure [ɪnˈkləuʒə*] *n* recinto

encompass [ɪnˈkʌmpəs] *vt* comprendere

encore [ɔŋˈkɔː*] *excl* bis ♦ *n* bis *m inv*

encounter [ɪnˈkauntə*] *n* incontro ♦ *vt* incontrare

encourage [ɪnˈkʌrɪdʒ] *vt* incoraggiare; **~ment** *n* incoraggiamento

encroach [ɪnˈkrəutʃ] *vi*: **to ~ (up)on** (*rights*) usurpare; (*time*) abusare di; (*land*) oltrepassare i limiti di

encumber [ɪnˈkʌmbə*] *vt*: **to be ~ed with** essere carico(a) di

encyclop(a)edia [ɛnsaɪkləuˈpiːdɪə] *n* enciclopedia

end [ɛnd] *n* fine *f*; (*aim*) fine *m*; (*of table*) bordo estremo; (*of pointed object*) punta ♦ *vt* finire; (*also: bring to an ~, put an ~ to*) mettere fine a ♦ *vi* finire; **in the ~** alla fine; **on ~** (*object*) ritto(a); **to stand on ~** (*hair*) rizzarsi; **for hours on ~** per ore ed

ore; ~ up *vi*: to ~ up in finire in
endanger [ɪn'deɪndʒə*] *vt* mettere in
pericolo
endearing [ɪn'dɪərɪŋ] *adj* accattivante
endeavour [ɪn'dɛvə*] (*US* **endeavor**) *n*
sforzo, tentativo ♦ *vi*: to ~ to do cercare
or sforzarsi di fare
ending ['ɛndɪŋ] *n* fine *f*, conclusione *f*;
(*LING*) desinenza
endive ['ɛndaɪv] *n* (*curly*) indivia (riccia);
(*smooth, flat*) indivia belga
endless ['ɛndlɪs] *adj* senza fine
endorse [ɪn'dɔːs] *vt* (*cheque*) girare;
(*approve*) approvare, appoggiare; **~ment**
n approvazione *f*; (*on driving licence*)
contravvenzione registrata sulla patente
endow [ɪn'dau] *vt* (*provide with money*)
devolvere denaro a; (*equip*): to ~ with
fornire di, dotare di
endurance [ɪn'djuərəns] *n* resistenza;
pazienza
endure [ɪn'djuə*] *vt* sopportare, resistere
a ♦ *vi* durare
enemy ['ɛnəmɪ] *adj, n* nemico(a)
energetic [ɛnə'dʒɛtɪk] *adj* energico(a),
attivo(a)
energy ['ɛnədʒɪ] *n* energia
enforce [ɪn'fɔːs] *vt* (*LAW*) applicare, far
osservare
engage [ɪn'geɪdʒ] *vt* (*hire*) assumere;
(*lawyer*) incaricare; (*attention, interest*)
assorbire; (*TECH*): to ~ gear/the clutch
innestare la marcia/la frizione ♦ *vi* (*TECH*)
ingranare; to ~ in impegnarsi in; **~d** *adj*
(*BRIT: busy, in use*) occupato(a); (*betrothed*)
fidanzato(a); to get ~d fidanzarsi; **~d**
tone (*BRIT*) *n* (*TEL*) segnale *m* di occupato;
~ment *n* impegno, obbligo;
appuntamento; (*to marry*) fidanzamento;
~ment ring *n* anello di fidanzamento
engaging [ɪn'geɪdʒɪŋ] *adj* attraente
engender [ɪn'dʒɛndə*] *vt* produrre,
causare
engine ['ɛndʒɪn] *n* (*AUT*) motore *m*; (*RAIL*)
locomotiva; ~ **driver** *n* (*of train*)
macchinista *m*
engineer [ɛndʒɪ'nɪə*] *n* ingegnere *m*;
(*BRIT: for repairs*) tecnico; (*on ship, US:
RAIL*) macchinista *m*; **~ing** *n* ingegneria

England ['ɪŋglənd] *n* Inghilterra
English ['ɪŋglɪʃ] *adj* inglese ♦ *n* (*LING*)
inglese *m*; **the ~** *npl* gli Inglesi; **the ~**
Channel *n* la Manica; **~man/woman** *n*
inglese *m/f*
engraving [ɪn'greɪvɪŋ] *n* incisione *f*
engrossed [ɪn'grəust] *adj*: ~ **in**
assorbito(a) da, preso(a) da
engulf [ɪn'gʌlf] *vt* inghiottire
enhance [ɪn'hɑːns] *vt* accrescere
enjoy [ɪn'dʒɔɪ] *vt* godere; (*have: success,
fortune*) avere; to ~ **o.s.** godersela,
divertirsi; **~able** *adj* piacevole; **~ment** *n*
piacere *m*, godimento
enlarge [ɪn'lɑːdʒ] *vt* ingrandire ♦ *vi*: to ~
on (*subject*) dilungarsi su
enlighten [ɪn'laɪtn] *vt* illuminare; dare
schiarimenti a; **~ed** *adj* illuminato(a);
~ment *n*: the E~ment (*HISTORY*)
l'Illuminismo
enlist [ɪn'lɪst] *vt* arruolare; (*support*)
procurare ♦ *vi* arruolarsi
enmity ['ɛnmɪtɪ] *n* inimicizia
enormous [ɪ'nɔːməs] *adj* enorme
enough [ɪ'nʌf] *adj, n*: ~ **time/books**
assai tempo/libri; **have you got ~?** ne ha
abbastanza *or* a sufficienza? ♦ *adv*: **big ~**
abbastanza grande; **he has not worked ~**
non ha lavorato abbastanza; **~! basta!**;
that's ~, thanks basta così, grazie; **I've**
had ~ of him ne ho abbastanza di lui; ...
which, funnily *or* **oddly ~** ... che, strano
a dirsi
enquire [ɪn'kwaɪə*] *vt, vi* = **inquire**
enrage [ɪn'reɪdʒ] *vt* fare arrabbiare
enrich [ɪn'rɪtʃ] *vt* arricchire
enrol [ɪn'rəul] *vt* iscrivere ♦ *vi* iscriversi;
~ment *n* iscrizione *f*
ensue [ɪn'sjuː] *vi* seguire, risultare
ensure [ɪn'ʃuə*] *vt* assicurare; garantire
entail [ɪn'teɪl] *vt* comportare
entangled [ɪn'tæŋgld] *adj*: to become ~
(in) impigliarsi (in)
enter ['ɛntə*] *vt* entrare in; (*army*)
arruolarsi in; (*competition*) partecipare a;
(*sb for a competition*) iscrivere; (*write
down*) registrare; (*COMPUT*) inserire ♦ *vi*
entrare; ~ **for** *vt fus* iscriversi a; ~ **into**
vt fus (*explanation*) cominciare a dare;

(*debate*) partecipare a; (*agreement*) concludere

enterprise ['ɛntəpraɪz] *n* (*undertaking, company*) impresa; (*spirit*) iniziativa; **free ~** liberalismo economico; **private ~** iniziativa privata

enterprising ['ɛntəpraɪzɪŋ] *adj* intraprendente

entertain [ɛntə'teɪn] *vt* divertire; (*invite*) ricevere; (*idea, plan*) nutrire; **~er** *n* comico/a; **~ing** *adj* divertente; **~ment** *n* (*amusement*) divertimento; (*show*) spettacolo

enthralled [ɪn'θrɔːld] *adj* affascinato(a)

enthusiasm [ɪn'θuːzɪæzəm] *n* entusiasmo

enthusiast [ɪn'θuːzɪæst] *n* entusiasta *m/ f*; **~ic** [-'æstɪk] *adj* entusiasta, entusiastico(a); **to be ~ic about sth/sb** essere appassionato(a) di qc/entusiasta di qn

entice [ɪn'taɪs] *vt* allettare, sedurre

entire [ɪn'taɪə*] *adj* intero(a); **~ly** *adv* completamente, interamente; **~ty** [ɪn'taɪərətɪ] *n*: **in its ~ty** nel suo complesso

entitle [ɪn'taɪtl] *vt* (*give right*) **to ~ sb to sth/to do** dare diritto a qn a qc/a fare; **~d** *adj* (*book*) che si intitola; **to be ~d to do** avere il diritto di fare

entrails ['ɛntreɪlz] *npl* interiora *fpl*

entrance [*n* 'ɛntrns, *vb* ɪn'trɑːns] *n* entrata, ingresso; (*of person*) entrata ♦ *vt* incantare, rapire; **to gain ~ to** (*university etc*) essere ammesso a; **~ examination** *n* esame *m* di ammissione; **~ fee** *n* tassa d'iscrizione; (*to museum etc*) prezzo d'ingresso; **~ ramp** (*US*) *n* (*AUT*) rampa di accesso

entrant ['ɛntrnt] *n* partecipante *m/f*; concorrente *m/f*

entreat [ɛn'triːt] *vt* supplicare

entrenched [ɛn'trɛntʃt] *adj* radicato(a)

entrepreneur [ɔntrəprə'nəː*] *n* imprenditore *m*

entrust [ɪn'trʌst] *vt*: **to ~ sth to** affidare qc a

entry ['ɛntrɪ] *n* entrata; (*way in*) entrata, ingresso; (*item: on list*) iscrizione *f*; (*in*

dictionary) voce *f*; **no ~** vietato l'ingresso; (*AUT*) divieto di accesso; **~ form** *n* modulo d'iscrizione; **~ phone** *n* citofono

envelop [ɪn'vɛləp] *vt* avvolgere, avviluppare

envelope ['ɛnvələup] *n* busta

envious ['ɛnvɪəs] *adj* invidioso(a)

environment [ɪn'vaɪərnmənt] *n* ambiente *m*; **~al** [-'mɛntl] *adj* ecologico(a); ambientale; **~-friendly** *adj* che rispetta l'ambiente

envisage [ɪn'vɪzɪdʒ] *vt* immaginare; prevedere

envoy ['ɛnvɔɪ] *n* inviato/a

envy ['ɛnvɪ] *n* invidia ♦ *vt* invidiare; **to ~ sb sth** invidiare qn per qc

epic ['ɛpɪk] *n* poema *m* epico ♦ *adj* epico(a)

epidemic [ɛpɪ'dɛmɪk] *n* epidemia

epilepsy ['ɛpɪlɛpsɪ] *n* epilessia

episode ['ɛpɪsəud] *n* episodio

epistle [ɪ'pɪsl] *n* epistola

epitome [ɪ'pɪtəmɪ] *n* epitome *f*; quintessenza; **epitomize** *vt* (*fig*) incarnare

equable ['ɛkwəbl] *adj* uniforme; equilibrato(a)

equal ['iːkwl] *adj* uguale ♦ *n* pari *m/f inv* ♦ *vt* uguagliare; **~ to** (*task*) all'altezza di; **~ity** [iː'kwɔlɪtɪ] *n* uguaglianza; **~ize** *vi* pareggiare; **~ly** *adv* ugualmente

equanimity [ɛkwə'nɪmɪtɪ] *n* serenità

equate [ɪ'kweɪt] *vt*: **to ~ sth with** considerare qc uguale a; (*compare*) paragonare qc con; **equation** [ɪ'kweɪʃən] *n* (*MATH*) equazione *f*

equator [ɪ'kweɪtə*] *n* equatore *m*

equilibrium [iːkwɪ'lɪbrɪəm] *n* equilibrio

equip [ɪ'kwɪp] *vt* equipaggiare, attrezzare; **to ~ sb/sth with** fornire qn/qc di; **to be well ~ped** (*office etc*) essere ben attrezzato(a); **he is well ~ped for the job** ha i requisiti necessari per quel lavoro; **~ment** *n* attrezzatura; (*electrical etc*) apparecchiatura

equitable ['ɛkwɪtəbl] *adj* equo(a), giusto(a)

equities ['ɛkwɪtɪz] (*BRIT*) *npl* (*COMM*) azioni *fpl* ordinarie

equivalent [ɪ'kwɪvəlnt] *adj* equivalente
♦ *n* equivalente *m*; **to be ~ to**
equivalere a

equivocal [ɪ'kwɪvəkl] *adj* equivoco(a);
(*open to suspicion*) dubbio(a)

era ['ɪərə] *n* era, età *f inv*

eradicate [ɪ'rædɪkeɪt] *vt* sradicare

erase [ɪ'reɪz] *vt* cancellare; **~r** n gomma

erect [ɪ'rɛkt] *adj* eretto(a) ♦ *vt* costruire;
(*assemble*) montare; **~ion** [ɪ'rɛkʃən] *n*
costruzione *f*; montaggio; (*PHYSIOL*)
erezione *f*

ERM *n* (= *Exchange Rate Mechanism*)
ERM *m*

ermine ['ə:mɪn] *n* ermellino

erode [ɪ'rəud] *vt* erodere; (*metal*)
corrodere

erotic [ɪ'rɔtɪk] *adj* erotico(a)

err [ə:*] *vi* errare

errand ['ɛrnd] *n* commissione *f*

erratic [ɪ'rætɪk] *adj* imprevedibile;
(*person, mood*) incostante

error ['ɛrə*] *n* errore *m*

erupt [ɪ'rʌpt] *vi* (*volcano*) mettersi (*or*
essere) in eruzione; (*war, crisis*)
scoppiare; **~ion** [ɪ'rʌpʃən] *n* eruzione *f*;
scoppio

escalate ['ɛskəleɪt] *vi* intensificarsi

escalator ['ɛskəleɪtə*] *n* scala mobile

escapade [ɛskə'peɪd] *n* scappatella;
avventura

escape [ɪ'skeɪp] *n* evasione *f*; fuga; (*of
gas etc*) fuga, fuoriuscita ♦ *vi* fuggire;
(*from jail*) evadere, scappare; (*leak*) uscire
♦ *vt* sfuggire a; **to ~ from** (*place*) fuggire
da; (*person*) sfuggire a; **escapism** *n*
evasione *f* (dalla realtà)

escort [*n* 'ɛskɔ:t, *vb* ɪ'skɔ:t] *n* scorta;
(*male companion*) cavaliere *m* ♦ *vt*
scortare; accompagnare

Eskimo ['ɛskɪməu] *n* eschimese *m/f*

especially [ɪ'spɛʃlɪ] *adv* specialmente;
soprattutto; espressamente

espionage ['ɛspɪənɑ:ʒ] *n* spionaggio

esplanade [ɛsplə'neɪd] *n* lungomare *m
inv*

Esq. *abbr* = **Esquire**

Esquire [ɪ'skwaɪə*] *n*: **J. Brown, ~**
Signor J. Brown

essay ['ɛseɪ] *n* (*SCOL*) composizione *f*;
(*LITERATURE*) saggio

essence ['ɛsns] *n* essenza

essential [ɪ'sɛnʃl] *adj* essenziale ♦ *n*
elemento essenziale; **~ly** *adv*
essenzialmente

establish [ɪ'stæblɪʃ] *vt* stabilire;
(*business*) mettere su; (*one's power etc*)
affermare; **~ed** *adj* (*business etc*)
affermato(a); **~ment** *n* stabilimento; **the
E~ment** la classe dirigente,
l'establishment *m*

estate [ɪ'steɪt] *n* proprietà *f inv*; beni
mpl, patrimonio; (*BRIT: also: housing ~*)
complesso edilizio; **~ agent** (*BRIT*) *n*
agente *m* immobiliare; **~ car** (*BRIT*) *n*
giardiniera

esteem [ɪ'sti:m] *n* stima ♦ *vt* (*think
highly of*) stimare; (*consider*) considerare

esthetic [ɪs'θɛtɪk] (*US*) *adj* = **aesthetic**

estimate [*n* 'ɛstɪmət, *vb* 'ɛstɪmeɪt] *n*
stima; (*COMM*) preventivo ♦ *vt* stimare,
valutare; **estimation** [-'meɪʃən] *n* stima;
opinione *f*

estranged [ɪ'streɪndʒd] *adj* separato(a)

etc *abbr* (= *et cetera*) etc, ecc

etching ['ɛtʃɪŋ] *n* acquaforte *f*

eternal [ɪ'tə:nl] *adj* eterno(a)

eternity [ɪ'tə:nɪtɪ] *n* eternità *f*

ether ['i:θə*] *n* etere *m*

ethical ['ɛθɪkl] *adj* etico(a), morale

ethics ['ɛθɪks] *n* etica ♦ *npl* morale *f*

Ethiopia [i:θɪ'əupɪə] *n* Etiopia

ethnic ['ɛθnɪk] *adj* etnico(a)

ethos ['i:θɔs] *n* norma di vita

etiquette ['ɛtɪkɛt] *n* etichetta

Eurocheque ['juərəutʃɛk] *n* eurochèque
m inv

Europe ['juərəp] *n* Europa; **~an** [-'pi:ən]
adj, n europeo(a)

evacuate [ɪ'vækjueɪt] *vt* evacuare

evade [ɪ'veɪd] *vt* (*tax*) evadere; (*duties etc*)
sottrarsi a; (*person*) schivare

evaluate [ɪ'væljueɪt] *vt* valutare

evaporate [ɪ'væpəreɪt] *vi* evaporare; **~d
milk** *n* latte *m* concentrato

evasion [ɪ'veɪʒən] *n* evasione *f*

evasive [ɪ'veɪsɪv] *adj* evasivo(a)

eve [i:v] *n*: **on the ~ of** alla vigilia di

even ['iːvn] *adj* regolare; (*number*) pari *inv* ♦ *adv* anche, perfino; ~ **if**, ~ **though** anche se; ~ **more** ancora di più; ~ **so** ciò nonostante; **not** ~ nemmeno; **to get** ~ **with sb** dare la pari a qn; ~ **out** *vi* pareggiare

evening ['iːvnɪŋ] *n* sera; (*as duration, event*) serata; **in the** ~ la sera; ~ **class** *n* corso serale; ~ **dress** *n* (*woman's*) abito da sera; **in** ~ **dress** (*man*) in abito scuro; (*woman*) in abito lungo

event [ɪ'vɛnt] *n* avvenimento; (*SPORT*) gara; **in the** ~ **of** in caso di; ~**ful** *adj* denso(a) di eventi

eventual [ɪ'vɛntʃuəl] *adj* finale; ~**ity** [-'ælɪtɪ] *n* possibilità *f inv*, eventualità *f inv*; ~**ly** *adv* alla fine

ever ['ɛvə*] *adv* mai; (*at all times*) sempre; **the best** ~ il migliore che ci sia mai stato; **have you** ~ **seen it?** l'ha mai visto?; ~ **since** *adv* da allora ♦ *conj* sin da quando; ~ **so pretty** così bello(a); ~**green** *n* sempreverde *m*; ~**lasting** *adj* eterno(a)

every ['ɛvrɪ] *adj* ogni; ~ **day** tutti i giorni, ogni giorno; ~ **other/third day** ogni due/tre giorni; ~ **other car** una macchina su due; ~ **now and then** ogni tanto, di quando in quando; ~**body** *pron* = ~**one**; ~**day** *adj* quotidiano(a); di ogni giorno; ~**one** *pron* ognuno, tutti *pl*; ~**thing** *pron* tutto, ogni cosa; ~**where** *adv* (*gen*) dappertutto; (*wherever*) ovunque

evict [ɪ'vɪkt] *vt* sfrattare

evidence ['ɛvɪdns] *n* (*proof*) prova; (*of witness*) testimonianza; (*sign*): **to show** ~ **of** dare segni di; **to give** ~ deporre

evident ['ɛvɪdnt] *adj* evidente; ~**ly** *adv* evidentemente

evil ['iːvl] *adj* cattivo(a), maligno(a) ♦ *n* male *m*

evoke [ɪ'vəuk] *vt* evocare

evolution [iːvə'luːʃən] *n* evoluzione *f*

evolve [ɪ'vɔlv] *vt* elaborare ♦ *vi* sviupparsi, evolversi

ewe [juː] *n* pecora

ex- [ɛks] *prefix* ex

exacerbate [ɛks'æsəbeɪt] *vt* aggravare

exact [ɪg'zækt] *adj* esatto(a) ♦ *vt*: **to** ~ **sth** (**from**) estorcere qc (da); esigere qc

(da); ~**ing** *adj* esigente; (*work*) faticoso(a); ~**ly** *adv* esattamente

exaggerate [ɪg'zædʒəreɪt] *vt*, *vi* esagerare; **exaggeration** [-'reɪʃən] *n* esagerazione *f*

exalted [ɪg'zɔːltɪd] *adj* esaltato(a); elevato(a)

exam [ɪg'zæm] *n abbr* (*SCOL*) = **examination**

examination [ɪgzæmɪ'neɪʃən] *n* (*SCOL*) esame *m*; (*MED*) controllo

examine [ɪg'zæmɪn] *vt* esaminare; ~**r** *n* esaminatore/trice

example [ɪg'zɑːmpl] *n* esempio; **for** ~ ad *or* per esempio

exasperate [ɪg'zɑːspəreɪt] *vt* esasperare; **exasperating** *adj* esasperante; **exasperation** [-'reɪʃən] *n* esasperazione *f*

excavate ['ɛkskəveɪt] *vt* scavare

exceed [ɪk'siːd] *vt* superare; (*one's powers, time limit*) oltrepassare; ~**ingly** *adv* eccessivamente

excellent ['ɛksələnt] *adj* eccellente

except [ɪk'sɛpt] *prep* (*also*: ~ **for**, ~**ing**) salvo, all'infuori di, eccetto ♦ *vt* escludere; ~ **if/when** salvo se/quando; ~ **that** salvo che; ~**ion** [ɪk'sɛpʃən] *n* eccezione *f*; **to take** ~**ion to** trovare a ridire su; ~**ional** [ɪk'sɛpʃənl] *adj* eccezionale

excerpt ['ɛksəːpt] *n* estratto

excess [ɪk'sɛs] *n* eccesso; ~ **baggage** *n* bagaglio in eccedenza; ~ **fare** *n* supplemento; ~**ive** *adj* eccessivo(a)

exchange [ɪks'tʃeɪndʒ] *n* scambio; (*also: telephone* ~) centralino ♦ *vt*: **to** ~ (**for**) scambiare (con); ~ **rate** *n* tasso di cambio

Exchequer [ɪks'tʃɛkə*] *n*: **the** ~ (*BRIT*) lo Scacchiere, ≈ il ministero delle Finanze

excise ['ɛksaɪz] *n* imposta, dazio

excite [ɪk'saɪt] *vt* eccitare; **to get** ~**d** eccitarsi; ~**ment** *n* eccitazione *f*; agitazione *f*; **exciting** *adj* avventuroso(a); (*film, book*) appassionante

exclaim [ɪk'skleɪm] *vi* esclamare; **exclamation** [ɛksklə'meɪʃən] *n* esclamazione *f*; **exclamation mark** *n* punto esclamativo

exclude [ɪk'skluːd] *vt* escludere

exclusive [ɪkˈskluːsɪv] *adj* esclusivo(a); ~ **of VAT** I.V.A. esclusa

excommunicate [ɛkskəˈmjuːnɪkeɪt] *vt* scomunicare

excruciating [ɪkˈskruːʃɪeɪtɪŋ] *adj* straziante, atroce

excursion [ɪkˈskəːʃən] *n* escursione *f*, gita

excuse [*n* ɪkˈskjuːs, *vb* ɪkˈskjuːz] *n* scusa ♦ *vt* scusare; **to ~ sb from** (*activity*) dispensare qn da; **~ me!** mi scusi!; **now, if you will ~ me ...** ora, mi scusi ma ....

ex-directory (*BRIT*) *adj* (*TEL*): **to be ~** non essere sull'elenco

execute [ˈɛksɪkjuːt] *vt* (*prisoner*) giustiziare; (*plan etc*) eseguire

execution [ɛksɪˈkjuːʃən] *n* esecuzione *f*; **~er** *n* boia *m inv*

executive [ɪgˈzɛkjutɪv] *n* (*COMM*) dirigente *m*; (*POL*) esecutivo ♦ *adj* esecutivo(a)

exemplify [ɪgˈzɛmplɪfaɪ] *vt* esemplificare

exempt [ɪgˈzɛmpt] *adj* esentato(a) ♦ *vt*: **to ~ sb from** esentare qn da; **~ion** [ɪgˈzɛmpʃən] *n* esenzione *f*

exercise [ˈɛksəsaɪz] *n* (*keep fit*) moto; (*SCOL, MIL etc*) esercizio ♦ *vt* esercitare; (*patience*) usare; (*dog*) portar fuori ♦ *vi* (*also: take ~*) fare del moto; **~bike** *n* cyclette *f inv*; **~ book** *n* quaderno

exert [ɪgˈzəːt] *vt* esercitare; **to ~ o.s.** sforzarsi; **~ion** [-ʃən] *n* sforzo

exhale [ɛksˈheɪl] *vt, vi* espirare

exhaust [ɪgˈzɔːst] *n* (*also: ~ fumes*) scappamento; (*also: ~ pipe*) tubo di scappamento ♦ *vt* esaurire; **~ed** *adj* esaurito(a); **~ion** [ɪgˈzɔːstʃən] *n* esaurimento; **nervous ~ion** *n* sovraffaticamento mentale; **~ive** *adj* esauriente

exhibit [ɪgˈzɪbɪt] *n* (*ART*) oggetto esposto; (*LAW*) documento *or* oggetto esibito ♦ *vt* esporre; (*courage, skill*) dimostrare; **~ion** [ɛksɪˈbɪʃən] *n* mostra, esposizione *f*

exhilarating [ɪgˈzɪləreɪtɪŋ] *adj* esilarante; stimolante

exhort [ɪgˈzɔːt] *vt* esortare

exile [ˈɛksaɪl] *n* esilio; (*person*) esiliato/a ♦ *vt* esiliare

exist [ɪgˈzɪst] *vi* esistere; **~ence** *n* esistenza; **~ing** *adj* esistente

exit [ˈɛksɪt] *n* uscita ♦ *vi* (*THEATRE, COMPUT*) uscire; **~ poll** *n* exit poll *m inv*; **~ ramp** (*US*) *n* (*AUT*) rampa di uscita

exodus [ˈɛksədəs] *n* esodo

exonerate [ɪgˈzɔnəreɪt] *vt*: **to ~ from** discolpare da

exotic [ɪgˈzɔtɪk] *adj* esotico(a)

expand [ɪkˈspænd] *vt* espandere; estendere; allargare ♦ *vi* (*business, gas*) espandersi; (*metal*) dilatarsi

expanse [ɪkˈspæns] *n* distesa, estensione *f*

expansion [ɪkˈspænʃən] *n* (*gen*) espansione *f*; (*of town, economy*) sviluppo; (*of metal*) dilatazione *f*

expect [ɪkˈspɛkt] *vt* (*anticipate*) prevedere, aspettarsi, prevedere *or* aspettarsi che + *sub*; (*require*) richiedere, esigere; (*suppose*) supporre; (*await, also baby*) aspettare ♦ *vi*: **to be ~ing** essere in stato interessante; **to ~ sb to do** aspettarsi che qn faccia; **~ancy** *n* (*anticipation*) attesa; **life ~ancy** probabilità *fpl* di vita; **~ant mother** *n* gestante *f*; **~ation** [ɛkspɛkˈteɪʃən] *n* aspettativa; speranza

expedience [ɪkˈspiːdɪəns] *n* convenienza

expediency [ɪkˈspiːdɪənsɪ] *n* convenienza

expedient [ɪkˈspiːdɪənt] *adj* conveniente; vantaggioso(a) ♦ *n* espediente *m*

expedition [ɛkspəˈdɪʃən] *n* spedizione *f*

expel [ɪkˈspɛl] *vt* espellere

expend [ɪkˈspɛnd] *vt* spendere; (*use up*) consumare; **~able** *adj* sacrificabile; **~iture** [ɪkˈspɛndɪtʃə*] *n* spesa

expense [ɪkˈspɛns] *n* spesa; (*high cost*) costo; **~s** *npl* (*COMM*) spese *fpl*, indennità *fpl*; **at the ~ of** a spese di; **~ account** *n* conto *m* spese *inv*

expensive [ɪkˈspɛnsɪv] *adj* caro(a), costoso(a)

experience [ɪkˈspɪərɪəns] *n* esperienza ♦ *vt* (*pleasure*) provare; (*hardship*) soffrire; **~d** *adj* esperto(a)

experiment [*n* ɪkˈspɛrɪmənt, *vb* ɪkˈspɛrɪmɛnt] *n* esperimento, esperienza ♦ *vi*: **to ~ (with/on)** fare esperimenti

(con/su)

expert ['ɛkspəːt] *adj, n* esperto(a); **~ise** [-'tiːz] *n* competenza

expire [ɪk'spaɪə*] *vi* (*period of time, licence*) scadere; **expiry** *n* scadenza

explain [ɪk'spleɪn] *vt* spiegare; **explanation** [ɛksplə'neɪʃən] *n* spiegazione *f*; **explanatory** [ɪk'splænətrɪ] *adj* esplicativo(a)

explicit [ɪk'splɪsɪt] *adj* esplicito(a)

explode [ɪk'spləud] *vi* esplodere

exploit [*n* 'ɛksplɔɪt, *vb* ɪk'splɔɪt] *n* impresa ♦ *vt* sfruttare; **~ation** [-'teɪʃən] *n* sfruttamento

exploratory [ɪk'splɔrətrɪ] *adj* esplorativo(a)

explore [ɪk'splɔː*] *vt* esplorare; (*possibilities*) esaminare; **~r** *n* esploratore/trice

explosion [ɪk'spləuʒən] *n* esplosione *f*

explosive [ɪk'spləusɪv] *adj* esplosivo(a) ♦ *n* esplosivo

exponent [ɪk'spəunənt] *n* esponente *m/f*

export [*vb* ɛk'spɔːt, *n* 'ɛkspɔːt] *vt* esportare ♦ *n* esportazione *f*; articolo di esportazione ♦ *cpd* d'esportazione; **~er** *n* esportatore *m*

expose [ɪk'spəuz] *vt* esporre; (*unmask*) smascherare; **~d** *adj* (*position*) esposto(a)

exposure [ɪk'spəuʒə*] *n* esposizione *f*; (*PHOT*) posa; (*MED*) assideramento; **~ meter** *n* esposimetro

expound [ɪk'spaund] *vt* esporre

express [ɪk'sprɛs] *adj* (*definite*) chiaro(a), espresso(a); (*BRIT: letter etc*) espresso *inv* ♦ *n* (*train*) espresso ♦ *vt* esprimere; **~ion** [ɪk'sprɛʃən] *n* espressione *f*; **~ive** *adj* espressivo(a); **~ly** *adv* espressamente; **~way** (*US*) *n* (*urban motorway*) autostrada che attraversa la città

exquisite [ɛk'skwɪzɪt] *adj* squisito(a)

extend [ɪk'stɛnd] *vt* (*visit*) protrarre; (*road, deadline*) prolungare; (*building*) ampliare; (*offer*) offrire, porgere ♦ *vi* (*land, period*) estendersi

extension [ɪk'stɛnʃən] *n* (*of road, term*) prolungamento; (*of contract, deadline*) proroga; (*building*) annesso; (*to wire, table*) prolunga; (*telephone*) interno; (: *in*

private house) apparecchio supplementare

extensive [ɪk'stɛnsɪv] *adj* esteso(a), ampio(a); (*damage*) su larga scala; (*coverage, discussion*) esauriente; (*use*) grande; **~ly** *adv*: **he's travelled ~ly** ha viaggiato molto

extent [ɪk'stɛnt] *n* estensione *f*; **to some ~** fino a un certo punto; **to such an ~ that ...** a un tal punto che ...; **to what ~?** fino a che punto?; **to the ~ of ...** fino al punto di ...

extenuating [ɪks'tɛnjueɪtɪŋ] *adj*: **~ circumstances** attenuanti *fpl*

exterior [ɛk'stɪərɪə*] *adj* esteriore, esterno(a) ♦ *n* esteriore *m*, esterno; aspetto (esteriore)

exterminate [ɪk'stəːmɪneɪt] *vt* sterminare

external [ɛk'stəːnl] *adj* esterno(a), esteriore

extinct [ɪk'stɪŋkt] *adj* estinto(a)

extinguish [ɪk'stɪŋgwɪʃ] *vt* estinguere; **~er** *n* estintore *m*

extort [ɪk'stɔːt] *vt*: **to ~ sth (from)** estorcere qc (da); **~ionate** [ɪk'stɔːʃnət] *adj* esorbitante

extra ['ɛkstrə] *adj* extra *inv*, supplementare ♦ *adv* (*in addition*) di più ♦ *n* extra *m inv*; (*surcharge*) supplemento; (*CINEMA, THEATRE*) comparsa

extra... ['ɛkstrə] *prefix* extra...

extract [*vb* ɪk'strækt, *n* 'ɛkstrækt] *vt* estrarre; (*money, promise*) strappare ♦ *n* estratto; (*passage*) brano

extracurricular ['ɛkstrəkə'rɪkjulə*] *adj* extrascolastico(a)

extradite ['ɛkstrədaɪt] *vt* estradare

extramarital [ɛkstrə'mærɪtl] *adj* extraconiugale

extramural [ɛkstrə'mjuərl] *adj* fuori dell'università

extraordinary [ɪk'strɔːdnrɪ] *adj* straordinario(a)

extravagance [ɪk'strævəgəns] *n* sperpero; stravaganza

extravagant [ɪk'strævəgənt] *adj* (*lavish*) prodigo(a); (*wasteful*) dispendioso(a)

extreme [ɪk'striːm] *adj* estremo(a) ♦ *n* estremo; **~ly** *adv* estremamente

extricate ['ɛkstrɪkeɪt] *vt*: **to ~ sth (from)** districare qc (da)

extrovert ['ɛkstrəvəːt] *n* estroverso/a

exude [ɪgˈzjuːd] *vt* trasudare; (*fig*) emanare

eye [aɪ] *n* occhio; (*of needle*) cruna ♦ *vt* osservare; **to keep an ~ on** tenere d'occhio; **~ball** *n* globo dell'occhio; **~bath** *n* occhino; **~brow** *n* sopracciglio; **~brow pencil** *n* matita per le sopracciglia; **~drops** *npl* gocce *fpl* oculari, collirio; **~lash** *n* ciglio; **~lid** *n* palpebra; **~ liner** *n* eye-liner *m inv*; **~-opener** *n* rivelazione *f*; **~shadow** *n* ombretto; **~sight** *n* vista; **~sore** *n* pugno nell'occhio; **~ witness** *n* testimone *m/f* oculare

F

F [ɛf] *n* (*MUS*) fa *m*

fable ['feɪbl] *n* favola

fabric ['fæbrɪk] *n* stoffa, tessuto

fabrication [fæbrɪˈkeɪʃən] *n* fabbricazione *f*; falsificazione *f*

fabulous ['fæbjuləs] *adj* favoloso(a); (*super*) favoloso(a), fantastico(a)

façade [fəˈsɑːd] *n* (*also fig*) facciata

face [feɪs] *n* faccia, viso, volto; (*expression*) faccia; (*of clock*) quadrante *m*; (*of building*) facciata ♦ *vt* essere di fronte a; (*facts, situation*) affrontare; **~ down** a faccia in giù; **to make** *or* **pull a ~** fare una smorfia; **in the ~ of** (*difficulties etc*) di fronte a; **on the ~ of it** a prima vista; **~ to ~** faccia a faccia; **~ up to** *vt fus* affrontare, far fronte a; **~ cloth** (*BRIT*) *n* guanto di spugna; **~ cream** *n* crema per il viso; **~ lift** *n* lifting *m inv*; (*of façade etc*) ripulita; **~ powder** *n* cipria; **~-saving** *adj* per salvare la faccia

facet ['fæsɪt] *n* sfaccettatura

facetious [fəˈsiːʃəs] *adj* faceto(a)

face value *n* (*of coin*) valore *m* facciale *or* nominale; **to take sth at ~** (*fig*) giudicare qc dalle apparenze

facial ['feɪʃəl] *adj* del viso

facile ['fæsaɪl] *adj* superficiale

facilities [fəˈsɪlɪtɪz] *npl* attrezzature *fpl*;

credit ~ facilitazioni *fpl* di credito

facing ['feɪsɪŋ] *prep* di fronte a

facsimile [fækˈsɪmɪlɪ] *n* facsimile *m inv*; **~ machine** *n* telecopiatrice *f*

fact [fækt] *n* fatto; **in ~** infatti

factor ['fæktə*] *n* fattore *m*

factory ['fæktərɪ] *n* fabbrica, stabilimento

factual ['fæktjuəl] *adj* che si attiene ai fatti

faculty ['fækəltɪ] *n* facoltà *f inv*; (*US*) corpo insegnante

fad [fæd] *n* mania; capriccio

fade [feɪd] *vi* sbiadire, sbiadirsi; (*light, sound, hope*) attenuarsi, affievolirsi; (*flower*) appassire

fag [fæg] (*BRIT: inf*) *n* (*cigarette*) cicca

fail [feɪl] *vt* (*exam*) non superare; (*candidate*) bocciare; (*subj: courage, memory*) mancare a ♦ *vi* fallire; (*student*) essere respinto(a); (*eyesight, health, light*) venire a mancare; **to ~ to do sth** (*neglect*) mancare di fare qc; (*be unable*) non riuscire a fare qc; **without ~** senza fallo; certamente; **~ing** *n* difetto ♦ *prep* in mancanza di; **~ure** ['feɪljə*] *n* fallimento; (*person*) fallito/a; (*mechanical etc*) guasto

faint [feɪnt] *adj* debole; (*recollection*) vago(a); (*mark*) indistinto(a) ♦ *n* (*MED*) svenimento ♦ *vi* svenire; **to feel ~** sentirsi svenire

fair [fɛə*] *adj* (*person, decision*) giusto(a), equo(a); (*quite large, quite good*) discreto(a); (*hair etc*) biondo(a); (*skin, complexion*) chiaro(a); (*weather*) bello(a), clemente ♦ *adv* (*play*) lealmente ♦ *n* fiera; (*BRIT: funfair*) luna park *m inv*; **~ly** *adv* equamente; (*quite*) abbastanza; **~ness** *n* equità, giustizia; **~ play** *n* correttezza

fairy ['fɛərɪ] *n* fata; **~ tale** *n* fiaba

faith [feɪθ] *n* fede *f*; (*trust*) fiducia; (*sect*) religione *f*, fede *f*; **~ful** *adj* fedele; **~fully** *adv* fedelmente; **yours ~fully** (*BRIT: in letters*) distinti saluti

fake [feɪk] *n* imitazione *f*; (*picture*) falso; (*person*) impostore/a ♦ *adj* falso(a) ♦ *vt* (*accounts*) falsificare; (*illness*) fingere; (*painting*) contraffare

falcon ['fɔːlkən] *n* falco, falcone *m*

fall [fɔːl] (*pt* **fell**, *pp* **fallen**) *n* caduta; (*in* *temperature*) abbassamento; (*in price*) ribasso; (*US: autumn*) autunno ♦ *vi* cadere; (*temperature, price, night*) scendere; ~s *npl* (*waterfall*) cascate *fpl*; to ~ flat (*on one's face*) cadere bocconi; (*joke*) fare cilecca; (*plan*) fallire; ~ back *vi* (*retreat*) indietreggiare; (*MIL*) ritirarsi; ~ back on *vt fus* (*remedy etc*) ripiegare su; ~ behind *vi* rimanere indietro; ~ down *vi* (*person*) cadere; (*building*) crollare; ~ for *vt fus* (*person*) prendere una cotta per; to ~ for a trick (*or a story etc*) cascarci; ~ in *vi* crollare; (*MIL*) mettersi in riga; ~ off *vi* cadere; (*diminish*) diminuire, abbassarsi; ~ out *vi* (*hair, teeth*) cadere; (*friends etc*) litigare; ~ through *vi* (*plan, project*) fallire

fallacy ['fæləsɪ] *n* errore *m*

fallen ['fɔːlən] *pp of* **fall**

fallout ['fɔːlaut] *n* fall-out *m*; ~ shelter *n* rifugio antiatomico

fallow ['fæləu] *adj* incolto(a), a maggese

false [fɔːls] *adj* falso(a); under ~ pretences *con l'inganno*; ~ teeth (*BRIT*) *npl* denti *mpl* finti

falter ['fɔːltə*] *vi* esitare, vacillare

fame [feɪm] *n* fama, celebrità

familiar [fə'mɪlɪə*] *adj* familiare; (*close*) intimo(a); to be ~ with (*subject*) conoscere; ~ize [fə'mɪlɪəraɪz] *vt*: to ~ize o.s. with familiarizzare con

family ['fæmɪlɪ] *n* famiglia; ~ business *n* ditta a conduzione familiare

famine ['fæmɪn] *n* carestia

famished ['fæmɪʃt] *adj* affamato(a)

famous ['feɪməs] *adj* famoso(a); ~ly *adv* (*get on*) a meraviglia

fan [fæn] *n* (*folding*) ventaglio; (*ELEC*) ventilatore *m*; (*person*) ammiratore/trice; tifoso/a ♦ *vt* far vento a; (*fire, quarrel*) alimentare; ~ out *vi* spargersi (a ventaglio)

fanatic [fə'nætɪk] *n* fanatico/a

fan belt *n* cinghia del ventilatore

fanciful ['fænsɪful] *adj* fantasioso(a)

fancy ['fænsɪ] *n* immaginazione *f*, fantasia; (*whim*) capriccio ♦ *adj* (*hat*) stravagante; (*hotel, food*) speciale ♦ *vt*

(*feel like, want*) aver voglia di; (*imagine, think*) immaginare; to take a ~ to incapricciarsi di; he fancies her (*inf*) gli piace; ~ dress *n* costume *m* (per maschera); ~-dress ball *n* ballo in maschera

fang [fæŋ] *n* zanna; (*of snake*) dente *m*

fantastic [fæn'tæstɪk] *adj* fantastico(a)

fantasy ['fæntəsɪ] *n* fantasia, immaginazione *f*; fantasticheria; chimera

far [fɑː*] *adj* lontano(a) ♦ *adv* lontano; (*much, greatly*) molto; ~ away, ~ off lontano, distante; ~ better assai migliore; ~ from lontano da; by ~ di gran lunga; go as ~ as the farm vada fino alla fattoria; as ~ as I know per quel che so; how ~? quanto lontano?; (*referring to activity etc*) fino a dove?; ~away *adj* lontano(a)

farce [fɑːs] *n* farsa

farcical ['fɑːsɪkəl] *adj* farsesco(a)

fare [fɛə*] *n* (*on trains, buses*) tariffa; (*in taxi*) prezzo della corsa; (*food*) vitto, cibo; half ~ metà tariffa; full ~ tariffa intera

Far East *n*: the ~ l'Estremo Oriente *m*

farewell [fɛə'wel] *excl*, *n* addio

farm [fɑːm] *n* fattoria, podere *m* ♦ *vt* coltivare; ~er *n* coltivatore/trice; agricoltore/trice; ~hand *n* bracciante *m* agricolo; ~house *n* fattoria; ~ing *n* (*gen*) agricoltura; (*of crops*) coltivazione *f*; (*of animals*) allevamento; ~land *n* terreno coltivabile; ~ worker *n* = ~hand; ~yard *n* aia

far-reaching [-'riːtʃɪŋ] *adj* di vasta portata

fart [fɑːt] (*inf!*) *vi* scoreggiare (*!*)

farther ['fɑːðə*] *adv* più lontano ♦ *adj* più lontano(a)

farthest ['fɑːðɪst] *superl of* **far**

fascinate ['fæsɪneɪt] *vt* affascinare; **fascinating** *adj* affascinante; **fascination** [-'neɪʃən] *n* fascino

fascism ['fæʃɪzəm] *n* fascismo

fashion ['fæʃən] *n* moda; (*manner*) maniera, modo ♦ *vt* foggiare, formare; in ~ alla moda; out of ~ passato(a) di moda; ~able *adj* alla moda, di moda; ~ show *n* sfilata di moda

fast [fɑːst] *adj* rapido(a), svelto(a), veloce; (*clock*): **to be ~** andare avanti; (*dye, colour*) solido(a) ♦ *adv* rapidamente; (*stuck, held*) saldamente ♦ *n* digiuno ♦ *vi* digiunare; **~ asleep** profondamente addormentato

fasten ['fɑːsn] *vt* chiudere, fissare; (*coat*) abbottonare, allacciare ♦ *vi* chiudersi, fissarsi; abbottonarsi, allacciarsi; **~er** *n* fermaglio, chiusura; **~ing** *n* = **~er**

fast food *n* fast food *m*

fastidious [fæs'tɪdɪəs] *adj* esigente, difficile

fat [fæt] *adj* grasso(a); (*book, profit etc*) grosso(a) ♦ *n* grasso

fatal ['feɪtl] *adj* fatale; mortale; disastroso(a); **~ity** [fə'tælɪtɪ] *n* (*road death etc*) morto/a, vittima; **~ly** *adv* a morte

fate [feɪt] *n* destino; (*of person*) sorte *f*; **~ful** *adj* fatidico(a)

father ['fɑːðə*] *n* padre *m*; **~-in-law** *n* suocero; **~ly** *adj* paterno(a)

fathom ['fæðəm] *n* braccio (= *1828 mm*) ♦ *vt* (*mystery*) penetrare, sondare

fatigue [fə'tiːg] *n* stanchezza

fatten ['fætn] *vt, vi* ingrassare

fatty ['fætɪ] *adj* (*food*) grasso(a) ♦ *n* (*inf*) ciccione/a

fatuous ['fætjʊəs] *adj* fatuo(a)

faucet ['fɔːsɪt] (*US*) *n* rubinetto

fault [fɔːlt] *n* colpa; (*TENNIS*) fallo; (*defect*) difetto; (*GEO*) faglia ♦ *vt* criticare; **it's my ~** è colpa mia; **to find ~ with** trovare da ridire su; **at ~** in fallo; **~y** *adj* difettoso(a)

fauna ['fɔːnə] *n* fauna

faux pas ['fəʊ'pɑː] *n* gaffe *f inv*

favour ['feɪvə*] (*US* **favor**) *n* favore *m* ♦ *vt* (*proposition*) favorire, essere favorevole a; (*pupil etc*) favorire; (*team, horse*) dare per vincente; **to do sb a ~** fare un favore *or* una cortesia a qn; **to find ~ with** (*subj: person*) entrare nelle buone grazie di; (: *suggestion*) avere l'approvazione di; **in ~ of** in favore di; **~able** *adj* favorevole; **~ite** [-rɪt] *adj, n* favorito(a)

fawn [fɔːn] *n* daino ♦ *adj* (*also:* **~-coloured**) marrone chiaro *inv* ♦ *vi*: **to ~ (up)on** adulare servilmente

fax [fæks] *n* (*document*) facsimile *m inv*, telecopia; (*machine*) telecopiatrice *f* ♦ *vt* telecopiare, trasmettere in facsimile

FBI (*US*) *n abbr* (= *Federal Bureau of Investigation*) F.B.I. *f*

fear [fɪə*] *n* paura, timore *m* ♦ *vt* aver paura di, temere; **for ~ of** per paura di; **~ful** *adj* pauroso(a); (*sight, noise*) terribile, spaventoso(a)

feasible ['fiːzəbl] *adj* possibile, realizzabile

feast [fiːst] *n* festa, banchetto; (*REL: also:* **~ day**) festa ♦ *vi* banchettare

feat [fiːt] *n* impresa, fatto insigne

feather ['feðə*] *n* penna

feature ['fiːtʃə*] *n* caratteristica; (*PRESS, TV*) articolo ♦ *vt* (*subj: film*) avere come protagonista ♦ *vi* figurare; **~s** *npl* (*of face*) fisionomia; **~ film** *n* film *m inv* principale

February ['fɛbruərɪ] *n* febbraio

fed [fɛd] *pt, pp of* **feed**

federal ['fɛdərəl] *adj* federale

fed-up *adj*: **to be ~** essere stufo(a)

fee [fiː] *n* pagamento; (*of doctor, lawyer*) onorario; (*for examination*) tassa d'esame; **school ~s** tasse *fpl* scolastiche

feeble ['fiːbl] *adj* debole

feed [fiːd] (*pt, pp* **fed**) *n* (*of baby*) pappa; (*of animal*) mangime *m*; (*on printer*) meccanismo di alimentazione ♦ *vt* nutrire; (*baby*) allattare; (*horse etc*) dare da mangiare a; (*fire, machine*) alimentare; (*data, information*): **to ~ into** inserire in; **~ on** *vt fus* nutrirsi di; **~back** *n* feedback *m*; **~ing bottle** (*BRIT*) *n* biberon *m inv*

feel [fiːl] (*pt, pp* **felt**) *n* consistenza; (*sense of touch*) tatto ♦ *vt* toccare; palpare; tastare; (*cold, pain, anger*) sentire; (*think, believe*): **to ~ (that)** pensare che; **to ~ hungry/cold** aver fame/freddo; **to ~ lonely/better** sentirsi solo/meglio; **I don't ~ well** non mi sento bene; **it ~s soft** è morbido al tatto; **to ~ like** (*want*) aver voglia di; **to ~ about** *or* **around for** cercare a tastoni; **~er** *n* (*of insect*) antenna; **to put out a ~er** *or* **~ers** (*fig*) fare un sondaggio; **~ing** *n* sensazione *f*;

(*emotion*) sentimento

feet [fiːt] *npl of* **foot**

feign [feɪn] *vt* fingere, simulare

fell [fɛl] *pt of* **fall** ♦ *vt* (*tree*) abbattere

fellow ['fɛləʊ] *n* individuo, tipo; compagno; (*of learned society*) membro ♦ *cpd*: ~ **citizen** *n* concittadino/a; ~ **countryman** *n* compatriota *m*; ~ **men** *npl* simili *mpl*; ~**ship** *n* associazione *f*; compagnia; *specie di borsa di studio universitaria*

felony ['fɛlənɪ] *n* reato, crimine *m*

felt [fɛlt] *pt*, *pp of* **feel** ♦ *n* feltro; ~-**tip pen** *n* pennarello

female ['fiːmeɪl] *n* (*ZOOL*) femmina; (*pej: woman*) donna, femmina ♦ *adj* (*BIOL*, *ELEC*) femmina *inv*; (*sex, character*) femminile; (*vote etc*) di donne

feminine ['fɛmɪnɪn] *adj* femminile

feminist ['fɛmɪnɪst] *n* femminista *m/f*

fence [fɛns] *n* recinto ♦ *vt* (*also*: ~ **in**) recingere ♦ *vi* (*SPORT*) tirare di scherma; **fencing** *n* (*SPORT*) scherma

fend [fɛnd] *vi*: **to** ~ **for o.s.** arrangiarsi; ~ **off** *vt* (*attack, questions*) respingere, difendersi da

fender ['fɛndə*] *n* parafuoco; (*on boat*) parabordo; (*US*) parafango; paraurti *m inv*

ferment [*vb* fə'mɛnt, *n* 'fəːmɛnt] *vi* fermentare ♦ *n* (*fig*) agitazione *f*, eccitazione *f*

fern [fəːn] *n* felce *f*

ferocious [fə'rəʊʃəs] *adj* feroce

ferret ['fɛrɪt] *n* furetto; ~ **out** *vt* (*information*) scovare

ferry ['fɛrɪ] *n* (*small*) traghetto; (*large: also*: ~**boat**) nave *f* traghetto *inv* ♦ *vt* traghettare

fertile ['fəːtaɪl] *adj* fertile; (*BIOL*) fecondo(a); **fertilizer** ['fəːtɪlaɪzə*] *n* fertilizzante *m*

fester ['fɛstə*] *vi* suppurare

festival ['fɛstɪvəl] *n* (*REL*) festa; (*ART, MUS*) festival *m inv*

festive ['fɛstɪv] *adj* di festa; **the ~ season** (*BRIT: Christmas*) il periodo delle feste

festivities [fɛs'tɪvɪtɪz] *npl* festeggiamenti *mpl*

festoon [fɛs'tuːn] *vt*: **to** ~ **with** ornare di

fetch [fɛtʃ] *vt* andare a prendere; (*sell for*) essere venduto(a) per

fetching ['fɛtʃɪŋ] *adj* attraente

fête [feɪt] *n* festa

fetish ['fɛtɪʃ] *n* feticcio

fetus ['fiːtəs] (*US*) *n* = **foetus**

feud [fjuːd] *n* contesa, lotta

feudal ['fjuːdl] *adj* feudale

fever ['fiːvə*] *n* febbre *f*; ~**ish** *adj* febbrile

few [fjuː] *adj* pochi(e); **a** ~ *adj* qualche *inv* ♦ *pron* alcuni(e); ~**er** *adj* meno *inv*; meno numerosi(e); ~**est** *adj* il minor numero di

fiancé [fɪ'ɑːnseɪ] *n* fidanzato; ~**e** *n* fidanzata

fib [fɪb] *n* piccola bugia

fibre ['faɪbə*] (*US* **fiber**) *n* fibra; **F~-glass** ® *n* fibra di vetro

fickle ['fɪkl] *adj* incostante, capriccioso(a)

fiction ['fɪkʃən] *n* narrativa, romanzi *mpl*; (*sth made up*) finzione *f*; ~**al** *adj* immaginario(a)

fictitious [fɪk'tɪʃəs] *adj* fittizio(a)

fiddle ['fɪdl] *n* (*MUS*) violino; (*cheating*) imbroglio; truffa ♦ *vt* (*BRIT: accounts*) falsificare, falsare; ~ **with** *vt fus* gingillarsi con

fidelity [fɪ'dɛlɪtɪ] *n* fedeltà; (*accuracy*) esattezza

fidget ['fɪdʒɪt] *vi* agitarsi

field [fiːld] *n* campo; ~ **marshal** *n* feldmaresciallo; ~**work** *n* ricerche *fpl* esterne

fiend [fiːnd] *n* demonio; ~**ish** ['fiːndɪʃ] *adj* (*person, problem*) diabolico(a)

fierce [fɪəs] *adj* (*animal, person, fighting*) feroce; (*loyalty*) assoluto(a); (*wind*) furioso(a); (*heat*) intenso(a)

fiery ['faɪərɪ] *adj* ardente; infocato(a)

fifteen [fɪf'tiːn] *num* quindici

fifth [fɪfθ] *num* quinto(a)

fifty ['fɪftɪ] *num* cinquanta; ~-~ *adj*: **a ~-~ chance** una possibilità su due ♦ *adv* fifty-fifty, metà per ciascuno

fig [fɪg] *n* fico

fight [faɪt] (*pt, pp* **fought**) *n* zuffa, rissa; (*MIL*) battaglia, combattimento; (*against* *cancer etc*) lotta ♦ *vt (person)* azzuffarsi con; *(enemy: also: MIL)* combattere; *(cancer, alcoholism, emotion)* lottare contro, combattere; *(election)* partecipare a ♦ *vi* combattere; **~er** *n* combattente *m*; *(plane)* aeroplano da caccia; **~ing** *n* combattimento

figment ['fɪgmənt] *n*: **a ~ of the imagination** un parto della fantasia

figurative ['fɪgjurətɪv] *adj* figurato(a)

figure ['fɪgə*] *n* figura; *(number, cipher)* cifra ♦ *vt (think: esp US)* pensare ♦ *vi (appear)* figurare; **~ out** *vt* riuscire a capire; calcolare; **~head** *n (NAUT)* polena; *(pej)* prestanome *m/f inv*; **~ of speech** *n* figura retorica

filch [fɪltʃ] *(inf) vt* sgraffignare

file [faɪl] *n (tool)* lima; *(dossier)* incartamento; *(folder)* cartellina; *(COMPUT)* archivio; *(row)* fila ♦ *vt (nails, wood)* limare; *(papers)* archiviare; *(LAW: claim)* presentare; passare agli atti; **~ in/out** *vi* entrare/uscire in fila

filing cabinet ['faɪlɪŋ-] *n* casellario

fill [fɪl] *vt* riempire; *(job)* occupare ♦ *n*: **to eat one's ~** mangiare a sazietà; **~ in** *vt (hole)* riempire; *(form)* compilare; **~ up** *vt* riempire ♦ *vi (AUT)* fare il pieno

fillet ['fɪlɪt] *n* filetto; **~ steak** *n* bistecca di filetto

filling ['fɪlɪŋ] *n (CULIN)* impasto, ripieno; *(for tooth)* otturazione *f*; **~ station** *n* stazione *f* di rifornimento

film [fɪlm] *n (CINEMA)* film *m inv*; *(PHOT)* pellicola; *(of powder, liquid)* sottile strato ♦ *vt, vi* girare; **~ star** *n* divo/a dello schermo; **~ strip** *n* filmina

filter ['fɪltə*] *n* filtro ♦ *vt* filtrare; **~ lane** *(BRIT) n (AUT)* corsia di svincolo; **~-tipped** *adj* con filtro

filth [fɪlθ] *n* sporcizia; **~y** *adj* lordo(a), sozzo(a); *(language)* osceno(a)

fin [fɪn] *n (of fish)* pinna

final ['faɪnl] *adj* finale, ultimo(a); definitivo(a) ♦ *n (SPORT)* finale *f*; **~s** *npl (SCOL)* esami *mpl* finali

finale [fɪ'nɑːlɪ] *n* finale *m*

finalize ['faɪnəlaɪz] *vt* mettere a punto

finally ['faɪnəlɪ] *adv (lastly)* alla fine;

(eventually) finalmente

finance [faɪ'næns] *n* finanza; *(capital)* capitale *m* ♦ *vt* finanziare; **~s** *npl (funds)* finanze *fpl*

financial [faɪ'nænʃəl] *adj* finanziario(a)

financier [faɪ'nænsɪə*] *n* finanziatore *m*

find [faɪnd] *(pt, pp* **found)** *vt* trovare; *(lost object)* ritrovare ♦ *n* trovata, scoperta; **to ~ sb guilty** *(LAW)* giudicare qn colpevole; **~ out** *vt (truth, secret)* scoprire; *(person)* cogliere in fallo; **to ~ out about** informarsi su; *(by chance)* scoprire; **~ings** *npl (LAW)* sentenza, conclusioni *fpl*; *(of report)* conclusioni

fine [faɪn] *adj* bello(a); ottimo(a); *(thin, subtle)* fine ♦ *adv (well)* molto bene ♦ *n (LAW)* multa ♦ *vt (LAW)* multare; **to be ~** *(person)* stare bene; *(weather)* far bello; **~ arts** *npl* belle arti *fpl*

finery ['faɪnərɪ] *n* abiti *mpl* eleganti

finger ['fɪŋgə*] *n* dito ♦ *vt* toccare, tastare; **little/index ~** mignolo/(dito) indice *m*; **~nail** *n* unghia; **~print** *n* impronta digitale; **~tip** *n* punta del dito

finicky ['fɪnɪkɪ] *adj* esigente, pignolo(a); minuzioso(a)

finish ['fɪnɪʃ] *n* fine *f*; *(polish etc)* finitura ♦ *vt, vi* finire; **to ~ doing sth** finire di fare qc; **to ~ third** arrivare terzo(a); **~ off** *vt* compiere; *(kill)* uccidere; **~ up** *vi, vt* finire; **~ing line** *n* linea d'arrivo; **~ing school** *n* scuola privata di perfezionamento *(per signorine)*

finite ['faɪnaɪt] *adj* limitato(a); *(verb)* finito(a)

Finland ['fɪnlənd] *n* Finlandia

Finn [fɪn] *n* finlandese *m/f*; **~ish** *adj* finlandese ♦ *n (LING)* finlandese *m*

fir [fəː*] *n* abete *m*

fire [faɪə*] *n* fuoco; *(destructive)* incendio; *(gas ~, electric ~)* stufa ♦ *vt (gun)* far fuoco con; *(arrow)* sparare; *(fig)* infiammare; *(inf: dismiss)* licenziare ♦ *vi* sparare, far fuoco; **on ~** in fiamme; **~ alarm** *n* allarme *m* d'incendio; **~arm** *n* arma da fuoco; **~ brigade** *(US* **~ department)** *n* (corpo dei) pompieri *mpl*; **~ engine** *n* autopompa; **~ escape** *n* scala di sicurezza; **~ extinguisher** *n* estintore *m*; **~guard** *n* parafuoco; **~man** *n* pompiere *m*; **~place** *n* focolare *m*; **~side** *n* angolo del focolare; **~ station** *n* caserma dei pompieri; **~wood** *n* legna; **~works** *npl* fuochi *mpl* d'artificio

firing squad ['faɪərɪŋ-] *n* plotone *m* d'esecuzione

firm [fəːm] *adj* fermo(a) ♦ *n* ditta, azienda; **~ly** *adv* fermamente

first [fəːst] *adj* primo(a) ♦ *adv* (*before others*) il primo, la prima; (*before other things*) per primo; (*when listing reasons etc*) per prima cosa ♦ *n* (*person: in race*) primo/a; (*BRIT: SCOL*) laurea con lode; (*AUT*) prima; **at ~** dapprima, all'inizio; **~ of all** prima di tutto; **~ aid** *n* pronto soccorso; **~-aid kit** *n* cassetta pronto soccorso; **~-class** *adj* di prima classe; **~-hand** *adj* di prima mano; **~ lady** (*US*) *n* moglie *f* del presidente; **~ly** *adv* in primo luogo; **~ name** *n* prenome *m*; **~-rate** *adj* di prima qualità, ottimo(a)

fish [fɪʃ] *n inv* pesce *m* ♦ *vt* (*river, area*) pescare in ♦ *vi* pescare; **to go ~ing** andare a pesca; **~erman** *n* pescatore *m*; **~ farm** *n* vivaio; **~ fingers** (*BRIT*) *npl* bastoncini *mpl* di pesce (surgelati); **~ing boat** *n* barca da pesca; **~ing line** *n* lenza; **~ing rod** *n* canna da pesca; **~monger** *n* pescivendolo; **~monger's (shop)** *n* pescheria; **~ sticks** (*US*) *npl* = **~ fingers**; **~y** (*inf*) *adj* (*tale, story*) sospetto(a)

fist [fɪst] *n* pugno

fit [fɪt] *adj* (*MED, SPORT*) in forma; (*proper*) adatto(a), appropriato(a); conveniente ♦ *vt* (*subj: clothes*) stare bene a; (*put in, attach*) mettere; installare; (*equip*) fornire, equipaggiare ♦ *vi* (*clothes*) stare bene; (*parts*) andare bene, adattarsi; (*in space, gap*) entrare ♦ *n* (*MED*) accesso, attacco; **~ to** in grado di; **~ for** adatto(a) a; degno(a) di; **a ~ of anger** un accesso d'ira; **this dress is a good ~** questo vestito sta bene; **by ~s and starts** a sbalzi; **~ in** *vi* accordarsi; adattarsi; **~ful** *adj* saltuario(a); **~ment** *n* componibile *m*; **~ness** *n* (*MED*) forma fisica; **~ted carpet** *n* moquette *f*; **~ted kitchen** *n* cucina

componibile; **~ter** *n* aggiustatore *m or* montatore *m* meccanico; **~ting** *adj* appropriato(a) ♦ *n* (*of dress*) prova; (*of piece of equipment*) montaggio, aggiustaggio; **~tings** *npl* (*in building*) impianti *mpl*; **~ting room** *n* camerino

five [faɪv] *num* cinque; **~r** (*inf*) *n* (*BRIT*) biglietto da cinque sterline; (*US*) biglietto da cinque dollari

fix [fɪks] *vt* fissare; (*mend*) riparare; (*meal, drink*) preparare ♦ *n*: **to be in a ~** essere nei guai; **~ up** *vt* (*meeting*) fissare; **to ~ sb up with sth** procurare qc a qn; **~ation** *n* fissazione *f*; **~ed** [fɪkst] *adj* (*prices etc*) fisso(a); **~ture** ['fɪkstʃə*] *n* impianto (fisso); (*SPORT*) incontro (del calendario sportivo)

fizzle out ['fɪzl-] *vi* finire in nulla

fizzy ['fɪzɪ] *adj* frizzante; gassato(a)

flabbergasted ['flæbəgɑːstɪd] *adj* sbalordito(a)

flabby ['flæbɪ] *adj* flaccido(a)

flag [flæg] *n* bandiera; (*also: ~stone*) pietra da lastricare ♦ *vi* stancarsi; affievolirsi; **~ down** *vt* fare segno (di fermarsi) a

flagpole ['flægpəul] *n* albero

flagship ['flægʃɪp] *n* nave *f* ammiraglia

flair [flɛə*] *n* (*for business etc*) fiuto; (*for languages etc*) facilità; (*style*) stile *m*

flak [flæk] *n* (*MIL*) fuoco d'artiglieria; (*inf: criticism*) critiche *fpl*

flake [fleɪk] *n* (*of rust, paint*) scaglia; (*of snow, soap powder*) fiocco ♦ *vi* (*also: ~ off*) sfaldarsi

flamboyant [flæm'bɔɪənt] *adj* sgargiante

flame [fleɪm] *n* fiamma

flamingo [flə'mɪŋgəu] *n* fenicottero, fiammingo

flammable ['flæməbl] *adj* infiammabile

flan [flæn] (*BRIT*) *n* flan *m inv*

flank [flæŋk] *n* fianco ♦ *vt* fiancheggiare

flannel ['flænl] *n* (*BRIT: also: face ~*) guanto di spugna; (*fabric*) flanella; **~s** *npl* (*trousers*) pantaloni *mpl* di flanella

flap [flæp] *n* (*of pocket*) patta; (*of envelope*) lembo ♦ *vt* (*wings*) battere ♦ *vi* (*sail, flag*) sbattere; (*inf: also: be in a ~*) essere in agitazione

flare [flɛə*] *n* razzo; (*in skirt etc*) svasatura; ~ **up** *vi* andare in fiamme; (*fig: person*) infiammarsi di rabbia; (: *revolt*) scoppiare

flash [flæʃ] *n* vampata; (*also: news ~*) notizia *f* lampo *inv*; (*PHOT*) flash *m inv* ♦ *vt* accendere e spegnere; (*send: message*) trasmettere; (: *look, smile*) lanciare ♦ *vi* brillare; (*light on ambulance, eyes etc*) lampeggiare; **in a** ~ in un lampo; **to** ~ **one's headlights** lampeggiare; **he** ~**ed by** or **past** ci passò davanti come un lampo; ~**bulb** *n* cubo *m* flash *inv*; ~**cube** *n* flash *m inv*; ~**light** *n* lampadina tascabile

flashy ['flæʃɪ] (*pej*) *adj* vistoso(a)

flask [flɑːsk] *n* fiasco; (*also: vacuum ~*) thermos *m inv* ®

flat [flæt] *adj* piatto(a); (*tyre*) sgonfio(a), a terra; (*battery*) scarico(a); (*beer*) svampito(a); (*denial*) netto(a); (*MUS*) bemolle *inv*; (: *voice*) stonato(a); (*rate, fee*) unico(a) ♦ *n* (*BRIT: rooms*) appartamento; (*AUT*) pneumatico sgonfio; (*MUS*) bemolle *m*; **to work** ~ **out** lavorare a più non posso; ~**ly** *adv* categoricamente; ~**-screen** *adj* a schermo piatto; ~**ten** *vt* (*also: ~ten out*) appiattire; (*building, city*) spianare

flatter ['flætə*] *vt* lusingare; ~**ing** *adj* lusinghiero(a); (*dress*) che dona; ~**y** *n* adulazione *f*

flaunt [flɔːnt] *vt* fare mostra di

flavour ['fleɪvə*] (*US* **flavor**) *n* gusto ♦ *vt* insaporire, aggiungere sapore a; **strawberry-**~**ed** al gusto di fragola; ~**ing** *n* essenza (artificiale)

flaw [flɔː] *n* difetto

flax [flæks] *n* lino; ~**en** *adj* biondo(a)

flea [fliː] *n* pulce *f*

fleck [flɛk] *n* (*mark*) macchiolina; (*pattern*) screziatura

fled [flɛd] *pt, pp of* **flee**

flee [fliː] (*pt, pp* **fled**) *vt* fuggire da ♦ *vi* fuggire, scappare

fleece [fliːs] *n* vello ♦ *vt* (*inf*) pelare

fleet [fliːt] *n* flotta; (*of lorries etc*) convoglio; parco

fleeting ['fliːtɪŋ] *adj* fugace, fuggitivo(a); (*visit*) volante

Flemish ['flɛmɪʃ] *adj* fiammingo(a)

flesh [flɛʃ] *n* carne *f*; (*of fruit*) polpa; ~ **wound** *n* ferita superficiale

flew [fluː] *pt of* **fly**

flex [flɛks] *n* filo (flessibile) ♦ *vt* flettere; (*muscles*) contrarre; ~**ible** *adj* flessibile

flick [flɪk] *n* colpetto; scarto ♦ *vt* dare un colpetto a; ~ **through** *vt fus* sfogliare

flicker ['flɪkə*] *vi* tremolare

flier ['flaɪə*] *n* aviatore *m*

flight [flaɪt] *n* volo; (*escape*) fuga; (*also: ~ of steps*) scalinata; ~ **attendant** (*US*) *n* steward *m inv*, hostess *f inv*; ~ **deck** *n* (*AVIAT*) cabina di controllo; (*NAUT*) ponte *m* di comando

flimsy ['flɪmzɪ] *adj* (*shoes, clothes*) leggero(a); (*building*) poco solido(a); (*excuse*) che non regge

flinch [flɪntʃ] *vi* ritirarsi; **to** ~ **from** tirarsi indietro di fronte a

fling [flɪŋ] (*pt, pp* **flung**) *vt* lanciare, gettare

flint [flɪnt] *n* selce *f*; (*in lighter*) pietrina

flip [flɪp] *vt* (*switch*) far scattare; (*coin*) lanciare in aria

flippant ['flɪpənt] *adj* senza rispetto, irriverente

flipper ['flɪpə*] *n* pinna

flirt [flɜːt] *vi* flirtare ♦ *n* civetta

flit [flɪt] *vi* svolazzare

float [fləʊt] *n* galleggiante *m*; (*in procession*) carro; (*money*) somma ♦ *vi* galleggiare

flock [flɔk] *n* (*of sheep, REL*) gregge *m*; (*of birds*) stormo ♦ *vi*: **to** ~ **to** accorrere in massa a

flog [flɔg] *vt* flagellare

flood [flʌd] *n* alluvione *m*; (*of letters etc*) marea ♦ *vt* allagare; (*subj: people*) invadere ♦ *vi* (*place*) allagarsi; (*people*): **to** ~ **into** riversarsi in; ~**ing** *n* inondazione *f*; ~**light** *n* riflettore *m* ♦ *vt* illuminare a giorno

floor [flɔː*] *n* pavimento; (*storey*) piano; (*of sea, valley*) fondo ♦ *vt* (*subj: blow*) atterrare; (: *question*) ridurre al silenzio; **ground** ~, (*US*) **first** ~ pianterreno; **first** ~, (*US*) **second** ~ primo piano; ~**board** *n* tavellone *m* di legno; ~ **show** *n* spettacolo di varietà

flop [flɔp] *n* fiasco ♦ *vi* far fiasco; *(fall)* lasciarsi cadere

floppy ['flɔpɪ] *adj* floscio(a), molle; ~ **(disk)** *n* (COMPUT) floppy disk *m inv*

flora ['flɔːrə] *n* flora

Florence ['flɔrəns] *n* Firenze *f*; **Florentine** ['flɔrəntaɪn] *adj* fiorentino(a)

florid ['flɔrɪd] *adj* (*complexion*) florido(a); (*style*) fiorito(a)

florist ['flɔrɪst] *n* fioraio/a

flounce [flauns] *n* balzo; ~ **out** *vi* uscire stizzito(a)

flounder ['flaundə*] *vi* annaspare ♦ *n* (ZOOL) passera di mare

flour ['flauə*] *n* farina

flourish ['flʌrɪʃ] *vi* fiorire ♦ *n* (*bold gesture*): **with a ~** con ostentazione; ~**ing** *adj* florido(a)

flout [flaut] *vt* (*order*) contravvenire a

flow [fləu] *n* flusso; circolazione *f* ♦ *vi* fluire; (*traffic, blood in veins*) circolare; (*hair*) scendere; ~ **chart** *n* schema *m* di flusso

flower ['flauə*] *n* fiore *m* ♦ *vi* fiorire; ~ **bed** *n* aiuola; ~**pot** *n* vaso da fiori; ~**y** *adj* (*perfume*) di fiori; (*pattern*) a fiori; (*speech*) fiorito(a)

flown [fləun] *pp of* **fly**

flu [fluː] *n* influenza

fluctuate ['flʌktjueɪt] *vi* fluttuare, oscillare

fluent ['fluːənt] *adj* (*speech*) facile, sciolto(a); corrente; **he speaks ~ Italian, he's ~ in Italian** parla l'italiano correntemente

fluff [flʌf] *n* lanugine *f*; ~**y** *adj* lanuginoso(a); (*toy*) di peluche

fluid ['fluːɪd] *adj* fluido(a) ♦ *n* fluido

fluke [fluːk] (*inf*) *n* colpo di fortuna

flung [flʌŋ] *pt, pp of* **fling**

fluoride ['fluəraɪd] *n* fluoruro; ~ **toothpaste** dentifricio al fluoro

flurry ['flʌrɪ] *n* (*of snow*) tempesta; **a ~ of activity** uno scoppio di attività

flush [flʌʃ] *n* rossore *m*; (*fig: of youth, beauty etc*) rigoglio, pieno vigore ♦ *vt* ripulire con un getto d'acqua ♦ *vi* arrossire ♦ *adj*: ~ **with** a livello di, pari a; **to ~ the toilet** tirare l'acqua; ~ **out** *vt*

(*birds*) far alzare in volo; (*animals, fig*) stanare; ~**ed** *adj* tutto(a) rosso(a)

flustered ['flʌstəd] *adj* sconvolto(a)

flute [fluːt] *n* flauto

flutter ['flʌtə*] *n* agitazione *f*; (*of wings*) battito ♦ *vi* (*bird*) battere le ali

flux [flʌks] *n*: **in a state of ~** in continuo mutamento

fly [flaɪ] (*pt* **flew**, *pp* **flown**) *n* (*insect*) mosca; (*on trousers: also: flies*) chiusura ♦ *vt* pilotare; (*passengers, cargo*) trasportare (in aereo); (*distances*) percorrere ♦ *vi* volare; (*passengers*) andare in aereo; (*escape*) fuggire; (*flag*) sventolare; ~ **away** *or* **off** *vi* volare via; ~**ing** *n* (*activity*) aviazione *f*; (*action*) volo ♦ *adj*: ~**ing visit** visita volante; **with ~ing colours** con risultati brillanti; ~**ing saucer** *n* disco volante; ~**ing start** *n*: **to get off to a ~ing start** partire come un razzo; ~**over** (BRIT) *n* (*bridge*) cavalcavia *m inv*; ~**sheet** *n* (*for tent*) soprattetto

foal [fəul] *n* puledro

foam [fəum] *n* schiuma; (*also*: ~ **rubber**) gommapiuma ® ♦ *vi* schiumare; (*soapy water*) fare la schiuma

fob [fɔb] *vt*: **to ~ sb off with** rifilare a qn

focus ['fəukəs] (*pl* ~**es**) *n* fuoco; (*of interest*) centro ♦ *vt* (*field glasses etc*) mettere a fuoco ♦ *vi*: **to ~ on** (*with camera*) mettere a fuoco; (*person*) fissare lo sguardo su; **in ~** a fuoco; **out of ~** sfocato(a)

fodder ['fɔdə*] *n* foraggio

foe [fəu] *n* nemico

foetus ['fiːtəs] (US **fetus**) *n* feto

fog [fɔg] *n* nebbia; ~**gy** *adj*: **it's ~gy** c'è nebbia; ~ **lamp** (US ~ **light**) *n* (AUT) faro *m* antinebbia *inv*

foil [fɔɪl] *vt* confondere, frustrare ♦ *n* lamina di metallo; (*kitchen* ~) foglio di alluminio; (*FENCING*) fioretto; **to act as a ~ to** (*fig*) far risaltare

fold [fəuld] *n* (*bend, crease*) piega; (AGR) ovile *m*; (*fig*) gregge *m* ♦ *vt* piegare; (*arms*) incrociare; ~ **up** *vi* (*map, bed, table*) piegarsi; (*business*) crollare ♦ *vt* (*map etc*) piegare, ripiegare; ~**er** *n* (*for papers*) cartella; cartellina; ~**ing** *adj* (*chair, bed*) pieghevole

foliage ['fəʊlɪdʒ] *n* fogliame *m*

folk [fəʊk] *npl* gente *f* ♦ *adj* popolare; ~**s** *npl* (*family*) famiglia; ~**lore** ['fəʊklɔ:*] *n* folclore *m*; ~ **song** *n* canto popolare

follow ['fɔləʊ] *vt* seguire ♦ *vi* seguire; (*result*) conseguire, risultare; **to ~ suit** fare lo stesso; ~ **up** *vt* (*letter, offer*) fare seguito a; (*case*) seguire; ~**er** *n* seguace *m/f*, discepolo/a; ~**ing** *adj* seguente ♦ *n* seguito, discepoli *mpl*

folly ['fɔlɪ] *n* pazzia, follia

fond [fɔnd] *adj* (*memory, look*) tenero(a), affettuoso(a); **to be ~ of sb** volere bene a qn; **he's ~ of walking** gli piace fare camminate

fondle ['fɔndl] *vt* accarezzare

font [fɔnt] *n* (*in church*) fonte *m* battesimale; (*TYP*) caratteri *mpl*

food [fu:d] *n* cibo; ~ **mixer** *n* frullatore *m*; ~ **poisoning** *n* intossicazione *f*; ~ **processor** *n* tritatutto *m inv* elettrico; ~**stuffs** *npl* generi *fpl* alimentari

fool [fu:l] *n* sciocco/a; (*CULIN*) frullato ♦ *vt* ingannare ♦ *vi* (*gen:* ~ *around*) fare lo sciocco; ~**hardy** *adj* avventato(a); ~**ish** *adj* scemo(a), stupido(a); imprudente; ~**proof** *adj* (*plan etc*) sicurissimo(a)

foot [fʊt] (*pl* **feet**) *n* piede *m*; (*measure*) piede (= 304 *mm*; 12 *inches*); (*of animal*) zampa ♦ *vt* (*bill*) pagare; **on ~** a piedi; ~**age** *n* (*CINEMA: length*) ≈ metraggio; (: *material*) sequenza; ~**ball** *n* pallone *m*; (*sport: BRIT*) calcio; (: *US*) football *m* americano; ~**ball player** *n* (*BRIT: also*: ~*baller*) calciatore *m*; (*US*) giocatore *m* di football americano; ~**brake** *n* freno a pedale; ~**bridge** *n* passerella; ~**hills** *npl* contrafforti *fpl*; ~**hold** *n* punto d'appoggio; ~**ing** *n* (*fig*) posizione *f*; **to lose one's ~ing** mettere un piede in fallo; ~**lights** *npl* luci *fpl* della ribalta; ~**man** *n* lacchè *m inv*; ~**note** *n* nota (a piè di pagina); ~**path** *n* sentiero *m*; (*in street*) marciapiede *m*; ~**print** *n* orma, impronta; ~**step** *n* passo; (~*print*) orma, impronta; ~**wear** *n* calzatura

---

KEYWORD

for [fɔ:*] *prep* **1** (*indicating destination, intention, purpose*) per; **the train ~ London** il treno per Londra; **he went ~ the paper** è andato a prendere il giornale; **it's time ~ lunch** è ora di pranzo; **what's it ~?** a che serve?; **what ~?** (*why*) perché?

2 (*on behalf of, representing*) per; **to work ~ sb/sth** lavorare per qn/qc; **I'll ask him ~ you** glielo chiederò a nome tuo; **G ~ George** G come George

3 (*because of*) per, a causa di; ~ **this reason** per questo motivo

4 (*with regard to*) per; **it's cold ~ July** è freddo per luglio; ~ **everyone who voted yes, 50 voted no** per ogni voto a favore ce n'erano 50 contro

5 (*in exchange for*) per; **I sold it ~ £5** l'ho venduto per 5 sterline

6 (*in favour of*) per, a favore di; **are you ~ or against us?** è con noi o contro di noi?; **I'm all ~ it** sono completamente a favore

7 (*referring to distance, time*) per; **there are roadworks ~ 5 km** ci sono lavori in corso per 5 km; **he was away ~ 2 years** è stato via per 2 anni; **she will be away ~ a month** starà via un mese; **it hasn't rained ~ 3 weeks** non piove da 3 settimane; **can you do it ~ tomorrow?** può farlo per domani?

8 (*with infinitive clauses*): **it is not ~ me to decide** non sta a me decidere; **it would be best ~ you to leave** sarebbe meglio che lei se ne andasse; **there is still time ~ you to do it** ha ancora tempo per farlo; ~ **this to be possible ...** perché ciò sia possibile ...

9 (*in spite of*) nonostante; ~ **all his complaints, he's very fond of her** nonostante tutte le sue lamentele, le vuole molto bene

♦ *conj* (*since, as: rather formal*) dal momento che, poiché

---

forage ['fɔrɪdʒ] *vi*: **to ~ (for)** andare in cerca (di)

foray ['fɔreɪ] *n* incursione *f*

forbad(e) [fə'bæd] *pt of* **forbid**

forbid [fə'bɪd] (*pt* **forbad(e)**, *pp* **forbidden**) *vt* vietare, interdire; **to ~ sb to do sth** proibire a qn di fare qc; **~den** *pp of* **forbid**; **~ding** *adj* minaccioso(a)

force [fɔːs] *n* forza ♦ *vt* forzare; **the F~s** (*BRIT*) *npl* le forze armate; **to ~ o.s. to do** costringersi a fare; **in ~** (*in large numbers*) in gran numero; (*law*) in vigore; **~d** *adj* forzato(a); **~-feed** *vt* (*animal, prisoner*) sottoporre ad alimentazione forzata; **~ful** *adj* forte, vigoroso(a)

forceps ['fɔːsɛps] *npl* forcipe *m*

forcibly ['fɔːsəblɪ] *adv* con la forza; (*vigorously*) vigorosamente

ford [fɔːd] *n* guado

fore [fɔː*] *n*: **to come to the ~** mettersi in evidenza

forearm ['fɔːrɑːm] *n* avambraccio

foreboding [fɔː'bəudɪŋ] *n* cattivo presagio

forecast ['fɔːkɑːst] (*irreg: like* **cast**) *n* previsione *f* ♦ *vt* prevedere

forecourt ['fɔːkɔːt] *n* (*of garage*) corte *f* esterna

forefathers ['fɔːfɑːðəz] *npl* antenati *mpl*, avi *mpl*

forefinger ['fɔːfɪŋgə*] *n* (dito) indice *m*

forefront ['fɔːfrʌnt] *n*: **in the ~ of** all'avanguardia in

forego [fɔː'gəu] (*irreg: like* **go**) *vt* rinunciare a

foregone [fɔː'gɔn] *pp of* **forego** ♦ *adj*: **it's a ~ conclusion** è una conclusione scontata

foreground ['fɔːgraund] *n* primo piano

forehead ['fɔrɪd] *n* fronte *f*

foreign ['fɔrɪn] *adj* straniero(a); (*trade*) estero(a); (*object, matter*) estraneo(a); **~er** *n* straniero/a; **~ exchange** *n* cambio con l'estero; (*currency*) valuta estera; **F~ Office** (*BRIT*) *n* Ministero degli Esteri; **F~ Secretary** (*BRIT*) *n* ministro degli Affari esteri

foreleg ['fɔːlɛg] *n* zampa anteriore

foreman ['fɔːmən] *n* caposquadra *m*

foremost ['fɔːməust] *adj* principale; più in vista ♦ *adv*: **first and ~** innanzitutto

forensic [fə'rɛnsɪk] *adj*: **~ medicine** medicina legale

forerunner ['fɔːrʌnə*] *n* precursore *m*

foresaw [fɔː'sɔː] *pt of* **foresee**

foresee [fɔː'siː] (*irreg: like* **see**) *vt* prevedere; **~able** *adj* prevedibile: **foreseen** *pp of* **foresee**

foreshadow [fɔː'ʃædəu] *vt* presagire, far prevedere

foresight ['fɔːsaɪt] *n* previdenza

forest ['fɔrɪst] *n* foresta

forestall [fɔː'stɔːl] *vt* prevenire

forestry ['fɔrɪstrɪ] *n* silvicoltura

foretaste ['fɔːteɪst] *n* pregustazione *f*

foretell [fɔː'tɛl] (*irreg: like* **tell**) *vt* predire; **foretold** [fɔː'təuld] *pt, pp of* **foretell**

forever [fə'rɛvə*] *adv* per sempre; (*endlessly*) sempre, di continuo

forewent [fɔː'wɛnt] *pt of* **forego**

foreword ['fɔːwəːd] *n* prefazione *f*

forfeit ['fɔːfɪt] *vt* perdere; (*one's happiness, health*) giocarsi

forgave [fə'geɪv] *pt of* **forgive**

forge [fɔːdʒ] *n* fucina ♦ *vt* (*signature, money*) contraffare, falsificare; (*wrought iron*) fucinare, foggiare; **~ ahead** *vi* tirare avanti; **~r** *n* contraffattore *m*; **~ry** *n* falso; (*activity*) contraffazione *f*

forget [fə'gɛt] (*pt* **forgot**, *pp* **forgotten**) *vt, vi* dimenticare; **~ful** *adj* di corta memoria; **~ful of** dimentico(a) di; **~-me-not** *n* nontiscordardimé *m inv*

forgive [fə'gɪv] (*pt* **forgave**, *pp* **forgiven**) *vt* perdonare; **to ~ sb for sth** perdonare qc a qn; **forgiven** *pp of* **forgive**; **~ness** *n* perdono

forgo [fɔː'gəu] = **forego**

forgot [fə'gɔt] *pt of* **forget**

forgotten [fə'gɔtn] *pp of* **forget**

fork [fɔːk] *n* (*for eating*) forchetta; (*for gardening*) forca; (*of roads, rivers, railways*) biforcazione *f* ♦ *vi* (*road etc*) biforcarsi; **~ out** (*inf*) *vt* (*pay*) sborsare; **~-lift truck** *n* carrello elevatore

forlorn [fə'lɔːn] *adj* (*person*) sconsolato(a); (*place*) abbandonato(a); (*attempt*) disperato(a); (*hope*) vano(a)

form [fɔːm] *n* forma; (*SCOL*) classe *f*; (*questionnaire*) scheda ♦ *vt* formare; **in top ~** in gran forma

formal ['fɔːməl] *adj* formale; (*gardens*) simmetrico(a), regolare; **~ly** *adv* formalmente

format ['fɔːmæt] *n* formato ♦ *vt* (*COMPUT*) formattare

formation [fɔː'meɪʃən] *n* formazione *f*

formative ['fɔːmətɪv] *adj*: **~ years** anni *mpl* formativi

former ['fɔːmə*] *adj* vecchio(a) (*before n*), ex *inv* (*before n*); **the ~ ... the latter** quello ... questo; **~ly** *adv* in passato

formula ['fɔːmjulə] *n* formula

forsake [fə'seɪk] (*pt* **forsook**, *pp* **forsaken**) *vt* abbandonare; **forsaken** *pp of* **forsake**; **forsook** [fə'suk] *pt of* **forsake**

fort [fɔːt] *n* forte *m*

forth [fɔːθ] *adv* in avanti; **back and ~** avanti e indietro; **and so ~** e così via; **~coming** *adj* (*event*) prossimo(a); (*help*) disponibile; (*character*) aperto(a), comunicativo(a); **~right** *adj* franco(a), schietto(a); **~with** *adv* immediatamente, subito

fortify ['fɔːtɪfaɪ] *vt* (*city*) fortificare; (*person*) armare

fortitude ['fɔːtɪtjuːd] *n* forza d'animo

fortnight ['fɔːtnaɪt] (*BRIT*) *n* quindici giorni *mpl*, due settimane *fpl*; **~ly** *adj* bimensile ♦ *adv* ogni quindici giorni

fortress ['fɔːtrɪs] *n* fortezza, rocca

fortunate ['fɔːtʃənɪt] *adj* fortunato(a); **it is ~ that** è una fortuna che; **~ly** *adv* fortunatamente

fortune ['fɔːtʃən] *n* fortuna; **~teller** *n* indovino/a

forty ['fɔːtɪ] *num* quaranta

forum ['fɔːrəm] *n* foro

forward ['fɔːwəd] *adj* (*ahead of schedule*) in anticipo; (*movement, position*) in avanti; (*not shy*) aperto(a); diretto(a) ♦ *n* (*SPORT*) avanti *m inv* ♦ *vt* (*letter*) inoltrare; (*parcel, goods*) spedire; (*career, plans*) promuovere, appoggiare; **to move ~** avanzare; **~(s)** *adv* avanti

fossil ['fɔsl] *adj* fossile ♦ *n* fossile *m*

foster ['fɔstə*] *vt* incoraggiare, nutrire; (*child*) avere in affidamento; **~ child** *n* bambino(a) preso(a) in affidamento

fought [fɔːt] *pt, pp of* **fight**

foul [faul] *adj* (*smell, food, temper etc*) cattivo(a); (*weather*) brutto(a); (*language*) osceno(a) ♦ *n* (*SPORT*) fallo ♦ *vt* sporcare; **~ play** *n* (*LAW*): **the police suspect ~ play** la polizia sospetta un atto criminale

found [faund] *pt, pp of* **find** ♦ *vt* (*establish*) fondare; **~ation** [-'deɪʃən] *n* (*act*) fondazione *f*; (*base*) base *f*; (*also*: **~ation cream**) fondo tinta; **~ations** *npl* (*of building*) fondamenta *fpl*

founder ['faundə*] *n* fondatore/trice ♦ *vi* affondare

foundry ['faundrɪ] *n* fonderia

fountain ['fauntɪn] *n* fontana; **~ pen** *n* penna stilografica

four [fɔː*] *num* quattro; **on all ~s** a carponi; **~-poster** *n* (*also*: **~-poster bed**) letto a quattro colonne; **~some** ['fɔːsəm] *n* partita a quattro; uscita in quattro; **~teen** *num* quattordici; **~th** *num* quarto(a)

fowl [faul] *n* pollame *m*; volatile *m*

fox [fɔks] *n* volpe *f* ♦ *vt* confondere

foyer ['fɔɪeɪ] *n* atrio; (*THEATRE*) ridotto

fraction ['frækʃən] *n* frazione *f*

fracture ['fræktʃə*] *n* frattura

fragile ['frædʒaɪl] *adj* fragile

fragment ['frægmənt] *n* frammento

fragrant ['freɪɡrənt] *adj* fragrante, profumato(a)

frail [freɪl] *adj* debole, delicato(a)

frame [freɪm] *n* (*of building*) armatura; (*of human, animal*) ossatura, corpo; (*of picture*) cornice *f*; (*of door, window*) telaio; (*of spectacles: also*: **~s**) montatura ♦ *vt* (*picture*) incorniciare; **~ of mind** *n* stato d'animo; **~work** *n* struttura

France [frɑːns] *n* Francia

franchise ['fræntʃaɪz] *n* (*POL*) diritto di voto; (*COMM*) concessione *f*

frank [fræŋk] *adj* franco(a), aperto(a) ♦ *vt* (*letter*) affrancare; **~ly** *adv* francamente, sinceramente

frantic ['fræntɪk] *adj* frenetico(a)

fraternity [frə'təːnɪtɪ] *n* (*club*)

associazione f; (*spirit*) fratellanza

fraud [frɔːd] n truffa; (*LAW*) frode f; (*person*) impostore/a

fraught [frɔːt] adj: ~ **with** pieno(a) di, intriso(a) da

fray [freɪ] n baruffa ♦ vt logorare ♦ vi logorarsi; **her nerves were ~ed** aveva i nervi a pezzi

freak [friːk] n fenomeno, mostro

freckle ['frɛkl] n lentiggine f

free [friː] adj libero(a); (*gratis*) gratuito(a) ♦ vt (*prisoner, jammed person*) liberare; (*jammed object*) districare; ~ (**of charge**), **for** ~ gratuitamente; **~dom** ['friːdəm] n libertà; **~-for-all** n parapiglia m generale; ~ **gift** n regalo, omaggio; **~hold** n proprietà assoluta; ~ **kick** n calcio libero; **~lance** adj indipendente; **~ly** adv liberamente; (*liberally*) liberalmente; **F~mason** n massone m; **F~post** ® n affrancatura a carico del destinatario; **~-range** adj (*hen*) ruspante; (*eggs*) di gallina ruspante; **~style** n (*SPORT*) stile m libero; ~ **trade** n libero scambio; **~way** (*US*) n superstrada; ~ **will** n libero arbitrio; **of one's own** ~ **will** di spontanea volontà

freeze [friːz] (*pt* froze, *pp* frozen) vi gelare ♦ vt gelare; (*food*) congelare; (*prices, salaries*) bloccare ♦ n gelo; blocco; **~-dried** adj liofilizzato(a); **~r** n congelatore m

freezing ['friːzɪŋ] adj (*wind, weather*) gelido(a); ~ **point** n punto di congelamento; **3 degrees below ~ point** 3 gradi sotto zero

freight [freɪt] n (*goods*) merce f, merci fpl; (*money charged*) spese fpl di trasporto; ~ **train** (*US*) n treno m merci inv

French [frɛntʃ] adj francese ♦ n (*LING*) francese m; **the** ~ npl i Francesi; ~ **bean** n fagiolino; ~ **fried potatoes** (*US* ~ **fries**) npl patate fpl fritte; **~man** n francese m; ~ **window** n portafinestra; **~woman** n francese f

frenzy ['frɛnzɪ] n frenesia

frequent [adj 'friːkwənt, vb frɪ'kwɛnt] adj frequente ♦ vt frequentare; **~ly** adv

frequentemente, spesso

fresco ['frɛskəʊ] n affresco

fresh [frɛʃ] adj fresco(a); (*new*) nuovo(a); (*cheeky*) sfacciato(a); **~en** vi (*wind, air*) rinfrescare; **~en up** vi rinfrescarsi; **~er** (*BRIT: inf*) n (*SCOL*) matricola; **~ly** adv di recente, di fresco; **~man** (*US*) n = **~er**; **~ness** n freschezza; **~water** adj (*fish*) d'acqua dolce

fret [frɛt] vi agitarsi, affliggersi

friar ['fraɪə*] n frate m

friction ['frɪkʃən] n frizione f, attrito

Friday ['fraɪdɪ] n venerdì m inv

fridge [frɪdʒ] (*BRIT*) n frigo, frigorifero

fried [fraɪd] pt, pp of **fry** ♦ adj fritto(a)

friend [frɛnd] n amico/a; **~ly** adj amichevole; **~ly fire** n (*MIL*) fuoco amico; **~ship** n amicizia

frieze [friːz] n fregio

fright [fraɪt] n paura, spavento; **to take ~** spaventarsi; **~en** vt spaventare, far paura a; **~ened** adj spaventato(a); **~ening** adj spaventoso(a), pauroso(a); **~ful** adj orribile

frigid ['frɪdʒɪd] adj (*woman*) frigido(a)

frill [frɪl] n balza

fringe [frɪndʒ] n (*decoration, BRIT: of hair*) frangia; (*edge: of forest etc*) margine m; ~ **benefits** npl vantaggi mpl

frisk [frɪsk] vt perquisire

frisky ['frɪskɪ] adj vivace, vispo(a)

fritter ['frɪtə*] n frittella; ~ **away** vt sprecare

frivolous ['frɪvələs] adj frivolo(a)

frizzy ['frɪzɪ] adj crespo(a)

fro [frəʊ] see **to**

frock [frɔk] n vestito

frog [frɔg] n rana; **~man** n uomo m rana inv

frolic ['frɔlɪk] vi sgambettare

KEYWORD

from [frɔm] prep **1** (*indicating starting place, origin etc*) da; **where do you come ~?, where are you ~?** da dove viene?, di dov'è?; ~ **London to Glasgow** da Londra a Glasgow; **a letter ~ my sister** una lettera da mia sorella; **tell him ~ me that ...** gli dica da parte mia che ...

2 (*indicating time*) da; ~ **one o'clock to**
or **until** or **till two** dall'una alle due; ~
January (on) da gennaio, a partire da
gennaio
3 (*indicating distance*) da; **the hotel is 1**
km ~ **the beach** l'albergo è a 1 km dalla
spiaggia
4 (*indicating price, number etc*) da; **prices**
range ~ **£10 to £50** i prezzi vanno dalle
10 alle 50 sterline
5 (*indicating difference*) da; **he can't tell**
red ~ **green** non sa distinguere il rosso
dal verde
6 (*because of, on the basis of*): ~ **what he**
says da quanto dice lui; **weak** ~ **hunger**
debole per la fame

front [frʌnt] *n* (*of house, dress*) davanti *m*
inv; (*of train*) testa; (*of book*) copertina;
(*promenade: also: sea* ~) lungomare *m*;
(MIL, POL, METEOR) fronte *f* ♦ *adj* primo(a); anteriore, davanti *inv*; **in** ~ **of** davanti a;
~**age** *n* facciata; ~ **door** *n* porta
d'entrata; (*of car*) sportello anteriore; ~**ier**
['frʌntɪə*] *n* frontiera; ~ **page** *n* prima
pagina; ~ **room** (BRIT) *n* salotto; ~-**wheel**
drive *n* trasmissione *f* anteriore

frost [frɔst] *n* gelo; (*also: hoar*~) brina;
~**bite** *n* congelamento; ~**ed** *adj* (*glass*)
smerigliato(a); ~**y** *adj* (*weather, look*)
gelido(a)

froth ['frɔθ] *n* spuma; schiuma

frown [fraun] *vi* accigliarsi

froze [frəuz] *pt of* **freeze**; **frozen** *pp of*
freeze

fruit [fruːt] *n inv* (*also fig*) frutto;
(*collectively*) frutta; ~**erer** *n* fruttivendolo;
~**erer's (shop)** *n*: **at the** ~**erer's (shop)**
dal fruttivendolo; ~**ful** *adj* fruttuoso(a);
~**ion** [fruːˈɪʃən] *n*: **to come to** ~**ion**
realizzarsi; ~ **juice** *n* succo di frutta; ~
machine (BRIT) *n* macchina *f* mangiasoldi
inv; ~ **salad** *n* macedonia

frustrate [frʌsˈtreɪt] *vt* frustrare

fry [fraɪ] (*pt, pp* **fried**) *vt* friggere; *see also*
small; ~**ing pan** *n* padella

ft. *abbr* = **foot**; **feet**

fuddy-duddy ['fʌdɪdʌdɪ] *n* matusa

fudge [fʌdʒ] *n* (CULIN) specie di caramella
a base di latte, burro e zucchero

fuel [fjuəl] *n* (*for heating*) combustibile *m*;
(*for propelling*) carburante *m*; ~ **tank** *n*
deposito *m* nafta *inv*; (*on vehicle*)
serbatoio (della benzina)

fugitive ['fjuːdʒɪtɪv] *n* fuggitivo/a,
profugo/a

fulfil [fulˈfɪl] *vt* (*function*) compiere;
(*order*) eseguire; (*wish, desire*) soddisfare,
appagare; ~**ment** *n* (*of wishes*)
soddisfazione *f*, appagamento; **sense of**
~**ment** soddisfazione

full [ful] *adj* pieno(a); (*details, skirt*)
ampio(a) ♦ *adv* (*very*): **to know** ~ **well that**
sapere benissimo che; **I'm** ~ **(up)** sono
pieno; **a** ~ **two hours** due ore intere; **at** ~
speed a tutta velocità; **in** ~ per intero; ~
employment *n* piena occupazione; ~-
length *adj* (*film*) a lungometraggio; (*coat,*
novel) lungo(a); (*portrait*) in piedi; ~
moon *n* luna piena; ~-**scale** *adj* (*attack,*
war) su larga scala; (*model*) in grandezza
naturale; ~ **stop** *n* punto; ~-**time** *adj,*
adv (*work*) a tempo pieno; ~**y** *adv*
interamente, pienamente, completamente;
(*at least*) almeno; ~**y-fledged** *adj*
(*teacher, member etc*) a tutti gli effetti

fulsome ['fulsəm] (*pej*) *adj* (*praise,*
compliments) esagerato(a)

fumble ['fʌmbl] *vi*: **to** ~ **with sth**
armeggiare con qc

fume [fjuːm] *vi* essere furioso(a); ~**s** *npl*
esalazioni *fpl*, vapori *mpl*

fun [fʌn] *n* divertimento, spasso; **to have**
~ divertirsi; **for** ~ per scherzo; **to make**
~ **of** prendersi gioco di

function ['fʌŋkʃən] *n* funzione *f*;
cerimonia, ricevimento ♦ *vi* funzionare;
~**al** *adj* funzionale

fund [fʌnd] *n* fondo, cassa; (*source*) fondo;
(*store*) riserva; ~**s** *npl* (*money*) fondi *mpl*

fundamental [fʌndəˈmɛntl] *adj*
fondamentale

funeral ['fjuːnərəl] *n* funerale *m*; ~
parlour *n* impresa di pompe funebri; ~
service *n* ufficio funebre

fun fair (BRIT) *n* luna park *m inv*

fungi ['fʌŋgaɪ] *npl of* **fungus**

fungus ['fʌŋgəs] (*pl* **fungi**) *n* fungo; (*mould*) muffa

funnel ['fʌnl] *n* imbuto; (*of ship*) ciminiera

funny ['fʌnɪ] *adj* divertente, buffo(a); (*strange*) strano(a), bizzarro(a)

fur [fə:*] *n* pelo; pelliccia; (*BRIT: in kettle etc*) deposito calcare; **~ coat** *n* pelliccia

furious ['fjʊərɪəs] *adj* furioso(a); (*effort*) accanito(a)

furlong ['fə:lɔŋ] *n = 201.17 m* (*termine ippico*)

furlough ['fə:ləu] *n* congedo, permesso

furnace ['fə:nɪs] *n* fornace *f*

furnish ['fə:nɪʃ] *vt* ammobiliare; (*supply*) fornire; **~ings** *npl* mobili *mpl*, mobilia

furniture ['fə:nɪtʃə*] *n* mobili *mpl*; **piece of ~** mobile *m*

furrow ['fʌrəu] *n* solco

furry ['fə:rɪ] *adj* (*animal*) peloso(a)

further ['fə:ðə*] *adj* supplementare, altro(a); nuovo(a); più lontano(a) ♦ *adv* più lontano; (*more*) di più; (*moreover*) inoltre ♦ *vt* favorire, promuovere; **college of ~ education** *n* istituto statale con corsi specializzati (*di formazione professionale, aggiornamento professionale etc*); **~more** [fə:ðə'mɔ:*] *adv* inoltre, per di più

furthest ['fə:ðɪst] *superl* of **far**

fury ['fjʊərɪ] *n* furore *m*

fuse [fju:z] *n* fusibile *m*; (*for bomb etc*) miccia, spoletta ♦ *vt* fondere ♦ *vi* fondersi; **to ~ the lights** (*BRIT: ELEC*) far saltare i fusibili; **~ box** *n* cassetta dei fusibili

fuselage ['fju:zəlɑ:ʒ] *n* fusoliera

fuss [fʌs] *n* agitazione *f*; (*complaining*) storie *fpl*; **to make a ~** fare delle storie; **~y** *adj* (*person*) puntiglioso(a), esigente; che fa le storie; (*dress*) carico(a) di fronzoli; (*style*) elaborato(a)

future ['fju:tʃə*] *adj* futuro(a) ♦ *n* futuro, avvenire *m*; (*LING*) futuro; **in ~** in futuro

fuze [fju:z] (*US*) = **fuse**

fuzzy ['fʌzɪ] *adj* (*PHOT*) indistinto(a), sfocato(a); (*hair*) crespo(a)

G

G [dʒi:] *n* (*MUS*) sol *m*

G7 *abbr* (= *Group of Seven*) G7

gabble ['gæbl] *vi* borbottare; farfugliare

gable ['geɪbl] *n* frontone *m*

gadget ['gædʒɪt] *n* aggeggio

Gaelic ['geɪlɪk] *adj* gaelico(a) ♦ *n* (*LING*) gaelico

gag [gæg] *n* bavaglio; (*joke*) facezia, scherzo ♦ *vt* imbavagliare

gaiety ['geɪɪtɪ] *n* gaiezza

gaily ['geɪlɪ] *adv* allegramente

gain [geɪn] *n* guadagno, profitto ♦ *vt* guadagnare ♦ *vi* (*clock, watch*) andare avanti; (*benefit*): **to ~ (from)** trarre beneficio (da); **to ~ 3lbs (in weight)** aumentare di 3 libbre; **to ~ on sb** (*in race etc*) guadagnare su qn

gait [geɪt] *n* andatura

gal. *abbr* = **gallon**

galaxy ['gæləksɪ] *n* galassia

gale [geɪl] *n* vento forte; burrasca

gallant ['gælənt] *adj* valoroso(a); (*towards ladies*) galante, cortese

gall bladder ['gɔ:l-] *n* cistifellea

gallery ['gælərɪ] *n* galleria

galley ['gælɪ] *n* (*ship's kitchen*) cambusa

gallon ['gælən] *n* gallone *m* (= *8 pints*; *BRIT* = 4.543*l*; *US* = 3.785*l*)

gallop ['gæləp] *n* galoppo ♦ *vi* galoppare

gallows ['gæləuz] *n* forca

gallstone ['gɔ:lstəun] *n* calcolo biliare

galore [gə'lɔ:*] *adv* a iosa, a profusione

galvanize ['gælvənaɪz] *vt* galvanizzare

gambit ['gæmbɪt] *n* (*fig*): **(opening) ~** prima mossa

gamble ['gæmbl] *n* azzardo, rischio calcolato ♦ *vt*, *vi* giocare; **to ~ on** (*fig*) giocare su; **~r** *n* giocatore/trice d'azzardo; **gambling** *n* gioco d'azzardo

game [geɪm] *n* gioco; (*event*) partita; (*TENNIS*) game *m* *inv*; (*CULIN, HUNTING*) selvaggina ♦ *adj* (*ready*): **to be ~ (for sth/to do)** essere pronto(a) (a qc/a fare); **big ~** selvaggina grossa; **~keeper** *n* guardacaccia *m* *inv*

gammon ['gæmən] n (*bacon*) quarto di maiale; (*ham*) prosciutto affumicato

gamut ['gæmət] n gamma

gang [gæŋ] n banda, squadra ♦ vi: to ~ **up on sb** far combutta contro qn

gangrene ['gæŋgriːn] n cancrena

gangster ['gæŋstə*] n gangster m inv

gangway ['gæŋweɪ] n passerella; (*BRIT: of bus*) corridoio

gaol [dʒeɪl] (*BRIT*) n, vt = **jail**

gap [gæp] n (*space*) buco; (*in time*) intervallo; (*difference*): ~ **(between)** divario (tra)

gape [geɪp] vi (*person*) restare a bocca aperta; (*shirt, hole*) essere spalancato(a); **gaping** adj spalancato(a)

garage ['gærɑːʒ] n garage m inv

garbage ['gɑːbɪdʒ] n (*US*) immondizie fpl, rifiuti mpl; (*inf*) sciocchezze fpl; ~ **can** (*US*) n bidone m della spazzatura

garbled ['gɑːbld] adj deformato(a); ingarbugliato(a)

garden ['gɑːdn] n giardino; ~s npl (*public park*) giardini pubblici; ~**er** n giardiniere/a; ~**ing** n giardinaggio

gargle ['gɑːgl] vi fare gargarismi

garish ['gɛərɪʃ] adj vistoso(a)

garland ['gɑːlənd] n ghirlanda; corona

garlic ['gɑːlɪk] n aglio

garment ['gɑːmənt] n indumento

garnish ['gɑːnɪʃ] vt (*food*) guarnire

garrison ['gærɪsn] n guarnigione f

garrulous ['gærjuləs] adj ciarliero(a), loquace

garter ['gɑːtə*] n giarrettiera

gas [gæs] n gas m inv; (*US: gasoline*) benzina ♦ vt asfissiare con il gas; ~ **cooker** (*BRIT*) n cucina a gas; ~ **cylinder** n bombola del gas; ~ **fire** (*BRIT*) n radiatore m a gas

gash [gæʃ] n sfregio ♦ vt sfregiare

gasket ['gæskɪt] n (*AUT*) guarnizione f

gas mask n maschera f antigas inv

gas meter n contatore m del gas

gasoline ['gæsəliːn] (*US*) n benzina

gasp [gɑːsp] n respiro affannoso, ansito ♦ vi ansare, ansimare; (*in surprise*) restare senza fiato; ~ **out** vt dire affannosamente

gas station (*US*) n distributore m di benzina

gassy ['gæsɪ] adj gassoso(a)

gate [geɪt] n cancello; (*at airport*) uscita; ~**crash** (*BRIT*) vt partecipare senza invito a; ~**way** n porta

gather ['gæðə*] vt (*flowers, fruit*) cogliere; (*pick up*) raccogliere; (*assemble*) radunare; raccogliere; (*understand*) capire; (*SEWING*) increspare ♦ vi (*assemble*) radunarsi; to ~ **speed** acquistare velocità; ~**ing** n adunanza

gauche [ɡəʊʃ] adj goffo(a), maldestro(a)

gaudy ['ɡɔːdɪ] adj vistoso(a)

gauge [geɪdʒ] n (*instrument*) indicatore m ♦ vt misurare; (*fig*) valutare

gaunt [ɡɔːnt] adj scarno(a); (*grim, desolate*) desolato(a)

gauntlet ['ɡɔːntlɪt] n guanto; (*fig*): to **run the ~ through an angry crowd** passare sotto il fuoco di una folla ostile; **to throw down the ~** gettare il guanto

gauze [ɡɔːz] n garza

gave [ɡeɪv] pt of **give**

gay [ɡeɪ] adj (*homosexual*) omosessuale; (*cheerful*) gaio(a), allegro(a); (*colour*) vivace, vivo(a)

gaze [ɡeɪz] n sguardo fisso ♦ vi: to ~ **at** guardare fisso

gazetteer [ɡæzɪˈtɪə*] n indice m dei nomi geografici

GB abbr = **Great Britain**

GCE (*BRIT*) n abbr (= *General Certificate of Education*) ≈ maturità

GCSE (*BRIT*) n abbr = *General Certificate of Secondary Education*

gear [ɡɪə*] n attrezzi mpl, equipaggiamento; (*TECH*) ingranaggio; (*AUT*) marcia ♦ vt (*fig: adapt*): to ~ **sth to** adattare qc a; **in top** or (*US*) **high/low** ~ in quarta (or quinta)/seconda; **in** ~ in marcia; ~ **box** n scatola del cambio; ~ **lever** (*US* ~ **shift**) n leva del cambio

geese [ɡiːs] npl of **goose**

gel [dʒel] n gel m inv

gelignite ['dʒelɪɡnaɪt] n nitroglicerina

gem [dʒem] n gemma

Gemini ['dʒemɪnaɪ] n Gemelli mpl

gender ['dʒendə*] n genere m

general ['dʒɛnərl] *n* generale *m* ♦ *adj*
generale; **in ~** in genere; **~ delivery** (*US*)
n fermo posta *m*; **~ election** *n* elezioni
fpl generali; **~ly** *adv* generalmente

general practitioner *n* medico generico

generate ['dʒɛnəreɪt] *vt* generare

generation [dʒɛnə'reɪʃən] *n* generazione
f

generator ['dʒɛnəreɪtə*] *n* generatore
m

generosity [dʒɛnə'rɒsɪtɪ] *n* generosità

generous ['dʒɛnərəs] *adj* generoso(a);
(*copious*) abbondante

genetic engineering [dʒɪ'nɛtɪkɛndʒɪ-
'nɪərɪŋ] *n* ingegneria genetica

genetic fingerprinting *n* rilevamento
delle impronte genetiche

Geneva [dʒɪ'niːvə] *n* Ginevra

genial ['dʒiːnɪəl] *adj* geniale, cordiale

genitals ['dʒɛnɪtlz] *npl* genitali *mpl*

genius ['dʒiːnɪəs] *n* genio

Genoa ['dʒɛnəuə] *n* Genova

gent [dʒɛnt] *n abbr* = **gentleman**

genteel [dʒɛn'tiːl] *adj* raffinato(a),
distinto(a)

gentle ['dʒɛntl] *adj* delicato(a); (*person*)
dolce

gentleman ['dʒɛntlmən] *n* signore *m*;
(*well-bred man*) gentiluomo

gently ['dʒɛntlɪ] *adv* delicatamente

gentry ['dʒɛntrɪ] *n* nobiltà minore

gents [dʒɛnts] *n* W.C. *m* (per signori)

genuine ['dʒɛnjuɪn] *adj* autentico(a);
sincero(a)

geography [dʒɪ'ɒgrəfɪ] *n* geografia

geology [dʒɪ'ɒlədʒɪ] *n* geologia

geometric(al) [dʒɪə'mɛtrɪk(l)] *adj*
geometrico(a)

geometry [dʒɪ'ɒmɛtrɪ] *n* geometria

geranium [dʒɪ'reɪnjəm] *n* geranio

geriatric [dʒɛrɪ'ætrɪk] *adj* geriatrico(a)

germ [dʒɜːm] *n* (*MED*) microbo; (*BIOL*, *fig*)
germe *m*

German ['dʒɜːmən] *adj* tedesco(a) ♦ *n*
tedesco/a; (*LING*) tedesco; **~ measles**
(*BRIT*) *n* rosolia

Germany ['dʒɜːmənɪ] *n* Germania

gesture ['dʒɛstjə*] *n* gesto

KEYWORD

get [gɛt] (*pt*, *pp* **got**, (*US*) *pp* **gotten**) *vi* **1**
(*become*, *be*) diventare, farsi; **to ~ old**
invecchiare; **to ~ tired** stancarsi; **to ~
drunk** ubriacarsi; **to ~ killed** venire *or*
rimanere ucciso(a); **when do I ~ paid?**
quando mi pagate?; **it's ~ting late** si sta
facendo tardi

2 (*go*): **to ~ to/from** andare a/da; **to ~
home** arrivare *or* tornare a casa; **how
did you ~ here?** come sei venuto?

3 (*begin*) mettersi a, cominciare a; **to ~
to know sb** incominciare a conoscere qn;
let's ~ going *or* **started** muoviamoci

4 (*modal aux vb*): **you've got to do it**
devi farlo

♦ *vt* **1**: **to ~ sth done** (*do*) fare qc; (*have
done*) far fare qc; **to ~ one's hair cut**
farsi tagliare i capelli; **to ~ sb to do sth**
far fare qc a qn

2 (*obtain*: *money*, *permission*, *results*)
ottenere; (*find*: *job*, *flat*) trovare; (*fetch*:
person, *doctor*) chiamare; (: *object*)
prendere; **to ~ sth for sb** prendere *or*
procurare qc a qn; **~ me Mr Jones,
please** (*TEL*) mi passi il signor Jones, per
favore; **can I ~ you a drink?** le posso
offrire da bere?

3 (*receive*: *present*, *letter*, *prize*) ricevere;
(*acquire*: *reputation*) farsi; **how much did
you ~ for the painting?** quanto ti hanno
dato per il quadro?

4 (*catch*) prendere; (*hit*: *target etc*) colpire;
to ~ sb by the arm/throat afferrare qn
per un braccio/alla gola; **~ him!**
prendetelo!

5 (*take*, *move*) portare; **to ~ sth to sb** far
avere qc a qn; **do you think we'll ~ it
through the door?** pensi che riusciremo
a farlo passare per la porta?

6 (*catch*, *take*: *plane*, *bus etc*) prendere

7 (*understand*) afferrare; (*hear*) sentire;
I've got it! ci sono arrivato!, ci sono!; **I'm
sorry, I didn't ~ your name** scusi, non
ho capito (*or* sentito) il suo nome

8 (*have*, *possess*): **to have got** avere; **how
many have you got?** quanti ne ha?

get about *vi* muoversi; (*news*)

diffondersi

get along *vi* (*agree*) andare d'accordo; (*depart*) andarsene; (*manage*) = **get by**

get at *vt fus* (*attack*) prendersela con; (*reach*) raggiungere, arrivare a

get away *vi* partire, andarsene; (*escape*) scappare

get away with *vt fus* cavarsela; farla franca

get back *vi* (*return*) ritornare, tornare ♦ *vt* riottenere, riavere

get by *vi* (*pass*) passare; (*manage*) farcela

get down *vi, vt fus* scendere ♦ *vt* far scendere; (*depress*) buttare giù

get down to *vt fus* (*work*) mettersi a (fare)

get in *vi* entrare; (*train*) arrivare; (*arrive home*) ritornare, tornare

get into *vt fus* entrare in; **to ~ into a rage** incavolarsi

get off *vi* (*from train etc*) scendere; (*depart: person, car*) andare via; (*escape*) cavarsela ♦ *vt* (*remove: clothes, stain*) levare ♦ *vt fus* (*train, bus*) scendere da

get on *vi* (*at exam etc*) andare; (*agree*): **to ~ on (with)** andare d'accordo (con) ♦ *vt fus* montare in; (*horse*) montare su

get out *vi* uscire; (*of vehicle*) scendere ♦ *vt* tirar fuori, far uscire

get out of *vt fus* uscire da; (*duty etc*) evitare

get over *vt fus* (*illness*) riaversi da

get round *vt fus* aggirare; (*fig: person*) rigirare

get through *vi* (TEL) avere la linea

get through to *vt fus* (TEL) parlare a

get together *vi* riunirsi ♦ *vt* raccogliere; (*people*) adunare

get up *vi* (*rise*) alzarsi ♦ *vt fus* salire su per

get up to *vt fus* (*reach*) raggiungere; (*prank etc*) fare

getaway ['gɛtəweɪ] *n* fuga

geyser ['giːzə*] *n* (BRIT) scaldabagno; (GEO) geyser *m inv*

Ghana ['gɑːnə] *n* Ghana *m*

ghastly ['gɑːstlɪ] *adj* orribile, orrendo(a); (*pale*) spettrale

gherkin ['gəːkɪn] *n* cetriolino

ghetto blaster ['gɛtəʊblɑːstə*] *n* maxistereo *m inv* portatile

ghost [gəʊst] *n* fantasma *m*, spettro

giant ['dʒaɪənt] *n* gigante *m* ♦ *adj* gigantesco(a), enorme

gibberish ['dʒɪbərɪʃ] *n* parole *fpl* senza senso

gibe [dʒaɪb] *n* = **jibe**

giblets ['dʒɪblɪts] *npl* frattaglie *fpl*

Gibraltar [dʒɪˈbrɔːltə*] *n* Gibilterra

giddy ['gɪdɪ] *adj* (*dizzy*): **to be ~** aver le vertigini

gift [gɪft] *n* regalo; (*donation, ability*) dono; **~ed** *adj* dotato(a); **~ token** *n* buono *m* omaggio *inv*; **~ voucher** *n* = **~ token**

gigantic [dʒaɪˈgæntɪk] *adj* gigantesco(a)

giggle ['gɪgl] *vi* ridere scioccamente

gill [dʒɪl] *n* (*measure*) = 0.25 pints (BRIT = 0.148l, US = 0.118l)

gills [gɪlz] *npl* (*of fish*) branchie *fpl*

gilt [gɪlt] *n* doratura ♦ *adj* dorato(a); **~-edged** *adj* (COMM) della massima sicurezza

gimmick ['gɪmɪk] *n* trucco

gin [dʒɪn] *n* (*liquor*) gin *m inv*

ginger ['dʒɪndʒə*] *n* zenzero; **~ ale** *n* bibita gassosa allo zenzero; **~ beer** *n* = **~ ale**; **~bread** *n* pan *m* di zenzero

gingerly ['dʒɪndʒəlɪ] *adv* cautamente

gipsy ['dʒɪpsɪ] *n* zingaro/a

giraffe [dʒɪˈrɑːf] *n* giraffa

girder ['gəːdə*] *n* trave *f*

girdle ['gəːdl] *n* (*corset*) guaina

girl [gəːl] *n* ragazza; (*young unmarried woman*) signorina; (*daughter*) figlia, figliola; **~friend** *n* (*of girl*) amica; (*of boy*) ragazza; **~ish** *adj* da ragazza

giro ['dʒaɪrəʊ] *n* (*bank ~*) versamento bancario; (*post office ~*) postagiro; (BRIT: *welfare cheque*) assegno del sussidio di assistenza sociale

girth [gəːθ] *n* circonferenza; (*of horse*) cinghia

gist [dʒɪst] *n* succo

give [gɪv] (*pt* **gave**, *pp* **given**) *vt* dare ♦ *vi* cedere; **to ~ sb sth**, **~ sth to sb** dare qc a

qn; **I'll ~ you £5 for it** te lo pago 5
sterline; **to ~ a cry/sigh** emettere un
grido/sospiro; **to ~ a speech** fare un
discorso; **~ away** *vt* dare via; (*disclose*)
rivelare; (*bride*) **~ back** *vt* rendere; **~ in** *vi* cedere ♦ *vt*
consegnare; **~ off** *vt* emettere; **~ out** *vt*
distribuire; annunciare; **~ up** *vi*
rinunciare ♦ *vt* rinunciare a; **to ~ up
smoking** smettere di fumare; **to ~ up
o.s. up** arrendersi; **~ way** *vi* cedere; (*BRIT:
AUT*) dare la precedenza; **given** *pp of* **give**

glacier ['glæsɪə*] *n* ghiacciaio
glad [glæd] *adj* lieto(a), contento(a)
gladly ['glædlɪ] *adv* volentieri
glamorous ['glæmərəs] *adj* affascinante,
seducente
glamour ['glæmə*] *n* fascino
glance [glɑːns] *n* occhiata, sguardo ♦ *vi*:
to ~ at dare un'occhiata a; **to ~ off**
(*bullet*) rimbalzare su; **glancing** *adj*
(*blow*) che colpisce di striscio
gland [glænd] *n* ghiandola
glare [glɛə*] *n* (*of anger*) sguardo furioso;
(*of light*) riverbero, luce *f* abbagliante; (*of
publicity*) chiasso ♦ *vi* abbagliare; **to ~ at**
guardare male; **glaring** *adj* (*mistake*)
madornale
glass [glɑːs] *n* (*substance*) vetro; (*tumbler*)
bicchiere *m*; **~es** *npl* (*spectacles*) occhiali
mpl; **~house** *n* serra; **~ware** *n* vetrame
m; **~y** *adj* (*eyes*) vitreo(a)
glaze [gleɪz] *vt* (*door*) fornire di vetri;
(*pottery*) smaltare ♦ *n* smalto; **~d** *adj*
(*eyes*) vitreo(a); (*pottery*) smaltato(a)
glazier ['gleɪzɪə*] *n* vetraio
gleam [gliːm] *vi* luccicare
glean [gliːn] *vt* (*information*) racimolare
glee [gliː] *n* allegrezza, gioia
glen [glɛn] *n* valletta
glib [glɪb] *adj* dalla parola facile; facile
glide [glaɪd] *vi* scivolare; (*AVIAT, birds*)
planare; **~r** *n* (*AVIAT*) aliante *m*; **gliding** *n*
(*AVIAT*) volo a vela
glimmer ['glɪmə*] *n* barlume *m*
glimpse [glɪmps] *n* impressione *f* fugace
♦ *vt* vedere al volo
glint [glɪnt] *vi* luccicare
glisten ['glɪsn] *vi* luccicare

glitter ['glɪtə*] *vi* scintillare
gloat [gləut] *vi*: **to ~ (over)** gongolare di
piacere (per)
global ['gləubl] *adj* globale; **~ warming**
n riscaldamento dell'atmosfera terrestre
globe [gləub] *n* globo, sfera
gloom [gluːm] *n* oscurità, buio; (*sadness*)
tristezza, malinconia; **~y** *adj* scuro(a);
fosco(a), triste
glorious ['glɔːrɪəs] *adj* glorioso(a);
magnifico(a)
glory ['glɔːrɪ] *n* gloria; splendore *m*
gloss [glɔs] *n* (*shine*) lucentezza; (*also: ~
paint*) vernice *f* a olio; **~ over** *vt fus*
scivolare su
glossary ['glɔsərɪ] *n* glossario
glossy ['glɔsɪ] *adj* lucente
glove [glʌv] *n* guanto; **~ compartment**
n (*AUT*) vano portaoggetti
glow [gləu] *vi* ardere; (*face*) essere
luminoso(a)
glower ['glauə*] *vi*: **to ~ (at sb)** guardare
(qn) in cagnesco
glue [gluː] *n* colla ♦ *vt* incollare
glum [glʌm] *adj* abbattuto(a)
glut [glʌt] *n* eccesso
glutton ['glʌtn] *n* ghiottone/a; **a ~ for
work** un(a) patito(a) del lavoro
gnarled [nɑːld] *adj* nodoso(a)
gnat [næt] *n* moscerino
gnaw [nɔː] *vt* rodere
go [gəu] (*pt* **went**, *pp* **gone**; *pl* **~es**) *vi*
andare; (*depart*) partire, andarsene;
(*work*) funzionare; (*time*) passare; (*break
etc*) rompersi; (*be sold*): **to ~ for £10**
essere venduto per 10 sterline; (*fit, suit*):
to ~ with andare bene con; (*become*): **to ~
pale** diventare pallido(a); **to ~ mouldy**
ammuffire ♦ *n*: **to have a ~ (at)** provare;
to be on the ~ essere in moto; **whose ~
is it?** a chi tocca?; **he's going to do** sta
per fare; **to ~ for a walk** andare a fare
una passeggiata; **to ~ dancing/shopping**
andare a ballare/fare la spesa; **just then
the bell went** proprio allora suonò il
campanello; **how did it ~?** com'è andato?;
to ~ round the back/by the shop
passare da dietro/davanti al negozio; **~
about** *vi* (*also: ~ round: rumour*) correre,

circolare ♦ *vt fus*: **how do I ~ about this?** qual'è la prassi per questo?; **~ ahead** *vi* andare avanti; **~ along** *vi* andare, avanzare ♦ *vt fus* percorrere; **to ~ along with** (*plan, idea*) appoggiare; **~ away** *vi* partire, andarsene; **~ back** *vi* tornare, ritornare; **~ back on** *vt fus* (*promise*) non mantenere; **~ by** *vi* (*years, time*) scorrere ♦ *vt fus* attenersi a, seguire (alla lettera); prestar fede a; **~ down** *vi* scendere; (*ship*) affondare; (*sun*) tramontare ♦ *vt fus* scendere; **~ for** *vt fus* (*fetch*) andare a prendere; (*like*) andar matto(a) per; (*attack*) attaccare; saltare addosso a; **~ in** *vi* entrare; **~ in for** *vt fus* (*competition*) iscriversi a; (*be interested in*) interessarsi di; **~ into** *vt fus* entrare in; (*investigate*) indagare, esaminare; (*embark on*) lanciarsi in; **~ off** *vi* partire, andar via; (*food*) guastarsi; (*explode*) esplodere, scoppiare; (*event*) passare ♦ *vt fus*: **I've gone off chocolate** la cioccolata non mi piace più; **the gun went off** il fucile si scaricò; **~ on** *vi* continuare; (*happen*) succedere; **to ~ on doing** continuare a fare; **~ out** *vi* uscire; (*couple*): **they went out for 3 years** sono stati insieme per 3 anni; (*fire, light*) spegnersi; **~ over** *vi* (*ship*) ribaltarsi ♦ *vt fus* (*check*) esaminare; **~ through** *vt fus* (*town etc*) attraversare; (*files, papers*) passare in rassegna; (*examine: list etc*) leggere da cima a fondo; **~ up** *vi* salire ♦ *vt fus* fare a meno di

goad [gəud] *vt* spronare

go-ahead *adj* intraprendente ♦ *n* via *m*

goal [gəul] *n* (SPORT) gol *m*, rete *f*; (: *place*) porta; (*fig: aim*) fine *m*, scopo; **~keeper** *n* portiere *m*; **~-post** *n* palo (della porta)

goat [gəut] *n* capra

gobble ['gɔbl] *vt* (*also*: ~ **down**, ~ **up**) ingoiare

go-between *n* intermediario/a

god [gɔd] *n* dio; **G~** *n* Dio; **~child** *n* figlioccio/a; **~daughter** *n* figlioccia; **~dess** *n* dea; **~father** *n* padrino; **~forsaken** *adj* desolato(a), sperduto(a); **~mother** *n* madrina; **~send** *n* dono del cielo; **~son** *n* figlioccio

goggles ['gɔglz] *npl* occhiali *mpl* (di protezione)

going ['gəuiŋ] *n* (*conditions*) andare *m*, stato del terreno ♦ *adj*: **the ~ rate** la tariffa in vigore

gold [gəuld] *n* oro ♦ *adj* d'oro; **~en** *adj* (*made of ~*) d'oro; (~ *in colour*) dorato(a); **~fish** *n* pesce *m* dorato *or* rosso; **~mine** *n* (*also fig*) miniera d'oro; **~-plated** *adj* placcato(a) oro *inv*; **~smith** *n* orefice *m*, orafo

golf [gɔlf] *n* golf *m*; **~ ball** *n* (*for game*) pallina da golf; (*on typewriter*) pallina; **~ club** *n* circolo di golf; (*stick*) bastone *m or* mazza da golf; **~ course** *n* campo di golf; **~er** *n* giocatore/trice di golf

gondola ['gɔndələ] *n* gondola

gone [gɔn] *pp of* go ♦ *adj* partito(a)

gong [gɔŋ] *n* gong *m inv*

good [gud] *adj* buono(a); (*kind*) buono(a), gentile; (*child*) bravo(a) ♦ *n* bene *m*; **~s** *npl* (COMM *etc*) beni *mpl*; merci *fpl*; **~!** bene!, ottimo!; **to be ~ at** essere bravo(a) in; **to be ~ for** andare bene per; **it's ~ for you** fa bene; **would you be ~ enough to ...?** avrebbe la gentilezza di ...?; **a ~ deal (of)** molto(a), una buona quantità (di); **a ~ many** molti(e); **to make ~** (*loss, damage*) compensare; **it's no ~ complaining** brontolare non serve a niente; **for ~** per sempre, definitivamente; **~ morning!** buon giorno!; **~ afternoon/evening!** buona sera!; **~ night!** buona notte!; **~bye** *excl* arrivederci!; **G~ Friday** *n* Venerdì Santo; **~-looking** *adj* bello(a); **~-natured** *adj* affabile; **~ness** *n* (*of person*) bontà; **for ~ness sake!** per amor di Dio!; **~ness gracious!** santo cielo!, mamma mia!; **~s train** (BRIT) *n* treno *m* merci *inv*; **~will** *n* amicizia, benevolenza

goose [gu:s] *n* (*pl* **geese**) oca

gooseberry ['guzbəri] *n* uva spina; **to play ~** (BRIT) tenere la candela

gooseflesh ['gu:sfleʃ] *n* pelle *f* d'oca

goose pimples *npl* pelle *f* d'oca

gore [gɔ:*] *vt* incornare ♦ *n* sangue *m* (coagulato)

gorge [gɔ:dʒ] *n* gola ♦ *vt*: **to ~ o.s. (on)**

ingozzarsi (di)
gorgeous ['gɔːdʒəs] *adj* magnifico(a)
gorilla [gə'rɪlə] *n* gorilla *m inv*
gorse [gɔːs] *n* ginestrone *m*
gory ['gɔːrɪ] *adj* sanguinoso(a)
go-slow (*BRIT*) *n* rallentamento dei lavori
(*per agitazione sindacale*)
gospel ['gɔspl] *n* vangelo
gossip ['gɔsɪp] *n* chiacchiere *fpl*;
pettegolezzi *mpl*; (*person*) pettegolo/a ♦ *vi*
chiacchierare
got [gɔt] *pt, pp of* **get**; **~ten** (*US*) *pp of* **get**
gout [gaut] *n* gotta
govern ['gʌvən] *vt* governare
governess ['gʌvənɪs] *n* governante *f*
government ['gʌvnmənt] *n* governo
governor ['gʌvənə*] *n* (*of state, bank*)
governatore *m*; (*of school, hospital*)
amministratore *m*; (*BRIT: of prison*)
direttore/trice
gown [gaun] *n* vestito lungo; (*of teacher,*
BRIT: of judge) toga
G.P. *n abbr* = **general practitioner**
grab [græb] *vt* afferrare, arraffare;
(*property, power*) impadronirsi di ♦ *vi*: **to**
~ at cercare di afferrare
grace [greɪs] *n* grazia ♦ *vt* onorare; **5**
days' ~ dilazione *f* di 5 giorni; **~ful** *adj*
elegante, aggraziato(a); **gracious**
['greɪʃəs] *adj* grazioso(a); misericor-
dioso(a)
grade [greɪd] *n* (*COMM*) qualità *f inv*;
classe *f*; categoria; (*in hierarchy*) grado;
(*SCOL: mark*) voto; (*US: school class*) classe
♦ *vt* classificare; ordinare; graduare; **~**
crossing (*US*) *n* passaggio a livello; **~**
school (*US*) *n* scuola elementare
gradient ['greɪdɪənt] *n* pendenza,
inclinazione *f*
gradual ['grædjuəl] *adj* graduale; **~ly** *adv*
man mano, a poco a poco
graduate [*n* 'grædjuɪt, *vb* 'grædjueɪt] *n* (*of*
university) laureato/a; (*US: of high school*)
diplomato/a ♦ *vi* laurearsi; diplomarsi;
graduation [-'eɪʃən] *n* (*ceremony*)
consegna delle lauree (*or* dei diplomi)
graffiti [grə'fiːtɪ] *npl* graffiti *mpl*
graft [grɑːft] *n* (*AGR, MED*) innesto;
(*bribery*) corruzione *f*; (*BRIT: hard work*):

it's hard **~** è un lavoraccio ♦ *vt* innestare
grain [greɪn] *n* grano; (*of sand*) granello;
(*of wood*) venatura
gram [græm] *n* grammo
grammar ['græmə*] *n* grammatica; **~**
school (*BRIT*) *n* ≈ liceo
grammatical [grə'mætɪkl] *adj*
grammaticale
gramme [græm] *n* = **gram**
grand [grænd] *adj* grande, magnifico(a);
grandioso(a); **~children** *npl* nipoti *mpl*;
~dad (*inf*) *n* nonno; **~daughter** *n* nipote
f; **~eur** ['grændjə*] *n* grandiosità;
~father *n* nonno; **~ma** (*inf*) *n* nonna;
~mother *n* nonna; **~pa** (*inf*) *n* = **~dad**;
~parents *npl* nonni *mpl*; **~ piano** *n*
pianoforte *m* a coda; **~son** *n* nipote *m*;
~stand (*SPORT*) *n* tribuna
granite ['grænɪt] *n* granito
granny ['grænɪ] (*inf*) *n* nonna
grant [grɑːnt] *vt* accordare; (*a request*)
accogliere; (*admit*) ammettere, concedere
♦ *n* (*SCOL*) borsa; (*ADMIN*) sussidio,
sovvenzione *f*; **to take sth for ~ed** dare
qc per scontato; **to take sb for ~ed** dare
per scontata la presenza di qn
granulated ['grænjuleɪtɪd] *adj*: **~ sugar**
zucchero cristallizzato
granule ['grænjuːl] *n* granello
grape [greɪp] *n* chicco d'uva, acino
grapefruit ['greɪpfruːt] *n* pompelmo
graph [grɑːf] *n* grafico; **~ic** *adj* grafico(a);
(*vivid*) vivido(a); **~ics** *n* grafica ♦ *npl*
illustrazioni *fpl*
grapple ['græpl] *vi*: **to ~ with** essere alle
prese con
grasp [grɑːsp] *vt* afferrare ♦ *n* (*grip*)
presa; (*fig*) potere *m*; comprensione *f*;
~ing *adj* avido(a)
grass [grɑːs] *n* erba; **~hopper** *n*
cavalletta; **~-roots** *adj* di base
grate [greɪt] *n* graticola (del focolare)
♦ *vi* cigolare, stridere ♦ *vt* (*CULIN*)
grattugiare
grateful ['greɪtful] *adj* grato(a),
riconoscente
grater ['greɪtə*] *n* grattugia
grating ['greɪtɪŋ] *n* (*iron bars*) grata
♦ *adj* (*noise*) stridente, stridulo(a)

gratitude ['grætɪtjuːd] *n* gratitudine *f*

gratuity [grə'tjuːɪtɪ] *n* mancia

grave [greɪv] *n* tomba ♦ *adj* grave, serio(a)

gravel ['grævl] *n* ghiaia

gravestone ['greɪvstəun] *n* pietra tombale

graveyard ['greɪvjɑːd] *n* cimitero

gravity ['grævɪtɪ] *n* (*PHYSICS*) gravità; pesantezza; (*seriousness*) gravità, serietà

gravy ['greɪvɪ] *n* intingolo della carne; salsa

gray [greɪ] *adj* = grey

graze [greɪz] *vi* pascolare, pascere ♦ *vt* (*touch lightly*) sfiorare; (*scrape*) escoriare ♦ *n* (*MED*) escoriazione *f*

grease [griːs] *n* (*fat*) grasso; (*lubricant*) lubrificante *m* ♦ *vt* ingrassare; lubrificare; **~proof paper** (*BRIT*) *n* carta oleata; **greasy** *adj* grasso(a), untuoso(a)

great [greɪt] *adj* grande; (*inf*) magnifico(a), meraviglioso(a); **G~ Britain** *n* Gran Bretagna; **~-grandfather** *n* bisnonno; **~-grandmother** *n* bisnonna; **~ly** *adv* molto; **~ness** *n* grandezza

Greece [griːs] *n* Grecia

greed [griːd] *n* (*also*: ~iness) avarizia; (*for food*) golosità, ghiottoneria; **~y** *adj* avido(a); goloso(a), ghiotto(a)

Greek [griːk] *adj* greco(a) ♦ *n* greco/a; (*LING*) greco

green [griːn] *adj* verde; (*inexperienced*) inesperto(a), ingenuo(a) ♦ *n* verde *m*; (*stretch of grass*) prato; (*on golf course*) green *m inv*; **~s** *npl* (*vegetables*) verdura; **~ belt** *n* (*round town*) cintura di verde; **~ card** *n* (*BRIT*: *AUT*) carta verde; (*US*: *ADMIN*) permesso di soggiorno e di lavoro; **~ery** *n* verde *m*; **~grocer** (*BRIT*) *n* fruttivendolo/a, erbivendolo/a; **~house** *n* serra; **~house effect** *n* effetto serra; **~house gas** *n* gas responsabile dell'effetto serra; **~ish** *adj* verdastro(a)

Greenland ['griːnlənd] *n* Groenlandia

greet [griːt] *vt* salutare; **~ing** *n* saluto; **~ing(s) card** *n* cartolina d'auguri

gregarious [grə'gɛərɪəs] *adj* (*person*) socievole

grenade [grə'neɪd] *n* (*also*: hand ~) granata

grew [gruː] *pt of* **grow**

grey [greɪ] *adj* grigio(a); **~-haired** *adj* dai capelli grigi; **~hound** *n* levriere *m*

grid [grɪd] *n* grata; (*ELEC*) rete *f*

gridlock ['grɪdlɒk] *n* (*traffic jam*) paralisi *f inv* del traffico

grief [griːf] *n* dolore *m*

grievance ['griːvəns] *n* lagnanza

grieve [griːv] *vi* addolorarsi; rattristarsi ♦ *vt* addolorare; **to ~ for sb** (*dead person*) piangere qn

grievous ['griːvəs] *adj*: **~ bodily harm** (*LAW*) aggressione *f*

grill [grɪl] *n* (*on cooker*) griglia; (*also*: mixed ~) grigliata mista ♦ *vt* (*BRIT*) cuocere ai ferri; (*inf*: *question*) interrogare senza sosta

grille [grɪl] *n* grata; (*AUT*) griglia

grim [grɪm] *adj* sinistro(a), brutto(a)

grimace [grɪ'meɪs] *n* smorfia ♦ *vi* fare smorfie; fare boccacce

grime [graɪm] *n* sudiciume *m*

grin [grɪn] *n* sorriso smagliante ♦ *vi* fare un gran sorriso

grind [graɪnd] (*pt, pp* **ground**) *vt* macinare; (*make sharp*) arrotare ♦ *n* (*work*) sgobbata

grip [grɪp] *n* impugnatura; presa; (*holdall*) borsa da viaggio ♦ *vt* (*object*) afferrare; (*attention*) catturare; **to come to ~s with** affrontare; cercare di risolvere

gripping ['grɪpɪŋ] *adj* avvincente

grisly ['grɪzlɪ] *adj* macabro(a), orrido(a)

gristle ['grɪsl] *n* cartilagine *f*

grit [grɪt] *n* ghiaia; (*courage*) fegato ♦ *vt* (*road*) coprire di sabbia; **to ~ one's teeth** stringere i denti

groan [grəun] *n* gemito ♦ *vi* gemere

grocer ['grəusə*] *n* negoziante *m* di generi alimentari; **~ies** *npl* provviste *fpl*; **~'s (shop)** *n* negozio di (generi) alimentari

groggy ['grɒgɪ] *adj* barcollante

groin [grɔɪn] *n* inguine *m*

groom [gruːm] *n* palafreniere *m*; (*also*: bride~) sposo ♦ *vt* (*horse*) strigliare; (*fig*): **to ~ sb for** avviare qn a; **well-~ed** (*person*) curato(a)

groove [gru:v] *n* scanalatura, solco

grope [grəup] *vi*: **to ~ for** cercare a tastoni

gross [grəus] *adj* grossolano(a); (*COMM*) lordo(a); **~ly** *adv* (*greatly*) molto

grotesque [grəu'tɛsk] *adj* grottesco(a)

grotto ['grɔtəu] *n* grotta

grotty ['grɔtɪ] (*inf*) *adj* terribile

ground [graund] *pt, pp of* **grind** ♦ *n* suolo, terra; (*land*) terreno; (*SPORT*) campo; (*reason: gen pl*) ragione *f*; (*US: also:* **~ wire**) terra ♦ *vt* (*plane*) tenere a terra; (*US: ELEC*) mettere la presa a terra a; **~s** *npl* (*of coffee etc*) fondi *mpl*; (*gardens etc*) terreno, giardini *mpl*; **on/to the ~** per/a terra; **to gain/lose ~** guadagnare/perdere terreno; **~ cloth** (*US*) *n* = **~sheet**; **~ing** *n* (*in education*) basi *fpl*; **~less** *adj* infondato(a); **~sheet** (*BRIT*) *n* telone *m* impermeabile; **~ staff** *n* personale *m* di terra; **~ swell** *n* (*fig*) movimento; **~work** *n* preparazione *f*

group [gru:p] *n* gruppo ♦ *vt* (*also:* **~ together**) raggruppare ♦ *vi* (*also:* **~ together**) raggrupparsi

grouse [graus] *n inv* (*bird*) tetraone *m* ♦ *vi* (*complain*) brontolare

grove [grəuv] *n* boschetto

grovel ['grɔvl] *vi* (*fig*): **to ~ (before)** strisciare (di fronte a)

grow [grəu] (*pt* **grew**, *pp* **grown**) *vi* crescere; (*increase*) aumentare; (*develop*) svilupparsi; (*become*): **to ~ rich/weak** arricchirsi/indebolirsi ♦ *vt* coltivare, far crescere; **~ up** *vi* farsi grande, crescere; **~er** *n* coltivatore/trice; **~ing** *adj* (*fear, amount*) crescente

growl [graul] *vi* ringhiare

grown [grəun] *pp of* **grow**; **~-up** *n* adulto/a, grande *m/f*

growth [grəuθ] *n* crescita, sviluppo; (*what has grown*) crescita; (*MED*) escrescenza, tumore *m*

grub [grʌb] *n* larva; (*inf: food*) roba (da mangiare)

grubby ['grʌbɪ] *adj* sporco(a)

grudge [grʌdʒ] *n* rancore *m* ♦ *vt*: **to ~ sb sth** dare qc a qn di malavoglia; invidiare qc a qn; **to bear sb a ~ (for)** serbar

rancore a qn (per)

gruelling ['gruəlɪŋ] *adj* estenuante

gruesome ['gru:səm] *adj* orribile

gruff [grʌf] *adj* rozzo(a)

grumble ['grʌmbl] *vi* brontolare, lagnarsi

grumpy ['grʌmpɪ] *adj* scorbutico(a)

grunt [grʌnt] *vi* grugnire

G-string *n* tanga *m inv*

guarantee [gærən'ti:] *n* garanzia ♦ *vt* garantire

guard [gɑ:d] *n* guardia; (*one man*) guardia, sentinella; (*BRIT: RAIL*) capotreno; (*on machine*) schermo protettivo; (*also:* **fire~**) parafuoco ♦ *vt* fare la guardia a; (*protect*): **to ~ (against)** proteggere (da); **to be on one's ~** stare in guardia; **~ against** *vt fus* guardarsi da; **~ed** *adj* (*fig*) cauto(a), guardingo(a); **~ian** *n* custode *m*; (*of minor*) tutore/trice; **~'s van** (*BRIT*) *n* (*RAIL*) vagone *m* di servizio

guerrilla [gə'rɪlə] *n* guerrigliero

guess [gɛs] *vi* indovinare ♦ *vt* indovinare; (*US*) credere, pensare ♦ *n*: **to take** *or* **have a ~** provare a indovinare; **~work** *n*: **I got the answer by ~work** ho azzeccato la risposta

guest [gɛst] *n* ospite *m/f*; (*in hotel*) cliente *m/f*; **~-house** *n* pensione *f*; **~ room** *n* camera degli ospiti

guffaw [gʌ'fɔ:] *vi* scoppiare in una risata sonora

guidance ['gaɪdəns] *n* guida, direzione *f*

guide [gaɪd] *n* (*person, book etc*) guida; (*BRIT: also:* **girl ~**) giovane esploratrice *f* ♦ *vt* guidare; **~book** *n* guida; **~ dog** *n* cane *m* guida *inv*; **~lines** *npl* (*fig*) indicazioni *fpl*, linee *fpl* direttive

guild [gɪld] *n* arte *f*, corporazione *f*; associazione *f*

guile [gaɪl] *n* astuzia

guillotine ['gɪlətiːn] *n* ghigliottina; (*for paper*) taglierina

guilt [gɪlt] *n* colpevolezza; **~y** *adj* colpevole

guinea pig ['gɪnɪ-] *n* cavia

guise [gaɪz] *n* maschera

guitar [gɪ'tɑ:*] *n* chitarra

gulf [gʌlf] *n* golfo; (*abyss*) abisso

gull [gʌl] *n* gabbiano

gullet ['gʌlɪt] *n* gola
gullible ['gʌlɪbl] *adj* credulo(a)
gully ['gʌlɪ] *n* burrone *m*; gola; canale *m*
gulp [gʌlp] *vi* deglutire; (*from emotion*) avere il nodo in gola ♦ *vt* (*also:* ~ **down**) tracannare, inghiottire
gum [gʌm] *n* (ANAT) gengiva; (*glue*) colla; (*also:* ~**drop**) caramella gommosa; (*also: chewing* ~) chewing-gum *m* ♦ *vt*: **to** ~ **(together)** incollare; ~**boots** (BRIT) *npl* stivali *mpl* di gomma
gumption ['gʌmpʃən] *n* spirito d'iniziativa, buonsenso
gun [gʌn] *n* fucile *m*; (*small*) pistola, rivoltella; (*rifle*) carabina; (*shotgun*) fucile da caccia; (*cannon*) cannone *m*; ~**boat** *n* cannoniera; ~**fire** *n* spari *mpl*; ~**man** *n* bandito armato; ~**point** *n*: **at** ~**point** sotto minaccia di fucile; ~**powder** *n* polvere *f* da sparo; ~**shot** *n* sparo
gurgle ['gə:gl] *vi* gorgogliare
guru ['guru:] *n* guru *m inv*
gush [gʌʃ] *vi* sgorgare; (*fig*) abbandonarsi ad effusioni
gusset ['gʌsɪt] *n* gherone *m*
gust [gʌst] *n* (*of wind*) raffica; (*of smoke*) buffata
gusto ['gʌstəu] *n* entusiasmo
gut [gʌt] *n* intestino, budello; ~**s** *npl* (ANAT) interiora *fpl*; (*courage*) fegato
gutter ['gʌtə*] *n* (*of roof*) grondaia; (*in street*) cunetta
guy [gaɪ] *n* (*inf: man*) tipo, elemento; (*also:* ~**rope**) cavo *or* corda di fissaggio; (*figure*) effigie di Guy Fawkes
guzzle ['gʌzl] *vt* trangugiare
gym [dʒɪm] *n* (*also: gymnasium*) palestra; (*also: gymnastics*) ginnastica
gymnast ['dʒɪmnæst] *n* ginnasta *m/f*; ~**ics** [-'næstɪks] *n, npl* ginnastica
gym shoes *npl* scarpe *fpl* da ginnastica
gym slip (BRIT) *n* grembiule *m* da scuola (*per ragazze*)
gynaecologist [gaɪnɪ'kɔlədʒɪst] (US **gynecologist**) *n* ginecologo/a
gypsy ['dʒɪpsɪ] *n* = **gipsy**
gyrate [dʒaɪ'reɪt] *vi* girare

H

haberdashery ['hæbə'dæʃərɪ] (BRIT) *n* merceria
habit ['hæbɪt] *n* abitudine *f*; (*costume*) abito; (REL) tonaca
habitual [hə'bɪtjuəl] *adj* abituale; (*drinker, liar*) inveterato(a)
hack [hæk] *vt* tagliare, fare a pezzi ♦ *n* (*pej: writer*) scribacchino/a
hacker ['hækə*] *n* (COMPUT) pirata *m* informatico
hackneyed ['hæknɪd] *adj* comune, trito(a)
had [hæd] *pt, pp of* **have**
haddock ['hædək] (*pl* ~ *or* ~**s**) *n* eglefino
hadn't ['hædnt] = **had not**
haemorrhage ['hemərɪdʒ] (US **hemorrhage**) *n* emorragia
haemorrhoids ['hemərɔɪdz] (US **hemorrhoids**) *npl* emorroidi *fpl*
haggard ['hægəd] *adj* smunto(a)
haggle ['hægl] *vi* mercanteggiare
Hague [heɪg] *n*: **The** ~ L'Aia
hail [heɪl] *n* grandine *f*; (*of criticism etc*) pioggia ♦ *vt* (*call*) chiamare; (*flag down: taxi*) fermare; (*greet*) salutare ♦ *vi* grandinare, ~**stone** *n* chicco di grandine
hair [heə*] *n* capelli *mpl*; (*single hair: on head*) capello; (: *on body*) pelo; **to do one's** ~ pettinarsi; ~**brush** *n* spazzola per capelli; ~**cut** *n* taglio di capelli; ~**do** ['heədu:] *n* acconciatura, pettinatura; ~**dresser** *n* parrucchiere/a; ~**dryer** *n* asciugacapelli *m inv*; ~ **grip** *n* forcina; ~**net** *n* retina per capelli; ~**pin** *n* forcina; ~**pin bend** (US ~**pin curve**) *n* tornante *m*; ~**raising** *adj* orripilante; ~ **removing cream** *n* crema depilatoria; ~ **spray** *n* lacca per capelli; ~**style** *n* pettinatura, acconciatura; ~**y** *adj* irsuto(a); peloso(a); (*inf: frightening*) spaventoso(a)
hake [heɪk] (*pl* ~ *or* ~**s**) *n* nasello
half [hɑːf] (*pl* **halves**) *n* mezzo, metà *f inv* ♦ *adj* mezzo(a) ♦ *adv* a mezzo, a metà; ~ **an hour** mezz'ora; ~ **a dozen** mezza dozzina; ~ **a pound** mezza libbra; **two**

and a ~ due e mezzo; **a week and a ~** una settimana e mezza; ~ **(of it)** la metà; ~ **(of)** la metà di; **to cut sth in ~** tagliare qc in due; ~ **asleep** mezzo(a) addormentato(a); ~**-baked** *adj* (*scheme*) che non sta in piedi; ~**-caste** *n* meticcio/a; ~**-hearted** *adj* tiepido(a); ~**-hour** *n* mezz'ora; ~**-mast**: **at** ~**-mast** *adv* (*flag*) a mezz'asta; ~**penny** ['heɪpnɪ] (*BRIT*) *n* mezzo penny *m inv*; ~**-price** *adj, adv* a metà prezzo; ~ **term** (*BRIT*) *n* (*SCOL*) vacanza a *or* di metà trimestre; ~**-time** *n* (*SPORT*) intervallo; ~**-way** *adv* a metà strada

halibut ['hælɪbət] *n inv* ippoglosso

hall [hɔːl] *n* sala, salone *m*; (*entrance way*) entrata; ~ **of residence** (*BRIT*) *n* casa dello studente

hallmark ['hɔːlmɑːk] *n* marchio di garanzia; (*fig*) caratteristica

hallo [hə'ləu] *excl* = **hello**

Hallowe'en [hæləu'iːn] *n* vigilia d'Ognissanti

hallucination [həluːsɪ'neɪʃən] *n* allucinazione *f*

hallway ['hɔːlweɪ] *n* corridoio; (*entrance*) ingresso

halo ['heɪləu] *n* (*of saint etc*) aureola

halt [hɔːlt] *n* fermata ♦ *vt* fermare ♦ *vi* fermarsi

halve [hɑːv] *vt* (*apple etc*) dividere a metà; (*expense*) ridurre di metà

halves [hɑːvz] *npl of* **half**

ham [hæm] *n* prosciutto

hamburger ['hæmbəːgə*] *n* hamburger *m inv*

hamlet ['hæmlɪt] *n* paesetto

hammer ['hæmə*] *n* martello ♦ *vt* martellare ♦ *vi*: **to** ~ **on** *or* **at the door** picchiare alla porta

hammock ['hæmək] *n* amaca

hamper ['hæmpə*] *vt* impedire ♦ *n* cesta

hamster ['hæmstə*] *n* criceto

hand [hænd] *n* mano *f*; (*of clock*) lancetta; (*handwriting*) scrittura; (*at cards*) mano; (: *game*) partita; (*worker*) operaio/a ♦ *vt* dare, passare; **to give sb a** ~ dare una mano a qn; **at** ~ a portata di mano; **in** ~ a disposizione; (*work*) in corso; **on** ~

(*person*) disponibile; (*services*) pronto(a) a intervenire; **to** ~ (*information etc*) a portata di mano; **on the one** ~ **...**, **on the other** ~ da un lato ..., dall'altro; ~ **in** *vt* consegnare; ~ **out** *vt* distribuire; ~ **over** *vt* passare; cedere; ~**bag** *n* borsetta; ~**book** *n* manuale *m*; ~**brake** *n* freno a mano; ~**cuffs** *npl* manette *fpl*; ~**ful** *n* manciata, pugno

handicap ['hændɪkæp] *n* handicap *m inv* ♦ *vt* handicappare; **to be physically** ~**ped** essere handicappato(a); **to be mentally** ~**ped** essere un(a) handicappato(a) mentale

handicraft ['hændɪkrɑːft] *n* lavoro d'artigiano

handiwork ['hændɪwəːk] *n* opera

handkerchief ['hæŋkətʃɪf] *n* fazzoletto

handle ['hændl] *n* (*of door etc*) maniglia; (*of cup etc*) ansa; (*of knife etc*) impugnatura; (*of saucepan*) manico; (*for winding*) manovella ♦ *vt* toccare, maneggiare; (*deal with*) occuparsi di; (*treat: people*) trattare; "~ **with care**" "fragile"; **to fly off the** ~ (*fig*) perdere le staffe, uscire dai gangheri; ~**bar(s)** *n(pl)* manubrio

hand: ~ **luggage** *n* bagagli *mpl* a mano; ~**made** *adj* fatto(a) a mano; ~**out** *n* (*money, food*) elemosina; (*leaflet*) volantino; (*at lecture*) prospetto; ~**rail** *n* corrimano; ~**shake** *n* stretta di mano

handsome ['hænsəm] *adj* bello(a); (*profit, fortune*) considerevole

handwriting ['hændraɪtɪŋ] *n* scrittura

handy ['hændɪ] *adj* (*person*) bravo(a); (*close at hand*) a portata di mano; (*convenient*) comodo(a); ~**man** *n* tuttofare *m inv*

hang [hæŋ] (*pt, pp* **hung**) *vt* appendere; (*criminal: pt, pp* **hanged**) impiccare ♦ *vi* (*painting*) essere appeso(a); (*hair*) scendere; (*drapery*) cadere; **to get the** ~ **of sth** (*inf*) capire come qc funziona; ~ **about** *or* **around** *vi* bighellonare, ciondolare; ~ **on** *vi* (*wait*) aspettare; ~ **up** *vi* (*TEL*) riattaccare ♦ *vt* appendere

hangar ['hæŋə*] *n* hangar *m inv*

hanger ['hæŋə*] *n* gruccia

hanger-on → *hatch*

hanger-on *n* parassita *m*

hang-gliding ['-glaɪdɪŋ] *n* volo col deltaplano

hangover ['hæŋəuvə*] *n* (after drinking) postumi *mpl* di sbornia

hang-up *n* complesso

hanker ['hæŋkə*] *vi*: to ~ after bramare

hankie ['hæŋkɪ] *n abbr* = **handkerchief**

hanky ['hæŋkɪ] *n abbr* = **handkerchief**

haphazard [hæp'hæzəd] *adj* a casaccio, alla carlona

happen ['hæpən] *vi* accadere, succedere; (chance): to ~ to do sth fare qc per caso; as it ~s guarda caso; **~ing** *n* avvenimento

happily ['hæpɪlɪ] *adv* felicemente; fortunatamente

happiness ['hæpɪnɪs] *n* felicità, contentezza

happy ['hæpɪ] *adj* felice, contento(a); ~ **with** (arrangements etc) soddisfatto(a) di; to be ~ **to do** (willing) fare volentieri; ~ **birthday!** buon compleanno!; **~-go-lucky** *adj* spensierato(a)

harangue [hə'ræŋ] *vt* arringare

harass ['hærəs] *vt* molestare; **~ment** *n* molestia

harbour ['hɑːbə*] (US **harbor**) *n* porto ♦ *vt* (hope, fear) nutrire; (criminal) dare rifugio a

hard [hɑːd] *adj* duro(a) ♦ *adv* (work) sodo; (think, try) bene; **to look ~ at** guardare fissamente; esaminare attentamente; **no ~ feelings!** senza rancore!; **to be ~ of hearing** essere duro(a) d'orecchio; **to be ~ done by** essere trattato(a) ingiustamente; **~back** *n* libro rilegato; ~ **cash** *n* denaro in contanti; ~ **disk** *n* (COMPUT) disco rigido; **~en** *vt, vi* indurire; **~-headed** *adj* pratico(a); ~ **labour** *n* lavori forzati *mpl*

hardly ['hɑːdlɪ] *adv* (scarcely) appena; **it's ~ the case** non è proprio il caso; ~ **anyone/anywhere** quasi nessuno/da nessuna parte; ~ **ever** quasi mai

hardship ['hɑːdʃɪp] *n* avversità *f inv*; privazioni *fpl*

hard-up (inf) *adj* al verde

hardware ['hɑːdwɛə*] *n* ferramenta *fpl*; (COMPUT) hardware *m*; (MIL) armamenti *mpl*; ~ **shop** *n* (negozio di) ferramenta *fpl*

hard-wearing [-'wɛərɪŋ] *adj* resistente; (shoes) robusto(a)

hard-working [-'wəːkɪŋ] *adj* lavoratore(trice)

hardy ['hɑːdɪ] *adj* robusto(a); (plant) resistente al gelo

hare [hɛə*] *n* lepre *f*; **~-brained** *adj* folle; scervellato(a)

harm [hɑːm] *n* male *m*; (wrong) danno ♦ *vt* (person) fare male a; (thing) danneggiare; **out of ~'s way** al sicuro; **~ful** *adj* dannoso(a); **~less** *adj* innocuo(a); inoffensivo(a)

harmonica [hɑː'mɔnɪkə] *n* armonica

harmonious [hɑː'məunɪəs] *adj* armonioso(a)

harmony ['hɑːmənɪ] *n* armonia

harness ['hɑːnɪs] *n* (for horse) bardatura, finimenti *mpl*; (for child) briglie *fpl*; (safety ~) imbracatura ♦ *vt* (horse) bardare; (resources) sfruttare

harp [hɑːp] *n* arpa ♦ *vi*: to ~ **on about** insistere tediosamente su

harpoon [hɑː'puːn] *n* arpione *m*

harrowing ['hærəuɪŋ] *adj* straziante

harsh [hɑːʃ] *adj* (life, winter) duro(a); (judge, criticism) severo(a), (sound) rauco(a); (light) violento(a)

harvest ['hɑːvɪst] *n* raccolto, (of grapes) vendemmia ♦ *vt* fare il raccolto di, raccogliere; vendemmiare

has [hæz] *vb see* **have**

hash [hæʃ] *n* (CULIN) specie di spezzatino fatto con carne già cotta; (fig: mess) pasticcio

hashish ['hæʃɪʃ] *n* hascisc *m*

hasn't ['hæznt] = **has not**

hassle ['hæsl] (inf) *n* sacco di problemi

haste [heɪst] *n* fretta; precipitazione *f*; **~n** ['heɪsn] *vt* affrettare ♦ *vi*: to **~n (to)** affrettarsi (a); **hastily** *adv* in fretta; precipitosamente; **hasty** *adj* affrettato(a); precipitoso(a)

hat [hæt] *n* cappello

hatch [hætʃ] *n* (NAUT: also: **~way**) boccaporto; (also: service ~) portello di servizio ♦ *vi* (*bird*) uscire dal guscio; (*egg*) schiudersi

hatchback [ˈhætʃbæk] *n* (AUT) tre (or cinque) porte *f inv*

hatchet [ˈhætʃɪt] *n* accetta

hate [heɪt] *vt* odiare, detestare ♦ *n* odio; **~ful** *adj* odioso(a), detestabile

hatred [ˈheɪtrɪd] *n* odio

haughty [ˈhɔːtɪ] *adj* altero(a), arrogante

haul [hɔːl] *vt* trascinare, tirare ♦ *n* (*of fish*) pescata; (*of stolen goods etc*) bottino; **~age** *n* trasporto; autotrasporto; **~ier** (US **~er**) *n* trasportatore *m*

haunch [hɔːntʃ] *n* anca; (*of meat*) coscia

haunt [hɔːnt] *vt* (*subj: fear*) pervadere; (: *person*) frequentare ♦ *n* rifugio; **this house is ~ed** questa casa è abitata da un fantasma

---

KEYWORD

have [hæv] (*pt, pp* **had**) *aux vb* **1** (*gen*) avere; essere; **to ~ arrived/gone** essere arrivato(a)/andato(a); **to ~ eaten/slept** avere mangiato/dormito; **he has been kind/promoted** è stato gentile/promosso; **having finished** *or* **when he had finished**, he left dopo aver finito, se n'è andato

2 (*in tag questions*): **you've done it, ~n't you?** l'hai fatto, (non è vero?); **he hasn't done it, has he?** non l'ha fatto, vero?

3 (*in short answers and questions*): **you've made a mistake — no I ~n't/so I ~** ha fatto un errore — ma no, niente affatto/sì, è vero; **we ~n't paid — yes we ~!** non abbiamo pagato — ma sì che abbiamo pagato!; **I've been there before, ~ you?** ci sono già stato, e lei?

♦ *modal aux vb* (*be obliged*): **to ~ (got) to do sth** dover fare qc; **I ~n't got** *or* **I don't ~ to wear glasses** non ho bisogno di portare gli occhiali

♦ *vt* **1** (*possess, obtain*) avere; **he has (got) blue eyes/dark hair** ha gli occhi azzurri/i capelli scuri; **do you ~** *or* **~ you got a car/phone?** ha la macchina/il telefono?; **may I ~ your address?** potrebbe darmi il suo indirizzo?; **you can ~ it for £5** te lo lascio per 5 sterline

2 (+ *noun*: *take, hold etc*): **to ~ breakfast/a swim/a bath** fare colazione/una nuotata/un bagno; **to ~ lunch** pranzare; **to ~ dinner** cenare; **to ~ a drink** bere qualcosa; **to ~ a cigarette** fumare una sigaretta

3: **to ~ sth done** far fare qc; **to ~ one's hair cut** farsi tagliare i capelli; **to ~ sb do sth** far fare qc a qn

4 (*experience, suffer*) avere; **to ~ a cold/ flu** avere il raffreddore/l'influenza; **she had her bag stolen** le hanno rubato la borsa

5 (*inf: dupe*): **you've been had!** ci sei cascato!

have out *vt*: **to ~ it out with sb** (*settle a problem etc*) mettere le cose in chiaro con qn

haven [ˈheɪvn] *n* porto; (*fig*) rifugio

haven't [ˈhævnt] = **have not**

haversack [ˈhævəsæk] *n* zaino

havoc [ˈhævək] *n* caos *m*

hawk [hɔːk] *n* falco

hay [heɪ] *n* fieno; **~ fever** *n* febbre *f* da fieno; **~stack** *n* pagliaio

haywire [ˈheɪwaɪə*] (*inf*) *adj*: **to go ~** impazzire

hazard [ˈhæzəd] *n* azzardo, ventura; pericolo, rischio ♦ *vt* (*guess etc*) azzardare; **~ous** *adj* pericoloso(a); **~ (warning) lights** *npl* (AUT) luci *fpl* di emergenza

haze [heɪz] *n* foschia

hazelnut [ˈheɪzlnʌt] *n* nocciola

hazy [ˈheɪzɪ] *adj* fosco(a); (*idea*) vago(a)

he [hiː] *pronoun* lui, egli; **it is ~ who ...** è lui che ....

head [hɛd] *n* testa; (*leader*) capo; (*of school*) preside *m/f* ♦ *vt* (*list*) essere in testa a; (*group*) essere a capo di; **~s** (or **tails**) testa (o croce), pari (o dispari); **~ first** a capofitto, di testa; **~ over heels in love** pazzamente innamorato(a); **to ~ the ball** colpire una palla di testa; **~ for** *vt fus* dirigersi verso; **~ache** *n* mal *m* di testa; **~dress** (BRIT) *n* (*of bride*) acconciatura; **~ing** *n* titolo; intestazione *f*; **~lamp** (BRIT) *n* = **~light**; **~land** *n* promontorio; **~light** n fanale m; **~line** n titolo; **~long** adv (fall) a capofitto; (rush) precipitosamente; **~master/mistress** n preside m/f; **~ office** n sede f (centrale); **~-on** adj (collision) frontale; **~phones** npl cuffia; **~quarters** npl ufficio centrale; (MIL) quartiere m generale; **~-rest** n poggiacapo; **~room** n (in car) altezza dell'abitacolo; (under bridge) altezza limite; **~scarf** n foulard m inv; **~strong** adj testardo(a); **~ waiter** n capocameriere m; **~way** n: to make ~way fare progressi; **~wind** n controvento; **~y** adj (experience, period) inebriante

heal [hi:l] vt, vi guarire

health [hɛlθ] n salute f; **~ centre** (BRIT) n poliambulatorio; **~ food(s)** n(pl) cibo macrobiotico; **~ food store** n negozio di alimenti dietetici e macrobiotici; **the H~ Service** (BRIT) n ≈ il Servizio Sanitario Statale; **~y** adj (person) sano(a), in buona salute; (climate) salubre; (appetite, economy etc) sano(a)

heap [hi:p] n mucchio ♦ vt (stones, sand): to ~ (up) ammucchiare; (plate, sink): to ~ sth with riempire qc di; **~s of** (inf) un mucchio di

hear [hɪə*] (pt, pp heard) vt sentire; (news) ascoltare ♦ vi sentire; to ~ about avere notizie di; sentire parlare di; to ~ from sb ricevere notizie da qn; **heard** [hɜ:d] pt, pp of hear; **~ing** n (sense) udito; (of witnesses) audizione f; (of a case) udienza; **~ing aid** n apparecchio acustico; **~say** n dicerie fpl, chiacchiere fpl

hearse [hɜ:s] n carro funebre

heart [hɑ:t] n cuore m; **~s** npl (CARDS) cuori mpl; to lose ~ scoraggiarsi; to take ~ farsi coraggio; at ~ in fondo; by ~ (learn, know) a memoria; **~ attack** n attacco di cuore; **~beat** n battito del cuore; **~breaking** adj straziante; **~broken** adj: to be ~broken avere il cuore spezzato; **~burn** n bruciore m di stomaco; **~ failure** n arresto cardiaco; **~felt** adj sincero(a)

hearth [hɑ:θ] n focolare m

heartland ['hɑ:tlænd] n regione f centrale

heartless ['hɑ:tlɪs] adj senza cuore

hearty ['hɑ:tɪ] adj caloroso(a); robusto(a), sano(a); vigoroso(a)

heat [hi:t] n calore m; (fig) ardore m; fuoco; (SPORT: also: qualifying ~) prova eliminatoria ♦ vt scaldare; **~ up** vi (liquids) scaldarsi; (room) riscaldarsi ♦ vt riscaldare; **~ed** adj riscaldato(a); (argument) acceso(a); **~er** n radiatore m; (stove) stufa

heath [hi:θ] (BRIT) n landa

heathen ['hi:ðn] n pagano/a

heather ['hɛðə*] n erica

heating ['hi:tɪŋ] n riscaldamento

heat-seeking adj termoguidato(a)

heatstroke ['hi:tstrəuk] n colpo di sole

heatwave ['hi:tweɪv] n ondata di caldo

heave [hi:v] vt (pull) tirare (con forza); (push) spingere (con forza); (lift) sollevare (con forza) ♦ vi sollevarsi; (retch) aver conati di vomito ♦ n (push) grande spinta; to ~ a sigh emettere un sospiro

heaven ['hɛvn] n paradiso, cielo; **~ly** adj divino(a), celeste

heavily ['hɛvɪlɪ] adv pesantemente; (drink, smoke) molto

heavy ['hɛvɪ] adj pesante; (sea) grosso(a); (rain, blow) forte; (weather) afoso(a); (drinker, smoker) gran (before noun); **~ goods vehicle** n veicolo per trasporti pesanti; **~weight** n (SPORT) peso massimo

Hebrew ['hi:bru:] adj ebreo(a) ♦ n (LING) ebraico

Hebrides ['hɛbrɪdi:z] npl: the ~ le Ebridi

heckle ['hɛkl] vt interpellare e dare noia a (un oratore)

hectic ['hɛktɪk] adj movimentato(a)

he'd [hi:d] = he would; he had

hedge [hɛdʒ] n siepe f ♦ vi essere elusivo(a); to ~ one's bets (fig) coprirsi dai rischi

hedgehog ['hɛdʒhɔg] n riccio

heed [hi:d] vt (also: take ~ of) badare a, far conto di; **~less** adj: ~less (of) sordo(a) (a)

heel [hi:l] n (ANAT) calcagno; (of shoe) tacco ♦ vt (shoe) rifare i tacchi a

hefty ['hɛftɪ] adj (person) robusto(a);

(*parcel*) pesante; (*profit*) grosso(a)
heifer ['hɛfə*] *n* giovenca
height [haɪt] *n* altezza; (*high ground*) altura; (*fig: of glory*) apice *m*; (: *of stupidity*) colmo; **~en** *vt* (*fig*) accrescere
heir [ɛə*] *n* erede *m*; **~ess** *n* erede *f*; **~loom** *n* mobile *m* (*or* gioiello *or* quadro) di famiglia
held [hɛld] *pt, pp of* **hold**
helicopter ['hɛlɪkɔptə*] *n* elicottero
heliport ['hɛlɪpɔːt] *n* eliporto
helium ['hiːlɪəm] *n* elio
hell [hɛl] *n* inferno; **~!** (*inf*) porca miseria!, accidenti!
he'll [hiːl] = **he will**; **he shall**
hellish ['hɛlɪʃ] (*inf*) *adj* infernale
hello [hə'ləu] *excl* buon giorno!; ciao! (*to sb one addresses as "tu"*); (*surprise*) ma guarda!
helm [hɛlm] *n* (*NAUT*) timone *m*
helmet ['hɛlmɪt] *n* casco
help [hɛlp] *n* aiuto; (*charwoman*) donna di servizio ♦ *vt* aiutare; **~!** aiuto!; **~ yourself (to bread)** si serva (del pane); **he can't ~ it** non ci può far niente; **~er** *n* aiutante *m/f*, assistente *m/f*; **~ful** *adj* di grande aiuto; (*useful*) utile; **~ing** *n* porzione *f*; **~less** *adj* impotente; debole
hem [hɛm] *n* orlo ♦ *vt* fare l'orlo a; **~ in** *vt* cingere
hemisphere ['hɛmɪsfɪə*] *n* emisfero
hemorrhage ['hɛmərɪdʒ] (*US*) *n* = **haemorrhage**
hemorrhoids ['hɛmərɔɪdz] (*US*) *npl* = **haemorrhoids**
hen [hɛn] *n* gallina; (*female bird*) femmina
hence [hɛns] *adv* (*therefore*) dunque; **2 years ~** di qui a 2 anni; **~forth** *adv* d'ora in poi
henchman ['hɛntʃmən] (*pej*) *n* caudatario
henpecked ['hɛnpɛkt] *adj* dominato dalla moglie
hepatitis [hɛpə'taɪtɪs] *n* epatite *f*
her [həː*] *pron* (*direct*) la, l' + *vowel*; (*indirect*) le; (*stressed, after prep*) lei ♦ *adj* il(la) suo(a), i(le) suoi(sue); *see also* **me**; **my**

herald ['hɛrəld] *n* araldo ♦ *vt* annunciare
heraldry ['hɛrəldrɪ] *n* araldica
herb [həːb] *n* erba
herd [həːd] *n* mandria
here [hɪə*] *adv* qui, qua ♦ *excl* ehi!; **~!** (*at roll call*) presente!; **~ is/are** ecco; **~ he/ she is** eccolo/eccola; **~after** *adv* in futuro; dopo questo; **~by** *adv* (*in letter*) con la presente
hereditary [hɪ'rɛdɪtrɪ] *adj* ereditario(a)
heresy ['hɛrəsɪ] *n* eresia
heretic ['hɛrətɪk] *n* eretico/a
heritage ['hɛrɪtɪdʒ] *n* eredità; (*fig*) retaggio
hermetically [həː'mɛtɪklɪ] *adv*: **~ sealed** ermeticamente chiuso(a)
hermit ['həːmɪt] *n* eremita *m*
hernia ['həːnɪə] *n* ernia
hero ['hɪərəu] (*pl* **~es**) *n* eroe *m*
heroin ['hɛrəuɪn] *n* eroina
heroine ['hɛrəuɪn] *n* eroina
heron ['hɛrən] *n* airone *m*
herring ['hɛrɪŋ] *n* aringa
hers [həːz] *pron* il(la) suo(a), i(le) suoi(sue); *see also* **mine**[1]
herself [həː'sɛlf] *pron* (*reflexive*) si; (*emphatic*) lei stessa; (*after prep*) se stessa, sé; *see also* **oneself**
he's [hiːz] = **he is**; **he has**
hesitant ['hɛzɪtənt] *adj* esitante, indeciso(a)
hesitate ['hɛzɪteɪt] *vi*: **to ~ (about/to do)** esitare (su/a fare); **hesitation** [-'teɪʃən] *n* esitazione *f*
heterosexual ['hɛtərəu'sɛksjuəl] *adj, n* eterosessuale *m/f*
hew [hjuː] *vt* (*stone*) scavare; (*wood*) tagliare
hexagonal [hɛk'sægənəl] *adj* esagonale
heyday ['heɪdeɪ] *n*: **the ~ of** i bei giorni di, l'età d'oro di
HGV *n abbr* = **heavy goods vehicle**
hi [haɪ] *excl* ciao!
hiatus [haɪ'eɪtəs] *n* vuoto; (*LING*) iato
hibernate ['haɪbəneɪt] *vi* ibernare
hiccough ['hɪkʌp] *vi* singhiozzare; **~s** *npl*: **to have ~s** avere il singhiozzo
hiccup ['hɪkʌp] = **hiccough**
hid [hɪd] *pt of* **hide**; **~den** ['hɪdn] *pp of*

hide

hide [haɪd] (*pt* **hid**, *pp* **hidden**) *n* (*skin*) pelle *f* ♦ *vt*: to ~ **sth** (**from sb**) nascondere qc (a qn) ♦ *vi*: to ~ (**from sb**) nascondersi (da qn); **~-and-seek** *n* rimpiattino; **~away** *n* nascondiglio

hideous ['hɪdɪəs] *adj* laido(a); orribile

hiding ['haɪdɪŋ] *n* (*beating*) bastonata; to **be in** ~ (*concealed*) tenersi nascosto(a)

hierarchy ['haɪərɑːkɪ] *n* gerarchia

hi-fi ['haɪfaɪ] *n* stereo ♦ *adj* ad alta fedeltà, hi-fi *inv*

high [haɪ] *adj* alto(a); (*speed, respect, number*) grande; (*wind*) forte; (*voice*) acuto(a) ♦ *adv* alto, in alto; **20m** ~ alto(a) 20m; **~brow** *adj, n* intellettuale *m/f*; **~chair** *n* seggiolone *m*; **~er education** *n* studi *mpl* superiori; **~-handed** *adj* prepotente; **~-heeled** *adj* con i tacchi alti; ~ **jump** *n* (SPORT) salto in alto; **the H~lands** *npl* le Highlands scozzesi; **~light** *n* (*fig: of event*) momento culminante; (*in hair*) colpo di sole ♦ *vt* mettere in evidenza; **~ly** *adv* molto; to **speak ~ly of** parlare molto bene di; **~ly strung** *adj* teso(a) di nervi, eccitabile; **~ness** *n*: **Her H~ness** Sua Altezza; **~-pitched** *adj* acuto(a); **~-rise block** *n* palazzone *m*; **~ school** *n* scuola secondaria; (US) istituto superiore d'istruzione; ~ **season** (BRIT) *n* alta stagione; ~ **street** (BRIT) *n* strada principale

highway ['haɪweɪ] *n* strada maestra; **H~ Code** (BRIT) *n* codice *m* della strada

hijack ['haɪdʒæk] *vt* dirottare; **~er** *n* dirottatore/trice

hike [haɪk] *vi* fare un'escursione a piedi ♦ *n* escursione *f* a piedi; **~r** *n* escursionista *m/f*

hilarious [hɪ'lɛərɪəs] *adj* (*behaviour, event*) spassosissimo(a)

hill [hɪl] *n* collina, colle *m*; (*fairly high*) montagna; (*on road*) salita; **~side** *n* fianco della collina; **~y** *adj* collinoso(a); montagnoso(a)

hilt [hɪlt] *n* (*of sword*) elsa; to **the ~** (*fig: support*) fino in fondo

him [hɪm] *pron* (*direct*) lo, l' + *vowel*; (*indirect*) gli; (*stressed, after prep*) lui; *see also* **me**; **~self** *pron* (*reflexive*) si; (*emphatic*) lui stesso; (*after prep*) se stesso, sé; *see also* **oneself**

hind [haɪnd] *adj* posteriore

hinder ['hɪndə*] *vt* ostacolare; **hindrance** ['hɪndrəns] *n* ostacolo, impedimento

hindsight ['haɪndsaɪt] *n*: **with** ~ con il senno di poi

Hindu ['hɪnduː] *n* indù *m/f inv*

hinge [hɪndʒ] *n* cardine *m* ♦ *vi* (*fig*): to ~ **on** dipendere da

hint [hɪnt] *n* (*suggestion*) allusione *f*; (*advice*) consiglio; (*sign*) accenno ♦ *vt*: to ~ **that** lasciar capire che ♦ *vi*: to ~ **at** alludere a

hip [hɪp] *n* anca, fianco

hippopotami [hɪpə'pɔtəmaɪ] *npl of* **hippopotamus**

hippopotamus [hɪpə'pɔtəməs] (*pl* **~es** *or* **hippopotami**) *n* ippopotamo

hire ['haɪə*] *vt* (BRIT: *car, equipment*) noleggiare; (*worker*) assumere, dare lavoro a ♦ *n* nolo, noleggio; **for** ~ da nolo; (*taxi*) libero(a); ~ **purchase** (BRIT) *n* acquisto (*or* vendita) rateale

his [hɪz] *adj, pron* il(la) suo(sua), i(le) suoi(sue); *see also* **my**; **mine**[1]

hiss [hɪs] *vi* fischiare; (*cat, snake*) sibilare

historic(al) [hɪ'stɔrɪk(l)] *adj* storico(a)

history ['hɪstərɪ] *n* storia

hit [hɪt] (*pt, pp* **hit**) *vt* colpire, picchiare; (*knock against*) battere; (*reach: target*) raggiungere; (*collide with: car*) urtare contro; (*fig: affect*) colpire; (*find: problem etc*) incontrare ♦ *n* colpo; (*success, song*) successo; to ~ **it off with sb** andare molto d'accordo con qn; **~-and-run driver** *n* pirata *m* della strada

hitch [hɪtʃ] *vt* (*fasten*) attaccare; (*also:* ~ *up*) tirare su ♦ *n* (*difficulty*) intoppo, difficoltà *f inv*; to ~ **a lift** fare l'autostop

hitch-hike *vi* fare l'autostop; **~r** *n* autostoppista *m/f*

hi-tech ['haɪtɛk] *adj* di alta tecnologia ♦ *n* alta tecnologia

hitherto [hɪðə'tuː] *adv* in precedenza

HIV *abbr*: **HIV-negative/-positive** *adj* sieronegativo(a)/sieropositivo(a)

hive [haɪv] *n* alveare *m*; ~ **off** *vt* separare

H.M.S. *abbr* = **His(Her) Majesty's Ship**

hoard [hɔːd] *n* (*of food*) provviste *fpl*; (*of money*) gruzzolo ♦ *vt* ammassare

hoarding ['hɔːdɪŋ] (*BRIT*) *n* (*for posters*) tabellone *m* per affissioni

hoarse [hɔːs] *adj* rauco(a)

hoax [həʊks] *n* scherzo; falso allarme

hob [hɔb] *n* piastra (con fornelli)

hobble ['hɔbl] *vi* zoppicare

hobby ['hɔbɪ] *n* hobby *m inv*, passatempo; ~**-horse** *n* (*fig*) chiodo fisso

hobo ['həʊbəʊ] (*US*) *n* vagabondo

hockey ['hɔkɪ] *n* hockey *m*

hoe [həʊ] *n* zappa

hog [hɔg] *n* maiale *m* ♦ *vt* (*fig*) arraffare; **to go the whole** ~ farlo fino in fondo

hoist [hɔɪst] *n* paranco ♦ *vt* issare

hold [həʊld] (*pt, pp* **held**) *vt* tenere; (*contain*) contenere; (*keep back*) trattenere; (*believe*) mantenere; considerare; (*possess*) avere, possedere; detenere ♦ *vi* (*withstand pressure*) tenere; (*be valid*) essere valido(a) ♦ *n* presa; (*control*): **to have a** ~ **over** avere controllo su; (*NAUT*) stiva; ~ **the line!** (*TEL*) resti in linea!; **to** ~ **one's own** (*fig*) difendersi bene; **to catch** *or* **get (a)** ~ **of** afferrare; ~ **back** *vt* trattenere; (*secret*) tenere celato(a); ~ **down** *vt* (*person*) tenere a terra; (*job*) tenere; ~ **off** *vt* tener lontano; ~ **on** *vi* tener fermo; (*wait*) aspettare; ~ **on!** (*TEL*) resti in linea!; ~ **on to** *vt fus* tenersi stretto(a) a; (*keep*) conservare; ~ **out** *vt* offrire ♦ *vi* (*resist*) resistere; ~ **up** *vt* (*raise*) alzare; (*support*) sostenere; (*delay*) ritardare; (*rob*) assaltare; ~**all** (*BRIT*) *n* borsone *m*; ~**er** *n* (*container*) contenitore *m*; (*of ticket, title*) possessore/posseditrice; (*of office etc*) incaricato/a; (*of record*) detentore/trice; ~**ing** *n* (*share*) azioni *fpl*, titoli *mpl*; (*farm*) podere *m*, tenuta; ~**up** *n* (*robbery*) rapina a mano armata; (*delay*) ritardo; (*BRIT: in traffic*) blocco

hole [həʊl] *n* buco, buca ♦ *vt* bucare

holiday ['hɔlədɪ] *n* vacanza; (*day off*) giorno di vacanza; (*public*) giorno festivo; **on** ~ in vacanza; ~ **camp** (*BRIT*) *n* (*also*: ~

centre) ≈ villaggio (di vacanze); ~**-maker** (*BRIT*) *n* villeggiante *m/f*; ~ **resort** *n* luogo di villeggiatura

holiness ['həʊlɪnɪs] *n* santità

Holland ['hɔlənd] *n* Olanda

hollow ['hɔləʊ] *adj* cavo(a); (*container, claim*) vuoto(a); (*laugh, sound*) cupo(a) ♦ *n* cavità *f inv*; (*in land*) valletta, depressione *f* ♦ *vt*: **to** ~ **out** scavare

holly ['hɔlɪ] *n* agrifoglio

holocaust ['hɔləkɔːst] *n* olocausto

holster ['həʊlstə*] *n* fondina (di pistola)

holy ['həʊlɪ] *adj* santo(a); (*bread*) benedetto(a), consacrato(a); (*ground*) consacrato(a)

homage ['hɔmɪdʒ] *n* omaggio; **to pay** ~ **to** rendere omaggio a

home [həʊm] *n* casa; (*country*) patria; (*institution*) casa, ricovero ♦ *cpd* familiare; (*cooking etc*) casalingo(a); (*ECON, POL*) nazionale, interno(a); (*SPORT*) di casa ♦ *adv* a casa; in patria; (*right in: nail etc*) fino in fondo; **at** ~ a casa; (*in situation*) a proprio agio; **to go** (*or* **come**) ~ tornare a casa (*or* in patria); **make yourself at** ~ si metta a suo agio; ~ **address** *n* indirizzo di casa; ~**land** *n* patria; ~**less** *adj* senza tetto; spatriato(a); ~**ly** *adj* semplice, alla buona; accogliente; ~**-made** *adj* casalingo(a); **H**~ **Office** (*BRIT*) *n* ministero degli Interni; ~ **rule** *n* autogoverno; **H**~ **Secretary** (*BRIT*) *n* ministro degli Interni; ~**sick** *adj*: **to be** ~**sick** avere la nostalgia; ~ **town** *n* città *f inv* natale; ~**ward** ['həʊmwəd] *adj* (*journey*) di ritorno; ~**work** *n* compiti *mpl* (per casa)

homicide ['hɔmɪsaɪd] (*US*) *n* omicidio

homogeneous [hɔməʊ'dʒiːnɪəs] *adj* omogeneo(a)

homosexual [hɔməʊ'sɛksjʊəl] *adj*, *n* omosessuale *m/f*

honest ['ɔnɪst] *adj* onesto(a); sincero(a); ~**ly** *adv* onestamente; sinceramente; ~**y** *n* onestà

honey ['hʌnɪ] *n* miele *m*; ~**comb** *n* favo; ~**moon** *n* luna di miele, viaggio di nozze; ~**suckle** *n* (*BOT*) caprifoglio

honk [hɔŋk] *vi* suonare il clacson

honorary ['ɔnərərɪ] *adj* onorario(a);

(*duty, title*) onorifico(a)

honour ['ɔnə*] (*US* **honor**) *vt* onorare ♦ *n* onore *m*; **~able** *adj* onorevole; **~s degree** *n* (*SCOL*) *laurea specializzata*

hood [hud] *n* cappuccio; (*on cooker*) cappa; (*BRIT: AUT*) capote *f*; (*US: AUT*) cofano

hoodlum ['hu:dləm] *n* teppista *m/f*

hoodwink ['hudwɪŋk] *vt* infinocchiare

hoof [hu:f] (*pl* **hooves**) *n* zoccolo

hook [huk] *n* gancio; (*for fishing*) amo ♦ *vt* uncinare; (*dress*) agganciare

hooligan ['hu:lɪgən] *n* giovinastro, teppista *m*

hoop [hu:p] *n* cerchio

hooray [hu:'reɪ] *excl* = **hurray**

hoot [hu:t] *vi* (*AUT*) suonare il clacson; (*siren*) ululare; (*owl*) gufare; **~er** *n* (*BRIT: AUT*) clacson *m inv*; (*NAUT*) sirena

hoover ['hu:və*] ® (*BRIT*) *n* aspirapolvere *m inv* ♦ *vt* pulire con l'aspirapolvere

hooves [hu:vz] *npl of* **hoof**

hop [hɔp] *vi* saltellare, saltare; (*on one foot*) saltare su una gamba

hope [həup] *vt*: **to ~ that/to do** sperare che/di fare ♦ *vi* sperare ♦ *n* speranza; **I ~ so/not** spero di sì/no; **~ful** *adj* (*person*) pieno(a) di speranza; (*situation*) promettente; **~fully** *adv* con speranza; **~fully he will recover** speriamo che si riprenda; **~less** *adj* senza speranza, disperato(a); (*useless*) inutile

hops [hɔps] *npl* luppoli *mpl*

horde [hɔ:d] *n* orda

horizon [hə'raɪzn] *n* orizzonte *m*; **~tal** [hɔrɪ'zɔntl] *adj* orizzontale

hormone ['hɔ:məun] *n* ormone *m*

horn [hɔ:n] *n* (*ZOOL, MUS*) corno; (*AUT*) clacson *m inv*

hornet ['hɔ:nɪt] *n* calabrone *m*

horny ['hɔ:nɪ] (*inf*) *adj* arrapato(a)

horoscope ['hɔrəskəup] *n* oroscopo

horrendous [hə'rɛndəs] *adj* orrendo(a)

horrible ['hɔrɪbl] *adj* orribile, tremendo(a)

horrid ['hɔrɪd] *adj* orrido(a); (*person*) odioso(a)

horrify ['hɔrɪfaɪ] *vt* scandalizzare

horror ['hɔrə*] *n* orrore *m*; **~ film** *n* film *m inv* dell'orrore

hors d'œuvre [ɔ:'də:vrə] *n* antipasto

horse [hɔ:s] *n* cavallo; **~back: on ~back** *adj, adv* a cavallo; **~ chestnut** *n* ippocastano; **~man** *n* cavaliere *m*; **~power** *n* cavallo (vapore); **~-racing** *n* ippica; **~radish** *n* rafano; **~shoe** *n* ferro di cavallo; **~woman** *n* amazzone *f*

horticulture ['hɔ:tɪkʌltʃə*] *n* orticoltura

hose [həuz] *n* (*also*: **~pipe**) tubo; (*also*: *garden* **~**) tubo per annaffiare

hosiery ['həuʒərɪ] *n* maglieria

hospice ['hɔspɪs] *n* ricovero, ospizio

hospitable [hɔs'pɪtəbl] *adj* ospitale

hospital ['hɔspɪtl] *n* ospedale *m*

hospitality [hɔspɪ'tælɪtɪ] *n* ospitalità

host [həust] *n* ospite *m*; (*REL*) ostia; (*large number*): **a ~ of** una schiera di

hostage ['hɔstɪdʒ] *n* ostaggio/a

hostel ['hɔstl] *n* ostello; (*also*: *youth* **~**) ostello della gioventù

hostess ['həustɪs] *n* ospite *f*; (*BRIT*: *air* **~**) hostess *f inv*

hostile ['hɔstaɪl] *adj* ostile

hostility [hɔ'stɪlɪtɪ] *n* ostilità *f inv*

hot [hɔt] *adj* caldo(a); (*as opposed to only warm*) molto caldo(a); (*spicy*) piccante; (*fig*) accanito(a); ardente; violento(a), focoso(a); **to be ~** (*person*) aver caldo; (*object*) essere caldo(a); (*weather*) far caldo; **~bed** *n* (*fig*) focolaio; **~ dog** *n* hot dog *m inv*

hotel [həu'tɛl] *n* albergo; **~ier** *n* albergatore/trice

hot: **~headed** *adj* focoso(a), eccitabile; **~house** *n* serra; **~ line** *n* (*POL*) telefono rosso; **~ly** *adv* violentemente; **~plate** *n* (*on cooker*) piastra riscaldante; **~-water bottle** *n* borsa dell'acqua calda

hound [haund] *vt* perseguitare ♦ *n* segugio

hour ['auə*] *n* ora; **~ly** *adj* all'ora

house [*n* haus, *pl* 'hauzɪz, *vb* hauz] *n* (*also*: *firm*) casa; (*POL*) camera; (*THEATRE*) sala; pubblico; spettacolo; (*dynasty*) casata ♦ *vt* (*person*) ospitare, alloggiare; **on the ~** (*fig*) offerto(a) dalla casa; **~ arrest** *n* arresti *mpl* domiciliari; **~boat** *n* house boat *f inv*; **~bound** *adj* confinato(a) in casa; **~breaking** *n* furto con scasso;

~coat *n* vestaglia; **~hold** *n* famiglia; casa; **~keeper** *n* governante *f*; **~keeping** *n* (*work*) governo della casa; (*money*) soldi *mpl* per le spese di casa; **~-warming party** *n* festa per inaugurare la casa nuova; **~wife** *n* massaia, casalinga; **~work** *n* faccende *fpl* domestiche

housing ['hauzɪŋ] *n* alloggio; **~ development** (*BRIT* ~ **estate**) *n* zona *residenziale con case popolari e/o private*

hovel ['hɔvl] *n* casupola

hover ['hɔvə*] *vi* (*bird*) librarsi; **~craft** *n* hovercraft *m inv*

how [hau] *adv* come; **~ are you?** come sta?; **~ do you do?** piacere!; **~ far is it to the river?** quanto è lontano il fiume?; **~ long have you been here?** da quando è qui?; **~ lovely!/awful!** che bello!/orrore!; **~ many?** quanti(e)?; **~ much?** quanto(a)?; **~ much milk?** quanto latte?; **~ many people?** quante persone?; **~ old are you?** quanti anni ha?; **~ever** *adv* in qualsiasi modo *or* maniera che; (+ *adjective*) per quanto + *sub*; (*in questions*) come ♦ *conj* comunque, però

howl [haul] *vi* ululare; (*baby, person*) urlare

H.P. *abbr* = **hire purchase**; **horsepower**

h.p. *n abbr* = **H.P.**

HQ *n abbr* = **headquarters**

hub [hʌb] *n* (*of wheel*) mozzo; (*fig*) fulcro

hubbub ['hʌbʌb] *n* baccano

hubcap ['hʌbkæp] *n* coprimozzo

huddle ['hʌdl] *vi*: **to ~ together** rannicchiarsi l'uno contro l'altro

hue [hju:] *n* tinta; **~ and cry** *n* clamore *m*

huff [hʌf] *n*: **in a ~** stizzito(a)

hug [hʌg] *vt* abbracciare; (*shore, kerb*) stringere

huge [hju:dʒ] *adj* enorme, immenso(a)

hulk [hʌlk] *n* (*ship*) nave *f* in disarmo; (*building, car*) carcassa; (*person*) mastodonte *m*

hull [hʌl] *n* (*of ship*) scafo

hullo [hə'ləu] *excl* = **hello**

hum [hʌm] *vt* (*tune*) canticchiare ♦ *vi* canticchiare; (*insect, plane, tool*) ronzare

human ['hju:mən] *adj* umano(a) ♦ *n* essere *m* umano

humane [hju:'meɪn] *adj* umanitario(a)

humanitarian [hju:mænɪ'tɛərɪən] *adj* umanitario(a)

humanity [hju:'mænɪtɪ] *n* umanità

humble ['hʌmbl] *adj* umile, modesto(a) ♦ *vt* umiliare

humbug ['hʌmbʌg] *n* sciocchezze *fpl*; (*BRIT: sweet*) caramella alla menta

humdrum ['hʌmdrʌm] *adj* monotono(a), tedioso(a)

humid ['hju:mɪd] *adj* umido(a)

humiliate [hju:'mɪlɪeɪt] *vt* umiliare; **humiliation** [-'eɪʃən] *n* umiliazione *f*

humility [hju:'mɪlɪtɪ] *n* umiltà

humorous ['hju:mərəs] *adj* umoristico(a); (*person*) buffo(a)

humour ['hju:mə*] (*US* **humor**) *n* umore *m* ♦ *vt* accontentare

hump [hʌmp] *n* gobba; **~backed** *adj*: **~backed bridge** ponte *m* a schiena d'asino

hunch [hʌntʃ] *n* (*premonition*) intuizione *f*; **~back** *n* gobbo/a; **~ed** *adj* incurvato(a)

hundred ['hʌndrəd] *num* cento; **~s of** centinaia *fpl* di; **~weight** *n* (*BRIT*) = 50.8 *kg; 112 lb*; (*US*) = 45.3 *kg; 100 lb*

hung [hʌŋ] *pt, pp of* **hang**

Hungary ['hʌŋgərɪ] *n* Ungheria

hunger ['hʌŋgə*] *n* fame *f* ♦ *vi*: **to ~ for** desiderare ardentemente; **~ strike** *n* sciopero della fame

hungry ['hʌŋgrɪ] *adj* affamato(a); (*avid*): **~ for** avido(a) di; **to be ~** aver fame

hunk [hʌŋk] *n* (*of bread etc*) bel pezzo

hunt [hʌnt] *vt* (*seek*) cercare; (*SPORT*) cacciare ♦ *vi*: **to ~ (for)** andare a caccia (di) ♦ *n* caccia; **~er** *n* cacciatore *m*; **~ing** *n* caccia

hurdle ['hə:dl] *n* (*SPORT, fig*) ostacolo

hurl [hə:l] *vt* lanciare con violenza

hurrah [hu'rɑ:] *excl* = **hurray**

hurray [hu'reɪ] *excl* urrà!, evviva!

hurricane ['hʌrɪkən] *n* uragano

hurried ['hʌrɪd] *adj* affrettato(a); (*work*) fatto(a) in fretta; **~ly** *adv* in fretta

hurry ['hʌrɪ] *n* fretta ♦ *vi* (*also:* **~ up**) affrettarsi ♦ *vt* (*also:* **~ up**: *person*) affrettare; (*: work*) far in fretta; **to be in**

a ~ aver fretta

hurt [həːt] (*pt, pp* **hurt**) *vt* (*cause pain to*) far male a; (*injure, fig*) ferire ♦ *vi* far male; **~ful** *adj* (*remark*) che ferisce

hurtle ['həːtl] *vi*: **to ~ past/down** passare/scendere a razzo

husband ['hʌzbənd] *n* marito

hush [hʌʃ] *n* silenzio, calma ♦ *vt* zittire; **~!** zitto(a)!; **~ up** *vt* (*scandal*) mettere a tacere

husk [hʌsk] *n* (*of wheat*) cartoccio; (*of rice, maize*) buccia

husky ['hʌskɪ] *adj* roco(a) ♦ *n* cane *m* eschimese

hustle ['hʌsl] *vt* spingere, incalzare ♦ *n*: **~ and bustle** trambusto

hut [hʌt] *n* rifugio; (*shed*) ripostiglio

hutch [hʌtʃ] *n* gabbia

hyacinth ['haɪəsɪnθ] *n* giacinto

hybrid ['haɪbrɪd] *n* ibrido

hydrant ['haɪdrənt] *n* (*also*: **fire ~**) idrante *m*

hydraulic [haɪ'drɔːlɪk] *adj* idraulico(a)

hydroelectric [haɪdrəʊ'lektrɪk] *adj* idroelettrico(a)

hydrofoil ['haɪdrəfɔɪl] *n* aliscafo

hydrogen ['haɪdrədʒən] *n* idrogeno

hyena [haɪ'iːnə] *n* iena

hygiene ['haɪdʒiːn] *n* igiene *f*

hymn [hɪm] *n* inno; cantica

hype [haɪp] (*inf*) *n* campagna pubblicitaria

hypermarket ['haɪpəmɑːkɪt] (*BRIT*) *n* ipermercato

hyphen ['haɪfn] *n* trattino

hypnotism ['hɪpnətɪzm] *n* ipnotismo

hypnotize ['hɪpnətaɪz] *vt* ipnotizzare

hypocrisy [hɪ'pɒkrɪsɪ] *n* ipocrisia

hypocrite ['hɪpəkrɪt] *n* ipocrita *m/f*; **hypocritical** [-'krɪtɪkl] *adj* ipocrita

hypothermia [haɪpəʊ'θəːmɪə] *n* ipotermia

hypotheses [haɪ'pɒθɪsiːz] *npl of* **hypothesis**

hypothesis [haɪ'pɒθɪsɪs] (*pl* **hypotheses**) *n* ipotesi *f inv*

hypothetical [haɪpəʊ'θetɪkl] *adj* ipotetico(a)

hysterical [hɪ'sterɪkl] *adj* isterico(a)

hysterics [hɪ'sterɪks] *npl* accesso di isteria; (*laughter*) attacco di riso

I

I [aɪ] *pron* io

ice [aɪs] *n* ghiaccio; (*on road*) gelo; (**~ cream**) gelato ♦ *vt* (*cake*) glassare ♦ *vi* (*also*: **~ over**) ghiacciare; (*also*: **~ up**) gelare; **~berg** *n* iceberg *m inv*; **~box** *n* (*US*) frigorifero; (*BRIT*) reparto ghiaccio; (*insulated box*) frigo portatile; **~ cream** *n* gelato; **~ hockey** *n* hockey *m* su ghiaccio

Iceland ['aɪslənd] *n* Islanda

ice: ~ lolly (*BRIT*) *n* ghiacciolo; **~ rink** *n* pista di pattinaggio; **~ skating** *n* pattinaggio sul ghiaccio

icicle ['aɪsɪkl] *n* ghiacciolo

icing ['aɪsɪŋ] *n* (*CULIN*) glassa; **~ sugar** (*BRIT*) *n* zucchero a velo

icy ['aɪsɪ] *adj* ghiacciato(a); (*weather, temperature*) gelido(a)

I'd [aɪd] = **I would**; **I had**

idea [aɪ'dɪə] *n* idea

ideal [aɪ'dɪəl] *adj* ideale ♦ *n* ideale *m*

identical [aɪ'dentɪkl] *adj* identico(a)

identification [aɪdentɪfɪ'keɪʃən] *n* identificazione *f*; (**means of**) ~ carta d'identità

identify [aɪ'dentɪfaɪ] *vt* identificare

identikit picture [aɪ'dentɪkɪt-] *n* identikit *m inv*

identity [aɪ'dentɪtɪ] *n* identità *f inv*; **~ card** *n* carta d'identità

idiom ['ɪdɪəm] *n* idioma *m*; (*phrase*) espressione *f* idiomatica

idiot ['ɪdɪət] *n* idiota *m/f*; **~ic** [-'ɔtɪk] *adj* idiota

idle ['aɪdl] *adj* inattivo(a); (*lazy*) pigro(a), ozioso(a); (*unemployed*) disoccupato(a); (*question, pleasures*) ozioso(a) ♦ *vi* (*engine*) girare al minimo; **~ away** *vt*: **to ~ away the time** buttar via il tempo

idol ['aɪdl] *n* idolo; **~ize** *vt* idoleggiare

i.e. *adv abbr* (= *that is*) cioè

if [ɪf] *conj* se; **~ I were you ...** se fossi in te ..., io al tuo posto ...; **~ so** se è così; **~ not** se no; **~ only** se solo *or* soltanto

ignite [ɪgˈnaɪt] *vt* accendere ♦ *vi* accendersi

ignition [ɪgˈnɪʃən] *n* (AUT) accensione *f*; **to switch on/off the** ~ accendere/spegnere il motore; **~ key** *n* (AUT) chiave *f* dell'accensione

ignorant [ˈɪgnərənt] *adj* ignorante; **to be ~ of** (*subject*) essere ignorante in; (*events*) essere ignaro(a) di

ignore [ɪgˈnɔː*] *vt* non tener conto di; (*person, fact*) ignorare

I'll [aɪl] = **I will**; **I shall**

ill [ɪl] *adj* (*sick*) malato(a); (*bad*) cattivo(a) ♦ *n* male *m* ♦ *adv*: **to speak** *etc* ~ **of sb** parlare *etc* male di qn; **to take** *or* **be taken** ~ ammalarsi; **~-advised** *adj* (*decision*) poco giudizioso(a); (*person*) mal consigliato(a); **~-at-ease** *adj* a disagio

illegal [ɪˈliːgl] *adj* illegale

illegible [ɪˈlɛdʒɪbl] *adj* illeggibile

illegitimate [ɪlɪˈdʒɪtɪmət] *adj* illegittimo(a)

ill-fated [ɪlˈfeɪtɪd] *adj* nefasto(a)

ill feeling *n* rancore *m*

illiterate [ɪˈlɪtərət] *adj* analfabeta, illetterato(a); (*letter*) scorretto(a)

ill-mannered [ɪlˈmænəd] *adj* maleducato(a)

illness [ˈɪlnɪs] *n* malattia

ill-treat *vt* maltrattare

illuminate [ɪˈluːmɪneɪt] *vt* illuminare; **illumination** [-ˈneɪʃən] *n* illuminazione *f*; **illuminations** *npl* (*decorative*) luminarie *fpl*

illusion [ɪˈluːʒən] *n* illusione *f*

illustrate [ˈɪləstreɪt] *vt* illustrare; **illustration** [-ˈstreɪʃən] *n* illustrazione *f*

ill will *n* cattiva volontà

I'm [aɪm] = **I am**

image [ˈɪmɪdʒ] *n* immagine *f*; (*public face*) immagine (pubblica); **~ry** *n* immagini *fpl*

imaginary [ɪˈmædʒɪnərɪ] *adj* immaginario(a)

imagination [ɪmædʒɪˈneɪʃən] *n* immaginazione *f*, fantasia

imaginative [ɪˈmædʒɪnətɪv] *adj* immaginoso(a)

imagine [ɪˈmædʒɪn] *vt* immaginare

imbalance [ɪmˈbæləns] *n* squilibrio

imbue [ɪmˈbjuː] *vt*: **to ~ sb/sth with** permeare qn/qc di

imitate [ˈɪmɪteɪt] *vt* imitare; **imitation** [-ˈteɪʃən] *n* imitazione *f*

immaculate [ɪˈmækjulət] *adj* immacolato(a); (*dress, appearance*) impeccabile

immaterial [ɪməˈtɪərɪəl] *adj* immateriale, indifferente

immature [ɪməˈtjuə*] *adj* immaturo(a)

immediate [ɪˈmiːdɪət] *adj* immediato(a); **~ly** *adv* (*at once*) subito, immediatamente; **~ly next to** proprio accanto a

immense [ɪˈmɛns] *adj* immenso(a); enorme

immerse [ɪˈməːs] *vt* immergere

immersion heater [ɪˈməːʃən-] (BRIT) *n* scaldaacqua *m inv* a immersione

immigrant [ˈɪmɪgrənt] *n* immigrante *m/f*; immigrato/a

immigration [ɪmɪˈgreɪʃən] *n* immigrazione *f*

imminent [ˈɪmɪnənt] *adj* imminente

immoral [ɪˈmɔrl] *adj* immorale

immortal [ɪˈmɔːtl] *adj, n* immortale *m/f*

immune [ɪˈmjuːn] *adj*: ~ **(to)** immune (da); **immunity** *n* immunità

imp [ɪmp] *n* folletto, diavoletto; (*child*) diavoletto

impact [ˈɪmpækt] *n* impatto

impair [ɪmˈpɛə*] *vt* danneggiare

impale [ɪmˈpeɪl] *vt* infilzare

impart [ɪmˈpaːt] *vt* (*make known*) comunicare; (*bestow*) impartire

impartial [ɪmˈpaːʃl] *adj* imparziale

impassable [ɪmˈpaːsəbl] *adj* insuperabile; (*road*) impraticabile

impassive [ɪmˈpæsɪv] *adj* impassibile

impatience [ɪmˈpeɪʃəns] *n* impazienza

impatient [ɪmˈpeɪʃənt] *adj* impaziente; **to get** *or* **grow** ~ perdere la pazienza

impeccable [ɪmˈpɛkəbl] *adj* impeccabile

impede [ɪmˈpiːd] *vt* impedire

impediment [ɪmˈpɛdɪmənt] *n* impedimento; (*also: speech* ~) difetto di pronuncia

impending [ɪmˈpɛndɪŋ] *adj* imminente

imperative [ɪmˈpɛrətɪv] *adj* impe-

rativo(a); necessario(a), urgente; (*voice*) imperioso(a) ♦ *n* (*LING*) imperativo
imperfect [ɪmˈpəːfɪkt] *adj* imperfetto(a); (*goods etc*) difettoso(a) ♦ *n* (*LING*: *also*: ~ *tense*) imperfetto
imperial [ɪmˈpɪərɪəl] *adj* imperiale; (*measure*) legale
impersonal [ɪmˈpəːsənl] *adj* impersonale
impersonate [ɪmˈpəːsəneɪt] *vt* impersonare; (*THEATRE*) fare la mimica di
impertinent [ɪmˈpəːtɪnənt] *adj* insolente, impertinente
impervious [ɪmˈpəːvɪəs] *adj* (*fig*): ~ **to** insensibile a; impassibile di fronte a
impetuous [ɪmˈpɛtjuəs] *adj* impetuoso(a), precipitoso(a)
impetus [ˈɪmpətəs] *n* impeto
impinge on [ɪmˈpɪndʒ-] *vt fus* (*person*) colpire; (*rights*) ledere
implement [*n* ˈɪmplɪmənt, *vb* ˈɪmplɪment] *n* attrezzo; (*for cooking*) utensile *m* ♦ *vt* effettuare
implicit [ɪmˈplɪsɪt] *adj* implicito(a); (*complete*) completo(a)
imply [ɪmˈplaɪ] *vt* insinuare; suggerire
impolite [ɪmpəˈlaɪt] *adj* scortese
import [*vb* ɪmˈpɔːt, *n* ˈɪmpɔːt] *vt* importare ♦ *n* (*COMM*) importazione *f*
importance [ɪmˈpɔːtns] *n* importanza
important [ɪmˈpɔːtnt] *adj* importante; **it's not ~** non ha importanza
importer [ɪmˈpɔːtə*] *n* importatore/trice
impose [ɪmˈpəuz] *vt* imporre ♦ *vi*: **to ~ on sb** sfruttare la bontà di qn
imposing [ɪmˈpəuzɪŋ] *adj* imponente
imposition [ɪmpəˈzɪʃən] *n* (*of tax etc*) imposizione *f*; **to be an ~ on** (*person*) abusare della gentilezza di
impossibility [ɪmpɔsəˈbɪlɪtɪ] *n* impossibilità
impossible [ɪmˈpɔsɪbl] *adj* impossibile
impotent [ˈɪmpətnt] *adj* impotente
impound [ɪmˈpaund] *vt* confiscare
impoverished [ɪmˈpɔvərɪʃt] *adj* impoverito(a)
impracticable [ɪmˈpræktɪkəbl] *adj* inattuabile
impractical [ɪmˈpræktɪkl] *adj* non pratico(a)

impregnable [ɪmˈprɛgnəbl] *adj* (*fortress*) inespugnabile
impress [ɪmˈprɛs] *vt* impressionare; (*mark*) imprimere, stampare; **to ~ sth on sb** far capire qc a qn
impression [ɪmˈprɛʃən] *n* impressione *f*; **to be under the ~ that** avere l'impressione che
impressive [ɪmˈprɛsɪv] *adj* notevole
imprint [ˈɪmprɪnt] *n* (*of hand etc*) impronta; (*PUBLISHING*) sigla editoriale
imprison [ɪmˈprɪzn] *vt* imprigionare; **~ment** *n* imprigionamento
improbable [ɪmˈprɔbəbl] *adj* improbabile; (*excuse*) inverosimile
impromptu [ɪmˈprɔmptjuː] *adj* improvvisato(a)
improper [ɪmˈprɔpə*] *adj* scorretto(a); (*unsuitable*) inadatto(a), improprio(a); sconveniente, indecente
improve [ɪmˈpruːv] *vt* migliorare ♦ *vi* migliorare; (*pupil etc*) fare progressi; **~ment** *n* miglioramento; progresso
improvise [ˈɪmprəvaɪz] *vt, vi* improvvisare
impudent [ˈɪmpjudnt] *adj* impudente, sfacciato(a)
impulse [ˈɪmpʌls] *n* impulso; **on ~** d'impulso, impulsivamente
impulsive [ɪmˈpʌlsɪv] *adj* impulsivo(a)

KEYWORD

in [ɪn] *prep* **1** (*indicating place, position*) in; ~ **the house/garden** in casa/giardino; ~ **the box** nella scatola; ~ **the fridge** nel frigorifero; **I have it** ~ **my hand** ce l'ho in mano; ~ **town/the country** in città/campagna; ~ **school** a scuola; ~ **here/there** qui/lì dentro
2 (*with place names: of town, region, country*): ~ **London** a Londra; ~ **England** in Inghilterra; ~ **the United States** negli Stati Uniti; ~ **Yorkshire** nello Yorkshire
3 (*indicating time: during, in the space of*) in; ~ **spring/summer** in primavera/estate; ~ **1988** nel 1988; ~ **May** in *or* a maggio; **I'll see you** ~ **July** ci vediamo a luglio; ~ **the afternoon** nel pomeriggio; **at 4 o'clock** ~ **the afternoon** alle 4 del

pomeriggio; **I did it ~ 3 hours/days** l'ho fatto in 3 ore/giorni; **I'll see you ~ 2 weeks** *or* **~ 2 weeks' time** ci vediamo tra 2 settimane

4 (*indicating manner etc*) a; **~ a loud/soft voice** a voce alta/bassa; **~ pencil** a matita; **~ English/French** in inglese/francese; **the boy ~ the blue shirt** il ragazzo con la camicia blu

5 (*indicating circumstances*): **~ the sun** al sole; **~ the shade** all'ombra; **~ the rain** sotto la pioggia; **a rise ~ prices** un aumento dei prezzi

6 (*indicating mood, state*): **~ tears** in lacrime; **~ anger** per la rabbia; **~ despair** disperato(a); **~ good condition** in buono stato, in buone condizioni; **to live ~ luxury** vivere nel lusso

7 (*with ratios, numbers*): **1 ~ 10** 1 su 10; **20 pence ~ the pound** 20 pence per sterlina; **they lined up ~ twos** si misero in fila a due a due

8 (*referring to people, works*) in; **the disease is common ~ children** la malattia è comune nei bambini; **~ (the works of) Dickens** in Dickens

9 (*indicating profession etc*) in; **to be ~ teaching** fare l'insegnante, insegnare; **to be ~ publishing** essere nell'editoria

10 (*after superlative*) di; **the best ~ the class** il migliore della classe

11 (*with present participle*): **~ saying this** dicendo questo, nel dire questo
♦ *adv*: **to be ~** (*person: at home, work*) esserci; (*train, ship, plane*) essere arrivato(a); (*in fashion*) essere di moda; **to ask sb ~** invitare qn ad entrare; **to run/limp** *etc* **~** entrare di corsa/zoppicando *etc*
♦ *n*: **the ~s and outs of the problem** tutti i particolari del problema

in. *abbr* = **inch**
inability [ɪnə'bɪlɪtɪ] *n*: **~ (to do)** incapacità (di fare)
inaccurate [ɪn'ækjʊrət] *adj* inesatto(a), impreciso(a)
inadequate [ɪn'ædɪkwət] *adj* insufficiente

inadvertently [ɪnəd'vɜːtntlɪ] *adv* senza volerlo
inadvisable [ɪnəd'vaɪzəbl] *adj* consigliabile
inane [ɪ'neɪn] *adj* vacuo(a), stupido(a)
inanimate [ɪn'ænɪmət] *adj* inanimato(a)
inappropriate [ɪnə'prəʊprɪət] *adj* non adatto(a); (*word, expression*) improprio(a)
inarticulate [ɪnɑː'tɪkjʊlət] *adj* (*person*) che si esprime male; (*speech*) inarticolato(a)
inasmuch as [ɪnəz'mʌtʃæz] *adv* in quanto che; (*insofar as*) poiché
inaudible [ɪn'ɔːdɪbl] *adj* che non si riesce a sentire
inauguration [ɪnɔːgjʊ'reɪʃən] *n* inaugurazione *f*; insediamento in carica
in-between *adj* fra i (*or* le) due
inborn [ɪn'bɔːn] *adj* innato(a)
inbred [ɪn'brɛd] *adj* innato(a); (*family*) connaturato(a)
Inc. (*US*) *abbr* (= *incorporated*) S.A
incapable [ɪn'keɪpəbl] *adj* incapace
incapacitate [ɪnkə'pæsɪteɪt] *vt*: **to ~ sb from doing** rendere qn incapace di fare
incense [*n* 'ɪnsɛns, *vb* ɪn'sɛns] *n* incenso
♦ *vt* (*anger*) infuriare
incentive [ɪn'sɛntɪv] *n* incentivo
incessant [ɪn'sɛsnt] *adj* incessante; **~ly** *adv* di continuo, senza sosta
inch [ɪntʃ] *n* pollice *m* (= *25 mm*; *12 in a foot*); **within an ~ of** a un pelo da; **he didn't give an ~** non ha ceduto di un millimetro; **~ forward** *vi* avanzare pian piano
incidence ['ɪnsɪdns] *n* (*of crime, disease*) incidenza
incident ['ɪnsɪdnt] *n* incidente *m*; (*in book*) episodio
incidental [ɪnsɪ'dɛntl] *adj* accessorio(a), d'accompagnamento; (*unplanned*) incidentale; **~ to** marginale a; **~ly** [-'dɛntlɪ] *adv* (*by the way*) a proposito
inclination [ɪnklɪ'neɪʃən] *n* inclinazione *f*
incline [*n* 'ɪnklaɪn, *vb* ɪn'klaɪn] *n* pendenza, pendio ♦ *vt* inclinare ♦ *vi* (*surface*) essere inclinato(a); **to be ~d to do** tendere a fare; essere propenso(a) a fare
include [ɪn'kluːd] *vt* includere,

comprendere; **including** *prep*
compreso(a), incluso(a)
inclusive [ɪn'kluːsɪv] *adj* incluso(a),
compreso(a); ~ **of tax** *etc* tasse *etc*
comprese
incoherent [ɪnkəu'hɪərənt] *adj*
incoerente
income ['ɪnkʌm] *n* reddito; ~ **tax** *n*
imposta sul reddito
incoming ['ɪnkʌmɪŋ] *adj* (*flight, mail*) in
arrivo; (*government*) subentrante; (*tide*)
montante
incompetent [ɪn'kɔmpɪtnt] *adj*
incompetente, incapace
incomplete [ɪnkəm'pliːt] *adj*
incompleto(a)
incongruous [ɪn'kɔŋgruəs] *adj* poco
appropriato(a); (*remark, act*) incongruo(a)
inconsiderate [ɪnkən'sɪdərət] *adj*
sconsiderato(a)
inconsistency [ɪnkən'sɪstənsɪ] *n*
incoerenza
inconsistent [ɪnkən'sɪstənt] *adj*
incoerente; ~ **with** non coerente con
inconspicuous [ɪnkən'spɪkjuəs] *adj*
incospicuo(a); (*colour*) poco appariscente;
(*dress*) dimesso(a)
inconvenience [ɪnkən'viːnjəns] *n*
inconveniente *m*; (*trouble*) disturbo ♦ *vt*
disturbare
inconvenient [ɪnkən'viːnjənt] *adj*
scomodo(a)
incorporate [ɪn'kɔːpəreɪt] *vt* incorporare;
(*contain*) contenere; ~ **d** *adj*: ~ **d company**
(*US*) società *f inv* anonima
incorrect [ɪnkə'rekt] *adj* scorretto(a);
(*statement*) inesatto(a)
increase [*n* 'ɪnkriːs, *vb* ɪn'kriːs] *n* aumento
♦ *vi, vt* aumentare
increasing [ɪn'kriːsɪŋ] *adj* (*number*)
crescente; ~ **ly** *adv* sempre più
incredible [ɪn'kredɪbl] *adj* incredibile
incredulous [ɪn'kredjuləs] *adj*
incredulo(a)
increment ['ɪnkrɪmənt] *n* aumento,
incremento
incriminate [ɪn'krɪmɪneɪt] *vt*
compromettere
incubator ['ɪnkjubeɪtə*] *n* incubatrice *f*

incumbent [ɪn'kʌmbənt] *n* titolare *m/f*
♦ *adj*: **to be** ~ **on sb** spettare a qn
incur [ɪn'kə:*] *vt* (*expenses*) incorrere;
(*anger, risk*) esporsi a; (*debt*) contrarre;
(*loss*) subire
indebted [ɪn'detɪd] *adj*: **to be** ~ **to sb**
(**for**) essere obbligato(a) verso qn (per)
indecent [ɪn'diːsnt] *adj* indecente; ~
assault (*BRIT*) *n* aggressione *f* a scopo di
violenza sessuale; ~ **exposure** *n* atti *mpl*
osceni in luogo pubblico
indecisive [ɪndɪ'saɪsɪv] *adj* indeciso(a)
indeed [ɪn'diːd] *adv* infatti; veramente;
yes ~! certamente!
indefinite [ɪn'defɪnɪt] *adj* indefinito(a);
(*answer*) vago(a); (*period, number*)
indeterminato(a); ~ **ly** *adv* (*wait*)
indefinitamente
indemnity [ɪn'demnɪtɪ] *n* (*insurance*)
assicurazione *f*; (*compensation*) indennità,
indennizzo
independence [ɪndɪ'pendns] *n*
indipendenza
independent [ɪndɪ'pendnt] *adj*
indipendente
index ['ɪndeks] (*pl* ~**es**) *n* (*in book*) indice
m; (: *in library etc*) catalogo; (*pl* **indices**:
ratio, sign) indice *m*; ~ **card** *n* scheda; ~
finger *n* (dito) indice *m*; ~ **-linked** (*US*
~ **ed**) *adj* legato(a) al costo della vita
India ['ɪndɪə] *n* India; ~ **n** *adj, n*
indiano(a); **Red** ~ **n** pellerossa *m/f*
indicate ['ɪndɪkeɪt] *vt* indicare;
indication [-'keɪʃən] *n* indicazione *f*,
segno
indicative [ɪn'dɪkətɪv] *adj*: ~ **of**
indicativo(a) di ♦ *n* (*LING*) indicativo
indicator ['ɪndɪkeɪtə*] *n* indicatore *m*;
(*AUT*) freccia
indices ['ɪndɪsiːz] *npl of* **index**
indictment [ɪn'daɪtmənt] *n* accusa
indifference [ɪn'dɪfrəns] *n* indifferenza
indifferent [ɪn'dɪfrənt] *adj* indifferente;
(*poor*) mediocre
indigenous [ɪn'dɪdʒɪnəs] *adj* indigeno(a)
indigestion [ɪndɪ'dʒestʃən] *n*
indigestione *f*
indignant [ɪn'dɪgnənt] *adj*: ~ (**at sth/**
with sb) indignato(a) (per qc/contro qn)

indignity [ɪnˈdɪɡnɪtɪ] *n* umiliazione *f*
indigo [ˈɪndɪɡəu] *n* indaco
indirect [ɪndɪˈrɛkt] *adj* indiretto(a)
indiscreet [ɪndɪˈskriːt] *adj* indiscreto(a);
(*rash*) imprudente
indiscriminate [ɪndɪˈskrɪmɪnət] *adj*
indiscriminato(a)
indisputable [ɪndɪˈspjuːtəbl] *adj*
incontestabile, indiscutibile
individual [ɪndɪˈvɪdjuəl] *n* individuo
♦ *adj* individuale; (*characteristic*) particolare, originale; **~ist** *n* individualista *m/f*
indoctrination [ɪndɔktrɪˈneɪʃən] *n*
indottrinamento
Indonesia [ɪndəˈniːzɪə] *n* Indonesia
indoor [ˈɪndɔː*] *adj* da interno; (*plant*)
d'appartamento; (*swimming pool*)
coperto(a); (*sport, games*) fatto(a) al
coperto; **~s** [ɪnˈdɔːz] *adv* all'interno
induce [ɪnˈdjuːs] *vt* persuadere; (*bring
about, MED*) provocare; **~ment** *n*
incentivo
indulge [ɪnˈdʌldʒ] *vt* (*whim*) compiacere,
soddisfare; (*child*) viziare ♦ *vi*: **to ~ in**
sth concedersi qc; abbandonarsi a qc;
~nce *n* lusso (che uno si permette);
(*leniency*) indulgenza; **~nt** *adj* indulgente
industrial [ɪnˈdʌstrɪəl] *adj* industriale;
(*injury*) sul lavoro; **~ action** *n* azione *f*
rivendicativa; **~ estate** (*BRIT*) *n* zona
industriale; **~ park** (*US*) *n* = **~ estate**
industrious [ɪnˈdʌstrɪəs] *adj*
industrioso(a), assiduo(a)
industry [ˈɪndəstrɪ] *n* industria;
(*diligence*) operosità
inebriated [ɪˈniːbrɪeɪtɪd] *adj* ubriaco(a)
inedible [ɪnˈedɪbl] *adj* immangiabile;
(*poisonous*) non commestibile
ineffective [ɪnɪˈfɛktɪv] *adj* inefficace;
incompetente
ineffectual [ɪnɪˈfɛktʃuəl] *adj* inefficace;
incompetente
inefficiency [ɪnɪˈfɪʃənsɪ] *n* inefficienza
inefficient [ɪnɪˈfɪʃənt] *adj* inefficiente
inept [ɪˈnept] *adj* inetto(a)
inequality [ɪnɪˈkwɔlɪtɪ] *n* ineguaglianza
inescapable [ɪnɪˈskeɪpəbl] *adj* inevitabile
inevitable [ɪnˈɛvɪtəbl] *adj* inevitabile;
inevitably *adv* inevitabilmente

inexact [ɪnɪɡˈzækt] *adj* inesatto(a)
inexcusable [ɪnɪksˈkjuːzəbl] *adj*
ingiustificabile
inexpensive [ɪnɪkˈspɛnsɪv] *adj* poco
costoso(a)
inexperienced [ɪnɪksˈpɪərɪənst] *adj*
inesperto(a), senza esperienza
infallible [ɪnˈfælɪbl] *adj* infallibile
infamous [ˈɪnfəməs] *adj* infame
infancy [ˈɪnfənsɪ] *n* infanzia
infant [ˈɪnfənt] *n* bambino/a; **~ school**
(*BRIT*) scuola elementare (*per bambini
dall'età di 5 a 7 anni*)
infantry [ˈɪnfəntrɪ] *n* fanteria
infatuated [ɪnˈfætjueɪtɪd] *adj*: **~ with**
infatuato(a) di
infatuation [ɪnfætjuˈeɪʃən] *n*
infatuazione *f*
infect [ɪnˈfɛkt] *vt* infettare; **~ion**
[ɪnˈfɛkʃən] *n* infezione *f*; **~ious** [ɪnˈfɛkʃəs]
adj (*disease*) infettivo(a), contagioso(a);
(*person, fig: enthusiasm*) contagioso(a)
infer [ɪnˈfəː*] *vt* inferire, dedurre
inferior [ɪnˈfɪərɪə*] *adj* inferiore; (*goods*)
di qualità scadente ♦ *n* inferiore *m/f*; (*in
rank*) subalterno/a; **~ity** [ɪnfɪərɪˈɔrətɪ] *n*
inferiorità; **~ity complex** *n* complesso di
inferiorità
inferno [ɪnˈfəːnəu] *n* rogo
infertile [ɪnˈfəːtaɪl] *adj* sterile
in-fighting [ˈɪnfaɪtɪŋ] *n* lotte *fpl* intestine
infiltrate [ˈɪnfɪltreɪt] *vt* infiltrarsi in
infinite [ˈɪnfɪnɪt] *adj* infinito(a)
infinitive [ɪnˈfɪnɪtɪv] *n* infinito
infinity [ɪnˈfɪnɪtɪ] *n* infinità; (*also MATH*)
infinito
infirmary [ɪnˈfəːmərɪ] *n* ospedale *m*; (*in
school, factory*) infermeria
infirmity [ɪnˈfəːmɪtɪ] *n* infermità *f inv*
inflamed [ɪnˈfleɪmd] *adj* infiammato(a)
inflammable [ɪnˈflæməbl] *adj*
infiammabile
inflammation [ɪnfləˈmeɪʃən] *n*
infiammazione *f*
inflatable [ɪnˈfleɪtəbl] *adj* gonfiabile
inflate [ɪnˈfleɪt] *vt* (*tyre, balloon*) gonfiare;
(*fig*) esagerare; gonfiare; **inflation**
[ɪnˈfleɪʃən] *n* (*ECON*) inflazione *f*;
inflationary [ɪnˈfleɪʃnərɪ] *adj*

inflazionistico(a)

inflict [ɪn'flɪkt] *vt*: **to ~ on** infliggere a

influence ['ɪnfluəns] *n* influenza ♦ *vt* influenzare; **under the ~ of alcohol** sotto l'effetto dell'alcool

influential [ɪnflu'ɛnʃl] *adj* influente

influenza [ɪnflu'ɛnzə] *n* (*MED*) influenza

influx ['ɪnflʌks] *n* afflusso

inform [ɪn'fɔːm] *vt*: **to ~ sb (of)** informare qn (di) ♦ *vi*: **to ~ on sb** denunciare qn

informal [ɪn'fɔːml] *adj* informale; (*announcement, invitation*) non ufficiale; **~ity** [-'mælɪtɪ] *n* informalità; carattere *m* non ufficiale

informant [ɪn'fɔːmənt] *n* informatore/ trice

information [ɪnfə'meɪʃən] *n* informazioni *fpl*; particolari *mpl*; **a piece of ~** un'informazione; **~ office** *n* ufficio *m* informazioni *inv*

informative [ɪn'fɔːmətɪv] *adj* istruttivo

informer [ɪn'fɔːmə*] *n* (*also: police ~*) informatore/trice

infringe [ɪn'frɪndʒ] *vt* infrangere ♦ *vi*: **to ~ on** calpestare; **~ment** *n* infrazione *f*

infuriating [ɪn'fjuərɪeɪtɪŋ] *adj* molto irritante

ingenious [ɪn'dʒiːnjəs] *adj* ingegnoso(a)

ingenuity [ɪndʒɪ'njuːɪtɪ] *n* ingegnosità

ingenuous [ɪn'dʒɛnjuəs] *adj* ingenuo(a)

ingot ['ɪŋgət] *n* lingotto

ingrained [ɪn'greɪnd] *adj* radicato(a)

ingratiate [ɪn'greɪʃɪeɪt] *vt*: **to ~ o.s. with sb** ingraziarsi qn

ingredient [ɪn'griːdɪənt] *n* ingrediente *m*; elemento

inhabit [ɪn'hæbɪt] *vt* abitare

inhabitant [ɪn'hæbɪtnt] *n* abitante *m/f*

inhale [ɪn'heɪl] *vt* inalare ♦ *vi* (*in smoking*) aspirare

inherent [ɪn'hɪərənt] *adj*: **~ (in or to)** inerente (a)

inherit [ɪn'herɪt] *vt* ereditare; **~ance** *n* eredità

inhibit [ɪn'hɪbɪt] *vt* (*PSYCH*) inibire; **~ion** [-'bɪʃən] *n* inibizione *f*

inhospitable [ɪnhɔs'pɪtəbl] *adj* inospitale

inhuman [ɪn'hjuːmən] *adj* inumano(a)

initial [ɪ'nɪʃl] *adj* iniziale ♦ *n* iniziale *f* ♦ *vt* siglare; **~s** *npl* (*of name*) iniziali *fpl*; (*as signature*) sigla; **~ly** *adv* inizialmente, all'inizio

initiate [ɪ'nɪʃɪeɪt] *vt* (*start*) avviare; intraprendere; iniziare; (*person*) iniziare; **to ~ sb into a secret** mettere qn a parte di un segreto; **to ~ proceedings against sb** (*LAW*) intentare causa contro qn

initiative [ɪ'nɪʃətɪv] *n* iniziativa

inject [ɪn'dʒɛkt] *vt* (*liquid*) iniettare; (*patient*): **to ~ sb with sth** fare a qn un'iniezione di qc; (*funds*) immettere; **~ion** [ɪn'dʒɛkʃən] *n* iniezione *f*, puntura

injure ['ɪndʒə*] *vt* ferire; (*damage: reputation etc*) nuocere a; **~d** *adj* ferito(a)

injury ['ɪndʒərɪ] *n* ferita; **~ time** *n* (*SPORT*) tempo di ricupero

injustice [ɪn'dʒʌstɪs] *n* ingiustizia

ink [ɪŋk] *n* inchiostro

inkling ['ɪŋklɪŋ] *n* sentore *m*, vaga idea

inlaid ['ɪnleɪd] *adj* incrostato(a); (*table etc*) intarsiato(a)

inland [*adj* 'ɪnlənd, *adv* ɪn'lænd] *adj* interno(a) ♦ *adv* all'interno; **I~ Revenue** (*BRIT*) *n* Fisco

in-laws ['ɪnlɔːz] *npl* suoceri *mpl*; famiglia del marito (*or* della moglie)

inlet ['ɪnlɛt] *n* (*GEO*) insenatura, baia

inmate ['ɪnmeɪt] *n* (*in prison*) carcerato/ a; (*in asylum*) ricoverato/a

inn [ɪn] *n* locanda

innate [ɪ'neɪt] *adj* innato(a)

inner ['ɪnə*] *adj* interno(a), interiore; **~ city** *n* centro di una zona urbana; **~ tube** *n* camera d'aria

innings ['ɪnɪŋz] *n* (*CRICKET*) turno di battuta

innocence ['ɪnəsns] *n* innocenza

innocent ['ɪnəsnt] *adj* innocente

innocuous [ɪ'nɔkjuəs] *adj* innocuo(a)

innuendo [ɪnju'ɛndəu] (*pl* **~es**) *n* insinuazione *f*

innumerable [ɪ'njuːmrəbl] *adj* innumerevole

inordinately [ɪ'nɔːdɪnətlɪ] *adv* smoderatamente

in-patient *n* ricoverato/a

input ['ɪnput] *n* input *m*

inquest ['ɪnkwɛst] *n* inchiesta

inquire [ɪn'kwaɪə*] *vi* informarsi ♦ *vt* domandare, informarsi su; **~ about** *vt fus* informarsi di *or* su; **~ into** *vt fus* fare indagini su; **inquiry** *n* domanda; (*LAW*) indagine *f*, investigazione *f*; **inquiry office** (*BRIT*) *n* ufficio *m* informazioni *inv*

inquisitive [ɪn'kwɪzɪtɪv] *adj* curioso(a)

inroads ['ɪnrəudz] *npl*: **to make ~ into** (*savings etc*) intaccare (pesantemente)

ins. *abbr* = **inches**

insane [ɪn'seɪn] *adj* matto(a), pazzo(a); (*MED*) alienato(a)

insanity [ɪn'sænɪtɪ] *n* follia; (*MED*) alienazione *f* mentale

inscription [ɪn'skrɪpʃən] *n* iscrizione *f*, dedica

inscrutable [ɪn'skruːtəbl] *adj* imperscrutabile

insect ['ɪnsɛkt] *n* insetto; **~icide** [ɪn'sɛktɪsaɪd] *n* insetticida *m*

insecure [ɪnsɪ'kjuə*] *adj* malsicuro(a); (*person*) insicuro(a)

insemination [ɪnsɛmɪ'neɪʃən] *n*: **artificial ~** fecondazione *f* artificiale

insensible [ɪn'sɛnsɪbl] *adj* (*unconscious*) privo(a) di sensi

insensitive [ɪn'sɛnsɪtɪv] *adj* insensibile

insert [ɪn'səːt] *vt* inserire, introdurre; **~ion** [ɪn'səːʃən] *n* inserzione *f*

in-service *adj* (*training, course*) durante l'orario di lavoro

inshore [ɪn'ʃɔː*] *adj* costiero(a) ♦ *adv* presso la riva; verso la riva

inside ['ɪn'saɪd] *n* interno, parte *f* interiore ♦ *adj* interno(a), interiore ♦ *adv* dentro, all'interno ♦ *prep* dentro, all'interno di; (*of time*): **~ 10 minutes** entro 10 minuti; **~s** *npl* (*inf: stomach*) ventre *m*; **~ forward** *n* (*SPORT*) mezzala, interno; **~ lane** *n* (*AUT*) corsia di marcia; **~ out** *adv* (*turn*) a rovescio; (*know*) a fondo

insider dealing [ɪn'saɪdə'diːlɪŋ] *n* insider dealing *m inv*

insider trading [ɪn'saɪdə'treɪdɪŋ] *n* insider trading *m inv*

insight ['ɪnsaɪt] *n* acume *m*, perspicacia;

(*glimpse, idea*) percezione *f*

insignia [ɪn'sɪgnɪə] *npl* insegne *fpl*

insignificant [ɪnsɪg'nɪfɪknt] *adj* insignificante

insincere [ɪnsɪn'sɪə*] *adj* insincero(a)

insinuate [ɪn'sɪnjueɪt] *vt* insinuare

insist [ɪn'sɪst] *vi* insistere; **to ~ on doing** insistere per fare; **to ~ that** insistere perché + *sub*; (*claim*) sostenere che; **~ent** *adj* insistente

insole ['ɪnsəul] *n* soletta

insolent ['ɪnsələnt] *adj* insolente

insomnia [ɪn'sɔmnɪə] *n* insonnia

inspect [ɪn'spɛkt] *vt* ispezionare; (*BRIT: ticket*) controllare; **~ion** [ɪn'spɛkʃən] *n* ispezione *f*; controllo; **~or** *n* ispettore/trice; (*BRIT: on buses, trains*) controllore *m*

inspire [ɪn'spaɪə*] *vt* ispirare; **~ation** [ɪnstə'leɪʃən] *n* installazione *f*

install [ɪn'stɔːl] *vt* installare; **~ation** [ɪnstə'leɪʃən] *n* installazione *f*

instalment [ɪn'stɔːlmənt] (*US* **installment**) *n* rata; (*of TV serial etc*) puntata; **in ~s** (*pay*) a rate; (*receive*) una parte per volta; (: *publication*) a fascicoli

instance ['ɪnstəns] *n* esempio, caso; **for ~** per *or* ad esempio; **in the first ~** in primo luogo

instant ['ɪnstənt] *n* istante *m*, attimo ♦ *adj* immediato(a); urgente; (*coffee, food*) in polvere; **~ly** *adv* immediatamente, subito

instead [ɪn'stɛd] *adv* invece; **~ of** invece di

instep ['ɪnstɛp] *n* collo del piede; (*of shoe*) collo della scarpa

instil [ɪn'stɪl] *vt*: **to ~ (into)** inculcare (in)

instinct ['ɪnstɪŋkt] *n* istinto

institute ['ɪnstɪtjuːt] *n* istituto ♦ *vt* istituire, stabilire; (*inquiry*) avviare; (*proceedings*) iniziare

institution [ɪnstɪ'tjuːʃən] *n* istituzione *f*; (*educational ~, mental ~*) istituto

instruct [ɪn'strʌkt] *vt*: **to ~ sb in sth** insegnare qc a qn; **to ~ sb to do** dare ordini a qn di fare; **~ion** [ɪn'strʌkʃən] *n* istruzione *f*; **~ions (for use)** istruzioni per l'uso; **~or** *n* istruttore/trice; (*for skiing*) maestro/a

instrument ['ɪnstrəmənt] *n* strumento; **~al** [-'mɛntl] *adj* (*MUS*) strumentale; **to be**

~al in essere d'aiuto in; ~ panel *n* quadro *m* portastrumenti *inv*

insufferable [ɪnˈsʌfərəbl] *adj* insopportabile

insufficient [ɪnsəˈfɪʃənt] *adj* insufficiente

insular [ˈɪnsjulə*] *adj* insulare; (*person*) di mente ristretta

insulate [ˈɪnsjuleɪt] *vt* isolare; insulating tape *n* nastro isolante; insulation [-ˈleɪʃən] *n* isolamento

insulin [ˈɪnsjulɪn] *n* insulina

insult [*n* ˈɪnsʌlt, *vb* ɪnˈsʌlt] *n* insulto, affronto ♦ *vt* insultare; ~ing *adj* offensivo(a), ingiurioso(a)

insuperable [ɪnˈsjuːprəbl] *adj* insormontabile, insuperabile

insurance [ɪnˈʃuərəns] *n* assicurazione *f*; fire/life ~ assicurazione contro gli incendi/sulla vita; ~ policy *n* polizza d'assicurazione

insure [ɪnˈʃuə*] *vt* assicurare

intact [ɪnˈtækt] *adj* intatto(a)

intake [ˈɪnteɪk] *n* (*TECH*) immissione *f*; (*of food*) consumo; (*BRIT: of pupils etc*) afflusso

integral [ˈɪntɪgrəl] *adj* integrale; (*part*) integrante

integrate [ˈɪntɪgreɪt] *vt* integrare ♦ *vi* integrarsi

integrity [ɪnˈtegrɪtɪ] *n* integrità

intellect [ˈɪntəlekt] *n* intelletto; ~ual [-ˈlektjuəl] *adj, n* intellettuale *m/f*

intelligence [ɪnˈtelɪdʒəns] *n* intelligenza; (*MIL etc*) informazioni *fpl*; ~ service *n* servizio segreto

intelligent [ɪnˈtelɪdʒənt] *adj* intelligente

intend [ɪnˈtend] *vt* (*gift etc*): to ~ sth for destinare qc a; to ~ to do aver l'intenzione di fare; ~ed *adj* (*effect*) voluto(a)

intense [ɪnˈtens] *adj* intenso(a); (*person*) di forti sentimenti; ~ly *adv* intensamente; profondamente

intensive [ɪnˈtensɪv] *adj* intensivo(a); ~ care unit *n* reparto terapia intensiva

intent [ɪnˈtent] *n* intenzione *f* ♦ *adj*: ~ (on) intento(a) (a), immerso(a) (in); to all ~s and purposes a tutti gli effetti; to be ~ on doing sth essere deciso a fare qc

intention [ɪnˈtenʃən] *n* intenzione *f*; ~al

adj intenzionale, deliberato(a); ~ally *adv* apposta

intently [ɪnˈtentlɪ] *adv* attentamente

interact [ɪntərˈækt] *vi* interagire

interactive *adj* (*COMPUT*) interattivo(a)

interchange [ˈɪntətʃeɪndʒ] *n* (*exchange*) scambio; (*on motorway*) incrocio pluridirezionale; ~able [-ˈtʃeɪndʒəbl] *adj* intercambiabile

intercom [ˈɪntəkɔm] *n* interfono

intercourse [ˈɪntəkɔːs] *n* rapporti *mpl*

interest [ˈɪntrɪst] *n* interesse *m*; (*COMM: stake, share*) interessi *mpl* ♦ *vt* interessare; ~ed *adj* interessato(a); to be ~ed in interessarsi di; ~ing *adj* interessante; ~ rate *n* tasso di interesse

interface [ˈɪntəfeɪs] *n* (*COMPUT*) interfaccia

interfere [ɪntəˈfɪə*] *vi*: to ~ in (*quarrel, other people's business*) immischiarsi in; to ~ with (*object*) toccare; (*plans, duty*) interferire con

interference [ɪntəˈfɪərəns] *n* interferenza

interim [ˈɪntərɪm] *adj* provvisorio(a) ♦ *n*: in the ~ nel frattempo

interior [ɪnˈtɪərɪə*] *n* interno; (*of country*) entroterra ♦ *adj* interno(a); (*minister*) degli Interni; ~ designer *n* arredatore/trice

interlock [ɪntəˈlɔk] *vi* ingranarsi

interloper [ˈɪntələupə*] *n* intruso/a

interlude [ˈɪntəluːd] *n* intervallo; (*THEATRE*) intermezzo

intermarry [ɪntəˈmærɪ] *vi* fare un matrimonio misto

intermediate [ɪntəˈmiːdɪət] *adj* intermedio(a)

intermission [ɪntəˈmɪʃən] *n* pausa; (*THEATRE, CINEMA*) intermissione *f*, intervallo

intern [*vb* ɪnˈtəːn, *n* ˈɪntəːn] *vt* internare ♦ *n* (*US*) medico interno

internal [ɪnˈtəːnl] *adj* interno(a); ~ly *adv*: "not to be taken ~ly" "per uso esterno"; I~ Revenue Service (*US*) *n* Fisco

international [ɪntəˈnæʃənl] *adj* internazionale ♦ *n* (*BRIT: SPORT*) incontro internazionale

interplay [ˈɪntəpleɪ] *n* azione e reazione *f*

interpret [ɪnˈtəːprɪt] *vt* interpretare ♦ *vi* fare da interprete; **~er** *n* interprete *m/f*

interrelated [ɪntərɪˈleɪtɪd] *adj* correlato(a)

interrogate [ɪnˈtɛrəʊgeɪt] *vt* interrogare; **interrogation** [-ˈgeɪʃən] *n* interrogazione *f*; (*of suspect etc*) interrogatorio; **interrogative** [ɪntəˈrɔgətɪv] *adj* interrogativo(a)

interrupt [ɪntəˈrʌpt] *vt*, *vi* interrompere; **~ion** [-ˈrʌpʃən] *n* interruzione *f*

intersect [ɪntəˈsɛkt] *vi* (*roads*) incrociarsi; **~ion** [-ˈsɛkʃən] *n* intersezione *f*; (*of roads*) incrocio

intersperse [ɪntəˈspəːs] *vt*: **to ~ with** costellare di

intertwine [ɪntəˈtwaɪn] *vi* intrecciarsi

interval [ˈɪntəvl] *n* intervallo; **at ~s** a intervalli

intervene [ɪntəˈviːn] *vi* (*time*) intercorrere; (*event, person*) intervenire; **intervention** [-ˈvɛnʃən] *n* intervento

interview [ˈɪntəvjuː] *n* (*RADIO, TV etc*) intervista; (*for job*) colloquio ♦ *vt* intervistare; avere un colloquio con; **~er** *n* intervistatore/trice

intestine [ɪnˈtɛstɪn] *n* intestino

intimacy [ˈɪntɪməsɪ] *n* intimità

intimate [*adj* ˈɪntɪmət, *vb* ˈɪntɪmeɪt] *adj* intimo(a); (*knowledge*) profondo(a) ♦ *vt* lasciar capire

into [ˈɪntuː] *prep* dentro, in; **come ~ the house** entra in casa; **he worked late ~ the night** lavorò fino a tarda notte; **~ Italian** in italiano

intolerable [ɪnˈtɔlərəbl] *adj* intollerabile

intolerance [ɪnˈtɔlərns] *n* intolleranza

intolerant [ɪnˈtɔlərnt] *adj*: **~ of** intollerante di

intoxicated [ɪnˈtɔksɪkeɪtɪd] *adj* inebriato(a)

intoxication [ɪntɔksɪˈkeɪʃən] *n* ebbrezza

intractable [ɪnˈtræktəbl] *adj* intrattabile

intransitive [ɪnˈtrænsɪtɪv] *adj* intransitivo(a)

intravenous [ɪntrəˈviːnəs] *adj* endovenoso(a)

in-tray *n* contenitore *m* per la corrispondenza in arrivo

intricate [ˈɪntrɪkət] *adj* intricato(a), complicato(a)

intrigue [ɪnˈtriːg] *n* intrigo ♦ *vt* affascinare; **intriguing** *adj* affascinante

intrinsic [ɪnˈtrɪnsɪk] *adj* intrinseco(a)

introduce [ɪntrəˈdjuːs] *vt* introdurre; **to ~ sb (to sb)** presentare qn (a qn); **to ~ sb to** (*pastime, technique*) iniziare qn a; **introduction** [-ˈdʌkʃən] *n* introduzione *f*; (*of person*) presentazione *f*; (*to new experience*) iniziazione *f*; **introductory** *adj* introduttivo(a)

intrude [ɪnˈtruːd] *vi* (*person*): **to ~ (on)** intromettersi (in); **~r** *n* intruso/a

intuition [ɪntjuːˈɪʃən] *n* intuizione *f*

inundate [ˈɪnʌndeɪt] *vt*: **to ~ with** inondare di

invade [ɪnˈveɪd] *vt* invadere

invalid [*n* ˈɪnvəlɪd, *adj* ɪnˈvælɪd] *n* malato/a; (*with disability*) invalido/a ♦ *adj* (*not valid*) invalido(a), non valido(a)

invaluable [ɪnˈvæljuəbl] *adj* prezioso(a); inestimabile

invariably [ɪnˈvɛərɪəblɪ] *adv* invariabilmente; sempre

invasion [ɪnˈveɪʒən] *n* invasione *f*

invent [ɪnˈvɛnt] *vt* inventare; **~ion** [ɪnˈvɛnʃən] *n* invenzione *f*; **~ive** *adj* inventivo(a); **~or** *n* inventore *m*

inventory [ˈɪnvəntrɪ] *n* inventario

invert [ɪnˈvəːt] *vt* invertire; (*cup, object*) rovesciare; **~ed commas** (*BRIT*) *npl* virgolette *fpl*

invest [ɪnˈvɛst] *vt* investire ♦ *vi*: **to ~ (in)** investire (in)

investigate [ɪnˈvɛstɪgeɪt] *vt* investigare, indagare; (*crime*) fare indagini su; **investigation** [-ˈgeɪʃən] *n* investigazione *f*; (*of crime*) indagine *f*

investment [ɪnˈvɛstmənt] *n* investimento

investor [ɪnˈvɛstə*] *n* investitore/trice; azionista *m/f*

invidious [ɪnˈvɪdɪəs] *adj* odioso(a); (*task*) spiacevole

invigilator [ɪnˈvɪdʒɪleɪtə*] *n* (*in exam*) sorvegliante *m/f*

invigorating [ɪnˈvɪgəreɪtɪŋ] *adj* stimolante; vivificante

invisible [ɪn'vɪzɪbl] *adj* invisibile
invitation [ɪnvɪ'teɪʃən] *n* invito
invite [ɪn'vaɪt] *vt* invitare; (*opinions etc*)
sollecitare; **inviting** *adj* invitante,
attraente
invoice ['ɪnvɔɪs] *n* fattura ♦ *vt* fatturare
involuntary [ɪn'vɔləntrɪ] *adj*
involontario(a)
involve [ɪn'vɔlv] *vt* (*entail*) richiedere,
comportare; (*associate*): **to ~ sb (in)**
implicare qn (in); coinvolgere qn (in); **~d**
adj involuto(a), complesso(a); **to be ~d in**
essere coinvolto(a) in; **~ment** *n*
implicazione *f*; coinvolgimento
inward ['ɪnwəd] *adj* (*movement*) verso
l'interno; (*thought, feeling*) interiore,
intimo(a); **~(s)** *adv* verso l'interno
I/O *abbr* (COMPUT: = *input/output*) I/O
iodine ['aɪədiːn] *n* iodio
ioniser ['aɪənaɪzə*] *n* ionizzatore *m*
iota [aɪ'əutə] *n* (*fig*) briciolo
IOU *n abbr* (= *I owe you*) pagherò *m inv*
IQ *n abbr* (= *intelligence quotient*)
quoziente *m* d'intelligenza
IRA *n abbr* (= *Irish Republican Army*)
IRA *f*
Iran [ɪ'rɑːn] *n* Iran *m*; **~ian** *adj, n*
iraniano(a)
Iraq [ɪ'rɑːk] *n* Iraq *m*; **~i** *adj, n*
iracheno(a)
irate [aɪ'reɪt] *adj* adirato(a)
Ireland ['aɪələnd] *n* Irlanda
iris ['aɪrɪs] (*pl* **~es**) *n* iride *f*; (BOT)
giaggiolo, iride
Irish ['aɪrɪʃ] *adj* irlandese ♦ *npl*: **the ~** gli
Irlandesi; **~man** *n* irlandese *m*; **~ Sea** *n*
Mar *m* d'Irlanda; **~woman** *n* irlandese *f*
irksome ['əːksəm] *adj* seccante
iron ['aɪən] *n* ferro; (*for clothes*) ferro da
stiro ♦ *adj* di *or* in ferro ♦ *vt* (*clothes*)
stirare; **~ out** *vt* (*crease*) appianare; (*fig*)
spianare; far sparire; **the I~ Curtain** *n* la
cortina di ferro
ironic(al) [aɪ'rɔnɪk(l)] *adj* ironico(a)
ironing ['aɪənɪŋ] *n* (*act*) stirare *m*;
(*clothes*) roba da stirare; **~ board** *n* asse *f*
da stiro
ironmonger's (shop) ['aɪənmʌŋɡəz-]
(BRIT) *n* negozio di ferramenta

irony ['aɪrənɪ] *n* ironia
irrational [ɪ'ræʃənl] *adj* irrazionale
irregular [ɪ'reɡjulə*] *adj* irregolare
irrelevant [ɪ'reləvənt] *adj* non pertinente
irreplaceable [ɪrɪ'pleɪsəbl] *adj*
insostituibile
irrepressible [ɪrɪ'presəbl] *adj*
irrefrenabile
irresistible [ɪrɪ'zɪstɪbl] *adj* irresistibile
irrespective [ɪrɪ'spektɪv]: **~ of** *prep*
senza riguardo a
irresponsible [ɪrɪ'spɔnsɪbl] *adj*
irresponsabile
irrigate ['ɪrɪɡeɪt] *vt* irrigare; **irrigation**
[-'ɡeɪʃən] *n* irrigazione *f*
irritable ['ɪrɪtəbl] *adj* irritabile
irritate ['ɪrɪteɪt] *vt* irritare; **irritating** *adj*
(*person, sound etc*) irritante; **irritation**
[-'teɪʃən] *n* irritazione *f*
IRS (US) *n abbr* = **Internal Revenue
Service**
is [ɪz] *vb see* **be**
Islam ['ɪzlɑːm] *n* Islam *m*
island ['aɪlənd] *n* isola; **~er** *n* isolano/a
isle [aɪl] *n* isola
isn't ['ɪznt] = **is not**
isolate ['aɪsəleɪt] *vt* isolare; **~d** *adj*
isolato(a); **isolation** [-'leɪʃən] *n*
isolamento
Israel ['ɪzreɪl] *n* Israele *m*; **~i** [ɪz'reɪlɪ] *adj,
n* israeliano(a)
issue ['ɪʃuː] *n* questione *f*, problema *m*;
(*of banknotes etc*) emissione *f*; (*of newspaper etc*) numero ♦ *vt* (*statement*)
rilasciare; (*rations, equipment*)
distribuire; (*book*) pubblicare; (*banknotes,
cheques, stamps*) emettere; **at ~** in gioco,
in discussione; **to take ~ with sb (over
sth)** prendere posizione contro qn
(riguardo a qc); **to make an ~ of sth** fare
un problema di qc
isthmus ['ɪsməs] *n* istmo

KEYWORD

it [ɪt] *pron* **1** (*specific: subject*) esso(a);
(: *direct object*) lo(la), l'; (: *indirect object*)
gli(le); **where's my book?** — **~'s on the
table** dov'è il mio libro? — è sulla tavola;
I can't find ~ non lo (*or* la) trovo; **give ~**

to me dammelo (*or* dammela); **about/from/of** ~ ne; **I spoke to him about** ~ gliene ho parlato; **what did you learn from** ~? quale insegnamento ne hai tratto?; **I'm proud of** ~ ne sono fiero; **did you go to** ~? ci sei andato?; **put the book in** ~ mettici il libro
2 (*impers*): ~**'s raining** piove; ~**'s Friday tomorrow** domani è venerdì; ~**'s 6 o'clock** sono le 6; **who is** ~? — ~**'s me** chi è? — sono io

Italian [ɪ'tæljən] *adj* italiano(a) ♦ *n* italiano/a; (*LING*) italiano; **the** ~**s** gli Italiani
italics [ɪ'tæliks] *npl* corsivo
Italy ['ɪtəlɪ] *n* Italia
itch [ɪtʃ] *n* prurito ♦ *vi* (*person*) avere il prurito; (*part of body*) prudere; **to** ~ **to do sth** aver una gran voglia di fare qc; ~**y** *adj* che prude; **to be** ~**y** = **to** ~
it'd ['ɪtd] = **it would**; **it had**
item ['aɪtəm] *n* articolo; (*on agenda*) punto; (*also: news* ~) notizia; ~**ize** *vt* specificare, dettagliare
itinerant [ɪ'tɪnərənt] *adj* ambulante
itinerary [aɪ'tɪnərərɪ] *n* itinerario
it'll ['ɪtl] = **it will**; **it shall**
its [ɪts] *adj* il(la) suo(a), i(le) suoi(sue)
it's [ɪts] = **it is**; **it has**
itself [ɪt'sɛlf] *pron* (*emphatic*) esso(a) stesso(a); (*reflexive*) si
ITV *n* (*BRIT*) *n abbr* (= *Independent Television*) rete televisiva in concorrenza con la BBC
I.U.D. *n abbr* (= *intra-uterine device*) spirale *f*
I've [aɪv] = **I have**
ivory ['aɪvərɪ] *n* avorio
ivy ['aɪvɪ] *n* edera

J

jab [dʒæb] *vt* dare colpetti a ♦ *n* (*MED: inf*) puntura; **to** ~ **sth into** affondare *or* piantare qc dentro
jack [dʒæk] *n* (*AUT*) cricco; (*CARDS*) fante *m*; ~ **up** *vt* sollevare col cricco

jackal ['dʒækl] *n* sciacallo
jackdaw ['dʒækdɔː] *n* taccola
jacket ['dʒækɪt] *n* giacca; (*of book*) copertura
jack-knife *vi*: **the lorry** ~**d** l'autotreno si è piegato su se stesso
jack plug *n* (*ELEC*) jack *m inv*
jackpot ['dʒækpɔt] *n* primo premio (in denaro)
jade [dʒeɪd] *n* (*stone*) giada
jaded ['dʒeɪdɪd] *adj* sfinito(a), spossato(a)
jagged ['dʒægɪd] *adj* seghettato(a); (*cliffs etc*) frastagliato(a)
jail [dʒeɪl] *n* prigione *f* ♦ *vt* mandare in prigione
jam [dʒæm] *n* marmellata; (*also: traffic* ~) ingorgo; (*inf*) pasticcio ♦ *vt* (*passage etc*) ingombrare, ostacolare; (*mechanism, drawer etc*) bloccare; (*RADIO*) disturbare con interferenze ♦ *vi* incepparsi; **to** ~ **sth into** forzare qc dentro; infilare qc a forza dentro
Jamaica [dʒə'meɪkə] *n* Giamaica
jangle ['dʒæŋgl] *vi* risuonare; (*bracelet*) tintinnare
janitor ['dʒænɪtə*] *n* (*caretaker*) portiere *m*; (*: SCOL*) bidello
January ['dʒænjuərɪ] *n* gennaio
Japan [dʒə'pæn] *n* Giappone *m*; ~**ese** [dʒæpə'niːz] *adj* giapponese ♦ *n inv* giapponese *m/f*; (*LING*) giapponese *m*
jar [dʒɑː*] *n* (*glass*) barattolo, vasetto ♦ *vi* (*sound*) stridere; (*colours etc*) stonare
jargon ['dʒɑːgən] *n* gergo
jasmin(e) ['dʒæzmɪn] *n* gelsomino
jaundice ['dʒɔːndɪs] *n* itterizia; ~**d** *adj* (*fig*) cupo(a)
jaunt [dʒɔːnt] *n* gita; ~**y** *adj* vivace; disinvolto(a)
javelin ['dʒævlɪn] *n* giavellotto
jaw [dʒɔː] *n* mascella
jay [dʒeɪ] *n* ghiandaia
jaywalker ['dʒeɪwɔːkə*] *n* pedone(a) indisciplinato(a)
jazz [dʒæz] *n* jazz *m*; ~ **up** *vt* rendere vivace
jealous ['dʒɛləs] *adj* geloso(a); ~**y** *n* gelosia
jeans [dʒiːnz] *npl* (blue-)jeans *mpl*

jeer [dʒɪə*] vi: **to ~ (at)** fischiare; beffeggiare

jelly ['dʒɛlɪ] n gelatina; **~fish** n medusa

jeopardy ['dʒɛpədɪ] n: **in ~** in pericolo

jerk [dʒəːk] n sobbalzo, scossa; sussulto; (inf: idiot) tonto/a ♦ vt dare una scossa a ♦ vi (vehicles) sobbalzare

jerkin ['dʒəːkɪn] n giubbotto

jersey ['dʒəːzɪ] n maglia; (fabric) jersey m

jest [dʒɛst] n scherzo

Jesus ['dʒiːzəs] n Gesù m

jet [dʒɛt] n (of gas, liquid) getto; (AVIAT) aviogetto; **~-black** adj nero(a) come l'ebano, corvino(a); **~ engine** n motore m a reazione; **~ lag** n (problemi mpl dovuti allo) sbalzo dei fusi orari

jettison ['dʒɛtɪsn] vt gettare in mare

jetty ['dʒɛtɪ] n molo

Jew [dʒuː] n ebreo

jewel ['dʒuːəl] n gioiello; **~ler** (US **~er**) n orefice m, gioielliere/a; **~(l)er's (shop)** n oreficeria, gioielleria; **~lery** (US **~ery**) n gioielli mpl

Jewess ['dʒuːɪs] n ebrea

Jewish ['dʒuːɪʃ] adj ebreo(a), ebraico(a)

jibe [dʒaɪb] n beffa

jiffy ['dʒɪfɪ] (inf) n: **in a ~** in un batter d'occhio

jig [dʒɪɡ] n giga

jigsaw ['dʒɪɡsɔː] n (also: **~ puzzle**) puzzle m inv

jilt [dʒɪlt] vt piantare in asso

jingle ['dʒɪŋɡl] n (for advert) sigla pubblicitaria ♦ vi tintinnare, scampanellare

jinx [dʒɪŋks] n iettatura; (person) iettatore/trice

jitters ['dʒɪtəz] (inf) npl: **to get the ~** aver fifa

job [dʒɔb] n lavoro; (employment) impiego, posto; **it's not my ~** (duty) non è compito mio; **it's a good ~ that ...** meno male che ...; **just the ~!** proprio quello che ci vuole; **~ centre** (BRIT) n ufficio di collocamento; **~less** adj senza lavoro, disoccupato(a)

jockey ['dʒɔkɪ] n fantino, jockey m inv ♦ vi: **to ~ for position** manovrare per una posizione di vantaggio

jocular ['dʒɔkjulə*] adj gioviale; scherzoso(a)

jog [dʒɔɡ] vt urtare ♦ vi (SPORT) fare footing, fare jogging; **to ~ sb's memory** rinfrescare la memoria a qn; **to ~ along** trottare; (fig) andare avanti piano piano; **~ging** n footing m, jogging m

join [dʒɔɪn] vt unire, congiungere; (become member of) iscriversi a; (meet) raggiungere; riunirsi a ♦ vi (roads, rivers) confluire ♦ n giuntura; **~ in** vi partecipare ♦ vt fus unirsi a; **~ up** vi incontrarsi; (MIL) arruolarsi

joiner ['dʒɔɪnə*] (BRIT) n falegname m

joint [dʒɔɪnt] n (TECH) giuntura; giunto; (ANAT) articolazione f, giuntura; (BRIT: CULIN) arrosto; (inf: place) locale m; (: of cannabis) spinello ♦ adj comune; **~ account** n (at bank etc) conto in partecipazione, conto comune

joist [dʒɔɪst] n trave f

joke [dʒəuk] n scherzo; (funny story) barzelletta; (also: **practical ~**) beffa ♦ vi scherzare; **to play a ~ on sb** fare uno scherzo a qn; **~r** n (CARDS) matta, jolly m inv

jolly ['dʒɔlɪ] adj allegro(a), gioioso(a) ♦ adv (BRIT: inf) veramente, proprio

jolt [dʒəult] n scossa, sobbalzo ♦ vt urtare

Jordan ['dʒɔːdən] n (country) Giordania; (river) Giordano

jostle ['dʒɔsl] vt spingere coi gomiti

jot [dʒɔt] n: **not one ~** nemmeno un po'; **~ down** vt annotare in fretta, buttare giù; **~ter** (BRIT) n blocco

journal ['dʒəːnl] n giornale m; rivista; diario; **~ism** n giornalismo; **~ist** n giornalista m/f

journey ['dʒəːnɪ] n viaggio; (distance covered) tragitto

joy [dʒɔɪ] n gioia; **~ful** adj gioioso(a), allegro(a); **~rider** n chi ruba un'auto per farvi un giro; **~stick** n (AVIAT) barra di comando; (COMPUT) joystick m inv

JP n abbr = **Justice of the Peace**

Jr abbr = **junior**

jubilant ['dʒuːbɪlnt] adj giubilante; trionfante

jubilee ['dʒuːbɪliː] *n* giubileo; **silver ~** venticinquesimo anniversario

judge [dʒʌdʒ] *n* giudice *m/f* ♦ *vt* giudicare; **judg(e)ment** *n* giudizio

judicial [dʒuːˈdɪʃl] *adj* giudiziale, giudiziario(a)

judiciary [dʒuːˈdɪʃɪərɪ] *n* magistratura

judo ['dʒuːdəu] *n* judo

jug [dʒʌg] *n* brocca, bricco

juggernaut ['dʒʌgənɔːt] (*BRIT*) *n* (*huge truck*) bestione *m*

juggle ['dʒʌgl] *vi* fare giochi di destrezza; **~r** *n* giocoliere/a

Jugoslav *etc* ['juːgəuslɑːv] = **Yugoslav** *etc*

juice [dʒuːs] *n* succo

juicy ['dʒuːsɪ] *adj* succoso(a)

jukebox ['dʒuːkbɔks] *n* juke-box *m inv*

July [dʒuːˈlaɪ] *n* luglio

jumble ['dʒʌmbl] *n* miscuglio ♦ *vt* (*also: ~ up*) mischiare; **~ sale** (*BRIT*) *n* vendita di oggetti per beneficenza

jumbo (jet) ['dʒʌmbəu-] *n* jumbo-jet *m inv*

jump [dʒʌmp] *vi* saltare, balzare; (*start*) sobbalzare; (*increase*) rincarare ♦ *vt* saltare ♦ *n* salto, balzo; sobbalzo

jumper ['dʒʌmpə*] *n* (*BRIT*: *pullover*) maglione *m*, pullover *m inv*; (*US*: *dress*) scamiciato; **~ cables** (*US*) *npl* = **jump leads**

jump leads (*BRIT*) *npl* cavi *mpl* per batteria

jumpy ['dʒʌmpɪ] *adj* nervoso(a), agitato(a)

Jun. *abbr* = **junior**

junction ['dʒʌŋkʃən] *n* (*BRIT*: *of roads*) incrocio; (*of rails*) nodo ferroviario

juncture ['dʒʌŋktʃə*] *n*: **at this ~** in questa congiuntura

June [dʒuːn] *n* giugno

jungle ['dʒʌŋgl] *n* giungla

junior ['dʒuːnɪə*] *adj, n*: **he's ~ to me (by 2 years)**, **he's my ~ (by 2 years)** è più giovane di me (di 2 anni); **he's ~ to me** (*seniority*) è al di sotto di me, ho più anzianità di lui; **~ school** (*BRIT*) *n* scuola elementare (*da 8 a 11 anni*)

junk [dʒʌŋk] *n* cianfrusaglie *fpl*; (*cheap goods*) robaccia; **~ bond** *n* (*COMM*) junk bond *m inv*; titolo *m* spazzatura *inv*; **~ food** *n* porcherie *fpl*

junkie ['dʒʌŋkɪ] (*inf*) *n* drogato/a

junk mail *n* stampe *fpl* pubblicitarie

junk shop *n* chincaglieria

Junr *abbr* = **junior**

juror ['dʒuərə*] *n* giurato/a

jury ['dʒuərɪ] *n* giuria

just [dʒʌst] *adj* giusto(a) ♦ *adv*: **he's ~ done it/left** lo ha appena fatto/è appena partito; **~ right** proprio giusto; **~ 2 o'clock** le 2 precise; **she's ~ as clever as you** è in gamba proprio quanto te; **it's ~ as well that ...** meno male che ...; **~ as I arrived** proprio mentre arrivavo; **it was ~ before/enough/here** era poco prima/ appena assai/proprio qui; **it's ~ me** sono solo io; **~ missed/caught** appena perso/ preso; **~ listen to this!** senta un po' questo!

justice ['dʒʌstɪs] *n* giustizia; **J~ of the Peace** *n* giudice *m* conciliatore

justify ['dʒʌstɪfaɪ] *vt* giustificare

jut [dʒʌt] *vi* (*also: ~ out*) sporgersi

juvenile ['dʒuːvənaɪl] *adj* giovane, giovanile; (*court*) dei minorenni; (*books*) per ragazzi ♦ *n* giovane *m/f*, minorenne *m/f*

juxtapose ['dʒʌkstəpəuz] *vt* giustapporre

K

K *abbr* (= *one thousand*) mille; (= *kilobyte*) K

Kampuchea [kæmpuˈtʃɪə] *n* Cambogia

kangaroo [kæŋgəˈruː] *n* canguro

karate [kəˈrɑːtɪ] *n* karatè *m*

kebab [kəˈbæb] *n* spiedino

keel [kiːl] *n* chiglia; **on an even ~** (*fig*) in uno stato normale

keen [kiːn] *adj* (*interest, desire*) vivo(a); (*eye, intelligence*) acuto(a); (*competition*) serrato(a); (*edge*) affilato(a); (*eager*) entusiasta; **to be ~ to do** *or* **on doing sth** avere una gran voglia di fare qc; **to be ~ on sth** essere appassionato(a) di qc; **to be ~ on sb** avere un debole per qn

keep [kiːp] (*pt, pp* **kept**) *vt* tenere; (*hold back*) trattenere; (*feed: one's family etc*) mantenere, sostentare; (*a promise*) mantenere; (*chickens, bees, pigs etc*) allevare ♦ *vi* (*food*) mantenersi; (*remain: in a certain state or place*) restare ♦ *n* (*of castle*) maschio; (*food etc*): **enough for his ~** abbastanza per vitto e alloggio; (*inf*): **for ~s** per sempre; **to ~ doing sth** continuare a fare qc; fare qc di continuo; **to ~ sb from doing** impedire a qn di fare; **to ~ busy/a place tidy** tenere qn occupato(a)/un luogo in ordine; **to ~ sth to o.s.** tenere qc per sé; **to ~ sth (back) from sb** celare qc a qn; **to ~ time** (*clock*) andar bene; **~ on** *vi*: **to ~ on doing** continuare a fare; **to ~ on (about sth)** continuare a insistere (su qc); **~ out** *vt* tener fuori; **"~ out"** "vietato l'accesso"; **~ up** *vt* continuare, mantenere ♦ *vi*: **to ~ up with** tener dietro a, andare di pari passo con; (*work etc*) farcela a seguire; **~er** *n* custode *m/f*, guardiano/a; **~-fit** *n* ginnastica; **~ing** *n* (*care*) custodia; **in ~ing with** in armonia con; in accordo con; **~sake** *n* ricordo

kennel ['kɛnl] *n* canile *m*; **to put a dog in ~s** mettere un cane al canile

kept [kɛpt] *pt, pp of* **keep**

kerb [kəːb] (*BRIT*) *n* orlo del marciapiede

kernel ['kəːnl] *n* nocciolo

kettle ['kɛtl] *n* bollitore *m*

kettle drum *n* timpano

key [kiː] *n* (*gen, MUS*) chiave *f*; (*of piano, typewriter*) tasto ♦ *adj* chiave *inv* ♦ *vt* (*also:* ~ **in**) digitare; **~board** *n* tastiera; **~ed up** *adj* (*person*) agitato(a); **~hole** *n* buco della serratura; **~note** *n* (*MUS*) tonica; *key* nota dominante; **~ ring** *n* portachiavi *m inv*

khaki ['kɑːkɪ] *adj* cachi ♦ *n* cachi *m*

kick [kɪk] *vt* calciare, dare calci a; (*inf: habit etc*) liberarsi di ♦ *vi* (*horse*) tirar calci ♦ *n* calcio; (*thrill*): **he does it for ~s** lo fa giusto per il piacere di farlo; **~ off** *vi* (*SPORT*) dare il primo calcio

kid [kɪd] *n* (*inf: child*) ragazzino/a; (*animal, leather*) capretto ♦ *vi* (*inf*) scherzare

kidnap ['kɪdnæp] *vt* rapire, sequestrare; **~per** *n* rapitore/trice; **~ping** *n* sequestro (di persona)

kidney ['kɪdnɪ] *n* (*ANAT*) rene *m*; (*CULIN*) rognone *m*

kill [kɪl] *vt* uccidere, ammazzare ♦ *n* uccisione *f*; **~er** *n* uccisore *m*, killer *m inv*; assassino/a; **~ing** *n* assassinio; **to make a ~ing** (*inf*) fare un bel colpo; **~joy** *n* guastafeste *m/f inv*

kiln [kɪln] *n* forno

kilo ['kiːləʊ] *n* chilo; **~byte** *n* (*COMPUT*) kilobyte *m inv*; **~gram(me)** ['kɪləʊgræm] *n* chilogrammo; **~metre** ['kɪləmiːtə*] (*US* **~meter**) *n* chilometro; **~watt** ['kɪləʊwɔt] *n* chilowatt *m inv*

kilt [kɪlt] *n* gonnellino scozzese

kin [kɪn] *n see* **next**; **kith**

kind [kaɪnd] *adj* gentile, buono(a) ♦ *n* sorta, specie *f*; (*species*) genere *m*; **to be two of a ~** essere molto simili; **in ~** (*COMM*) in natura

kindergarten ['kɪndəgɑːtn] *n* giardino d'infanzia

kind-hearted [-'hɑːtɪd] *adj* di buon cuore

kindle ['kɪndl] *vt* accendere, infiammare

kindly ['kaɪndlɪ] *adj* pieno(a) di bontà, benevolo(a) ♦ *adv* con bontà, gentilmente; **will you ~ ...** vuole ... per favore

kindness ['kaɪndnɪs] *n* bontà, gentilezza

kindred ['kɪndrɪd] *adj*: **~ spirit** spirito affine

king [kɪŋ] *n* re *m inv*; **~dom** *n* regno, reame *m*; **~fisher** *n* martin *m inv* pescatore; **~-size** *adj* super *inv*; gigante

kinky ['kɪŋkɪ] (*pej*) *adj* eccentrico(a); dai gusti particolari

kiosk ['kiːɔsk] *n* edicola, chiosco; (*BRIT: TEL*) cabina (telefonica)

kipper ['kɪpə*] *n* aringa affumicata

kiss [kɪs] *n* bacio ♦ *vt* baciare; **to ~ (each other)** baciarsi; **~ of life** *n* respirazione *f* bocca a bocca

kit [kɪt] *n* equipaggiamento, corredo; (*set of tools etc*) attrezzi *mpl*; (*for assembly*) scatola di montaggio

kitchen ['kɪtʃɪn] *n* cucina; **~ sink** *n* acquaio

kite [kaɪt] *n* (*toy*) aquilone *m*

kith [kɪθ] *n*: ~ **and kin** amici e parenti *mpl*

kitten ['kɪtn] *n* gattino/a, micino/a

kitty ['kɪtɪ] *n* (*money*) fondo comune

knack [næk] *n*: **to have the** ~ **of** avere l'abilità di

knapsack ['næpsæk] *n* zaino, sacco da montagna

knead [niːd] *vt* impastare

knee [niː] *n* ginocchio; ~**cap** *n* rotula

kneel [niːl] (*pt, pp* **knelt**) *vi* (*also:* ~ *down*) inginocchiarsi; **knelt** [nɛlt] *pt, pp of* **kneel**

knew [njuː] *pt of* **know**

knickers ['nɪkəz] (*BRIT*) *npl* mutandine *fpl*

knife [naɪf] (*pl* **knives**) *n* coltello ♦ *vt* accoltellare, dare una coltellata a

knight [naɪt] *n* cavaliere *m*; (*CHESS*) cavallo; ~**hood** (*BRIT*) *n* (*title*): **to get a** ~**hood** essere fatto cavaliere

knit [nɪt] *vt* fare a maglia ♦ *vi* lavorare a maglia; (*broken bones*) saldarsi; **to** ~ **one's brows** aggrottare le sopracciglia; ~**ting** *n* lavoro a maglia; ~**ting machine** *n* macchina per maglieria; ~**ting needle** *n* ferro (da calza); ~**wear** *n* maglieria

knives [naɪvz] *npl of* **knife**

knob [nɔb] *n* bottone *m*, manopola

knock [nɔk] *vt* colpire; urtare; (*fig: inf*) criticare ♦ *vi* (*at door etc*): **to** ~ **at/on** bussare a ♦ *n* bussata; colpo, botta; ~ **down** *vt* abbattere; ~ **off** *vi* (*inf: finish*) smettere (di lavorare) ♦ *vt* (*from price*) far abbassare; (*inf: steal*) sgraffignare; ~ **out** *vt* stendere; (*BOXING*) mettere K.O.; (*defeat*) battere; ~ **over** *vt* (*person*) investire; (*object*) far cadere; ~**er** *n* (*on door*) battente *m*; ~**out** *n* (*BOXING*) knock out *m inv* ♦ *cpd* a eliminazione

knot [nɔt] *n* nodo ♦ *vt* annodare; ~**ty** *adj* (*fig*) spinoso(a)

know [nəu] (*pt* **knew**, *pp* **known**) *vt* sapere; (*person, author, place*) conoscere; **to** ~ **how to do** sapere fare; **to** ~ **about** *or* **of sth/sb** conoscere qc/qn; ~-**all** *n* sapientone/a; ~-**how** *n* tecnica; pratica; ~**ing** *adj* (*look etc*) d'intesa; ~**ingly** *adv* (*purposely*) consapevolmente; (*smile, look*) con aria d'intesa

knowledge ['nɔlɪdʒ] *n* consapevolezza; (*learning*) conoscenza, sapere *m*; ~**able** *adj* ben informato(a)

known [nəun] *pp of* **know**

knuckle ['nʌkl] *n* nocca

Koran [kɔ'rɑːn] *n* Corano

Korea [kə'rɪə] *n* Corea

kosher ['kəuʃə*] *adj* kasher *inv*

L

L (*BRIT*) *abbr* = **learner driver**

lab [læb] *n abbr* (= *laboratory*) laboratorio

label ['leɪbl] *n* etichetta, cartellino; (*brand: of record*) casa ♦ *vt* etichettare

labor *etc* ['leɪbə*] (*US*) = **labour** *etc*

laboratory [lə'bɔrətərɪ] *n* laboratorio

labour ['leɪbə*] (*US* **labor**) *n* (*task*) lavoro; (*workmen*) manodopera; (*MED*): **to be in** ~ avere le doglie ♦ *vi*: **to** ~ (**at**) lavorare duro (a); **L~, the L~ party** (*BRIT*) il partito laburista, i laburisti; **hard** ~ lavori *mpl* forzati; ~**ed** *adj* (*breathing*) affannoso(a); ~**er** *n* manovale *m*; **farm** ~**er** *n* lavoratore *m* agricolo

lace [leɪs] *n* merletto, pizzo; (*of shoe etc*) laccio ♦ *vt* (*shoe: also:* ~ **up**) allacciare

lack [læk] *n* mancanza ♦ *vt* mancare di; **through** *or* **for** ~ **of** per mancanza di; **to be** ~**ing** mancare; **to be** ~**ing in** mancare di

lackadaisical [lækə'deɪzɪkl] *adj* disinteressato(a), noncurante

lacquer ['lækə*] *n* lacca

lad [læd] *n* ragazzo, giovanotto

ladder ['lædə*] *n* scala; (*BRIT: in tights*) smagliatura

laden ['leɪdn] *adj*: ~ (**with**) carico(a) *or* caricato(a) (di)

ladle ['leɪdl] *n* mestolo

lady ['leɪdɪ] *n* signora; dama; **L~ Smith** lady Smith; **the ladies' (room)** i gabinetti per signore; ~**bird** (*US* ~**bug**) *n* coccinella; ~**like** *adj* da signora, distinto(a); ~**ship** *n*: **your** ~**ship** signora contessa (*or* baronessa *etc*)

lag [læg] n (of time) lasso, intervallo ♦ vi (also: ~ **behind**) trascinarsi ♦ vt (pipes) rivestire di materiale isolante

lager ['lɑːɡə*] n lager m inv

lagoon [lə'ɡuːn] n laguna

laid [leɪd] pt, pp of **lay**; ~ **back** (inf) adj rilassato(a), tranquillo(a); ~ **up** adj: ~ **up** (**with**) costretto(a) a letto (da)

lain [leɪn] pp of **lie**

lair [lɛə*] n covo, tana

lake [leɪk] n lago

lamb [læm] n agnello

lame [leɪm] adj zoppo(a); (excuse etc) zoppicante

lament [lə'ment] n lamento ♦ vt lamentare, piangere

laminated ['læmɪneɪtɪd] adj laminato(a)

lamp [læmp] n lampada

lamppost ['læmppəʊst] (BRIT) n lampione m

lampshade ['læmpʃeɪd] n paralume m

lance [lɑːns] n lancia ♦ vt (MED) incidere

land [lænd] n (as opposed to sea) terra (ferma); (country) paese m; (soil) terreno; suolo; (estate) terreni mpl, terre fpl ♦ vi (from ship) sbarcare; (AVIAT) atterrare; (fig: fall) cadere ♦ vt (passengers) sbarcare; (goods) scaricare; **to ~ sb with sth** affibbiare qc a qn; ~ **up** vi andare a finire; ~**fill site** n discarica; ~**ing** n atterraggio; (of staircase) pianerottolo; ~**ing gear** n carrello di atterraggio; ~**ing strip** n pista di atterraggio; ~**lady** n padrona or proprietaria di casa; ~**locked** adj senza sbocco sul mare; ~**lord** n padrone m or proprietario di casa; (of pub etc) padrone m; ~**mark** n punto di riferimento; (fig) pietra miliare; ~**owner** n proprietario(a) terriero(a)

landscape ['lænskeɪp] n paesaggio

landslide ['lændslaɪd] n (GEO) frana; (fig: POL) valanga

lane [leɪn] n stradina; (AUT, in race) corsia

language ['læŋɡwɪdʒ] n lingua; (way one speaks) linguaggio; **bad** ~ linguaggio volgare; ~ **laboratory** n laboratorio linguistico

languid ['læŋɡwɪd] adj languido(a)

lank [læŋk] adj (hair) liscio(a) e opaco(a)

lanky ['læŋkɪ] adj allampanato(a)

lantern ['læntn] n lanterna

lap [læp] n (of track) giro; (of body): **in or on one's** ~ in grembo ♦ vt (also: ~ **up**) papparsi, leccare ♦ vi (waves) sciabordare; ~ **up** vt (fig) bearsi di

lapel [lə'pel] n risvolto

Lapland ['læplænd] n Lapponia

lapse [læps] n lapsus m inv; (longer) caduta ♦ vi (law) cadere; (membership, contract) scadere; **to ~ into bad habits** pigliare cattive abitudini; ~ **of time** spazio di tempo

laptop (computer) ['læp,tɔp-] n laptop m inv

larceny ['lɑːsənɪ] n furto

larch [lɑːtʃ] n larice m

lard [lɑːd] n lardo

larder ['lɑːdə*] n dispensa

large [lɑːdʒ] adj grande; (person, animal) grosso(a); **at** ~ (free) in libertà; (generally) in generale; nell'insieme; ~**ly** adv in gran parte

largesse [lɑː'ʒes] n generosità

lark [lɑːk] n (bird) allodola; (joke) scherzo, gioco; ~ **about** vi fare lo stupido

laryngitis [lærɪn'dʒaɪtɪs] n laringite f

laser ['leɪzə*] n laser m; ~ **printer** n stampante f laser inv

lash [læʃ] n frustata; (also: eye~) ciglio ♦ vt frustare; (tie): **to ~ to/together** legare a insieme; ~ **out** vi: **to ~ out** (**at** or **against sb**) attaccare violentemente (qn)

lass [læs] n ragazza

lasso [læ'suː] n laccio

last [lɑːst] adj ultimo(a); (week, month, year) scorso(a), passato(a) ♦ adv per ultimo ♦ vi durare; ~ **week** la settimana scorsa; ~ **night** ieri sera, la notte scorsa; **at** ~ finalmente, alla fine; ~ **but one** penultimo(a); ~**-ditch** adj (attempt) estremo(a); ~**ing** adj durevole; ~**ly** adv infine, per finire; ~**-minute** adj fatto(a) (or preso(a) etc) all'ultimo momento

latch [lætʃ] n chiavistello

late [leɪt] adj (not on time) in ritardo; (far on in day etc) tardi inv; tardo(a); (former) ex; (dead) defunto(a) ♦ adv tardi; (behind *time, schedule*) in ritardo; **of** ~ di recente; **in the** ~ **afternoon** nel tardo pomeriggio; **in** ~ **May** verso la fine di maggio; ~**comer** *n* ritardatario/a; ~**ly** *adv* recentemente

later ['leɪtə*] *adj* (*date etc*) posteriore; (*version etc*) successivo(a) ♦ *adv* più tardi; ~ **on** più avanti

lateral ['lætərl] *adj* laterale

latest ['leɪtɪst] *adj* ultimo(a), più recente; **at the** ~ al più tardi

lathe [leɪð] *n* tornio

lather ['lɑːðə*] *n* schiuma di sapone ♦ *vt* insaponare

Latin ['lætɪn] *n* latino ♦ *adj* latino(a); ~ **America** *n* America Latina; ~-**American** *adj*, *n* sudamericano(a)

latitude ['lætɪtjuːd] *n* latitudine *f*; (*fig*) libertà d'azione

latter ['lætə*] *adj* secondo(a); più recente ♦ *n*: **the** ~ quest'ultimo, il secondo; ~**ly** *adv* recentemente, negli ultimi tempi

lattice ['lætɪs] *n* traliccio; graticolato

laudable ['lɔːdəbl] *adj* lodevole

laugh [lɑːf] *n* risata ♦ *vi* ridere; ~ **at** *vt fus* (*misfortune etc*) ridere di; ~ **off** *vt* prendere alla leggera; ~**able** *adj* ridicolo(a); ~**ing stock** *n*: **the** ~**ing stock of** lo zimbello di; ~**ter** *n* riso; risate *fpl*

launch [lɔːntʃ] *n* (*of rocket, COMM*) lancio; (*of new ship*) varo; (*also*: *motor* ~) lancia ♦ *vt* (*rocket, COMM*) lanciare; (*ship, plan*) varare; ~ **into** *vt fus* lanciarsi in; ~**(ing) pad** *n* rampa di lancio

launder ['lɔːndə*] *vt* lavare e stirare

launderette [lɔːn'drɛt] (*BRIT*) *n* lavanderia (automatica)

laundromat ['lɔːndrəmæt] (*US*: ®) *n* lavanderia automatica

laundry ['lɔːndrɪ] *n* lavanderia; (*clothes*) biancheria; (: *dirty*) panni *mpl* da lavare

laureate ['lɔːrɪət] *adj see* **poet**

laurel ['lɔrl] *n* lauro

lava ['lɑːvə] *n* lava

lavatory ['lævətərɪ] *n* gabinetto

lavender ['lævəndə*] *n* lavanda

lavish ['lævɪʃ] *adj* copioso(a); abbondante; (*giving freely*): ~ **with** prodigo(a) di, largo(a) in ♦ *vt*: **to** ~ **sth on sb** colmare

qn di qc

law [lɔː] *n* legge *f*; **civil/criminal** ~ diritto civile/penale; ~-**abiding** *adj* ubbidiente alla legge; ~ **and order** *n* l'ordine *m* pubblico; ~ **court** *n* tribunale *m*, corte *f* di giustizia; ~**ful** *adj* legale; lecito(a); ~**less** *adj* che non conosce nessuna legge

lawn [lɔːn] *n* tappeto erboso; ~ **mower** *n* tosaerba *m or f inv*; ~ **tennis** *n* tennis *m* su prato

law school *n* facoltà *f inv* di legge

lawsuit ['lɔːsuːt] *n* processo, causa

lawyer ['lɔːjə*] *n* (*for sales, wills etc*) ≈ notaio; (*partner, in court*) ≈ avvocato/ essa

lax [læks] *adj* rilassato(a); negligente

laxative ['læksətɪv] *n* lassativo

lay [leɪ] (*pt, pp* **laid**) *pt of* **lie** ♦ *adj* laico(a); (*not expert*) profano(a) ♦ *vt* posare, mettere; (*eggs*) fare; (*trap*) tendere; (*plans*) fare, elaborare; **to** ~ **the table** apparecchiare la tavola; ~ **aside** *or* **by** *vt* mettere da parte; ~ **down** *vt* mettere giù; (*rules etc*) formulare, fissare; **to** ~ **down the law** dettar legge; **to** ~ **down one's life** dare la propria vita; ~ **off** *vt* (*workers*) licenziare; ~ **on** *vt* (*provide*) fornire; ~ **out** *vt* (*display*) presentare, disporre; ~**about** *n* sfaccendato/a, fannullone/a; ~-**by** (*BRIT*) *n* piazzola (di sosta)

layer ['leɪə*] *n* strato

layman ['leɪmən] *n* laico; profano

layout ['leɪaʊt] *n* lay-out *m inv*, disposizione *f*; (*PRESS*) impaginazione *f*

laze [leɪz] *vi* oziare

lazy ['leɪzɪ] *adj* pigro(a)

lb. *abbr* = **pound** (*weight*)

lead[1] [liːd] (*pt, pp* **led**) *n* (*front position*) posizione *f* di testa; (*distance, time ahead*) vantaggio; (*clue*) indizio; (*ELEC*) filo (elettrico); (*for dog*) guinzaglio; (*THEATRE*) parte *f* principale ♦ *vt* guidare, condurre; (*induce*) indurre; (*be leader of*) essere a capo di ♦ *vi* condurre; (*SPORT*) essere in testa; **in the** ~ in testa; **to** ~ **the way** fare strada; ~ **away** *vt* condurre via; ~ **back** *vt*: **to** ~ **back to** ricondurre a; ~ **on** *vt* (*tease*) tenere sulla corda; ~ **to** *vt fus* condurre a; portare a; ~ **up to** *vt fus* portare a

lead² [lɛd] *n* (*metal*) piombo; (*in pencil*) mina

leaden ['lɛdn] *adj* (*sky, sea*) plumbeo(a)

leader ['li:də*] *n* capo; leader *m inv*; (*in newspaper*) articolo di fondo; (*SPORT*) chi è in testa; **~ship** *n* direzione *f*; capacità di comando

leading ['li:dɪŋ] *adj* primo(a); principale; ~ **light** *n* (*person*) personaggio di primo piano; ~ **man/lady** *n* (*THEATRE*) primo attore/prima attrice

lead singer *n cantante alla testa di un gruppo*

leaf [li:f] (*pl* **leaves**) *n* foglia ♦ *vi*: **to ~ through sth** sfogliare qc; **to turn over a new ~** cambiar vita

leaflet ['li:flɪt] *n* dépliant *m inv*; (*POL, REL*) volantino

league [li:g] *n* lega; (*FOOTBALL*) campionato; **to be in ~ with** essere in lega con

leak [li:k] *n* (*out*) fuga; (*in*) infiltrazione *f*; (*security* ~) fuga d'informazioni ♦ *vi* (*roof, bucket*) perdere; (*liquid*) uscire; (*shoes*) lasciar passare l'acqua ♦ *vt* (*information*) divulgare; ~ **out** *vi* uscire; (*information*) trapelare

lean [li:n] (*pt, pp* **leaned** *or* **leant**) *adj* magro(a) ♦ *vt*: **to ~ sth on sth** appoggiare qc su qc ♦ *vi* (*slope*) pendere; (*rest*): **to ~ against** appoggiarsi contro; essere appoggiato(a) a; **to ~ on** appoggiarsi a; ~ **back/forward** *vi* sporgersi indietro/in avanti; ~ **out** *vi* sporgersi; ~ **over** *vi* inclinarsi; **~ing** *n*: **~ing (towards)** propensione *f* (per); **leant** [lɛnt] *pt, pp of* **lean**

leap [li:p] (*pt, pp* **leaped** *or* **leapt**) *n* salto, balzo ♦ *vi* saltare, balzare; **~frog** *n* gioco della cavallina; **leapt** [lɛpt] *pt, pp of* **leap**; ~ **year** *n* anno bisestile

learn [lə:n] (*pt, pp* **learned** *or* **learnt**) *vt, vi* imparare; **to ~ about sth** (*hear, read*) apprendere qc; **to ~ to do sth** imparare a fare qc; **~ed** ['lə:nɪd] *adj* erudito(a), dotto(a); **~er** *n* principiante *m/f*;

apprendista *m/f*; (*BRIT*: *also*: ~**er driver**) guidatore/trice principiante; **~ing** *n* erudizione *f*, sapienza; **learnt** *pt, pp of* **learn**

lease [li:s] *n* contratto d'affitto ♦ *vt* affittare

leash [li:ʃ] *n* guinzaglio

least [li:st] *adj*: **the ~** (+ *noun*) il(la) più piccolo(a), il(la) minimo(a); (*smallest amount of*) il(la) meno ♦ *adv* (+ *verb*) meno; **the ~** (+ *adjective*): **the ~ beautiful girl** la ragazza meno bella; **the ~ possible effort** il minimo sforzo possibile; **I have the ~ money** ho meno denaro di tutti; **at ~** almeno; **not in the ~** affatto, per nulla

leather ['lɛðə*] *n* cuoio

leave [li:v] (*pt, pp* **left**) *vt* lasciare; (*go away from*) partire da ♦ *vi* partire, andarsene; (*bus, train*) partire ♦ *n* (*time off*) congedo; (*MIL, also: consent*) licenza; **to be left** rimanere; **there's some milk left over** c'è rimasto del latte; **on ~** in congedo; ~ **behind** *vt* (*person, object*) lasciare; (: *forget*) dimenticare; ~ **out** *vt* omettere, tralasciare; ~ **of absence** *n* congedo

leaves [li:vz] *npl of* **leaf**

Lebanon ['lɛbənən] *n* Libano

lecherous ['lɛtʃərəs] *adj* lascivo(a), lubrico(a)

lecture ['lɛktʃə*] *n* conferenza; (*SCOL*) lezione *f* ♦ *vi* fare conferenze; fare lezioni ♦ *vt* (*scold*): **to ~ sb on** *or* **about sth** rimproverare qn *or* fare una ramanzina a qn per qc; **to give a ~ on** tenere una conferenza su

lecturer ['lɛktʃərə*] (*BRIT*) *n* (*at university*) professore/essa, docente *m/f*

led [lɛd] *pt, pp of* **lead**

ledge [lɛdʒ] *n* (*of window*) davanzale *m*; (*on wall etc*) sporgenza; (*of mountain*) cornice *f*, cengia

ledger ['lɛdʒə*] *n* libro maestro, registro

lee [li:] *n* lato sottovento

leech [li:tʃ] *n* sanguisuga

leek [li:k] *n* porro

leer [lɪə*] *vi*: **to ~ at sb** gettare uno sguardo voglioso (*or* maligno) su qn

leeway ['li:weɪ] *n* (*fig*): **to have some ~** avere una certa libertà di azione

left [lɛft] *pt, pp of* **leave** ♦ *adj* sinistro(a) ♦ *adv* a sinistra ♦ *n* sinistra; **on the ~, to the ~** a sinistra; **the L~** (*POL*) la sinistra; **~-handed***adj* mancino(a); **~-hand side** *n* lato *or* fianco sinistro; **~ luggage (office)** (*BRIT*) *n* deposito *m* bagagli *inv*; **~overs***npl* avanzi *mpl*, resti *mpl*; **~-wing***adj* (*POL*) di sinistra

leg [lɛg] *n* gamba; (*of animal*) zampa; (*of furniture*) piede *m*; (*CULIN*: *of chicken*) coscia; (*of journey*) tappa; **1st/2nd ~** (*SPORT*) partita di andata/ritorno

legacy ['lɛgəsɪ] *n* eredità *f inv*

legal ['li:gl] *adj* legale; **~ holiday** (*US*) *n* giorno festivo, festa nazionale; **~ tender** *n* moneta legale

legend ['lɛdʒənd] *n* leggenda

legislation [lɛdʒɪs'leɪʃən] *n* legislazione *f*; **legislature** ['lɛdʒɪslətʃə*] *n* corpo legislativo

legitimate [lɪ'dʒɪtɪmət] *adj* legittimo(a)

leg-room*n* spazio per le gambe

leisure ['lɛʒə*] *n* agio, tempo libero; ricreazioni *fpl*; **at ~** con comodo; **~ centre***n* centro di ricreazione; **~ly***adj* tranquillo(a); fatto(a) con comodo *or* senza fretta

lemon ['lɛmən] *n* limone *m*; **~ade** [-'neɪd] *n* limonata; **~ tea***n* tè *m inv* al limone

lend [lɛnd] (*pt, pp* **lent**) *vt*: **to ~ sth (to sb)** prestare qc (a qn); **~ing library***n* biblioteca che consente prestiti di libri

length [lɛŋθ] *n* lunghezza; (*distance*) distanza; (*section: of road, pipe etc*) pezzo, tratto; (*of time*) periodo; **at ~** (*at last*) finalmente, alla fine; (*lengthily*) a lungo; **~en***vt* allungare, prolungare ♦ *vi* allungarsi; **~ways***adv* per il lungo; **~y** *adj* molto lungo(a)

lenient ['li:nɪənt] *adj* indulgente, clemente

lens [lɛnz] *n* lente *f*; (*of camera*) obiettivo

Lent [lɛnt] *n* Quaresima

lent [lɛnt] *pt, pp of* **lend**

lentil ['lɛntl] *n* lenticchia

Leo ['li:əu] *n* Leone *m*

leotard ['li:əta:d] *n* calzamaglia

leprosy ['lɛprəsɪ] *n* lebbra

lesbian ['lɛzbɪən] *n* lesbica

less [lɛs] *adj, pron, adv* meno ♦ *prep*: **~ tax/10% discount** meno tasse/il 10% di sconto; **~ than ever** meno che mai; **~ than half** meno della metà; **~ and ~** sempre meno; **the ~ he works ...** meno lavora ....

lessen ['lɛsn] *vi* diminuire, attenuarsi ♦ *vt* diminuire, ridurre

lesser ['lɛsə*] *adj* minore, più piccolo(a); **to a ~ extent** in grado *or* misura minore

lesson ['lɛsn] *n* lezione *f*; **to teach sb a ~** dare una lezione a qn

lest [lɛst] *conj* per paura di + *infinitive*, per paura che + *sub*

let [lɛt] (*pt, pp* **let**) *vt* lasciare; (*BRIT*: *lease*) dare in affitto; **to ~ sb do sth** lasciar fare qc a qn, lasciare che qn faccia qc; **to ~ sb know sth** far sapere qc a qn; **~'s go** andiamo; **~ him come** lo lasci venire; **"to ~"** "affittasi"; **~ down***vt* (*lower*) abbassare; (*dress*) allungare; (*hair*) sciogliere; (*tyre*) sgonfiare; (*disappoint*) deludere; **~ go***vt, vi* mollare; **~ in***vt* lasciare entrare; (*visitor etc*) far entrare; **~ off***vt* (*allow to go*) lasciare andare; (*firework etc*) far partire; **~ on** (*inf*) *vi* dire; **~ out***vt* lasciare uscire; (*scream*) emettere; **~ up***vi* diminuire

lethal ['li:θl] *adj* letale, mortale

lethargic [lɛ'θɑ:dʒɪk] *adj* letargico(a)

letter ['lɛtə*] *n* lettera; **~ bomb***n* lettera esplosiva; **~-box** (*BRIT*) *n* buca delle lettere; **~ing***n* iscrizione *f*; caratteri *mpl*

lettuce ['lɛtɪs] *n* lattuga, insalata

let-up*n* pausa

leukaemia [lu:'ki:mɪə] (*US* **leukemia**) *n* leucemia

level ['lɛvl] *adj* piatto(a), piano(a); orizzontale ♦ *adv*: **to draw ~ with** mettersi alla pari di ♦ *n* livello ♦ *vt* livellare, spianare; **to be ~ with** essere alla pari di; **A ~s** (*BRIT*) *npl* ≈ esami *mpl* di maturità; **O ~s** (*BRIT*) *npl* esami *fatti* in Inghilterra all'età di 16 anni; **on the ~** piatto(a); (*fig*) onesto(a); **~ off** *or* **out***vi* (*prices etc*) stabilizzarsi; **~ crossing** (*BRIT*) *n* passaggio a livello; **~-headed***adj* equilibrato(a)

lever ['liːvə*] *n* leva; **~age***n*: ~**age** (**on** or **with**) forza (su); (*fig*) ascendente *m* (su)

levity ['lɛvɪtɪ] *n* leggerezza, frivolezza

levy ['lɛvɪ] *n* tassa, imposta ♦ *vt* imporre

lewd [luːd] *adj* osceno(a), lascivo(a)

liability [laɪə'bɪlətɪ] *n* responsabilità *f inv*; (*handicap*) peso; **liabilities***npl* debiti *mpl*; (*on balance sheet*) passivo

liable ['laɪəbl] *adj* (*subject*): ~ **to** soggetto(a) a; passibile di; (*responsible*): ~ (**for**) responsabile (di); (*likely*): ~ **to do** propenso(a) a fare

liaise [liː'eɪz] *vi*: **to** ~ (**with**) mantenere i contatti (con)

liaison [liː'eɪzɔn] *n* relazione *f*; (*MIL*) collegamento

liar ['laɪə*] *n* bugiardo/a

libel ['laɪbl] *n* libello, diffamazione *f* ♦ *vt* diffamare

liberal ['lɪbərl] *adj* liberale; (*generous*): **to be** ~ **with** distribuire liberalmente

liberty ['lɪbətɪ] *n* libertà *f inv*; **at** ~ (*criminal*) in libertà; **at** ~ **to do** libero(a) di fare

Libra ['liːbrə] *n* Bilancia

librarian [laɪ'brɛərɪən] *n* bibliotecario/a

library ['laɪbrərɪ] *n* biblioteca

Libya ['lɪbɪə] *n* Libia; ~*nadj*, *n* libico(a)

lice [laɪs] *npl of* **louse**

licence ['laɪsns] (*US* **license**) *n* autorizzazione *f*, permesso; (*COMM*) licenza; (*RADIO, TV*) canone *m*, abbonamento; (*also*: *driving* ~, (*US*) *driver's* ~) patente *f* da guida; (*excessive freedom*) licenza; ~ **number***n* numero di targa; ~ **plate***n* targa

license ['laɪsns] *n* (*US*) = **licence** ♦ *vt* dare una licenza a; ~**d***adj* (*for alcohol*) che ha la licenza di vendere bibite alcoliche

lick [lɪk] *vt* leccare; (*inf: defeat*) stracciare; **to** ~ **one's lips** (*fig*) leccarsi i baffi

licorice ['lɪkərɪs] (*US*) *n* = **liquorice**

lid [lɪd] *n* coperchio; (*eye*~) palpebra

lie [laɪ] (*pt* lay, *pp* lain) *vi* (*rest*) giacere; star disteso(a); (*of object: be situated*) trovarsi, essere; (*tell lies: pt, pp* lied)

mentire, dire bugie ♦ *n* bugia, menzogna; **to** ~ **low** (*fig*) latitare; ~ **about**or **around***vi* (*things*) essere in giro; (*person*) bighellonare; **~-down**(*BRIT*) *n*: **to have a ~-down** sdraiarsi, riposarsi; **~-in**(*BRIT*) *n*: **to have a ~-in** rimanere a letto

lieu [luː]: **in** ~ **of** *prep* invece di, al posto di

lieutenant [lɛf'tɛnənt, (*US*) luː'tɛnənt] *n* tenente *m*

life [laɪf] (*pl* lives) *n* vita ♦ *cpd* di vita; della vita; a vita; **to come to** ~ rianimarsi; ~ **assurance**(*BRIT*) *n* = ~ **insurance**; **~belt**(*BRIT*) *n* salvagente *m*; **~boat***n* scialuppa di salvataggio; **~guard***n* bagnino; ~ **imprisonment***n* carcere *m* a vita; ~ **insurance***n* assicurazione *f* sulla vita; ~ **jacket***n* giubbotto di salvataggio; **~less***adj* senza vita; **~like***adj* verosimile; rassomigliante; **~line***n*: **it was his ~line** era vitale per lui; **~long***adj* per tutta la vita; ~ **preserver**(*US*) *n* salvagente *m*; giubbotto di salvataggio; ~ **sentence***n* ergastolo; **~-size(d)***adj* a grandezza naturale; ~ **span***n* (durata della) vita; **~style***n* stile *m* di vita; ~ **support system***n* respiratore *m* automatico; **~time***n*: **in his ~time** durante la sua vita; **once in a ~time** una volta nella vita

lift [lɪft] *vt* sollevare; (*ban, rule*) levare ♦ *vi* (*fog*) alzarsi ♦ *n* (*BRIT: elevator*) ascensore *m*; **to give sb a** ~ (*BRIT*) dare un passaggio a qn; **~-off***n* decollo

light [laɪt] (*pt, pp* lighted *or* lit) *n* luce *f*, lume *m*; (*daylight*) luce *f*, giorno; (*lamp*) lampada; (*AUT: rear*) ~) luce *f* di posizione; (: *headlamp*) fanale *m*; (*for cigarette etc*): **have you got a** ~? ha da accendere?; **~s** *npl* (*AUT: traffic* ~s) semaforo ♦ *vt* (*candle, cigarette, fire*) accendere; (*room*): **to be lit by** essere illuminato(a) da ♦ *adj* (*room, colour*) chiaro(a); (*not heavy, also fig*) leggero(a); **to come to** ~ venire alla luce, emergere; ~ **up***vi* illuminarsi ♦ *vt* illuminare; ~ **bulb***n* lampadina; **~en***vt* (*make less heavy*) alleggerire; **~er***n* (*also: cigarette* ~er) accendino; **~-headed***adj* stordito(a); **~-hearted***adj* gioioso(a),

gaio(a); **~house** *n* faro; **~ing** *n*
illuminazione *f*; **~ly** *adv* leggermente; **to
get off ~ly** cavarsela a buon mercato;
~ness *n* chiarezza; (*in weight*) leggerezza

lightning ['laɪtnɪŋ] *n* lampo, fulmine *m*;
~ conductor (*US* **~ rod**) *n* parafulmine *m*

light pen *n* penna ottica

lightweight ['laɪtweɪt] *adj* (*suit*)
leggero(a) ♦ *n* (*BOXING*) peso leggero

light year *n* anno *m* luce *inv*

like [laɪk] *vt* (*person*) volere bene a;
(*activity, object, food*): **I ~ swimming/
that book/chocolate** mi piace nuotare/
quel libro/il cioccolato ♦ *prep* come ♦ *adj*
simile, uguale ♦ *n*: **the ~** uno(a) uguale;
his ~s and dislikes i suoi gusti; **I would
~, I'd ~** mi piacerebbe, vorrei; **would
you ~ a coffee?** gradirebbe un caffè?; **to
be/look ~ sb/sth** somigliare a qn/qc;
what does it look/taste ~? che aspetto/
gusto ha?; **what does it sound ~?** come
fa?; **that's just ~ him** è proprio da lui;
do it ~ this fallo così; **it is nothing ~ ...**
non è affatto come ...; **~able** *adj*
simpatico(a)

likelihood ['laɪklɪhud] *n* probabilità

likely ['laɪklɪ] *adj* probabile; plausibile;
he's ~ to leave probabilmente partirà, è
probabile che parta; **not ~!** neanche per
sogno!

likeness ['laɪknɪs] *n* somiglianza

likewise ['laɪkwaɪz] *adv* similmente,
nello stesso modo

liking ['laɪkɪŋ] *n*: **~ (for)** debole *m* (per);
to be to sb's ~ piacere a qn

lilac ['laɪlək] *n* lilla *m inv*

lily ['lɪlɪ] *n* giglio; **~ of the valley** *n*
mughetto

limb [lɪm] *n* arto

limber up ['lɪmbə*-] *vi* riscaldarsi i
muscoli

limbo ['lɪmbəu] *n*: **to be in ~** (*fig*) essere
lasciato(a) nel dimenticatoio

lime [laɪm] *n* (*tree*) tiglio; (*fruit*) limetta;
(*GEO*) calce *f*

limelight ['laɪmlaɪt] *n*: **in the ~** (*fig*) alla
ribalta, in vista

limerick ['lɪmərɪk] *n* poesiola umoristica
di 5 versi

limestone ['laɪmstəun] *n* pietra calcarea;
(*GEO*) calcare *m*

limit ['lɪmɪt] *n* limite *m* ♦ *vt* limitare;
~ed *adj* limitato(a), ristretto(a); **to be
~ed to** limitarsi a; **~ed (liability)
company** (*BRIT*) *n* ≈ società *f inv* a
responsabilità limitata

limp [lɪmp] *n*: **to have a ~** zoppicare ♦ *vi*
zoppicare ♦ *adj* floscio(a), flaccido(a)

limpet ['lɪmpɪt] *n* patella

line [laɪn] *n* linea; (*rope*) corda; (*for
fishing*) lenza; (*wire*) filo; (*of power*) verso;
(*row, series*) fila, riga; coda; (*on face*) ruga
♦ *vt* (*clothes*): **to ~ (with)** foderare (di);
(*box*): **to ~ (with)** rivestire *or* foderare
(di); (*subj: trees, crowd*) fiancheggiare; **~
of business** settore *m or* ramo d'attività;
in ~ with in linea con; **~ up** *vi*
allinearsi, mettersi in fila ♦ *vt* mettere in
fila; (*event, celebration*) preparare

lined [laɪnd] *adj* (*face*) rugoso(a); (*paper*) a
righe, rigato(a)

linen ['lɪnɪn] *n* biancheria, panni *mpl*;
(*cloth*) tela di lino

liner ['laɪnə*] *n* nave *f* di linea; (*for bin*)
sacchetto

linesman ['laɪnzmən] *n* guardalinee *m
inv*

line-up *n* allineamento, fila; (*SPORT*)
formazione *f* di gioco

linger ['lɪŋgə*] *vi* attardarsi; indugiare;
(*smell, tradition*) persistere

lingerie ['lænʒəri:] *n* biancheria intima
femminile

lingo ['lɪŋgəu] (*pl* **~es**) (*pej*) *n* gergo

linguistics [lɪŋ'gwɪstɪks] *n* linguistica

lining ['laɪnɪŋ] *n* fodera

link [lɪŋk] *n* (*of a chain*) anello;
(*relationship*) legame *m*; (*connection*)
collegamento ♦ *vt* collegare, unire,
congiungere; (*associate*): **to ~ with** *or* **to
~ to** collegare a; **~s** *npl* (*GOLF*) pista *or* terreno
da golf; **~ up** *vt* collegare, unire ♦ *vi*
riunirsi; associarsi

lino ['laɪnəu] *n* = **linoleum**

linoleum [lɪ'nəuliəm] *n* linoleum *m inv*

lion ['laɪən] *n* leone *m*; **~ess** *n* leonessa

lip [lɪp] *n* labbro; (*of cup etc*) orlo

liposuction ['lɪpəusʌkʃən] *n*

liposuzione f

lip: **~read** vi leggere sulle labbra; **~ salve** n burro di cacao; **~ service** n: **to pay ~ service to sth** essere favorevole a qc solo a parole; **~stick** n rossetto

liqueur [lɪˈkjuə*] n liquore m

liquid [ˈlɪkwɪd] n liquido ♦ adj liquido(a)

liquidize [ˈlɪkwɪdaɪz] vt (CULIN) passare al frullatore; **~r** n frullatore m (a brocca)

liquor [ˈlɪkə*] n alcool m

liquorice [ˈlɪkərɪs] (BRIT) n liquirizia

liquor store (US) n negozio di liquori

lisp [lɪsp] n pronuncia blesa della "s"

list [lɪst] n lista, elenco ♦ vt (write down) mettere in lista; fare una lista di; (enumerate) elencare; **~ed building** (BRIT) n edificio sotto la protezione delle Belle Arti

listen [ˈlɪsn] vi ascoltare; **to ~ to** ascoltare; **~er** n ascoltatore/trice

listless [ˈlɪstlɪs] adj apatico(a)

lit [lɪt] pt, pp of **light**

liter [ˈliːtə*] (US) n = **litre**

literacy [ˈlɪtərəsɪ] n il sapere leggere e scrivere

literal [ˈlɪtərl] adj letterale

literary [ˈlɪtərərɪ] adj letterario(a)

literate [ˈlɪtərət] adj che sa leggere e scrivere

literature [ˈlɪtərɪtʃə*] n letteratura; (brochures etc) materiale m

lithe [laɪð] adj agile, snello(a)

litigation [lɪtɪˈgeɪʃən] n causa

litre [ˈliːtə*] (US **liter**) n litro

litter [ˈlɪtə*] n (rubbish) rifiuti mpl; (young animals) figliata; **~ bin** (BRIT) n cestino per rifiuti; **~ed** adj: **~ed with** coperto(a) di

little [ˈlɪtl] adj (small) piccolo(a); (not much) poco(a) ♦ adv poco; **a ~** un po' (di); **a ~ bit** un pochino; **~ by ~** a poco a poco; **~ finger** n mignolo

live[1] [lɪv] vi vivere; (reside) vivere, abitare; **~ down** vt far dimenticare (alla gente); **~ on** vt fus (food) vivere di; **~ together** vi vivere insieme, convivere; **~ up to** vt fus tener fede a, non venir meno a

live[2] [laɪv] adj (animal) vivo(a); (wire)

sotto tensione; (bullet, missile) inesploso(a); (broadcast) diretto(a); (performance) dal vivo

livelihood [ˈlaɪvlɪhud] n mezzi mpl di sostentamento

lively [ˈlaɪvlɪ] adj vivace, vivo(a)

liven up [ˈlaɪvnˈʌp] vt (discussion, evening) animare ♦ vi ravvivarsi

liver [ˈlɪvə*] n fegato

lives [laɪvz] npl of **life**

livestock [ˈlaɪvstɔk] n bestiame m

livid [ˈlɪvɪd] adj livido(a); (furious) livido(a) di rabbia, furibondo(a)

living [ˈlɪvɪŋ] adj vivo(a), vivente ♦ n: **to earn** or **make a ~** guadagnarsi la vita; **~ conditions** npl condizioni fpl di vita; **~ room** n soggiorno; **~ standards** npl tenore m di vita; **~ wage** n salario sufficiente per vivere

lizard [ˈlɪzəd] n lucertola

load [ləud] n (weight) peso; (thing carried) carico ♦ vt (also: **~ up**): **to ~ (with)** (lorry, ship) caricare (di); (gun, camera, COMPUT) caricare (con); **a ~ of, ~s of** (fig) un sacco di; **~ed** adj (vehicle): **~ed (with)** carico(a) (di); (question) capzioso(a); (inf: rich) carico(a) di soldi

loaf [ləuf] (pl **loaves**) n pane m, pagnotta

loan [ləun] n prestito ♦ vt dare in prestito; **on ~** in prestito

loath [ləuθ] adj: **to be ~ to do** essere restio(a) a fare

loathe [ləuð] vt detestare, aborrire

loaves [ləuvz] npl of **loaf**

lobby [ˈlɔbɪ] n atrio, vestibolo; (POL: pressure group) gruppo di pressione ♦ vt fare pressione su

lobster [ˈlɔbstə*] n aragosta

local [ˈləukl] adj locale ♦ n (BRIT: pub) ≈ bar m inv all'angolo; **the ~s** npl (local inhabitants) la gente della zona; **~ authority** n ente m locale; **~ call** n (TEL) telefonata urbana; **~ government** n amministrazione f locale

locality [ləuˈkælɪtɪ] n località f inv; (position) posto, luogo

locally [ˈləukəlɪ] adv da queste parti; nel vicinato

locate [ləuˈkeɪt] vt (find) trovare; (situate)

collocare; situare
location [ləu'keɪʃən] *n* posizione *f*; **on ~**
(*CINEMA*) all'esterno
loch [lɔx] *n* lago
lock [lɔk] *n* (*of door, box*) serratura; (*of
canal*) chiusa; (*of hair*) ciocca, riccio ♦ *vt*
(*with key*) chiudere a chiave ♦ *vi* (*door
etc*) chiudersi; (*wheels*) bloccarsi,
incepparsi; **~ in** *vt* chiudere dentro (a
chiave); **~ out** *vt* chiudere fuori; **~ up** *vt*
(*criminal, mental patient*) rinchiudere;
(*house*) chiudere (a chiave) ♦ *vi* chiudere
tutto (a chiave)
locker ['lɔkə*] *n* armadietto
locket ['lɔkɪt] *n* medaglione *m*
locksmith ['lɔksmɪθ] *n* magnano
lock-up (*US*) *n* prigione *f*; guardina
locomotive [ləukə'məutɪv] *n* locomotiva
locum ['ləukəm] *n* (*MED*) medico sostituto
locust ['ləukəst] *n* locusta
lodge [lɔdʒ] *n* casetta, portineria;
(*hunting ~*) casino di caccia ♦ *vi* (*person*):
to ~ (*with*) essere a pensione (presso *or*
da); (*bullet etc*) conficcarsi ♦ *vt* (*appeal
etc*) presentare, fare; **to ~ a complaint**
presentare un reclamo; **~r** *n* affittuario/a;
(*with room and meals*) pensionante *m/f*
lodgings ['lɔdʒɪŋz] *npl* camera d'affitto;
camera ammobiliata
loft [lɔft] *n* solaio, soffitta
lofty ['lɔftɪ] *adj* alto(a); (*haughty*)
altezzoso(a)
log [lɔg] *n* (*of wood*) ceppo; (*book*)
= **logbook** ♦ *vt* registrare
logbook ['lɔgbuk] *n* (*NAUT, AVIAT*) diario di
bordo; (*AUT*) libretto di circolazione
loggerheads ['lɔgəhedz] *npl*: **at ~** (*with*)
ai ferri corti (con)
logic ['lɔdʒɪk] *n* logica; **~al** *adj* logico(a)
loin [lɔɪn] *n* (*CULIN*) lombata
loiter ['lɔɪtə*] *vi* attardarsi
loll [lɔl] *vi* (*also*: **~ about**) essere
stravaccato(a)
lollipop ['lɔlɪpɔp] *n* lecca lecca *m inv*; **~
man/lady** (*BRIT*) *n* impiegato/a che aiuta
*i bambini ad attraversare la strada in
vicinanza di scuole*
London ['lʌndən] *n* Londra; **~er** *n*
londinese *m/f*

lone [ləun] *adj* solitario(a)
loneliness ['ləunlɪnɪs] *n* solitudine *f*,
isolamento
lonely ['ləunlɪ] *adj* solo(a); solitario(a),
isolato(a)
long [lɔŋ] *adj* lungo(a) ♦ *adv* a lungo, per
molto tempo ♦ *vi*: **to ~ for sth/to do**
desiderare qc/di fare; avere l'ora di
aver qc/di fare; **so** *or* **as ~ as** (*while*)
finché; (*provided that*) sempre che + *sub*;
don't be ~! fai presto!; **how ~ is this
river/course?** quanto è lungo questo
fiume/corso?; **6 metres ~** lungo 6 metri; **6
months ~** che dura 6 mesi, di 6 mesi; **all
night ~** tutta la notte; **he no ~er comes**
non viene più; **~ before** molto tempo
prima; **before ~** (+*future*) presto, fra
poco; (+*past*) poco tempo dopo; **at ~ last**
finalmente; **~-distance** *adj* (*race*) di
fondo; (*call*) interurbano(a); **~-haired** *adj*
dai capelli lunghi; **~hand** *n* scrittura
normale; **~ing** *n* desiderio, voglia, brama
longitude ['lɔŋgɪtjuːd] *n* longitudine *f*
long: **~ jump** *n* salto in lungo; **~-life** *adj*
(*milk*) a lunga conservazione; (*batteries*)
di lunga durata; **~-lost** *adj* perduto(a) da
tempo; **~-playing record** *n* (disco) 33
giri *m inv*; **~-range** *adj* a lunga portata;
~-sighted *adj* presbite; **~-standing** *adj*
di vecchia data; **~-suffering** *adj* estremamente paziente; infinitamente tollerante;
~-term *adj* a lungo termine; **~ wave** *n*
onde *fpl* lunghe; **~-winded** *adj*
prolisso(a), interminabile
loo [luː] (*BRIT*: *inf*) *n* W.C. *m inv*, cesso
look [luk] *vi* guardare; (*seem*) sembrare,
parere; (*building etc*): **to ~ south/on to
the sea** dare a sud/sul mare ♦ *n* sguardo;
(*appearance*) aspetto, aria; **~s** *npl* (*good
~s*) bellezza; **~ after** *vt fus* occuparsi di,
prendere cura di; (*keep an eye on*)
guardare, badare a; **~ at** *vt fus* guardare;
~ back *vi*: **to ~ back on** (*event etc*)
ripensare a; **~ down on** *vt fus* (*fig*)
guardare dall'alto, disprezzare; **~ for** *vt
fus* cercare; **~ forward to** *vt fus* non
veder l'ora di; (*in letters*): **we ~ forward
to hearing from you** in attesa di una
vostra gentile risposta; **~ into** *vt fus*

esaminare; ~ **on** *vi* fare da spettatore; ~ **out** *vi* (*beware*): **to ~ out** (*for*) stare in guardia (per); ~ **out for** *vt fus* cercare; ~ **round** *vi* (*turn*) girarsi, voltarsi; (*in shop*) dare un'occhiata; ~ **to** *vt fus* (*rely on*) contare su; ~ **up** *vi* alzare gli occhi; (*improve*) migliorare ♦ *vt* (*word*) cercare; (*friend*) andare a trovare; ~ **up to** *vt fus* avere rispetto per; ~**out** *n* posto d'osservazione; guardia; **to be on the ~-out** (**for**) stare in guardia (per)

loom [luːm] *n* telaio ♦ *vi* (*also:* ~ **up**) apparire minaccioso(a) imminente

loony ['luːnɪ] (*inf*) *n* pazzo/a

loop [luːp] *n* cappio ♦ *vt:* **to ~ sth round sth** passare qc intorno a qc; ~**hole** *n* via d'uscita; scappatoia

loose [luːs] *adj* (*knot*) sciolto(a); (*screw*) allentato(a); (*stone*) cadente; (*clothes*) ampio(a), largo(a); (*animal*) in libertà, scappato(a); (*life, morals*) dissoluto(a) ♦ *n:* **to be on the ~** essere in libertà; ~ **change** *n* spiccioli *mpl*, moneta; ~ **chippings** *npl* (*on road*) ghiaino; ~ **end** *n:* **to be at a ~ end** (*BRIT*) *or* **at ~ ends** (*US*) non saper che fare; ~**ly** *adv* senza stringere; approssimativamente; ~**n** *vt* sciogliere; (*belt etc*) allentare

loot [luːt] *n* bottino ♦ *vt* saccheggiare

lop [lɒp] *vt* (*also:* ~ **off**) tagliare via, recidere

lop-sided ['lɒp'saɪdɪd] *adj* non equilibrato(a), asimmetrico(a)

lord [lɔːd] *n* signore *m*; **L~ Smith** lord Smith; **the L~** il Signore; **good L~!** buon Dio!; **the (House of) L~s** (*BRIT*) la Camera dei Lord; ~**ship** *n:* **your L~ship** Sua Eccellenza

lore [lɔː*] *n* tradizioni *fpl*

lorry ['lɒrɪ] (*BRIT*) *n* camion *m inv*; ~ **driver** (*BRIT*) *n* camionista *m*

lose [luːz] (*pt, pp* **lost**) *vt* perdere ♦ *vi* perdere; **to ~ (time)** (*clock*) ritardare; ~**r** *n* perdente *m/f*

loss [lɒs] *n* perdita; **to be at a ~** essere perplesso(a)

lost [lɒst] *pt, pp of* **lose** ♦ *adj* perduto(a); ~ **property** (*US* ~ **and found**) *n* oggetti *mpl* smarriti

lot [lɒt] *n* (*at auctions*) lotto; (*destiny*) destino, sorte *f*; **the ~** tutto(a) quanto(a); tutti(e) quanti(e); **a ~** molto; **a ~ of** una gran quantità di, un sacco di; ~**s of** molto(a); **to draw ~s (for sth)** tirare a sorte (per qc)

lotion ['ləʊʃən] *n* lozione *f*

lottery ['lɒtərɪ] *n* lotteria

loud [laʊd] *adj* forte, alto(a); (*gaudy*) vistoso(a), sgargiante ♦ *adv* (*speak etc*) forte; **out ~** (*read etc*) ad alta voce; ~**hailer** (*BRIT*) *n* portavoce *m inv*; ~**ly** *adv* fortemente, ad alta voce; ~**speaker** *n* altoparlante *m*

lounge [laʊndʒ] *n* salotto, soggiorno; (*at airport, station*) sala d'attesa; (*BRIT: also:* ~ **bar**) bar *m inv* con servizio a tavolino ♦ *vi* oziare; **out** *or* **around** *vi* starsene colle mani in mano; ~ **suit** (*BRIT*) *n* completo da uomo

louse [laʊs] (*pl* **lice**) *n* pidocchio

lousy ['laʊzɪ] (*inf*) *adj* orrendo(a), schifoso(a); **to feel ~** stare da cani

lout [laʊt] *n* zoticone *m*

lovable ['lʌvəbl] *adj* simpatico(a), carino(a); amabile

love [lʌv] *n* amore *m* ♦ *vt* amare; voler bene a; **to ~ to do: I ~ to do** mi piace fare; **to be/fall in ~ with** essere innamorato(a)/innamorarsi di; **to make ~** fare l'amore; **"15 ~"** (*TENNIS*) "15 a zero"; ~ **affair** *n* relazione *f*; ~ **life** *n* vita sentimentale

lovely ['lʌvlɪ] *adj* bello(a); (*delicious: smell, meal*) buono(a)

lover ['lʌvə*] *n* amante *m/f*; (*person in love*) innamorato/a; (*amateur*): **a ~ of** un(un')amante di; un(un')appassionato(a) di

loving ['lʌvɪŋ] *adj* affettuoso(a)

low [ləʊ] *adj* basso(a) ♦ *adv* in basso ♦ *n* (*METEOR*) depressione *f*; **to be ~ on** (*supplies etc*) avere scarsità di; **to feel ~** sentirsi giù; ~**alcohol** *adj* a basso contenuto alcolico; ~**cut** *adj* (*dress*) scollato(a); ~**er** *adj* (*bottom: of 2 things*) più basso; (*less important*) meno importante ♦ *vt* calare; (*prices, eyes, voice*) abbassare; **~-fat** *adj* magro(a); **~lands** *npl* (GEO) pianura; **~ly** *adj* umile, modesto(a)

loyal ['lɔɪəl] *adj* fedele, leale; **~ty** *n* fedeltà, lealtà

lozenge ['lɔzɪndʒ] *n* (MED) pastiglia

L.P. *n abbr* = **long-playing record**

L-plates (BRIT) *npl* cartelli sui veicoli dei guidatori principianti

Ltd *abbr* (= **limited**) ≈ S.r.l.

lubricate ['lu:brɪkeɪt] *vt* lubrificare

luck [lʌk] *n* fortuna, sorte *f*; **bad** ~ sfortuna, mala sorte; **good** ~! buona fortuna!; **~ily** *adv* fortunatamente, per fortuna; **~y** *adj* fortunato(a); (*number etc*) che porta fortuna

ludicrous ['lu:dɪkrəs] *adj* ridicolo(a)

lug [lʌg] (*inf*) *vt* trascinare

luggage ['lʌgɪdʒ] *n* bagagli *mpl*; ~ **rack** *n* portabagagli *m inv*

lukewarm ['lu:kwɔ:m] *adj* tiepido(a)

lull [lʌl] *n* intervallo di calma ♦ *vt*: **to ~ sb to sleep** cullare qn finché si addormenta; **to be ~ed into a false sense of security** illudersi che tutto vada bene

lullaby ['lʌləbaɪ] *n* ninnananna

lumbago [lʌm'beɪgəu] *n* lombaggine *f*

lumber ['lʌmbə*] *n* (*wood*) legname *m*; (*junk*) roba vecchia; ~ **with** *vt*: **to be ~ed with sth** doversi sorbire qc; **~jack** *n* boscaiolo

luminous ['lu:mɪnəs] *adj* luminoso(a)

lump [lʌmp] *n* pezzo; (*in sauce*) grumo; (*swelling*) gonfiore *m*; (*also: sugar* ~) zolletta ♦ *vt* (*also:* ~ *together*) riunire, mettere insieme; **a ~ sum** una somma globale; **~y** *adj* (*sauce*) pieno(a) di grumi; (*bed*) bitorzoluto(a)

lunatic ['lu:nətɪk] *adj* pazzo(a), matto(a)

lunch [lʌntʃ] *n* pranzo, colazione *f*

luncheon ['lʌntʃən] *n* pranzo; ~ **meat** *n* ≈ mortadella; ~ **voucher** (BRIT) *n* buono *m* pasto *inv*

lunch time *n* ora di pranzo

lung [lʌŋ] *n* polmone *m*

lunge [lʌndʒ] *vi* (*also:* ~ *forward*) fare un balzo in avanti; **to ~ at** balzare su

lurch [lə:tʃ] *vi* vacillare, barcollare ♦ *n*

scatto improvviso; **to leave sb in the ~** piantare in asso qn

lure [luə*] *n* richiamo; lusinga ♦ *vt* attirare (con l'inganno)

lurid ['luərɪd] *adj* sgargiante; (*details etc*) impressionante

lurk [lə:k] *vi* stare in agguato

luscious ['lʌʃəs] *adj* succulento(a); delizioso(a)

lush [lʌʃ] *adj* lussureggiante

lust [lʌst] *n* lussuria; cupidigia; desiderio; (*fig*): ~ **for** sete *f* di; ~ **after** *or* **for** *vt fus* bramare, desiderare

lusty ['lʌstɪ] *adj* vigoroso(a), robusto(a)

Luxembourg ['lʌksəmbə:g] *n* (*state*) Lussemburgo *m*; (*city*) Lussemburgo *f*

luxuriant [lʌg'zjuərɪənt] *adj* lussureggiante; (*hair*) folto(a)

luxurious [lʌg'zjuərɪəs] *adj* sontuoso(a), di lusso

luxury ['lʌkʃərɪ] *n* lusso ♦ *cpd* di lusso

lying ['laɪɪŋ] *n* bugie *fpl*, menzogne *fpl* ♦ *adj* bugiardo(a)

lynch [lɪntʃ] *vt* linciare

lyrical ['lɪrɪkl] *adj* lirico(a); (*fig*) entusiasta

lyrics ['lɪrɪks] *npl* (*of song*) parole *fpl*

M

m. *abbr* = **metre**; **mile**; **million**

M.A. *abbr* = **Master of Arts**

mac [mæk] (BRIT) *n* impermeabile *m*

macaroni [mækə'rəunɪ] *n* maccheroni *mpl*

machine [mə'ʃi:n] *n* macchina ♦ *vt* (TECH) lavorare a macchina; (*dress etc*) cucire a macchina; ~ **gun** *n* mitragliatrice *f*; **~ry** *n* macchinario, macchine *fpl*; (*fig*) macchina

mackerel ['mækrl] *n inv* sgombro

mackintosh ['mækɪntɔʃ] (BRIT) *n* impermeabile *m*

mad [mæd] *adj* matto(a), pazzo(a); (*foolish*) sciocco(a); (*angry*) furioso(a); **to be ~ about** (*keen*) andare pazzo(a) per

madam ['mædəm] *n* signora

madden ['mædn] *vt* fare infuriare

made [meɪd] *pt, pp of* **make**

Madeira [mə'dɪərə] *n* (*GEO*) Madera; (*wine*) madera

made-to-measure (*BRIT*) *adj* fatto(a) su misura

madly ['mædlɪ] *adv* follemente

madman ['mædmən] *n* pazzo, alienato

madness ['mædnɪs] *n* pazzia

magazine [mægə'ziːn] *n* (*PRESS*) rivista; (*RADIO, TV*) rubrica

maggot ['mægət] *n* baco, verme *m*

magic ['mædʒɪk] *n* magia ♦ *adj* magico(a); **~al** *adj* magico(a); **~ian** [mə'dʒɪʃən] *n* mago/a

magistrate ['mædʒɪstreɪt] *n* magistrato; giudice *m/f*

magnet ['mægnɪt] *n* magnete *m*, calamita; **~ic** [-'nɛtɪk] *adj* magnetico(a)

magnificent [mæg'nɪfɪsnt] *adj* magnifico(a)

magnify ['mægnɪfaɪ] *vt* ingrandire; **~ing glass** *n* lente *f* d'ingrandimento

magnitude ['mægnɪtjuːd] *n* grandezza; importanza

magpie ['mægpaɪ] *n* gazza

mahogany [mə'hɒgənɪ] *n* mogano

maid [meɪd] *n* domestica; (*in hotel*) cameriera; **old ~** (*pej*) vecchia zitella

maiden ['meɪdn] *n* fanciulla ♦ *adj* (*aunt etc*) nubile; (*speech, voyage*) inaugurale; **~ name** *n* nome *m* da nubile *or* da ragazza

mail [meɪl] *n* posta ♦ *vt* spedire (per posta); **~box** (*US*) *n* cassetta delle lettere; **~ing list** *n* elenco d'indirizzi; **~-order** *n* vendita (*or* acquisto) per corrispondenza

maim [meɪm] *vt* mutilare

main [meɪn] *adj* principale ♦ *n* (*pipe*) conduttura principale; **the ~s** *npl* (*ELEC*) la linea principale; **in the ~** nel complesso, nell'insieme; **~frame** *n* (*COMPUT*) mainframe *m inv*; **~land** *n* continente *m*; **~ly** *adv* principalmente, soprattutto; **~ road** *n* strada principale; **~stay** *n* (*fig*) sostegno principale; **~stream** *n* (*fig*) corrente *f* principale

maintain [meɪn'teɪn] *vt* mantenere; (*affirm*) sostenere; **maintenance** ['meɪntənəns] *n* manutenzione *f*; (*alimony*) alimenti *mpl*

maize [meɪz] *n* granturco, mais *m*

majestic [mə'dʒɛstɪk] *adj* maestoso(a)

majesty ['mædʒɪstɪ] *n* maestà *f inv*

major ['meɪdʒə*] *n* (*MIL*) maggiore *m* ♦ *adj* (*greater, MUS*) maggiore; (*in importance*) principale, importante

Majorca [mə'jɔːkə] *n* Maiorca

majority [mə'dʒɒrɪtɪ] *n* maggioranza

make [meɪk] (*pt, pp* made) *vt* fare; (*manufacture*) fare, fabbricare; (*cause to be*): **to ~ sb sad** *etc* rendere qn triste *etc*; (*force*): **to ~ sb do sth** costringere qn a fare qc, far fare qc a qn; (*equal*): **2 and 2 ~ 4** 2 più 2 fa 4 ♦ *n* fabbricazione *f*; (*brand*) marca; **to ~ a fool of sb** far fare a qn la figura dello scemo; **to ~ a profit** realizzare un profitto; **to ~ a loss** subire una perdita; **to ~ it** (*arrive*) arrivare; (*achieve sth*) farcela; **what time do you ~ it?** che ora fai?; **to ~ do with** arrangiarsi con; **~ for** *vt fus* (*place*) avviarsi verso; **~ out** *vt* (*write out*) scrivere; (: *cheque*) emettere; (*understand*) capire; (*see*) distinguere; (: *numbers*) decifrare; **~ up** *vt* (*constitute*) formare; (*invent*) inventare; (*parcel*) fare ♦ *vi* conciliarsi; (*with cosmetics*) truccarsi; **~ up for** *vt fus* compensare; ricuperare; **~-believe** *n*: **a world of ~-believe** un mondo di favole; **it's just ~-believe** è tutta un'invenzione; **~r** *n* (*of programme etc*) creatore/trice; (*manufacturer*) fabbricante *m*; **~shift** *adj* improvvisato(a); **~-up** *n* trucco; **~-up remover** *n* struccatore *m*

making ['meɪkɪŋ] *n* (*fig*): **in the ~** in formazione; **to have the ~s of** (*actor, athlete etc*) avere la stoffa di

maladjusted [mælə'dʒʌstɪd] *adj* disadattato(a)

malaise [mæ'leɪz] *n* malessere *m*

malaria [mə'lɛərɪə] *n* malaria

Malaya [mə'leɪə] *n* Malesia

male [meɪl] *n* (*BIOL*) maschio ♦ *adj* maschile; maschio(a)

malfunction [mæl'fʌŋkʃən] *n* funzione *f* difettosa

malice ['mælɪs] *n* malevolenza; **malicious** [mə'lɪʃəs] *adj* malevolo(a); (*LAW*) doloso(a)

malign [mə'laɪn] *vt* malignare su; calunniare

malignant [mə'lɪgnənt] *adj* (*MED*) maligno(a)

mall [mɔːl] *n* (*also: shopping* ~) centro commerciale

mallet ['mælɪt] *n* maglio

malnutrition [mælnjuː'trɪʃən] *n* denutrizione *f*

malpractice [mæl'præktɪs] *n* prevaricazione *f*; negligenza

malt [mɔːlt] *n* malto

Malta ['mɔːltə] *n* Malta

mammal ['mæml] *n* mammifero

mammoth ['mæməθ] *n* mammut *m inv* ♦ *adj* enorme, gigantesco(a)

man [mæn] (*pl* **men**) *n* uomo ♦ *vt* fornire d'uomini; stare a; **an old ~** un vecchio; ~ **and wife** marito e moglie

manage ['mænɪdʒ] *vi* farcela ♦ *vt* (*be in charge of*) occuparsi di; gestire; **to ~ to do sth** riuscire a far qc; **~able***adj* maneggevole; fattibile; **~ment***n* amministrazione *f*, direzione *f*; **~r***n* direttore *m*; (*of shop, restaurant*) gerente *m*; (*of artist, SPORT*) manager *m inv*; **~ress** [-ə'res] *n* direttrice *f*; gerente *f*; **~rial** [-ə'dʒɪərɪəl] *adj* dirigenziale; **managing director***n* amministratore *m* delegato

mandarin ['mændərɪn] *n* (*person, fruit*) mandarino

mandatory ['mændətərɪ] *adj* obbligatorio(a); ingiuntivo(a)

mane [meɪn] *n* criniera

maneuver *etc* [mə'nuːvə*] (*US*) = **manoeuvre** *etc*

manfully ['mænfəlɪ] *adv* valorosamente

mangle ['mæŋgl] *vt* straziare; mutilare

mango ['mæŋgəu] (*pl* **~es**) *n* mango

mangy ['meɪndʒɪ] *adj* rognoso(a)

manhandle ['mænhændl] *vt* malmenare

manhole ['mænhəul] *n* botola stradale

manhood ['mænhud] *n* età virile; virilità

man-hour*n* ora di lavoro

manhunt ['mænhʌnt] *n* caccia all'uomo

mania ['meɪnɪə] *n* mania; **~c** ['meɪnɪæk] *n* maniaco/a

manic ['mænɪk] *adj* (*behaviour, activity*) maniacale

manicure ['mænɪkjuə*] *n* manicure *f inv*; **~ set***n* trousse *f inv* della manicure

manifest ['mænɪfest] *vt* manifestare ♦ *adj* manifesto(a), palese

manifesto [mænɪ'festəu] *n* manifesto

manipulate [mə'nɪpjuleɪt] *vt* manipolare

mankind [mæn'kaɪnd] *n* umanità, genere *m* umano

manly ['mænlɪ] *adj* virile; coraggioso(a)

man-made*adj* sintetico(a); artificiale

manner ['mænə*] *n* maniera, modo; (*behaviour*) modo di fare; (*type, sort*): **all ~ of things** ogni genere di cosa; **~s** *npl* (*conduct*) maniere *fpl*; **bad ~s** maleducazione *f*; **~ism***n* vezzo, tic *m inv*

manoeuvre [mə'nuːvə*] (*US* **maneuver**) *vt* manovrare ♦ *vi* far manovre ♦ *n* manovra

manor ['mænə*] *n* (*also:* ~ *house*) maniero

manpower ['mænpauə*] *n* manodopera

mansion ['mænʃən] *n* casa signorile

manslaughter ['mænslɔːtə*] *n* omicidio preterintenzionale

mantelpiece ['mæntlpiːs] *n* mensola del caminetto

manual ['mænjuəl] *adj* manuale ♦ *n* manuale *m*

manufacture [mænju'fæktʃə*] *vt* fabbricare ♦ *n* fabbricazione *f*, manifattura; **~r***n* fabbricante *m*

manure [mə'njuə*] *n* concime *m*

manuscript ['mænjuskrɪpt] *n* manoscritto

many ['menɪ] *adj* molti(e) ♦ *pron* molti(e); **a great ~** moltissimi(e), un gran numero (di); ~ **a time** molte volte

map [mæp] *n* carta (geografica); ~ **out***vt* tracciare un piano di

maple ['meɪpl] *n* acero

mar [mɑː*] *vt* sciupare

marathon ['mærəθən] *n* maratona

marauder [mə'rɔːdə*] *n* saccheggiatore *m*

marble ['mɑːbl] *n* marmo; (*toy*) pallina, bilia

March [mɑːtʃ] *n* marzo

march [mɑːtʃ] *vi* marciare; sfilare ♦ *n* marcia

mare [mɛə*] *n* giumenta

margarine [maːdʒəˈriːn] *n* margarina

margin [ˈmaːdʒɪn] *n* margine *m*; **~al (seat)** *n* (*POL*) seggio elettorale ottenuto con una stretta maggioranza

marigold [ˈmærɪgəʊld] *n* calendola

marijuana [mærɪˈwaːnə] *n* marijuana

marine [məˈriːn] *adj* (*animal, plant*) marino(a); (*forces, engineering*) marittimo(a) ♦ *n* (*BRIT*) fante *m* di marina; (*US*) marine *m inv*

marital [ˈmærɪtl] *adj* maritale, coniugale; **~ status** stato coniugale

mark [maːk] *n* segno; (*stain*) macchia; (*of skid etc*) traccia; (*BRIT: SCOL*) voto; (*SPORT*) bersaglio; (*currency*) marco ♦ *vt* segnare; (*stain*) macchiare; (*indicate*) indicare; (*BRIT: SCOL*) dare un voto a; correggere; **to ~ time** segnare il passo; **~ed** *adj* spiccato(a), chiaro(a); **~er** *n* (*sign*) segno; (*bookmark*) segnalibro

market [ˈmaːkɪt] *n* mercato ♦ *vt* (*COMM*) mettere in vendita; **~ garden** (*BRIT*) *n* orto industriale; **~ing** *n* marketing *m*; **~ place** *n* piazza del mercato; (*COMM*) piazza, mercato; **~ research** *n* indagine *f or* ricerca di mercato

marksman [ˈmaːksmən] *n* tiratore *m* scelto

marmalade [ˈmaːməleɪd] *n* marmellata d'arance

maroon [məˈruːn] *vt* (*also fig*): **to be ~ed (in *or* at)** essere abbandonato(a) (in) ♦ *adj* bordeaux *inv*

marquee [maːˈkiː] *n* padiglione *m*

marquess [ˈmaːkwɪs] *n* = **marquis**

marquis [ˈmaːkwɪs] *n* marchese *m*

marriage [ˈmærɪdʒ] *n* matrimonio; **~ bureau** *n* agenzia matrimoniale; **~ certificate** *n* certificato di matrimonio

married [ˈmærɪd] *adj* sposato(a); (*life, love*) coniugale, matrimoniale

marrow [ˈmærəʊ] *n* midollo; (*vegetable*) zucca

marry [ˈmærɪ] *vt* sposare, sposarsi con; (*subj: father, priest etc*) dare in matrimonio ♦ *vi* (*also: get married*) sposarsi

Mars [maːz] *n* (*planet*) Marte *m*

marsh [maːʃ] *n* palude *f*

marshal [ˈmaːʃl] *n* maresciallo; (*US: fire*) capo; (*: police*) capitano ♦ *vt* (*thoughts, support*) ordinare; (*soldiers*) adunare

martyr [ˈmaːtə*] *n* martire *m/f*; **~dom** *n* martirio

marvel [ˈmaːvl] *n* meraviglia ♦ *vi*: **to ~ (at)** meravigliarsi (di); **~lous** (*US* **~ous**) *adj* meraviglioso(a)

Marxist [ˈmaːksɪst] *adj, n* marxista *m/f*

marzipan [ˈmaːzɪpæn] *n* marzapane *m*

mascara [mæsˈkaːrə] *n* mascara *m*

masculine [ˈmæskjulɪn] *adj* maschile; (*woman*) mascolino(a)

mash [mæʃ] *vt* passare, schiacciare; **~ed potatoes** *npl* purè *m* di patate

mask [maːsk] *n* maschera ♦ *vt* mascherare

mason [ˈmeɪsn] *n* (*also: stone~*) scalpellino; (*also: free~*) massone *m*; **~ry** *n* muratura

masquerade [mæskəˈreɪd] *vi*: **to ~ as** farsi passare per

mass [mæs] *n* moltitudine *f*, massa; (*PHYSICS*) massa; (*REL*) messa ♦ *cpd* di massa ♦ *vi* ammassarsi; **the ~es** *npl* (*ordinary people*) le masse; **~es of** (*inf*) una montagna di

massacre [ˈmæsəkə*] *n* massacro

massage [ˈmæsɑːʒ] *n* massaggio

masseur [mæˈsɜː*] *n* massaggiatore *m*; **masseuse** [-ˈsɜːz] *n* massaggiatrice *f*

massive [ˈmæsɪv] *adj* enorme, massiccio(a)

mass media *npl* mass media *mpl*

mass-production *n* produzione *f* in serie

mast [maːst] *n* albero

master [ˈmaːstə*] *n* padrone *m*; (*ART etc, teacher: in primary school*) maestro; (*: in secondary school*) professore *m*; (*title for boys*): **M~ X** Signorino X ♦ *vt* domare; (*learn*) imparare a fondo; (*understand*) conoscere a fondo; **~ key** *n* chiave *f* maestra; **~ly** *adj* magistrale; **~mind** *n* mente *f* superiore ♦ *vt* essere il cervello di; **M~ of Arts/Science** *n* Master *m inv* in lettere/scienze; **~piece** *n* capolavoro; **~y** *n* dominio; padronanza

mat [mæt] *n* stuoia; (*also: door~*) stoino, zerbino; (*also: table ~*) sottopiatto ♦ *adj* = **matt**

match [mætʃ] *n* fiammifero; (*game*) partita, incontro; (*fig*) uguale *m/f*; matrimonio; partito ♦ *vt* intonare; (*go well with*) andare benissimo con; (*equal*) uguagliare; (*correspond to*) corrispondere a; (*pair: also: ~ up*) accoppiare ♦ *vi* combaciare; **to be a good ~** andare bene; **~box** *n* scatola per fiammiferi; **~ing** *adj* ben assortito(a)

mate [meit] *n* compagno/a di lavoro; (*inf: friend*) amico/a; (*animal*) compagno/a; (*in merchant navy*) secondo ♦ *vi* accoppiarsi

material [mə'tiəriəl] *n* (*substance*) materiale *m*, materia; (*cloth*) stoffa ♦ *adj* materiale; **~s** *npl* (*equipment*) materiali *mpl*

maternal [mə'tə:nl] *adj* materno(a)

maternity [mə'tə:niti] *n* maternità; **~ dress** *n* vestito *m* pre-maman *inv*; **~ hospital** *n* ≈ clinica ostetrica

math [mæθ] (*US*) *n* = **maths**

mathematical [mæθə'mætikl] *adj* matematico(a)

mathematics [mæθə'mætiks] *n* matematica

maths [mæθs] (*US* **math**) *n* matematica

matinée ['mætinei] *n* matinée *f inv*

mating call ['meitiŋ-] *n* richiamo sessuale

matriculation [mətrikju'leiʃən] *n* immatricolazione *f*

matrimonial [mætri'məuniəl] *adj* matrimoniale, coniugale

matrimony ['mætriməni] *n* matrimonio

matron ['meitrən] *n* (*in hospital*) capoinfermiera; (*in school*) infermiera

mat(t) [mæt] *adj* opaco(a)

matted ['mætid] *adj* ingarbugliato(a)

matter ['mætə*] *n* questione *f*; (*PHYSICS*) materia, sostanza; (*content*) contenuto; (*MED: pus*) pus *m* ♦ *vi* importare; **it doesn't ~** non importa; (*I don't mind*) non fa niente; **what's the ~?** che cosa c'è?; **no ~ what** qualsiasi cosa accada; **as a ~ of course** come cosa naturale; **as a ~ of fact** in verità; **~-of-fact** *adj* prosaico(a)

mattress ['mætris] *n* materasso

mature [mə'tjuə*] *adj* maturo(a); (*cheese*) stagionato(a) ♦ *vi* maturare; stagionare

maul [mɔ:l] *vt* lacerare

mauve [məuv] *adj* malva *inv*

maverick ['mævərik] *n* chi sta fuori dal branco

maxim ['mæksim] *n* massima

maxima ['mæksimə] *npl of* **maximum**

maximum ['mæksiməm] (*pl* **maxima**) *adj* massimo(a) ♦ *n* massimo

May [mei] *n* maggio

may [mei] (*conditional:* **might**) *vi* (*indicating possibility*): **he ~ come** può darsi che venga; (*be allowed to*): **~ I smoke?** posso fumare?; (*wishes*): **~ God bless you!** Dio la benedica!; **you ~ as well go** tanto vale che tu te ne vada

maybe ['meibi:] *adv* forse, può darsi; **~ he'll ...** può darsi che lui ... + *sub*, forse lui ....

May Day *n* il primo maggio

mayhem ['meihem] *n* cagnara

mayonnaise [meiə'neiz] *n* maionese *f*

mayor [mɛə*] *n* sindaco; **~ess** *n* sindaco (*donna*); moglie *f* del sindaco

maze [meiz] *n* labirinto, dedalo

M.D. *abbr* = **Doctor of Medicine**

me [mi:] *pron* mi, m' + *vowel or silent "h"*; (*stressed, after prep*) me; **he heard ~** mi ha *or* m'ha sentito; **give ~ a book** dammi (*or* mi dia) un libro; **it's ~** sono io; **with ~** con me; **without ~** senza di me

meadow ['mɛdəu] *n* prato

meagre ['mi:gə*] (*US* **meager**) *adj* magro(a)

meal [mi:l] *n* pasto; (*flour*) farina; **~time** *n* l'ora di mangiare

mean [mi:n] (*pt, pp* **meant**) *adj* (*with money*) avaro(a), gretto(a); (*unkind*) meschino(a), maligno(a); (*shabby*) misero(a); (*average*) medio(a) ♦ *vt* (*signify*) significare, voler dire; (*intend*): **to ~ to do** aver l'intenzione di fare ♦ *n* mezzo; (*MATH*) media; **~s** *npl* (*way, money*) mezzi *mpl*; **by ~s of** per mezzo di; **by all ~s** ma certo, prego; **to be meant for** essere destinato(a) a; **do you ~ it?** dice sul serio?; **what do you ~?** che cosa vuol dire?

meander [mɪ'ændə*] *vi* far meandri

meaning ['mi:nɪŋ] *n* significato, senso; **~ful** *adj* significativo(a); **~less** *adj* senza senso

meant [mɛnt] *pt, pp of* **mean**

meantime ['mi:ntaɪm] *adv* (*also: in the ~*) nel frattempo

meanwhile ['mi:nwaɪl] *adv* nel frattempo

measles ['mi:zlz] *n* morbillo

measly ['mi:zlɪ] (*inf*) *adj* miserabile

measure ['mɛʒə*] *vt, vi* misurare ♦ *n* misura; (*also: tape ~*) metro; **~ments** *npl* (*size*) misure *fpl*

meat [mi:t] *n* carne *f*; **cold ~** affettato; **~ball** *n* polpetta di carne; **~ pie** *n* pasticcio di carne in crosta

Mecca ['mɛkə] *n* (*also fig*) la Mecca

mechanic [mɪ'kænɪk] *n* meccanico; **~al** *adj* meccanico(a); **~s** *n* meccanica ♦ *npl* meccanismo

mechanism ['mɛkənɪzəm] *n* meccanismo

medal ['mɛdl] *n* medaglia; **~lion** [mɪ'dælɪən] *n* medaglione *m*; **~list** (*US* **~ist**) *n* (*SPORT*): **to be a gold ~list** essere medaglia d'oro

meddle ['mɛdl] *vi*: **to ~ in** immischiarsi in, mettere le mani in; **to ~ with** toccare

media ['mi:dɪə] *npl* media *mpl*

mediaeval [mɛdɪ'i:vl] *adj* = **medieval**

median ['mi:dɪən] (*US*) *n* (*also: ~ strip*) banchina *f* spartitraffico

mediate ['mi:dɪeɪt] *vi* fare da mediatore/ trice

Medicaid ['mɛdɪkeɪd] (*US*) *n* assistenza *medica ai poveri*

medical ['mɛdɪkl] *adj* medico(a) ♦ *n* visita medica

Medicare ['mɛdɪkɛə*] (*US*) *n* assistenza *medica agli anziani*

medication [mɛdɪ'keɪʃən] *n* medicinali *mpl*, farmaci *mpl*

medicine ['mɛdsɪn] *n* medicina

medieval [mɛdɪ'i:vl] *adj* medievale

mediocre [mi:dɪ'əukə*] *adj* mediocre

meditate ['mɛdɪteɪt] *vi*: **to ~ (on)** meditare (su)

Mediterranean [mɛdɪtə'reɪnɪən] *adj* mediterraneo(a); **the ~ (Sea)** il (mare) Mediterraneo

medium ['mi:dɪəm] (*pl* **media**) *adj* medio(a) ♦ *n* (*means*) mezzo; (*pl* **mediums**: *person*) medium *m inv*; **~ wave** *n* onde *fpl* medie

medley ['mɛdlɪ] *n* selezione *f*; (*MUS*) potpourri *m inv*

meek [mi:k] *adj* dolce, umile

meet [mi:t], (*pt, pp* **met**) *vt* incontrare; (*for the first time*) fare la conoscenza di; (*go and fetch*) andare a prendere; (*fig*) affrontare; soddisfare; raggiungere ♦ *vi* incontrarsi; (*in session*) riunirsi; (*join: objects*) unirsi; **~ with** *vt fus* incontrare; **~ing** *n* incontro; (*session: of club etc*) riunione *f*; (*interview*) intervista; **she's at a ~ing** (*COMM*) è in riunione

megabyte ['mɛgəbaɪt] *n* (*COMPUT*) megabyte *m inv*

megaphone ['mɛgəfəun] *n* megafono

melancholy ['mɛlənkəlɪ] *n* malinconia ♦ *adj* malinconico(a)

mellow ['mɛləu] *adj* (*wine, sound*) ricco(a); (*light*) dolce; (*colour*) caldo(a) ♦ *vi* (*person*) addolcirsi

melody ['mɛlədɪ] *n* melodia

melon ['mɛlən] *n* melone *m*

melt [mɛlt] *vi* (*gen*) sciogliersi, struggersi; (*metals*) fondersi ♦ *vt* sciogliere, struggere; fondere; **~ down** *vt* fondere; **~down** *n* (*in nuclear reactor*) fusione *f* (dovuta a surriscaldamento); **~ing pot** *n* (*fig*) crogiolo

member ['mɛmbə*] *n* membro; **M~ of the European Parliament** (*BRIT*) *n* eurodeputato; **M~ of Parliament** (*BRIT*) *n* deputato; **~ship** *n* iscrizione *f*; (*numero d'iscritti*) *mpl*, membri *mpl*; **~ship card** *n* tessera (di iscrizione)

memento [mə'mɛntəu] *n* ricordo, souvenir *m inv*

memo ['mɛməu] *n* appunto; (*COMM etc*) comunicazione *f* di servizio

memoirs ['mɛmwɑ:z] *npl* memorie *fpl*, ricordi *mpl*

memoranda [mɛmə'rændə] *npl of* **memorandum**

memorandum [mɛmə'rændəm] (*pl* **memoranda**) *n* appunto; (*COMM etc*) comunicazione *f* di servizio

memorial [mɪ'mɔːrɪəl] *n* monumento commemorativo ♦ *adj* commemorativo(a)

memorize ['mɛmərɑɪz] *vt* memorizzare

memory ['mɛmərɪ] *n* (*also COMPUT*) memoria; (*recollection*) ricordo

men [mɛn] *npl of* **man**

menace ['mɛnəs] *n* minaccia ♦ *vt* minacciare

mend [mɛnd] *vt* aggiustare, riparare; (*darn*) rammendare ♦ *n*: **on the ~** in via di guarigione; **to ~ one's ways** correggersi

menial ['miːnɪəl] *adj* da servo, domestico(a); umile

meningitis [mɛnɪn'dʒɑɪtɪs] *n* meningite *f*

menopause ['mɛnəupɔːz] *n* menopausa

menstruation [mɛnstru'eɪʃən] *n* mestruazione *f*

mental ['mɛntl] *adj* mentale

mentality [mɛn'tælɪtɪ] *n* mentalità *f inv*

menthol ['mɛnθɔl] *n* mentolo

mention ['mɛnʃən] *n* menzione *f* ♦ *vt* menzionare, far menzione di; **don't ~ it!** non c'è di che!, prego!

menu ['mɛnjuː] *n* (*set* ~, *COMPUT*) menù *m inv*; (*printed*) carta

MEP *n abbr* = **Member of the European Parliament**

mercenary ['məːsɪnərɪ] *adj* venale ♦ *n* mercenario

merchandise ['məːtʃəndɑɪz] *n* merci *fpl*

merchant ['məːtʃənt] *n* mercante *m*, commerciante *m*; **~ bank** (*BRIT*) *n* banca d'affari; **~ navy** (*US* ~ **marine**) *n* marina mercantile

merciful ['məːsɪful] *adj* pietoso(a), clemente

merciless ['məːsɪlɪs] *adj* spietato(a)

mercury ['məːkjurɪ] *n* mercurio

mercy ['məːsɪ] *n* pietà; (*REL*) misericordia; **at the ~ of** alla mercè di

mere [mɪə*] *adj* semplice; **by a ~ chance** per mero caso; **~ly** *adv* semplicemente, non ... che

merge [məːdʒ] *vt* unire ♦ *vi* fondersi, unirsi; (*COMM*) fondersi; **~r** *n* (*COMM*) fusione *f*

meringue [mə'ræŋ] *n* meringa

merit ['mɛrɪt] *n* merito, valore *m* ♦ *vt* meritare

mermaid ['məːmeɪd] *n* sirena

merry ['mɛrɪ] *adj* gaio(a), allegro(a); **M~ Christmas!** Buon Natale!; **~-go-round** *n* carosello

mesh [mɛʃ] *n* maglia; rete *f*

mesmerize ['mɛzmərɑɪz] *vt* ipnotizzare; affascinare

mess [mɛs] *n* confusione *f*, disordine *m*; (*fig*) pasticcio; (*dirt*) sporcizia; (*MIL*) mensa; **~ about** (*inf*) *vi* (*also:* ~ **around**) trastullarsi; **~ about with** (*inf*) *vt fus* (*also:* ~ **around with**) gingillarsi con; (*plans*) fare un pasticcio di; **~ up** *vt* sporcare; fare un pasticcio; rovinare

message ['mɛsɪdʒ] *n* messaggio

messenger ['mɛsɪndʒə*] *n* messaggero/a

Messrs ['mɛsəz] *abbr* (*on letters*) Spett

messy ['mɛsɪ] *adj* sporco(a); disordinato(a)

met [mɛt] *pt, pp of* **meet**

metal ['mɛtl] *n* metallo; **~lic** [-'tælɪk] *adj* metallico(a)

metaphor ['mɛtəfə*] *n* metafora

mete [miːt]: **to ~ out** *vt* infliggere

meteorology [miːtɪə'rɔlədʒɪ] *n* meteorologia

meter ['miːtə*] *n* (*instrument*) contatore *m*; (*parking* ~) parchimetro; (*US: unit*) = **metre**

method ['mɛθəd] *n* metodo; **~ical** [mɪ'θɔdɪkl] *adj* metodico(a)

Methodist ['mɛθədɪst] *n* metodista *m/f*

meths [mɛθs] (*BRIT*) *n* = **methylated spirit**

methylated spirit ['mɛθɪleɪtɪd-] (*BRIT*) *n* alcool *m* denaturato

metre ['miːtə*] (*US* **meter**) *n* metro

metric ['mɛtrɪk] *adj* metrico(a)

metropolitan [mɛtrə'pɔlɪtən] *adj* metropolitano(a); **the M~ Police** (*BRIT*) *n* la polizia di Londra

mettle ['mɛtl] *n*: **to be on one's ~** essere pronto(a) a dare il meglio di se stesso(a)

mew [mjuː] *vi* (*cat*) miagolare

mews [mjuːz] (*BRIT*) *n*: **~ flat**

appartamento ricavato da un'antica
scuderia
Mexico ['mɛksɪkəʊ] *n* Messico
miaow [miː'aʊ] *vi* miagolare
mice [maɪs] *npl of* **mouse**
micro... ['maɪkrəʊ] *prefix* micro...; **~chip**
n microcircuito integrato; **~(computer)**
n microcomputer *m inv*; **~film** *n*
microfilm *m inv*; **~phone** *n* microfono;
~scope *n* microscopio; **~wave** *n* (*also:*
~wave oven) forno a microonde
mid [mɪd] *adj:* **~ May** metà maggio; **~**
afternoon metà pomeriggio; **in ~ air** a
mezz'aria; **~day** *n* mezzogiorno
middle [mɪdl] *n* mezzo; centro; (*waist*)
vita ♦ *adj* di mezzo; **in the ~ of the**
night nel bel mezzo della notte; **~-aged**
adj di mezza età; **the M~ Ages** *npl* il
Medioevo; **~-class** *adj* ≈ borghese; **the ~**
class(es) *n(pl)* ≈ la borghesia; **M~ East**
n Medio Oriente *m*; **~man** *n*
intermediario; agente *m* rivenditore; **~**
name *n* secondo nome *m*; **~-of-the-road**
adj moderato(a); **~weight** *n* (*BOXING*) peso
medio
middling ['mɪdlɪŋ] *adj* medio(a)
midge [mɪdʒ] *n* moscerino
midget ['mɪdʒɪt] *n* nano/a
Midlands ['mɪdləndz] *npl contee del*
centro dell'Inghilterra
midnight ['mɪdnaɪt] *n* mezzanotte *f*
midriff ['mɪdrɪf] *n* diaframma *m*
midst [mɪdst] *n:* **in the ~ of** in mezzo a
midsummer [mɪd'sʌmə*] *n* mezza *or*
piena estate *f*
midway [mɪd'weɪ] *adj, adv:* **~ (between)**
a mezza strada (fra); **~ (through)** a metà
(di)
midweek [mɪd'wiːk] *adv* a metà
settimana
midwife ['mɪdwaɪf] (*pl* **midwives**) *n*
levatrice *f*
midwinter [mɪd'wɪntə*] *n:* **in ~** in pieno
inverno
midwives ['mɪdwaɪvz] *npl of* **midwife**
might [maɪt] *vb see* **may** ♦ *n* potere *m*,
forza; **~y** *adj* forte, potente
migraine ['miːgreɪn] *n* emicrania
migrant ['maɪgrənt] *adj* (*bird*)

migratore(trice); (*worker*) emigrato(a)
migrate [maɪ'greɪt] *vi* (*bird*) migrare;
(*person*) emigrare
mike [maɪk] *n abbr* (= *microphone*)
microfono
Milan [mɪ'læn] *n* Milano *f*
mild [maɪld] *adj* mite; (*person, voice*)
dolce; (*flavour*) delicato(a); (*illness*)
leggero(a); (*interest*) blando(a)
mildew ['mɪldjuː] *n* muffa
mildly ['maɪldlɪ] *adv* mitemente;
dolcemente; delicatamente; leggermente;
blandamente; **to put it ~** a dire poco
mile [maɪl] *n* miglio; **~age** *n* distanza in
miglia, ≈ chilometraggio
mileometer [maɪ'lɔmɪtə*] *n* ≈
contachilometri *m inv*
milestone ['maɪlstəʊn] *n* pietra miliare
milieu ['miːljəː] *n* ambiente *m*
militant ['mɪlɪtnt] *adj* militante
military ['mɪlɪtərɪ] *adj* militare
militate ['mɪlɪteɪt] *vi:* **to ~ against** essere
d'ostacolo a
milk [mɪlk] *n* latte *m* ♦ *vt* (*cow*) mungere;
(*fig*) sfruttare; **~ chocolate** *n* cioccolato
al latte; **~man** *n* lattaio; **~ shake** *n*
frappé *m inv*; **~y** *adj* lattiginoso(a);
(*colour*) latteo(a); **M~y Way** *n* Via Lattea
mill [mɪl] *n* mulino; (*small: for coffee,*
pepper etc) macinino; (*factory*) fabbrica;
(*spinning ~*) filatura ♦ *vt* macinare ♦ *vi*
(*also: ~ about*) brulicare
miller ['mɪlə*] *n* mugnaio
milli... ['mɪlɪ] *prefix:* **~gram(me)** *n*
milligrammo; **~metre** (*US* **~meter**) *n*
millimetro
millinery ['mɪlɪnərɪ] *n* modisteria
million ['mɪljən] *n* milione *m*; **~aire** *n*
milionario, ≈ miliardario
milometer [maɪ'lɔmɪtə*] *n*
= **mileometer**
mime [maɪm] *n* mimo ♦ *vt, vi* mimare
mimic ['mɪmɪk] *n* imitatore/trice ♦ *vt*
fare la mimica di
min. *abbr* = **minute(s)**; **minimum**
mince [mɪns] *vt* tritare, macinare ♦ *vi* (*in*
walking) camminare a passettini ♦ *n*
(*BRIT: CULIN*) carne *f* tritata *or* macinata;
~meat *n* frutta secca tritata per uso in

pasticceria; (*US*) carne *f* tritata *or* macinata; ~ **pie** *n specie di torta con frutta secca*; ~**r** *n* tritacarne *m inv*
mind [maɪnd] *n* mente *f* ♦ *vt* (*attend to, look after*) badare a, occuparsi di; (*be careful*) fare attenzione a, stare attento(a) a; (*object to*): **I don't ~ the noise** il rumore non mi dà alcun fastidio; **I don't ~** non m'importa; **it is on my ~** mi preoccupa; **to my ~** secondo me, a mio parere; **to be out of one's ~** essere uscito(a) di mente; **to keep** *or* **bear sth in ~** non dimenticare qc; **to make up one's ~** decidersi; ~ **you, ...** sì, però va detto che ...; **never** ~ non importa, non fa niente; (*don't worry*) non preoccuparti; "~ **the step**" "attenzione allo scalino"; ~**er** *n* (*child ~er*) bambinaia; (*bodyguard*) guardia del corpo; ~**ful** *adj*: ~**ful of** attento(a) a; memore di; ~**less** *adj* idiota
mine[1] [maɪn] *pron* il(la) mio(a), *pl* i(le) miei(mie); **that book is** ~ quel libro è mio; **yours is red,** ~ **is green** il tuo è rosso, il mio è verde; **a friend of** ~ un mio amico
mine[2] [maɪn] *n* miniera; (*explosive*) mina ♦ *vt* (*coal*) estrarre; (*ship, beach*) minare; ~**field** *n* (*also fig*) campo minato
miner [ˈmaɪnə*] *n* minatore *m*
mineral [ˈmɪnərəl] *adj* minerale ♦ *n* minerale *m*; ~**s** *npl* (*BRIT: soft drinks*) bevande *fpl* gasate; ~ **water** *n* acqua minerale
mingle [ˈmɪŋgl] *vi*: **to ~ with** mescolarsi a, mischiarsi con
miniature [ˈmɪnətʃə*] *adj* in miniatura ♦ *n* miniatura
minibus [ˈmɪnɪbʌs] *n* minibus *m inv*
minim [ˈmɪnɪm] *n* (*MUS*) minima
minima [ˈmɪnɪmə] *npl of* **minimum**
minimum [ˈmɪnɪməm] (*pl* **minima**) *n* minimo ♦ *adj* minimo(a)
mining [ˈmaɪnɪŋ] *n* industria mineraria
miniskirt [ˈmɪnɪskə:t] *n* minigonna
minister [ˈmɪnɪstə*] *n* (*BRIT: POL*) ministro; (*REL*) pastore *m* ♦ *vi*: **to ~ to sb** assistere qn; **to ~ to sb's needs** provvedere ai bisogni di qn; ~**ial** [-ˈtɪərɪəl] (*BRIT*) *adj* (*POL*) ministeriale

ministry [ˈmɪnɪstrɪ] *n* (*BRIT: POL*) ministero; (*REL*): **to go into the ~** diventare pastore
mink [mɪŋk] *n* visone *m*
minnow [ˈmɪnəu] *n* pesciolino d'acqua dolce
minor [ˈmaɪnə*] *adj* minore, di poca importanza; (*MUS*) minore ♦ *n* (*LAW*) minorenne *m/f*
minority [maɪˈnɔrɪtɪ] *n* minoranza
mint [mɪnt] *n* (*plant*) menta; (*sweet*) pasticca di menta ♦ *vt* (*coins*) battere; **the (Royal) M~** (*BRIT*), **the (US) M~** (*US*) la Zecca; **in ~ condition** come nuovo(a) di zecca
minus [ˈmaɪnəs] *n* (*also*: ~ **sign**) segno meno ♦ *prep* meno
minute [*adj* maɪˈnju:t, *n* ˈmɪnɪt] *adj* minuscolo(a); (*detail*) minuzioso(a) ♦ *n* minuto; ~**s** *npl* (*of meeting*) verbale *m*
miracle [ˈmɪrəkl] *n* miracolo
mirage [ˈmɪrɑ:ʒ] *n* miraggio
mirror [ˈmɪrə*] *n* specchio; (*in car*) specchietto
mirth [mə:θ] *n* ilarità
misadventure [mɪsədˈventʃə*] *n* disavventura; **death by ~** morte *f* accidentale
misapprehension [ˈmɪsæprɪˈhenʃən] *n* malinteso
misappropriate [mɪsəˈprəuprɪeɪt] *vt* appropriarsi indebitamente di
misbehave [mɪsbɪˈheɪv] *vi* comportarsi male
miscarriage [ˈmɪskærɪdʒ] *n* (*MED*) aborto spontaneo; ~ **of justice** errore *m* giudiziario
miscellaneous [mɪsɪˈleɪnɪəs] *adj* (*items*) vario(a); (*selection*) misto(a)
mischance [mɪsˈtʃɑ:ns] *n* sfortuna
mischief [ˈmɪstʃɪf] *n* (*naughtiness*) birichineria; (*maliciousness*) malizia; **mischievous** *adj* birichino(a)
misconception [ˈmɪskənˈsepʃən] *n* idea sbagliata
misconduct [mɪsˈkɔndʌkt] *n* cattiva condotta; **professional ~** reato professionale
misdemeanour [mɪsdɪˈmi:nə*] (*US*

misdemeanor) *n* misfatto; infrazione *f*
miser ['maizə*'] *n* avaro
miserable ['mizərəbl] *adj* infelice;
(*wretched*) miserabile; (*weather*)
deprimente; (*offer, failure*) misero(a)
miserly ['maizəli] *adj* avaro(a)
misery ['mizəri] *n* (*unhappiness*)
tristezza; (*wretchedness*) miseria
misfire [mis'faiə*'] *vi* far cilecca; (*car engine*) perdere colpi
misfit ['misfit] *n* (*person*) spostato/a
misfortune [mis'fɔːtʃən] *n* sfortuna
misgiving [mis'givin] *n* apprensione *f*; **to have ~s about** avere dei dubbi per quanto riguarda
misguided [mis'gaidid] *adj* sbagliato(a); poco giudizioso(a)
mishandle [mis'hændl] *vt* (*mismanage*) trattare male
mishap ['mishæp] *n* disgrazia
misinterpret [misin'tə:prit] *vt* interpretare male
misjudge [mis'dʒʌdʒ] *vt* giudicare male
mislay [mis'lei] (*irreg*) *vt* smarrire
mislead [mis'li:d] (*irreg*) *vt* sviare; **~ing** *adj* ingannevole
mismanage [mis'mænidʒ] *vt* gestire male
misnomer [mis'nəumə*'] *n* termine *m* sbagliato *or* improprio
misplace [mis'pleis] *vt* smarrire
misprint ['misprint] *n* errore *m* di stampa
Miss [mis] *n* Signorina
miss [mis] *vt* (*fail to get*) perdere; (*fail to hit*) mancare; (*fail to see*): **you can't ~ it** non puoi non vederlo; (*regret the absence of*): **I ~ him** sento la sua mancanza ♦ *vi* mancare ♦ *n* (*shot*) colpo mancato; **~ out** (*BRIT*) *vt* omettere
misshapen [mis'ʃeipən] *adj* deforme
missile ['misail] *n* (*MIL*) missile *m*; (*object thrown*) proiettile *m*
missing ['misin] *adj* perso(a), smarrito(a); (*person*) scomparso(a); (*: after disaster, MIL*) disperso(a); (*removed*) mancante; **to be ~** mancare
mission ['miʃən] *n* missione *f*; **~ary** *n* missionario/a

misspent ['mis'spent] *adj*: **his ~ youth** la sua gioventù sciupata
mist [mist] *n* nebbia, foschia ♦ *vi* (*also: ~ over, ~ up*) annebbiarsi; (*: BRIT: windows*) appannarsi
mistake [mis'teik] (*irreg: like take*) *n* sbaglio, errore *m* ♦ *vt* sbagliarsi di; fraintendere; **to make a ~** fare uno sbaglio, sbagliare; **by ~** per sbaglio; **to ~ for** prendere per; **mistaken** *pp of* **mistake** ♦ *adj* (*idea etc*) sbagliato(a); **to be mistaken** sbagliarsi
mister ['mistə*'] (*inf*) *n* signore *m*; *see* **Mr**
mistletoe ['misltəu] *n* vischio
mistook [mis'tuk] *pt of* **mistake**
mistress ['mistris] *n* padrona; (*lover*) amante *f*; (*BRIT: SCOL*) insegnante *f*
mistrust [mis'trʌst] *vt* diffidare di
misty ['misti] *adj* nebbioso(a), brumoso(a)
misunderstand [misʌndə'stænd] (*irreg*) *vt, vi* capire male, fraintendere; **~ing** *n* malinteso, equivoco
misuse [*n* mis'ju:s, *vb* mis'ju:z] *n* cattivo uso; (*of power*) abuso ♦ *vt* far cattivo uso di; abusare di
mitigate ['mitigeit] *vt* mitigare
mitt(en) ['mit(n)] *n* mezzo guanto; manopola
mix [miks] *vt* mescolare ♦ *vi* (*people*): **to ~ with** avere a che fare con ♦ *n* mescolanza; preparato; **~ up** *vt* mescolare; (*confuse*) confondere; **~ed** *adj* misto(a); **~ed-up** *adj* (*confused*) confuso(a); **~er** *n* (*for food: electric*) frullatore *m*; (*: hand*) frullino; (*person*): **he is a good ~er** è molto socievole; **~ture** *n* mescolanza; (*blend: of tobacco etc*) miscela; (*MED*) sciroppo; **~-up** *n* confusione *f*
moan [məun] *n* gemito ♦ *vi* (*inf: complain*): **to ~ (about)** lamentarsi (di)
moat [məut] *n* fossato
mob [mɔb] *n* calca ♦ *vt* accalcarsi intorno a
mobile ['məubail] *adj* mobile ♦ *n* (*decoration*) mobile *m*; **~ home** *n* grande roulotte *f inv* (utilizzata come domicilio); **~ phone** telefono portatile, telefonino
mock [mɔk] *vt* deridere, burlarsi di ♦ *adj*

falso(a); **~ery** *n* derisione *f*; **to make a ~ery of** burlarsi di; (*exam*) rendere una farsa; **~-up** *n* modello

mod [mɔd] *adj see* **convenience**

mode [məud] *n* modo

model ['mɔdl] *n* modello; (*person: for fashion*) indossatore/trice; (: *for artist*) modello/a ♦ *adj* (*small-scale: railway etc*) in miniatura; (*child, factory*) modello *inv* ♦ *vt* modellare ♦ *vi* fare l'indossatore (*or* l'indossatrice); **to ~ clothes** presentare degli abiti

modem ['məudɛm] *n* modem *m inv*

moderate [*adj* 'mɔdərət, *vb* 'mɔdəreɪt] *adj* moderato(a) ♦ *vi* moderarsi, placarsi ♦ *vt* moderare

modern ['mɔdən] *adj* moderno(a); **~ize** *vt* modernizzare

modest ['mɔdɪst] *adj* modesto(a); **~y** *n* modestia

modicum ['mɔdɪkəm] *n*: **a ~ of** un minimo di

modify ['mɔdɪfaɪ] *vt* modificare

mogul ['məugl] *n* (*fig*) magnate *m*, pezzo grosso

mohair ['məuhɛə*] *n* mohair *m*

moist [mɔɪst] *adj* umido(a); **~en** ['mɔɪsn] *vt* inumidire; **~ure** ['mɔɪstʃə*] *n* umidità; (*on glass*) goccioline *fpl* di vapore; **~urizer** ['mɔɪstʃəraɪzə*] *n* idratante *f*

molar ['məulə*] *n* molare *m*

mold [məuld] (*US*) *n*, *vt* = **mould**

mole [məul] *n* (*animal, fig*) talpa; (*spot*) neo

molest [məu'lɛst] *vt* molestare

mollycoddle ['mɔlɪkɔdl] *vt* coccolare, vezzeggiare

molt [məult] (*US*) *vi* = **moult**

molten ['məultən] *adj* fuso(a)

mom [mɔm] (*US*) *n* = **mum**

moment ['məumənt] *n* momento, istante *m*; **at that ~** in quel momento; **at the ~** al momento, in questo momento; **~ary** *adj* momentaneo(a), passeggero(a); **~ous** [-'mɛntəs] *adj* di grande importanza

momentum [məu'mɛntəm] *n* (*PHYSICS*) momento; (*fig*) impeto; **to gather ~** aumentare di velocità

mommy ['mɔmɪ] (*US*) *n* = **mummy**

Monaco ['mɔnəkəu] *n* Principato di Monaco

monarch ['mɔnək] *n* monarca *m*; **~y** *n* monarchia

monastery ['mɔnəstərɪ] *n* monastero

Monday ['mʌndɪ] *n* lunedì *m inv*

monetary ['mʌnɪtərɪ] *adj* monetario(a)

money ['mʌnɪ] *n* denaro, soldi *mpl*; **~ order** *n* vaglia *m inv*; **~-spinner** (*inf*) *n* miniera d'oro (*fig*)

mongol ['mɔŋgəl] *adj, n* (*MED*) mongoloide *m/f*

mongrel ['mʌŋgrəl] *n* (*dog*) cane *m* bastardo

monitor ['mɔnɪtə*] *n* (*TV, COMPUT*) monitor *m inv* ♦ *vt* controllare

monk [mʌŋk] *n* monaco

monkey ['mʌŋkɪ] *n* scimmia; **~ nut** (*BRIT*) *n* nocciolina americana; **~ wrench** *n* chiave *f* a rullino

mono ['mɔnəu] *adj* (*recording*) (in) mono *inv*

monopoly [mə'nɔpəlɪ] *n* monopolio

monotone ['mɔnətəun] *n* pronunzia (*or* voce *f*) monotona

monotonous [mə'nɔtənəs] *adj* monotono(a)

monsoon [mɔn'suːn] *n* monsone *m*

monster ['mɔnstə*] *n* mostro

monstrous ['mɔnstrəs] *adj* mostruoso(a); (*huge*) gigantesco(a)

montage [mɔn'tɑːʒ] *n* montaggio

month [mʌnθ] *n* mese *m*; **~ly** *adj* mensile ♦ *adv* al mese; ogni mese

monument ['mɔnjumənt] *n* monumento

moo [muː] *vi* muggire, mugghiare

mood [muːd] *n* umore *m*; **to be in a good/bad ~** essere di buon/cattivo umore; **~y** *adj* (*variable*) capriccioso(a), lunatico(a); (*sullen*) imbronciato(a)

moon [muːn] *n* luna; **~light** *n* chiaro di luna; **~lighting** *n* lavoro nero; **~lit** *adj*: **a ~lit night** una notte rischiarata dalla luna

Moor [muə*] *n* moro/a

moor [muə*] *n* brughiera ♦ *vt* (*ship*) ormeggiare ♦ *vi* ormeggiarsi

moorland ['muələnd] *n* brughiera

moose [muːs] *n inv* alce *m*

mop [mɔp] *n* lavapavimenti *m inv*; (*also:* ~ *of hair*) zazzera ♦ *vt* lavare con lo straccio; (*face*) asciugare; ~ **up** *vt* asciugare con uno straccio

mope [məup] *vi* fare il broncio

moped ['məuped] *n* (*BRIT*) ciclomotore *m*

moral ['mɔrl] *adj* morale ♦ *n* morale *f*; ~**s** *npl* (*principles*) moralità

morale [mɔ'rɑːl] *n* morale *m*

morality [mə'rælɪtɪ] *n* moralità

morass [mə'ræs] *n* palude *f*, pantano

morbid ['mɔːbɪd] *adj* morboso(a)

KEYWORD

more [mɔː*] *adj* **1** (*greater in number etc*) più; ~ **people/letters than we expected** più persone/lettere di quante ne aspettavamo; **I have** ~ **wine/money than you** ho più vino/soldi di te; **I have** ~ **wine than beer** ho più vino che birra **2** (*additional*) altro(a), ancora; **do you want (some)** ~ **tea?** vuole dell'altro tè?, vuole ancora del tè?; **I have no** *or* **I don't have any** ~ **money** non ho più soldi
♦ *pron* **1** (*greater amount*) più; ~ **than 10** più di 10; **it cost** ~ **than we expected** ha costato più di quanto ci aspettavamo **2** (*further or additional amount*) ancora; **is there any** ~? ce n'è ancora?; **there's no** ~ non ce n'è più; **a little** ~ ancora un po'; **many/much** ~ molti(e)/molto(a) di più
♦ *adv*: ~ **dangerous/easily (than)** più pericoloso/facilmente (di); ~ **and** ~ sempre di più; ~ **and** ~ **difficult** sempre più difficile; ~ **or less** più o meno; ~ **than ever** più che mai

moreover [mɔː'rəuvə*] *adv* inoltre, di più

morgue [mɔːg] *n* obitorio

morning ['mɔːnɪŋ] *n* mattina, mattino; (*duration*) mattinata ♦ *cpd* del mattino; **in the** ~ la mattina; **7 o'clock in the** ~ le 7 di *or* della mattina; ~ **sickness** *n* nausee *fpl* mattutine

Morocco [mə'rɔkəu] *n* Marocco

moron ['mɔːrɔn] (*inf*) *n* deficiente *m/f*

morose [mə'rəus] *adj* cupo(a), tetro(a)

Morse [mɔːs] *n* (*also:* ~ *code*) alfabeto Morse

morsel ['mɔːsl] *n* boccone *m*

mortal ['mɔːtl] *adj* mortale ♦ *n* mortale *m*

mortar ['mɔːtə*] *n* mortaio; (*CONSTR*) malta

mortgage ['mɔːgɪdʒ] *n* ipoteca; (*loan*) prestito ipotecario ♦ *vt* ipotecare; ~ **company** (*US*) *n* società *f inv* di credito immobiliare

mortuary ['mɔːtjuərɪ] *n* camera mortuaria; obitorio

mosaic [məu'zeɪɪk] *n* mosaico

Moscow ['mɔskəu] *n* Mosca

Moslem ['mɔzləm] *adj, n* = **Muslim**

mosque [mɔsk] *n* moschea

mosquito [mɔs'kiːtəu] (*pl* ~**es**) *n* zanzara

moss [mɔs] *n* muschio

most [məust] *adj* (*almost all*) la maggior parte di; (*largest, greatest*): **who has (the)** ~ **money?** chi ha più soldi di tutti?
♦ *pron* la maggior parte ♦ *adv* più; (*work, sleep etc*) di più; (*very*) molto, estremamente; **the** ~ (*also:* + *adjective*) il(la) più; ~ **of** la maggior parte di; ~ **of them** quasi tutti; **I saw (the)** ~ ho visto più io; **at the (very)** ~ al massimo; **to make the** ~ **of** trarre il massimo vantaggio da; **a** ~ **interesting book** un libro estremamente interessante; ~**ly** *adv* per lo più

MOT (*BRIT*) *n abbr* (= *Ministry of Transport*): **the** ~ (**test**) *revisione annuale obbligatoria degli autoveicoli*

motel [məu'tɛl] *n* motel *m inv*

moth [mɔθ] *n* farfalla notturna; tarma; ~**ball** *n* pallina di naftalina

mother ['mʌðə*] *n* madre *f* ♦ *vt* (*care for*) fare da madre a; ~**hood** *n* maternità; ~-**in-law** *n* suocera; ~**ly** *adj* materno(a); ~-**of-pearl** *n* madreperla; ~-**to-be** *n* futura mamma; ~ **tongue** *n* madrelingua

motion ['məuʃən] *n* movimento, moto; (*gesture*) gesto; (*at meeting*) mozione *f* ♦ *vt, vi*: **to** ~ (**to**) **sb to do** fare cenno a qn di fare; ~**less** *adj* immobile; ~ **picture** *n* film *m inv*

motivated ['məutɪveɪtɪd] *adj* motivato(a)

motive ['məutɪv] *n* motivo
motley ['mɔtlɪ] *adj* eterogeneo(a), molto vario(a)
motor ['məutə*] *n* motore *m*; (*BRIT: inf: vehicle*) macchina ♦ *cpd* automobilistico(a); **~bike** *n* moto *f inv*; **~boat** *n* motoscafo; **~car** (*BRIT*) *n* automobile *f*; **~cycle** *n* motocicletta; **~cyclist** *n* motociclista *m/f*; **~ing** (*BRIT*) *n* turismo automobilistico; **~ist** *n* automobilista *m/f*; **~ racing** (*BRIT*) *n* corse *fpl* automobilistiche; **~way** (*BRIT*) *n* autostrada
mottled ['mɔtld] *adj* chiazzato(a), marezzato(a)
motto ['mɔtəu] (*pl* **~es**) *n* motto
mould [məuld] (*US* **mold**) *n* forma, stampo; (*mildew*) muffa ♦ *vt* formare; (*fig*) foggiare; **~y** *adj* ammuffito(a); (*smell*) di muffa
moult [məult] (*US* **molt**) *vi* far la muta
mound [maund] *n* rialzo, collinetta; (*heap*) mucchio
mount [maunt] *n* (*GEO*) monte *m* ♦ *vt* montare; (*horse*) montare a ♦ *vi* (*increase*) aumentare; **~ up** *vi* (*build up*) accumularsi
mountain ['mauntɪn] *n* montagna ♦ *cpd* di montagna; **~ bike** *n* mountain bike *f inv*; **~eer** [-'nɪə*] *n* alpinista *m/f*; **~eering** [-'nɪərɪŋ] *n* alpinismo; **~ous** *adj* montagnoso(a); **~ rescue team** *n* squadra di soccorso alpino; **~side** *n* fianco della montagna
mourn [mɔːn] *vt* piangere, lamentare ♦ *vi*: **to ~ (for sb)** piangere (la morte di qn); **~er** *n* parente *m/f or* amico/a del defunto; **~ful** *adj* triste, lugubre; **~ing** *n* lutto; **in ~ing** in lutto
mouse [maus] (*pl* **mice**) *n* topo; (*COMPUT*) mouse *m inv*; **~trap** *n* trappola per i topi
mousse [muːs] *n* mousse *f inv*
moustache [məs'tɑːʃ] (*US* **mustache**) *n* baffi *mpl*
mousy ['mausɪ] *adj* (*hair*) né chiaro(a) né scuro(a)
mouth [mauθ, *pl* mauðz] *n* bocca; (*of river*) bocca, foce *f*; (*opening*) orifizio; **~ful**

n boccata; **~ organ** *n* armonica; **~piece** *n* (*of musical instrument*) imboccatura, bocchino; (*spokesman*) portavoce *m/f inv*; **~wash** *n* collutorio; **~-watering** *adj* che fa venire l'acquolina in bocca
movable ['muːvəbl] *adj* mobile
move [muːv] *n* (*movement*) movimento; (*in game*) mossa; (: *turn to play*) turno; (*change: of house*) trasloco; (: *of job*) cambiamento ♦ *vt* muovere, spostare; (*emotionally*) commuovere; (*POL: resolution etc*) proporre ♦ *vi* (*gen*) muoversi, spostarsi; (*also*: **~ house**) cambiar casa, traslocare; **to get a ~ on** affrettarsi, sbrigarsi; **to ~ sb to do sth** indurre or spingere qn a fare qc; **to ~ towards** andare verso; **~ about** *or* **around** *vi* spostarsi; **~ along** *vi* muoversi avanti; **~ away** *vi* allontanarsi, andarsene; **~ back** *vi* (*return*) ritornare; **~ forward** *vi* avanzare; **~ in** *vi* (*to a house*) entrare (in una nuova casa); (*police etc*) intervenire; **~ on** *vi* riprendere la strada; **~ out** *vi* (*of house*) sgombrare; **~ over** *vi* spostarsi; **~ up** *vi* avanzare
moveable ['muːvəbl] *adj* = **movable**
movement ['muːvmənt] *n* (*gen*) movimento; (*gesture*) gesto; (*of stars, water, physical*) moto
movie ['muːvɪ] *n* film *m inv*; **the ~s** il cinema
moviecamera *n* cinepresa
moving ['muːvɪŋ] *adj* mobile; (*causing emotion*) commovente
mow [məu] (*pt* **mowed**, *pp* **mowed** *or* **mown**) *vt* (*grass*) tagliare; (*corn*) mietere; **~ down** *vt* falciare; **~er** *n* (*also*: *lawnmower*) tagliaerba *m inv*; **mown** *pp* of **mow**
MP *n abbr* = **Member of Parliament**
m.p.h. *n abbr* = *miles per hour* (*60 m.p.h.* = *96 km/h*)
Mr ['mɪstə*] (*US* **Mr.**) *n*: **~ X** Signor X, Sig. X
Mrs ['mɪsɪz] (*US* **Mrs.**) *n*: **~ X** Signora X, Sig.ra X
Ms [mɪz] (*US* **Ms.**) *n* (= *Miss or Mrs*): **~ X** ≈ Signora X, Sig.ra X
M.Sc. *abbr* = **Master of Science**

---

much [mʌtʃ] *adj, pron* molto(a); **he's done so ~ work** ha lavorato così tanto; I have as **~ money as you** ho tanti soldi quanti ne hai tu; **how ~ is it?** quant'è?; it costs too **~** costa troppo; **as ~ as you want** quanto vuoi

♦ *adv* **1** (*greatly*) molto, tanto; **thank you very ~** molte grazie; **he's very ~ the gentleman** è il vero gentiluomo; **I read as ~ as I can** leggo quanto posso; **as ~ as you** tanto quanto te

2 (*by far*) molto; **it's ~ the biggest company in Europe** è di gran lunga la più grossa società in Europa

3 (*almost*) grossomodo, praticamente; **they're ~ the same** sono praticamente uguali

---

muck [mʌk] *n* (*dirt*) sporcizia; **~ about** *or* **around** (*inf*) *vi* fare lo stupido; (*waste time*) gingillarsi; **~ up** (*inf*) *vt* (*ruin*) rovinare

mud [mʌd] *n* fango

muddle ['mʌdl] *n* confusione *f*, disordine *m*; pasticcio ♦ *vt* (*also*: ~ **up**) confondere; **~ through** *vi* cavarsela alla meno peggio

muddy ['mʌdi] *adj* fangoso(a)

mudguard ['mʌdgɑːd] *n* parafango

muesli ['mjuːzli] *n* muesli *m*

muffin ['mʌfin] *n* specie di pasticcino soffice da tè

muffle ['mʌfl] *vt* (*sound*) smorzare, attutire; (*against cold*) imbacuccare

muffler ['mʌflə*] (*US*) *n* (*AUT*) marmitta; (: *on motorbike*) silenziatore *m*

mug [mʌg] *n* (*cup*) tazzone *m*; (*for beer*) boccale *m*; (*inf: face*) muso; (: *fool*) scemo/a ♦ *vt* (*assault*) assalire; **~ging** *n* assalto

muggy ['mʌgi] *adj* afoso(a)

mule [mjuːl] *n* mulo

mull over [mʌl-] *vt* rimuginare

multi-level ['mʌlti-] (*US*) *adj* = **multistorey**

multiple ['mʌltipl] *adj* multiplo(a); molteplice ♦ *n* multiplo; **~ sclerosis** *n* sclerosi *f* a placche

multiplication [mʌltiplɪ'keiʃən] *n* moltiplicazione *f*

multiply ['mʌltiplai] *vt* moltiplicare ♦ *vi* moltiplicarsi

multistorey ['mʌltɪ'stɔːri] (*BRIT*) *adj* (*building, car park*) a più piani

mum [mʌm] (*BRIT: inf*) *n* mamma ♦ *adj*: **to keep ~** non aprire bocca

mumble ['mʌmbl] *vt, vi* borbottare

mummy ['mʌmi] *n* (*BRIT: mother*) mamma; (*embalmed*) mummia

mumps [mʌmps] *n* orecchioni *mpl*

munch [mʌntʃ] *vt, vi* sgranocchiare

mundane [mʌn'dein] *adj* terra a terra *inv*

municipal [mjuː'nisipl] *adj* municipale

mural ['mjuərl] *n* dipinto murale

murder ['məːdə*] *n* assassinio, omicidio ♦ *vt* assassinare; **~er** *n* omicida *m*, assassino; **~ous** *adj* omicida

murky ['məːki] *adj* tenebroso(a)

murmur ['məːmə*] *n* mormorio ♦ *vt, vi* mormorare

muscle ['mʌsl] *n* muscolo; (*fig*) forza; **~ in** *vi* immischiarsi

muscular ['mʌskjulə*] *adj* muscolare; (*person, arm*) muscoloso(a)

muse [mjuːz] *vi* meditare, sognare ♦ *n* musa

museum [mjuː'ziəm] *n* museo

mushroom ['mʌʃrum] *n* fungo ♦ *vi* crescere in fretta

music ['mjuːzik] *n* musica; **~al** *adj* musicale; (*person*) portato(a) per la musica ♦ *n* (*show*) commedia musicale; **~al instrument** *n* strumento musicale; **~ hall** *n* teatro di varietà; **~ian** [-'ziʃən] *n* musicista *m/f*

musk [mʌsk] *n* muschio

Muslim ['mʌzlim] *adj, n* musulmano(a)

muslin ['mʌzlin] *n* mussola

mussel ['mʌsl] *n* cozza

must [mʌst] *aux vb* (*obligation*): **I ~ do it** devo farlo; (*probability*): **he ~ be there by now** dovrebbe essere arrivato ormai; **I ~ have made a mistake** devo essermi sbagliato ♦ *n*: **it's a ~** è d'obbligo

mustache ['mʌstæʃ] (*US*) *n* = **moustache**

mustard ['mʌstəd] *n* senape *f*, mostarda

muster ['mʌstə*] *vt* radunare

mustn't ['mʌsnt] = **must not**

musty ['mʌstɪ] *adj* che sa di muffa *or* di rinchiuso

mute [mju:t] *adj, n* muto(a)

muted ['mju:tɪd] *adj* smorzáto(a)

mutiny ['mju:tɪnɪ] *n* ammutinamento

mutter ['mʌtə*] *vt, vi* borbottare, brontolare

mutton ['mʌtn] *n* carne *f* di montone

mutual ['mju:tʃuəl] *adj* mutuo(a), reciproco(a); **~ly** *adv* reciprocamente

muzzle ['mʌzl] *n* muso; (*protective device*) museruola; (*of gun*) bocca ♦ *vt* mettere la museruola a

my [maɪ] *adj* il(la) mio(a), *pl* i(le) miei(mie); ~ **house** la mia casa; ~ **books** i miei libri; ~ **brother** mio fratello; **I've washed ~ hair/cut ~ finger** mi sono lavato i capelli/tagliato il dito

myself [maɪ'self] *pron* (*reflexive*) mi; (*emphatic*) io stesso(a); (*after prep*) me; *see also* **oneself**

mysterious [mɪs'tɪərɪəs] *adj* misterioso(a)

mystery ['mɪstərɪ] *n* mistero

mystify ['mɪstɪfaɪ] *vt* mistificare; (*puzzle*) confondere

mystique [mɪs'ti:k] *n* fascino

myth [mɪθ] *n* mito; **~ology** [mɪ'θɔlədʒɪ] *n* mitologia

N

n/a *abbr* = **not applicable**

nag [næg] *vt* tormentare ♦ *vi* brontolare in continuazione; **~ging** *adj* (*doubt, pain*) persistente

nail [neɪl] *n* (*human*) unghia; (*metal*) chiodo ♦ *vt* inchiodare; **to ~ sb down to (doing) sth** costringere qn a (fare) qc; **~brush** *n* spazzolino da *or* per unghie; **~file** *n* lima da *or* per unghie; **~ polish** *n* smalto da *or* per unghie; **~ polish remover** *n* acetone *m*, solvente *m*; **~ scissors** *npl* forbici *fpl* da *or* per unghie; **~ varnish** (*BRIT*) *n* = **~ polish**

naïve [naɪ'i:v] *adj* ingenuo(a)

naked ['neɪkɪd] *adj* nudo(a)

name [neɪm] *n* nome *m*; (*reputation*) nome, reputazione *f* ♦ *vt* (*baby etc*) chiamare; (*plant, illness*) nominare; (*person, object*) identificare; (*price, date*) fissare; **what's your ~?** come si chiama?; **by ~** di nome; **she knows them all by ~** li conosce tutti per nome; **~less** *adj* senza nome; **~ly** *adv* cioè; **~sake** *n* omonimo

nanny ['nænɪ] *n* bambinaia

nap [næp] *n* (*sleep*) pisolino; (*of cloth*) peluria; **to be caught ~ping** essere preso alla sprovvista

nape [neɪp] *n*: ~ **of the neck** nuca

napkin ['næpkɪn] *n* (*also:* table ~) tovagliolo

nappy ['næpɪ] (*BRIT*) *n* pannolino; ~ **rash** *n* arrossamento (causato dal pannolino)

narcissi [nɑ:'sɪsaɪ] *npl of* **narcissus**

narcissus [nɑ:'sɪsəs] (*pl* **narcissi**) *n* narciso

narcotic [nɑ:'kɔtɪk] *n* narcotico ♦ *adj* narcotico(a)

narrative ['nærətɪv] *n* narrativa

narrow ['nærəu] *adj* stretto(a); (*fig*) limitato(a), ristretto(a) ♦ *vi* stringersi; **to have a ~ escape** farcela per un pelo; **to ~ sth down to** ridurre qc a; **~ly** *adv* per un pelo; (*time*) per poco; **~-minded** *adj* meschino(a)

nasty ['nɑ:stɪ] *adj* (*person, remark*: *unpleasant*) cattivo(a); (: *rude*) villano(a); (*smell, wound, situation*) brutto(a)

nation ['neɪʃən] *n* nazione *f*

national ['næʃənl] *adj* nazionale ♦ *n* cittadino/a; ~ **dress** *n* costume *m* nazionale; **N~ Health Service** (*BRIT*) *n* servizio nazionale di assistenza sanitaria, ≈ S.A.U.B. *f*; **N~ Insurance** (*BRIT*) *n* ≈ Previdenza Sociale; **~ism** *n* nazionalismo; **~ity** [-'nælɪtɪ] *n* nazionalità *f inv*; **~ize** *vt* nazionalizzare; **~ly** *adv* a livello nazionale

nationwide ['neɪʃənwaɪd] *adj* diffuso(a) in tutto il paese ♦ *adv* in tutto il paese

native ['neɪtɪv] *n* abitante *m/f* del paese; (*of tribe etc*) indigeno/a ♦ *adj* indigeno(a); (*country*) natio(a); (*ability*) innato(a); **a ~ of Russia** un nativo della Russia; **a ~**

speaker of French una persona di madrelingua francese; **N~ American** *n discendente di tribù dell'America settentrionale*; **~ language** *n* madrelingua

Nativity [nə'tɪvɪtɪ] *n*: **the ~** la Natività

NATO ['neɪtəu] *n abbr* (= *North Atlantic Treaty Organization*) N.A.T.O. *f*

natural ['nætʃrəl] *adj* naturale; (*ability*) innato(a); (*manner*) semplice; **~ gas** *n* gas *m* metano; **~ize** *vt* naturalizzare; **to become ~ized** (*person*) naturalizzarsi; (*plant*) acclimatarsi; **~ly** *adv* naturalmente; (*by nature: gifted*) di natura

nature ['neɪtʃə*] *n* natura; (*character*) natura, indole *f*; **by ~** di natura

naught [nɔ:t] *n* = **nought**

naughty ['nɔ:tɪ] *adj* (*child*) birichino(a), cattivello(a); (*story, film*) spinto(a)

nausea ['nɔ:sɪə] *n* (*MED*) nausea; (*fig: disgust*) schifo; **~te** ['nɔ:sɪeɪt] *vt* nauseare; far schifo a

nautical ['nɔ:tɪkl] *adj* nautico(a)

naval ['neɪvl] *adj* navale; **~ officer** *n* ufficiale *m* di marina

nave [neɪv] *n* navata centrale

navel ['neɪvl] *n* ombelico

navigate ['nævɪgeɪt] *vt* percorrere navigando ♦ *vi* navigare; (*AUT*) fare da navigatore; **navigation** [-'geɪʃən] *n* navigazione *f*; **navigator** *n* (*NAUT, AVIAT*) ufficiale *m* di rotta; (*explorer*) navigatore *m*; (*AUT*) copilota *m/f*

navvy ['nævɪ] (*BRIT*) *n* manovale *m*

navy ['neɪvɪ] *n* marina; **~(-blue)** *adj* blu scuro *inv*

Nazi ['nɑ:tsɪ] *n* nazista *m/f*

NB *abbr* (= *nota bene*) N.B.

near [nɪə*] *adj* vicino(a); (*relation*) prossimo(a) ♦ *adv* vicino ♦ *prep* (*also: ~ to*) vicino a, presso; (: *time*) verso ♦ *vt* avvicinarsi a; **~by** [nɪə'baɪ] *adj* vicino(a) ♦ *adv* vicino; **~ly** *adv* quasi; **I ~ly fell** per poco non sono caduto; **~ miss** *n*: **that was a ~ miss** c'è mancato poco; **~side** *n* (*AUT: in Britain*) lato sinistro; (: *in US, Europe etc*) lato destro; **~-sighted** *adj* miope

neat [ni:t] *adj* (*person, room*) ordinato(a);

(*work*) pulito(a); (*solution, plan*) ben indovinato(a), azzeccato(a); (*spirits*) liscio(a); **~ly** *adv* con ordine; (*skilfully*) abilmente

necessarily ['nɛsɪsrɪlɪ] *adv* necessariamente

necessary ['nɛsɪsrɪ] *adj* necessario(a)

necessity [nɪ'sɛsɪtɪ] *n* necessità *f inv*

neck [nɛk] *n* collo; (*of garment*) colletto ♦ *vi* (*inf*) pomiciare, sbaciucchiarsi; **~ and ~** testa a testa

necklace ['nɛklɪs] *n* collana

neckline ['nɛklaɪn] *n* scollatura

necktie ['nɛktaɪ] *n* cravatta

née [neɪ] *adj*: **~ Scott** nata Scott

need [ni:d] *n* bisogno ♦ *vt* aver bisogno di; **to ~ to do** dover fare; aver bisogno di fare; **you don't ~ to go** non devi andare, non c'è bisogno che tu vada

needle ['ni:dl] *n* ago; (*on record player*) puntina ♦ *vt* punzecchiare

needless ['ni:dlɪs] *adj* inutile

needlework ['ni:dlwə:k] *n* cucito

needn't ['ni:dnt] = **need not**

needy ['ni:dɪ] *adj* bisognoso(a)

negative ['nɛgətɪv] *n* (*LING*) negazione *f*; (*PHOT*) negativo ♦ *adj* negativo(a)

neglect [nɪ'glɛkt] *vt* trascurare ♦ *n* (*of person, duty*) negligenza; (*of child, house etc*) scarsa cura, **state of ~** stato di abbandono

negligee ['nɛglɪʒeɪ] *n* négligé *m inv*

negligence ['nɛglɪdʒəns] *n* negligenza

negligible ['nɛglɪdʒɪbl] *adj* insignificante, trascurabile

negotiable [nɪ'gəuʃɪəbl] *adj* (*cheque*) trasferibile

negotiate [nɪ'gəuʃɪeɪt] *vi*: **to ~ (with)** negoziare (con) ♦ *vt* (*COMM*) negoziare; (*obstacle*) superare; **negotiation** [-'eɪʃən] *n* negoziato, trattativa

Negress ['ni:grɪs] *n* negra

Negro ['ni:grəu] (*pl* **~es**) *adj, n* negro(a)

neigh [neɪ] *vi* nitrire

neighbour ['neɪbə*] (*US* **neighbor**) *n* vicino/a; **~hood** *n* vicinato; **~ing** *adj* vicino(a); **~ly** *adj*: **he is a ~ly person** è un buon vicino

neither ['naɪðə*] *adj, pron* né l'uno(a) né

l'altro(a), nessuno(a) dei(delle) due ♦ *conj* neanche, nemmeno, neppure ♦ *adv*: ~ **good nor bad** né buono né cattivo; **I didn't move and ~ did Claude** io non mi mossi e nemmeno Claude; ..., ~ **did I refuse** ..., ma non ho nemmeno rifiutato

neon ['ni:ɔn] *n* neon *m*; ~ **light** *n* luce *f* al neon

nephew ['nɛvju:] *n* nipote *m*

nerve [nə:v] *n* nervo; *(fig)* coraggio; *(impudence)* faccia tosta; **a fit of ~s** una crisi di nervi; ~-**racking** *adj* che spezza i nervi

nervous ['nə:vəs] *adj* nervoso(a); *(anxious)* agitato(a), in apprensione; ~ **breakdown** *n* esaurimento nervoso

nest [nɛst] *n* nido ♦ *vi* fare il nido, nidificare; ~ **egg** *n* (*fig*) gruzzolo

nestle ['nɛsl] *vi* accoccolarsi

net [nɛt] *n* rete *f* ♦ *adj* netto(a) ♦ *vt* (*fish etc*) prendere con la rete; (*profit*) ricavare un utile netto di; ~**ball** *n* specie di *pallacanestro*; ~ **curtains** *npl* tende *fpl* di tulle

Netherlands ['nɛðələndz] *npl*: **the ~** i Paesi Bassi

nett [nɛt] *adj* = **net**

netting ['nɛtɪŋ] *n* (*for fence etc*) reticolato

nettle ['nɛtl] *n* ortica

network ['nɛtwə:k] *n* rete *f*

neurotic [njuə'rɔtɪk] *adj*, *n* nevrotico(a)

neuter ['nju:tə*] *adj* neutro(a) ♦ *vt* (*cat etc*) castrare

neutral ['nju:trəl] *adj* neutro(a); (*person, nation*) neutrale ♦ *n* (*AUT*): **in ~** in folle; ~**ize** *vt* neutralizzare

never ['nɛvə*] *adv* (non...) mai; ~ **again** mai più; **I'll ~ go there again** non ci vado più; ~ **in my life** mai in vita mia; *see also* **mind**; ~-**ending** *adj* interminabile; ~**theless** [nɛvəðə'lɛs] *adv* tuttavia, ciò nonostante, ciò nondimeno

new [nju:] *adj* nuovo(a); (*brand new*) nuovo(a) di zecca; **N~ Age** *n* New Age *f inv*; ~**born** *adj* neonato(a); ~**comer** ['nju:kʌmə*] *n* nuovo(a) venuto(a); ~-**fangled** ['nju:fæŋgld] (*pej*) *adj* stramoderno(a); ~-**found** *adj* nuovo(a); ~**ly** *adv* di recente; ~**ly-weds** *npl* sposini

mpl, sposi *mpl* novelli

news [nju:z] *n* notizie *fpl*; (*RADIO*) giornale *m* radio; (*TV*) telegiornale *m*; **a piece of ~** una notizia; ~ **agency** *n* agenzia di stampa; ~**agent** (*BRIT*) *n* giornalaio; ~**caster** *n* (*RADIO, TV*) annunciatore/trice; ~**dealer** (*US*) *n* = ~**agent**; ~ **flash** *n* notizia *f* lampo *inv*; ~**letter** *n* bollettino; ~**paper** *n* giornale *m*; ~**print** *n* carta da giornale; ~**reader** *n* = ~**caster**; ~**reel** *n* cinegiornale *m*; ~ **stand** *n* edicola

newt [nju:t] *n* tritone *m*

New Year *n* Anno Nuovo; ~'**s Day** *n* il Capodanno; ~'**s Eve** *n* la vigilia di Capodanno

New York [-'jɔ:k] *n* New York *f*

New Zealand [-'zi:lənd] *n* Nuova Zelanda; ~**er** *n* neozelandese *m/f*

next [nɛkst] *adj* prossimo(a) ♦ *adv* accanto; (*in time*) dopo; **the ~ day** il giorno dopo, l'indomani; ~ **time** la prossima volta; ~ **year** l'anno prossimo; **when do we meet ~?** quando ci rincontriamo?; ~ **to** accanto a; ~ **to nothing** quasi niente; ~ **please!** (avanti) il prossimo!; ~ **door** *adv, adj* accanto *inv*; ~-**of-kin** *n* parente *m/f* prossimo(a)

NHS *n abbr* = **National Health Service**

nib [nɪb] *n* (*of pen*) pennino

nibble ['nɪbl] *vt* mordicchiare

Nicaragua [nɪkə'ræɡjuə] *n* Nicaragua *m*

nice [naɪs] *adj* (*holiday, trip*) piacevole; (*flat, picture*) bello(a); (*person*) simpatico(a), gentile; ~**ly** *adv* bene

niceties ['naɪsɪtɪz] *npl* finezze *fpl*

nick [nɪk] *n* taglietto; tacca ♦ *vt* (*inf*) rubare; **in the ~ of time** appena in tempo

nickel ['nɪkl] *n* nichel *m*; (*US*) moneta da cinque centesimi di dollaro

nickname ['nɪkneɪm] *n* soprannome *m* ♦ *vt* soprannominare

niece [ni:s] *n* nipote *f*

Nigeria [naɪ'dʒɪərɪə] *n* Nigeria

niggling ['nɪɡlɪŋ] *adj* insignificante; (*annoying*) irritante

night [naɪt] *n* notte *f*; (*evening*) sera; **at ~** la sera; **by ~** di notte; **the ~ before last** l'altro ieri notte (*or* sera); ~**cap** *n*

bicchierino prima di andare a letto; ~
club *n* locale *m* notturno; **~dress** *n*
camicia da notte; **~fall** *n* crepuscolo;
~gown *n* = **~dress**; **~ie** ['naɪtɪ] *n* =
~dress

nightingale ['naɪtɪŋgeɪl] *n* usignolo

nightlife ['naɪtlaɪf] *n* vita notturna

nightly ['naɪtlɪ] *adj* di ogni notte *or* sera;
(*by night*) notturno(a) ♦ *adv* ogni notte *or*
sera

nightmare ['naɪtmeə*] *n* incubo

night: ~ **porter** *n* portiere *m* di notte; ~
school *n* scuola serale; ~ **shift** *n* turno
di notte; **~-time** *n* notte *f*

nil [nɪl] *n* nulla *m*; (*BRIT: SPORT*) zero

Nile [naɪl] *n*: the ~ il Nilo

nimble ['nɪmbl] *adj* agile

nine [naɪn] *num* nove; **~teen** *num*
diciannove; **~ty** *num* novanta

ninth [naɪnθ] *adj* nono(a)

nip [nɪp] *vt* pizzicare; (*bite*) mordere

nipple ['nɪpl] *n* (*ANAT*) capezzolo

nitrogen ['naɪtrədʒən] *n* azoto

KEYWORD
---

no [nəu] (*pl* ~**es**) *adv* (*opposite of "yes"*)
no; **are you coming?** — ~ (**I'm not**)
viene? — no (non vengo); **would you like
some more?** — ~ **thank you** ne vuole
ancora un po'? — no, grazie
♦ *adj* (*not any*) nessuno(a); **I have** ~
money/time/books non ho soldi/tempo/
libri; ~ **student would have done it**
nessuno studente lo avrebbe fatto; "**~
parking**" "divieto di sosta"; "**~
smoking**" "vietato fumare"
♦ *n* no *m inv*

nobility [nəu'bɪlɪtɪ] *n* nobiltà

noble ['nəubl] *adj* nobile

nobody ['nəubədɪ] *pron* nessuno

nod [nɔd] *vi* accennare col capo, fare un
cenno; (*in agreement*) annuire con un
cenno del capo; (*sleep*) sonnecchiare ♦ *vt*:
to ~ one's head fare di sì col capo ♦ *n*
cenno; ~ **off** *vi* assopirsi

noise [nɔɪz] *n* rumore *m*; (*din, racket*)
chiasso; **noisy** *adj* (*street, car*)
rumoroso(a); (*person*) chiassoso(a)

nominal ['nɔmɪnl] *adj* nominale; (*rent*)
simbolico(a)

nominate ['nɔmɪneɪt] *vt* (*propose*)
proporre come candidato; (*elect*) nominare

nominee [nɔmɪ'niː] *n* persona nominata;
candidato/a

non... [nɔn] *prefix* non...; **~-alcoholic** *adj*
analcolico(a); **~-aligned** *adj* non
allineato(a)

nonchalant ['nɔnʃələnt] *adj*
disinvolto(a), noncurante

non-committal ['nɔnkə'mɪtl] *adj*
evasivo(a)

nondescript ['nɔndɪskrɪpt] *adj*
qualunque *inv*

none [nʌn] *pron* (*not one thing*) niente;
(*not one person*) nessuno(a); ~ **of you**
nessuno(a) di voi; **I've ~ left** non ne ho
più; **he's ~ the worse for it** non ne ha
risentito

nonentity [nɔ'nentɪtɪ] *n* persona
insignificante

nonetheless [nʌnðə'les] *adv* nondimeno

non-existent [-ɪg'zɪstənt] *adj* inesistente

non-fiction *n* saggistica

nonplussed [nɔn'plʌst] *adj*
sconcertato(a)

nonsense ['nɔnsəns] *n* sciocchezze *fpl*

non: **~-smoker** *n* non fumatore/trice; **~-
stick** *adj* antiaderente, antiadesivo(a); **~-
stop** *adj* continuo(a); (*train, bus*)
direttissimo(a) ♦ *adv* senza sosta

noodles ['nuːdlz] *npl* taglierini *mpl*

nook [nuk] *n*: **~s and crannies** angoli
mpl

noon [nuːn] *n* mezzogiorno

no one ['nəuwʌn] *pron* = **nobody**

noose [nuːs] *n* nodo scorsoio;
(*hangman's*) cappio

nor [nɔː*] *conj* = **neither** ♦ *adv see*
neither

norm [nɔːm] *n* norma

normal ['nɔːml] *adj* normale; **~ly** *adv*
normalmente

north [nɔːθ] *n* nord *m*, settentrione *m* ♦
adj nord *inv*, del nord, settentrionale
♦ *adv* verso nord; **N~ America** *n*
America del Nord; **~-east** *n* nord-est *m*;
~erly ['nɔːðəlɪ] *adj* (*point, direction*) verso

nord; **~ern** ['nɔːðən] *adj* del nord, settentrionale; **N~ern Ireland** *n* Irlanda del Nord; **N~ Pole** *n* Polo Nord; **N~ Sea** *n* Mare *m* del Nord; **~ward(s)** ['nɔːθwəd(z)] *adv* verso nord; **~-west** *n* nord-ovest *m*

Norway ['nɔːweɪ] *n* Norvegia
Norwegian [nɔː'wiːdʒən] *adj* norvegese ♦ *n* norvegese *m/f*; (*LING*) norvegese *m*
nose [nəuz] *n* naso; (*of animal*) muso ♦ *vi*: **to ~ about** aggirarsi; **~bleed** *n* emorragia nasale; **~-dive** *n* picchiata; **~y** (*inf*) *adj* = **nosy**
nostalgia [nɔs'tældʒɪə] *n* nostalgia
nostril ['nɔstrɪl] *n* narice *f*; (*of horse*) frogia
nosy ['nəuzɪ] (*inf*) *adj* curioso(a)
not [nɔt] *adv* non; **he is ~** *or* **isn't here** non è qui, non c'è; **you must ~** *or* **you mustn't do that** non devi fare quello; **it's too late, isn't it** *or* **is it ~?** è troppo tardi, vero?; **~ that I don't like him** non che (lui) non mi piaccia; **~ yet/now** non ancora/ora; *see also* **all; only**
notably ['nəutəblɪ] *adv* (*markedly*) notevolmente; (*particularly*) in particolare
notary ['nəutərɪ] *n* notaio
notch [nɔtʃ] *n* tacca; (*in saw*) dente *m*
note [nəut] *n* nota; (*letter, banknote*) biglietto ♦ *vt* (*also*: **~ down**) prendere nota di; **to take ~s** prendere appunti; **~book** *n* taccuino; **~d** ['nəutɪd] *adj* celebre; **~pad** *n* bloc-notes *m inv*; **~paper** *n* carta da lettere
nothing ['nʌθɪŋ] *n* nulla *m*, niente *m*; (*zero*) zero; **he does ~** non fa niente; **~ new/much** *etc* niente di nuovo/speciale *etc*; **for ~** per niente
notice ['nəutɪs] *n* avviso; (*of leaving*) preavviso ♦ *vt* notare, accorgersi di; **to take ~ of** fare attenzione a; **to bring sth to sb's ~** far notare qc a qn; **at short ~** con un breve preavviso; **until further ~** fino a nuovo avviso; **to hand in one's ~** licenziarsi; **~able** *adj* evidente; **~ board** (*BRIT*) *n* tabellone *m* per affissi
notify ['nəutɪfaɪ] *vt*: **to ~ sth to sb** far sapere qc a qn; **to ~ sb of sth** avvisare qn di qc

notion ['nəuʃən] *n* idea; (*concept*) nozione *f*
notorious [nəu'tɔːrɪəs] *adj* famigerato(a)
notwithstanding [nɔtwɪθ'stændɪŋ] *adv* nondimeno ♦ *prep* nonostante, malgrado
nougat ['nuːgɑː] *n* torrone *m*
nought [nɔːt] *n* zero
noun [naun] *n* nome *m*, sostantivo
nourish ['nʌrɪʃ] *vt* nutrire
novel ['nɔvl] *n* romanzo ♦ *adj* nuovo(a); **~ist** *n* romanziere/a; **~ty** *n* novità *f inv*
November [nəu'vembə*] *n* novembre *m*
novice ['nɔvɪs] *n* principiante *m/f*; (*REL*) novizio/a
now [nau] *adv* ora, adesso ♦ *conj*: **~ (that)** adesso che, ora che; **by ~** ormai; **just ~** proprio ora; **right ~** subito, immediatamente; **~ and then, ~ and again** ogni tanto; **from ~ on** da ora in poi; **~adays** ['nauədeɪz] *adv* oggidì
nowhere ['nəuwɛə*] *adv* in nessun luogo, da nessuna parte
nozzle ['nɔzl] *n* (*of hose etc*) boccaglio; (*of fire extinguisher*) lancia
nuance ['njuːɑ̃ːns] *n* sfumatura
nuclear ['njuːklɪə*] *adj* nucleare
nuclei ['njuːklɪaɪ] *npl of* **nucleus**
nucleus ['njuːklɪəs] (*pl* **nuclei**) *n* nucleo
nude [njuːd] *adj* nudo(a) ♦ *n* (*ART*) nudo; **in the ~** tutto(a) nudo(a)
nudge [nʌdʒ] *vt* dare una gomitata a
nudist ['njuːdɪst] *n* nudista *m/f*
nuisance ['njuːsns] *n*: **it's a ~** è una seccatura; **he's a ~** è uno scocciatore
null [nʌl] *adj*: **~ and void** nullo(a)
numb [nʌm] *adj*: **~ (with)** intorpidito(a) (da); (*with fear*) impietrito(a) (da); **~ with cold** intirizzito(a) (dal freddo)
number ['nʌmbə*] *n* numero ♦ *vt* numerare; (*include*) contare; **a ~ of** un certo numero di; **to be ~ed among** venire annoverato(a) tra; **they were 10 in ~** erano in tutto 10; **~ plate** (*BRIT*) *n* (*AUT*) targa
numeral ['njuːmərəl] *n* numero, cifra
numerate ['njuːmərɪt] *adj*: **to be ~** avere nozioni di aritmetica
numerical [njuː'merɪkl] *adj* numerico(a)
numerous ['njuːmərəs] *adj* numeroso(a)

nun [nʌn] *n* suora, monaca

nurse [nəːs] *n* infermiere/a; (*also*: ~*maid*) bambinaia ♦ *vt* (*patient, cold*) curare; (*baby*: *BRIT*) cullare; (: *US*) allattare, dare il latte a

nursery ['nəːsərɪ] *n* (*room*) camera dei bambini; (*institution*) asilo; (*for plants*) vivaio; ~ **rhyme** *n* filastrocca; ~ **school** *n* scuola materna; ~ **slope** (*BRIT*) *n* (*SKI*) pista per principianti

nursing ['nəːsɪŋ] *n* (*profession*) professione *f* di infermiere (*or* di infermiera); (*care*) cura; ~ **home** *n* casa di cura

nurture ['nəːtʃə*] *vt* allevare; nutrire

nut [nʌt] *n* (*of metal*) dado; (*fruit*) noce *f*; ~**crackers** *npl* schiaccianoci *m inv*

nutmeg ['nʌtmɛg] *n* noce *f* moscata

nutritious [njuː'trɪʃəs] *adj* nutriente

nuts [nʌts] (*inf*) *adj* matto(a)

nutshell ['nʌtʃɛl] *n*: **in a** ~ in poche parole

nylon ['naɪlɔn] *n* nailon *m* ♦ *adj* di nailon

O

oak [əuk] *n* quercia ♦ *adj* di quercia

O.A.P. (*BRIT*) *n abbr* = **old age pensioner**

oar [ɔː*] *n* remo

oasis [əu'eɪsɪs] (*pl* **oases**) *n* oasi *f inv*

oath [əuθ] *n* giuramento; (*swear word*) bestemmia

oatmeal ['əutmiːl] *n* farina d'avena

oats [əuts] *npl* avena

obedience [ə'biːdɪəns] *n* ubbidienza

obedient [ə'biːdɪənt] *adj* ubbidiente

obey [ə'beɪ] *vt* ubbidire a; (*instructions, regulations*) osservare

obituary [ə'bɪtjuərɪ] *n* necrologia

object [*n* 'ɔbdʒɪkt, *vb* əb'dʒɛkt] *n* oggetto; (*purpose*) scopo, intento; (*LING*) complemento oggetto ♦ *vi*: **to ~ to** (*attitude*) disapprovare; (*proposal*) protestare contro, sollevare delle obiezioni contro; **expense is no** ~ non si bada a spese; **to ~ that** obiettare che; **I ~!** mi oppongo!; ~**ion** [əb'dʒɛkʃən] *n* obiezione *f*; ~**ionable** [əb'dʒɛkʃənəbl] *adj*

antipatico(a); (*language*) scostumato(a); ~**ive** *n* obiettivo

obligation [ɔblɪ'geɪʃən] *n* obbligo, dovere *m*; **without** ~ senza impegno

oblige [ə'blaɪdʒ] *vt* (*force*): **to ~ sb to do** costringere qn a fare; (*do a favour*) fare una cortesia a; **to be ~d to sb for sth** essere grato a qn per qc; **obliging** *adj* servizievole, compiacente

oblique [ə'bliːk] *adj* obliquo(a); (*allusion*) indiretto(a)

obliterate [ə'blɪtəreɪt] *vt* cancellare

oblivion [ə'blɪvɪən] *n* oblio

oblivious [ə'blɪvɪəs] *adj*: ~ **of** incurante di; inconscio(a) di

oblong ['ɔblɔŋ] *adj* oblungo(a) ♦ *n* rettangolo

obnoxious [əb'nɔkʃəs] *adj* odioso(a); (*smell*) disgustoso(a), ripugnante

oboe ['əubəu] *n* oboe *m*

obscene [əb'siːn] *adj* osceno(a)

obscure [əb'skjuə*] *adj* oscuro(a) ♦ *vt* oscurare; (*hide*: *sun*) nascondere

observant [əb'zəːvnt] *adj* attento(a)

observation [ɔbzə'veɪʃən] *n* osservazione *f*; (*by police etc*) sorveglianza

observatory [əb'zəːvətrɪ] *n* osservatorio

observe [əb'zəːv] *vt* osservare; (*remark*) fare osservare; ~**r** *n* osservatore/trice

obsess [əb'sɛs] *vt* ossessionare; ~**ive** *adj* ossessivo(a)

obsolescence [ɔbsə'lɛsns] *n* obsolescenza

obsolete ['ɔbsəliːt] *adj* obsoleto(a)

obstacle ['ɔbstəkl] *n* ostacolo

obstinate ['ɔbstɪnɪt] *adj* ostinato(a)

obstruct [əb'strʌkt] *vt* (*block*) ostruire, ostacolare; (*halt*) fermare; (*hinder*) impedire

obtain [əb'teɪn] *vt* ottenere; ~**able** *adj* ottenibile

obvious ['ɔbvɪəs] *adj* ovvio(a), evidente; ~**ly** *adv* ovviamente; certo

occasion [ə'keɪʒən] *n* occasione *f*; (*event*) avvenimento; ~**al** *adj* occasionale; ~**ally** *adv* ogni tanto

occupation [ɔkju'peɪʃən] *n* occupazione *f*; (*job*) mestiere *m*, professione *f*; ~**al hazard** *n* rischio del mestiere

occupier ['ɔkjupaɪə*] *n* occupante *m/f*
occupy ['ɔkjupaɪ] *vt* occupare; **to ~ o.s.
in doing** occuparsi a fare
occur [ə'kə:*] *vi* accadere, capitare; **to ~
to sb** venire in mente a qn; **~rence** *n*
caso, fatto; presenza
ocean ['əuʃən] *n* oceano; **~-going** *adj*
d'alto mare
o'clock [ə'klɔk] *adv*: **it is 5 ~** sono le 5
OCR *n abbr* (= *optical character
recognition*) lettura ottica; (= *optical
character reader*) lettore *m* ottico
octave ['ɔktɪv] *n* ottavo
October [ɔk'təubə*] *n* ottobre *m*
octopus ['ɔktəpəs] *n* polpo, piovra
odd [ɔd] *adj* (*strange*) strano(a),
bizzarro(a); (*number*) dispari *inv*; (*not of a
set*) spaiato(a); **60-~** 60 e oltre; **at ~ times**
di tanto in tanto; **the ~ one out**
l'eccezione *f*; **~ity** *n* bizzarria; (*person*)
originale *m*; **~-job man** *n* tuttofare *m
inv*; **~ jobs** *npl* lavori *mpl* occasionali;
~ly *adv* stranamente; **~ments** *npl* (*COMM*)
rimanenze *fpl*; **~s** *npl* (*in betting*) quota;
~s and ends *npl* avanzi *mpl*; **it makes
no ~s** non importa; **at ~s** in contesa
odometer [ɔ'dɔmɪtə*] *n* odometro
odour ['əudə*] (*US* **odor**) *n* odore *m*;
(*unpleasant*) cattivo odore

---

of [ɔv, əv] *prep* **1** (*gen*) di; **a boy ~ 10** un
ragazzo di 10 anni; **a friend ~ ours** un
nostro amico; **that was kind ~ you** è
stato molto gentile da parte sua
2 (*expressing quantity, amount, dates etc*)
di; **a kilo ~ flour** un chilo di farina; **how
much ~ this do you need?** quanto gliene
serve?; **there were 3 ~ them** (*people*) erano in 3; (*objects*) ce n'erano 3; **3 ~ us
went** 3 di noi sono andati; **the 5th ~
July** il 5 luglio
3 (*from, out of*) di, in; **made ~ wood**
(fatto) di *or* in legno

---

off [ɔf] *adv* **1** (*distance, time*): **it's a long
way ~** è lontano; **the game is 3 days ~**
la partita è tra 3 giorni
2 (*departure, removal*) via; **to go ~ to
Paris** andarsene a Parigi; **I must be ~**
devo andare via; **to take ~ one's coat**
togliersi il cappotto; **the button came ~**
il bottone è venuto via *or* si è staccato;
10% ~ con lo sconto del 10%
3 (*not at work*): **to have a day ~** avere
un giorno libero; **to be ~ sick** essere
assente per malattia
♦ *adj* (*engine*) spento(a); (*tap*) chiuso(a);
(*cancelled*) sospeso(a); (*BRIT*: *food*)
andato(a) a male; **on the ~ chance** nel
caso; **to have an ~ day** non essere in
forma
♦ *prep* **1** (*motion, removal etc*) da; (*distant
from*) a poca distanza da; **a street ~ the
square** una strada che parte dalla piazza
2: **to be ~ meat** non mangiare più la
carne

offal ['ɔfl] *n* (*CULIN*) frattaglie *fpl*
off-colour (*BRIT*) *adj* (*ill*) malato(a),
indisposto(a)
offence [ə'fɛns] *n* (*LAW*)
contravvenzione *f*; (: *more serious*) reato;
to take ~ at offendersi per
offend [ə'fɛnd] *vt* (*person*) offendere; **~er**
n delinquente *m/f*; (*against regulations*)
contravventore/trice
offense [ə'fɛns] (*US*) *n* = **offence**
offensive [ə'fɛnsɪv] *adj* offensivo(a);
(*smell etc*) sgradevole, ripugnante ♦ *n*
(*MIL*) offensiva
offer ['ɔfə*] *n* offerta, proposta ♦ *vt*
offrire; **"on ~"** (*COMM*) "in offerta
speciale"; **~ing** *n* offerta
offhand [ɔf'hænd] *adj* disinvolto(a),
noncurante ♦ *adv* su due piedi
office ['ɔfɪs] *n* (*place*) ufficio; (*position*)
carica; **doctor's ~** (*US*) studio; **to take ~**
entrare in carica; **~ automation** *n*
automazione *f* dell'ufficio; burotica; **~ block**
(*US* **~ building**) *n* complesso di uffici; **~
hours** *npl* orario d'ufficio; (*US*: *MED*)
orario di visite
officer ['ɔfɪsə*] *n* (*MIL etc*) ufficiale *m*;
(*also*: **police ~**) agente *m* di polizia; (*of
organization*) funzionario

office worker *n* impiegato/a d'ufficio
official [ə'fɪʃl] *adj* (*authorized*) ufficiale
♦ *n* ufficiale *m*; (*civil servant*) impiegato/a
statale; funzionario; ~**dom** (*pej*) *n*
burocrazia
officiate [ə'fɪʃɪeɪt] *vi* presenziare
officious [ə'fɪʃəs] *adj* invadente
offing ['ɔfɪŋ] *n*: **in the** ~ (*fig*) in vista
off: ~**-licence** (*BRIT*) *n* (*shop*) spaccio di
bevande alcoliche; ~**-line** *adj*, *adv*
(*COMPUT*) off-line *inv*, fuori linea;
(: *switched off*) spento(a); ~**-peak** *adj*
(*ticket, heating etc*) a tariffa ridotta; (*time*)
non di punta; ~**-putting** (*BRIT*) *adj*
sgradevole, antipatico(a); ~**-season** *adj*,
adv fuori stagione
offset ['ɔfsɛt] (*irreg*) *vt* (*counteract*)
controbilanciare, compensare
offshoot ['ɔfʃuːt] *n* (*fig*) diramazione *f*
offshore [ɔf'ʃɔː*] *adj* (*breeze*) di terra;
(*island*) vicino alla costa; (*fishing*)
costiero(a)
offside ['ɔf'saɪd] *adj* (*SPORT*) fuori gioco;
(*AUT: in Britain*) destro(a); (: *in Italy etc*)
sinistro(a)
offspring ['ɔfsprɪŋ] *n inv* prole *f*,
discendenza
off: ~**stage** *adv* dietro le quinte; ~**-the-
peg** (*US* ~**-the-rack**) *adv* prêt-à-porter; ~**-
white** *adj* bianco sporco *inv*
often ['ɔfn] *adv* spesso; **how** ~ **do you
go?** quanto spesso ci vai?
ogle ['əugl] *vt* occhieggiare
oh [əu] *excl* oh!
oil [ɔɪl] *n* olio; (*petroleum*) petrolio; (*for
central heating*) nafta ♦ *vt* (*machine*)
lubrificare; ~**can** *n* oliatore *m* a mano;
(*for storing*) latta da olio; ~**field** *n*
giacimento petrolifero; ~ **filter** *n* (*AUT*)
filtro dell'olio; ~ **painting** *n* quadro a
olio; ~ **refinery** *n* raffineria di petrolio; ~
rig *n* derrick *m inv*; (*at sea*) piattaforma
per trivellazioni subacquee; ~**skins**
indumenti *mpl* di tela cerata; ~ **tanker** *n*
(*ship*) petroliera; (*truck*) autocisterna per
petrolio; ~ **well** *n* pozzo petrolifero; ~**y**
adj unto(a), oleoso(a); (*food*) grasso(a)
ointment ['ɔɪntmənt] *n* unguento
O.K. ['əu'keɪ] *excl* d'accordo! ♦ *adj* non

male *inv* ♦ *vt* approvare; **is it** ~**?, are
you** ~**?** tutto bene?
okay ['əu'keɪ] *excl, adj, vt* = **O.K**
old [əuld] *adj* vecchio(a); (*ancient*)
antico(a), vecchio(a); (*person*) vecchio(a),
anziano(a); **how** ~ **are you?** quanti anni
ha?; **he's 10 years** ~ ha 10 anni; ~**er
brother** fratello maggiore; ~ **age** *n*
vecchiaia; ~ **age pensioner** (*BRIT*) *n*
pensionato/a; ~**-fashioned** *adj*
antiquato(a), fuori moda; (*person*) all'antica
olive ['ɔlɪv] *n* (*fruit*) oliva; (*tree*) olivo
♦ *adj* (*also*: ~**-green**) verde oliva *inv*; ~ **oil**
n olio d'oliva
Olympic [əu'lɪmpɪk] *adj* olimpico(a); **the**
~ **Games, the** ~**s** i giochi olimpici, le
Olimpiadi
omelet(te) ['ɔmlɪt] *n* omelette *f inv*
omen ['əumən] *n* presagio, augurio
ominous ['ɔmɪnəs] *adj* minaccioso(a);
(*event*) di malaugurio
omit [əu'mɪt] *vt* omettere

KEYWORD

on [ɔn] *prep* **1** (*indicating position*) su; ~
the wall sulla parete; ~ **the left** a *or*
sulla sinistra
2 (*indicating means, method, condition
etc*): ~ **foot** a piedi; ~ **the train/plane** in
treno/aereo; ~ **the telephone** al telefono;
~ **the radio/television** alla radio/
televisione; **to be** ~ **drugs** drogarsi; ~
holiday in vacanza
3 (*referring to time*): ~ **Friday** venerdì; ~
Fridays il *or* di venerdì; ~ **June 20th** il
20 giugno; ~ **Friday, June 20th** venerdì,
20 giugno; **a week** ~ **Friday** venerdì a
otto; ~ **his arrival** al suo arrivo; ~
seeing this vedendo ciò
4 (*about, concerning*) su, di; **information**
~ **train services** informazioni sui
collegamenti ferroviari; **a book** ~
Goldoni/physics un libro su Goldoni/di
or sulla fisica
♦ *adv* **1** (*referring to dress, covering*): **to
have one's coat** ~ avere indosso il
cappotto; **to put one's coat** ~ mettersi il
cappotto; **what's she got** ~**?** cosa

indossa?; **she put her boots/gloves/hat
~** si mise gli stivali/i guanti/il cappello;
screw the lid ~ tightly avvita bene il
coperchio
2 (*further, continuously*): **to walk ~, go ~**
etc continuare, proseguire *etc*; **to read ~**
continuare a leggere; **~ and off** ogni
tanto
♦ *adj* **1** (*in operation: machine, TV, light*)
acceso(a); (: *tap*) aperto(a); (: *brake*)
inserito(a); **is the meeting still ~?** (*in
progress*) la riunione è ancora in corso?;
(*not cancelled*) è confermato l'incontro?;
there's a good film ~ at the cinema
danno un buon film al cinema
2 (*inf*): **that's not ~!** (*not acceptable*) non
si fa così!; (*not possible*) non se ne parla
neanche!

once [wʌns] *adv* una volta ♦ *conj* non
appena, quando; **~ he had left/it was
done** dopo che se n'era andato/fu fatto;
at ~ subito; (*simultaneously*) a un tempo;
~ a week una volta per settimana; **~
more** ancora una volta; **~ and for all**
una volta per sempre; **~ upon a time**
c'era una volta

oncoming [ˈɔnkʌmɪŋ] *adj* (*traffic*) che
viene in senso opposto

one [wʌn] *num* uno(a); **~ hundred and
fifty** centocinquanta; **~ day** un giorno
♦ *adj* **1** (*sole*) unico(a); **the ~ book which**
l'unico libro che; **the ~ man who** l'unico
che
2 (*same*) stesso(a); **they came in the ~
car** sono venuti nella stessa macchina
♦ *pron* **1** : **this ~** questo/a; **that ~** quello/
a; **I've already got ~/a red ~** ne ho già
uno/uno rosso; **~ by ~** uno per uno
2 : **~ another** l'un l'altro; **to look at ~
another** guardarsi; **to help ~ another**
aiutarsi l'un l'altro *or* a vicenda
3 (*impersonal*) si; **~ never knows** non si
sa mai; **to cut ~'s finger** tagliarsi un
dito; **~ needs to eat** bisogna mangiare

one: ~-day excursion (*US*) *n* biglietto

giornaliero di andata e ritorno; **~-man**
adj (*business*) diretto(a) *etc* da un solo
uomo; **~-man band** *n* suonatore
ambulante con vari strumenti; **~-off** (*BRIT:
inf*) *n* fatto eccezionale

oneself [wʌnˈsɛlf] *pron* (*reflexive*) si;
(*after prep*) se stesso(a), sé; **to do sth (by)
~** fare qc da sé; **to hurt ~** farsi male; **to
keep sth for ~** tenere qc per sé; **to talk
to ~** parlare da solo

one: ~-sided *adj* (*argument*) unilaterale; **~-
to-~** *adj* (*relationship*) univoco(a); **~-
upmanship** [-ˈʌpmənʃɪp] *n* l'arte di fare
sempre meglio degli altri; **~-way** *adj*
(*street, traffic*) a senso unico

ongoing [ˈɔngəʊɪŋ] *adj* in corso; in
attuazione

onion [ˈʌnjən] *n* cipolla

on-line *adj, adv* (*COMPUT*) on-line *inv*

onlooker [ˈɔnlʊkə*] *n* spettatore/trice

only [ˈəʊnlɪ] *adv* solo, soltanto ♦ *adj*
solo(a), unico(a) ♦ *conj* solo che, ma; **an ~
child** un figlio unico; **not ~ ... but also**
non solo ... ma anche

onset [ˈɔnsɛt] *n* inizio

onshore [ˈɔnʃɔː*] *adj* (*wind*) di mare

onslaught [ˈɔnslɔːt] *n* attacco, assalto

onto [ˈɔntu] *prep* = **on to**

onus [ˈəʊnəs] *n* onere *m*, peso

onward(s) [ˈɔnwəd(z)] *adv* (*move*) in
avanti; **from that time ~** da quella volta
in poi

onyx [ˈɔnɪks] *n* onice *f*

ooze [uːz] *vi* stillare

OPEC [ˈəʊpɛk] *n abbr* (= *Organization of
Petroleum-Exporting Countries*) O.P.E.C. *f*

open [ˈəʊpn] *adj* aperto(a); (*road*)
libero(a); (*meeting*) pubblico(a) ♦ *vt* aprire
♦ *vi* (*eyes, door, debate*) aprirsi; (*flower*)
sbocciare; (*shop, bank, museum*) aprire;
(*book etc: commence*) cominciare; **in the ~
(air)** all'aperto; **~ on to** *vt fus* (*subj:
room, door*) dare su; **~ up** *vt* aprire;
(*blocked road*) sgombrare ♦ *vi* (*shop,
business*) aprire; **~ing** *adj* (*speech*) di
apertura ♦ *n* apertura; (*opportunity*)
occasione *f*, opportunità *f inv*; sbocco; **~
learning centre** *n* sistema educativo nel
quale lo studente ha maggiore controllo e

gestione delle modalità di apprendimento; **~ly** *adv* apertamente; **~-minded** *adj* che ha la mente aperta; **~-necked** *adj* col collo slacciato; **~-plan** *adj* senza pareti divisorie

opera ['ɔpərə] *n* opera

operate ['ɔpəreɪt] *vt* (*machine*) azionare, far funzionare; (*system*) usare ♦ *vi* funzionare; (*drug*) essere efficace; **to ~ on sb (for)** (*MED*) operare qn (di)

operatic [ɔpə'rætɪk] *adj* dell'opera, lirico(a)

operating ['ɔpəreɪtɪŋ] *adj*: **~ table** tavolo operatorio; **~ theatre** sala operatoria

operation [ɔpə'reɪʃən] *n* operazione *f*; **to be in ~** (*machine*) essere in azione *or* funzionamento; (*system*) essere in vigore; **to have an ~** (*MED*) subire un'operazione; **~al** *adj* in funzione; d'esercizio

operative ['ɔpərətɪv] *adj* (*measure*) operativo(a)

operator ['ɔpəreɪtə*] *n* (*of machine*) operatore/trice; (*TEL*) centralinista *m/f*

opinion [ə'pɪnɪən] *n* opinione *f*, parere *m*; **in my ~** secondo me, a mio avviso; **~ated** *adj* dogmatico(a); **~ poll** *n* sondaggio di opinioni

opium ['əupɪəm] *n* oppio

opponent [ə'pəunənt] *n* avversario/a

opportunist [ɔpə'tjuːnɪst] *n* opportunista *m/f*

opportunity [ɔpə'tjuːnɪtɪ] *n* opportunità *f inv*, occasione *f*; **to take the ~ of doing** cogliere l'occasione per fare

oppose [ə'pəuz] *vt* opporsi a; **~d to** contrario(a) a; **as ~d to** in contrasto con; **opposing** *adj* opposto(a); (*team*) avversario(a)

opposite ['ɔpəzɪt] *adj* opposto(a); (*house etc*) di fronte ♦ *adv* di fronte, dirimpetto ♦ *prep* di fronte a ♦ *n*: **the ~** il contrario, l'opposto; **the ~ sex** l'altro sesso

opposition [ɔpə'zɪʃən] *n* opposizione *f*

oppress [ə'prɛs] *vt* opprimere

opt [ɔpt] *vi*: **to ~ for** optare per; **to ~ to do** scegliere di fare; **~ out** *vi*: **to ~ out of** ritirarsi da

optical ['ɔptɪkl] *adj* ottico(a)

optician [ɔp'tɪʃən] *n* ottico

optimist ['ɔptɪmɪst] *n* ottimista *m/f*; **~ic** [-'mɪstɪk] *adj* ottimistico(a)

optimum ['ɔptɪməm] *adj* ottimale

option ['ɔpʃən] *n* scelta; (*SCOL*) materia facoltativa; (*COMM*) opzione *f*; **~al** *adj* facoltativo(a); (*COMM*) a scelta

or [ɔː*] *conj* o, oppure; (*with negative*): **he hasn't seen ~ heard anything** non ha visto né sentito niente; **~ else** se no, altrimenti; oppure

oral ['ɔːrəl] *adj* orale ♦ *n* esame *m* orale

orange ['ɔrɪndʒ] *n* (*fruit*) arancia ♦ *adj* arancione

orator ['ɔrətə*] *n* oratore/trice

orbit ['ɔːbɪt] *n* orbita ♦ *vt* orbitare intorno a

orchard ['ɔːtʃəd] *n* frutteto

orchestra ['ɔːkɪstrə] *n* orchestra; (*US: seating*) platea

orchid ['ɔːkɪd] *n* orchidea

ordain [ɔː'deɪn] *vt* (*REL*) ordinare; (*decide*) decretare

ordeal [ɔː'diːl] *n* prova, travaglio

order ['ɔːdə*] *n* ordine *m*; (*COMM*) ordinazione *f* ♦ *vt* ordinare; **in ~** in ordine; (*of document*) in regola; **in (working) ~** funzionante; **in ~ to do** per fare; **in ~ that** affinché + *sub*; **on ~** (*COMM*) in ordinazione; **out of ~** non in ordine; (*not working*) guasto; **to ~ sb to do** ordinare a qn di fare; **~ form** *n* modulo d'ordinazione; **~ly** *n* (*MIL*) attendente *m*; (*MED*) inserviente *m* ♦ *adj* (*room*) in ordine; (*mind*) metodico(a); (*person*) ordinato(a), metodico(a)

ordinary ['ɔːdnrɪ] *adj* normale, comune; (*pej*) mediocre; **out of the ~** diverso dal solito, fuori dell'ordinario

Ordnance Survey ['ɔːdnəns-] (*BRIT*) *n* istituto cartografico britannico

ore [ɔː*] *n* minerale *m* grezzo

organ ['ɔːgən] *n* organo; **~ic** [ɔː'gænɪk] *adj* organico(a)

organization [ɔːgənaɪ'zeɪʃən] *n* organizzazione *f*

organize ['ɔːgənaɪz] *vt* organizzare; **~r** *n* organizzatore/trice

orgasm ['ɔːgæzəm] *n* orgasmo

orgy ['ɔːdʒɪ] *n* orgia

Orient ['ɔːrɪənt] *n*: **the ~** l'Oriente *m*;
oriental [-'ɛntl] *adj, n* orientale *m/f*

origin ['ɔrɪdʒɪn] *n* origine *f*

original [ə'rɪdʒɪnl] *adj* originale; (*earliest*)
originario(a) ♦ *n* originale *m*; **~ly** *adv* (*at
first*) all'inizio

originate [ə'rɪdʒɪneɪt] *vi*: **to ~ from**
essere originario(a) di; (*suggestion*)
provenire da; **to ~ in** avere origine in

Orkneys ['ɔːknɪz] *npl*: **the ~** (*also: the
Orkney Islands*) le Orcadi

ornament ['ɔːnəmənt] *n* ornamento;
(*trinket*) ninnolo; **~al** [-'mɛntl] *adj*
ornamentale

ornate [ɔː'neɪt] *adj* molto ornato(a)

orphan ['ɔːfn] *n* orfano/a; **~age** *n*
orfanotrofio

orthodox ['ɔːθədɔks] *adj* ortodosso(a)

orthopaedic [ɔːθə'piːdɪk] (*US*
orthopedic) *adj* ortopedico(a)

ostensibly [ɔs'tɛnsɪblɪ] *adv* all'apparenza

ostentatious [ɔstɛn'teɪʃəs] *adj*
pretenzioso(a); ostentato(a)

ostrich ['ɔstrɪtʃ] *n* struzzo

other ['ʌðə*] *adj* altro(a) ♦ *pron*: **the ~
(one)** l'altro(a); **~s** (~ *people*) altri *mpl*; **~
than** altro che; a parte; **~wise** *adv, conj*
altrimenti

otter ['ɔtə*] *n* lontra

ouch [autʃ] *excl* ohi!, ahi!

ought [ɔːt] (*pt* **ought**) *aux vb*: **I ~ to do
it** dovrei farlo; **this ~ to have been
corrected** questo avrebbe dovuto essere
corretto; **he ~ to win** dovrebbe vincere

ounce [auns] *n* oncia (= *28.35 g; 16 in a
pound*)

our ['auə*] *adj* il(la) nostro(a), *pl* i(le)
nostri(e); *see also* **my**; **~s** *pron* il(la)
nostro(a), *pl* i(le) nostri(e); *see also* **mine**;
~selves *pron pl* (*reflexive*) ci; (*after
preposition*) noi; (*emphatic*) noi stessi(e);
see also **oneself**

oust [aust] *vt* cacciare, espellere

KEYWORD

out [aut] *adv* (*gen*) fuori; **~ here/there**
qui/là fuori; **to speak ~ loud** parlare
forte; **to have a night ~** uscire una sera;
the boat was 10 km ~ la barca era a 10

km dalla costa; **3 days ~ from Plymouth**
a 3 giorni da Plymouth

♦ *adj*: **to be ~** (*gen*) essere fuori;
(*unconscious*) aver perso i sensi; (*style,
singer*) essere fuori moda; **before the
week was ~** prima che la settimana fosse
finita; **to be ~ to do sth** avere intenzione
di fare qc; **to be ~ in one's calculations**
aver sbagliato i calcoli

♦ *out of prep* **1** (*outside, beyond*) fuori di;
to go ~ of the house uscire di casa; **to
look ~ of the window** guardare fuori
dalla finestra

2 (*because of*) per

3 (*origin*) da; **to drink ~ of a cup** bere
da una tazza

4 (*from among*): **~ of 10** su 10

5 (*without*) senza; **~ of petrol** senza
benzina

out-and-out *adj* (*liar, thief etc*) vero(a) e
proprio(a)

outback ['autbæk] *n* (*in Australia*)
interno, entroterra

outboard ['autbɔːd] *n*: **~ (motor)**
(motore *m*) fuoribordo

outbreak ['autbreɪk] *n* scoppio; epidemia

outburst ['autbəːst] *n* scoppio

outcast ['autkɑːst] *n* esule *m/f*; (*socially*)
paria *m inv*

outcome ['autkʌm] *n* esito, risultato

outcrop ['autkrɔp] *n* (*of rock*)
affioramento

outcry ['autkraɪ] *n* protesta, clamore *m*

outdated [aut'deɪtɪd] *adj* (*custom,
clothes*) fuori moda; (*idea*) sorpassato(a)

outdo [aut'duː] (*irreg*) *vt* sorpassare

outdoor [aut'dɔː*] *adj* all'aperto; **~s** *adv*
fuori; all'aria aperta

outer ['autə*] *adj* esteriore; **~ space** *n*
spazio cosmico

outfit ['autfɪt] *n* (*clothes*) completo; (: *for
sport*) tenuta

outgoing ['autɡəuɪŋ] *adj* (*character*)
socievole; **~s** (*BRIT*) *npl* (*expenses*) spese
fpl, uscite *fpl*

outgrow [aut'ɡrəu] (*irreg*) *vt*: **he has ~n
his clothes** tutti i vestiti gli sono
diventati piccoli

outhouse ['authaus] *n* costruzione *f* annessa

outing ['autɪŋ] *n* gita; escursione *f*

outlandish [aut'lændɪʃ] *adj* strano(a)

outlaw ['autlɔ:] *n* fuorilegge *m/f* ♦ *vt* bandire

outlay ['autleɪ] *n* spese *fpl*; (*investment*) sborsa, spesa

outlet ['autlɛt] *n* (*for liquid etc*) sbocco, scarico; (*US: ELEC*) presa di corrente; (*also: retail ~*) punto di vendita

outline ['autlaɪn] *n* contorno, profilo; (*summary*) abbozzo, grandi linee *fpl* ♦ *vt* (*fig*) descrivere a grandi linee

outlive [aut'lɪv] *vt* sopravvivere a

outlook ['autluk] *n* prospettiva, vista

outlying ['autlaɪɪŋ] *adj* periferico(a)

outmoded [aut'məudɪd] *adj* passato(a) di moda; antiquato(a)

outnumber [aut'nʌmbə*] *vt* superare in numero

out-of-date *adj* (*passport*) scaduto(a); (*clothes*) fuori moda *inv*

out-of-the-way *adj* (*place*) fuori mano *inv*

outpatient ['autpeɪʃənt] *n* paziente *m/f* esterno(a)

outpost ['autpəust] *n* avamposto

output ['autput] *n* produzione *f*; (*COMPUT*) output *m inv*

outrage ['autreɪdʒ] *n* oltraggio; scandalo ♦ *vt* oltraggiare; **~ous** [-'reɪdʒəs] *adj* oltraggioso(a); scandaloso(a)

outright [*adv* aut'raɪt, *adj* 'autraɪt] *adv* completamente; schiettamente; apertamente; sul colpo ♦ *adj* completo(a); schietto(a) e netto(a)

outset ['autsɛt] *n* inizio

outside [aut'saɪd] *n* esterno, esteriore *m* ♦ *adj* esterno(a), esteriore ♦ *adv* fuori, all'esterno ♦ *prep* fuori di, all'esterno di; **at the ~** (*fig*) al massimo; **~ lane** *n* (*AUT*) corsia di sorpasso; **~ line** *n* (*TEL*) linea esterna; **~r** *n* (*in race etc*) outsider *m inv*; (*stranger*) estraneo/a

outsize ['autsaɪz] *adj* (*clothes*) per taglie forti

outskirts ['autskə:ts] *npl* sobborghi *mpl*

outspoken [aut'spəukən] *adj* molto franco(a)

outstanding [aut'stændɪŋ] *adj* eccezionale, di rilievo; (*unfinished*) non completo(a); non evaso(a); non regolato(a)

outstay [aut'steɪ] *vt*: **to ~ one's welcome** diventare un ospite sgradito

outstretched [aut'strɛtʃt] *adj* (*hand*) teso(a); (*body*) disteso(a)

outstrip [aut'strɪp] *vt* (*competitors, demand*) superare

out-tray *n* contenitore *m* per la corrispondenza in partenza

outward ['autwəd] *adj* (*sign, appearances*) esteriore; (*journey*) d'andata; **~ly** *adv* esteriormente; in apparenza

outweigh [aut'weɪ] *vt* avere maggior peso di

outwit [aut'wɪt] *vt* superare in astuzia

oval ['əuvl] *adj* ovale ♦ *n* ovale *m*

ovary ['əuvərɪ] *n* ovaia

oven ['ʌvn] *n* forno; **~proof** *adj* da forno

over ['əuvə*] *adv* al di sopra ♦ *adj* (*or adv*) (*finished*) finito(a), terminato(a); (*too*) troppo; (*remaining*) che avanza ♦ *prep* su; sopra; (*above*) al di sopra di; (*on the other side of*) di là di; (*more than*) più di; (*during*) durante; **~ here** qui; **~ there** là; **all ~** (*everywhere*) dappertutto; (*finished*) tutto(a) finito(a); **~ and ~ (again)** più e più volte; **~ and above** oltre (a); **to ask sb ~** invitare qn (a passare)

overall [*adj, n* 'əuvərɔ:l, *adv* əuvər'ɔ:l] *adj* totale ♦ *n* (*BRIT*) grembiule *m* ♦ *adv* nell'insieme, complessivamente; **~s** *npl* (*worker's ~s*) tuta (da lavoro)

overawe [əuvər'ɔ:] *vt* intimidire

overbalance [əuvə'bæləns] *vi* perdere l'equilibrio

overbearing [əuvə'bɛərɪŋ] *adj* imperioso(a), prepotente

overboard ['əuvəbɔ:d] *adv* (*NAUT*) fuori bordo, in mare

overbook [əuvə'buk] *vt*: **the hotel was ~ed** le prenotazioni all'albergo superavano i posti disponibili

overcast ['əuvəkɑ:st] *adj* coperto(a)

overcharge [əuvə'tʃɑ:dʒ] *vt*: **to ~ sb for sth** far pagare troppo caro a qn per qc

overcoat ['əuvəkəut] *n* soprabito,

cappotto

overcome [əuvə'kʌm] (*irreg*) *vt* superare; sopraffare

overcrowded [əuvə'kraudid] *adj* sovraffollato(a)

overdo [əuvə'du:] (*irreg*) *vt* esagerare; (*overcook*) cuocere troppo

overdose ['əuvədəus] *n* dose *f* eccessiva

overdraft ['əuvədrɑːft] *n* scoperto (di conto)

overdrawn [əuvə'drɔːn] *adj* (*account*) scoperto(a)

overdue [əuvə'djuː] *adj* in ritardo

overestimate [əuvər'ɛstimeit] *vt* sopravvalutare

overflow [*vb* əuvə'fləu, *n* 'əuvəfləu] *vi* traboccare ♦ *n* (*also*: ~ *pipe*) troppopieno

overgrown [əuvə'grəun] *adj* (*garden*) ricoperto(a) di vegetazione

overhaul [*vb* əuvə'hɔːl, *n* 'əuvəhɔːl] *vt* revisionare ♦ *n* revisione *f*

overhead [*adv* əuvə'hɛd, *adj, n* 'əuvəhɛd] *adv* di sopra ♦ *adj* aereo(a); (*lighting*) verticale ♦ *n* (*US*) = ~s; **~s** *npl* spese *fpl* generali

overhear [əuvə'hiə*] (*irreg*) *vt* sentire (per caso)

overheat [əuvə'hiːt] *vi* (*engine*) surriscaldare

overjoyed [əuvə'dʒɔid] *adj* pazzo(a) di gioia

overkill ['əuvəkil] *n* (*fig*) eccessi *mpl*

overlap [əuvə'læp] *vi* sovrapporsi

overleaf [əuvə'liːf] *adv* a tergo

overload [əuvə'ləud] *vt* sovraccaricare

overlook [əuvə'luk] *vt* (*have view of*) dare su; (*miss*) trascurare; (*forgive*) passare sopra a

overnight [əuvə'nait] *adv* (*happen*) durante la notte; (*fig*) tutto ad un tratto ♦ *adj* di notte; **he stayed there ~** ci ha passato la notte

overpass ['əuvəpɑːs] *n* cavalcavia *m inv*

overpower [əuvə'pauə*] *vt* sopraffare; **~ing** *adj* irresistibile; (*heat, stench*) soffocante

overrate [əuvə'reit] *vt* sopravvalutare

override [əuvə'raid] (*irreg: like* **ride**) *vt* (*order, objection*) passar sopra a; (*decision*)

annullare; **overriding** *adj* preponderante

overrule [əuvə'ruːl] *vt* (*decision*) annullare; (*claim*) respingere

overrun [əuvə'rʌn] (*irreg: like* **run**) *vt* (*country*) invadere; (*time limit*) superare

overseas [əuvə'siːz] *adv* oltremare; (*abroad*) all'estero ♦ *adj* (*trade*) estero(a); (*visitor*) straniero(a)

overshadow [əuvə'ʃædəu] *vt* far ombra su; (*fig*) eclissare

overshoot [əuvə'ʃuːt] (*irreg*) *vt* superare

oversight ['əuvəsait] *n* omissione *f*, svista

oversleep [əuvə'sliːp] (*irreg*) *vt* dormire troppo a lungo

overstate [əuvə'steit] *vt* esagerare

overstep [əuvə'stɛp] *vt*: **to ~ the mark** superare ogni limite

overt [əu'vɜːt] *adj* palese

overtake [əuvə'teik] (*irreg*) *vt* sorpassare

overthrow [əuvə'θrəu] (*irreg*) *vt* (*government*) rovesciare

overtime ['əuvətaim] *n* (*labour*) straordinario

overtone ['əuvətəun] *n* sfumatura

overture ['əuvətʃuə*] *n* (*MUS*) ouverture *f inv*; (*fig*) approccio

overturn [əuvə'tɜːn] *vt* rovesciare ♦ *vi* rovesciarsi

overweight [əuvə'weit] *adj* (*person*) troppo grasso(a)

overwhelm [əuvə'wɛlm] *vt* sopraffare; sommergere; schiacciare; **~ing** *adj* (*victory, defeat*) schiacciante; (*heat, desire*) intenso(a)

overwork [əuvə'wɜːk] *n* eccessivo lavoro

overwrought [əuvə'rɔːt] *adj* molto agitato(a)

owe [əu] *vt*: **to ~ sb sth, to ~ sth to sb** dovere qc a qn; **owing to** *prep* a causa di

owl [aul] *n* gufo

own [əun] *vt* possedere ♦ *adj* proprio(a); **a room of my ~** la mia propria camera; **to get one's ~ back** vendicarsi; **on one's ~** tutto(a) solo(a); **~ up** *vi* confessare; **~er** *n* proprietario/a; **~ership** *n* possesso

ox [ɔks] *pl* **oxen** *n* bue *m*

oxen ['ɔksn] *npl of* **ox**

oxtail ['ɔksteɪl] n: ~ **soup** minestra di coda di bue

oxygen ['ɔksɪdʒən] n ossigeno; ~ **mask/ tent** n maschera/tenda ad ossigeno

oyster ['ɔɪstə*] n ostrica

oz. abbr = **ounce(s)**

ozone ['əuzəun] n ozono; ~-**friendly** adj che non danneggia l'ozono; ~ **hole** n buco nell'ozono; ~ **layer** n strato di ozono

P

p [pi:] abbr = **penny; pence**

P.A. n abbr = **personal assistant; public address system**

p.a. abbr = **per annum**

pa [pɑ:] (inf) n papà m inv, babbo

pace [peɪs] n passo; (speed) passo; velocità ♦ vi: **to ~ up and down** camminare su e giù; **to keep ~ with** camminare di pari passo a; (events) tenersi al corrente di; ~**maker** n (MED) segnapasso; (SPORT: also: ~ **setter**) battistrada m inv

pacific [pə'sɪfɪk] n: **the P~ (Ocean)** il Pacifico, l'Oceano Pacifico

pacify ['pæsɪfaɪ] vt calmare, placare

pack [pæk] n pacco; (US: of cigarettes) pacchetto; (back~) zaino; (of hounds) muta; (of thieves etc) banda; (of cards) mazzo ♦ vt (in suitcase etc) mettere; (box) riempire; (cram) stipare, pigiare; **to ~ (one's bags)** fare la valigia; **to ~ sb off** spedire via qn; ~ **it in!** (inf) dacci un taglio!

package ['pækɪdʒ] n pacco; balla; (also: ~ **deal**) pacchetto; forfait m inv; ~ **holiday** n vacanza organizzata; ~ **tour** n viaggio organizzato

packed lunch n pranzo al sacco

packet ['pækɪt] n pacchetto

packing ['pækɪŋ] n imballaggio; ~ **case** n cassa da imballaggio

pact [pækt] n patto, accordo; trattato

pad [pæd] n blocco; (to prevent friction) cuscinetto; (inf: flat) appartamentino ♦ vt imbottire; ~**ding** n imbottitura

paddle ['pædl] n (oar) pagaia; (US: for table tennis) racchetta da ping-pong ♦ vi squazzare ♦ vt: **to ~ a canoe** etc vogare con la pagaia; ~ **steamer** n battello a ruote; **paddling pool** (BRIT) n piscina per bambini

paddock ['pædək] n prato recintato; (at racecourse) paddock m inv

paddy field ['pædɪ-] n risaia

padlock ['pædlɔk] n lucchetto

paediatrics [pi:dɪ'ætrɪks] (US **pediatrics**) n pediatria

pagan ['peɪgən] adj, n pagano(a)

page [peɪdʒ] n pagina; (also: ~ **boy**) paggio ♦ vt (in hotel etc) (far) chiamare

pageant ['pædʒənt] n spettacolo storico; grande cerimonia; ~**ry** n pompa

pager ['peɪdʒə*] n (TEL) cercapersone m inv

paging device ['peɪdʒɪŋ-] n (TEL) cercapersone m inv

paid [peɪd] pt, pp of **pay** ♦ adj (work, official) rimunerato(a); **to put ~ to** (BRIT) mettere fine a

pail [peɪl] n secchio

pain [peɪn] n dolore m; **to be in ~** soffrire, aver male; **to take ~s to do** mettercela tutta per fare; ~**ed** adj addolorato(a), afflitto(a); ~**ful** adj doloroso(a), che fa male; difficile, penoso(a); ~**fully** adv (fig: very) fin troppo; ~**killer** n antalgico, antidolorifico; ~**less** adj indolore

painstaking ['peɪnzteɪkɪŋ] adj (person) sollecito(a); (work) accurato(a)

paint [peɪnt] n vernice f, colore m ♦ vt dipingere; (walls, door etc) verniciare; **to ~ the door blue** verniciare la porta di azzurro; ~**brush** n pennello; ~**er** n (artist) pittore m; (decorator) imbianchino; ~**ing** n pittura; verniciatura; (picture) dipinto, quadro; ~**work** n tinta; (of car) vernice f

pair [pɛə*] n (of shoes, gloves etc) paio; (of people) coppia; duo m inv; **a ~ of scissors/trousers** un paio di forbici/ pantaloni

pajamas [pɪ'dʒɑːməz] (US) npl pigiama m

Pakistan [pɑːkɪ'stɑːn] n Pakistan m; ~**i** adj, n pakistano(a)

pal [pæl] (inf) n amico/a, compagno/a

palace ['pæləs] *n* palazzo
palatable ['pælɪtəbl] *adj* gustoso(a)
palate ['pælɪt] *n* palato
palatial [pə'leɪʃəl] *adj* sontuoso(a),
sfarzoso(a)
pale [peɪl] *adj* pallido(a) ♦ *n*: **to be
beyond the ~** aver oltrepassato ogni
limite
Palestine ['pælɪstaɪn] *n* Palestina;
Palestinian [-'tɪnɪən] *adj, n* palestinese
m/f
palette ['pælɪt] *n* tavolozza
palings ['peɪlɪŋz] *npl* (*fence*) palizzata
pall [pɔːl] *n* (*of smoke*) cappa ♦ *vi*: **to ~
(on)** diventare noioso(a) (a)
pallet ['pælɪt] *n* (*for goods*) paletta
pallid ['pælɪd] *adj* pallido(a), smorto(a)
pallor ['pælə*] *n* pallore *m*
palm [pɑːm] *n* (ANAT) palma, palmo; (*also:
~ tree*) palma ♦ *vt*: **to ~ sth off on sb**
(*inf*) rifilare qc a qn; **P~ Sunday** *n*
Domenica delle Palme
palpable ['pælpəbl] *adj* palpabile
paltry ['pɔːltrɪ] *adj* irrisorio(a);
insignificante
pamper ['pæmpə*] *vt* viziare, coccolare
pamphlet ['pæmflət] *n* dépliant *m inv*
pan [pæn] *n* (*also: sauce~*) casseruola;
(*also: frying ~*) padella
panache [pə'næʃ] *n* stile *m*
pancake ['pænkeɪk] *n* frittella
pancreas ['pæŋkrɪəs] *n* pancreas *m inv*
panda ['pændə] *n* panda *m inv*; **~ car**
(BRIT) *n* auto *f* della polizia
pandemonium [pændɪ'məʊnɪəm] *n*
pandemonio
pander ['pændə*] *vi*: **to ~ to** lusingare;
concedere tutto a
pane [peɪn] *n* vetro
panel ['pænl] *n* (*of wood, cloth etc*)
pannello; (RADIO, TV) giuria; **~ling** (US
~ing) *n* rivestimento a pannelli
pang [pæŋ] *n*: **a ~ of regret** un senso di
rammarico; **hunger ~s** morsi *mpl* della
fame
panic ['pænɪk] *n* panico ♦ *vi* perdere il
sangue freddo; **~ky** *adj* (*person*)
pauroso(a); **~-stricken** *adj* (*person*)
preso(a) dal panico, in preda al panico;

(*look*) terrorizzato(a)
pansy ['pænzɪ] *n* (BOT) viola del pensiero,
pensée *f inv*; (*inf: pej*) femminuccia
pant [pænt] *vi* ansare
panther ['pænθə*] *n* pantera
panties ['pæntɪz] *npl* slip *m*, mutandine
fpl
pantihose ['pæntɪhəʊz] (US) *n* collant *m
inv*
pantomime ['pæntəmaɪm] (BRIT) *n*
pantomima
pantry ['pæntrɪ] *n* dispensa
pants [pænts] *npl* mutande *fpl*, slip *m*;
(US: *trousers*) pantaloni *mpl*
papal ['peɪpəl] *adj* papale, pontificio(a)
paper ['peɪpə*] *n* carta; (*also: wall~*)
carta da parati, tappezzeria; (*also: news~*)
giornale *m*; (*study, article*) saggio; (*exam*)
prova scritta ♦ *adj* di carta ♦ *vt*
tappezzare; **~s** *npl* (*also: identity ~s*) carte
fpl, documenti *mpl*; **~back** *n* tascabile *m*;
edizione *f* economica; **~ bag** *n* sacchetto
di carta; **~ clip** *n* graffetta, clip *f inv*; **~
hankie** *n* fazzolettino di carta; **~weight**
n fermacarte *m inv*; **~work** *n* lavoro
amministrativo
papier-mâché ['pæpɪeɪ'mæʃeɪ] *n*
cartapesta
par [pɑː*] *n* parità, pari *f*; (GOLF) norma;
on a ~ with alla pari con
parable ['pærəbl] *n* parabola
parachute ['pærəʃuːt] *n* paracadute *m
inv*
parade [pə'reɪd] *n* parata ♦ *vt* (*fig*) fare
sfoggio di ♦ *vi* sfilare in parata
paradise ['pærədaɪs] *n* paradiso
paradox ['pærədɔks] *n* paradosso; **~ically**
[-'dɔksɪklɪ] *adv* paradossalmente
paraffin ['pærəfɪn] (BRIT) *n*: **~ (oil)**
paraffina
paragon ['pærəgən] *n* modello di
perfezione *or* di virtù
paragraph ['pærəgrɑːf] *n* paragrafo
parallel ['pærəlɛl] *adj* parallelo(a); (*fig*)
analogo(a) ♦ *n* (*line*) parallela; (*fig, GEO*)
parallelo
paralyse ['pærəlaɪz] (US **paralyze**) *vt*
paralizzare
paralysis [pə'rælɪsɪs] *n* paralisi *f inv*

paralyze ['pærəlaɪz] (*US*) *vt* = **paralyse**
paramount ['pærəmaunt] *adj*: **of ~ importance** di capitale importanza
paranoid ['pærənɔɪd] *adj* paranoico(a)
paraphernalia [pærəfə'neɪlɪə] *n* attrezzi *mpl*, roba
parasol ['pærəsɔl] *n* parasole *m*
paratrooper ['pærətru:pə*] *n* paracadutista *m* (*soldato*)
parcel ['pɑ:sl] *n* pacco, pacchetto ♦ *vt* (*also: ~ up*) impaccare
parch [pɑ:tʃ] *vt* riardere; **~ed** *adj* (*person*) assetato(a)
parchment ['pɑ:tʃmənt] *n* pergamena
pardon ['pɑ:dn] *n* perdono; grazia ♦ *vt* perdonare; (*LAW*) graziare; **~ me!** mi scusi!; **I beg your ~!** scusi!; **I beg your ~?** (*BRIT*), **~ me?** (*US*) prego?
parent ['pɛərənt] *n* genitore *m*; **~s** *npl* (*mother and father*) genitori *mpl*; **~al** [pə'rɛntl] *adj* dei genitori
parentheses [pə'rɛnθɪsi:z] *npl of* **parenthesis**
parenthesis [pə'rɛnθɪsɪs] (*pl* **parentheses**) *n* parentesi *f inv*
Paris ['pærɪs] *n* Parigi *f*
parish ['pærɪʃ] *n* parrocchia, (*BRIT: civil*) ≈ municipio
park [pɑ:k] *n* parco ♦ *vt*, *vi* parcheggiare
parka ['pɑ:kə] *n* eskimo
parking ['pɑ:kɪŋ] *n* parcheggio; **"no ~"** "sosta vietata"; **~ lot** (*US*) *n* posteggio, parcheggio; **~ meter** *n* parchimetro; **~ ticket** *n* multa per sosta vietata
parlance ['pɑ:ləns] *n* gergo
parliament ['pɑ:ləmənt] *n* parlamento; **~ary** [-'mɛntərɪ] *adj* parlamentare
parlour ['pɑ:lə*] (*US* **parlor**) *n* salotto
parochial [pə'rəukɪəl] (*pej*) *adj* provinciale
parody ['pærədɪ] *n* parodia
parole [pə'rəul] *n*: **on ~** in libertà per buona condotta
parrot ['pærət] *n* pappagallo
parry ['pærɪ] *vt* parare
parsley ['pɑ:slɪ] *n* prezzemolo
parsnip ['pɑ:snɪp] *n* pastinaca
parson ['pɑ:sn] *n* prete *m*; (*Church of England*) parroco

part [pɑ:t] *n* parte *f*; (*of machine*) pezzo; (*US: in hair*) scriminatura ♦ *adj* in parte ♦ *adv* = **partly** ♦ *vt* separare ♦ *vi* (*people*) separarsi; **to take ~ in** prendere parte a; **for my ~** per parte mia; **to take sth in good ~** prendere bene qc; **to take sb's ~** parteggiare per *or* prendere le parti di qn; **for the most ~** in generale; nella maggior parte dei casi; **~ with** *vt fus* separarsi da; rinunciare a; **~ exchange** (*BRIT*) *n*: **in ~ exchange** in pagamento parziale
partial ['pɑ:ʃl] *adj* parziale; **to be ~ to** avere un debole per
participate [pɑ:'tɪsɪpeɪt] *vi*: **to ~ (in)** prendere parte (a), partecipare (a); **participation** [-'peɪʃən] *n* partecipazione *f*
participle ['pɑ:tɪsɪpl] *n* participio
particle ['pɑ:tɪkl] *n* particella
particular [pə'tɪkjulə*] *adj* particolare; speciale; (*fussy*) difficile; meticoloso(a); **in ~** in particolare, particolarmente; **~ly** *adv* particolarmente; in particolare; **~s** *npl* particolari *mpl*, dettagli *mpl*; (*information*) informazioni *fpl*
parting ['pɑ:tɪŋ] *n* separazione *f*; (*BRIT: in hair*) scriminatura ♦ *adj* d'addio
partisan [pɑ:tɪ'zæn] *n* partigiano/a ♦ *adj* partigiano(a); di parte
partition [pɑ:'tɪʃən] *n* (*POL*) partizione *f*; (*wall*) tramezzo
partly ['pɑ:tlɪ] *adv* parzialmente; in parte
partner ['pɑ:tnə*] *n* (*COMM*) socio/a; (*wife, husband etc, SPORT*) compagno/a; (*at dance*) cavaliere/dama; **~ship** *n* associazione *f*; (*COMM*) società *f inv*
partridge ['pɑ:trɪdʒ] *n* pernice *f*
part-time *adj*, *adv* a orario ridotto
party ['pɑ:tɪ] *n* (*POL*) partito; (*group*) gruppo; (*LAW*) parte *f*; (*celebration*) ricevimento; serata; festa ♦ *cpd* (*POL*) del partito, di partito; **~ dress** *n* vestito della festa; **~ line** *n* (*TEL*) duplex *m inv*
pass [pɑ:s] *vt* (*gen*) passare; (*place*) passare davanti a; (*exam*) passare, superare; (*candidate*) promuovere; (*overtake, surpass*) sorpassare, superare; (*approve*) approvare ♦ *vi* passare ♦ *n*

(*permit*) lasciapassare *m inv*; permesso; (*in mountains*) passo, gola; (*SPORT*) passaggio; (*SCOL*): **to get a ~** prendere la sufficienza; **to ~ sth through a hole** *etc* far passare qc attraverso un buco *etc*; **to make a ~ at sb** (*inf*) fare delle proposte *or* delle avances a qn; **~ away** *vi* morire; **~ by** *vi* passare ♦ *vt* trascurare; **~ on** *vt* passare; **~ out** *vi* svenire; **~ up** *vt* (*opportunity*) lasciarsi sfuggire, perdere; **~able** *adj* (*road*) praticabile; (*work*) accettabile

passage ['pæsɪdʒ] *n* (*gen*) passaggio; (*also*: ~**way**) corridoio; (*in book*) brano, passo; (*by boat*) traversata

passbook ['pɑːsbʊk] *n* libretto di risparmio

passenger ['pæsɪndʒə*] *n* passeggero/a

passer-by ['pɑːsə'baɪ] *n* passante *m/f*

passing ['pɑːsɪŋ] *adj* (*fig*) fuggevole; **to mention sth in ~** accennare a qc di sfuggita; **~ place** *n* (*AUT*) piazzola di sosta

passion ['pæʃən] *n* passione *f*; amore *m*; **~ate** *adj* appassionato(a)

passive ['pæsɪv] *adj* (*also LING*) passivo(a); **~ smoking** *n* fumo passivo

Passover ['pɑːsəʊvə*] *n* Pasqua ebraica

passport ['pɑːspɔːt] *n* passaporto; **~ control** *n* controllo *m* passaporti *inv*

password ['pɑːswɜːd] *n* parola d'ordine

past [pɑːst] *prep* (*further than*) oltre, di là di; dopo; (*later than*) dopo ♦ *adj* passato(a); (*president etc*) ex *inv* ♦ *n* passato; **he's ~ forty** ha più di quarant'anni; **ten ~ eight** le otto e dieci; **for the ~ few days** da qualche giorno; in questi ultimi giorni; **to run ~** passare di corsa

pasta ['pæstə] *n* pasta

paste [peɪst] *n* (*glue*) colla; (*CULIN*) pâté *m inv*; pasta ♦ *vt* collare

pastel ['pæstl] *adj* pastello *inv*

pasteurized ['pæstəraɪzd] *adj* pastorizzato(a)

pastille ['pæstl] *n* pastiglia

pastime ['pɑːstaɪm] *n* passatempo

pastry ['peɪstrɪ] *n* pasta

pasture ['pɑːstʃə*] *n* pascolo

pasty¹ ['pæstɪ] *n* pasticcio di carne

pasty² ['peɪstɪ] *adj* (*face etc*) smorto(a)

pat [pæt] *vt* accarezzare, dare un colpetto (affettuoso) a

patch [pætʃ] *n* (*of material, on tyre*) toppa; (*eye ~*) benda; (*spot*) macchia ♦ *vt* (*clothes*) rattoppare; **(to go through) a bad ~** (attraversare) un brutto periodo; **~ up** *vt* rappezzare; (*quarrel*) appianare; **~y** *adj* irregolare

pâté ['pæteɪ] *n* pâté *m inv*

patent ['peɪtnt] *n* brevetto ♦ *vt* brevettare ♦ *adj* patente, manifesto(a); **~ leather** *n* cuoio verniciato

paternal [pə'tɜːnl] *adj* paterno(a)

path [pɑːθ] *n* sentiero, viottolo; viale *m*; (*fig*) via, strada; (*of planet, missile*) traiettoria

pathetic [pə'θetɪk] *adj* (*pitiful*) patetico(a); (*very bad*) penoso(a)

pathological [pæθə'lɒdʒɪkl] *adj* patologico(a)

pathway ['pɑːθweɪ] *n* sentiero

patience ['peɪʃns] *n* pazienza; (*BRIT: CARDS*) solitario

patient ['peɪʃnt] *n* paziente *m/f*; malato/a ♦ *adj* paziente

patio ['pætɪəʊ] *n* terrazza

patriot ['peɪtrɪət] *n* patriota *m/f*; **~ic** [pætrɪ'ɔtɪk] *adj* patriottico(a); **~ism** *n* patriottismo

patrol [pə'trəʊl] *n* pattuglia ♦ *vt* pattugliare; **~ car** *n* autoradio *f inv* (della polizia); **~man** (*US*) *n* poliziotto

patron ['peɪtrən] *n* (*in shop*) cliente *m/f*; (*of charity*) benefattore/trice; **~ of the arts** mecenate *m/f*; **~ize** ['pætrənaɪz] *vt* essere cliente abituale di; (*fig*) trattare dall'alto in basso

patter ['pætə*] *n* picchiettio; (*sales talk*) propaganda di vendita ♦ *vi* picchiettare; **a ~ of footsteps** un rumore di passi

pattern ['pætən] *n* modello; (*design*) disegno, motivo

paunch [pɔːntʃ] *n* pancione *m*

pauper ['pɔːpə*] *n* indigente *m/f*

pause [pɔːz] *n* pausa ♦ *vi* fare una pausa, arrestarsi

pave [peɪv] *vt* pavimentare; **to ~ the way for** aprire la via a

pavement ['peɪvmənt] (*BRIT*) *n*
marciapiede *m*

pavilion [pə'vɪliən] *n* (*SPORT*) *edificio
annesso a campo sportivo*

paving ['peɪvɪŋ] *n* pavimentazione *f*; ~
stone *n* lastra di pietra

paw [pɔː] *n* zampa

pawn [pɔːn] *n* (*CHESS*) pedone *m*; (*fig*)
pedina ♦ *vt* dare in pegno; ~**broker** *n*
prestatore *m* su pegno; ~**shop** *n* monte *m*
di pietà

pay [peɪ] (*pt, pp* **paid**) *n* stipendio; paga
♦ *vt* pagare ♦ *vi* (*be profitable*) rendere; **to
~ attention (to)** fare attenzione (a); **to ~
sb a visit** far visita a qn; **to ~ one's
respects to sb** porgere i propri rispetti a
qn; ~ **back** *vt* rimborsare; ~ **for** *vt fus*
pagare; ~ **in** *vt* versare; ~ **off** *vt* (*debt*)
saldare; (*person*) pagare; (*employee*)
pagare e licenziare ♦ *vi* (*scheme, decision*)
dare dei frutti; ~ **up** *vt* saldare; ~**able**
adj pagabile; ~**ee** *n* beneficiario/a; ~
envelope (*US*) *n* = ~**packet**; ~**ment** *n*
pagamento; versamento; saldo; ~ **packet**
(*BRIT*) *n* busta *f* paga *inv*; ~ **phone** *n*
cabina telefonica; ~**roll** *n* ruolo
(organico); ~ **slip** *n* foglio *m* paga *inv*; ~
television *n* televisione *f* a pagamento,
pay-tv *f inv*

PC *n abbr* = **personal computer**

p.c. *abbr* = **per cent**

pea [piː] *n* pisello

peace [piːs] *n* pace *f*; ~**ful** *adj* pacifico(a),
calmo(a)

peach [piːtʃ] *n* pesca

peacock ['piːkɔk] *n* pavone *m*

peak [piːk] *n* (*of mountain*) cima, vetta;
(*mountain itself*) picco; (*of cap*) visiera;
(*fig*) apice *m*, culmine *m*; ~ **hours** *npl* ore
fpl di punta; ~ **period** *n* = ~ **hours**

peal [piːl] *n* (*of bells*) scampanio, carillon
m inv; ~**s of laughter** scoppi *mpl* di risa

peanut ['piːnʌt] *n* arachide *f*, nocciolina
americana; ~ **butter** *n* burro di arachidi

pear [pɛə*] *n* pera

pearl [pəːl] *n* perla

peasant ['pɛznt] *n* contadino/a

peat [piːt] *n* torba

pebble ['pɛbl] *n* ciottolo

peck [pɛk] *vt* (*also:* ~ *at*) beccare ♦ *n*
colpo di becco; (*kiss*) bacetto; ~**ing order**
n ordine *m* gerarchico; ~**ish** (*BRIT: inf*)
adj: **I feel ~ish** ho un languorino

peculiar [pɪ'kjuːlɪə*] *adj* strano(a),
bizzarro(a); peculiare; ~ **to** peculiare di

pedal ['pɛdl] *n* pedale *m* ♦ *vi* pedalare

pedantic [pɪ'dæntɪk] *adj* pedantesco(a)

peddler ['pɛdlə*] *n* (*also: drugs* ~)
spacciatore/trice

pedestal ['pɛdəstl] *n* piedestallo

pedestrian [pɪ'dɛstrɪən] *n* pedone/a
♦ *adj* pedonale; (*fig*) prosaico(a), pedestre;
~ **crossing** (*BRIT*) *n* passaggio pedonale

pediatrics [piːdɪ'ætrɪks] (*US*) *n*
= **paediatrics**

pedigree ['pɛdɪgriː] *n* (*of animal*)
pedigree *m inv*; (*fig*) background *m inv*
♦ *cpd* (*animal*) di razza

pee [piː] (*inf*) *vi* pisciare

peek [piːk] *vi* guardare furtivamente

peel [piːl] *n* buccia; (*of orange, lemon*)
scorza ♦ *vt* sbucciare ♦ *vi* (*paint etc*)
staccarsi

peep [piːp] *n* (*BRIT: look*) sguardo furtivo,
sbirciata; (*sound*) pigolio ♦ *vi* (*BRIT*)
guardare furtivamente; ~ **out** *vi*
mostrarsi furtivamente; ~**hole** *n*
spioncino

peer [pɪə*] *vi*: **to ~ at** scrutare ♦ *n*
(*noble*) pari *m inv*; (*equal*) pari *m/f inv*,
uguale *m/f*; (*contemporary*) contempora-
neo/a; ~**age** *n* dignità di pari; pari *mpl*

peeved [piːvd] *adj* stizzito(a)

peevish ['piːvɪʃ] *adj* stizzoso(a)

peg [pɛg] *n* caviglia; (*for coat etc*)
attaccapanni *m inv*; (*BRIT: also: clothes* ~)
molletta

Peking [piː'kɪŋ] *n* Pechino *f*

pelican ['pɛlɪkən] *n* pellicano; ~
crossing (*BRIT*) *n* (*AUT*) attraversamento
*pedonale con semaforo a controllo
manuale*

pellet ['pɛlɪt] *n* pallottola, pallina

pelt [pɛlt] *vt*: **to ~ sb (with)** bombardare
qn (con) ♦ *vi* (*rain*) piovere a dirotto; (*inf:
run*) filare ♦ *n* pelle *f*

pelvis ['pɛlvɪs] *n* pelvi *f inv*, bacino

pen [pɛn] *n* penna; (*for sheep*) recinto

penal ['piːnl] *adj* penale; **~ize** *vt* punire; (*SPORT*, *fig*) penalizzare

penalty ['pɛnltɪ] *n* penalità *f inv*; sanzione *f* penale; (*fine*) ammenda; (*SPORT*) penalizzazione *f*; **~ (kick)** *n* (*SPORT*) calcio di rigore

penance ['pɛnəns] *n* penitenza

pence [pɛns] (*BRIT*) *npl of* **penny**

pencil ['pɛnsl] *n* matita; **~ case** *n* astuccio per matite; **~ sharpener** *n* temperamatite *m inv*

pendant ['pɛndnt] *n* pendaglio

pending ['pɛndɪŋ] *prep* in attesa di ♦ *adj* in sospeso

pendulum ['pɛndjuləm] *n* pendolo

penetrate ['pɛnɪtreɪt] *vt* penetrare

penfriend ['pɛnfrɛnd] (*BRIT*) *n* corrispondente *m/f*

penguin ['pɛŋgwɪn] *n* pinguino

penicillin [pɛnɪ'sɪlɪn] *n* penicillina

peninsula [pə'nɪnsjulə] *n* penisola

penis ['piːnɪs] *n* pene *m*

penitent ['pɛnɪtnt] *adj* penitente

penitentiary [pɛnɪ'tɛnʃərɪ] (*US*) *n* carcere *m*

penknife ['pɛnnaɪf] *n* temperino

pen name *n* pseudonimo

penniless ['pɛnɪlɪs] *adj* senza un soldo

penny ['pɛnɪ] (*pl* **pennies** *or* **pence** (*BRIT*)) *n* penny *m*; (*US*) centesimo

penpal ['pɛnpæl] *n* corrispondente *m/f*

pension ['pɛnʃən] *n* pensione *f*; **~er** (*BRIT*) *n* pensionato/a

pensive ['pɛnsɪv] *adj* pensoso(a)

penthouse ['pɛnthaus] *n* appartamento (di lusso) nell'attico

pent-up ['pɛntʌp] *adj* (*feelings*) represso(a)

people ['piːpl] *npl* gente *f*; persone *fpl*; (*citizens*) popolo ♦ *n* (*nation, race*) popolo; **4/several ~ came** 4/parecchie persone sono venute; **~ say that ...** si dice che ....

pep [pɛp] (*inf*) *n* dinamismo; **~ up** *vt* vivacizzare; (*food*) rendere più gustoso(a)

pepper ['pɛpə*] *n* pepe *m*; (*vegetable*) peperone *m* ♦ *vt* (*fig*): **to ~ with** spruzzare di; **~mint** *n* (*sweet*) pasticca di menta

peptalk ['pɛptɔːk] (*inf*) *n* discorso di incoraggiamento

per [pəː*] *prep* per; a; **~ hour** all'ora; **~ kilo** *etc* il chilo *etc*; **~ day** al giorno; **~ annum** *adv* all'anno; **~ capita** *adj, adv* pro capite *inv*

perceive [pə'siːv] *vt* percepire; (*notice*) accorgersi di

per cent [pəː'sɛnt] *adv* per cento

percentage [pə'sɛntɪdʒ] *n* percentuale *f*

perception [pə'sɛpʃən] *n* percezione *f*; sensibilità; perspicacia

perceptive [pə'sɛptɪv] *adj* percettivo(a); perspicace

perch [pəːtʃ] *n* (*fish*) pesce *m* persico; (*for bird*) sostegno, ramo ♦ *vi* appollaiarsi

percolator ['pəːkəleɪtə*] *n* (*also: coffee ~*) caffettiera a pressione; caffettiera elettrica

percussion [pə'kʌʃən] *n* percussione *f*; (*MUS*) strumenti *mpl* a percussione

peremptory [pə'rɛmptərɪ] *adj* perentorio(a)

perennial [pə'rɛnɪəl] *adj* perenne

perfect [*adj, n* 'pəːfɪkt, *vb* pə'fɛkt] *adj* perfetto(a) ♦ *n* (*also: ~ tense*) perfetto, passato prossimo ♦ *vt* perfezionare; mettere a punto; **~ly** *adv* perfettamente, alla perfezione

perforate ['pəːfəreɪt] *vt* perforare; **perforation** [-'reɪʃən] *n* perforazione *f*

perform [pə'fɔːm] *vt* (*carry out*) eseguire, fare; (*symphony etc*) suonare; (*play, ballet*) dare; (*opera*) fare ♦ *vi* suonare; recitare; **~ance** *n* esecuzione *f*; (*at theatre etc*) rappresentazione *f*, spettacolo; (*of an artist*) interpretazione *f*; (*of player etc*) performance *f*; (*of car, engine*) prestazione *f*; **~er** *n* artista *m/f*

perfume ['pəːfjuːm] *n* profumo

perfunctory [pə'fʌŋktərɪ] *adj* superficiale, per la forma

perhaps [pə'hæps] *adv* forse

peril ['pɛrɪl] *n* pericolo

perimeter [pə'rɪmɪtə*] *n* perimetro

period ['pɪərɪəd] *n* periodo; (*HISTORY*) epoca; (*SCOL*) lezione *f*; (*full stop*) punto; (*MED*) mestruazione *fpl* ♦ *adj* (*costume, furniture*) d'epoca; **~ic(al)** [-'ɔdɪk(l)] *adj* periodico(a); **~ical** [-'ɔdɪkl] *n* periodico

peripheral [pə'rɪfərəl] *adj* periferico(a)
♦ *n* (COMPUT) unità *f inv* periferica
perish ['perɪʃ] *vi* perire, morire; (*decay*)
deteriorarsi; **~able** *adj* deperibile
perjury ['pə:dʒərɪ] *n* spergiuro
perk [pə:k] (*inf*) *n* vantaggio; **~ up** *vi*
(*cheer up*) rianimarsi; **~y** *adj* (*cheerful*)
vivace, allegro(a)
perm [pə:m] *n* (*for hair*) permanente *f*
permanent ['pə:mənənt] *adj* permanente
permeate ['pə:mɪeɪt] *vi* penetrare ♦ *vt*
permeare
permissible [pə'mɪsɪbl] *adj* permissibile,
ammissibile
permission [pə'mɪʃən] *n* permesso
permissive [pə'mɪsɪv] *adj* permissivo(a)
permit [*n* 'pə:mɪt, *vb* pə'mɪt] *n* permesso
♦ *vt* permettere; **to ~ sb to do** permettere
a qn di fare
perpendicular [pə:pən'dɪkjulə*] *adj*
perpendicolare ♦ *n* perpendicolare *f*
perplex [pə'pleks] *vt* lasciare perplesso(a)
persecute ['pə:sɪkju:t] *vt* perseguitare
persevere [pə:sɪ'vɪə*] *vi* perseverare
Persian ['pə:ʃən] *adj* persiano(a) ♦ *n*
(LING) persiano; **the (~) Gulf** *n* il Golfo
Persico
persist [pə'sɪst] *vi*: **to ~ (in doing)**
persistere (nel fare); ostinarsi (a fare);
~ent *adj* persistente; ostinato(a)
person ['pə:sn] *n* persona; **in ~** di *or* in
persona, personalmente; **~al** *adj*
personale; individuale; **~al assistant** *n*
segretaria personale; **~al column** *n* ≈
messaggi *mpl* personali; **~al computer** *n*
personal computer *m inv*; **~ality** [-'nælɪtɪ]
n personalità *f inv*; **~ally** *adv*
personalmente; **to take sth ~ally**
prendere qc come una critica personale;
~al organizer *n* (*Filofax* ®) Fulltime ®;
(*electronic*) agenda elettronica; **~ stereo** *n*
Walkman ® *m inv*
personnel [pə:sə'nel] *n* personale *m*
perspective [pə'spektɪv] *n* prospettiva
Perspex ['pə:speks] ® (BRIT) *n* tipo di
resina termoplastica
perspiration [pə:spɪ'reɪʃən] *n*
traspirazione *f*, sudore *m*
persuade [pə'sweɪd] *vt*: **to ~ sb to do**

sth persuadere qn a fare qc
pertaining [pə:'teɪnɪŋ]: **~ to** *prep* che
riguarda
perturb [pə'tə:b] *vt* turbare
peruse [pə'ru:z] *vt* leggere
pervade [pə'veɪd] *vt* pervadere
pervert [*n* 'pə:və:t, *vb* pə'və:t] *n*
pervertito/a ♦ *vt* pervertire
pessimism ['pesɪmɪzəm] *n* pessimismo
pessimist ['pesɪmɪst] *n* pessimista *m/f*;
~ic [-'mɪstɪk] *adj* pessimistico(a)
pest [pest] *n* animale *m* (*or* insetto)
pestifero; (*fig*) peste *f*
pester ['pestə*] *vt* tormentare, molestare
pet [pet] *n* animale *m* domestico ♦ *cpd*
favorito(a) ♦ *vt* accarezzare ♦ *vi* (*inf*) fare
il petting; **teacher's ~** favorito/a del
maestro
petal ['petl] *n* petalo
peter ['pi:tə*]: **to ~ out** *vi* esaurirsi;
estinguersi
petite [pə'ti:t] *adj* piccolo(a) e
aggraziato(a)
petition [pə'tɪʃən] *n* petizione *f*
petrified ['petrɪfaɪd] *adj* (*fig*) morto(a) di
paura
petrol ['petrəl] (BRIT) *n* benzina; **two/
four-star ~** ≈ benzina normale/super; **~
can** *n* tanica per benzina
petroleum [pə'trəʊlɪəm] *n* petrolio
petrol: **~ pump** (BRIT) *n* (*in car, at
garage*) pompa di benzina; **~ station**
(BRIT) *n* stazione *f* di rifornimento; **~ tank**
(BRIT) *n* serbatoio della benzina
petticoat ['petɪkəʊt] *n* sottana
petty ['petɪ] *adj* (*mean*) meschino(a);
(*unimportant*) insignificante; **~ cash** *n*
piccola cassa; **~ officer** *n* sottufficiale *m*
di marina
petulant ['petjulənt] *adj* irritabile
pew [pju:] *n* panca (di chiesa)
pewter ['pju:tə*] *n* peltro
phallic ['fælɪk] *adj* fallico(a)
phantom ['fæntəm] *n* fantasma *m*
pharmaceutical [fɑ:mə'sju:tɪkl] *adj*
farmaceutico(a)
pharmacy ['fɑ:məsɪ] *n* farmacia
phase [feɪz] *n* fase *f*, periodo ♦ *vt*: **to ~
sth in/out** introdurre/eliminare qc

progressivamente

Ph.D. *n abbr* = **Doctor of Philosophy**

pheasant ['fɛznt] *n* fagiano

phenomena [fə'nɔmɪnə] *npl of*
phenomenon

phenomenon [fə'nɔmɪnən] (*pl*
phenomena) *n* fenomeno

Philippines ['fɪlɪpiːnz] *npl*: **the ~** le
Filippine

philosophical [fɪlə'sɔfɪkl] *adj*
filosofico(a)

philosophy [fɪ'lɔsəfɪ] *n* filosofia

phlegmatic [flɛg'mætɪk] *adj*
flemmatico(a)

phobia ['fəubjə] *n* fobia

phone [fəun] *n* telefono ♦ *vt* telefonare;
to be on the ~ avere il telefono; (*be
calling*) essere al telefono; **~ back** *vt, vi*
richiamare; **~ up** *vt* telefonare a ♦ *vi*
telefonare; **~ book** *n* guida del telefono,
elenco telefonico; **~ booth** *n* = **~ box**; **~
box** *n* cabina telefonica; **~ call** *n*
telefonata; **~card** *n* scheda telefonica; **~-
in** *n* (*BRIT: RADIO, TV*) trasmissione *f* a filo
diretto con gli ascoltatori

phonetics [fə'nɛtɪks] *n* fonetica

phoney ['fəunɪ] *adj* falso(a), fasullo(a)

phosphorus ['fɔsfərəs] *n* fosforo

photo ['fəutəu] *n* foto *f inv*

photo... ['fəutəu] *prefix*: **~copier** *n*
fotocopiatrice *f*; **~copy** *n* fotocopia ♦ *vt*
fotocopiare; **~graph** *n* fotografia ♦ *vt*
fotografare; **~grapher** [fə'tɔgrəfə*] *n*
fotografo; **~graphy** [fə'tɔgrəfɪ] *n*
fotografia

phrase [freɪz] *n* espressione *f*; (*LING*)
locuzione *f*; (*MUS*) frase *f* ♦ *vt* esprimere; **~
book** *n* vocabolarietto

physical ['fɪzɪkl] *adj* fisico(a); **~
education** *n* educazione *f* fisica; **~ly** *adv*
fisicamente

physician [fɪ'zɪʃən] *n* medico

physicist ['fɪzɪsɪst] *n* fisico

physics ['fɪzɪks] *n* fisica

physiology [fɪzɪ'ɔlədʒɪ] *n* fisiologia

physique [fɪ'ziːk] *n* fisico; costituzione *f*

pianist ['piːənɪst] *n* pianista *m/f*

piano [pɪ'ænəu] *n* pianoforte *m*

piccolo ['pɪkələu] *n* ottavino

pick [pɪk] *n* (*tool: also*: **~-axe**) piccone *m*
♦ *vt* scegliere; (*gather*) cogliere; (*remove*)
togliere; (*lock*) far scattare; **take your ~**
scelga; **the ~ of** il fior fiore di; **to ~ one's
nose** mettersi le dita nel naso; **to ~ one's
teeth** pulirsi i denti con lo stuzzicadenti;
to ~ a quarrel attaccar briga; **~ at** *vt
fus*: **to ~ at one's food** piluccare; **~ on** *vt
fus* (*person*) avercela con; **~ out** *vt*
scegliere; (*distinguish*) distinguere; **~ up**
vi (*improve*) migliorarsi ♦ *vt* raccogliere;
(*POLICE, RADIO*) prendere; (*collect*) passare a
prendere; (*AUT: give lift to*) far salire;
(*person: for sexual encounter*) rimorchiare;
(*learn*) imparare; **to ~ up speed**
acquistare velocità; **to ~ o.s. up** rialzarsi

picket ['pɪkɪt] *n* (*in strike*) scioperante
m/f che fa parte di un picchetto;
picchetto ♦ *vt* picchettare

pickle ['pɪkl] *n* (*also*: **~s**: *as condiment*)
sottaceti *mpl*; (*fig: mess*) pasticcio ♦ *vt*
mettere sottaceto; mettere in salamoia

pickpocket ['pɪkpɔkɪt] *n* borsaiolo

pickup ['pɪkʌp] *n* (*small truck*)
camioncino

picnic ['pɪknɪk] *n* picnic *m inv*

picture ['pɪktʃə*] *n* quadro; (*painting*)
pittura; (*photograph*) foto(grafia);
(*drawing*) disegno; (*film*) film *m inv* ♦ *vt*
raffigurarsi; **~s** (*BRIT*) *npl* (*cinema*): **the ~s**
il cinema; **~ book** *n* libro illustrato

picturesque [pɪktʃə'rɛsk] *adj*
pittoresco(a)

pie [paɪ] *n* torta; (*of meat*) pasticcio

piece [piːs] *n* pezzo; (*of land*)
appezzamento; (*item*): **a ~ of furniture/
advice** un mobile/consiglio ♦ *vt*: **to ~
together** mettere insieme; **to take to ~s**
smontare; **~meal** *adv* pezzo a pezzo, a
spizzico; **~work** *n* (lavoro a) cottimo

pie chart *n* grafico a torta

pier [pɪə*] *n* molo; (*of bridge etc*) pila

pierce [pɪəs] *vt* forare; (*with arrow etc*)
trafiggere

piercing ['pɪəsɪŋ] *adj* (*cry*) acuto(a); (*eyes*)
penetrante; (*wind*) pungente

pig [pɪg] *n* maiale *m*, porco

pigeon ['pɪdʒən] *n* piccione *m*; **~hole** *n*
casella

piggy bank ['pɪgɪ-] n salvadanaro

pigheaded ['pɪg'hɛdɪd] adj caparbio(a), cocciuto(a)

piglet ['pɪglɪt] n porcellino

pigskin ['pɪgskɪn] n cinghiale m

pigsty ['pɪgstaɪ] n porcile m

pigtail ['pɪgteɪl] n treccina

pike [paɪk] n (fish) luccio

pilchard ['pɪltʃəd] n specie di sardina

pile [paɪl] n (pillar, of books) pila; (heap) mucchio; (of carpet) pelo ♦ vt (also: ~ up) ammucchiare ♦ vi (also: ~ up) ammucchiarsi; **to ~ into** (car) stiparsi or ammucchiarsi

piles [paɪlz] npl emorroidi fpl

pileup ['paɪlʌp] n (AUT) tamponamento a catena

pilfering ['pɪlfərɪŋ] n rubacchiare m

pilgrim ['pɪlgrɪm] n pellegrino/a; **~age** n pellegrinaggio

pill [pɪl] n pillola; **the ~** la pillola

pillage ['pɪlɪdʒ] vt saccheggiare

pillar ['pɪlə*] n colonna; **~ box** (BRIT) n cassetta postale

pillion ['pɪljən] n: **to ride ~** (on motor cycle) viaggiare dietro

pillory ['pɪlərɪ] vt mettere alla berlina

pillow ['pɪləu] n guanciale m; **~case** n fodera

pilot ['paɪlət] n pilota m/f ♦ cpd (scheme etc) pilota inv ♦ vt pilotare; **~ light** n fiamma pilota

pimp [pɪmp] n mezzano

pimple ['pɪmpl] n foruncolo

pin [pɪn] n spillo; (TECH) perno ♦ vt attaccare con uno spillo; **~s and needles** formicolio; **to ~ sb down** (fig) obbligare qn a pronunziarsi; **to ~ sth on sb** (fig) addossare la colpa di qc a qn

pinafore ['pɪnəfɔː*] n (also: ~ dress) grembiule m (senza maniche)

pinball ['pɪnbɔːl] n flipper m inv

pincers ['pɪnsəz] npl pinzette fpl

pinch [pɪntʃ] n pizzicotto, pizzico ♦ vt pizzicare; (inf: steal) grattare; **at a ~** in caso di bisogno

pincushion ['pɪnkuʃən] n puntaspilli m inv

pine [paɪn] n (also: ~ tree) pino ♦ vi: **to ~**

for struggersi dal desiderio di; **~ away** vi languire

pineapple ['paɪnæpl] n ananas m inv

ping [pɪŋ] n (noise) tintinnio; **~-pong** ® n ping-pong m ®

pink [pɪŋk] adj rosa inv ♦ n (colour) rosa m inv; (BOT) garofano

PIN (number) [pɪn-] n abbr codice m segreto

pinpoint ['pɪnpɔɪnt] vt indicare con precisione

pint [paɪnt] n pinta (BRIT = 0.57l; US = 0.47l); (BRIT: inf) ≈ birra da mezzo

pioneer [paɪə'nɪə*] n pioniere/a

pious ['paɪəs] adj pio(a)

pip [pɪp] n (seed) seme m; (BRIT: time signal on radio) segnale m orario

pipe [paɪp] n tubo; (for smoking) pipa ♦ vt portare per mezzo di tubazione; **~s** npl (also: bag~s) cornamusa (scozzese); **~ down** (inf) vi calmarsi; **~ cleaner** n scovolino; **~ dream** n vana speranza; **~line** n conduttura; (for oil) oleodotto; **~r** n piffero; suonatore/trice di cornamusa

piping ['paɪpɪŋ] adv: **~ hot** caldo bollente

pique [piːk] n picca

pirate ['paɪərət] n pirata m ♦ vt riprodurre abusivamente

Pisces ['paɪsiːz] n Pesci mpl

piss [pɪs] (inf) vi pisciare; **~ed** (inf) adj (drunk) ubriaco(a) fradicio(a)

pistol ['pɪstl] n pistola

piston ['pɪstən] n pistone m

pit [pɪt] n buca, fossa; (also: coal ~) miniera; (quarry) cava ♦ vt: **to ~ sb against sb** opporre qn a qn; **~s** npl (AUT) box m

pitch [pɪtʃ] n (BRIT: SPORT) campo; (MUS) tono; (tar) pece f; (fig) grado, punto ♦ vt (throw) lanciare ♦ vi (fall) cascare; **to ~ a tent** piantare una tenda; **~ed battle** n battaglia campale

piteous ['pɪtɪəs] adj pietoso(a)

pitfall ['pɪtfɔːl] n trappola

pith [pɪθ] n (of plant) midollo; (of orange) parte f interna della scorza; (fig) essenza, succo; vigore m

pithy ['pɪθɪ] adj conciso(a); vigoroso(a)

pitiful ['pɪtɪful] adj (touching) pietoso(a)

pitiless ['pɪtɪlɪs] *adj* spietato(a)

pittance ['pɪtns] *n* miseria, magro salario

pity ['pɪtɪ] *n* pietà ♦ *vt* aver pietà di; **what a ~!** che peccato!

pivot ['pɪvət] *n* perno

pizza ['piːtsə] *n* pizza

placard ['plækɑːd] *n* affisso

placate [plə'keɪt] *vt* placare, calmare

place [pleɪs] *n* posto, luogo; (*proper position, rank, seat*) posto; (*house*) casa, alloggio; (*home*): **at/to his ~** a casa sua ♦ *vt* (*object*) posare, mettere; (*identify*) riconoscere; individuare; **to take ~** aver luogo; succedere; **to change ~s with sb** scambiare il posto con qn; **out of ~** (*not suitable*) inopportuno(a); **in the first ~** in primo luogo; **to ~ an order** dare un'ordinazione; **to be ~d** (*in race, exam*) classificarsi

placid ['plæsɪd] *adj* placido(a), calmo(a)

plagiarism ['pleɪdʒərɪzəm] *n* plagio

plague [pleɪg] *n* peste *f* ♦ *vt* tormentare

plaice [pleɪs] *n inv* pianuzza

plaid [plæd] *n* plaid *m inv*

plain [pleɪn] *adj* (*clear*) chiaro(a), palese; (*simple*) semplice; (*frank*) franco(a), aperto(a); (*not handsome*) bruttino(a); (*without seasoning etc*) scondito(a); naturale; (*in one colour*) tinta unita *inv* ♦ *adv* francamente, chiaramente ♦ *n* pianura; **~ chocolate** *n* cioccolato fondente; **~ clothes** *npl*: **in ~ clothes** (*police*) in borghese; **~ly** *adv* chiaramente; (*frankly*) francamente

plaintiff ['pleɪntɪf] *n* attore/trice

plaintive ['pleɪntɪv] *adj* (*cry, voice*) dolente, lamentoso(a)

plait [plæt] *n* treccia

plan [plæn] *n* pianta; (*scheme*) progetto, piano ♦ *vt* (*think in advance*) progettare; (*prepare*) organizzare ♦ *vi* far piani *or* progetti; **to ~ to do** progettare di fare

plane [pleɪn] *n* (*AVIAT*) aereo; (*tree*) platano; (*tool*) pialla; (*ART, MATH etc*) piano ♦ *adj* piano(a), piatto(a) ♦ *vt* (*with tool*) piallare

planet ['plænɪt] *n* pianeta *m*

plank [plæŋk] *n* tavola, asse *f*

planner ['plænə*] *n* pianificatore/trice

planning ['plænɪŋ] *n* progettazione *f*; **family ~** pianificazione *f* delle nascite; **~ permission** *n* permesso di costruzione

plant [plɑːnt] *n* pianta; (*machinery*) impianto; (*factory*) fabbrica ♦ *vt* piantare; (*bomb*) mettere

plantation [plæn'teɪʃən] *n* piantagione *f*

plaque [plæk] *n* placca

plaster ['plɑːstə*] *n* intonaco; (*also: ~ of Paris*) gesso; (*BRIT: also: sticking ~*) cerotto ♦ *vt* intonacare; ingessare; (*cover*): **to ~ with** coprire di; **~ed** (*inf*) *adj* ubriaco(a) fradicio(a)

plastic ['plæstɪk] *n* plastica ♦ *adj* (*made of ~*) di *or* in plastica; **~ bag** *n* sacchetto di plastica

Plasticine ['plæstɪsiːn] ® *n* plastilina ®

plastic surgery *n* chirurgia plastica

plate [pleɪt] *n* (*dish*) piatto; (*in book*) tavola; (*dental*) *n* dentiera; **gold/silver ~** vasellame *m* d'oro/d'argento

plateau ['plætəʊ] (*pl* **~s** *or* **~x**) *n* altipiano

plateaux ['plætəʊz] *npl of* **plateau**

plate glass *n* vetro piano

platform ['plætfɔːm] *n* (*stage, at meeting*) palco; (*RAIL*) marciapiede *m*; (*BRIT: of bus*) piattaforma

platinum ['plætɪnəm] *n* platino

platitude ['plætɪtjuːd] *n* luogo comune

platoon [plə'tuːn] *n* plotone *m*

platter ['plætə*] *n* piatto

plausible ['plɔːzɪbl] *adj* plausibile, credibile; (*person*) convincente

play [pleɪ] *n* gioco; (*THEATRE*) commedia ♦ *vt* (*game*) giocare a; (*team, opponent*) giocare contro; (*instrument, piece of music*) suonare; (*record, tape*) ascoltare; (*role, part*) interpretare; **to ~ safe** giocare sul sicuro; **~ down** *vt* minimizzare; **~ up** *vi* (*cause trouble*) fare i capricci; **~boy** *n* playboy *m inv*; **~er** *n* giocatore/trice; (*THEATRE*) attore/trice; (*MUS*) musicista *m/f*; **~ful** *adj* giocoso(a); **~ground** *n* (*in school*) cortile *m* per la ricreazione; (*in park*) parco *m* giochi *inv*; **~group** *n* giardino d'infanzia; **~ing card** *n* carta da gioco; **~ing field** *n* campo sportivo;

~**mate** n compagno/a di gioco; ~**-off** n (SPORT) bella; ~**pen** n box m inv; ~**thing** n giocattolo; ~**time** n (SCOL) ricreazione f; ~**wright** n drammaturgo/a

plc abbr (= public limited company) società per azioni a responsabilità limitata quotata in borsa

plea [pli:] n (request) preghiera, domanda; (LAW) (argomento di) difesa; ~ **bargaining** n (LAW) patteggiamento (della pena)

plead [pli:d] vt patrocinare; (give as excuse) addurre a pretesto ♦ vi (LAW) perorare la causa; (beg): **to ~ with sb** implorare qn

pleasant ['plɛznt] adj piacevole, gradevole; ~**ries** npl (polite remarks): **to exchange ~ries** scambiarsi i convenevoli

please [pli:z] excl per piacere!, per favore!; (acceptance): **yes, ~** sì, grazie ♦ vt piacere a ♦ vi piacere; (think fit): **do as you ~** faccia come le pare; ~ **yourself!** come ti (or le) pare!; ~**d** adj: ~**d** (with) contento(a) (di); ~**d to meet you!** piacere!; **pleasing** adj piacevole, che fa piacere

pleasure ['plɛʒə*] n piacere m; "**it's a ~**" "prego"; ~ **boat** n imbarcazione f da diporto

pleat [pli:t] n piega

pledge [plɛdʒ] n pegno; (promise) promessa ♦ vt impegnare; promettere

plentiful ['plɛntɪful] adj abbondante, copioso(a)

plenty ['plɛntɪ] n: ~ **of** tanto(a), molto(a); un'abbondanza di

pleurisy ['pluərɪsɪ] n pleurite f

pliable ['plaɪəbl] adj flessibile; (fig: person) malleabile

pliant [plaɪənt] adj = **pliable**

pliers ['plaɪəz] npl pinza

plight [plaɪt] n situazione f critica

plimsolls ['plɪmsəlz] (BRIT) npl scarpe fpl da tennis

plinth [plɪnθ] n plinto; piedistallo

plod [plɔd] vi camminare a stento; (fig) sgobbare

plonk [plɔŋk] (inf) n (BRIT: wine) vino da poco ♦ vt: **to ~ sth down** buttare giù qc

bruscamente

plot [plɔt] n congiura, cospirazione f; (of story, play) trama; (of land) lotto ♦ vt (mark out) fare la pianta di; rilevare; (: diagram etc) tracciare; (conspire) congiurare, cospirare ♦ vi congiurare; ~**ter** n (instrument) plotter m inv

plough [plaʊ] (US **plow**) n aratro ♦ vt (earth) arare; **to ~ money into** (company etc) investire denaro in; ~ **through** vt fus (snow etc) procedere a fatica in; ~**man's lunch** n (BRIT) n pasto a base di pane, formaggio e birra

ploy [plɔɪ] n stratagemma m

pluck [plʌk] vt (fruit) cogliere; (musical instrument) pizzicare; (bird) spennare; (hairs) togliere ♦ n coraggio, fegato; **to ~ up courage** farsi coraggio

plug [plʌg] n tappo; (ELEC) spina; (AUT: also: spark(ing) ~) candela ♦ vt (hole) tappare; (inf: advertise) spingere; ~ **in** vt (ELEC) attaccare a una presa

plum [plʌm] n (fruit) susina ♦ cpd: ~ **job** (inf) impiego ottimo or favoloso

plumb [plʌm] vt: **to ~ the depths** (fig) toccare il fondo

plumber ['plʌmə*] n idraulico

plumbing ['plʌmɪŋ] n (trade) lavoro di idraulico; (piping) tubature fpl

plume [plu:m] n piuma, penna; (decorative) pennacchio

plummet ['plʌmɪt] vi: **to ~ (down)** cadere a piombo

plump [plʌmp] adj grassoccio(a) ♦ vi: **to ~ for** (inf: choose) decidersi per; ~ **up** vt (cushion etc) sprimacciare

plunder ['plʌndə*] n saccheggio ♦ vt saccheggiare

plunge [plʌndʒ] n tuffo; (fig) caduta ♦ vt immergere ♦ vi (fall) cadere, precipitare; (dive) tuffarsi; **to take the ~** saltare il fosso; ~**r** n sturalavandini m inv; **plunging** adj (neckline) profondo(a)

pluperfect [plu:'pə:fɪkt] n piuccheperfetto

plural ['pluərl] adj plurale ♦ n plurale m

plus [plʌs] n (also: ~ **sign**) segno più ♦ prep più; **ten/twenty ~** più di dieci/ venti

plush [plʌʃ] *adj* lussuoso(a)

ply [plaɪ] *vt* (*a trade*) esercitare ♦ *vi* (*ship*) fare il servizio ♦ *n* (*of wool, rope*) capo; **to ~ sb with drink** dare di bere continuamente a qn; **~wood** *n* legno compensato

P.M. *n abbr* = **prime minister**

p.m. *adv abbr* (= *post meridiem*) del pomeriggio

pneumatic drill [njuˈmætɪk-] *n* martello pneumatico

pneumonia [njuːˈməʊnɪə] *n* polmonite *f*

poach [pəʊtʃ] *vt* (*cook: egg*) affogare; (: *fish*) cuocere in bianco; (*steal*) cacciare (*or* pescare) di frodo ♦ *vi* fare il bracconiere; **~er** *n* bracconiere *m*

P.O. Box *n abbr* = **Post Office Box**

pocket [ˈpɔkɪt] *n* tasca ♦ *vt* intascare; **to be out of ~** (*BRIT*) rimetterci; **~book** (*US*) *n* (*wallet*) portafoglio; **~ knife** *n* temperino; **~ money** *n* paghetta, settimana

pod [pɔd] *n* guscio

podgy [ˈpɔdʒɪ] *adj* grassoccio(a)

podiatrist [pɔˈdiːətrɪst] (*US*) *n* callista *m/f*, pedicure *m/f*

poem [ˈpəʊɪm] *n* poesia

poet [ˈpəʊɪt] *n* poeta/essa; **~ic** [-ˈɛtɪk] *adj* poetico(a); **~ laureate** *n* poeta *m* laureato (*nominato dalla Corte Reale*); **~ry** *n* poesia

poignant [ˈpɔɪnjənt] *adj* struggente

point [pɔɪnt] *n* (*gen*) punto; (*tip: of needle etc*) punta; (*in time*) punto, momento; (*SCOL*) voto; (*main idea, important part*) nocciolo; (*ELEC*) presa (di corrente); (*also: decimal ~*): **2 ~ 3 (2.3)** 2 virgola 3 (2,3) ♦ *vt* (*show*) indicare; (*gun etc*): **to ~ sth at** puntare qc contro ♦ *vi*: **to ~ at** mostrare a dito; **~s** *npl* (*AUT*) puntine *fpl*; (*RAIL*) scambio; **to be on the ~ of doing sth** essere sul punto di *or* stare per fare qc; **to make a ~** fare un'osservazione; **to get/miss the ~** capire/non capire; **to come to the ~** venire al fatto; **there's no ~ (in doing)** è inutile (fare); **~ out** *vt* far notare; **~ to** *vt fus* indicare; (*fig*) dimostrare; **~-blank** *adv* (*also: at ~-blank range*) a bruciapelo; (*fig*) categoricamente; **~ed** *adj* (*shape*) aguzzo(a), appuntito(a);

(*remark*) specifico(a); **~edly** *adv* in maniera inequivocabile; **~er** *n* (*needle*) lancetta; (*fig*) indicazione *f*, consiglio; **~less** *adj* inutile, vano(a); **~ of view** *n* punto di vista

poise [pɔɪz] *n* (*composure*) portamento; **~d** *adj*: **to be ~d to do** tenersi pronto(a) a fare

poison [ˈpɔɪzn] *n* veleno ♦ *vt* avvelenare; **~ous** *adj* velenoso(a)

poke [pəʊk] *vt* (*fire*) attizzare; (*jab with finger, stick etc*) punzecchiare; (*put*): **to ~ sth in(to)** spingere qc dentro; **~ about** *vi* frugare

poker [ˈpəʊkə*] *n* attizzatoio; (*CARDS*) poker *m*

poky [ˈpəʊkɪ] *adj* piccolo(a) e stretto(a)

Poland [ˈpəʊlənd] *n* Polonia

polar [ˈpəʊlə*] *adj* polare; **~ bear** *n* orso bianco

Pole [pəʊl] *n* polacco/a

pole [pəʊl] *n* (*of wood*) palo; (*ELEC, GEO*) polo; **~ bean** (*US*) *n* (*runner bean*) fagiolino; **~ vault** *n* salto con l'asta

police [pəˈliːs] *n* polizia ♦ *vt* mantenere l'ordine in; **~ car** *n* macchina della polizia; **~man** *n* poliziotto, agente *m* di polizia; **~ station** *n* posto di polizia; **~woman** *n* donna *f* poliziotto *inv*

policy [ˈpɔlɪsɪ] *n* politica; (*also: insurance ~*) polizza (d'assicurazione)

polio [ˈpəʊlɪəʊ] *n* polio *f*

Polish [ˈpəʊlɪʃ] *adj* polacco(a) ♦ *n* (*LING*) polacco

polish [ˈpɔlɪʃ] *n* (*for shoes*) lucido; (*for floor*) cera; (*for nails*) smalto; (*shine*) lucentezza, lustro; (*fig: refinement*) raffinatezza ♦ *vt* lucidare; (*fig: improve*) raffinare; **~ off** *vt* (*work*) sbrigare; (*food*) mangiarsi; **~ed** *adj* (*fig*) raffinato(a)

polite [pəˈlaɪt] *adj* cortese; **~ness** *n* cortesia

political [pəˈlɪtɪkl] *adj* politico(a); **~ly** *adv* politicamente

politician [pɔlɪˈtɪʃən] *n* politico

politics [ˈpɔlɪtɪks] *n* politica ♦ *npl* (*views, policies*) idee *fpl* politiche

poll [pəʊl] *n* scrutinio; (*votes cast*) voti *mpl*; (*also: opinion ~*) sondaggio

(d'opinioni) ♦ *vt* ottenere
pollen ['pɒlən] *n* polline *m*
polling day ['pəʊlɪŋ-] (*BRIT*) *n* giorno delle elezioni
polling station ['pəʊlɪŋ-] (*BRIT*) *n* sezione *f* elettorale
pollute [pə'luːt] *vt* inquinare
pollution [pə'luːʃən] *n* inquinamento
polo ['pəʊləʊ] *n* polo; **~-necked** *adj* a collo alto risvoltato; **~ shirt** *n* polo *f inv*
polyester [pɒlɪ'ɛstə*] *n* poliestere *m*
polystyrene [pɒlɪ'staɪriːn] *n* polistirolo
polytechnic [pɒlɪ'tɛknɪk] *n* (*college*) *istituto superiore ad indirizzo tecnologico*
polythene ['pɒliθiːn] *n* politene *m*; **~ bag** *n* sacco di plastica
pomegranate ['pɒmɪgrænɪt] *n* melagrana
pomp [pɒmp] *n* pompa, fasto
pompom ['pɒmpɒm] *n* pompon *m inv*
pompon ['pɒmpɒn] *n* = **pompom**
pompous ['pɒmpəs] *adj* pomposo(a)
pond [pɒnd] *n* pozza, stagno
ponder ['pɒndə*] *vt* ponderare, riflettere su; **~ous** *adj* ponderoso(a), pesante
pong [pɒŋ] (*BRIT*: *inf*) *n* puzzo
pony ['pəʊnɪ] *n* pony *m inv*; **~tail** *n* coda di cavallo; **~ trekking** (*BRIT*) *n* escursione *f* a cavallo
poodle ['puːdl] *n* barboncino, barbone *m*
pool [puːl] *n* (*puddle*) pozza; (*pond*) stagno; (*also: swimming ~*) piscina; (*fig: of light*) cerchio; (*billiards*) *specie di biliardo a buca* ♦ *vt* mettere in comune; **~s** *npl* (*football ~s*) ≈ totocalcio; **typing ~** servizio comune di dattilografia
poor [puə*] *adj* povero(a); (*mediocre*) mediocre, cattivo(a) ♦ *npl*: **the ~** i poveri; **~ in** povero(a) di; **~ly** *adv* poveramente, male ♦ *adj* indisposto(a), malato(a)
pop [pɒp] *n* (*noise*) schiocco; (*MUS*) musica pop; (*drink*) bibita gasata; (*US: inf: father*) babbo ♦ *vt* (*put*) mettere (in fretta) ♦ *vi* scoppiare; (*cork*) schioccare; **~ in** *vi* passare; **~ out** *vi* fare un salto fuori; **~ up** *vi* apparire, sorgere; **~corn** *n* pop-corn *m*
pope [pəʊp] *n* papa *m*
poplar ['pɒplə*] *n* pioppo

popper ['pɒpə*] *n* bottone *m* a pressione
poppy ['pɒpɪ] *n* papavero
popsicle ['pɒpsɪkl] (*US*: ®) *n* (*ice lolly*) ghiacciolo
populace ['pɒpjʊlɪs] *n* popolino
popular ['pɒpjʊlə*] *adj* popolare; (*fashionable*) in voga; **~ity** [-'lærɪtɪ] *n* popolarità; **~ize** *vt* divulgare; (*science*) volgarizzare
population [pɒpjʊ'leɪʃən] *n* popolazione *f*
porcelain ['pɔːslɪn] *n* porcellana
porch [pɔːtʃ] *n* veranda
porcupine ['pɔːkjupaɪn] *n* porcospino
pore [pɔː*] *n* poro ♦ *vi*: **to ~ over** essere immerso(a) in
pork [pɔːk] *n* carne *f* di maiale
pornographic [pɔːnə'græfɪk] *adj* pornografico(a)
pornography [pɔː'nɒgrəfɪ] *n* pornografia
porpoise ['pɔːpəs] *n* focena
porridge ['pɒrɪdʒ] *n* porridge *m*
port [pɔːt] *n* (*gen, wine*) porto; (*NAUT*: *left side*) babordo; **~ of call** (porto di) scalo
portable ['pɔːtəbl] *adj* portatile
porter ['pɔːtə*] *n* (*for luggage*) facchino, portabagagli *m inv*; (*doorkeeper*) portiere *m*, portinaio
portfolio [pɔːt'fəʊlɪəʊ] *n* (*case*) cartella; (*POL, FINANCE*) portafoglio; (*of artist*) raccolta dei propri lavori
porthole ['pɔːthəʊl] *n* oblò *m inv*
portion ['pɔːʃən] *n* porzione *f*
portly ['pɔːtlɪ] *adj* corpulento(a)
portrait ['pɔːtreɪt] *n* ritratto
portray [pɔː'treɪ] *vt* fare il ritratto di; (*character on stage*) rappresentare; (*in writing*) ritrarre
Portugal ['pɔːtjugl] *n* Portogallo
Portuguese [pɔːtju'giːz] *adj* portoghese ♦ *n inv* portoghese *m/f*; (*LING*) portoghese *m*
pose [pəʊz] *n* posa ♦ *vi* posare; (*pretend*): **to ~ as** atteggiarsi a, posare a ♦ *vt* porre
posh [pɒʃ] (*inf*) *adj* elegante; (*family*) per bene
position [pə'zɪʃən] *n* posizione *f*; (*job*) posto ♦ *vt* sistemare
positive ['pɒzɪtɪv] *adj* positivo(a); (*certain*) sicuro(a), certo(a); (*definite*)

preciso(a); definitivo(a)
posse ['pɔsɪ] (*US*) *n* drappello
possess [pə'zɛs] *vt* possedere; **~ion**
[pə'zɛʃən] *n* possesso; **~ions** *npl*
(*belongings*) beni *mpl*; **~ive** *adj*
possessivo(a)
possibility [pɔsɪ'bɪlɪtɪ] *n* possibilità *f inv*
possible ['pɔsɪbl] *adj* possibile; **as big as
~** il più grande possibile
possibly ['pɔsɪblɪ] *adv* (*perhaps*) forse; **if
you ~ can** se le è possibile; **I cannot ~
come** proprio non posso venire
post [pəust] *n* (*BRIT*) posta; (: *collection*)
levata; (*job, situation*) posto; (*MIL*)
postazione *f*; (*pole*) palo ♦ *vt* (*BRIT*: *send by
post*) impostare; (: *appoint*): **to ~ to**
assegnare a; **~age** *n* affrancatura; **~age
stamp** *n* francobollo; **~al order** *n* vaglia
m inv postale; **~box** (*BRIT*) *n* cassetta
postale; **~card** *n* cartolina; **~ code** (*BRIT*)
n codice *m* (di avviamento) postale
poster ['pəustə*] *n* manifesto, affisso
poste restante [pəust'rɛstɑ̃:nt] (*BRIT*) *n*
fermo posta *m*
postgraduate ['pəust'grædjuət] *n* lau-
reato/a che continua gli studi
posthumous ['pɔstjuməs] *adj*
postumo(a)
postman ['pəustmən] *n* postino
postmark ['pəustmɑ:k] *n* bollo *or* timbro
postale
post-mortem [-'mɔ:təm] *n* autopsia
post office *n* (*building*) ufficio postale;
(*organization*): **the Post Office** ≈ le Poste
e Telecomunicazioni; **Post Office Box** *n*
casella postale
postpone [pəs'pəun] *vt* rinviare
postscript ['pəustskrɪpt] *n* poscritto
posture ['pɔstʃə*] *n* portamento; (*pose*)
posa, atteggiamento
postwar ['pəust'wɔ:*] *adj* del dopoguerra
posy ['pəuzɪ] *n* mazzetto di fiori
pot [pɔt] *n* (*for cooking*) pentola,
casseruola; (*tea~*) teiera; (*coffee~*)
caffettiera; (*for plants, jam*) vaso; (*inf*:
marijuana) erba ♦ *vt* (*plant*) piantare in
vaso; **a ~ of tea for two** tè per due; **to go
to ~** (*inf*: *work, performance*) andare in
malora

potato [pə'teɪtəu] (*pl* **~es**) *n* patata; **~
peeler** *n* sbucciapatate *m inv*
potent ['pəutnt] *adj* potente, forte
potential [pə'tɛnʃl] *adj* potenziale ♦ *n*
possibilità *fpl*
pothole ['pɔthəul] *n* (*in road*) buca; (*BRIT*:
underground) caverna; **potholing** (*BRIT*)
n: **to go potholing** fare speleologia
potluck [pɔt'lʌk] *n*: **to take ~** tentare la
sorte
potted ['pɔtɪd] *adj* (*food*) in conserva;
(*plant*) in vaso; (*account etc*) condensato(a)
potter ['pɔtə*] *n* vasaio ♦ *vi*: **to ~
around**, **~ about** (*BRIT*) lavoracchiare; **~y**
n ceramiche *fpl*; (*factory*) fabbrica di
ceramiche
potty ['pɔtɪ] *adj* (*inf*: *mad*) tocco(a) ♦ *n*
(*child's*) vasino
pouch [pautʃ] *n* borsa; (*ZOOL*) marsupio
poultry ['pəultrɪ] *n* pollame *m*
pounce [pauns] *vi*: **to ~ (on)** piombare
(su)
pound [paund] *n* (*weight*) libbra; (*money*)
(lira) sterlina ♦ *vt* (*beat*) battere; (*crush*)
pestare, polverizzare ♦ *vi* (*beat*) battere,
martellare; **~ sterling** *n* sterlina (inglese)
pour [pɔ:*] *vt* versare ♦ *vi* riversarsi;
(*rain*) piovere a dirotto; **~ away** *vt*
vuotare; **~ in** *vi* affluire in gran quantità;
~ off *vt* vuotare; **~ out** *vi* (*people*) uscire
a fiumi ♦ *vt* vuotare; versare; (*fig*)
sfogare; **~ing** *adj*: **~ing rain** pioggia
torrenziale
pout [paut] *vi* sporgere le labbra; fare il
broncio
poverty ['pɔvətɪ] *n* povertà, miseria; **~-
stricken** *adj* molto povero(a), misero(a)
powder ['paudə*] *n* polvere *f* ♦ *vt*: **to ~
one's face** incipriarsi il viso; **~ compact**
n portacipria *m inv*; **~ed milk** *n* latte *m*
in polvere; **~ puff** *n* piumino della cipria;
~ room *n* toilette *f inv* (per signore)
power ['pauə*] *n* (*strength*) potenza,
forza; (*ability, POL*: *of party, leader*) potere
m; (*ELEC*) corrente *f*; **to be in ~** (*POL etc*)
essere al potere; **~ cut** (*BRIT*) *n*
interruzione *f or* mancanza di corrente;
~ed *adj*: **~ed by** azionato(a) da; **~ failure**
n interruzione *f* della corrente elettrica;

~ful adj potente, forte; **~less** adj
impotente; **~less to do** impossibilitato(a)
a fare; **~ point** (BRIT) n presa di corrente;
~ station n centrale f elettrica
p.p. abbr (= per procurationem): **~ J.
Smith** per J. Smith; (= pages) p.p.
PR abbr = **public relations**
practicable ['præktɪkəbl] adj (scheme)
praticabile
practical ['præktɪkl] adj pratico(a); **~ity**
[-'kælɪtɪ] (no pl) n (of situation etc) lato
pratico; **~ joke** n beffa; **~ly** adv
praticamente
practice ['præktɪs] n pratica; (of
profession) esercizio; (at football etc)
allenamento; (business) gabinetto;
clientela ♦ vt, vi (US) = **practise**; **in ~** (in
reality) in pratica; **out of ~** fuori
esercizio
practise ['præktɪs] (US **practice**) vt (work
at: piano, one's backhand etc) esercitarsi
a; (train for: skiing, running etc) allenarsi
a; (a sport, religion) praticare; (method)
usare; (profession) esercitare ♦ vi
esercitarsi; (train) allenarsi; (lawyer,
doctor) esercitare; **practising** adj
(Christian etc) praticante; (lawyer) che
esercita la professione
practitioner [præk'tɪʃənə*] n
professionista m/f
pragmatic [præg'mætɪk] adj
pragmatico(a)
prairie ['prɛərɪ] n prateria
praise [preɪz] n elogio, lode f ♦ vt
elogiare, lodare; **~worthy** adj lodevole
pram [præm] (BRIT) n carrozzina
prance [prɑːns] vi (person) camminare
pavoneggiandosi; (horse) caracollare
prank [præŋk] n burla
prawn [prɔːn] n gamberetto
pray [preɪ] vi pregare
prayer [prɛə*] n preghiera
preach [priːtʃ] vt, vi predicare
precarious [prɪ'kɛərɪəs] adj precario(a)
precaution [prɪ'kɔːʃən] n precauzione f
precede [prɪ'siːd] vt precedere
precedent ['prɛsɪdənt] n precedente m
precept ['priːsɛpt] n precetto
precinct ['priːsɪŋkt] n (US) circoscrizione

f; **~s** npl (of building) zona recintata;
pedestrian ~ (BRIT) zona pedonale;
shopping ~ (BRIT) centro commerciale
(chiuso al traffico)
precious ['prɛʃəs] adj prezioso(a)
precipitate [prɪ'sɪpɪteɪt] vt precipitare
precise [prɪ'saɪs] adj preciso(a); **~ly** adv
precisamente
preclude [prɪ'kluːd] vt precludere,
impedire
precocious [prɪ'kəʊʃəs] adj precoce
precondition [priːkən'dɪʃən] n
condizione f necessaria
predecessor ['priːdɪsɛsə*] n predeces-
sore/a
predicament [prɪ'dɪkəmənt] n situazione
f difficile
predict [prɪ'dɪkt] vt predire; **~able** adj
prevedibile
predominantly [prɪ'dɔmɪnəntlɪ] adv in
maggior parte; soprattutto
predominate [prɪ'dɔmɪneɪt] vi
predominare
pre-empt [priː'ɛmpt] vt pregiudicare
preen [priːn] vt: **to ~ itself** (bird) lisciarsi
le penne; **to ~ o.s.** agghindarsi
prefab ['priːfæb] n casa prefabbricata
preface ['prɛfəs] n prefazione f
prefect ['priːfɛkt] n (BRIT: in school)
studente/essa con funzioni disciplinari,
(French etc, Admin) prefetto
prefer [prɪ'fɜː*] vt preferire; **to ~ doing**
or **to do** preferire fare; **~ably** ['prɛfrəblɪ]
adv preferibilmente; **~ence** ['prɛfrəns] n
preferenza; **~ential** [prɛfə'rɛnʃəl] adj
preferenziale
prefix ['priːfɪks] n prefisso
pregnancy ['prɛgnənsɪ] n gravidanza
pregnant ['prɛgnənt] adj incinta af
prehistoric ['priːhɪs'tɔrɪk] adj
preistorico(a)
prejudice ['prɛdʒʊdɪs] n pregiudizio;
(harm) torto, danno; **~d** adj: **~d (against)**
prevenuto(a) (contro); **~d (in favour of)**
ben disposto(a) (verso)
preliminary [prɪ'lɪmɪnərɪ] adj
preliminare
premarital ['priː'mærɪtl] adj
prematrimoniale

premature ['prɛmətʃuə*] *adj*
prematuro(a)

premier ['prɛmɪə*] *adj* primo(a) ♦ *n* (*POL*)
primo ministro

première ['prɛmɪɛə*] *n* prima

premise ['prɛmɪs] *n* premessa; **~s** *npl* (*of
business, institution*) locale *m*; **on the ~s**
sul posto

premium ['priːmɪəm] *n* premio; **to be at
a ~** essere ricercatissimo; **~ bond** (*BRIT*)
n obbligazione *f* a premio

premonition [prɛmə'nɪʃən] *n*
premonizione *f*

preoccupied [priː'ɔkjupaɪd] *adj*
preoccupato(a)

prep [prɛp] *n* (*SCOL: study*) studio

prepaid [priː'peɪd] *adj* pagato(a) in
anticipo

preparation [prɛpə'reɪʃən] *n*
preparazione *f*; **~s** *npl* (*for trip, war*)
preparativi *mpl*

preparatory [prɪ'pærətərɪ] *adj*
preparatorio(a); **~ school** *n* scuola
elementare privata

prepare [prɪ'pɛə*] *vt* preparare ♦ *vi*: **to ~
for** prepararsi a; **~d to** pronto(a) a

preposition [prɛpə'zɪʃən] *n* preposizione
f

preposterous [prɪ'pɔstərəs] *adj*
assurdo(a)

prep school *n* = **preparatory school**

prerequisite [priː'rɛkwɪzɪt] *n* requisito
indispensabile

prescribe [prɪ'skraɪb] *vt* (*MED*)
prescrivere

prescription [prɪ'skrɪpʃən] *n*
prescrizione *f*; (*MED*) ricetta

presence ['prɛzns] *n* presenza; **~ of
mind** presenza di spirito

present [*adj, n* 'prɛznt, *vb* prɪ'zɛnt] *adj*
presente; (*wife, residence, job*) attuale ♦ *n*
(*actuality*): **the ~** il presente; (*gift*) regalo
♦ *vt* presentare; (*give*): **to ~ sb with sth**
offrire qc a qn; **to give sb a ~** fare un
regalo a qn; **at ~** al momento; **~ation**
[-'teɪʃən] *n* presentazione *f*; (*ceremony*)
consegna ufficiale; **~-day** *adj* attuale,
d'oggigiorno; **~er** *n* (*RADIO, TV*)
presentatore/trice; **~ly** *adv* (*soon*) fra

poco, presto; (*at present*) al momento

preservative [prɪ'zəːvətɪv] *n*
conservante *m*

preserve [prɪ'zəːv] *vt* (*keep safe*)
preservare, proteggere; (*maintain*)
conservare; (*food*) mettere in conserva
♦ *n* (*often pl: jam*) marmellata; (: *fruit*)
frutta sciroppata

preside [prɪ'zaɪd] *vi*: **to ~ (over)**
presiedere (a)

president ['prɛzɪdənt] *n* presidente *m*;
~ial [-'dɛnʃl] *adj* presidenziale

press [prɛs] *n* (*newspapers etc*): **the P~** la
stampa; (*tool, machine*) pressa; (*for wine*)
torchio ♦ *vt* (*push*) premere, pigiare;
(*squeeze*) spremere; (: *hand*) stringere;
(*clothes: iron*) stirare; (*pursue*) incalzare;
(*insist*): **to ~ sth on sb** far accettare qc da
qn ♦ *vi* premere; accalcare; **we are ~ed
for time** ci manca il tempo; **to ~ for sth**
insistere per avere qc; **~ on** *vi*
continuare; **~ conference** *n* conferenza *f*
stampa *inv*; **~ing** *adj* urgente; **~ stud**
(*BRIT*) *n* bottone *m* a pressione; **~-up** (*BRIT*)
n flessione *f* sulle braccia

pressure ['prɛʃə*] *n* pressione *f*; **to put ~
on sb (to do)** mettere qn sotto pressione
(affinché faccia); **~ cooker** *n* pentola a
pressione; **~ gauge** *n* manometro; **~
group** *n* gruppo di pressione

prestige [prɛs'tiːʒ] *n* prestigio

presumably [prɪ'zjuːməblɪ] *adv*
presumibilmente

presume [prɪ'zjuːm] *vt* supporre

presumption [prɪ'zʌmpʃən] *n*
presunzione *f*

presumptuous [prɪ'zʌmpʃəs] *adj*
presuntuoso(a)

pretence [prɪ'tɛns] (*US* **pretense**) *n*
(*claim*) pretesa; **to make a ~ of doing** far
finta di fare; **under false ~s** con
l'inganno

pretend [prɪ'tɛnd] *vt* (*feign*) fingere ♦ *vi*
far finta; **to ~ to do** far finta di fare

pretense [prɪ'tɛns] (*US*) *n* = **pretence**

pretentious [prɪ'tɛnʃəs] *adj*
pretenzioso(a)

pretext ['priːtɛkst] *n* pretesto

pretty ['prɪtɪ] *adj* grazioso(a), carino(a) ♦

adv abbastanza, assai

prevail [prɪ'veɪl] *vi* (*win, be usual*) prevalére; (*persuade*): **to ~ (up)on sb to do** persuadere qn a fare; **~ing** *adj* dominante

prevalent ['prɛvələnt] *adj* (*belief*) predominante; (*customs*) diffuso(a); (*fashion*) corrente; (*disease*) comune

prevent [prɪ'vɛnt] *vt*: **to ~ sb from doing** impedire a qn di fare; **to ~ sth from happening** impedire che qc succeda; **~ative** *adj* = **~ive**; **~ion** [-'vɛnʃən] *n* prevenzione *f*; **~ive** *adj* preventivo(a)

preview ['priːvjuː] *n* (*of film*) anteprima

previous ['priːvɪəs] *adj* precedente; anteriore; **~ly** *adv* prima

prewar ['priːwɔː*] *adj* anteguerra *inv*

prey [preɪ] *n* preda ♦ *vi*: **to ~ on** far preda di; **it was ~ing on his mind** lo stava ossessionando

price [praɪs] *n* prezzo ♦ *vt* (*goods*) fissare il prezzo di; valutare; **~less** *adj* inapprezzabile; **~ list** *n* listino (dei) prezzi

prick [prɪk] *n* puntura ♦ *vt* pungere; **to ~ up one's ears** drizzare gli orecchi

prickle ['prɪkl] *n* (*of plant*) spina; (*sensation*) pizzicore *m*

prickly ['prɪklɪ] *adj* spinoso(a), **~ heat** *n* sudamina

pride [praɪd] *n* orgoglio; superbia ♦ *vt*: **to ~ o.s. on** essere orgoglioso(a) di; vantarsi di

priest [priːst] *n* prete *m*, sacerdote *m*; **~hood** *n* sacerdozio

prig [prɪg] *n*: **he's a ~** è compiaciuto di se stesso

prim [prɪm] *adj* pudico(a); contegnoso(a)

primarily ['praɪmərɪlɪ] *adv* principalmente, essenzialmente

primary ['praɪmərɪ] *adj* primario(a); (*first in importance*) primo(a) ♦ *n* (*US: election*) primarie *fpl*; **~ school** (*BRIT*) *n* scuola elementare

prime [praɪm] *adj* primario(a), fondamentale; (*excellent*) di prima qualità ♦ *vt* (*wood*) preparare; (*fig*) mettere al corrente ♦ *n*: **in the ~ of life** nel fiore

della vita; **P~ Minister** *n* primo ministro

primeval [praɪ'miːvl] *adj* primitivo(a)

primitive ['prɪmɪtɪv] *adj* primitivo(a)

primrose ['prɪmrəʊz] *n* primavera

primus (stove) ['praɪməs(-)] ® (*BRIT*) *n* fornello a petrolio

prince [prɪns] *n* principe *m*

princess [prɪn'sɛs] *n* principessa

principal ['prɪnsɪpl] *adj* principale ♦ *n* (*headmaster*) preside *m*

principle ['prɪnsɪpl] *n* principio; **in ~** in linea di principio; **on ~** per principio

print [prɪnt] *n* (*mark*) impronta; (*letters*) caratteri *mpl*; (*fabric*) tessuto stampato; (*ART, PHOT*) stampa ♦ *vt* imprimere; (*publish*) stampare, pubblicare; (*write in capitals*) scrivere in stampatello; **out of ~** esaurito(a); **~ed matter** *n* stampe *fpl*; **~er** *n* tipografo; (*machine*) stampante *f*; **~ing** *n* stampa; **~-out** *n* (*COMPUT*) tabulato

prior ['praɪə*] *adj* precedente; (*claim etc*) più importante; **~ to doing** prima di fare

priority [praɪ'ɔrɪtɪ] *n* priorità *f inv*; precedenza

prise [praɪz] *vt*: **to ~ open** forzare

prison ['prɪzn] *n* prigione *f* ♦ *cpd* (*system*) carcerario(a); (*conditions, food*) nelle *or* delle prigioni; **~er** *n* prigioniero/a

pristine ['prɪstiːn] *adj* immacolato(a)

privacy ['prɪvəsɪ] *n* solitudine *f*, intimità

private ['praɪvɪt] *adj* privato(a); personale ♦ *n* soldato semplice; "**~**" (*on envelope*) "riservata"; (*on door*) "privato"; **in ~** in privato; **~ enterprise** *n* iniziativa privata; **~ eye** *n* investigatore *m* privato; **~ly** *adv* in privato; (*within oneself*) dentro di sé; **~ property** *n* proprietà privata; **privatize** *vt* privatizzare

privet ['prɪvɪt] *n* ligustro

privilege ['prɪvɪlɪdʒ] *n* privilegio

privy ['prɪvɪ] *adj*: **to be ~ to** essere al corrente di

prize [praɪz] *n* premio ♦ *adj* (*example, idiot*) perfetto(a); (*bull, novel*) premiato(a) ♦ *vt* apprezzare, pregiare; **~ giving** *n* premiazione *f*; **~winner** *n* premiato/a

pro [prəʊ] *n* (*SPORT*) professionista *m/f* ♦ *prep* pro; **the ~s and cons** il pro e il contro

probability [prɔbə'bɪlɪtɪ] *n* probabilità *f inv*; **in all ~** con tutta probabilità

probable ['prɔbəbl] *adj* probabile; **probably** *adv* probabilmente

probation [prə'beɪʃən] *n*: **on ~** (*employee*) in prova; (*LAW*) in libertà vigilata

probe [prəub] *n* (*MED, SPACE*) sonda; (*enquiry*) indagine *f*, investigazione *f* ♦ *vt* sondare, esplorare; indagare

problem ['prɔbləm] *n* problema *m*

procedure [prə'si:dʒə*] *n* (*ADMIN, LAW*) procedura; (*method*) metodo, procedimento

proceed [prə'si:d] *vi* (*go forward*) avanzare, andare avanti; (*go about it*) procedere; (*continue*): **to ~ (with)** continuare; **to ~ to** andare a; passare a; **to ~ to do** mettersi a fare; **~ings** *npl* misure *fpl*; (*LAW*) riunione *f*; (*records*) rendiconti *mpl*, atti *mpl*; **~s** ['prəusi:dz] *npl* profitto, incasso

process ['prəusɛs] *n* processo; (*method*) metodo, sistema *m* ♦ *vt* trattare; (*information*) elaborare; **~ing** *n* trattamento; elaborazione *f*

procession [prə'sɛʃən] *n* processione *f*, corteo; **funeral ~** corteo funebre

pro-choice [prəu'tʃɔɪs] *adj* per la libertà di scelta di gravidanza

proclaim [prə'kleɪm] *vt* proclamare, dichiarare

procrastinate [prəu'kræstɪneɪt] *vi* procrastinare

prod [prɔd] *vt* dare un colpetto a; pungolare ♦ *n* colpetto

prodigal ['prɔdɪgl] *adj* prodigo(a)

prodigy ['prɔdɪdʒɪ] *n* prodigio

produce [*n* 'prɔdju:s, *vb* prə'dju:s] *n* (*AGR*) prodotto, prodotti *mpl* ♦ *vt* produrre; (*to show*) esibire, mostrare; (*cause*) cagionare, causare; **~r** *n* (*THEATRE*) regista *m/f*; (*AGR, CINEMA*) produttore *m*

product ['prɔdʌkt] *n* prodotto

production [prə'dʌkʃən] *n* produzione *f*; **~ line** *n* catena di lavorazione

productivity [prɔdʌk'tɪvɪtɪ] *n* produttività

profane [prə'feɪn] *adj* profano(a); (*language*) empio(a)

profess [prə'fɛs] *vt* (*claim*) dichiarare; (*opinion etc*) professare

profession [prə'fɛʃən] *n* professione *f*; **~al** *n* professionista *m/f* ♦ *adj* professionale; (*work*) da professionista

professor [prə'fɛsə*] *n* professore *m* (*titolare di una cattedra*); (*US*) professore/essa

proficiency [prə'fɪʃənsɪ] *n* competenza, abilità

profile ['prəufaɪl] *n* profilo

profit ['prɔfɪt] *n* profitto; beneficio ♦ *vi*: **to ~ (by *or* from)** approfittare (di); **~ability** [-'bɪlɪtɪ] *n* redditività; **~able** *adj* redditizio(a)

profound [prə'faund] *adj* profondo(a)

profusely [prə'fju:slɪ] *adv* con grande effusione

programme ['prəugræm] (*US* **program**) *n* programma *m* ♦ *vt* programmare; **~r** (*US* **programer**) *n* programmatore/trice

progress [*n* 'prəugrɛs, *vb* prə'grɛs] *n* progresso ♦ *vi* avanzare, procedere; **in ~** in corso; **to make ~** far progressi; **~ive** [-'grɛsɪv] *adj* progressivo(a); (*person*) progressista

prohibit [prə'hɪbɪt] *vt* proibire, vietare; **~ion** [prəuɪ'bɪʃən] *n* proibizione *f*, divieto; (*US*): **P~** proibizionismo; **~ive** *adj* (*price etc*) proibitivo(a)

project [*n* 'prɔdʒɛkt, *vb* prə'dʒɛkt] *n* (*plan*) piano; (*venture*) progetto; (*SCOL*) studio ♦ *vt* proiettare ♦ *vi* (*stick out*) sporgere

projectile [prə'dʒɛktaɪl] *n* proiettile *m*

projector [prə'dʒɛktə*] *n* proiettore *m*

pro-life [prəu'laɪf] *adj* per il diritto alla vita

prolific [prə'lɪfɪk] *adj* (*artist etc*) fecondo(a)

prolong [prə'lɔŋ] *vt* prolungare

prom [prɔm] *n abbr* = **promenade**; (*US*: *ball*) ballo studentesco

promenade [prɔmə'nɑːd] *n* (*by sea*) lungomare *m*; **~ concert** *n* concerto (*con posti in piedi*)

prominent ['prɔmɪnənt] *adj* (*standing out*) prominente; (*important*) importante

promiscuous [prə'mɪskjuəs] *adj* (*sexually*) di facili costumi

promise ['prɔmɪs] *n* promessa ♦ *vt, vi* promettere; **to ~ sb sth, ~ sth to sb** promettere qc a qn; **to ~ (sb) that/to do sth** promettere (a qn) che/di fare qc; **promising** *adj* promettente

promote [prə'məʊt] *vt* promuovere; *(venture, event)* organizzare; **~r** *n* promotore/trice; *(of sporting event)* organizzatore/trice; **promotion** [-'məʊʃən] *n* promozione *f*

prompt [prɔmpt] *adj* rapido(a), svelto(a); puntuale; *(reply)* sollecito(a) ♦ *adv* *(punctually)* in punto ♦ *n* (COMPUT) prompt *m* ♦ *vt* incitare; provocare; (THEATRE) suggerire a; **to ~ sb to do** incitare qn a fare; **~ly** *adv* prontamente; puntualmente

prone [prəʊn] *adj* *(lying)* prono(a); **~ to** propenso(a) a, incline a

prong [prɔŋ] *n* rebbio, punta

pronoun ['prəʊnaʊn] *n* pronome *m*

pronounce [prə'naʊns] *vt* pronunciare

pronunciation [prənʌnsɪ'eɪʃən] *n* pronuncia

proof [pruːf] *n* prova; *(of book)* bozza; *(PHOT)* provino ♦ *adj*: **~ against** a prova di

prop [prɔp] *n* sostegno, appoggio ♦ *vt* *(also: ~ up)* sostenere, appoggiare; *(lean)*: **to ~ sth against** appoggiare qc contro *or* a

propaganda [prɔpə'gændə] *n* propaganda

propel [prə'pel] *vt* spingere (in avanti), muovere; **~ler** *n* elica

propensity [prə'pensɪtɪ] *n* tendenza

proper ['prɔpə*] *adj* *(suited, right)* adatto(a), appropriato(a); *(seemly)* decente; *(authentic)* vero(a); *(inf: real)* noun + vero(a) e proprio(a); **~ly** *adv* *(eat, study)* bene; *(behave)* come si deve; **~ noun** *n* nome *m* proprio

property ['prɔpətɪ] *n* *(things owned)* beni *mpl*; *(land, building)* proprietà *f inv*; *(CHEM etc: quality)* proprietà; **~ owner** *n* proprietario/a

prophecy ['prɔfɪsɪ] *n* profezia

prophesy ['prɔfɪsaɪ] *vt* predire

prophet ['prɔfɪt] *n* profeta *m*

proportion [prə'pɔːʃən] *n* proporzione *f*; *(share)* parte *f*; **~al** *adj* proporzionale; **~ate** *adj* proporzionato(a)

proposal [prə'pəʊzl] *n* proposta; *(plan)* progetto; *(of marriage)* proposta di matrimonio

propose [prə'pəʊz] *vt* proporre, suggerire ♦ *vi* fare una proposta di matrimonio; **to ~ to do** proporsi di fare, aver l'intenzione di fare

proposition [prɔpə'zɪʃən] *n* proposizione *f*; *(offer)* proposta

proprietor [prə'praɪətə*] *n* proprietario/a

propriety [prə'praɪətɪ] *n* *(seemliness)* decoro, rispetto delle convenienze sociali

pro rata ['prəʊ'rɑːtə] *adv* in proporzione

prose [prəʊz] *n* prosa

prosecute ['prɔsɪkjuːt] *vt* processare; **prosecution** [-'kjuːʃən] *n* processo; *(accusing side)* accusa; **prosecutor** *n* *(also: public prosecutor)* ≈ procuratore *m* della Repubblica

prospect [*n* 'prɔspekt, *vb* prə'spekt] *n* prospettiva; *(hope)* speranza ♦ *vi*: **to ~ for** cercare; **~s** *npl* *(for work etc)* prospettive *fpl*; **~ive** [-'spektɪv] *adj* possibile; futuro(a)

prospectus [prə'spektəs] *n* prospetto, programma *m*

prosperity [prɔ'sperɪtɪ] *n* prosperità

prostitute ['prɔstɪtjuːt] *n* prostituta; **male ~** uomo che si prostituisce

prostrate ['prɔstreɪt] *adj* bocconi *inv*

protect [prə'tekt] *vt* proteggere, salvaguardare; **~ion** *n* protezione *f*; **~ive** *adj* protettivo(a)

protégé ['prəʊtəʒeɪ] *n* protetto

protein ['prəʊtiːn] *n* proteina

protest [*n* 'prəʊtest, *vb* prə'test] *n* protesta ♦ *vt, vi* protestare

Protestant ['prɔtɪstənt] *adj, n* protestante *m/f*

protester [prə'testə*] *n* dimostrante *m/f*

prototype ['prəʊtətaɪp] *n* prototipo

protracted [prə'træktɪd] *adj* tirato(a) per le lunghe

protrude [prə'truːd] *vi* sporgere

proud [praʊd] *adj* fiero(a), orgoglioso(a); *(pej)* superbo(a)

prove [pruːv] *vt* provare, dimostrare ♦ *vi*:
to ~ (to be) correct *etc* risultare vero(a)
etc; to ~ o.s. mostrare le proprie capacità

proverb ['prɔvəːb] *n* proverbio

provide [prə'vaɪd] *vt* fornire, provvedere;
to ~ sb with sth fornire *or* provvedere
qn di qc; ~ for *vt fus* provvedere a;
(future event) prevedere; ~d (that) *conj*
purché + *sub*, a condizione che + *sub*

providing [prə'vaɪdɪŋ] *conj* purché + *sub*,
a condizione che + *sub*

province ['prɔvɪns] *n* provincia;
provincial [prə'vɪnʃəl] *adj* provinciale

provision [prə'vɪʒən] *n* *(supply)* riserva;
(supplying) provvista; rifornimento;
(stipulation) condizione *f*; ~s *npl* *(food)*
provviste *fpl*; ~al *adj* provvisorio(a)

proviso [prə'vaɪzəu] *n* condizione *f*

provocative [prə'vɔkətɪv] *adj*
(aggressive) provocatorio(a); *(thought-
provoking)* stimolante; *(seductive)*
provocante

provoke [prə'vəuk] *vt* provocare; incitare

prow [prau] *n* prua

prowess ['prauɪs] *n* prodezza

prowl [praul] *vi* *(also: ~ about, ~ around)*
aggirarsi ♦ *n*: to be on the ~ aggirarsi;
~er *n* tipo sospetto *(che s'aggira con
l'intenzione di rubare, aggredire etc)*

proximity [prɔk'sɪmɪtɪ] *n* prossimità

proxy ['prɔksɪ] *n*: by ~ per procura

prude [pruːd] *n* puritano/a

prudent ['pruːdnt] *adj* prudente

prudish ['pruːdɪʃ] *adj* puritano(a)

prune [pruːn] *n* prugna secca ♦ *vt* potare

pry [praɪ] *vi*: to ~ into ficcare il naso in

PS *abbr* (= *postscript*) P.S.

psalm [sɑːm] *n* salmo

pseudo- ['sjuːdəu] *prefix* pseudo...

pseudonym ['sjuːdənɪm] *n* pseudonimo

psyche ['saɪkɪ] *n* psiche *f*

psychiatric [saɪkɪ'ætrɪk] *adj*
psichiatrico(a)

psychiatrist [saɪ'kaɪətrɪst] *n* psichiatra
m/f

psychic ['saɪkɪk] *adj* *(also: ~al)*
psichico(a); *(person)* dotato(a) di qualità
telepatiche

psychoanalyst [saɪkəu'ænəlɪst] *n* psica-

nalista *m/f*

psychological [saɪkə'lɔdʒɪkl] *adj* psico-
logico(a)

psychologist [saɪ'kɔlədʒɪst] *n* psico-
logo/a

psychology [saɪ'kɔlədʒɪ] *n* psicologia

psychopath ['saɪkəupæθ] *n* psicopatico/a

P.T.O. *abbr* (= *please turn over*) v.r.

pub [pʌb] *n abbr* (= *public house*) pub *m
inv*

pubic ['pjuːbɪk] *adj* pubico(a), del pube

public ['pʌblɪk] *adj* pubblico(a) ♦ *n*
pubblico; **in ~** in pubblico; **~ address
system** *n* impianto di amplificazione

publican ['pʌblɪkən] *n* proprietario di un
pub

publication [pʌblɪ'keɪʃən] *n*
pubblicazione *f*

public: ~ company *n* società *f inv* per
azioni *(costituita tramite pubblica
sottoscrizione)*; **~ convenience** (*BRIT*) *n*
gabinetti *mpl*; **~ holiday** *n* giorno festivo,
festa nazionale; **~ house** (*BRIT*) *n* pub *m
inv*

publicity [pʌb'lɪsɪtɪ] *n* pubblicità

publicize ['pʌblɪsaɪz] *vt* rendere
pubblico(a)

publicly ['pʌblɪklɪ] *adv* pubblicamente

public: ~ opinion *n* opinione *f* pubblica;
~ relations *n* pubbliche relazioni *fpl*; **~
school** *n* (*BRIT*) scuola privata; (*US*) scuola
statale; **~-spirited** *adj* che ha senso
civico; **~ transport** *n* mezzi *mpl* pubblici

publish ['pʌblɪʃ] *vt* pubblicare; **~er** *n*
editore *m*; **~ing** *n* *(industry)* editoria; *(of
a book)* pubblicazione *f*

puce [pjuːs] *adj* marroncino rosato *inv*

pucker ['pʌkə*] *vt* corrugare

pudding ['pudɪŋ] *n* budino; (*BRIT*: *dessert*)
dolce *m*; **black ~** sanguinaccio

puddle ['pʌdl] *n* pozza, pozzanghera

puff [pʌf] *n* sbuffo ♦ *vt*: **~ one's pipe**
tirare sboccate di fumo ♦ *vi* *(pant)*
ansare; **~ out** *vt* *(cheeks etc)* gonfiare;
~ed *(inf)* *adj* *(out of breath)* senza fiato; **~
pastry** *n* pasta sfoglia; **~y** *adj* gonfio(a)

pull [pul] *n* *(tug)*: **to give sth a ~** tirare
su qc ♦ *vt* tirare; *(muscle)* strappare;
(trigger) premere ♦ *vi* tirare; **to ~ to**

pieces fare a pezzi; **to ~ one's punches** (*BOXING*) risparmiare l'avversario; **to ~ one's weight** dare il proprio contributo; **to ~ o.s. together** ricomporsi, riprendersi; **to ~ sb's leg** prendere in giro qn; **~ apart** *vt* (*break*) fare a pezzi; **~ down** *vt* (*house*) demolire; (*tree*) abbattere; **~ in** *vi* (*AUT: at the kerb*) accostarsi; (*RAIL*) entrare in stazione; **~ off** *vt* (*clothes*) togliere; (*deal etc*) portare a compimento; **~ out** *vi* partire; (*AUT: come out of line*) spostarsi sulla mezzeria ♦ *vt* staccare; far uscire; (*withdraw*) ritirare; **~ over** *vi* (*AUT*) accostare; **~ through** *vi* farcela; **~ up** *vi* (*stop*) fermarsi ♦ *vt* (*raise*) sollevare; (*uproot*) sradicare

pulley ['pulɪ] *n* puleggia, carrucola
pullover ['puləuvə*] *n* pullover *m inv*
pulp [pʌlp] *n* (*of fruit*) polpa
pulpit ['pulpɪt] *n* pulpito
pulsate [pʌl'seɪt] *vi* battere, palpitare
pulse [pʌls] *n* polso; (*BOT*) legume *m*
pummel ['pʌml] *vt* dare pugni a
pump [pʌmp] *n* pompa; (*shoe*) scarpetta ♦ *vt* pompare; **~ up** *vt* gonfiare
pumpkin ['pʌmpkɪn] *n* zucca
pun [pʌn] *n* gioco di parole
punch [pʌntʃ] *n* (*blow*) pugno; (*tool*) punzone *m*; (*drink*) ponce *m* ♦ *vt* (*hit*): **to ~ sb/sth** dare un pugno a qn/qc; **~ line** *n* (*of joke*) battuta finale; **~-up** (*BRIT: inf*) *n* rissa
punctual ['pʌŋktjuəl] *adj* puntuale
punctuation [pʌŋktju'eɪʃən] *n* interpunzione *f*, punteggiatura
puncture ['pʌŋktʃə*] *n* foratura ♦ *vt* forare
pundit ['pʌndɪt] *n* sapientone/a
pungent ['pʌndʒənt] *adj* pungente
punish ['pʌnɪʃ] *vt* punire; **~ment** *n* punizione *f*
punk [pʌŋk] *n* (*also: ~ rocker*) punk *m/f inv*; (*also: ~ rock*) musica punk, punk rock *m*; (*US: inf: hoodlum*) teppista *m*
punt [pʌnt] *n* (*boat*) barchino
punter ['pʌntə*] (*BRIT*) *n* (*gambler*) scommettitore/trice; (: *inf*) cliente *m/f*
puny ['pjuːnɪ] *adj* gracile

pup [pʌp] *n* cucciolo/a
pupil ['pjuːpl] *n* allievo/a; (*ANAT*) pupilla
puppet ['pʌpɪt] *n* burattino
puppy ['pʌpɪ] *n* cucciolo/a, cagnolino/a
purchase ['pəːtʃɪs] *n* acquisto, compera ♦ *vt* comprare; **~r** *n* compratore/trice
pure [pjuə*] *adj* puro(a)
purée ['pjuəreɪ] *n* (*of potatoes*) purè *m*; (*of tomatoes*) passato; (*of apples*) crema
purely ['pjuəlɪ] *adv* puramente
purge [pəːdʒ] *n* (*MED*) purga; (*POL*) epurazione *f* ♦ *vt* purgare
puritan ['pjuərɪtən] *adj*, *n* puritano(a)
purity ['pjuərɪtɪ] *n* purezza
purple ['pəːpl] *adj* di porpora; viola *inv*
purport [pəː'pɔːt] *vi*: **to ~ to be/do** pretendere di essere/fare
purpose ['pəːpəs] *n* intenzione *f*, scopo; **on ~** apposta; **~ful** *adj* deciso(a), risoluto(a)
purr [pəː*] *vi* fare le fusa
purse [pəːs] *n* (*BRIT*) borsellino; (*US*) borsetta ♦ *vt* contrarre
purser ['pəːsə*] *n* (*NAUT*) commissario di bordo
pursue [pə'sjuː] *vt* inseguire; (*fig: activity etc*) continuare con; (: *aim etc*) perseguire
pursuit [pə'sjuːt] *n* inseguimento; (*fig*) ricerca; (*pastime*) passatempo
push [puʃ] *n* spinta; (*effort*) grande sforzo; (*drive*) energia ♦ *vt* spingere; (*button*) premere; (*thrust*): **to ~ sth (into)** ficcare qc (in); (*fig*) fare pubblicità a ♦ *vi* spingere; premere; **to ~ for** (*fig*) insistere per; **~ aside** *vt* scostare; **~ off** (*inf*) *vi* filare; **~ on** *vi* (*continue*) continuare; **~ through** *vi* farsi largo spingendo ♦ *vt* (*measure*) far approvare; **~ up** *vt* (*total, prices*) far salire; **~chair** (*BRIT*) *n* passeggino; **~er** *n* (*drug ~er*) spacciatore/trice; **~over** (*inf*) *n*: **it's a ~over** è un lavoro da bambini; **~-up** (*US*) *n* (*press-up*) flessione *f* sulle braccia; **~y** (*pej*) *adj* opportunista
puss [pus] (*inf*) *n* = **pussy(-cat)**
pussy(-cat) ['pusɪ(-)] (*inf*) *n* micio
put [put] *vt* (*pt, pp put*) vt mettere, porre; (*say*) dire, esprimere; (*a question*) fare; (*estimate*) stimare; **~ about** *or* **around** *vt*

(*rumour*) diffondere; **~ across** *vt* (*ideas etc*) comunicare; far capire; **~ away** *vt* (*return*) mettere a posto; **~ back** *vt* (*replace*) rimettere (a posto); (*postpone*) rinviare; (*delay*) ritardare; **~ by** *vt* (*money*) mettere da parte; **~ down** *vt* (*parcel etc*) posare, mettere giù; (*pay*) versare; (*in writing*) mettere per iscritto; (*revolt, animal*) sopprimere; (*attribute*) attribuire; **~ forward** *vt* (*ideas*) avanzare, proporre; **~ in** *vt* (*application, complaint*) presentare; (*time, effort*) mettere; **~ off** *vt* (*postpone*) rimandare, rinviare; (*discourage*) dissuadere; **~ on** *vt* (*clothes, lipstick etc*) mettere; (*light etc*) accendere; (*play etc*) mettere in scena; (*food, meal*) mettere su; (*brake*) mettere; **to ~ on weight** ingrassare; **to ~ on airs** darsi delle arie; **~ out** *vt* mettere fuori; (*one's hand*) porgere; (*light etc*) spegnere; (*person: inconvenience*) scomodare; **~ through** *vt* (*TEL: call*) passare; (*: person*) mettere in comunicazione; (*plan*) far approvare; **~ up** *vt* (*raise*) sollevare, alzare; (*: umbrella*) aprire; (*: tent*) montare; (*pin up*) affiggere; (*hang*) appendere; (*build*) costruire, erigere; (*increase*) aumentare; (*accommodate*) alloggiare; **~ up with** *vt fus* sopportare

putt [pʌt] *n* colpo leggero; **~ing green** *n* green *m inv*; campo da putting

putty ['pʌtɪ] *n* stucco

puzzle ['pʌzl] *n* enigma *m*, mistero; (*jigsaw*) puzzle *m*; (*also: crossword ~*) parole *fpl* incrociate, cruciverba *m inv* ♦ *vt* confondere, rendere perplesso(a) ♦ *vi* scervellarsi

pyjamas [pɪ'dʒɑːməz] (*BRIT*) *npl* pigiama *m*

pylon ['paɪlən] *n* pilone *m*

pyramid ['pɪrəmɪd] *n* piramide *f*

Pyrenees [pɪrɪ'niːz] *npl*: **the ~** i Pirenei

Q

quack [kwæk] *n* (*of duck*) qua qua *m inv*; (*pej: doctor*) dottoruccio/a

quad [kwɒd] *n abbr* = **quadrangle**;

quadruplet

quadrangle ['kwɒdræŋgl] *n* (*courtyard*) cortile *m*

quadruple [kwɒ'druːpl] *vt* quadruplicare ♦ *vi* quadruplicarsi

quadruplets [kwɒ'druːplɪts] *npl* quattro gemelli *mpl*

quagmire ['kwægmaɪə*] *n* pantano

quail [kweɪl] *n* (*ZOOL*) quaglia ♦ *vi* (*person*): **to ~ at** *or* **before** perdersi d'animo davanti a

quaint [kweɪnt] *adj* bizzarro(a); (*old-fashioned*) antiquato(a); grazioso(a), pittoresco(a)

quake [kweɪk] *vi* tremare ♦ *n abbr* = **earthquake**

Quaker ['kweɪkə*] *n* quacchero/a

qualification [kwɒlɪfɪ'keɪʃən] *n* (*degree etc*) qualifica, titolo; (*ability*) competenza, qualificazione *f*; (*limitation*) riserva, restrizione *f*

qualified ['kwɒlɪfaɪd] *adj* qualificato(a); (*able*): **~ to** competente in, qualificato(a) a; (*limited*) condizionato(a)

qualify ['kwɒlɪfaɪ] *vt* abilitare; (*limit: statement*) modificare, precisare ♦ *vi*: **to ~ (as)** qualificarsi (come); **to ~ (for)** acquistare i requisiti necessari (per); (*SPORT*) qualificarsi (per *or* a)

quality ['kwɒlɪtɪ] *n* qualità *f inv*

qualm [kwɑːm] *n* dubbio; scrupolo

quandary ['kwɒndrɪ] *n*: **in a ~** in un dilemma

quantity ['kwɒntɪtɪ] *n* quantità *f inv*; **~ surveyor** *n* geometra *m* (*specializzato nel calcolare la quantità e il costo del materiale da costruzione*)

quarantine ['kwɒrntiːn] *n* quarantena

quarrel ['kwɒrl] *n* lite *f*, disputa ♦ *vi* litigare; **~some** *adj* litigioso(a)

quarry ['kwɒrɪ] *n* (*for stone*) cava; (*animal*) preda

quart [kwɔːt] *n* ≈ litro

quarter ['kwɔːtə*] *n* quarto, (*US: coin*) quarto di dollaro; (*of year*) trimestre *m*; (*district*) quartiere *m* ♦ *vt* dividere in quattro; (*MIL*) alloggiare; **~s** *npl* (*living ~s*) alloggio; (*MIL*) alloggi *mpl*, quadrato; **a ~ of an hour** un quarto d'ora; **~ final** *n*

quarto di finale; **~ly** *adj* trimestrale ♦ *adv* trimestralmente
quartet(te) [kwɔː'tɛt] *n* quartetto
quartz [kwɔːts] *n* quarzo
quash [kwɔʃ] *vt* (*verdict*) annullare
quaver ['kweɪvə*] *n* (*BRIT: MUS*) croma ♦ *vi* tremolare
quay [kiː] *n* (*also: ~side*) banchina
queasy ['kwiːzɪ] *adj* (*stomach*) delicato(a); **to feel ~** aver la nausea
queen [kwiːn] *n* (*gen*) regina, (*CARDS etc*) regina, donna; **~ mother** *n* regina madre
queer [kwɪə*] *adj* strano(a), curioso(a) ♦ *n* (*inf*) finocchio
quell [kwɛl] *vt* domare
quench [kwɛntʃ] *vt*: **to ~ one's thirst** dissetarsi
querulous ['kwɛrʊləs] *adj* querulo(a)
query ['kwɪərɪ] *n* domanda, questione *f* ♦ *vt* mettere in questione
quest [kwɛst] *n* cerca, ricerca
question ['kwɛstʃən] *n* domanda, questione *f* ♦ *vt* (*person*) interrogare; (*plan, idea*) mettere in questione *or* in dubbio; **it's a ~ of doing** si tratta di fare; **beyond ~** fuori di dubbio; **out of the ~** fuori discussione, impossibile; **~able** *adj* discutibile; **~ mark** *n* punto interrogativo
questionnaire [kwɛstʃə'nɛə*] *n* questionario
queue [kjuː] (*BRIT*) *n* coda, fila ♦ *vi* fare la coda
quibble ['kwɪbl] *vi* cavillare
quiche [kiːʃ] *n* torta salata a base di uova, formaggio, prosciutto o altro
quick [kwɪk] *adj* rapido(a), veloce; (*reply*) pronto(a); (*mind*) pronto(a), acuto(a) ♦ *n*: **cut to the ~** (*fig*) toccato(a) sul vivo; **be ~!** fa presto!; **~en** *vt* accelerare, affrettare ♦ *vi* accelerare, affrettarsi; **~ly** *adv* rapidamente, velocemente; **~sand** *n* sabbie *fpl* mobili; **~-witted** *adj* pronto(a) d'ingegno
quid [kwɪd] (*BRIT: inf*) *n inv* sterlina
quiet ['kwaɪət] *adj* tranquillo(a), quieto(a); (*ceremony*) semplice ♦ *n* tranquillità, calma ♦ *vt, vi* (*US*) = **~en**; **keep ~!** sta zitto!; **~en** (*also: ~en down*) *vi* calmarsi, chetarsi ♦ *vt* calmare, chetare;

~ly *adv* tranquillamente, calmamente; sommessamente
quilt [kwɪlt] *n* trapunta; (*continental ~*) piumino
quin [kwɪn] *n abbr* = **quintuplet**
quinine [kwɪ'niːn] *n* chinino
quintuplets [kwɪn'tjuːplɪts] *npl* cinque gemelli *mpl*
quip [kwɪp] *n* frizzo
quirk [kwəːk] *n* ghiribizzo
quit [kwɪt] (*pt, pp* **quit** *or* **quitted**) *vt* mollare; (*premises*) lasciare, partire da ♦ *vi* (*give up*) mollare; (*resign*) dimettersi
quite [kwaɪt] *adv* (*rather*) assai; (*entirely*) completamente, del tutto; **I ~ understand** capisco perfettamente; **that's not ~ big enough** non è proprio sufficiente; **~ a few of them** non pochi di loro; **~ (so)!** esatto!
quits [kwɪts] *adj*: **~ (with)** pari (con); **let's call it ~** adesso siamo pari
quiver ['kwɪvə*] *vi* tremare, fremere
quiz [kwɪz] *n* (*game*) quiz *m inv*; indovinello ♦ *vt* interrogare; **~zical** *adj* enigmatico(a)
quota ['kwəʊtə] *n* quota
quotation [kwəʊ'teɪʃən] *n* citazione *f*; (*of shares etc*) quotazione *f*; (*estimate*) preventivo; **~ marks** *npl* virgolette *fpl*
quote [kwəʊt] *n* citazione *f* ♦ *vt* (*sentence*) citare; (*price*) dare, fissare; (*shares*) quotare ♦ *vi*: **to ~ from** citare; **~s** *npl* = **quotation marks**

R

rabbi ['ræbaɪ] *n* rabbino
rabbit ['ræbɪt] *n* coniglio; **~ hutch** *n* conigliera
rabble ['ræbl] (*pej*) *n* canaglia, plebaglia
rabies ['reɪbiːz] *n* rabbia
RAC (*BRIT*) *n abbr* = **Royal Automobile Club**
raccoon [rə'kuːn] *n* procione *m*
race [reɪs] *n* razza; (*competition, rush*) corsa ♦ *vt* (*horse*) far correre ♦ *vi* correre; (*engine*) imballarsi; **~ car** (*US*) *n* = **racing car**; **~ car driver** (*US*) *n* = **racing**

driver; **~course** *n* campo di corse, ippodromo; **~horse** *n* cavallo da corsa; **~track** *n* pista

racial ['reɪʃl] *adj* razziale

racing ['reɪsɪŋ] *n* corsa; **~ car** (*BRIT*) *n* macchina da corsa; **~ driver** (*BRIT*) *n* corridore *m* automobilista

racism ['reɪsɪzəm] *n* razzismo; **racist** *adj*, *n* razzista *m/f*

rack [ræk] *n* rastrelliera; (*also: luggage ~*) rete *f*, portabagagli *m inv*; (*also: roof ~*) portabagagli; (*dish ~*) scolapiatti *m inv* ♦ *vt:* **~ed by** torturato(a) da; **to ~ one's brains** scervellarsi

racket ['rækɪt] *n* (*for tennis*) racchetta; (*noise*) fracasso; baccano; (*swindle*) imbroglio, truffa; (*organized crime*) racket *m inv*

racoon [rə'ku:n] *n* = **raccoon**

racquet ['rækɪt] *n* racchetta

racy ['reɪsɪ] *adj* brioso(a); piccante

radar ['reɪdɑː*] *n* radar *m*

radial ['reɪdɪəl] *adj* (*also: ~-ply*) radiale

radiant ['reɪdɪənt] *adj* raggiante; (*PHYSICS*) radiante

radiate ['reɪdɪeɪt] *vt* (*heat*) irraggiare, irradiare ♦ *vi* (*lines*) irradiarsi

radiation [reɪdɪ'eɪʃən] *n* irradiamento; (*radioactive*) radiazione *f*

radiator ['reɪdɪeɪtə*] *n* radiatore *m*

radical ['rædɪkl] *adj* radicale

radii ['reɪdɪaɪ] *npl of* **radius**

radio ['reɪdɪəu] *n* radio *f inv*; **on the ~** alla radio

radioactive [reɪdɪəu'æktɪv] *adj* radioattivo(a)

radio station *n* stazione *f* radio *inv*

radish ['rædɪʃ] *n* ravanello

radius ['reɪdɪəs] *n* (*pl* **radii**) *n* raggio

RAF *n abbr* = **Royal Air Force**

raffle ['ræfl] *n* lotteria

raft [rɑːft] *n* zattera; (*also: life ~*) zattera di salvataggio

rafter ['rɑːftə*] *n* trave *f*

rag [ræg] *n* straccio, cencio; (*pej: newspaper*) giornalaccio, bandiera; (*for charity*) iniziativa studentesca a scopo benefico; **~s** *npl* (*torn clothes*) stracci *mpl*, brandelli *mpl*; **~-and-bone man** (*BRIT*) *n*

= **ragman**; **~ doll** *n* bambola di pezza

rage [reɪdʒ] *n* (*fury*) collera, furia ♦ *vi* (*person*) andare su tutte le furie; (*storm*) infuriare; **it's all the ~** fa furore

ragged ['rægɪd] *adj* (*edge*) irregolare; (*clothes*) logoro(a); (*appearance*) pezzente

ragman ['rægmæn] *n* straccivendolo

raid [reɪd] *n* (*MIL*) incursione *f*; (*criminal*) rapina; (*by police*) irruzione *f* ♦ *vt* fare un'incursione in; rapinare; fare irruzione in

rail [reɪl] *n* (*on stair*) ringhiera; (*on bridge, balcony*) parapetto; (*of ship*) battagliola; **~s** *npl* (*for train*) binario, rotaie *fpl*; **by ~** per ferrovia; **~ing(s)** *n(pl)* ringhiere *fpl*; **~road** (*US*) *n* = **~way**; **~way** (*BRIT*) *n* ferrovia; **~way line** (*BRIT*) *n* linea ferroviaria; **~wayman** (*BRIT*) *n* ferroviere *m*; **~way station** (*BRIT*) *n* stazione *f* ferroviaria

rain [reɪn] *n* pioggia ♦ *vi* piovere; **in the ~** sotto la pioggia; **it's ~ing** piove; **~bow** *n* arcobaleno; **~coat** *n* impermeabile *m*; **~drop** *n* goccia di pioggia; **~fall** *n* pioggia; (*measurement*) piovosità; **~forest** *n* foresta pluviale; **~y** *adj* piovoso(a)

raise [reɪz] *n* aumento ♦ *vt* (*lift*) alzare; sollevare; (*increase*) aumentare; (*a protest, doubt, question*) sollevare; (*cattle, family*) allevare; (*crop*) coltivare; (*army, funds*) raccogliere; (*loan*) ottenere; **to ~ one's voice** alzare la voce

raisin ['reɪzn] *n* uva secca

rake [reɪk] *n* (*tool*) rastrello ♦ *vt* (*garden*) rastrellare; (*with machine gun*) spazzare

rally ['rælɪ] *n* (*POL etc*) riunione *f*; (*AUT*) rally *m inv*; (*TENNIS*) scambio ♦ *vt* riunire, radunare ♦ *vi* (*sick person, Stock Exchange*) riprendersi; **~ round** *vt fus* raggrupparsi intorno a; venire in aiuto di

RAM [ræm] *n abbr* (= *random access memory*) memoria ad accesso casuale

ram [ræm] *n* montone *m*, ariete *m* ♦ *vt* conficcare; (*crash into*) cozzare, sbattere contro; percuotere; speronare; **~ raiding** *n* il rapinare un negozio o una banca sfondandone la vetrina con un'auto-ariete

ramble ['ræmbl] *n* escursione *f* ♦ *vi* (*pej: also: ~ on*) divagare; **~r** *n* escursionista *m/f*; (*BOT*) rosa rampicante; **rambling** *adj* (*speech*) sconnesso(a); (*house*) tutto(a) a nicchie e corridoi; (*BOT*) rampicante

ramp [ræmp] *n* rampa; **on/off ~** (*US: AUT*) raccordo di entrata/uscita

rampage [ræm'peɪdʒ] *n*: **to go on the ~** scatenarsi in modo violento

rampant ['ræmpənt] *adj* (*disease etc*) che infierisce

rampart ['ræmpɑːt] *n* bastione *m*

ramshackle ['ræmʃækl] *adj* (*house*) cadente; (*car etc*) sgangherato(a)

ran [ræn] *pt of* **run**

ranch [rɑːntʃ] *n* ranch *m inv*; **~er** *n* proprietario di un ranch; cowboy *m inv*

rancid ['rænsɪd] *adj* rancido(a)

rancour ['ræŋkə*] (*US* **rancor**) *n* rancore *m*

random ['rændəm] *adj* fatto(a) *or* detto(a) per caso; (*COMPUT, MATH*) casuale ♦ *n*: **at ~** a casaccio; **~ access** *n* (*COMPUT*) accesso casuale

randy ['rændɪ] (*BRIT: inf*) *adj* arrapato(a); lascivo(a)

rang [ræŋ] *pt of* **ring**

range [reɪndʒ] *n* (*of mountains*) catena; (*of missile, voice*) portata; (*of proposals, products*) gamma; (*MIL: also: shooting ~*) campo di tiro; (*also: kitchen ~*) fornello, cucina economica ♦ *vt* disporre ♦ *vi*: **to ~ over** coprire; **to ~ from ... to** andare da ... a

ranger ['reɪndʒə*] *n* guardia forestale

rank [ræŋk] *n* fila; (*status, MIL*) grado; (*BRIT: also: taxi ~*) posteggio di taxi ♦ *vi*: **to ~ among** essere tra ♦ *adj* puzzolente; vero(a) e proprio(a); **the ~ and file** (*fig*) la gran massa

ransack ['rænsæk] *vt* rovistare; (*plunder*) saccheggiare

ransom ['rænsəm] *n* riscatto; **to hold sb to ~** (*fig*) esercitare pressione su qn

rant [rænt] *vi* vociare

rap [ræp] *vt* bussare a; picchiare su ♦ *n* (*music*) rap *m inv*

rape [reɪp] *n* violenza carnale, stupro; (*BOT*) ravizzone *m* ♦ *vt* violentare; **~(seed) oil** *n* olio di ravizzone

rapid ['ræpɪd] *adj* rapido(a); **~s** *npl* (*GEO*) rapida; **~ly** *adv* rapidamente

rapist ['reɪpɪst] *n* violentatore *m*

rapport [ræ'pɔː*] *n* rapporto

rapture ['ræptʃə*] *n* estasi *f inv*

rare [rɛə*] *adj* raro(a); (*CULIN: steak*) al sangue

rarely ['rɛəlɪ] *adv* raramente

raring ['rɛərɪŋ] *adj*: **to be ~ to go** (*inf*) non veder l'ora di cominciare

rascal ['rɑːskl] *n* mascalzone *m*

rash [ræʃ] *adj* imprudente, sconsidera-to(a) ♦ *n* (*MED*) eruzione *f*; (*of events etc*) scoppio

rasher ['ræʃə*] *n* fetta sottile (di lardo *or* prosciutto)

raspberry ['rɑːzbərɪ] *n* lampone *m*

rasping ['rɑːspɪŋ] *adj* stridulo(a)

rat [ræt] *n* ratto

rate [reɪt] *n* (*proportion*) tasso, percentuale *f*; (*speed*) velocità *f inv*; (*price*) tariffa ♦ *vt* giudicare; stimare; **~s** *npl* (*BRIT: property tax*) imposte *fpl* comunali; (*fees*) tariffe *fpl*; **to ~ sb/sth as** valutare qn/qc come; **~able value** (*BRIT*) *n* valore *m* imponibile *or* locativo (di una proprietà); **~payer** (*BRIT*) *n* contribuente *m/f* (che paga le imposte comunali)

rather ['rɑːðə*] *adv* piuttosto; **it's ~ expensive** è piuttosto caro; (*too*) è un po' caro; **there's ~ a lot** ce n'è parecchio; **I would** *or* **I'd ~ go** preferirei andare

ratify ['rætɪfaɪ] *vt* ratificare

rating ['reɪtɪŋ] *n* (*assessment*) valutazione *f*; (*score*) punteggio di merito; (*BRIT: NAUT: sailor*) marinaio semplice

ratio ['reɪʃɪəʊ] *n* proporzione *f*, rapporto

ration ['ræʃən] *n* (*gen pl*) razioni *fpl* ♦ *vt* razionare

rational ['ræʃənl] *adj* razionale, ragionevole; (*solution, reasoning*) logico(a); **~e** [-'nɑːl] *n* fondamento logico; giustificazione *f*; **~ize** *vt* razionalizzare

rat race *n* carrierismo, corsa al successo

rattle ['rætl] *n* tintinnio; (*louder*) strepito; (*for baby*) sonaglino ♦ *vi* risuonare, tintinnare; fare un rumore di ferraglia ♦ *vt* scuotere (con strepito); **~snake** *n* serpente *m* a sonagli

raucous ['rɔːkəs] *adj* rumoroso(a), fragoroso(a)

ravage ['rævɪdʒ] *vt* devastare; **~s** *npl* danni *mpl*

rave [reɪv] *vi* (*in anger*) infuriarsi; (*with enthusiasm*) andare in estasi; (*MED*) delirare

raven ['reɪvən] *n* corvo

ravenous ['rævənəs] *adj* affamato(a)

ravine [rə'viːn] *n* burrone *m*

raving ['reɪvɪŋ] *adj*: **~ lunatic** pazzo(a) furioso(a)

ravishing ['rævɪʃɪŋ] *adj* incantevole

raw [rɔː] *adj* (*uncooked*) crudo(a); (*not processed*) greggio(a); (*sore*) vivo(a); (*inexperienced*) inesperto(a); (*weather, day*) gelido(a); **~ deal** *n* (*inf*) bidonata; **~ material** *n* materia prima

ray [reɪ] *n* raggio; **a ~ of hope** un barlume di speranza

rayon ['reɪɔn] *n* raion *m*

raze [reɪz] *vt* radere, distruggere

razor ['reɪzə*] *n* rasoio; **~ blade** *n* lama di rasoio

Rd *abbr* = **road**

re [riː] *prep* con riferimento a

reach [riːtʃ] *n* portata; (*of river etc*) tratto ♦ *vt* raggiungere; arrivare a ♦ *vi* stendersi; **out of/within ~** fuori/a portata di mano; **within ~ of the shops/station** vicino ai negozi/alla stazione; **~ out** *vt* (*hand*) allungare ♦ *vi*: **to ~ out for** stendere la mano per prendere

react [riː'ækt] *vi* reagire; **~ion** [-'ækʃən] *n* reazione *f*

reactor [riː'æktə*] *n* reattore *m*

read [riːd, *pt, pp* rɛd] (*pt, pp* **read**) *vi* leggere ♦ *vt* leggere; (*understand*) intendere, interpretare; (*study*) studiare; **~ out** *vt* leggere ad alta voce; **~able** *adj* (*writing*) leggibile; (*book etc*) che si legge volentieri; **~er** *n* lettore/trice; (*book*) libro di lettura; (*BRIT: at university*) professore *con funzioni preminenti di ricerca*; **~ership** *n* (*of paper etc*) numero di lettori

readily ['rɛdɪlɪ] *adv* volentieri; (*easily*) facilmente; (*quickly*) prontamente

readiness ['rɛdɪnɪs] *n* prontezza; **in ~** (*prepared*) pronto(a)

reading ['riːdɪŋ] *n* lettura; (*understanding*) interpretazione *f*; (*on instrument*) indicazione *f*

readjust [riːə'dʒʌst] *vt* riaggiustare ♦ *vi* (*person*): **to ~ (to)** riadattarsi (a)

ready ['rɛdɪ] *adj* pronto(a); (*willing*) pronto(a), disposto(a); (*available*) disponibile ♦ *n*: **at the ~** (*MIL*) pronto a sparare; **to get ~** *vi* prepararsi ♦ *vt* preparare; **~-made** *adj* prefabbricato(a); (*clothes*) confezionato(a); **~ money** *n* denaro contante, contanti *mpl*; **~ reckoner** *n* prontuario di calcolo; **~-to-wear** *adj* prêt-à-porter *inv*

reaffirm [riːə'fəːm] *vt* riaffermare

real [rɪəl] *adj* reale; vero(a); **in ~ terms** in realtà; **~ estate** *n* beni *mpl* immobili; **~ism** *n* (*also ART*) realismo; **~ist** *n* realista *m/f*; **~istic** [-'lɪstɪk] *adj* realistico(a)

reality [riː'ælɪtɪ] *n* realtà *f inv*

realization [rɪəlaɪ'zeɪʃən] *n* presa di coscienza; realizzazione *f*

realize ['rɪəlaɪz] *vt* (*understand*) rendersi conto di; (*a project, COMM: asset*) realizzare

really ['rɪəlɪ] *adv* veramente, davvero; **~!** (*indicating annoyance*) oh, insomma!

realm [rɛlm] *n* reame *m*, regno

realtor ['rɪəltɔ:*] (*US: ®*) *n* agente *m* immobiliare

reap [riːp] *vt* mietere; (*fig*) raccogliere

reappear [riːə'pɪə*] *vi* ricomparire, riapparire

rear [rɪə*] *adj* di dietro; (*AUT: wheel etc*) posteriore ♦ *n* didietro, parte *f* posteriore ♦ *vt* (*cattle, family*) allevare ♦ *vi* (*also*: **~ up**: *animal*) impennarsi

rearmament [riː'ɑːməmənt] *n* riarmo

rearrange [riːə'reɪndʒ] *vt* riordinare

rear-view: **~ mirror** *n* (*AUT*) specchio retrovisore

reason ['riːzn] *n* ragione *f*; (*cause, motive*) ragione, motivo ♦ *vi*: **to ~ with sb** far ragionare qn; **it stands to ~ that** è ovvio che; **~able** *adj* ragionevole; (*not bad*) accettabile; **~ably** *adv* ragionevolmente; **~ed** *adj*: **a well-~ed argument** una forte argomentazione; **~ing** *n* ragionamento

reassurance [riːə'ʃuərəns] *n*

rassicurazione f

reassure [riːə'ʃuə*] vt rassicurare; **to ~ sb of** rassicurare qn di or su

rebate ['riːbeɪt] n (on tax etc) sgravio

rebel [n 'rɛbl, vb rɪ'bɛl] n ribelle m/f ♦ vi ribellarsi; **~lion** n ribellione f; **~lious** adj ribelle

rebound [vb rɪ'baund, n 'riːbaund] vi (ball) rimbalzare ♦ n: **on the ~** di rimbalzo

rebuff [rɪ'bʌf] n secco rifiuto

rebuke [rɪ'bjuːk] vt rimproverare

rebut [rɪ'bʌt] vt rifiutare

recall [rɪ'kɔːl] vt richiamare; (remember) ricordare, richiamare alla mente ♦ n richiamo

recant [rɪ'kænt] vi ritrattarsi; (REL) fare abiura

recap ['riːkæp] vt ricapitolare ♦ vi riassumere

recapitulate [riːkə'pɪtjuleɪt] vt, vi = **recap**

rec'd abbr = **received**

recede [rɪ'siːd] vi allontanarsi; ritirarsi; calare; **receding** adj (forehead, chin) sfuggente; **he's got a receding hairline** sta stempiando

receipt [rɪ'siːt] n (document) ricevuta; (act of receiving) ricevimento; **~s** npl (COMM) introiti mpl

receive [rɪ'siːv] vt ricevere; (guest) ricevere, accogliere

receiver [rɪ'siːvə*] n (TEL) ricevitore m; (RADIO, TV) apparecchio ricevente; (of stolen goods) ricettatore/trice; (COMM) curatore m fallimentare

recent ['riːsnt] adj recente; **~ly** adv recentemente

receptacle [rɪ'sɛptɪkl] n recipiente m

reception [rɪ'sɛpʃən] n ricevimento; (welcome) accoglienza; (TV etc) ricezione f; **~ desk** n (in hotel) reception f inv; (in hospital, at doctor's) accettazione f; (in offices etc) portineria; **~ist** n receptionist m/f inv

receptive [rɪ'sɛptɪv] adj ricettivo(a)

recess [rɪ'sɛs] n (in room, secret place) alcova; (POL etc: holiday) vacanze fpl; **~ion** [-'sɛʃən] n recessione f

recharge [riː'tʃɑːdʒ] vt (battery)

ricaricare

recipe ['rɛsɪpɪ] n ricetta

recipient [rɪ'sɪpɪənt] n beneficiario/a; (of letter) destinatario/a

recital [rɪ'saɪtl] n recital m inv

recite [rɪ'saɪt] vt (poem) recitare

reckless ['rɛkləs] adj (driver etc) spericolato(a); (spending) folle

reckon ['rɛkən] vt (count) calcolare; (think): **I ~ that ...** penso che ...; **~ on** vt fus contare su; **~ing** n conto; stima

reclaim [rɪ'kleɪm] vt (demand back) richiedere, reclamare; (land) bonificare; (materials) recuperare; **reclamation** [rɛklə'meɪʃən] n bonifica

recline [rɪ'klaɪn] vi stare sdraiato(a); **reclining** adj (seat) ribaltabile

recognition [rɛkəg'nɪʃən] n riconoscimento; **transformed beyond ~** irriconoscibile

recognize ['rɛkəgnaɪz] vt: **to ~ (by/as)** riconoscere (a or da/come)

recoil [rɪ'kɔɪl] vi (person): **to ~ from doing sth** rifuggire dal fare qc ♦ n (of gun) rinculo

recollect [rɛkə'lɛkt] vt ricordare; **~ion** [-'lɛkʃən] n ricordo

recommend [rɛkə'mɛnd] vt raccomandare; (advise) consigliare

reconcile ['rɛkənsaɪl] vt (two people) riconciliare; (two facts) conciliare, quadrare; **to ~ o.s. to** rassegnarsi a

recondition [riːkən'dɪʃən] vt rimettere a nuovo

reconnaissance [rɪ'kɔnɪsns] n (MIL) ricognizione f

reconnoitre [rɛkə'nɔɪtə*] (US **reconnoiter**) vt (MIL) fare una ri-cognizione di

reconstruct [riːkən'strʌkt] vt ricostruire

record [n 'rɛkɔːd, vb rɪ'kɔːd] n ricordo, documento; (of meeting etc) nota, verbale m; (register) registro; (file) pratica, dossier m inv; (COMPUT) record m inv; (also: criminal ~) fedina penale sporca; (MUS: disc) disco; (SPORT) record m inv, primato ♦ vt (set down) prendere nota di, registrare; (MUS: song etc) registrare; **in ~ time** a tempo di record; **off the ~** adj ufficioso(a) ♦ *adv* ufficiosamente; ~ **card** *n* (*in file*) scheda; **~ed delivery** (*BRIT*) *n* (*POST*): **~ed delivery letter** *etc* lettera *etc* raccomandata; **~er** *n* (*MUS*) flauto diritto; ~ **holder** *n* (*SPORT*) primatista *m/f*; **~ing** *n* (*MUS*) registrazione *f*; ~ **player** *n* giradischi *m inv*

recount [rɪ'kaunt] *vt* raccontare, narrare

re-count [n 'riːkaunt, vb riː'kaunt] *n* (*POL: of votes*) nuovo computo ♦ *vt* ricontare

recoup [rɪ'kuːp] *vt* ricuperare

recourse [rɪ'kɔːs] *n*: **to have ~ to** ricorrere a, far ricorso a

recover [rɪ'kʌvə*] *vt* ricuperare ♦ *vi*: **to ~ (from)** riprendersi (da)

recovery [rɪ'kʌvərɪ] *n* ricupero; ristabilimento; ripresa

recreation [rɛkrɪ'eɪʃən] *n* ricreazione *f*; svago; **~al** *adj* ricreativo(a); **~al drug** *n* sostanza stupefacente usata a scopo ricreativo

recrimination [rɪkrɪmɪ'neɪʃən] *n* recriminazione *f*

recruit [rɪ'kruːt] *n* recluta; (*in company*) nuovo(a) assunto(a) ♦ *vt* reclutare

rectangle [rɛk'tæŋgl] *n* rettangolo; **rectangular** [-'tæŋgjulə*] *adj* rettangolare

rectify ['rɛktɪfaɪ] *vt* (*error*) rettificare; (*omission*) riparare

rector ['rɛktə*] *n* (*REL*) parroco (*anglicano*); **~y** *n* presbiterio

recuperate [rɪ'kjuːpəreɪt] *vi* ristabilirsi

recur [rɪ'kɔː*] *vi* riaccadere; (*symptoms*) ripresentarsi; **~rent** *adj* ricorrente, periodico(a)

recycle [riː'saɪkl] *vt* riciclare

red [rɛd] *n* rosso; (*POL: pej*) rosso/a ♦ *adj* rosso(a); **in the ~** (*account*) scoperto; (*business*) in deficit; ~ **carpet treatment** *n* cerimonia col gran pavese; **R~ Cross** *n* Croce *f* Rossa; **~currant** *n* ribes *m inv*; **~den** *vt* arrossare ♦ *vi* arrossire; **~dish** *adj* rossiccio(a)

redeem [rɪ'diːm] *vt* (*debt*) riscattare; (*sth in pawn*) ritirare; (*fig, also REL*) redimere; **~ing** *adj*: **~ing feature** unico aspetto positivo

redeploy [riːdɪ'plɔɪ] *vt* (*resources*) riorganizzare

red-haired [-'hɛəd] *adj* dai capelli rossi

red-handed [-'hændɪd] *adj*: **to be caught ~** essere preso(a) in flagrante *or* con le mani nel sacco

redhead ['rɛdhɛd] *n* rosso/a

red herring *n* (*fig*) falsa pista

red-hot *adj* arroventato(a)

redirect [riːdaɪ'rɛkt] *vt* (*mail*) far seguire

red light *n*: **to go through a ~** (*AUT*) passare col rosso; **red-light district** *n* quartiere *m* a luci rosse

redo [riː'duː] (*irreg*) *vt* rifare

redolent ['rɛdələnt] *adj*: **~ of** che sa di; (*fig*) che ricorda

redouble [riː'dʌbl] *vt*: **to ~ one's efforts** raddoppiare gli sforzi

redress [rɪ'drɛs] *n* riparazione *f* ♦ *vt* riparare

Red Sea *n*: **the ~** il Mar Rosso

redskin ['rɛdskɪn] *n* pellerossa *m/f*

red tape *n* (*fig*) burocrazia

reduce [rɪ'djuːs] *vt* ridurre; (*lower*) ridurre, abbassare; "**~ speed now**" (*AUT*) "rallentare"; **at a ~d price** scontato(a); **reduction** [rɪ'dʌkʃən] *n* riduzione *f*; (*of price*) ribasso; (*discount*) sconto

redundancy [rɪ'dʌndənsɪ] *n* licenziamento

redundant [rɪ'dʌndnt] *adj* (*worker*) licenziato(a); (*detail, object*) superfluo(a); **to be made ~** essere licenziato (per eccesso di personale)

reed [riːd] *n* (*BOT*) canna; (*MUS: of clarinet etc*) ancia

reef [riːf] *n* (*at sea*) scogliera

reek [riːk] *vi*: **to ~ (of)** puzzare (di)

reel [riːl] *n* bobina, rocchetto; (*FISHING*) mulinello; (*CINEMA*) rotolo; (*dance*) danza veloce scozzese ♦ *vi* (*sway*) barcollare; ~ **in** *vt* tirare su

ref [rɛf] (*inf*) *n abbr* (= *referee*) arbitro

refectory [rɪ'fɛktərɪ] *n* refettorio

refer [rɪ'fə:*] *vt*: **to ~ sth to** (*dispute, decision*) deferire qc a; **to ~ sb to** (*inquirer, MED: patient*) indirizzare qn a; (*reader: to text*) rimandare qn a ♦ *vi*: ~ **to** (*allude to*) accennare a; (*consult*) rivolgersi a

referee [rɛfə'riː] *n* arbitro; (*BRIT: for job application*) referenza ♦ *vt* arbitrare

reference ['rɛfrəns] *n* riferimento; (*mention*) menzione *f*, allusione *f*; (*for job application*) referenza ♦ *vi*, **with ~ to** (*COMM: in letter*) in or con riferimento a; **~ book** *n* libro di consultazione; **~ number** *n* numero di riferimento

referenda [rɛfə'rɛndə] *npl of* **referendum**

referendum [rɛfə'rɛndəm] (*pl* **referenda**) *n* referendum *m inv*

refill [*vb* riː'fɪl, *n* 'riːfɪl] *vt* riempire di nuovo; (*pen, lighter etc*) ricaricare ♦ *n* (*for pen etc*) ricambio

refine [rɪ'faɪn] *vt* raffinare; **~d** *adj* (*person, taste*) raffinato(a)

reflect [rɪ'flɛkt] *vt* (*light, image*) riflettere; (*fig*) rispecchiare ♦ *vi* (*think*) riflettere, considerare; **it ~s badly/well on him** si ripercuote su di lui in senso negativo/ positivo; **~ion** [-'flɛkʃən] *n* riflessione *f*; (*image*) riflesso; (*criticism*): **~ion on** giudizio su; attacco a; **on ~ion** pensandoci sopra

reflex ['riːflɛks] *adj* riflesso(a) ♦ *n* riflesso; **~ive** [rɪ'flɛksɪv] *adj* (*LING*) riflessivo(a)

reform [rɪ'fɔːm] *n* (*of sinner etc*) correzione *f*; (*of law etc*) riforma ♦ *vt* correggere; riformare; **the R~ation** [rɛfə'meɪʃən] *n* la Riforma; **~atory** (*US*) *n* riformatorio

refrain [rɪ'freɪn] *vi*: **to ~ from doing** trattenersi dal fare ♦ *n* ritornello

refresh [rɪ'frɛʃ] *vt* rinfrescare; (*subj: food, sleep*) ristorare; **~er course** (*BRIT*) *n* corso di aggiornamento; **~ing** *adj* (*drink*) rinfrescante; (*sleep*) riposante, ristoratore(trice); **~ments** *npl* rinfreschi *mpl*

refrigerator [rɪ'frɪdʒəreɪtə*] *n* frigorifero

refuel [riː'fjuəl] *vi* far rifornimento (di carburante)

refuge ['rɛfjuːdʒ] *n* rifugio; **to take ~ in** rifugiarsi in

refugee [rɛfju'dʒiː] *n* rifugiato/a, profugo/a

refund [*n* 'riːfʌnd, *vb* rɪ'fʌnd] *n* rimborso ♦ *vt* rimborsare

refurbish [riː'fəːbɪʃ] *vt* rimettere a nuovo

refusal [rɪ'fjuːzəl] *n* rifiuto; **to have first ~ on** avere il diritto d'opzione su

refuse [*n* 'rɛfjuːs, *vb* rɪ'fjuːz] *n* rifiuti *mpl* ♦ *vt, vi* rifiutare; **to ~ to do** rifiutare di fare; **~ collection** *n* raccolta di rifiuti

refute [rɪ'fjuːt] *vt* confutare

regain [rɪ'ɡeɪn] *vt* riguadagnare; riacquistare, ricuperare

regal ['riːɡl] *adj* regale; **~ia** [rɪ'ɡeɪlɪə] *n* insegne *fpl* regie

regard [rɪ'ɡɑːd] *n* riguardo, stima ♦ *vt* considerare, stimare; **to give one's ~s to** porgere i suoi saluti a; **"with kindest ~s"** "cordiali saluti"; **~ing, as ~s, with ~ to** riguardo a; **~less** *adv* lo stesso; **~less of** a dispetto di, nonostante

regenerate [rɪ'dʒɛnəreɪt] *vt* rigenerare

régime [reɪ'ʒiːm] *n* regime *m*

regiment ['rɛdʒɪmənt] *n* reggimento; **~al** [-'mɛntl] *adj* reggimentale

region ['riːdʒən] *n* regione *f*; **in the ~ of** (*fig*) all'incirca di; **~al** *adj* regionale

register ['rɛdʒɪstə*] *n* registro; (*also: electoral ~*) lista elettorale ♦ *vt* registrare; (*vehicle*) immatricolare; (*letter*) assicurare; (*subj: instrument*) segnare ♦ *vi* iscriversi; (*at hotel*) firmare il registro; (*make impression*) entrare in testa; **~ed** (*BRIT*) *adj* (*letter*) assicurato(a); **~ed trademark** *n* marchio depositato

registrar ['rɛdʒɪstrɑː*] *n* ufficiale *m* di stato civile; segretario

registration [rɛdʒɪs'treɪʃən] *n* (*act*) registrazione *f*; iscrizione *f*; (*AUT: also: ~ number*) numero di targa

registry ['rɛdʒɪstrɪ] *n* ufficio del registro; **~ office** (*BRIT*) *n* anagrafe *f*; **to get married in a ~ office** ≈ sposarsi in municipio

regret [rɪ'ɡrɛt] *n* rimpianto, rincrescimento ♦ *vt* rimpiangere; **~fully** *adv* con rincrescimento; **~table** *adj* deplorevole

regular ['rɛɡjulə*] *adj* regolare; (*usual*) abituale, normale; (*soldier*) dell'esercito regolare ♦ *n* (*client etc*) cliente *m/f* abituale; **~ly** *adv* regolarmente

regulate ['regjuleɪt] *vt* regolare;
regulation [-'leɪʃən] *n* regolazione *f*;
(*rule*) regola, regolamento
rehabilitation ['riːhəbɪlɪ'teɪʃən] *n* (*of offender*) riabilitazione *f*; (*of disabled*) riadattamento
rehearsal [rɪ'həːsəl] *n* prova
rehearse [rɪ'həːs] *vt* provare
reign [reɪn] *n* regno ♦ *vi* regnare
reimburse [riːɪm'bəːs] *vt* rimborsare
rein [reɪn] *n* (*for horse*) briglia
reindeer ['reɪndɪə*] *n inv* renna
reinforce [riːɪn'fɔːs] *vt* rinforzare; **~d concrete** *n* cemento armato; **~ment** *n* rinforzo; **~ments** *npl* (*MIL*) rinforzi *mpl*
reinstate [riːɪn'steɪt] *vt* reintegrare
reiterate [riː'ɪtəreɪt] *vt* reiterare, ripetere
reject [*n* 'riːdʒɛkt, *vb* rɪ'dʒɛkt] *n* (*COMM*) scarto ♦ *vt* rifiutare, respingere; (*COMM*: *goods*) scartare; **~ion** [rɪ'dʒɛkʃən] *n* rifiuto
rejoice [rɪ'dʒɔɪs] *vi*: **to ~ (at** *or* **over)** provare diletto in
rejuvenate [rɪ'dʒuːvəneɪt] *vt* ringiovanire
relapse [rɪ'læps] *n* (*MED*) ricaduta
relate [rɪ'leɪt] *vt* (*tell*) raccontare; (*connect*) collegare ♦ *vi*: **to ~ to** (*connect*) riferirsi a; (*get on with*) stabilire un rapporto con; **~d** *adj*: **~ (to)** imparentato(a) (con); collegato(a) *or* connesso(a) (a); **relating to** che riguarda, rispetto a
relation [rɪ'leɪʃən] *n* (*person*) parente *m/f*; (*link*) rapporto, relazione *f*; **~ship** *n* rapporto; (*personal ties*) rapporti *mpl*, relazioni *fpl*; (*also*: *family* ~*ship*) legami *mpl* di parentela
relative ['rɛlətɪv] *n* parente *m/f* ♦ *adj* relativo(a); (*respective*) rispettivo(a)
relax [rɪ'læks] *vi* rilasciarsi; (*person*: *unwind*) rilassarsi ♦ *vt* rilasciare; (*mind*, *person*) rilassare; **~ation** [riːlæk'seɪʃən] *n* rilasciamento; rilassamento; (*entertainment*) ricreazione *f*, svago; **~ed** *adj* rilassato(a); **~ing** *adj* rilassante
relay ['riːleɪ] *n* (*SPORT*) corsa a staffetta ♦ *vt* (*message*) trasmettere
release [rɪ'liːs] *n* (*from prison*) rilascio;

(*from obligation*) liberazione *f*; (*of gas etc*) emissione *f*; (*of film etc*) distribuzione *f*; (*record*) disco; (*device*) disinnesto ♦ *vt* (*prisoner*) rilasciare; (*from obligation*, *wreckage etc*) liberare; (*book*, *film*) fare uscire; (*news*) rendere pubblico(a); (*gas etc*) emettere; (*TECH*: *catch*, *spring etc*) disinnestare
relegate ['rɛləgeɪt] *vt* relegare; (*BRIT*: *SPORT*): **to be ~d** essere retrocesso(a)
relent [rɪ'lɛnt] *vi* cedere; **~less** *adj* implacabile
relevant ['rɛləvənt] *adj* pertinente; (*chapter*) in questione; **~ to** pertinente a
reliability [rɪlaɪə'bɪlɪtɪ] *n* (*of person*) serietà; (*of machine*) affidabilità
reliable [rɪ'laɪəbl] *adj* (*person*, *firm*) fidato(a), che dà affidamento; (*method*) sicuro(a); (*machine*) affidabile; **reliably** *adv*: **to be reliably informed** sapere da fonti sicure
reliance [rɪ'laɪəns] *n*: **~ (on)** fiducia (in); bisogno (di)
relic ['rɛlɪk] *n* (*REL*) reliquia; (*of the past*) resto
relief [rɪ'liːf] *n* (*from pain*, *anxiety*) sollievo; (*help*, *supplies*) soccorsi *mpl*; (*ART*, *GEO*) rilievo
relieve [rɪ'liːv] *vt* (*pain*, *patient*) sollevare; (*bring help*) soccorrere; (*take over from*: *gen*) sostituire; (: *guard*) rilevare; **to ~ sb of sth** (*load*) alleggerire qn di qc; **to ~ o.s.** fare i propri bisogni
religion [rɪ'lɪdʒən] *n* religione *f*; **religious** *adj* religioso(a)
relinquish [rɪ'lɪŋkwɪʃ] *vt* abbandonare; (*plan*, *habit*) rinunziare a
relish ['rɛlɪʃ] *n* (*CULIN*) condimento; (*enjoyment*) gran piacere *m* ♦ *vt* (*food etc*) godere; **to ~ doing** adorare fare
relocate ['riːləu'keɪt] *vt* trasferire ♦ *vi* trasferirsi
reluctance [rɪ'lʌktəns] *n* riluttanza
reluctant [rɪ'lʌktənt] *adj* riluttante, mal disposto(a); **~ly** *adv* di mala voglia, a malincuore
rely [rɪ'laɪ]: **to ~ on** *vt fus* contare su; (*be dependent*) dipendere da
remain [rɪ'meɪn] *vi* restare, rimanere;

~der *n* resto; (*COMM*) rimanenza; **~ing** *adj* che rimane; **~s** *npl* resti *mpl*

remand [rɪ'mɑːnd] *n*: **on ~** in detenzione preventiva ♦ *vt*: **to ~ in custody** rinviare in carcere; trattenere a disposizione della legge; **~ home** (*BRIT*) *n* riformatorio, casa di correzione

remark [rɪ'mɑːk] *n* osservazione *f* ♦ *vt* osservare, dire; **~able** *adj* notevole; eccezionale

remedial [rɪ'miːdɪəl] *adj* (*tuition, classes*) di riparazione; (*exercise*) correttivo(a)

remedy ['rɛmədɪ] *n*: **~ (for)** rimedio (per) ♦ *vt* rimediare a

remember [rɪ'mɛmbə*] *vt* ricordare, ricordarsi di; **~ me to him** salutalo da parte mia; **remembrance** *n* memoria; ricordo

remind [rɪ'maɪnd] *vt*: **to ~ sb of sth** ricordare qc a qn; **to ~ sb to do** ricordare a qn di fare; **~er** *n* richiamo; (*note etc*) promemoria *m inv*

reminisce [rɛmɪ'nɪs] *vi*: **to ~ (about)** abbandonarsi ai ricordi (di)

reminiscent [rɛmɪ'nɪsnt] *adj*: **~ of** che fa pensare a, che richiama

remiss [rɪ'mɪs] *adj* negligente

remission [rɪ'mɪʃən] *n* remissione *f*

remit [rɪ'mɪt] *vt* (*send: money*) rimettere; **~tance** *n* rimessa

remnant ['rɛmnənt] *n* resto, avanzo; **~s** *npl* (*COMM*) scampoli *mpl*; fine *f* serie

remorse [rɪ'mɔːs] *n* rimorso; **~ful** *adj* pieno(a) di rimorsi; **~less** *adj* (*fig*) spietato(a)

remote [rɪ'məut] *adj* remoto(a), lontano(a); (*person*) distaccato(a); **~ control** *n* telecomando; **~ly** *adv* remotamente; (*slightly*) vagamente

remould ['riːməuld] (*BRIT*) *n* (*tyre*) gomma rivestita

removable [rɪ'muːvəbl] *adj* (*detachable*) staccabile

removal [rɪ'muːvəl] *n* (*taking away*) rimozione *f*; soppressione *f*; (*BRIT: from house*) trasloco; (*from office: dismissal*) destituzione *f*; (*MED*) ablazione *f*; **~ van** (*BRIT*) *n* furgone *m* per traslochi

remove [rɪ'muːv] *vt* togliere, rimuovere;

(*employee*) destituire; (*stain*) far sparire; (*doubt, abuse*) sopprimere, eliminare; **~rs** (*BRIT*) *npl* (*company*) ditta *or* impresa di traslochi

Renaissance [rɪ'neɪsɑːns] *n*: **the ~** il Rinascimento

render ['rɛndə*] *vt* rendere; **~ing** *n* (*MUS etc*) interpretazione *f*

rendez-vous ['rɔndɪvuː] *n* appuntamento; (*place*) luogo d'incontro; (*meeting*) incontro

renegade ['rɛnɪgeɪd] *n* rinnegato/a

renew [rɪ'njuː] *vt* rinnovare; (*negotiations*) riprendere; **~able** *adj* rinnovabile; **~al** *n* rinnovo; ripresa

renounce [rɪ'nauns] *vt* rinunziare a

renovate ['rɛnəveɪt] *vt* rinnovare; (*art work*) restaurare; **renovation** [-'veɪʃən] *n* rinnovamento; restauro

renown [rɪ'naun] *n* rinomanza; **~ed** *adj* rinomato(a)

rent [rɛnt] *n* affitto ♦ *vt* (*take for ~*) prendere in affitto; (*also*: **~ out**) dare in affitto; **~al** *n* (*for television, car*) fitto

renunciation [rɪnʌnsɪ'eɪʃən] *n* rinunzia

rep [rɛp] *n abbr* (*COMM*: = *representative*) rappresentante *m/f*; (*THEATRE*: = *repertory*) teatro di repertorio

repair [rɪ'pɛə*] *n* riparazione *f* ♦ *vt* riparare; **in good/bad ~** in buone/cattive condizioni; **~ kit** *n* corredo per riparazioni

repatriate [riː'pætrɪeɪt] *vt* rimpatriare

repay [riː'peɪ] (*irreg*) *vt* (*money, creditor*) rimborsare, ripagare; (*sb's efforts*) ricompensare; (*favour*) ricambiare; **~ment** *n* pagamento; rimborso

repeal [rɪ'piːl] *n* (*of law*) abrogazione *f* ♦ *vt* abrogare

repeat [rɪ'piːt] *n* (*RADIO, TV*) replica ♦ *vt* ripetere; (*pattern*) riprodurre; (*promise, attack, also COMM: order*) rinnovare ♦ *vi* ripetere; **~edly** *adv* ripetutamente, spesso

repel [rɪ'pɛl] *vt* respingere; (*disgust*) ripugnare a; **~lent** *adj* repellente ♦ *n*: **insect ~lent** prodotto *m* anti-insetti *inv*

repent [rɪ'pɛnt] *vi*: **to ~ (of)** pentirsi (di); **~ance** *n* pentimento

repertoire ['rɛpətwɑː*] *n* repertorio

repertory ['rɛpətərɪ] n (*also:* ~ *theatre*) teatro di repertorio

repetition [rɛpɪ'tɪʃən] n ripetizione f

repetitive [rɪ'pɛtɪtɪv] adj (*movement*) che si ripete; (*work*) monotono(a); (*speech*) pieno(a) di ripetizioni

replace [rɪ'pleɪs] vt (*put back*) rimettere a posto; (*take the place of*) sostituire; **~ment** n rimessa; sostituzione f; (*person*) sostituto/a

replay ['riːpleɪ] n (*of match*) partita ripetuta; (*of tape, film*) replay m *inv*

replenish [rɪ'plɛnɪʃ] vt (*glass*) riempire; (*stock etc*) rifornire

replete [rɪ'pliːt] adj (*well-fed*) sazio(a)

replica ['rɛplɪkə] n replica, copia

reply [rɪ'plaɪ] n risposta ♦ vi rispondere; ~ **coupon** n buono di risposta

report [rɪ'pɔːt] n rapporto; (*PRESS etc*) cronaca; (*BRIT: also:* school ~) pagella; (*of gun*) sparo ♦ vt riportare; (*PRESS etc*) fare una cronaca su; (*bring to notice: occurrence*): segnalare; (: *person*) denunciare ♦ vi (*make a report*) fare un rapporto (*or* una cronaca); (*present o.s.*): to ~ **(to sb)** presentarsi (a qn); ~ **card** (*US, SCOTTISH*) n pagella; **~edly** adv stando a quanto si dice; **he ~edly told them to** ... avrebbe detto loro di ...; **~er** n reporter m *inv*

repose [rɪ'pəuz] n: **in** ~ (*face, mouth*) in riposo

reprehensible [rɛprɪ'hɛnsɪbl] adj riprovevole

represent [rɛprɪ'zɛnt] vt rappresentare; **~ation** [-'teɪʃən] n rappresentazione f; (*petition*) rappresentanza; **~ations** npl (*protest*) protesta; **~ative** n rappresentante m/f; (*US: POL*) deputato/a ♦ adj rappresentativo(a)

repress [rɪ'prɛs] vt reprimere; **~ion** [-'prɛʃən] n repressione f

reprieve [rɪ'priːv] n (*LAW*) sospensione f dell'esecuzione della condanna; (*fig*) dilazione f

reprimand ['rɛprɪmɑːnd] n rimprovero ♦ vt rimproverare

reprint ['riːprɪnt] n ristampa

reprisal [rɪ'praɪzl] n rappresaglia

reproach [rɪ'prəutʃ] n rimprovero ♦ vt: to ~ **sb for sth** rimproverare qn di qc; **~ful** adj di rimprovero

reproduce [riːprə'djuːs] vt riprodurre ♦ vi riprodursi; **reproduction** [-'dʌkʃən] n riproduzione f

reproof [rɪ'pruːf] n riprovazione f

reprove [rɪ'pruːv] vt: to ~ (**for**) biasimare (per)

reptile ['rɛptaɪl] n rettile m

republic [rɪ'pʌblɪk] n repubblica, **~an** adj, n repubblicano(a)

repudiate [rɪ'pjuːdɪeɪt] vt (*accusation*) respingere

repulse [rɪ'pʌls] vt respingere

repulsive [rɪ'pʌlsɪv] adj ripugnante, ripulsivo(a)

reputable ['rɛpjutəbl] adj di buona reputazione; (*occupation*) rispettabile

reputation [rɛpju'teɪʃən] n reputazione f

reputed [rɪ'pjuːtɪd] adj reputato(a); **~ly** adv secondo quanto si dice

request [rɪ'kwɛst] n domanda; (*formal*) richiesta ♦ vt: to ~ (**of** *or* **from sb**) chiedere (a qn); ~ **stop** (*BRIT*) n (*for bus*) fermata facoltativa *or* a richiesta

require [rɪ'kwaɪə*] vt (*need: subj: person*) aver bisogno di; (: *thing, situation*) richiedere; (*want*) volere; esigere; (*order*): to ~ **sb to do sth** ordinare a qn di fare qc; **~ment** n esigenza; bisogno; requisito

requisite ['rɛkwɪzɪt] n cosa necessaria ♦ adj necessario(a)

requisition [rɛkwɪ'zɪʃən] n: ~ (**for**) richiesta (di) ♦ vt (*MIL*) requisire

rescue ['rɛskjuː] n salvataggio; (*help*) soccorso ♦ vt salvare; ~ **party** n squadra di salvataggio; **~r** n salvatore/trice

research [rɪ'səːtʃ] n ricerca, ricerche fpl ♦ vt fare ricerche su; **~er** n ricercatore/trice

resemblance [rɪ'zɛmbləns] n somiglianza

resemble [rɪ'zɛmbl] vt assomigliare a

resent [rɪ'zɛnt] vt risentirsi di; **~ful** adj pieno(a) di risentimento; **~ment** n risentimento

reservation [rɛzə'veɪʃən] n (*booking*) prenotazione f; (*doubt*) dubbio; (*protected* *area*) riserva; (*BRIT: on road: also: central ~*) spartitraffico *m inv*

reserve [rɪˈzəːv] *n* riserva ♦ *vt* (*seats etc*) prenotare; **~s** *npl* (*MIL*) riserve *fpl*; **in ~** in serbo; **~d** *adj* (*shy*) riservato(a)

reservoir [ˈrɛzəvwɑː*] *n* serbatoio

reshuffle [riːˈʃʌfl] *n*: **Cabinet ~** (*POL*) rimpasto governativo

reside [rɪˈzaɪd] *vi* risiedere

residence [ˈrɛzɪdəns] *n* residenza; **~ permit** (*BRIT*) *n* permesso di soggiorno

resident [ˈrɛzɪdənt] *n* residente *m/f*; (*in hotel*) cliente *m/f* fisso(a) ♦ *adj* residente; (*doctor*) fisso(a); (*course, college*) a tempo pieno con pernottamento; **~ial** [-ˈdɛnʃəl] *adj* di residenza; (*area*) residenziale

residue [ˈrɛzɪdjuː] *n* resto; (*CHEM, PHYSICS*) residuo

resign [rɪˈzaɪn] *vt* (*one's post*) dimettersi da ♦ *vi* dimettersi; **to ~ o.s. to** rassegnarsi a; **~ation** [rɛzɪgˈneɪʃən] *n* dimissioni *fpl*; rassegnazione *f*; **~ed** *adj* rassegnato(a)

resilience [rɪˈzɪlɪəns] *n* (*of material*) elasticità, resilienza; (*of person*) capacità di recupero

resilient [rɪˈzɪlɪənt] *adj* elastico(a); (*person*) che si riprende facilmente

resin [ˈrɛzɪn] *n* resina

resist [rɪˈzɪst] *vt* resistere a; **~ance** *n* resistenza

resolution [rɛzəˈluːʃən] *n* risoluzione *f*

resolve [rɪˈzɔlv] *n* risoluzione *f* ♦ *vi* (*decide*): **to ~ to do** decidere di fare ♦ *vt* (*problem*) risolvere

resort [rɪˈzɔːt] *n* (*town*) stazione *f*; (*recourse*) ricorso ♦ *vi*: **to ~ to** aver ricorso a; **in the last ~** come ultima risorsa

resound [rɪˈzaund] *vi*: **to ~ (with)** risonare (di); **~ing** *adj* risonante; (*fig*) clamoroso(a)

resource [rɪˈsɔːs] *n* risorsa; **~s** *npl* (*coal, iron etc*) risorse *fpl*; **~ful** *adj* pieno(a) di risorse, intraprendente

respect [rɪsˈpɛkt] *n* rispetto ♦ *vt* rispettare; **~s** *npl* (*greetings*) ossequi *mpl*; **with ~ to** rispetto a, riguardo a; **in this ~** per questo riguardo; **~able** *adj* rispettabile; **~ful** *adj* rispettoso(a)

respective [rɪsˈpɛktɪv] *adj* rispettivo(a)

respite [ˈrɛspaɪt] *n* respiro, tregua

resplendent [rɪsˈplɛndənt] *adj* risplendente

respond [rɪsˈpɔnd] *vi* rispondere

response [rɪsˈpɔns] *n* risposta

responsibility [rɪspɔnsɪˈbɪlɪtɪ] *n* responsabilità *f inv*

responsible [rɪsˈpɔnsɪbl] *adj* (*trustworthy*) fidato(a); (*job*) di (grande) responsabilità; **~ (for)** responsabile (di)

responsive [rɪsˈpɔnsɪv] *adj* che reagisce

rest [rɛst] *n* riposo; (*stop*) sosta, pausa; (*MUS*) pausa; (*object: to support sth*) appoggio, sostegno; (*remainder*) resto, avanzi *mpl* ♦ *vi* riposarsi; (*remain*) rimanere, restare; (*be supported*): **to ~ on** appoggiarsi su ♦ *vt* (far) riposare; (*lean*): **to ~ sth on/against** appoggiare qc su/contro; **the ~ of them** gli altri; **it ~s with him to decide** sta a lui decidere

restaurant [ˈrɛstərɔŋ] *n* ristorante *m*; **~ car** (*BRIT*) *n* vagone *m* ristorante

restful [ˈrɛstful] *adj* riposante

rest home *n* casa di riposo

restitution [rɛstɪˈtjuːʃən] *n*: **to make ~ to sb for sth** compensare qn di qc

restive [ˈrɛstɪv] *adj* agitato(a), impaziente

restless [ˈrɛstlɪs] *adj* agitato(a), irrequieto(a)

restoration [rɛstəˈreɪʃən] *n* restauro; restituzione *f*

restore [rɪˈstɔː*] *vt* (*building, to power*) restaurare; (*sth stolen*) restituire; (*peace, health*) ristorare

restrain [rɪsˈtreɪn] *vt* (*feeling, growth*) contenere, frenare; (*person*): **to ~ (from doing)** trattenere (dal fare); **~ed** *adj* (*style*) contenuto(a), sobrio(a); (*person*) riservato(a); **~t** *n* (*restriction*) limitazione *f*; (*moderation*) ritegno; (*of style*) contenutezza

restrict [rɪsˈtrɪkt] *vt* restringere, limitare; **~ion** [-kʃən] *n*: **~ (on)** restrizione *f* (di), limitazione *f*

rest room (*US*) *n* toletta

restructure [riːˈstrʌktʃə*] *vt* ristrutturare

result [rɪ'zʌlt] *n* risultato ♦ *vi*: **to ~ in** avere per risultato; **as a ~ of** in *or* di conseguenza a, in seguito a

resume [rɪ'zjuːm] *vt*, *vi* (*work*, *journey*) riprendere

résumé ['reɪzjuːmeɪ] *n* riassunto; (*US*) curriculum *m inv* vitae

resumption [rɪ'zʌmpʃən] *n* ripresa

resurgence [rɪ'səːdʒəns] *n* rinascita

resurrection [rɛzə'rɛkʃən] *n* risurrezione *f*

resuscitate [rɪ'sʌsɪteɪt] *vt* (*MED*) risuscitare; **resuscitation** [-'teɪʃən] *n* rianimazione *f*

retail ['riːteɪl] *adj*, *adv* al minuto ♦ *vt* vendere al minuto; **~er** *n* commerciante *m/f* al minuto, dettagliante *m/f*; **~ price** *n* prezzo al minuto

retain [rɪ'teɪn] *vt* (*keep*) tenere, serbare; **~er** *n* (*fee*) onorario

retaliate [rɪ'tælɪeɪt] *vi*: **to ~ (against)** vendicarsi (di); **retaliation** [-'eɪʃən] *n* rappresaglie *fpl*

retarded [rɪ'tɑːdɪd] *adj* ritardato(a)

retch [rɛtʃ] *vi* aver conati di vomito

retire [rɪ'taɪə*] *vi* (*give up work*) andare in pensione; (*withdraw*) ritirarsi, andarsene; (*go to bed*) andare a letto, ritirarsi; **~d** *adj* (*person*) pensionato(a); **~ment** *n* pensione *f*; (*act*) pensionamento; **retiring** *adj* (*leaving*) uscente; (*shy*) riservato(a)

retort [rɪ'tɔːt] *vi* rimbeccare

retrace [riː'treɪs] *vt*: **to ~ one's steps** tornare sui passi

retract [rɪ'trækt] *vt* (*statement*) ritrattare; (*claws*, *undercarriage*, *aerial*) ritrarre, ritirare

retrain [riː'treɪn] *vt* (*worker*) riaddestrare

retread ['riːtrɛd] *n* (*tyre*) gomma rigenerata

retreat [rɪ'triːt] *n* ritirata; (*place*) rifugio ♦ *vi* battere in ritirata

retribution [rɛtrɪ'bjuːʃən] *n* castigo

retrieval [rɪ'triːvəl] *n* (*see vb*) ricupero; riparazione *f*

retrieve [rɪ'triːv] *vt* (*sth lost*) ricuperare, ritrovare; (*situation*, *honour*) salvare; (*error*, *loss*) rimediare a; **~r** *n* cane *m* da

riporto

retrospect ['rɛtrəspɛkt] *n*: **in ~** guardando indietro; **~ive** [-'spɛktɪv] *adj* retrospettivo(a); (*law*) retroattivo(a)

return [rɪ'təːn] *n* (*going or coming back*) ritorno; (*of sth stolen etc*) restituzione *f*; (*FINANCE: from land, shares*) profitto, reddito ♦ *cpd* (*journey*, *match*) di ritorno; (*BRIT: ticket*) di andata e ritorno ♦ *vi* tornare, ritornare ♦ *vt* rendere, restituire; (*bring back*) riportare; (*send back*) mandare indietro; (*put back*) rimettere; (*POL: candidate*) eleggere; **~s** *npl* (*COMM*) incassi *mpl*; profitti *mpl*; **in ~ (for)** in cambio (di); **by ~ of post** a stretto giro di posta; **many happy ~s (of the day)!** cento di questi giorni!

reunion [riː'juːnɪən] *n* riunione *f*

reunite [riːjuː'naɪt] *vt* riunire

rev [rɛv] *n abbr* (*AUT*: = *revolution*) giro ♦ *vt* (*also*: **~ up**) imballare

revamp ['riː'væmp] *vt* (*firm*) riorganizzare

reveal [rɪ'viːl] *vt* (*make known*) rivelare, svelare; (*display*) rivelare, mostrare; **~ing** *adj* rivelatore(trice); (*dress*) scollato(a)

reveille [rɪ'vælɪ] *n* (*MIL*) sveglia

revel ['rɛvl] *vi*: **to ~ in sth/in doing** dilettarsi di qc/a fare

revelation [rɛvə'leɪʃən] *n* rivelazione *f*

revelry ['rɛvlrɪ] *n* baldoria

revenge [rɪ'vɛndʒ] *n* vendetta ♦ *vt* vendicare; **to take ~ on** vendicarsi di

revenue ['rɛvənjuː] *n* reddito

reverberate [rɪ'vəːbəreɪt] *vi* (*sound*) rimbombare; (*light*) riverberarsi; (*fig*) ripercuotersi

revere [rɪ'vɪə*] *vt* venerare

reverence ['rɛvərəns] *n* venerazione *f*, riverenza

Reverend ['rɛvərənd] *adj* (*in titles*) reverendo(a)

reverie ['rɛvərɪ] *n* fantasticheria

reversal [rɪ'vəːsl] *n* capovolgimento

reverse [rɪ'vəːs] *n* contrario, opposto; (*back*, *defeat*) rovescio; (*AUT*: *also*: **~ gear**) marcia indietro ♦ *adj* (*order*, *direction*) contrario(a), opposto(a) ♦ *vt* (*turn*) invertire, rivoltare; (*change*) capovolgere, rovesciare; (*LAW: judgment*) cassare; (*car*) fare marcia indietro con ♦ *vi* (*BRIT: AUT, person etc*) fare marcia indietro; **~d charge call** (*BRIT*) *n* (*TEL*) telefonata con addebito al ricevente; **reversing lights** (*BRIT*) *npl* (*AUT*) luci *fpl* per la retromarcia

revert [rɪ'vɜːt] *vi*: **to ~** tornare a

review [rɪ'vjuː] *n* rivista; (*of book, film*) recensione *f*; (*of situation*) esame *m* ♦ *vt* passare in rivista; fare la recensione di; fare il punto di; **~er** *n* recensore/a

revile [rɪ'vaɪl] *vt* insultare

revise [rɪ'vaɪz] *vt* (*manuscript*) rivedere, correggere, (*opinion*) emendare, modificare; (*study: subject, notes*) ripassare; **revision** [rɪ'vɪʒən] *n* revisione *f*; ripasso

revitalize [riː'vaɪtəlaɪz] *vt* ravvivare

revival [rɪ'vaɪvəl] *n* ripresa; ristabilimento; (*of faith*) risveglio

revive [rɪ'vaɪv] *vt* (*person*) rianimare; (*custom*) far rivivere; (*hope, courage, economy*) ravvivare; (*play, fashion*) riesumare ♦ *vi* (*person*) rianimarsi; (*hope*) ravvivarsi; (*activity*) riprendersi

revolt [rɪ'vəult] *n* rivolta, ribellione *f* ♦ *vi* rivoltarsi, ribellarsi ♦ *vt* (far) rivoltare; **~ing** *adj* ripugnante

revolution [revə'luːʃən] *n* rivoluzione *f*; (*of wheel etc*) rivoluzione, giro; **~ary** *adj, n* rivoluzionario(a)

revolve [rɪ'vɔlv] *vi* girare

revolver [rɪ'vɔlvə*] *n* rivoltella

revolving [rɪ'vɔlvɪŋ] *adj* girevole

revue [rɪ'vjuː] *n* (*THEATRE*) rivista

revulsion [rɪ'vʌlʃən] *n* ripugnanza

reward [rɪ'wɔːd] *n* ricompensa, premio ♦ *vt*: **to ~** (**for**) ricompensare (per); **~ing** *adj* (*fig*) gratificante

rewind [riː'waɪnd] (*irreg*) *vt* (*watch*) ricaricare; (*ribbon etc*) riavvolgere

rewire [riː'waɪə*] *vt* (*house*) rifare l'impianto elettrico di

reword [riː'wɜːd] *vt* formulare *or* esprimere con altre parole

rheumatism ['ruːmətɪzəm] *n* reumatismo

Rhine [raɪn] *n*: **the ~** il Reno

rhinoceros [raɪ'nɔsərəs] *n* rinoceronte *m*

rhododendron [rəudə'dendrən] *n* rododendro

Rhone [rəun] *n*: **the ~** il Rodano

rhubarb ['ruːbɑːb] *n* rabarbaro

rhyme [raɪm] *n* rima; (*verse*) poesia

rhythm ['rɪðm] *n* ritmo

rib [rɪb] *n* (*ANAT*) costola ♦ *vt* (*tease*) punzecchiare

ribbon ['rɪbən] *n* nastro; **in ~s** (*torn*) a brandelli

rice [raɪs] *n* riso; **~ pudding** *n* budino di riso

rich [rɪtʃ] *adj* ricco(a); (*clothes*) sontuoso(a); (*abundant*): **~ in** ricco(a) di; **the ~** *npl* (*wealthy people*) i ricchi; **~es** *npl* ricchezze *fpl*; **~ly** *adv* riccamente; (*dressed*) sontuosamente; (*deserved*) pienamente

rickets ['rɪkɪts] *n* rachitismo

rickety ['rɪkɪtɪ] *adj* traballante

rickshaw ['rɪkʃɔː] *n* risciò *m inv*

ricochet ['rɪkəʃeɪ] *vi* rimbalzare

rid [rɪd] (*pt, pp* rid) *vt*: **to ~ sb of** sbarazzare *or* liberare qn di; **to get ~ of** sbarazzarsi di

ridden ['rɪdn] *pp of* ride

riddle ['rɪdl] *n* (*puzzle*) indovinello ♦ *vt*: **to be ~d with** (*holes*) essere crivellato(a) di; (*doubts*) essere pieno(a) di

ride [raɪd] (*pt* rode, *pp* ridden) *n* (*on horse*) cavalcata; (*outing*) passeggiata; (*distance covered*) cavalcata; corsa ♦ *vi* (*as sport*) cavalcare; (*go somewhere: on horse, bicycle*) andare (a cavallo *or* in bicicletta etc); (*journey: on bicycle, motorcycle, bus*) andare, viaggiare ♦ *vt* (*a horse*) montare, cavalcare; **to take sb for a ~** (*fig*) prendere in giro qn; fregare qn; **to ~ a horse/bicycle/camel** montare a cavallo/ in bicicletta/in groppa a un cammello; **~r** *n* cavalcatore/trice; (*in race*) fantino; (*on bicycle*) ciclista *m/f*; (*on motorcycle*) motociclista *m/f*

ridge [rɪdʒ] *n* (*of hill*) cresta; (*of roof*) colmo; (*on object*) riga (in rilievo)

ridicule ['rɪdɪkjuːl] *n* ridicolo; scherno ♦ *vt* mettere in ridicolo

ridiculous [rɪ'dɪkjuləs] *adj* ridicolo(a)

riding ['raɪdɪŋ] *n* equitazione *f*; **~ school**

n scuola d'equitazione

rife [raɪf] *adj* diffuso(a); **to be ~ with** abbondare di

riffraff ['rɪfræf] *n* canaglia

rifle ['raɪfl] *n* carabina ♦ *vt* vuotare; ~ **through** *vt fus* frugare tra; ~ **range** *n* campo di tiro; (*at fair*) tiro a segno

rift [rɪft] *n* fessura, crepatura; (*fig: disagreement*) incrinatura, disaccordo

rig [rɪg] *n* (*also: oil ~: on land*) derrick *m inv*; (: *at sea*) piattaforma di trivellazione ♦ *vt* (*election etc*) truccare; ~ **out** (*BRIT*) *vt*: **to ~ out as/in** vestire da/in; ~ **up** *vt* allestire; ~**ging** *n* (*NAUT*) attrezzatura

right [raɪt] *adj* giusto(a); (*suitable*) appropriato(a); (*not left*) destro(a) ♦ *n* giusto; (*title, claim*) diritto; (*not left*) destra ♦ *adv* (*answer*) correttamente; (*not on the left*) a destra ♦ *vt* raddrizzare; (*fig*) riparare ♦ *excl* bene!; **to be ~** (*person*) aver ragione; (*answer*) essere giusto(a) *or* corretto(a); **by ~s** di diritto; **on the ~** a destra; **to be in the ~** aver ragione, essere nel giusto; ~ **now** proprio adesso; subito; ~ **away** subito; ~ **angle** *n* angolo retto; ~**eous** ['raɪtʃəs] *adj* retto(a), virtuoso(a); (*anger*) giusto(a), giustificato(a); ~**ful** *adj* (*heir*) legittimo(a); ~-**handed** *adj* (*person*) che adopera la mano destra; ~-**hand man** *n* braccio destro; ~-**hand side** *n* il lato destro; ~**ly** *adv* bene, correttamente; (*with reason*) a ragione; ~ **of way** *n* diritto di passaggio; (*AUT*) precedenza; ~-**wing** *adj* (*POL*) di destra

rigid ['rɪdʒɪd] *adj* rigido(a); (*principle*) rigoroso(a)

rigmarole ['rɪgmərəul] *n* tiritera; commedia

rile [raɪl] *vt* irritare, seccare

rim [rɪm] *n* orlo; (*of spectacles*) montatura; (*of wheel*) cerchione *m*

rind [raɪnd] *n* (*of bacon*) cotenna; (*of lemon etc*) scorza

ring [rɪŋ] (*pt* **rang**, *pp* **rung**) *n* anello; (*of people, objects*) cerchio; (*of spies*) giro; (*of smoke etc*) spirale *m*; (*arena*) pista, arena; (*for boxing*) ring *m inv*; (*sound of bell*) scampanio ♦ *vi* (*person, bell, telephone*) suonare; (*also: ~ out: voice, words*) risuonare; (*TEL*) telefonare; (*ears*) fischiare ♦ *vt* (*BRIT: TEL*) telefonare a; (*bell, doorbell*) suonare; **to give sb a ~** (*BRIT: TEL*) dare un colpo di telefono a qn; ~ **back** *vt, vi* (*TEL*) richiamare; ~ **off** (*BRIT*) *vi* (*TEL*) mettere giù, riattaccare; ~ **up** (*BRIT*) *vt* (*TEL*) telefonare a; ~**ing** *n* (*of bell*) scampanio; (*of telephone*) squillo; (*in ears*) ronzio; ~**ing tone** (*BRIT*) *n* (*TEL*) segnale *m* di libero; ~**leader** *n* (*of gang*) capobanda *m*

ringlets ['rɪŋlɪts] *npl* boccoli *mpl*

ring road (*BRIT*) *n* raccordo anulare

rink [rɪŋk] *n* (*also: ice ~*) pista di pattinaggio

rinse [rɪns] *n* risciacquatura; (*hair tint*) cachet *m inv* ♦ *vt* sciacquare

riot ['raɪət] *n* sommossa, tumulto; (*of colours*) orgia ♦ *vi* tumultuare; **to run ~** creare disordine; ~**ous** *adj* tumultuoso(a); (*living*) sfrenato(a); (*party*) scatenato(a)

rip [rɪp] *n* strappo ♦ *vt* strappare ♦ *vi* strapparsi; ~**cord** *n* cavo di sfilamento

ripe [raɪp] *adj* (*fruit, grain*) maturo(a); (*cheese*) stagionato(a); ~**n** *vt* maturare ♦ *vi* maturarsi

ripple ['rɪpl] *n* increspamento, ondulazione *f*; mormorio ♦ *vi* incresparsi

rise [raɪz] (*pt* **rose**, *pp* **risen**) *n* (*slope*) salita, pendio; (*hill*) altura; (*increase: in wages: BRIT*) aumento; (: *in prices, temperature*) rialzo, aumento; (*fig: to power etc*) ascesa ♦ *vi* alzarsi, levarsi; (*prices*) aumentare; (*waters, river*) crescere; (*sun, wind, person: from chair, bed*) levarsi; (*also: ~ up: building*) ergersi; (: *rebel*) insorgere; ribellarsi; (*in rank*) salire; **to give ~ to** provocare, dare origine a; **to ~ to the occasion** essere all'altezza; **risen** ['rɪzn] *pp of* **rise**; **rising** *adj* (*increasing: number*) sempre crescente; (: *prices*) in aumento; (*tide*) montante; (*sun, moon*) nascente, che sorge

risk [rɪsk] *n* rischio; pericolo ♦ *vt* rischiare; **to take** *or* **run the ~ of doing** correre il rischio di fare; **at ~** in pericolo; **at one's own ~** a proprio rischio e pericolo; ~**y** *adj* rischioso(a)

risqué ['riːskeɪ] *adj* (*joke*) spinto(a)

rissole ['rɪsəul] n crocchetta

rite [raɪt] n rito; **last ~s** l'estrema unzione

ritual ['rɪtjuəl] adj rituale ♦ n rituale m

rival ['raɪvl] n rivale m/f; (in business) concorrente m/f ♦ adj rivale; che fa concorrenza ♦ vt essere in concorrenza con; **to ~ sb/sth in** competere con qn/qc in; **~ry** n rivalità; concorrenza

river ['rɪvə*] n fiume m ♦ cpd (port, traffic) fluviale; **up/down ~** a monte/valle; **~bank** n argine m; **~bed** n letto di fiume

rivet ['rɪvɪt] n ribattino, rivetto ♦ vt (fig) concentrare, fissare

Riviera [rɪvɪ'eərə] n: **the (French) ~** la Costa Azzurra; **the Italian ~** la Riviera

road [rəud] n strada; (small) cammino; (in town) via ♦ cpd stradale; **major/minor ~** strada con/senza diritto di precedenza; **~block** n blocco stradale; **~hog** n guidatore m egoista e spericolato; **~ map** n carta stradale; **~ safety** n sicurezza sulle strade; **~side** n margine m della strada; **~sign** n cartello stradale; **~ user** n chi usa la strada; **~way** n carreggiata; **~works** npl lavori mpl stradali; **~worthy** adj in buono stato di marcia

roam [rəum] vi errare, vagabondare

roar [rɔː*] n ruggito; (of crowd) tumulto; (of thunder, storm) muggito; (of laughter) scoppio ♦ vi ruggire; tumultuare; muggire; **to ~ with laughter** scoppiare dalle risa; **to do a ~ing trade** fare affari d'oro

roast [rəust] n arrosto ♦ vt arrostire; (coffee) tostare, torrefare; **~ beef** n arrosto di manzo

rob [rɔb] vt (person) rubare; (bank) svaligiare; **to ~ sb of sth** derubare qn di qc; (fig: deprive) privare qn di qc; **~ber** n ladro; (armed) rapinatore m; **~bery** n furto; rapina

robe [rəub] n (for ceremony etc) abito; (also: bath ~) accappatoio; (US: also: lap ~) coperta

robin ['rɔbɪn] n pettirosso

robot ['rəubɔt] n robot m inv

robust [rəu'bʌst] adj robusto(a); (economy) solido(a)

rock [rɔk] n (substance) roccia; (boulder) masso; roccia; (in sea) scoglio; (US: pebble) ciottolo; (BRIT: sweet) zucchero candito ♦ vt (swing gently: cradle) dondolare; (: child) cullare; (shake) scrollare, far tremare ♦ vi dondolarsi; scrollarsi, tremare; **on the ~s** (drink) col ghiaccio; (marriage etc) in crisi; **~ and roll** n rock and roll m; **~-bottom** adj bassissimo(a); **~ery** n giardino roccioso

rocket ['rɔkɪt] n razzo

rock fall n parete f della roccia

rocking ['rɔkɪŋ]: **~ chair** n sedia a dondolo; **~ horse** n cavallo a dondolo

rocky ['rɔkɪ] adj (hill) roccioso(a); (path) sassoso(a); (marriage etc) instabile

rod [rɔd] n (metallic, TECH) asta; (wooden) bacchetta; (also: fishing ~) canna da pesca

rode [rəud] pt of **ride**

rodent ['rəudnt] n roditore m

rodeo ['rəudɪəu] n rodeo

roe [rəu] n (species: also: ~ deer) capriolo; (of fish, also: hard ~) uova fpl di pesce; **soft ~** latte m di pesce

rogue [rəug] n mascalzone m

role [rəul] n ruolo

roll [rəul] n rotolo; (of banknotes) mazzo; (also: bread ~) panino; (register) lista; (sound: of drums etc) rullo ♦ vt rotolare; (also: ~ up: string) aggomitolare; (also: ~ up: sleeves) rimboccare; (cigarettes) arrotolare; (eyes) roteare; (also: ~ out: pastry) stendere; (lawn, road etc) spianare ♦ vi rotolare; (wheel) girare; (drum) rullare; (vehicle: also: ~ along) avanzare; (ship) rollare; **~ about** or **around** vi rotolare qua e là; (person) rotolarsi; **~ by** vi (time) passare; **~ in** vi (mail, cash) arrivare a fiumi; **~ over** vi rivoltarsi; **~ up** (inf) vi (arrive) arrivare ♦ vt (carpet) arrotolare; **~ call** n appello; **~er** n rullo; (wheel) rotella; (for hair) bigodino; **~er coaster** n montagne fpl russe; **~er skates** npl pattini mpl a rotelle

rolling ['rəulɪŋ] adj (landscape) ondulato(a); **~ pin** n matterello; **~ stock** n (RAIL) materiale m rotabile

ROM [rɔm] n abbr (= read only memory) memoria di sola lettura

Roman [ˈrəumən] *adj, n* romano(a); **~ Catholic** *adj, n* cattolico(a)

romance [rəˈmæns] *n* storia (*or* avventura *or* film *m inv*) romantico(a); (*charm*) poesia; (*love affair*) idillio

Romania [rəuˈmeɪnɪə] *n* = **Rumania**

Roman numeral *n* numero romano

romantic [rəˈmæntɪk] *adj* romantico(a); sentimentale

Rome [rəum] *n* Roma

romp [rɔmp] *n* gioco rumoroso ♦ *vi* (*also:* ~ *about*) far chiasso, giocare in un modo rumoroso

rompers [ˈrɔmpəz] *npl* pagliaccetto

roof [ruːf] *n* tetto; (*of tunnel, cave*) volta ♦ *vt* coprire (con un tetto); ~ **of the mouth** palato; **~ing** *n* materiale *m* per copertura; ~ **rack** *n* (*AUT*) portabagagli *m inv*

rook [ruk] *n* (*bird*) corvo nero; (*CHESS*) torre *f*

room [ruːm] *n* (*in house*) stanza; (*bed~, in hotel*) camera; (*in school etc*) sala; (*space*) posto, spazio; **~s** *npl* (*lodging*) alloggio; "**~s to let**" (*BRIT*), "**~s for rent**" (*US*) "si affittano camere"; **there is ~ for improvement** si potrebbe migliorare; **~ing house** (*US*) *n* casa in cui si affittano camere o appartamentini ammobiliati; **~mate** *n* compagno/a di stanza; ~ **service** *n* servizio da camera; **~y** *adj* spazioso(a); (*garment*) ampio(a)

roost [ruːst] *vi* appollaiarsi

rooster [ˈruːstə*] *n* gallo

root [ruːt] *n* radice *f* ♦ *vi* (*plant, belief*) attecchire; ~ **about** *vi* (*fig*) frugare; ~ **for** *vt fus* fare il tifo per; ~ **out** *vt* estirpare

rope [rəup] *n* corda, fune *f*; (*NAUT*) cavo ♦ *vt* (*box*) legare; (*climbers*) legare in cordata; (*area: also:* ~ *off*) isolare cingendo con cordoni; **to know the ~s** (*fig*) conoscere i trucchi del mestiere; ~ **in** *vt* (*fig*) coinvolgere; ~ **ladder** *n* scala a corda

rosary [ˈrəuzərɪ] *n* rosario; roseto

rose [rəuz] *pt of* **rise** ♦ *n* rosa; (*also:* ~ *bush*) rosaio; (*on watering can*) rosetta

rosé [ˈrəuzeɪ] *n* vino rosato

rosebud [ˈrəuzbʌd] *n* bocciolo di rosa

rosebush [ˈrəuzbuʃ] *n* rosaio

rosemary [ˈrəuzmərɪ] *n* rosmarino

rosette [rəuˈzɛt] *n* coccarda

roster [ˈrɔstə*] *n*: **duty ~** ruolino di servizio

rostrum [ˈrɔstrəm] *n* tribuna

rosy [ˈrəuzɪ] *adj* roseo(a)

rot [rɔt] *n* (*decay*) putrefazione *f*; (*inf: nonsense*) stupidaggini *fpl* ♦ *vt, vi* imputridire, marcire

rota [ˈrəutə] *n* tabella dei turni

rotary [ˈrəutərɪ] *adj* rotante

rotate [rəuˈteɪt] *vt* (*revolve*) far girare; (*change round: jobs*) fare a turno ♦ *vi* (*revolve*) girare; **rotating** *adj* (*movement*) rotante

rote [rəut] *n*: **by ~** (*by heart*) a memoria; (*mechanically*) meccanicamente

rotten [ˈrɔtn] *adj* (*decayed*) putrido(a), marcio(a); (*dishonest*) corrotto(a); (*inf: bad*) brutto(a); (: *action*) vigliacco(a); **to feel ~** (*ill*) sentirsi da cani

rouble [ˈruːbl] (*US* **ruble**) *n* rublo

rouge [ruːʒ] *n* belletto

rough [rʌf] *adj* (*skin, surface*) ruvido(a); (*terrain, road*) accidentato(a); (*voice*) rauco(a); (*person, manner: coarse*) rozzo(a), aspro(a); (: *violent*) brutale; (*district*) malfamato(a); (*weather*) cattivo(a); (*sea*) mosso(a); (*plan*) abbozzato(a); (*guess*) approssimativo(a) ♦ *n* (*GOLF*) macchia; **to ~ it** far vita dura; **to sleep ~** (*BRIT*) dormire all'addiaccio; **~age** *n* alimenti *mpl* ricchi in cellulosa; **~-and-ready** *adj* rudimentale; **~cast** *n* intonaco grezzo; ~ **copy** *n* brutta copia; **~ly** *adv* (*handle*) rudemente, brutalmente; (*make*) grossolanamente; (*speak*) bruscamente; (*approximately*) approssimativamente; **~ness** *n* ruvidità; (*of manner*) rozzezza

roulette [ruːˈlet] *n* roulette *f*

Roumania [ruːˈmeɪnɪə] *n* = **Rumania**

round [raund] *adj* rotondo(a); (*figures*) tondo(a) ♦ *n* (*BRIT: of toast*) fetta; (*duty: of policeman, milkman etc*) giro; (: *of doctor*) visite *fpl*; (*game: of cards, golf, in competition*) partita; (*of ammunition*) cartuccia; (*BOXING*) round *m inv*; (*of talks*) serie *f inv* ♦ *vt* (*corner*) girare; (*bend*) prendere ♦ *prep* intorno a ♦ *adv*: **all ~** tutt'attorno; **to go the long way ~** fare il giro più lungo; **all the year ~** tutto l'anno; **it's just ~ the corner** (*also fig*) è dietro l'angolo; **~ the clock** ininterrottamente; **to go ~ to sb's house** andare da qn; **go ~ the back** passi dietro; **to go ~ a house** visitare una casa; **enough to go ~** abbastanza per tutti; **~ of applause** applausi *mpl*; **~ of drinks** giro di bibite; **~ of sandwiches** sandwich *m inv*; **~ off** *vt* (*speech etc*) finire; **~ up** *vt* radunare; (*criminals*) fare una retata di; (*prices*) arrotondare; **~about** *n* (*BRIT: AUT*) rotatoria; (: *at fair*) giostra ♦ *adj* (*route, means*) indiretto(a); **~ers** *npl* (*game*) gioco simile al baseball; **~ly** *adv* (*fig*) chiaro e tondo; **~-shouldered** *adj* dalle spalle tonde; **~ trip** *n* (*viaggio di*) andata e ritorno; **~up** *n* raduno; (*of criminals*) retata

rouse [rauz] *vt* (*wake up*) svegliare; (*stir up*) destare; provocare; risvegliare; **rousing** *adj* (*speech, applause*) entusiastico(a)

rout [raut] *n* (*MIL*) rotta ♦ *vt* (*defeat*) mettere in rotta

route [ru:t] *n* itinerario; (*of bus*) percorso; **~ map** (*BRIT*) *n* (*for journey*) cartina di itinerario

routine [ru:'ti:n] *adj* (*work*) corrente, abituale; (*procedure*) solito(a) ♦ *n* (*pej*) routine *f*, tran tran *m*; (*THEATRE*) numero

rove [rəuv] *vt* vagabondare per

row[1] [rəu] *n* (*line*) riga, fila; (*KNITTING*) ferro; (*behind one another: of cars, people*) fila; (*in boat*) remata ♦ *vi* (*in boat*) remare; (*as sport*) vogare ♦ *vt* (*boat*) manovrare a remi; **in a ~** (*fig*) di fila

row[2] [rau] *n* (*racket*) baccano, chiasso; (*dispute*) lite *f*; (*scolding*) sgridata ♦ *vi* (*argue*) litigare

rowboat ['rəubəut] (*US*) *n* barca a remi

rowdy ['raudɪ] *adj* chiassoso(a); turbolento(a) ♦ *n* teppista *m/f*

rowing ['rəuɪŋ] *n* canottaggio; **~ boat** (*BRIT*) *n* barca a remi

royal ['rɔɪəl] *adj* reale; **R~ Air Force** *n* aeronautica militare britannica

royalty ['rɔɪəltɪ] *n* (*royal persons*) (membri *mpl* della) famiglia reale; (*payment: to author*) diritti *mpl* d'autore

r.p.m. *abbr* (= *revolutions per minute*) giri/min

R.S.V.P. *abbr* (= *répondez s'il vous plaît*) R.S.V.P.

Rt Hon. (*BRIT*) *abbr* (= *Right Honourable*) ≈ Onorevole

rub [rʌb] *n*: **to give sth a ~** strofinare qc; (*sore place*) massaggiare qc ♦ *vt* strofinare; massaggiare; (*hands: also: ~ together*) sfregarsi; **to ~ sb up** (*BRIT*) *or* **~ sb the wrong way** (*US*) lisciare qn contro pelo; **~ off** *vi* andare via; **~ off on** *vt fus* lasciare una traccia su; **~ out** *vt* cancellare

rubber ['rʌbə*] *n* gomma; **~ band** *n* elastico; **~ plant** *n* ficus *m inv*; **~y** *adj* gommoso(a)

rubbish ['rʌbɪʃ] *n* (*from household*) immondizie *fpl*, rifiuti *mpl*; (*fig: pej*) cose *fpl* senza valore; robaccia; sciocchezze *fpl*; **~ bin** (*BRIT*) *n* pattumiera; **~ dump** *n* (*in town*) immondezzaio

rubble ['rʌbl] *n* macerie *fpl*; (*smaller*) pietrisco

ruble ['ru:bl] (*US*) *n* = **rouble**

ruby ['ru:bɪ] *n* rubino

rucksack ['rʌksæk] *n* zaino

rudder ['rʌdə*] *n* timone *m*

ruddy ['rʌdɪ] *adj* (*face*) rubicondo(a); (*inf: damned*) maledetto(a)

rude [ru:d] *adj* (*impolite: person*) scortese, rozzo(a); (: *word, manners*) grossolano(a), rozzo(a); (*shocking*) indecente; **~ness** *n* scortesia; grossolanità

rueful ['ru:ful] *adj* mesto(a), triste

ruffian ['rʌfɪən] *n* briccone *m*, furfante *m*

ruffle ['rʌfl] *vt* (*hair*) scompigliare; (*clothes, water*) increspare; (*fig: person*) turbare

rug [rʌg] *n* tappeto; (*BRIT: for knees*) coperta

rugby ['rʌgbɪ] *n* (*also: ~ football*) rugby *m*

rugged ['rʌgɪd] *adj* (*landscape*) aspro(a); (*features, determination*) duro(a); (*character*) brusco(a)

rugger ['rʌgə*] (*BRIT*: *inf*) *n* rugby *m*
ruin ['ruːɪn] *n* rovina ♦ *vt* rovinare; **~s**
npl (*of building, castle etc*) rovine *fpl*,
ruderi *mpl*; **~ous** *adj* rovinoso(a);
(*expenditure*) inverosimile
rule [ruːl] *n* regola; (*regulation*)
regolamento, regola; (*government*)
governo; (~*r*) riga ♦ *vt* (*country*)
governare; (*person*) dominare ♦ *vi*
regnare; decidere; (*LAW*) dichiarare; **as a ~**
normalmente; **~ out** *vt* escludere; **~d** *adj*
(*paper*) vergato(a); **~r** *n* (*sovereign*)
sovrano/a; (*for measuring*) regolo, riga;
ruling *adj* (*party*) al potere; (*class*)
dirigente ♦ *n* (*LAW*) decisione *f*
rum [rʌm] *n* rum *m*
Rumania [ruːˈmeɪnɪə] *n* Romania
rumble ['rʌmbl] *n* rimbombo; brontolio
♦ *vi* rimbombare; (*stomach, pipe*)
brontolare
rummage ['rʌmɪdʒ] *vi* frugare
rumour ['ruːmə*] (*US* **rumor**) *n* voce *f*
♦ *vt*: **it is ~ed that** corre voce che
rump [rʌmp] *n* groppa; **~ steak** *n*
bistecca di girello
rumpus ['rʌmpəs] (*inf*) *n* baccano;
(*quarrel*) rissa
run [rʌn] (*pt* **ran**, *pp* **run**) *n* corsa;
(*outing*) gita (in macchina); (*distance
travelled*) percorso, tragitto; (*SKI*) pista;
(*CRICKET, BASEBALL*) meta; (*series*) serie *f*;
(*THEATRE*) periodo di rappresentazione; (*in
tights, stockings*) smagliatura ♦ *vt*
(*distance*) correre; (*operate: business*)
gestire, dirigere; (*: competition, course*)
organizzare; (*: hotel*) gestire; (*: house*)
governare; (*COMPUT*) eseguire; (*water,
bath*) far scorrere; (*force through: rope,
pipe*) **to ~ sth through** far passare qc
attraverso; (*pass: hand, finger*) **to ~ sth
over** passare qc su; (*PRESS: feature*)
presentare ♦ *vi* correre; (*flee*) scappare;
(*pass: road etc*) passare; (*work: machine,
factory*) funzionare, andare; (*bus, train:
operate*) far servizio; (*: travel*) circolare;
(*continue: play, contract*) durare; (*slide:
drawer; flow: river, bath*) scorrere;
(*colours, washing*) stemperarsi; (*in
election*) presentarsi candidato; (*nose*)

colare; **there was a ~ on ...** c'era una
corsa a ...; **in the long ~** a lungo andare;
on the ~ in fuga; **to ~ a race** partecipare
ad una gara; **I'll ~ you to the station** la
porto alla stazione; **to ~ a risk** correre
un rischio; **~ about** *or* **around** *vi*
(*children*) correre qua e là; **~ across** *vt
fus* (*find*) trovare per caso; **~ away** *vi*
fuggire; **~ down** *vt* (*production*) ridurre
gradualmente; (*factory*) rallentare
l'attività di; (*AUT*) investire; (*criticize*)
criticare; **to be ~ down** (*person: tired*)
essere esausto(a); **~ in** (*BRIT*) *vt* (*car*)
rodare, fare il rodaggio di; **~ into** *vt fus*
(*meet: person*) incontrare per caso;
(*: trouble*) incontrare, trovare; (*collide
with*) andare a sbattere contro; **~ off** *vi*
fuggire ♦ *vt* (*water*) far scolare; (*copies*)
fare; **~ out** *vi* (*person*) uscire di corsa;
(*liquid*) colare; (*lease*) scadere; (*money*)
esaurirsi; **~ out of** *vt fus* rimanere a
corto di; **~ over** *vt* (*AUT*) investire,
mettere sotto ♦ *vt fus* (*revise*) rivedere; **~
through** *vt fus* (*instructions*) dare una
scorsa a; (*rehearse: play*) riprovare,
ripetere; **~ up** *vt* (*debt*) lasciar
accumulare; **to ~ up against** (*difficulties*)
incontrare; **~away** *adj* (*person*)
fuggiasco(a); (*horse*) in libertà; (*truck*)
fuori controllo
rung [rʌŋ] *pp of* **ring** ♦ *n* (*of ladder*) piolo
runner ['rʌnə*] *n* (*in race*) corridore *m*;
(*: horse*) partente *m/f*; (*on sledge*) pattino;
(*for drawer etc*) guida; **~ bean** (*BRIT*) *n*
fagiolo rampicante; **~-up** *n* secondo(a)
arrivato(a)
running ['rʌnɪŋ] *n* corsa; direzione *f*;
organizzazione *f*; funzionamento ♦ *adj*
(*water*) corrente; (*commentary*)
simultaneo(a); **to be in/out of the ~ for
sth** essere/non essere più in lizza per qc;
6 days ~ 6 giorni di seguito; **~ costs** *npl*
costi *mpl* d'esercizio; (*of car*) spese *fpl* di
mantenimento
runny ['rʌnɪ] *adj* che cola
run-of-the-mill *adj* solito(a), banale
runt [rʌnt] *n* (*also pej*) omuncolo; (*ZOOL*)
animale *m* più piccolo del normale
run-through *n* prova

run-up *n*: ~ **to** (*election etc*) periodo che precede

runway ['rʌnweɪ] *n* (*AVIAT*) pista (di decollo)

rupee [ru:'pi:] *n* rupia

rupture ['rʌptʃə*] *n* (*MED*) ernia

rural ['ruərəl] *adj* rurale

ruse [ru:z] *n* trucco

rush [rʌʃ] *n* corsa precipitosa; (*hurry*) furia, fretta; (*sudden demand*): ~ **for** corsa a; (*current*) flusso; (*of emotion*) impeto; (*BOT*) giunco ♦ *vt* mandare or spedire velocemente; (*attack: town etc*) prendere d'assalto ♦ *vi* precipitarsi; ~ **hour** *n* ora di punta

rusk [rʌsk] *n* biscotto

Russia ['rʌʃə] *n* Russia; **~n** *adj* russo(a) ♦ *n* russo/a; (*LING*) russo

rust [rʌst] *n* ruggine *f* ♦ *vi* arrugginirsi

rustic ['rʌstɪk] *adj* rustico(a)

rustle ['rʌsl] *vi* frusciare ♦ *vt* (*paper*) far frusciare; (*US: cattle*) rubare

rustproof ['rʌstpru:f] *adj* inossidabile

rusty ['rʌstɪ] *adj* arrugginito(a)

rut [rʌt] *n* solco; (*ZOOL*) fregola; **to get into a** ~ (*fig*) adagiarsi troppo

ruthless ['ru:θlɪs] *adj* spietato(a)

rye [raɪ] *n* segale *f*; ~ **bread** *n* pane *m* di segale

S

Sabbath ['sæbəθ] *n* (*Jewish*) sabato; (*Christian*) domenica

sabotage ['sæbətɑ:ʒ] *n* sabotaggio ♦ *vt* sabotare

saccharin(e) ['sækərɪn] *n* saccarina

sachet ['sæʃeɪ] *n* bustina

sack [sæk] *n* (*bag*) sacco ♦ *vt* (*dismiss*) licenziare, mandare a spasso; (*plunder*) saccheggiare; **to get the** ~ essere mandato a spasso; **~ing** *n* tela di sacco; (*dismissal*) licenziamento

sacrament ['sækrəmənt] *n* sacramento

sacred ['seɪkrɪd] *adj* sacro(a)

sacrifice ['sækrɪfaɪs] *n* sacrificio ♦ *vt* sacrificare

sad [sæd] *adj* triste

saddle ['sædl] *n* sella ♦ *vt* (*horse*) sellare; **to be ~d with sth** (*inf*) avere qc sulle spalle; **~bag** *n* (*on bicycle*) borsa

sadistic [sə'dɪstɪk] *adj* sadico(a)

sadness ['sædnɪs] *n* tristezza

s.a.e. *n abbr* = **stamped addressed envelope**

safe [seɪf] *adj* sicuro(a); (*out of danger*) salvo(a), al sicuro; (*cautious*) prudente ♦ *n* cassaforte *f*; ~ **from** al sicuro da; ~ **and sound** sano(a) e salvo(a); **(just) to be on the** ~ **side** per non correre rischi; **~-conduct** *n* salvacondotto; **~-deposit** *n* (*vault*) caveau *m inv*; (*box*) cassetta di sicurezza; **~guard** *n* salvaguardia ♦ *vt* salvaguardare; **~keeping** *n* custodia; **~ly** *adv* sicuramente; sano(a) e salvo(a); prudentemente; ~ **sex** *n* sesso sicuro

safety ['seɪftɪ] *n* sicurezza; ~ **belt** *n* cintura di sicurezza; ~ **pin** *n* spilla di sicurezza; ~ **valve** *n* valvola di sicurezza

saffron ['sæfrən] *n* zafferano

sag [sæg] *vi* incurvarsi; afflosciarsi

sage [seɪdʒ] *n* (*herb*) salvia; (*man*) saggio

Sagittarius [sædʒɪ'tɛərɪəs] *n* Sagittario

Sahara [sə'hɑ:rə] *n*: **the** ~ (**Desert**) il (deserto del) Sahara

said [sɛd] *pt, pp of* **say**

sail [seɪl] *n* (*on boat*) vela; (*trip*): **to go for a** ~ fare un giro in barca a vela ♦ *vt* (*boat*) condurre, governare ♦ *vi* (*travel: ship*) navigare; (: *passenger*) viaggiare per mare; (*set off*) salpare; (*sport*) fare della vela; **they ~ed into Genoa** entrarono nel porto di Genova; ~ **through** *vt fus* (*fig*) superare senza difficoltà; **~boat** (*US*) *n* barca a vela; **~ing** (*sport*) vela; **to go ~ing** fare della vela; **~ing boat** *n* barca a vela; **~ing ship** *n* veliero; **~or** *n* marinaio

saint [seɪnt] *n* santo/a; **~ly** *adj* santo(a)

sake [seɪk] *n*: **for the** ~ **of** per, per amore di

salad ['sæləd] *n* insalata; ~ **bowl** *n* insalatiera; ~ **cream** (*BRIT*) *n* (tipo di) maionese *f*; ~ **dressing** *n* condimento per insalata

salami [sə'lɑ:mɪ] *n* salame *m*

salary ['sælərɪ] *n* stipendio

sale [seɪl] *n* vendita; (*at reduced prices*) svendita, liquidazione *f*; (*auction*) vendita all'asta; **"for ~"** "in vendita"; **on ~** in vendita; **on ~ or return** da vendere o rimandare; **~room** *n* sala delle aste; **~s assistant** (*US* **~s clerk**) *n* commesso/a; **~sman/swoman** *n* commesso/a; (*representative*) rappresentante *m/f*

sallow ['sæləu] *adj* giallastro(a)

salmon ['sæmən] *n inv* salmone *m*

saloon [sə'lu:n] *n* (*US*) saloon *m inv*, bar *m inv*; (*BRIT: AUT*) berlina; (*ship's lounge*) salone *m*

salt [sɔlt] *n* sale *m* ♦ *vt* salare; **~ cellar** *n* saliera; **~water** *adj* di mare; **~y** *adj* salato(a)

salute [sə'lu:t] *n* saluto ♦ *vt* salutare

salvage ['sælvɪdʒ] *n* (*saving*) salvataggio; (*things saved*) beni *mpl* salvati *or* recuperati ♦ *vt* salvare, mettere in salvo

salvation [sæl'veɪʃən] *n* salvezza; **S~ Army** *n* Esercito della Salvezza

same [seɪm] *adj* stesso(a), medesimo(a) ♦ *pron*: **the ~** lo(la) stesso(a), gli(le) stessi(e); **the ~ book as** lo stesso libro di (*o* che); **at the ~ time** allo stesso tempo; **all** *or* **just the ~** tuttavia; **to do the ~ as sb** fare come qn; **the ~ to you!** altrettanto a te!

sample ['sɑ:mpl] *n* campione *m* ♦ *vt* (*food*) assaggiare; (*wine*) degustare

sanctimonious [sæŋktɪ'məunɪəs] *adj* bigotto(a), bacchettone(a)

sanction ['sæŋkʃən] *n* sanzione *f* ♦ *vt* sancire, sanzionare

sanctity ['sæŋktɪtɪ] *n* santità

sanctuary ['sæŋktjuərɪ] *n* (*holy place*) santuario; (*refuge*) rifugio; (*for wildlife*) riserva

sand [sænd] *n* sabbia ♦ *vt* (*also*: ~ **down**) cartavetrare

sandal ['sændl] *n* sandalo

sandbox ['sændbɔks] (*US*) *n* = **sandpit**

sandcastle ['sændkɑ:sl] *n* castello di sabbia

sandpaper ['sændpeɪpə*] *n* carta vetrata

sandpit ['sændpɪt] *n* (*for children*) buca di sabbia

sandstone ['sændstəun] *n* arenaria

sandwich ['sændwɪtʃ] *n* tramezzino, panino, sandwich *m inv* ♦ *vt*: **~ed between** incastrato(a) fra; **cheese/ham ~** sandwich al formaggio/prosciutto; **~ course** (*BRIT*) *n* corso di formazione professionale

sandy ['sændɪ] *adj* sabbioso(a); (*colour*) color sabbia *inv*, biondo(a) rossiccio(a)

sane [seɪn] *adj* (*person*) sano(a) di mente; (*outlook*) sensato(a)

sang [sæŋ] *pt of* **sing**

sanitary ['sænɪtərɪ] *adj* (*system, arrangements*) sanitario(a); (*clean*) igienico(a); **~ towel** (*US* **~ napkin**) *n* assorbente *m* (igienico)

sanitation [sænɪ'teɪʃən] *n* (*in house*) impianti *mpl* sanitari; (*in town*) fognature *fpl*; **~ department** (*US*) *n* nettezza urbana

sanity ['sænɪtɪ] *n* sanità mentale; (*common sense*) buon senso

sank [sæŋk] *pt of* **sink**

Santa Claus [sæntə'klɔ:z] *n* Babbo Natale

sap [sæp] *n* (*of plants*) linfa ♦ *vt* (*strength*) fiaccare

sapling ['sæplɪŋ] *n* alberello

sapphire ['sæfaɪə*] *n* zaffiro

sarcasm ['sɑ:kæzm] *n* sarcasmo

sardine [sɑ:'di:n] *n* sardina

Sardinia [sɑ:'dɪnɪə] *n* Sardegna

sash [sæʃ] *n* fascia

sat [sæt] *pt, pp of* **sit**

Satan ['seɪtən] *n* Satana *m*

satchel ['sætʃl] *n* cartella

satellite ['sætəlaɪt] *adj* satellite ♦ *n* satellite *m*; **~ dish** *n* antenna parabolica; **~ television** *n* televisione *f* via satellite

satin ['sætɪn] *n* raso ♦ *adj* di raso

satire ['sætaɪə*] *n* satira

satisfaction [sætɪs'fækʃən] *n* soddisfazione *f*

satisfactory [sætɪs'fæktərɪ] *adj* soddisfacente

satisfy ['sætɪsfaɪ] *vt* soddisfare; (*convince*) convincere; **~ing** *adj* soddisfacente

Saturday ['sætədɪ] *n* sabato

sauce [sɔ:s] *n* salsa; (*containing meat, fish*) sugo; **~pan** *n* casseruola

saucer ['sɔːsə*] n sottocoppa m, piattino

saucy ['sɔːsɪ] adj impertinente

Saudi ['saudɪ]: **~ Arabia** n Arabia Saudita; **~ (Arabian)** adj, n arabo(a) saudita

sauna ['sɔːnə] n sauna

saunter ['sɔːntə*] vi andare a zonzo, bighellonare

sausage ['sɔsɪdʒ] n salsiccia; **~ roll** n rotolo di pasta sfoglia ripieno di salsiccia

sauté ['sauteɪ] adj: **~ potatoes** patate fpl saltate in padella

savage ['sævɪdʒ] adj (cruel, fierce) selvaggio(a), feroce; (primitive) primitivo(a) ♦ n selvaggio/a ♦ vt attaccare selvaggiamente

save [seɪv] vt (person, belongings, COMPUT) salvare; (money) risparmiare, mettere da parte; (time) risparmiare; (food) conservare; (avoid: trouble) evitare; (SPORT) parare ♦ vi (also: ~ up) economizzare ♦ n (SPORT) parata ♦ prep salvo, a eccezione di

saving ['seɪvɪŋ] n risparmio ♦ adj: **the ~ grace** of l'unica cosa buona di; **~s** npl (money) risparmi mpl; **~s account** n libretto di risparmio; **~s bank** n cassa di risparmio

saviour ['seɪvjə*] (US **savior**) n salvatore m

savour ['seɪvə*] (US **savor**) vt gustare; **~y** adj (dish: not sweet) salato(a)

saw [sɔː] (pt **sawed**, pp **sawed** or **sawn**) pt of **see** ♦ n (tool) sega ♦ vt segare; **~dust** n segatura; **~mill** n segheria; **sawn** pp of **saw**; **~n-off shotgun** n fucile m a canne mozze

saxophone ['sæksəfəun] n sassofono

say [seɪ] (pt, pp **said**) n: **to have one's ~** fare sentire il proprio parere; **to have a** or **some ~** avere voce in capitolo ♦ vt dire; **could you ~ that again?** potrebbe ripeterlo?; **that goes without ~ing** va da sé; **~ing** n proverbio, detto

scab [skæb] n crosta; (pej) crumiro/a

scaffold ['skæfəuld] n (gallows) patibolo; **~ing** n impalcatura

scald [skɔːld] n scottatura ♦ vt scottare

scale [skeɪl] n scala; (of fish) squama ♦ vt (mountain) scalare; **~s** npl (for weighing) bilancia; **on a large ~** su vasta scala; **~ of charges** tariffa; **~ down** vt ridurre (proporzionalmente)

scallop ['skɔləp] n (ZOOL) pettine m; (SEWING) smerlo

scalp [skælp] n cuoio capelluto ♦ vt scotennare

scalpel ['skælpl] n bisturi m inv

scamper ['skæmpə*] vi: **to ~ away,** **~ off** darsela a gambe

scampi ['skæmpɪ] npl scampi mpl

scan [skæn] vt scrutare; (glance at quickly) scorrere, dare un'occhiata a; (TV) analizzare; (RADAR) esplorare ♦ n (MED) ecografia

scandal ['skændl] n scandalo; (gossip) pettegolezzi mpl

Scandinavia [skændɪ'neɪvɪə] n Scandinavia; **~n** adj, n scandinavo(a)

scant [skænt] adj scarso(a); **~y** adj insufficiente; (swimsuit) ridotto(a)

scapegoat ['skeɪpgəut] n capro espiatorio

scar [skɑː] n cicatrice f ♦ vt sfregiare

scarce [skɛəs] adj scarso(a); (copy, edition) raro(a); **to make o.s. ~** (inf) squagliarsela; **~ly** adv appena; **scarcity** n scarsità, mancanza

scare [skɛə*] n spavento; panico ♦ vt spaventare, atterrire; **there was a bomb ~ at the bank** hanno evacuato la banca per paura di un attentato dinamitardo; **to ~ sb stiff** spaventare a morte qn; **~ off** or **away** vt mettere in fuga; **~crow** n spaventapasseri m inv; **~d** adj: **to be ~d** aver paura

scarf [skɑːf] (pl **scarves** or **~s**) n (long) sciarpa; (square) fazzoletto da testa, foulard m inv

scarlet ['skɑːlɪt] adj scarlatto(a); **~ fever** n scarlattina

scarves [skɑːvz] npl of **scarf**

scary ['skɛərɪ] adj che spaventa

scathing ['skeɪðɪŋ] adj aspro(a)

scatter ['skætə*] vt spargere; (crowd) disperdere ♦ vi disperdersi; **~brained** adj sbadato(a)

scavenger ['skævəndʒə*] n (person)

accattone/a
scenario [sɪ'nɑːrɪəu] *n* (THEATRE, CINEMA) copione *m*; (*fig*) situazione *f*
scene [siːn] *n* (THEATRE, fig etc) scena; (*of crime, accident*) scena, luogo; (*sight, view*) vista, veduta; ~**ry** *n* (THEATRE) scenario; (*landscape*) panorama *m*; **scenic** *adj* scenico(a); panoramico(a)
scent [sɛnt] *n* profumo; (*sense of smell*) olfatto, odorato; (*fig: track*) pista
sceptical ['skɛptɪkəl] (US **skeptical**) *adj* scettico(a)
sceptre ['sɛptə*] (US **scepter**) *n* scettro
schedule ['ʃɛdjuːl, (US) 'skɛdjuːl] *n* programma *m*, piano; (*of trains*) orario; (*of prices etc*) lista, tabella ♦ *vt* fissare; **on ~** in orario; **to be ahead of/behind ~** essere in anticipo/ritardo sul previsto; ~**d flight** *n* volo di linea
scheme [skiːm] *n* piano, progetto; (*method*) sistema *m*; (*dishonest plan, plot*) intrigo, trama; (*arrangement*) disposizione *f*, sistemazione *f*; (*pension ~ etc*) programma *m* ♦ *vi* fare progetti; (*intrigue*) complottare; **scheming** *adj* intrigante ♦ *n* intrighi *mpl*, macchinazioni *fpl*
schism ['skɪzəm] *n* scisma *m*
scholar ['skɔlə*] *n* erudito/a; (*pupil*) scolaro/a; ~**ly** *adj* dotto(a), erudito(a); ~**ship** *n* erudizione *f*; (*grant*) borsa di studio
school [skuːl] *n* (*primary, secondary*) scuola; (*university: US*) università *f inv* ♦ *cpd* scolare, scolastico(a) ♦ *vt* (*animal*) addestrare; ~ **age** *n* età scolare; ~**bag** *n* cartella; ~**book** *n* libro scolastico; ~**boy** *n* scolaro; ~**children** *npl* scolari *mpl*; ~**days** *npl* giorni *mpl* di scuola; ~**girl** *n* scolara; ~**ing** *n* istruzione *f*; ~**master** *n* (*primary*) maestro; (*secondary*) insegnante *m*; ~**mistress** *n* maestra; insegnante *f*; ~**teacher** *n* insegnante *m/f*, docente *m/f*; (*primary*) maestro/a
sciatica [saɪ'ætɪkə] *n* sciatica
science ['saɪəns] *n* scienza; ~ **fiction** *n* fantascienza; **scientific** [-'tɪfɪk] *adj* scientifico(a); **scientist** *n* scienziato/a
scissors ['sɪzəz] *npl* forbici *fpl*

scoff [skɔf] *vt* (BRIT: inf: eat) trangugiare, ingozzare ♦ *vi*: **to ~ (at)** (*mock*) farsi beffe (di)
scold [skəuld] *vt* rimproverare
scone [skɔn] *n* focaccina da tè
scoop [skuːp] *n* mestolo; (*for ice cream*) cucchiaio dosatore; (PRESS) colpo giornalistico, notizia (in) esclusiva; ~ **out** *vt* scavare; ~ **up** *vt* tirare su, sollevare
scooter ['skuːtə*] *n* (*motor cycle*) motoretta, scooter *m inv*; (*toy*) monopattino
scope [skəup] *n* (*capacity: of plan, undertaking*) portata; (: *of person*) capacità *fpl*; (*opportunity*) possibilità *fpl*
scorch [skɔːtʃ] *vt* (*clothes*) strinare, bruciacchiare; (*earth, grass*) seccare, bruciare
score [skɔː*] *n* punti *mpl*, punteggio; (MUS) partitura, spartito; (*twenty*) venti ♦ *vt* (*goal, point*) segnare, fare; (*success*) ottenere ♦ *vi* segnare; (FOOTBALL) fare un goal; (*keep score*) segnare i punti; ~**s of** (*very many*) un sacco di; **on that ~** a questo riguardo; **to ~ 6 out of 10** prendere 6 su 10; ~ **out** *vt* cancellare con un segno; ~**board** *n* tabellone *m* segnapunti
scorn [skɔːn] *n* disprezzo ♦ *vt* disprezzare
scornful ['skɔːnful] *adj* sprezzante
Scorpio ['skɔːpɪəu] *n* Scorpione *m*
scorpion ['skɔːpɪən] *n* scorpione *m*
Scot [skɔt] *n* scozzese *m/f*
scotch [skɔtʃ] *vt* (*rumour etc*) soffocare; **S~** *n* whisky *m* scozzese, scotch *m*
scot-free *adv*: **to get off ~** farla franca
Scotland ['skɔtlənd] *n* Scozia
Scots [skɔts] *adj* scozzese; ~**man/woman** *n* scozzese *m/f*
Scottish ['skɔtɪʃ] *adj* scozzese
scoundrel ['skaundrl] *n* farabutto/a; (*child*) furfantello/a
scour ['skauə*] *vt* (*search*) battere, perlustrare
scourge [skəːdʒ] *n* flagello
scout [skaut] *n* (MIL) esploratore *m*; (*also: boy ~*) giovane esploratore, scout *m inv*; ~ **around** *vi* cercare in giro; **girl ~** (*US*) *n* giovane esploratrice *f*

scowl [skaul] *vi* accigliarsi, aggrottare le sopracciglia; **to ~ at** guardare torvo

scrabble ['skræbl] *vi* (*claw*): **to ~ (at)** graffiare, grattare; (*also: ~ around*: *search*) cercare a tentoni ♦ *n*: **S~** ® Scarabeo ®

scraggy ['skrægɪ] *adj* scarno(a), molto magro(a)

scram [skræm] (*inf*) *vi* filare via

scramble ['skræmbl] *n* arrampicata ♦ *vi* inerpicarsi; **to ~ out** *etc* uscire *etc* in fretta; **to ~ for** azzuffarsi per; **~d eggs** *npl* uova *fpl* strapazzate

scrap [skræp] *n* pezzo, pezzetto; (*fight*) zuffa; (*also: ~ iron*) rottami *mpl* di ferro, ferraglia ♦ *vt* demolire; (*fig*) scartare ♦ *vi*: **to ~ (with sb)** fare a botte (con qn); **~s** *npl* (*waste*) scarti *mpl*; **~book** *n* album *m inv* di ritagli; **~ dealer** *n* commerciante *m* di ferraglia

scrape [skreɪp] *vt, vi* raschiare, grattare ♦ *n*: **to get into a ~** cacciarsi in un guaio; **~ through** *vi* farcela per un pelo; **~ together** *vt* (*money*) raggranellare; **~r** *n* raschietto

scrap: **~ heap** *n*: **on the ~ heap** (*fig*) nel dimenticatoio; **~ merchant** (*BRIT*) *n* commerciante *m* di ferraglia; **~ paper** *n* cartaccia

scrappy ['skræpɪ] *adj* frammentario(a), sconnesso(a)

scratch [skrætʃ] *n* graffio ♦ *cpd*: **~ team** squadra raccogliticcia ♦ *vt* graffiare, rigare ♦ *vi* grattare; (*paint, car*) graffiare; **to start from ~** cominciare *or* partire da zero; **to be up to ~** essere all'altezza

scrawl [skrɔːl] *n* scarabocchio ♦ *vi* scarabocchiare

scrawny ['skrɔːnɪ] *adj* scarno(a), pelle e ossa *inv*

scream [skriːm] *n* grido, urlo ♦ *vi* urlare, gridare

scree [skriː] *n* ghiaione *m*

screech [skriːtʃ] *vi* stridere

screen [skriːn] *n* schermo; (*fig*) muro, cortina, velo ♦ *vt* schermare, fare schermo a; (*from the wind etc*) riparare; (*film*) proiettare; (*book*) adattare per lo schermo; (*candidates etc*) selezionare;

~ing *n* (*MED*) dépistage *m inv*; **~play** *n* sceneggiatura

screw [skruː] *n* vite *f* ♦ *vt* avvitare; **~ up** *vt* (*paper etc*) spiegazzare; (*inf: ruin*) rovinare; **to ~ up one's eyes** strizzare gli occhi; **~driver** *n* cacciavite *m*

scribble ['skrɪbl] *n* scarabocchio ♦ *vt* scribacchiare in fretta ♦ *vi* scarabocchiare

script [skrɪpt] *n* (*CINEMA etc*) copione *m*; (*in exam*) elaborato *or* compito d'esame

scripture(s) ['skrɪptʃə(z)] *n(pl)* sacre Scritture *fpl*

scroll [skrəul] *n* rotolo di carta

scrounge [skraundʒ] (*inf*) *vt*: **to ~ sth (off *or* from sb)** scroccare qc (a qn) ♦ *n*: **on the ~** a sbafo

scrub [skrʌb] *n* (*land*) boscaglia ♦ *vt* pulire strofinando; (*reject*) annullare

scruff [skrʌf] *n*: **by the ~ of the neck** per la collottola

scruffy ['skrʌfɪ] *adj* sciatto(a)

scrum(mage) ['skrʌm(ɪdʒ)] *n* mischia

scruple ['skruːpl] *n* scrupolo

scrutiny ['skruːtɪnɪ] *n* esame *m* accurato

scuff [skʌf] *vt* (*shoes*) consumare strascicando

scuffle ['skʌfl] *n* baruffa, tafferuglio

sculptor ['skʌlptə*] *n* scultore *m*

sculpture ['skʌlptʃə*] *n* scultura

scum [skʌm] *n* schiuma; (*pej: people*) feccia

scupper ['skʌpə*] (*BRIT: inf*) *vt* far naufragare

scurrilous ['skʌrɪləs] *adj* scurrile, volgare

scurry ['skʌrɪ] *vi* sgambare, affrettarsi; **~ off** *vi* andarsene a tutta velocità

scuttle ['skʌtl] *n* (*also: coal ~*) secchio del carbone ♦ *vt* (*ship*) autoaffondare ♦ *vi* (*scamper*): **to ~ away, ~ off** darsela a gambe, scappare

scythe [saɪð] *n* falce *f*

SDP (*BRIT*) *n abbr* = **Social Democratic Party**

sea [siː] *n* mare *m* ♦ *cpd* marino(a), del mare; (*bird, fish*) di mare; (*route, transport*) marittimo(a); **by ~** (*travel*) per mare; **on the ~** (*boat*) in mare; (*town*) di mare; **to be all at ~** (*fig*) non sapere che pesci pigliare; **out to ~** al largo; **(out) at ~ in** mare; **~board** n costa; **~food** n frutti *mpl* di mare; **~ front** n lungomare m; **~gull** n gabbiano

seal [siːl] n (*animal*) foca; (*stamp*) sigillo; (*impression*) impronta del sigillo ♦ vt sigillare; **~ off** vt (*close*) sigillare; (*forbid entry to*) bloccare l'accesso a

sea level n livello del mare

seam [siːm] n cucitura; (*of coal*) filone m

seaman ['siːmən] n marinaio

seamy ['siːmɪ] adj orribile

seance ['seɪɔns] n seduta spiritica

seaplane ['siːpleɪn] n idrovolante m

seaport ['siːpɔːt] n porto di mare

search [səːtʃ] n ricerca; (*LAW: at sb's home*) perquisizione f ♦ vt frugare ♦ vi: **~ for** ricercare; **in ~ of** alla ricerca di; **~ through** vt fus frugare; **~ing** adj minuzioso(a); penetrante; **~light** n proiettore m; **~ party** n squadra di soccorso; **~ warrant** n mandato di perquisizione

seashore ['siːʃɔː*] n spiaggia

seasick ['siːsɪk] adj che soffre il mal di mare

seaside ['siːsaɪd] n spiaggia; **~ resort** n stazione f balneare

season ['siːzn] n stagione f ♦ vt condire, insaporire; **~al** adj stagionale; **~ed** adj (*fig*) con esperienza; **~ing** n condimento; **~ ticket** n abbonamento

seat [siːt] n sedile m; (*in bus, train: place*) posto; (*PARLIAMENT*) seggio; (*buttocks*) didietro; (*of trousers*) fondo ♦ vt far sedere; (*have room for*) avere or essere fornito(a) di posti a sedere per; **to be ~ed** essere seduto(a); **~ belt** n cintura di sicurezza

sea water n acqua di mare

seaweed ['siːwiːd] n alghe *fpl*

seaworthy ['siːwəːðɪ] adj atto(a) alla navigazione

sec. *abbr* = **second(s)**

secluded [sɪ'kluːdɪd] adj isolato(a), appartato(a)

seclusion [sɪ'kluːʒən] n isolamento

second¹ [sɪ'kɔnd] (*BRIT*) vt (*worker*) distaccare

second² ['sɛkənd] num secondo(a) ♦ adv (*in race etc*) al secondo posto ♦ n (*unit of time*) secondo; (*AUT: also: ~ gear*) seconda; (*COMM: imperfect*) scarto; (*BRIT: SCOL: degree*) laurea con punteggio discreto ♦ vt (*motion*) appoggiare; **~ary** adj secondario(a); **~ary school** n scuola secondaria; **~-class** adj di seconda classe ♦ adv in seconda classe; **~er** n sostenitore/trice; **~hand** adj di seconda mano, usato(a); **~ hand** n (*on clock*) lancetta dei secondi; **~ly** adv in secondo luogo; **~-rate** adj scadente; **~ thoughts** *npl* ripensamenti *mpl*; **on ~ thoughts** (*BRIT*) or **thought** (*US*) ripensandoci bene

secrecy ['siːkrəsɪ] n segretezza

secret ['siːkrɪt] adj segreto(a) ♦ n segreto; **in ~** in segreto

secretarial [sɛkrɪ'tɛərɪəl] adj di segretario(a)

secretariat [sɛkrɪ'tɛərɪət] n segretariato

secretary ['sɛkrətrɪ] n segretario/a; **S~ of State (for)** (*BRIT: POL*) ministro (di)

secretive ['siːkrətɪv] adj riservato(a)

sect [sɛkt] n setta; **~arian** [-'tɛərɪən] adj settario(a)

section ['sɛkʃən] n sezione f

sector ['sɛktə*] n settore m

secure [sɪ'kjuə*] adj sicuro(a); (*firmly fixed*) assicurato(a), ben fermato(a); (*in safe place*) al sicuro ♦ vt (*fix*) fissare, assicurare; (*get*) ottenere, assicurarsi

security [sɪ'kjuərɪtɪ] n sicurezza; (*for loan*) garanzia

sedan [sɪ'dæn] (*US*) n (*AUT*) berlina

sedate [sɪ'deɪt] adj posato(a); calmo(a) ♦ vt calmare

sedation [sɪ'deɪʃən] n (*MED*) effetto dei sedativi

sedative ['sɛdɪtɪv] n sedativo, calmante m

seduce [sɪ'djuːs] vt sedurre; **seduction** [-'dʌkʃən] n seduzione f; **seductive** [-'dʌktɪv] adj seducente

see [siː] (*pt saw, pp seen*) vt vedere; (*accompany*): **to ~ sb to the door** accompagnare qn alla porta ♦ vi vedere; (*understand*) capire ♦ n sede f vescovile;

to ~ **that** (*ensure*) badare che + *sub*, fare in modo che + *sub*; ~ **you soon!** a presto!; ~ **about** *vt fus* occuparsi di; ~ **off** *vt* salutare alla partenza; ~ **through** *vt* portare a termine ♦ *vt fus* non lasciarsi ingannare da; ~ **to** *vt fus* occuparsi di

seed [si:d] *n* seme *m*; (*fig*) germe *m*; (*TENNIS*) testa di serie; **to go to ~** fare seme; (*fig*) scadere; ~**ling** *n* piantina di semenzaio; ~**y** *adj* (*shabby: person*) sciatto(a); (: *place*) cadente

seeing ['si:ɪŋ] *conj*: ~ **(that)** visto che

seek [si:k] (*pt, pp* **sought**) *vt* cercare

seem [si:m] *vi* sembrare, parere; **there ~s to be ...** sembra che ci sia ...; ~**ingly** *adv* apparentemente

seen [si:n] *pp of* **see**

seep [si:p] *vi* filtrare, trapelare

seesaw ['si:sɔ:] *n* altalena a bilico

seethe [si:ð] *vi* ribollire; **to ~ with anger** fremere di rabbia

see-through *adj* trasparente

segregate ['sɛɡrɪɡeɪt] *vt* segregare, isolare

seize [si:z] *vt* (*grasp*) afferrare; (*take possession of*) impadronirsi di; (*LAW*) sequestrare; ~ **(up)on** *vt fus* ricorrere a; ~ **up** *vi* (*TECH*) grippare

seizure ['si:ʒə*] *n* (*MED*) attacco; (*LAW*) confisca, sequestro

seldom ['sɛldəm] *adv* raramente

select [sɪ'lɛkt] *adj* scelto(a) ♦ *vt* scegliere, selezionare; ~**ion** [-'lɛkʃən] *n* selezione *f*, scelta

self [sɛlf] *n*: **the ~** l'io *m* ♦ *prefix* auto...; ~**-assured** *adj* sicuro(a) di sé; ~**-catering** (*BRIT*) *adj* in cui ci si cucina da sé; ~**-centred** (*US* ~**-centered**) *adj* egocentrico(a); ~**-confidence** *n* sicurezza di sé; ~**-conscious** *adj* timido(a); ~**-contained** (*BRIT*) *adj* (*flat*) indipendente; ~**-control** *n* autocontrollo; ~**-defence** (*US* ~**-defense**) *n* autodifesa; (*LAW*) legittima difesa; ~**-discipline** *n* autodisciplina; ~**-employed** *adj* che lavora in proprio; ~**-evident** *adj* evidente; ~**-governing** *adj* autonomo(a); ~**-indulgent** *adj* indulgente verso se stesso(a); ~**-interest** *n* interesse *m* personale; ~**ish** *adj* egoista; ~**ishness**

n egoismo; ~**less** *adj* dimentico(a) di sé, altruista; ~**-pity** *n* autocommiserazione *f*; ~**-portrait** *n* autoritratto; ~**-possessed** *adj* controllato(a); ~**-preservation** *n* istinto di conservazione; ~**-respect** *n* rispetto di sé, amor proprio; ~**-righteous** *adj* soddisfatto(a) di sé; ~**-sacrifice** *n* abnegazione *f*; ~**-satisfied** *adj* compiaciuto(a) di sé; ~**-service** *n* autoservizio, self-service *m*; ~**-sufficient** *adj* autosufficiente; ~**-taught** *adj* autodidatta

sell [sɛl] (*pt, pp* **sold**) *vt* vendere ♦ *vi* vendersi; **to ~ at** *or* **for 1000 lire** essere in vendita a 1000 lire; ~ **off** *vt* svendere, liquidare; ~ **out** *vi*: **to ~ out (of sth)** esaurire (qc); **the tickets are all sold out** i biglietti sono esauriti; ~**-by date** *n* data di scadenza; ~**er** *n* venditore/trice; ~**ing price** *n* prezzo di vendita

sellotape ['sɛləʊteɪp] ® (*BRIT*) *n* nastro adesivo, scotch *m* ®

selves [sɛlvz] *npl of* **self**

semaphore ['sɛməfɔ:*] *n* segnalazioni *fpl* con bandierine; (*RAIL*) semaforo (ferroviario)

semblance ['sɛmbləns] *n* parvenza, apparenza

semen ['si:mən] *n* sperma *m*

semester [sɪ'mɛstə*] (*US*) *n* semestre *m*

semi... ['sɛmɪ] *prefix* semi...; ~**circle** *n* semicerchio; ~**colon** *n* punto e virgola; ~**detached (house)** (*BRIT*) *n* casa gemella; ~**final** *n* semifinale *f*

seminar ['sɛmɪnɑ:*] *n* seminario

seminary ['sɛmɪnərɪ] *n* (*REL*) seminario

semiskilled ['sɛmɪ'skɪld] *adj* (*worker*) parzialmente qualificato(a); (*work*) che richiede una qualificazione parziale

senate ['sɛnɪt] *n* senato; **senator** *n* senatore/trice

send [sɛnd] (*pt, pp* **sent**) *vt* mandare; ~ **away** *vt* (*letter, goods*) spedire; (*person*) mandare via; ~ **away for** *vt fus* richiedere per posta, farsi spedire; ~ **back** *vt* rimandare; ~ **for** *vt fus* mandare a chiamare, far venire; ~ **off** *vt* (*goods*) spedire; (*BRIT: SPORT: player*) espellere; ~ **out** *vt* (*invitation*) diramare; ~ **up** *vt* (*person, price*) far salire; (*BRIT: parody*) mettere in ridicolo; **~er** *n* mittente *m/f*; **~-off** *n*: **to give sb a good ~-off** festeggiare la partenza di qn

senior ['si:nɪə*] *adj* (*older*) più vecchio(a); (*of higher rank*) di grado più elevato; **~ citizen** *n* persona anziana; **~ity** [-'ɔrɪtɪ] *n* anzianità

sensation [sɛn'seɪʃən] *n* sensazione *f*; **~al** *adj* sensazionale; (*marvellous*) eccezionale

sense [sɛns] *n* senso; (*feeling*) sensazione *f*, senso; (*meaning*) senso, significato; (*wisdom*) buonsenso ♦ *vt* sentire, percepire; **it makes ~** ha senso; **~less** *adj* sciocco(a); (*unconscious*) privo(a) di sensi

sensible ['sɛnsɪbl] *adj* sensato(a), ragionevole

sensitive ['sɛnsɪtɪv] *adj* sensibile; (*skin, question*) delicato(a)

sensual ['sɛnsjuəl] *adj* sensuale

sensuous ['sɛnsjuəs] *adj* sensuale

sent [sɛnt] *pt, pp of* **send**

sentence ['sɛntns] *n* (*LING*) frase *f*; (*LAW: judgment*) sentenza; (*: punishment*) condanna ♦ *vt*: **to ~ sb to death/to 5 years** condannare qn a morte/a 5 anni

sentiment ['sɛntɪmənt] *n* sentimento; (*opinion*) opinione *f*; **~al** [-'mɛntl] *adj* sentimentale

sentry ['sɛntrɪ] *n* sentinella

separate [*adj* 'sɛprɪt, *vb* 'sɛpəreɪt] *adj* separato(a) ♦ *vt* separare ♦ *vi* separarsi; **~ly** *adv* separatamente; **~s** *npl* (*clothes*) coordinati *mpl*; **separation** [-'reɪʃən] *n* separazione *f*

September [sɛp'tɛmbə*] *n* settembre *m*

septic ['sɛptɪk] *adj* settico(a); (*wound*) infettato(a); **~ tank** *n* fossa settica

sequel ['si:kwl] *n* conseguenza; (*of story*) seguito; (*of film*) sequenza

sequence ['si:kwəns] *n* (*series*) serie *f*; (*order*) ordine *m*

sequin ['si:kwɪn] *n* lustrino, paillette *f inv*

serene [sə'ri:n] *adj* sereno(a), calmo(a)

sergeant ['sɑ:dʒənt] *n* sergente *m*; (*POLICE*) brigadiere *m*

serial ['sɪərɪəl] *n* (*PRESS*) romanzo a puntate; (*RADIO, TV*) trasmissione *f* a puntate, serial *m inv*; **~ize** *vt* pubblicare (*or* trasmettere) a puntate; **~ killer** *n* serial-killer *m/f inv*; **~ number** *n* numero di serie

series ['sɪərɪ:z] *n inv* serie *f inv*; (*PUBLISHING*) collana

serious ['sɪərɪəs] *adj* serio(a), grave; **~ly** *adv* seriamente

sermon ['sə:mən] *n* sermone *m*

serrated [sɪ'reɪtɪd] *adj* seghettato(a)

serum ['sɪərəm] *n* siero

servant ['sə:vənt] *n* domestico/a

serve [sə:v] *vt* (*employer etc*) servire, essere a servizio di; (*purpose*) servire a; (*customer, food, meal*) servire; (*apprenticeship*) fare; (*prison term*) scontare ♦ *vi* (*also TENNIS*) servire; (*be useful*): **to ~ as/for/to do** servire da/per/per fare ♦ *n* (*TENNIS*) servizio; **it ~s him right** ben gli sta, se l'è meritata; **~ out** *vt* (*food*) servire; **~ up** *vt* = **~ out**

service ['sə:vɪs] *n* servizio; (*AUT: maintenance*) assistenza, revisione *f* ♦ *vt* (*car, washing machine*) revisionare; **the S~s** le forze armate; **to be of ~ to sb** essere d'aiuto a qn; **~able** *adj* pratico(a), utile; **~ charge** (*BRIT*) *n* servizio; **~man** *n* militare *m*; **~ station** *n* stazione *f* di servizio

serviette [sə:vɪ'ɛt] (*BRIT*) *n* tovagliolo

session ['sɛʃən] *n* (*sitting*) seduta, sessione *f*; (*SCOL*) anno scolastico (*or* accademico)

set [sɛt] (*pt, pp* set) *n* serie *f inv*; (*of cutlery etc*) servizio; (*RADIO, TV*) apparecchio; (*TENNIS*) set *m inv*; (*group of people*) mondo, ambiente *m*; (*CINEMA*) scenario; (*THEATRE: stage*) scene *fpl*; (*: scenery*) scenario; (*MATH*) insieme *m*; (*HAIRDRESSING*) messa in piega ♦ *adj* (*fixed*) stabilito(a), determinato(a); (*ready*) pronto(a) ♦ *vt* (*place*) posare, mettere; (*arrange*) sistemare; (*fix*) fissare; (*adjust*) regolare; (*decide: rules etc*) stabilire, fissare ♦ *vi* (*sun*) tramontare; (*jam, jelly*) rapprendersi; (*concrete*) fare presa; **to be ~ on doing** essere deciso a fare; **to ~ to**

settee → sham

music mettere in musica; **to ~ on fire** dare fuoco a; **to ~ free** liberare; **to ~ sth going** mettere in moto qc; **to ~ sail** prendere il mare; **~ about** vt fus (task) intraprendere, mettersi a; **~ aside** vt mettere da parte; **~ back** vt (in time): **to ~ back (by)** mettere indietro (di); (inf: cost): **it ~ me back £5** mi è costato la bellezza di 5 sterline; **~ off** vi partire ♦ vt (bomb) far scoppiare; (cause to start) mettere in moto; (show up well) dare risalto a; **~ out** vi partire ♦ vt (arrange) disporre; (state) esporre, presentare; **to ~ out to do** proporsi di fare; **~ up** vt (organization) fondare, costituire; **~back** n (hitch) contrattempo, inconveniente m; **~ menu** n menù m inv fisso

settee [sɛˈtiː] n divano, sofà m inv

setting [ˈsɛtɪŋ] n (background) ambiente m; (of controls) posizione f; (of sun) tramonto; (of jewel) montatura

settle [ˈsɛtl] vt (argument, matter) appianare; (accounts) regolare; (MED: calm) calmare ♦ vi (bird, dust etc) posarsi; (sediment) depositarsi; (also: ~ down) sistemarsi, stabilirsi; calmarsi; **to ~ for sth** accontentarsi di qc; **to ~ on sth** decidersi per qc; **~ in** vi sistemarsi; **~ up** vi: **to ~ up with sb** regolare i conti con qn; **~ment** n (payment) pagamento, saldo; (agreement) accordo; (colony) colonia; (village etc) villaggio, comunità f inv; **~r** n colonizzatore/trice

setup [ˈsɛtʌp] n (arrangement) sistemazione f; (situation) situazione f

seven [ˈsɛvn] num sette; **~teen** num diciassette; **~th** num settimo(a); **~ty** num settanta

sever [ˈsɛvə*] vt recidere, tagliare; (relations) troncare

several [ˈsɛvərl] adj, pron alcuni(e), diversi(e); **~ of us** alcuni di noi

severance [ˈsɛvərəns] n (of relations) rottura; **~ pay** n indennità di licenziamento

severe [sɪˈvɪə*] adj severo(a); (serious) serio(a), grave; (hard) duro(a); (plain) semplice, sobrio(a); **severity** [sɪˈvɛrɪtɪ] n severità; gravità; (of weather) rigore m

sew [səu] (pt **sewed**, pp **sewn**) vt, vi cucire; **~ up** vt ricucire

sewage [ˈsuːɪdʒ] n acque fpl di scolo

sewer [ˈsuːə*] n fogna

sewing [ˈsəuɪŋ] n cucitura; cucito; **~ machine** n macchina da cucire

sewn [səun] pp of **sew**

sex [sɛks] n sesso; **to have ~ with** avere rapporti sessuali con; **~ist** adj, n sessista m/f

sexual [ˈsɛksjuəl] adj sessuale

sexy [ˈsɛksɪ] adj provocante, sexy inv

shabby [ˈʃæbɪ] adj malandato(a); (behaviour) vergognoso(a)

shack [ʃæk] n baracca, capanna

shackles [ˈʃæklz] npl ferri mpl, catene fpl

shade [ʃeɪd] n ombra; (for lamp) paralume m; (of colour) tonalità f inv; (small quantity): **a ~ (more/too large)** un po' (di più/troppo grande) ♦ vt ombreggiare, fare ombra a; **in the ~** all'ombra

shadow [ˈʃædəu] n ombra ♦ vt (follow) pedinare; **~ cabinet** n (BRIT) (POL) governo m ombra inv; **~y** adj ombreggiato(a), ombroso(a); (dim) vago(a), indistinto(a)

shady [ˈʃeɪdɪ] adj ombroso(a); (fig: dishonest) losco(a), equivoco(a)

shaft [ʃɑːft] n (of arrow, spear) asta; (AUT, TECH) albero; (of mine) pozzo; (of lift) tromba; (of light) raggio

shaggy [ˈʃægɪ] adj ispido(a)

shake [ʃeɪk] (pt **shook**, pp **shaken**) vt scuotere; (bottle, cocktail) agitare ♦ vi tremare; **to ~ one's head** (in refusal, dismay) scuotere la testa; **to ~ hands with sb** stringere or dare la mano a qn; **~ off** vt scrollare (via); (fig) sbarazzarsi di; **~ up** vt scuotere; **~n** pp of **shake**; **shaky** adj (hand, voice) tremante; (building) traballante

shall [ʃæl] aux vb: **I ~ go** andrò; **~ I open the door?** apro io la porta?; **I'll get some, ~ I?** ne prendo un po', va bene?

shallow [ˈʃæləu] adj poco profondo(a); (fig) superficiale

sham [ʃæm] n finzione f, messinscena;

(*jewellery*, *furniture*) imitazione *f*

shambles ['ʃæmblz] *n* confusione *f*, baraonda, scompiglio

shame [ʃeɪm] *n* vergogna ♦ *vt* far vergognare; **it is a ~ (that/to do)** è un peccato (che + *sub*/fare); **what a ~!** che peccato!; **~faced** *adj* vergognoso(a); **~ful** *adj* vergognoso(a); **~less** *adj* sfrontato(a); (*immodest*) spudorato(a)

shampoo [ʃæm'puː] *n* shampoo *m inv* ♦ *vt* fare lo shampoo a; **~ and set** *n* shampoo e messa in piega

shamrock ['ʃæmrɔk] *n* trifoglio (*simbolo nazionale dell'Irlanda*)

shandy ['ʃændɪ] *n* birra con gassosa

shan't [ʃɑːnt] = **shall not**

shanty town ['ʃæntɪ-] *n* bidonville *f inv*

shape [ʃeɪp] *n* forma ♦ *vt* formare; (*statement*) formulare; (*sb's ideas*) condizionare; **to take ~** prendere forma; **~ up** *vi* (*events*) andare, mettersi; (*person*) cavarsela; **-shaped** *suffix*: **heart-shaped** a forma di cuore; **~less** *adj* senza forma, informe; **~ly** *adj* ben proporzionato(a)

share [ʃɛə*] *n* (*thing received*, *contribution*) parte *f*; (*COMM*) azione *f* ♦ *vt* dividere; (*have in common*) condividere, avere in comune; **~ out** *vi* dividere; **~holder** *n* azionista *m/f*

shark [ʃɑːk] *n* squalo, pescecane *m*

sharp [ʃɑːp] *adj* (*razor*, *knife*) affilato(a); (*point*) acuto(a), acuminato(a); (*nose*, *chin*) aguzzo(a); (*outline*, *contrast*) netto(a); (*cold*, *pain*) pungente; (*voice*) stridulo(a); (*person*: *quick-witted*) sveglio(a); (: *unscrupulous*) disonesto(a); (*MUS*) **C ~** do diesis ♦ *n* (*MUS*) diesis *m inv* ♦ *adv*: **at 2 o'clock ~** alle due in punto; **~en** *vt* affilare; (*pencil*) fare la punta a; (*fig*) acuire; **~ener** *n* (*also: pencil ~ener*) temperamatite *m inv*; **~-eyed** *adj* dalla vista acuta; **~ly** *adv* (*turn*, *stop*) bruscamente; (*stand out*, *contrast*) nettamente; (*criticize*, *retort*) duramente, aspramente

shatter ['ʃætə*] *vt* mandare in frantumi, frantumare; (*fig*: *upset*) distruggere; (: *ruin*) rovinare ♦ *vi* frantumarsi, andare in pezzi

shave [ʃeɪv] *vt* radere, rasare ♦ *vi* radersi, farsi la barba ♦ *n*: **to have a ~** farsi la barba; **~r** *n* (*also: electric ~r*) rasoio elettrico

shaving ['ʃeɪvɪŋ] *n* (*action*) rasatura; **~s** *npl* (*of wood etc*) trucioli *mpl*; **~ brush** *n* pennello da barba; **~ cream** *n* crema da barba; **~ foam** *n* = **~ cream**

shawl [ʃɔːl] *n* scialle *m*

she [ʃiː] *pron* ella, lei; **~-cat** *n* gatta; **~-elephant** *n* elefantessa

sheaf [ʃiːf] (*pl* **sheaves**) *n* covone *m*; (*of papers*) fascio

shear [ʃɪə*] (*pt* **~ed**, *pp* **~ed** *or* **shorn**) *vt* (*sheep*) tosare; **~ off** *vi* spezzarsi; **~s** *npl* (*for hedge*) cesoie *fpl*

sheath [ʃiːθ] *n* fodero, guaina; (*contraceptive*) preservativo

sheaves [ʃiːvz] *npl of* **sheaf**

shed [ʃɛd] (*pt*, *pp* **shed**) *n* capannone *m* ♦ *vt* (*leaves*, *fur etc*) perdere; (*tears*, *blood*) versare; (*workers*) liberarsi di

she'd [ʃiːd] = **she had**; **she would**

sheen [ʃiːn] *n* lucentezza

sheep [ʃiːp] *n inv* pecora; **~dog** *n* cane *m* da pastore; **~ish** *adj* vergognoso(a), timido(a); **~skin** *n* pelle *f* di pecora

sheer [ʃɪə*] *adj* (*utter*) vero(a) (e proprio(a)); (*steep*) a picco, perpendicolare; (*almost transparent*) sottile ♦ *adv* a picco

sheet [ʃiːt] *n* (*on bed*) lenzuolo; (*of paper*) foglio; (*of glass*, *ice*) lastra; (*of metal*) foglio, lamina; **~ lightning** *n* lampo diffuso

sheik(h) [ʃeɪk] *n* sceicco

shelf [ʃɛlf] (*pl* **shelves**) *n* scaffale *m*, mensola

shell [ʃɛl] *n* (*on beach*) conchiglia; (*of egg*, *nut etc*) guscio; (*explosive*) granata; (*of building*) scheletro ♦ *vt* (*peas*) sgranare; (*MIL*) bombardare; **~ suit** *n* (*lightweight*) tuta di acetato; (*heavier*) tuta di trilobato

she'll [ʃiːl] = **she will**; **she shall**

shellfish ['ʃɛlfɪʃ] *n inv* (*crab etc*) crostaceo; (*scallop etc*) mollusco; (*pl*: *as food*) crostacei; molluschi

shelter ['ʃɛltə*] *n* riparo, rifugio ♦ *vt* riparare, proteggere; (*give lodging to*) dare rifugio *or* asilo a ♦ *vi* ripararsi, mettersi al riparo; **~ed** *adj* riparato(a); **~ed housing** (BRIT) *n* alloggi dotati di strutture per anziani o handicappati

shelve [ʃɛlv] *vt* (*fig*) accantonare, rimandare; **~s** *npl of* **shelf**

shepherd ['ʃɛpəd] *n* pastore *m* ♦ *vt* (*guide*) guidare; **~'s pie** (BRIT) *n* timballo di carne macinata e purè di patate

sheriff ['ʃɛrɪf] (US) *n* sceriffo

sherry ['ʃɛrɪ] *n* sherry *m inv*

she's [ʃiːz] = **she is**; **she has**

Shetland ['ʃɛtlənd] *n* (*also:* **the ~s, the ~ Isles**) le isole Shetland, le Shetland

shield [ʃiːld] *n* scudo; (*trophy*) scudetto; (*protection*) schermo ♦ *vt*: **to ~ (from)** riparare (da), proteggere (da *or* contro)

shift [ʃɪft] *n* (*change*) cambiamento; (*of workers*) turno ♦ *vt* spostare, muovere; (*remove*) rimuovere ♦ *vi* spostarsi, muoversi; **~less** *adj*: **a ~less person** un(a) fannullone(a); **~ work** *n* lavoro a squadre; **~y** *adj* ambiguo(a); (*eyes*) sfuggente

shilling ['ʃɪlɪŋ] (BRIT) *n* scellino (= *12 old pence; 20 in a pound*)

shilly-shally ['ʃɪlɪʃælɪ] *vi* tentennare, esitare

shimmer ['ʃɪmə*] *vi* brillare, luccicare

shin [ʃɪn] *n* tibia

shine [ʃaɪn] (*pt, pp* **shone**) *n* splendore *m*, lucentezza ♦ *vi* (ri)splendere, brillare ♦ *vt* far brillare, far risplendere; (*torch*): **to ~ sth on** puntare qc verso

shingle ['ʃɪŋgl] *n* (*on beach*) ciottoli *mpl*; **~s** *n* (MED) herpes zoster *m*

shiny ['ʃaɪnɪ] *adj* lucente, lucido(a)

ship [ʃɪp] *n* nave *f* ♦ *vt* trasportare (via mare); (*send*) spedire (via mare); **~building** *n* costruzione *f* navale; **~ment** *n* carico; **~ping** *n* (*ships*) naviglio; (*traffic*) navigazione *f*; **~shape** *adj* in perfetto ordine; **~wreck** *n* relitto; (*event*) naufragio ♦ *vt*: **to be ~wrecked** naufragare, fare naufragio; **~yard** *n* cantiere *m* navale

shire ['ʃaɪə*] (BRIT) *n* contea

shirk [ʃəːk] *vt* sottrarsi a, evitare

shirt [ʃəːt] *n* camicia; **in ~ sleeves** in maniche di camicia

shit [ʃɪt] (*inf!*) *excl* merda (!)

shiver ['ʃɪvə*] *n* brivido ♦ *vi* rabbrividire, tremare

shoal [ʃəul] *n* (*of fish*) banco; (*fig*) massa

shock [ʃɔk] *n* (*impact*) urto, colpo; (ELEC) scossa; (*emotional*) colpo, shock *m inv*; (MED) shock ♦ *vt* colpire, scioccare; scandalizzare; **~ absorber** *n* ammortizzatore *m*; **~ing** *adj* scioccante, traumatizzante; scandaloso(a)

shod [ʃɔd] *pt, pp of* **shoe**

shoddy ['ʃɔdɪ] *adj* scadente

shoe [ʃuː] *n* (*pt, pp* **shod**) scarpa; (*also:* **horse~**) ferro di cavallo ♦ *vt* (*horse*) ferrare; **~brush** *n* spazzola per scarpe; **~lace** *n* stringa; **~ polish** *n* lucido per scarpe; **~shop** *n* calzoleria; **~string** *n* (*fig*): **on a ~string** con quattro soldi

shone [ʃɔn] *pt, pp of* **shine**

shoo [ʃuː] *excl* sciò!, via!

shook [ʃuk] *pt of* **shake**

shoot [ʃuːt] (*pt, pp* **shot**) *n* (*on branch, seedling*) germoglio ♦ *vt* (*game*) cacciare, andare a caccia di; (*person*) sparare a; (*execute*) fucilare; (*film*) girare ♦ *vi* (*with gun*): **to ~ (at)** sparare (a), fare fuoco (su); (*with bow*): **to ~ (at)** tirare (su); (FOOTBALL) sparare, tirare (forte); **~ down** *vt* (*plane*) abbattere; **~ in/out** *vi* entrare/ uscire come una freccia; **~ up** *vi* (*fig*) salire alle stelle; **~ing** *n* (*shots*) sparatoria; (HUNTING) caccia; **~ing star** *n* stella cadente

shop [ʃɔp] *n* negozio; (*workshop*) officina ♦ *vi* (*also:* **go ~ping**) fare spese; **~ assistant** (BRIT) *n* commesso/a; **~ floor** *n* officina; (BRIT: *fig*) operai *mpl*, maestranze *fpl*; **~keeper** *n* negoziante *m/f*, bottegaio/a; **~lifting** *n* taccheggio; **~per** *n* compratore/trice; **~ping** *n* (*goods*) spesa, acquisti *mpl*; **~ping bag** *n* borsa per la spesa; **~ping centre** (US **~ping center**) *n* centro commerciale; **~-soiled** *adj* sciupato(a) a forza di stare in vetrina; **~ steward** (BRIT) *n* (INDUSTRY) rappresentante *m* sindacale; **~ window** *n* vetrina

shore [ʃɔː*] *n* (*of sea*) riva, spiaggia; (*of*

lake) riva ♦ *vt*: **to ~ (up)** puntellare; **on ~** a riva

shorn [ʃɔːn] *pp of* **shear**

short [ʃɔːt] *adj* (*not long*) corto(a); (*soon finished*) breve; (*person*) basso(a); (*curt*) brusco(a), secco(a); (*insufficient*) insufficiente ♦ *n* (*also: ~ film*) cortometraggio; **(a pair of) ~s** (i) calzoncini *m*; **to be ~ of sth** essere a corto *di or* mancare di qc; **in ~** in breve; **~ of doing** a meno che non si faccia; **everything ~ of** tutto fuorché; **it is ~ for** è l'abbreviazione *or* il diminutivo di; **to cut ~** (*speech, visit*) accorciare, abbreviare; **to fall ~ of** venir meno a; non soddisfare; **to run ~ of** rimanere senza; **to stop ~** fermarsi di colpo; **to stop ~ of** non arrivare fino a; **~age** *n* scarsezza, carenza; **~bread** *n* biscotto di pasta frolla; **~-change** *vt*: **to ~-change sb** imbrogliare qn sul resto; **~-circuit** *n* cortocircuito; **~coming** *n* difetto; **~(crust) pastry** (*BRIT*) *n* pasta frolla; **~cut** *n* scorciatoia; **~en** *vt* accorciare, ridurre; **~fall** *n* deficit *m*; **~hand** (*BRIT*) *n* stenografia; **~hand typist** (*BRIT*) *n* stenodattilografo/a; **~ list** (*BRIT*) *n* (*for job*) rosa dei candidati; **~-lived** *adj* di breve durata; **~ly** *adv* fra poco; **~-sighted** (*BRIT*) *adj* miope; **~-staffed** *adj* a corto di personale; **~ story** *n* racconto, novella; **~-tempered** *adj* irascibile; **~-term** *adj* (*effect*) di *or* a breve durata; (*borrowing*) a breve scadenza; **~wave** *n* (*RADIO*) onde *fpl* corte

shot [ʃɔt] *pt, pp of* **shoot** ♦ *n* sparo, colpo; (*try*) prova; (*FOOTBALL*) tiro; (*injection*) iniezione *f*; (*PHOT*) foto *f inv*; **like a ~** come un razzo; (*very readily*) immediatamente; **~gun** *n* fucile *m* da caccia

should [ʃud] *aux vb*: **I ~ go now** dovrei andare ora; **he ~ be there now** dovrebbe essere arrivato ora; **I ~ go if I were you** se fossi in te andrei; **I ~ like to** mi piacerebbe

shoulder [ˈʃəʊldə*] *n* spalla; (*BRIT: of road*): **hard ~** banchina ♦ *vt* (*fig*) addossarsi, prendere sulle proprie spalle;

~ bag *n* borsa a tracolla; **~ blade** *n* scapola; **~ strap** *n* bretella, spallina

shouldn't [ˈʃudnt] = **should not**

shout [ʃaut] *n* urlo, grido ♦ *vt* gridare ♦ *vi* (*also: ~ out*) urlare, gridare; **~ down** *vt* zittire gridando; **~ing** *n* urli *mpl*

shove [ʃʌv] *vt* spingere; (*inf: put*): **to ~ sth in** ficcare qc in; **~ off** (*inf*) *vi* sloggiare, smammare

shovel [ˈʃʌvl] *n* pala ♦ *vt* spalare

show [ʃəʊ] (*pt* **~ed**, *pp* **shown**) *n* (*of emotion*) dimostrazione *f*, manifestazione *f*; (*semblance*) apparenza; (*exhibition*) mostra, esposizione *f*; (*THEATRE, CINEMA*) spettacolo ♦ *vt* far vedere, mostrare; (*courage etc*) dimostrare, dar prova di; (*exhibit*) esporre ♦ *vi* vedersi, essere visibile; **for ~** per fare scena; **on ~** (*exhibits etc*) esposto(a); **~ in** *vt* (*person*) far entrare; **~ off** *vi* (*pej*) esibirsi, mettersi in mostra ♦ *vt* (*display*) mettere in risalto; (*pej*) mettere in mostra; **~ out** *vt* (*person*) accompagnare alla porta; **~ up** *vi* (*stand out*) essere ben visibile; (*inf: turn up*) farsi vedere ♦ *vt* mettere in risalto; **~ business** *n* industria dello spettacolo; **~down** *n* prova di forza

shower [ˈʃaʊə*] *n* (*rain*) acquazzone *m*; (*of stones etc*) pioggia; (*also: ~bath*) doccia ♦ *vi* fare la doccia ♦ *vt*: **to ~ sb with** (*gifts, abuse etc*) coprire qn di; (*missiles*) lanciare contro qn una pioggia di; **to have a ~** fare la doccia; **~proof** *adj* impermeabile

showing [ˈʃəʊɪŋ] *n* (*of film*) proiezione *f*

show jumping *n* concorso ippico (di salto ad ostacoli)

shown [ʃəʊn] *pp of* **show**

show-off (*inf*) *n* (*person*) esibizionista *m/f*

showpiece [ˈʃəʊpiːs] *n* pezzo forte

showroom [ˈʃəʊrum] *n* sala d'esposizione

shrank [ʃræŋk] *pt of* **shrink**

shrapnel [ˈʃræpnl] *n* shrapnel *m*

shred [ʃred] *n* (*gen pl*) brandello ♦ *vt* fare a brandelli; (*CULIN*) sminuzzare, tagliuzzare; **~der** *n* (*vegetable ~der*) grattugia; (*document ~der*) distruttore *m*

di documenti
shrewd [ʃruːd] *adj* astuto(a), scaltro(a)
shriek [ʃriːk] *n* strillo ♦ *vi* strillare
shrill [ʃrɪl] *adj* acuto(a), stridulo(a),
stridente
shrimp [ʃrɪmp] *n* gamberetto
shrine [ʃraɪn] *n* reliquario; (*place*)
santuario
shrink [ʃrɪŋk] (*pt* **shrank**, *pp* **shrunk**) *vi*
restringersi; (*fig*) ridursi; (*also*: ~ *away*)
ritrarsi ♦ *vt* (*wool*) far restringere ♦ *n*
(*inf*: *pej*) psicanalista *m/f*; **to ~ from
doing sth** rifuggire dal fare qc; **~age** *n*
restringimento; **~wrap** *vt* confezionare
con pellicola di plastica
shrivel [ʃrɪvl] (*also*: ~ *up*) *vt* raggrinzare,
avvizzire ♦ *vi* raggrinzirsi, avvizzire
shroud [ʃraud] *n* lenzuolo funebre ♦ *vt*:
~**ed in mystery** avvolto(a) nel mistero
Shrove Tuesday [ʃrəuv-] *n* martedì *m*
grasso
shrub [ʃrʌb] *n* arbusto; **~bery** *n* arbusti
mpl
shrug [ʃrʌg] *n* scrollata di spalle ♦ *vt*, *vi*:
to ~ (one's shoulders) alzare le spalle,
fare spallucce; **~ off** *vt* passare sopra a
shrunk [ʃrʌŋk] *pp of* **shrink**
shudder [ʃʌdə*] *n* brivido ♦ *vi*
rabbrividire
shuffle [ʃʌfl] *vt* (*cards*) mescolare; **to ~
(one's feet)** strascicare i piedi
shun [ʃʌn] *vt* sfuggire, evitare
shunt [ʃʌnt] *vt* (*RAIL*: *direct*) smistare;
(: *divert*) deviare; (*object*) spostare
shut [ʃʌt] (*pt*, *pp* **shut**) *vt* chiudere ♦ *vi*
chiudersi, chiudere; **~ down** *vt*, *vi*
chiudere definitivamente; **~ off** *vt*
fermare, bloccare; **~ up** *vi* (*inf*: *keep
quiet*) stare zitto(a), fare silenzio ♦ *vt*
(*close*) chiudere; (*silence*) far tacere; **~ter**
n imposta; (*PHOT*) otturatore *m*
shuttle [ʃʌtl] *n* spola, navetta; (*space ~*)
navetta spaziale; (*also*: ~ *service*)
servizio *m* navetta *inv*
shuttlecock [ʃʌtlkɔk] *n* volano
shuttle diplomacy *n la gestione dei
rapporti diplomatici caratterizzata da
frequenti viaggi e incontri dei
rappresentanti del governo*

shy [ʃaɪ] *adj* timido(a)
sibling [sɪblɪŋ] *n* fratello/sorella
Sicily [sɪsɪlɪ] *n* Sicilia
sick [sɪk] *adj* (*ill*) malato(a); (*vomiting*): **to
be ~** vomitare; (*humour*) macabro(a); **to
feel ~** avere la nausea; **to be ~ of** (*fig*)
averne abbastanza di; **~ bay** *n*
infermeria; **~en** *vt* nauseare ♦ *vi*: **to be
~ening for sth** (*cold etc*) covare qc
sickle [sɪkl] *n* falcetto
sick: **~ leave** *n* congedo per malattia; **~ly**
adj malaticcio(a); (*causing nausea*)
nauseante; **~ness** *n* malattia; (*vomiting*)
vomito; **~ pay** *n* sussidio per malattia
side [saɪd] *n* lato; (*of lake*) riva; (*team*)
squadra ♦ *cpd* (*door, entrance*) laterale
♦ *vi*: **to ~ with sb** parteggiare per qn,
prendere le parti di qn; **by the ~ of** a
fianco di; (*road*) sul ciglio di; **~ by ~**
fianco a fianco; **from ~ to ~** da una parte
all'altra; **to take ~s (with)** schierarsi
(con); **~board** *n* credenza; **~burns** (*BRIT*
~boards) *npl* (*whiskers*) basette *fpl*; **~
effect** *n* (*MED*) effetto collaterale; **~light** *n*
(*AUT*) luce *f* di posizione; **~line** *n* (*SPORT*)
linea laterale; (*fig*) attività secondaria;
~long *adj* obliquo(a); **~saddle** *adv*
all'amazzone; **~ show** *n* attrazione *f*;
~step *vt* (*question*) eludere; (*problem*)
scavalcare; **~ street** *n* traversa; **~track**
vt (*fig*) distrarre; **~walk** (*US*) *n*
marciapiede *m*; **~ways** *adv* (*move*) di
lato, di fianco
siding [saɪdɪŋ] *n* (*RAIL*) binario di
raccordo
sidle [saɪdl] *vi*: **to ~ up (to)** avvicinarsi
furtivamente (a)
siege [siːdʒ] *n* assedio
sieve [sɪv] *n* setaccio ♦ *vt* setacciare
sift [sɪft] *vt* passare al crivello; (*fig*)
vagliare
sigh [saɪ] *n* sospiro ♦ *vi* sospirare
sight [saɪt] *n* (*faculty*) vista; (*spectacle*)
spettacolo; (*on gun*) mira ♦ *vt* avvistare;
in ~ in vista; **on ~** a vista; **out of ~** non
visibile; **~seeing** *n* giro turistico; **to go
~seeing** visitare una località
sign [saɪn] *n* segno; (*with hand etc*) segno,
gesto; (*notice*) insegna, cartello ♦ *vt*

firmare; (*player*) ingaggiare; ~ **on** *vi* (*MIL*) arruolarsi; (*as unemployed*) iscriversi sulla lista (dell'ufficio di collocamento); ♦ *vt* (*MIL*) arruolare; (*employee*) assumere; ~ **over** *vt*: **to** ~ **sth over to sb** cedere qc con scrittura legale a qn; ~ **up** *vi* (*MIL*) arruolarsi; (*for course*) iscriversi ♦ *vt* (*player*) ingaggiare; (*recruits*) reclutare

signal ['sɪgnl] *n* segnale *m* ♦ *vi* (*AUT*) segnalare, mettere la freccia ♦ *vt* (*person*) fare segno a; (*message*) comunicare per mezzo di segnali; **~man** *n* (*RAIL*) deviatore *m*

signature ['sɪgnətʃə*] *n* firma; ~ **tune** *n* sigla musicale

signet ring ['sɪgnət-] *n* anello con sigillo

significance [sɪg'nɪfɪkəns] *n* significato; importanza

significant [sɪg'nɪfɪkənt] *adj* significativo(a)

sign language *n* linguaggio dei muti

signpost ['saɪnpəust] *n* cartello indicatore

silence ['saɪlns] *n* silenzio ♦ *vt* far tacere, ridurre al silenzio; **~r** *n* (*on gun*, *BRIT*: *AUT*) silenziatore *m*

silent ['saɪlnt] *adj* silenzioso(a); (*film*) muto(a); **to remain** ~ tacere, stare zitto; ~ **partner** *n* (*COMM*) socio inattivo

silhouette [sɪlu:'ɛt] *n* silhouette *f inv*

silicon chip ['sɪlɪkən-] *n* piastrina di silicio

silk [sɪlk] *n* seta ♦ *adj* di seta; **~y** *adj* di seta

silly ['sɪlɪ] *adj* stupido(a), sciocco(a)

silt [sɪlt] *n* limo

silver ['sɪlvə*] *n* argento; (*money*) monete da 5, 10 or 50 pence; (*also*: ~*ware*) argenteria ♦ *adj* d'argento; ~ **paper** (*BRIT*) *n* carta argentata, (carta) stagnola; **~-plated** *adj* argentato(a); **~smith** *n* argentiere *m*; **~y** *adj* (*colour*) argenteo(a); (*sound*) argentino(a)

similar ['sɪmɪlə*] *adj*: ~ **(to)** simile (a); **~ly** *adv* allo stesso modo; così pure

simile ['sɪmɪlɪ] *n* similitudine *f*

simmer ['sɪmə*] *vi* cuocere a fuoco lento

simpering ['sɪmpərɪŋ] *adj* lezioso(a), smorfioso(a)

simple ['sɪmpl] *adj* semplice; **simplicity** [-'plɪsɪtɪ] *n* semplicità; **simply** *adv* semplicemente

simultaneous [sɪməl'teɪnɪəs] *adj* simultaneo(a)

sin [sɪn] *n* peccato ♦ *vi* peccare

since [sɪns] *adv* da allora ♦ *prep* da ♦ *conj* (*time*) da quando; (*because*) poiché, dato che; ~ **then, ever** ~ da allora

sincere [sɪn'sɪə*] *adj* sincero(a); **~ly** *adv*: **yours ~ly** (*in letters*) distinti saluti; **sincerity** [-'serɪtɪ] *n* sincerità

sinew ['sɪnju:] *n* tendine *m*

sinful ['sɪnful] *adj* peccaminoso(a)

sing [sɪŋ] (*pt* **sang**, *pp* **sung**) *vt*, *vi* cantare

singe [sɪndʒ] *vt* bruciacchiare

singer ['sɪŋə*] *n* cantante *m/f*

singing ['sɪŋɪŋ] *n* canto

single ['sɪŋgl] *adj* solo(a), unico(a); (*unmarried*: *man*) celibe; (: *woman*) nubile; (*not double*) semplice ♦ *n* (*BRIT*: *also*: ~ *ticket*) biglietto di (sola) andata; (*record*) 45 giri *m*; **~s** *n* (*TENNIS*) singolo; ~ **out** *vt* scegliere; (*distinguish*) distinguere; **~-breasted** *adj* a un petto; ~ **file** *n*: **in ~ file** in fila indiana; **~-handed** *adv* senza aiuto, da solo(a); **~-minded** *adj* tenace, risoluto(a); ~ **room** *n* camera singola

singly ['sɪŋglɪ] *adv* separatamente

singular ['sɪŋgjulə*] *adj* (*exceptional*, *LING*) singolare ♦ *n* (*LING*) singolare *m*

sinister ['sɪnɪstə*] *adj* sinistro(a)

sink [sɪŋk] (*pt* **sank**, *pp* **sunk**) *n* lavandino, acquaio ♦ *vt* (*ship*) (fare) affondare, colare a picco; (*foundations*) scavare; (*piles etc*): **to ~ sth into** conficcare qc in ♦ *vi* affondare, andare a fondo; (*ground etc*) cedere, avvallarsi; **my heart sank** mi sentii venir meno; ~ **in** *vi* penetrare

sinner ['sɪnə*] *n* peccatore/trice

sinus ['saɪnəs] *n* (*ANAT*) seno

sip [sɪp] *n* sorso ♦ *vt* sorseggiare

siphon ['saɪfən] *n* sifone *m*; ~ **off** *vt* travasare (con un sifone)

sir [sə*] *n* signore *m*; **S~ John Smith** Sir John Smith; **yes ~** sì, signore

siren ['saɪərn] *n* sirena

sirloin ['sə:lɔɪn] *n* controfiletto
sissy ['sɪsɪ] *(inf) n* femminuccia
sister ['sɪstə*] *n* sorella; *(nun)* suora; *(BRIT: nurse)* infermiera *f* caposala *inv*; **~-in-law** *n* cognata
sit [sɪt] *(pt, pp sat) vi* sedere, sedersi; *(assembly)* essere in seduta; *(for painter)* posare ♦ *vt (exam)* sostenere, dare; **~ down** *vi* sedersi; **~ in on** *vt fus* assistere a; **~ up** *vi* tirarsi su a sedere; *(not go to bed)* stare alzato(a) fino a tardi
sitcom ['sɪtkɔm] *n abbr* (= *situation comedy*) commedia di situazione; *(TV)* telefilm *m inv* comico d'interni
site [saɪt] *n* posto; *(also: building ~)* cantiere *m* ♦ *vt* situare
sit-in *n (demonstration)* sit-in *m inv*
sitting ['sɪtɪŋ] *n (of assembly etc)* seduta; *(in canteen)* turno; **~ room** *n* soggiorno
situated ['sɪtjueɪtɪd] *adj* situato(a)
situation [sɪtju'eɪʃən] *n* situazione *f*; *(job)* lavoro; *(location)* posizione *f*; "**~s vacant**" *(BRIT)* "offerte *fpl* di impiego"
six [sɪks] *num* sei; **~teen** *num* sedici; **~th** *num* sesto(a); **~ty** *num* sessanta
size [saɪz] *n* dimensioni *fpl*; *(of clothing)* taglia, misura; *(of shoes)* numero; *(glue)* colla; **~ up** *vt* giudicare, farsi un'idea di; **~able** *adj* considerevole
sizzle ['sɪzl] *vi* sfrigolare
skate [skeɪt] *n* pattino; *(fish: pl inv)* razza ♦ *vi* pattinare; **~board** *n* skateboard *m inv*; **~r** *n* pattinatore/trice; **skating** *n* pattinaggio; **skating rink** *n* pista di pattinaggio
skeleton ['skelɪtn] *n* scheletro; **~ staff** *n* personale *m* ridotto
skeptical ['skeptɪkl] *(US) adj* = **sceptical**
sketch [sketʃ] *n (drawing)* schizzo, abbozzo; *(THEATRE)* scenetta comica, sketch *m inv* ♦ *vt* abbozzare, schizzare; **~ book** *n* album *m inv* per schizzi; **~y** *adj* incompleto(a), lacunoso(a)
skewer ['skju:ə*] *n* spiedo
ski [ski:] *n* sci *m inv* ♦ *vi* sciare; **~ boot** *n* scarpone *m* da sci
skid [skɪd] *n* slittamento ♦ *vi* slittare
skier ['ski:ə*] *n* sciatore/trice
skiing ['ski:ɪŋ] *n* sci *m*

ski jump *n (ramp)* trampolino; *(event)* salto con gli sci
skilful ['skɪlful] *(US* **skillful***) adj* abile
ski lift ['ski:lɪft] *n* sciovia
skill [skɪl] *n* abilità *f inv*, capacità *f inv*; **~ed** *adj* esperto(a); *(worker)* qualificato(a), specializzato(a); **~ful** *(US) adj* = **skilful**
skim [skɪm] *vt (milk)* scremare; *(glide over)* sfiorare ♦ *vi:* **to ~ through** *(fig)* scorrere, dare una scorsa a; **~med milk** *n* latte *m* scremato
skimp [skɪmp] *vt (work: also:* ~ *on)* fare alla carlona; *(cloth etc)* lesinare; **~y** *adj* misero(a); striminzito(a); frugale
skin [skɪn] *n* pelle *f* ♦ *vt (fruit etc)* sbucciare; *(animal)* scuoiare, spellare; **~ cancer** *n* cancro alla pelle; **~-deep** *adj* superficiale; **~ diving** *n* nuoto subacqueo; **~ny** *adj* molto magro(a), pelle e ossa *inv*; **~tight** *adj (dress etc)* aderente
skip [skɪp] *n* saltello, balzo; *(BRIT: container)* benna ♦ *vi* saltare; *(with rope)* saltare la corda ♦ *vt* saltare
ski pants *npl* pantaloni *mpl* da sci
ski pole *n* racchetta (da sci)
skipper ['skɪpə*] *n (NAUT, SPORT)* capitano
skipping rope ['skɪpɪŋ-] *(BRIT) n* corda per saltare
skirmish ['skə:mɪʃ] *n* scaramuccia
skirt [skə:t] *n* gonna, sottana ♦ *vt* fiancheggiare, costeggiare; **~ing board** *(BRIT) n* zoccolo
ski slope *n* pista da sci
ski suit *n* tuta da sci
skit [skɪt] *n* parodia; scenetta satirica
skittle ['skɪtl] *n* birillo; **~s** *n (game)* (gioco dei) birilli *mpl*
skive [skaɪv] *(BRIT: inf) vi* fare il lavativo
skulk [skʌlk] *vi* muoversi furtivamente
skull [skʌl] *n* cranio, teschio
skunk [skʌŋk] *n* moffetta
sky [skaɪ] *n* cielo; **~light** *n* lucernario; **~scraper** *n* grattacielo
slab [slæb] *n* lastra; *(of cake, cheese)* fetta
slack [slæk] *adj (loose)* allentato(a); *(slow)* lento(a); *(careless)* negligente; **~en** *(also:* ~**en off***) vi* rallentare, diminuire ♦ *vt* allentare; *(speed)* diminuire; **~s** *npl*

(*trousers*) pantaloni *mpl*

slag heap [slæg-] *n* ammasso di scorie

slag off [slæg-] (*BRIT: inf*) *vt* sparlare di

slain [sleɪn] *pp* of **slay**

slam [slæm] *vt* (*door*) sbattere; (*throw*) scaraventare; (*criticize*) stroncare ♦ *vi* sbattere

slander ['slɑːndə*] *n* calunnia; diffamazione *f*

slang [slæŋ] *n* gergo, slang *m*

slant [slɑːnt] *n* pendenza, inclinazione *f*; (*fig*) angolazione *f*, punto di vista; **~ed** *adj* in pendenza, inclinato(a); (*eyes*) obliquo(a); **~ing** *adj* = **~ed**

slap [slæp] *n* manata, pacca; (*on face*) schiaffo ♦ *vt* dare una manata a; schiaffeggiare ♦ *adv* (*directly*) in pieno; ~ **a coat of paint on it** dagli una mano di vernice; **~dash** *adj* negligente; (*work*) raffazzonato(a); **~stick** *n* (*comedy*) farsa grossolana; **~-up** (*BRIT*) *adj*: **a ~-up meal** un pranzo (*or* una cena) coi fiocchi

slash [slæʃ] *vt* tagliare; (*face*) sfregiare; (*fig: prices*) ridurre drasticamente, tagliare

slat [slæt] *n* (*of wood*) stecca; (*of plastic*) lamina

slate [sleɪt] *n* ardesia; (*piece*) lastra di ardesia ♦ *vt* (*fig: criticize*) stroncare, distruggere

slaughter ['slɔːtə*] *n* strage *f*, massacro ♦ *vt* (*animal*) macellare; (*people*) trucidare, massacrare

slave [sleɪv] *n* schiavo/a ♦ *vi* (*also: ~ away*) lavorare come uno schiavo; **~ry** *n* schiavitù *f*; **slavish** *adj* servile; (*copy*) pedissequo/a

slay [sleɪ] (*pt* **slew**, *pp* **slain**) *vt* (*formal*) uccidere

sleazy ['sliːzɪ] *adj* trasandato(a)

sledge [slɛdʒ] *n* slitta; **~hammer** *n* mazza, martello da fabbro

sleek [sliːk] *adj* (*hair, fur*) lucido(a), lucente; (*car, boat*) slanciato(a), affusolato(a)

sleep [sliːp] (*pt, pp* **slept**) *n* sonno ♦ *vi* dormire; **to go to ~** addormentarsi; **~ around** *vi* andare a letto con tutti; **~ in** *vi* (*oversleep*) dormire fino a tardi; **~er**

(*BRIT*) *n* (*RAIL: on track*) traversina; (: *train*) treno di vagoni letto; **~ing bag** *n* sacco a pelo; **~ing car** *n* vagone *m* letto *inv*, carrozza *f* letto *inv*; **~ing partner** (*BRIT*) *n* (*COMM*) socio inattivo; **~ing pill** *n* sonnifero; **~less** *adj*: **a ~less night** una notte in bianco; **~walker** *n* sonnambulo/a; **~y** *adj* assonnato(a), sonnolento(a); (*fig*) addormentato(a)

sleet [sliːt] *n* nevischio

sleeve [sliːv] *n* manica; (*of record*) copertina

sleigh [sleɪ] *n* slitta

sleight [slaɪt] *n*: ~ **of hand** gioco di destrezza

slender ['slɛndə*] *adj* snello(a), sottile; (*not enough*) scarso(a), esiguo(a)

slept [slɛpt] *pt, pp* of **sleep**

slew [sluː] *pt* of **slay** ♦ *vi* (*BRIT*) girare

slice [slaɪs] *n* fetta ♦ *vt* affettare, tagliare a fette

slick [slɪk] *adj* (*skilful*) brillante; (*clever*) furbo(a) ♦ *n* (*also: oil ~*) chiazza di petrolio

slide [slaɪd] (*pt, pp* **slid**) *n* scivolone *m*; (*in playground*) scivolo; (*PHOT*) diapositiva; (*BRIT: also: hair ~*) fermaglio (per capelli) ♦ *vt* far scivolare ♦ *vi* scivolare; ~ **rule** *n* regolo calcolatore; **sliding** *adj* (*door*) scorrevole; **sliding scale** *n* scala mobile

slight [slaɪt] *adj* (*slim*) snello(a), sottile; (*frail*) delicato(a), fragile; (*trivial*) insignificante; (*small*) piccolo(a) ♦ *n* offesa, affronto; **not in the ~est** affatto, neppure per sogno; **~ly** *adv* lievemente, un po'

slim [slɪm] *adj* magro(a), snello(a) ♦ *vi* dimagrire; fare (*or* seguire) una dieta dimagrante

slime [slaɪm] *n* limo, melma; viscidume *m*

slimming ['slɪmɪŋ] *adj* (*diet*) dimagrante; (*food*) ipocalorico(a)

sling [slɪŋ] (*pt, pp* **slung**) *n* (*MED*) fascia al collo; (*for baby*) marsupio ♦ *vt* lanciare, tirare

slip [slɪp] *n* scivolata, scivolone *m*; (*mistake*) errore *m*, sbaglio; (*underskirt*) sottoveste *f*; (*of paper*) striscia di carta; tagliando, scontrino ♦ *vt* (*slide*) far scivolare ♦ *vi* (*slide*) scivolare; (*move smoothly*): **to ~ into/out of** scivolare in/fuori da; (*decline*) declinare; **to ~ sth on/off** infilarsi/togliersi qc; **to give sb the ~** sfuggire qn; **a ~ of the tongue** un lapsus linguae; **~ away** *vi* svignarsela; **~ in** *vt* infilare ♦ *vi* (*error*) scivolare; **~ out** *vi* scivolare fuori; **~ up** *vi* sbagliarsi; **~ped disc** *n* spostamento delle vertebre

slipper ['slɪpə*] *n* pantofola

slippery ['slɪpərɪ] *adj* scivoloso(a)

slip road (BRIT) *n* (*to motorway*) rampa di accesso

slipshod ['slɪpʃɔd] *adj* sciatto(a), trasandato(a)

slip-up *n* granchio (*fig*)

slipway ['slɪpweɪ] *n* scalo di costruzione

slit [slɪt] (*pt, pp* **slit**) *n* fessura, fenditura; (*cut*) taglio ♦ *vt* fendere; tagliare

slither ['slɪðə*] *vi* scivolare, sdrucciolare

sliver ['slɪvə*] *n* (*of glass, wood*) scheggia; (*of cheese etc*) fettina

lob [slɔb] (*inf*) *n* sciattone/a

slog [slɔg] (BRIT) *n* faticata ♦ *vi* lavorare con accanimento, sgobbare

slogan ['sləʊgən] *n* motto, slogan *m inv*

slop [slɔp] *vi* (*also*: ~ **over**) traboccare; versarsi ♦ *vt* versare

slope [sləʊp] *n* pendio; (*side of mountain*) versante *m*; (*ski ~*) pista; (*of roof*) pendenza; (*of floor*) inclinazione *f* ♦ *vi*: **to ~ down** declinare; **to ~ up** essere in salita; **sloping** *adj* inclinato(a)

sloppy ['slɔpɪ] *adj* (*work*) tirato(a) via; (*appearance*) sciatto(a)

slot [slɔt] *n* fessura ♦ *vt*: **to ~ sth into** infilare qc in

sloth [sləʊθ] *n* (*laziness*) pigrizia, accidia

slot machine *n* (BRIT: *vending machine*) distributore *m* automatico; (*for gambling*) slot-machine *f inv*

slouch [slaʊtʃ] *vi* (*when walking*) camminare dinoccolato(a); **she was ~ing in a chair** era sprofondata in una poltrona

Slovenia [sləʊ'viːnɪə] *n* Slovenia

slovenly ['slʌvənlɪ] *adj* sciatto(a), trasandato(a)

slow [sləʊ] *adj* lento(a); (*watch*): **to be ~** essere indietro ♦ *adv* lentamente ♦ *vt, vi* (*also*: ~ **down**, ~ **up**) rallentare; **"~"** (*road sign*) "rallentare"; **~ly** *adv* lentamente; **~ motion** *n*: **in ~ motion** al rallentatore

sludge [slʌdʒ] *n* fanghiglia

slue [sluː] (*US*) *vi* = **slew**

slug [slʌg] *n* lumaca; (*bullet*) pallottola; **~gish** *adj* lento(a); (*trading*) stagnante

sluice [sluːs] *n* chiusa

slum [slʌm] *n* catapecchia

slumber ['slʌmbə*] *n* sonno

slump [slʌmp] *n* crollo, caduta; (*economic*) depressione *f*, crisi *f inv* ♦ *vi* crollare

slung [slʌŋ] *pt, pp of* **sling**

slur [sləː*] *n* (*fig*): ~ **(on)** calunnia (su) ♦ *vt* pronunciare in modo indistinto

slush [slʌʃ] *n* neve *f* mista a fango; ~ **fund** *n* fondi *mpl* neri

slut [slʌt] *n* donna trasandata, sciattona

sly [slaɪ] *adj* (*smile, remark*) sornione(a); (*person*) furbo(a)

smack [smæk] *n* (*slap*) pacca; (*on face*) schiaffo ♦ *vt* schiaffeggiare; (*child*) picchiare ♦ *vi*: **to ~ of** puzzare di

small [smɔːl] *adj* piccolo(a); ~ **ads** (BRIT) *npl* piccola pubblicità; ~ **change** *n* moneta, spiccioli *mpl*; ~ **fry** *npl* pesci *mpl* piccoli; **~-holder** *n* piccolo proprietario; ~ **hours** *npl*: **in the ~ hours** alle ore piccole; **~pox** *n* vaiolo; ~ **talk** *n* chiacchiere *fpl*

smart [smɑːt] *adj* elegante; (*fashionable*) alla moda; (*clever*) intelligente, sveglio(a) ♦ *vi* bruciare; **~en up** *vi* farsi bello(a) ♦ *vt* (*people*) fare bello(a); (*things*) abbellire

smash [smæʃ] *n* (*also*: ~**-up**) scontro, collisione *f*; (~ *hit*) successone *m* ♦ *vt* frantumare, fracassare; (SPORT: *record*) battere ♦ *vi* frantumarsi, andare in pezzi; **~ing** (*inf*) *adj* favoloso(a), formidabile

smattering ['smætərɪŋ] *n*: **a ~ of** un'infarinatura di

smear [smɪə*] *n* macchia; (MED) striscio ♦ *vt* spalmare; (*make dirty*) sporcare; ~ **campaign** *n* campagna diffamatoria

smell [smɛl] (*pt, pp* **smelt** *or* **smelled**) *n* odore *m*; (*sense*) olfatto, odorato ♦ *vt* sentire (l')odore di ♦ *vi* (*food etc*): **to ~ (of)** avere odore (di); (*pej*) puzzare, avere un cattivo odore; **~y** *adj* puzzolente

smile [smaɪl] *n* sorriso ♦ *vi* sorridere

smirk [smə:k] *n* sorriso furbo; sorriso compiaciuto

smithy ['smɪðɪ] *n* fucina

smock [smɔk] *n* grembiule *m*, camice *m*; (*US*) tuta

smog [smɔg] *n* smog *m*

smoke [sməʊk] *n* fumo ♦ *vt, vi* fumare; **~d** *adj* (*bacon, glass*) affumicato(a); **~r** *n* (*person*) fumatore/trice; (*RAIL*) carrozza per fumatori; **~ screen** *n* (*MIL*) cortina fumogena *or* di fumo; (*fig*) copertura; **smoking** *n* fumo; **"no smoking"** (*sign*) "vietato fumare"; **smoky** *adj* fumoso(a); (*taste*) affumicato(a)

smolder ['sməʊldə*] (*US*) *vi* = **smoulder**

smooth [smu:ð] *adj* liscio(a); (*sauce*) omogeneo(a); (*flavour, whisky*) amabile; (*movement*) regolare; (*person*) mellifluo(a) ♦ *vt* (*also: ~ out*) lisciare, spianare; (: *difficulties*) appianare

smother ['smʌðə*] *vt* soffocare

smoulder ['sməʊldə*] (*US* **smolder**) *vi* covare sotto la cenere

smudge [smʌdʒ] *n* macchia; sbavatura ♦ *vt* imbrattare, sporcare

smug [smʌg] *adj* soddisfatto(a), compiaciuto(a)

smuggle ['smʌgl] *vt* contrabbandare; **~r** *n* contrabbandiere/a; **smuggling** *n* contrabbando

smutty ['smʌtɪ] *adj* (*fig*) osceno(a), indecente

snack [snæk] *n* spuntino; **~ bar** *n* tavola calda, snack bar *m inv*

snag [snæg] *n* intoppo, ostacolo imprevisto

snail [sneɪl] *n* chiocciola

snake [sneɪk] *n* serpente *m*

snap [snæp] *n* (*sound*) schianto, colpo secco; (*photograph*) istantanea ♦ *adj* improvviso(a) ♦ *vt* (far) schioccare; (*break*) spezzare di netto ♦ *vi* spezzarsi con un rumore secco; (*fig: person*) parlare con tono secco; **to ~ shut** chiudersi di scatto; **~ at** *vt fus* (*subj: dog*) cercare di mordere; **~ off** *vt* (*break*) schiantare; **~ up** *vt* afferrare; **~py** (*inf*) *adj* (*answer, slogan*) d'effetto; **make it ~py!** (*hurry up*) sbrigati!, svelto!; **~shot** *n* istantanea

snare [snɛə*] *n* trappola

snarl [snɑ:l] *vi* ringhiare

snatch [snætʃ] *n* (*small amount*) frammento ♦ *vt* strappare (con violenza); (*fig*) rubare

sneak [sni:k] (*pt* (*US*) **snuck**) *vi*: **to ~ in/ out** entrare/uscire di nascosto ♦ *n* spione/a; **to ~ up on sb** avvicinarsi quatto quatto a qn; **~ers** *npl* scarpe *fpl* da ginnastica

sneer [snɪə*] *vi* sogghignare; **to ~ at** farsi beffe di

sneeze [sni:z] *n* starnuto ♦ *vi* starnutire

sniff [snɪf] *n* fiutata, annusata ♦ *vi* tirare su col naso ♦ *vt* fiutare, annusare

snigger ['snɪgə*] *vi* ridacchiare, ridere sotto i baffi

snip [snɪp] *n* pezzetto; (*bargain*) (buon) affare *m*, occasione *f* ♦ *vt* tagliare

sniper ['snaɪpə*] *n* (*marksman*) franco tiratore *m*, cecchino

snippet ['snɪpɪt] *n* frammento

snivelling ['snɪvlɪŋ] *adj* (*whimpering*) piagnucoloso(a)

snob [snɔb] *n* snob *m/f inv*; **~bery** *n* snobismo; **~bish** *adj* snob *inv*

snooker ['snu:kə*] *n* tipo di gioco del biliardo

snoop ['snu:p] *vi*: **to ~ about** curiosare

snooty ['snu:tɪ] *adj* borioso(a), snob *inv*

snooze [snu:z] *n* sonnellino, pisolino ♦ *v* fare un sonnellino

snore [snɔ:*] *vi* russare

snorkel ['snɔ:kl] *n* (*of swimmer*) respiratore *m* a tubo

snort [snɔ:t] *n* sbuffo ♦ *vi* sbuffare

snout [snaʊt] *n* muso

snow [snəʊ] *n* neve *f* ♦ *vi* nevicare; **~ball** *n* palla di neve ♦ *vi* (*fig*) crescere a vista d'occhio; **~bound** *adj* bloccato(a) dalla neve; **~drift** *n* cumulo di neve (ammucchiato dal vento); **~drop** *n* bucaneve *m inv*; **~fall** *n* nevicata; **~flake**

n fiocco di neve; **~man** *n* pupazzo di neve; **~plough** (*US* **~plow**) *n* spazzaneve *m inv*; **~shoe** *n* racchetta da neve; **~storm** *n* tormenta

snub [snʌb] *vt* snobbare ♦ *n* offesa, affronto; **~-nosed** *adj* dal naso camuso

snuff [snʌf] *n* tabacco da fiuto

snug [snʌg] *adj* comodo(a); (*room, house*) accogliente, comodo(a)

snuggle ['snʌgl] *vi*: **to ~ up to sb** stringersi a qn

KEYWORD

so [səu] *adv* **1** (*thus, likewise*) così; **if ~ se** è così, quand'è così; **I didn't do it — you did ~!** non l'ho fatto io — sì che l'hai fatto!; **~ do I, ~ am I** *etc* anch'io; **it's 5 o'clock — ~ it is!** sono le 5 — davvero!; **I hope ~** lo spero; **I think ~** penso di sì; **~ far** finora, fin qui; (*in past*) fino ad allora

2 (*in comparisons etc: to such a degree*) così; **~ big (that)** così grande (che); **she's not ~ clever as her brother** lei non è (così) intelligente come suo fratello

3: **~ much** *adj* tanto(a) ♦ *adv* tanto; **I've got ~ much work/money** ho tanto lavoro/tanti soldi; **I love you ~ much** ti amo tanto; **~ many** tanti(e)

4 (*phrases*): **10 or ~** circa 10; **~ long!** (*inf: goodbye*) ciao!, ci vediamo!

♦ *conj* **1** (*expressing purpose*): **~ as to do** in modo *or* così da fare; **we hurried ~ as not to be late** ci affrettammo per non fare tardi; **~ (that)** affinché + *sub*, perché + *sub*

2 (*expressing result*): **he didn't arrive ~ I left** non è venuto così me ne sono andata; **~ you see, I could have gone** vedi, sarei potuto andare

soak [səuk] *vt* inzuppare; (*clothes*) mettere a mollo ♦ *vi* (*clothes etc*) essere a mollo; **~ in** *vi* penetrare; **~ up** *vt* assorbire

soap [səup] *n* sapone *m*; **~flakes** *npl* sapone *m* in scaglie; **~ opera** *n* soap opera *f inv*; **~ powder** *n* detersivo; **~y** *adj* insaponato(a)

soar [sɔː*] *vi* volare in alto; (*price etc*)

salire alle stelle; (*building*) ergersi

sob [sɔb] *n* singhiozzo ♦ *vi* singhiozzare

sober ['səubə*] *adj* sobrio(a); (*not drunk*) non ubriaco(a); (*moderate*) moderato(a); **~ up** *vt* far passare la sbornia a ♦ *vi* farsi passare la sbornia

so-called ['səu'kɔːld] *adj* cosiddetto(a)

soccer ['sɔkə*] *n* calcio

sociable ['səuʃəbl] *adj* socievole

social ['səuʃl] *adj* sociale ♦ *n* festa, serata; **~ club** *n* club *m inv* sociale; **~ism** *n* socialismo; **~ist** *adj*, *n* socialista *m/f*; **~ize** *vi*: **to ~ize (with)** socializzare (con); **~ security** (*BRIT*) *n* previdenza sociale; **~ work** *n* servizio sociale; **~ worker** *n* assistente *m/f* sociale

society [sə'saɪətɪ] *n* società *f inv*; (*club*) società, associazione *f*; (*also: high ~*) alta società

sociology [səusɪ'ɔlədʒɪ] *n* sociologia

sock [sɔk] *n* calzino

socket ['sɔkɪt] *n* cavità *f inv*; (*of eye*) orbita; (*BRIT: ELEC: also: wall ~*) presa di corrente

sod [sɔd] *n* (*of earth*) zolla erbosa; (*BRIT: inf!*) bastardo/a (!)

soda ['səudə] *n* (*CHEM*) soda; (*also: ~ water*) acqua di seltz; (*US: also: ~ pop*) gassosa

sodden ['sɔdn] *adj* fradicio(a)

sodium ['səudɪəm] *n* sodio

sofa ['səufə] *n* sofà *m inv*

soft [sɔft] *adj* (*not rough*) morbido(a); (*not hard*) soffice; (*not loud*) sommesso(a); (*not bright*) tenue; (*kind*) gentile; **~ drink** *n* analcolico; **~en** ['sɔfn] *vt* ammorbidire; addolcire; attenuare ♦ *vi* ammorbidirsi; addolcirsi; attenuarsi; **~ly** *adv* dolcemente; morbidamente; **~ness** *n* dolcezza; morbidezza; **~ spot** *n*: **to have a ~ spot for sb** avere un debole per qn

software ['sɔftwɛə*] *n* (*COMPUT*) software *m*

soggy ['sɔgɪ] *adj* inzuppato(a)

soil [sɔɪl] *n* terreno ♦ *vt* sporcare

solace ['sɔlɪs] *n* consolazione *f*

solar ['səulə*] *adj* solare; **~ panel** *n* pannello solare; **~ power** *n* energie solare

sold [səʊld] *pt, pp of* **sell**; **~ out** *adj*
(COMM) esaurito(a)

solder ['səʊldə*] *vt* saldare ♦ *n* saldatura

soldier ['səʊldʒə*] *n* soldato, militare *m*

sole [səʊl] *n* (*of foot*) pianta (del piede);
(*of shoe*) suola; (*fish: pl inv*) sogliola ♦ *adj*
solo(a), unico(a)

solemn ['sɔləm] *adj* solenne

sole trader *n* (COMM) commerciante *m* in
proprio

solicit [sə'lɪsɪt] *vt* (*request*) richiedere,
sollecitare ♦ *vi* (*prostitute*) adescare i
passanti

solicitor [sə'lɪsɪtə*] (BRIT) *n* (*for wills etc*)
≈ notaio; (*in court*) ≈ avvocato

solid ['sɔlɪd] *adj* solido(a); (*not hollow*)
pieno(a); (*meal*) sostanzioso(a) ♦ *n* solido

solidarity [sɔlɪ'dærɪtɪ] *n* solidarietà

solitaire [sɔlɪ'tɛə*] *n* (*games, gem*)
solitario

solitary ['sɔlɪtərɪ] *adj* solitario(a); **~
confinement** *n* (LAW) isolamento

solo ['səʊləʊ] *n* assolo; **~ist** *n* solista *m/f*

soluble ['sɔljʊbl] *adj* solubile

solution [sə'luːʃən] *n* soluzione *f*

solve [sɔlv] *vt* risolvere

solvent ['sɔlvənt] *adj* (COMM) solvibile ♦
n (CHEM) solvente *m*

sombre ['sɔmbə*] (US **somber**) *adj*
scuro(a); (*mood, person*) triste

KEYWORD

some [sʌm] *adj* **1** (*a certain amount or
number of*): **~ tea/water/cream** del tè/
dell'acqua/della panna; **~ children/
apples** dei bambini/delle mele
2 (*certain: in contrasts*) certo(a); **~ people
say that ...** alcuni dicono che ..., certa
gente dice che ...
3 (*unspecified*) un(a) certo(a), qualche; **~
woman was asking for you** una tale
chiedeva di lei; **~ day** un giorno; **~ day
next week** un giorno della prossima
settimana
♦ *pron* **1** (*a certain number*) alcuni(e),
certi(e); **I've got ~** (*books etc*) ne ho
alcuni; **~ (of them) have been sold**
alcuni sono stati venduti
2 (*a certain amount*) un po'; **I've got ~**

(*money, milk*) ne ho un po'; **I've read ~
of the book** ho letto parte del libro
♦ *adv*: **~ 10 people** circa 10 persone

somebody ['sʌmbədɪ] *pron* = **someone**

somehow ['sʌmhaʊ] *adv* in un modo o
nell'altro, in qualche modo; (*for some
reason*) per qualche ragione

someone ['sʌmwʌn] *pron* qualcuno

someplace ['sʌmpleɪs] (US) *adv*
= **somewhere**

somersault ['sʌməsɔːlt] *n* capriola; salto
mortale ♦ *vi* fare una capriola (*or* un
salto mortale); (*car*) cappottare

something ['sʌmθɪŋ] *pron* qualcosa,
qualche cosa; **~ nice** qualcosa di bello; **~
to do** qualcosa da fare

sometime ['sʌmtaɪm] *adv* (*in future*) un
volta o l'altra; (*in past*): **~ last month**
durante il mese scorso

sometimes ['sʌmtaɪmz] *adv* qualche
volta

somewhat ['sʌmwɔt] *adv* piuttosto

somewhere ['sʌmwɛə*] *adv* in *or* da
qualche parte

son [sʌn] *n* figlio

song [sɔŋ] *n* canzone *f*

sonic ['sɔnɪk] *adj* (*boom*) sonico(a)

son-in-law *n* genero

sonnet ['sɔnɪt] *n* sonetto

sonny ['sʌnɪ] (*inf*) *n* ragazzo mio

soon [suːn] *adv* presto, fra poco; (*early, o
short time after*) presto; **~ afterwards**
poco dopo; *see also* **as**; **~er** *adv* (*time*)
prima; (*preference*): **I would ~er do**
preferirei fare; **~er or later** prima o poi

soot [sʊt] *n* fuliggine *f*

soothe [suːð] *vt* calmare

sophisticated [sə'fɪstɪkeɪtɪd] *adj*
sofisticato(a); raffinato(a); complesso(a)

sophomore ['sɔfəmɔː*] (US) *n* studente/
essa del secondo anno

sopping ['sɔpɪŋ] *adj* (*also*: **~ wet**)
bagnato(a) fradicio(a)

soppy ['sɔpɪ] (*pej*) *adj* sentimentale

soprano [sə'prɑːnəʊ] *n* (*voice*) soprano *n*
(*singer*) soprano *m/f*

sorcerer ['sɔːsərə*] *n* stregone *m*, mago

sore [sɔː*] *adj* (*painful*) dolorante ♦ *n*

piaga; **~ly** *adv* (*tempted*) fortemente

sorrow ['sɔrəu] *n* dolore *m*; **~ful** *adj* doloroso(a)

sorry ['sɔrɪ] *adj* spiacente; (*condition, excuse*) misero(a); **~!** scusa! (*or* scusi! *or* scusate!); **to feel ~ for sb** rincrescersi per qn

sort [sɔːt] *n* specie *f*, genere *m* ♦ *vt* (*also*: **~ out**: *papers*) classificare; ordinare; (: *letters etc*) smistare; (: *problems*) risolvere; **~ing office** *n* ufficio *m* smistamento *inv*

SOS *n abbr* (= *save our souls*) S.O.S. *m inv*

so-so *adv* così così

sought [sɔːt] *pt, pp of* **seek**

soul [səul] *n* anima; **~-destroying** *adj* demoralizzante; **~ful** *adj* pieno(a) di sentimento

sound [saund] *adj* (*healthy*) sano(a); (*safe, not damaged*) solido(a), in buono stato; (*reliable, not superficial*) solido(a); (*sensible*) giudizioso(a), di buon senso ♦ *adv*: **~ asleep** profondamente addormentato ♦ *n* suono; (*noise*) rumore *m*; (GEO) stretto ♦ *vt* (*alarm*) suonare ♦ *vi* suonare; (*fig*: *seem*) sembrare; **to ~ like** rassomigliare a; **~ out** *vt* sondare; **~ barrier** *n* muro del suono; **~bite** *n* dichiarazione breve ed incisiva (*trasmessa per radio o per TV*); **~ effects** *npl* effetti sonori; **~ly** *adv* (*sleep*) profondamente; (*beat*) duramente; **~proof** *adj* insonorizzato(a), isolato(a) acusticamente; **~track** *n* (*of film*) colonna sonora

soup [suːp] *n* minestra; brodo; zuppa; **in the ~** (*fig*) nei guai; **~ plate** *n* piatto fondo; **~spoon** *n* cucchiaio da minestra

sour ['sauə*] *adj* aspro(a); (*fruit*) acerbo(a); (*milk*) acido(a); (*fig*) arcigno(a); acido(a); **it's ~ grapes** è soltanto invidia

source [sɔːs] *n* fonte *f*, sorgente *f*; (*fig*) fonte

south [sauθ] *n* sud *m*, meridione *m*, mezzogiorno ♦ *adj* del sud, sud *inv*, meridionale ♦ *adv* verso sud; **S~ Africa** *n* Sudafrica *m*; **S~ African** *adj, n* sudafricano(a); **S~ America** *n* Sudamerica *m*, America del sud; **S~**

American *adj, n* sudamericano(a); **~-east** *n* sud-est *m*; **~erly** ['sʌðəlɪ] *adj* del sud; **~ern** ['sʌðən] *adj* del sud, meridionale; esposto(a) a sud; **S~ Pole** *n* Polo Sud; **~ward(s)** *adv* verso sud; **~-west** *n* sud-ovest *m*

souvenir [suːvə'nɪə*] *n* ricordo, souvenir *m inv*

sovereign ['sɔvrɪn] *adj, n* sovrano(a)

soviet ['səuvɪət] *adj* sovietico(a); **the S~ Union** l'Unione *f* Sovietica

sow[1] [səu] (*pt* **~ed**, *pp* **sown**) *vt* seminare

sow[2] [sau] *n* scrofa

sown [səun] *pp of* **sow**

soy [sɔɪ] (US) *n* = **soya**

soya ['sɔɪə] (US **soy**) *n*: **~ bean** *n* seme *m* di soia; **~ sauce** *n* salsa di soia

spa [spɑː] *n* (*resort*) stazione *f* termale; (US: *also*: **health ~**) centro di cure estetiche

space [speɪs] *n* spazio; (*room*) posto; spazio; (*length of time*) intervallo ♦ *cpd* spaziale ♦ *vt* (*also*: **~ out**) distanziare; **~craft** *n inv* veicolo spaziale; **~man/woman** *n* astronauta *m/f*, cosmonauta *m/f*; **~ship** *n* = **~craft**; **spacing** *n* spaziatura

spacious ['speɪʃəs] *adj* spazioso(a), ampio(a)

spade [speɪd] *n* (*tool*) vanga; pala; (*child's*) paletta; **~s** *npl* (CARDS) picche *fpl*

Spain [speɪn] *n* Spagna

span [spæn] *n* (*of bird, plane*) apertura alare; (*of arch*) campata; (*in time*) periodo; durata ♦ *vt* attraversare; (*fig*) abbracciare

Spaniard ['spænjəd] *n* spagnolo/a

spaniel ['spænjəl] *n* spaniel *m inv*

Spanish ['spænɪʃ] *adj* spagnolo(a) ♦ *n* (LING) spagnolo; **the ~** *npl* gli Spagnoli

spank [spæŋk] *vt* sculacciare

spanner ['spænə*] (BRIT) *n* chiave *f* inglese

spar [spɑː*] *n* asta, palo ♦ *vi* (BOXING) allenarsi

spare [spɛə*] *adj* di riserva, di scorta; (*surplus*) in più, d'avanzo ♦ *n* (*part*) pezzo di ricambio ♦ *vt* (*do without*) fare a meno di; (*afford to give*) concedere; (*refrain from hurting, using*) risparmiare; **to ~**

(*surplus*) d'avanzo; ~ **part** n pezzo di
ricambio; ~ **time** n tempo libero; ~
wheel n (*AUT*) ruota di scorta
sparing ['spɛərɪŋ] *adj*: **to be ~ with sth**
risparmiare qc; **~ly** *adv* moderatamente
spark [spɑːk] n scintilla; **~(ing) plug** n
candela
sparkle ['spɑːkl] n scintillio, sfavillio ♦ *vi*
scintillare, sfavillare; **sparkling** *adj*
scintillante, sfavillante; (*conversation,
wine, water*) frizzante
sparrow ['spærəu] n passero
sparse [spɑːs] *adj* sparso(a), rado(a)
spartan ['spɑːtən] *adj* (*fig*) spartano(a)
spasm ['spæzəm] n (*MED*) spasmo; (*fig*)
accesso, attacco; **~odic** [spæz'mɔdɪk] *adj*
spasmodico(a); (*fig*) intermittente
spastic ['spæstɪk] n spastico/a
spat [spæt] *pt, pp* of **spit**
spate [speɪt] n (*fig*): ~ **of** diluvio *or* fiume
m di
spatter ['spætə*] *vt, vi* schizzare
spawn [spɔːn] *vi* deporre le uova ♦ n
uova *fpl*
speak [spiːk] (*pt* **spoke**, *pp* **spoken**) *vt*
(*language*) parlare; (*truth*) dire ♦ *vi*
parlare; **to ~ to sb/of** *or* **about sth**
parlare a qn/di qc; ~ **up!** parla più forte!;
~er n (*in public*) oratore/trice; (*also:
loud~er*) altoparlante *m*; (*POL*): **the S~er** il
presidente della Camera dei Comuni (*BRIT*)
or dei Rappresentanti (*US*)
spear [spɪə*] n lancia ♦ *vt* infilzare;
~head *vt* (*attack etc*) condurre
spec [spɛk] (*inf*) n: **on ~** sperando bene
special ['spɛʃl] *adj* speciale; **~ist** n
specialista *m/f*; **~ity** [spɛʃɪ'ælɪtɪ] n
specialità *f inv*; **~ize** *vi*: **to ~ize (in)**
specializzarsi (in); **~ly** *adv* specialmente,
particolarmente; **~ty** n = **speciality**
species ['spiːʃiːz] n *inv* specie *f inv*
specific [spə'sɪfɪk] *adj* specifico(a);
preciso(a); **~ally** *adv* esplicitamente;
(*especially*) appositamente
specimen ['spɛsɪmən] n esemplare *m*,
modello; (*MED*) campione *m*
speck [spɛk] n puntino, macchiolina;
(*particle*) granello
speckled ['spɛkld] *adj* macchiettato(a)

specs [spɛks] (*inf*) *npl* occhiali *mpl*
spectacle ['spɛktəkl] n spettacolo; **~s** *npl*
(*glasses*) occhiali *mpl*; **spectacular**
[-'tækjulə*] *adj* spettacolare
spectator [spɛk'teɪtə*] n spettatore *m*
spectra ['spɛktrə] *npl* of **spectrum**
spectre ['spɛktə*] (*US* **specter**) n spettro
spectrum ['spɛktrəm] (*pl* **spectra**) n
spettro
speculation [spɛkju'leɪʃən] n
speculazione *f*; congettura *fpl*
speech [spiːtʃ] n (*faculty*) parola; (*talk,
THEATRE*) discorso; (*manner of speaking*)
parlata; **~less** *adj* ammutolito(a), muto(a)
speed [spiːd] n velocità *f inv*;
(*promptness*) prontezza; **at full** *or* **top ~** a
tutta velocità; ~ **up** *vi, vt* accelerare;
~boat n motoscafo; **~ily** *adv*
velocemente; prontamente; **~ing** n (*AUT*)
eccesso di velocità; ~ **limit** n limite *m* di
velocità; **~ometer** [spɪ'dɔmɪtə*] n
tachimetro; **~way** n (*sport*) corsa
motociclistica (su pista); **~y** *adj* veloce,
rapido(a); pronto(a)
spell [spɛl] (*pt, pp* **spelt** (*BRIT*) *or* **~ed**) n
(*also: magic ~*) incantesimo; (*period of
time*) (breve) periodo ♦ *vt* (*in writing*)
scrivere (lettera per lettera); (*aloud*) dire
lettera per lettera; (*fig*) significare; **to
cast a ~ on sb** fare un incantesimo a qn;
he can't ~ fa errori di ortografia;
~bound *adj* incantato(a); affascinato(a);
~ing n ortografia; **spelt** (*BRIT*) *pt, pp* of
spell
spend [spɛnd] (*pt, pp* **spent**) *vt* (*money*)
spendere; (*time, life*) passare; **~thrift** n
spendaccione/a; **spent** *pt, pp* of **spend**
sperm [spəːm] n sperma *m*
spew [spjuː] *vt* vomitare
sphere [sfɪə*] n sfera
spice [spaɪs] n spezia ♦ *vt* aromatizzare
spick-and-span ['spɪkən'spæn] *adj*
impeccabile
spicy ['spaɪsɪ] *adj* piccante
spider ['spaɪdə*] n ragno
spike [spaɪk] n punta
spill [spɪl] (*pt, pp* **spilt** *or* **~ed**) *vt* versare
rovesciare ♦ *vi* versarsi, rovesciarsi; ~
over *vi* (*liquid*) versarsi; (*crowd*)

riversarsi; **spilt** *pt, pp of* **spill**

spin [spɪn] (*pt, pp* **spun**) *n* (*revolution of wheel*) rotazione *f*; (AVIAT) avvitamento; (*trip in car*) giretto ♦ *vt* (*wool etc*) filare; (*wheel*) far girare ♦ *vi* girare; ~ **out** *vt* far durare

spinach ['spɪnɪtʃ] *n* spinacio; (*as food*) spinaci *mpl*

spinal ['spaɪnl] *adj* spinale; ~ **cord** *n* midollo spinale

spindly ['spɪndlɪ] *adj* lungo(a) e sottile, filiforme

spin doctor *n pierre addetto alla difesa di provvedimenti impopolari con interviste, interventi in TV ecc.*

spin-dryer (BRIT) *n* centrifuga

spine [spaɪn] *n* spina dorsale; (*thorn*) spina

spinning ['spɪnɪŋ] *n* filatura; ~ **top** *n* trottola; ~ **wheel** *n* filatoio

spin-off *n* (*product*) prodotto secondario

spinster ['spɪnstə*] *n* nubile *f*; zitella

spiral ['spaɪərl] *n* spirale *f* ♦ *vi* (*fig*) salire a spirale; ~ **staircase** *n* scala a chiocciola

spire ['spaɪə*] *n* guglia

spirit ['spɪrɪt] *n* spirito; (*ghost*) spirito, fantasma *m*; (*mood*) stato d'animo, umore *m*; (*courage*) coraggio; ~**s** *npl* (*drink*) alcolici *mpl*; **in good ~s** di buon umore; ~**ed** *adj* vivace, vigoroso(a); (*horse*) focoso(a); ~ **level** *n* livella a bolla (d'aria)

spiritual ['spɪrɪtjuəl] *adj* spirituale

spit [spɪt] (*pt, pp* **spat**) *n* (*for roasting*) spiedo; (*saliva*) sputo; saliva ♦ *vi* sputare; (*fire, fat*) scoppiettare

spite [spaɪt] *n* dispetto ♦ *vt* contrariare, far dispetto a; **in ~ of** nonostante, malgrado; ~**ful** *adj* dispettoso(a)

spittle ['spɪtl] *n* saliva; sputo

splash [splæʃ] *n* spruzzo; (*sound*) splash *m inv*; (*of colour*) schizzo ♦ *vt* spruzzare ♦ *vi* (*also*: ~ *about*) sguazzare

spleen [spliːn] *n* (ANAT) milza

splendid ['splendɪd] *adj* splendido(a), magnifico(a)

splint [splɪnt] *n* (MED) stecca

splinter ['splɪntə*] *n* scheggia ♦ *vi* scheggiarsi

split [splɪt] (*pt, pp* **split**) *n* spaccatura; (*fig: division, quarrel*) scissione *f* ♦ *vt* spaccare; (*party*) dividere; (*work, profits*) spartire, ripartire ♦ *vi* (*divide*) dividersi; ~ **up** *vi* (*couple*) separarsi, rompere; (*meeting*) sciogliersi

splutter ['splʌtə*] *vi* farfugliare; sputacchiare

spoil [spɔɪl] (*pt, pp* **spoilt** *or* ~**ed**) *vt* (*damage*) rovinare, guastare; (*mar*) sciupare; (*child*) viziare; ~**s** *npl* bottino; ~**sport** *n* guastafeste *m/f inv*; **spoilt** *pt, pp of* **spoil**

spoke [spəuk] *pt of* **speak** ♦ *n* raggio

spoken ['spəukn] *pp of* **speak**

spokesman ['spəuksmən] *n* portavoce *m inv*

spokeswoman ['spəukswumən] *n* portavoce *f inv*

sponge [spʌndʒ] *n* spugna; (*also*: ~ *cake*) pan *m* di spagna ♦ *vt* spugnare, pulire con una spugna ♦ *vi*: **to ~ off** *or* **on** scroccare a; ~ **bag** (BRIT) *n* nécessaire *m inv*

sponsor ['spɒnsə*] *n* (RADIO, TV, SPORT *etc*) sponsor *m inv*; (POL: *of bill*) promotore/trice ♦ *vt* sponsorizzare; (*bill*) presentare; ~**ship** *n* sponsorizzazione *f*

spontaneous [spɒn'teɪnɪəs] *adj* spontaneo(a)

spooky ['spuːkɪ] (*inf*) *adj* che fa accapponare la pelle

spool [spuːl] *n* bobina

spoon [spuːn] *n* cucchiaio; ~**-feed** *vt* nutrire con il cucchiaio; (*fig*) imboccare; ~**ful** *n* cucchiaiata

sport [spɔːt] *n* sport *m inv*; (*person*) persona di spirito ♦ *vt* sfoggiare; ~**ing** *adj* sportivo(a); **to give sb a ~ing chance** dare a qn una possibilità (di vincere); ~ **jacket** (US) *n* = ~**s jacket**; ~**s car** *n* automobile *f* sportiva; ~**s jacket** (BRIT) *n* giacca sportiva; ~**sman** *n* sportivo; ~**smanship** *n* spirito sportivo; ~**swear** *n* abiti *mpl* sportivi; ~**swoman** *n* sportiva; ~**y** *adj* sportivo(a)

spot [spɒt] *n* punto; (*mark*) macchia; (*dot: on pattern*) pallino; (*pimple*) foruncolo; (*place*) posto; (RADIO, TV) spot *m inv*; (*small* *amount*): **a ~ of** un po' di ♦ *vt* (*notice*) individuare, distinguere; **on the ~** sul posto; (*immediately*) su due piedi; (*in difficulty*) nei guai; **~ check** *n* controllo senza preavviso; **~less** *adj* immacolato(a); **~light** *n* proiettore *m*; (*AUT*) faro ausiliario; **~ted** *adj* macchiato(a); a puntini, a pallini; **~ty** *adj* (*face*) foruncoloso(a)

spouse [spauz] *n* sposo/a

spout [spaut] *n* (*of jug*) beccuccio; (*of pipe*) scarico ♦ *vi* zampillare

sprain [sprein] *n* storta, distorsione *f* ♦ *vt*: **to ~ one's ankle** storcersi una caviglia

sprang [sprǽŋ] *pt of* **spring**

sprawl [sprɔːl] *vi* sdraiarsi (in modo scomposto); (*place*) estendersi (disordinatamente)

spray [sprei] *n* spruzzo; (*container*) nebulizzatore *m*, spray *m inv*; (*of flowers*) mazzetto ♦ *vt* spruzzare; (*crops*) irrorare

spread [spred] (*pt, pp* **spread**) *n* diffusione *f*; (*distribution*) distribuzione *f*; (*CULIN*) pasta (da spalmare); (*inf: food*) banchetto ♦ *vt* (*cloth*) stendere, distendere; (*butter etc*) spalmare; (*disease, knowledge*) propagare, diffondere ♦ *vi* stendersi, distendersi; spalmarsi; propagarsi, diffondersi; **~ out** *vi* (*move apart*) separarsi; **~-eagled** ['spredi:gld] *adj* a gambe e braccia aperte; **~sheet** *n* (*COMPUT*) foglio elettronico ad espansione

spree [spriː] *n*: **to go on a ~** fare baldoria

sprightly ['spraitli] *adj* vivace

spring [spriŋ] (*pt* **sprang**, *pp* **sprung**) *n* (*leap*) salto, balzo; (*coiled metal*) molla; (*season*) primavera; (*of water*) sorgente *f* ♦ *vi* saltare, balzare; **~ up** *vi* (*problem*) presentarsi; **~board** *n* trampolino; **~-clean(ing)** *n* grandi pulizie *fpl* di primavera; **~time** *n* primavera

sprinkle ['spriŋkl] *vt* spruzzare; spargere; **to ~ water etc on, ~ with water etc** spruzzare dell'acqua *etc* su; **~r** *n* (*for lawn*) irrigatore *m*; (*to put out fire*) sprinkler *m inv*

sprint [sprint] *n* scatto ♦ *vi* scattare; **~er** *n* (*SPORT*) velocista *m/f*

sprout [spraut] *vi* germogliare; **~s** *npl* (*also: Brussels ~s*) cavolini *mpl* di Bruxelles

spruce [spruːs] *n inv* abete *m* rosso ♦ *adj* lindo(a); azzimato(a)

sprung [sprʌŋ] *pp of* **spring**

spry [sprai] *adj* arzillo(a), sveglio(a)

spun [spʌn] *pt, pp of* **spin**

spur [spəː*] *n* sperone *m*; (*fig*) sprone *m*, incentivo ♦ *vt* (*also: ~ on*) spronare; **on the ~ of the moment** lì per lì

spurious ['spjuəriəs] *adj* falso(a)

spurn [spəːn] *vt* rifiutare con disprezzo, sdegnare

spurt [spəːt] *n* (*of water*) getto; (*of energy*) scatto ♦ *vi* sgorgare

spy [spai] *n* spia ♦ *vi*: **to ~ on** spiare ♦ *vt* (*see*) scorgere; **~ing** *n* spionaggio

sq. *abbr* = **square**

squabble ['skwɔbl] *vi* bisticciarsi

squad [skwɔd] *n* (*MIL*) plotone *m*; (*POLICE*) squadra

squadron ['skwɔdrn] *n* (*MIL*) squadrone *m*; (*AVIAT, NAUT*) squadriglia

squalid ['skwɔlid] *adj* squallido(a)

squall [skwɔːl] *n* raffica; burrasca

squalor ['skwɔlə*] *n* squallore *m*

squander ['skwɔndə*] *vt* dissipare

square [skwɛə*] *n* quadrato; (*in town*) piazza ♦ *adj* quadrato(a); (*inf: ideas, person*) di vecchio stampo ♦ *vt* (*arrange*) regolare; (*MATH*) elevare al quadrato; (*reconcile*) conciliare; **all ~** pari; **a ~ meal** un pasto abbondante; **2 metres ~** di 2 metri per 2; **1 ~ metre** 1 metro quadrato; **~ly** *adv* diritto; fermamente

squash [skwɔʃ] *n* (*SPORT*) squash *m*; (*BRIT: drink*): **lemon/orange ~** sciroppo di limone/arancia; (*US*) zucca; (*SPORT*) squash *m* ♦ *vt* schiacciare

squat [skwɔt] *adj* tarchiato(a), tozzo(a) ♦ *vi* (*also: ~ down*) accovacciarsi; **~ter** *n* occupante *m/f* abusivo(a)

squawk [skwɔːk] *vi* emettere strida rauche

squeak [skwiːk] *vi* squittire

squeal [skwiːl] *vi* strillare

squeamish ['skwiːmiʃ] *adj* schizzinoso(a); disgustato(a)

squeeze [skwi:z] *n* pressione *f*; (*also ECON*) stretta ♦ *vt* premere; (*hand, arm*) stringere; ~ **out***vt* spremere

squelch [skwɛltʃ] *vi* fare ciac; sguazzare

squid [skwɪd] *n* calamaro

squiggle ['skwɪgl] *n* ghirigoro

squint [skwɪnt] *vi* essere strabico(a) ♦ *n*: **he has a** ~ è strabico

squire ['skwaɪə*] (*BRIT*) *n* proprietario terriero

squirm [skwəːm] *vi* contorcersi

squirrel ['skwɪrəl] *n* scoiattolo

squirt [skwəːt] *vi* schizzare; zampillare ♦ *vt* spruzzare

Sr *abbr* = **senior**

St *abbr* = **saint**; **street**

stab [stæb] *n* (*with knife etc*) pugnalata; (*of pain*) fitta; (*inf: try*): **to have a** ~ **at (doing) sth** provare (a fare) qc ♦ *vt* pugnalare

stable ['steɪbl] *n* (*for horses*) scuderia; (*for cattle*) stalla ♦ *adj* stabile

stack [stæk] *n* catasta, pila ♦ *vt* accatastare, ammucchiare

stadium ['steɪdɪəm] *n* stadio

staff [stɑːf] *n* (*work force: gen*) personale *m*; (: *BRIT: SCOL*) personale insegnante ♦ *vt* fornire di personale

stag [stæg] *n* cervo

stage [steɪdʒ] *n* palcoscenico; (*profession*): **the** ~ il teatro, la scena; (*point*) punto; (*platform*) palco ♦ *vt* (*play*) allestire, mettere in scena; (*demonstration*) organizzare; **in** ~**s** per gradi; a tappe; ~**coach** *n* diligenza; ~ **manager** *n* direttore *m* di scena

stagger ['stægə*] *vi* barcollare ♦ *vt* (*person*) sbalordire; (*hours, holidays*) scaglionare; ~**ing** *adj* (*amazing*) sbalorditivo(a)

stagnate [stæg'neɪt] *vi* stagnare

stag party *n* festa di addio al celibato

staid [steɪd] *adj* posato(a), serio(a)

stain [steɪn] *n* macchia; (*colouring*) colorante *m* ♦ *vt* macchiare; (*wood*) tingere; ~**ed glass window** *n* vetrata; ~**less** *adj* (*steel*) inossidabile; ~ **remover** *n* smacchiatore *m*

stair [stɛə*] *n* (*step*) gradino; ~**s** *npl*

(*flight of* ~s) scale *fpl*, scala; ~**case** *n* scale *fpl*, scala; ~**way** *n* = ~**case**

stake [steɪk] *n* palo, piolo; (*COMM*) interesse *m*; (*BETTING*) puntata, scommessa ♦ *vt* (*bet*) scommettere; (*risk*) rischiare; **to be at** ~ essere in gioco

stale [steɪl] *adj* (*bread*) raffermo(a); (*food*) stantio(a); (*air*) viziato(a); (*beer*) svaporato(a); (*smell*) di chiuso

stalemate ['steɪlmeɪt] *n* stallo; (*fig*) punto morto

stalk [stɔːk] *n* gambo, stelo ♦ *vt* inseguire; ~ **off** *vi* andarsene impettito(a)

stall [stɔːl] *n* bancarella; (*in stable*) box *m inv* di stalla ♦ *vt* (*AUT*) far spegnere; (*fig*) bloccare ♦ *vi* (*AUT*) spegnersi, fermarsi; (*fig*) temporeggiare; ~**s** *npl* (*BRIT: in cinema, theatre*) platea

stallion ['stæljən] *n* stallone *m*

stalwart ['stɔːlwət] *adj* fidato(a); risoluto(a)

stamina ['stæmɪnə] *n* vigore *m*, resistenza

stammer ['stæmə*] *n* balbuzie *f* ♦ *vi* balbettare

stamp [stæmp] *n* (*postage* ~) francobollo; (*implement*) timbro; (*mark, also fig*) marchio, impronta; (*on document*) bollo; timbro ♦ *vi* (*also*: ~ *one's foot*) battere il piede ♦ *vt* battere; (*letter*) affrancare; (*mark with a* ~) timbrare; ~ **album** *n* album *m inv* per francobolli; ~ **collecting** *n* filatelia

stampede [stæm'piːd] *n* fuggi fuggi *m inv*

stance [stæns] *n* posizione *f*

stand [stænd] (*pt, pp* **stood**) *n* (*position*) posizione *f*; (*for taxis*) posteggio; (*structure*) supporto, sostegno; (*at exhibition*) stand *m inv*; (*in shop*) banco; (*at market*) bancarella; (*booth*) chiosco; (*SPORT*) tribuna ♦ *vi* stare in piedi; (*rise*) alzarsi in piedi; (*be placed*) trovarsi ♦ *vt* (*place*) mettere, porre; (*tolerate, withstand*) resistere, sopportare; (*treat*) offrire; **to make a** ~ prendere posizione; **to** ~ **for parliament** (*BRIT*) presentarsi come candidato (per il parlamento); ~ **by** *vi* (*be ready*) tenersi pronto(a) ♦ *vt fus* (*opinion*)

sostenere; ~ **down** *vi* (*withdraw*)
ritirarsi; ~ **for** *vt fus* (*signify*)
rappresentare, significare; (*tolerate*)
sopportare, tollerare; ~ **in for** *vt fus*
sostituire; ~ **out** *vi* (*be prominent*)
spiccare; ~ **up** *vi* (*rise*) alzarsi in piedi; ~
up for *vt fus* difendere; ~ **up to** *vt fus*
tener testa a, resistere a
standard ['stændəd] *n* modello, standard
m inv; (*level*) livello; (*flag*) stendardo
♦ *adj* (*size etc*) normale, standard *inv*; **~s**
npl (*morals*) principi *mpl*, valori *mpl*; ~
lamp (*BRIT*) *n* lampada a stelo; ~ **of**
living *n* livello di vita
stand-by *n* riserva, sostituto; **to be on** ~
(*gen*) tenersi pronto(a); (*doctor*) essere di
guardia; ~ **ticket** *n* (*AVIAT*) biglietto senza
garanzia
stand-in *n* sostituto/a
standing ['stændɪŋ] *adj* diritto(a), in
piedi; (*permanent*) permanente ♦ *n* rango,
condizione *f*, posizione *f*; **of many years'**
~ che esiste da molti anni; ~ **joke** *n*
barzelletta; ~ **order** (*BRIT*) *n* (*at bank*)
ordine *m* di pagamento (permanente); ~
room *n* posto all'impiedi
standoffish [stænd'ɔfɪʃ] *adj* scostante,
freddo(a)
standpoint ['stændpɔɪnt] *n* punto di
vista
standstill ['stændstɪl] *n*: **at a** ~ fermo(a);
(*fig*) a un punto morto; **to come to a** ~
fermarsi; giungere a un punto morto
stank [stæŋk] *pt of* **stink**
staple ['steɪpl] *n* (*for papers*) graffetta ♦
adj (*food etc*) di base ♦ *vt* cucire; **~r** *n*
cucitrice *f*
star [staː*] *n* stella; (*celebrity*) divo/a ♦ *vi*:
to ~ (**in**) essere il (*or* la) protagonista (di)
♦ *vt* (*CINEMA*) essere interpretato(a) da
starboard ['staːbəd] *n* dritta
starch [staːtʃ] *n* amido
stardom ['staːdəm] *n* celebrità
stare [stɛə*] *n* sguardo fisso ♦ *vi*: **to** ~ **at**
fissare
starfish ['staːfɪʃ] *n* stella di mare
stark [staːk] *adj* (*bleak*) desolato(a) ♦ *adv*:
~ **naked** completamente nudo(a)
starling ['staːlɪŋ] *n* storno

starry ['staːrɪ] *adj* stellato(a); **~-eyed** *adj*
(*innocent*) ingenuo(a)
start [staːt] *n* inizio; (*of race*) partenza;
(*sudden movement*) sobbalzo; (*advantage*)
vantaggio ♦ *vt* cominciare, iniziare; (*car*)
mettere in moto ♦ *vi* cominciare; (*on*
journey) partire, mettersi in viaggio;
(*jump*) sobbalzare; **to** ~ **doing** *or* **to do**
sth (in)cominciare a fare qc; ~ **off** *vi*
cominciare; (*leave*) partire; ~ **up** *vi*
cominciare; (*car*) avviare ♦ *vt* iniziare;
(*car*) avviare; **~er** *n* (*AUT*) motorino
d'avviamento; (*SPORT: official*) starter *m*
inv; (*BRIT: CULIN*) primo piatto; **~ing point**
n punto di partenza
startle ['staːtl] *vt* far trasalire; **startling**
adj sorprendente
starvation [staː'veɪʃən] *n* fame *f*, inedia
starve [staːv] *vi* morire di fame; soffrire
la fame ♦ *vt* far morire di fame, affamare
state [steɪt] *n* stato ♦ *vt* dichiarare,
affermare; annunciare; **the S~s** (*USA*) gli
Stati Uniti; **to be in a** ~ essere agitato(a);
~ly *adj* maestoso(a), imponente; **~ment** *n*
dichiarazione *f*; **~sman** *n* statista *m*
static ['stætɪk] *n* (*RADIO*) scariche *fpl*
♦ *adj* statico(a)
station ['steɪʃən] *n* stazione *f* ♦ *vt*
collocare, disporre
stationary ['steɪʃənərɪ] *adj* fermo(a),
immobile
stationer ['steɪʃənə*] *n* cartolaio/a; **~'s**
(**shop**) *n* cartoleria; **~y** *n* articoli *mpl* di
cancelleria
station master *n* (*RAIL*) capostazione *m*
station wagon (*US*) *n* giardinetta
statistic [stə'tɪstɪk] *n* statistica; **~s** *n*
(*science*) statistica
statue ['stætjuː] *n* statua
status ['steɪtəs] *n* posizione *f*, condizione
f sociale; prestigio; stato; ~ **symbol** *n*
simbolo di prestigio
statute ['stætjuːt] *n* legge *f*; **statutory**
adj stabilito(a) dalla legge, statutario(a)
staunch [stɔːntʃ] *adj* fidato(a), leale
stave [steɪv] *vt*: **to** ~ **off** (*attack*)
respingere; (*threat*) evitare
stay [steɪ] *n* (*period of time*) soggiorno,
permanenza ♦ *vi* rimanere; (*reside*)

alloggiare, stare; (*spend some time*) trattenersi, soggiornare; **to ~ put** non muoversi; **to ~ the night** fermarsi per la notte; **~ behind** *vi* restare indietro; **~ in** *vi* (*at home*) restare, rimanere; **~ out** *vi* (*of house*) rimanere fuori (di casa); **~ up** *vi* (*at night*) rimanere alzato(a); **~ing power** *n* capacità di resistenza

stead [stɛd] *n*: **in sb's ~** al posto di qn; **to stand sb in good ~** essere utile a qn

steadfast ['stɛdfɑːst] *adj* fermo(a), risoluto(a)

steadily ['stɛdɪlɪ] *adv* (*firmly*) saldamente; (*constantly*) continuamente; (*fixedly*) fisso; (*walk*) con passo sicuro

steady ['stɛdɪ] *adj* (*not wobbling*) fermo(a); (*regular*) costante; (*person, character*) serio(a); (: *calm*) calmo(a), tranquillo(a) ♦ *vt* stabilizzare; calmare

steak [steɪk] *n* (*meat*) bistecca; (*fish*) trancia

steal [stiːl] (*pt* **stole**, *pp* **stolen**) *vt* rubare ♦ *vi* rubare; (*move*) muoversi furtivamente

stealth [stɛlθ] *n*: **by ~** furtivamente; **~y** *adj* furtivo(a)

steam [stiːm] *n* vapore *m* ♦ *vt* (*CULIN*) cuocere a vapore ♦ *vi* fumare; **~ engine** *n* macchina a vapore; (*RAIL*) locomotiva a vapore; **~er** *n* piroscafo, vapore *m*; **~roller** *n* rullo compressore; **~ship** *n* = **~er**; **~y** *adj* (*room*) pieno(a) di vapore; (*window*) appannato(a)

steel [stiːl] *n* acciaio ♦ *adj* di acciaio; **~works** *n* acciaieria

steep [stiːp] *adj* ripido(a), scosceso(a); (*price*) eccessivo(a) ♦ *vt* inzuppare; (*washing*) mettere a mollo

steeple ['stiːpl] *n* campanile *m*

steer [stɪə*] *vt* guidare ♦ *vi* (*NAUT: person*) governare; (*car*) guidarsi; **~ing** *n* (*AUT*) sterzo; **~ing wheel** *n* volante *m*

stem [stɛm] *n* (*of flower, plant*) stelo; (*of tree*) fusto; (*of glass*) gambo; (*of fruit, leaf*) picciolo ♦ *vt* contenere, arginare; **~ from** *vt fus* provenire da, derivare da

stench [stɛntʃ] *n* puzzo, fetore *m*

stencil ['stɛnsl] *n* (*of metal, cardboard*) stampino, mascherina; (*in typing*) matrice *f* ♦ *vt* disegnare con stampino

stenographer [stɛ'nɔgrəfə*] (*US*) *n* stenografo/a

step [stɛp] *n* passo, (*stair*) gradino, scalino; (*action*) mossa, azione *f* ♦ *vi*: **to ~ forward/back** fare un passo avanti/indietro; **~s** *npl* (*BRIT*) = **stepladder**; **to be in/out of ~ (with)** stare/non stare al passo (con); **~ down** *vi* (*fig*) ritirarsi; **~ on** *vt fus* calpestare; **~ up** *vt* aumentare; intensificare; **~brother** *n* fratellastro; **~daughter** *n* figliastra; **~father** *n* patrigno; **~ladder** *n* scala a libretto; **~mother** *n* matrigna; **~ping stone** *n* pietra di un guado; **~sister** *n* sorellastra; **~son** *n* figliastro

stereo ['stɛrɪəʊ] *n* (*system*) sistema *m* stereofonico; (*record player*) stereo *m inv* ♦ *adj* (*also*: **~phonic**) stereofonico(a)

sterile ['stɛraɪl] *adj* sterile; **sterilize** ['stɛrɪlaɪz] *vt* sterilizzare

sterling ['stəːlɪŋ] *adj* (*gold, silver*) di buona lega ♦ *n* (*ECON*) (lira) sterlina; **a pound ~** una lira sterlina

stern [stəːn] *adj* severo(a) ♦ *n* (*NAUT*) poppa

stew [stjuː] *n* stufato ♦ *vt* cuocere in umido

steward ['stjuːəd] *n* (*AVIAT, NAUT, RAIL*) steward *m inv*; (*in club etc*) dispensiere *m*; **~ess** *n* assistente *f* di volo, hostess *f inv*

stick [stɪk] (*pt*, *pp* **stuck**) *n* bastone *m*; (*of rhubarb, celery*) gambo; (*of dynamite*) candelotto ♦ *vt* (*glue*) attaccare; (*thrust*): **to ~ sth into** conficcare *or* piantare *or* infiggere qc in; (*inf: put*) ficcare; (*inf: tolerate*) sopportare ♦ *vi* attaccarsi; (*remain*) restare, rimanere; **~ out** *vi* sporgere, spuntare; **~ up** *vi* sporgere, spuntare; **~ up for** *vt fus* difendere; **~er** *n* cartellino adesivo; **~ing plaster** *n* cerotto adesivo

stickler ['stɪklə*] *n*: **to be a ~ for** essere pignolo(a) su, tenere molto a

stick-up (*inf*) *n* rapina a mano armata

sticky ['stɪkɪ] *adj* attaccaticcio(a), vischioso(a); (*label*) adesivo(a); (*fig: situation*) difficile

stiff [stɪf] *adj* rigido(a), duro(a); *(muscle)* legato(a), indolenzito(a); *(difficult)* difficile, arduo(a); *(cold)* freddo(a), formale; *(strong)* forte; *(high: price)* molto alto(a) ♦ *adv*: **bored** ~ annoiato(a) a morte; **~en** *vt* irrigidire; rinforzare ♦ *vi* irrigidirsi; indurirsi; ~ **neck** *n* torcicollo

stifle ['staɪfl] *vt* soffocare

stigma ['stɪgmə] *n (fig)* stigma *m*

stile [staɪl] *n* cavalcasiepe *m*; cavalcasteccato

stiletto [stɪ'lɛtəu] *(BRIT) n (also:* ~ *heel)* tacco a spillo

still [stɪl] *adj* fermo(a); silenzioso(a) ♦ *adv (up to this time, even)* ancora; *(nonetheless)* tuttavia, ciò nonostante; **~born** *adj* nato(a) morto(a); ~ **life** *n* natura morta

stilt [stɪlt] *n* trampolo; *(pile)* palo

stilted ['stɪltɪd] *adj* freddo(a), formale; artificiale

stimulate ['stɪmjuleɪt] *vt* stimolare

stimuli ['stɪmjulaɪ] *npl of* **stimulus**

stimulus ['stɪmjuləs] *(pl* **stimuli**) *n* stimolo

sting [stɪŋ] *(pt, pp* **stung**) *n* puntura; *(organ)* pungiglione *m* ♦ *vt* pungere

stingy ['stɪndʒɪ] *adj* spilorcio(a), tirchio(a)

stink [stɪŋk] *(pt* **stank**, *pp* **stunk**) *n* fetore *m*, puzzo ♦ *vi* puzzare; **~ing** *(inf) adj (fig):* **a ~ing ...** uno schifo di ..., un(a) maledetto(a) ....

stint [stɪnt] *n* lavoro, compito ♦ *vi*: **to ~ on** lesinare su

stir [stə:*] *n* agitazione *f*, clamore *m* ♦ *vt* mescolare; *(fig)* risvegliare ♦ *vi* muoversi; ~ **up** *vt* provocare, suscitare

stirrup ['stɪrəp] *n* staffa

stitch [stɪtʃ] *n (SEWING)* punto; *(KNITTING)* maglia; *(MED)* punto (di sutura); *(pain)* fitta ♦ *vt* cucire, attaccare; suturare

stoat [stəut] *n* ermellino

stock [stɔk] *n* riserva, provvista; *(COMM)* giacenza, stock *m inv*; *(AGR)* bestiame *m*; *(CULIN)* brodo; *(descent)* stirpe *f*; *(FINANCE)* titoli *mpl*, azioni *fpl* ♦ *adj (fig: reply etc)* consueto(a); classico(a) ♦ *vt (have in stock)* avere, vendere; ~**s and shares**

valori *mpl* di borsa; **in** ~ in magazzino; **out of** ~ esaurito(a); ~ **up** *vi*: **to** ~ **up (with)** fare provvista (di)

stockbroker ['stɔkbrəukə*] *n* agente *m* di cambio

stock cube *(BRIT) n* dado

stock exchange *n* Borsa (valori)

stocking ['stɔkɪŋ] *n* calza

stockist ['stɔkɪst] *(BRIT) n* fornitore *m*

stock: ~ **market** *n* Borsa, mercato finanziario; ~ **phrase** *n* cliché *m inv*; ~**pile** *n* riserva ♦ *vt* accumulare riserve di; ~**taking** *(BRIT) n (COMM)* inventario

stocky ['stɔkɪ] *adj* tarchiato(a), tozzo(a)

stodgy ['stɔdʒɪ] *adj* pesante, indigesto(a)

stoke [stəuk] *vt* alimentare

stole [stəul] *pt of* **steal** ♦ *n* stola

stolen ['stəuln] *pp of* **steal**

stolid ['stɔlɪd] *adj* impassibile

stomach ['stʌmək] *n* stomaco; *(belly)* pancia ♦ *vt* sopportare, digerire; ~ **ache** *n* mal *m* di stomaco

stone [stəun] *n* pietra; *(pebble)* sasso, ciottolo; *(in fruit)* nocciolo; *(MED)* calcolo; *(BRIT: weight)* = 6.348 *kg.*; 14 *libbre* ♦ *adj* di pietra ♦ *vt* lapidare; *(fruit)* togliere il nocciolo a; ~**-cold** *adj* gelido(a); ~**-deaf** *adj* sordo(a) come una campana; ~**work** *n* muratura; **stony** *adj* sassoso(a); *(fig)* di pietra

stood [stud] *pt, pp of* **stand**

stool [stu:l] *n* sgabello

stoop [stu:p] *vi (also: have a ~)* avere una curvatura; *(also:* ~ *down)* chinarsi, curvarsi

stop [stɔp] *n* arresto; *(stopping place)* fermata; *(in punctuation)* punto ♦ *vt* arrestare, fermare; *(break off)* interrompere; *(also: put a ~ to)* porre fine a ♦ *vi* fermarsi; *(rain, noise etc)* cessare, finire; **to ~ doing sth** cessare *or* finire di fare qc; **to ~ dead** fermarsi di colpo; ~ **off** *vi* sostare brevemente; ~ **up** *vt (hole)* chiudere, turare; ~**gap** *n* tappabuchi *m inv*; ~**over** *n* breve sosta; *(AVIAT)* scalo

stoppage ['stɔpɪdʒ] *n* arresto, fermata; *(of pay)* trattenuta; *(strike)* interruzione *f* del lavoro

stopper ['stɔpə*] *n* tappo

stop press *n* ultimissime *fpl*

stopwatch ['stɔpwɔtʃ] *n* cronometro

storage ['stɔːrɪdʒ] *n* immagazzinamento; **~ heater** *n* radiatore *m* elettrico che accumula calore

store [stɔː*] *n* provvista, riserva; (*depot*) deposito; (*BRIT: department ~*) grande magazzino; (*US: shop*) negozio ♦ *vt* immagazzinare; **~s** *npl* (*provisions*) rifornimenti *mpl*, scorte *fpl*; **in ~** di riserva; in serbo; **~ up** *vt* conservare; mettere in serbo; **~room** *n* dispensa

storey ['stɔːrɪ] (*US* **story**) *n* piano

stork [stɔːk] *n* cicogna

storm [stɔːm] *n* tempesta, temporale *m*, burrasca; uragano ♦ *vi* (*fig*) infuriarsi ♦ *vt* prendere d'assalto; **~y** *adj* tempestoso(a), burrascoso(a)

story ['stɔːrɪ] *n* storia; favola; racconto; (*US*) = **storey**; **~book** *n* libro di racconti

stout [staut] *adj* solido(a), robusto(a); (*friend, supporter*) tenace; (*fat*) corpulento(a), grasso(a) ♦ *n* birra scura

stove [stəuv] *n* (*for cooking*) fornello; (*: small*) fornelletto; (*for heating*) stufa

stow [stəu] *vt* (*also: ~ away*) mettere via; **~away** *n* passeggero(a) clandestino(a)

straddle ['strædl] *vt* stare a cavalcioni di; (*fig*) essere a cavallo di

straggle ['strægl] *vi* crescere (*or* estendersi) disordinatamente; trascinarsi; rimanere indietro; **straggly** *adj* (*hair*) in disordine

straight [streɪt] *adj* dritto(a); (*frank*) onesto(a), franco(a); (*simple*) semplice ♦ *adv* diritto; (*drink*) liscio; **to put** *or* **get ~** mettere in ordine, mettere ordine in; **~ away**, **~ off** (*at once*) immediatamente; **~en** *vt* (*also: ~en out*) raddrizzare; **~-faced** *adj* impassibile, imperturbabile; **~forward** *adj* semplice; onesto(a), franco(a)

strain [streɪn] *n* (*TECH*) sollecitazione *f*; (*physical*) sforzo; (*mental*) tensione *f*; (*MED*) strappo; distorsione *f*; (*streak, trace*) tendenza; elemento ♦ *vt* tendere; (*muscle*) sforzare; (*ankle*) storcere; (*resources*) pesare su; (*food*) colare; passare; **~s** *npl* (*MUS*) note *fpl*; **~ed** *adj* (*muscle*) stirato(a);

(*laugh etc*) forzato(a); (*relations*) teso(a); **~er** *n* passino, colino

strait [streɪt] *n* (*GEO*) stretto; **~s** *npl*: **to be in dire ~s** (*fig*) essere nei guai; **~jacket** *n* camicia di forza; **~-laced** *adj* bacchettone(a)

strand [strænd] *n* (*of thread*) filo; **~ed** *adj* nei guai; senza mezzi di trasporto

strange [streɪndʒ] *adj* (*not known*) sconosciuto(a); (*odd*) strano(a), bizzarro(a); **~ly** *adv* stranamente; **~r** *n* sconosciuto/a; estraneo/a

strangle ['stræŋgl] *vt* strangolare; **~hold** *n* (*fig*) stretta (mortale)

strap [stræp] *n* cinghia; (*of slip, dress*) spallina, bretella

strapping ['stræpɪŋ] *adj* ben piantato(a)

strategic [strə'tiːdʒɪk] *adj* strategico(a)

strategy ['strætɪdʒɪ] *n* strategia

straw [strɔː] *n* paglia; (*drinking ~*) cannuccia; **that's the last ~!** è la goccia che fa traboccare il vaso!

strawberry ['strɔːbərɪ] *n* fragola

stray [streɪ] *adj* (*animal*) randagio(a); (*bullet*) vagante; (*scattered*) sparso(a) ♦ *vi* perdersi

streak [striːk] *n* striscia; (*of hair*) mèche *f inv* ♦ *vt* striare, screziare ♦ *vi*: **to ~ past** passare come un fulmine

stream [striːm] *n* ruscello, corrente *f*; (*of people, smoke etc*) fiume *m* ♦ *vt* (*SCOL*) dividere in livelli di rendimento ♦ *vi* scorrere; **to ~ in/out** entrare/uscire a fiotti

streamer ['striːmə*] *n* (*of paper*) stella filante

streamlined ['striːmlaɪnd] *adj* aerodinamico(a), affusolato(a)

street [striːt] *n* strada, via; **~car** (*US*) *n* tram *m inv*; **~ lamp** *n* lampione *m*; **~ plan** *n* pianta (di una città); **~wise** (*inf*) *adj* esperto(a) dei bassifondi

strength [streŋθ] *n* forza; **~en** *vt* rinforzare; fortificare; consolidare

strenuous ['strenjuəs] *adj* vigoroso(a), energico(a); (*tiring*) duro(a), pesante

stress [stres] *n* (*force, pressure*) pressione *f*; (*mental strain*) tensione *f*; (*accent*) accento ♦ *vt* insistere su, sottolineare;

accentare

stretch [stretʃ] *n* (*of sand etc*) distesa ♦ *vi* stirarsi; (*extend*): **to ~ to** *or* **as far as** estendersi fino a ♦ *vt* tendere, allungare; (*spread*) distendere; (*al massimo*); **~ out** *vi* allungarsi, estendersi ♦ *vt* (*arm etc*) allungare, tendere; (*to spread*) distendere

stretcher ['stretʃə*] *n* barella, lettiga

strewn [struːn] *adj*: **~ with** cosparso(a) di

stricken ['strɪkən] *adj* (*person*) provato(a); (*city, industry etc*) colpito(a); **~ with** (*disease etc*) colpito(a) da

strict [strɪkt] *adj* (*severe*) rigido(a), severo(a); (*precise*) preciso(a), stretto(a)

stridden ['strɪdn] *pp of* **stride**

stride [straɪd] (*pt* **strode**, *pp* **stridden**) *n* passo lungo ♦ *vi* camminare a grandi passi

strife [straɪf] *n* conflitto; litigi *mpl*

strike [straɪk] (*pt, pp* **struck**) *n* sciopero; (*of oil etc*) scoperta; (*attack*) attacco ♦ *vt* colpire; (*oil etc*) scoprire, trovare (*bargain*) fare; (*fig*): **the thought** *or* **it ~s me that ...** mi viene in mente che ... ♦ *vi* scioperare; (*attack*) attaccare; (*clock*) suonare; **on ~** (*workers*) in sciopero; **to ~ a match** accendere un fiammifero; **~ down** *vt* (*fig*) atterrare; **~ up** *vt* (*MUS, conversation*) attaccare; **to ~ up a friendship** *with* fare amicizia con; **~r** *n* scioperante *m/f*; (*SPORT*) attaccante *m*; **striking** *adj* che colpisce

string [strɪŋ] (*pt, pp* **strung**) *n* spago; (*row*) fila; sequenza; catena; (*MUS*) corda ♦ *vt*: **to ~ out** disporre di fianco a; **to ~ together** (*words, ideas*) mettere insieme; **the ~s** *npl* (*MUS*) gli archi; **to pull ~s for sb** (*fig*) raccomandare qn; **~ bean** *n* fagiolino; **~(ed) instrument** *n* (*MUS*) strumento a corda

stringent ['strɪndʒənt] *adj* rigoroso(a)

strip [strɪp] *n* striscia ♦ *vt* spogliare; (*paint*) togliere; (*also*: **~ down**: *machine*) smontare ♦ *vi* spogliarsi; **~ cartoon** *n* fumetto

stripe [straɪp] *n* striscia, riga; (*MIL, POLICE*) gallone *m*; **~d** *adj* a strisce *or* righe

strip lighting *n* illuminazione *f* al neon

stripper ['strɪpə*] *n* spogliarellista *m/f*

striptease ['strɪptiːz] *n* spogliarello

strive [straɪv] (*pt* **strove**, *pp* **striven**) *vi*: **to ~ to do** sforzarsi di fare; **striven** ['strɪvn] *pp of* **strive**

strode [strəʊd] *pt of* **stride**

stroke [strəʊk] *n* colpo; (*SWIMMING*) bracciata; (: *style*) stile *m*; (*MED*) colpo apoplettico ♦ *vt* accarezzare; **at a ~** in un attimo

stroll [strəʊl] *n* giretto, passeggiatina ♦ *vi* andare a spasso; **~er** (*US*) *n* passeggino

strong [strɒŋ] *adj* (*gen*) forte; (*sturdy: table, fabric etc*) robusto(a); **they are 50 ~** sono in 50; **~box** *n* cassaforte *f*; **~hold** *n* (*also fig*) roccaforte *f*; **~ly** *adv* fortemente, con forza; energicamente; vivamente; **~room** *n* camera di sicurezza

strove [strəʊv] *pt of* **strive**

struck [strʌk] *pt, pp of* **strike**

structural ['strʌktʃərəl] *adj* strutturale

structure ['strʌktʃə*] *n* struttura; (*building*) costruzione *f*, fabbricato

struggle ['strʌgl] *n* lotta ♦ *vi* lottare

strum [strʌm] *vt* (*guitar*) strimpellare

strung [strʌŋ] *pt, pp of* **string**

strut [strʌt] *n* sostegno, supporto ♦ *vi* pavoneggiarsi

stub [stʌb] *n* mozzicone *m*; (*of ticket etc*) matrice *f*, tallloncino ♦ *vt*: **to ~ one's toe** urtare *or* sbattere il dito del piede; **~ out** *vt* schiacciare

stubble ['stʌbl] *n* stoppia; (*on chin*) barba ispida

stubborn ['stʌbən] *adj* testardo(a), ostinato(a)

stuck [stʌk] *pt, pp of* **stick** ♦ *adj* (*jammed*) bloccato(a); **~-up** *adj* presuntuoso(a)

stud [stʌd] *n* bottoncino; borchia; (*also*: **~ earring**) orecchino a pressione; (*also*: **~ farm**) scuderia, allevamento di cavalli; (*also*: **~ horse**) stallone *m* ♦ *vt* (*fig*): **~ded with** tempestato(a) di

student ['stjuːdənt] *n* studente/essa ♦ *cpd* studentesco(a); universitario(a); degli studenti; **~ driver** (*US*) *n* conducente *m/f* principiante

studio ['stju:dɪəʊ] *n* studio; **~ flat** (*US* **~ apartment**) *n* monolocale *m*

studious ['stju:dɪəs] *adj* studioso(a); (*studied*) studiato(a), voluto(a); **~ly** *adv* (*carefully*) deliberatamente, di proposito

study ['stʌdɪ] *n* studio ♦ *vt* studiare; esaminare ♦ *vi* studiare

stuff [stʌf] *n* roba; (*substance*) sostanza, materiale *m* ♦ *vt* imbottire; (*CULIN*) farcire; (*dead animal*) impagliare; (*inf: push*) ficcare; **~ing** *n* imbottitura; (*CULIN*) ripieno; **~y** *adj* (*room*) mal ventilato(a), senz'aria; (*ideas*) antiquato(a)

stumble ['stʌmbl] *vi* inciampare; **to ~ across** (*fig*) imbattersi in; **stumbling block** *n* ostacolo, scoglio

stump [stʌmp] *n* ceppo; (*of limb*) moncone *m* ♦ *vt*: **to be ~ed** essere sconcertato(a)

stun [stʌn] *vt* stordire; (*amaze*) sbalordire

stung [stʌŋ] *pt, pp of* **sting**

stunk [stʌŋk] *pp of* **stink**

stunning ['stʌnɪŋ] *adj* sbalorditivo(a); (*girl etc*) fantastico(a)

stunt [stʌnt] *n* bravata; trucco pubblicitario; **~ed** *adj* stentato(a), rachitico(a); **~man** *n* cascatore *m*

stupefy ['stju:pɪfaɪ] *vt* stordire; intontire; (*fig*) stupire

stupendous [stju:'pɛndəs] *adj* stupendo(a), meraviglioso(a)

stupid ['stju:pɪd] *adj* stupido(a); **~ity** [-'pɪdɪtɪ] *n* stupidità *f inv*, stupidaggine *f*

stupor ['stju:pə*] *n* torpore *m*

sturdy ['stɜ:dɪ] *adj* robusto(a), vigoroso(a); solido(a)

stutter ['stʌtə*] *n* balbuzie *f* ♦ *vi* balbettare

sty [staɪ] *n* (*of pigs*) porcile *m*

stye [staɪ] *n* (*MED*) orzaiolo

style [staɪl] *n* stile *m*; (*distinction*) eleganza, classe *f*; **stylish** *adj* elegante

stylus ['staɪləs] *n* (*of record player*) puntina

suave [swɑ:v] *adj* untuoso(a)

sub... [sʌb] *prefix* sub..., sotto...; **~conscious** *adj* subcosciente ♦ *n* subcosciente *m*; **~contract** *vt*

subappaltare

subdue [səb'dju:] *vt* sottomettere, soggiogare; **~d** *adj* pacato(a); (*light*) attenuato(a)

subject [*n* 'sʌbdʒɪkt, *vb* səb'dʒɛkt] *n* soggetto; (*citizen etc*) cittadino/a; (*SCOL*) materia ♦ *vt*: **to ~ to** sottomettere a; esporre a; **to be ~ to** (*law*) essere sottomesso(a) a; (*disease*) essere soggetto(a) a; **~ive** [-'dʒɛktɪv] *adj* soggettivo(a); **~ matter** *n* argomento; contenuto

subjunctive [səb'dʒʌŋktɪv] *n* congiuntivo

sublet [sʌb'lɛt] *vt* subaffittare

submachine gun ['sʌbmə'ʃi:n-] *n* mitra *m inv*

submarine [sʌbmə'ri:n] *n* sommergibile *m*

submerge [səb'mɜ:dʒ] *vt* sommergere; immergere ♦ *vi* immergersi

submission [səb'mɪʃən] *n* sottomissione *f*; (*claim*) richiesta

submissive [səb'mɪsɪv] *adj* remissivo(a)

submit [səb'mɪt] *vt* sottomettere ♦ *vi* sottomettersi

subnormal [sʌb'nɔ:məl] *adj* subnormale

subordinate [sə'bɔ:dɪnət] *adj, n* subordinato(a)

subpoena [səb'pi:nə] *n* (*LAW*) citazione *f*, mandato di comparizione

subscribe [səb'skraɪb] *vi* contribuire; **to ~ to** (*opinion*) approvare, condividere; (*fund*) sottoscrivere a; (*newspaper*) abbonarsi a; essere abbonato(a) a; **~r** *n* (*to periodical, telephone*) abbonato/a

subscription [səb'skrɪpʃən] *n* sottoscrizione *f*; abbonamento

subsequent ['sʌbsɪkwənt] *adj* successivo(a), seguente; conseguente; **~ly** *adv* in seguito, successivamente

subside [səb'saɪd] *vi* cedere, abbassarsi; (*flood*) decrescere; (*wind*) calmarsi; **~nce** [-'saɪdns] *n* cedimento, abbassamento

subsidiarity [səbsɪdɪ'ærɪtɪ] *n* (*POL*) principio del decentramento del potere

subsidiary [səb'sɪdɪərɪ] *adj* sussidiario(a); accessorio(a) ♦ *n* (*also*: **~ company**) filiale *f*

subsidize ['sʌbsɪdaɪz] *vt* sovvenzionare

subsidy ['sʌbsɪdɪ] *n* sovvenzione *f*

subsistence [səb'sɪstəns] *n* esistenza; mezzi *mpl* di sostentamento; **~ allowance** *n* indennità *f inv* di trasferta

substance ['sʌbstəns] *n* sostanza

substantial [səb'stænʃl] *adj* solido(a); (*amount, progress etc*) notevole; (*meal*) sostanzioso(a)

substantiate [səb'stænʃɪeɪt] *vt* comprovare

substitute ['sʌbstɪtjuːt] *n* (*person*) sostituto/a; (*thing*) succedaneo, surrogato ♦ *vt*: **to ~ sth/sb for** sostituire qc/qn a

subterfuge ['sʌbtəfjuːdʒ] *n* sotterfugio

subterranean [sʌbtə'reɪnɪən] *adj* sotterraneo(a)

subtitle ['sʌbtaɪtl] *n* (*CINEMA*) sottotitolo

subtle ['sʌtl] *adj* sottile; **~ty** *n* sottigliezza

subtotal [sʌb'təʊtl] *n* somma parziale

subtract [səb'trækt] *vt* sottrarre; **~ion** [-'trækʃən] *n* sottrazione *f*

suburb ['sʌbəːb] *n* sobborgo; **the ~s** la periferia; **~an** [sə'bəːbən] *adj* suburbano(a); **~ia** *n* periferia, sobborghi *mpl*

subversive [səb'vəːsɪv] *adj* sovversivo(a)

subway ['sʌbweɪ] *n* (*US: underground*) metropolitana; (*BRIT: underpass*) sottopassaggio

succeed [sək'siːd] *vi* riuscire; avere successo ♦ *vt* succedere a; **to ~ in doing** riuscire a fare; **~ing** *adj* (*following*) successivo(a)

success [sək'sɛs] *n* successo; **~ful** *adj* (*venture*) coronato(a) da successo, riuscito(a); **to be ~ful (in doing)** riuscire (a fare); **~fully** *adv* con successo

succession [sək'sɛʃən] *n* successione *f*

successive [sək'sɛsɪv] *adj* successivo(a); consecutivo(a)

succumb [sə'kʌm] *vi* soccombere

such [sʌtʃ] *adj* tale; (*of that kind*): **~ a book** un tale libro, un libro del genere; **~ books** tali libri, libri del genere; (*so much*): **~ courage** tanto coraggio ♦ *adv* talmente, così; **~ a long trip** un viaggio così lungo; **~ a lot of** talmente *or* così

tanto(a); **~ as** (*like*) come; **as ~** come *or* in quanto tale; **~-and-~** *adj* tale (*after noun*)

suck [sʌk] *vt* succhiare; (*breast, bottle*) poppare; **~er** *n* (*ZOOL, TECH*) ventosa; (*inf*) gonzo/a, babbeo/a

suction ['sʌkʃən] *n* succhiamento; (*TECH*) aspirazione *f*

sudden ['sʌdn] *adj* improvviso(a); **all of a ~** improvvisamente, all'improvviso; **~ly** *adv* bruscamente, improvvisamente, di colpo

suds [sʌdz] *npl* schiuma (di sapone)

sue [suː] *vt* citare in giudizio

suede [sweɪd] *n* pelle *f* scamosciata

suet ['suɪt] *n* grasso di rognone

suffer ['sʌfə*] *vt* soffrire, patire; (*bear*) sopportare, tollerare ♦ *vi* soffrire; **to ~ from** soffrire di; **~er** *n* malato/a; **~ing** *n* sofferenza

suffice [sə'faɪs] *vi* essere sufficiente, bastare

sufficient [sə'fɪʃənt] *adj* sufficiente; **~ money** abbastanza soldi; **~ly** *adv* sufficientemente, abbastanza

suffocate ['sʌfəkeɪt] *vi* (*have difficulty breathing*) soffocare; (*die through lack of air*) asfissiare

suffused [sə'fjuːzd] *adj*: **~ with** (*colour*) tinto(a) di; **the room was ~ with light** nella stanza c'era una luce soffusa

sugar ['ʃʊgə*] *n* zucchero ♦ *vt* zuccherare; **~ beet** *n* barbabietola da zucchero; **~ cane** *n* canna da zucchero

suggest [sə'dʒɛst] *vt* proporre, suggerire; indicare; **~ion** [-'dʒɛstʃən] *n* suggerimento, proposta; indicazione *f*; **~ive** (*pej*) *adj* indecente

suicide ['suɪsaɪd] *n* (*person*) suicida *m/f*; (*act*) suicidio; *see also* **commit**

suit [suːt] *n* (*man's*) vestito; (*woman's*) completo, tailleur *m inv*; (*LAW*) causa; (*CARDS*) seme *m*, colore *m* ♦ *vt* andar bene a *or* per; essere adatto(a) a *or* per; (*adapt*): **to ~ sth to** adattare qc a; **well ~ed** ben assortito(a); **~able** *adj* adatto(a); appropriato(a); **~ably** *adv* (*dress*) in modo adatto; (*impressed*) favorevolmente

suitcase ['suːtkeɪs] *n* valigia

suite [swiːt] *n* (*of rooms*) appartamento;

(*MUS*) suite *f inv*; (*furniture*): **bedroom/ dining room** ~ arredo *or* mobilia per la camera da letto/sala da pranzo

suitor ['su:tə*] *n* corteggiatore *m*, spasimante *m*

sulfur ['sʌlfə*] (*US*) *n* = **sulphur**

sulk [sʌlk] *vi* fare il broncio; **~y** *adj* imbronciato(a)

sullen ['sʌlən] *adj* scontroso(a); cupo(a)

sulphur ['sʌlfə*] (*US* **sulfur**) *n* zolfo

sultana [sʌl'tɑ:nə] *n* (*fruit*) uva (secca) sultanina

sultry ['sʌltrɪ] *adj* afoso(a)

sum [sʌm] *n* somma; (*SCOL etc*) addizione *f*; ~ **up** *vt*, *vi* riassumere

summarize ['sʌməraɪz] *vt* riassumere, riepilogare

summary ['sʌmərɪ] *n* riassunto

summer ['sʌmə*] *n* estate *f* ♦ *cpd* d'estate, estivo(a); ~ **holidays** *npl* vacanze *fpl* estive; **~house** *n* (*in garden*) padiglione *m*; **~time** *n* (*season*) estate *f*; ~ **time** *n* (*by clock*) ora legale (estiva)

summit ['sʌmɪt] *n* cima, sommità; (*POL*) vertice *m*

summon ['sʌmən] *vt* chiamare, convocare; ~ **up** *vt* raccogliere, fare appello a; **~s** *n* ordine *m* di comparizione ♦ *vt* citare

sump [sʌmp] (*BRIT*) *n* (*AUT*) coppa dell'olio

sumptuous ['sʌmptjuəs] *adj* sontuoso(a)

sun [sʌn] *n* sole *m*; **~bathe** *vi* prendere un bagno di sole; **~burn** *n* (*painful*) scottatura; **~burnt** *adj* abbronzato(a); (*painfully*) scottato(a)

Sunday ['sʌndɪ] *n* domenica; ~ **school** *n* ≈ scuola di catechismo

sundial ['sʌndaɪəl] *n* meridiana

sundown ['sʌndaun] *n* tramonto

sundry ['sʌndrɪ] *adj* vari(e), diversi(e); **all and** ~ tutti quanti; **sundries** *npl* articoli diversi, cose diverse

sunflower ['sʌnflauə*] *n* girasole *m*

sung [sʌŋ] *pp of* **sing**

sunglasses ['sʌnglɑ:sɪz] *npl* occhiali *mpl* da sole

sunk [sʌŋk] *pp of* **sink**

sun: **~light** *n* (luce *f* del) sole *m*; **~lit** *adj* soleggiato(a); **~ny** *adj* assolato(a),

soleggiato(a); (*fig*) allegro(a), felice; **~rise** *n* levata del sole, alba; ~ **roof** *n* (*AUT*) tetto apribile; **~set** *n* tramonto; **~shade** *n* parasole *m*; **~shine** *n* (luce *f* del) sole *m*; **~stroke** *n* insolazione *f*, colpo di sole; **~tan** *n* abbronzatura; **~tan lotion** *n* lozione *f* solare; **~tan oil** *n* olio solare

super ['su:pə*] (*inf*) *adj* fantastico(a)

superannuation [su:pərænju'eɪʃən] *n* contributi *mpl* pensionistici; pensione *f*

superb [su:'pə:b] *adj* magnifico(a)

supercilious [su:pə'sɪlɪəs] *adj* sprezzante, sdegnoso(a)

superficial [su:pə'fɪʃəl] *adj* superficiale

superhuman [su:pə'hju:mən] *adj* sovrumano(a)

superimpose ['su:pərɪm'pəuz] *vt* sovrapporre

superintendent [su:pərɪn'tɛndənt] *n* direttore/trice; (*POLICE*) ≈ commissario (capo)

superior [su'pɪərɪə*] *adj*, *n* superiore *m/f*; **~ity** [-'ɔrɪtɪ] *n* superiorità

superlative [su'pə:lətɪv] *adj* superlativo(a), supremo(a) ♦ *n* (*LING*) superlativo

superman ['su:pəmæn] *n* superuomo

supermarket ['su:pəmɑ:kɪt] *n* supermercato

supernatural [su:pə'nætʃərəl] *adj* soprannaturale ♦ *n* soprannaturale *m*

superpower ['su:pəpauə*] *n* (*POL*) superpotenza

supersede [su:pə'si:d] *vt* sostituire, soppiantare

superstitious [su:pə'stɪʃəs] *adj* superstizioso(a)

supertanker ['su:pətæŋkə*] *n* superpetroliera

supervise ['su:pəvaɪz] *vt* (*person etc*) sorvegliare; (*organization*) soprintendere a; **supervision** [-'vɪʒən] *n* sorveglianza; supervisione *f*; **supervisor** *n* sorvegliante *m/f*; soprintendente *m/f*; (*in shop*) capocommesso/a

supine ['su:paɪn] *adj* supino(a)

supper ['sʌpə*] *n* cena

supplant [sə'plɑ:nt] *vt* (*person, thing*) soppiantare

supple ['sʌpl] *adj* flessibile; agile
supplement [*n* 'sʌplɪmənt, *vb* sʌplɪ'mɛnt]
n supplemento ♦ *vt* completare, integrare;
~ary [-'mɛntərɪ] *adj* supplementare
supplier [sə'plaɪə*] *n* fornitore *m*
supply [sə'plaɪ] *vt* (*provide*) fornire;
(*equip*): **to ~ (with)** approvvigionare (di);
attrezzare (con) ♦ *n* riserva, provvista;
(*supplying*) approvvigionamento; (*TECH*)
alimentazione *f*; **supplies** *npl* (*food*) viveri
mpl; (*MIL*) sussistenza; **~ teacher** (*BRIT*) *n*
supplente *m/f*
support [sə'pɔ:t] *n* (*moral, financial etc*)
sostegno, appoggio; (*TECH*) supporto ♦ *vt*
sostenere; (*financially*) mantenere;
(*uphold*) sostenere, difendere; **~er** *n* (*POL
etc*) sostenitore/trice, fautore/trice; (*SPORT*)
tifoso/a
suppose [sə'pəuz] *vt* supporre;
immaginare; **to be ~d to do** essere
tenuto/a a fare; **~dly** [sə'pəuzɪdlɪ] *adv*
presumibilmente; **supposing** *conj* se,
ammesso che + *sub*
suppress [sə'prɛs] *vt* reprimere;
sopprimere; occultare
supreme [su'pri:m] *adj* supremo(a)
surcharge ['sə:tʃɑ:dʒ] *n* supplemento
sure [ʃuə*] *adj* sicuro(a); (*definite,
convinced*) sicuro(a), certo(a); **~!** (*of
course*) senz'altro!, certo!; **~ enough**
infatti; **to make ~ of sth/ that**
assicurarsi di qc/che; **~-footed** *adj* dal
passo sicuro; **~ly** *adv* sicuramente;
certamente
surety ['ʃuərətɪ] *n* garanzia
surf [sə:f] *n* (*waves*) cavalloni *mpl*; (*foam*)
spuma
surface ['sə:fɪs] *n* superficie *f* ♦ *vt* (*road*)
asfaltare ♦ *vi* risalire alla superficie; (*fig:
news, feeling*) venire a galla; **~ mail** *n*
posta ordinaria
surfboard ['sə:fbɔ:d] *n* tavola per surfing
surfeit ['sə:fɪt] *n*: **a ~ of** un eccesso di;
un'indigestione di
surfing ['sə:fɪŋ] *n* surfing *m*
surge [sə:dʒ] *n* (*strong movement*) ondata;
(*of feeling*) impeto ♦ *vi* gonfiarsi; (*people*)
riversarsi
surgeon ['sə:dʒən] *n* chirurgo

surgery ['sə:dʒərɪ] *n* chirurgia; (*BRIT:
room*) studio *or* gabinetto medico,
ambulatorio; (: *also*: **~ hours**) orario delle
visite *or* di consultazione; **to undergo ~**
subire un intervento chirurgico
surgical ['sə:dʒɪkl] *adj* chirurgico(a); **~
spirit** (*BRIT*) *n* alcool *m* denaturato
surly ['sə:lɪ] *adj* scontroso(a), burbero(a)
surname ['sə:neɪm] *n* cognome *m*
surpass [sə:'pɑ:s] *vt* superare
surplus ['sə:pləs] *n* eccedenza; (*ECON*)
surplus *m inv* ♦ *adj* eccedente, d'avanzo
surprise [sə'praɪz] *n* sorpresa;
(*astonishment*) stupore *m* ♦ *vt*
sorprendere; stupire; **surprising** *adj*
sorprendente, stupefacente; **surprisingly**
adv (*easy, helpful*) sorprendentemente
surrender [sə'rɛndə*] *n* resa,
capitolazione *f* ♦ *vi* arrendersi
surreptitious [sʌrəp'tɪʃəs] *adj* furtivo(a)
surrogate ['sʌrəgɪt] *n* surrogato; **~
mother** *n* madre *f* provetta
surround [sə'raund] *vt* circondare; (*MIL
etc*) accerchiare; **~ing** *adj* circostante;
~ings *npl* dintorni *mpl*; (*fig*) ambiente *m*
surveillance [sə:'veɪləns] *n* sorveglianza,
controllo
survey [*n* 'sə:veɪ, *vb* sə:'veɪ] *n* quadro
generale; (*study*) esame *m*; (*in
housebuying etc*) perizia; (*of land*)
rilevamento, rilievo topografico ♦ *vt*
osservare; esaminare; valutare; rilevare;
~or *n* perito; geometra *m*; (*of land*)
agrimensore *m*
survival [sə'vaɪvl] *n* sopravvivenza; (*relic*)
reliquia, vestigio
survive [sə'vaɪv] *vi* sopravvivere ♦ *vt*
sopravvivere a; **survivor** *n* superstite *m/
f*, sopravvissuto/a
susceptible [sə'sɛptəbl] *adj*: **~ (to)**
sensibile (a); (*disease*) predisposto(a) (a)
suspect [*adj, n* 'sʌspɛkt, *vb* səs'pɛkt] *adj*
sospetto(a) ♦ *n* persona sospetta ♦ *vt*
sospettare; (*think likely*) supporre; (*doubt*)
dubitare
suspend [səs'pɛnd] *vt* sospendere; **~ed
sentence** *n* condanna con la
condizionale; **~er belt** *n* reggicalze *m inv*;
~ers *npl* (*BRIT*) giarrettiere *fpl*; (*US*)

bretelle *fpl*

suspense [səs'pɛns] *n* apprensione *f*; (*in film etc*) suspense *m*; **to keep sb in ~** tenere qn in sospeso

suspension [səs'pɛnʃən] *n* (*gen AUT*) sospensione *f*; (*of driving licence*) ritiro temporaneo; **~ bridge** *n* ponte *m* sospeso

suspicion [səs'pɪʃən] *n* sospetto

suspicious [səs'pɪʃəs] *adj* (*suspecting*) sospettoso(a); (*causing suspicion*) sospetto(a)

sustain [səs'teɪn] *vt* sostenere; sopportare; (*LAW: charge*) confermare; (*suffer*) subire; **~able** *adj* sostenibile; **~ed** *adj* (*effort*) prolungato(a)

sustenance [ˈsʌstɪnəns] *n* nutrimento; mezzi *mpl* di sostentamento

swab [swɔb] *n* (*MED*) tampone *m*

swagger [ˈswæɡə*] *vi* pavoneggiarsi

swallow [ˈswɔləu] *n* (*bird*) rondine *f* ♦ *vt* inghiottire; (*fig: story*) bere; **~ up** *vt* inghiottire

swam [swæm] *pt of* **swim**

swamp [swɔmp] *n* palude *f* ♦ *vt* sommergere

swan [swɔn] *n* cigno

swap [swɔp] *vt*: **to ~ (for)** scambiare (con)

swarm [swɔːm] *n* sciame *m* ♦ *vi* (*bees*) sciamare; (*place*): **to be ~ing with** brulicare di

swarthy [ˈswɔːðɪ] *adj* di carnagione scura

swastika [ˈswɔstɪkə] *n* croce *f* uncinata, svastica

swat [swɔt] *vt* schiacciare

sway [sweɪ] *vi* (*tree*) ondeggiare; (*person*) barcollare ♦ *vt* (*influence*) influenzare, dominare

swear [swɛə*] (*pt* **swore**, *pp* **sworn**) *vi* (*curse*) bestemmiare, imprecare ♦ *vt* (*promise*) giurare; **~word** *n* parolaccia

sweat [swɛt] *n* sudore *m*, traspirazione *f* ♦ *vi* sudare

sweater [ˈswɛtə*] *n* maglione *m*

sweatshirt [ˈswɛtʃəːt] *n* felpa

sweaty [ˈswɛtɪ] *adj* sudato(a); bagnato(a) di sudore

Swede [swiːd] *n* svedese *m/f*

swede [swiːd] *n* (*BRIT*) rapa svedese

Sweden [ˈswiːdn] *n* Svezia

Swedish [ˈswiːdɪʃ] *adj* svedese ♦ *n* (*LING*) svedese *m*

sweep [swiːp] (*pt, pp* **swept**) *n* spazzata; (*also: chimney ~*) spazzacamino ♦ *vt* spazzare, scopare; (*current*) spazzare ♦ *vi* (*hand*) muoversi con gesto ampio; (*wind*) infuriare; **~ away** *vt* spazzare via; trascinare via; **~ past** *vi* sfrecciare accanto; passare accanto maestosamente; **~ up** *vt, vi* spazzare; **~ing** *adj* (*gesture*) ampio(a); circolare; a **~ing statement** un'affermazione generica

sweet [swiːt] *n* (*BRIT: pudding*) dolce *m*; (*candy*) caramella ♦ *adj* dolce; (*fresh*) fresco(a); (*fig*) piacevole; delicato(a), grazioso(a); gentile; **~corn** *n* granturco dolce; **~en** *vt* addolcire; zuccherare; **~heart** *n* innamorato/a; **~ness** *n* sapore *m* dolce; dolcezza; **~ pea** *n* pisello odoroso

swell [swɛl] (*pt* **~ed**, *pp* **swollen**, **~ed**) *n* (*of sea*) mare *m* lungo ♦ *adj* (*US: inf: excellent*) favoloso(a) ♦ *vt* gonfiare, ingrossare; aumentare ♦ *vi* gonfiarsi, ingrossarsi; (*sound*) crescere; (*also: ~ up*) gonfiarsi; **~ing** *n* (*MED*) tumefazione *f*, gonfiore *m*

sweltering [ˈswɛltərɪŋ] *adj* soffocante

swept [swɛpt] *pt, pp of* **sweep**

swerve [swəːv] *vi* deviare; (*driver*) sterzare; (*boxer*) scartare

swift [swɪft] *n* (*bird*) rondone *m* ♦ *adj* rapido(a), veloce

swig [swɪɡ] (*inf*) *n* (*drink*) sorsata

swill [swɪl] *vt* (*also: ~ out, ~ down*) risciacquare

swim [swɪm] (*pt* **swam**, *pp* **swum**) *n*: **to go for a ~** andare a fare una nuotata ♦ *vi* nuotare; (*SPORT*) fare del nuoto; (*head, room*) girare ♦ *vt* (*river, channel*) attraversare *or* percorrere a nuoto; (*length*) nuotare; **~mer** *n* nuotatore/trice; **~ming** *n* nuoto; **~ming cap** *n* cuffia; **~ming costume** (*BRIT*) *n* costume *m* da bagno; **~ming pool** *n* piscina; **~ming trunks** *npl* costume *m* da bagno (da uomo); **~suit** *n* costume *m* da bagno

swindle [ˈswɪndl] *n* truffa ♦ *vt* truffare

swine [swaɪn] (*inf!*) *n inv* porco (*!*)
swing [swɪŋ] (*pt, pp* swung) *n* altalena; (*movement*) oscillazione *f*; (*MUS*) ritmo; swing *m* ♦ *vt* dondolare, far oscillare; (*also:* ~ *round*) far girare ♦ *vi* oscillare, dondolare; (*also:* ~ *round: object*) roteare; (: *person*) girarsi, voltarsi; **to be in full** ~ (*activity*) essere in piena attività; (*party etc*) essere nel pieno; ~ **door** (*US* ~**ing door**) *n* porta battente
swingeing ['swɪndʒɪŋ] *adj* (*BRIT: defeat*) violento(a); (: *cuts*) enorme
swipe [swaɪp] *vt* (*hit*) colpire con forza; dare uno schiaffo a; (*inf: steal*) sgraffignare
swirl [swəːl] *vi* turbinare, far mulinello
swish [swɪʃ] *vi* sibilare
Swiss [swɪs] *adj, n inv* svizzero(a)
switch [swɪtʃ] *n* (*for light, radio etc*) interruttore *m*; (*change*) cambiamento ♦ *vt* (*change*) cambiare; scambiare; ~ **off** *vt* spegnere; ~ **on** *vt* accendere; (*engine, machine*) mettere in moto, avviare; ~**board** *n* (*TEL*) centralino
Switzerland ['swɪtsələnd] *n* Svizzera
swivel ['swɪvl] *vi* (*also:* ~ *round*) girare
swollen ['swəʊlən] *pp of* swell
swoon [swuːn] *vi* venire
swoop [swuːp] *n* incursione *f* ♦ *vi* (*also:* ~ *down*) scendere in picchiata, piombare
swop [swɔp] *n, vt* = swap
sword [sɔːd] *n* spada; ~**fish** *n* pesce *m* spada *inv*
swore [swɔː*] *pt of* swear
sworn [swɔːn] *pp of* swear ♦ *adj* giurato(a)
swot [swɔt] *vi* sgobbare
swum [swʌm] *pp of* swim
swung [swʌŋ] *pt, pp of* swing
syllable ['sɪləbl] *n* sillaba
syllabus ['sɪləbəs] *n* programma *m*
symbol ['sɪmbl] *n* simbolo
symmetry ['sɪmɪtrɪ] *n* simmetria
sympathetic [sɪmpə'θɛtɪk] *adj* (*showing pity*) compassionevole; (*kind*) comprensivo(a); ~ **towards** ben disposto(a) verso
sympathize ['sɪmpəθaɪz] *vi*: **to** ~ **with** (*person*) compatire; partecipare al dolore

di; (*cause*) simpatizzare per; ~**r** *n* (*POL*) simpatizzante *m/f*
sympathy ['sɪmpəθɪ] *n* compassione *f*; **sympathies** *npl* (*support, tendencies*) simpatie *fpl*; **in** ~ **with** (*strike*) per solidarietà con; **with our deepest** ~ con le nostre più sincere condoglianze
symphony ['sɪmfənɪ] *n* sinfonia
symptom ['sɪmptəm] *n* sintomo; indizio
synagogue ['sɪnəgɔg] *n* sinagoga
syndicate ['sɪndɪkɪt] *n* sindacato
synonym ['sɪnənɪm] *n* sinonimo
synopses [sɪ'nɔpsiːz] *npl of* synopsis
synopsis [sɪ'nɔpsɪs] (*pl* synopses) *n* sommario, sinossi *f inv*
syntax ['sɪntæks] *n* sintassi *f inv*
syntheses ['sɪnθəsiːz] *npl of* synthesis
synthesis ['sɪnθəsɪs] (*pl* syntheses) *n* sintesi *f inv*
synthetic [sɪn'θɛtɪk] *adj* sintetico(a)
syphilis ['sɪfɪlɪs] *n* sifilide *f*
syphon ['saɪfən] *n, vb* = siphon
Syria ['sɪrɪə] *n* Siria
syringe [sɪ'rɪndʒ] *n* siringa
syrup ['sɪrəp] *n* sciroppo; (*also: golden* ~) melassa raffinata
system ['sɪstəm] *n* sistema *m*; (*order*) metodo; (*ANAT*) organismo; ~**atic** [-'mætɪk] *adj* sistematico(a); metodico(a); ~ **disk** *n* (*COMPUT*) disco del sistema; ~**s analyst** *n* analista *m* di sistemi

T

ta [tɑː] (*BRIT: inf*) *excl* grazie!
tab [tæb] *n* (*loop on coat etc*) laccetto; (*label*) etichetta; **to keep** ~**s on** (*fig*) tenere d'occhio
tabby ['tæbɪ] *n* (*also:* ~ *cat*) (gatto) soriano, gatto tigrato
table ['teɪbl] *n* tavolo, tavola; (*MATH, CHEM etc*) tavola ♦ *vt* (*BRIT: motion etc*) presentare; **to lay** *or* **set the** ~ apparecchiare *or* preparare la tavola; ~**cloth** *n* tovaglia; ~ **of contents** *n* indice *m*; ~ **d'hôte** [tɑːbl'dəut] *adj* (*meal*) a prezzo fisso; ~ **lamp** *n* lampada da tavolo; ~**mat** *n* sottopiatto; ~**spoon** *n*

cucchiaio da tavola; (*also: ~spoonful: as measurement*) cucchiaiata

tablet ['tæblɪt] *n* (MED) compressa; (*of stone*) targa

table: ~ **tennis** *n* tennis *m* da tavolo, ping-pong *m* ®; ~ **wine** *n* vino da tavola

tabulate ['tæbjuleɪt] *vt* (*data, figures*) tabulare, disporre in tabelle

tacit ['tæsɪt] *adj* tacito(a)

tack [tæk] *n* (*nail*) bulletta; (*fig*) approccio ♦ *vt* imbullettare; imbastire ♦ *vi* bordeggiare

tackle ['tækl] *n* attrezzatura, equipaggiamento; (*for lifting*) paranco; (FOOTBALL) contrasto; (RUGBY) placcaggio ♦ *vt* (*difficulty*) affrontare; (FOOTBALL) contrastare; (RUGBY) placcare

tacky ['tækɪ] *adj* appiccicaticcio(a); (*pej*) scadente

tact [tækt] *n* tatto; **~ful** *adj* delicato(a), discreto(a)

tactical ['tæktɪkl] *adj* tattico(a)

tactics ['tæktɪks] *n, npl* tattica

tactless ['tæktlɪs] *adj* che manca di tatto

tadpole ['tædpəʊl] *n* girino

taffy ['tæfɪ] (US) *n* caramella *f* mou *inv*

tag [tæg] *n* etichetta; ~ **along** *vi* seguire

tail [teɪl] *n* coda; (*of shirt*) falda ♦ *vt* (*follow*) seguire, pedinare; ~ **away** *vi* = ~ **off**; ~ **off** *vi* (*in size, quality etc*) diminuire gradatamente; **~back** (BRIT) *n* (AUT) ingorgo; ~ **end** *n* (*of train, procession etc*) coda; (*of meeting etc*) fine *f*; **~gate** *n* (AUT) portellone *m* posteriore

tailor ['teɪlə*] *n* sarto; **~ing** *n* (*cut*) stile *m*; (*craft*) sartoria; **~-made** *adj* (*also fig*) fatto(a) su misura

tailwind ['teɪlwɪnd] *n* vento di coda

tainted ['teɪntɪd] *adj* (*food*) guasto(a); (*water, air*) infetto(a); (*fig*) corrotto(a)

take [teɪk] (*pt* **took**, *pp* **taken**) *vt* prendere; (*gain: prize*) ottenere, vincere; (*require: effort, courage*) occorrere, volerci; (*tolerate*) accettare, sopportare; (*hold: passengers etc*) contenere; (*accompany*) accompagnare; (*bring, carry*) portare; (*exam*) sostenere, presentarsi a; **to ~ a photo/a shower** fare una fotografia/una doccia; **I ~ it that**

suppongo che; ~ **after** *vt fus* assomigliare a; ~ **apart** *vt* smontare; ~ **away** *vt* portare via; togliere; ~ **back** *vt* (*return*) restituire; riportare; (*one's words*) ritirare; ~ **down** *vt* (*building*) demolire; (*letter etc*) scrivere; ~ **in** *vt* (*deceive*) imbrogliare, abbindolare; (*understand*) capire; (*include*) comprendere, includere; (*lodger*) prendere, ospitare; ~ **off** *vi* (AVIAT) decollare; (*go away*) andarsene ♦ *vt* (*remove*) togliere; ~ **on** *vt* (*work*) accettare, intraprendere; (*employee*) assumere; (*opponent*) sfidare, affrontare; ~ **out** *vt* portare fuori; (*remove*) togliere; (*licence*) prendere, ottenere; **to ~ sth out of sth** (*drawer, pocket etc*) tirare qc fuori da qc; estrarre qc da qc; ~ **over** *vt* (*business*) rilevare ♦ *vi*: **to ~ over from sb** prendere le consegne *or* il controllo da qn; ~ **to** *vt fus* (*person*) prendere in simpatia; (*activity*) prendere gusto a; ~ **up** *vt* (*dress*) accorciare; (*occupy: time, space*) occupare; (*engage in: hobby etc*) mettersi a; **to ~ sb up on sth** accettare qc da qn; **~away** (BRIT) *n* (*shop etc*) ≈ rosticceria; (*food*) pasto per asporto; **~off** *n* (AVIAT) decollo; **~out** (US) *n* = **~away**; **~over** *n* (COMM) assorbimento

takings ['teɪkɪnz] *npl* (COMM) incasso

talc [tælk] *n* (*also: ~um powder*) talco

tale [teɪl] *n* racconto, storia; **to tell ~s** (*fig: to teacher, parent etc*) fare la spia

talent ['tælnt] *n* talento; **~ed** *adj* di talento

talk [tɔːk] *n* discorso; (*gossip*) chiacchiere *fpl*; (*conversation*) conversazione *f*; (*interview*) discussione *f* ♦ *vi* parlare; ~**s** *npl* (POL etc) colloqui *mpl*; **to ~ about** parlare di; **to ~ sb out of/into doing** dissuadere qn da/convincere qn a fare; **to ~ shop** parlare di lavoro *or* di affari; ~ **over** *vt* discutere; **~ative** *adj* loquace, ciarliero(a); ~ **show** *n* conversazione *f* televisiva, talk show *m inv*

tall [tɔːl] *adj* alto(a); **to be 6 feet ~** ≈ essere alto 1 metro e 80; ~ **story** *n* panzana, frottola

tally ['tælɪ] *n* conto, conteggio ♦ *vi*: **to ~ (with)** corrispondere (a)

talon ['tælən] *n* artiglio

tambourine [tæmbə'ri:n] *n* tamburello

tame [teɪm] *adj* addomesticato(a); (*fig*: *story, style*) insipido(a), scialbo(a)

tamper ['tæmpə*] *vi*: **to ~ with** manomettere

tampon ['tæmpɔn] *n* tampone *m*

tan [tæn] *n* (*also: sun~*) abbronzatura ♦ *vi* abbronzarsi ♦ *adj* (*colour*) marrone rossiccio *inv*

tang [tæŋ] *n* odore *m* penetrante; sapore *m* piccante

tangent ['tændʒənt] *n* (*MATH*) tangente *f*; **to go off at a ~** (*fig*) partire per la tangente

tangerine [tændʒə'ri:n] *n* mandarino

tangle ['tæŋgl] *n* groviglio; **to get into a ~** aggrovigliarsi; (*fig*) combinare un pasticcio

tank [tæŋk] *n* serbatoio; (*for fish*) acquario; (*MIL*) carro armato

tanker ['tæŋkə*] *n* (*ship*) nave *f* cisterna *inv*; (*truck*) autobotte *f*, autocisterna

tanned [tænd] *adj* abbronzato(a)

tantalizing ['tæntəlaɪzɪŋ] *adj* allettante

tantamount ['tæntəmaunt] *adj*: **~ to** equivalente a

tantrum ['tæntrəm] *n* accesso di collera

tap [tæp] *n* (*on sink etc*) rubinetto; (*gentle blow*) colpetto ♦ *vt* dare un colpetto a; (*resources*) sfruttare, utilizzare; (*telephone*) mettere sotto controllo; **on ~** (*fig*: *resources*) a disposizione; **~ dancing** *n* tip tap *m*

tape [teɪp] *n* nastro; (*also: magnetic ~*) nastro (magnetico); (*sticky ~*) nastro adesivo ♦ *vt* (*record*) registrare (su nastro); (*stick*) attaccare con nastro adesivo; **~ deck** *n* piastra; **~ measure** *n* metro a nastro

taper ['teɪpə*] *n* candelina ♦ *vi* assottigliarsi

tape recorder *n* registratore *m* (a nastro)

tapestry ['tæpɪstrɪ] *n* arazzo; tappezzeria

tar [tɑ:*] *n* catrame *m*

target ['tɑ:gɪt] *n* bersaglio; (*fig*: *objective*) obiettivo

tariff ['tærɪf] *n* tariffa

tarmac ['tɑ:mæk] *n* (*BRIT*: *on road*) macadam *m* al catrame; (*AVIAT*) pista di decollo

tarnish ['tɑ:nɪʃ] *vt* offuscare, annerire; (*fig*) macchiare

tarpaulin [tɑ:'pɔ:lɪn] *n* tela incatramata

tarragon ['tærəgən] *n* dragoncello

tart [tɑ:t] *n* (*CULIN*) crostata; (*BRIT*: *inf*: *pej*: *woman*) sgualdrina ♦ *adj* (*flavour*) aspro(a), agro(a); **~ up** (*inf*) *vt* agghindare

tartan ['tɑ:tn] *n* tartan *m inv*

tartar ['tɑ:tə*] *n* (*on teeth*) tartaro; **~(e) sauce** *n* salsa tartara

task [tɑ:sk] *n* compito; **to take to ~** rimproverare; **~ force** *n* (*MIL, POLICE*) unità operativa

tassel ['tæsl] *n* fiocco

taste [teɪst] *n* gusto; (*flavour*) sapore *m*, gusto; (*sample*) assaggio; (*fig*: *glimpse*, *idea*) idea ♦ *vt* gustare; (*sample*) assaggiare ♦ *vi*: **to ~ of** *or* **like** (*fish etc*) sapere *or* avere sapore di; **you can ~ the garlic (in it)** (ci) si sente il sapore dell'aglio; **in good/bad ~** di buon/cattivo gusto; **~ful** *adj* di buon gusto; **~less** *adj* (*food*) insipido(a); (*remark*) di cattivo gusto; **tasty** *adj* saporito(a), gustoso(a)

tatters ['tætəz] *npl*: **in ~** a brandelli

tattoo [tə'tu:] *n* tatuaggio; (*spectacle*) parata militare ♦ *vt* tatuare

tatty ['tætɪ] *adj* malridotto(a)

taught [tɔ:t] *pt, pp of* **teach**

taunt [tɔ:nt] *n* scherno ♦ *vt* schernire

Taurus ['tɔ:rəs] *n* Toro

taut [tɔ:t] *adj* teso(a)

tax [tæks] *n* (*on goods*) imposta; (*on services*) tassa; (*on income*) imposte *fpl*, tasse *fpl* ♦ *vt* tassare; (*fig*: *strain*: *patience etc*) mettere alla prova; **~able** *adj* (*income*) imponibile; **~ation** [-'seɪʃən] *n* tassazione *f*; tasse *fpl*, imposte *fpl*; **~ avoidance** *n* elusione *f* fiscale; **~ disc** (*BRIT*) *n* (*AUT*) ≈ bollo; **~ evasion** *n* evasione *f* fiscale; **~-free** *adj* esente da imposte

taxi ['tæksɪ] *n* taxi *m inv* ♦ *vi* (*AVIAT*) rullare; **~ driver** *n* tassista *m/f*; **~ rank** (*BRIT*) *n* = **~ stand**; **~ stand** *n* posteggio dei taxi

tax: ~ **payer** *n* contribuente *m/f*; ~ **relief** *n* agevolazioni *fpl* fiscali; ~ **return** *n* dichiarazione *f* dei redditi

TB *n abbr* = **tuberculosis**

tea [tiː] *n* tè *m inv*; (*BRIT: snack: for children*) merenda; **high** ~ (*BRIT*) cena leggera (*presa nel tardo pomeriggio*); ~ **bag** *n* bustina di tè; ~ **break** (*BRIT*) *n* intervallo per il tè

teach [tiːtʃ] (*pt, pp* **taught**) *vt*: **to** ~ **sb sth**, ~ **sth to sb** insegnare qc a qn ♦ *vi* insegnare; ~**er** *n* insegnante *m/f*; (*in secondary school*) professore/essa; (*in primary school*) maestro/a; ~**ing** *n* insegnamento

tea cosy *n* copriteiera *m inv*

teacup ['tiːkʌp] *n* tazza da tè

teak [tiːk] *n* teak *m*

tea leaves *npl* foglie *fpl* di tè

team [tiːm] *n* squadra; (*of animals*) tiro; ~**work** *n* lavoro di squadra

teapot ['tiːpɔt] *n* teiera

tear[1] [tɛə*] (*pt* **tore**, *pp* **torn**) *n* strappo ♦ *vt* strappare ♦ *vi* strapparsi; ~ **along** *vi* (*rush*) correre all'impazzata; ~ **up** *vt* (*sheet of paper etc*) strappare

tear[2] [tɪə*] *n* lacrima; **in** ~**s** in lacrime; ~**ful** *adj* piangente, lacrimoso(a); ~ **gas** *n* gas *m* lacrimogeno

tearoom ['tiːruːm] *n* sala da tè

tease [tiːz] *vt* canzonare; (*unkindly*) tormentare

tea set *n* servizio da tè

teaspoon ['tiːspuːn] *n* cucchiaino da tè; (*also*: ~*ful: as measurement*) cucchiaino

teat [tiːt] *n* capezzolo

teatime ['tiːtaɪm] *n* ora del tè

tea towel (*BRIT*) *n* strofinaccio (per i piatti)

technical ['tɛknɪkl] *adj* tecnico(a); ~ **college** (*BRIT*) *n* ≈ istituto tecnico; ~**ity** [-'kælɪtɪ] *n* tecnicità; (*detail*) dettaglio tecnico; (*legal*) cavillo

technician [tɛk'nɪʃən] *n* tecnico/a

technique [tɛk'niːk] *n* tecnica

technological [tɛknə'lɔdʒɪkl] *adj* tecnologico(a)

technology [tɛk'nɔlədʒɪ] *n* tecnologia

teddy (bear) ['tɛdɪ-] *n* orsacchiotto

tedious ['tiːdɪəs] *adj* noioso(a), tedioso(a)

tee [tiː] *n* (*GOLF*) tee *m inv*

teem [tiːm] *vi*: **to** ~ **with** brulicare di; **it is** ~**ing (with rain)** piove a dirotto

teenage ['tiːneɪdʒ] *adj* (*fashions etc*) per giovani, per adolescenti; ~**r** *n* adolescente *m/f*

teens [tiːnz] *npl*: **to be in one's** ~ essere adolescente

tee-shirt ['tiːʃəːt] *n* = **T-shirt**

teeter ['tiːtə*] *vi* barcollare, vacillare

teeth [tiːθ] *npl of* **tooth**

teethe [tiːð] *vi* mettere i denti

teething ring ['tiːðɪŋ-] *n* dentaruolo

teething troubles ['tiːðɪŋ-] *npl* (*fig*) difficoltà *fpl* iniziali

teetotal ['tiː'təutl] *adj* astemio(a)

telegram ['tɛlɪgræm] *n* telegramma *m*

telegraph ['tɛlɪgrɑːf] *n* telegrafo

telepathy [tə'lɛpəθɪ] *n* telepatia

telephone ['tɛlɪfəun] *n* telefono ♦ *vt* (*person*) telefonare a; (*message*) comunicare per telefono; ~ **booth** (*BRIT* ~ **box**) *n* cabina telefonica; ~ **call** *n* telefonata; ~ **directory** *n* elenco telefonico; ~ **number** *n* numero di telefono; **telephonist** [tə'lɛfənɪst] (*BRIT*) *n* telefonista *m/f*

telescope ['tɛlɪskəup] *n* telescopio

television ['tɛlɪvɪʒən] *n* televisione *f*; **on** ~ alla televisione; ~ **set** *n* televisore *m*

telex ['tɛlɛks] *n* telex *m inv* ♦ *vt* trasmettere per telex; **to** ~ **sb** contattare qn via telex

tell [tɛl] (*pt, pp* **told**) *vt* dire; (*relate: story*) raccontare; (*distinguish*): **to** ~ **sth from** distinguere qc da ♦ *vi* (*talk*): **to** ~ **(of)** parlare (di); (*have effect*) farsi sentire, avere effetto; **to** ~ **sb to do** dire a qn di fare; ~ **off** *vt* rimproverare, sgridare; ~**er** *n* (*in bank*) cassiere/a; ~**ing** *adj* (*remark, detail*) rivelatore(trice); ~**tale** *adj* (*sign*) rivelatore(trice)

telly ['tɛlɪ] (*BRIT: inf*) *n abbr* (= **television**) tivù *f inv*

temerity [tə'mɛrɪtɪ] *n* temerarietà

temp [tɛmp] *n abbr* (= **temporary**) segretaria temporanea

temper ['tɛmpə*] *n* (*nature*) carattere *m*;

(*mood*) umore m; (*fit of anger*) collera ♦ *vt*
(*moderate*) temperare, moderare; **to be in
a ~** essere in collera; **to lose one's ~**
andare in collera

temperament ['tɛmprəmənt] *n* (*nature*)
temperamento; **~al** [-'mɛntl] *adj*
capriccioso(a)

temperate ['tɛmprət] *adj* moderato(a);
(*climate*) temperato(a)

temperature ['tɛmprətʃə*] *n*
temperatura; **to have** *or* **run a ~** avere la
febbre

tempest ['tɛmpɪst] *n* tempesta

template ['tɛmplɪt] *n* sagoma

temple ['tɛmpl] *n* (*building*) tempio;
(*ANAT*) tempia

temporary ['tɛmpərəri] *adj*
temporaneo(a); (*job, worker*) avventizio(a),
temporaneo(a)

tempt [tɛmpt] *vt* tentare; **to ~ sb into
doing** indurre qn a fare; **~ation** [-'teɪʃən]
n tentazione *f*; **~ing** *adj* allettante

ten [tɛn] *num* dieci

tenacity [tə'næsɪti] *n* tenacia

tenancy ['tɛnənsi] *n* affitto; condizione *f*
di inquilino

tenant ['tɛnənt] *n* inquilino/a

tend [tɛnd] *vt* badare a, occuparsi di ♦ *vi*:
to ~ to do tendere a fare

tendency ['tɛndənsi] *n* tendenza

tender ['tɛndə*] *adj* tenero(a); (*sore*)
dolorante ♦ *n* (*COMM: offer*) offerta;
(*money*): **legal ~** moneta in corso legale
♦ *vt* offrire

tendon ['tɛndən] *n* tendine m

tenement ['tɛnəmənt] *n* casamento

tenet ['tɛnət] *n* principio

tennis ['tɛnɪs] *n* tennis m; **~ ball** *n* palla
da tennis; **~ court** *n* campo da tennis; **~
player** *n* tennista m/f; **~ racket** *n*
racchetta da tennis; **~ shoes** *npl* scarpe
fpl da tennis

tenor ['tɛnə*] *n* (*MUS*) tenore m

tenpin bowling ['tɛnpɪn-] *n* bowling m

tense [tɛns] *adj* teso(a) ♦ *n* (*LING*) tempo

tension ['tɛnʃən] *n* tensione *f*

tent [tɛnt] *n* tenda

tentative ['tɛntətɪv] *adj* esitante,
incerto(a); (*conclusion*) provvisorio(a)

tenterhooks ['tɛntəhuks] *npl*: **on ~** sulle
spine

tenth [tɛnθ] *num* decimo(a)

tent: **~ peg** *n* picchetto da tenda; **~ pole**
n palo da tenda, montante m

tenuous ['tɛnjuəs] *adj* tenue

tenure ['tɛnjuə*] *n* (*of property*) possesso;
(*of job*) permanenza; titolarità

tepid ['tɛpɪd] *adj* tiepido(a)

term [tə:m] *n* termine m; (*SCOL*) trimestre
m; (*LAW*) sessione *f* ♦ *vt* chiamare,
definire; **~s** *npl* (*conditions*) condizioni *fpl*;
(*COMM*) prezzi *mpl*, tariffe *fpl*; **in the
short/long ~** a breve/lunga scadenza; **to
be on good ~s with sb** essere in buoni
rapporti con qn; **to come to ~s with**
(*problem*) affrontare

terminal ['tə:mɪnl] *adj* finale, terminale;
(*disease*) terminale ♦ *n* (*ELEC*) morsetto;
(*COMPUT*) terminale m; (*AVIAT, for oil, ore
etc*) terminal m *inv*; (*BRIT: also: coach ~*)
capolinea m

terminate ['tə:mɪneɪt] *vt* mettere fine a

termini ['tə:mɪnaɪ] *npl of* **terminus**

terminus ['tə:mɪnəs] (*pl* **termini**) *n* (*for
buses*) capolinea m; (*for trains*) stazione *f*
terminale

terrace ['tɛrəs] *n* terrazza; (*BRIT: row of
houses*) fila di case a schiera; **the ~s** *npl*
(*BRIT: SPORT*) le gradinate; **~d** *adj* (*garden*)
a terrazze

terracotta ['tɛrə'kɔtə] *n* terracotta

terrain [tɛ'reɪn] *n* terreno

terrible ['tɛrɪbl] *adj* terribile; **terribly**
adv terribilmente; (*very badly*) malissimo

terrier ['tɛrɪə*] *n* terrier m *inv*

terrific [tə'rɪfɪk] *adj* incredibile,
fantastico(a); (*wonderful*) formidabile,
eccezionale

terrify ['tɛrɪfaɪ] *vt* terrorizzare

territory ['tɛrɪtəri] *n* territorio

terror ['tɛrə*] *n* terrore m; **~ism** *n*
terrorismo; **~ist** *n* terrorista m/f

terse [tə:s] *adj* (*style*) conciso(a); (*reply*)
laconico(a)

Terylene ['tɛrəli:n] ® *n* terital m ®,
terilene m ®

test [tɛst] *n* (*trial, check, of courage etc*)
prova; (*MED*) esame m; (*CHEM*) analisi *f*

inv; (*exam: of intelligence etc*) test *m inv*;
(: *in school*) compito in classe; (*also: driving* ~) esame *m* di guida ♦ *vt* provare;
esaminare; analizzare; sottoporre ad
esame; **to** ~ **sb in history** esaminare qn
in storia

testament['tɛstəmənt] *n* testamento;
the Old/New T~ il Vecchio/Nuovo
testamento

testicle['tɛstɪkl] *n* testicolo

testify['tɛstɪfaɪ] *vi* (*LAW*) testimoniare,
deporre; **to** ~ **to sth** (*LAW*) testimoniare
qc; (*gen*) comprovare *or* dimostrare qc

testimony['tɛstɪmənɪ] *n* (*LAW*)
testimonianza, deposizione *f*

test: ~ **match***n* (*CRICKET, RUGBY*) partita
internazionale; ~ **pilot***n* pilota *m*
collaudatore; ~ **tube***n* provetta

tetanus['tɛtənəs] *n* tetano

tether['tɛðə*] *vt* legare ♦ *n*: **at the end
of one's** ~ al limite (della pazienza)

text[tɛkst] *n* testo; ~**book***n* libro di
testo

textiles['tɛkstaɪlz] *npl* tessuti *mpl*;
(*industry*) industria tessile

texture['tɛkstʃə*] *n* tessitura; (*of skin,
paper etc*) struttura

Thames[tɛmz] *n*: **the** ~ il Tamigi

than[ðæn, ðən] *conj* (*in comparisons*)
che; (*with numerals, pronouns, proper
names*) di; **more** ~ **10/once** più di 10/una
volta; **I have more/less** ~ **you** ne ho
più/meno di te; **I have more pens** ~
pencils ho più penne che matite; **she is
older** ~ **you think** è più vecchia di
quanto tu (non) pensi

thank[θæŋk] *vt* ringraziare; ~ **you (very
much)** grazie (tante); ~**s***npl*
ringraziamenti *mpl*, grazie *fpl* ♦ *excl*
grazie!; ~**s to** grazie a; ~**ful***adj*: ~**ful
(for)** riconoscente (per); ~**less***adj*
ingrato(a); **T~sgiving (Day)***n* giorno del
ringraziamento

that[ðæt] (*pl* **those**) *adj* (*demonstrative*)
quel(quell', quello) *m*; quella(quell') *f*; ~
man/woman/book quell'uomo/quella
donna/quel libro; (*not "this"*)

quell'uomo/quella donna/quel libro là; ~
one quello(a) là
♦ *pron* **1**(*demonstrative*) ciò; (*not "this
one"*) quello(a); **who's** ~? chi è?; **what's**
~? cos'è quello?; **is** ~ **you?** sei tu?; **I
prefer this to** ~ preferisco questo a
quello; ~**'s what he said** questo è ciò che
ha detto; **what happened after** ~? che è
successo dopo?; ~ **is (to say)** cioè
2(*relative: direct*) che; (: *indirect*) cui; **the
book (**~**) I read** il libro che ho letto; **the
box (**~**) I put it in** la scatola in cui l'ho
messo; **the people (**~**) I spoke to** le
persone con cui *or* con le quali ho parlato
3(*relative: of time*) in cui; **the day (**~**) he
came** il giorno in cui è venuto
♦ *conj* che; **he thought** ~ **I was ill**
pensava che io fossi malato
♦ *adv* (*demonstrative*) così; **I can't work**
~ **much** non posso lavorare (così) tanto;
~ **high** così alto; **the wall's about** ~
high and ~ **thick** il muro è alto circa
così e spesso circa così

thatched[θætʃt] *adj* (*roof*) di paglia; ~
cottage*n* cottage *m inv* col tetto di
paglia

thaw[θɔː] *n* disgelo ♦ *vi* (*ice*) sciogliersi;
(*food*) scongelarsi ♦ *vt* (*food: also*: ~ **out**)
(fare) scongelare

the[ðiː, ðə] *def art* **1**(*gen*) il(lo, l') *m*;
la(l') *f*; i(gli) *mpl*; le *fpl*; ~ **boy/girl/ink** il
ragazzo/la ragazza/l'inchiostro; ~ **books/
pencils** i libri/le matite; ~ **history of** ~
world la storia del mondo; **give it to** ~
postman dallo al postino; **I haven't** ~
time/money non ho tempo/soldi; ~ **rich
and** ~ **poor** i ricchi e i poveri
2(*in titles*): **Elizabeth** ~ **First** Elisabetta
prima; **Peter** ~ **Great** Pietro il grande
3(*in comparisons*): ~ **more he works,** ~
more he earns più lavora più guadagna

theatre['θɪətə*] (*US* **theater**) *n* teatro;
(*also: lecture* ~) aula magna; (*also:
operating* ~) sala operatoria; ~**-goer***n*
frequentatore/trice di teatri

theatrical [θɪˈætrɪkl] *adj* teatrale

theft [θɛft] *n* furto

their [ðɛə*] *adj* il(la) loro, *pl* i(le) loro; **~s** *pron* il(la) loro, *pl* i(le) loro; *see also* **my; mine**

them [ðɛm, ðəm] *pron* (*direct*) li(le); (*indirect*) gli, loro (*after vb*); (*stressed, after prep: people*) loro; (: *people, things*) essi(e); *see also* **me**

theme [θiːm] *n* tema *m*; **~ park** *n* parco di divertimenti (*intorno a un tema centrale*); **~ song** *n* tema musicale

themselves [ðəmˈsɛlvz] *pl pron* (*reflexive*) si; (*emphatic*) loro stessi(e); (*after prep*) se stessi(e)

then [ðɛn] *adv* (*at that time*) allora; (*next*) poi, dopo; (*and also*) e poi ♦ *conj* (*therefore*) perciò, dunque, quindi ♦ *adj*: **the ~ president** il presidente di allora; **by ~** allora; **from ~ on** da allora in poi

theology [θɪˈɔlədʒɪ] *n* teologia

theorem [ˈθɪərəm] *n* teorema *m*

theoretical [θɪəˈrɛtɪkl] *adj* teorico(a)

theory [ˈθɪərɪ] *n* teoria

therapy [ˈθɛrəpɪ] *n* terapia

KEYWORD
---

there [ðɛə*] *adv* **1**: **~ is, ~ are** c'è, ci sono; **~ are 3 of them** (*people*) sono in 3; (*things*) ce ne sono 3; **~ is no-one here** non c'è nessuno qui; **~ has been an accident** c'è stato un incidente
2 (*referring to place*) là, lì; **up/in/down ~** lassù/là dentro/laggiù; **he went ~ on Friday** ci è andato venerdì; **I want that book ~** voglio quel libro là *or* lì; **~ he is!** eccolo!
3: **~, ~,** (*esp to child*) su, su

thereabouts [ðɛərəˈbauts] *adv* (*place*) nei pressi, da quelle parti; (*amount*) giù di lì, all'incirca

thereafter [ðɛərˈɑːftə*] *adv* da allora in poi

thereby [ðɛəˈbaɪ] *adv* con ciò

therefore [ˈðɛəfɔː*] *adv* perciò, quindi

there's [ðɛəz] = **there is; there has**

thermal [ˈθəːml] *adj* termico(a)

thermometer [θəˈmɔmɪtə*] *n* termometro

Thermos [ˈθəːməs] ® *n* (*also:* **~ flask**) thermos *m inv* ®

thesaurus [θɪˈsɔːrəs] *n* dizionario dei sinonimi

these [ðiːz] *pl pron, adj* questi(e)

theses [ˈθiːsiːz] *npl of* **thesis**

thesis [ˈθiːsɪs] (*pl* **theses**) *n* tesi *f inv*

they [ðeɪ] *pl pron* essi(esse); (*people only*) loro; **~ say that ...** (*it is said that*) si dice che ...; **~'d** = **they had; they would; ~'ll** = **they shall; they will; ~'re** = **they are; ~'ve** = **they have**

thick [θɪk] *adj* spesso(a); (*crowd*) compatto(a); (*stupid*) ottuso(a), lento(a) ♦ *n*: **in the ~ of** nel folto di; **it's 20 cm ~** ha uno spessore di 20 cm; **~en** *vi* ispessire ♦ *vt* (*sauce etc*) ispessire, rendere più denso(a); **~ly** *adv* (*spread*) a strati spessi; (*cut*) a fette grosse; (*populated*) densamente; **~ness** *n* spessore *m*; **~set** *adj* tarchiato(a), tozzo(a); **~-skinned** *adj* (*fig*) insensibile

thief [θiːf] (*pl* **thieves**) *n* ladro/a

thieves [θiːvz] *npl of* **thief**

thigh [θaɪ] *n* coscia

thimble [ˈθɪmbl] *n* ditale *m*

thin [θɪn] *adj* sottile; (*person*) magro(a); (*soup*) poco denso(a) ♦ *vt*: **to ~ (down)** (*sauce, paint*) diluire

thing [θɪŋ] *n* cosa; (*object*) oggetto; (*mania*): **to have a ~ about** essere fissato con; **~s** *npl* (*belongings*) cose *fpl*; **poor ~** poverino(a); **the best ~ would be to** la cosa migliore sarebbe di; **how are ~s?** come va?

think [θɪŋk] (*pt, pp* **thought**) *vi* pensare, riflettere ♦ *vt* pensare, credere; (*imagine*) immaginare; **to ~ of** pensare a; **what did you ~ of them?** cosa ne ha pensato?; **to ~ about sth/sb** pensare a qc/qn; **I'll ~ about it** ci penserò; **to ~ of doing** pensare di fare; **I ~ so/not** penso di sì/ no; **to ~ well of** avere una buona opinione di; **~ out** *vt* (*plan*) elaborare; (*solution*) trovare; **~ over** *vt* riflettere su; **~ through** *vt* riflettere a fondo su; **~ up** *vt* ideare; **~ tank** *n* commissione *f* di esperti

third [θəːd] *num* terzo(a) ♦ *n* terzo/a; (*fraction*) terza, terza parte *f*; (*AUT*) terza; (*BRIT: SCOL: degree*) laurea col minimo dei voti; **~ly** *adv* in terzo luogo; **~ party insurance** (*BRIT*) *n* assicurazione *f* contro terzi; **~-rate** *adj* di qualità scadente; **the T~ World** *n* il Terzo Mondo

thirst [θəːst] *n* sete *f*; **~y** *adj* (*person*) assetato(a), che ha sete

thirteen [θəː'tiːn] *num* tredici

thirty ['θəːti] *num* trenta

KEYWORD

this [ðis] (*pl* these) *adj* (*demonstrative*) questo(a); **~ man/woman/book** quest'uomo/questa donna/questo libro; (*not "that"*) quest'uomo/questa donna/ questo libro qui; **~ one** questo(a) qui ♦ *pron* (*demonstrative*) questo(a); (*not "that one"*) questo(a) qui; **who/what is ~?** chi è/che cos'è questo?; **I prefer ~ to that** preferisco questo a quello; **~ is where I live** è qui abito qui; **~ is what he said** questo è ciò che ha detto; **~ is Mr Brown** (*in introductions, photo*) questo è il signor Brown; (*on telephone*) sono il signor Brown
♦ *adv* (*demonstrative*): **~ high/long etc** alto/lungo *etc* così; **I didn't know things were ~ bad** non sapevo andasse così male

thistle ['θisl] *n* cardo

thong [θɒŋ] *n* cinghia

thorn [θɔːn] *n* spina; **~y** *adj* spinoso(a)

thorough ['θʌrə] *adj* (*search*) minuzioso(a); (*knowledge, research*) approfondito(a), profondo(a); (*person*) coscienzioso(a); (*cleaning*) a fondo; **~bred** *n* (*horse*) purosangue *m/f inv*; **~fare** *n* strada transitabile; **"no ~fare"** "divieto di transito"; **~ly** *adv* (*search*) minuziosamente; (*wash, study*) a fondo; (*very*) assolutamente

those [ðəuz] *pl pron* quelli(e) ♦ *pl a* quei(quegli) *mpl*; quelle *fpl*

though [ðəu] *conj* benché, sebbene ♦ *adv* comunque

thought [θɔːt] *pt, pp of* **think** ♦ *n*

pensiero; (*opinion*) opinione *f*; **~ful** *adj* pensieroso(a), pensoso(a); (*considerate*) premuroso(a); **~less** *adj* sconsiderato(a); (*behaviour*) scortese

thousand ['θauzənd] *num* mille; **one ~** mille; **~s of** migliaia di; **~th** *num* millesimo(a)

thrash [θræʃ] *vt* picchiare; bastonare; (*defeat*) battere; **~ about** *vi* dibattersi; **~ out** *vt* dibattere

thread [θrɛd] *n* filo; (*of screw*) filetto ♦ *vt* (*needle*) infilare; **~bare** *adj* consumato(a), logoro(a)

threat [θrɛt] *n* minaccia; **~en** *vi* (*storm*) minacciare ♦ *vt*: **to ~en sb with/to do** minacciare qn con/di fare

three [θriː] *num* tre; **~-dimensional** *adj* tridimensionale; (*film*) stereoscopico(a); **~-piece suit** *n* completo (con gilè); **~-piece suite** *n* salotto comprendente un divano e due poltrone; **~-ply** *adj* (*wool*) a tre fili

thresh [θrɛʃ] *vt* (*AGR*) trebbiare

threshold ['θrɛʃhəuld] *n* soglia

threw [θruː] *pt of* **throw**

thrifty ['θrifti] *adj* economico(a)

thrill [θril] *n* brivido ♦ *vt* (*audience*) elettrizzare; **to be ~ed** (*with gift etc*) essere elettrizzato(a); **~er** *n* thriller *m inv*; **~ing** *adj* (*book*) pieno(a) di suspense; (*news, discovery*) elettrizzante

thrive [θraiv] (*pt* **thrived** *or* **throve**, *pp* **thrived** *or* **thriven**) *vi* crescere *or* svilupparsi bene; (*business*) prosperare; **he ~s on it** gli fa bene, ne gode; **thriven** ['θrivn] *pp of* **thrive**; **thriving** *adj* fiorente

throat [θrəut] *n* gola; **to have a sore ~** avere (un *or* il) mal di gola

throb [θrɒb] *n* (*of heart*) palpito; (*of wound*) pulsazione *f*; (*of engine*) vibrazione *f* ♦ *vi* palpitare; pulsare; vibrare

throes [θrəuz] *npl*: **in the ~ of** alle prese con; in preda a

thrombosis [θrɒm'bəusis] *n* trombosi *f*

throne [θrəun] *n* trono

throng [θrɒŋ] *n* moltitudine *f* ♦ *vt* affollare

throttle ['θrɔtl] n (AUT) valvola a farfalla ♦ vt strangolare

through [θruː] prep attraverso; (time) per, durante; (by means of) per mezzo di; (owing to) a causa di ♦ adj (ticket, train, passage) diretto(a) ♦ adv attraverso; **to put sb ~ to sb** (TEL) passare qn a qn; **to be ~** (TEL) ottenere la comunicazione; (have finished) essere finito(a); **"no ~ road"** (BRIT) "strada senza sbocco"; **~out** prep (place) dappertutto in; (time) per or durante tutto(a) ♦ adv dappertutto; sempre

throve [θrəuv] pt of **thrive**

throw [θrəu] (pt **threw**, pp **thrown**) n (SPORT) lancio, tiro ♦ vt tirare, gettare; (SPORT) lanciare, tirare; (rider) disarcionare; (fig) confondere; **to ~ a party** dare una festa; **~ away** vt gettare or buttare via; **~ off** vt sbarazzarsi di; **~ out** vt buttare fuori; (reject) respingere; **~ up** vi vomitare; **~away** adj da buttare; **~-in** n (SPORT) rimessa in gioco; **thrown** pp of **throw**

thru [θruː] (US) prep, adj, adv = **through**

thrush [θrʌʃ] n tordo

thrust [θrʌst] (pt, pp **thrust**) n (TECH) spinta ♦ vt spingere con forza; (push in) conficcare

thud [θʌd] n tonfo

thug [θʌg] n delinquente m

thumb [θʌm] n (ANAT) pollice m; **to ~ a lift** fare l'autostop; **~ through** vt fus (book) sfogliare; **~tack** (US) n puntina da disegno

thump [θʌmp] n colpo forte; (sound) tonfo ♦ vt (person) picchiare; (object) battere su ♦ vi picchiare; battere

thunder ['θʌndə*] n tuono ♦ vi tuonare; (train etc): **to ~ past** passare con un rombo; **~bolt** n fulmine m; **~clap** n rombo di tuono; **~storm** n temporale m; **~y** adj temporalesco(a)

Thursday ['θɜːzdɪ] n giovedì m inv

thus [ðʌs] adv così

thwart [θwɔːt] vt contrastare

thyme [taɪm] n timo

thyroid ['θaɪrɔɪd] n (also: ~ gland) tiroide f

tiara [tɪ'ɑːrə] n (woman's) diadema m

Tiber ['taɪbə*] n: **the ~** il Tevere

tick [tɪk] n (sound: of clock) tic tac m inv; (mark) segno; spunta; (ZOOL) zecca; (BRIT: inf): **in a ~** in un attimo ♦ vi fare tic tac ♦ vt spuntare; **~ off** vt spuntare; (person) sgridare; **~ over** vi (engine) andare al minimo; (fig) andare avanti come al solito

ticket ['tɪkɪt] n biglietto; (in shop: on goods) etichetta; (parking ~) multa; (for library) scheda; **~ collector** n bigliettaio; **~ office** n biglietteria

tickle ['tɪkl] vt fare il solletico a; (fig) solleticare ♦ vi: **it ~s me** (or gli etc) fa il solletico; **ticklish** [-lɪʃ] adj che soffre il solletico; (problem) delicato(a)

tidal ['taɪdl] adj di marea; (estuary) soggetto(a) alla marea; **~ wave** n onda anomala

tidbit ['tɪdbɪt] (US) n (food) leccornia; (news) notizia ghiotta

tiddlywinks ['tɪdlɪwɪŋks] n gioco della pulce

tide [taɪd] n marea; (fig: of events) corso; **high/low ~** alta/bassa marea; **~ over** vt dare una mano a

tidy ['taɪdɪ] adj (room) ordinato(a), lindo(a); (dress, work) curato(a), in ordine; (person) ordinato(a) ♦ vt (also: ~ up) riordinare, mettere in ordine

tie [taɪ] n (string etc) legaccio; (BRIT: also: neck~) cravatta; (fig: link) legame m; (SPORT: draw) pareggio ♦ vt (parcel) legare; (ribbon) annodare ♦ vi (SPORT) pareggiare; **to ~ sth in a bow** annodare qc; **to ~ a knot in sth** fare un nodo a qc; **~ down** vt legare; (to price etc) costringere ad accettare; **~ up** vt (parcel, dog) legare; (boat) ormeggiare; (arrangements) concludere; **to be ~d up** (busy) essere occupato(a) or preso(a)

tier [tɪə*] n fila; (of cake) piano, strato

tiger ['taɪgə*] n tigre f

tight [taɪt] adj (rope) teso(a), tirato(a); (money) poco(a); (clothes, budget, bend etc) stretto(a); (control) severo(a), fermo(a); (inf: drunk) sbronzo(a) ♦ adv (squeeze) fortemente; (shut) ermeticamente; **~s** (BRIT) npl collant m inv; **~en** vt (rope) tendere; (*screw*) stringere; (*control*) rinforzare ♦ *vi* tendersi; stringersi; ~-**fisted** *adj* avaro(a); ~**ly** *adv* (*grasp*) bene, saldamente; ~**rope** *n* corda (da acrobata)

tile [taɪl] *n* (*on roof*) tegola; (*on wall or floor*) piastrella, mattonella; ~**d** *adj* di tegole; a piastrelle, a mattonelle

till [tɪl] *n* registratore *m* di cassa ♦ *vt* (*land*) coltivare ♦ *prep, conj* = **until**

tiller ['tɪlə*] *n* (*NAUT*) barra del timone

tilt [tɪlt] *vt* inclinare, far pendere ♦ *vi* inclinarsi, pendere

timber ['tɪmbə*] *n* (*material*) legname *m*; (*trees*) alberi *mpl* da legname

time [taɪm] *n* tempo; (*epoch: often pl*) epoca, tempo; (*by clock*) ora; (*moment*) momento; (*occasion*) volta; (*MUS*) tempo ♦ *vt* (*race*) cronometrare; (*programme*) calcolare la durata di; (*fix moment for*) programmare; (*remark etc*) dire (*or* fare) al momento giusto; **a long** ~ molto tempo; **for the** ~ **being** per il momento; 4 **at a** ~ 4 *per* alla volta; **from** ~ **to** ~ ogni tanto; **at** ~s a volte; **in** ~ (*soon enough*) in tempo; (*after some* ~) col tempo; (*MUS*) a tempo; **in a week's** ~ fra una settimana; **in no** ~ in un attimo; **any** ~ in qualsiasi momento; **on** ~ puntualmente; **5** ~ **s 5** 5 volte 5, 5 per 5; **what** ~ **is it?** che ora è?, che ore sono?; **to have a good** ~ divertirsi; ~ **bomb** *n* bomba a orologeria; ~**less** *adj* eterno(a); ~**ly** *adj* opportuno(a); ~ **off** *n* tempo libero; ~ *r n* (~ *switch*) temporizzatore *m*; (*in kitchen*) contaminuti *m inv*; ~ **scale** *n* periodo; ~**share** *adj*: ~**share apartment/villa** appartamento/villa in multiproprietà; ~ **switch** (*BRIT*) *n* temporizzatore *m*; ~**table** *n* orario; ~ **zone** *n* fuso orario

timid ['tɪmɪd] *adj* timido(a); (*easily scared*) pauroso(a)

timing ['taɪmɪŋ] *n* (*SPORT*) cronometraggio; (*fig*) scelta del momento opportuno

timpani ['tɪmpənɪ] *npl* timpani *mpl*

tin [tɪn] *n* stagno; (*also: ~ plate*) latta; (*container*) scatola; (*BRIT: can*) barattolo (di latta), lattina; ~**foil** *n* stagnola

tinge [tɪndʒ] *n* sfumatura ♦ *vt*: ~**d with** tinto(a) di

tingle ['tɪŋgl] *vi* pizzicare

tinker ['tɪŋkə*]: ~ **with** *vt fus* armeggiare intorno a; cercare di riparare

tinned [tɪnd] (*BRIT*) *adj* (*food*) in scatola

tin opener ['-əupnə*] (*BRIT*) *n* apriscatole *m inv*

tinsel ['tɪnsl] *n* decorazioni *fpl* natalizie (*argentate*)

tint [tɪnt] *n* tinta; ~**ed** *adj* (*hair*) tinto(a); (*spectacles, glass*) colorato(a)

tiny ['taɪnɪ] *adj* minuscolo(a)

tip [tɪp] *n* (*end*) punta; (*gratuity*) mancia; (*BRIT: for rubbish*) immondezzaio; (*advice*) suggerimento ♦ *vt* (*waiter*) dare la mancia a; (*tilt*) inclinare; (*overturn: also:* ~ *over*) capovolgere; (*empty: also:* ~ *out*) scaricare; ~-**off** *n* (*hint*) soffiata; ~**ped** (*BRIT*) *adj* (*cigarette*) col filtro

Tipp-Ex ['tɪpɛks] ® *n* correttore *m*

tipsy ['tɪpsɪ] *adj* brillo(a)

tiptoe ['tɪptəu] *n*: **on** ~ in punta di piedi

tiptop ['tɪp'tɔp] *adj*: **in** ~ **condition** in ottime condizioni

tire ['taɪə*] *n* (*US*) = **tyre** ♦ *vt* stancare ♦ *vi* stancarsi; ~**d** *adj* stanco(a); **to be** ~**d of** essere stanco *or* stufo di; ~**less** *adj* instancabile; ~**some** *adj* noioso(a); **tiring** *adj* faticoso(a)

tissue ['tɪʃuː] *n* tessuto; (*paper handkerchief*) fazzoletto di carta; ~ **paper** *n* carta velina

tit [tɪt] *n* (*bird*) cinciallegra; **to give** ~ **for tat** rendere pan per focaccia

titbit ['tɪtbɪt] (*BRIT*) *n* (*food*) leccornia; (*news*) notizia ghiotta

title ['taɪtl] *n* titolo; ~ **deed** *n* (*LAW*) titolo di proprietà; ~ **role** *n* ruolo *or* parte *f* principale

titter ['tɪtə*] *vi* ridere scioccamente

TM *abbr* = **trademark**

KEYWORD

to [tuː, tə] *prep* **1** (*direction*) a; **to go** ~ **France/London/school** andare in Francia/a Londra/a scuola; **to go** ~ **Paul's/the doctor's** andare da Paul/dal dottore; **the road** ~ **Edinburgh** la strada per Edimburgo; ~ **the left/right** a sinistra/destra

2 (*as far as*) (fino) a; **from here ~ London** da qui a Londra; **to count ~ 10** contare fino a 10; **from 40 ~ 50 people** da 40 a 50 persone

3 (*with expressions of time*): **a quarter ~ 5** le 5 meno un quarto; **it's twenty ~ 3** sono le 3 meno venti

4 (*for, of*): **the key ~ the front door** la chiave della porta d'ingresso; **a letter ~ his wife** una lettera per la moglie

5 (*expressing indirect object*) a; **to give sth ~ sb** dare qc a qn; **to talk ~ sb** parlare a qn; **to be a danger ~ sb/sth** rappresentare un pericolo per qn/qc

6 (*in relation to*) a; **3 goals ~ 2** 3 goal a 2; **30 miles ~ the gallon** ≈ 11 chilometri con un litro

7 (*purpose, result*): **to come ~ sb's aid** venire in aiuto a qn; **to sentence sb ~ death** condannare a morte qn; **~ my surprise** con mia sorpresa

♦ *with vb* **1** (*simple infinitive*): ~ **go/eat** *etc* andare/mangiare *etc*

2 (*following another vb*): **to want/try/start ~ do** volere/cercare di/cominciare a fare

3 (*with vb omitted*): **I don't want ~** non voglio (farlo); **you ought ~** devi (farlo)

4 (*purpose, result*) per; **I did it ~ help you** l'ho fatto per aiutarti

5 (*equivalent to relative clause*): **I have things ~ do** ho da fare; **the main thing is ~ try** la cosa più importante è provare

6 (*after adjective etc*): **ready ~ go** pronto a partire; **too old/young ~ ...** troppo vecchio/giovane per ...

♦ *adv*: **to push the door ~** accostare la porta

toad [təud] *n* rospo; **~stool** *n* fungo (velenoso)

toast [təust] *n* (*CULIN*) pane *m* tostato; (*drink, speech*) brindisi *m inv* ♦ *vt* (*CULIN*) tostare; (*drink to*) brindare a; **a piece** *or* **slice of ~** una fetta di pane tostato; **~er** *n* tostapane *m inv*

tobacco [tə'bækəu] *n* tabacco; **~nist** *n*

tabaccaio/a; **~nist's (shop)** *n* tabaccheria

toboggan [tə'bɔgən] *n* toboga *m inv*

today [tə'deɪ] *adv* oggi ♦ *n* (*also fig*) oggi *m*

toddler ['tɔdlə*] *n* bambino/a che impara a camminare

to-do *n* (*fuss*) storie *fpl*

toe [təu] *n* dito del piede; (*of shoe*) punta; **to ~ the line** (*fig*) stare in riga, conformarsi; **~nail** *n* unghia del piede

toffee ['tɔfɪ] *n* caramella; **~ apple** *n* mela caramellata

toga ['təugə] *n* toga

together [tə'gɛðə*] *adv* insieme; (*at same time*) allo stesso tempo; **~ with** insieme a

toil [tɔɪl] *n* travaglio, fatica ♦ *vi* affannarsi; sgobbare

toilet ['tɔɪlət] *n* (*BRIT: lavatory*) gabinetto ♦ *cpd* (*bag, soap etc*) da toletta; **~ paper** *n* carta igienica; **~ries** *npl* articoli *mpl* da toletta; **~ roll** *n* rotolo di carta igienica; **~ water** *n* acqua di colonia

token ['təukən] *n* (*sign*) segno; (*substitute coin*) gettone *m*; **book/record/gift ~** (*BRIT*) buono-libro/disco/regalo

told [təuld] *pt, pp of* **tell**

tolerable ['tɔlərəbl] *adj* (*bearable*) tollerabile; (*fairly good*) passabile

tolerant ['tɔlərnt] *adj*: **~ (of)** tollerante (nei confronti di)

tolerate ['tɔləreɪt] *vt* sopportare; (*MED, TECH*) tollerare

toll [təul] *n* (*tax, charge*) pedaggio ♦ *vi* (*bell*) suonare; **the accident ~ on the roads** il numero delle vittime della strada

tomato [tə'mɑːtəu] (*pl* **~es**) *n* pomodoro

tomb [tuːm] *n* tomba

tomboy ['tɔmbɔɪ] *n* maschiaccio

tombstone ['tuːmstəun] *n* pietra tombale

tomcat ['tɔmkæt] *n* gatto

tomorrow [tə'mɔrəu] *adv* domani ♦ *n* (*also fig*) domani *m inv*; **the day after ~** dopodomani; **~ morning** domani mattina

ton [tʌn] *n* tonnellata (*BRIT* = 1016 *kg*; *US* = 907 *kg*; *metric* = 1000 *kg*); **~s of** (*inf*) un mucchio *or* sacco di

tone [təun] *n* tono ♦ *vi* (*also*: ~ *in*) intonarsi; **~ down** *vt* (*colour, criticism, sound*) attenuare; **~ up** *vt* (*muscles*) tonificare; **~-deaf** *adj* che non ha orecchio (musicale)

tongs [tɒŋz] *npl* tenaglie *fpl*; (*for coal*) molle *fpl*; (*for hair*) arricciacapelli *m inv*

tongue [tʌŋ] *n* lingua; **~ in cheek** (*say, speak*) ironicamente; **~-tied** *adj* (*fig*) muto(a); **~-twister** *n* scioglilingua *m inv*

tonic ['tɒnɪk] *n* (*MED*) tonico; (*also*: ~ *water*) acqua tonica

tonight [tə'naɪt] *adv* stanotte; (*this evening*) stasera ♦ *n* questa notte; questa sera

tonnage ['tʌnɪdʒ] *n* (*NAUT*) tonnellaggio, stazza

tonsil ['tɒnsl] *n* tonsilla; **~litis** [-'laɪtɪs] *n* tonsillite *f*

too [tu:] *adv* (*excessively*) troppo; (*also*) anche; **~ much** *adv* troppo ♦ *adj* troppo(a); **~ many** troppi(e)

took [tuk] *pt of* **take**

tool [tu:l] *n* utensile *m*, attrezzo; **~ box** *n* cassetta *f* portautensili

toot [tu:t] *n* (*of horn*) colpo di clacson; (*of whistle*) fischio ♦ *vi* suonare; (*with car horn*) suonare il clacson

tooth [tu:θ] (*pl* **teeth**) *n* (*ANAT, TECH*) dente *m*; **~ache** *n* mal *m* di denti, **~brush** *n* spazzolino da denti; **~paste** *n* dentifricio; **~pick** *n* stuzzicadenti *m inv*

top [tɒp] *n* (*of mountain, page, ladder*) cima; (*of box, cupboard, table*) sopra *m inv*, parte *f* superiore; (*lid: of box, jar*) coperchio; (*: of bottle*) tappo; (*blouse etc*) sopra *m inv*; (*toy*) trottola ♦ *adj* più alto(a); (*in rank*) primo(a); (*best*) migliore ♦ *vt* (*exceed*) superare; (*be first in*) essere in testa a; **on ~** sopra, in cima a; (*in addition to*) oltre a; **from ~ to bottom** da cima a fondo; **~ up** (*US* **~ off**) *vt* riempire; (*salary*) integrare; **~ floor** *n* ultimo piano; **~ hat** *n* cilindro; **~-heavy** *adj* (*object*) con la parte superiore troppo pesante

topic ['tɒpɪk] *n* argomento; **~al** *adj* d'attualità

top: ~less *adj* (*bather etc*) col seno

scoperto; **~-level** *adj* (*talks*) ad alto livello; **~most** *adj* il(la) più alto(a)

topple ['tɒpl] *vt* rovesciare, far cadere ♦ *vi* cadere; traballare

top-secret *adj* segretissimo(a)

topsy-turvy ['tɒpsɪ'tə:vɪ] *adj, adv* sottosopra *inv*

torch [tɔ:tʃ] *n* torcia; (*BRIT: electric*) lampadina tascabile

tore [tɔ:*] *pt of* **tear**[1]

torment [*n* 'tɔ:mɛnt, *vb* tɔ:'mɛnt] *n* tormento ♦ *vt* tormentare

torn [tɔ:n] *pp of* **tear**[1]

torpedo [tɔ:'pi:dəu] (*pl* ~**es**) *n* siluro

torrent ['tɒrnt] *n* torrente *m*

torrid ['tɒrɪd] *adj* torrido(a); (*love affair*) infuocato(a)

tortoise ['tɔ:təs] *n* tartaruga; **~shell** ['tɔ:təʃɛl] *adj* di tartaruga

torture ['tɔ:tʃə*] *n* tortura ♦ *vt* torturare

Tory ['tɔ:rɪ] (*BRIT: POL*) *adj* dei tories, conservatore(trice) ♦ *n* tory *m/f inv*, conservatore/trice

toss [tɒs] *vt* gettare, lanciare; (*one's head*) scuotere; **to ~ a coin** fare a testa o croce; **to ~ up for sth** fare a testa o croce per qc; **to ~ and turn** (*in bed*) girarsi e rigirarsi

tot [tɒt] *n* (*BRIT: drink*) bicchierino; (*child*) bimbo/a

total ['təutl] *adj* totale ♦ *n* totale *m* ♦ *vt* (*add up*) sommare; (*amount to*) ammontare a

totally ['təutəlɪ] *adv* completamente

totter ['tɒtə*] *vi* barcollare

touch [tʌtʃ] *n* tocco, (*sense*) tatto; (*contact*) contatto ♦ *vt* toccare; **a ~ of** (*fig*) un tocco di; un pizzico di; **to get in ~ with** mettersi in contatto con; **to lose ~** (*friends*) perdersi di vista; **~ on** *vt fus* (*topic*) sfiorare, accennare a; **~ up** *vt* (*paint*) ritoccare; **~-and-go** *adj* incerto(a); **~down** *n* atterraggio; (*on sea*) ammaraggio; (*US: FOOTBALL*) meta; **~ed** *adj* commosso(a); **~ing** *adj* commovente; **~line** *n* (*SPORT*) linea laterale; **~y** *adj* (*person*) suscettibile

tough [tʌf] *adj* duro(a); (*resistant*) resistente; **~en** *vt* rinforzare

toupee ['tu:peɪ] *n* parrucchino
tour ['tuə*] *n* viaggio; (*also: package* ~)
viaggio organizzato *or* tutto compreso; (*of
town, museum*) visita; (*by artist*) tournée *f
inv* ♦ *vt* visitare; **~ing** *n* turismo
tourism ['tuərɪzəm] *n* turismo
tourist ['tuərɪst] *n* turista *m/f* ♦ *adv*
(*travel*) in classe turistica ♦ *cpd*
turistico(a); **~ office** *n* pro loco *f inv*
tournament ['tuənəmənt] *n* torneo
tousled ['tauzld] *adj* (*hair*) arruffato(a)
tout [taut] *vi*: **to ~ for** procacciare,
raccogliere; cercare clienti per ♦ *n* (*also:
ticket* ~) bagarino
tow [təu] *vt* rimorchiare; **"on ~"** (*BRIT*),
"in ~" (*US*) "veicolo rimorchiato"
toward(s) [tə'wɔ:d(z)] *prep* verso; (*of
attitude*) nei confronti di; (*of purpose*) per
towel ['tauəl] *n* asciugamano; (*also: tea
~*) strofinaccio; **~ling** *n* (*fabric*) spugna; ~
rail (*US* ~ **rack**) *n* portasciugamano
tower ['tauə*] *n* torre *f*; **~ block** (*BRIT*) *n*
palazzone *m*; **~ing** *adj* altissimo(a),
imponente
town [taun] *n* città *f inv*; **to go to ~**
andare in città; (*fig*) mettercela tutta; ~
centre *n* centro (città); **~ council** *n*
consiglio comunale; **~ hall** *n*
≈ municipio; **~ plan** *n* pianta della città;
~ planning *n* urbanistica
towrope ['təurəup] *n* (cavo da)
rimorchio
tow truck (*US*) *n* carro *m* attrezzi *inv*
toxic ['tɔksɪk] *adj* tossico(a)
toy [tɔɪ] *n* giocattolo; **~ with** *vt fus*
giocare con; (*idea*) accarezzare,
trastullarsi con; **~ shop** *n* negozio di
giocattoli
trace [treɪs] *n* traccia ♦ *vt* (*draw*)
tracciare; (*follow*) seguire; (*locate*)
rintracciare; **tracing paper** *n* carta da
ricalco
track [træk] *n* (*of person, animal*) traccia;
(*on tape, SPORT, path: gen*) pista; (: *of
bullet etc*) traiettoria; (: *of suspect, animal*)
pista, tracce *fpl*; (*RAIL*) binario, rotaie *fpl*
♦ *vt* seguire le tracce di; **to keep ~ of**
seguire; **~ down** *vt* (*prey*) scovare,
snidare; (*sth lost*) rintracciare; **~suit** *n*

tuta sportiva
tract [trækt] *n* (*GEO*) tratto, estensione *f*;
(*pamphlet*) opuscolo, libretto
tractor ['træktə*] *n* trattore *m*
trade [treɪd] *n* commercio; (*skill, job*)
mestiere *m* ♦ *vi* commerciare ♦ *vt*: **to ~
sth (for sth)** barattare qc (con qc); **to ~
with/in** commerciare con/in; **~ in** *vt* (*old
car etc*) dare come pagamento parziale; ~
fair *n* fiera commerciale; **~mark** *n*
marchio di fabbrica; **~ name** *n* marca,
nome *m* depositato; **~r** *n* commerciante
m/f; **~sman** *n* fornitore *m*; (*shopkeeper*)
negoziante *m*; **~ union** *n* sindacato; ~
unionist *n* sindacalista *m/f*
tradition [trə'dɪʃən] *n* tradizione *f*; **~al**
adj tradizionale
traffic ['træfɪk] *n* traffico ♦ *vi*: **to ~ in**
(*pej: liquor, drugs*) trafficare in; **~ circle**
(*US*) *n* isola rotatoria; **~ jam** *n* ingorgo
(del traffico); **~ lights** *npl* semaforo; ~
warden *n* addetto/a al controllo del
traffico e del parcheggio
tragedy ['trædʒədɪ] *n* tragedia
tragic ['trædʒɪk] *adj* tragico(a)
trail [treɪl] *n* (*tracks*) tracce *fpl*, pista;
(*path*) sentiero; (*of smoke etc*) scia ♦ *vt*
trascinare, strascicare; (*follow*) seguire
♦ *vi* essere al traino; (*dress etc*)
strusciare; (*plant*) arrampicarsi;
strisciare; (*in game*) essere in svantaggio;
~ behind *vi* essere al traino; **~er** *n* (*AUT*)
rimorchio; (*US*) roulotte *f inv*; (*CINEMA*)
prossimamente *m inv*; **~er truck** (*US*) *n*
(*articulated lorry*) autoarticolato
train [treɪn] *n* treno; (*of dress*) coda,
strascico ♦ *vt* (*apprentice, doctor etc*)
formare; (*sportsman*) allenare; (*dog*)
addestrare; (*memory*) esercitare; (*point:
gun etc*): **to ~ sth on** puntare qc contro
♦ *vi* formarsi; allenarsi; **one's ~ of
thought** il filo dei propri pensieri; **~ed**
adj qualificato(a); allenato(a);
addestrato(a); **~ee** [treɪ'ni:] *n* (*in trade*)
apprendista *m/f*; **~er** *n* (*SPORT*)
allenatore/trice; (: *shoe*) scarpa da
ginnastica ♦ *n* (*of dogs etc*) addestratore/
trice; **~ing** *n* formazione *f*; allenamento;
addestramento; **in ~ing** (*SPORT*) in

allenamento; **~ing college** n istituto professionale; *(for teachers)* ≈ istituto magistrale; **~ing shoes** npl scarpe fpl da ginnastica

traipse [treɪps] vi girovagare, andare a zonzo

trait [treɪt] n tratto

traitor ['treɪtə*] n traditore m

tram [træm] *(BRIT)* n *(also: ~car)* tram m inv

tramp [træmp] n *(person)* vagabondo/a; *(inf: pej: woman)* sgualdrina ♦ vi camminare con passo pesante

trample ['træmpl] vt: **to ~ (underfoot)** calpestare

trampoline ['træmpəliːn] n trampolino

tranquil ['træŋkwɪl] adj tranquillo(a); **~lizer** n *(MED)* tranquillante m

transact [træn'zækt] vt *(business)* trattare; **~ion** [-'zækʃən] n transazione f

transatlantic ['trænzət'læntɪk] adj transatlantico(a)

transcript ['trænskrɪpt] n trascrizione f

transfer [n 'trænsfə*, vb træns'fə*] n *(gen, also SPORT)* trasferimento; *(POL: of power)* passaggio; *(picture, design)* decalcomania; *: stick-on)* autoadesivo ♦ vt trasferire; passare; **to ~ the charges** *(BRIT: TEL)* fare una chiamata a carico del destinatario

transform [træns'fɔːm] vt trasformare

transfusion [træns'fjuːʒən] n trasfusione f

transient ['trænzɪənt] adj transitorio(a), fugace

transistor [træn'zɪstə*] n *(ELEC)* transistor m inv; *(also: ~ radio)* radio f inv a transistor

transit ['trænzɪt] n: **in ~** in transito

transitive ['trænzɪtɪv] adj *(LING)* transitivo(a)

translate [trænz'leɪt] vt tradurre; **translation** [-'leɪʃən] n traduzione f; **translator** n traduttore/trice

transmission [trænz'mɪʃən] n trasmissione f

transmit [trænz'mɪt] vt trasmettere; **~ter** n trasmettitore m

transparency [træns'pɛərənsɪ] n trasparenza; *(BRIT: PHOT)* diapositiva

transparent [træns'pærnt] adj trasparente

transpire [træn'spaɪə*] vi *(happen)* succedere; *(turn out)*: **it ~d that** si venne a sapere che

transplant [vb træns'plɑːnt, n 'trænsplɑːnt] vt trapiantare ♦ n *(MED)* trapianto

transport [n 'trænspɔːt, vb træns'pɔːt] n trasporto ♦ vt trasportare; **~ation** [-'teɪʃən] n *(mezzo di)* trasporto; **~ café** *(BRIT)* n trattoria per camionisti

trap [træp] n *(snare, trick)* trappola; *(carriage)* calesse m ♦ vt prendere in trappola, intrappolare; **~ door** n botola

trapeze [trə'piːz] n trapezio

trappings ['træpɪŋz] npl ornamenti mpl; indoratura, sfarzo

trash [træʃ] *(pej)* n *(goods)* ciarpame m; *(nonsense)* sciocchezze fpl; **~ can** *(US)* n secchio della spazzatura

trauma ['trɔːmə] n trauma m; **~tic** [-'mætɪk] adj traumatico(a)

travel ['trævl] n viaggio; viaggi mpl ♦ vi viaggiare ♦ vt *(distance)* percorrere; **~ agency** n agenzia (di) viaggi; **~ agent** n agente m di viaggio; **~ler** *(US* **~er)** n viaggiatore/trice; **~ler's cheque** *(US* **~er's check)** n assegno turistico; **~ling** *(US* **~ing)** n viaggi mpl; **~ sickness** n mal m d'auto *(or* di mare *or* d'aria)

travesty ['trævəstɪ] n parodia

trawler ['trɔːlə*] n peschereccio (a strascico)

tray [treɪ] n *(for carrying)* vassoio; *(on desk)* vaschetta

treacherous ['tretʃərəs] adj infido(a)

treachery ['tretʃərɪ] n tradimento

treacle ['triːkl] n melassa

tread [trɛd] *(pt trod, pp trodden)* n passo; *(sound)* rumore m di passi; *(of stairs)* pedata; *(of tyre)* battistrada m inv ♦ vi camminare; **~ on** vt fus calpestare

treason ['triːzn] n tradimento

treasure ['trɛʒə*] n tesoro ♦ vt *(value)* tenere in gran conto, apprezzare molto; *(store)* custodire gelosamente

treasurer ['trɛʒərə*] n tesoriere/a

treasury ['trɛʒərɪ] n: **the T~** *(BRIT)*, **the T~ Department** *(US)* il ministero del

Tesoro

treat [triːt] *n* regalo ♦ *vt* trattare; (*MED*) curare; **to ~ sb to sth** offrire qc a qn

treatment ['triːtmənt] *n* trattamento

treaty ['triːtɪ] *n* patto, trattato

treble ['trɛbl] *adj* triplo(a), triplice ♦ *vt* triplicare ♦ *vi* triplicarsi; **~ clef** *n* chiave *f* di violino

tree [triː] *n* albero; **~ trunk** *n* tronco d'albero

trek [trɛk] *n* escursione *f* a piedi; escursione *f* in macchina; (*tiring walk*) camminata sfiancante ♦ *vi* (*as holiday*) fare dell'escursionismo

trellis ['trɛlɪs] *n* graticcio

tremble ['trɛmbl] *vi* tremare

tremendous [trɪ'mɛndəs] *adj* (*enormous*) enorme; (*excellent*) meraviglioso(a), formidabile

tremor ['trɛmə*] *n* tremore *m*, tremito; (*also: earth ~*) scossa sismica

trench [trɛntʃ] *n* trincea

trend [trɛnd] *n* (*tendency*) tendenza; (*of events*) corso; (*fashion*) moda; **~y** *adj* (*idea*) di moda; (*clothes*) all'ultima moda

trepidation [trɛpɪ'deɪʃən] *n* trepidazione *f*, agitazione *f*

trespass ['trɛspəs] *vi*: **to ~ on** entrare abusivamente in; **"no ~ing"** "proprietà privata", "vietato l'accesso"

trestle ['trɛsl] *n* cavalletto

trial ['traɪəl] *n* (*LAW*) processo; (*test: of machine etc*) collaudo; **~s** *npl* (*unpleasant experiences*) dure prove *fpl*; **on ~** (*LAW*) sotto processo; **by ~ and error** a tentoni; **~ period** periodo di prova

triangle ['traɪæŋgl] *n* (*MATH, MUS*) triangolo

tribe [traɪb] *n* tribù *f inv*; **~sman** *n* membro di tribù

tribunal [traɪ'bjuːnl] *n* tribunale *m*

tributary ['trɪbjutərɪ] *n* (*river*) tributario, affluente *m*

tribute ['trɪbjuːt] *n* tributo, omaggio; **to pay ~** to rendere omaggio a

trick [trɪk] *n* trucco; (*joke*) tiro; (*CARDS*) presa ♦ *vt* imbrogliare, ingannare; **to play a ~ on sb** giocare un tiro a qn; **that should do the ~** vedrai che funziona;

~ery *n* inganno

trickle ['trɪkl] *n* (*of water etc*) rivolo; gocciolio ♦ *vi* gocciolare

tricky ['trɪkɪ] *adj* difficile, delicato(a)

tricycle ['traɪsɪkl] *n* triciclo

trifle ['traɪfl] *n* sciocchezza; (*BRIT: CULIN*) ≈ zuppa inglese ♦ *adv*: **a ~ long** un po' lungo; **trifling** *adj* insignificante

trigger ['trɪgə*] *n* (*of gun*) grilletto; **~ off** *vt* dare l'avvio a

trim [trɪm] *adj* (*house, garden*) ben tenuto(a); (*figure*) snello(a) ♦ *n* (*haircut etc*) spuntata, regolata; (*embellishment*) finiture *fpl*; (*on car*) guarnizioni *fpl* ♦ *vt* spuntare; (*decorate*): **to ~ (with)** decorare (con); (*NAUT: a sail*) orientare; **~mings** *npl* decorazioni *fpl*; (*extras: gen CULIN*) guarnizione *f*

trinket ['trɪŋkɪt] *n* gingillo; (*piece of jewellery*) ciondolo

trip [trɪp] *n* viaggio; (*excursion*) gita, escursione *f*; (*stumble*) passo falso ♦ *vi* inciampare; (*go lightly*) camminare con passo leggero; **on a ~** in viaggio; **~ up** *vi* inciampare ♦ *vt* fare lo sgambetto a

tripe [traɪp] *n* (*CULIN*) trippa; (*pej: rubbish*) sciocchezze *fpl*, fesserie *fpl*

triple ['trɪpl] *adj* triplo(a)

triplets ['trɪplɪts] *npl* bambini(e) trigemini(e)

triplicate ['trɪplɪkət] *n*: **in ~** in triplice copia

tripod ['traɪpɔd] *n* treppiede *m*

trite [traɪt] *adj* banale, trito(a)

triumph ['traɪʌmf] *n* trionfo ♦ *vi*: **to ~ (over)** trionfare (su)

trivia ['trɪvɪə] *npl* banalità *fpl*

trivial ['trɪvɪəl] *adj* insignificante; (*commonplace*) banale

trod [trɔd] *pt of* **tread**; **~den** *pp of* **tread**

trolley ['trɔlɪ] *n* carrello; **~ bus** *n* filobus *m inv*

trombone [trɔm'bəun] *n* trombone *m*

troop [truːp] *n* gruppo; (*MIL*) squadrone *m*; **~s** *npl* (*MIL*) truppe *fpl*; **~ in/out** *vi* entrare/uscire a frotte; **~ing the colour** *n* (*ceremony*) sfilata della bandiera

trophy ['trəufɪ] *n* trofeo

tropic ['trɔpɪk] *n* tropico; **~al** *adj*

tropicale

trot [trɔt] *n* trotto ♦ *vi* trottare; **on the ~** (*BRIT: fig*) di fila, uno(a) dopo l'altro(a)

trouble ['trʌbl] *n* difficoltà *f inv*, problema *m*; difficoltà *fpl*, problemi; (*worry*) preoccupazione *f*; (*bother, effort*) sforzo; (*POL*) conflitti *mpl*, disordine *m*; (*MED*): **stomach** *etc* ~ disturbi *mpl* gastrici *etc* ♦ *vt* disturbare; (*worry*) preoccupare ♦ *vi*: **to ~ to do** disturbarsi a fare; **~s** *npl* (*POL etc*) disordini *mpl*; **to be in ~** avere dei problemi; **it's no ~!** di niente!; **what's the ~?** cosa c'è che non va?; **~d** *adj* (*person*) preoccupato(a), inquieto(a); (*epoch, life*) agitato(a), difficile; **~maker** *n* elemento disturbatore, agitatore/trice; (*child*) disloco/a; **~shooter** *n* (*in conflict*) conciliatore *m*; **~some** *adj* fastidioso(a), seccante

trough [trɔf] *n* (*also: drinking ~*) abbeveratoio; (*also: feeding ~*) trogolo, mangiatoia; (*channel*) canale *m*

trousers ['trauzəz] *npl* pantaloni *mpl*, calzoni *mpl*; **short ~** calzoncini *mpl*

trousseau ['tru:səu] (*pl* **~x** *or* **~s**) *n* corredo da sposa

trousseaux ['tru:səuz] *npl of* **trousseau**

trout [traut] *n inv* trota

trowel ['trauəl] *n* cazzuola

truant ['truənt] (*BRIT*) *n*: **to play ~** marinare la scuola

truce [tru:s] *n* tregua

truck [trʌk] *n* autocarro, camion *m inv*; (*RAIL*) carro merci aperto; (*for luggage*) carrello *m* portabagagli *inv*; **~ driver** *n* camionista *m/f*; **~ farm** (*US*) *n* orto industriale

trudge [trʌdʒ] *vi* (*also: ~ along*) trascinarsi pesantemente

true [tru:] *adj* vero(a); (*accurate*) accurato(a), esatto(a); (*genuine*) reale; (*faithful*) fedele; **to come ~** avverarsi

truffle ['trʌfl] *n* tartufo

truly ['tru:lɪ] *adv* veramente; (*truthfully*) sinceramente; (*faithfully*): **yours ~** (*in letter*) distinti saluti

trump [trʌmp] *n* (*also: ~ card*) atout *m inv*; **~ed-up** *adj* inventato(a)

trumpet ['trʌmpɪt] *n* tromba

truncheon ['trʌntʃən] *n* sfollagente *m inv*

trundle ['trʌndl] *vt* far rotolare rumorosamente ♦ *vi*: **to ~ along** rotolare rumorosamente

trunk [trʌŋk] *n* (*of tree, person*) tronco; (*of elephant*) proboscide *f*; (*case*) baule *m*; (*US: AUT*) bagagliaio; **~s** *npl* (*also: swimming ~s*) calzoncini *mpl* da bagno

truss [trʌs] *n* (*MED*) cinto erniario; **~ (up)** *vt* (*CULIN*) legare

trust [trʌst] *n* fiducia; (*LAW*) amministrazione *f* fiduciaria; (*COMM*) trust *m inv* ♦ *vt* (*rely on*) contare su; (*hope*) sperare; (*entrust*): **to ~ sth to sb** affidare qc a qn; **~ed** *adj* fidato(a); **~ee** [trʌs'ti:] *n* (*LAW*) amministratore(trice) fiduciario(a); (*of school etc*) amministratore/trice; **~ful** *adj* fiducioso(a); **~ing** *adj* = **~ful**; **~worthy** *adj* fidato(a), degno(a) di fiducia

truth [tru:θ, *pl* tru:ðz] *n* verità *f inv*; **~ful** *adj* (*person*) sincero(a); (*description*) veritiero(a), esatto(a)

try [traɪ] *n* prova, tentativo; (*RUGBY*) meta ♦ *vt* (*LAW*) giudicare; (*test: also: ~ out*) provare; (*strain*) mettere alla prova ♦ *vi* provare; **to have a ~** fare un tentativo; **to ~ to do** (*seek*) cercare di fare; **~ on** *vt* (*clothes*) provare; **~ing** *adj* (*day, experience*) logorante, pesante; (*child*) difficile, insopportabile

tsar [zɑ:*] *n* zar *m inv*

T-shirt ['ti:-] *n* maglietta

T-square ['ti:-] *n* riga a T

tub [tʌb] *n* tinozza; mastello; (*bath*) bagno

tuba ['tju:bə] *n* tuba

tubby ['tʌbɪ] *adj* grassoccio(a)

tube [tju:b] *n* tubo; (*BRIT: underground*) metropolitana, metrò *m inv*; (*for tyre*) camera d'aria; **~ station** (*BRIT*) *n* stazione *f* della metropolitana

tubular ['tju:bjulə*] *adj* tubolare

TUC (*BRIT*) *n abbr* (= *Trades Union Congress*) confederazione *f* dei sindacati britannici

tuck [tʌk] *vt* (*put*) mettere; **~ away** *vt* riporre; (*building*): **to be ~ed away** essere in un luogo isolato; **~ in** *vt* mettere dentro; (*child*) rimboccare ♦ *vi* (*eat*) mangiare di buon appetito; abbuffarsi; **~ up** *vt* (*child*) rimboccare le coperte a; **~ shop** *n* negozio di pasticceria (*in una scuola*)

Tuesday ['tjuːzdɪ] *n* martedì *m inv*

tuft [tʌft] *n* ciuffo

tug [tʌg] *n* (*ship*) rimorchiatore *m* ♦ *vt* tirare con forza; **~-of-war** *n* tiro alla fune

tuition [tjuː'ɪʃən] *n* (*BRIT*) lezioni *fpl*; (: *private* ~) lezioni *fpl* private; (*US: school fees*) tasse *fpl* scolastiche

tulip ['tjuːlɪp] *n* tulipano

tumble ['tʌmbl] *n* (*fall*) capitombolo ♦ *vi* capitombolare, ruzzolare; **to ~ to sth** (*inf*) realizzare qc; **~down** *adj* cadente, diroccato(a); **~ dryer** (*BRIT*) *n* asciugatrice *f*

tumbler ['tʌmblə*] *n* bicchiere *m* (senza stelo)

tummy ['tʌmɪ] (*inf*) *n* pancia

tumour ['tjuːmə*] (*US* **tumor**) *n* tumore *m*

tuna ['tjuːnə] *n inv* (*also*: ~ *fish*) tonno

tune [tjuːn] *n* (*melody*) melodia, aria ♦ *vt* (*MUS*) accordare; (*RADIO, TV, AUT*) regolare, mettere a punto; **to be in/out of ~** (*instrument*) essere accordato(a)/scordato(a); (*singer*) essere intonato(a)/stonato(a); **~ in** *vi*: **to ~ in (to)** (*RADIO, TV*) sintonizzarsi (su); **~ up** *vi* (*musician*) accordare lo strumento; **~ful** *adj* melodioso(a); **~r** *n*: **piano ~r** accordatore *m*

tunic ['tjuːnɪk] *n* tunica

Tunisia [tjuː'nɪzɪə] *n* Tunisia

tunnel ['tʌnl] *n* galleria ♦ *vi* scavare una galleria

turban ['təːbən] *n* turbante *m*

turbulence ['təːbjuləns] *n* (*AVIAT*) turbolenza

tureen [tə'riːn] *n* zuppiera

turf [təːf] *n* terreno erboso; (*clod*) zolla ♦ *vt* coprire di zolle erbose; **~ out** (*inf*) *vt* buttar fuori

turgid ['təːdʒɪd] *adj* (*speech*) ampolloso(a), pomposo(a)

Turin [tjuə'rɪn] *n* Torino *f*

Turk [təːk] *n* turco/a

Turkey ['təːkɪ] *n* Turchia

turkey ['təːkɪ] *n* tacchino

Turkish ['təːkɪʃ] *adj* turco(a) ♦ *n* (*LING*) turco

turmoil ['təːmɔɪl] *n* confusione *f*, tumulto

turn [təːn] *n* giro; (*change*) cambiamento; (*in road*) curva; (*tendency: of mind, events*) tendenza; (*performance*) numero; (*chance*) turno; (*MED*) crisi *f inv*, attacco ♦ *vt* girare, voltare; (*change*): **to ~ sth into** trasformare qc in ♦ *vi* girare; (*person: look back*) girarsi, voltarsi; (*reverse direction*) voltare; (*change*) cambiare; (*milk*) andare a male; (*become*) diventare; **a good ~** un buon servizio; **it gave me quite a ~** mi ha fatto prendere un bello spavento; **"no left ~"** (*AUT*) "divieto di svolta a sinistra"; **it's your ~** tocca a lei; **in ~** a sua volta; a turno; **to take ~s (at sth)** fare (qc) a turno; **~ away** *vi* girarsi (dall'altra parte) ♦ *vt* mandare via; **~ back** *vi* ritornare, tornare indietro ♦ *vt* far tornare indietro; (*clock*) spostare indietro; **~ down** *vt* (*refuse*) rifiutare; (*reduce*) abbassare; (*fold*) ripiegare; **~ in** *vi* (*inf: go to bed*) andare a letto ♦ *vt* (*fold*) voltare in dentro; **~ off** *vi* (*from road*) girare, voltare ♦ *vt* (*light, radio, engine etc*) spegnere; **~ on** *vt* (*light, radio etc*) accendere; **~ out** *vt* (*light, gas*) chiudere; spegnere ♦ *vi* (*voters*) presentarsi; **to ~ out to be ...** rivelarsi ..., risultare ...; **~ over** *vi* (*person*) girarsi ♦ *vt* girare; **~ round** *vi* girare; (*person*) girarsi; **~ up** *v* (*person*) arrivare, presentarsi; (*lost object*) saltar fuori ♦ *vt* (*collar, sound*) alzare; **~ing** *n* (*in road*) curva; **~ing point** *n* (*fig*) svolta decisiva

turnip ['təːnɪp] *n* rapa

turnout ['təːnaut] *n* presenza, affluenza

turnover ['təːnəuvə*] *n* (*COMM*) turnover *m inv*

turnpike ['təːnpaɪk] (*US*) *n* autostrada a pedaggio

turnstile ['təːnstaɪl] *n* tornella

turntable ['təːnteɪbl] *n* (*on record player*) piatto

turn-up (*BRIT*) *n* (*on trousers*) risvolto

turpentine ['təːpəntaɪn] *n* (*also*: **turps**)

acqua ragia

turquoise ['tə:kwɔɪz] *n* turchese *m* ♦ *adj* turchese

turret ['tʌrɪt] *n* torretta

turtle ['tə:tl] *n* testuggine *f*; **~neck (sweater)** *n* maglione *m* con il collo alto

Tuscany ['tʌskənɪ] *n* Toscana

tusk [tʌsk] *n* zanna

tussle ['tʌsl] *n* baruffa, mischia

tutor ['tju:tə*] *n* (*in college*) docente *m/f* (*responsabile di un gruppo di studenti*); (*private teacher*) precettore *m*; **~ial** [-'tɔ:rɪəl] *n* (*SCOL*) lezione *f* con discussione (*a un gruppo limitato*)

tuxedo [tʌk'si:dəu] (*US*) *n* smoking *m inv*

TV [ti:'vi:] *n abbr* (= television) tivù *f inv*

twang [twæŋ] *n* (*of instrument*) suono vibrante; (*of voice*) accento nasale

tweed [twi:d] *n* tweed *m inv*

tweezers ['twi:zəz] *npl* pinzette *fpl*

twelfth [twelfθ] *num* dodicesimo(a)

twelve [twelv] *num* dodici; **at ~ (o'clock)** alle dodici, a mezzogiorno; (*midnight*) a mezzanotte

twentieth ['twentɪıθ] *num* ventesimo(a)

twenty ['twentɪ] *num* venti

twice [twaɪs] *adv* due volte; **~ as much** due volte tanto

twiddle ['twɪdl] *vt, vi*: **to ~ (with) sth** giocherellare con qc; **to ~ one's thumbs** (*fig*) girarsi i pollici

twig [twɪg] *n* ramoscello ♦ *vt, vi* (*inf*) capire

twilight ['twaɪlaɪt] *n* crepuscolo

twin [twɪn] *adj, n* gemello(a) ♦ *vt*: **to ~ one town with another** fare il gemellaggio di una città con un'altra; **~-bedded room** *n* stanza con letti gemelli

twine [twaɪn] *n* spago, cordicella ♦ *vi* attorcigliarsi

twinge [twɪndʒ] *n* (*of pain*) fitta; **a ~ of conscience/regret** un rimorso/rimpianto

twinkle ['twɪŋkl] *vi* scintillare; (*eyes*) brillare

twirl [twə:l] *vt* far roteare ♦ *vi* roteare

twist [twɪst] *n* torsione *f*; (*in wire, flex*) piega; (*in road*) curva; (*in story*) colpo di scena ♦ *vt* attorcigliare; (*ankle*) slogare; (*weave*) intrecciare; (*roll around*)

arrotolare; (*fig*) distorcere ♦ *vi* (*road*) serpeggiare

twit [twɪt] (*inf*) *n* cretino(a)

twitch [twɪtʃ] *n* tiratina; (*nervous*) tic *m inv* ♦ *vi* contrarsi

two [tu:] *num* due; **to put ~ and ~ together** (*fig*) fare uno più uno; **~-door** *adj* (*AUT*) a due porte; **~-faced** (*pej*) *adj* (*person*) falso(a); **~fold** *adv*: **to increase ~fold** aumentare del doppio; **~-piece (suit)** *n* due pezzi *m inv*; **~-piece (swimsuit)** *n* (costume *m* da bagno a) due pezzi *m inv*; **~some** *n* (*people*) coppia; **~-way** *adj* (*traffic*) a due sensi

tycoon [taɪ'ku:n] *n*: **(business) ~** magnate *m*

type [taɪp] *n* (*category*) genere *m*; (*model*) modello; (*example*) tipo; (*TYP*) tipo, carattere *m* ♦ *vt* (*letter etc*) battere (a macchina), dattilografare; **~-cast** *adj* (*actor*) a ruolo fisso; **~face** *n* carattere *m* tipografico; **~script** *n* dattiloscritto; **~writer** *n* macchina da scrivere; **~written** *adj* dattiloscritto(a), battuto(a) a macchina

typhoid ['taɪfɔɪd] *n* tifoidea

typhoon [taɪ'fu:n] *n* tifone *m*

typical ['tɪpɪkl] *adj* tipico(a)

typify ['tɪpɪfaɪ] *vt* caratterizzare; (*person*) impersonare

typing ['taɪpɪŋ] *n* dattilografia

typist ['taɪpɪst] *n* dattilografo/a

tyrant ['taɪərnt] *n* tiranno

tyre ['taɪə*] (*US* **tire**) *n* pneumatico, gomma; **~ pressure** *n* pressione *f* (delle gomme)

tzar [zɑ:*] *n* = **tsar**

U

U-bend ['ju:'-] *n* (*in pipe*) sifone *m*

ubiquitous [ju:'bɪkwɪtəs] *adj* onnipresente

udder ['ʌdə*] *n* mammella

UFO ['ju:fəu] *n abbr* (= unidentified flying object) UFO *m inv*

ugh [ə:h] *excl* puah!

ugly ['ʌglɪ] *adj* brutto(a)

UK *n abbr* = **United Kingdom**

ulcer ['ʌlsə*] *n* ulcera; (*also: mouth ~*) afta

Ulster ['ʌlstə*] *n* Ulster *m*

ulterior [ʌl'tɪərɪə*] *adj* ulteriore; **~ motive** *n* secondo fine *m*

ultimate ['ʌltɪmət] *adj* ultimo(a), finale; (*authority*) massimo(a), supremo(a); **~ly** *adv* alla fine; in definitiva, in fin dei conti

ultrasound [ʌltrə'saund] *n* (*MED*) ultrasuono

umbilical cord [ʌmbɪ'laɪkl-] *n* cordone *m* ombelicale

umbrella [ʌm'brelə] *n* ombrello

umpire ['ʌmpaɪə*] *n* arbitro

umpteen [ʌmp'tiːn] *adj* non so quanti(e); **for the ~th time** per l'ennesima volta

UN *n abbr* (= *United Nations*) ONU *f*

unable [ʌn'eɪbl] *adj*: **to be ~ to** non potere, essere nell'impossibilità di; essere incapace di

unaccompanied [ʌnə'kʌmpənɪd] *adj* (*child, lady*) non accompagnato(a)

unaccountably [ʌnə'kauntəblɪ] *adv* inesplicabilmente

unaccustomed [ʌnə'kʌstəmd] *adj*: **to be ~ to sth** non essere abituato a qc

unanimous [juː'nænɪməs] *adj* unanime; **~ly** *adv* all'unanimità

unarmed [ʌn'ɑːmd] *adj* (*without a weapon*) disarmato(a); (*combat*) senz'armi

unashamed [ʌnə'ʃeɪmd] *adj* sfacciato(a)

unassuming [ʌnə'sjuːmɪŋ] *adj* modesto(a), senza pretese

unattached [ʌnə'tætʃt] *adj* senza legami, libero(a)

unattended [ʌnə'tendɪd] *adj* (*car, child, luggage*) incustodito(a)

unattractive [ʌnə'træktɪv] *adj* poco attraente

unauthorized [ʌn'ɔːθəraɪzd] *adj* non autorizzato(a)

unavoidable [ʌnə'vɔɪdəbl] *adj* inevitabile

unaware [ʌnə'wɛə*] *adj*: **to be ~ of** non sapere, ignorare; **~s** *adv* di sorpresa, alla sprovvista

unbalanced [ʌn'bælənst] *adj* squilibrato(a)

unbearable [ʌn'bɛərəbl] *adj* insopportabile

unbeknown(st) [ʌnbɪ'nəun(st)] *adv*: **~ to** all'insaputa di

unbelievable [ʌnbɪ'liːvəbl] *adj* incredibile

unbend [ʌn'bend] (*irreg: like bend*) *vi* distendersi ♦ *vt* (*wire*) raddrizzare

unbias(s)ed [ʌn'baɪəst] *adj* (*person, report*) obiettivo(a), imparziale

unborn [ʌn'bɔːn] *adj* non ancora nato(a)

unbreakable [ʌn'breɪkəbl] *adj* infrangibile

unbroken [ʌn'brəukən] *adj* intero(a); (*series*) continuo(a); (*record*) imbattuto(a)

unbutton [ʌn'bʌtn] *vt* sbottonare

uncalled-for [ʌn'kɔːld-] *adj* (*remark*) fuori luogo *inv*; (*action*) ingiustificato(a)

uncanny [ʌn'kænɪ] *adj* misterioso(a), strano(a)

unceasing [ʌn'siːsɪŋ] *adj* incessante

unceremonious [ʌnserɪ'məunɪəs] *adj* (*abrupt, rude*) senza tante cerimonie

uncertain [ʌn'səːtn] *adj* incerto(a); dubbio(a); **~ty** *n* incertezza

unchanged [ʌn'tʃeɪndʒd] *adj* invariato(a)

unchecked [ʌn'tʃekt] *adj* incontrollato(a)

uncivilized [ʌn'sɪvɪlaɪzd] *adj* (*gen*) selvaggio(a); (*fig*) incivile, barbaro(a)

uncle ['ʌŋkl] *n* zio

uncomfortable [ʌn'kʌmfətəbl] *adj* scomodo(a); (*uneasy*) a disagio, agitato(a); (*unpleasant*) fastidioso(a)

uncommon [ʌn'kɔmən] *adj* raro(a), insolito(a), non comune

uncompromising [ʌn'kɔmprəmaɪzɪŋ] *adj* intransigente, inflessibile

unconcerned [ʌnkən'səːnd] *adj*: **to be ~ (about)** non preoccuparsi (di *or* per)

unconditional [ʌnkən'dɪʃənl] *adj* incondizionato(a), senza condizioni

unconscious [ʌn'kɔnʃəs] *adj* privo(a) di sensi, svenuto(a); (*unaware*) inconsapevole, inconscio(a) ♦ *n*: **the ~** l'inconscio; **~ly** *adv* inconsciamente

uncontrollable [ʌnkən'trəuləbl] *adj* incontrollabile; indisciplinato(a)

unconventional [ʌnkən'venʃənl] *adj*

poco convenzionale

uncouth [ʌnˈkuːθ] *adj* maleducato(a), grossolano(a)

uncover [ʌnˈkʌvə*] *vt* scoprire

undecided [ʌndɪˈsaɪdɪd] *adj* indeciso(a)

under [ˈʌndə*] *prep* sotto; (*less than*) meno di; al disotto di; (*according to*) secondo, in conformità a ♦ *adv* (al) disotto; ~ **there** là sotto; ~ **repair** in riparazione

under... [ˈʌndə*] *prefix* sotto..., sub...; ~**age** *adj* minorenne; ~**carriage** (*BRIT*) *n* carrello (d'atterraggio); ~**charge** *vt* far pagare di meno a; ~**clothes** *npl* biancheria (intima); ~**coat** *n* (*paint*) mano *f* di fondo; ~**cover** *adj* segreto(a), clandestino(a); ~**current** *n* corrente *f* sottomarina; ~**cut** *vt irreg* vendere a prezzo minore di; ~**developed** *adj* sottosviluppato(a); ~**dog** *n* oppresso/a; ~**done** *adj* (*CULIN*) al sangue; (*pej*) poco cotto(a); ~**estimate** *vt* sottovalutare; ~**fed** *adj* denutrito(a); ~**foot** *adv* sotto i piedi; ~**go** *vt irreg* subire; (*treatment*) sottoporsi a; ~**graduate** *n* studente(essa) universitario(a); ~**ground** *n* (*BRIT*: *railway*) metropolitana; (*POL*) movimento clandestino ♦ *adj* sotterraneo(a); (*fig*) clandestino(a) ♦ *adv* sotterra; **to go** ~**ground** (*fig*) darsi alla macchia; ~**growth** *n* sottobosco; ~**hand(ed)** *adj* (*fig*) furtivo(a), subdolo(a); ~**lie** *vt irreg* essere alla base di; ~**line** *vt* sottolineare; ~**ling** [ˈʌndəlɪŋ] (*pej*) *n* subalterno/a, tirapiedi *m/f inv*; ~**mine** *vt* minare; ~**neath** [ʌndəˈniːθ] *adv* sotto, disotto ♦ *prep* sotto, al di sotto di; ~**paid** *adj* sottopagato(a); ~**pants** *npl* mutande *fpl*, slip *m inv*; ~**pass** (*BRIT*) *n* sottopassaggio; ~**privileged** *adj* non abbiente; meno favorito(a); ~**rate** *vt* sottovalutare; ~**shirt** (*US*) *n* maglietta; ~**shorts** (*US*) *npl* mutande *fpl*, slip *m inv*; ~**side** *n* disotto; ~**skirt** (*BRIT*) *n* sottoveste *f*

understand [ʌndəˈstænd] (*irreg: like* **stand**) *vt, vi* capire, comprendere; **I** ~ **that ...** sento che ...; credo di capire che ...; ~**able** *adj* comprensibile; ~**ing** *adj* comprensivo(a) ♦ *n* comprensione *f*;

(*agreement*) accordo

understatement [ʌndəˈsteɪtmənt] *n*: **that's an ~!** a dire poco!

understood [ʌndəˈstud] *pt, pp of* **understand** ♦ *adj* inteso(a); (*implied*) sottinteso(a)

understudy [ˈʌndəstʌdɪ] *n* sostituto/a, attore/trice supplente

undertake [ʌndəˈteɪk] (*irreg: like* **take**) *vt* intraprendere; **to** ~ **to do sth** impegnarsi a fare qc

undertaker [ˈʌndəteɪkə*] *n* impresario di pompe funebri

undertaking [ʌndəˈteɪkɪŋ] *n* impresa; (*promise*) promessa

undertone [ˈʌndətəun] *n*: **in an** ~ a mezza voce, a voce bassa

underwater [ʌndəˈwɔːtə*] *adv* sott'acqua ♦ *adj* subacqueo(a)

underwear [ˈʌndəwɛə*] *n* biancheria (intima)

underworld [ˈʌndəwəːld] *n* (*of crime*) malavita

underwriter [ˈʌndəraɪtə*] *n* (*INSURANCE*) sottoscrittore/trice

undesirable [ʌndɪˈzaɪərəbl] *adj* sgradevole

undies [ˈʌndɪz] (*inf*) *npl* biancheria intima da donna

undo [ʌnˈduː] *vt irreg* disfare; ~**ing** *n* rovina, perdita

undoubted [ʌnˈdautɪd] *adj* sicuro(a), certo(a); ~**ly** *adv* senza alcun dubbio

undress [ʌnˈdrɛs] *vi* spogliarsi

undue [ʌnˈdjuː] *adj* eccessivo(a)

undulating [ˈʌndjuleɪtɪŋ] *adj* ondeggiante; ondulato(a)

unduly [ʌnˈdjuːlɪ] *adv* eccessivamente

unearth [ʌnˈəːθ] *vt* dissotterrare; (*fig*) scoprire

unearthly [ʌnˈəːθlɪ] *adj* (*hour*) impossibile

uneasy [ʌnˈiːzɪ] *adj* a disagio; (*worried*) preoccupato(a); (*peace*) precario(a)

uneconomic(al) [ˈʌnɪkəˈnɔmɪk(l)] *adj* antieconomico(a)

unemployed [ʌnɪmˈplɔɪd] *adj* disoccupato(a) ♦ *npl*: **the** ~ i disoccupati

unemployment [ʌnɪmˈplɔɪmənt] *n*

disoccupazione f

unending [ʌn'endɪŋ] *adj* senza fine

unerring [ʌn'əːrɪŋ] *adj* infallibile

uneven [ʌn'iːvn] *adj* ineguale; irregolare

unexpected [ʌnɪk'spɛktɪd] *adj*
inatteso(a), imprevisto(a); **~ly** *adv*
inaspettatamente

unfailing [ʌn'feɪlɪŋ] *adj* (*supply*, *energy*)
inesauribile; (*remedy*) infallibile

unfair [ʌn'fɛə*] *adj*: ~ **(to)** ingiusto(a)
(nei confronti di)

unfaithful [ʌn'feɪθful] *adj* infedele

unfamiliar [ʌnfə'mɪlɪə*] *adj*
sconosciuto(a), strano(a); **to be ~ with**
non avere familiarità con

unfashionable [ʌn'fæʃnəbl] *adj* (*clothes*)
fuori moda; (*district*) non alla moda

unfasten [ʌn'fɑːsn] *vt* slacciare;
sciogliere

unfavourable [ʌn'feɪvərəbl] (*US*
unfavorable) *adj* sfavorevole

unfeeling [ʌn'fiːlɪŋ] *adj* insensibile,
duro(a)

unfinished [ʌn'fɪnɪʃt] *adj* incompleto(a)

unfit [ʌn'fɪt] *adj* (*ill*) malato(a), in cattiva
salute; (*incompetent*): ~ **(for)**
incompetente (in); (: *work*, *MIL*) inabile (a)

unfold [ʌn'fəuld] *vt* spiegare ♦ *vi* (*story*,
plot) svelarsi

unforeseen ['ʌnfɔː'siːn] *adj*
imprevisto(a)

unforgettable [ʌnfə'gɛtəbl] *adj*
indimenticabile

unfortunate [ʌn'fɔːtʃnət] *adj*
sfortunato(a); (*event*, *remark*) infelice; **~ly**
adv sfortunatamente, purtroppo

unfounded [ʌn'faundɪd] *adj* infondato(a)

unfriendly [ʌn'frɛndlɪ] *adj* poco
amichevole, freddo(a)

ungainly [ʌn'geɪnlɪ] *adj* goffo(a),
impacciato(a)

ungodly [ʌn'gɔdlɪ] *adj*: **at an ~ hour** a
un'ora impossibile

ungrateful [ʌn'greɪtful] *adj* ingrato(a)

unhappiness [ʌn'hæpɪnɪs] *n* infelicità

unhappy [ʌn'hæpɪ] *adj* infelice; ~
about/with (*arrangements* etc)
insoddisfatto(a) di

unharmed [ʌn'hɑːmd] *adj* incolume,

sano(a) e salvo(a)

unhealthy [ʌn'hɛlθɪ] *adj* (*gen*)
malsano(a); (*person*) malaticcio(a)

unheard-of [ʌn'hɔːdɔv] *adj* inaudito(a),
senza precedenti

unhurt [ʌn'hɔːt] *adj* illeso(a)

uniform ['juːnɪfɔːm] *n* uniforme *f*, divisa
♦ *adj* uniforme

uninhabited [ʌnɪn'hæbɪtɪd] *adj*
disabitato(a)

unintentional [ʌnɪn'tɛnʃənəl] *adj*
involontario(a)

union ['juːnjən] *n* unione *f*; (*also: trade*
~) sindacato ♦ *cpd* sindacale, dei
sindacati; **U~ Jack** *n* bandiera nazionale
britannica

unique [juː'niːk] *adj* unico(a)

unit ['juːnɪt] *n* unità *f inv*; (*section: of*
furniture etc) elemento; (*team*, *squad*)
reparto, squadra

unite [juː'naɪt] *vt* unire ♦ *vi* unirsi; **~d**
adj unito(a); unificato(a); (*efforts*)
congiunto(a); **U~d Kingdom** *n* Regno
Unito; **U~d Nations (Organization)** *n*
(Organizzazione *f* delle) Nazioni Unite;
U~d States (of America) *n* Stati *mpl*
Uniti (d'America)

unit trust (*BRIT*) *n* fondo d'investimento

unity ['juːnɪtɪ] *n* unità

universal [juːnɪ'vəːsl] *adj* universale

universe ['juːnɪvəːs] *n* universo

university [juːnɪ'vəːsɪtɪ] *n* università *f*
inv

unjust [ʌn'dʒʌst] *adj* ingiusto(a)

unkempt [ʌn'kɛmpt] *adj* trasandato(a);
spettinato(a)

unkind [ʌn'kaɪnd] *adj* scortese; crudele

unknown [ʌn'nəun] *adj* sconosciuto(a)

unlawful [ʌn'lɔːful] *adj* illecito(a),
illegale

unleaded [ʌn'lɛdɪd] *adj* (*petrol*, *fuel*)
verde, senza piombo

unleash [ʌn'liːʃ] *vt* (*fig*) scatenare

unless [ʌn'lɛs] *conj* a meno che (non)
+ *sub*

unlike [ʌn'laɪk] *adj* diverso(a) ♦ *prep* a
differenza di, contrariamente a

unlikely [ʌn'laɪklɪ] *adj* improbabile

unlisted [ʌn'lɪstɪd] (*US*) *adj* (*TEL*): **to be ~**

non essere sull'elenco
unload [ʌn'ləud] *vt* scaricare
unlock [ʌn'lɔk] *vt* aprire
unlucky [ʌn'lʌkɪ] *adj* sfortunato(a); *(object, number)* che porta sfortuna
unmarried [ʌn'mærɪd] *adj* non sposato(a); *(man only)* scapolo, celibe; *(woman only)* nubile
unmistakable [ʌnmɪs'teɪkəbl] *adj* inconfondibile
unmitigated [ʌn'mɪtɪgeɪtɪd] *adj* non mitigato(a), assoluto(a), vero(a) e proprio(a)
unnatural [ʌn'nætʃrəl] *adj* innaturale; contro natura
unnecessary [ʌn'nesəsərɪ] *adj* inutile, superfluo(a)
unnoticed [ʌn'nəutɪst] *adj*: **(to go) ~** (passare) inosservato(a)
UNO ['juːnəu] *n abbr* (= *United Nations Organization*) ONU *f*
unobtainable [ʌnəb'teɪnəbl] *adj* (*TEL*) non ottenibile
unobtrusive [ʌnəb'truːsɪv] *adj* discreto(a)
unofficial [ʌnə'fɪʃl] *adj* non ufficiale; *(strike)* non dichiarato(a) dal sindacato
unpack [ʌn'pæk] *vi* disfare la valigia (*or* le valigie) ♦ *vt* disfare
unpalatable [ʌn'pælətəbl] *adj* sgradevole
unparalleled [ʌn'pærəleld] *adj* incomparabile, impareggiabile
unpleasant [ʌn'pleznt] *adj* spiacevole
unplug [ʌn'plʌg] *vt* staccare
unpopular [ʌn'pɔpjulə*] *adj* impopolare
unprecedented [ʌn'presɪdəntɪd] *adj* senza precedenti
unpredictable [ʌnprɪ'dɪktəbl] *adj* imprevedibile
unprofessional [ʌnprə'feʃənl] *adj* poco professionale
unqualified [ʌn'kwɔlɪfaɪd] *adj* (*teacher*) non abilitato(a); *(success)* assoluto(a), senza riserve
unravel [ʌn'rævl] *vt* dipanare, districare
unreal [ʌn'rɪəl] *adj* irreale
unrealistic [ʌnrɪə'lɪstɪk] *adj* non realistico(a)
unreasonable [ʌn'riːznəbl] *adj* irragionevole
unrelated [ʌnrɪ'leɪtɪd] *adj*: **~ (to)** senza rapporto (con); non imparentato(a) (con)
unrelenting [ʌnrɪ'lentɪŋ] *adj* senza tregua
unreliable [ʌnrɪ'laɪəbl] *adj* (*person, machine*) che non dà affidamento; *(news, source of information*) inattendibile
unremitting [ʌnrɪ'mɪtɪŋ] *adj* incessante
unreservedly [ʌnrɪ'zəːvɪdlɪ] *adv* senza riserve
unrest [ʌn'rest] *n* agitazione *f*
unroll [ʌn'rəul] *vt* srotolare
unruly [ʌn'ruːlɪ] *adj* indisciplinato(a)
unsafe [ʌn'seɪf] *adj* pericoloso(a), rischioso(a)
unsaid [ʌn'sed] *adj*: **to leave sth ~** passare qc sotto silenzio
unsatisfactory ['ʌnsætɪs'fæktərɪ] *adj* che lascia a desiderare, insufficiente
unsavoury [ʌn'seɪvərɪ] *(US unsavory) adj (fig: person, place)* losco(a)
unscathed [ʌn'skeɪðd] *adj* incolume
unscrew [ʌn'skruː] *vt* svitare
unscrupulous [ʌn'skruːpjuləs] *adj* senza scrupoli
unsettled [ʌn'setld] *adj* (*person*) turbato(a); indeciso(a); *(weather)* instabile
unshaven [ʌn'ʃeɪvn] *adj* non rasato(a)
unsightly [ʌn'saɪtlɪ] *adj* brutto(a), sgradevole a vedersi
unskilled [ʌn'skɪld] *adj* non specializzato(a)
unspeakable [ʌn'spiːkəbl] *adj* (*indescribable*) indicibile; *(awful)* abominevole
unstable [ʌn'steɪbl] *adj* (*gen*) instabile; *(mentally)* squilibrato(a)
unsteady [ʌn'stedɪ] *adj* instabile, malsicuro(a)
unstuck [ʌn'stʌk] *adj*: **to come ~** scollarsi; *(fig)* fare fiasco
unsuccessful [ʌnsək'sesful] *adj* (*writer, proposal*) che non ha successo; *(marriage, attempt*) mal riuscito(a), fallito(a); **to be ~** *(in attempting sth)* non avere successo
unsuitable [ʌn'suːtəbl] *adj* inadatto(a);

unsure [ʌnˈʃuə*] *adj* incerto(a); **to be ~ of o.s.** essere insicuro(a)
unsuspecting [ʌnsəˈspɛktɪŋ] *adj* che non sospetta nulla
unsympathetic [ʌnsɪmpəˈθɛtɪk] *adj* (*person*) antipatico(a); (*attitude*) poco incoraggiante
untapped [ʌnˈtæpt] *adj* (*resources*) non sfruttato(a)
unthinkable [ʌnˈθɪŋkəbl] *adj* impensabile, inconcepibile
untidy [ʌnˈtaɪdɪ] *adj* (*room*) in disordine; (*appearance*) trascurato(a); (*person*) disordinato(a)
untie [ʌnˈtaɪ] *vt* (*knot, parcel*) disfare; (*prisoner, dog*) slegare
until [ʌnˈtɪl] *prep* fino a; (*after negative*) prima di ♦ *conj* finché, fino a quando; (*in past, after negative*) prima che + *sub*, prima di + *infinitive*; ~ **he comes** finché *or* fino a quando non arriva; ~ **now** finora; ~ **then** fino ad allora
untimely [ʌnˈtaɪmlɪ] *adj* intempestivo(a), inopportuno(a); (*death*) prematuro(a)
untold [ʌnˈtəʊld] *adj* (*story*) mai rivelato(a); (*wealth*) incalcolabile; (*joy, suffering*) indescrivibile
untoward [ʌntəˈwɔːd] *adj* sfortunato(a), sconveniente
unused [ʌnˈjuːzd] *adj* nuovo(a)
unusual [ʌnˈjuːʒuəl] *adj* insolito(a), eccezionale, raro(a)
unveil [ʌnˈveɪl] *vt* scoprire; svelare
unwanted [ʌnˈwɒntɪd] *adj* (*clothing*) smesso(a); (*child*) non desiderato(a)
unwavering [ʌnˈweɪvərɪŋ] *adj* fermo(a), incrollabile
unwelcome [ʌnˈwɛlkəm] *adj* non gradito(a)
unwell [ʌnˈwɛl] *adj* indisposto(a); **to feel ~** non sentirsi bene
unwieldy [ʌnˈwiːldɪ] *adj* poco maneggevole
unwilling [ʌnˈwɪlɪŋ] *adj*: **to be ~ to do** non voler fare; **~ly** *adv* malvolentieri
unwind [ʌnˈwaɪnd] (*irreg: like* wind[1]) *vt* svolgere, srotolare ♦ *vi* (*relax*) rilassarsi
unwise [ʌnˈwaɪz] *adj* poco saggio(a)

unwitting [ʌnˈwɪtɪŋ] *adj* involontario(a)
unworkable [ʌnˈwəːkəbl] *adj* (*plan*) inattuabile
unworthy [ʌnˈwəːðɪ] *adj* indegno(a)
unwrap [ʌnˈræp] *vt* disfare; aprire
unwritten [ʌnˈrɪtn] *adj* (*agreement*) tacito(a); (*law*) non scritto(a)

KEYWORD
---

up [ʌp] *prep*: **he went ~ the stairs/the hill** è salito su per le scale/sulla collina; **the cat was ~ a tree** il gatto era su un albero; **they live further ~ the street** vivono un po' più su nella stessa strada
♦ *adv* **1** (*upwards, higher*) su, in alto; ~ **in the sky/the mountains** su nel cielo/in montagna; ~ **there** lassù; ~ **above** su in alto
2: **to be ~** (*out of bed*) essere alzato(a); (*prices, level*) essere salito(a)
3: ~ **to** (*as far as*) fino a; **to now** finor
4: **to be ~ to** (*depending on*): **it's ~ to you** sta a lei, dipende da lei; (*equal to*): **he's not ~ to it** (*job, task etc*) non ne è all'altezza; (*inf: be doing*): **what is he ~ to?** cosa sta combinando?
♦ *n*: ~**s and downs** alti e bassi *mpl*

upbringing [ˈʌpbrɪŋɪŋ] *n* educazione *f*
update [ʌpˈdeɪt] *vt* aggiornare
upgrade [ʌpˈgreɪd] *vt* (*house, job*) migliorare; (*employee*) avanzare di grado
upheaval [ʌpˈhiːvl] *n* sconvolgimento; tumulto
uphill [ʌpˈhɪl] *adj* in salita; (*fig: task*) difficile ♦ *adv*: **to go ~** andare in salita, salire
uphold [ʌpˈhəʊld] (*irreg: like* hold) *vt* approvare; sostenere
upholstery [ʌpˈhəʊlstərɪ] *n* tappezzeria
upkeep [ˈʌpkiːp] *n* manutenzione *f*
upon [əˈpɒn] *prep* su
upper [ˈʌpə*] *adj* superiore ♦ *n* (*of shoe*) tomaia; **~-class** *adj* dell'alta borghesia; ~ **hand** *n*: **to have the ~ hand** avere il coltello dalla parte del manico; **~most** *adj* il(la) più alto(a); predominante
upright [ˈʌpraɪt] *adj* diritto(a); verticale; (*fig*) diritto(a), onesto(a)

prising [ˈʌpraızıŋ] n insurrezione f, rivolta

proar [ˈʌprɔ:*] n tumulto, clamore m

proot [ʌpˈru:t] vt sradicare

pset [n ˈʌpset, vb, adj ʌpˈset] (irreg: like set) n (to plan etc) contrattempo; (stomach ~) disturbo ♦ vt (glass etc) rovesciare; (plan, stomach) scombussolare; (person: offend) contrariare; (: grieve) addolorare; sconvolgere ♦ adj contrariato(a); addolorato(a); (stomach) scombussolato(a)

pshot [ˈʌpʃɔt] n risultato

pside down [ˈʌpsaid-] adv sottosopra

pstairs [ʌpˈstɛəz] adv, adj di sopra, al piano superiore ♦ n piano di sopra

pstart [ˈʌpstɑ:t] n parvenu m inv

pstream [ʌpˈstri:m] adv a monte

ptake [ˈʌpteɪk] n: he is quick/slow on the ~ è pronto/lento di comprendonio

ptight [ʌpˈtaɪt] (inf) adj teso(a)

p-to-date adj moderno(a); aggiornato(a)

pturn [ˈʌptə:n] n (in luck) svolta favorevole, (COMM: in trade) rialzo

pward [ˈʌpwəd] adj ascendente; verso l'alto; **~(s)** adv in su, verso l'alto

rban [ˈə:bən] adj urbano(a)

rbane [ə:ˈbeɪn] adj civile, urbano(a), educato(a)

rchin [ˈə:tʃɪn] n monello

rge [ə:dʒ] n impulso; stimolo; forte desiderio ♦ vt: to ~ sb to do esortare qn a fare, spingere qn a fare; raccomandare a qn di fare

rgency [ˈə:dʒənsɪ] n urgenza; (of tone) insistenza

rgent [ˈə:dʒənt] adj urgente; (voice) insistente

rinate [ˈjuərɪneɪt] vi orinare

rine [ˈjuərɪn] n orina

rn [ə:n] n urna; (also: tea ~) bollitore m per il tè

s [ʌs] pron ci; (stressed, after prep) noi; see also **me**

S(A) n abbr (= United States (of America)) USA mpl

sage [ˈju:zɪdʒ] n uso ♦

se [n ju:s, vb ju:z] n uso; impiego; utilizzazione f ♦ vt usare, utilizzare, servirsi di; **in ~** in uso; **out of ~** fuori

uso; **to be of ~** essere utile, servire; **it's no ~** non serve, è inutile; **she ~d to do it** lo faceva (una volta), era solita farlo; **to be ~d to** avere l'abitudine di; **~ up** vt consumare; esaurire; **~d** adj (object, car) usato(a); **~ful** adj utile; **~fulness** n utilità; **~less** adj inutile; (person) inetto(a); **~r** n utente m/f; **~r-friendly** adj (computer) di facile uso

usher [ˈʌʃə*] n usciere m; **~ette** [-ˈrɛt] n (in cinema) maschera

USSR n: **the ~** l'URSS f

usual [ˈju:ʒuəl] adj solito(a); **as ~** come al solito, come d'abitudine; **~ly** adv di solito

utensil [ju:ˈtɛnsl] n utensile m; **kitchen ~s** utensili da cucina

uterus [ˈju:tərəs] n utero

utility [ju:ˈtɪlɪtɪ] n utilità; (also: public ~) servizio pubblico; **~ room** n locale adibito alla stiratura dei panni etc

utmost [ˈʌtməust] adj estremo(a) ♦ n: to do one's ~ fare il possibile or di tutto

utter [ˈʌtə*] adj assoluto(a), totale ♦ vt pronunciare, proferire; emettere; **~ance** n espressione f; parole fpl; **~ly** adv completamente, del tutto

U-turn [ˈju:ˈtə:n] n inversione f a U

V

v. abbr = **verse**; **versus**; **volt**; (= vide) vedi, vedere

vacancy [ˈveɪkənsɪ] n (BRIT: job) posto libero; (room) stanza libera

vacant [ˈveɪkənt] adj (job, seat etc) libero(a); (expression) assente; **~ lot** (US) n terreno non occupato; (for sale) terreno in vendita

vacate [vəˈkeɪt] vt lasciare libero(a)

vacation [vəˈkeɪʃən] (esp US) n vacanze fpl

vaccinate [ˈvæksɪneɪt] vt vaccinare

vacuum [ˈvækjum] n vuoto; **~ cleaner** n aspirapolvere m inv; **~-packed** adj confezionato(a) sottovuoto

vagina [vəˈdʒaɪnə] n vagina

vagrant [ˈveɪgrnt] n vagabondo/a

vague [veɪg] adj vago(a); (blurred: photo,

memory) sfocato(a); **~ly** *adv* vagamente

vain [veɪn] *adj (useless)* inutile, vano(a); *(conceited)* vanitoso(a); **in ~** inutilmente, invano

valentine ['væləntaɪn] *n (also:* ~ *card)* cartolina *or* biglietto di San Valentino; *(person)* innamorato/a

valet ['væleɪ] *n* cameriere *m* personale

valiant ['væliənt] *adj* valoroso(a), coraggioso(a)

valid ['vælɪd] *adj* valido(a), valevole; *(excuse)* valido(a)

valley ['vælɪ] *n* valle *f*

valour ['vælə*] *(US* **valor)** *n* valore *m*

valuable ['væljuəbl] *adj (jewel)* di (grande) valore; *(time, help)* prezioso(a); **~s** *npl* oggetti *mpl* di valore

valuation [vælju'eɪʃən] *n* valutazione *f*, stima

value ['vælju:] *n* valore *m* ♦ *vt (fix price)* valutare, dare un prezzo a; *(cherish)* apprezzare, tenere a; **~ added tax** *(BRIT) n* imposta sul valore aggiunto; **~d** *adj (appreciated)* stimato(a), apprezzato(a)

valve [vælv] *n* valvola

van [væn] *n (AUT)* furgone *m*; *(BRIT: RAIL)* vagone *m*

vandal ['vændl] *n* vandalo/a; **~ism** *n* vandalismo

vanilla [və'nɪlə] *n* vaniglia ♦ *cpd (ice cream)* alla vaniglia

vanish ['vænɪʃ] *vi* svanire, scomparire

vanity ['vænɪtɪ] *n* vanità

vantage ['vɑ:ntɪdʒ] *n*: **~ point** posizione *f or* punto di osservazione; *(fig)* posizione vantaggiosa

vapour ['veɪpə*] *(US* **vapor)** *n* vapore *m*

variable ['vɛərɪəbl] *adj* variabile; *(mood)* mutevole

variance ['vɛərɪəns] *n*: **to be at ~ (with)** essere in disaccordo (con); *(facts)* essere in contraddizione (con)

varicose ['værɪkəus] *adj*: **~ veins** vene *fpl* varicose

varied ['vɛərɪd] *adj* vario(a), diverso(a)

variety [və'raɪətɪ] *n* varietà *f inv*; *(quantity)* quantità, numero; **~ show** *n* varietà *m inv*

various ['vɛərɪəs] *adj* vario(a), diverso(a);

(several) parecchi(e), molti(e)

varnish ['vɑ:nɪʃ] *n* vernice *f*; *(nail* ~) smalto ♦ *vt* verniciare; mettere lo smalto su

vary ['vɛərɪ] *vt, vi* variare, mutare

vase [vɑ:z] *n* vaso

Vaseline ['væsɪli:n] ® *n* vaselina

vast [vɑ:st] *adj* vasto(a); *(amount, success)* enorme

VAT [væt] *n abbr (= value added tax)* I.V.A. *f*

vat [væt] *n* tino

Vatican ['vætɪkən] *n*: **the ~** il Vaticano

vault [vɔ:lt] *n (of roof)* volta; *(tomb)* tomba; *(in bank)* camera blindata ♦ *vt (also:* ~ *over)* saltare (d'un balzo)

vaunted ['vɔ:ntɪd] *adj*: **much-~** tanto celebrato(a)

VCR *n abbr* = **video cassette recorder**

VD *n abbr* = **venereal disease**

VDU *n abbr* = **visual display unit**

veal [vi:l] *n* vitello

veer [vɪə*] *vi* girare; virare

vegeburger ['vedʒɪbз:gз*] *n* hamburger *m inv* vegetariano

vegetable ['vedʒtəbl] *n* verdura, ortaggi ♦ *adj* vegetale

vegetarian [vedʒɪ'tɛərɪən] *adj, n* vegetariano/a

vehement ['vi:ɪmənt] *adj* veemente, violento(a)

vehicle ['vi:ɪkl] *n* veicolo

veil [veɪl] *n* velo; **~ed** *adj (fig: threat)* velato(a)

vein [veɪn] *n* vena; *(on leaf)* nervatura

velvet ['vɛlvɪt] *n* velluto ♦ *adj* di velluto

vending machine ['vɛndɪŋ-] *n* distributore *m* automatico

vendor ['vɛndə*] *n* venditore/trice

veneer [və'nɪə*] *n* impiallacciatura; *(fig)* vernice *f*

venereal [vɪ'nɪərɪəl] *adj*: **~ disease** malattia venerea

Venetian [vɪ'ni:ʃən] *adj* veneziano(a); **~ blind** *n* (tenda alla) veneziana

vengeance ['vɛndʒəns] *n* vendetta; **with a ~** *(fig)* davvero; furiosamente

Venice ['vɛnɪs] *n* Venezia

venison ['vɛnɪsn] *n* carne *f* di cervo

venom ['vɛnəm] n veleno

vent [vɛnt] n foro, apertura; (in dress, jacket) spacco ♦ vt (fig: one's feelings) sfogare, dare sfogo a

ventilate ['vɛntɪleɪt] vt (room) dare aria a, arieggiare; **ventilator** n ventilatore m

ventriloquist [vɛn'trɪləkwɪst] n ventriloquo/a

venture ['vɛntʃə*] n impresa (rischiosa) ♦ vt rischiare, azzardare ♦ vi avventurarsi; **business ~** iniziativa commerciale

venue ['vɛnjuː] n luogo (designato) per l'incontro

verb [vəːb] n verbo; **~al** adj verbale; (translation) orale

verbatim [vəː'beɪtɪm] adj, adv parola per parola

verdict ['vəːdɪkt] n verdetto

verge [vəːdʒ] (BRIT) n bordo, orlo; **"soft ~s"** (BRIT: AUT) banchine fpl cedevoli; **on the ~ of doing** sul punto di fare; **~ on** vt fus rasentare

veritable ['vɛrɪtəbl] adj vero(a)

vermin ['vəːmɪn] npl animali mpl nocivi; (insects) insetti mpl parassiti

vermouth ['vəːməθ] n vermut m inv

versatile ['vəːsətaɪl] adj (person) versatile; (machine, tool etc) (che si presta) a molti usi

verse [vəːs] n versi mpl; (stanza) stanza, strofa; (in Bible) versetto

versed [vəːst] adj: **(well-)~ in** pratico(a) di

version ['vəːʃən] n versione f

versus ['vəːsəs] prep contro

vertical ['vəːtɪkl] adj verticale ♦ n verticale m; **~ly** adv verticalmente

vertigo ['vəːtɪɡəʊ] n vertigine f

verve [vəːv] n brio; entusiasmo

very ['vɛrɪ] adv molto ♦ adj: **the ~ book which** proprio il libro che; **the ~ last** proprio l'ultimo; **at the ~ least** almeno; **~ much** moltissimo

vessel ['vɛsl] n (ANAT) vaso; (NAUT) nave f; (container) recipiente m

vest [vɛst] n (BRIT) maglia; (: sleeveless) canottiera; (US: waistcoat) gilè m inv

vested interests ['vɛstɪd-] npl (COMM) diritti mpl acquisiti

vet [vɛt] n abbr (BRIT: = veterinary surgeon) veterinario ♦ vt esaminare minuziosamente

veteran ['vɛtərn] n (also: war ~) veterano

veterinary ['vɛtrɪnərɪ] adj veterinario(a); **~ surgeon** (US **veterinarian**) n veterinario

veto ['viːtəu] (pl ~es) n veto ♦ vt opporre il veto a

vex [vɛks] vt irritare, contrariare; **~ed** adj (question) controverso(a), dibattuto(a)

via ['vaɪə] prep (by way of) via; (by means of) tramite

viable ['vaɪəbl] adj attuabile; vitale

viaduct ['vaɪədʌkt] n viadotto

vibrant ['vaɪbrənt] adj (lively, bright) vivace; (voice) vibrante

vibrate [vaɪ'breɪt] vi: **to ~ (with)** vibrare (di); (resound) risonare (di)

vicar ['vɪkə*] n pastore m; **~age** n presbiterio

vicarious [vɪ'kɛərɪəs] adj indiretto(a)

vice [vaɪs] n (evil) vizio; (TECH) morsa

vice- [vaɪs] prefix vice...

vice squad n (squadra del) buon costume f

vice versa ['vaɪsɪ'vəːsə] adv viceversa

vicinity [vɪ'sɪnɪtɪ] n vicinanze fpl

vicious ['vɪʃəs] adj (remark, dog) cattivo(a); (blow) violento(a); **~ circle** n circolo vizioso

victim ['vɪktɪm] n vittima

victor ['vɪktə*] n vincitore m

Victorian [vɪk'tɔːrɪən] adj vittoriano(a)

victory ['vɪktərɪ] n vittoria

video ['vɪdɪəu] cpd video... ♦ n (~ film) video m inv; (also: ~ cassette) videocassetta; (also: ~ cassette recorder) videoregistratore m; **~ tape** n videotape m inv

vie [vaɪ] vi: **to ~ with** competere con, rivaleggiare con

Vienna [vɪ'ɛnə] n Vienna

Vietnam [vjɛt'næm] n Vietnam m; **~ese** adj, n inv vietnamita m/f

view [vjuː] n vista, veduta; (opinion) opinione f ♦ vt (look at: also fig) considerare; (house) visitare; **on ~** (in *museum etc*) esposto(a); **in full** ~ **of** sotto gli occhi di; **in** ~ **of the weather/the fact that** considerato il tempo/che; **in my** ~ a mio parere; **~er** *n* spettatore/trice; **~finder** *n* mirino; **~point** *n* punto di vista; (*place*) posizione *f*

vigil ['vɪdʒɪl] *n* veglia

vigorous ['vɪgərəs] *adj* vigoroso(a)

vile [vaɪl] *n* (*action*) vile; (*smell*) disgustoso(a), nauseante; (*temper*) pessimo(a)

villa ['vɪlə] *n* villa

village ['vɪlɪdʒ] *n* villaggio; **~r** *n* abitante *m/f* di villaggio

villain ['vɪlən] *n* (*scoundrel*) canaglia; (*BRIT: criminal*) criminale *m*; (*in novel etc*) cattivo

vindicate ['vɪndɪkeɪt] *vt* comprovare; giustificare

vindictive [vɪn'dɪktɪv] *adj* vendicativo(a)

vine [vaɪn] *n* vite *f*; (*climbing plant*) rampicante *m*

vinegar ['vɪnɪgə*] *n* aceto

vineyard ['vɪnjɑːd] *n* vigna, vigneto

vintage ['vɪntɪdʒ] *n* (*year*) annata, produzione *f* ♦ *cpd* d'annata; **~ car** *n* auto *f inv* d'epoca; **~ wine** *n* vino d'annata

vinyl ['vaɪnl] *n* vinile *m*

violate ['vaɪəleɪt] *vt* violare

violence ['vaɪələns] *n* violenza

violent ['vaɪələnt] *adj* violento(a)

violet ['vaɪələt] *adj* (*colour*) viola *inv*, violetto(a) ♦ *n* (*plant*) violetta; (*colour*) violetto

violin [vaɪə'lɪn] *n* violino; **~ist** *n* violinista *m/f*

VIP *n abbr* (= *very important person*) V.I.P. *m/f inv*

virgin ['vəːdʒɪn] *n* vergine *f* ♦ *adj* vergine *inv*

Virgo ['vəːgəu] *n* (*sign*) Vergine *f*

virile ['vɪraɪl] *adj* virile

virtual reality ['vəːtʃuəl -] *n* (*COMPUT*) realtà virtuale

virtually ['vəːtjuəlɪ] *adv* (*almost*) praticamente

virtue ['vəːtjuː] *n* virtù *f inv*; (*advantage*) pregio, vantaggio; **by** ~ **of** grazie a

virtuous ['vəːtjuəs] *adj* virtuoso(a)

virus ['vaɪərəs] *n* (*also COMPUT*) virus *m inv*

visa ['viːzə] *n* visto

vis-à-vis [viːzə'viː] *prep* rispetto a, nei riguardi di

visibility [vɪzɪ'bɪlɪtɪ] *n* visibilità

visible ['vɪzəbl] *adj* visibile

vision ['vɪʒən] *n* (*sight*) vista; (*foresight, in dream*) visione *f*

visit ['vɪzɪt] *n* visita; (*stay*) soggiorno ♦ *vt* (*person: US also:* ~ **with**) andare a trovare; (*place*) visitare; **~ing hours** *npl* (*in hospital etc*) orario delle visite; **~or** *n* visitatore/trice; (*guest*) ospite *m/f*

visor ['vaɪzə*] *n* visiera

vista ['vɪstə] *n* vista, prospettiva

visual ['vɪzjuəl] *adj* visivo(a); visuale; ottico(a); ~ **aid** *n* sussidio visivo; ~ **display unit** *n* visualizzatore *m*

visualize ['vɪzjuəlaɪz] *vt* immaginare, figurarsi; (*foresee*) prevedere

vital ['vaɪtl] *adj* vitale; **~ly** *adv* estremamente; ~ **statistics** *npl* (*fig*) misure *fpl*

vitamin ['vɪtəmɪn] *n* vitamina

vivacious [vɪ'veɪʃəs] *adj* vivace

vivid ['vɪvɪd] *adj* vivido(a); **~ly** *adv* (*describe*) vividamente; (*remember*) con precisione

V-neck ['viːnɛk] *n* maglione *m* con lo scollo a V

vocabulary [vəu'kæbjulərɪ] *n* vocabolario

vocal ['vəukl] *adj* (*MUS*) vocale; (*communication*) verbale; ~ **cords** *npl* corde *fpl* vocali

vocation [vəu'keɪʃən] *n* vocazione *f*; **~al** *adj* professionale

vociferous [və'sɪfərəs] *adj* rumoroso(a)

vodka ['vɔdkə] *n* vodka *f inv*

vogue [vəug] *n* moda; (*popularity*) popolarità, voga

voice [vɔɪs] *n* voce *f* ♦ *vt* (*opinion*) esprimere

void [vɔɪd] *n* vuoto ♦ *adj* (*invalid*) nullo(a); (*empty*): ~ **of** privo(a) di

volatile ['vɔlətaɪl] *adj* volatile; (*fig*) volubile

volcano [vɔl'keɪnəu] (*pl* ~**es**) *n* vulcano

volition [vəˈlɪʃən] *n*: of one's own ~ di sua volontà

volley [ˈvɒlɪ] *n* (*of gunfire*) salva; (*of stones, questions etc*) raffica; (*TENNIS etc*) volata; **~ball** *n* pallavolo *f*

volt [vəʊlt] *n* volt *m inv*; **~age** *n* tensione *f*, voltaggio

voluble [ˈvɒljʊbl] *adj* loquace, ciarliero(a)

volume [ˈvɒljuːm] *n* volume *m*

voluntarily [ˈvɒləntrɪlɪ] *adv* volontariamente; gratuitamente

voluntary [ˈvɒləntərɪ] *adj* volontario(a); (*unpaid*) gratuito(a), non retribuito(a)

volunteer [vɒlənˈtɪə*] *n* volontario/a ♦ *vt* offrire volontariamente ♦ *vi* (*MIL*) arruolarsi volontario; **to ~ to do** offrire (volontariamente) di fare

voluptuous [vəˈlʌptjʊəs] *adj* voluttuoso(a)

vomit [ˈvɒmɪt] *n* vomito ♦ *vt*, *vi* vomitare

vote [vəʊt] *n* voto, suffragio; (*cast*) voto; (*franchise*) diritto di voto ♦ *vt*: **to be ~d chairman** *etc* venir eletto presidente *etc*; (*propose*): **to ~ that** approvare la proposta che ♦ *vi* votare; **~ of thanks** discorso di ringraziamento; **~r** *n* elettore/trice; **voting** *n* scrutinio

vouch [vaʊtʃ]: **to ~ for** *vt fus* farsi garante di

voucher [ˈvaʊtʃə*] *n* (*for meal, petrol etc*) buono

vow [vaʊ] *n* voto, promessa solenne ♦ *vt*: **to ~ to do/that** giurare di fare/che

vowel [ˈvaʊəl] *n* vocale *f*

voyage [ˈvɔɪdʒ] *n* viaggio per mare, traversata

V-sign [ˈviː-] (*BRIT*) *n* gesto volgare con le dita

vulgar [ˈvʌlgə*] *adj* volgare

vulnerable [ˈvʌlnərəbl] *adj* vulnerabile

vulture [ˈvʌltʃə*] *n* avvoltoio

W

wad [wɒd] *n* (*of cotton wool, paper*) tampone *m*; (*of banknotes etc*) fascio

waddle [ˈwɒdl] *vi* camminare come una papera

wade [weɪd] *vi*: **to ~ through** camminare a stento in; (*fig*: *book*) leggere con fatica

wafer [ˈweɪfə*] *n* (*CULIN*) cialda

waffle [ˈwɒfl] *n* (*CULIN*) cialda; (*inf*) ciance *fpl* ♦ *vi* cianciare

waft [wɒft] *vt* portare ♦ *vi* diffondersi

wag [wæg] *vt* agitare, muovere ♦ *vi* agitarsi

wage [weɪdʒ] *n* (*also*: ~s) salario, paga ♦ *vt*: **to ~ war** fare la guerra; **~ earner** *n* salariato/a; **~ packet** *n* busta *f* paga *inv*

wager [ˈweɪdʒə*] *n* scommessa

waggle [ˈwægl] *vt* dimenare, agitare

wag(g)on [ˈwægən] *n* (*horse-drawn*) carro; (*BRIT*: *RAIL*) vagone *m* (merci)

wail [weɪl] *n* gemito; (*of siren*) urlo ♦ *vi* gemere; urlare

waist [weɪst] *n* vita, cintola; **~coat** (*BRIT*) *n* panciotto, gilè *m inv*; **~line** *n* (giro di) vita

wait [weɪt] *n* attesa ♦ *vi* aspettare, attendere; **to lie in ~ for** stare in agguato a; **to ~ for** aspettare; **I can't ~ to** (*fig*) non vedo l'ora di; **~ behind** *vi* rimanere (ad aspettare); **~ on** *vt fus* servire; **~er** *n* cameriere *m*; **~ing** *n*: "**no ~ing**" (*BRIT*: *AUT*) "divieto di sosta"; **~ing list** *n* lista di attesa; **~ing room** *n* sala d'aspetto *or* d'attesa; **~ress** *n* cameriera

waive [weɪv] *vt* rinunciare a, abbandonare

wake [weɪk] (*pt* woke, ~d, *pp* woken, ~d) *vt* (*also*: ~ up) svegliare ♦ *vi* (*also*: ~ up) svegliarsi ♦ *n* (*for dead person*) veglia funebre; (*NAUT*) scia; **waken** *vt*, *vi* = **wake**

Wales [weɪlz] *n* Galles *m*

walk [wɔːk] *n* passeggiata; (*short*) giretto; (*gait*) passo, andatura; (*path*) sentiero; (*in park etc*) sentiero, vialetto ♦ *vi* camminare; (*for pleasure, exercise*) passeggiare ♦ *vt* (*distance*) fare *or* percorrere a piedi; (*dog*) accompagnare, portare a passeggiare; **10 minutes' ~ from** 10 minuti di cammino *or* a piedi da; **from all ~s of life** di tutte le condizioni sociali; **~ out** *vi* (*audience*) andarsene; (*workers*) scendere in sciopero; **~ out on** (*inf*) *vt fus* piantare in asso; **~er** *n*

(*person*) camminatore/trice; **~ie-talkie**
['wɔːkɪ'tɔːkɪ] *n* walkie-talkie *m inv*; **~ing**
n camminare *m*; **~ing shoes** *npl* pedule
fpl; **~ing stick** *n* bastone *m* da passeggio;
~out *n* (*of workers*) sciopero senza
preavviso *or* a sorpresa; **~over** (*inf*) *n*
vittoria facile, gioco da ragazzi; **~way** *n*
passaggio pedonale

wall [wɔːl] *n* muro; (*internal, of tunnel,*
cave) parete *f*; **~ed** *adj* (*city*) fortificato(a);
(*garden*) cintato(a)

wallet ['wɔlɪt] *n* portafoglio

wallflower ['wɔːlflauə*] *n* violacciocca;
to be a ~ (*fig*) fare da tappezzeria

wallop ['wɔləp] (*inf*) *vt* pestare

wallow ['wɔləu] *vi* sguazzare

wallpaper ['wɔːlpeɪpə*] *n* carta da parati
♦ *vt* (*room*) mettere la carta da parati in

wally ['wɔlɪ] (*inf*) *n* imbecille *m/f*

walnut ['wɔːlnʌt] *n* noce *f*; (*tree, wood*)
noce *m*

walrus ['wɔːlrəs] (*pl* ~ *or* ~**es**) *n* tricheco

waltz [wɔːlts] *n* valzer *m inv* ♦ *vi* ballare
il valzer

wan [wɔn] *adj* pallido(a), smorto(a); triste

wand [wɔnd] *n* (*also: magic* ~) bacchetta
(magica)

wander ['wɔndə*] *vi* (*person*) girare
senza meta, girovagare; (*thoughts*) vagare
♦ *vt* girovagare per

wane [weɪn] *vi* calare

wangle [wæŋgl] (*BRIT: inf*) *vt* procurare
con l'astuzia

want [wɔnt] *vt* volere; (*need*) aver
bisogno di ♦ *n*: **for ~ of** per mancanza di;
~s *npl* (*needs*) bisogni *mpl*; **to ~ to do**
volere fare; **to ~ sb to do** volere che qn
faccia; **~ed** *adj* (*criminal*) ricercato(a);
"**~ed**" (*in adverts*) "cercasi"; **~ing** *adj*: **to**
be found ~ing non risultare all'altezza

wanton ['wɔntn] *adj* sfrenato(a); senza
motivo

war [wɔː*] *n* guerra; **to make ~ (on)** far
guerra (a)

ward [wɔːd] *n* (*in hospital: room*) corsia;
(: *section*) reparto; (*POL*) circoscrizione *f*;
(*LAW: child: also:* ~ *of court*) pupillo/a; **~**
off *vt* parare, schivare

warden ['wɔːdn] *n* (*of park, game reserve,*

youth hostel) guardiano/a; (*BRIT: of*
institution) direttore/trice; (*BRIT: also:*
traffic ~) addetto/a al controllo del
traffico e del parcheggio

warder ['wɔːdə*] (*BRIT*) *n* guardia
carceraria

wardrobe ['wɔːdrəub] *n* (*cupboard*)
guardaroba *m inv*, armadio; (*clothes*)
guardaroba; (*CINEMA, THEATRE*) costumi *mpl*

warehouse ['wɛəhaus] *n* magazzino

wares [wɛəz] *npl* merci *fpl*

warfare ['wɔːfɛə*] *n* guerra

warhead ['wɔːhɛd] *n* (*MIL*) testata

warily ['wɛərɪlɪ] *adv* cautamente, con
prudenza

warlike ['wɔːlaɪk] *adj* bellicoso(a)

warm [wɔːm] *adj* caldo(a); (*thanks,*
welcome, applause) caloroso(a); (*person*)
cordiale; **it's** ~ fa caldo; **I'm** ~ ho caldo; ~
up *vi* scaldarsi, riscaldarsi ♦ *vt* scaldare,
riscaldare; (*engine*) far scaldare; **~-**
hearted *adj* affettuoso(a); **~ly** *adv*
(*applaud, welcome*) calorosamente; (*dress*)
con abiti pesanti; **~th** *n* calore *m*

warn [wɔːn] *vt*: **to ~ sb that/(not) to**
do/of avvertire *or* avvisare qn che/di
(non) fare/di; **~ing** *n* avvertimento;
(*notice*) avviso; (*signal*) segnalazione *f*;
~ing light *n* spia luminosa; **~ing**
triangle *n* (*AUT*) triangolo

warp [wɔːp] *vi* deformarsi ♦ *vt* (*fig*)
corrompere

warrant ['wɔrnt] *n* (*voucher*) buono; (*LAW:*
to arrest) mandato di cattura; (: *to search*)
mandato di perquisizione

warranty ['wɔrəntɪ] *n* garanzia

warren ['wɔrən] *n* (*of rabbits*) tana; (*fig:*
of streets etc) dedalo

warrior ['wɔrɪə*] *n* guerriero/a

Warsaw ['wɔːsɔː] *n* Varsavia

warship ['wɔːʃɪp] *n* nave *f* da guerra

wart [wɔːt] *n* verruca

wartime ['wɔːtaɪm] *n*: **in ~** in tempo di
guerra

wary ['wɛərɪ] *adj* prudente

was [wɔz] *pt of* **be**

wash [wɔʃ] *vt* lavare ♦ *vi* lavarsi; (*sea*):
to ~ over/against sth infrangersi su/
contro qc ♦ *n* lavaggio; (*of ship*) scia; **to**

give sth a ~ lavare qc, dare una lavata a qc; **to have a ~** lavarsi; **~ away***vt* (*stain*) togliere lavando; (*subj: river*) trascinare via; **~ off***vi* andare via con il lavaggio; **~ up***vi* (*BRIT*) lavare i piatti; (*US*) darsi una lavata; **~able***adj* lavabile; **~basin** (*US* **~bowl**) *n* lavabo; **~cloth** (*US*) *n* pezzuola (per lavarsi); **~er** *n* (*TECH*) rondella; **~ing** *n* (*linen etc*) bucato; **~ing machine** *n* lavatrice *f*; **~ing powder** (*BRIT*) *n* detersivo (in polvere)

Washington ['wɔʃɪŋtən] *n* Washington *f*

wash: ~ing up *n* rigovernatura, lavatura dei piatti; **~ing-up liquid** *n* detersivo liquido (per stoviglie); **~-out** (*inf*) *n* disastro; **~room** *n* gabinetto

wasn't ['wɔznt] = **was not**

wasp [wɔsp] *n* vespa

wastage ['weɪstɪdʒ] *n* spreco; (*in manufacturing*) scarti *mpl*; **natural ~** diminuzione *f* di manodopera (*per pensionamento, decesso etc*)

waste [weɪst] *n* spreco; (*of time*) perdita; (*rubbish*) rifiuti *mpl*; (*also: household ~*) immondizie *fpl* ♦ *adj* (*material*) di scarto; (*food*) avanzato(a); (*land*) incolto(a) ♦ *vt* sprecare; **~s** *npl* (*area of land*) distesa desolata; **~ away** *vi* deperire; **~ disposal unit** (*BRIT*) *n* eliminatore *m* di rifiuti; **~ful** *adj* sprecone(a); (*process*) dispendioso(a); **~ ground** (*BRIT*) *n* terreno incolto *or* abbandonato; **~paper basket** *n* cestino per la carta straccia; **~pipe** *n* tubo di scarico

watch [wɔtʃ] *n* (*also: wrist ~*) orologio (da polso); (*act of watching, vigilance*) sorveglianza; (*guard*: MIL, NAUT) guardia; (*NAUT: spell of duty*) quarto ♦ *vt* (*look at*) osservare, guardare; (*: match, programme*) guardare; (*spy on, guard*) sorvegliare, tenere d'occhio; (*be careful of*) fare attenzione a ♦ *vi* osservare, guardare; (*keep guard*) fare *or* montare la guardia; **~ out** *vi* fare attenzione; **~dog** *n* (*also fig*) cane *m* da guardia; **~ful** *adj* attento(a), vigile; **~maker** *n* orologiaio/a; **~man** *n see* **night**; **~ strap** *n* cinturino per orologio

water ['wɔːtə*] *n* acqua ♦ *vt* (*plant*) annaffiare ♦ *vi* (*eyes*) lacrimare; (*mouth*):

to make sb's mouth ~ far venire l'acquolina in bocca a qn; **in British ~s** nelle acque territoriali britanniche; **~ down** *vt* (*milk*) diluire; (*fig: story*) edulcorare; **~ cannon** *n* idrante *m*; **~ closet** (*BRIT*) *n* water *m inv*; **~colour** *n* acquerello; **~cress** *n* crescione *m*; **~fall** *n* cascata; **~ heater** *n* scaldabagno; **~ing can** *n* annaffiatoio; **~ lily** *n* ninfea; **~line** *n* (*NAUT*) linea di galleggiamento; **~logged** *adj* saturo(a) d'acqua; imbevuto(a) d'acqua; (*football pitch etc*) allagato(a); **~ main** *n* conduttura dell'acqua; **~melon** *n* anguria, cocomero; **~proof** *adj* impermeabile; **~shed** *n* (GEO, *fig*) spartiacque *m*; **~-skiing** *n* sci *m* acquatico; **~tight** *adj* stagno(a); **~way** *n* corso d'acqua navigabile; **~works** *npl* impianto idrico; **~y** *adj* (*colour*) slavato(a); (*coffee*) acquoso(a); (*eyes*) umido(a)

watt [wɔt] *n* watt *m inv*

wave [weɪv] *n* onda; (*of hand*) gesto, segno; (*in hair*) ondulazione *f*; (*fig: surge*) ondata ♦ *vi* fare un cenno con la mano; (*branches, grass*) ondeggiare; (*flag*) sventolare ♦ *vt* (*hand*) fare un gesto con; (*handkerchief*) sventolare; (*stick*) brandire; **~length** *n* lunghezza d'onda

waver ['weɪvə*] *vi* esitare; (*voice*) tremolare

wavy ['weɪvɪ] *adj* ondulato(a); ondeggiante

wax [wæks] *n* cera ♦ *vt* dare la cera a; (*car*) lucidare ♦ *vi* (*moon*) crescere; **~works** *npl* cere *fpl* ♦ *n* museo delle cere

way [weɪ] *n* via, strada; (*path, access*) passaggio; (*distance*) distanza; (*direction*) parte *f*, direzione *f*; (*manner*) modo, stile *m*; (*habit*) abitudine *f*; **which ~? - this ~** da che parte *or* in quale direzione? – da questa parte *or* per di qua; **on the ~** (*en route*) per strada; **to be on one's ~** essere in cammino *or* sulla strada; **to be in the ~** bloccare il passaggio; (*fig*) essere tra i piedi *or* d'impiccio; **to go out of one's ~ to do** (*fig*) mettercela tutta *or* fare di tutto per fare; **under ~** (*project*) in corso; **to lose one's ~** perdere la strada; **in a ~**

in un certo senso; **in some ~s** sotto certi aspetti; **no ~!** (*inf*) neanche per idea!; **by the ~ ...** a proposito ...; **"~ in"** (*BRIT*) "entrata", "ingresso"; **"~ out"** (*BRIT*) "uscita"; **the ~ back** la strada del ritorno; **"give ~"** (*BRIT: AUT*) "dare la precedenza"

waylay [weɪ'leɪ] (*irreg: like* lay) *vt* tendere un agguato a; attendere al passaggio

wayward ['weɪwəd] *adj* capriccioso(a); testardo(a)

W.C. ['dʌblju:'si:] (*BRIT*) *n* W.C. *m inv*, gabinetto

we [wi:] *pl pron* noi

weak [wi:k] *adj* debole; (*health*) precario(a); (*beam etc*) fragile; (*tea*) leggero(a); **~en** *vi* indebolirsi ♦ *vt* indebolire; **~ling** ['wi:klɪŋ] *n* smidollato/a; debole *m/f*; **~ness** *n* debolezza; (*fault*) punto debole, difetto; **to have a ~ness for** avere un debole per

wealth [welθ] *n* (*money, resources*) ricchezza, ricchezze *fpl*; (*of details*) abbondanza, profusione *f*; **~y** *adj* ricco(a)

wean [wi:n] *vt* svezzare

weapon ['wepən] *n* arma

wear [wɛə*] (*pt* wore, *pp* worn) *n* (*use*) uso; (*damage through use*) logorio, usura; (*clothing*): **sports/baby ~** abbigliamento sportivo/per neonati ♦ *vt* (*clothes*) portare; (*put on*) mettersi; (*damage: through use*) consumare ♦ *vi* (*last*) durare; (*rub etc through*) consumarsi; **evening ~** abiti *mpl* or tenuta da sera; **~ away** *vt* consumare; erodere ♦ *vi* consumarsi; essere eroso(a); **~ down** *vt* consumare; (*strength*) esaurire; **~ off** *vi* sparire lentamente; **~ out** *vt* consumare; (*person, strength*) esaurire; **~ and tear** *n* usura, consumo

weary ['wɪərɪ] *adj* stanco(a) ♦ *vi*: **to ~ of** stancarsi di

weasel ['wi:zl] *n* (*ZOOL*) donnola

weather ['wɛðə*] *n* tempo ♦ *vt* (*storm, crisis*) superare; **under the ~** (*fig: ill*) poco bene; **~-beaten** *adj* (*face, skin*) segnato(a) dalle intemperie; (*building*) logorato(a) dalle intemperie; **~cock** *n*

banderuola; **~ forecast** *n* previsioni *fpl* del tempo, bollettino meteorologico; **~man** (*inf*) *n* meteorologo; **~ vane** *n* = **~cock**

weave [wi:v] (*pt* wove, *pp* woven) *vt* (*cloth*) tessere; (*basket*) intrecciare; **~r** *n* tessitore/trice; **weaving** *n* tessitura

web [web] *n* (*of spider*) ragnatela; (*on foot*) palma; (*fabric, also fig*) tessuto

wed [wed] (*pt, pp* wedded) *vt* sposare ♦ *vi* sposarsi

we'd [wi:d] = **we had**; **we would**

wedding ['wedɪŋ] *n* matrimonio; **silver/ golden ~** (*anniversary*) *n* nozze *fpl* d'argento/d'oro; **~ day** *n* giorno delle nozze o del matrimonio; **~ dress** *n* abito nuziale; **~ ring** *n* fede *f*

wedge [wedʒ] *n* (*of wood etc*) zeppa; (*of cake*) fetta ♦ *vt* (*fix*) fissare con zeppe; (*pack tightly*) incastrare

Wednesday ['wednzdɪ] *n* mercoledì *m inv*

wee [wi:] (*SCOTTISH*) *adj* piccolo(a)

weed [wi:d] *n* erbaccia ♦ *vt* diserbare; **~killer** *n* diserbante *m*; **~y** *adj* (*person*) allampanato/a

week [wi:k] *n* settimana; **a ~ today/on Friday** oggi/venerdì a otto; **~day** *n* giorno feriale; (*COMM*) giornata lavorativa; **~end** *n* fine settimana *m or f inv*, weekend *m inv*; **~ly** *adv* ogni settimana, settimanalmente ♦ *adj* settimanale ♦ *n* settimanale *m*

weep [wi:p] (*pt, pp* wept) *vi* (*person*) piangere; **~ing willow** *n* salice *m* piangente

weigh [weɪ] *vt, vi* pesare; **to ~ anchor** salpare l'ancora; **~ down** *vt* (*branch*) piegare; (*fig: with worry*) opprimere, caricare; **~ up** *vt* valutare

weight [weɪt] *n* peso; **to lose/put on ~** dimagrire/ingrassare; **~ing** *n* (*allowance*) indennità; **~ lifter** *n* pesista *m*; **~y** *adj* pesante; (*fig*) importante, grave

weir [wɪə*] *n* diga

weird [wɪəd] *adj* strano(a), bizzarro(a); (*eerie*) soprannaturale

welcome ['welkəm] *adj* benvenuto(a) ♦ *n* accoglienza, benvenuto ♦ *vt* dare il

benvenuto a; (*be glad of*) rallegrarsi di;
thank you – you're ~! grazie – prego!
weld [wɛld] *n* saldatura ♦ *vt* saldare
welfare ['welfɛə*] *n* benessere *m*; **~
state** *n* stato assistenziale; **~ work** *n*
assistenza sociale
well [wɛl] *n* pozzo ♦ *adv* bene ♦ *adj*: **to
be ~** (*person*) stare bene ♦ *excl* allora!;
ma!; ebbene!; **as ~** anche; **as ~ as** così
come; oltre a; **~ done!** bravo(a)!; **get ~
soon!** guarisci presto!; **to do ~** andare
bene; **~ up** *vi* sgorgare
we'll [wi:l] = **we will; we shall**
well: **~-behaved** *adj* ubbidiente; **~-
being** *n* benessere *m*; **~-built** *adj*
(*person*) ben fatto(a); **~-deserved** *adj*
meritato(a); **~-dressed** *adj* ben vestito(a),
vestito(a) bene; **~-heeled** (*inf*) *adj*
(*wealthy*) agiato(a), facoltoso(a)
wellingtons ['welɪŋtənz] *npl* (*also*:
wellington boots) stivali *mpl* di gomma
well: **~-known** *adj* noto(a), famoso(a); **~-
mannered** *adj* ben educato(a); **~-
meaning** *adj* ben intenzionato(a); **~-off**
adj benestante, danaroso(a); **~-read** *adj*
colto(a); **~-to-do** *adj* abbiente,
benestante; **~-wisher** *n* ammiratore/trice
Welsh [wɛlʃ] *adj* gallese ♦ *n* (*LING*) gallese
m; **the ~** *npl* i Gallesi; **~man/woman** *n*
gallese *m/f*; **~ rarebit** *n* crostino al
formaggio
went [wɛnt] *pt of* **go**
wept [wɛpt] *pt, pp of* **weep**
were [wə:*] *pt of* **be**
we're [wɪə*] = **we are**
weren't [wə:nt] = **were not**
west [wɛst] *n* ovest *m*, occidente *m*,
ponente *m* ♦ *adj* (a) ovest *inv*, occidentale
♦ *adv* verso ovest; **the W~** l'Occidente *m*;
the W~ Country (*BRIT*) *n* il sud-ovest
dell'Inghilterra; **~erly** *adj* (*point*) a ovest;
(*wind*) occidentale, da ovest; **~ern** *adj*
occidentale, dell'ovest ♦ *n* (*CINEMA*)
western *m inv*; **W~ Germany** *n*
Germania Occidentale; **W~ Indian** *adj*
delle Indie Occidentali ♦ *n* abitante *m/f*
delle Indie Occidentali; **W~ Indies** *npl*
Indie *fpl* Occidentali; **~ward(s)** *adv* verso
ovest

wet [wɛt] *adj* umido(a), bagnato(a);
(*soaked*) fradicio(a); (*rainy*) piovoso(a) ♦ *n*
(*BRIT: POL*) politico moderato; **to get ~**
bagnarsi; **"~ paint"** "vernice fresca"; **~
blanket** *n* (*fig*) guastafeste *m/f*; **~ suit** *n*
tuta da sub
we've [wi:v] = **we have**
whack [wæk] *vt* picchiare, battere
whale [weɪl] *n* (*ZOOL*) balena
wharf [wɔ:f] (*pl* **wharves**) *n* banchina
wharves [wɔ:vz] *npl of* **wharf**

KEYWORD

what [wɔt] *adv* **1** (*in direct/indirect
questions*) che; quale; **~ size is it?** che
taglia è?; **~ colour is it?** di che colore è?;
~ books do you want? quali *or* che libri
vuole?
2 (*in exclamations*) che; **~ a mess!** che
disordine!
♦ *pron* **1** (*interrogative*) che cosa, cosa,
che; **~ are you doing?** che *or* (che) cosa
fai?; **~ are you talking about?** di che
cosa parli?; **~ is it called?** come si
chiama?; **~ about me?** e io?; **~ about
doing ...?** e se facessimo ...?
2 (*relative*) ciò che, quello che; **I saw ~
you did/was on the table** ho visto
quello che hai fatto/quello che era sul
tavolo
3 (*indirect use*) (che) cosa; **he asked me
~ she had said** mi ha chiesto che cosa
avesse detto; **tell me ~ you're thinking
about** dimmi a cosa stai pensando
♦ *excl* (*disbelieving*) cosa!, come!

whatever [wɔt'ɛvə*] *adj*: **~ book**
qualunque *or* qualsiasi libro + *sub*
♦ *pron*: **do ~ is necessary/you want**
faccia qualunque *or* qualsiasi cosa sia
necessaria/lei voglia; **~ happens**
qualunque cosa accada; **no reason ~ *or*
whatsoever** nessuna ragione affatto *or* al
mondo; **nothing ~** proprio niente
whatsoever [wɔtsəu'ɛvə*] *adj* =
whatever
wheat [wi:t] *n* grano, frumento
wheedle ['wi:dl] *vt*: **to ~ sb into doing
sth** convincere qn a fare qc (con

lusinghe); **to ~ sth out of sb** ottenere qc
da qn (con lusinghe)

wheel [wi:l] *n* ruota; (*AUT: also: steering
~*) volante *m*; (*NAUT*) (ruota del) timone *m*
♦ *vt* spingere ♦ *vi* (*birds*) roteare; (*also: ~
round*) girare; **~barrow** *n* carriola;
~chair *n* sedia a rotelle; **~ clamp** *n* (*AUT*)
*morsa che blocca la ruota di una vettura
in sosta vietata*

wheeze [wi:z] *vi* ansimare

KEYWORD

when [wɛn] *adv* quando; **~ did it
happen?** quando è successo?
♦ *conj* **1** (*at, during, after the time that*)
quando; **she was reading ~ I came in**
quando sono entrato lei leggeva; **that
was ~ I needed you** era allora che avevo
bisogno di te
2 (*on, at which*): **on the day ~ I met him**
il giorno in cui l'ho incontrato; **one day
~ it was raining** un giorno che pioveva
3 (*whereas*) quando, mentre; **you said I
was wrong ~ in fact I was right** mi hai
detto che avevo torto, quando in realtà
avevo ragione

whenever [wɛn'ɛvə*] *adv* quando mai
♦ *conj* quando; (*every time that*) ogni volta
che

where [wɛə*] *adv, conj* dove; **this is ~** è
qui che; **~abouts** *adv* dove ♦ *n*: **sb's
~abouts** luogo dove qn si trova; **~as** *conj*
mentre; **~by** *pron* per cui; **~upon** *conj* al
che; **wherever** [-'ɛvə*] *conj* dovunque
+ *sub*; (*interrogative*) dove mai; **~withal**
n mezzi *mpl*

whet [wɛt] *vt* (*appetite etc*) stimolare

whether ['wɛðə*] *conj* se; **I don't know
~ to accept or not** non so se accettare o
no; **it's doubtful ~** è poco probabile che;
~ you go or not che lei vada o no

KEYWORD

which [wɪtʃ] *adj* **1** (*interrogative: direct,
indirect*) quale; **~ picture do you want?**
quale quadro vuole?; **~ one?** quale?; **~
one of you did it?** chi di voi lo ha fatto?
2: **in ~ case** nel qual caso

♦ *pron* **1** (*interrogative*) quale; **~ (of
these) are yours?** quali di questi sono
suoi?; **~ of you are coming?** chi di voi
viene?
2 (*relative*) che; (: *indirect*) cui, il (la)
quale; **the apple ~ you ate/~ is on the
table** la mela che hai mangiato/che è sul
tavolo; **the chair on ~ you are sitting** la
sedia sulla quale *or* su cui sei seduto; **he
said he knew, ~ is true** ha detto che lo
sapeva, il che è vero; **after ~** dopo di che

whichever [wɪtʃ'ɛvə*] *adj*: **take ~ book
you prefer** prenda qualsiasi libro che
preferisce; **~ book you take** qualsiasi
libro prenda

whiff [wɪf] *n* soffio; sbuffo; odore *m*

while [waɪl] *n* momento ♦ *conj* mentre;
(*as long as*) finché; (*although*) sebbene
+ *sub*; per quanto + *sub*; **for a ~** per un
po'; **~ away** *vt* (*time*) far passare

whim [wɪm] *n* capriccio

whimper ['wɪmpə*] *n* piagnucolio ♦ *vi*
piagnucolare

whimsical ['wɪmzɪkl] *adj* (*person*)
capriccioso(a); (*look*) strano(a)

whine [waɪn] *n* gemito ♦ *vi* gemere;
uggiolare; piagnucolare

whip [wɪp] *n* frusta; (*for riding*) frustino;
(*POL: person*) capogruppo (*che sovrintende
alla disciplina dei colleghi di partito*) ♦ *vt*
frustare; (*cream, eggs*) sbattere; **~ped
cream** *n* panna montata; **~-round** (*BRIT*)
n colletta

whirl [wə:l] *vt* (far) girare rapidamente;
(far) turbinare ♦ *vi* (*dancers*) volteggiare;
(*leaves, water*) sollevarsi in vortice;
~pool *n* mulinello; **~wind** *n* turbine *m*

whirr [wə:*] *vi* ronzare; rombare; frullare

whisk [wɪsk] *n* (*CULIN*) frusta; frullino ♦
vt sbattere, frullare; **to ~ sb away** *or* **off**
portar via qn a tutta velocità

whiskers ['wɪskəz] *npl* (*of animal*) baffi
mpl; (*of man*) favoriti *mpl*

whisky ['wɪskɪ] (*US, IRELAND* **whiskey**) *n*
whisky *m inv*

whisper ['wɪspə*] *n* sussurro ♦ *vt, vi*
sussurrare

whist [wɪst] *n* whist *m*

whistle ['wɪsl] *n* (*sound*) fischio; (*object*) fischietto ♦ *vi* fischiare

white [waɪt] *adj* bianco(a); (*with fear*) pallido(a) ♦ *n* bianco; (*person*) bianco/a; ~ **coffee** (*BRIT*) *n* caffellatte *m inv*; ~**collar worker** *n* impiegato; ~ **elephant** *n* (*fig*) oggetto (*or* progetto) costoso ma inutile; ~ **lie** *n* bugia pietosa; ~**ness** *n* bianchezza; ~ **paper** *n* (*POL*) libro bianco; ~**wash** *n* (*paint*) bianco di calce ♦ *vt* imbiancare; (*fig*) coprire

whiting ['waɪtɪŋ] *n inv* (*fish*) merlango

Whitsun ['wɪtsn] *n* Pentecoste *f*

whittle ['wɪtl] *vt*: **to ~ away, ~ down** ridurre, tagliare

whizz [wɪz] *vi*: **to ~ past** *or* **by** passare sfrecciando; ~ **kid** (*inf*) *n* prodigio

who [hu:] *pron* **1** (*interrogative*) chi; ~ **is it?, ~'s there?** chi è?

2 (*relative*) che; **the man ~ spoke to me** l'uomo che ha parlato con me; **those ~ can swim** quelli che sanno nuotare

whodunit [hu:'dʌnɪt] (*inf*) *n* giallo

whoever [hu:'evə*] *pron*: ~ **finds it** chiunque lo trovi; **ask ~ you like** lo chieda a chiunque vuole; ~ **she marries** chiunque sposerà, non importa chi sposerà; ~ **told you that?** chi mai gliel'ha detto?

whole [həʊl] *adj* (*complete*) tutto(a), completo(a); (*not broken*) intero(a), intatto(a) ♦ *n* (*all*): **the ~ of** tutto(a) il(la); (*entire unit*) tutto; (*not broken*) tutto; **the ~ of the town** tutta la città, la città intera; **on the ~, as a ~** nel complesso, nell'insieme; ~ **food(s)** *n(pl)* cibo integrale; ~**hearted** *adj* sincero(a); ~**meal** *adj* (*bread, flour*) integrale; ~**sale** *n* commercio *or* vendita all'ingrosso ♦ *adj* all'ingrosso; (*destruction*) totale; ~**saler** *n* grossista *m/f*; ~**some** *adj* sano(a); salutare; ~**wheat** *adj* = ~**meal**; **wholly** *adv* completamente, del tutto

whom [hu:m] *pron* **1** (*interrogative*) chi;

~ **did you see?** chi hai visto?; **to ~ did you give it?** a chi lo hai dato?

2 (*relative*) che, *prep* +il (la) quale (*check syntax of Italian verb used*); **the man ~ I saw/to ~ I spoke** l'uomo che ho visto/al quale ho parlato

whooping cough ['hu:pɪŋ-] *n* pertosse *f*

whore [hɔː*] (*inf: pej*) *n* puttana

whose [hu:z] *adj* **1** (*possessive: interrogative*) di chi; ~ **book is this?, ~ is this book?** di chi è questo libro?; ~ **daughter are you?** di chi sei figlia?

2 (*possessive: relative*): **the man ~ son you rescued** l'uomo il cui figlio hai salvato; **the girl ~ sister you were speaking to** la ragazza alla cui sorella stavi parlando

♦ *pron* di chi; ~ **is this?** di chi è questo?; **I know ~ it is** so di chi è

why [waɪ] *adv, conj* perché ♦ *excl* (*surprise*) ma guarda un po'!; (*remonstrating*) ma (via)!; (*explaining*) ebbene!; ~ **not?** perché no?; ~ **not do it now?** perché non farlo adesso?; **that's not ~ I'm here** non è questo il motivo per cui sono qui; **the reason ~** il motivo per cui; ~**ever** *adv* perché mai

wicked ['wɪkɪd] *adj* cattivo(a), malvagio(a); maligno(a); perfido(a)

wickerwork ['wɪkəwɜːk] *adj* di vimini ♦ *n* articoli *mpl* di vimini

wicket ['wɪkɪt] *n* (*CRICKET*) porta; area tra le due porte

wide [waɪd] *adj* largo(a); (*area, knowledge*) vasto(a); (*choice*) ampio(a) ♦ *adv*: **to open** ~ spalancare; **to shoot** ~ tirare a vuoto *or* fuori bersaglio; ~**angle lens** *n* grandangolare *m*; ~**awake** *adj* completamente sveglio(a); ~**ly** *adv* (*differing*) molto, completamente; (*travelled, spaced*) molto; (*believed*) generalmente; ~**n** *vt* allargare, ampliare; ~ **open** *adj* spalancato(a); ~**spread** *adj* (*belief etc*) molto *or* assai diffuso(a)

widow ['wɪdəʊ] *n* vedova; ~**ed** *adj*: **to be**

~**ed** restare vedovo(a); ~**er** *n* vedovo
width [wɪdθ] *n* larghezza
wield [wiːld] *vt* (*sword*) maneggiare;
(*power*) esercitare
wife [waɪf] (*pl* **wives**) *n* moglie *f*
wig [wɪg] *n* parrucca
wiggle ['wɪgl] *vt* dimenare, agitare
wild [waɪld] *adj* selvatico(a); selvaggio(a);
(*sea, weather*) tempestoso(a); (*idea, life*)
folle; stravagante; (*applause*) frenetico(a);
~**s** *npl* regione *f* selvaggia; ~**erness**
['wɪldənɪs] *n* deserto; ~ **goose chase** *n*
(*fig*) pista falsa; ~**life** *n* natura; ~**ly** *adv*
selvaggiamente; (*applaud*) freneticamente;
(*hit, guess*) a casaccio; (*happy*) follemente
wilful ['wɪlful] (*US* **willful**) *adj* (*person*)
testardo(a), ostinato(a); (*action*)
intenzionale; (*crime*) premeditato(a)

KEYWORD
---

will [wɪl] (*pt, pp* ~**ed**) *aux vb* **1** (*forming
future tense*): **I ~ finish it tomorrow** lo
finirò domani; **I ~ have finished it by
tomorrow** lo finirò entro domani; ~ **you
do it?** – **yes I ~/no I won't** lo farai? – sì
(lo farò)/no (non lo farò)
2 (*in conjectures, predictions*): **he ~** *or*
he'll be there by now dovrebbe essere
arrivato ora; **that ~ be the postman** sarà
il postino
3 (*in commands, requests, offers*): ~ **you
be quiet!** vuoi stare zitto?; ~ **you come?**
vieni anche tu?; ~ **you help me?** mi
aiuti?, mi puoi aiutare?; ~ **you have a
cup of tea?** vorrebbe una tazza di tè?; **I
won't put up with it!** non lo accetterò!
♦ *vt*: **to ~ sb to do** volere che qn faccia;
he ~ed himself to go on continuò grazie
a un grande sforzo di volontà
♦ *n* volontà; testamento

---

willful ['wɪlful] (*US*) *adj* = **wilful**
willing ['wɪlɪŋ] *adj* volonteroso(a); ~ **to
do** disposto(a) a fare; ~**ly** *adv* volentieri;
~**ness** *n* buona volontà
willow ['wɪləu] *n* salice *m*
will power *n* forza di volontà
willy-nilly [wɪlɪ'nɪlɪ] *adv* volente o
nolente

wilt [wɪlt] *vi* appassire ·
wily ['waɪlɪ] *adj* furbo(a)
win [wɪn] (*pt, pp* **won**) *n* (*in sports etc*)
vittoria ♦ *vt* (*battle, prize, money*) vincere;
(*popularity*) conquistare ♦ *vi* vincere; ~
over *vt* convincere; ~ **round** (*BRIT*) *vt*
convincere
wince [wɪns] *vi* trasalire
winch [wɪntʃ] *n* verricello, argano
wind¹ [waɪnd] (*pt, pp* **wound**) *vt*
attorcigliare; (*wrap*) avvolgere; (*clock, toy*)
caricare ♦ *vi* (*road, river*) serpeggiare; ~
up *vt* (*clock*) caricare; (*debate*) concludere
wind² [wɪnd] *n* vento; (*MED*) flatulenza;
(*breath*) respiro, fiato ♦ *vt* (*take breath
away*) far restare senza fiato; ~**fall** *n*
(*money*) guadagno insperato; ~ **power**
energia eolica
winding ['waɪndɪŋ] *adj* (*road*)
serpeggiante; (*staircase*) a chiocciola
wind instrument *n* (*MUS*) strumento a
fiato
windmill ['wɪndmɪl] *n* mulino a vento
window ['wɪndəu] *n* finestra; (*in car,
train*) finestrino; (*in shop etc*) vetrina;
(*also*: ~ **pane**) vetro; ~ **box** *n* cassetta da
fiori; ~ **cleaner** *n* (*person*) pulitore *m* di
finestre; ~ **envelope** *n* busta a finestra;
~ **ledge** *n* davanzale *m*; ~ **pane** *n* vetro;
~-**shopping** *n*: **to go** ~-**shopping** andare
a vedere le vetrine; ~**sill** *n* davanzale *m*
windpipe ['wɪndpaɪp] *n* trachea
windscreen ['wɪndskriːn] *n* parabrezza
m inv; ~ **washer** *n* lavacristallo; ~
wiper *n* tergicristallo
windshield ['wɪndʃiːld] (*US*) *n*
= **windscreen**
windswept ['wɪndswɛpt] *adj* spazzato(a)
dal vento
windy ['wɪndɪ] *adj* ventoso(a); **it's ~** c'è
vento
wine [waɪn] *n* vino; ~ **bar** *n* bar *m inv*
(*con licenza per alcolici*); ~ **cellar** *n*
cantina; ~ **glass** *n* bicchiere *m* da vino; ~
list *n* lista dei vini; ~ **merchant** *n*
commerciante *m* di vini; ~ **tasting** *n*
degustazione *f* dei vini; ~ **waiter** *n*
sommelier *m inv*
wing [wɪŋ] *n* ala; (*AUT*) fiancata; ~**s** *npl*

(*THEATRE*) quinte *fpl*; **~er** *n* (*SPORT*) ala
wink [wɪŋk] *n* ammiccamento ♦ *vi*
ammiccare, fare l'occhiolino; (*light*)
balugīnare
winner ['wɪnə*] *n* vincitore/trice
winning ['wɪnɪŋ] *adj* (*team, goal*)
vincente; (*smile*) affascinante; **~s** *npl*
vincite *fpl*
winter ['wɪntə*] *n* inverno; **~ sports** *npl*
sport *mpl* invernali
wintry ['wɪntrɪ] *adj* invernale
wipe [waɪp] *n* pulita, passata ♦ *vt* pulire
(strofinando); (*erase: tape*) cancellare; **~
off** *vt* cancellare; (*stains*) togliere
strofinando; **~ out** *vt* (*debt*) pagare,
liquidare; (*memory*) cancellare; (*destroy*)
annientare; **~ up** *vt* asciugare
wire ['waɪə*] *n* filo; (*ELEC*) filo elettrico;
(*TEL*) telegramma *m* ♦ *vt* (*house*) fare
l'impianto elettrico di; (*also: ~ up*)
collegare, allacciare; (*person*) telegrafare a
wireless ['waɪəlɪs] (*BRIT*) *n* (*set*)
(apparecchio *m*) radio *f inv*
wiring ['waɪərɪŋ] *n* impianto elettrico
wiry ['waɪərɪ] *adj* magro(a) e
nerboruto(a); (*hair*) ispido(a)
wisdom ['wɪzdəm] *n* saggezza; (*of action*)
prudenza; **~ tooth** *n* dente *m* del giudizio
wise [waɪz] *adj* saggio(a); prudente;
giudizioso(a)
...wise [waɪz] *suffix*: **time~** per quanto
riguarda il tempo, in termini di tempo
wisecrack ['waɪzkræk] *n* battuta di
spirito
wish [wɪʃ] *n* (*desire*) desiderio; (*specific
desire*) richiesta ♦ *vt* desiderare, volere;
best ~es (*on birthday etc*) i migliori
auguri; **with best ~es** (*in letter*) cordiali
saluti, con i migliori saluti; **to ~ to
do/sb to do** desiderare *or* volere fare/che
qn faccia; **to ~ for** desiderare; **~ful** *adj*:
it's ~ful thinking è prendere i desideri
per realtà
wishy-washy [wɪʃɪ'wɔʃɪ] (*inf*) *adj*
(*colour*) slavato(a); (*ideas, argument*)
insulso(a)
wisp [wɪsp] *n* ciuffo, ciocca; (*of smoke*)

filo
wistful ['wɪstful] *adj* malinconico(a)
wit [wɪt] *n* (*also: ~s*) intelligenza;
presenza di spirito; (*wittiness*) spirito,
arguzia; (*person*) bello spirito
witch [wɪtʃ] *n* strega

KEYWORD

with [wɪð, wɪθ] *prep* **1** (*in the company
of*) con; **I was ~ him** ero con lui; **we
stayed ~ friends** siamo stati da amici;
I'll be ~ you in a minute vengo subito
2 (*descriptive*) con; **a room ~ a view** una
stanza con vista sul mare (*or* sulle
montagne *etc*); **the man ~ the grey hat/
blue eyes** l'uomo con il cappello grigio/
gli occhi blu
3 (*indicating manner, means, cause*): **~
tears in her eyes** con le lacrime agli
occhi; **red ~ anger** rosso dalla rabbia; **to
shake ~ fear** tremare di paura
4: **I'm ~ you** (*I understand*) la seguo; **to
be ~ it** (*inf: up-to-date*) essere alla moda;
(: *alert*) essere sveglio(a)

withdraw [wɪθ'drɔː] (*irreg: like* draw) *vt*
ritirare; (*money from bank*) ritirare;
prelevare ♦ *vi* ritirarsi; **~al** *n* ritiro;
prelievo; (*of army*) ritirata; (*~al
symptoms* (*MED*) crisi *f* di astinenza; **~n**
adj (*person*) distaccato(a)
wither ['wɪðə*] *vi* appassire
withhold [wɪθ'həuld] (*irreg: like* hold) *vt*
(*money*) trattenere; (*permission*): **to ~
(from)** rifiutare (a); (*information*): **to ~
(from)** nascondere (a)
within [wɪð'ɪn] *prep* all'interno; (*in time,
distances*) entro ♦ *adv* all'interno, dentro;
~ reach (of) alla portata (di); **~ sight (of)**
in vista (di); **~ a mile of** entro un miglio
da; **~ the week** prima della fine della
settimana
without [wɪð'aut] *prep* senza; **to go ~
sth** fare a meno di qc
withstand [wɪθ'stænd] (*irreg: like* stand)
vt resistere a
witness ['wɪtnɪs] *n* (*person, also LAW*)
testimone *m/f* ♦ *vt* (*event*) essere
testimone di; (*document*) attestare

l'autenticità di; ~ **box**(US ~ **stand**) n
banco dei testimoni
witticism ['wɪtɪsɪzm] n spiritosaggine f
witty ['wɪtɪ] adj spiritoso(a)
wives [waɪvz] npl of **wife**
wizard ['wɪzəd] n mago
wkabbr = **week**
wobble ['wɔbl] vi tremare; (chair)
traballare
woe [wəu] n dolore m; disgrazia
woke [wəuk] pt of **wake**; **woken**pp of
wake
wolf [wulf] (pl **wolves**) n lupo
wolves [wulvz] npl of **wolf**
woman ['wumən] (pl **women**) n donna; ~
doctorn dottoressa; **women's lib**(inf)
n movimento femminista
womb [wu:m] n (ANAT) utero
women ['wɪmɪn] npl of **woman**
won [wʌn] pt, pp of **win**
wonder ['wʌndə*] n meraviglia ♦ vi: **to**
~ **whether/why** domandarsi se/perché;
to ~ **at** essere sorpreso(a) di;
meravigliarsi di; **to** ~ **about** domandarsi
di; pensare a; **it's no** ~ **that** c'è poco or
non c'è da meravigliarsi che + sub; ~**ful**
adj meraviglioso(a)
won't [wəunt] = **will not**
woo [wu:] vt (woman, audience) cercare
di conquistare
wood [wud] n legno; (timber) legname m;
(forest) bosco; ~ **carving**n scultura in
legno, intaglio; ~**ed**adj boschivo(a);
boscoso(a); ~**en**adj di legno; (fig)
rigido(a); inespressivo(a); ~**pecker**n
picchio; ~**wind**npl (MUS): **the** ~**wind** i
legni; ~**work**n (craft, subject)
falegnameria; ~**worm**n tarlo del legno
wool [wul] n lana; **to pull the** ~ **over**
sb's eyes (fig) imbrogliare qn; ~**len** (US
~**en**) adj di lana; (industry) laniero(a);
~**lens**npl indumenti mpl di lana; ~**ly** (US
~**y**) adj di lana; (fig: ideas) confuso(a)
word [wə:d] n parola; (news) notizie fpl ♦
vt esprimere, formulare; **in other** ~**s** in
altre parole; **to break/keep one's** ~ non
mantenere/mantenere la propria parola;
to have ~**s with sb** avere un diverbio
con qn; ~**ing**n formulazione f; ~

processingn elaborazione f di testi,
word processing m; ~ **processor**n word
processor m inv
wore [wɔ:*] pt of **wear**
work [wə:k] n lavoro; (ART, LITERATURE)
opera ♦ vi lavorare; (mechanism, plan etc)
funzionare; (medicine) essere efficace ♦ vt
(clay, wood etc) lavorare; (mine etc)
sfruttare; (machine) far funzionare; (cause:
effect, miracle) fare; **to be out of** ~ essere
disoccupato(a); ~**s** n (BRIT: factory)
fabbrica ♦ npl (of clock, machine)
meccanismo; **to** ~ **loose** allentarsi; ~ **on**
vt fus lavorare a; (person) lavorarsi;
(principle) basarsi su; ~ **out**vi (plans etc)
riuscire, andare bene ♦ vt (problem)
risolvere; (plan) elaborare; **it** ~**s out at**
£100 fa 100 sterline; ~ **up**vt: **to get** ~**ed**
up andare su tutte le furie; eccitarsi;
~**able**adj (solution) realizzabile; ~**aholic**
n maniaco/a del lavoro; ~**er**n
lavoratore/trice, operaio/a; ~**force**n
forza lavoro; ~**ing class**n classe f
operaia; ~**ing-class**adj operaio(a); ~**ing**
ordern: **in** ~**ing order** funzionante;
~**man**n operaio; ~**manship**n abilità;
~**sheet**n foglio col programma di lavoro;
~**shop**n officina; (practical session)
gruppo di lavoro; ~ **station**n stazione f
di lavoro; ~**-to-rule** (BRIT) n sciopero
bianco
world [wə:ld] n mondo ♦ cpd (champion)
del mondo; (power, war) mondiale; **to**
think the ~ **of sb** (fig) pensare un gran
bene di qn; ~**ly**adj di questo mondo;
(knowledgeable) di mondo; ~**-wide**adj
universale
worm [wə:m] n (also: earth~) verme m
worn [wɔ:n] pp of **wear** ♦ adj usato(a);
~**-out**adj (object) consumato(a), logoro(a);
(person) sfinito(a)
worried ['wʌrɪd] adj preoccupato(a)
worry ['wʌrɪ] n preoccupazione f ♦ vt
preoccupare ♦ vi preoccuparsi
worse [wə:s] adj peggiore ♦ adv, n
peggio; **a change for the** ~ un
peggioramento; ~**n**vt, vi peggiorare; ~
offadj in condizioni (economiche)
peggiori

worship ['wəːʃɪp] n culto ♦ vt (God) adorare, venerare; (person) adorare; **Your W~** (BRIT: to mayor) signor sindaco; (: to judge) signor giudice

worst [wəːst] adj il(la) peggiore ♦ adv, n peggio; **at ~** al peggio, per male che vada

worth [wəːθ] n valore m ♦ adj: **to be ~** valere; **it's ~ it** ne vale la pena; **it is ~ one's while (to do)** vale la pena (fare); **~less** adj di nessun valore; **~while** adj (activity) utile; (cause) lodevole

worthy ['wəːðɪ] adj (person) degno(a); (motive) lodevole; **~ of** degno di

KEYWORD

would [wud] aux vb **1** (conditional tense): **if you asked him he ~ do it** se glielo chiedesse lo farebbe; **if you had asked him he ~ have done it** se glielo avesse chiesto lo avrebbe fatto

2 (in offers, invitations, requests): **~ you like a biscuit?** vorrebbe or vuole un biscotto?; **~ you ask him to come in?** lo faccia entrare, per cortesia; **~ you open the window please?** apra la finestra, per favore

3 (in indirect speech): **I said I ~ do it** ho detto che l'avrei fatto

4 (emphatic): **it WOULD have to snow today!** doveva proprio nevicare oggi!

5 (insistence): **she ~n't do it** non ha voluto farlo

6 (conjecture): **it ~ have been midnight** sarà stato mezzanotte; **it ~ seem so** sembrerebbe proprio di sì

7 (indicating habit): **he ~ go there on Mondays** andava lì ogni lunedì

would-be (pej) adj sedicente
wouldn't ['wudnt] = **would not**
wound[1] [waund] pt, pp of **wind**[1]
wound[2] [wuːnd] n ferita ♦ vt ferire
wove [wəuv] pt of **weave**; **woven** pp of **weave**
wrangle ['ræŋgl] n litigio
wrap [ræp] n (stole) scialle m; (cape) mantellina ♦ vt avvolgere; (pack: also: ~ up) incartare; **~per** n (on chocolate) carta; (BRIT: of book) copertina; **~ping paper** n

carta da pacchi; (for gift) carta da regali
wrath [rɔθ] n collera, ira
wreak [riːk] vt (havoc) portare, causare; **to ~ vengeance on** vendicarsi su
wreath [riːθ, pl riːðz] n corona
wreck [rɛk] n (sea disaster) naufragio; (ship) relitto; (pej: person) rottame m ♦ vt demolire; (ship) far naufragare; (fig) rovinare; **~age** n (of car) rottami mpl; (of building) macerie fpl; (of ship) relitti mpl
wren [rɛn] n (ZOOL) scricciolo
wrench [rɛntʃ] n (TECH) chiave f; (tug) torsione f brusca; (fig) strazio ♦ vt strappare; storcere; **to ~ sth from** strappare qc a or da
wrestle ['rɛsl] vi: **to ~ (with sb)** lottare (con qn); **~r** n lottatore/trice; **wrestling** n lotta
wretched ['rɛtʃɪd] adj disgraziato(a); (inf: weather, holiday) orrendo(a), orribile; (: child, dog) pestifero(a)
wriggle ['rɪgl] vi (also: ~ about) dimenarsi; (: snake, worm) serpeggiare, muoversi serpeggiando
wring [rɪŋ] (pt, pp **wrung**) vt torcere; (wet clothes) strizzare; (fig): **to ~ sth out of** strappare qc a
wrinkle ['rɪŋkl] n (on skin) ruga; (on paper etc) grinza ♦ vt (nose) torcere; (forehead) corrugare ♦ vi (skin, paint) raggrinzirsi
wrist [rɪst] n polso; **~watch** n orologio da polso
writ [rɪt] n ordine m; mandato
write [raɪt] (pt **wrote**, pp **written**) vt, vi scrivere; **~ down** vt annotare; (put in writing) mettere per iscritto; **~ off** vt (debt, plan) cancellare; **~ out** vt mettere per iscritto; (cheque, receipt) scrivere; **~ up** vt redigere; **~-off** n perdita completa; **~r** n autore/trice, scrittore/trice
writhe [raɪð] vi contorcersi
writing ['raɪtɪŋ] n scrittura; (of author) scritto, opera; **in ~** per iscritto; **~ paper** n carta da lettere
written ['rɪtn] pp of **write**
wrong [rɔŋ] adj sbagliato(a); (not suitable) inadatto(a); (wicked) cattivo(a); (unfair) ingiusto(a) ♦ adv in modo

sbagliato, erroneamente ♦ *n* (*injustice*) torto ♦ *vt* fare torto a; **you are ~ to do it** ha torto a farlo; **you are ~ about that, you've got it ~** si sbaglia; **what's ~?** cosa c'è che non va?; **to go ~** (*person*) sbagliarsi; (*plan*) fallire, non riuscire; (*machine*) guastarsi; **~ful** *adj* illegittimo(a); ingiusto(a); **~ly** *adv* (*incorrectly, by mistake*) in modo sbagliato

wrote [rəut] *pt of* **write**

wrought [rɔːt] *adj*: **~ iron** ferro battuto

wrung [rʌŋ] *pt, pp of* **wring**

wry [raɪ] *adj* storto(a)

X

Xmas ['ɛksməs] *n abbr* = **Christmas**

X-ray ['ɛks'reɪ] *n* raggio X; (*photograph*) radiografia ♦ *vt* radiografare

xylophone ['zaɪləfəun] *n* xilofono

Y

yacht [jɔt] *n* panfilo, yacht *m inv*; **~ing** *n* yachting *m*, sport *m* della vela

Yank [jæŋk] (*pej*) *n* yankee *m/f inv*

Yankee ['jæŋkɪ] (*pej*) *n* = **Yank**

yap [jæp] *vi* (*dog*) guaire

yard [jɑːd] *n* (*of house etc*) cortile *m*; (*measure*) iarda (= *914 mm; 3 feet*); **~stick** *n* (*fig*) misura, criterio

yarn [jɑːn] *n* filato; (*tale*) lunga storia

yawn [jɔːn] *n* sbadiglio ♦ *vi* sbadigliare; **~ing** *adj* (*gap*) spalancato(a)

yd. *abbr* = **yard(s)**

yeah [jɛə] (*inf*) *adv* sì

year [jɪə*] *n* anno; (*referring to harvest, wine etc*) annata; **he is 8 ~s old** ha 8 anni; **an eight-~-old child** un(a) bambino/a di otto anni; **~ly** *adj* annuale ♦ *adv* annualmente

yearn [jəːn] *vi*: **to ~ for sth/to do** desiderare ardentemente qc/di fare

yeast [jiːst] *n* lievito

yell [jɛl] *n* urlo ♦ *vi* urlare

yellow ['jɛləu] *adj* giallo(a)

yelp [jɛlp] *vi* guaire, uggiolare

yeoman ['jəumən] *n*: **~ of the guard** guardiano della Torre di Londra

yes [jɛs] *adv* sì ♦ *n* sì *m inv*; **to say/ answer ~** dire/rispondere di sì

yesterday ['jɛstədɪ] *adv* ieri ♦ *n* ieri *m inv*; **~ morning/evening** ieri mattina/ sera; **all day ~** ieri per tutta la giornata

yet [jɛt] *adv* ancora; già ♦ *conj* ma, tuttavia; **it is not finished ~** non è ancora finito; **the best ~** finora il migliore; **as ~** finora

yew [juː] *n* tasso (*albero*)

yield [jiːld] *n* produzione *f*, resa; reddito ♦ *vt* produrre, rendere; (*surrender*) cedere ♦ *vi* cedere; (*US: AUT*) dare la precedenza

YMCA *n abbr* (= *Young Men's Christian Association*) Y.M.C.A. *m*

yog(h)ourt ['jəugət] *n* = **yog(h)urt**

yog(h)urt ['jəugət] *n* iogurt *m inv*

yoke [jəuk] *n* (*also fig*) giogo

yolk [jəuk] *n* tuorlo, rosso d'uovo

---KEYWORD---

you [juː] *pron* **1** (*subject*) tu; (*: polite form*) lei; (*: pl*) voi; (*: very formal*) loro; **~ Italians enjoy your food** a voi Italiani piace mangiare bene; **~ and I will go** tu ed io *or* lei ed io andiamo
2 (*object: direct*) ti; la; vi; loro (*after vb*); (*: indirect*) ti; le; vi; loro (*after vb*); **I know ~** ti *or* la *or* vi conosco; **I gave it to ~** te l'ho dato; gliel'ho dato; ve l'ho dato; l'ho dato loro
3 (*stressed, after prep, in comparisons*) te; lei; voi; loro; **I told YOU to do it** ho detto a TE (*or a* LEI *etc*) di farlo; **she's younger than ~** è più giovane di te (*or lei etc*)
4 (*impers: one*) si; **fresh air does ~ good** l'aria fresca fa bene; **~ never know** non si sa mai

you'd [juːd] = **you had**; **you would**

you'll [juːl] = **you will**; **you shall**

young [jʌŋ] *adj* giovane ♦ *npl* (*of animal*) piccoli *mpl*; (*people*): **the ~** i giovani, la gioventù; **~er** *adj* più giovane; (*brother*) minore, più giovane; **~ster** *n* giovanotto, ragazzo; (*child*) bambino/a

your [jɔː*] adj il(la) tuo(a), pl i(le) tuoi(tue); il(la) suo(a), pl i(le) suoi(sue); il(la) vostro(a), pl i(le) vostri(e); il(la) loro, pl i(le) loro; *see also* **my**

you're [juə*] = **you are**

yours [jɔːz] pron il(la) tuo(a), pl i(le) tuoi(tue); (*polite form*) il(la) suo(a), pl i(le) suoi(sue); (*pl*) il(la) vostro(a), pl i(le) vostri(e); (: *very formal*) il(la) loro, pl i(le) loro; *see also* **mine**; **faithfully**; **sincerely**

yourself [jɔː'sɛlf] pron (*reflexive*) ti; si; (*after prep*) te; sé; (*emphatic*) tu stesso(a); lei stesso(a); **yourselves** pl pron (*reflexive*) vi; si; (*after prep*) voi; loro;

(*emphatic*) voi stessi(e); loro stessi(e); *see also* **oneself**

youth [juːθ, pl juːðz] n gioventù f; (*young man*) giovane m, ragazzo; ~ **club** n centro giovanile; **~ful** adj giovane; da giovane; giovanile; ~ **hostel** n ostello della gioventù

you've [juːv] = **you have**

Yugoslav ['juːgəu'slɑːv] adj, n jugoslavo(a)

Yugoslavia ['juːgəu'slɑːvɪə] n Jugoslavia

yuppie ['jʌpɪ] (*inf*) n, adj yuppie m/f inv

YWCA n abbr (= *Young Women's Christian Association*) Y.W.C.A. m

Z

zany ['zeɪnɪ] adj un po' pazzo(a)

zap [zæp] vt (*COMPUT*) cancellare

zeal [ziːl] n zelo; entusiasmo

zebra ['ziːbrə] n zebra; ~ **crossing** (*BRIT*) n (passaggio pedonale a) strisce fpl, zebre fpl

zero ['zɪərəu] n zero

zest [zɛst] n gusto; (*CULIN*) buccia

zigzag ['zɪgzæg] n zigzag m inv ♦ vi zigzagare

Zimbabwe [zɪm'bɑːbwɪ] n Zimbabwe m

zinc [zɪŋk] n zinco

zip [zɪp] n (*also*: ~ *fastener*, (*US*) ~*per*) chiusura f or cerniera f lampo inv ♦ vt

(*also*: ~ *up*) chiudere con una cerniera lampo; ~ **code** (*US*) n codice m di avviamento postale

zodiac ['zəudɪæk] n zodiaco

zombie ['zɔmbɪ] n (*fig*): **like a** ~ come un morto che cammina

zone [zəun] n (*also MIL*) zona

zoo [zuː] n zoo m inv

zoology [zuː'ɔlədʒɪ] n zoologia

zoom [zuːm] vi: **to** ~ **past** sfrecciare; ~ **lens** n zoom m inv, obiettivo a focale variabile

zucchini [zuː'kiːnɪ] (*US*) npl (*courgettes*) zucchine fpl

ITALIAN VERBS

1 Gerundio *2* Participio passato *3* Presente *4* Imperfetto *5* Passato remoto *6* Futur
7 Condizionale *8* Congiuntivo presente *9* Congiuntivo passato *10* Imperativo

andare *3* vado, vai, va, andiamo, andate, vanno *6* andrò *etc 8* vada *10* va'!, vada!, andate!, vadano!

apparire *2* apparso *3* appaio, appari *o* apparisci, appare *o* apparisce, appaiono *o* appariscono *5* apparvi *o* apparsi, apparisti, apparve *o* apparì *o* apparse, apparvero *o* apparirono *o* apparsero *8* appaia *o* apparisca

aprire *2* aperto *3* apro *5* aprii *o* apersi, apristi *8* apra

AVERE *3* ho, hai, ha, abbiamo, avete, hanno *5* ebbi, avesti, ebbe, avemmo, aveste, ebbero *6* avrò *etc 8* abbia *etc 10* abbi!, abbia!, abbiate!, abbiano!

bere *1* bevendo *2* bevuto *3* bevo *etc 4* bevevo *etc 8* beva *etc 9* bevessi *etc*

cadere *5* caddi, cadesti *6* cadrò *etc*

cogliere *2* colto *3* colgo, colgono *5* colsi, cogliesti *8* colga

correre *2* corso *5* corsi, corresti

cuocere *2* cotto *3* cuocio, cociamo, cuociono *5* cossi, cocesti

dare *3* do, dai, dà, diamo, date, danno *5* diedi *o* detti, desti *6* darò *etc 8* dia *etc 9* dessi *etc 10* da'!, dia!, date!, diano!

dire *1* dicendo *2* detto *3* dico, dici, dice, diciamo, dite, dicono *4* dicevo *etc 5* dissi, dicesti *6* dirò *etc 8* dica, diciate, dicano *9* dicessi *etc 10* di'!, dica!, dite!, dicano!

dolere *3* dolgo, duoli, duole, dolgono *5* dolsi, dolesti *6* dorrò *etc 8* dolga

dovere *3* devo *o* debbo, devi, deve, dobbiamo, dovete, devono *o* debbono *6* dovrò *etc 8* debba, dobbiamo, dobbiate, devano *o* debbano

ESSERE *2* stato *3* sono, sei, è, siamo, siete, sono *4* ero, eri, era, eravamo, eravate, erano *5* fui, fosti, fu, fummo, foste, furono *6* sarò *etc 8* sia *etc 9* fossi, fossi, fosse, fossimo, foste, fossero *10* sii!, sia!, siate!, siano!

fare *1* facendo *2* fatto *3* faccio, fai, f facciamo, fate, fanno *4* facevo *etc* feci, facesti *6* farò *etc 8* faccia *etc* facessi *etc 10* fa'!, faccia!, fate facciano!

FINIRE *1* finendo *2* finito *3* finisc finisci, finisce, finiamo, finit finiscono *4* finivo, finivi, finiv finivamo, finivate, finivano *5* fin finisti, finì, finimmo, finiste, finiror *6* finirò, finirai, finirà, finirem finirete, finiranno *7* finirei, finires finirebbe, finiremmo, finireste, finir bbero *8* finisca, finisca, finisc finiamo, finiate, finiscano *9* finiss finissi, finisse, finissimo, finiss finissero *10* finisci!, finisca!, finit finiscano!

giungere *2* giunto *5* giunsi, giungesti

leggere *2* letto *5* lessi, leggesti

mettere *2* messo *5* misi, mettesti

morire *2* morto *3* muoio, muor muore, moriamo, morite, muoiono morirò *o* morrò *etc 8* muoia

muovere *2* mosso *5* mossi, movesti

nascere *2* nato *5* nacqui, nascesti

nuocere *2* nuociuto *3* nuoccio, nuo nuoce, nociamo *o* nuociamo, nuoce nuocciono *4* nuocevo *etc 5* nocqu nuocesti *6* nuocerò *etc 7* nuoccia

offrire *2* offerto *3* offro *5* offersi *o* offr offristi *8* offra

parere *2* parso *3* paio, paiamo, paionc parvi *o* parsi, paresti *6* parrò *etc* paia, paiamo, paiate, paiano

PARLARE *1* parlando *2* parlato *3* par parli, parla, parliamo, parla parlano *4* parlavo, parlavi, parlav parlavamo, parlavate, parlavano parlai, parlasti, parlò, parlamm parlaste, parlarono *6* parlerò, parler parlerà, parleremo, parlere parleranno *7* parlerei, parleres

1

parlerebbe, parleremmo, parlereste, parlerebbero *8* parli, parli, parli, parliamo, parliate, parlino *9* parlassi, parlassi, parlasse, parlassimo, parlaste, parlassero *10* parla!, parli!, parlate!, parlino!

iacere *2* piaciuto *3* piaccio, piacciamo, piacciono *5* piacqui, piacesti *8* piaccia *etc*

orre *1* ponendo *2* posto *3* pongo, poni, pone, poniamo, ponete, pongono *4* ponevo *etc* *5* posi, ponesti *6* porrò *etc* *8* ponga, poniamo, poniate, pongano *9* ponessi *etc*

otere *3* posso, puoi, può, possiamo, potete, possono *6* potrò *etc* *8* possa, possiamo, possiate, possano

rendere *2* preso *5* presi, prendesti

durre *1* riducendo *2* ridotto *3* riduco *etc* *4* riducevo *etc* *5* ridussi, riducesti *6* ridurrò *etc* *8* riduca *etc* *9* riducessi *etc*

empire *1* riempiendo *3* riempio, riempi, riempie, riempiono

manere *2* rimasto *3* rimango, rimangono *5* rimasi, rimanesti *6* rimarrò *etc* *8* rimanga

spondere *2* risposto *5* risposi, rispondesti

alire *3* salgo, sali, salgono *8* salga

apere *3* so, sai, sa, sappiamo, sapete, sanno *5* seppi, sapesti *6* saprò *etc* *8* sappia *etc* *10* sappi!, sappia!, sappiate!, sappiano!

crivere *2* scritto *5* scrissi, scrivesti

edere *3* siedo, siedi, siede, siedono *8* sieda

egnere *2* spento *3* spengo, spengono *5* spensi, spegnesti *8* spenga

are *2* stato *3* sto, stai, sta, stiamo, state, stanno *5* stetti, stesti *6* starò *etc*

8 stia *etc* *9* stessi *etc* *10* sta'!, stia!, state!, stiano!

tacere *2* taciuto *3* taccio, tacciono *5* tacqui, tacesti *8* taccia

tenere *3* tengo, tieni, tiene, tengono *5* tenni, tenesti *6* terrò *etc* *8* tenga

trarre *1* traendo *2* tratto *3* traggo, trai, trae, traiamo, traete, traggono *4* traevo *etc* *5* trassi, traesti *6* trarrò *etc* *8* tragga *9* traessi *etc*

udire *3* odo, odi, ode, odono *8* oda

uscire *3* esco, esci, esce, escono *8* esca

valere *2* valso *3* valgo, valgono *5* valsi, valesti *6* varrò *etc* *8* valga

vedere *2* visto *o* veduto *5* vidi, vedesti *6* vedrò *etc*

VENDERE *1* vendendo *2* venduto *3* vendo, vendi, vende, vendiamo, vendete, vendono *4* vendevo, vendevi, vendeva, vendevamo, vendevate, vendevano *5* vendei *o* vendetti, vendesti, vendé *o* vendette, vendemmo, vendeste, venderono *o* vendettero *6* venderò, venderai, venderà, venderemo, venderete, venderanno *7* venderei, venderesti, venderebbe, venderemmo, vendereste, venderebbero *8* venda, venda, venda, vendiamo, vendiate, vendano *9* vendessi, vendessi, vendesse, vendessimo, vendeste, vendessero *10* vendi!, venda!, vendete!, vendano!

venire *2* venuto *3* vengo, vieni, viene, vengono *5* venni, venisti *6* verrò *etc* *8* venga

vivere *2* vissuto *5* vissi, vivesti

volere *3* voglio, vuoi, vuole, vogliamo, volete, vogliono *5* volli, volesti *6* vorrò *etc* *8* voglia *etc* *10* vogli!, voglia!, vogliate!, vogliano!

VERBI INGLESI

present	pt	pp	present	pt	pp
arise	arose	arisen	feed	fed	fed
awake	awoke	awoken	feel	felt	felt
be (am, is, are; being)	was, were	been	fight	fought	fought
			find	found	found
bear	bore	born(e)	flee	fled	fled
beat	beat	beaten	fling	flung	flung
become	became	become	fly (flies)	flew	flown
begin	began	begun	forbid	forbade	forbidden
behold	beheld	beheld	forecast	forecast	forecast
bend	bent	bent	forego	forewent	foregone
beseech	besought	besought	foresee	foresaw	foreseen
beset	beset	beset	foretell	foretold	foretold
bet	bet, betted	bet, betted	forget	forgot	forgotten
bid	bid, bade	bid, bidden	forgive	forgave	forgiven
bind	bound	bound	forsake	forsook	forsaken
bite	bit	bitten	freeze	froze	frozen
bleed	bled	bled	get	got	got, (US) gotten
blow	blew	blown			
break	broke	broken	give	gave	given
breed	bred	bred	go (goes)	went	gone
bring	brought	brought	grind	ground	ground
build	built	built	grow	grew	grown
burn	burnt, burned	burnt, burned	hang	hung, hanged	hung, hanged
burst	burst	burst	have (has; having)	had	had
buy	bought	bought			
can	could	(been able)	hear	heard	heard
cast	cast	cast	hide	hid	hidden
catch	caught	caught	hit	hit	hit
choose	chose	chosen	hold	held	held
cling	clung	clung	hurt	hurt	hurt
come	came	come	keep	kept	kept
cost	cost	cost	kneel	knelt, kneeled	knelt, kneeled
creep	crept	crept			
cut	cut	cut	know	knew	known
deal	dealt	dealt	lay	laid	laid
dig	dug	dug	lead	led	led
do (3rd person: he/she/it does)	did	done	lean	leant, leaned	leant, leaned
			leap	leapt, leaped	leapt, leaped
draw	drew	drawn			
dream	dreamed, dreamt	dreamed, dreamt	learn	learnt, learned	learnt, learned
drink	drank	drunk	leave	left	left
drive	drove	driven	lend	lent	lent
dwell	dwelt	dwelt	let	let	let
eat	ate	eaten	lie (lying)	lay	lain
fall	fell	fallen	light	lit, lighted	lit, lighted

3

present	pt	pp	present	pt	pp
lose	lost	lost	**spell**	spelt, spelled	spelt, spelled
make	made	made	**spend**	spent	spent
may	might	—	**spill**	spilt, spilled	spilt, spilled
mean	meant	meant	**spin**	spun	spun
meet	met	met	**spit**	spat	spat
mistake	mistook	mistaken	**split**	split	split
mow	mowed	mown, mowed	**spoil**	spoiled, spoilt	spoiled, spoilt
must	(had to)	(had to)			
pay	paid	paid	**spread**	spread	spread
put	put	put	**spring**	sprang	sprung
quit	quit, quitted	quit, quitted	**stand**	stood	stood
			steal	stole	stolen
read	read	read	**stick**	stuck	stuck
rid	rid	rid	**sting**	stung	stung
ride	rode	ridden	**stink**	stank	stunk
ring	rang	rung	**stride**	strode	stridden
rise	rose	risen	**strike**	struck	struck, stricken
run	ran	run			
saw	sawed	sawn	**strive**	strove	striven
say	said	said	**swear**	swore	sworn
see	saw	seen	**sweep**	swept	swept
seek	sought	sought	**swell**	swelled	swollen, swelled
sell	sold	sold			
send	sent	sent	**swim**	swam	swum
set	set	set	**swing**	swung	swung
shake	shook	shaken	**take**	took	taken
shall	should	—	**teach**	taught	taught
shear	sheared	shorn, sheared	**tear**	tore	torn
shed	shed	shed	**tell**	told	told
shine	shone	shone	**think**	thought	thought
shoot	shot	shot	**throw**	threw	thrown
show	showed	shown	**thrust**	thrust	thrust
shrink	shrank	shrunk	**tread**	trod	trodden
shut	shut	shut	**wake**	woke	woken
sing	sang	sung	**waylay**	waylaid	waylaid
sink	sank	sunk	**wear**	wore	worn
sit	sat	sat	**weave**	wove, weaved	woven, weaved
slay	slew	slain			
sleep	slept	slept	**wed**	wedded, wed	wedded, wed
slide	slid	slid			
sling	slung	slung	**weep**	wept	wept
slit	slit	slit	**win**	won	won
smell	smelt, smelled	smelt, smelled	**wind**	wound	wound
sow	sowed	sown, sowed	**wring**	wrung	wrung
speak	spoke	spoken	**write**	wrote	written
speed	sped, speeded	sped, speeded			

I NUMERI

NUMBERS

uno(a)	1	one
due	2	two
tre	3	three
quattro	4	four
cinque	5	five
sei	6	six
sette	7	seven
otto	8	eight
nove	9	nine
dieci	10	ten
undici	11	eleven
dodici	12	twelve
tredici	13	thirteen
quattordici	14	fourteen
quindici	15	fifteen
sedici	16	sixteen
diciassette	17	seventeen
diciotto	18	eighteen
diciannove	19	nineteen
venti	20	twenty
ventuno	21	twenty-one
ventidue	22	twenty-two
ventitré	23	twenty-three
ventotto	28	twenty-eight
trenta	30	thirty
quaranta	40	forty
cinquanta	50	fifty
sessanta	60	sixty
settanta	70	seventy
ottanta	80	eighty
novanta	90	ninety
cento	100	a hundred, one hundred
cento uno	101	a hundred and one
duecento	200	two hundred
mille	1 000	a thousand, one thousand
milleduecentodue	1 202	one thousand two hundred and two
cinquemila	5 000	five thousand
un milione	1 000 000	a million, one million

primo(a), 1º		first, 1st
secondo(a), 2º		second, 2nd
terzo(a), 3º		third, 3rd
quarto(a)		fourth, 4th
quinto(a)		fifth, 5th
sesto(a)		sixth, 6th

NUMERI

ettimo(a)	seventh
tavo(a)	eighth
ono(a)	ninth
ecimo(a)	tenth
ndicesimo(a)	eleventh
odicesimo(a)	twelfth
edicesimo(a)	thirteenth
uattordicesimo(a)	fourteenth
uindicesimo(a)	fifteenth
edicesimo(a)	sixteenth
ciassettesimo(a)	seventeenth
ciottesimo(a)	eighteenth
ciannovesimo(a)	nineteenth
entesimo(a)	twentieth
entunesimo(a)	twenty-first
entiduesimo(a)	twenty-second
entitreesimo(a)	twenty-third
entottesimo(a)	twenty-eighth
entesimo(a)	thirtieth
ntesimo(a)	hundredth
ntunesimo(a)	hundred-and-first
illesimo(a)	thousandth
ilionesimo(a)	millionth

razioni etc

ezzo	half
rzo	third
ue terzi	two thirds
uarto	quarter
uinto	fifth
ro virgola cinque, 0,5	(nought) point five, 0.5
e virgola quattro, 3,4	three point four, 3.4
eci per cento	ten per cent
nto per cento	a hundred per cent

sempi

ita al numero dieci	he lives at number 10
trova nel capitolo sette, a agina sette	it's in chapter 7, on page 7
ita al terzo piano	he lives on the 3rd floor
rivò quarto	he came in 4th
ala uno a venticinquemila	scale 1:25,000

NUMBERS

Fractions etc

Examples

L'ORA

THE TIME

che ora è?, che ore sono?	*what time is it?*
è ..., sono ...	*it is ...*
mezzanotte	midnight, twelve p.m.
l'una (della mattina)	one o'clock (in the morning), one (a.m.)
l'una e cinque	five past one
l'una e dieci	ten past one
l'una e un quarto, l'una e quindici	a quarter past one, one fifteen
l'una e venticinque	twenty-five past one, one twenty-five
l'una e mezzo *or* mezza, l'una e trenta	half-past one, one thirty
le due meno venticinque, l'una e trentacinque	twenty-five to two, one thirty-five
le due meno venti, l'una e quaranta	twenty to two, one forty
le due meno un quarto, l'una e quarantacinque	a quarter to two, one forty-five
le due meno dieci, l'una e cinquanta	ten to two, one fifty
mezzogiorno	twelve o'clock, midday, noon
l'una, le tredici	one o'clock (in the afternoon), one (p.m.)
le sette (di sera), le diciannove	seven o'clock (in the evening), seven (p.m.)
a che ora?	*at what time?*
a mezzanotte	at midnight
all'una, alle tredici	at one o'clock
fra venti minuti	in twenty minutes
venti minuti fa	twenty minutes ago

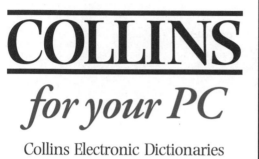